Y0-DDR-550

THE XEROX INTERMEDIATE DICTIONARY

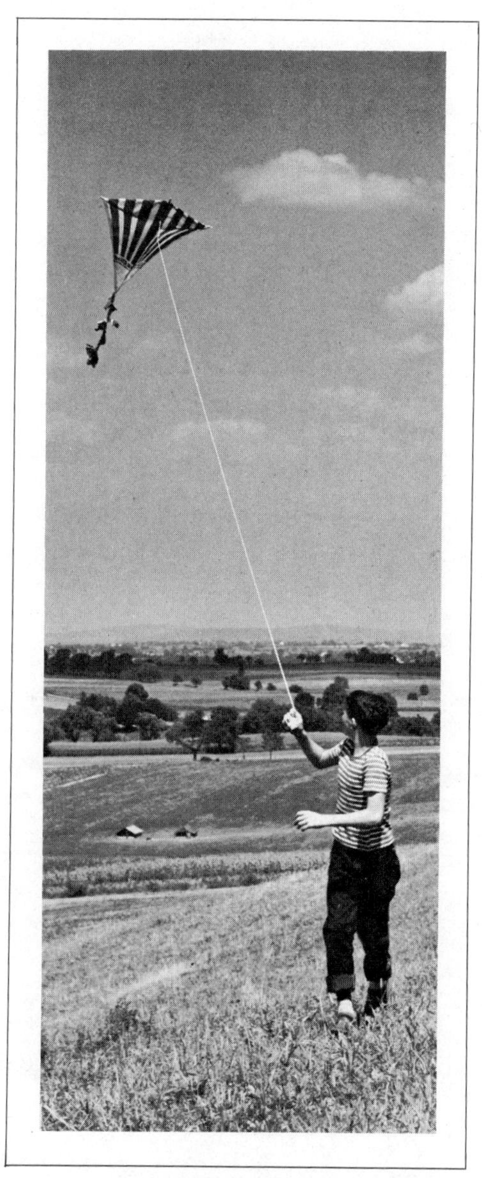

The Xerox Intermediate Dictionary is also published for school and library use as *The Ginn Intermediate Dictionary* by Ginn and Company, a Xerox Company.

THE XEROX INTERMEDIATE DICTIONARY

WILLIAM MORRIS
Editor in Chief

GROSSET & DUNLAP, INC. · Publishers · New York
A NATIONAL GENERAL COMPANY

Grosset & Dunlap Edition
Published by Arrangement with
Xerox Family Education Services
XEROX® is a trademark of Xerox Corporation
Printed in the United States of America.
Published simultaneously in Canada
Library of Congress Catalog Card Number: 73-75574
ISBN: 0-448-02849-2 (Trade Edition)
ISBN: 0-448-02905-7 (Deluxe Edition)

Contents

Staff and Consultants.

Editor in Chief

William Morris, Editor in Chief of *The American Heritage Dictionary* and of *Grolier Universal Encyclopedia;* author of *Your Heritage of Words* and, with Mary Morris, of *Dictionary of Word and Phrase Origins* and the internationally syndicated newspaper column "Words, Wit and Wisdom."

Advisory Board

Linguistics: Dr. Roger W. Shuy, Professor of Linguistics and Director, Sociolinguistics Program, Georgetown University.

Language Arts: Dr. Thomas L. Faix, Associate Professor of Education, Macalester College, Saint Paul, Minnesota.

Social Studies: Dr. Robert W. Saunders, Professor of Education and Education Curriculum Coordinator, State University College, Oneonta, New York.

Mathematics: Dr. David Rappaport, Professor of Mathematics Education, Northeastern Illinois University, Chicago.

Science: Dr. David P. Butts, Professor, Science Education Center, The University of Texas at Austin.

Elementary Curriculum: Margaret D. Parks, intermediate team teacher and language arts specialist, Worthington (Ohio) City Schools.

Editorial Staff for Mr. Morris

Executive Editor: Mary Morris, lexicographer, editor, columnist, and co-author (with William Morris) of books including *The Word Game Book* and *Dictionary of Word and Phrase Origins.*

Consulting Editor: Norman Hoss, lexicographer, Managing Editor of *The American Heritage Dictionary.*

Editorial Staff for Xerox Family Education Services

Publisher: John E. Schmid

Editorial Director: George H. Wolfson

Managing Editor: Mary Lou Kennedy

Assistant to the Managing Editor: Regina Grant

Definers: Evelyn Drimmer, Adele French, Earl French, Leo Grant, Walter Scott Houston, Ruth Wolfe Harley, Ruth Kahn, Joanna Morris, Jerome Wyckoff

Copy Editors and Proofreaders: Jo Ashley Bacon, Sharon Dykas, Susan Fernandez, Virginia Frecking, Karen Klingel, Florence Munat, Sharon Rasmussen, Germaine Schumacher, Jan Spegele

Research and Production Assistants: Antoinette Bondi, Barbara Freudenstein, June Goodrich, Marion Kardok, Anne Kennedy

Design and Production

Book Designer and Art Director: Jos. Trautwein

Artist: Ken Martin

Photo and Permissions Researchers: Betty Zuraw, Vivian Larson, Deborah Blish Thomas, Peter Thomas

Book Production Manager: William Miller

Teacher Contributors

Special appreciation and recognition go to the following elementary teachers who, with their students, participated in nationwide research on the words that children use in everyday speech and in the classroom.

Mary C. Andersen, *L. H. Tanglen Elementary School, Minnetonka, Minnesota;* Miriam C. Avore, *Roger Wolcott School, Windsor, Connecticut;* Virginia F. Barbery, *Ashley Park School, Charlotte, North Carolina;* Virginia T. Bernard, *K. A. Brennan School, New Haven, Connecticut;* Nancy Boreske, *Wickliffe School, Columbus, Ohio;* Joan Bryant, *Fishinger Elementary School, Columbus, Ohio;* Margaret S. Callahan, *Barrow Elementary School, Athens, Georgia;* Elizabeth Carey, *John F. Kennedy Elementary School, Butte, Montana;* Ada Carney, *George Gray School, Wilmington, Delaware;* Dietria L. Cobb, *K. A. Brennan School, New Haven, Connecticut;* Naoma Cousins, *John Fitch School, Windsor, Connecticut;* Florence E. Cozza, *Poquonock School, Windsor, Connecticut;* Dorothy O. Davis, *Gordon Elementary School, Bellaire, Texas;* Norma Dodd, *Highland Springs Elementary School, Highland Springs, Virginia;* A. L. Donato, *Albion Street Elementary School, Los Angeles, California;* Joyce B. Edelson, *Nathan Hale School, Mount Vernon, New York;* Mildred Erickson, *Saybrook Elementary School, Ashtabula, Ohio;* Joseph A. Ginnetti, *K. A. Brennan School, New Haven, Connecticut;* A. H. Gosselin, *K. A. Brennan School, New Haven, Connecticut;* Anne C. Gossett, *Jefferson Elementary School, Walla Walla, Washington;* Catherine M. Hansen, *Harrison School, Trenton, New Jersey;* Elizabeth C. Harris, *Berea Elementary School, Greenville, South Carolina;* Conradine Henderson, *Barrow Elementary School, Athens, Georgia;* Thelma Hobbs, *Ainsworth School, Portland, Oregon;* Martha C. Hodge, *Berea Elementary School, Greenville, South Carolina;* Agnes J. Homan, *Coral Gables Elementary School, Coral Gables, Florida;* George M. Ilko, Jr., *Lyon School, St. Louis, Missouri;* Vera N. Johnson, *Linden School, South Bend, Indiana;* John Kanakis, *William F. Harrity School, Philadelphia, Pennsylvania;* Louise Kimzey, *Ainsworth School, Portland, Oregon;* Susan Kleinkauf, *Albion Street Elementary School, Los Angeles, California;* Mary Reitz Koehneke, *Rose Park School, Salt Lake City, Utah;* Florence Leonard, *Harrison School, Trenton, New Jersey;* Gloria Levine, *Oliver Ellsworth School, Windsor, Connecticut;* Sally Liechty, *Adams School, Des Moines, Iowa;* Martha S. Lindner, *Tremont Elementary School, Columbus, Ohio;* Karin Markus, *L. H. Tanglen Elementary School, Hopkins, Minnesota;* Mrs. R. Pennington Moore, *Leinkauf Elementary School, Mobile, Alabama;* Mary E. O'Hare, *Prince Elementary School, Boston, Massachusetts;* Maureen Onofrio, *K. A. Brennan School, New Haven, Connecticut;* Margaret D. Parks, *Evening Street Elementary School; Worthington, Ohio;* Theda Price, *Leinkauf Elementary School, Mobile, Alabama;* Fran Stein, *P. S. 72, New York, New York;* Beverly R. Stocker, *Paine Elementary School, Walla Walla, Washington;* Christine W. Stuckey, *Liberty-Eylan Elementary School, Texarkana, Texas;* Sally Swearingen, *Sacramento Elementary School, Alamogordo, New Mexico;* Dorothy Taylor, *Courville School, Detroit, Michigan;* Larry R. Thomson, *Paine Elementary School, Walla Walla, Washington;* Lynne Tillotson, *P. S. 72, New York, New York;* Gloria Verdin, *Lyon School, St. Louis, Missouri;* Janelle Weber, *Windermere School, Columbus, Ohio;* Tressie White, *Nathan Hale School, Mount Vernon, New York;* Mary E. Wong, *Prince Elementary School, Boston, Massachusetts.*

Introduction

by William Morris

Welcome to the world of words! You may wonder at that particular greeting, because, of course, you have been using words ever since you learned to talk. But now—with the help of this dictionary—you will find a whole new world of excitement and fun in the language you use every day at home, on the playground, and in school.

For many people the dictionary is simply a useful tool, a book that you look at when you need help in spelling or pronouncing a word. And it's quite true that many dictionaries are dull-looking and not really much more interesting to read than a telephone book or a calendar.

But *The Xerox Intermediate Dictionary* is a brand-new kind of dictionary. Just glance through the pages and you will see what we mean. In this dictionary you will find not just words and definitions but hundreds on hundreds of pictures, most of them specially drawn or photographed for this book. Now you will no longer have to puzzle over what a certain bird or animal or flower looks like. In these pages you will find pictures that will bring them all to life for you. And these pictures, many of them in two colors, are not crowded in with the text, as they are in most dictionaries. Here they are set out in the margins, so that there is plenty of room to give you a clear picture of every creature or object that we have illustrated.

And that is not all. The editors have made every effort to write the definitions of words in clear, simple language, so that you will grasp the meanings immediately. Wherever it seemed helpful, they have added sample sentences or phrases to make clear to you exactly how each word and phrase is used.

Another remarkable thing about this dictionary is that many hundreds of young people helped to choose the words that are most important to you at this stage of your schooling. Before any of this dictionary was written, we wrote to teachers in every part of this country and asked them to have their pupils tell us what words they use every day—but can't find in their dictionaries. From these suggestions made by young people just like you we found words like *tacos, Chicano, hoagie, busted play,* and many more. These are words that some of you in some parts of the country know perfectly well but, because they may be unfamiliar to young people in other areas, they need to be put in the dictionary and explained.

We have also made every effort to keep the dictionary up-to-date, including many slang expressions such as *up tight, yak, meathead, drag,* and *cool it.* You will see, when you look these up in the dictionary, that each is marked "Slang." That is your warning not to use these words in papers or reports you write for your teacher unless you are using the words in a story in which they are needed to show the kind of person you are writing about.

Most of all, though, we have tried to make a dictionary that you will enjoy using, a dictionary that will prove to you that words can be fun. Leaf through the pages, whether you are looking for a particular word or not. If a word or picture catches your eye—and a lot of them will—stop and read about it. Browse around through the book—the word *browse* itself might be a good place to start. You'll find that it has at least one meaning that you probably didn't know before. You will find that a deer can browse just as well as you can. The difference is that the deer gets real food from its browsing, while you get food for thought.

So here you have a dictionary that is not dull, a word book that you can enjoy. As you use it day after day, try to keep in mind the fact that you should be looking for the exact words to say what you want to say in precisely the right way. Remember what Mark Twain once said: "The difference between the right word and the almost right word is the difference between lightning and the lightning bug."

How To Use Your Dictionary

Your new dictionary will serve you best if you take time now to review all its working parts. The illustration below shows you the major items in a typical main entry:

1. Main Entry Word. The main entry word, **an·chor,** is printed in **bold-faced** type. You will notice that it is set out slightly to the left of the other lines in the entry.

2. Syllabication Dot. The entry word is divided into parts, or syllables, by a centered dot.

3. Respelling as a Guide to Pronunciation. Next (within parentheses) comes the respelling of the entry word. (You will find a guide to pronunciation on page 19.)

4. Part of Speech. The labels *noun* and *verb,* printed in *italic* type, tell you that the entry word is used as two parts of speech.

5. Definition. The number *1* introduces a definition of the first meaning of *anchor.* Definitions are numbered in any entry where a word has more than one meaning. You will see that *anchor* has two noun meanings and two verb meanings.

6. Sample Sentence or Phrase. Some meanings of a word become clearer when you see the word used in a phrase or sentence. So examples are used to expand or reinforce the meanings of many words. Note that the main entry word appears in *italic* type within the sample sentence or phrase.

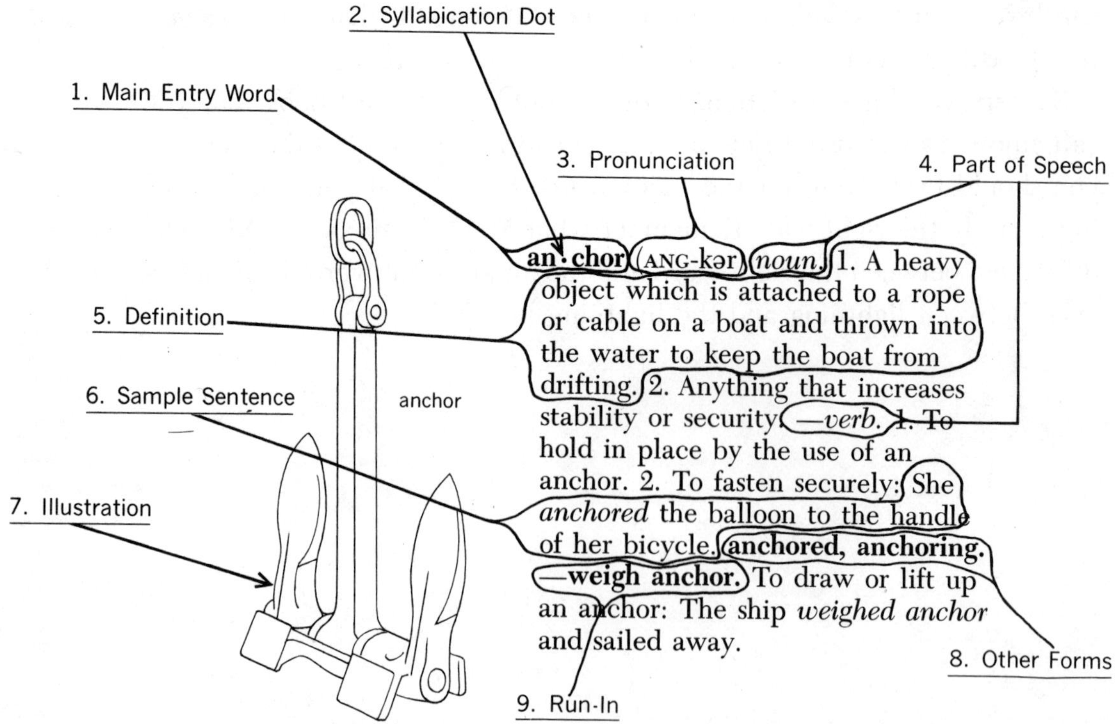
2. Syllabication Dot
1. Main Entry Word
3. Pronunciation
4. Part of Speech
5. Definition
6. Sample Sentence
anchor
7. Illustration
an·chor (ANG-kər) noun 1. A heavy object which is attached to a rope or cable on a boat and thrown into the water to keep the boat from drifting. 2. Anything that increases stability or security. —verb. 1. To hold in place by the use of an anchor. 2. To fasten securely: She anchored the balloon to the handle of her bicycle. anchored, anchoring. —weigh anchor. To draw or lift up an anchor: The ship weighed anchor and sailed away.
8. Other Forms
9. Run-In

7. Illustration. Photographs, drawings, maps, charts, and diagrams are used by the hundreds throughout this dictionary as still another way to enlarge your understanding of words.

8. Other Forms. Shown here are two forms of the verb *to anchor.* You can read more on pages 15–16 about the varying forms of different parts of speech.

9. Phrasal Run-In. Certain entry words, when used in combination with one or more other words, take on a special meaning. *Weigh anchor* is such a combination with a particular meaning. As you can see, it doesn't mean to find out how much an anchor weighs. Read more on page 13 about the phrases that are run in at the end of many entries.

FINDING WORDS IN YOUR DICTIONARY

All main entries are listed alphabetically on pages 29 through 795. To use this dictionary, therefore, you must know the order of letters in the English alphabet. Refer to the list at right whenever you need to refresh your memory of alphabetical order. To test your memory now, try this "missing letter" puzzle. In each of the four lists below, the alphabet is given in order but with some letters missing. See if you can find, in each list, the word spelled by the missing letters. (Answers on page 16.)

1. *a-c-d-f-g-h-i-j-k-m-n-o-p-q-r-s-u-v-w-x-y-z*
2. *a-b-c-e-f-g-h-j-k-l-m-n-o-p-q-s-u-v-w-x-z*
3. *a-b-c-d-e-f-g-h-i-j-l-m-p-q-r-s-u-v-w-x-y-z*
4. *a-b-d-e-f-g-i-j-k-l-m-n-q-r-t-u-v-w-x-y-z*

If you know alphabetical order, the first letter of a word tells you where to start looking for it in the dictionary. With practice you can locate any word quickly in three easy steps.

Step 1—Opening the Dictionary

Decide in which part of the alphabet you will find the first letter of the word you want to look up. Is it toward the beginning, like *b*? In the middle, like *l* or *m*? Or at the end, like *z*? To find a word beginning with *h*, you would open your dictionary a little before the middle of the book. If you open by chance in the *j*'s, you know you have to go backward to *h*. If your first opening puts you in the *f*'s, leaf forward more pages.

Step 2—Using the Guide Words

Always use the guide words at the top of each page to speed your search for a word. The left-hand guide word is the same as the first entry on that page. The right-hand guide word tells you what entry begins at the end of the page. By watching just the guide words, you can quickly flip through many pages until you reach those where guide words begin with the same letter as the word you are looking up. For each word in the left column below, find in the right column the pair of guide words that would come at the top of the page on which each entry is found. Number 1 will fall between the words lettered E. Write down the other pairs of numbers and words and check the answers on page 16.

1. **fudge**	A. **I—idea**
2. **chocolate**	B. **Jell-O—jigger**
3. **dessert**	C. **chipmunk—chord**
4. **ice cream**	D. **ginger ale—glad**
5. **Jell-O**	E. **fruitful—fumigate**
6. **gingerbread**	F. **despite—deter**

Step 3—Finding Alphabetical Order Beyond the First Letters of Words

To find the exact page on which words are listed you have to look beyond their first letters to the alphabetical order of the second or third letters and often even beyond the fourth. The order in which two words fall alphabetically is decided by whichever letter in one word is first found to be different from a letter in the other word. That letter might be the first in each word or it might be the sixth or the tenth. See for yourself how this works in the following pairs of words that are arranged alphabetically.

A a
B b
C c
D d
E e
F f
G g
H h
I i
J j
K k
L l
M m
N n
O o
P p
Q q
R r
S s
T t
U u
V v
W w
X x
Y y
Z z

insight **knife**	The **first** letter of *insight* comes before the first letter of *knife.*
insight **island**	The **second** letter of *insight* comes before the second letter of *island.*
insight **intent**	The **third** letter of *insight* comes before the third letter of *intent.*
insight **insure**	The **fourth** letter of *insight* comes before the fourth letter of *insure.*
insight **insist**	The **fifth** letter of *insight* comes before the fifth letter of *insist.*
insight **insignia**	The **sixth** letter of *insight* comes before the sixth letter of *insignia.*
insight **insights**	The **seventh** letter is the same in both words, but *insights* has one more letter than *insight* and follows it in alphabetical order.

The guide words on page 190 of this dictionary are **covert-crack.** How many of the following words will you find listed on this page: *cow, coy, cram, crab, cozy, craft, cover, court, corner, cracker?*

Using Cross References

You may already have discovered that certain words in the English language can be spelled in two ways (or even more). Usually one spelling is used more often than the other and is called the "preferred spelling." In this dictionary the main entry for such a word is alphabetized according to the preferred spelling. Thus the main entry describing a color between black and white is **gray.** Perhaps you have spelled this word as **grey** and look for it under the words beginning *gre* . . . . You will find:

grey (GRAY) *noun. See* **gray.**

This cross reference tells you to look back to words beginning *gra* . . . . There you find:

gray Also **grey** . . . .

Cross references such as this are usually provided when the variant spelling of a word does not fall in close alphabetical order with the preferred spelling. Cross references are not given, however, when the variant spellings are very close together in alphabetical sequence. You will not, for example, find separate entries for **bogy** or **bogie,** the variant spellings for **bogey** (all beginning *bog* . . .). But you will find at **cosy** (beginning *cos* . . .) a cross reference to **cozy** (beginning *coz* . . .).

Cross references are also used throughout this book for irregular verb forms. Consider the verbs in the following sentence. "When I *was* on vacation, I *bought* souvenirs and *went* to a museum." You will find the meanings of these three verbs given under a main entry at the verb form that shows present time. For the verb forms in the sentence, the following cross references appear:

was (WUHZ) *verb. See* **be.**
bought (BAWT) *verb. See* **buy.**
went *verb. See* **go.**

A third kind of helpful reference comes at the end of certain entries, such as **rabies.** This entry ends, "Also called 'hydrophobia'." This kind of signal lets you know whenever one thing is commonly known by more than one name.

Occasionally you will find a cross reference from one entry to an illustration in a different part of the dictionary. For example, pictures of both an alligator and a crocodile are shown together at **alligator** for comparison of the shapes of their heads. The entry for crocodile carries this cross reference: "*See* illustration at **alligator.**"

Finding a Word That Is Not a Main Entry

Most of the words you look up in this dictionary will be found in alphabetical order among the main entries. Sometimes, however, you will find the word or phrase you want within an entry for a slightly different form of the word. This happens in the following cases:

1. *Different Forms of Entry Words.* The plurals of some nouns, different forms of verbs, and degrees of certain adjectives are not found as separate entries. You will find them listed in **boldface** *within* the entries for their base words. (See pages 15–16 for how these different forms are made and used.)

2. *Different Parts of Speech.* At the end of the entry **foolish** you find two words in boldface. **Foolishly** is the adverb formed by adding **-ly** to the adjective **foolish. Foolishness** is the noun formed by adding the suffix **-ness** to the adjective **foolish.** Printing these different parts of speech at the end of a main entry is a way of saving space in the dictionary.

3. *Phrasal Run-Ins.* At the end of the entry for **foot,** you will notice three phrases:—**put one's best foot forward;—put one's foot down;—put one's foot in one's mouth.**

Phrases such as these, often used in everyday speech, are called *idioms.* **Pass the buck** and **in the same boat** are other samples of such phrases. You will find them listed at the end of the entry for the key word in any phrase. Thus **blow a fuse** comes at the end of the entry **blow. Keep the faith** falls under **faith.**

FINDING THE MEANINGS OF WORDS

Many words in our language have just one meaning. This is true for the names of such animals as *gnu, zebra,* and *giraffe.* But what about *rat, chicken, monkey, dove,* and *hawk?* Can you think of two (or even more) meanings for each of these names?

Whenever an entry word has more than one meaning, each meaning is given a separate, numbered definition. The most common or important meaning usually comes first. When you see the number *1* in any entry, it can be a signal that the definition that follows is the most common but not the *only* meaning of that word. Some words have more than one widely used meaning. In an entry for this kind of word the order of the definitions does not necessarily show which meaning is most widely used.

Test Meaning by Substitution

If you're not sure which meaning of a word applies, try substituting all the meanings in the same sentence. For example, what does *consume* mean in this sentence? "Time will consume the strongest cord." Test each of the meanings from the entry for *consume* (below).

1. Time will *use up, spend, or waste* the strongest cord.
2. Time will *eat up* the strongest cord.
3. Time will *destroy* the strongest cord.
4. Time will *take up the attention of* the strongest cord.

All four substitutions make sentences of a sort. But the third sentence makes the most sense.

The sample entry on **head** (below) shows more of the ways in which your dictionary helps you understand the meanings of

> **con·sume** (kən-SOOM or kən-SYOOM) *verb.* 1. To use up; to spend or waste: Mary's homework *consumed* an hour of her time. 2. To eat or drink up. 3. To destroy. 4. To fill up or take up the attention of: The athlete was *consumed* with the desire to become a champion. **consumed, consuming.**

> **head** (HED) *noun.* 1. The top part of the body containing (in man and some animals) the brain, eyes, ears, nose, and mouth. 2. The mind. 3. Control; calm: When Liz saw the mouse, she lost her *head.* 4. (Usually plural) The side of a coin that has the more important design; the opposite of tails. 5. The first position: at the *head* of the class. 6. Each member of a set or group: count *heads.* 7. The leader; the most important or powerful one. 8. A plant part that has leaves formed into a ball: a *head* of lettuce. 9. The part of something that is at the top: the *head* of a hammer. —*verb.* 1. To go toward: *head* home. 2. To be in charge of. **headed, heading. —head off.** To get in front of; to cut off. **—out of one's head.** Crazy; out of control. **—over one's head.** Beyond one's ability to do or understand.

words. After some definitions you will find a full sentence in which the entry word is used. For example: "3. Control; calm: When Liz saw the mouse, she lost her *head*." Substituting the definition in this sentence, you understand that Liz lost her control or calm.

For still other definitions, a short phrase may be used to illustrate meaning: "a *head* of lettuce" (noun meaning #8); "*head* for home" (verb meaning #1). See how well you can match different meanings of *head* with their definitions. For each sentence below select the correct definition from one of the following meanings: *noun*—1, 2, 4, 7, 8, 9; *verb*–1, 2.

1. *Heads* I win, tails you lose.
2. There are 12 *heads* of cabbage in my garden.
3. Hit the nail on the *head*.
4. The President is the *head* of our country.
5. The President *heads* our country.
6. My *head* aches.
7. I can't get that memory out of my *head*.
8. In case of fire, *head* for the exit.

Homographs and Homophones

Anyone learning the English language is often puzzled by words that are spelled exactly alike but have completely different meanings and sometimes different pronunciations. Adding to the puzzle are still other words that sound the same but are spelled differently. These two classes of words are called *homographs* and *homophones*.

Homo- means "the same"; *-graph* means "something written or drawn." So *homograph* means "something written the same." The two sample entries for *desert* (right) show two homographs. Notice the small numbers [1] and [2] before the entry words. Such a number at the start of an entry signals that you may have to search through two (or more) separate entries to find the particular meaning you're after. How does [1]**desert** differ from [2]**desert** in meaning?

Now compare the sample entry for **dessert** with the entry for [1]**desert.** These two words are not spelled the same, but they are both pronounced the same way (di-ZERT).

[1]**de·sert** (di-ZERT) *verb.* 1. To leave behind, forsake. 2. To leave the army without permission and with no plan to return. **deserted, deserting.** —*noun.* (Usually plural) Something deserved, either reward or punishment: The lazy grasshopper got its just *deserts.*

[2]**de·sert** (DEZ-ərt) *noun.* A dry, usually sandy region where there are few people, animals, or plants because of lack of water.

des·sert (di-ZERT) *noun.* A sweet dish served after the main meal.

They are homophones. As noted, *homo-* means "the same." *-Phone* means "a sound or something that makes a sound." So *homophone* means "something that sounds the same."

Finding the Meanings of Words Not in This Dictionary

Some common words that you use every day are not listed because their meanings should be clear from the meanings of other words that *are* in the dictionary, words or word parts that combine to make other words. For example, if you know one of the meanings for *court* and *room,* you probably know what a *courtroom* is. You can find *fight* as an entry, plus another entry that tells you the suffix *-er* means "someone who." So you know that a *fighter* is "someone who fights."

If you understand the meaning of *back* as "to the rear," you don't need a dictionary for the meaning of *backstairs.* But you will find in this dictionary the word *backlog,* because its special meaning is not easily grasped from the words *back* and *log.*

Starting on page 22 is a fascinating discussion of root words, prefixes, and suffixes and other word elements from the Latin and Greek languages. The more time you spend with these pages, the better you will be able to spell and to recognize the parts and the meanings of many words.

SPELLING AND USING WORDS CORRECTLY

You have now seen the ways in which your dictionary can help you discover the meanings of words. It is also a valuable tool in helping you spell, pronounce, and use words correctly.

Capitalization

1. If a word always begins with a capital letter, its main entry word also starts with a capital letter. This is true for such proper names as *January, Central America,* and *Chicano.*

2. If a word only sometimes begins with a capital letter, its main entry word begins with a small letter. You must then look inside the entry for clues to when the word should be spelled with a capital letter.

a. The first meaning of *genesis* (with a small letter) is "birth, beginning, creation." The second meaning is marked [Capital G]. This tells you to start the word with a capital letter if you are referring to the first book of the Bible.

b. Other clues within an entry are [Usually capital] or [Sometimes capital]. Thus, the entry for *east* tells you that you would usually capitalize *the East* to mean the countries of eastern Asia.

Syllabication

All entry words of more than one syllable are divided by dots to show the parts that stand for syllables. When printers set type for a book, they sometimes find that they must start a word on one line and end it on the next. So they follow rules of syllabication to decide where a word can be divided into parts. Perhaps you have studied some of these rules in school. If so, you know that it's sometimes hard to remember which rules apply to certain words.

Here's where your dictionary can help. If, in your own writing, you need to split a word, the dots show you how to divide it into the parts that stand for its syllables.

Plurals

A plural indicates more than one of something. In the English language, most plurals are formed by adding *s* to the singular noun. Thus *roots* is the plural form of *root.* If the plural of a word is formed regularly by merely adding *s* to the singular, its plural form usually will not be listed in this dictionary. It *is* given, however, for any word when there might be some doubt about its plural form, as with words ending in vowels (*radios, caches*). And it is also given for many words that form their plurals by adding *es* (*churches*) or where *y* is replaced by *i* before *es* is added (*stories*).

You will also find listed the plurals of words that are formed in an irregular way: *children* (the plural of *child*); *men* (the plural of *man*). Such plurals will be found at the end of the noun definitions. At the beginning or in the middle of certain noun definitions come other guidelines on plurals:

1. *Noun, plural* tells you that an entry word should be used with a plural verb form: "These *groceries are* heavy to carry." (not *groceries is*).

2. *Noun, plural in form but used with a singular verb* applies to a word like *checkers.* You would say, "*Checkers is* my favorite game." (not *checkers are*).

3. (Plural) or (Usually plural) before a particular definition of a noun tells you to switch to the plural form: "Coffee *grounds are* at the bottom of the cup." (not coffee *ground is*).

Degrees of Adjectives and Adverbs

"I am *happy* to play indoors in winter. I am *happier* when spring comes. I am *happiest* when I go away on a trip." *Happy* is the positive degree of the adjective. *Happier,* the comparative degree, means "more happy." *Happiest,* the superlative degree, means "most happy." *More happily* and *most happily* are degrees of the adverb *happily.*

The most commonly used degrees of adjectives are given in this dictionary. When they do not appear, it usually means one of two things:

1. The comparative and superlative forms are made by using "more" or "most" and not by adding *-er* or *-est* (*more anxious,* not *anxiouser*).

2. The adjective has only one degree. Something that is *unique* is the only one of its kind. Therefore, it cannot be *more unique* or *most unique.*

Verb Forms

Following most verb definitions are two *regular* verb forms. The first, ending in *-ed,* indicates time past: I *played.* I have *played.* The second is the *-ing* form of the verb: I was *playing.* For *irregular* verbs, however, you will find more than two forms listed: I *get;* I *got;* I have *gotten,* I am *getting.* And it takes a special chart (page 91) to show all the forms of *to be.*

(*Special note:* In your particular school, you may have learned that *be* is not truly a verb like other verbs. For dictionary purposes, however, it is labeled as a verb.)

Usage Labels

When you are traveling by car, you look for signposts to tell you which roads to take. "Scenic Route" means that a road may not be the quickest or most direct way but it offers a lovely landscape. If you want to bypass a town, you follow the thruway. But if you're hunting for a bank or store, you might turn off at a sign that says "To Business District."

In much the same way, your dictionary signals you which words to use for either general or special purposes. Words in wide general use are not labeled. But those used in special ways have the following labels in parentheses:

1. (Music), (Sports), (Grammar). Labels such as these pinpoint studies or fields in which one meaning of a word has a special or unique application.

2. (Informal). This label identifies words that are used mostly in everyday or colloquial speech. *Gobbledygook, gumption, go-getter, hassle,* and *hooky* are examples of words often used in informal conversation or writing.

3. (Slang). This label is a signal somewhat like a blinking amber caution light in traffic. It is not always a red stoplight that says, "Stop, don't ever use this word." Rather, it tells you: "Stop for a minute and think whether this is *really* a word you want to use." Slang words are colorful but common. We may use them in talking with friends or in such casual writing as a personal letter. You might even want to use terms like *hang-up* or *cop out* in the dialogue of a realistic play or short story. But stop for the caution signal before you use slang in writing or in talking with people you don't know well.

Most of the phrasal run-ins at the end of entries are not labeled. Because they are mostly idioms, however, you should consider them as informal.

4. (British). This label on one of the meanings for *lift* tells you that it is only in Great Britain that an elevator is known as a lift.

5. (Rare). This label tells you that a word like *unto* is old-fashioned, or archaic. Such a label is used for words that are seldom used in present-day speech but are found in poetry, the Bible, and other literary works of an earlier time.

Answers to Word Puzzles. *Missing Letters:* 1, belt; 2, dirty; 3, knot; 4, chops. *Guide Words:* 1, E; 2, C; 3, F; 4, A; 5, B; 6, D.

Guide to Pronunciation

by Norman Hoss

You can't remember learning to talk, can you? Nobody can. But you can bet you were talking a blue streak before you started to learn to read and write. Every language was spoken for a long time before anybody figured out how to write a message in it so that anybody else could receive it without the sound of a voice. Some languages still haven't been written down by the people who speak them, but no group of people has ever been reported on who didn't talk. And the most primitive people we know anything about speak languages just as complicated as our American English—often having even more rules and exceptions to rules.

You have already learned, better than you may realize, the most complicated system you are likely to learn in your life—your own language. It's easy to learn new words, because you have learned patterns of words. You may not be able to describe the patterns—professors have trouble with that—but we all have stored in our brains patterns that help us fit new words into the language we already know.

Reading and writing seem harder than listening and talking, which we learned before we knew what "hard" was. "Hard" turns out to be matching the sounds we know with the spellings we're trying to learn. In English we quickly come up against the fact that some sounds can be represented by more than one spelling and some spellings stand for more than one sound. It's easy to jump to the conclusion that written English has no rhyme nor reason. Its reason we can leave to professors, who tell us the spelling of English works better in the long run than if there were only one spelling to one sound, because it shows how words are related to each other. Let's think about rhyme rather than reason.

Pit rhymes with *bit*, *pet* rhymes with *bet*, *pat* rhymes with *bat*. You couldn't say any of them wrong once you had learned to read English at all. And *pay* rhymes with *bay*. O.K., but so does *weigh*. If you hadn't seen and heard the word *weigh* you wouldn't know that, but if you saw the word *way* you couldn't miss; it will probably rhyme with *pay*. So, to tell you that *weigh* rhymes with *pay*, we simply respell *weigh* (WAY). Of course, in the dictionary you first learn to spell *weigh*. If you wrote *way* for *weigh*, people wouldn't know what you were writing about. Right after the printed form of the word **weigh,** in bold type as you see it here, we show you how to say it by spelling (WAY) surrounded by parentheses, those curved marks. This is the way it looks:

weigh (WAY) . . .

When the rhyme of a word is highly likely, as with the word *way*, we don't bother to repeat the spelling. Of course, with long words, you can't rhyme the whole thing with one other word, so long words are broken into the parts that stand for their syllables, which can be pronounced as if they were a series of short words, like this:

kid·nap (KID-nap)

It's easy to hear that *pit* doesn't quite rhyme with *pet* or *pat*, but they sound something alike. They begin and end the same, but the sound in the middle is different. *Pat* and *tap* come closer to rhyming, because the sound in the middle is the same. The sound in the middle of all these is the vowel sound. The beginning and ending sounds are consonant sounds. There can't be an English word without a vowel sound. There are short words like *a* and *I* and *oh* without consonant sounds. If you think of language as a stream, the vowels are the unbroken flow and the consonants interrupt the flow or divert it from one vowel channel to another. Consonant sounds are really just ways of beginning or separating vowel sounds. To make a consonant sound, the lips or tongue *do* something that marks a beginning, an end, or a change. A simple vowel sound can be carried on, as in a song, for as long as you have breath without changing the position of any part of your mouth. (You've heard a mother call "Paaaaat" for little Patrick.)

We've been saying vowel *sounds* and consonant *sounds* because the letters of the alphabet are traditionally called vowels and consonants and we haven't been talking about letters. You may have memorized that *a, e, i, o, u,* and sometimes *y* are vowels and the rest are consonants, but this doesn't tell us much about sounds. It just says that these letters are usually used in spelling to *represent* vowel or consonant *sounds.* There are many more vowel sounds, for example, than there are vowel letters in the alphabet, so the vowel letters are used with other letters, both vowels and some that are usually called consonants, to make spellings that stand for the vowel sounds. For example, *a* and *y* go together to stand for the vowel sound in the word *pay.*

When we talked about rhymes we were talking about matching sounds. In the pronunciations we have matched sounds among words by respelling words as necessary so that each vowel and consonant sound is represented by the letter or combination of letters that nearly always matches the same sound when it appears in the spelling of any English word. Of course, there are often other letters or combinations that may match the same sound, but if such a spelling matches one sound as often as another, it is avoided. For example, we never use the letter (c) to show pronunciations because it can stand for the first sound in *cut* and the last sound in *nice,* while (k) can stand only for the first sound in *cut,* and (ss) only for the last sound in *nice.*

CONSONANT SOUNDS

Let's look at the consonant sounds first, because most of them are represented in only one way in English spelling, and they are therefore simpler.

There are 25 consonant sounds; this is more than there are consonant letters in the alphabet, so some are shown by combinations. Fifteen of them are represented by spellings that could hardly be misread as any other sound: b, d, f, h, j, k, m, p, r, sh, t, v, w, y, z. A little explanation may be helpful for the others:

The spelling (ch) is always used for the sound in *church,* never for the sound in *Christmas,* where (k) is used: (KRISS-məss).

The letter (g) never stands for the sound that (j) usually represents; it is always the g in *go.*

The spelling (hw) is not familiar from printed words, but it accurately describes what we may do in pronouncing *wh* as in *when* (HWEN). In the speech of many Americans there is no difference in the sound of the words *which* and *witch,* but the dictionary shows the pronunciation used by those who do say them differently (HWICH) for *which* and (WICH) for *witch.*

The letter (l) turns up in two ways in the respellings; it stands for the sound in *lip* and *pal,* and it also sometimes stands for a syllable all by itself. This happens only after certain consonant sounds. The reason there is no vowel is that the tip of the tongue stays in the same place to make the sound for *l.* An example is the last syllable of *needle* (NEED-l).

The same thing is true of (n), which can also stand for a syllable by itself after the same consonant sounds. For example, *button* is pronounced (BUHT-n). Here the last vowel goes up the nose rather than out the mouth. The letter *n* is also involved in another

Key to Pronunciation

Letter Symbol for a Sound	Key Word and Its Respelling	Letter Symbol for a Sound	Key Word and Its Respelling
(a)	pat (PAT)	(ng)	thing (THING)
	barrel (BA-rəl)		finger (FING-gər)
(ah)	far (FAHR)	(o)	pot (POT)
(ai)	air (AIR)	(oh)	oh, boat (BOHT)
(aw)	jaw (JAW)	(oi)	oil (OIL)
(ay)	pay (PAY)	(oo)	boot, rule (ROOL)
(b)	bib (BIB)	(or)	for (FOR)
(ch)	church (CHURCH)	(ow)	power (POW-ər)
(d)	dad (DAD)	(p)	pop (POP)
(e)	pet (PET)	(r)	rear (RIHR)
(ee)	bee (BEE)	(s)	sits (SITS)
(ehr)	berry (BEHR-ee)	(sh)	shoe (SHOO)
(er)	term (TERM)	(ss)	case (KAYSS)
(f)	fifteen (fif-TEEN)	(t)	tapped (TAPT)
(g)	gag (GAG)	(th)	thing (THING)
(h)	hit (HIT)	(t̲h̲)	this (T̲H̲IS)
(hw)	when (HWEN)	(u)	put, book (BUK)
(i)	pit (PIT)	(uh)	cut (KUHT)
(igh)	sigh (SIGH)	(v)	valve (VALV)
(ihr)	pier (PIHR)	(w)	win (WIN)
(j)	judge (JUHJ)	(y)	yet (YET)
(k)	kick (KIK)	(y)	is also used in place of (igh) before two consonant letters as in child (CHYLD)
(ks)	mix (MIKS)	(z)	zippers (ZIP-ərz)
(kw)	quick (KWIK)	(zh)	pleasure (PLEZH-ər)
(l)	lip (LIP)		rouge (ROOZH)
	needle (NEED-l)	(ə)	represents the sound of any vowel spelling when a syllable is sounded very weakly, as in the first syllable of *a*bout, or the last syllables of it*e*m, gal-l*o*p, or foc*u*s, or the middle syllable of char*i*ty.
(m)	mum (MUHM)		
(n)	no (NOH)		
	button (BUHT-n)		

sound called an "eng." We show it by the letters (ng) as in *finger* (FING-gər). Here the g is repeated because it stands for the beginning of the last syllable, in addition to helping to represent the "eng." But there is only one sound for g in the word *hanger* (HANG-ər). (By the way, you have to say each example out loud wherever examples are given, or you may not hear what we're talking about.)

Because the letter *s* at the end of some words can stand for a sound like (z) as in *daisies* (DAY-ZEEZ), the spelling (ss) is sometimes used to stand for the sound in a word like *mass*.

Two sounds are represented by the letters *th* in the English spelling. We represent the sound in the word *thing* in the ordinary way, and for the sound in the word *this*, we underline the (th): (THISS).

The spelling (zh) is not one you will find in many words, but when you see it in the respellings it's easy to know by comparing it with the familiar combination (sh) that it stands for the sound in *pleasure* (PLEZH-ər).

VOWEL SOUNDS

Vowel sounds are often called short and long, not according to how they are spelled but according to how they sound. In making a short or unglided vowel sound, the tongue and mouth don't move, so there is just one sound. In a long or glided vowel sound, the tongue or the lips move during the sound, so there is a "glide" from one position to another. You don't need to know a short from a long vowel sound to use the dictionary, but we'll describe them separately.

There's not much to say about the short or unglided vowel sounds in the words *pit*, *pet*, *pat*, and *pot*. They present no questions in spellings, but there are two other short or unglided vowel sounds whose spellings overlap and need to be clarified. The vowel sound in the word *cut* is different from the vowel sound in *put*, even though they are both represented by *u*.

To show the difference, we have used in the pronunciations a simple difference in spelling. When we see the spelling *uh* by itself we automatically think of the vowel sound in *cut* (KUHT), so this vowel sound is always shown that way. The vowel sound in the word *put* may be represented in other ways, as in the words *could* and *book*, which have the same vowel sound. To keep it simple we stick with the (u) for this sound. So *could* is (KUD) and *book* is (BUK).

The long or glided vowel sounds are each represented in the respellings by two or more letters together. They are seen in more different spellings than the short or unglided vowel sounds, but there is one spelling in each case that can hardly be misread. The vowel sounds in *bee*, *pay*, *jaw*, and *oil* don't present any questions when they are spelled that way in the respellings.

The only thing to remember about the spelling (oo) for the vowel sound in *boot* is that in the respellings it never stands for the sound in *book*. When the (oo) spelling is preceded by the letter *y* (yoo), it is obvious that it matches the vowel sound of the word *you*. This sound can be represented by other spellings, as in the words *few* (FYOO) and *cute* (KYOOT).

The sound of the word *oh!* is obvious, so we always use that spelling for the same sound in other words, as in the word *boat* (BOHT).

Similarly, the sound for the syllable *ah* is obvious. It's what the doctor asks you to say when he looks down your throat. It is used in words like *father* (FAH-ther) and *far* (FAHR).

When somebody pinches you, you may say *ow!* This is the vowel sound in *owl*. It is also used to stand for the vowel sound in words that may be spelled with *ou*, such as the word *out* (OWT).

The vowel sound in *night* is represented by the spelling (igh) in the respellings. It often appears in words formed like *bite* (BIGHT). Because this three-letter combination may be hard to read when it comes before two or more consonant letters, we substitute (y) for the same sound in such words as *child* (CHYLD).

When you make a consonant such as (t) after a vowel sound, you stop the vowel sound suddenly. (Such a consonant sound is called a "stop" because of this.) But when you end a vowel sound with (r), the movement of the tongue changes the vowel sound a little because the tongue starts moving while the vowel sound is still occurring. Normal spelling reflects this fact, so we have to represent some vowel sounds followed by (r) in different ways in the respellings.

The vowel sound in *fairy* is the same as the vowel sound in *air*, so this presents no problem, even though we do not use the spelling (ai) except before (r). The first vowel sound in the word *barrel* is separated in the respellings from the (r) thus (BA-rəl) so you won't be led to pronounce it with the vowel sound in *far*, which is (FAHR). The first vowel sound in the word *berry* is represented by (BEHR) so you will pronounce it like the syllable *eh* rather than like the vowel sound in *term*. The vowel sound in *pier* is represented as in (PIHR) so you won't say it like the vowel sound in *fir*.

The syllable *or* is pronounced differently in different words by people in different places, but all the various sounds are represented in the pronunciations as (or). Some people say the words *horse* and *hoarse* differently. Also some people say the first syllable of *forest* differently from the word *for*. But many people say these the same, so they are all shown the same: *horse* and *hoarse* (HORSS); *forest* as (FOR-ist), not (FAHR-ist), which is one pronunciation.

Anyone can tell that Americans don't all speak alike. The purpose of the respellings is not to have everybody say a word exactly the same, but to show you how to say it in the way of talking you have grown up with. If a Southerner interprets the respellings the way they look to him, he may not make the same sounds as a person from Chicago, but they will both be right for their part of the country. There is no such thing as a single Southern accent. Some Southerners saying (SOR) for the word *sore* may sound to the Chicagoan as if they were saying *so-uh*, but that's O.K. The "dropping of the r," as it is called, is done by educated people in several parts of the country.

Finally there is one more vowel sound; you'll see the symbol for it more often in the respellings than any other. It is represented by an upside-down *e*, thus (ə). (It is called "schwa" (SHWAH), but you don't need to know that to use it.) The reason you see this symbol more often is that any of the vowel spellings may stand for this sound when it is in a syllable pronounced weakly and briefly and another syllable in the word is loud. It is the vowel sound produced when the mouth is relaxed and the tongue is neither high nor low nor forward nor backward. You can hear the sound in the first syllable of the word *about* (ə-BOWT), or in the last syllables of *item* (IGH-təm), *gallop* (GAL-əp), or *focus* (FOH-kəss), and the middle syllable of *charity* (CHA-rə-tee).

In the key, the letter symbol for each sound is shown first in parentheses. Following the sample, or key word comes the pronunciation in parentheses.

The part of the word that stands for the syllable that is spoken most loudly is shown in SMALL CAPITAL letters, as (PROM-i-nənt) for *prominent*.

Latin and Greek Roots

by Margaret D. Parks

As you have probably discovered, many of our so-called "English" words have been borrowed from other languages. The earliest beginnings of what we call English were the languages of the Angles, Saxons, and Jutes, tribes who came from what is now Germany to settle in England more than 1,500 years ago. Later many words were taken directly into our everyday speech from French, Spanish, American Indian, and other languages, with little or no change in spelling or pronunciation.

A much larger group of words has developed from the Latin and Greek languages. Here something quite different happened—something more important than the mere borrowing of a word (such as *patio* from Spanish, *cafe* from the French language, and *raccoon* from American Indian).

The important difference is that the Latin words we borrowed are mostly *parts,* or *roots,* to which we have added prefixes and suffixes, thus creating many words and shades of meaning from one root. In addition, two roots are often combined to meet a need for a new word.

Our list of words has multiplied as many new words have been developed from a single Latin root. From Latin we have taken the word *manus,* meaning "hand," and today this root and its meaning appear in such words as: *manicure, manual, manufacture, manuscript, manner,* and *manipulate.* When *manu* is combined with the Latin root *script* (writing), we get the word *manuscript* (handwriting). When *manu* is combined with the Latin root *fact* (to make) and the ending *ure* (the act of), we have the word *manufacture,* meaning "make by hand."

The Latin root *memor,* meaning "mindful," can be recognized in these words: *memory, remember, memorial, memorandum, memorize,* and *remembrance.* In each of these words, the meaning "keep in mind" can be found.

An even greater multiplication of words occurs when the roots are combined with prefixes to make words with new meanings. The Latin root *fuse* (to pour) joins with prefixes to form such words as:

refuse	(re = back)
confuse	(con = together)
effuse	(ef = out of)
transfuse	(trans = across)

We increase the number of our words even more with the addition of appropriate endings. The root *dict,* meaning "to say or tell," can take the prefix *pre* (ahead), making the word *predict* (to tell ahead). This root can also add suffixes to become these words: *prediction, predictable,* and *predictive.*

A knowledge of some of the most frequently used Latin roots can be an important tool in increasing your vocabulary. Together with a study of prefixes and suffixes, recognizing roots helps make clear the meaning of many new words.

A study of Latin roots, prefixes, and suffixes is a valuable aid in understanding meaning and in spelling and syllabication. But only by using a dictionary can the student learn exact definitions for words, correct usage, placement of accent, and any changes in spelling that may occur when an ending is added.

The examples given below will serve to show how Latin roots are used to form many more words related in meaning.

In the first section of examples that follow, Latin roots are used to form English words with various endings, making nouns, verbs, and adjectives. These words are used in sentences that help to explain their meanings.

The second group of examples shows how Latin roots are combined with prefixes to create new meanings.

The third section contains a list of additional roots, each Latin root with a list of words built from it. With the aid of a dictionary, you can gain valuable practice and understanding by using each word in a sentence of your own.

A list of frequently used Greek roots with examples follows this section and can be used by you to write your own definitions.

Meanings of prefixes are listed separately for reference. You should always check the dictionary for the correct spelling of a new word, since slight spelling changes of a root may occur when suffixes are added.

Meanings of Some Common Latin Roots and Related Words

ACT (do, drive)

The *action* (doing) of the wind operates a windmill.

An *active* (doing) person is usually healthy.

How do you *react* to that idea? (*re* = back)

CAPT (take, hold)

The criminal was soon *captured* (taken).

A *captive* (taken) bird will sometimes refuse to sing.

The prisoner begged his *captor* (one who took him) for release.

CREAT (make)

The children *create* puppets to tell stories.

Charles Schulz is the *creator* of Snoopy.

His *creative* ideas are always interesting.

The *creation* of a work of art is often difficult.

A shrew is a tiny mouse-like *creature*.

DICT (say, speak, tell)

Her *diction* (way of speaking words) is very pleasant.

Can you *predict* (tell ahead) the weather? (*pre* = before)

A *dictator* tells people what they can do.

Please *dictate* (say the words) the letter you want written.

A *dictionary* is an important reference.

It is not polite to *contradict* (speak against) another person's opinion. (*contra* = against)

EQU (same)

In an *equation* both parts have the same value.

An *equal* sign separates the two parts.

Four quarters are the *equivalent* of a dollar.

An *equinox* occurs twice a year, when days and nights are the same length.

The *equator* is an imaginary line that divides the earth into equal parts.

An *equilateral* triangle has sides that are the same in length.

Equality of people's rights is guaranteed by law in our country.

LECT (read)

The speaker's *lecture* was made from written notes.

The papers were on a *lectern* as he spoke.

LOC (place)

The best *location* (place) for a store is one that has enough parking space.

Can you *locate* (find the place) Lake Erie on the map?

The *local* (placed nearby) drugstore sells magazines.

PED (foot)

Pedestrians (foot travelers) must stay in the crosswalk when crossing the street.

The bicycle *pedal* (part operated by foot) needs to be repaired.

Statues are often placed on tall *pedestals* (feet or bases).

LIBER (free)

The campers were given the *liberty* (freedom) to choose their activities.

The coach was *liberal* (free) with praise for the team.

The *liberated* (made free) prisoners wept with joy.

VAC (empty, free from)

There was no *vacancy* (empty space) at the motel.

The flood victims were *evacuated* (emptied) from the town. (*e* = from)

A *vacation* (free time) from our usual work is welcome.

This old house has been *vacant* (empty) for many years.

Dirt is pulled into the empty space in a *vacuum* cleaner.

An elected official must *vacate* (make empty) his office at the end of his term.

VIS (see)

The moon is *visible* (can be seen) on a clear night.

He *visited* (went to see) Europe last year.

The travelers had a *vista* (distant sight or view) of the Rocky Mountains.

An eagle's *vision* (ability to see) is excellent.

It might be fun to be *invisible* (not seen).

Visual aids can help to explain an idea.

UNI (one, single)

The fifty states are *united* (as one) to make one nation.

The team made a *united* effort to win.

Her idea was *unique* (only one of its kind).

The children's choir sang in *unison* (one sound together).

The appearance of his writing is *uniform* (one form).

Astronomers study the *universe* (all things together as one).

It is not easy to ride a *unicycle* (one-wheeled vehicle).

Two sets can be joined to make a *union.*

The broken *unit* (one part) cannot be used again.

Adding Prefixes and Suffixes Can Make New Words

DUCT (lead, take)

Furnace *ducts* (pipes leading out) carry hot or cold air to rooms in a house.

The club will *conduct* (lead together) a program. (*con* = together)

Wheat is a *product* (thing taken forth) of the Great Plains. (*pro* = forth)

A narrow canal called an *aqueduct* leads water to places where it is needed. (*aqua* = water)

This money can be *deducted* (taken away) from your income tax. (*de* = away)

FER (carry, bring)

Transfer (carry across) the package from the car to the plane. (*trans* = across)

My question *refers* (carries back) to your first statement. (*re* = back)

The leaders will *confer* (come together) with each other about the problem. (*con* = with, together)

They plan to *defer* (hold away) judgment until later. (*de* = away)

Some people *prefer* (hold in first place) living in a city. (*pre* = before)

FLEX (bend)

The thin copper wire is quite *flexible.* (easy to bend)

A *reflection* in a mirror bends the light back to show an image.

When the doctor tapped his patient's knee, *reflex* action caused the leg to move.

FUSE (pour)

The surgeon ordered blood *transfused* to the patient. (*trans* = across)

He *refused* to accept the offer. (*re* = back)

The facts were *confused* and hard to put together. (*con* = together)

Ink mixed with water *diffuses* to a lighter color. (*dif* = apart)

GRESS (step, go)

She was praised for *progress* in her studies. (*pro* = forward)

The cave's *ingress* was narrow. (*in* = into)

Instead of improving, he seemed to *regress.* (*re* = back)

An *aggressive* person may try to bully others. (*ag* = toward)

To save time, do not *digress* from the subject. (*di* = away)

They were warned not to *transgress* the rules. (trans = across, against)

HABIT (live)

A tiger's usual *habitat* is the jungle.

The people who *inhabit* these islands are friendly.

JECT (throw)

A machine is used to *project* a picture on a screen. (*pro* = before)

You can *reject* the idea if it does not please you. (*re* = back)

A doctor can *inject* medicine through your skin. (*in* = into)

Do you *object* to that idea? (*ob* = against)

Ripe seeds are *ejected* by most plants. (*e* = out)

MIT (send, go)

The radio can *transmit* messages for great distances. (*trans* = across)

This ticket will *permit* you to enter. (*per* = through)

The group *committed* itself to the project. (*com* = together)

Submit the plan to the committee. (*sub* = under)

A pass will *admit* you to the show. (*ad* = to)

Chimneys *emit* smoke from material which is burning. (*e* = out)

MOT (move)

The *motion* of the boat stopped when the *motor* was shut off.

What was his *motive* (reason, cause to move) for doing that?

The manager was *promoted* to president. (*pro* = ahead)

His assistant was *demoted* to a lower position. (*de* = down)

PEL (push, drive)

Gasoline engines *propel* the cars. (*pro* = forward)

There was a campaign to *expel* the traitors. (*ex* = out)

We tried to *compel* them to leave. (*com* = together)

A spray is used to *repel* insects. (*re* = back)

Strong winds arose to *dispel* the clouds. (*dis* = away)

PEND (hang)

A lovely *pendant* hung from a chain around her neck.

You can *depend* on his promise. (*de* = from)

Lightning signaled the *impending* storm. (*im* = over)

Suspend the ornaments from the Christmas tree. (*sus* = under)

PLI (fold)

Leather is *pliable* when it is soft.

A *duplicate* copy can be made with carbon paper. (*du* = twice)

Events in the mystery story became *complicated.* (*com* = together)

The accused person was *implicated* in several crimes. (*im* = in)

PORT (carry)

Some hotels have *porters* to carry luggage.

A *portable* radio is a great convenience.

The campers carried their canoes on a *portage* between lakes.

The spy was *deported* from the country. (*de* = away)

Bananas are *imported* to the United States. (*im* = in)

Coffee is *exported* from South America. (*ex* = out)

Vegetables are *transported* to the city in trucks. (*trans* = across)

POS (e) (put, place)

Compose a letter telling what you want. (*com* = together)

Money *deposited* in a bank earns more money in interest. (*de* = away, aside)

The *opposing* team won the toss. (*op* = against)

Used paper is *disposed* of in trash cans. (*dis* = away)

The speaker *proposed* a new plan. (*pro* = forward)

Skin *exposed* to the sun will tan or burn. (*ex* = out)

PRESS (push, squeeze)

Steam makes *pressure* to run engines.

The car stopped when the driver *depressed* the brake pedal. (*de* = down)

Wood pulp is *compressed* to make paper. (*com* = together)

The performer tried to *impress* her audience. (*im* = in)

It was hard for the speaker to *express* his feelings. (*ex* = out)

People ruled by others may feel *oppressed.* (*op* = against)

RUPT (break)

A *rupture* in the water pipe flooded the street.

The volcano is expected to *erupt.* (*e* = out)

Delays *disrupted* the schedule. (*dis* = apart)

A news flash *interrupted* the program. (*inter* = between)

A *bankrupt* business has no money.

SCRIPT (write)

The author's *description* is exciting. (*de* = down)

A *postscript* was added to her letter. (*post* = after)

The *inscription* on the monument was a poem. (*in* = in)

A doctor's *prescription* is needed before a drug is given. (*pre* = before)

SECT (divide, cut)

A *section* of the audience remained standing.

Highways *intersect* at a cloverleaf. (*inter* = across)

A square can be *bisected,* making two triangles. (*bi* = two)

The instructor showed how to *dissect* a frog. (*dis* = apart)

SPECT (look, see)

Spectators cheered the winning team.

The Grand Canyon is one of nature's *spectacles.*

A *specimen* of moon rock is studied carefully.

Firemen *inspect* buildings for safety. (*in* = into)

Farmers *expect* a good corn crop. (*ex* = forward to)

The *suspect* was kept under close watch. (*sus* = under)

Prospects seem good for a fishing trip. (*pro* = ahead)

In *retrospect,* it seems to us that the trip was successful. (*retro* = back)

STRICT (hold tight)

Some of the rules seem very *strict.*

Swimming is *restricted* to certain hours. (*re* = back)

The travelers moved single file through the *constricted* passageway. (*con* = together)

STRUCT (build)

The *structure* at the corner is an office building.

Two girls worked to *construct* a playhouse. (*con* = together)

An iron gate *obstructs* the entrance. (*ob* = against)

The hurricane caused *destruction* of property. (*de* = down)

If he is well-*instructed*, he can work out the problem. (*in* = into)

TORT (twist)

A *tortuous* path led to the mountaintop.

His face was *contorted* with pain. (*con* = together)

The kidnappers planned to *extort* money from the victim's family. (*ex* = out of)

TRACT (draw, pull)

A *tractor* moved the heavy logs.

The wheels lost *traction* on the ice.

The show *attracted* a large crowd. (*at* = toward)

The amount *subtracted* should leave a balance. (*sub* = down)

A *protractor* is used to extend lines. (*pro* = ahead of)

The cat purred and *retracted* its claws. (*re* = back)

Orange juice can be *extracted* and frozen. (*ex* = out)

The *contraction* for "I am" is "I'm." (*con* = together)

VENT (come)

A storm *prevented* the plane from landing. (*pre* = before)

The *convention* was held in a hotel. (*con* = together)

It was difficult to *circumvent* the muddy field. (*circum* = around)

VERT (turn)

A loud noise *diverted* her attention from her book. (*di* = away)

Banks and some stores will *convert* checks into cash. (*con* = into, together)

The property *reverts* to its original owner. (*re* = back)

A Study List of Additional Latin Roots

AQUA (water): aqualung, aquanaut, aquaplane, aquarium, aquatic, aquamarine, aquacade, aqueduct

BENE (good): benefit, benefactor, benevolent, beneficial, benediction

CED (to go): proceed, succeed, exceed, procedure, recede

CENT (hundred): cent, century, centipede, percent, centennial

CEPT (to take): accept, except, concept, deceptive

CHORUS (song, dance): choral, chorale, choreographer, chorus

CHRON (time): chronicle, chronic, chronometer, chronology

CIVI (citizen): civil, civilization, civic, civilian

CLUDE (to shut, close): conclude, include, preclude, exclude

CRED (belief, faith): credit, discredit, credentials, credible, incredulous, credibility

CUMUL (heap, mass): cumulus, accumulate, cumulative

CYCL (circle): cyclone, bicycle, cyclotron, encyclopedia

DONUM (gift): donor, donate, donation

DURA (lasting for a length of time): durable, endure, obdurate, during, duration

FLICT (to strike): inflict, conflict, afflict

FRACT (to break): fraction, fracture, fractious, fragile, fragment, refract, infraction

FUSE (pour): refuse, transfuse, confuse, diffuse, effusive

GRAD (step): grade, graduate, gradual, degrade, upgrade

LEGIS (law): legal, legacy, legislature, legitimate

LITTERA (written letter): literal, literary, literature, illiterate

MAL (bad): malice, malignant, malign, malevolent, malefactor, malediction, malfeasance

MANU (hand): manual, manufacture, manuscript, manner, manicure, manipulate

MARE (sea): marine, mariner, submarine, aquamarine, maritime

MEMOR (mindful): memory, remember, memorial, memorandum, memorize, remembrance

NOM (name): nominee, nominate, denomination, denominator

OPERA (works): opera, operetta, operate, operable, cooperate, operative

PRIMUS (first rank, most important): primer, primary, primate, prime, primeval, primitive

SEQU (to follow): sequel, sequence, consequent, subsequent

SIMIL (like): similar, simile, simulation

SOLV (to loosen, release, unbind): solution, solve, solvent, dissolve, resolve, resolution

SPIR (to breathe): aspire, expire, respire, perspire, transpire, inspire, conspire, conspirator, conspiracy

TRIBU (to give): contribute, tributary, attribute, distribute, tribe

Frequently Used Greek Roots

From the Greek language we have also borrowed parts of words and frequently put two or more Greek words together to create new ones. Three Greek words are combined here:

auto (self) + bio (life) + graph (writing) = autobiography (a story of one's own life)

A number of our words related to science have been built this way. For example:

micro(small) + scope(see) = microscope (an instrument for looking at small things)

See how many English words you can think of that contain the following Greek roots.

astro (star)	mono (one, single)
auto (self)	naut (seaman)
bio (life)	ology, logy (study)
geo (earth)	para (beside, along) with)
gram (small)	phone (sound, voice)
graph (writing)	photo (light)
gyro (circle)	plane (flat, level)
hemi (halt)	poly (much, many)
hydro (water)	scope (see)
kine (move)	sphere (ball, globe)
meter (measure)	tele (far away)
micro (small)	

The meanings listed above will help to define the following words:

astro + logy	hydro + plane
astro + naut	kine + scope
auto + graph	mono + graph
bio + graph + y	micro + phone
bio + logy	para + graph
bio + scope	photo + graph
geo + graph + y	poly + graph
geo + met (ry)	tele + gram
geo + logy	tele + met (ry)
gyro + scope	tele + phone
hemi + sphere	tele + scope

Latin Prefixes

ab (a, abs): from, away

ad (ac, af, ag, al, an, ap, ar, as, at): to, toward

circum: around

com (co, col, con, cor): with, together

contra: against

de: from, away, down

dis (di, dif): apart, away, not

ex (e, ef): from, out, out from, out of

in (il, im): in, into

in (il, im): not

inter: among, between

intro: within

non: not

ob (oc, of, op): against

per: through

post: after

pre: before, ahead

pro: before, in front of, forth, forward, out, ahead of

re (red): again, back

retro: back

sub (sus): under, down

trans (tra): across

These are the most common meanings of Latin prefixes. Meanings may change slightly according to use in English words.

A, a (AY) *noun.* 1. The first letter of the English alphabet. 2. In some grading systems, the mark representing the best grade: She received an "A" in spelling. 3. In music the sixth note in the C scale. —(uh or ə) *indefinite article.* One or any: Pick *a* piece of candy from the box.

a- *prefix.* 1. On, in, to, or at, as in *a*top and *a*shore. 2. In the act or condition of, as in *a*sleep and *a*drift.

aard·vark (AHRD-vahrk) *noun.* A warm-blooded burrowing animal of Africa, with long ears, tongue, and snout.

ab- *prefix.* From, away from, or off: *ab*normal.

A.B. Also **B.A.** *abbreviation.* Bachelor of Arts.

a·back (ə-BAK) *adverb* or *adjective.* (Rare) Backward, toward the back. —**taken aback.** Surprised, startled.

ab·a·cus (AB-ə-kəss) *noun.* A device with rows of beads set in a frame, used for mathematical problems. **abacuses.**

a·ban·don (ə-BAN-dən) *verb.* 1. To desert; leave or withdraw from completely: The passengers *abandoned* the sinking ship. 2. To give up or discontinue: The search for the plane was *abandoned* after two weeks. **abandoned, abandoning.** —*noun.* Recklessness; lack of care.

a·bash (ə-BASH) *verb.* To embarrass or shame: News of his failure *abashed* John. **abashed, abashing.**

a·bate (ə-BAYT) *verb.* To make or become less in amount, strength, or degree: His pain *abated* after treatment. **abated, abating.**

ab·bey (AB-ee) *noun.* A place where monks or nuns live; a monastery or convent.

ab·bot (AB-ət) *noun.* The head or superior of a monastery.

abbr. *abbreviation.* Abbreviation.

ab·bre·vi·ate (ə-BREE-vee-ayt) *verb.* To make shorter; especially to make a word shorter by leaving out letters: She *abbreviated* "avenue" to "ave." **abbreviated, abbreviating.**

ab·bre·vi·a·tion (ə-bree-vee-AY-shən) *noun.* A shortened form, especially of a word.

ABC's *noun, plural.* 1. The alphabet: My little brother just learned his *ABC's*. 2. The basic facts of any subject.

ab·di·cate (AB-di-kayt) *verb.* To resign; give up officially (a position or power): The king has *abdicated* his throne; he is no longer king. **abdicated, abdicating.**

ab·do·men (AB-də–mən or ab-DOH-mən) *noun.* 1. The belly; the front part of the body between the ribs and the pelvis, containing the stomach and intestines. 2. In insects and some other animals, the rear section of the body.

ab·dom·i·nal (ab-DOM-ə-nl) *adjective.* Of or related to the stomach or intestines. —**abdominally** *adverb.*

ab·duct (ab-DUHKT) *verb.* To take away by force; kidnap: The official was *abducted* and held for ransom. **abducted, abducting.**

ab·er·ra·tion (ab-ə-RAY-shən) *noun.* 1. A departure from the usual way. 2. A slight mental upset. 3. (Astronomy) The difference (caused partly by the motion of the earth) between a star's true position and the position it seems to occupy when viewed from the earth.

aardvark

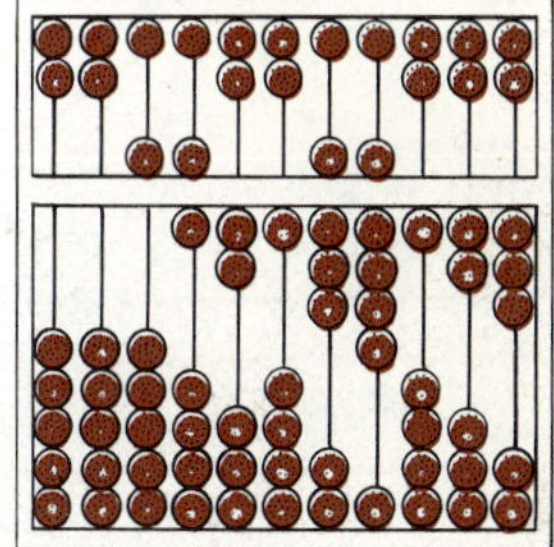

abacus

ab·hor (ab-HOR) *verb.* To detest; feel extreme dislike or loathing for: My friend *abhors* snakes and spiders. **abhorred, abhorring.**

ab·hor·rent (ab-HOR-ənt) *adjective.* Causing extreme dislike or loathing; detestable. —**abhorrently** *adverb.*

a·bide (ə-BIGHD) *verb.* 1. To stay or remain somewhere. 2. To tolerate; put up with: The coach cannot *abide* laziness in his players. 3. (Used with *by*) To obey or follow: *abide* by the rules. **abode** (ə-BOHD) or **abided, abiding.**

aborigine

a·bil·i·ty (ə-BIL-ə-tee) *noun.* Skill or power to do something: Jay has the *ability* to learn very fast. **abilities.**

a·blaze (ə-BLAYZ) *adjective.* 1. On fire: The leaves were set *ablaze* by the match. 2. Glowing brilliantly: The house was *ablaze* with lights.

a·ble (AY-bəl) *adjective.* 1. Having the ability (to do something): Raccoons are *able* to climb trees. 2. Skillful; talented: The violinist is an *able* musician; he plays well. **abler, ablest.** —**ably** *adverb.*

-able *suffix.* Indicates: 1. Able to, capable of, or possible to: eras*able*, mov*able*. 2. Deserving of: charit*able*, favor*able*. Also **-ble, -ible.** When used to form adverbs, **-ably.**

ab·nor·mal (ab-NOR-məl) *adjective.* Not normal or usual; irregular: Hot weather in winter would be *abnormal* in Alaska. —**abnormally** *adverb.*

a·board (ə-BORD) *adverb.* On board; on or within a ship, plane, train, or other transport: He came *aboard* when the ship docked. —*preposition.* On; in: Only ten passengers were *aboard* the bus.

a·bol·ish (ə-BOL-ish) *verb.* To do away with; cancel: The new law will *abolish* the tax on jewelry. **abolished, abolishing.**

ab·o·li·tion (ab-ə-LISH-ən) *noun.* 1. The act of doing away with; cancellation: He voted for the *abolition* of the sales tax. 2. [Capital A] The official ending of slavery in the U.S.

A-bomb (AY-bom) *noun. See* **atomic bomb.**

a·bom·i·na·ble (ə-BOM-ə-nə-bəl) *adjective.* 1. Detestable; hateful: Murder is an *abominable* crime. 2. Very bad or unpleasant; gross: Don't go to that restaurant; the food and service are *abominable.* —**abominably** *adverb.*

Abominable Snowman. A large, hairy creature, which is reported to resemble man and to live in the Himalayas.

ab·o·rig·i·ne (ab-ə-RIJ-ə-nee) *noun.* One of the earliest dwellers known to have lived in an area or country. **aborigines.**

a·bort (ə-BORT) *verb.* 1. To stop; discontinue. 2. To cancel one or more planned operations of a spacecraft, usually because of equipment failures. **aborted, aborting.**

a·bor·tion (ə-BOR-shən) *noun.* 1. The loss or removal of a developing child or offspring from a female before the normal time of birth. 2. Anything that ends or fails before it is completed.

a·bound (ə-BOWND) *verb.* To be numerous or plentiful: Salmon *abound* in this river. **abounded, abounding.**

a·bout (ə-BOWT) *preposition.* 1. Concerning; having to do with: The story is *about* horses. 2. All around: She strolled *about* the park. 3. In or around: The dog is somewhere *about* the house. 4. Related to: There is something strange *about* him. —*adverb.* 1. Around; all around: The child wandered *about.* 2. Almost; nearly: Linda is *about* ready. 3. In the opposite direction: The ship turned *about* and returned to port.

4. Approximately; nearly: The box weighs *about* ten pounds. —*adjective.* Moving around: Dad was up and *about* at sunrise. —**about to.** Ready, on the verge of.

about face. A military command to face the rear. —**about-face** *noun.* A complete change to the opposite direction: Dad did an *about-face* in his decision not to raise my allowance.

a·bove (ə-BUHV) *preposition.* 1. In or toward a place higher than; over: She cleaned the shelves *above* the desk. 2. Higher in rank or position than: A general is *above* a major. 3. Greater in amount or number than: Remove any packages *above* ten pounds. 4. Superior to in character or importance: An honest student is *above* cheating. —*adverb.* 1. Overhead; toward a higher place: The plane climbed *above.* 2. Earlier in a written work: Look *above* in this dictionary to find the word "abacus."

a·bove·board (ə-BUHV-bord) *adverb* or *adjective.* Clearly in sight, without tricks: The action in the game was *aboveboard;* there were no unfair plays.

a·breast (ə-BREST) *adverb* or *adjective.* 1. Side by side: The marines marched four *abreast.* 2. Keeping up with in awareness or development: Sandra is *abreast* of the latest styles.

a·bridge (ə-BRIJ) *verb.* To condense; shorten, especially a written work: The story was *abridged* from six to four pages. **abridged, abridging.**

a·bridg·ment (ə-BRIJ-mənt) Also **abridgement** *noun.* 1. A story, book, or other work that is a shortened form of a longer work; a condensation. 2. The act or process of abridging or shortening; the state of being abridged.

a·broad (ə-BRAWD) *adverb.* 1. Beyond one's own country: My teacher traveled *abroad* last summer to study in Italy. 2. Far and wide; extensively: The news of the victory spread *abroad* in the country. 3. Beyond one's usual dwelling place: The hungry wolves left their dens and prowled *abroad.*

a·brupt (ə-BRUHPT) *adjective.* 1. Sudden; unexpected: The army's *abrupt* retreat shocked the people. 2. Blunt or curt in manner: Her *abrupt* response showed that she was angry. 3. Steep: The hikers came to an *abrupt* rise in the trail. —**abruptly** *adverb.*

ab·scess (AB-sess) *noun.* A collection of pus in any part of the body, usually caused by infection. **abscesses.**

ab·sence (AB-sənss) *noun.* 1. A state or period of being away: Dad's note explained Tom's *absence* from school. 2. A lack: The *absence* of moisture caused the plant to wither. **absences.**

ab·sent (AB-sənt) *adjective.* 1. Not present; away. 2. Lacking. —(ab-SENT) *verb.* To keep oneself away: He *absented* himself from the meeting because he was ill. **absented, absenting.** —**absently** *adverb.*

ab·sent-mind·ed (AB-sənt-MIGHN-did) *adjective.* Forgetful; distracted; lost in thought: The *absent-minded* old man forgot to eat lunch. —**absent-mindedly** *adverb.*

ab·so·lute (AB-sə-loot) *adjective.* 1. Complete; without flaw: He trusted in the lawyer's *absolute* honesty. 2. Positive; certain: The detective has *absolute* proof of her guilt. 3. Unlimited; unrestrained: The tyrant possessed *absolute* power over his country. —**absolutely** *adverb.*

absolute zero. In theory the lowest possible temperature that a material could have, $-273.15°$C. or $-459.67°$F.

ab·solve (əb-ZOLV) *verb.* 1. To pardon; free from blame or guilt: The judge *absolved* the motorist of responsibility for the accident. 2. To release from a duty or obligation: Mother *absolved* Jane from her promise to wash the dishes. **absolved, absolving.**

ab·sorb (ab-SORB) *verb.* 1. To draw in; soak up (a liquid): The sponge *absorbed* the spilled water. 2. To take in without reflecting or rebounding: Drapes help to *absorb* sound in a room. 3. To hold the attention of; interest greatly. **absorbed, absorbing.**

ab·sorp·tion (ab-SORP-shən) *noun.* The process or act of absorbing, of drawing in or sucking up: The *absorption* of water by the sponge was rapid.

ab·stain (ab-STAYN) *verb.* To do without (something); refrain: Because he is overweight, Leo *abstains* from desserts. **abstained, abstaining.**

ab·sti·nence (AB-stə-nənss) *noun.* The act or condition of doing without (something): *Abstinence* from sugar is required by his diet.

ab·stract (ab-STRAKT) *adjective.* 1. Difficult or impossible to see, touch, measure, or understand: "Love" is a much more *abstract* word than "hug." 2. A style of art or design, usually modern. —(AB-strakt) *noun.* A summary: This *abstract* presents the main ideas of his speech. —*verb.* To summarize. **abstracted, abstracting.**

ab·surd (ab-SERD) *adjective.* Ridiculous; very silly: The belief that the moon is made of cheese is *absurd.* —**absurdly** *adverb.*

a·bun·dance (ə-BUHN-dənss) *noun.* A great quantity; an amount larger than needed: We had such an *abundance* of candy that we gave some away.

a·bun·dant (ə-BUHN-dənt) *adjective.* Very plentiful; more than needed: The huge forest provided us with an *abundant* supply of firewood. —**abundantly** *adverb.*

a·buse (ə-BYOOZ) *verb.* 1. To use improperly; misuse: By speeding, some motorists *abuse* the privilege of driving. 2. To mistreat; treat cruelly: He *abused* the dog by not giving it enough food. 3. To insult; speak harshly to: The angry player *abused* the umpire with his rude remarks. **abused, abusing.** —(ə-BYOOSS) *noun.* 1. An improper use; a misuse. 2. Bad treatment. 3. Insulting or extremely harsh language. **abuses.**

a·bu·sive (ə-BYOO-siv) *adjective.* 1. Insulting; harsh: Dad was angered by the rude fellow's *abusive* language. 2. Cruel; mean: The boy was scolded for his *abusive* treatment of his dog. —**abusively** *adverb.*

a·but·ment (ə-BUHT-mənt) *noun.* 1. The act of bordering or being next to. 2. The point at which two things make contact with each other, as the *abutment* of property to a road. 3. The foundation that supports and secures the end of a bridge or bridge cables.

a·byss (ə-BISS) *noun.* 1. A very deep chasm or space. 2. Something without end or limit: The comet streaked through the *abyss* of space. **abysses.**

ac *abbreviation.* Alternating current.

a·cad·e·my (ə-KAD-ə-mee) *noun.* 1. A school, usually a private school. 2. A school for special studies or instruction: She attends an *academy* of art. **academies.**

ac·cel·er·ate (ak-SEL-ə-rayt) *verb.* 1. To increase (a rate of speed): The driver *accelerated* when he wanted to pass the car ahead. 2. To increase or speed up (a process or development): The fertilizer *accelerated* the growth of the plant. **accelerated, accelerating.**

ac·cel·er·a·tion (ak-sel-ə-RAY-shən) *noun.* 1. An increase of speed or the rate at which speed changes. 2. The act of speeding up (a process).

ac·cel·er·a·tor (ak-SEL-ə-ray-tər) *noun.* A device for increasing speed, especially the gas pedal in an automobile.

ac·cent (AK-sent) *noun.* 1. The stress in speaking given to, or required by, a word or syllable: This dictionary shows *accent* by printing a syllable in small capital letters. 2. A mark that indicates which syllable in a word receives vocal emphasis or stress. 3. A special manner of speaking associated with a region or country: Julie has a Southern *accent.* —*verb.* 1. To pronounce with an emphasis or stress on a word or syllable: He *accents* his name on the second syllable. 2. To emphasize: make noticeable: The spices *accented* the flavor of the soup. **accented, accenting.**

ac·cept (ak-SEPT) *verb.* 1. To receive; take (something that is offered): Mother *accepted* the package from the mailman. 2. To believe in: I *accept* the doctor's explanation of my illness. 3. To approve of; receive with pleasure: The popular girl was *accepted* by her new playmates. **accepted, accepting.**

ac·cept·a·ble (ak-SEP-tə-bəl) *adjective.* 1. Satisfactory; worthy to be received or believed: Her homework was *acceptable.* 2. Appropriate or agreeable: That waltz will be *acceptable* for one dance. —**acceptably** *adverb.*

ac·cep·tance (ak-SEP-tənss) *noun.* 1. The act of receiving: His *acceptance* of the medal was greeted with cheers. 2. Believing or having confidence in: Further study led to his *acceptance* of the professor's ideas. 3. Approving of or receiving with pleasure: The new pitcher was delighted by the other players' *acceptance* of him.

ac·cess (AK-sess) *noun.* 1. An approach or way to a place: Rugged mountains and dense forests made *access* to the village difficult. 2. The permission or ability to enter or use: Our teacher has *access* to a tape recorder only on one day each week. **accesses.**

ac·ces·si·ble (ak-SESS-ə-bəl) *adjective.* Able to be approached, entered, or used; available: The fishing camp is *accessible* by boat. —**accessibly** *adverb.*

ac·ces·so·ry (ak-SESS-ə-ree) *noun.* 1. Something added to that which is basic, to provide convenience or improvement: Power steering and a spotlight are *accessories* on my automobile. 2. One who aids another in committing a crime: He was arrested as an *accessory* to the crime. **accessories.**

ac·ci·dent (AK-sə-dənt) *noun.* 1. An unexpected event or occurrence, especially one that involves damage, harm, or injury: Ted's arm was broken in the automobile *accident.* 2. Chance; luck: Ed was lucky; he found the trail by *accident.*

ac·ci·den·tal (ak-sə-DEN-tl) *adjective.* Happening by chance: Don't blame the driver; the breakdown of the bus was *accidental.* —**accidentally** *adverb.*

ac·claim (ə-KLAYM) *noun.* Spirited approval; applause: The election of the popular candidate was greeted with *acclaim.* —*verb.* To greet with approval; cheer for or applaud: The crowd at the parade *acclaimed* the hero as he passed by. **acclaimed, acclaiming.**

ac·cli·mate (ə-KLIGH-mət or AK-le-mayt) *verb.* To be, or become, accustomed to a new climate or new surroundings: The man from Florida is not yet *acclimated* to the weather in Alaska. **acclimated, acclimating.**

ac·com·mo·date (ə-KOM-ə-dayt) *verb.* 1. To supply with lodging or other services: The motel can easily *accommodate* all four of us for the first week of our vacation. 2. To hold; have a capacity for: The bus can *accommodate* 32 people. 3. To do a favor for; help out: I would like to *accommodate* you with a loan, but I don't have any money. **accommodated, accommodating.**

ac·com·mo·da·tion (ə-kom-ə-DAY-shən) *noun.* 1. (Plural) Room or lodging, as in a hotel, or a place aboard a train, ship, or other transport: The travel agent arranged for *accommodations* for us on the plane from New York. 2. An adjustment or settlement of differences: An *accommodation* was made so that both hostile nations could agree to the treaty. 3. The act or process of aiding, supplying, or holding.

ac·com·pa·ni·ment (ə-KUHM-pə-nee-mənt or ə-KUHMP-nee-mənt) *noun.* 1. Something which is added to a main thing or event: We are going to have a pep rally as an *accompaniment* to the big game. 2. Instrumental music which serves as background for the main voice or another instrument: Theresa always has piano *accompaniment* when she sings.

accordion

ac·com·pa·ny (ə-KUHM-pə-nee or ə-KUMP-nee) *verb.* 1. To join; go along with: Mary's lamb *accompanied* her to school. 2. To occur with; to be associated with: Smoke usually *accompanies* fire. 3. To play a musical accompaniment for: Helen sang and Ronald *accompanied* her on the piano. **accompanied, accompanying.**

ac·com·plice (ə-KOM-pliss) *noun.* One who aids another in committing a crime: He was arrested as the robber's *accomplice.* **accomplices.**

ac·com·plish (ə-KOM-plish) *verb.* To succeed in doing; finish; complete: Pat *accomplished* her plan to design a new dress. **accomplished, accomplishing. —accomplishment** *noun.*

ac·cord (ə-KORD) *noun.* Agreement; harmony: His account of the incident is in *accord* with that of the policeman. *—verb.* 1. To be in agreement or harmony. 2. To grant, present, or confer: The general *accorded* to the heroic soldier all the honors he deserved. **accorded, according.**

ac·cord·ance (ə-KOR-dənss) *noun.* Agreement; harmony: The judge's decision was in *accordance* with the law.

ac·cord·ing·ly (ə-KOR-ding-lee) *adverb.* 1. In harmony or accord with what has been established: School begins at 9 A.M.; *accordingly,* each child must be in his place at that time. 2. Therefore; hence: Ralph is on a diet; *accordingly,* he eats less than usual. **—according to.** 1. In harmony or accord with: The selection of honor students will be made *according to* the quality of the work done by the students over the past year. 2. As stated by; on the authority of: *According to* the map, we still have 20 miles to go.

ac·cor·di·on (ə-KOR-dee-ən) *noun.* A musical instrument with a row of keys resembling piano keys, and a pleated bellows that is squeezed to force air over metal reeds.

ac·count (ə-KOWNT) *noun.* 1. A detailed explanation or report: Our school newspaper gave an interesting *account* of the basketball game. 2. A record of finances; a detailed explanation of business dealings: Judy's bank *account* showed that she had $100. 3. Worth; importance: They looked down on the tramp as a man of little *account.* *—verb.* 1. To provide an explanation or give reasons for: Mrs.

Rossi *accounted* for Mary's absence. 2. To give a detailed explanation of business or financial dealings: The treasurer *accounted* for the spending of the class dues. **accounted, accounting.** —**take into account.** To consider; make allowance for: The teacher *took* Joan's illness *into account* when making up her final grade. —**of no account.** Having little or no importance; worthless: Money is *of no account* to someone lost in the woods.

ac·count·ant (ə-KOWNT-ənt) *noun.* A person whose job it is to keep or inspect financial records.

ac·cu·mu·late (ə-KYOOM-yə-layt) *verb.* 1. To collect; gather together: The campers *accumulated* piles of wood for the fire. 2. To increase; add onto: Rust began to *accumulate* on the bottom of the old ship. **accumulated, accumulating.**

ac·cu·mu·la·tion (ə-kyoom-yə-LAY-shən) *noun.* 1. A quantity or mass that develops or is gathered together: The *accumulation* of trash filled three baskets. 2. The process of collecting or gathering together: the *accumulation* of wealth.

ac·cu·ra·cy (AK-yər-ə-see) *noun.* The state of being correct or precise; exactness: Albert was careful to perform the experiment with *accuracy;* he wanted no mistakes.

ac·cu·rate (AK-yər-it) *adjective.* 1. Correct; precise; without mistake: His additions and subtractions were *accurate;* therefore, the teacher gave him an "A." 2. Close to or able to come close to a target or mark: Tex was very *accurate;* he hit the center of the target five times with six shots. —**accurately** *adverb.*

ac·cu·sa·tion (ak-yoo-ZAY-shən) *noun.* A charge of wrongdoing.

ac·cuse (ə-KYOOZ) *verb.* To charge with wrongdoing or misconduct; to blame: The policeman *accused* Ted of playing hooky. **accused, accusing.**

ac·cus·tom (ə-KUHSS-təm) *verb.* To make familiar with through experience or habit: If you practice every day, you can *accustom* yourself to your new skates. **accustomed, accustoming.**

ac·cus·tomed (ə-KUHSS-təmd) *adjective.* 1. Used to; in the habit of: Susan is *accustomed* to doing her homework before dinner. 2. Usual; normal: The little boy fell asleep at his *accustomed* bedtime.

ace (AYSS) *noun.* 1. An expert; a highly skilled person: The tennis *ace* has won many trophies and medals. 2. A playing card with one mark or spot, usually the card highest in value. —*verb.* (Slang) To get an A as a school grade: I *aced* that test. **aced, acing.**

ace

ache (AYK) *noun.* Pain; continuous hurting: Otto got a stomach *ache* from eating too much candy. **aches.** —*verb.* To have a dull or lasting pain: Paul's shoulder *ached* where it was struck with the baseball. **ached, aching.**

a·chieve (ə-CHEEV) *verb.* 1. To succeed in doing; to complete; accomplish: The committee *achieved* all of its goals for the year. 2. To gain or win: Henry *achieved* the highest rank in his class. **achieved, achieving.**

a·chieve·ment (ə-CHEEV-mənt) *noun.* Whatever is accomplished, completed, or gained: Edgar's winning the trophy was a great *achievement* for him.

ac·id (ASS-id) *noun.* 1. A chemical compound which usually has a bitter or sour taste and which turns blue litmus paper red when dissolved in water. 2. (Slang) LSD, a strong drug which can be harmful. —*adjective.* Tart; sharp tasting. —**acidly** *adverb.*

ac·knowl·edge (ak-NOL-ij) *verb.* 1. To admit to be true or correct: Alex *acknowledged* that he was responsible for the damage. 2. To give recognition to the authority of: The prince *acknowledged* the king to be his ruler. 3. To respond or reply to (a greeting or message): Sam *acknowledged* my greeting with a wave of his hand. 4. To show gratitude or give praise for (a favor, gift, or service). **acknowledged, acknowledging.**

ac·knowl·edg·ment (ak-NOL-ij-mənt) *noun.* 1. Something said or done in recognition of a message, service, greeting, or favor: The company awarded Dad a watch as an *acknowledgment* of his years of service. 2. An act of recognition of truth: Tim freely gave an *acknowledgment* of his faults.

acorn

ac·ne (AK-nee) *noun.* A type of skin disease accompanied by the appearance of pimples, especially on the face.

a·corn (AY-korn) *noun.* The nut of an oak tree.

a·cous·tic (ə-KOO-stik) *adjective.* Related or pertaining to sound or the sense of hearing: *Acoustic* tiles on a ceiling absorb sound and help to make a room quiet. —*noun.* (Plural) 1. The study of sound. 2. The way in which sound carries, especially throughout an enclosed room. —**acoustically** *adverb.*

acropolis

ac·quaint (ə-KWAYNT) *verb.* To make familiar with; make known or accustomed: Jack *acquainted* the new student with the rules of the school. **acquainted, acquainting.**

ac·quain·tance (ə-KWAYN-tənss) *noun.* 1. A person one knows who is not a close friend; a casual friend. 2. Familiarity with or knowledge of: I have no *acquaintance* with the rules of tennis. **acquaintances.**

ac·qui·esce (ak-wee-ESS) *verb.* To consent or submit (to) as necessary or unavoidable: Because he feared a strike, the employer *acquiesced* to the demands of the workers. **acquiesced, acquiescing.**

ac·quire (ə-KWIGHR) *verb.* To gain or earn for oneself; achieve. **acquired, acquiring.**

ac·qui·si·tion (ak-wə-ZISH-ən) *noun.* 1. Something that is gained or achieved: A new playground and a parking lot were two *acquisitions* of the school board. 2. The act or process of gaining or achieving: The *acquisition* of wealth usually requires years of hard work.

ac·quit (ə-KWIT) *verb.* 1. To proclaim not guilty; free from a charge of crime or misconduct or from an obligation: When the real thief confessed, the judge *acquitted* the other man. 2. To conduct (oneself); perform or behave. **acquitted, acquitting.** —**acquittal** *noun.*

a·cre (AY-kər) *noun.* A measure of land equal to 43,560 square feet, or 160 square rods. **acres.**

a·cre·age (AY-kər-ij) *noun.* Amount of land counted in acres.

ac·rid (AK-rid) *adjective.* 1. Sharp or stinging in smell or taste; bitter or irritating: The *acrid* smoke made the fireman's eyes water. 2. Sharp or bitter in speech or manner; very severe: Hal's *acrid* comments showed what a nasty person he is.

ac·ro·bat (AK-rə-bat) *noun.* A performer with superb balance, strength, and muscle control: The tightrope walker was the best *acrobat* at the circus.

ac·ro·nym (AK-rə-nim) *noun.* A word formed from the first letter or letters in a group of words: "Scuba" is an *acronym* for "self-contained underwater breathing apparatus."

a·crop·o·lis (ə-KROP-ə-liss) *noun.* A fortified hill used by the ancient Greeks as a stronghold against attacking armies.

a·cross (ə-KRAWSS) *preposition.* 1. From one side of to the other: I walked *across* the room to open the window. 2. On the other side of: Europe is *across* the Atlantic Ocean from America. 3. In contact with: I came *across* some old books in the attic. —*adverb.* From one side to the other: The bridge is safe; you can drive *across.*

act (AKT) *noun.* 1. Something done; a deed: Frank's rescue of the child was a brave *act.* 2. The process of doing: The policeman caught him in the *act* of committing a theft. 3. A law; formal decision: That practice was forbidden by an *act* of Congress. 4. A major division or part of a play or other long performance: Each of Shakespeare's plays is divided into five *acts.* 5. A performance, usually short, by an entertainer: The clown performed a juggling *act.* 6. A deception, a bluff: I think he is faking; his sickness is just an *act* to get attention. —*verb.* 1. To behave; function: The spoiled child *acted* badly. 2. To do something: When the child fell in the lake, we *acted* quickly to save her. 3. To perform before an audience, camera, or microphone. 4. To have an effect on or cause a reaction: When the medicine began to *act,* Pete's cold began to go away. 5. To deceive; bluff: I don't think Joe is really sorry; he is just *acting* as if he were. **acted, acting.** —**act up.** To perform, operate, or behave poorly: The teacher punished those students who *acted up* in class.

ac·tion (AK-shən) *noun.* 1. Something done; an act. 2. The doing of something: We observed the *action* of the carpenter as he sawed the lumber. 3. The series of events or deeds in a story or drama: The *action* of the novel involves the discovery of buried treasure. 4. A way of working, functioning, or producing an effect: The *action* of the engine became smoother when it was oiled. 5. Combat; warfare.

ac·tive (AK-tiv) *adjective.* 1. Busy; moving: Football is an *active* sport. 2. Working or functioning: Lava spouted from the *active* volcano. 3. Energetic; full of vitality: My grandmother is still *active* at 85; she does all her own housework. 4. (Grammar) Describing a verb that expresses an action performed by, rather than upon, its subject; the opposite of passive: In "Tom kicked the ball," the verb is *active.* —**actively** *adverb.*

ac·tiv·ist (AK-tiv-ist) *noun.* A person who works for changes in society by such direct actions as picketing or marching in the streets.

ac·tiv·i·ty (ak-TIV-ə-tee) *noun.* 1. The state of working or acting; the state of being active: The students were in a state of great *activity* preparing for the school play. 2. Action in a special area of interest: Of Sue's after-school *activities,* skating was her favorite. **activities.**

ac·tor (AK-tər) *noun.* A man who acts or performs before an audience, camera, or microphone.

ac·tress (AK-triss) *noun.* A female actor. **actresses.**

ac·tu·al (AK-choo-əl) *adjective.* Real; existing in reality: The Battle of Gettysburg was an *actual* event, not an imaginary one. —**actually** *adverb.*

ac·u·punc·ture (AK-yoo-puhngk-chər) *noun.* A healing process, developed in China, in which the body is punctured with needles.

a·cute (ə-KYOOT) *adjective.* 1. Very severe or intense: an *acute* attack of appendicitis. 2. Very keen or sharp in one of the senses: an *acute* sense of smell. 3. Sharp in understanding or insight; alert. 4. Pointed or sharp; having less than a 90-degree angle. —**acutely** *adverb.*

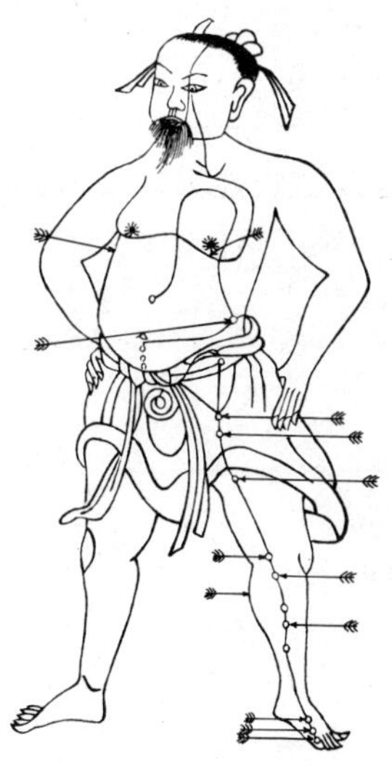
acupuncture

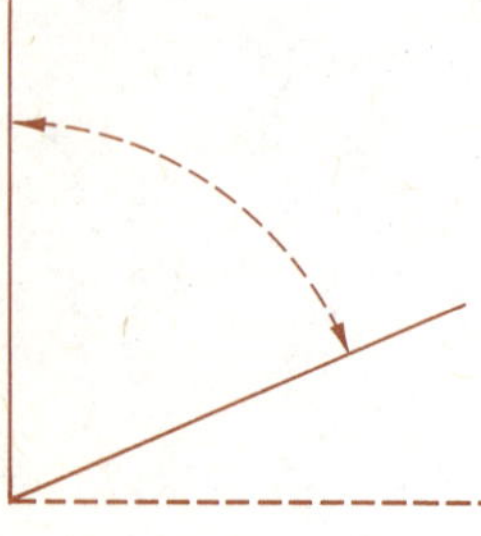
acute angle

adder

acute angle. Any angle less than 90 degrees.

ad *noun.* An advertisement.

A.D. *abbreviation.* "In the year of our Lord." Used to indicate dates after the birth of Christ.

ad·age (AD-ij) *noun.* A common or well-known saying; a proverb: "A penny saved is a penny earned" is a useful *adage.* **adages.**

a·dapt (ə-DAPT) *verb.* 1. To make appropriate; to adjust: The adult novel was *adapted* into a shorter story for children. 2. To adjust oneself to new conditions or surroundings: The new student finally *adapted* to our school. **adapted, adapting.**

a·dapt·a·ble (ə-DAP-tə-bəl) *adjective.* 1. Able to be changed or adjusted: The Skellys' summer cottage is *adaptable* to year-round living. 2. Able to adjust oneself to new conditions or surroundings: George is *adaptable;* he will be able to adjust to the changes of army life. —**adaptably** *adverb.*

ad·ap·ta·tion (ad-ap-TAY-shən) *noun.* 1. The act or process of adjusting or changing: *Adaptation* to the cold weather of Alaska requires careful planning and common sense. 2. That which is the result of an adjustment or change: The new hit tune is an *adaptation* of an old folk song.

add (AD) *verb.* 1. To put with or join to so as to increase: Mother *added* a box of cookies to our picnic lunch. 2. To combine into a total; find the sum of: If you *add* 12 and 12, you get 24. 3. To state or write further: The guide completed his description of the park and *added* that maps were available at the ranger's office. **added, adding.**

ad·dend (AD-end) *noun.* A number that when added to another number forms a sum: The sum of three and two is five; three and two are both *addends.*

ad·der (AD-ər) *noun.* 1. A type of small, harmless snake found mainly in North America. 2. A type of small, poisonous snake found mainly in Europe and Australia.

ad·dict (ə-DIKT) *verb.* To cause to become enslaved or given over to a habit: Regular use of narcotics will soon *addict* the user. **addicted, addicting.** —(AD-ikt) *noun.* A person enslaved by or given over to a habit, especially to the taking of drugs.

ad·dic·tion (ə-DIK-shən) *noun.* The state of being enslaved by a habit.

ad·di·tion (ə-DISH-ən) *noun.* 1. The act or process of adding, as in arithmetic. 2. Something added: The *addition* on our house gave us two more bedrooms.

ad·di·tion·al (ə-DISH-ən-l) *adjective.* Added; extra: The classroom didn't have enough chalk and erasers; the teacher had to order *additional* supplies. —**additionally** *adverb.*

ad·di·tive (AD-ə-tiv) *noun.* What is added; anything added to preserve or strengthen: Vitamins are often *additives* in cereal. **additives.**

ad·dress (ə-DRESS or AD-ress) *noun.* 1. The place where a person lives or a business is located; the place where mail is sent to a person or business: The little girl forgot her *address;* she could not find her home. 2. A formal speech: President Lincoln's *address* at Gettysburg is a famous speech. **addresses.** —(ə-DRESS) *verb.* 1. To make a formal speech: The President *addressed* the nation on television. 2. To write or indicate the destination on a letter or package: Timmy *addressed* the letter and mailed it. 3. To direct one's efforts or attentions to; apply oneself: Grandmother *addressed* herself to the job of completing her knitting. 4. To refer to or call by a special name or title: The lawyer *addressed* the judge as "Your Honor." **addressed, addressing.**

ad·e·noids (AD-n-oidz) *noun, plural.* Growths in the nose that hinder breathing when they become swollen or infected.

ad·ept (ə-DEPT) *adjective.* Highly skilled or accomplished; expert: Vince is an *adept* skier. —**adeptly** *adverb.*

ad·e·quate (AD-i-kwit) *adjective.* Sufficient; satisfactory; enough: One hamburger each will be *adequate;* we are not very hungry. —**adequately** *adverb.*

ad·here (ad-HIHR) *verb.* 1. To stick or cling (to): The gum *adhered* to the sole of Pat's shoe. 2. To be faithful (to); follow or observe: My Dad *adhered* to his promise; he took us to the beach. **adhered, adhering.**

ad·he·sive (ad-HEE-siv) *adjective.* Having the quality of clinging or sticking to: The bandage was attached with *adhesive* tape. —*noun.* A sticking or clinging material or substance: Glue is an *adhesive.* **adhesives.**

a·di·os (ah-dee-OHSS) *interjection.* A Spanish word used to say good-bye, though it actually means "to God": "*Adios,* amigos" is what a Spaniard says when he means "Good-bye, friends."

adj. *abbreviation.* Adjective.

ad·ja·cent (ə-JAY-sənt) *adjective.* Next to; near or adjoining: The playground is *adjacent* to the school.

ad·jec·tive (AJ-ik-tiv) *noun.* A word that is used to describe a person, place, or thing: *old* man, *calm* lake, *red* book, *train* track. **adjectives.**

ad·join (ə-JOIN) *verb.* To be next to or close to: Our garage *adjoins* our house. **adjoined, adjoining.**

ad·journ (ə-JERN) *verb.* To stop or discontinue for a time: At 11 A.M. the chairman *adjourned* the meeting until 2 P.M. —**adjourned, adjourning.**

ad·just (ə-JUHST) *verb.* 1. To change or alter to fit a need or situation: The schedule was *adjusted* so that all students could attend the assembly. 2. To regulate; make accurate: Tony *adjusted* the TV to make the color sharper. **adjusted, adjusting.**

ad·just·ment (ə-JUHST-mənt) *noun.* A change or an alteration: The store made an *adjustment* on the bill after Mother pointed out an error.

ad-lib (ad-LIB) *verb.* To talk or act without practice or preparation: When Eric forgot the speech he had prepared, he *ad-libbed* a new one. **ad-libbed, ad-libbing.** —*noun.* An unpracticed act, speech, or remark: The comedian used *ad-libs* onstage instead of a practiced act.

ad·min·is·ter (ad-MIN-iss-tər) *verb.* 1. To manage or have charge of: As chairman he *administered* the project for improving our neighborhood. 2. To give out, apply, or perform: A parent may *administer* a spanking to a naughty child. **administered, administering.**

ad·min·is·trate (ad-MIN-iss-trayt) *verb.* To manage or direct. **administrated, administrating.** —**administrator** *noun.*

ad·min·is·tra·tion (ad-min-iss-TRAY-shən) *noun.* 1. The management or direction of a business organization or office: The *administration* of a summer camp requires a thorough knowledge of children and children's activities. 2. A group of directors or administrators working together; the time during which they serve: The Korean War began during President Truman's *administration.*

ad·mi·ra·ble (AD-mər-ə-bəl) *adjective.* Deserving or worthy of praise; excellent: James has an *admirable* school record. —**admirably** *adverb.*

ad·mi·ral (AD-mər-əl) *noun.* A high-ranking officer in the Navy.

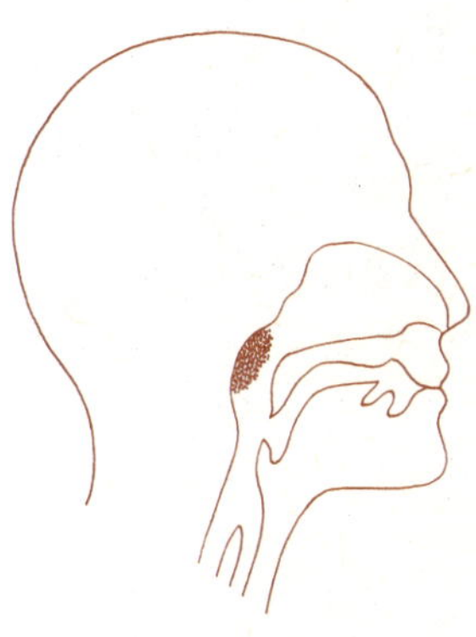

adenoids

ad·mi·ra·tion (ad-mə-RAY-shən) *noun.* High regard or respect, often with feelings of wonder or delight: Our class showed its *admiration* for the astronauts by writing essays in their honor.

ad·mire (ad-MIGHR) *verb.* To regard or respect highly, often with feelings of wonder or delight: Sandra *admired* the beautiful statue. **admired, admiring.**

ad·mis·sion (ad-MISH-ən) *noun.* 1. The act of permitting to enter; letting in: *Admission* to the zoo will begin at noon. 2. Entrance or acceptance into; the right or permission to enter a place, organization, or position: Jose's *admission* to the club delighted him. 3. A fee paid to enter a place or activity: *Admission* to the game is 50 cents. 4. A confession or acknowledgment of something: Victor's bold *admission* of guilt shocked the principal.

ad·mit (ad-MIT) *verb.* 1. To accept or to permit to enter: Our club *admitted* a new member. 2. To confess or concede: The soldier *admitted* that he was scared. **admitted, admitting.**

ad·mon·ish (ad-MON-ish) *verb.* To warn mildly; advise or caution about one's behavior or obligations: The teacher *admonished* the lazy student about his need for improvement. **admonished, admonishing.**

adobe

ad·mo·ni·tion (ad-mə-NISH-ən) *noun.* A mild warning; an expression of advice or caution about one's behavior or obligations: The policeman's *admonition* made the bus driver slow down.

a·do (ə-DOO) *noun.* Fuss; brisk activity; bother: There was much *ado* when the mouse appeared at the girls' party.

a·do·be (ə-DOH-bee) *noun.* 1. A sun-baked brick. 2. A building made of sun-baked brick: Many people in Mexico live in *adobes.* **adobes.**

ad·o·les·cence (ad-ə-LESS-nss) *noun.* The period between childhood and adulthood; the process of developing from a child to an adult.

ad·o·les·cent (ad-ə-LESS-ənt) *noun.* A person between childhood and adulthood. *—adjective.* 1. Growing up. 2. Youthful.

a·dopt (ə-DOPT) *verb.* 1. To accept or put to use as one's own: The students *adopted* that famous saying for their school motto. 2. To take or accept legally (another person's child) as your own: My aunt and uncle *adopted* a baby from the orphanage. **adopted, adopting.**

a·dop·tion (ə-DOP-shən) *noun.* 1. The acceptance or use (of something) as one's own: The *adoption* of the famous tune for the school song was a popular decision. 2. The legal acceptance (of another person's child) as one's own.

a·dor·a·ble (ə-DOR-ə-bəl) *adjective.* 1. Worthy of great devotion, love, or honor. 2. Deserving of worship or divine honor. 3. (Informal) Very charming, desirable, or attractive: **—adorably** *adverb.*

a·dore (ə-DOR) *verb.* 1. To give great devotion, love, or honor to. 2. To worship or give divine honor to: The shepherds *adored* the infant Jesus at Bethlehem. 3. (Informal) To regard as charming, desirable, or attractive: Marcia *adores* chocolate cake. **adored, adoring. —adoration** *noun.*

a·dorn (ə-DORN) *verb.* To decorate or serve as a decoration for: Betsy *adorned* the Christmas tree with tinsel. **adorned, adorning.**

a·drift (ə-DRIFT) *adverb* or *adjective.* Floating without control over movement or direction; drifting; not moored or anchored: When the raft was untied, it went *adrift* on the river.

a·droit (ə-DROIT) *adjective.* Skillful; capable; having a specific ability, especially in the use of the hands: Barbara is an *adroit* typist; she types without error. —**adroitly** *adverb.*

ad·u·la·tion (aj-u-LAY-shən) *noun.* Flattery; excessive praise or devotion.

a·dult (ə-DUHLT or AD-uhlt) *noun.* 1. A grownup; a mature man or woman. 2. A full-grown animal or plant: Its huge size showed us that the bear was an *adult.* —*adjective.* 1. Of or for adults: The grownups were having an *adult* conversation. 2. Grown-up; mature; full-grown: The huge tracks were those of an *adult* bear. —**adultly** *adverb.*

a·dul·ter·ate (ə-DUHL-tə-rayt) *verb.* To weaken or make less valuable by adding an inferior substance: The lemonade was *adulterated* by the addition of too much water. **adulterated, adulterating.**

a·dul·ter·y (ə-DUHL-tər-ee) *noun.* Sexual relations between a married person and another who is not the husband or wife of the first. **adulteries.**

adv. *abbreviation.* 1. Adverb. 2. Advertisement.

ad·vance (ad-VANSS) *verb.* 1. To move oneself forward or to move something forward: The principal *advanced* John to a higher class. 2. To increase; move upward: The cost of food *advanced* year after year. 3. To raise in rank or position: The captain *advanced* the private to the rank of corporal. 4. To suggest or submit, as an opinion or plan: The idea that Jane *advanced* at the meeting was a good one. 5. To lend; give credit or a loan to: The manager *advanced* him $20 until next Friday. 6. To aid a cause; help with; support: His donation *advanced* the cause of better education. **advanced, advancing.** —*noun.* 1. A movement forward. 2. An improvement: This car is an *advance* over last year's model. 3. An increase; upward movement. 4. A loan; something given before payment is due: Dad gave me an *advance* on next week's allowance. **advances.**

ad·vance·ment (ad-VANSS-mənt) *noun.* 1. A moving forward, progression, or improvement: The *advancement* of medical knowledge has saved many lives. 2. A promotion: Uncle Paul was delighted with his *advancement* from major to colonel.

ad·van·tage (ad-VAN-tij) *noun.* 1. A favorable circumstance, benefit, or blessing: Dad enjoyed the *advantage* of a good education. 2. Superiority in situation or position: My tennis practice gave me an *advantage* over my opponent. **advantages.**

ad·van·ta·geous (ad-van-TAY-jəss) *adjective.* Beneficial; profitable; favorable: Ralph's knowledge of French was *advantageous* during his visit to Paris. —**advantageously** *adverb.*

ad·ven·ture (ad-VEN-chər) *noun.* 1. A thrilling occurrence or undertaking, usually involving risks or danger: The soldier's escape from the enemy was a daring *adventure.* 2. An especially interesting or unusual experience. **adventures.**

ad·ven·tur·ous (ad-VEN-chər-əss) *adjective.* 1. Filled with a desire for unusual and daring deeds or undertakings: Columbus must have had an *adventurous* spirit. 2. Involving risks and difficulties: The rescue of the pilot will be an *adventurous* undertaking. —**adventurously** *adverb.*

ad·verb (AD-verb) *noun.* (Grammar) A word that is used to modify verbs, adjectives, or other adverbs: *Adverbs* usually answer when, where, how, or how much.

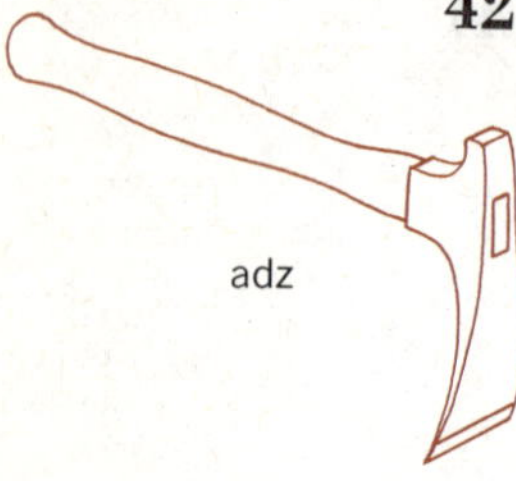
adz

ad·ver·sar·y (AD-vər-sehr-ee) *noun.* 1. An opponent in a contest or competition: Central was our school's *adversary* in the football game. 2. An enemy: The Americans and British were *adversaries* at the Battle of Bunker Hill. **adversaries.**

ad·verse (ad-VERSS) *adjective.* 1. Hostile; unfriendly; displeasing: Pablo was upset by the *adverse* comments about his painting. 2. Acting against; opposed to; conflicting: The *adverse* weather conditions forced the picnickers to go home. —**adversely** *adverb.*

aerial

ad·ver·si·ty (ad-VER-sə-tee) *noun.* A state or condition of conflict or opposition; misfortune: War and famine brought a period of *adversity* to that country. **adversities.**

ad·ver·tise (AD-vər-tighz) *verb.* To call general attention to; emphasize or announce something, especially the good qualities of a product for sale to the public: To increase sales, the company *advertised* its soap products on television. **advertised, advertising.**

aerialist

ad·ver·tise·ment (ad-vər-TIGHZ-mənt or ad-VER-tiss-mənt) *noun.* A public notice or announcement, especially of the good qualities of a product for sale: An *advertisement* for the new cereal was in this morning's newspaper.

ad·vice (ad-VIGHSS) *noun.* An opinion or suggestion about an action or the way something should be done: My doctor's *advice* was for me to get more sleep.

ad·vis·a·ble (ad-VIGH-zə-bəl) *adjective.* To be recommended; wise; desirable: It is not *advisable* to go sailing in bad weather. —**advisably** *adverb.*

ad·vise (ad-VIGHZ) *verb.* 1. To offer an opinion or suggestion about an action or the way something should be done: The teacher *advised* us to start studying for the test. 2. To inform: The pilot was *advised* of bad weather ahead. **advised, advising.**

ad·vis·er (ad-VIGH-zər) Also **advisor** *noun.* One who gives suggestions or opinions on certain subjects: Our school has an *adviser* to help the students with their problems.

ad·vo·cate (AD-və-kayt) *verb.* To support or speak in favor of; recommend: The students *advocated* an end to exams. **advocated, advocating.** —(AD-və-kit) *noun.* A person who supports or speaks in favor (of a cause or person): The principal is an *advocate* of better education. **advocates.**

adz Also **adze** *noun.* A heavy, curved tool similar to an ax, used for trimming lumber. **adzes.**

aer·ate (AIR-ayt) *verb.* 1. To expose to or supply with air: Judy *aerated* the water in her fish tank. 2. To mix or charge a liquid with air or another gas: Ginger ale is *aerated* to make it fizz. **aerated, aerating.**

aer·i·al (AIR-ee-əl) *noun.* A wire, rod, or other metal device used for receiving or sending radio or television broadcasts; an antenna. —*adjective.* Related to or operating in or from the air or an aircraft: The town was destroyed by an *aerial* bombardment.

aer·i·al·ist (AIR-ee-əl-ist) *noun.* An acrobat who works high up on a trapeze, tightrope, or other aerial equipment.

aero-, aer- *prefix.* Of or related to aircraft, air, or gases: *aero*nautics, *aero*sol, *aer*ate.

aer·o·nau·tics (air-ə-NAW-tiks) *noun.* The science or study of flight or of the design and operation of aircraft.

aer·o·sol (AIR-ə-sawl) *noun.* A liquified substance sealed in a container under pressure so that it can be released in a spray or foam: Shaving cream and deodorant are products often manufactured as *aerosols.*

aer·o·space (AIR-oh-spayss) *noun.* The air around the earth and outer space considered together.

af·fa·ble (AF-ə-bəl) *adjective.* Pleasant; friendly; easy to get along with. —**affably** *adverb.*

af·fair (ə-FAIR) *noun.* 1. An event or occurrence: The school dance was an *affair* Sue will always remember. 2. A matter of personal or business concern; a duty: The mayor studied the *affairs* that required his attention. 3. A relationship involving love or affection.

af·fect (ə-FEKT) *verb.* 1. To influence; cause a change in: Rainfall *affects* the growth of plants. 2. To stir the emotions or spirit: The sad story *affected* Ruth so much that she cried. 3. To feign; fake or pretend: He *affected* a limp so that he would not have to run in the race. **affected, affecting.**

af·fec·tion (ə-FEK-shən) *noun.* Warm feeling or fondness: The students had *affection* for the popular teacher.

af·fec·tion·ate (ə-FEK-shən-it) *adjective.* Showing or having warm feelings of fondness or love: At his graduation Paul received an *affectionate* hug from his sister. —**affectionately** *adverb.*

af·firm (ə-FERM) *verb.* To state firmly; declare to be true: The teacher *affirmed* that all the students passed the test. **affirmed, affirming.**

af·firm·a·tive (ə-FER-mə-tiv) *adjective.* Indicating consent or agreement; indicating an answer of yes: When Bob asked if Greenland is an island, the teacher's answer was *affirmative.* —**affirmatively** *adverb.*

af·fix (ə-FIKS) *verb.* To add to; fasten or attach: Dad *affixed* a label to my suitcase. **affixed, affixing.** —(AF-iks) *noun.* A prefix, suffix, or other part added to a word to form a new word. **affixes.**

af·flict (ə-FLIKT) *verb.* To cause pain or distress; trouble greatly: Mary is *afflicted* with a case of the measles. **afflicted, afflicting.**

af·flic·tion (ə-FLIK-shən) *noun.* 1. Suffering or distress: Poverty and hunger are great *afflictions* of mankind. 2. A cause or source of suffering or distress: The doctor cured the *affliction* that had caused Kevin's pain.

af·flu·ence (AF-loo-ənss) *noun.* Wealth; riches: The person who owns the hotel is a man of *affluence.*

af·flu·ent (AF-loo-ənt) *adjective.* Wealthy; rich: Veronica lives in an *affluent* neighborhood. —**affluently** *adverb.*

af·ford (ə-FORD) *verb.* 1. To be able to purchase or bear the expense of: We have enough money; we can *afford* to buy sodas. 2. To be able to bear the results of: I need my sleep; I cannot *afford* to stay up late. 3. To provide; make available to: The large window *affords* us a beautiful view of the sea. **afforded, affording.**

af·front (ə-FRUHNT) *verb.* To insult or offend deliberately: Agnes was *affronted* by the nasty remark. **affronted, affronting.** —*noun.* A deliberate insult or offense: The senator's refusal to shake hands was an *affront* to the judge.

a·field (ə-FEELD) *adverb.* 1. Away; not at home or nearby: The children wandered *afield.* 2. Away from what is important, known, or significant: Simon did not stick to his subject; his speech went *afield.*

a·fire (ə-FIGHR) *adjective.* Ablaze, on fire: The forest was set *afire* by a careless smoker's cigarette.

a·foot (ə-FOOT) *adverb* or *adjective.* 1. On foot; by walking: The parents arrived in cars but the children came *afoot.* 2. Going on; in progress: Secret meetings were *afoot* throughout the school.

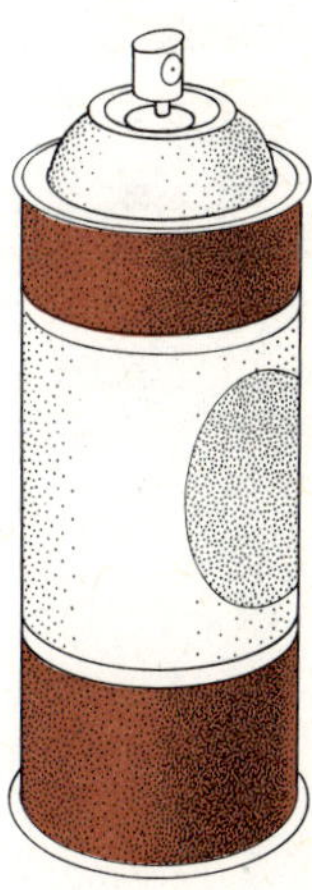

aerosol container

a·fore·said (ə-FOR-sed) *adjective.* Mentioned earlier; said before: The *aforesaid* plan must be understood before we continue.

a·fraid (ə-FRAYD) *adjective.* 1. Frightened; full of fear: Jane is *afraid* of spiders. 2. Sorry; regretful: I'm *afraid* that I can't stay longer.

aft *adverb.* At or toward the stern or rear part of a ship: The sailor went *aft* to cast off a line from the stern.

af·ter (AF-tər) *preposition.* 1. Behind; following: *After* the last boxcar came the caboose. 2. Later than: You may play *after* dinner. 3. In pursuit or search of: The dog ran *after* the rabbit. 4. Behind in position or rank: That player is rated *after* Jim in importance to the team. 5. In imitation or honor of: They named the baby *after* George Washington. 6. Because of; as a result of: *After* the warning about speeding, the driver slowed down. 7. In spite of: *After* all Dad's efforts the car still would not start. *—adverb.* 1. Following; later. 2. Behind or below in place or position: The cavalry rode ahead; the infantry followed *after.* *—conjunction.* Later than the time when: *After* the dishes were done, we all relaxed. **—take after.** To resemble in appearance or manner; to look like: Rusty *takes after* his father; both have red hair and freckles.

agate

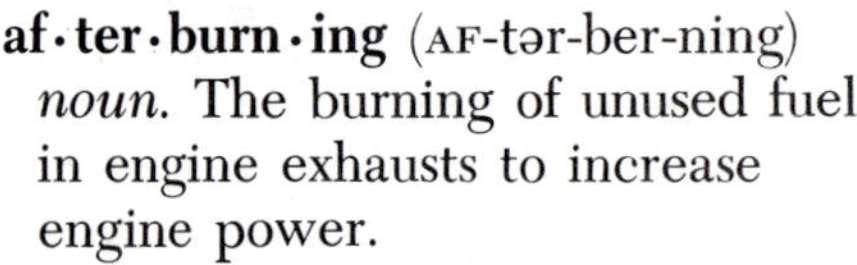

af·ter·burn·ing (AF-tər-ber-ning) *noun.* The burning of unused fuel in engine exhausts to increase engine power.

af·ter·ef·fect (AF-tər-ə-fekt) *noun.* A result or effect that occurs following a first or main effect: The pill cured Bob's headache, but he got a rash as an *aftereffect.*

af·ter·glow (AF-tər-gloh) *noun.* 1. A glow often seen in the sky following a sunset. 2. A pleasant feeling or memory that follows an enjoyable experience: The *afterglow* from the dance remained with Dorothy for several days.

af·ter·math (AF-tər-math) *noun.* A result or effect, especially an unfortunate one: The *aftermath* of Sally's day at the beach was a bad sunburn.

af·ter·noon (af-tər-NOON) *noun.* The period of the day from noon until evening.

af·ter·ward (AF-tər-wərd) Also **afterwards** *adverb.* Later; in a following time: We worked during the morning and went swimming *afterward.*

a·gain (ə-GEN) *adverb.* Once more; another time: Please sing that song *again.*

a·gainst (ə-GENST) *preposition.* 1. In opposition to: The British fought *against* the French in 1815. 2. Upon; in contact with: Herman bounced the ball *against* the wall. 3. Next to: The ladder is *against* the house. 4. In contrast with: The general considered one plan *against* the other. 5. In preparation for: The settlers gathered fuel *against* the cold weather.

ag·ate (AG-it) *noun.* A type of stone having varied colors in layers or swirls: Johnny's marbles are made of *agate.* **agates.**

age (AYJ) *noun.* 1. A specific time in a life: At the *age* of 18 he joined the Navy. 2. A period in history; an era: The Stone *Age* was many centuries ago. 3. The length of time a thing or person exists: The *age* of that old turtle is very great. 4. A specific period in the life of a person or thing: Old *age* should be a time for relaxation. 5. The condition of being old: *Age* has caused Grandfather to retire. 6. A long time: It has been an *age* since I last saw you. **ages.** *—verb.* 1. To grow old: Grandfather has *aged* since he retired. 2. To make old; to produce the effects of being old:

Sickness and worry *aged* him rapidly. **aged, aging.**

-age *suffix.* Indicates: 1. Action or process: anchor*age.* 2. Collection: leaf*age.* 3. Rate of: leak*age.* 4. A state or condition: marri*age.* 5. A fee or charge: post*age.* 6. Result of: break*age.* 7. Place: orphan*age.*

a·gen·cy (AY-jən-see) *noun.* 1. A business or firm that provides a service or represents another organization or person: I got a summer job through an employment *agency.* 2. A special government department or organization: The senator suggested the establishment of an *agency* to stop smuggling. 3. Aid, power, or assistance: Our visit to the ship was arranged through the *agency* of my uncle, the admiral. **agencies.**

a·gen·da (ə-JEN-də) *noun, plural in form but used with a singular verb.* Things that must be done or considered: The *agenda* for the next meeting was prepared by our committee.

a·gent (AY-jənt) *noun.* 1. A person who represents another person or an organization: Mr. Jones is an *agent* for the insurance company. 2. A member of a special government department or organization: My uncle was an *agent* with the FBI. 3. A person or thing that acts or causes an effect: Soap and bleach are *agents* for cleaning clothes.

ag·gra·vate (AG-rə-vayt) *verb.* 1. To make worse: Walter's sore throat was *aggravated* by a bad cough. 2. (Informal) To annoy; bother: The loud noise *aggravated* grandfather. **aggravated, aggravating.**

ag·gra·va·tion (ag-ra-VAY-shən) *noun.* 1. The condition or process of making worse or more serious. 2. (Informal) Annoyance; the condition or process of being bothered.

ag·gre·gate (AG-rə-git) *noun.* A combination, collection, or total: That garden is an *aggregate* of many different flowers and shrubs. **aggregates.** —*adjective.* Formed by combining or gathering together: Concrete is an *aggregate* material; it contains cement, sand, and stone.

ag·gres·sion (ə-GRESH-ən) *noun.* 1. An attack or assault, usually unprovoked. 2. The quality or act of being hostile or disagreeably forward.

ag·gres·sive (ə-GRESS-iv) *adjective.* 1. Showing hostility or forwardness: Tom's *aggressive* nature made him always fight to be first in the cafeteria line. 2. Warlike; attacking: That country's *aggressive* policies may cause a war. 3. Energetic; inclined to make progress or move ahead boldly: John is certainly *aggressive* in getting more customers for his paper route. —**aggressively** *adverb.*

ag·gres·sor (ə-GRESS-ər) *noun.* A person, group, or nation that causes or starts a quarrel, conflict, or war: Tom was the *aggressor;* he hit Charles first.

a·ghast (ə-GAST) *adjective.* Shocked; filled with horror or amazement: Sandra was *aghast* at the news that her baby brother was lost.

ag·ile (AJ-əl) *adjective.* 1. Able to move quickly and nimbly; spry: Monkeys are *agile* climbers. 2. Alert; clever: An understanding of algebra requires an *agile* mind. —**agilely** *adverb.*

a·gil·i·ty (ə-JIL-ə-tee) *noun.* The ability to move swiftly and nimbly: We admired the dancer's *agility.*

ag·i·tate (AJ-ə-tayt) *verb.* 1. To arouse or disturb: Mother was *agitated* by Johnny's crying. 2. To cause to shake briskly, tumble, or move about: The water was *agitated* by the ship's propeller. 3. To try to gain public attention or support: The strikers *agitated* for higher wages. **agitated, agitating.**

ag·i·ta·tor (AJ-ə-tay-tər) *noun.* 1. Someone who stirs things up, particularly one who tries to involve others in political or social problems. 2. Any device used for mixing up or stirring about, as a washing machine *agitator.*

a·go (ə-GOH) *adjective.* Past; gone by: Years *ago* she was a great star. —*adverb.* In an earlier time: He died long *ago.*

ag·o·ny (AG-ə-nee) *noun.* Extreme suffering of body or mind. **agonies.**

a·gree (ə-GREE) *verb.* 1. To share the same opinion or idea: The boys *agreed* that stealing is a crime. 2. To consent: The teacher *agreed* to help us after school. 3. To reach an understanding or settlement: They finally *agreed* on a place for their vacation. 4. To be in harmony or conformity: My watch *agrees* with his. 5. To be suitable for a person's health or comfort: His stomach aches because red peppers do not *agree* with him. **agreed, agreeing.**

a·gree·a·ble (ə-GREE-ə-bəl) *adjective.* 1. Pleasant, friendly, or pleasing. 2. Willing to consent: Angela was *agreeable* to the new plan. —**agreeably** *adverb.*

aileron

a·gree·ment (ə-GREE-mənt) *noun.* 1. Harmony of ideas or opinions: Mother and Dad are in *agreement* about the value of education. 2. An understanding; a written or spoken arrangement or contract between people or nations.

ag·ri·cul·ture (AG-ri-kuhl-chər) *noun.* Farming; raising crops and livestock. —**agricultural** *adjective.*

a·gron·o·my (ə-GRON-ə-mee) *noun.* The science of growing crops and of preserving and enriching soil for farming.

ah *interjection.* An exclamation expressing an attitude or feeling like surprise, pleasure, pity, or regret.

a·ha (ah-HAH) *interjection.* An exclamation expressing surprise, discovery, or ridicule.

a·head (ə-HED) *adverb.* 1. In advance in place or achievement: That bright girl ranks *ahead* of me in spelling and math. 2. Forward; onward in progress or movement: When the light changed, Dad drove *ahead.* 3. For the future: Plan *ahead* for your vacation.

a·hoy (ə-HOI) *interjection.* A word called out by sailors to attract attention.

aid (AYD) *noun.* 1. Help; assistance; support: Ed raised the front of the automobile with the *aid* of a jack. 2. An assistant or helper. *See* **aide.** —*verb.* To help; assist; support: Edna *aided* her mother with the housework. **aided, aiding.**

aide (AYD) *noun.* 1. A military officer who aids or assists a superior. 2. Any person who aids or assists someone in a position of importance: a nurse's *aide.* **aides.**

ail (AYL) *verb.* 1. To cause distress to; bother: He seems gloomy; what *ails* him? 2. To be ill or in pain. **ailed, ailing.**

ai·le·ron (AY-lə-ron) *noun.* A small movable section at the rear edge of an airplane wing that is raised or lowered to control balance and enable the pilot to bank the plane when turning.

ail·ment (AYL-mənt) *noun.* An illness; a mild sickness.

aim (AYM) *verb.* 1. To point or direct toward a target, as a gun, arrow, or blow: He *aimed* his rifle at the bear. 2. To direct (one's efforts or words) in order to influence or affect: The teacher *aimed* her criticism at the lazy student. 3. To try; strive; intend: He *aimed* to finish his homework by seven o'clock. **aimed, aiming** —*noun.* 1. The act of pointing or directing toward a target: The hunter's *aim* was steady. 2. An intention; purpose: Joe's *aim* in life is to be a lawyer.

aim·less (AYM-liss) *adjective.* Without point, purpose, or reason: It was an *aimless* walk; Jimmy and I just wandered along the beach. —**aimlessly** *adverb.*

air *noun.* 1. The invisible mixture of gases that surrounds the earth: All of us breathe *air.* 2. The space above the earth. 3. An outward appearance; a suggested quality: The meetings had an *air* of mystery. 4. Transportation in an aircraft: We traveled to Chicago by *air.* 5. Public expression; publicity: Margaret gave *air* to her complaints. 6. A piece of music; a principal melody or singing part: The opera star sang a famous *air.* 7. (Plural) Exaggerated or artificial manners: Jacqueline's *airs* made the other children laugh. —*verb.* 1. To expose to air: Mother *aired* the old clothes by hanging them outdoors. 2. To publicize; bring to public attention: The workers *aired* their complaints. **aired, airing.** —**on the air.** Sending (a program) by radio or TV. —**up in the air.** Not settled or decided; undetermined: Plans for our vacation are still *up in the air.* —**walk on air.** To be very happy or delighted.

air base. A military airport.

air-con·di·tion (AIR-kən-DISH-ən) *verb.* To supply with a system or machine for regulating temperature, especially cooling and cleaning the air: It cost thousands of dollars to *air-condition* the theater. **air-conditioned, air-conditioning.**

air conditioner. A machine for controlling temperature inside a building, especially by cooling and cleaning air from outside.

air·craft (AIR-kraft) *noun.* Any or all of the airplanes, balloons, helicopters, and other devices that can be floated or flown through the air. —**aircraft** *plural.*

aircraft carrier. A naval ship with a deck that allows aircraft to take off and land.

air·drome (AIR-drohm) *noun.* An airport or airplane hangar. **airdromes.**

air·field (AIR-feeld) *noun.* A level area, usually with paved landing strips, on which airplanes take off and land.

air force. 1. A military organization responsible for conducting or being prepared for air warfare. 2. [Capital A and F] The air division of the U.S. Department of Defense.

air lane. A regular route used by airplanes in flying from one place to another.

air·line (AIR-lighn) *noun.* A system of people and equipment that provides air transportation for passengers and cargo. **airlines.**

air·lin·er (AIR-ligh-nər) *noun.* A large passenger plane.

air·mail (AIR-mayl) *noun.* 1. A system for sending mail by airplane: The letter arrived by *airmail.* 2. Mail sent by airplane.

air·plane (AIR-playn) *noun.* A flying machine driven by engines and kept aloft by the forces of air acting on its wings. **airplanes.**

air conditioner

aircraft carrier

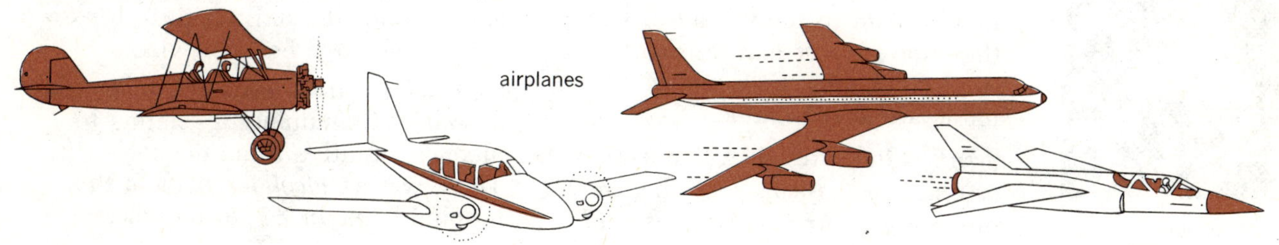

airplanes

airport

Alabama
★capital: Montgomery

Alaska
★capital: Juneau

albatross

air·port (AIR-port) *noun.* A place where aircraft take off, land, and are serviced; usually with shops, restaurants, and lounges.

air pressure. Pressure exerted by the earth's atmosphere or by air in a closed space, as in bicycle tires.

air·ship (AIR-ship) *noun.* A balloon, blimp, or similar aircraft which is lighter than air, moves under its own power, and can be steered.

air·tight (AIR-tight) *adjective.* 1. Closed or sealed so tight that no air can leave or enter: The cookies are kept in an *airtight* jar. 2. Having no flaws or weaknesses: He has an *airtight* excuse for not working yesterday.

air·way (AIR-way) *noun.* A route established for the flight of airplanes.

air·y (AIR-ee) *adjective.* 1. Breezy; well-ventilated. 2. Like air, especially in movement or lightness: Cotton candy is *airy.* 3. Lighthearted; gay: He was delighted by Marilyn's *airy* conversation. 4. Unreal; imaginary: A fairy is not real; it is an *airy* creature of make-believe. **airier, airiest.** —**airily** *adverb.*

aisle (IGHL) *noun.* The space for walking between rows of seats in a classroom, auditorium, or church.

a·jar (ə-JAHR) *adverb.* Opened a little way, usually said of a door: The door was left *ajar.*

a·kim·bo (ə-KIM-boh) *adjective* or *adverb.* With hand on the hip and elbow out from the body.

a·kin (ə-KIN) *adjective.* 1. Of the same family, group, or tribe: The mink is *akin* to the weasel. 2. Of the same type or nature; sharing similar qualities: Felix's ideas about music are *akin* to mine.

-al *suffix.* Indicates: 1. A connection or relation: music*al,* continu*al.* 2. A process or action: refus*al,* dispos*al.*

Al·a·bam·a (al-ə-BAM-ə) *noun.* A south central state of the United States, 22nd to join the Union (1819). —**Ala.** *abbreviation.* Also **AL** for Zip Codes.

a·larm (ə-LAHRM) *noun.* 1. A fear caused by a feeling of danger. 2. A bell or other noisemaker used to give warning or to awaken. —*verb.* 1. To give a warning. 2. To frighten suddenly. **alarmed, alarming.**

alarm clock. A clock which has a bell or buzzer which can be set to ring or buzz at a particular time.

a·las (ə-LASS) *interjection.* An expression used to show sadness or despair.

A·las·ka (ə-LASS-kə) *noun.* A Pacific state of the United States, 49th to join the Union (1959). —**Alas.** *abbreviation.* Also **AK** for Zip Codes.

al·ba·tross (AL-bə-trawss) *noun.* A type of large web-footed sea bird which can fly great distances: The Ancient Mariner believed his killing an *albatross* was the cause of his bad luck. —**albatross** or **albatrosses** *plural.*

al·bi·no (al-BIGH-noh) *noun.* A person or animal with very white skin, pale hair, and pink or light-colored eyes. **albinos.**

al·bum (AL-bəm) *noun.* 1. A book of blank pages used for keeping stamps, photographs, and other collections: an autograph *album.* 2. A long-playing record of several numbers: That singer's first *album* is my favorite. 3. A folder in which records are kept.

al·co·hol (AL-kə-hawl) *noun.* A colorless liquid made from sugars and starches; used in drugs and cleaning liquids, and found in drinks such as whiskey, beer, or wine.

al·co·hol·ic (al-kə-HAWL-ik) *adjective.* Containing or relating to alcohol; resulting from alcohol: There was an *alcoholic* odor in the hospital. —*noun.* A person whose desire or need for alcohol is an illness.

al·co·hol·ism (AL-kə-hawl-iz-əm) *noun.* An illness which results in or from excessive, uncontrolled drinking of alcoholic beverages.

al·cove (AL-kohv) *noun.* A hollow or indented recess in a wall of a room, often containing furniture. **alcoves.**

al·der (AHL-dər) *noun.* A tree of the birch family which grows in damp ground in the cold or temperate regions of the world.

al·der·man (AWL-dər-mən) *noun.* A member of the lawmaking body of a town or city government. **aldermen.**

ale (AYL) *noun.* A beer-like beverage made from malt. **ales.**

a·lert (ə-LERT) *verb.* To warn, caution: The police *alerted* the townspeople that a lion had escaped from the zoo. **alerted, alerting.** —*adjective.* Wide-awake, watchful: She is an *alert* student. —*noun.* A warning, a signal which means danger: Sound the *alert!* —**alertly** *adverb.*

al·fal·fa (al-FAL-fə) *noun.* A grass grown for feeding cattle or other animals.

al·gae (AL-jee) *noun, plural.* Green plants such as seaweed which grow in water. —**al·ga** (AL-gə) *singular.*

al·ge·bra (AL-jə-brə) *noun.* A mathematical system in which letters and other symbols are used to represent unknown numbers.

al·go·rism (AL-gə-riz-əm) *noun.* The decimal system; the Arabic number system using the numbers one through nine plus zero.

a·li·as (AY-lee-əss) *noun.* A false name usually used to hide identity: The smuggler used an *alias* to get a passport. **aliases.**

al·i·bi (AL-ə-bigh) *noun.* 1. The claim by an accused person that he was not at the scene of the crime. 2. (Informal) Any excuse: He gave an *alibi* for not cleaning his room.

a·li·en (AY-lee-ən) *noun.* Anyone who lives in a country but is not a citizen of it. —*adjective.* Foreign; strange; peculiar: Smoking is *alien* to my family's health habits.

al·ien·ate (AYL-yə-nayt) *verb.* To take away affection or interest. **alienated, alienating.**

al·ien·a·tion (ayl-yən-AY-shən or ay-lee-ən-AY-shən) *noun.* A state or feeling of separation (from friendship or deep human ties).

a·light (ə-LIGHT) *verb.* 1. To get off a horse or out of a car or other vehicle. 2. To land: The bird *alighted* after a short flight. **alighted** or **alit, alighting.** —*adjective.* Aflame; giving off light: The cake was *alight* with candles.

a·like (ə-LIGHK) *adjective.* The same; close in appearance or manner. —*adverb.* In the same way; equally: The traffic officer treats all the children *alike;* he has no favorites.

al·i·men·ta·ry (al-ə-MEN-tree) *adjective.* Of or about food.

alimentary canal. The channel which food follows through the body as it is eaten, digested, and eliminated.

al·i·mo·ny (AL-ə-moh-nee) *noun.* (Law) The money a divorced man pays to his ex-wife by order of the court: In some states husbands can receive *alimony.*

a·live (ə-LIGHV) *adjective.* 1. Living; full of life; not dead. 2. Covered with moving bodies: *alive* with ants. 3. Aware; knowing: He was *alive* to the message of the song. 4. In high spirits.

al·ka·li (AL-kə-ligh) *noun.* Any chemical base which changes acids to salts: *Alkalis* are bases; they turn litmus paper blue.

al·ka·line (AL-kə-lin) *adjective.* Of or like an alkali; basic.

alder

alfalfa

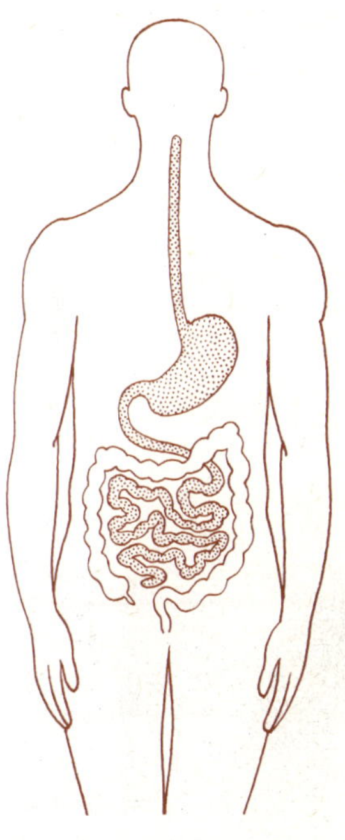

alimentary canal

all (AWL) *adjective.* 1. Everything, everyone: *All* the guests had a good time. 2. The whole, entire: *All* summer the ducks swam around the little pond. *—adverb.* Entirely, completely: She was *all* alone. *—pronoun.* 1. Each one, everybody: *All* are present. 2. Everything: We thought the books were lost, but *all* were found in the carton. *—noun.* 1. Everything a person has: Nathan Hale gave his *all* for his country. 2. The whole; the complete amount.

allosaurus

All-American (awl-ə-MEHR-i-kən) *noun.* (Sports) A member of a U.S. team selected as best in a particular sport.

al·lay (ə-LAY) *verb.* To relieve; calm; ease. **allayed, allaying.**

al·lege (ə-LEJ) *verb.* 1. To claim without proof: Mary *alleged* that Tom took her pencil. 2. To say with sureness. **alleged, alleging.**

al·le·giance (ə-LEE-jənss) *noun.* Loyalty to a government, ruler, or a cause: "I pledge *allegiance* to the flag . . ." (Bellamy).

al·ler·gic (ə-LER-jik) *adjective.* Affected badly or irritated by certain substances: John is *allergic* to cat fur; it makes him sneeze.

al·ler·gy (AL-ər-jee) *noun.* Sensitiveness to or irritation from pollen, dust, fur, or other materials: His sneezing and rash were caused by an *allergy.* **allergies.**

al·ley (AL-ee) *noun.* 1. A walkway between buildings. 2. A narrow passageway or street. 3. A long, narrow, enclosed area with a wooden floor used for bowling.

alligator

crocodile

al·li·ance (ə-LIGH-ənss) *noun.* 1. An agreement based on common interest, usually between governments of different countries. 2. The nations making such an agreement. **alliances.**

al·li·ga·tor (AL-ə-gay-tər) *noun.* 1. A large reptile with a broad nose, long tail, scaly hide, and sharp teeth: *Alligators* live in swamps and rivers of Southeastern United States. 2. Leather made from alligator hide.

al·lit·er·a·tion (ə-lit-ə-RAY-shən) *noun.* A literary device of repeating words beginning with the same letter or sound, for example: "She sells seashells by the seashore."

al·lo·sau·rus (al-ə-SAWR-uhss) *noun.* A dinosaur; a meat-eating prehistoric animal of the reptile family.

al·lot (ə-LOT) *verb.* 1. To give shares: The farmer *allotted* his land to his five sons. 2. To give as a portion: The teacher *allotted* ten minutes for review. 3. To assign for a purpose: The mayor *allotted* money for a new playground. **allotted, allotting.**

al·lot·ment (ə-LOT-mənt) *noun.* 1. That which is given in a portion or a lot: Each child was given his *allotment* of paper and pencils for the exam. 2. The act of giving such a portion: The teacher made the *allotment* of supplies for the year.

all-out (AWL-OWT) *adjective.* Complete; total: The team made an *all-out* effort to win the game.

al·low (ə-LOW) *verb.* 1. To give permission: Mother will *allow* me to paint my bicycle. 2. To not prevent: Mary *allowed* weeds to grow in her garden. 3. To make room for; plan for extra: Let's *allow* some spare time in case we lose our way. **allowed, allowing.**

al·low·ance (ə-LOW-ənss) *noun.* 1. A fixed sum of money given at regular intervals: Mandy gets her *allowance* every Thursday. 2. A rebate or discount: The salesman gave my mother an *allowance* of 20 dollars on her old vacuum cleaner. 3. Consideration: awareness: Timmy makes *allowance* for his baby sister's slowness. **allowances.**

al·loy (AL-oi) *noun.* A mixture of metals designed for greater strength, hardness, or reduced cost: Brass is an *alloy* of copper and zinc.

all-round (AWL-ROWND) Also **all-around** *adjective.* Having a variety of skills, talents, or uses: Tim can play any position on the team; he is an *all-round* athlete.

all-star (AWL-stahr) *noun.* An athlete of a very special ability; a star player. —*adjective.* Describing athletes of very special ability or those elected to play in special games.

al·lude (ə-LOOD) *verb.* To refer to; hint at; mention in a casual way. **alluded, alluding.**

al·lure (ə-LUR) *verb.* To attract or tempt. **allured, alluring.** —*noun.* Attractiveness, charm.

al·lu·sion (ə-LOO-zhən) *noun.* A casual mention; suggestion; hint: Grace made an *allusion* to her party; she didn't say who was invited.

al·ly (AL-igh or ə-LIGH) *noun.* 1. One who is joined or united with another. 2. Partner in a common cause. **allies.** —(ə-LIGH or AL-igh) *verb.* To join in a treaty, agreement, or common cause. **allied, allying.**

al·ma·nac (AWL-mə-nak) *noun.* A book published each year which contains calendars with the positions of the sun and the moon, weather forecasts, and other useful information.

al·mighty (awl-MIGH-tee) *adjective.* 1. Having all power. 2. (Informal) Great; tremendous. —*noun.* [Capital A] God: the *Almighty.*

al·mond (AH-mənd) *noun.* 1. A nut, oval in shape and light tan in color. 2. The tree on which this nut grows. 3. (Also *adjective*) A pale, golden-brown color. —*adjective.* Shaped like an almond, as *almond* eyes.

al·most (AWL-mohst) *adverb.* Very nearly; just short of: We are *almost* home.

a·loft (ə-LAWFT) *adverb.* 1. Above; over: He held his hand *aloft* and waved. 2. In the air. 3. At or near the upper rigging of a ship.

a·lone (ə-LOHN) *adjective.* By oneself; not with others: Jane was *alone* all day. —*adverb.* Singly, solely: You can play this game *alone.*

a·long (ə-LAWNG) *preposition.* By the side of: The children played *along* the river bank. —*adverb.* 1. Ahead; forward: Move *along* now! 2. In company; together: He went *along* with his father.

a·long·side (ə-LAWNG-SIGHD) *adverb.* Along, to the side of: They drove their car *alongside* ours at the drive-in.

a·loof (ə-LOOF) *adjective.* Apart in an unsympathetic way; not interested: He remained *aloof* from the arguments of his classmates.

a·loud (ə-LOWD) *adverb.* 1. Spoken so as to be heard; out loud: She read the story *aloud* in class. 2. With a loud voice; noisily: He shrieked *aloud* at the funny story.

al·pac·a (al-PAK-ə) *noun.* 1. A South American animal with long, soft hair. 2. The hair or wool of the alpaca. 3. Fabric made from the wool of the alpaca. **alpacas.**

al·pha·bet (AL-fə-bet) *noun.* The letters of a language listed in a particular order.

al·pha·bet·i·cal (al-fə-BET-ə-kəl) *adjective.* Arranged in the same order as the letters of an alphabet: Roll call was taken by our last names in *alphabetical* order.

al·pha·bet·ize (AL-fə-bə-tighz) *verb.* To arrange according to the order of letters in an alphabet. **alphabetized, alphabetizing.**

al·read·y (awl-RED-ee) *adverb.* Before now; by now: I have *already* washed my hands.

alpaca

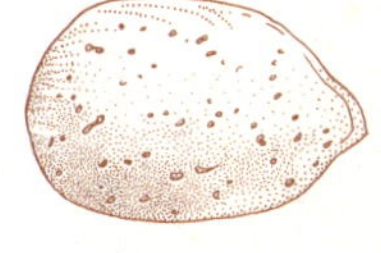
almond

al·so (AWL-soh) *adverb.* In addition to; as well as.

altar

al·tar (AWL-tər) *noun.* A raised block or table, usually at the front of a church, at which religious services are held.

al·ter (AWL-tər) *verb.* To change or make different in some way: Marge's new hairdo *altered* her appearance. **altered, altering.**

al·ter·a·tion (awl-tər-AY-shən) *noun.* A change: The store is closed for *alterations.*

al·ter·nate (AWL-tər-nayt) *verb.* To switch from one to another; take turns. **alternated, alternating.** —(AWL-ter-nit) *adjective.* 1. Coming in turns, rotating. 2. Every other one in a series. 3. Substitute: If I can't have pie, my *alternate* choice is cake. —**alternately** *adverb.*

alternating current. (Electricity) A current that reverses its direction at regular times.

al·ter·na·tive (awl-TER-nə-tiv) *noun.* A choice between two things: Martin had the *alternative* of visiting his grandfather's farm or going to summer camp. **alternatives.**

al·though (awl-THOH) *conjunction.* Even if; in spite of the fact that: *Although* he was not hungry he managed to eat another cupcake.

al·tim·e·ter (al-TIM-ə-tər) *noun.* An instrument used to measure altitude: *Altimeters* are used in aircraft to record elevation above sea level.

al·ti·tude (AL-tə-tood or AL-tə-tyood) *noun.* The height from sea level to any point in space above. **altitudes.**

al·to (AL-toh) *noun.* One of the ranges of the human voice, usually a woman's lowest singing voice.

al·to·geth·er (awl-tə-GETH-ər) *adverb.* 1. All things considered; by and large: *Altogether,* we were pleased with our costumes. 2. Thoroughly; entirely: Joe was not *altogether* truthful.

al·um (AL-əm) *noun.* A whitish mineral, frequently used in medicine and in dyeing fabrics.

aluminium. British form of **aluminum.**

a·lu·mi·num (ə-LOO-mə-nəm) *noun.* A silver-white, lightweight metal that does not readily tarnish.

alumna (ə-LUM-nə) *noun.* A female who attended or is a graduate of a school or college. —**alumnae** (ə-LUM-nee) *plural.*

a·lum·nus (ə-LUM-nəss) *noun.* A male who attended or is a graduate of a school or college. —**alumni** (ə-LUM-nigh) *plural.*

al·ways (AWL-wayz) *adverb.* 1. Forever; without end; everlasting; perpetual; ceaseless; never stopping. 2. Every time; at all times: Jack *always* forgets his spelling book.

A.M. *abbreviation.* Also **a.m.** Before noon.

am *verb. See* **be.**

am·a·ni·ta (əm-ə-NEE-tə) *noun.* A type of mushroom, usually poisonous.

a·mass (ə-MASS) *verb.* To collect in great quantity; gather in a pile. **amassed, amassing.**

am·a·teur (AM-ə-chər) *noun.* 1. A person who uses his talent or skill for fun and not to make money. 2. An athlete who has never received money for playing.

a·maze (ə-MAYZ) *verb.* To fill with surprise; astound: The news so *amazed* her that she was left speechless. **amazed, amazing.** —**amazingly** *adverb.*

a·maze·ment (ə-MAYZ-mənt) *noun.* Surprise; astonishment.

am·bas·sa·dor (am-BASS-ə-dər) *noun.* 1. A person usually appointed by the head of a government to serve the interests of his country in another nation. 2. A person appointed to carry out a special mission: U.S. athletes are *ambassadors* of good will.

am·ber (AM-bər) *noun.* 1. A substance of yellow-brown color used in costume jewelry. 2. (Also *adjective*). A yellow-brown color.

am·bi- *prefix.* Indicates both, more than one: *ambi*dextrous.

am·bi·dex·trous (am-bi-DEK-strəss) *adjective.* Able to use either hand with equal ease.

am·big·u·ous (am-BIG-yoo-əss) *adjective.* Open to doubt; having more than one possible meaning: Jim's *ambiguous* reply left me unsure as to what he meant.

am·bi·tion (am-BISH-ən) *noun.* 1. Great desire to achieve a goal. 2. The goal itself.

am·bi·tious (am-BISH-əss) *adjective.* Wanting to achieve a goal or aim.

am·ble (AM-bəl) *verb.* To walk leisurely; to stroll. **ambled, ambling.** —*noun.* The gait of a horse when lifting his two legs on one side and then lifting his two legs on the other side.

am·bro·sia (am-BROH-zhə) *noun.* 1. The traditional food for the ancient Greek and Roman gods. 2. Anything that smells or tastes particularly good. 3. A dessert usually made from sliced oranges and bananas with shredded coconut.

am·bu·lance (AM-byə-lənss) *noun.* A vehicle equipped with a stretcher and instruments of first aid, used to carry sick or injured persons to the hospital. **ambulances.**

am·bush (AM-bush) *verb.* To attack without warning from a hidden place. **ambushed, ambushing.** —*noun.* 1. An attack from a hidden place. 2. The hidden place itself.

a·men (ay-MEN or ah-MEN) *interjection.* 1. The final word used at the end of a prayer. 2. (Informal) Indicates there is no more to be said or done: *Amen* to that lesson; let's move on to the next. 3. Used to express agreement; yes, truly.

a·mend (ə-MEND) *verb.* To change; improve: The U.S. Constitution was *amended* to guarantee greater freedom. **amended, amending.**

a·mend·ment (ə-MEND-mənt) *noun.* 1. A change for improvement. 2. A section added to a law or document to clarify or improve: The first ten *amendments* to the U.S. Constitution are called the Bill of Rights.

A·mer·i·ca (ə-MEHR-ə-kə) *noun.* 1. The Western Hemisphere. 2. The United States. —**American** *adjective.*

am·e·thyst (AM-ə-thist) *noun.* 1. A light purple quartz used for jewelry. 2. The color of amethyst.

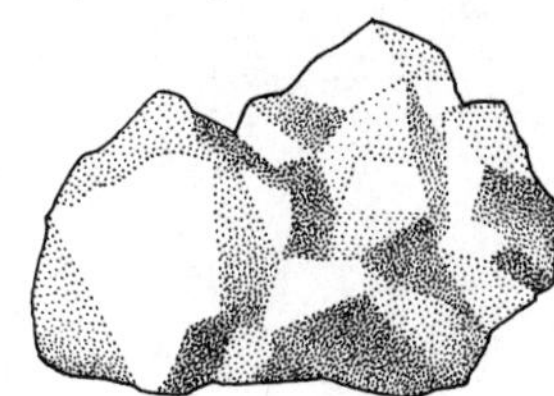

amethyst

a·mi·able (AY-mee-ə-bəl) *adjective.* Friendly, cheerful, good tempered: The janitor always had an *amiable* smile for everyone. —**amiably** *adverb.*

a·mid (ə-MID) *preposition.* In the middle of; surrounded by; in the center of; among.

a·mid·ships (ə-MID-ships) *adverb.* At the middle of a boat or ship.

a·mi·go (ah-MEE-goh) *noun.* A Spanish word for friend: Pancho and Cisco were *amigos;* they liked each other very much. **amigos.**

a·miss (ə-MISS) *adjective.* Wrong; not as it should be; in error: Mother knew something was *amiss* when Jimmy did not arrive home on time.

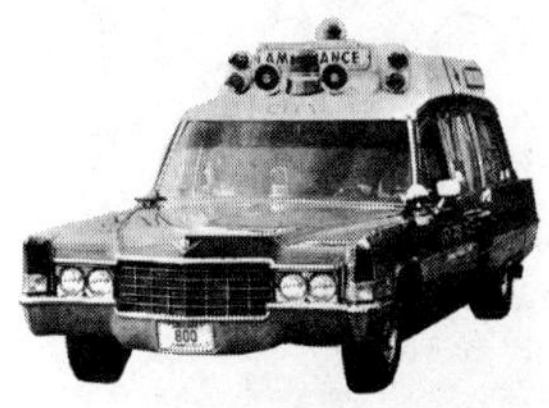

ambulance

am·me·ter (AM-mee-tər) *noun.* A device for measuring the strength of electrical current.

am·mo·ni·a (ə-MOHN-yə) *noun.* 1. A colorless gas used to make many chemical products. 2. A harsh-smelling cleaning liquid made from ammonia gas and water: Housewives use *ammonia* for cleaning.

am·mu·ni·tion (am-yə-NISH-ən) *noun.* Bullets, bombs, shells, charges, and other missiles or explosives used as weapons.

am·ne·sia (am-NEE-zhə) *noun.* Loss of memory: My aunt had *amnesia* and could not remember her name.

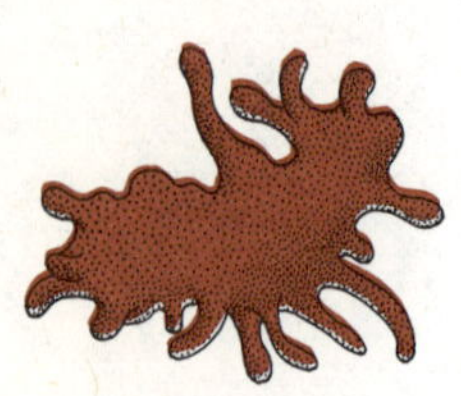
amoeba

a·moe·ba (ə-MEE-bə) *noun.* Single cell form of life, which reproduces by splitting in half. —**amoebas** or **amoebae** (ə-MEE-bee) *plural.*

a·mong (ə-MUHNG) *preposition.* 1. Along with: *Among* other things, I want to learn to swim this summer. 2. In the middle or midst of: He was *among* the shouting boys. 3. With a share to each of: divide candy *among* the children.

a·mor·al (ay-MOR-əl) *adjective.* Not concerned about or aware of standards of right or wrong.

a·mount (ə-MOWNT) *noun.* 1. Total; sum: Dad paid the full *amount* of his car repair bill. 2. Quantity: No *amount* of scolding will make the child stop crying. —*verb.* Equal; come to: The damages *amounted* to $100. **amounted, amounting.**

amphibian

am·pere (AM-pihr) *noun.* A unit used to measure the strength of an electric current. **amperes.**

am·phet·a·mine (am-FET-ə-meen) *noun.* A drug that stimulates or speeds up the working of the nervous system.

am·phib·i·an (am-FIB-ee-ən) *noun.* 1. An animal that can live on land and in the water. 2. An airplane or other vehicle able to operate from water as well as from land.

anaconda

am·phib·i·ous (am-FIB-ee-əss) *adjective.* Capable of living, or being used, on land and in water.

am·ple (AM-pəl) *adjective.* 1. More than needed; plentiful: We shared what was left of our *ample* Halloween treats. 2. Sufficient; enough: There was *ample* food for everyone, with no waste.

am·pli·fy (AM-plə-figh) *verb.* 1. Increase; add more to; make larger: A loudspeaker system was added to *amplify* the sound. 2. Explain more fully; talk at length: The speaker will have time to *amplify* his remarks. **amplified, amplifying.**

am·pu·tate (AM-pyoo-tayt) *verb.* To cut off a part of the body, as an arm or a leg. **amputated, amputating.**

am·u·let (AM-yə-lət) *noun.* A charm or other object that is supposed to bring good luck, or keep away bad luck, often worn around the neck.

a·muse (ə-MYOOZ) *verb.* 1. To make happy or cheerful; to entertain: The clown *amused* the children; they giggled with delight. 2. To make time pass pleasantly for: The television programs *amused* Bob while he was sick in bed. **amused, amusing.**

a·muse·ment (ə-MYOOZ-mənt) *noun.* 1. State of being entertained or amused: I couldn't hide my *amusement* at Mother's new hat; I burst out laughing. 2. Any device or practice that provides fun or entertainment: Rodeos are a popular *amusement.*

an *indefinite article.* One; any. Used with a noun that begins with a vowel or vowel sound: *an* orange, *an* hour.

-an *suffix.* Connected with, belonging to, referring to, or believing in: Mexic*an*, electrici*an*.

an·a·con·da (ən-ə-KON-də) *noun.* A huge, nonpoisonous South American snake that crushes its victims to death. **anacondas.**

an·a·gram (AN-ə-gram) *noun.* 1. A game of switching around letters in a word to form another word or words. 2. A word formed in this manner: "Owl" is an *anagram* for "low."

a·nal·o·gy (ə-NAL-ə-jee) *noun.* The comparison of two things which have a certain feature or features in common: One can make an *analogy* between a kite and an airplane because both can fly. **analogies.**

a·nal·y·sis (ə-NAL-ə-siss) *noun.* Breaking down anything into its basic parts so that each part can be examined: The scientists made an *analysis* of the moon rocks. —**analyses** (ə-NAL-ə-seez) *plural.*

an·a·lyze (AN-ə-lighz) *verb.* Take apart to examine; break down to basic parts: In science class the students *analyzed* the structure of leaves. **analyzed, analyzing.**

an·ar·chist (AN-ər-kist) *noun.* A person who believes in doing away with all laws and rules for society.

an·ar·chy (AN-ər-kee) noun. 1. A society with no laws, rules, or government. 2. State of disorder: When the teacher left the noisy classroom, *anarchy* resulted. **anarchies.**

a·nat·o·my (ə-NAT-ə-mee) *noun.* 1. Basic structure of anything. 2. Science of basic structures of plants and animals. 3. Skeleton. **anatomies.**

-ance *suffix.* Indicates a quality, an action, or a condition: import*ance.*

an·ces·tor (AN-sess-tər) *noun.* Any person from whom one is descended in a direct line: *Ancestors* include parents and grandparents.

an·ces·try (AN-sess-tree) *noun.* One's background; the line of people from whom one descends. **ancestries.**

an·chor (ANG-kər) *noun.* 1. A heavy object which is attached to a rope or cable on a boat and thrown into the water to keep the boat from drifting. 2. Anything that increases stability or security. *—verb.* 1. To hold in place by the use of an anchor. 2. To fasten securely: She *anchored* the balloon to the handle of her bicycle. **anchored, anchoring.** **—weigh anchor.** To draw or lift up an anchor: The ship *weighed anchor* and sailed away.

an·chor·age (ANG-kər-ij) *noun.* A place where ships are anchored.

anchor man. 1. The most dependable one on a team, as in sports. 2. The man who makes the final lap in a relay race. 3. A radio or TV announcer who is the main speaker on a program with other reporters.

an·cient (AYN-shənt) *adjective.* 1. Very old: Her great-grandmother's wrinkled face looked *ancient.* 2. Belonging to the distant past: In *ancient* times men lived in caves.

-ancy *suffix.* State or quality of being: const*ancy.*

and (ənd or AND) *conjunction.* 1. Also; as well as: "Jack *and* Jill went up the hill." 2. Plus; in addition to: Two *and* five are seven.

and·i·ron (AND-igh-ərn) *noun.* One of two supports for logs in a fireplace: An *andiron* is usually made of metal with a short, upright post in front.

andirons

an·ec·dote (AN-ik-doht) *noun.* A brief story about an unusual or interesting incident: The comedian told amusing *anecdotes* about his boyhood. **anecdotes.**

a·ne·mia (ə-NEE-mee-ə) *noun.* An illness caused by lack of enough oxygen-carrying material in the blood. **—anemic** *adjective.*

an·e·mom·e·ter (an-ə-MOM-ə-tər) *noun.* An instrument that measures the speed of the wind.

a·nem·o·ne (ə-NEM-ə-nee) *noun.* A small plant with white flowers. **anemones.**

an·er·oid (AN-ə-roid) *adjective.* Having no fluid.

aneroid barometer. An instrument for measuring air pressure.

an·es·the·sia (an-iss-THEE-zhə) *noun.* A state of feeling no sensation, especially of feeling no pain.

anesthetic (an-iss-THET-ik) *noun.* A substance that causes a loss of consciousness or sensitivity to pain.

anesthetize (ə-NESS-thə-tighz) *verb.* To bring on or cause a state of no pain or sensation.

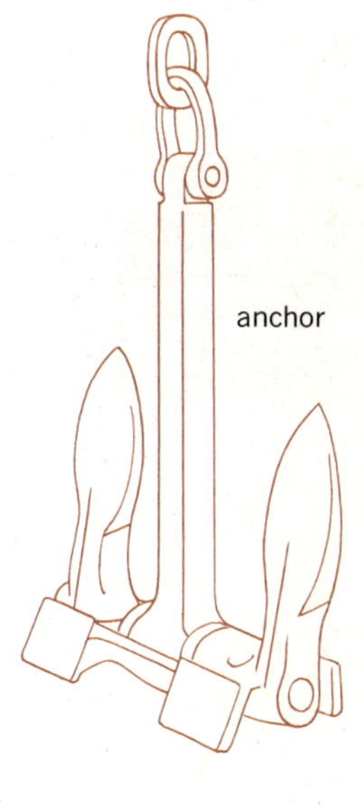
anchor

a·new (ə-NOO or ə-NYOO) *adverb.* Over again, once more: The little boy's sand castle fell down but he began to build it *anew.*

an·gel (AYN-jəl) *noun.* 1. Messenger of God, a spiritual being. 2. (Informal) A good, kind person: You're an *angel* to help Mother take care of the baby.

an·ger (ANG-gər) *noun.* A strong feeling of annoyance, irritation, or displeasure: Father showed his *anger* when he saw the car's broken headlight. —*verb.* 1. To annoy or displease very much. 2. To become upset. **angered, angering.**

an·gle (ANG-gəl) *noun.* 1. The shape or space formed by two lines meeting at one point. 2. Viewpoint: Looking at the problem from another *angle* may help you understand it better. **angles.** —*verb.* 1. To bend in an angle. 2. To move or adjust at an angle: If you *angle* the couch a little bit to the right, you will be able to get it around the corner. **angled, angling.**

angleworm

an·gle·worm (ANG-gəl-werm) *noun.* A common type of worm; an earthworm: John dug up *angleworms* to use as bait for fishing.

an·gry (ANG-gree) *adjective.* 1. Irate; feeling extremely bothered. 2. Showing annoyance: Sheila's *angry* look showed how she felt about failing the test. 3. Harsh, stormy. **angrier, angriest.** —**angrily** *adverb.*

an·guish (ANG-gwish) *noun.* 1. Worry, heartache: Mother felt a great deal of *anguish* until the police found her missing purse. 2. Pain: The injured skier writhed in *anguish.*

an·gu·lar (ANG-gyə-lər) *adjective.* 1. Having an angle or angles. 2. Thin, bony: The skinny boy had an *angular* face.

an·i·mal (AN-ə-məl) *noun.* 1. A living thing or being other than a plant: *Animals* have the ability to move, unlike plants. 2. A beast, especially a four-footed one such as a cow or an elephant.

an·i·mate (AN-ə-mayt) *verb.* 1. To bring to life, to put life into. 2. To make appear to move: Story characters are often *animated* in cartoons at the movies. **animated, animating.**

an·i·ma·tion (an-ə-MAY-shən) *noun.* Liveliness: The *animation* of the child after we gave him the ice cream was amazing; he ran and shouted with glee.

an·i·mos·i·ty (an-ə-MOSS-ə-tee) *noun.* Feeling of ill-will, hatred: His *animosity* toward the principal had changed to good will by the end of the year. **animosities.**

an·kle (ANG-kəl) *noun.* The narrow part of the leg; the joint connecting the foot and lower leg. **ankles.**

an·nex (ə-NEKS) *verb.* To add on: They *annexed* the garage to the house. **annexed, annexing.** —(AN-eks) *noun.* An addition: The new *annex* to the library will be built soon.

an·ni·hi·late (ə-NIGH-ə-layt) *verb.* To ruin so that nothing is left; destroy entirely: The town was *annihilated* by the explosion; nothing remains. **annihilated, annihilating.**

an·ni·ver·sa·ry (an-ə-VER-sər-ee) *noun.* 1. The return of a yearly date of special importance: Today is my parents' wedding *anniversary;* they have been married for 15 years. 2. The celebration of such a date. **anniversaries.**

an·nounce (ə-NOWNSS) *verb.* 1. To make public in a formal way: They *announced* my sister's engagement in the newspaper. 2. To tell, reveal: She *announced* that the class would visit the zoo. **announced, announcing.**

an·nounce·ment (ə-NOWNSS-mənt) *noun.* 1. A public or formal message or notice: The *announcement* of the school closing on Thursday was made over the public address system. 2. The act of announcing.

an·nounc·er (ə-NOWN-sər) *noun.* A person who announces or makes messages public: The radio *announcer* said that all the beaches are very crowded.

an·noy (ə-NOI) *verb.* To bother, irritate, make displeased: The buzzing of that fly *annoys* me. **annoyed, annoying.**

an·noy·ance (ə-NOI-ənss) *noun.* 1. That which bothers or irritates. 2. The feeling of being irritated. 3. The act of bothering or annoying.

an·nu·al (AN-yoo-əl) *adjective.* 1. Happening once a year: Chanukah is an *annual* holiday for people of the Jewish faith. 2. Happening or done during a year: the *annual* change of seasons. 3. Living for one year: Those are *annual* flowers; they must be replanted each year. —*noun.* A book or paper which is published once a year. —**annually** *adverb.*

an·ode (AN-ohd) *noun.* In a battery or other source of electric current, the electrode or terminal with a positive charge: This battery has two terminals, one an *anode* with a positive charge, the other a cathode with a negative charge. **anodes.**

a·noint (ə-NOINT) *verb.* 1. To put oil on: He *anointed* himself with suntan oil until his body glistened. 2. To apply oil in a religious ceremony. **anointed, anointing.**

anon. *abbreviation.* Anonymous.

a·non·y·mous (ə-NON-ə-məss) *adjective.* Unknown, unnamed: The gift was from an *anonymous* person. —**anonymously** *adverb.*

an·oth·er (ə-NUTH-ər) *adjective.* 1. One more, additional: Are we having *another* guest for dinner? 2. Not the same, different: Please give me *another* pen; this one does not work.

an·swer (AN-sər) *verb.* 1. To reply to (a question) either by speaking or by writing. 2. To reply to (a call or a signal): Jane, please *answer* the doorbell. 3. To be enough, to serve as (used with *for*): The candy bar *answered* for Jimmy's lunch. 4. To fill; conform to or be like: The little lamb *answered* the description of one of Bo Peep's lost sheep. **answered, answering.** —*noun.* 1. A reply. 2. A correct reply to a test of knowledge: Six is the *answer* for the question "What is three plus three?" 3. An action which serves as a reply: The playful boy's *answer* was to throw a snowball.

ant *noun.* A tiny red or black crawling insect that lives in colonies.

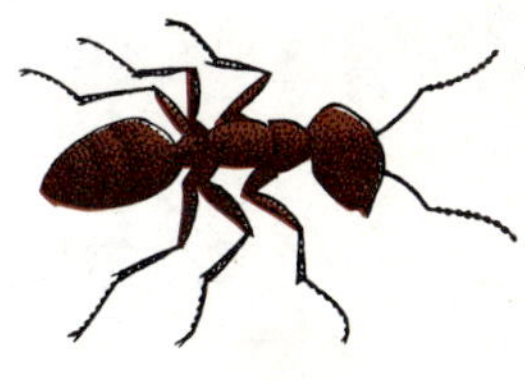
ant

ant- *prefix.* A form of the prefix "anti" used before a vowel or a silent *h* to denote being opposed to, opposite of, or against: *ant*arctic.

-ant *suffix.* Indicates: 1. One who does a certain act: serv*ant.* 2. Being in or performing a certain act: deodor*ant.*

an·tag·o·nism (an-TAG-ə-niz-əm) *noun.* Hostility, open dislike: The boy felt *antagonism* toward the man who threatened his dog. —**antagonistic** (an-tag-ə-NISS-tik) *adjective.* —**antagonistically** *adverb.*

an·tag·o·nist (an-TAG-ə-nist) *noun.* Anything or anyone in conflict or opposition with another: The boxer knocked out his *antagonist.*

an·tag·o·nize (an-TAG-ə-nighz) *verb.* To provoke, cause hostile feelings in: She purposely *antagonized* her mother by throwing her clothes on the floor. **antagonized, antagonizing.**

ant·arc·tic (ant-AHRK-tik) *adjective* (and *noun,* used with *the*). [Often capital A] Related to the South Pole region.

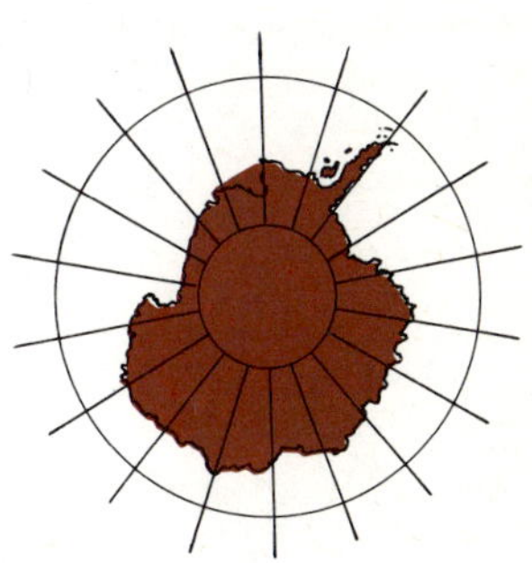
Antarctic

an·te- *prefix.* Indicates before, preceding: *ante*date, *ante*cedent.

anteater

antelope

ant·eat·er (ANT-ee-tər) *noun.* An animal with a long snout and a sticky tongue with which it catches ants.

an·te·ce·dent (an-tə-SEED-ənt) *noun.* 1. Something that precedes or comes before: The accident was the *antecedent* to the forming of the safety patrol. 2. A word or phrase which is later referred to by a pronoun: John took off his coat. "John" is the *antecedent* of "his."

an·te·lope (an-tə-LOHP) *noun.* A graceful, swift animal with long curved horns: The *antelope* is of the goat family but looks like a deer. **antelopes.**

an·ten·na (an-TEN-ə) *noun.* 1. One of two feelers on certain animals and insects. —**antennae** (an-TEN-ee) *plural.* 2. An aerial that sends or receives radio or TV signals. **antennas.**

an·them (AN-thəm) *noun.* A patriotic or sacred hymn of praise: The crowd rose to sing our national *anthem,* "The Star-Spangled Banner."

an·ther (AN-thər) *noun.* On a flower, the part of the stamen which holds the pollen.

an·thol·o·gy (an-THOL-ə-jee) *noun.* A collection of writings, stories, or poems: The book is an *anthology* of ghost stories. **anthologies.**

an·thra·cite (AN-thrə-sight) *noun.* A hard coal that burns with little smoke and bright, clean flame.

an·thro·poid (AN-thrə-poid) *adjective.* Resembling man: The gorilla is *anthropoid* because it looks something like a man.

an·thro·pol·o·gy (an-thrə-POL-ə-jee) *noun.* The study of the origins and customs of man. —**anthropologist** (an-thrə-POL-ə-jist) *noun.*

anti- *prefix.* Indicates against, opposite of, not, in opposition to: *anti*freeze, *anti*slavery.

an·ti·bi·ot·ic (an-ti-bigh-OT-ik) *noun.* A substance made from certain bacteria and fungi that has the ability to fight disease: Doctors give penicillin, an *antibiotic,* to prevent or stop infection.

an·ti·bod·y (AN-ti-bod-ee) *noun.* A chemical substance made by the blood that fights bacteria, viruses, poisons, and other substances foreign to the body. **antibodies.**

an·tic (AN-tik) *noun.* [Usually plural] A playful or silly act: The baby loved the *antics* of the kitten.

an·tic·i·pate (an-TISS-ə-payt) *verb.* 1. To look forward to, expect: She *anticipated* many adventures at summer camp. 2. To understand ahead of time; do in advance of: Leonardo da Vinci *anticipated* the invention of airplanes 500 years ago. **anticipated, anticipating.**

an·tic·i·pa·tion (an-tiss-ə-PAY-shən) *noun.* Expectation, act of looking forward to: He brought an umbrella in *anticipation* of a rainstorm.

an·ti·co·lo·ni·al·ism (ant-i-kə-LOH-nee-ə-liz-əm) *noun.* A feeling or movement against a nation which controls or conquers other lands and territories.

an·ti·dote (AN-ti-doht) *noun.* 1. Any substance or treatment given to oppose the effects of poison: Raw eggs are used as an *antidote* for certain poisons. 2. Anything that is a cure: Studying is an *antidote* for poor marks. **antidotes.**

an·ti·his·ta·mine (an-ti-HISS-tə-meen) *noun.* A drug that acts against certain allergies and colds: The doctor gave Ruth some *antihistamines* for her hay fever. **antihistamines.**

an·ti·quat·ed (AN-tə-kway-tid) *adjective.* Outdated, old-fashioned: The *antiquated* car could not keep up with the new models on the highway.

an·tique (an-TEEK) *noun.* An object, usually valuable, that is very old: This desk is a priceless *antique* that has been in our family for generations. **antiques.** *—adjective.* Old, of long ago: The *antique* rocker belonged to my grandmother.

an·tiq·ui·ty (an-TIK-wə-tee) *noun.* 1. Oldness: The building is of great *antiquity;* it was built in Caesar's time. 2. Ancient times: Homer is a poet of *antiquity.* **antiquities.**

an·ti·sep·tic (an-tə-SEP-tik) *noun.* A substance that fights disease by killing germs. *—adjective.* Free from germs: Equipment in a hospital must be kept *antiseptic.*

an·ti·so·cial (an-ti-SOH-shəl) *adjective.* 1. Unfriendly; not caring to be with people: The *antisocial* man stayed inside his house and never had visitors. 2. Harmful to society: Robbery is an *antisocial* act.

an·ti·tox·in (an-ti-TOK-sin) *noun.* A chemical made in the blood that acts against poisons and infection in the body.

ant·ler (ANT-lər) *noun.* One of two large branched horns on the head of an animal of the deer family.

an·to·nym (AN-tə-nim) *noun.* A word meaning the opposite of another word: "Heavy" is the *antonym* of "light."

a·nus (AY-nəss) *noun.* The lower opening of the alimentary canal through which solid wastes are excreted. **anuses.**

an·vil (AN-vil) *noun.* A heavy block on which metal is molded: Blacksmiths shape horseshoes on *anvils.*

anx·i·e·ty (ang-ZIGH-ə-tee) *noun.* Worry; uneasy fearful feelings: Her *anxiety* was calmed when the children returned. **anxieties.**

anx·ious (ANGK-shəss) *adjective.* 1. Worried or upset about what might happen: Dad is *anxious* about Dora's grades; he thinks she might fail. 2. Excited, eager: Gerard is very *anxious* to please his teacher. **—anxiously** *adverb.*

an·y (EN-ee) *adjective.* 1. Not a particular one: Pick *any* of those flowers and bring it to Mother. 2. Every, all: *Any* boat on the lake would be fun to sail. 3. Some: Aren't there *any* basketballs left in the gym?

an·y·bod·y (EN-ee-bod-ee) *pronoun.* 1. Any person, anyone: *Anybody* can come to the school picnic. 2. Somebody: Is *anybody* home? 3. Person of worth, value. You'll never be *anybody* if you don't stop sleeping in class.

an·y·how (EN-ee-how) *adverb.* 1. Anyway, in spite of that: I have a headache but I'll go to school *anyhow.* 2. In any manner or way: There isn't enough cake *anyhow* you slice it.

an·y·one (EN-ee-wuhn) *pronoun.* No certain person, anybody: *Anyone* in the class can come to my party.

an·y·thing (EN-ee-thing) *pronoun.* 1. No certain thing, any of an unnamed number of objects: You can bring *anything* you want on the picnic. 2. Something: Is there *anything* left in her desk?

an·y·way (EN-ee-way) *adverb.* 1. In any case, nevertheless: It may rain but let's start our picnic *anyway.* 2. Also **any way.** In any manner or method.

an·y·where (EN-ee-hwair) *adverb.* Someplace, no certain place: You have to go to a special store for that ice cream; you can't find it just *anywhere.*

a·or·ta (ay-OR-tə) *noun.* The main artery that carries blood from the heart to other, smaller arteries. **aortas.**

AP *abbreviation.* Associated Press.

a·part (ə-PAHRT) *adverb.* 1. Separate from, not together: Keep the cat and the dog *apart.* 2. Into parts or pieces: He took the toy airplane *apart.* 3. Aside, to the side: He stood in the corner of the playground, *apart* from the other children.

antlers

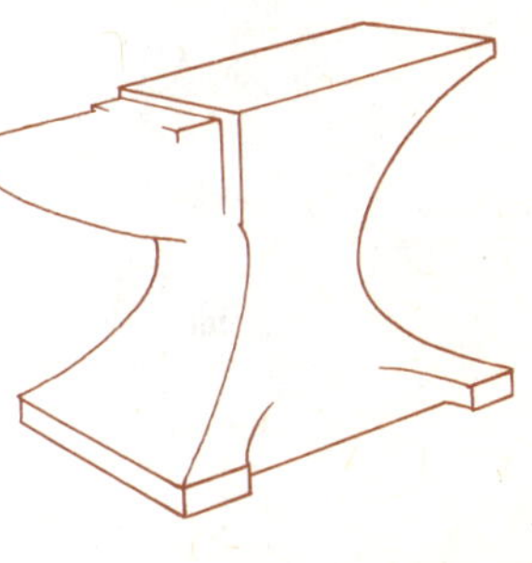
anvil

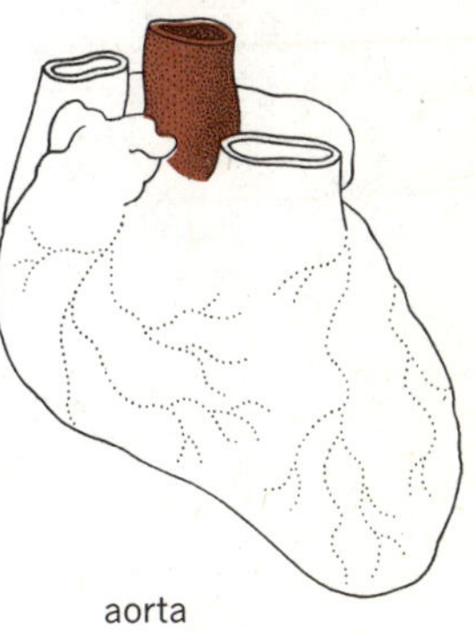
aorta

a·part·heid (ə-PAHRT-hight) *noun.* Segregation; an official policy of keeping colored races apart from and subordinate to whites in the Republic of South Africa.

a·part·ment (ə-PAHRT-mənt) *noun.* A room or group of rooms serving as living quarters in one part of a building: There are 16 *apartments* in our building.

ap·a·thy (AP-ə-thee) *noun.* Lack of feeling, interest, or emotion: The students' *apathy* showed in poor attendance at school events. **—apathetic** (ap-ə-THET-ik) *adjective.*

ape (AYP) *noun.* A powerful tailless animal of the monkey family that can walk on two legs like a man. *—verb.* To imitate, to copy: The boy *aped* the clown. **aped, aping.**

ap·er·ture (AP-ər-chər) *noun.* An opening, hole, or crack: There was an *aperture* in the fence so we could see into the yard. **apertures.**

a·pex (AY-peks) *noun.* The highest point of something: The mountain is 5,000 feet high at its *apex.* **—apexes** or **apices** (AY-pə-seez) *plural.*

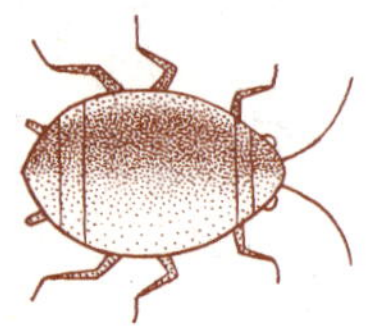

aphid

a·phid (AY-fid) *noun.* A small, crawling insect that lives by sucking juices from plants: *Aphids* are kept as "cows" by some ants.

a·piece (ə-PEESS) *adverb.* Each, for each: He gave the children an apple *apiece.*

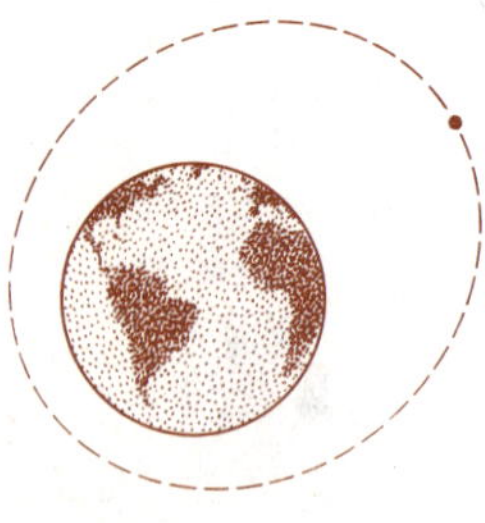

apogee

ap·o·gee (AP-ə-jee) *noun.* The point in the orbit of the moon or man-made satellite at which that body is farthest from the earth. **apogees.**

a·pol·o·get·ic (ə-pol-ə-JET-ik) *adjective.* Sorry, ready to make an apology: The boy was *apologetic* for coming home with ripped clothes.

a·pol·o·gize (ə-POL-ə-jighz) *verb.* To say that one is sorry; make an apology. **apologized, apologizing.**

a·pol·o·gy (ə-POL-ə-jee) *noun.* 1. A statement of regret: She made an *apology* for being late. 2. An explanation: He wrote an *apology* for the cost of building the playground. **apologies.**

a·pos·tle (ə-POSS-l) *noun.* 1. [Usually capital A] One of the 12 men who followed Jesus and spread his teachings. 2. One who is a teacher or missionary for a Christian religion. 3. One who starts a new or reform movement. 4. One of the 12 members of the administrative council of the Mormon Church. **apostles.**

a·pos·tro·phe (ə-POSS-trə-fee) *noun.* A punctuation mark (') that is used to show possession, as in *John's* hat. It also replaces a letter or letters in shortened or combined words: *bo's'n* (for *boatswain*). **apostrophes.**

ap·pall (ə-PAWL) *verb.* To horrify, frighten: She was *appalled* by the horrible Halloween mask. **appalled, appalling. —appallingly** *adverb.*

ap·pa·ra·tus (ap-ə-RAY-təss or ap-ə-RAT-əss) *noun.* Equipment or tools for a certain job: Our garage does not have the *apparatus* needed for towing a car. **—apparatus** or **apparatuses** *plural.*

ap·par·el (ə-PA-rəl) *noun.* Clothing: Her *apparel* for the weekend included jeans and a bathing suit.

ap·par·ent (ə-PA-rənt) *adjective.* Appearing real, obvious: It is *apparent* that Dad is in a bad mood this morning. **—apparently** *adverb.*

ap·pa·ri·tion (ap-ə-RISH-ən) *noun.* A ghost; a strange image: Some say that house is haunted by the *apparition* of its former owner.

ap·peal (ə-PEEL) *verb.* 1. To make a request (as for help): They *appealed* to the Coast Guard to rescue the sailors. 2. To attract, to interest: I would like to play tennis; the sport *appeals* to me. 3. (Used with *to*) To try to arouse: She *appealed* to her mother's good nature by looking sad. 4. (Law) To take a case to a higher court. **appealed, appealing.** —*noun.* 1. A call or request for help. 2. A request to take a legal case to a higher court for review.

ap·peal·ing (ə-PEEL-ing) *adjective.* Causing interest, affection, or appeal; attractive: The women were attracted by the *appealing* display in the shop window. —**appealingly** *adverb.*

ap·pear (ə-PIHR) *verb.* 1. To come into view: When the leaves *appeared,* we knew it was spring. 2. To give the outward appearance of: Their dog *appears* friendly but he can be very mean. 3. To come before the public: The actor has *appeared* on television. **appeared, appearing.**

ap·pear·ance (ə-PIHR-ənss) *noun.* 1. The act of being visible: Her sudden *appearance* in the room startled us. 2. Coming before the public: The singer will make an *appearance* at the school. 3. One's condition; the way someone looks. **appearances.**

ap·pease (ə-PEEZ) *verb.* 1. To calm, to still: The angry bear was *appeased* when the zoo keeper returned the cubs. 2. To satisfy: Her thirst was *appeased* by the cold lemonade. **appeased, appeasing.** —**appeasement** *noun.*

ap·pen·dage (ə-PEN-dij) *noun.* A limb, a part attached to the main body of something: A leg is an *appendage;* so is the branch of a tree. **appendages.**

ap·pen·di·ci·tis (ə-pen-də-SIGH-tiss) *noun.* A condition in which the appendix is inflamed and sore.

ap·pen·dix (ə-PEN-diks) *noun.* 1. A short, narrow growth from the large intestine. 2. An addition at the end of a book containing additional information. —**appendixes** or **appendices** (ə-PEN-də-seez) *plural.*

ap·pe·tite (AP-ə-tight) *noun.* 1. Desire, need for food. 2. Desire, longing, need: Jim's *appetite* for learning is great; he reads every day. **appetites.**

ap·pe·tiz·er (AP-ə-tighz-ər) *noun.* Food eaten before the main part of a meal.

ap·plaud (ə-PLAWD) *verb.* 1. To clap, show approval: The audience *applauded* the dancers. 2. To show appreciation, admiration: We *applaud* his efforts to study harder. **applauded, applauding.**

ap·plause (ə-PLAWZ) *noun.* 1. The act of showing approval by clapping or other sounds. 2. The sound made by clapping.

ap·ple (AP-əl) *noun.* A round red, yellow, or green fleshy fruit; the tree on which this fruit grows. **apples.**

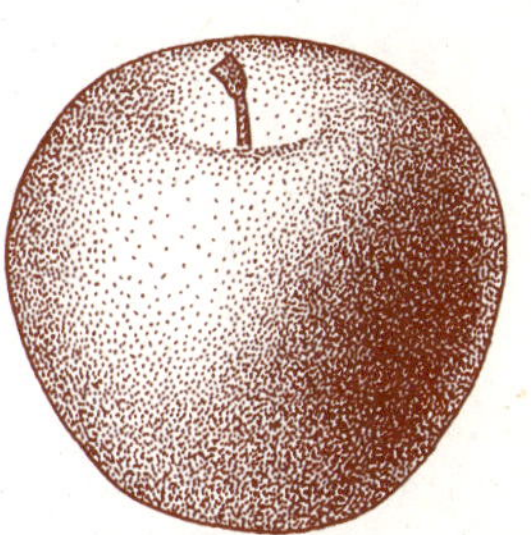

apple

apple-polish (AP-əl-pol-ish) *verb.* (Slang) To seek approval with flattery, often insincere. **apple-polished, apple-polishing.**

ap·ple·sauce (ap-əl-SAWSS) *noun.* 1. A sweet sauce made with stewed apples, sugar, and cinnamon. 2. (Slang) Nonsense!

ap·pli·ance (ə-PLIGH-ənss) *noun.* A tool or other device for doing a job, usually in the home: A stove is an *appliance* and so is an electric mixer. **appliances.**

ap·pli·cant (AP-lə-kənt) *noun.* A person who formally writes or asks for a position: The new *applicant* for the swim team was asked to try out today.

ap·pli·ca·tion (ap-lə-KAY-shən) *noun.* 1. A formal request for something or for some position: Jerry filled out an *application* so that he could go to summer camp. 2. Putting or rubbing something on: *Application* of extra wax made our car shine. 3. The substance that is applied or put on. 4. Putting to use: Dad's *application* of common sense solved our family argument. 5. Attention, effort: His *application* to his job makes him a good worker.

ap·ply (ə-PLIGH) *verb.* 1. To request formally: He *applied* for a position on the school newspaper. 2. To put or spread on: Jim *applied* two coats of paint to the house. 3. To relate (to): Traffic rules *apply* to everyone. 4. To devote; put effort into: He *applied* himself to the drawing because he wanted to be an artist. **applied, applying.**

ap·point (ə-POINT) *verb.* 1. To pick, choose: The teacher *appointed* Diane to clean the blackboards. 2. To select, decide, set: Saturday is *appointed* as the day for the picnic. **appointed, appointing.**

ap·point·ment (ə-POINT-mənt) *noun.* 1. A set or planned meeting: He made an *appointment* to go to the dentist. 2. The selection or naming of one to a certain position: Karen worked hard so she would get an *appointment* to the dance committee.

ap·praise (ə-PRAYZ) *verb.* 1. To find the value of: He *appraised* the car and said that it was worth a thousand dollars. 2. To seek the nature of: Ellen *appraised* her father's mood before asking for an increased allowance. **appraised, appraising.**

ap·pre·ci·able (ə-PREE-shə-bəl) *adjective.* Marked, notable; able to be felt or seen: There was an *appreciable* amount of water in the basement after the storm.

ap·pre·ci·ate (ə-PREE-shee-ayt) *verb.* 1. To be thankful for: Elizabeth *appreciated* the big chocolate cake Grandma made for her. 2. To know, understand: Her first trip to the city made her *appreciate* the difficulty of finding a place to park. 3. To see the value or worth in: Diane *appreciates* friendship. **appreciated, appreciating.** —**appreciation** *noun.*

ap·pre·hend (AP-ri-hend) *verb.* 1. To arrest or catch: The police *apprehended* the car thief. 2. To understand. 3. To look forward to with uncertainty. **apprehended, apprehending.**

ap·pre·hen·sion (ap-ri-HEN-shən) *noun.* 1. Uneasiness, fear: She had a feeling of *apprehension* as she entered the gloomy old house. 2. Understanding: His *apprehension* of math problems is excellent. 3. The act of arresting or stopping.

ap·pren·tice (ə-PREN-tiss) *noun.* A beginner, an assistant; one who assists in a certain trade in order to learn that trade: As an *apprentice,* Jack learned new skills from the carpenter. **apprentices.**

ap·proach (ə-PROHCH) *verb.* 1. To come near, verge on: We could see them more clearly as they *approached* our house. 2. To come close to in manner, amount, or quality: His skill in basketball does not *approach* Bill's. **approached, approaching.** —*noun.* 1. The act of coming close: Birds could hear the cat's *approach* because of the bell on its collar. 2. Way of entering or reaching (someone or something): The only *approach* to the farmhouse was a dirt road. **approaches.**

ap·pro·pri·ate (ə-PROH-pree-it) *adjective.* Proper or suitable: Blue jeans are not *appropriate* for a formal occasion. —(ə-PROH-pree-ayt) *verb.* 1. To set aside for a special purpose: The committee has *appropriated* funds to be used for education. 2. To take for one's own use: Wally *appropriated* the camp's only boat; now the rest of us are stranded. **appropriated, appropriating.** —**appropriately** *adverb.*

ap·pro·pri·a·tion (ə-proh-pree-AY-shən) *noun.* 1. Anything, especially money, set aside for a special purpose: The library was given an *appropriation* of 500 dollars for new magazines and books. 2. The act or process of setting something aside for a special purpose or taking for one's own use: The boy was punished for his *appropriation* of school property.

ap·prov·al (ə-PROOV-əl) *noun.* 1. The act of approving or thinking well of; acceptance: Sally's efforts to make the party cheerful met with everyone's *approval.* 2. Permission or consent: The principal gave her *approval* for our class party. **—on approval.** Without obligation to purchase unless satisfied after examination and use: My dad bought the radio after having it for one week *on approval.*

ap·prove (ə-PROOV) *verb.* 1. To think well of: Mother *approved* of my new friends. 2. To accept as good or satisfactory: I'm glad that the teacher *approved* your choice of a book for a history report. 3. To give consent to: Mother *approved* our request for a new bike. **approved, approving.**

ap·prox·i·mate (ə-PROK-sə-mit) *adjective.* Nearly correct; almost exact: The *approximate* price is $10; the exact price is $9.98. —(ə-PROK-sə-mayt) *verb.* To be similar to or almost the same as: The statue *approximates* the appearance of Abraham Lincoln. **approximated, approximating. —approximately** *adverb.*

a·pri·cot (AY-pri-kot or AP-ri-kot) *noun.* 1. A sweet, rosy-yellow or orange-colored fruit, resembling a small peach. 2. The tree on which apricots grow. 3. (Also *adjective*) A rosy-yellow color.

A·pril (AY-prəl) *noun.* The fourth month of the year: There are 30 days in *April.* **—Apr.** *abbreviation.*

April fool. A person who is the object of a joke or trick on April 1st, April Fool's Day.

a·pron (AY-prən) *noun.* 1. A garment worn over the front part of the body to protect one's clothing. 2. A section or area, usually forming an edge or border of a flat surface like a stage, platform, or roadway.

ap·ro·pos (ap-rə-POH) *adjective.* Significant; relevant; appropriate: Steve's remarks were *apropos;* he didn't wander off the subject. —*adverb.* With reference to: Priscilla's comments were made *apropos* our problem.

apt *adjective.* 1. Likely; inclined: That vicious dog is *apt* to bite someone. 2. Appropriate; suitable: The teacher was pleased by Harriet's *apt* reply. 3. Bright; alert; quick to learn: Billy is an *apt* pupil; he learns quickly. **—aptly** *adverb.*

ap·ti·tude (AP-tə-tood) *noun.* 1. A natural talent or ability for something: Mark has an *aptitude* for drawing. 2. Quickness to learn: Albert amazed us by his *aptitude* in science class. **aptitudes.**

Aq·ua-Lung (AK-wə-luhng) *trademark.* An underwater breathing device for skin divers, consisting of an air tank connected to air hose and mouthpiece. *See* **scuba.**

aq·ua·naut (AK-wə-nawt) *noun.* A man or woman who is trained to live in an underwater base and to do scientific research there.

aq·ua·plane (AK-wə-playn) *noun.* A wide, smooth board on which a person can be towed by a motorboat for sport or recreation: Leo likes to use the water skis; I prefer the *aquaplane.* **aquaplanes.** —*verb.* To ride on an aquaplane. **aquaplaned, aquaplaning.**

a·quar·i·um (ə-KWAIR-ee-əm) *noun.* 1. A glass tank, bowl, or pond used to contain collections of fish and other water animals and plants. 2. A building or area where collections of fish and other water animals and plants, especially rare or unusual ones, are displayed.

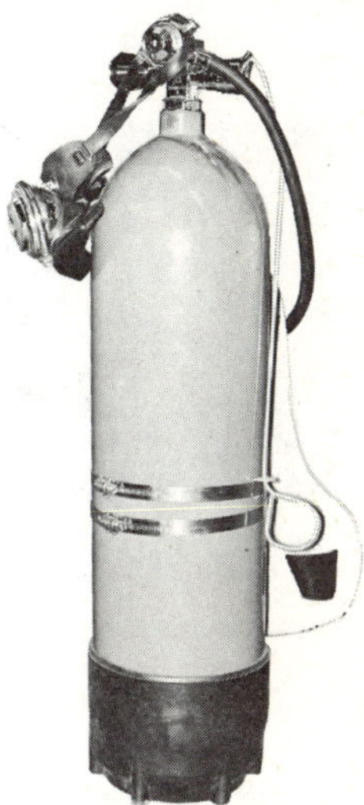
Aqua-Lung

apricot

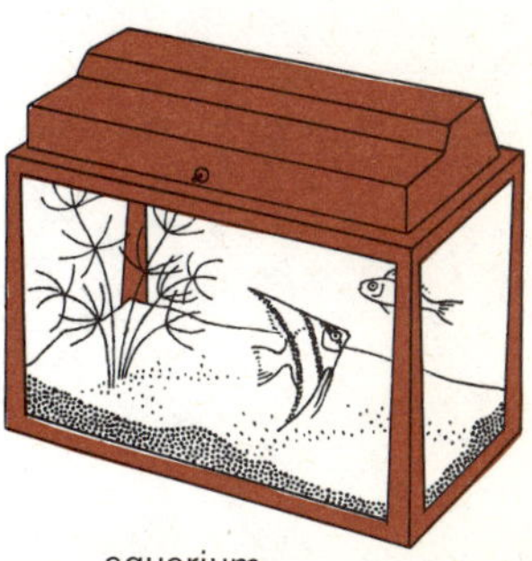
aquarium

Aquarius

aqueduct

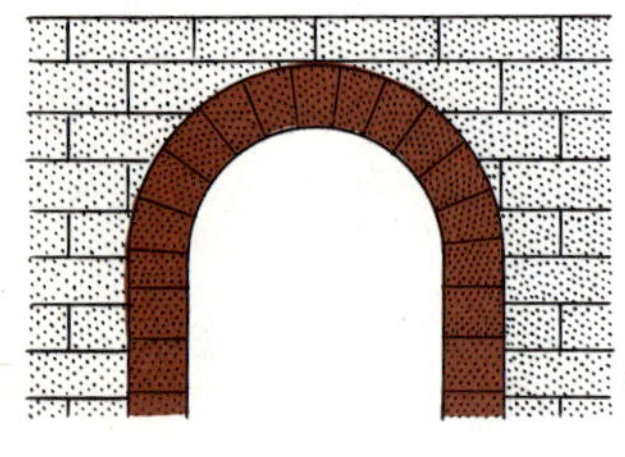
arch

A·quar·i·us (ə-KWAIR-ee-əss) *noun.* The 11th sign of the zodiac, also known as the "Water Bearer." The time of this sign is from January 20 through February 18.

a·quat·ic (ə-KWOT-ik) *adjective.* 1. Existing in water: Seaweed is a type of *aquatic* plant. 2. Performed in or on water.

aq·ue·duct (AK-wə-duhkt) *noun.* 1. A large pipe, canal, or other carrier used to bring water a long distance. 2. A structure that supports a pipe or similar water carrier across a valley or river.

aq·ui·fer (AK-wə-fər) *noun.* An underground bed of rock or sand through which water can move easily.

-ar *suffix.* Indicates being related to, similar, or like: pol*ar*, cellul*ar*.

Ar·a·bic nu·mer·als (A-rə-bik NOO-mər-əlz) *noun.* The numbers 0, 1, 2, 3, 4, 5, 6, 7, 8, 9.

ar·a·ble (A-rə-bəl) *adjective.* Suitable for growing crops: A desert region contains little *arable* land.

ar·bi·trar·y (AHR-bə-trehr-ee) *adjective.* 1. According to one's own choice, wishes, or mood rather than to rules or law: Howard's decision to end the ball game was an *arbitrary* one; we wanted to keep playing. 2. Unjustified; fickle.

ar·bi·trate (AHR-bə-trayt) *verb.* 1. To settle an argument or disagreement between two sides by accepting the decision of a third person or group. 2. To act as the judge in a dispute. **arbitrated, arbitrating.**

ar·bi·tra·tion (ahr-bə-TRAY-shən) *noun.* The process of reaching a settlement in a dispute by having another person or persons decide or judge the differences involved: The boys' argument was settled by the teacher's *arbitration.*

ar·bor (AHR-bər) *noun.* A shady place formed by overhanging branches or vines often supported by a wooden or metal frame: Roses grow over the *arbor* in our garden.

Arbor Day. (U.S.) A special day for planting trees, set aside in most states in late spring.

ar·bo·re·tum (ahr-bə-REE-təm) *noun.* A place where trees and shrubs are grown to be admired or studied. —**arboretums** or **arboreta** *plural.*

arc (AHRK) *noun.* 1. A curved line: The rocket left an *arc* of smoke in the sky. 2. Part of a circle: Two *arcs* are formed when a circle is cut in half. 3. A band of bright light or sparks formed when an electric current jumps between two conductors. —*verb.* To move or shoot in a curve: The golfer *arced* the ball over the trees. **arced** or **arcked, arcing** or **arcking.**

ar·cade (ahr-KAYD) *noun.* 1. A row of arches supported by columns. 2. An arched or covered street or passageway, usually lined with shops. **arcades.**

¹arch (AHRCH) *noun.* 1. A curved structure designed to support a heavy weight above a door, window, or other opening. 2. Anything in the shape of an arch, especially a monument. 3. The upper part of the foot; instep: Shoes are laced over the *arch* of the foot. **arches.** —*verb.* 1. To curve; to put into the form of an arch: The swan *arched* its neck. 2. To cover with an arch; to span: "By the rude bridge that *arched* the flood. . . ." (Emerson). **arched, arching.**

²arch *adjective.* 1. Chief; principal: Nino was defeated by his *arch* rival. 2. Sly; mischievous: Lee's *arch* expression made me suspicious. —**archly** *adverb.*

arch- *prefix.* Indicates foremost or chief: *arch*bishop.

ar·chae·ol·o·gist (ahr-kee-OL-ə-jist) Also **archeologist** *noun.* A person who studies ancient people and cultures by examining tools, pottery, pictures, clothing, and other relics.

ar·chae·ol·o·gy (ahr-kee-OL-ə-jee) Also **archeology** *noun.* The science or study of ancient peoples or cultures through the examination of their relics or remains.

arch·bish·op (ahrch-BISH-əp) *noun.* Highest in rank among bishops, the leader in charge of a number of church districts.

arch·di·o·cese (ahrch-DIGH-ə-siss) *noun.* A district in which members of a religion are ruled over by an archbishop.

arch·er (AHR-chər) *noun.* A person who shoots with bow and arrows.

arch·er·y (AHR-chər-ee) *noun.* The sport of shooting with bow and arrows.

ar·chi·pel·a·go (ahr-kə-PEL-ə-goh) *noun.* 1. A group of islands. 2. A body of water with many islands in it. **archipelagos** or **archipelagoes.**

ar·chi·tect (AHR-kə-tekt) *noun.* 1. A person who designs buildings or other structures and supervises their construction. 2. Any planner or designer.

ar·chi·tec·ture (AHR-kə-tek-chər) *noun.* 1. The art or profession of designing and constructing buildings and other structures. 2. A specific style of construction: The old cathedral is an example of Roman *architecture.* 3. Buildings and other structures considered in general: The *architecture* of Athens is a mixture of classical Greek and later styles.

ar·chives (AHR-kighvz) *noun, plural.* 1. A place for storing such records as census and tax facts or historical documents. 2. The records and legal papers themselves.

-archy *suffix.* Indicates rule or governing: mon*archy*, patri*archy*.

arc·tic (AHRK-tik or AHR-tik) *noun.* 1. [Often capital A] The geographic area around the North Pole. 2. [Capital A] The Arctic Ocean. —*adjective.* 1. Related to, from, or of the area around the North Pole: An *arctic* fox turns white in winter. 2. Very cold; frigid: The farmers feared an *arctic* winter.

ar·dent (AHR-dənt) *adjective.* Intensely devoted or eager; enthusiastic: Irene is an *ardent* admirer of that author; she has read all his books. —**ardently** *adverb.*

ar·dor (AHR-dər) *noun.* Intense devotion or enthusiasm; eagerness: The *ardor* with which Tom studied amazed his parents.

ar·du·ous (AHR-joo-əss) *adjective.* Very difficult; hard to do: Ted finds doing his homework an *arduous* task. —**arduously** *adverb.*

are (AHR) *verb. See* **be.**

ar·e·a (AIR-ee-ə) *noun.* 1. A region; territory: The boys searched the wooded *area* for their lost ball. 2. Range; field; scope: History is Winston's favorite *area* of study. 3. The extent or amount of a surface, measured in square units: The *area* of this floor is 140 square feet. 4. A yard or any other open space of land.

archipelago

area code. The three digits which precede a local telephone number to identify a particular area of a state or a country: To dial a long distance call to New York City, one must use a "212" *area code.*

a·re·na (ə-REE-nə) *noun.* 1. A place for holding sporting events or other entertainments, especially a building for such a purpose: A crowd of 10,000 filled the *arena* to watch the football game. 2. Any area or place of conflict or competition: The jungle was the army's *arena* for battle.

aren't (AHRNT) *contraction.* A shortened form of the words *are not:* These girls are playing hopscotch, those girls *aren't.*

Arizona
★capital: Phoenix

ark

Aries

Arkansas
★capital: Little Rock

ar·gon (AHR-gon) *noun.* An inactive gas, with no color or smell, used in electric and fluorescent lights.

ar·gue (AHR-gyoo) *verb.* 1. To dispute or have a disagreement with: The boys *argued* with the umpire about his call. 2. To present another side of a discussion: Leonard *argued* against taking piano lessons. **argued, arguing.**

ar·gu·ment (AHR-gyə-mənt) *noun.* 1. A disagreement, debate, or dispute: The two players had an *argument* about the rules of the card game. 2. A reason offered for or against something: Joe's *argument* for less homework is a good one. 3. A summary of the main idea of a speech or written work.

ar·id (A-rid) *adjective.* 1. Dry; without life: A desert is an *arid* region. 2. Boring; uninteresting.

Ar·ies (AIR-eez) *noun.* The first sign of the zodiac, also called the "Ram." The time of this sign is from March 21 through April 19.

a·rise (ə-RIGHZ) *verb.* 1. To stand: Everyone must *arise* when a judge enters the courtroom. 2. To travel skyward: Smoke will *arise* from the burning leaves. 3. To come into being, especially as the result of something: Herb's errors on the tests *arise* from carelessness. **arose, arisen, arising.**

ar·is·toc·ra·cy (a-riss-TOK-rə-see) *noun.* 1. A form of government in which a select few, usually the highest in rank, rule. 2. The group that rules such a government. 3. A country ruled by a select few. 4. Persons who have a very high rank and special privileges, especially those who have noble titles: Dukes, countesses and earls are members of the *aristocracy.* 5. Persons regarded as above others because of wealth, intelligence, or achievement. **aristocracies.**

a·ris·to·crat (ə-RISS-tə-krat) *noun.* 1. A member of a select group, especially a member of the nobility. 2. A person who has aristocratic dignity or bearing.

a·rith·me·tic (ə-RITH-mə-tik) *noun.* The study of numbers; process of solving problems with numbers. —**arithmetic** (a-rith-MET-ik) *adjective.*

arithmetic mean. An average found by dividing the sum of a set of quantities by the number of quantities in that set.

Ar·i·zo·na (a-rə-ZOH-nə) *noun.* A western state of the United States, 48th to join the Union (1912). —**Ariz.** *abbreviation.* Also **AZ** for Zip Codes.

ark (AHRK) *noun.* 1. The boat on which Noah and his family survived the flood described in the Old Testament. 2. A chest containing the Ten Commandments and other relics of God's agreement with the Israelites. 3. Any big and roomy boat.

Ar·kan·sas (AHR-kən-saw) *noun.* A south central state of the United States, 25th to join the Union (1836). —**Ark.** *abbreviation.* Also **AR** for Zip Codes.

arm (AHRM) *noun.* 1. The part of the human body that connects the shoulder to the wrist and the hand. 2. Something that resembles or is used like a human arm: the *arm* of a chair. 3. (Usually plural) Weapons: The hardware store sold rifles and other *arms.* —*verb.* 1. To provide oneself or others with weapons; prepare for battle. 2. To strengthen oneself against temptation or difficulty: Paul *armed* himself with oranges and candy bars before the long hike. **armed, arming.** —**at arm's length.** At a distance; not close; not in a friendly way: The boys held their new classmate *at arm's length.* —**up in arms.** Very angry; outraged. —**with open arms.** With a hearty welcome.

ar·ma·da (ahr-MAH-də) *noun.* 1. A large fleet of armed ships or planes. 2. [Capital A] The powerful naval force sent by Spain against England in 1588; the Spanish Armada.

ar·ma·dil·lo (ahr-mə-DIL-oh) *noun.* A small, burrowing mammal with a covering of bony plates, found mainly in South America and southern North America. **armadillos.**

ar·ma·ment (AHR-mə-mənt) *noun.* Equipment for waging war, especially the amount of military equipment possessed by a specific unit, ship, plane, tank, or other vehicle.

ar·ma·ture (AHR-mə-chur) *noun.* 1. A protective covering; armor. 2. A moving part of an electric motor or dynamo. **armatures.**

arm·chair (AHRM-chair) *noun.* A chair with supports on the sides for a person's arms. —*adjective.* Looking on from outside; being concerned about actions in which one has no part: My uncle is an *armchair* quarterback; he thinks he knows more than the ballplayers.

armed forces. All the naval, military and air forces of a country considered together: Sailors, marines, soldiers, and airmen are all members of the *armed forces.*

ar·mi·stice (AHR-mə-stiss) *noun.* A halt in a war or a military action by a pact between the hostile parties; a truce. **armistices.**

arm·load (AHRM-lohd) *noun.* The quantity that can be taken up in one or both arms; an armful.

ar·mor (AHR-mər) *noun.* 1. Any protective covering: The turtle carries a shell of *armor.* 2. A suit of protective material, usually metal, worn in battle: knights in shining *armor.* 3. A mechanized unit of the armed forces: When the major requested more *armor,* the general sent him a column of tanks. —*verb.* To cover or plate with metal or some other protective material. **armored, armoring.**

ar·mor·y (AHR-mər-ee) *noun.* 1. A place where weapons are stored; an arsenal. 2. A place where weapons are made. 3. A building in which reserve units of the armed forces drill. **armories.**

armour. British form of **armor.**

arm·pit (AHRM-pit) *noun.* The part of the human body under the arm at the shoulder.

ar·my (AHR-mee) *noun.* 1. A number of men brought together and trained for land combat. 2. [Capital A] The U.S. Army. 3. Any large number or group of persons, animals or things, especially a group united for a common cause: An *army* of grasshoppers swept through the field. **armies.**

a·ro·ma (ə-ROH-mə) *noun.* A fragrance; a pleasing odor: The hot apple pie had a delightful *aroma.*

ar·o·mat·ic (a-rə-MAT-ik) *adjective.* Fragrant; having a pleasing odor. —**aromatically** *adverb.*

a·rose (ə-ROHZ) *verb. See* **arise.**

a·round (ə-ROWND) *preposition.* 1. Circling about; on all sides of: Alice walked *around* the tree. 2. Encircling; on all sides: He placed the ring *around* her finger. 3. Here and there in: I'll see you *around* town. 4. Near: He is *around* here someplace. 5. Nearly; about: Bob weighs *around* 120 pounds. —*adverb.* 1. In a circle: The skater spun *around* rapidly. 2. On every side: The children began to gather *around.* 3. In the opposite direction: Close your eyes and turn *around.*

a·rouse (ə-ROWZ) *verb.* 1. To excite to action or enthusiasm: The coach's pep talk *aroused* the tired team. 2. To wake up; awaken: The loud noise *aroused* Susie from her nap. **aroused, arousing.**

armadillo

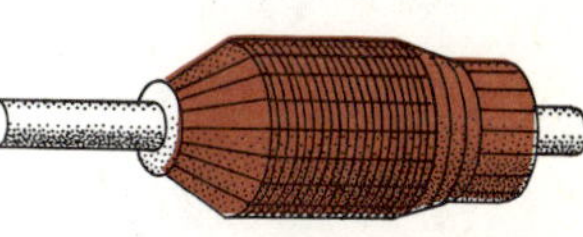
armature

armchair

armor

ar·range (ə-RAYNJ) *verb.* 1. To plan or prepare: The girls *arranged* our class picnic. 2. To put into correct order: Dan *arranged* the names in alphabetical order. 3. To adapt or adjust a work of music for a particular style, instrument, or performer: The composer *arranged* the classical music to suit the singer. **arranged, arranging.**

ar·range·ment (ə-RAYNJ-mənt) *noun.* 1. A plan or preparation: The *arrangements* for the class trip were made by our teacher. 2. A putting into correct order: The *arrangement* of our seats in class was done on the first day of school. 3. The order or shape into which something is put: The *arrangement* of the flowers was very pleasing. 4. An agreement or settlement: Tommy worked out an *arrangement* with Dad for an allowance. 5. A special adaptation or version of a musical work.

ar·ray (ə-RAY) *noun.* 1. An orderly arrangement, especially of persons: The soldiers were drawn up in battle *array.* 2. An impressive and orderly display: An *array* of flowers decorated the table. 3. Clothing, especially rich clothing: The queen was dressed in beautiful *array.* 4. (Math) a. Numbers arranged in rows going both across and up and down. b. A series of numbers or terms arranged according to value or size. —*verb.* 1. To put in order; arrange. 2. To dress, especially in rich clothing. **arrayed, arraying.**

ar·rest (ə-REST) *verb.* 1. To seize or delay by authority of the law: The policeman *arrested* the thief. 2. To attract or catch and hold: The display of beautiful dresses *arrested* Tammy's attention. 3. To stop or halt; to slow down: The new medicine *arrested* the spread of the disease. **arrested, arresting.** —*noun.* 1. A seizing or delaying by authority of the law. 2. A stopping or slowing down.

arrow

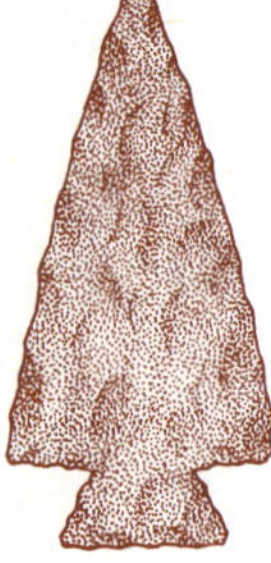

arrowhead

ar·ri·val (ə-RIGH-vəl) *noun.* 1. The act of reaching a place, position or conclusion: The *arrival* of the school bus is expected in five minutes. 2. Someone who reaches a place: The first *arrivals* at camp looked tired when they got off the bus.

ar·rive (ə-RIGHV) *verb.* 1. To come to; reach: The boys have just *arrived* at the party. 2. To come to or reach (a position or conclusion): Virginia and Jane *arrived* at an agreement; they would do the dishes together. 3. To come to be: The time to leave has *arrived.* **arrived, arriving.**

ar·ro·gance (A-rə-gənss) *noun.* Harsh pride; haughty or snobbish behavior.

ar·ro·gant (A-rə-gənt) *adjective.* Offensively proud, feeling important without good reason: The *arrogant* shopper interrupted Mother's talk with the sales clerk. —**arrogantly** *adverb.*

ar·row (A-roh) *noun.* 1. A slender, pointed shaft or rod, usually of wood, that is shot from a bow. 2. A line or mark with a point at one end used to indicate direction: The *arrow* on the road sign showed that the park was to the left.

ar·row·head (A-roh-hed) *noun.* The pointed tip or head of an arrow.

ar·roy·o (ə-ROI-oh) *noun.* A narrow, steep-sided gully or ditch which is usually dry except after heavy rainfall: *Arroyos* are usually found where the climate is dry and the land is rocky. **arroyos.**

ar·se·nal (AHR-sə-nəl) *noun.* 1. A building or place for storing, making, or repairing weapons and other military equipment. 2. A stock of military weapons.

ar·se·nic (AHR-sə-nik) *noun.* A gray-white substance that is a deadly poison.

ar·son (AHR-sən) *noun.* The crime of deliberately setting fire to a building or other property.

art (AHRT) *noun.* 1. The creation of beauty, especially in painting, drawing, and sculpture. 2. A field of activity devoted to creating beauty: Music is a universal *art.* 3. Works of beauty: The *art* of Michelangelo has been admired for centuries. 4. A craft or skill, especially one developed through experience: Carpentry and watchmaking are *arts.* 5. The ability, method or principles involved in a craft or skill: The *art* of being a good tailor takes years to acquire. 6. Skill or ability in conducting any social activity: Jean has acquired the *art* of pleasant conversation.

ar·ter·y (AHR-tər-ee) *noun.* 1. A vessel that carries blood from the heart to another part of the body. 2. A major roadway or other line of travel or transportation: The river and the turnpike are the two main *arteries* into the city. **arteries.** —**arterial** (ahr-TIHR-ee-əl) *adjective.*

ar·te·sian well. A deep man-made hole from which water flows by the force of underground pressure.

ar·ti·choke (AHR-tə-chohk) *noun.* A vegetable with a large flower head or the plant on which it grows. **artichokes.**

ar·ti·cle (AHR-ti-kəl) *noun.* 1. A particular item: Patty packed several *articles* of clothing in a suitcase. 2. One of several items of writing in a magazine, newspaper or book: Geraldine read an *article* about sewing in the magazine. 3. A specific section of a document: Strikes are forbidden by the third *article* of this contract. 4. (Grammar) One of the words *a, an,* or *the,* which are used to modify nouns. **articles.**

ar·tic·u·late (ahr-TIK-yə-lit) *adjective.* 1. Able to speak clearly or to express oneself effectively: The *articulate* speaker kept his audience very interested. 2. Clearly organized and expressed: The class praised Daniel's *articulate* speech. 3. Pronounced distinctly: We admired the actor's *articulate* reading of the story. —*verb.* (ahr-TIK-yə-layt) 1. To organize and express clearly. 2. To pronounce distinctly. **articulated, articulating.** —**articulately** *adverb.*

ar·ti·fact (AHR-tə-fakt) *noun.* A simple object made by human hands, particularly by men in prehistoric times.

ar·ti·fice (AHR-tə-fiss) *noun.* 1. Trickery; deception. 2. Skill, cleverness. **artifices.**

ar·ti·fi·cial (ahr-tə-FISH-əl) *adjective.* 1. Made by man rather than by nature: The plastic flowers look natural, but they are really *artificial.* 2. False; insincere. —**artificially** *adverb.*

ar·til·ler·y (ahr-TIL-ər-ee) *noun.* 1. Cannon and other heavy mounted guns. 2. The soldiers or branch of the Army involved in the use of artillery. **artilleries.**

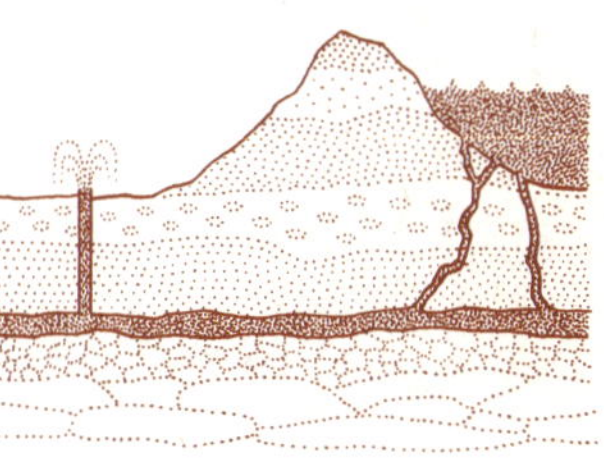

artesian well

art·ist (AHR-tist) *noun.* 1. A person who draws or paints pictures. 2. A person skilled in music, dancing, sculpture, or any of the other arts. 3. A person who possesses or practices a special skill: The old carpenter is an *artist.* 4. A performer; an entertainer.

ar·tis·tic (ahr-TISS-tik) *adjective.* 1. Of or related to art or artists. 2. Having good taste or liking for beauty. —**artistically** *adverb.*

art·less (AHRT-liss) *adjective.* Simple, natural; without slyness or falseness. —**artlessly** *adverb.*

-ary *suffix.* Indicates reference to or connection with: diction*ary,* element*ary.*

artichoke

as (AZ) *adverb.* 1. To the same point; equally: Our cat is as big *as* your dog. 2. For example: There are many green vegetables, *as* peas, string beans, or spinach. —*conjunction.* 1. During, while: The dwarfs whistled *as* they worked. 2. Because: She did not go to school *as* she was ill. 3. In the same way: Johnny goes home *as* I do, by bus. —**as is.** In the condition in which something is presently found: My mother bought on sale a table that was marked *as is;* it had scratches all over it.

as·bes·tos (as-BESS-təss or az-BESS-təss) *noun.* 1. A substance used for making fireproof items. 2. A type of fireproof fabric.

as·ca·rid (ASS-kə-rid) Also **ascaris** *noun.* A whitish, parasitic roundworm that infects animal and human intestines.

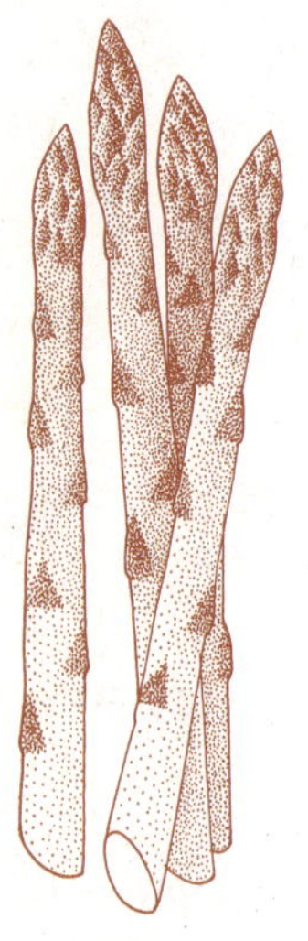

asparagus

as·cend (ə-SEND) *verb.* 1. To travel upward: The climbers *ascended* the mountain. 2. To rise to a higher rank or position: Herb *ascended* to the rank of Eagle Scout. **ascended, ascending.**

as·cent (ə-SENT) *noun.* 1. The process of rising or going up: The *ascent* of the plane was very rapid. 2. A climbing or rising in place or position: The major's *ascent* to colonel pleased his troops.

as·cer·tain (ass-ər-TAYN) *verb.* To get from a reliable source; to determine: Janet examined a dictionary to *ascertain* the correct spelling of the word. **ascertained, ascertaining.**

as·cribe (ə-SKRIGHB) *verb.* To attribute (to) or connect with a cause or source: Cliff's sickness was *ascribed* to a poor diet. **ascribed, ascribing.**

aspen

ash *noun.* 1. That which remains after something has been completely burned: The *ash* from his cigarette fell on the rug. 2. A type of shade tree or the tough wood from that tree. **ashes.**

a·shamed (ə-SHAYMD) *adjective.* Not proud; guilty or embarrassed: After the argument Tom was *ashamed* of his childish behavior. —**ashamedly** (ə-SHAY-mid-lee) *adverb.*

ash·en (ASH-ən) *adjective.* Gray or very pale; resembling the color of ashes.

a·shore (ə-SHOR) *adverb.* To or on the shore: The sailors rowed *ashore.*

a·side (ə-SIGHD) *adverb.* 1. To either side: Push the chair *aside.* 2. In reserve: Nelson spent some money and put the rest *aside.* 3. Apart from one's mind: Put your worries *aside* and relax. —*noun.* A comment made softly by an actor to the audience so that others on stage seem not to hear it. **asides.**

ask *verb.* 1. To request; to seek information: *Ask* how long we must wait. 2. To inquire of a person: Priscilla *asked* the teacher when the Pilgrims had landed. 3. To demand or require of: The teacher *asked* the students to turn in their exams. 4. To invite: Terry *asked* the girls to her party. **asked, asking.**

a·skance (ə-SKANSS) *adverb.* 1. With a sidewise glance: The dishonest student looked *askance* at the exam paper across the aisle. 2. With suspicion, disapproval, or distrust: Jane's mother looked *askance* at her daughter's new friends.

a·skew (ə-SKYOO) *adverb* or *adjective.* Crooked; out of line: The snowball knocked Barry's hat *askew.*

a·sleep (ə-SLEEP) *adjective.* 1. Sleeping. 2. Numb: My foot is *asleep.* —*adverb.* Into the state of sleep: The child closed his eyes and fell *asleep.*

as·par·a·gus (ə-SPA-rə-gəss) *noun.* A slender, green vegetable or the plant on which it grows.

as·pect (ASS-pekt) *noun.* 1. The appearance of a person or thing: Larry had a gloomy *aspect* after he failed the test. 2. A feature or characteristic of a subject: The expense of the trip is an *aspect* our club has to consider.

as·pen (ASS-pən) *noun.* A poplar tree

with delicate leaves. —*adjective.* Trembling; quivering.

as·phalt (ASS-fawlt) *noun.* A dark substance similar to tar that is used with sand or gravel to pave roads and cover roofs. —*verb.* To cover with asphalt: The builder promised to *asphalt* our driveway. **asphalted, asphalting.**

as·phyx·i·ate (ass-FIK-see-ayt) *verb.* To suffocate; make unconscious or cause to die from lack of oxygen or the breathing of harmful gases. **asphyxiated, asphyxiating.**

as·pic (ASS-pik) *noun.* A type of jelly usually containing meat, fish, or vegetables.

as·pire (ə-SPIGHR) *verb.* To desire or strive for a goal or for a position of importance or honor: Daniel *aspires* to be a lawyer. **aspired, aspiring.** —**as·pi·rant** (ASS-pər-ənt or ə-SPIGHR-ənt) *noun.*

as·pi·rin (ASS-pər-in) *noun.* A drug, usually in pill form, used to relieve colds, headaches, and other pains.

ass *noun.* 1. A donkey. 2. A stupid or silly person. **asses.**

as·sail (ə-SAYL) *verb.* 1. To attack physically with violence: Bobby was *assailed* by several boys throwing rocks. 2. To attack with harsh or insulting words: The angry fans *assailed* the umpire with insults. **assailed, assailing.**

as·sail·ant (ə-SAY-lənt) *noun.* A person who attacks another: Leaving his victim unconscious, the *assailant* fled.

as·sas·sin (ə-SASS-in) *noun.* A murderer, often hired, whose victim may be a person of special rank or importance: Martin Luther King was shot by an *assassin.*

as·sas·si·nate (ə-SASS-ə-nayt) *verb.* To murder, often by a planned and treacherous attack on a person of special rank or importance. **assassinated, assassinating.** —**assassination** (ə-sass-ə-NAY-shən) *noun.*

as·sault (ə-SAWLT) *noun.* A forceful attack: The *assault* on Fort Sumter was one of the immediate causes of the U.S. Civil War. —*verb.* To attack violently: The guard was *assaulted* by two men swinging clubs. **assaulted, assaulting.**

as·say (ASS-ay or ə-SAY) *verb.* 1. To evaluate or study; examine: After the storm, Sam *assayed* the damages to his boat. 2. To examine (a substance, especially an ore) to determine its value. **assayed, assaying.** —*noun.* An analysis of a substance, especially an ore: The *assay* showed that the ore contained only small amounts of gold.

as·sem·ble (ə-SEM-bəl) *verb.* 1. To gather; meet: The children *assembled* in front of the school. 2. To bring or fit together: Ted could not *assemble* the jigsaw puzzle. **assembled, assembling.**

as·sem·bly (ə-SEM-blee) *noun.* 1. A gathering together: The *assembly* of the troops took just two minutes. 2. A gathering or meeting of people for a common purpose: Today's student *assembly* will be a football rally. 3. [Capital A] A group or meeting of lawmakers: A vote was held in the General *Assembly* of the U.N. 4. A fitting together of parts: The *assembly* of the puzzle was difficult. **assemblies.**

as·sent (ə-SENT) *verb.* To agree to go along with: Dad *assented* to our plans for building a tree house. **assented, assenting.** —*noun.* Agreement; acceptance of a plan.

as·sert (ə-SERT) *verb.* 1. To state definitely; declare: The teacher *asserted* that her class was ready for the exam. 2. To call attention to or claim (as a right or privilege): The accused man *asserted* his right to a fair trial. 3. To advance oneself; insist on recognition: Terry was not shy; he *asserted* himself boldly. **asserted, asserting.** —**as·ser·tion** (ə-SER-shən) *noun.*

ass

as·sess (ə-SESS) *verb.* 1. To evaluate; judge the value or quality of something: The teacher *assessed* the student's painting and found it good. 2. To judge officially the value of property for tax purposes. 3. To set a fine, tax, or other charge. **assessed, assessing.**

as·sess·ment (ə-SESS-mənt) *noun.* 1. A judgment or evaluation. 2. The value of property for tax purposes. 3. An amount established for a tax.

as·set (ASS-et) *noun.* 1. A useful or valuable talent: Jane's sense of humor is a valuable *asset.* 2. Any of the items a person or organization owns that has value: Dad listed a gold watch, a car, and a house among his *assets.*

as·sid·u·ous (ə-SIJ-oo-əss) *adjective.* Careful; industrious; involving constant attention: The girls' *assiduous* preparations made the party a great success. —**assiduously** *adverb.*

as·sign (ə-SIGHN) *verb.* 1. To give as a task or requirement: The teacher *assigned* eight pages of reading for homework. 2. To name for a duty: Milly was *assigned* to be class monitor. 3. To set aside for a specific purpose: The principal *assigned* one classroom for teaching sewing. **assigned, assigning.**

as·sign·ment (ə-SIGHN-mənt) *noun.* 1. An appointment: The sailor's *assignment* to sea duty delighted him. 2. A requirement: The teacher gave a homework *assignment.*

as·sim·i·late (ə-SIM-ə-layt) *verb.* 1. To absorb; adopt as one's own: America has *assimilated* many foreign customs and traditions. 2. To digest: Our bodies must *assimilate* food in order for us to survive. **assimilated, assimilating.**

as·sist (ə-SIST) *verb.* To help or aid: His children *assisted* the farmer by picking apples. **assisted, assisting.** —*noun.* 1. An act of helping: Mother finished the dishes with an *assist* from Jean. 2. (Sports) An action that helps another player. —**as·sis·tance** (ə-SISS-tənss) *noun.*

as·sis·tant (ə-SISS-tnt) *noun.* One who helps or aids: Dad is looking for an *assistant* to help him lead our scout troop.

assn. *abbreviation.* Association.

as·so·ci·ate (ə-SOH-shee-ayt or ə-SOH-see-ayt) *verb.* 1. To join in one's thoughts: I always *associate* lions with Africa. 2. To unite in companionship or business: Dad *associates* with other salesmen when he travels. **associated, associating.** —(ə-SOH-shee-ət or ə-SOH-see-ət) *noun.* A friend, companion, or business acquaintance. **associates.** —*adjective.* 1. Related or allied by similar activities, interests, or authority: The two nurses were *associate* workers at the hospital. 2. Having fewer privileges or a less important position: The *associate* director assisted the director of the play.

as·so·ci·a·tion (ə-soh-see-AY-shən or ə-soh-shee-AY-shən) *noun.* 1. A group united for a special purpose: Frank belongs to an *association* dedicated to helping the poor. 2. Acquaintance; relationship: The *associations* one makes at school often last a lifetime. 3. A relationship in thought: Doug couldn't make an *association* between that name and anyone he knew.

as·so·ci·a·tive (ə-SOH-shee-ay-tiv, ə-SOH-see-ay-tiv or ə-SOH-shə-tiv) *adjective.* Describing a mathematical operation—in addition, for example—in which the result does not depend upon keeping all elements in their original grouping: $(3 + 4) + 2 = 3 + (4 + 2)$.

as·so·nance (ASS-ə-nənss) *noun.* 1. Agreement or similarity, especially of sounds. 2. Agreement in part or in general.

as·sor·ted (ə-SOR-tid) *adjective.* 1. Made up of mixed and different types: The salesgirl scooped *assorted* candies into a bag. 2. Arranged by kind; classified: Each of the *assorted* garden rows contained a different kind of plant.

as·sort·ment (ə-SORT-mənt) *noun.* 1. A selection of mixed and various kinds. 2. A selection arranged by kind: The candy *assortment* contained separate rows of caramels, chocolates, and creams.

asst. *abbreviation.* Assistant.

as·suage (ə-SWAYJ) *verb.* 1. To soothe; to calm; make milder: The soft music *assuaged* Dad's nervousness. 2. To satisfy or quench: The hot meal *assuaged* his hunger. **assuaged, assuaging.**

as·sume (ə-SOOM) *verb.* 1. To suppose; take for granted: We *assumed* that we would have homework as usual. 2. To bear the burden of, as a job or obligation: The man *assumed* his son's debts. 3. To develop: The argument *assumed* a new seriousness when punches were thrown. 4. To put on (an appearance) falsely; to fake: The guilty boy *assumed* an innocent look. **assumed, assuming.**

as·sump·tion (ə-SUMP-shən) *noun.* 1. A taking for granted; a supposition: Joan's *assumption* that the exam would be difficult was correct. 2. The act of assuming.

as·sur·ance (ə-SHUR-ənss) *noun.* 1. A statement meant to give certainty; a pledge: We received the owner's *assurance* that the dog would not bite. 2. Trust; surety: Believing their leader, the soldiers marched with *assurance.* **assurances.**

as·sure (ə-SHUR) *verb.* 1. To make confident or certain: Danny checked his compass to *assure* himself that he was not lost. 2. To inform with confidence: The clerk *assured* us that the eggs were fresh. **assured, assuring.**

as·sured (ə-SHURD) *adjective.* 1. Certain, sure: John said, "You may be *assured* that we will win the game." 2. Sure of oneself, confident: Walter is an *assured* boy; he never doubts his own ability. —**assuredly** (ə-SHUR-id-lee) *adverb.*

as·ter (ASS-tər) *noun.* A type of flower that resembles the daisy and may be any of a variety of colors.

aster

as·ter·isk (ASS-tə-risk) *noun.* A starlike mark (*) made in writing, typing, or printing to indicate omission of a word or to call attention to a footnote.

a·stern (ə-STERN) *adverb.* 1. Toward or in the rear of a ship. 2. Backward. —*adjective.* Behind or at the rear of a ship.

as·ter·oid (ASS-tə-roid) *noun.* 1. A relatively small, planetlike body in space, especially one of many that move in orbit about the sun between Mars and Jupiter. 2. A starfish.

asth·ma (AZ-mə) *noun.* A disease that causes coughing and difficulty in breathing.

a·stig·ma·tism (ə-STIG-mə-tiz-əm) *noun.* A defect of the eye which causes improper focus or distorted vision.

a·stir (ə-STER) *adjective.* 1. Moving: The leaves were *astir* from a light breeze. 2. Out of bed; arisen: By sunrise the farmer was already *astir.*

a·ston·ish (ə-STON-ish) *verb.* To fill with wonder: The discovery of the secret *astonished* us. **astonished, astonishing.**

a·ston·ish·ment (ə-STON-ish-mənt) *noun.* Amazement; wonder: Imagine Marian's *astonishment* when she found her piggy bank empty!

a·stound (ə-STOWND) *verb.* To amaze; astonish. **astounded, astounding.**

a·stray (ə-STRAY) *adverb.* 1. Not in the right place or direction: The camper wandered *astray* when he lost his compass. 2. Away from proper behavior: Dennis went *astray* because of a bad temper.

astro- *prefix.* Indicates: 1. Star: *astro*nomy. 2. Outer space: *astro*naut.

astronaut

as·trol·o·gy (ə-STROL-ə-jee) *noun.* A pseudo-science that is claimed by some to foretell future events and reveal the influence of heavenly bodies.

as·tro·naut (ASS-trə-nawt) *noun.* A pilot or other crew member of a spaceship.

as·tron·o·mer (ə-STRON-ə-mər) *noun.* One whose work is astronomy.

as·tro·nom·i·cal (ass-trə-NOM-i-kəl) Also **astronomic** *adjective.* 1. Having to do with the stars, the planets, and other areas of astronomy. 2. Extremely large: The sum of money needed to build a pool is *astronomical.* —**astronomically** *adverb.*

as·tron·o·my (ə-STRON-ə-mee) *noun.* The science that deals with outer space, with the characteristics of the moon, planets, stars, and other heavenly bodies.

as·tute (ə-STOOT or ə-STYOOT) *adjective.* 1. Bright; able to learn or understand quickly. 2. Crafty; cunning: The *astute* salesman made a large profit on the sale. —**astutely** *adverb.*

a·sun·der (ə-SUN-dər) *adverb* or *adjective.* 1. Into many pieces or parts: Spot knocked the vase *asunder.* 2. Separated; far apart: The leaves were scattered *asunder.*

a·sy·lum (ə-SIGH-ləm) *noun.* 1. A hospital-like place for the care of persons such as orphans, the handicapped, or the mentally ill. 2. Protection or refuge provided by an institution or by one country to a citizen of another, especially to a fugitive or exile: The Russian sailor asked for *asylum* in England.

at *preposition.* 1. To, toward, or through: Aim *at* the target. 2. Present in, on, or near: He is *at* school. 3. Involved in (a state, process or occupation): Dad is *at* work. 4. On or near (a time, degree, or condition): We will leave *at* noon. 5. As a result of: He laughed *at* the story. 6. For an amount of: The paint sold *at* three dollars a gallon.

ate (AYT) *verb. See* **eat.**

-ate *suffix.* 1. Affected by, acted upon, or provided with: hyphen*ate.* 2. (Chemistry) Indicates a compound that comes from another compound or element: nitr*ate.*

a·the·ism (AY-thee-iz-əm) *noun.* The belief that there is no God.

a·the·ist (AY-thee-ist) *noun.* A person who believes that there is no God. —**atheistic** *adjective.*

ath·lete (ATH-leet) *noun.* A trained, skilled person who competes seriously in sports that require qualities like speed and endurance. **athletes.** —**athletic** *adjective.*

ath·let·ics (ath-LET-ikss) *noun, plural in form but used with a singular verb.* Sports; competitive activities requiring qualities like speed, strength, and endurance: *Athletics* can help to strengthen the body.

-ation *suffix.* Indicates the action or state of: alter*ation,* exagger*ation.*

-ative *suffix.* Indicates a relationship or a leaning to: talk*ative.*

at·las (AT-ləss) *noun.* 1. A book of maps. 2. [Capital A] (Mythology) A giant who supported the heavens on his shoulders. **atlases.**

at·mos·phere (AT-mə-sfihr) *noun.* 1. The layer of air that surrounds the earth. 2. The influence, feeling, or mood experienced in a particular place or situation: An *atmosphere* of joy filled the circus tent. 3. The air in a particular place: The *atmosphere* was damp along the waterfront.

at·mos·pher·ic (at-mə-SFIHR-ik) Also **atmospherical** *adjective.* 1. Of or related to the layer of air that surrounds the earth. 2. Having or producing a special mood or feeling, especially a pleasant mood: The French restaurant was especially *atmospheric;* we felt as though we were in Paris. —**atmospherically** *adverb.*

a·toll (AT-ol) *noun.* An island or reef made of skeletons of tiny sea animals (coral) and enclosing a shallow body of water called a lagoon.

at·om (AT-əm) *noun.* 1. (Physics and Chemistry) The smallest part of an element that has all the properties of that element: *Atoms* are composed of a nucleus, protons, and electrons. 2. Anything thought to be the smallest possible thing of its kind, unable to be broken or divided into smaller parts. 3. A very small thing or amount.

a·tom·ic (ə-TOM-ik) *adjective.* 1. Of or referring to an atom, atoms, or atomic energy: An *atomic* submarine is one that is powered by energy from the splitting of atoms. 2. Very small. —**atomically** *adverb.*

atomic bomb. A bomb of tremendous explosive force created by the splitting of atoms.

a·tone (ə-TOHN) *verb.* To pay; make up: The man *atoned* for his early years of crime by working for the poor. **atoned, atoning.** —**atonement** *noun.*

a·top (ə-TOP) *preposition.* On the highest part of: The kitten sat *atop* the table.

a·tro·cious (ə-TROH-shəss) *adjective.* 1. Very wicked, vicious, or cruel: The enemy soldier was punished for his *atrocious* treatment of prisoners. 2. (Informal) Bad; poorly done; in bad taste: The movie was *atrocious.* —**atrociously** *adverb.*

a·troc·i·ty (ə-TROSS-ə-tee) *noun.* 1. An extremely wicked, vicious, or cruel act: The killing of the peasants was an *atrocity.* 2. (Informal) Something that is bad, poorly done, or in poor taste. **atrocities.**

at·tach (ə-TACH) *verb.* 1. To fasten; tie: She *attached* the ribbon to the package. 2. To stick to: The bur was *attached* to Jim's trousers. 3. To add or include: Dad *attached* his signature to the contract. 4. To join by affection or interest: The two neighbors were *attached* to each other. 5. To take all or part of a property or salary for legal reasons, especially for payment of a debt: The worker's salary was *attached* to pay off a debt that he owed. **attached, attaching.**

at·tach·ment (ə-TACH-mənt) *noun.* 1. Affection; devotion: We admired the boy's *attachment* for his young friend. 2. That which connects one thing to another: The picture fell when its *attachment* to the wall worked loose. 3. An accessory to a machine; a device used to change a machine for a special purpose: An *attachment* for the electric drill enables you to use it to polish things.

at·tack (ə-TAK) *verb.* 1. To assault; cause violent physical harm: The robbers *attacked* the guard with clubs. 2. To speak or write against: The senator was *attacked* in a newspaper article. 3. To raid; make a military advance or begin armed conflict: The troops *attacked* the fort. 4. To go at with enthusiasm: The hungry boy *attacked* his dinner. **attacked,**

atomic bomb

attacking. —*noun.* 1. A violent physical assault: The *attack* on the guard left him unconscious. 2. A criticism; a speaking or writing against. 3. A military assault; a raid. 4. A sudden onset of disease or harmful effects.

at·tain (ə-TAYN) *verb.* To arrive at or get: The artist *attained* great success. **attained, attaining.**

at·tain·ment (ə-TAYN-mənt) *noun.* 1. The act of accomplishing or reaching: *Attainment* of that merit badge took me six weeks. 2. An achievement or a skill obtained through effort.

at·tempt (ə-TEMPT) *verb.* To try, to endeavor. **attempted, attempting.** —*noun.* 1. A try or an effort: He made an *attempt* to climb the mountain. 2. A physical attack: The criminal made an *attempt* on the guard's life.

at·tend (ə-TEND) *verb.* 1. To go to: Bill *attended* the Boy Scout meeting. 2. To give one's efforts or attention (to): The mayor *attended* to the town's business. 3. To go along with: The sickness was *attended* by great pain. 4. To serve; care for. **attended, attending.**

at·ten·dance (ə-TEN-dnss) *noun.* 1. The number of people at a particular place or event: The *attendance* at the game was over 8,000. 2. The act of being present.

at·ten·dant (ə-TEN-dnt) *noun.* A person who waits on or takes care of (something): The *attendant* at the gas station checked our engine. —*adjective.* Going with: a sickness and its *attendant* pain.

at·ten·tion (ə-TEN-shən) *noun.* 1. A directing of one's thoughts or efforts: *Attention* is required for learning in school. 2. A military posture with body erect and eyes front: The sergeant stood at *attention* when the major arrived.

at·ten·tive (ə-TEN-tiv) *adjective.* 1. Alert; paying attention: The student was *attentive* during the history lesson. 2. Considerate of the needs and desires of others. —**attentively** *adverb.*

at·test (ə-TEST) *verb.* 1. To state or swear to be true. 2. To offer proof of. **attested, attesting.**

at·tic (AT-ik) *noun.* A room or other part of a house or building just below the roof.

at·tire (ə-TIGHR) *noun.* Clothing: The clown wore colorful *attire.* —*verb.* To clothe: She *attired* herself in a white gown. **attired, attiring.**

at·ti·tude (AT-ə-tood or AT-ə-tyood) *noun.* 1. A feeling or mood. 2. A bearing of the body indicating feeling: The *attitude* of the boy slumped down in his seat suggested a lack of interest. 3. The slant of an aircraft or spaceship in relation to the horizon or to some other reference point. **attitudes.**

at·tor·ney (ə-TER-nee) *noun.* A lawyer. **attorneys.**

at·tract (ə-TRAKT) *verb.* 1. To gain the interest of; appeal to: The red sign *attracted* our attention. 2. To cause to move closer or to attach: The magnet *attracted* the pieces of iron. **attracted, attracting.**

at·trac·tion (ə-TRAK-shən) *noun.* 1. Something that interests or appeals: The bears were the main *attraction* at the zoo. 2. The power to cause to move closer or to attach: The *attraction* of that magnet is very strong. 3. The act or process of attracting.

at·trac·tive (ə-TRAK-tiv) *adjective.* 1. Able to interest or to attract: The colorful poster is very *attractive.* 2. Charming; pleasing. —**attractively** *adverb.*

at·tri·bute (AT-rə-byoot) *noun.* A particular quality of a person or thing: Honesty is an *attribute* we expect of bankers. **attributes.** —(ə-TRIB-yoot) *verb.* 1. To believe to be a result of: The damage was *attributed* to an earthquake. 2. To believe to be natural to or appropriate: We usually *attribute* courage to soldiers. **attributed, attributing.**

at·tri·tion (ə-TRISH-ən) *noun.* A gradual wearing away; a decrease or lessening: The wind and rain caused *attrition* of the soil.

atty. *abbreviation.* Attorney.

au·burn (AW-bərn) *noun* (and *adjective*). A brown color with red and gold highlights.

auc·tion (AWK-shən) *noun.* A manner of selling by which bids, or money offerings, are made, the highest of which wins the item. *—verb.* To sell at an auction. **auctioned, auctioning.**

au·da·cious (aw-DAY-shəss) *adjective.* 1. Courageous; rash. 2. Rude; very fresh; insolent. —**audaciously** *adverb.*

au·dac·i·ty (aw-DASS-ə-tee) *noun.* 1. Rashness; fearlessness. 2. Rudeness; insolence: She had the *audacity* to use Joan's car without permission.

au·di·ble (AW-də-bəl) *adjective.* Loud enough or able to be heard: The music is not loud, but it is *audible.* —**audibly** *adverb.*

au·di·ence (AW-dee-ənss) *noun.* 1. All those gathered to hear or see someone or something: The *audience* listened attentively to the concert. 2. All those reached by a television or radio broadcast or by a publication. 3. The chance of being listened to: The committee gave Thelma an *audience* so that she could explain her project. 4. A formal meeting: an *audience* with the Queen. **audiences.**

au·di·o-vis·u·al (aw-dee-oh-VIZH-yoo-əl) *adjective.* Having to do with hearing and seeing: Television is *audio-visual;* we can both hear and see it.

au·di·tion (aw-DISH-ən) *noun.* A tryout; a chance for one to show off his talents: The dancer and the singer were offered jobs after their *auditions. —verb.* To take part in a tryout; to conduct a tryout. **auditioned, auditioning.**

au·di·tor (AW-də-tər) *noun.* 1. One who hears or listens. 2. A person who inspects financial records.

au·di·to·ri·um (aw-də-TOR-ee-əm) *noun.* 1. A large room or enclosed area used for an audience. 2. A building designed or used for performances like concerts, plays, and movies.

au·ger (AW-gər) *noun.* A tool used in carpentry for boring holes.

aug·ment (awg-MENT) *verb.* To make or become greater. **augmented, augmenting.**

au·gust (aw-GUHST) *adjective.* Inspiring awe; dignified: an *august* occasion.

Au·gust (AW-gəst) *noun.* The eighth month of the year: There are 31 days in *August.* —**Aug.** *abbreviation.*

auk (AWK) *noun.* A type of diving bird with webbed feet that lives in cold northern regions.

aunt (ANT or AHNT) *noun.* 1. One's father's or mother's sister. 2. One's uncle's wife.

au·ri·cle (OR-i·kəl) *noun.* One of two upper sections of the heart.

au·ro·ra bo·re·al·is (aw-ROR-ə bor-ee-AL-iss) *noun.* An unusual display of streaks or bands of light that can be seen at times in northern skies; "northern lights."

aus·pic·es (AW-spə-seez) *noun, plural.* Sponsorship; protection: The plan was developed under the *auspices* of the mayor.

aus·pi·cious (aw-SPISH-əss) *adjective.* Good; suggesting victory: The bright, sunny morning was an *auspicious* sign for our afternoon picnic. —**auspiciously** *adverb.*

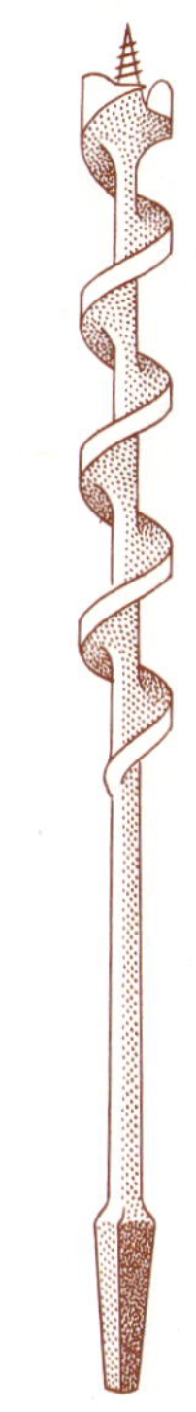

auger

auk

aus·tere (awss-TIHR) *adjective.* 1. Stern; harsh. 2. Extremely simple; without luxury: Prisoners' cells are very *austere* places. —**austerely** *adverb.* —**aus·ter·i·ty** (aw-STER-ə-tee) *noun.*

au·then·tic (aw-THEN-tik) *adjective.* 1. Dependable; worthy of trust or belief. 2. Real; valid: The art collector discovered an *authentic* masterpiece. —**authentically** *adverb.*

au·thor (AW-thər) *noun.* 1. The writer of a book, poem, or other literary work. 2. One who starts (something): the *author* of a rumor.

au·thor·i·tar·i·an (ə-thor-ə-TAIR-ee-ən) *adjective.* Related to the belief that obedience to central authority is more important than personal freedom.

au·thor·i·ta·tive (ə-THOR-ə-tay-tiv) *adjective.* 1. Having power; official: The general issued *authoritative* orders to the troops. 2. Reliable; worthy of belief.

au·thor·i·ty (ə-THOR-ə-tee) *noun.* 1. The ability or right to command or to make decisions. 2. An expert: Professor Jackson is an *authority* on ancient history. 3. Someone or something referred to in support of an argument or idea: The *authority* for his statement about Moses is the Bible. 4. Assurance; confidence. 5. An official, especially one who makes or enforces laws or decisions. **authorities.**

au·thor·ize (AW-thə-righz) *verb.* 1. To approve officially: The mayor *authorized* the hiring of four new policemen. 2. To give power or rights to: The owner *authorized* the manager to increase salaries. 3. To show to be acceptable; give permission: The school rules do not *authorize* visitors during class hours. **authorized, authorizing.**

au·to (AW-toh) *noun.* An automobile. **autos.**

auto- Also **aut-** *prefix.* Indicates "self" or "same": *auto*biography.

au·to·bi·og·ra·phy (aw-toh-bigh-OG-rə-fee) *noun.* The story of a person's life written by that same person. **autobiographies.**

au·to·crat (AW-tə-krat) *noun.* 1. A ruler with unlimited power. 2. A person who is thoughtless or arrogant in his use of power.

au·to·graph (AW-tə-graf) *noun.* 1. A person's signature. 2. A signature or short writing of a famous person kept as a souvenir. —*verb.* To write one's signature. **autographed, autographing.**

au·to·mat·ed (AW-tə-may-tid) *adjective.* Produced or operated under automatic control.

au·to·mat·ic (aw-tə-MAT-ik) *adjective.* 1. Operating by itself: Our washing machine is *automatic.* 2. Done by habit or without thinking: Yawning is *automatic.* —*noun.* A gun that fires several rounds on one pressure of the trigger. —**automatically** *adverb.*

au·to·ma·tion (aw-tə-MAY-shən) *noun.* A method by which the control of machinery or production is largely or completely automatic.

au·to·mo·bile (aw-tə-moh-BEEL or AW-tə-moh-beel) *noun.* A car; a passenger vehicle, usually with four wheels, that runs on its own power. **automobiles.**

automobiles

au·ton·o·my (aw-TON-ə-mee) *noun.* The condition of deciding one's own affairs; independence: Many American colonists preferred *autonomy* to rule by England.

au·tumn (AW-təm) *noun.* The season of the year that comes after summer and before winter; fall: In the Northern Hemisphere, *autumn* lasts from about September 21 to December 22.

aux·il·ia·ry (awg-ZIL-yə-ree) *adjective.* 1. Assisting; supporting: An *auxiliary* force aided the weary firemen. 2. Additional: The hospital has an *auxiliary* source of electricity in case the main power fails. —*noun.* A person or group that assists. **auxiliaries.**

a·vail (ə-VAYL) *verb.* To be of service or benefit to: Acting silly in class will *avail* you little in terms of earning a good grade. **availed, availing.** —*noun.* Service; profit; benefit: His pleading was of no *avail;* the jury convicted him.

a·vail·a·ble (ə-VAYL-ə-bəl) *adjective.* 1. Securable; able to be acquired: Tickets are *available* for the football game. 2. Employable; handy: The camper used a map to start the fire; it was the only paper *available.* —**availability** *noun.*

av·a·lanche (AV-ə-lanch) *noun.* 1. A huge mass of snow, earth, or rocks tumbling down a hillside or mountain. 2. Any great pouring forth of things: The star of the play received an *avalanche* of compliments. **avalanches.**

a·vant-garde (ah-vahnt-GAHRD) *noun.* Those persons who are most advanced, daring, or original in such fields as art, music, and literature.

av·a·rice (AV-ə-riss) *noun.* Extreme greed, especially for money.

Ave. *abbreviation.* Avenue.

a·venge (ə-VENJ) *verb.* To get revenge for. **avenged, avenging.**

av·e·nue (AV-ə-noo or AV-ə-nyoo) *noun.* 1. A street, especially a wide or heavily traveled one. 2. A way of entering or leaving: The window provides an *avenue* of escape in case of fire. **avenues.**

a·ver (ə-VER) *verb.* To state with surety; assert; affirm. **averred, averring.**

av·er·age (AV-rij or AV-ər-ij) *noun.* The number found by dividing a sum by the number of quantities added. The *average* of 3, 4, and 8 is 5. **averages.** —*adjective.* 1. Being the result of the division of a sum by the number of quantities added. 2. Usual; typical; normal. —*verb.* 1. To find a number by dividing a sum by the number of quantities added. 2. To do or have on a regular basis: The star player *averaged* 20 points a game. **averaged, averaging.**

a·verse (ə-VERSS) *adjective.* Against; having a dislike for. —**aversely** *adverb.*

a·ver·sion (ə-VER-zhən) *noun.* Strong dislike or opposition: She has an *aversion* to lying.

a·vert (ə-VERT) *verb.* 1. To turn away: The naughty child *averted* his face from his mother's look. 2. To prevent: The spread of the disease was *averted* when the medicine arrived in time. **averted, averting.**

a·vi·ar·y (AY-vee-ehr-ee) *noun.* A large cage or closed-in area in which many birds are kept. **aviaries.**

a·vi·a·tion (ay-vee-AY-shən) *noun.* The study or science of aircraft.

a·vi·a·tor (AY-vee-ay-tər) *noun.* The man who flies a plane; a pilot.

av·id (AV-id) *adjective.* 1. Eager; enthusiastic: Martin is an *avid* reader. 2. Very desirous of possessions. —**avidly** *adverb.*

av·o·ca·do (av-ə-KAH-doh) *noun.* A tropical, pear-shaped fruit or the tree on which it grows. **avocados.**

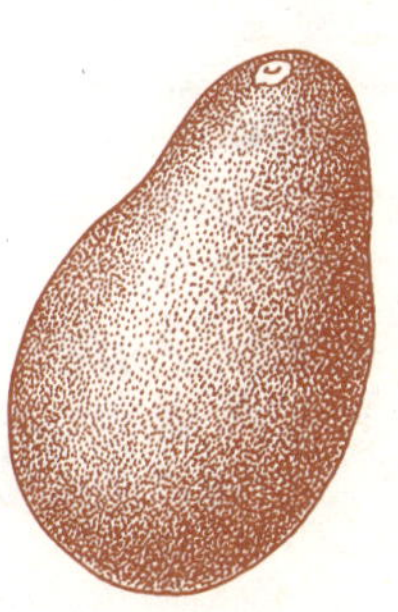
avocado

awning

axis

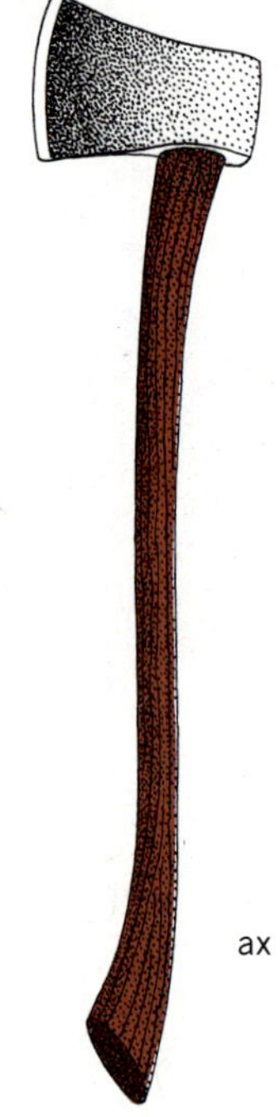
ax

azalea

av·o·ca·tion (av-ə-KAY-shən) *noun.* An activity other than one's main job; a hobby.

a·void (ə-VOID) *verb.* To refrain from; evade: The pilot *avoided* the storm by turning north. **avoided, avoiding.** —**avoidance** *noun.*

a·wait (ə-WAYT) *verb.* 1. To wait for; anticipate. 2. To be waiting for: Many benefits *await* those who work hard. **awaited, awaiting.**

a·wake (ə-WAYK) *verb.* 1. To wake up. 2. To awaken (someone); to alert: He will *awake* Dad at seven o'clock. **awoke** or **awaked, awaking.** —*adjective.* Not asleep; active or alert.

a·wak·en (ə-WAY-kən) *verb.* To awake; to arouse. **awakened, awakening.**

a·ward (ə-WAHRD) *noun.* 1. A prize or honor. 2. A legal grant or decision: The lawyer requested an *award* of $1,000 for the injured woman. —*verb.* 1. To give a prize or honor. 2. To grant by a legal decision. **awarded, awarding.**

a·ware (ə-WAIR) *adjective.* Informed; knowing: I was not *aware* that Tom had left. —**awareness** *noun.*

a·way (ə-WAY) *adverb.* 1. Aside; in another direction: He steered *away* from the broken glass. 2. From a place: They sailed *away* from the dock. 3. From one's use or possession: He gave *away* his pencil. 4. Out of existence: The light faded *away.* 5. Continually: Jack worked *away* on his project. —*adjective.* 1. Absent; gone: Linda is *away* for the summer. 2. Distant; far: The town is three miles *away.*

awe (AW) *noun.* Wonder; reverence; respectful fear: We were filled with *awe* by the magnificent view from the mountain. —*verb.* To fill with wonder: The inside of the cathedral *awed* the visitor. **awed, awing.** —**awesome** *adjective.*

aw·ful (AW-fəl) *adjective.* 1. Causing awe: He saw the *awful* eruption of the volcano. 2. (Informal) Terrible; bad or displeasing.

aw·ful·ly (AW-fəl-ee) *adverb.* (Informal) 1. In a manner causing distaste or disapproval: The team played *awfully.* 2. Very; greatly: She is an *awfully* kind woman.

a·while (ə-HWIGHL) *adverb.* For a brief time.

awk·ward (AWK-wərd) *adjective.* 1. Clumsy; not graceful: The girl learning to walk on stilts looked *awkward.* 2. Difficult to operate or make use of: A heavy bat can be *awkward* for a small boy to swing. 3. Causing discomfort: Making a speech can be *awkward* for a shy person. —**awkwardly** *adverb.*

awl *noun.* A pointed tool for poking holes in leather, wood, or other materials.

awn·ing (AWN-ing) *noun.* A cover of canvas or other material over the outside of a window or door for protection from sun and rain.

a·woke (ə-WOHK) *verb. See* **awake.**

ax (AKS) Also **axe** *noun.* A tool with a long handle and sharp metal head used mostly for chopping wood. **axes.** —**ax to grind.** (Slang) A selfish interest or goal.

ax·is (AK-siss) *noun.* A real or imaginary line about which an object turns or seems to turn: The *axis* of the earth passes through its center from the North to the South Pole. —**axes** (AK-seez) *plural.*

ax·le (AK-sl) *noun.* A rod or shaft connecting two wheels or on which a wheel or wheels turn. **axles.**

aye (IGH) *adverb.* Yes: "*Aye, aye,* sir," said the sailor. —*noun.* A vote of "yes": The *ayes* won over the nays. **ayes.**

a·zal·ea (ə-ZAYL-yə) *noun.* A type of fragrant, colorful flower or the shrub on which it grows.

B, b (BEE) *noun.* The second letter of the English alphabet.

b. *abbreviation.* Born.

B.A. *abbreviation.* Bachelor of Arts. Also **A.B.**

bab·ble (BAB-əl) *verb.* 1. To speak quickly or confusingly; to make sounds like a young child's meaningless noises. 2. To make a low murmuring sound: The brook *babbled* over the rocks. **babbled, babbling.** —*noun.* Speech that is confused or without meaning.

babe (BAYB) *noun.* 1. Short for baby. 2. Anyone who seems helpless. 3. (Slang) A woman. **babes.**

ba·boon (ba-BOON) *noun.* A fierce monkey with a pointed face like a dog, found in Africa and Arabia.

ba·by (BAY-bee) *noun.* 1. An infant. 2. The youngest one in a group: His little brother is the *baby* of the family. 3. A childish person: Stop that crying; don't be such a *baby.* **babies.** —*verb.* To treat as an infant; to coddle. **babied, babying.**

baby carriage. A small cart with a handle and four wheels, used for a baby.

baby sitter. A person hired to care for a child while its parents are away.

bach·e·lor (BACH-ə-lər) *noun.* A man who is not married.

ba·cil·lus (bə-SIL-əss) *noun.* A rod-shaped bacterium, or tiny organism. —**bacilli** (bə-SIL-igh) *plural.*

back (BAK) *noun.* 1. The part of a person's body from the neck to the buttocks; the spine side of the trunk. 2. Anything opposite to the front: *back* of the bus. 3. A position in football and similar games; a person who plays that position. —*verb.* 1. To move to the rear. 2. To support someone or something. **backed, backing.** —*adjective.* Last, rear, past: *back* pay, *back* seat. —**back down.** To give in, to relent. —**back out.** To stop before finished; fail to keep a promise or to go through with a plan. —**behind one's back.** Without informing some other person; secretly: The new pupil told lies about the teacher *behind her back.* —**go back on.** To fail to do or fulfill.

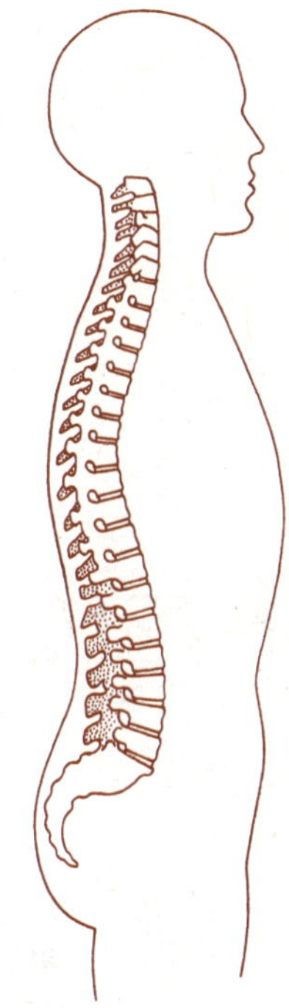

backbone

back·bone (BAK-bohn) *noun.* 1. The spine; the main bone in the back of humans and other animals. 2. Courage; firmness. 3. The base or foundation: The keel is the *backbone* of a ship. **backbones.**

back·field (BAK-feeld) *noun.* (Football) The players or the area behind the line of scrimmage.

baboons

back·ground (BAK-grownd) *noun.* 1. The parts of a picture or view that appear to be farthest away. 2. Past events that make up a person's experience: Mr. Grant's boyhood *background* in camping makes him a fine scout leader. 3. A place or position removed from the center of action: Jimmy is shy; he always stays in the *background.*

back·hand (BAK-hand) *noun.* 1. (Sports) A stroke in which the arm is brought from a position across the body to a forward and outward position, striking the ball with the back of the racket or paddle. 2. Handwriting which slants to the left. —*verb.* 1. To hit with the back of the hand. 2. To hit with a backhand stroke. **backhanded, backhanding.**

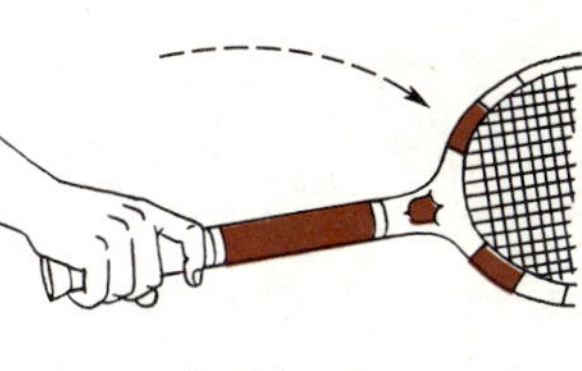

backhand

back·hand·ed (BAK-han-did) *adjective.* 1. Using a backhand. 2. (Handwriting) Slanting to the left. 3. Having two meanings, one of which is a somewhat hidden insult or jest: John's saying that Jean was the prettiest girl at the party was a *backhanded* compliment because Jean was the only girl at the party. —**backhandedly** *adverb.*

back·lash (BAK-lash) *noun.* 1. A quick backward movement. 2. A distrustful, often violent, reaction of a social or ethnic group against progress by another such group. **backlashes.**

badger

back·log (BAK-lawg) *noun.* 1. A piling up; a collection of something overdue: There was a *backlog* of work to do after vacation. 2. A supply; an extra amount: The farmer had a *backlog* of food for the long winter ahead. —*verb.* To store or pile up. **backlogged, backlogging.**

back·ward (BAK-wərd) Also **backwards** *adverb.* 1. Toward the back: Tim looked *backward* to the rear of the bus. 2. In an opposite manner to what is usual: Johnny did his math all *backward;* he added the subtraction problems and subtracted the addition. 3. With the back first: Marion walked into the closet *backward* and fell over the broom. —*adjective.* 1. Aimed toward the back: a *backward* look. 2. Slow to learn or progress: The *backward* student could not learn his multiplication tables. 3. Shy, bashful: The *backward* boy blushed and stammered when he spoke to the girls.

bagel

ba·con (BAY-kən) *noun.* Smoked, salted meat from the backside of a hog.

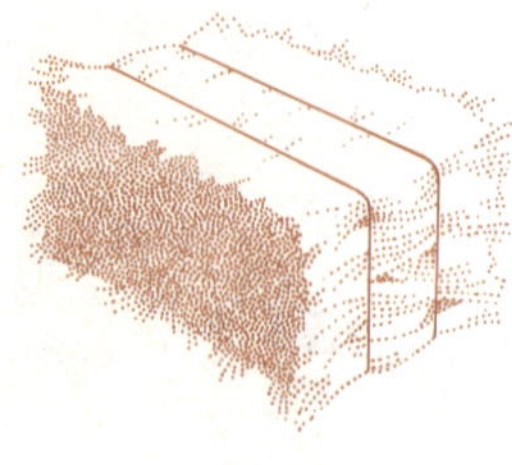
bale

bac·te·ri·a (bak-TIHR-ee-ə) *noun, plural.* Small one-cell plants which can be seen only under a microscope: *Bacteria* can be both useful and harmful; some *bacteria* help in making cheese, while others cause disease. —**bacterium** *singular.*

bad *adjective.* 1. Wicked; evil. 2. Defective; faulty: Two tomatoes in the package were *bad.* 3. Harmful: Smoking is *bad* for your health. 4. Severe: a *bad* accident. **worse, worst.** —**badly** *adverb.*

badge (BAJ) *noun.* 1. A button, emblem, or pin which shows a person's rank or position; an emblem or pin given as an award: A gold star is the sheriff's *badge* of office. 2. A sign or symbol: The warrior's scar was a *badge* of his courage. **badges.**

bade (BAD or BAYD) *verb. See* **bid.**

bad·ger (BAJ-ər) *noun.* A short-legged, furry animal that lives in a burrow, or hole, dug in the ground. —*verb.* To nag, pester, or bother. **badgered, badgering.**

bad·lands (BAD-landz) *noun, plural.* A stretch of dry, barren land marked by ragged rock and soil.

bad·min·ton (BAD-min-tn) *noun.* A game played by batting a feathered, ball-like object back and forth over a high net with long-handled rackets.

baf·fle (BAF-əl) *verb.* To confuse or fool; puzzle or prevent from understanding: The safe *baffled* the burglar; he could not open it. **baffled, baffling.** —*noun.* A wall, screen, or partition made to control the direction of light, air, or sound. **baffles.**

bag *noun.* 1. A sack or container, usually of paper, cloth, or plastic. 2. A purse, suitcase, or other container used to carry things. 3. (Slang) A special interest, skill, or favorite pastime: Mystery stories are my *bag.* —*verb.* 1. To catch or kill as in hunting: The hunter *bagged* two rabbits. 2. To pack into a bag or sack: The clerk *bagged* the groceries after Dad paid for them. **bagged, bagging.**

ba·gel (BAY-gəl) *noun.* A hard, round roll similar in shape to a doughnut.

bag·gage (BAG-ij) *noun.* Luggage; the bags that a traveler carries with him: Mother unpacked our *baggage* when we arrived at the motel.

bag·gy (BAG-ee) *adjective.* 1. Puffy, loose, hanging: a *baggy* chin. 2. Loose or ill-fitting (clothing): a *baggy* pair of pants.

bag·pipe (BAG-pighp) *noun.* A musical instrument made of a windbag and pipes and used primarily in Scotland. **bagpipes.**

bail (BAYL) *noun.* Money or goods handed over to a court by an arrested person as a promise to appear for trial. *—verb.* 1. To get an arrested person out of jail by putting up money. 2. To get (someone) out of trouble; save: She *bailed* me out by lending me her car. 3. To scoop water out of a boat with a bucket or other means. **bailed, bailing.** **—bail out.** To jump out of a plane; to parachute out; to get out of anything quickly. **—jump bail.** To lose bail by not appearing for trial.

bait (BAYT) *noun.* 1. Food placed on a hook or trap to attract and capture fish and other animals. 2. Something used to tempt a person: The money was left on the table as *bait* to catch the thief. *—verb.* 1. To place food on a hook or in a trap: Jim *baited* the hook with a worm. 2. To tease or torment: The boy *baited* the old dog by tossing pebbles at him. **baited, baiting.**

bake (BAYK) *verb.* 1. To cook food in an oven. 2. To dry out and harden with heat: Clay must be *baked* in order to make pottery. **baked, baking.**

bak·er (BAY-kər) *noun.* A person who bakes bread and pastries for a living.

baker's dozen. Thirteen instead of the usual twelve in a dozen.

bak·er·y (BAY-kə-ree) *noun.* A place where bread and other baked goods are made or sold. **bakeries.**

baking powder. A white powder added to dough to make it rise.

baking soda. A powder used in cooking and in making certain medicines; sodium bicarbonate.

bal·ance (BAL-ənss) *verb.* 1. To make steady or even: The waiter *balanced* the tray on one hand. 2. To compare the weight or value of things: The athlete *balanced* the hardship of practice against the joy of victory. **balanced, balancing.** *—noun.* 1. An instrument used for weighing; a scale. 2. Steadiness of body or mind: It is hard to keep your *balance* when you are dizzy. 3. A remainder; what is left: We spend part of the dollar for milk and the *balance* for candy. 4. Equality in weight or value: He knew there was a *balance* between hard work and success. **—in the balance.** Still to be determined; not yet decided.

bal·co·ny (BAL-kə-nee) *noun.* 1. A small porch or platform projecting from the upper floors of a building. 2. The seats above the main floor of a theater or arena. **balconies.**

bald (BAWLD) *adjective.* 1. Without hair, or having very little hair. 2. Lacking a natural covering: The *bald* rock had no plants on it. 3. Naked, bare, or plain: a *bald* fact. **balder, baldest.**

bald eagle. A powerful dark-bodied bird of North America with white feathers on its tail, neck, and head: The *bald eagle,* also called the "American eagle," is the national emblem of the U.S.

bale (BAYL) *noun.* A large bundle of hay or cotton wired together by hand or by machine. **bales.** *—verb.* To put into bales; bundle tightly with string or wire. **baled, baling.**

bagpipe

balcony

bald eagle

balloon

bale•ful (BAYL-fəl) *adjective.* Menacing, sinister: The man gave us a *baleful* look.

balk (BAWK) *verb.* To stop; refuse to continue; to block; to boycott: Roger *balked* at taking piano and violin lessons. **balked, balking.** —*noun.* 1. Something that stops, blocks, or hinders. 2. A fake pitch in baseball, usually an illegal move.

ball (BAWL) *noun.* 1. A round object that is thrown, kicked, or struck in certain games and sports —sometimes oval shaped, as a football. 2. Any round object; a sphere: The kitten played with a *ball* of yarn. 3. A dancing party: Cinderella lost her glass slipper after dancing at a *ball.* 4. Any game played with a ball. 5. A pitch in baseball that misses the strike zone and is not swung at by the batter. 6. (Slang) A good time: We had a *ball* at the party; it was great fun. —*verb.* To roll or form into a ball. **balled, balling. —on the ball.** (Slang) Sharp, keen, ready for action: Kathy was *on the ball* when the child fell into the pool; she jumped in and pulled him out.

bal•lad (BAL-əd) *noun.* 1. A song or poem that tells a story, usually sad or romantic. 2. Any simple love song that is popular.

bal•last (BAL-əst) *noun.* A heavy weight, such as rocks, to make a boat steady and stable: The empty boat needed *ballast* to keep it upright in the heavy winds.

ball bearing. One of a cluster of tiny steel balls used in machinery to reduce friction between fixed and moving parts.

ball control. In sports such as football and basketball, the ability to keep possession of the ball: Our team won with skillful *ball control* in the final minutes of the game; the visiting team could not get possession of the basketball in order to score.

bal•let (ba-LAY) *noun.* A graceful dance form that may tell a story and is usually presented on a stage.

bal•lis•tics (bə-LISS-tiks) *noun, plural in form but used with a singular verb.* 1. A science that studies how bullets, rockets, and bombs move and hit their targets. 2. The study of the insides of guns and how bullets are marked when fired.

bal•loon (bə-LOON) *noun.* 1. An airtight bag, usually very large, that can be inflated with hot air or gas to make it rise and float above the ground. 2. A toy that is an inflated, light rubber bag. —*verb.* To swell out; become enlarged: The sail on the boat *ballooned* forward when the wind shifted. **ballooned, ballooning.**

bal•lot (BAL-ət) *noun.* 1. A piece of paper on which a person votes, or a list of names with places to check off a vote: Mark your *ballot* for the candidate of your choice. 2. The system of voting by ballot. —*verb.* To vote by means of ballots. **balloted, balloting.**

ball•room (BAWL-room) *noun.* A large room where dances or large dinners are held.

balm•y (BAH-mee) *adjective.* 1. Soft, gentle; soothing, pleasant: *Balmy* breezes blow on tropical islands. 2. (Slang) Crazy, odd: That fellow is *balmy;* he's been sitting on that flagpole for three days. **balmier, balmiest.**

ba•lon•ey (bə-LOH-nee) Also **boloney** or **bologna** *noun.* 1. A sausage made of mixed meats, often used for sandwiches. 2. (Slang) Nonsense.

bal•sa (BAWL-sə) *noun.* 1. A tree found in tropical America. 2. The very lightweight wood of this tree.

bal•sam (BAWL-səm) *noun.* 1. The sap of certain trees used in making medicines and perfume. 2. Any plant or tree from which balsam is taken. 3. A kind of fir tree.

bam·boo (bam-BOO) *noun.* A thick tall tropical grass with long, stiff hollow stems of wood used in making furniture and houses.

bam·boo·zle (bam-BOO-zl) *verb.* (Informal) To persuade or coax by pressure, flattery, or deceit; fool: The fast-talking salesman *bamboozled* Dad into buying three shirts he really didn't need. **bamboozled, bamboozling.** —**bamboozlement, bamboozler** *nouns.*

ban *verb.* To forbid, refuse to allow; to outlaw: Fishing in that pond is *banned.* **banned, banning.** *—noun.* An act, law, or decision that forbids or outlaws certain actions or objects: There is a *ban* on cars in the park.

ba·nan·a (bə-NAN-ə) *noun.* 1. A fruit, usually with smooth yellow skin and a soft, creamy inside. 2. The tree-like plant on which bananas grow in the tropics.

[1]**band** *noun.* 1. A group; a gathering of people or animals: A *band* of outlaws raided the western town. 2. A group of musicians who play together. *—verb.* To gather together; unite: The Indians *banded* together to prepare for another attack. **banded, banding.**

[2]**band** *noun.* 1. A strip of material used for strengthening or binding: The crate was encircled with two *bands* of steel. 2. A stripe: The black dress had a *band* of red around the waist.

band·age (BAN-dij) *noun.* A piece of cotton, gauze, or plastic which is used to cover a wound or injury. **bandages.** *—verb.* To cover or dress a wound. **bandaged, bandaging.**

Band-Aid (BAND-ayd) *trademark.* A small packaged bandage used to protect cuts.

ban·dan·na (ban-DAN-ə) Also **bandana** *noun.* A large handkerchief or scarf.

ban·dit (BAN-dit) *noun.* An outlaw; robber.

band saw. A machine for cutting or sawing on which a band or loop of toothed metal is kept in motion by wheels that turn.

band·stand (BAND-stand) *noun.* A platform, often covered when outdoors, on which a band or orchestra performs.

band·wag·on (BAND-wag-ən) *noun.* 1. A popular cause, the popular side of a question: They jumped on the *bandwagon* and voted for Peter because everyone else wanted him to be class president. 2. A colorfully decorated wagon on which musicians ride in a parade.

bane (BAYN) *noun.* 1. A person or thing that harms or ruins something: The destructive dog was the *bane* of Mother's existence. 2. A poison.

bane·ful (BAYN-fəl) *adjective.* Destructive. —**banefully** *adverb.*

bang *noun.* 1. A loud and sudden noise: Dynamite explodes with a *bang.* 2. A hard, loud blow: The carpenter gave the nail one more *bang.* 3. (Slang) A thrill; excitement: Tim gets a *bang* out of watching parades. *—verb.* 1. To make a loud and sudden noise: The gun *banged* to start the race. 2. To strike; hit with hard, loud blows: We heard someone *banging* on the door. **banged, banging.**

bangs (BANGZ) *noun, plural.* Locks of short hair worn down across the forehead.

ban·ish (BAN-ish) *verb.* 1. To send or drive away; expel: The rude boy was *banished* from the classroom. 2. To send away from a country by order of some high authority. **banished, banishing.**

ban·ish·ment (BAN-ish-mənt) *noun.* The state of being ordered from a place or country by official command: "The Man Without a Country" is a story of a man in *banishment;* he could never return to his native land.

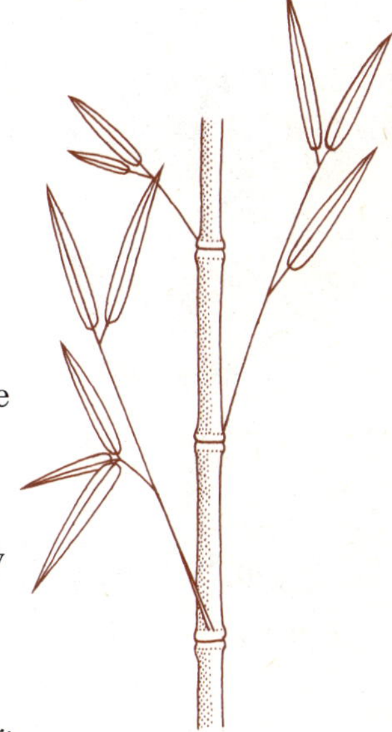

bamboo

bandanna

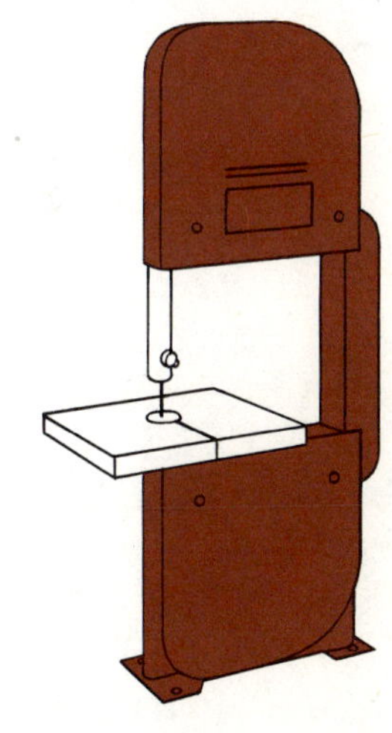

band saw

Band-Aid

banjo

ban·is·ter (BAN-i-stər) *noun.* A railing with supports, usually running alongside a stairway: The old man held on firmly to the *banister* as he climbed the stairs.

ban·jo (BAN-joh) *noun.* A stringed musical instrument similar to a guitar, played by strumming or plucking the strings. **banjos** or **banjoes.**

bank (BANGK) *noun.* 1. A place where money is kept and exchanged: Dad cashed his check and deposited fifty dollars at the *bank.* 2. A small container for saving money: Judy used a glass jar as a *bank* for her coins. 3. A slope; a long mound or mass: The boys hid behind a *bank* of sand. 4. The edge of land along a body of water: Uncle Joe sat fishing on the *bank* of the river. —*verb.* 1. To deposit or keep (money) in a bank. 2. To make a mound or pile: The boys *banked* the leaves along the wall. 3. To slant to one side from a level position: The pilot *banked* the plane to the left as he began the turn toward the airport. 4. To fix a fire so that it will burn for a long time. **banked, banking.**

bank·book (BANGK-buk) *noun.* A small book in which a record is kept of the money a person puts in and takes out of a bank.

ban·ker (BANG-kər) *noun.* 1. A person, especially an official, who works in a bank. 2. A player in a game who is in charge of the bank: When we play Monopoly, Walter likes to be the *banker.*

bank·rupt (BANGK-ruhpt) *adjective.* Unable to pay one's debts: The butcher is *bankrupt;* he has to close down because he cannot pay his bills. —*noun.* A person who is unable to pay his debts. —*verb.* To make a person bankrupt or unable to pay his debts: The damage caused by the flood *bankrupted* the owner of the store. **bankrupted, bankrupting.** —**bankruptcy** *noun.*

ban·ner (BAN-ər) *noun.* A flag or other symbol representing a country, organization, or person. —*adjective.* Outstanding; unusual: This has been a *banner* year for selling cars.

ban·quet (BANG-kwit) *noun.* A feast; a formal meal in honor of a person, group, or event.

ban·tam (BAN-təm) *noun.* 1. A very small chicken or other fowl. 2. A small, aggressive, or determined person.

ban·ter (BAN-tər) *noun.* Playful or teasing conversation. —*verb.* To talk, tease, or make fun of in a playful way. **bantered, bantering.**

bap·tism (BAP-tiz-əm) *noun.* A religious ceremony or sacrament in which a person is immersed in, or sprinkled with, water as a sign of his being cleansed from sin and received into a Christian church.

bap·tize (bap-TIGHZ or BAP-tighz) *verb.* 1. To perform the ceremony of baptism. 2. To give a name to a person when he receives baptism; christen: The infant was *baptized* James. **baptized, baptizing.**

bar (BAHR) *noun.* 1. A hard, oblong piece of material, usually metal: *Bars* of gold are stored at Fort Knox. 2. A rod used to lock, shut, or protect: The woman felt safer once she pushed the *bar* into place across the door. 3. Any object, condition, or situation that blocks or stops: The boy's age was a *bar* to his joining the Army. 4. A place where drinks, usually alcoholic, and snacks are served. 5. An official organization of lawyers; the legal profession. 6. (Music) An up and down line which divides a staff into equal parts or measures. —*verb.* 1. To set a rod in place in order to shut, lock, or protect. 2. To block, restrict, or shut off: The angry mob *barred* the entrance to the courtroom. 3. To prohibit or exclude. **barred, barring.**

barb (BAHRB) *noun.* 1. A point or sharp edge sticking backward from another point, as on a fishhook. 2. A sarcastic comment: Ed's *barb* about Joan's appearance annoyed her.

bar•bar•i•an (bahr-BAIR-ee-ən) *noun.* A primitive, uncivilized, or cruel human being: Roman civilization was destroyed when armies of *barbarians* invaded the Roman Empire.

bar•bar•ic (bahr-BA-rik) *adjective.* Typical of barbarians; crude, rough. **—barbarically** *adverb.*

bar•be•cue (BAHR-bi-kyoo) *noun.* 1. A pit or outdoor fireplace for roasting meat. 2. An outdoor meal or feast. 3. Meat or fish dish prepared with special, spiced sauces. **barbecues.** *—verb.* 1. To roast meat or a whole animal for a barbecue or feast. 2. To prepare meat or fish with barbecue sauce. **barbecued, barbecuing.**

barbed wire. Also **barbwire.** Wire with small, sharp spikes or points at regular distances from one another.

bar•ber (BAHR-bər) *noun.* A person whose job is giving haircuts and shaves for men. *—verb.* To perform the duties of a barber. **barbered, barbering.**

bare (BAIR) *adjective.* 1. Naked; not dressed. 2. Exposed; without covering: The gardener planted seeds in the *bare* spot on our lawn. 3. Empty; not stocked or equipped: Old Mother Hubbard's cupboard was *bare.* **barer, barest.** *—verb.* To reveal; uncover: The detective *bared* the plot of the robbers. **bared, baring.**

bare•back (BAIR-bak) *adverb* or *adjective.* On a horse's bare back without a saddle: American Indians rode their horses *bareback.*

bare•faced (BAIR-fayst) *adjective.* 1. Without a covering for the face. 2. Without shame or guilt; bold: Rather than admit his guilt, Jim told a *barefaced* lie.

bare•foot (BAIR-foot) *adjective* and *adverb.* With bare feet; without shoes and stockings.

bare•head•ed (BAIR-hed-id) *adjective* or *adverb.* Without a hat or covering for the head.

bare•ly (BAIR-lee) *adverb.* Scarcely; with little to spare: Jim was *barely* able to finish the long race.

bar•gain (BAHR-gin) *noun.* 1. Something that can be bought at less than the usual price. 2. An agreement made for a purchase, trade, or service: Dad made a *bargain* with the owner to buy the automobile. *—verb.* 1. To try to arrange for a purchase or sale at an advantage: Mildred *bargained* with the shopkeeper over the price of the radio. 2. To make an agreement for a purchase, trade, or service. **bargained, bargaining.**

barge (BAHRJ) *noun.* A large boat with a flat bottom, usually pushed or towed, used to carry freight, especially on inland waterways. **barges.** *—verb.* To move by a barge. **barged, barging. —barge in.** (Informal) To enter or intrude abruptly and without permission.

bar•i•tone (BA-rə-tohn) *noun.* 1. A male voice between bass and tenor in range. 2. A man with a baritone voice. **baritones.**

bark (BAHRK) *noun.* 1. The rough outside covering of trees. 2. The short, sharp noise or cry of a dog, or a similar sound made by other animals. 3. Also **barque.** A three-masted sailing vessel. *—verb.* 1. To make the short, sharp cry of a dog: The hound *barked* when he saw the fox. 2. To speak harshly; to shout: The drill sergeant *barked* orders at the new soldiers. **barked, barking.**

bark•er (BAHR-kər) *noun.* A circus, fair, or sideshow worker who calls to people passing by to come in and see the show.

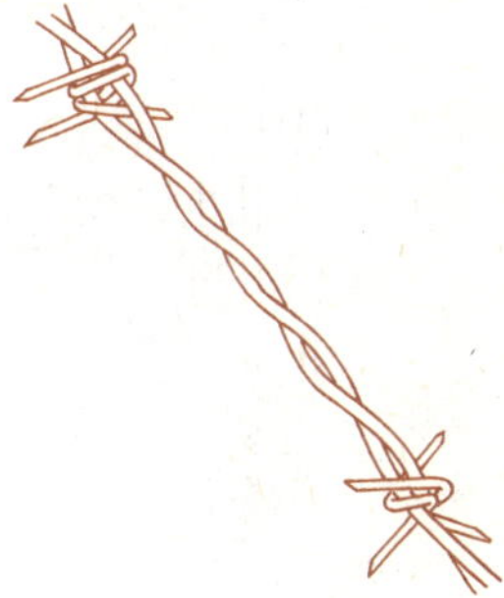

barbed wire

barge

bareback rider

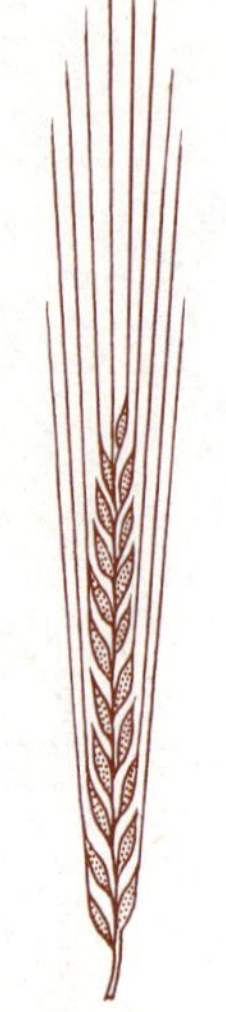
barley

barn

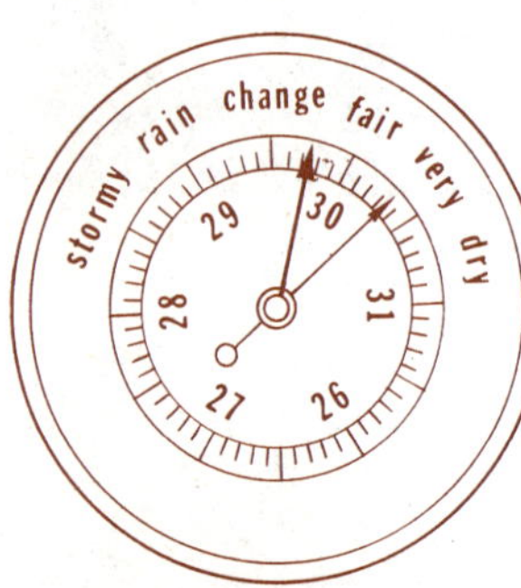

barometer

barrel

bar·ley (BAHR-lee) *noun.* A plant producing grain which is used for food and for the making of alcoholic beverages.

bar mitz·vah (bahr-MITS-və) Also **bar mitsvah** or **bar mizvah** [Often capital B and M] A religious ceremony of Judaism in which a boy is formally recognized as an adult member of the Jewish religion. —**bat** (baht) or **bas** (bahss) **mitzvah.** A ceremony for a girl similar to a boy's bar mitzvah.

barn (BAHRN) *noun.* A farm building used for sheltering livestock and storing grain.

bar·na·cle (BAHR-nə-kəl) *noun.* A small sea animal with a shell that attaches itself to the bottoms of ships and piers. **barnacles.**

barn·yard (BAHRN-yahrd) *noun.* The area, usually fenced in, next to a barn. —*adjective.* (Informal) Not in good taste; vulgar.

ba·rom·e·ter (bə-ROM-ə-tər) *noun.* 1. An instrument used to measure atmospheric or air pressure and to indicate changes in the weather. 2. Anything that indicates changes. —**barometric** (ba-rə-MET-rik) Also **barometrical** *adjective.*

bar·on (BA-ron) *noun.* 1. A nobleman of the lowest rank. 2. Very powerful or wealthy director of industry.

bar·racks (BA-rikss) *noun.* One or more buildings used to house soldiers.

bar·rel (BA-rəl) *noun.* 1. A large container of wood or heavy cardboard with curved sides and a flat top and bottom. 2. A unit of measure equal to thirty-one and one half gallons. 3. The cylinder that forms the forward part of a gun. 4. (Informal) A great amount: Charlie is a *barrel* of fun. —*verb.* 1. To put in barrels. 2. (Slang) To move forward rapidly or forcefully. **barreled** or **barrelled, barreling** or **barrelling.**

barrel organ. A musical instrument that resembles an organ in sound and is played by turning a handle.

bar·ren (BA-rən) *adjective.* 1. Not fertile; bare: No plants would grow in the *barren* desert area. 2. Not able to have children or produce offspring. 3. Uninteresting; dull.

bar·rette (bə-RET) *noun.* A clip for keeping a woman's hair in place. **barrettes.**

bar·ri·cade (BA-rə-kayd or ba-rə-KAYD) *noun.* A barrier; something that blocks the way or an advance. **barricades.** —*verb.* To block passage with a barricade. **barricaded, barricading.**

bar·ri·er (BA-ree-ər) *noun.* A barricade; something that blocks or hinders passage or movement.

barrier reef. A long narrow reef of rocks or the skeletons of tiny marine animals (coral) that is separated from the shore by a shallow lagoon of salt water.

bar·ri·o (BAH-ree-oh) *noun.* 1. A ward or section of a South American city. 2. A mostly Spanish-speaking area in a North American city. **barrios.**

bar·row (BA-roh) *noun.* 1. A cart with handles at the rear end. 2. A frame or support with handles at each end, used for carrying. 3. A large mound of earth; a hill.

bar·tend·er (BAHR-ten-dər) *noun.* A man who serves drinks at a bar.

bar·ter (BAHR-tər) *verb.* To trade or exchange one thing for another: Peter *bartered* his frog for Jack's penknife. **bartered, bartering.**

ba·salt (bə-SAWLT) *noun.* A hard rock of dark color which is formed from the lava of a volcano.

base (BAYSS) *noun.* 1. The bottom of anything; the part that ordinarily supports an object or structure. 2. A center of operation or supply; a settlement: The Vikings established *bases* along the coast of Ireland. 3. A basic content or essential element: Rover's food has a beef *base.* 4. A specific place or goal in certain sports oı games: The catcher ran to second *base.* 5. (Geometry) The side of a figure, as a triangle, on which the figure could rest; the horizontal side of a figure to which an altitude is, or can be, drawn. 6. (Math) A number that can be raised to various powers and that acts as the starting point for a number system. 7. (Chemistry) A compound that reacts with acid to form a salt. **bases.** —*verb.* To establish; rely upon: The scientist *based* his ideas on years of experiments. **based, basing.** —*adjective.* 1. Mean or vile in character or spirit: Lying and cheating are *base* activities. 2. Low or inferior in rank or value: a *base* metal like lead. **baser, basest.** —**basely** *adverb.*

base·ball (BAYSS-bawl) *noun.* 1. A team sport played with bat and ball on a field with four bases. 2. The ball used in the game of baseball.

base·ment (BAYSS-mənt) *noun.* A cellar; the story of a building beneath the main floor, usually underground.

base on balls. (Baseball) An automatic gaining of first base when a batter has received four balls from the pitcher.

bash·ful (BASH-fəl) *adjective.* Shy; timid: The *bashful* boy blushed when he was introduced to the visitors. —**bashfully** *adverb.*

ba·sic (BAY-sik) *adjective.* Main; essential; necessary or required: Food and water are *basic* needs for human life. —**basically** *adverb.*

ba·sin (BAY-sin) *noun.* 1. A shallow bowl that holds liquid, as a wash *basin.* 2. A sheltered area of water where boats dock or tie up. 3. The land drained by a river.

ba·sis (BAY-siss) *noun.* 1. A main or essential quality: Her respect for others is the *basis* for Joan's popularity. 2. The major ingredient: Iron forms the *basis* of steel. —**bases** (BAY-seez) *plural.*

bask *verb.* 1. To expose oneself to comfortable warmth. 2. To enjoy or find satisfaction in, as popularity or success: The team *basked* in the glory of their victory. **basked, basking.**

bas·ket (BASS-kit) *noun.* 1. A container made of thin strips of material that are woven or fastened together. 2. A hoop through which a ball is thrown in basketball. 3. A shot that goes through the hoop in basketball.

bas·ket·ball (BASS-kit-bawl) *noun.* 1. A game or sport in which two teams try to shoot a ball through hoops at the ends of a playing court. 2. The ball that is used in the game of basketball.

bas mitzvah. *See* **bar mitzvah.**

bas-re·lief (bah-ri-LEEF) *noun.* A sculpture in which figures stand out only slightly from a flat background.

[1]**bass** (BAYSS) *noun.* 1. A male voice of the lowest tone. 2. A man, instrument, or piece of music having a low, deep tone. **basses.**

[2]**bass** (BASS) *noun.* A kind of fish found in either fresh or salt water. **bass** or **basses.**

basset hound. A dog with short hair, short legs, and droopy ears.

bas·soon (bə-SOON) *noun.* A musical instrument of the woodwind family that has a deep, low sound.

bass viol. Also **double bass** or **bull fiddle.** The largest type of stringed instrument.

bas·tard (BASS-tərd) *noun.* A child of parents not legally married to each other.

baste (BAYST) *verb.* 1. To pour melted butter, fat, or a similar substance

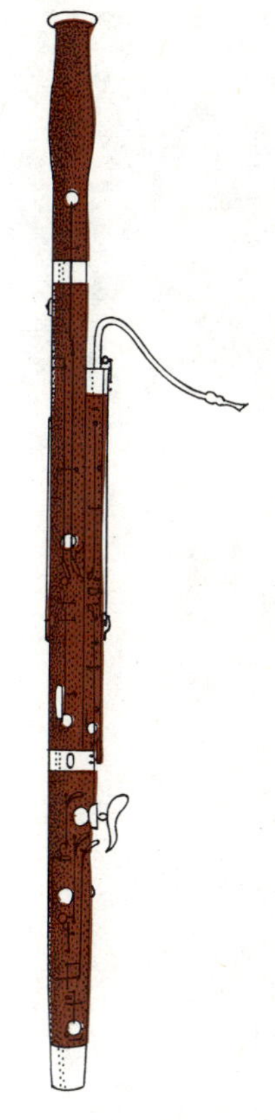
bassoon

bass viol

baton

bat

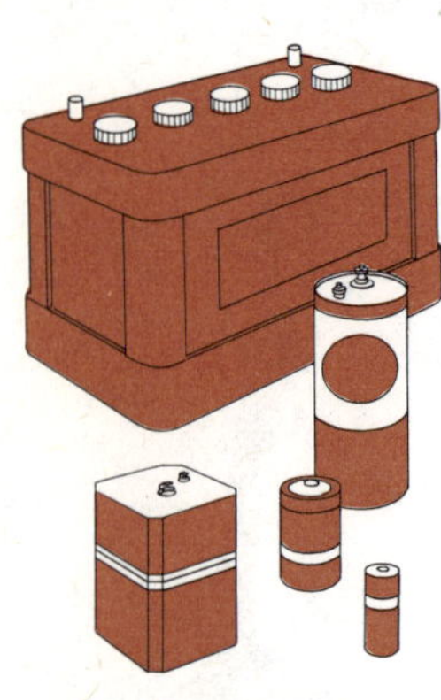
batteries

over meat or fish while it is being cooked. 2. To sew with large stitches to hold materials together for a short time. **basted, basting.**

[1]**bat** *noun.* A wooden club; especially the one used in baseball. —*verb.* To strike or hit, particularly with a club: The player *batted* the ball for a double. **batted, batting.** —**go to bat for.** (Informal) Stand up for; assist.

[2]**bat** *noun.* A small, flying, warm-blooded animal resembling a mouse with wings.

batch (BACH) *noun.* 1. A quantity made or produced at one time or in one process: Grandmother took the second *batch* of cookies out of the oven. 2. A group or collection of persons or things: Tom brought a *batch* of records to our party. **batches.**

bath *noun.* 1. A washing with water, especially of the body. 2. Water used for bathing: The mother prepared a *bath* for her baby. 3. A room for bathing.

bathe (BAYTH) *verb.* 1. To wash; give or take a bath. 2. To soak or cover with water or some other liquid. 3. To expose oneself to water or sunshine. 4. To cover; spread over: The moon *bathed* the trees with a silver light. **bathed, bathing.**

bathing suit. A garment worn for swimming.

bath·robe (BATH-rohb) *noun.* A garment for use after bathing or over nightclothes. **bathrobes.**

bath·room (BATH-room) *noun.* A room with a sink and toilet, and usually a bathtub or shower.

bath·tub (BATH-tuhb) *noun.* A tub used for bathing.

bath·y·sphere (BATH-i-sfihr) *noun.* A sturdy steel sphere in which men can be lowered into the ocean for underwater exploration. **bathyspheres.**

bat mitzvah. *See* **bar mitzvah.**

ba·ton (bə-TON) *noun.* 1. A thin stick or rod used by a conductor or leader to direct an orchestra or band. 2. A fancy rod carried or twirled by a drum major. 3. A short rod or cylinder passed from one teammate to another during a relay race. 4. A staff or rod that serves as a symbol of authority.

bat·tal·ion (bə-TAL-yən) *noun.* A large unit of soldiers, usually smaller than a regiment.

bat·ter (BAT-ər) *verb.* 1. To pound noisily and repeatedly: The soldiers *battered* on the door with their rifle butts. 2. To damage by blows or rough use: The waves *battered* the ship in the storm. **battered, battering.** —*noun.* 1. One who bats, especially in sports: The *batter* struck out. 2. A mixture of flour with milk or water and other ingredients that is cooked to make cake or similar food.

bat·ter·y (BAT-ə-ree) *noun.* 1. A device that is used to provide electric current by chemical reaction: There are two new *batteries* in the flashlight. 2. A group of persons or a set of similar things assembled for a common purpose: A *battery* of air conditioners kept the building cool. 3. A set of heavy guns: The shore *battery* opened fire on the enemy ship. 4. An attack upon another person. 5. The combination of a pitcher and catcher in baseball. **batteries.**

bat·tle (BAT-l) *noun.* 1. A conflict between armed forces: Gettysburg was a famous *battle* of the American Civil War. 2. A contest or struggle: The game was a thrilling *battle.* **battles.** —*verb.* To fight; struggle. **battled, battling.**

bat·tle·field (BAT-l-feeld) *noun.* The place where a battle is fought. "We are met on a great *battlefield* of that war." (Lincoln).

bat·tle·ground (BAT-l-grownd) *noun.* 1. A battlefield. 2. A place where any conflict occurs.

bat·tle·ship (BAT-l-ship) *noun.* A large, armed fighting ship.

baux·ite (BAWK-sight) *noun.* The main ore from which aluminum is made.

bawl *verb.* 1. To shout or call out loudly: The sergeant *bawled* his orders to the troops. 2. To cry aloud: The child *bawled* when he burned his fingers. **bawled, bawling.** —*noun.* A loud shout or cry.

bay *noun.* 1. A cove or inlet of a body of water. 2. A howl or deep bark: The hunter heard the *bay* of his hound. 3. A laurel tree or shrub. 4. (Also *adjective*). A reddish-brown color. —*verb.* To howl or bark: The wolf *bayed* at the moon. **bayed, baying. —at bay.** The condition of a hunted creature when he cannot escape his pursuers.

bay·o·net (BAY-ə-nit, BAY-ə-net or bay-ə-NET) *noun.* A knife or blade attached to the end of a rifle for fighting. —*verb.* To stab with such a blade. **bayoneted** or **bayonetted, bayoneting** or **bayonetting.**

bay·ou (BIGH-oo) *noun.* A swampy or marshy section of a lake, river, or other body of water. **bayous.**

ba·zaar (bə-ZAHR) Also **bazar** *noun.* 1. A fair or a festive occasion at which goods are sold and entertainment is provided to raise money for a special purpose. 2. A section of a town, especially in countries of the Orient, where goods are sold at shops or marketplaces.

BB gun *noun.* An air rifle which shoots round pellets.

B.C. *abbreviation.* 1. Before Christ. Used to indicate dates before the birth of Christ. 2. British Columbia.

be (BEE) *verb.* 1. To live; exist. 2. To have a certain quality or identity: Mother will *be* angry when she finds the cake gone. 3. To belong to a group or class: We want to *be* Girl Scouts. 4. To lie in a certain place: Dinner will *be* on the table when you get home.

Present Singular:	*Present Plural:*
I **am**	We **are**
You **are**	You **are**
He (she, it) **is**	They **are**
Past Singular:	*Past Plural:*
I **was**	We **were**
You **were**	You **were**
He (she, it) **was**	They **were**

Present participle: **being**
Past participle: **been**

be- *prefix.* Indicates: 1. A complete covering of: *be*fog. 2. An action causing a condition to occur: *be*witch.

beach (BEECH) *noun.* The sandy or pebbly shore of a body of water. **beaches.** —*verb.* To run a boat aground on a beach. **beached, beaching.**

bea·con (BEE-kən) *noun.* 1. A tower or other structure, like a lighthouse, on which there is a light to guide or warn. 2. A light used to guide or warn. 3. An electronic signal, like a radio or radar signal, used to guide ships and planes. 4. Anything used to warn, direct, or guide.

bead (BEED) *noun.* 1. One of many small pieces of glass or other material strung together to make jewelry or ornaments. 2. Any small, round item; a drop: A *bead* of water formed at the end of the faucet. —*verb.* To shape into beads or drops: The perspiration *beaded* on his forehead. **beaded, beading.**

bea·gle (BEE-gəl) *noun.* A small dog of the hound family with tan, white, and black markings, short legs and droopy ears. **beagles.**

beak (BEEK) *noun.* 1. The bill of a bird: The robin held the worm in its *beak.* 2. Something shaped like a beak, such as a spout: The *beak* on the pitcher was broken.

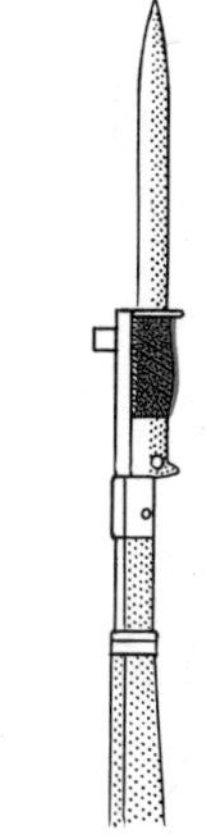
bayonet

beagle

beard

beak·er (BEE-kər) *noun.* 1. A large drinking cup. 2. A vessel or container of glass or metal, usually with a small lip, used in laboratory experiments.

beam (BEEM) *noun.* 1. A large, sturdy timber or piece of metal used to support or strengthen a building or structure. 2. A ray or shaft of light or electronic signal: A plane may be guided by a radar *beam* in bad weather. 3. The maximum width of a ship. —*verb.* 1. To smile. 2. To send out a ray of light or an electronic signal. **beamed, beaming.** —**off the beam.** (Informal) Inaccurate, incorrect: We were *off the beam* in our directions; we could not find the house. —**on the beam.** (Informal) Exact, correct: He was *on the beam* when he said that she would be an excellent student.

bean (BEEN) *noun.* 1. A large seed of certain plants used as food, or the plant or pod containing such seeds. 2. (Slang) The head. 3. (Slang, plural). A very small amount: Sarah doesn't know *beans* about sewing. —*verb.* (Slang) To hit on the head with something: The pitcher *beaned* the batter. **beaned, beaning.**

bean·bag (BEEN-bag) *noun.* A small bag, filled with dried beans, that is tossed about in games or play.

bean ball. (Baseball) A ball pitched with the intention of hitting the batter on the head.

bean·ie (BEE-nee) *noun.* A small cap. **beanies.**

bear

[1]**bear** (BAIR) *noun.* 1. A large, powerful animal with heavy coarse hair. 2. (Informal) A grouchy person.

[2]**bear** (BAIR) *verb.* 1. To hold; to support: This bridge can *bear* the weight of the truck. 2. To carry: The workman will *bear* his tools to the shed. 3. To endure; to withstand: Some animals cannot *bear* very cold weather. 4. To produce; to yield. 5. To give birth to: *bear* puppies. **bore, borne** or **born, bearing.**

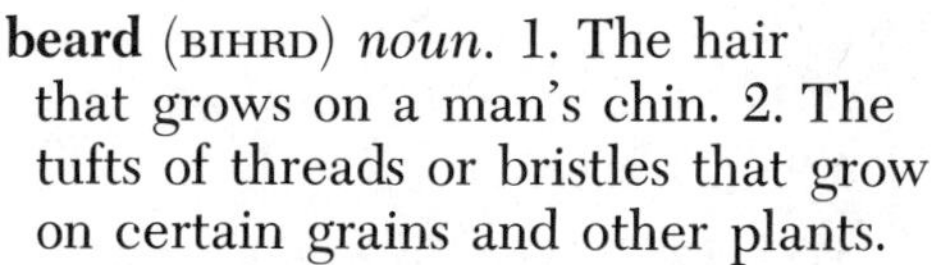

beard (BIHRD) *noun.* 1. The hair that grows on a man's chin. 2. The tufts of threads or bristles that grow on certain grains and other plants.

bear·ing (BAIR-ing) *noun.* 1. A way of conducting oneself in manner and posture: The courteous old gentleman is a person of noble *bearing.* 2. Relevance; effect: What *bearing* will the strike have on prices? 3. A machine part for making other parts move more easily. 4. (Usually plural). Direction or location in terms of other places: The hunter lost his *bearings* in the woods.

bear·skin (BAIR-skin) *noun.* The fur or pelt of a bear.

beast (BEEST) *noun.* 1. An animal. 2. A cruel person; one like a beast.

beast·ly (BEEST-lee) *adjective.* Like or typical of a beast; crude; disgusting: The public was shocked by the *beastly* deeds of the criminals. **beastlier, beastliest.**

beat (BEET) *verb.* 1. To hit again and again: The musician *beat* the drum. 2. To make a repeated noise or sound: Listen to the metronome as it *beats.* 3. To defeat: The champion *beat* the challenger. 4. To blend with vigor; whip: Mother *beat* the pancake batter. 5. (Slang) To confuse, to puzzle: It *beats* me how Timmy lost the race. **beat** or **beaten, beating.** —*noun.* 1. A stroke or sound that is repeated: I was so scared that I could feel the *beat* of my heart. 2. The scheduled patrol of a policeman or guard: The policeman's *beat* was Main Street from the factory to the river. —*adjective.* (Slang) Tired, exhausted: He was *beat* after hiking and swimming all day. —**beat it.** (Slang) Get out, leave immediately: "*Beat it,*" he yelled at the cat.

beau (BOH) *noun.* 1. A boyfriend or special male friend of a girl or woman. 2. A dandy. —**beaux** or **beaus** *plural.*

beau·ti·cian (byoo-TISH-ən) *noun.* A person whose job is to aid in the good grooming or attractive appearance of others: Ruth had her hair cut and waved by a *beautician.*

beau·ti·ful (BYOO-tə-fəl) *adjective.* Possessing beauty; lovely; delightful to behold. —**beautifully** *adverb.*

beau·ti·fy (BYOO-tə-figh) *verb.* To make beautiful; increase the loveliness of: Our town plans to *beautify* its park by planting more trees and flowers. **beautified, beautifying.**

beau·ty (BYOO-tee) *noun.* 1. The quality of being delightful to behold; loveliness: "A thing of *beauty* is a joy forever." (Keats). 2. Good looks: That actress certainly has *beauty.* 3. A beautiful person or thing. **beauties.**

bea·ver (BEE-vər) *noun.* 1. A water animal with a broad, flat tail and soft fur that is valuable for the making of clothing. 2. The fur or pelt of a beaver. —**eager beaver.** (Informal) A busy, hard-working person.

beaver

be·cause (bi-KAWZ) *conjunction.* Since; for the reason that: The hiker rested *because* he was tired.

beck·on (BEK-ən) *verb.* 1. To summon (someone) with a movement, as a wave or a nod: The customer *beckoned* the waiter to bring the food. 2. To attract or lure: When hunger *beckoned,* Dick ran to the refrigerator. **beckoned, beckoning.**

be·come (bi-KUHM) *verb.* 1. To come or grow to be: As Jim continues to work, he will *become* tired. 2. To look good on; be suitable: Alice's blue gown *becomes* her. **became, become, becoming.**

bed *noun.* 1. A piece of furniture or anything used to sleep or rest upon: The calf rested on a *bed* of straw. 2. A plot of ground where plants are grown: Stay out of the flower *bed;* seeds are planted there. 3. A flat surface that serves as a foundation: The house was built on a *bed* of rock. 4. The ground beneath a river or other body of water. —*verb.* To prepare a bed or shelter for; to put to bed. **bedded, bedding.**

bed·bug (BED-buhg) *noun.* A small insect pest that infests beds and similar places.

bed·clothes (BED-klohz) *noun, plural.* The sheets, blankets, and other covers that are spread on a bed.

bed·ding (BED-ing) *noun.* 1. Bedclothes. 2. A material used to provide a comfortable place to rest: The farmer used straw as *bedding* for his horse.

be·dev·il (bi-DEV-əl) *verb.* To be cruel to in a devilish manner; to trick: The nasty boys *bedeviled* the old man by throwing stones at his window. **bedeviled, bedeviling.**

bed·lam (BED-ləm) *noun.* A state of great confusion or disorder: The fire alarm in the store caused *bedlam* among the crowd of shoppers.

be·drag·gled (bi-DRAG-əld) *adjective.* Worn-out; soiled; limp, as with wetness: Bob's clothes looked *bedraggled* after his hike in the rain.

bed·rid·den (BED-rid-n) *adjective.* Confined to bed, usually for a long time: Ed is *bedridden* with a broken hip.

bed·rock (BED-rok) *noun.* 1. A solid layer of rock beneath other material, as soil. 2. A basis; that on which something is built or developed: Hard work has been the *bedrock* of Uncle Howard's success.

bed·room (BED-room) *noun.* A room where people sleep.

bed·side (BED-sighd) *noun.* The area next to or beside a bed: She sat at the sick child's *bedside.* **bedsides.**

bed·spread (BED-spred) *noun.* A decorative cover for a bed.

bee

beech leaf

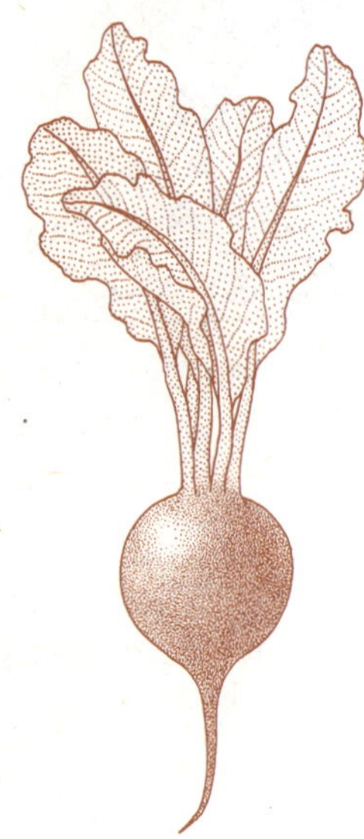
beet

beetle

bed·time (BED-tighm) *noun.* The time when a person goes or should go to bed: The child must be tired; it is past his *bedtime.* **bedtimes.**

bee *noun.* 1. A stinging insect that gathers the nectar of flowers, from which it makes honey. 2. A gathering for work or play; a contest: a spelling *bee.* **bees.**

beech *noun.* A nut-bearing tree or the wood from this tree. **beeches.**

beef *noun.* 1. The meat that comes from full-grown cattle. —**beeves** (BEEVZ) *plural.* 2. (Slang) A complaint. **beefs.** —*verb.* (Slang) To complain. **beefed, beefing.**

beef·steak (BEEF-stayk) *noun.* A cut or slab of beef.

bee·hive (BEE-highv) *noun.* 1. A place in which bees live and store honey. 2. (Slang) A very busy place: The drugstore is a *beehive* of activity after school. **beehives.**

bee·line (BEE-lighn) *noun.* The shortest or most direct route from one place to another: The hungry boys made a *beeline* to the dinner table. **beelines.**

been (BIN) *verb.* *See* **be.**

beep *noun.* A short, sudden sound like that made by an automobile horn. —*verb.* To make a short, sudden sound. **beeped, beeping.**

beer (BIHR) *noun.* 1. An alcoholic beverage made from grains and other ingredients. 2. A soft drink made from certain plants, as root *beer*, ginger *beer.*

beet *noun.* 1. A plant with a large red or white root used for food or as a source of sugar. 2. The root of a beet plant.

bee·tle (BEET-l) *noun.* An insect with a hard covering to protect its wings. **beetles.**

be·fall (bi-FAWL) *verb.* 1. To happen. 2. Happen to: No matter what evil *befalls* us, mankind will survive. **befell, befallen, befalling.**

be·fit (bi-FIT) *verb.* To be suitable for or appropriate: Laughter does not *befit* one in church. **befitted, befitting.**

be·fore (bi-FOR) *preposition.* 1. Earlier than; prior to: He arrived *before* the rest of the class. 2. In front of or ahead of: There is a great future *before* you. 3. In preference to: She would choose the red dress *before* the brown one. —*adverb.* Previously; earlier: We were here *before.* —*conjunction.* 1. Prior to a time when: Remember to turn off the radio *before* you study. 2. More willingly than: I would walk *before* I would accept a ride from a stranger.

be·fore·hand (bi-FOR-hand) *adverb.* Early; before the present time: To avoid a delay, Dad had the car filled with gas *beforehand.*

be·friend (bi-FREND) *verb.* To act as a friend to; aid: The kind woman *befriended* the lost child. **befriended, befriending.**

beg *verb.* 1. To ask charity: The poor old man *begged* for food. 2. To plead; request humbly: Sally *begged* her mother for another hour of playtime. **begged, begging.** —**beg off.** 1. To ask to be released from an obligation. 2. To make an excuse for not doing (something): Charles *begged off* going to the game with us because he was tired. —**go begging.** To be unwelcome or unwanted: We are all so full that half of Mother's cake must *go begging.*

beg·gar (BEG-ər) *noun.* A person who begs; one who lives by begging.

be·gin (bi-GIN) *verb.* 1. To start; do the first part of: The hikers will *begin* their trip at dawn. 2. To come into existence: "Liberty like charity must *begin* at home." (J. B. Conant). **began, begun, beginning.**

be·gin·ning (bi-GIN-ing) *noun.* A start; the first part of an action or thing: The *beginning* of the story is dull. *—adjective.* First; introductory: The *beginning* song of the concert is very popular.

be·gone (bi-GAWN) *interjection.* Go away; leave: *"Begone!"* shouted the watchman to the strangers.

be·go·nia (bi-GOHN-yə) *noun.* A tropical plant with waxy flowers.

be·half (bi-HAF) *noun.* Interest; benefit; support: Jim asked for a favor on Tom's *behalf.*

be·have (bi-HAYV) *verb.* 1. To act or function; conduct oneself: The child *behaved* badly. 2. To conduct oneself properly: If you don't *behave,* you will be punished. **behaved, behaving.**

be·hav·ior (bi-HAYV-yər) *noun.* 1. A person's manner of acting or conducting himself: The teacher scolded the boys for their disorderly *behavior.* 2. The reaction of something to conditions or surroundings: The scientist observed the *behavior* of the chemicals when they were heated.

be·hind (bi-HYND) *preposition.* 1. In back of; in the rear of: He hid *behind* the boulder. 2. Tardy in; not current with: The train was *behind* schedule. 3. Not as advanced as: Bob is *behind* Ted in math. *—adverb.* 1. At another place or time: When we travel we leave the dog *behind* with a neighbor. 2. In the rear. *—adjective.* Following; at the rear: The driver of the car *behind* honked its horn.

be·hold (bi-HOHLD) *verb.* To see; observe: "My heart leaps up when I *behold* a rainbow in the sky." (Wordsworth). **beheld, beholding.** *—interjection.* Look: *Behold!* The castle is on fire!

be·hold·en (bi-HOHL-dn) *adjective.* Owing a debt; obligated: The strangers were *beholden* to the farmer for his kindness and assistance.

beige (BAYZH) *noun* (Also *adjective*). A light tan or grayish-brown color.

be·ing (BEE-ing) *noun.* 1. A creature; that which exists: Man is a human *being.* 2. The state of existing: When television came into *being* children were happy. *—verb. See* **be.**

be·la·bor (bi-LAY-bər) *verb.* 1. To attack physically or with words; beat: The bully *belabored* the poor fellow with kicks and punches. 2. To spend too much time talking about or working on; overstress: There is no need to *belabor* the point; we know what you think. **belabored, belaboring.**

begonia

be·lat·ed (bi-LAY-tid) *adjective.* Delayed, late: We received the *belated* Christmas card in January. —**belatedly** *adverb.*

belch *verb.* 1. To expel or let out air or gas from the stomach through the mouth in a sudden, loud manner. 2. To erupt or give off in bursts: The chimney of the factory *belched* smoke. **belched, belching.** *—noun.* A sudden eruption, as of fire, smoke, or gas. **belches.**

bel·fry (BEL-free) *noun.* A tower in which a bell or bells are hung. **belfries.**

belfry

be·lief (bi-LEEF) *noun.* 1. That which a person believes in or regards as true: It was his *belief* that all men are created equal. 2. Trust; confidence: The general placed his *belief* in the courage of his troops.

be·liev·a·ble (bi-LEEV-ə-bəl) *adjective.* Able to be believed; worthy of belief. —**believably** *adverb.*

be·lieve (bi-LEEV) *verb.* 1. To hold or accept as true: He *believes* in the Bible. 2. To rely on the truth or honesty of another: I *believe* John; there is no reason to doubt him. 3. To have trust or confidence. **believed, believing.**

be·lit·tle (bi-LIT-l) *verb.* To make something seem less important than it is or appears to be: The jealous girl *belittled* Barbara's victory in the spelling contest. **belittled, belittling.**

bell (BEL) *noun.* 1. A cup-shaped object, usually of metal, that gives off a ringing sound when struck. 2. The sound of a bell. 3. On shipboard, a signal rung to indicate the passage of each half-hour.

bell-bot·toms (BEL-bot-əmz) *noun, plural.* Pants that flare at the bottom of the legs.

bell·boy (BEL-boi) *noun.* A male who carries luggage and does other jobs at a hotel.

bell·hop (BEL-hop) *noun.* Bellboy.

bel·lig·er·ent (bə-LIJ-ər-ənt) *adjective.* Inclined or tending to be hostile: My neighbor has a *belligerent* attitude; he is always looking for a fight. *—noun.* A person or nation engaged in fighting or warfare. —**belligerently** *adverb.*

bel·low (BEL-oh) *verb.* To make a loud, deep sound or outcry: The sergeant *bellowed* orders to the soldiers. **bellowed, bellowing.** *—noun.* A loud, deep shout.

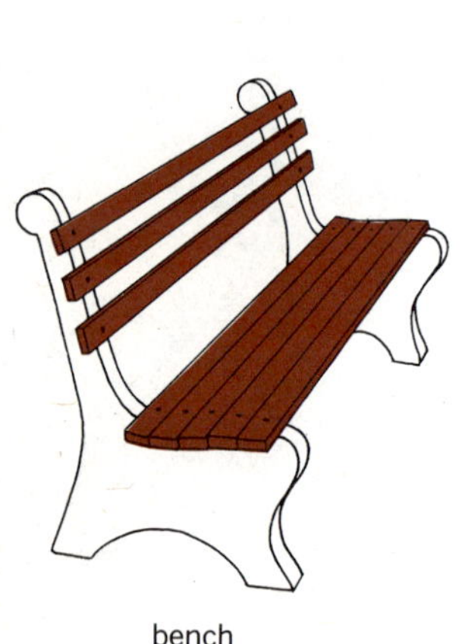

bench

bel·ly (BEL-ee) *noun.* 1. The front part of the body below the ribs, containing the stomach and the intestines; the abdomen. 2. The stomach. **bellies.** *—verb.* To fill out; bulge; swell: The sails *bellied* when the gust of wind reached them. **bellied, bellying.**

bel·ly·but·ton (BEL-ee-buht-n) *noun.* (Slang) The navel.

be·long (bi-LAWNG) *verb.* 1. To be owned by: The book *belongs* to Ed. 2. To be a member of: Mother *belongs* to the Red Cross. 3. To have a place with, or be part of (a set or group): That plate *belongs* with Mother's new set of dishes. **belonged, belonging.**

be·long·ings (bi-LAWNG-ingz) *noun, plural.* Those things that a person or group owns; possessions; property: The settlers packed all of their *belongings* on a wagon and moved west.

be·lov·ed (bi-LUHV-id or bi-LUHVD) *adjective.* Loved very much; dearly loved: The woman sent a gift to her *beloved* daughter. *—noun.* A person who is loved very much.

be·low (bi-LOH) *preposition.* 1. Beneath; under: My room was *below* Tom's. 2. Lower in value, rank, or degree than: A major is *below* a general. *—adverb.* 1. Toward a lower place; under: From the top of the building, we could see *below.* 2. On a lower level, floor, or deck: The captain ordered passengers to remain *below* during the storm. 3. Lower down on a page: The entry on "belt" comes *below.*

belt *noun.* 1. A strip or band, often of leather, used to hold clothing in place. 2. Any broad strip or band: The *belt* connecting the motor to the fan had to be repaired. 3. A region known for a particular characteristic or quality: The cotton *belt* is a section of the southern U.S. where that crop is grown in abundance. *—verb.* 1. To fasten or secure with a belt: The flier *belted* on his parachute. 2. (Slang) To strike; to hit: The boxer *belted* his opponent. **belted, belting.**

be·moan (bi-MOHN) *verb.* To express disappointment, pity, or sorrow; to lament; deplore: The man *bemoaned* the theft of his wallet. **bemoaned, bemoaning.**

bench *noun.* 1. A long seat, usually of wood, for more than one person. 2. A worktable: The carpenter's *bench* was piled with tools. 3. The judge or judges in a court or the place where they sit: The lawyer was asked to approach the *bench.* **benches.** *—verb.* In sports, to remove or keep from playing in a game: The coach *benched* the halfback when he dropped the pass. **benched, benching.**

bench warmer. In ball games, a player who stays on the bench and rarely is allowed to play.

bend *verb.* 1. To put a curve in; fold: He had to *bend* the plastic rod to make it fit into the closet. 2. To curve: The road *bends* around the hill. 3. To stoop: *bend* over to pick up a bucket. 4. To yield or to force to yield or submit: The tyrant could not *bend* the spirit of the loyal citizens. **bent, bending.** —*noun.* A curve.

bends (BENDZ) *noun, plural.* A sickness caused by the formation of air bubbles in the blood, created by a sudden change from high pressure to normal air pressure.

be·neath (bi-NEETH) *preposition.* 1. Under: The ball rolled *beneath* the porch. 2. Lower than in position or value. —*adverb.* Under; in a lower place.

ben·e·dic·tion (ben-ə-DIK-shən) *noun.* 1. Blessing: The Pilgrims asked for God's *benediction.* 2. A formal religious ceremony, usually short, at which prayers are offered for God's blessing.

ben·e·fac·tor (BEN-ə-fak-tər) *noun.* A person who provides money or some other aid or benefit: The equipment for the hospital was donated by a wealthy *benefactor.*

ben·e·fi·cial (ben-ə-FISH-əl) *adjective.* Helpful; providing a benefit or advantage: Exercise is *beneficial* to a person's health. —**beneficially** *adverb.*

ben·e·fit (BEN-ə-fit) *noun.* 1. Anything that is of help or advantage: Uncle George enjoyed the *benefit* of a good education. 2. A performance, as of a play or concert, that raises money for a special cause. —*verb.* 1. To receive help; to profit. 2. To give help; improve. **benefited, benefiting.**

be·nev·o·lence (bə-NEV-ə-lənss) *noun.* 1. Kindness; the inclination to do good or to be charitable: We all admired the *benevolence* of the helpful woman. 2. An act of kindness; a good deed.

be·nev·o·lent (bə-NEV-ə-lənt) *adjective.* 1. Kind; generous; inclined to do good: The children loved their *benevolent* teacher. 2. Operating for purposes of charity or aid to others: The Salvation Army is a *benevolent* organization. —**benevolently** *adverb.*

bent *adjective.* 1. Crooked; curved: The car's bumper was *bent* after the accident. 2. Determined; having one's mind set: Tim is *bent* on winning the race tomorrow. —*noun.* A desire for or interest in some action or condition: Martha shows a strong *bent* for becoming a doctor. —*verb.* See **bend.**

be·queath (bi-KWEETH) *verb.* 1. To leave or give over in a will: The old man *bequeathed* his land to his sons. 2. To pass on or hand down: Our ancestors in America *bequeathed* a love of freedom to us. **bequeathed, bequeathing.**

be·reave (bi-REEV) *verb.* 1. To deprive (of): The settlers were *bereaved* of hope by the crop failure. 2. To make sad or desolate: Sue was *bereaved* by the death of her father. **bereaved** or **bereft, bereaving.**

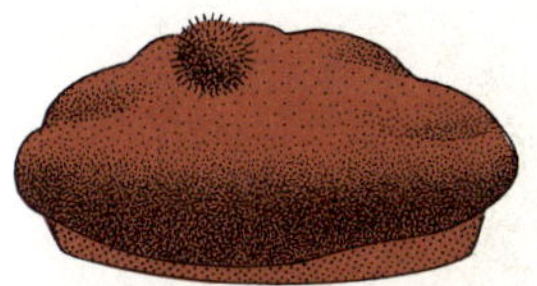
beret

be·ret (bə-RAY) *noun.* A round cloth cap without a brim or peak.

Bermuda shorts. Long shorts that almost reach the knee.

ber·ry (BEHR-ee) *noun.* A sweet, fleshy, juicy fruit. **berries.** —*verb.* To pick berries. **berried, berrying.**

berth *noun.* 1. A bunk or place for sleeping, as on a train or ship. 2. A place in a harbor where a ship anchors or ties up. 3. A job: Jim won a *berth* as second mate on an ocean liner. —*verb.* 1. To dock or be docked at a berth. 2. To provide a sleeping place or bunk on a train or ship. **berthed, berthing.**

be•seech (bi-SEECH) *verb.* To plead with; beg for. **besought** or **beseeched, beseeching.**

be•set (bi-SET) *verb.* To attack; surround; torment: Great dangers *beset* Columbus in exploring his new world. **beset, besetting.**

be•side (bi-SIGHD) *preposition.* 1. At or by the side of: I usually sit *beside* my mother at church. 2. In comparison with: My allowance looks good *beside* the one that Sally gets. 3. In addition to: No one else came *beside* the three girls.

be•sides (bi-SYDZ) *adverb.* In addition: We had cake and ice cream *besides.* —*preposition.* 1. In addition to. 2. Other than; except: No one offered to help *besides* us.

best *adjective.* The highest degree of *good;* most excellent; largest; of the highest quality. —*adverb.* In the most excellent manner: Ralph sings *best* of all the boys. —*noun.* That which is most excellent or of the highest quality. —*verb.* To defeat; overcome: Jack *bested* Carl in a game of chess. **bested, besting.** —**at best.** The best or most that can be done under certain conditions: The delayed train will arrive an hour late *at best.* —**get the best of.** To overcome; defeat. —**make the best of.** To do as well as one can under unfavorable conditions: When it rained, the boys *made the best of* their afternoon by playing indoors.

be•stow (bi-STOH) *verb.* 1. To give to, present: The award was *bestowed* upon Gloria for her excellent work in history. 2. To use or apply. **bestowed, bestowing.**

bet *noun.* A promise to pay (money or other goods) if one guesses wrong. —*verb.* 1. To make a bet: Joe *bet* his uncle a dollar that the champion would win. 2. To feel certain. **bet** or **betted, betting.**

be•tray (bi-TRAY) *verb.* 1. To be disloyal or unfaithful to: The boy *betrayed* his friend by telling his secret. 2. To turn over to an enemy: The traitor *betrayed* the fort to the enemy. 3. To reveal: The smoke *betrayed* the location of the campfire. **betrayed, betraying.**

bet•ter (BET-ər) *adjective.* 1. More excellent; larger; of a higher quality: John's radio is *better* than Harry's. 2. Healthier; in an improved condition: The patient feels *better* today. —*adverb.* In a more excellent manner: Mona dances *better* than Sheila does. —*noun.* That which is more excellent: The coach used the *better* of the two players as his fullback. —*verb.* To improve: Toby *bettered* his grades by studying harder. **bettered, bettering.**

be•tween (bi-TWEEN) *preposition.* 1. In the space, time, or degree separating two things: The price is *between* 10 and 15 cents. 2. Combining in action, effort, or possession: *Between* them they finished the job in an hour. 3. One or the other: She had to choose *between* the blue dress and the red one. —*adverb.* In the space, time, or degree separating two things: I will work Monday and Wednesday and rest *between.*

bev•el (BEV-əl) *noun.* 1. An angle wider than a right angle formed by one surface against another; a slanted edge. 2. An instrument used for measuring or making angles. —*verb.* To form a wide angle between two angles; to slant or slope: The carpenter *beveled* the edge of the table to make it more attractive. **beveled, beveling.**

bev•er•age (BEV-rij or BEV-ə-rij) *noun.* A liquid used for drinking: Coffee, tea, and soda are *beverages.* **beverages.**

be•ware (bi-WAIR) *verb.* Watch out; be careful: *Beware* of sudden storms. **bewared, bewaring.**

be•wil•der (bi-WIL-dər) *verb.* To confuse: The difficult instructions on the machine *bewildered* my sister. **bewildered, bewildering.**

be·witch (bi-WICH) *verb.* 1. To place under a magic spell. 2. To delight or enchant. **bewitched, bewitching.**

be·yond (bee-OND) *preposition.* 1. Farther than; on the other side of: The ball landed *beyond* the fence. 2. Higher or more than; superior to: Mother's skill in sewing is far *beyond* Mary's. 3. Outside of or greater than the limits or bounds of: Bob's success was *beyond* his greatest hopes and dreams. *—adverb.* Farther on; in a more distant place.

bi- *prefix.* 1. Two or twice: *bi*cycle, *bi*annual. 2. Once in every two: A *bi*monthly report appears just one time every two months.

bi·as (BIGH-əss) *noun.* 1. A diagonal or slanted line, as of a cut across the weave of a fabric. 2. An opinion based on personal preference or prejudice; a slanted viewpoint: Try to be fair; don't let *bias* influence your decision. **biases** *—verb.* To influence by appealing to personal preference or to prejudice: The dishonest politician tried to *bias* the voters with false stories about his opponent. **biased** or **biassed, biasing** or **biassing.**

bib *noun.* A cloth worn under the chin, especially by infants, to protect clothing while eating.

bi·ble (BIGH-bəl) *noun.* 1. [Capital B] The book that contains the sacred writings of the Christian religion; Scripture. 2. Any book containing especially useful or valuable information: This dictionary is my *bible* for doing school work. **bibles.** **—bib·li·cal** (BIB-li-kəl) *adjective.*

bib·li·og·ra·phy (bib-lee-OG-rə-fee) *noun.* A list of books or other written works that are about the same topic or by the same author. **bibliographies.**

bi·car·bon·ate of soda (bigh-KAHR-bə-nət). A powder used in cooking and in making certain medicines; baking soda.

bi·cen·ten·ni·al (bigh-sen-TEN-ee-əl) *adjective.* Happening one time in 200 years. *—noun.* The anniversary of 200 years.

bi·ceps (BIGH-seps) *noun.* The muscle that moves the elbow.

bick·er (BIK-ər) *verb.* To quarrel; argue, especially about minor details. **bickered, bickering.**

bi·cus·pid (bigh-KUSS-pid) *noun.* One of the eight teeth that are located between the canines and molars in humans and are used for tearing and grinding. *—adjective.* Having two points: The moon is *bicuspid* tonight; it is in the shape of a crescent.

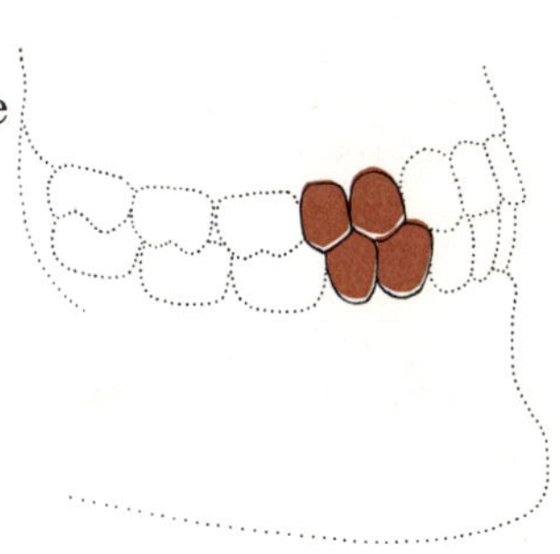

bicuspids

bi·cy·cle (BIGH-sik-əl) *noun.* A two-wheeled vehicle steered by turning handlebars and propelled by turning a set of pedals. **bicycles.** *—verb.* To travel by bicycle. **bicycled, bicycling.**

bid *verb.* 1. To offer: Jim *bid* five dollars for the chair at the auction. **bid, bidding.** 2. To order; command: Why did you *bid* me to stop? 3. To express: The sailor will *bid* farewell to his shipmates. **bade, bidden** or **bid, bidding.** *—noun.* 1. The offer made by a customer: Jim's *bid* failed to get the chair. 2. An attempt or effort.

bide (BIGHD) *verb.* To wait; remain; stay; continue: *bide* one's time. **bided** or **bode, biding.**

bi·en·ni·al (bigh-EN-ee-əl) *adjective.* 1. Occurring once every two years: The town's *biennial* celebration is held each odd-numbered year. 2. Lasting or living for two years. *—noun.* 1. An event occurring once every two years. 2. A plant that lives for two years. **—biennially** *adverb.*

bier (BIHR) *noun.* A stand that supports a coffin or dead body before burial.

big *adjective.* 1. Large in size or amount: Edward ate a *big* breakfast. 2. Significant; important: Graduation is a *big* day for students. 3. Grown up: When my little brother is *big*, he is going to be a doctor. **bigger, biggest.** —**big deal.** (Slang) 1. Something important. 2. Something less important than it appears to be: Jack said, "So you are the class monitor. *Big deal!*" —**big shot.** (Slang) Someone who is important or high-ranking. —**big top.** 1. The largest tent in a circus show. 2. A circus: The *big top* is coming to town with elephants and bears. —**big wheel.** (Slang) Important person, one in a high position: Jay is a *big wheel;* he is president of his class.

big·ot (BIG-ət) *noun.* A person who has little or no respect for opinions, creeds, or races other than his own; a prejudiced person.

bike (BIGHK) *noun.* (Informal) 1. A bicycle. 2. A motorcycle. **bikes.** —*verb.* To ride a bicycle. **biked, biking.**

bi·ki·ni (bi-KEE-nee) *noun.* A very brief two-piece bathing suit worn by women.

bi·lat·er·al (bigh-LAT-ər-əl) *adjective.* 1. Having two sides. 2. Affecting or binding two sides in the same way: The two countries made a *bilateral* agreement to call a truce. —**bilaterally** *adverb.*

bill (BIL) *noun.* 1. A record of what is owed by a person for purchases or services: The waitress added up our *bill* and placed it on the table. 2. A unit of paper money: A dollar *bill* is worth four quarters. 3. A matter that is presented to a legislature for the purpose of having it made a law. 4. A poster or printed notice: The men distributed *bills* praising their candidate for mayor. 5. A bird's beak. —*verb.* 1. To send a customer a record of the money owed for purchases or services. 2. To advertise; promote: Jo Jo was *billed* as the world's funniest clown. **billed, billing.**

bill·board (BIL-bord) *noun.* A large board or flat surface to which posters or advertisements can be attached.

bil·liards (BIL-yərdz) *noun, plural in form but used with a singular verb.* A game, played by tapping balls across a special table with a cue or long stick.

bil·lion (BIL-yən) *noun.* The cardinal number 1,000,000,000 in the United States or 1,000,000,000,000 in Great Britain.

bil·low (BIL-oh) *verb.* To fill, to bulge: The wind *billowed* the sails. **billowed, billowing.** —*noun.* 1. A large wave: The wind created *billows* which made the boat rock. 2. A moving mass that sweeps like a wave: *Billows* of smoke came from the chimney.

bin *noun.* A box or container for storing loose things like coal or potatoes.

bi·na·ry (BIGH-nə-ree) *adjective.* 1. Referring to or involving two. 2. Referring to the numerical system that has two as its base.

bind (BYND) *verb.* 1. To tie together: To prevent an escape, he must *bind* the captive's hands and feet. 2. To attach a border to something to strengthen or decorate it: The dressmaker plans to *bind* the bottom of the skirt with blue ribbon. 3. To fasten together in the form of a book: The class will *bind* its drawings into an album for the teacher. 4. To bandage. 5. To require or be required by association or law: The government *binds* citizens to pay taxes. **bound, binding.** —*noun.* (Informal) A difficult or embarrassing situation: Without money I am in a *bind* until my next pay day.

bin·go (BING-goh) *noun.* A game, usually played by a large number of people, in which each player tries to be first to cover a row of numbered spaces as a leader calls off numbers selected by chance.

bin·oc·u·lars (bə-NOK-yə-lərz) *noun, plural.* An instrument held to the eyes that makes distant objects appear to be closer; field glasses.

bio- *prefix.* Life: *bio*chemistry.

bi·o·de·grad·a·ble (bigh-oh-di-GRAYD-ə-bəl) *adjective.* Capable of decomposing through natural processes of decay and bacterial action: *Biodegradable* products do not become permanent piles of junk.

bi·og·ra·phy (bigh-OG-rə-fee) *noun.* A book or article that contains the story of a person's life. **biographies.**

bi·ol·o·gist (bigh-OL-ə-jist) *noun.* A scientist who is trained in biology, the science of all living things: *Biologists* study both plants and animals.

bi·ol·o·gy (bigh-OL-ə-jee) *noun.* The science of living things and the processes of life; the study of plants and animals.

birch (BERCH) *noun.* A tree with smooth (usually white) bark and hard wood; the wood from such a tree. **birches.**

bird (BERD) *noun.* A warm-blooded animal covered with feathers and having a pair of wings.

bird·bath (BERD-bath) *noun.* A man-made basin at which birds can drink or bathe.

bird·call (BERD-kawl) *noun.* 1. The sound or call of a bird. 2. A device used, especially by hunters, to imitate the call of a bird.

bird dog. 1. A dog specially trained to hunt or retrieve game birds. 2. (Slang) A person used as a spy or information seeker by another: We used Tim as a *bird dog* to find out what other classes were planning for the science fair.

bird of prey. A bird that catches and eats other birds and animals.

birds of a feather. Persons having similar interests or goals: The three athletes are *birds of a feather.*

birth (BERTH) *noun.* 1. The process by which a baby or offspring is born. 2. A beginning: The *birth* of space travel occurred in our own century. 3. Family background; ancestry; descent: Lincoln was a man of humble *birth.*

birth·day (BERTH-day) *noun.* The day on which a person was born or something originated; the anniversary of such a day.

birth·place (BERTH-playss) *noun.* The place where one is born or something begins. **birthplaces.**

birth·rate (BERTH-rayt) *noun.* The number of babies born over a certain period of time, usually a year. **birthrates.**

birth·right (BERTH-right) *noun.* A right or set of privileges that a person receives or inherits at the time of his birth: Citizenship is a *birthright* of anyone born in the United States.

bis·cuit (BISS-kit) *noun.* 1. A small, light bread made with baking powder or soda. 2. A cracker or, especially in Great Britain, a plain cookie.

bi·sect (BIGH-sekt or bigh-SEKT) *verb.* To divide into two equal parts. **bisected, bisecting.**

bish·op (BISH-əp) *noun.* 1. A high-ranking clergyman who usually has charge of a diocese, or area including a number of churches and other clergymen. 2. A piece in the game of chess that moves along any free diagonal row of the same color as the square in which the bishop starts.

bi·son (BIGH-sn) *noun.* A large animal of the ox family with short horns and a shaggy head; the American buffalo. —**bison** *plural.*

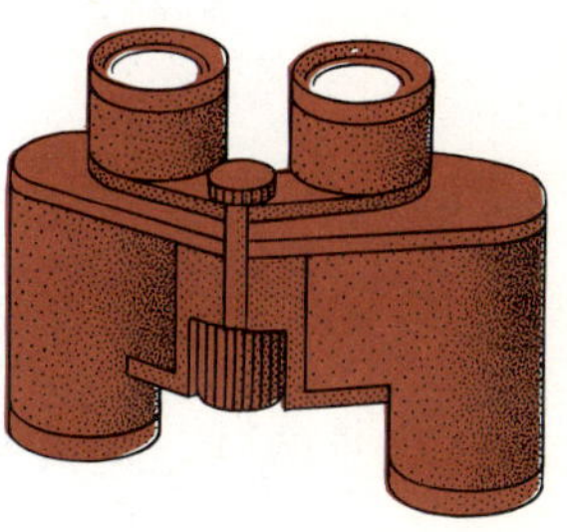
binoculars

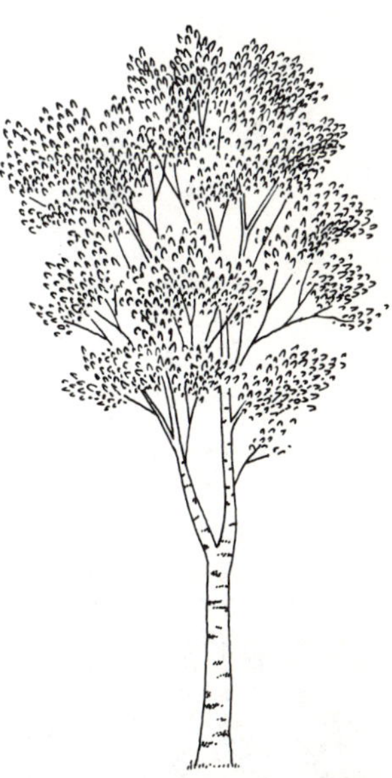
birch

bison

bit *noun.* 1. A very small part or amount: Jim tossed some *bits* of bread to the birds. 2. A tool or device used for drilling: As the *bit* turned, it cut into the wood. 3. A piece of metal attached to a bridle, inserted in a horse's mouth as a device to control him. 4. (Slang) Half of a quarter; 12½ cents: George bet two *bits* that his team would win. 5. (Computers) A single unit of basic information, or single character of a two-character computer language.

blackberries

bitch (BICH) *noun.* A female dog. **bitches.**

bite (BIGHT) *verb.* 1. To cut or grind with the teeth. 2. To wound with the teeth or a stinger: My dog may *bite* the mailman. 3. To cause discomfort or stinging pain: The cold wind will *bite* his nose and ears. 4. To take bait: The fishermen are delighted when the trout *bite.* 5. (Informal) To accept a lure or temptation; to be fooled: Money was left on the table to attract the thief, but he didn't *bite.* 6. To grip; hold: Our tires were too smooth to *bite* the snow on the road. **bit, bitten, biting.** *—noun.* 1. A cut made by the teeth. 2. A wound: A mosquito *bite* may cause illness. 3. The amount one cuts off with the teeth. 4. Discomfort or stinging pain: Mittens can protect your hands from the *bite* of the cold. 5. A grip or hold. 6. A light meal; snack: He enjoyed a *bite* between meals. **bites.**

blackbird

bit·ter (BIT-ər) *adjective.* 1. Sharply unpleasant to the taste: The child hated the taste of the *bitter* medicine. 2. Harsh; extreme: The *bitter* cold and wind forced them to seek shelter. 3. Difficult to accept or endure: He suffered a *bitter* defeat. 4. Severely resentful: The workman was *bitter* because he was fired. **bitterer, bitterest.** **—bitterly** *adverb.*

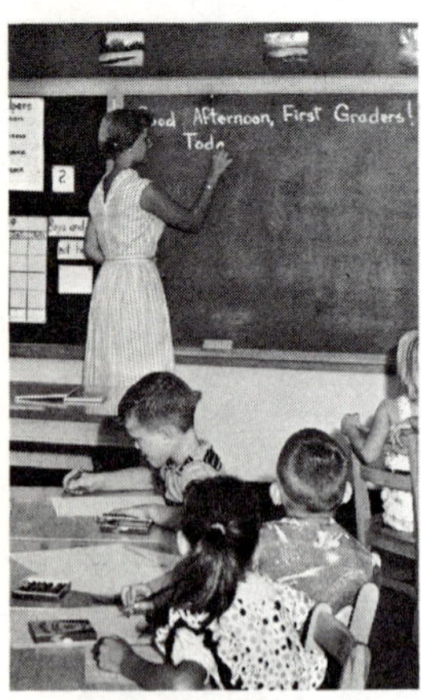

blackboard

bit·ter·ness (BIT-ər-ness) *noun.* 1. A condition of being sharply unpleasant to the taste. 2. Feelings of deep resentment or hostility.

bi·tu·mi·nous (bi-TOO-mə-nəs) *adjective.* Referring to soft coal.

biv·ou·ac (BIV-oo-ak or BIV-wak) *noun.* A camp without permanent shelter; a group of tents or other temporary dwellings.

black (BLAK) *adjective.* 1. The opposite of white insofar as color is described by the amount of light reflected: A *black* object reflects little or no light; it is much darker than a gray or white object. 2. Dark-skinned. 3. Gloomy, unhappy. 4. Angry. 5. Evil or mysterious, as in *black* magic. **blacker, blackest** *—noun.* 1. The darkest color value, reflecting little or no light. 2. A Negro; a member of a Negroid race.

black·ber·ry (BLAK-behr-ee) *noun.* A small, black or deep-purple fruit, or the plant on which it grows. **blackberries.**

black·bird (BLAK-berd) *noun.* Any of several kinds of birds that are all or mostly black.

black·board (BLAK-bord) *noun.* A sheet of dark, hard material on which one can write with chalk.

black·en (BLAK-ən) *verb.* 1. To make or become black or very dark: The sky *blackened* before the storm. 2. To slander; spoil: He *blackened* my reputation with his lies. **blackened, blackening.**

black-eyed pea (BLAK-ighd PEE) *noun.* A seed of the cowpea plant which is used as a food.

black·mail (BLAK-mayl) *noun.* Money or some other bribe forced from a person in exchange for not revealing some secret or misdeed. *—verb.* To force or extort money or some other bribe. **blackmailed, blackmailing.**

black·out (BLAK-owt) *noun.* 1. A loss or absence of light, as from an electrical power failure. 2. A stopping of news or communication: The strike caused a newspaper *blackout* for three weeks. 3. A loss of consciousness: The doctor revived the patient after her *blackout*.

Black Power. The force or influence shown by Negroes when they act together for some goal, as for better housing or education.

black·smith (BLAK-smith) *noun.* A man who forms things out of iron or repairs iron objects.

blad·der (BLAD-ər) *noun.* A sac in the body that holds urine.

blade (BLAYD) *noun.* 1. The cutting part of a knife or other sharp instrument: The *blade* of the carving knife cut through the roast beef. 2. A leaf of grass or the flat part of any other leaf. 3. A wide, thin surface or part: The *blades* of the old electric fan were rusty. 4. A spirited young man. **blades.**

blame (BLAYM) *verb.* To accuse of being responsible for a fault or error: The policeman *blamed* the truck driver for the accident. **blamed, blaming.** —*noun.* The responsibility for a fault or error.

bland *adjective.* 1. Mild, soothing, gentle: The *bland* salve made the rash feel better. 2. Dull, unexciting: The *bland* conversation made Dad fall asleep. —**blandly** *adverb.*

blank *noun.* 1. An empty space: The student left a *blank* where he should have written his answer. 2. A paper or form to be filled out: The coach has application *blanks* on his desk. 3. A cartridge not containing a bullet: *Blanks* were fired during the play, not real bullets. —*adjective.* 1. Without printing or writing; empty: One page was written on; the other was *blank*. 2. Without decoration or attractive features: The wall looked *blank* without any pictures. 3. Dull, without interest or enthusiasm: The bored student had a *blank* expression on his face. —**blankly** *adverb.*

blan·ket (BLANG-kit) *noun.* 1. A large, warm covering, especially for a sleeping person; a bed cover. 2. A covering; something resembling a bed cover: The ground was covered with a *blanket* of snow. —*verb.* To cover: Fallen leaves *blanketed* our yard. **blanketed, blanketing.**

blare (BLAIR) *verb.* To make a loud sound: The radio *blared* out music until Dad turned it down. **blared, blaring.** —*noun.* A loud or harsh noise.

blast *verb.* 1. To blow up; destroy. 2. To cause to wither or shrivel. 3. (Slang) To attack with words or actions: Dad really *blasted* me for breaking the window. **blasted, blasting.** —*noun.* 1. An explosion. 2. A sudden gust of wind. 3. A sudden, loud sound, especially that made by a horn. 4. (Slang) A wild or very spirited party or occasion: The party after the football game was a *blast*.

blast furnace. A large furnace, capable of very great heat, in which iron or other metal is melted from ore.

blast·off (BLAST-awf) Also, **blast-off** *noun.* 1. The moment of takeoff of a rocket or spacecraft. 2. The first few seconds of rocket flight.

blastoff

blaze (BLAYZ) *verb.* 1. To burn brightly and rapidly: Soon after they were lighted, the dry leaves *blazed*. 2. To gleam; show bright colors or lights: The skyscraper *blazed* with light at night. 3. To burst out in activity or feeling: The racer *blazed* with anger when his rival tripped him. 4. To mark or indicate the direction of (a trail), especially by cutting notches in trees: The pioneer used an ax to *blaze* a trail through the forest. **blazed, blazing.** —*noun.* 1. A brilliant fire; a bright burst of flame. 2. A bright display of color. 3. A sudden outburst of activity or feeling. 4. A mark, made by a knife or ax, on a tree. **blazes.**

blaz·er (BLAY-zər) *noun.* A sports jacket, usually with an emblem on the breast pocket.

bldg. *abbreviation.* Building.

bleach (BLEECH) *noun.* A substance used for removing color or making something white: Mother added *bleach* to the washing machine full of sheets. **bleaches.** —*verb.* To make lighter or whiter, as with sunlight or a chemical substance. **bleached, bleaching.**

bleak (BLEEK) *adjective.* 1. Bare and lonely: The seashore is *bleak* in February. 2. Cold; chilling: A *bleak* wind made hiking unpleasant. 3. Depressing; cheerless. **bleaker, bleakest.** —**bleakly** *adverb.*

bleat (BLEET) *noun.* The noise or cry made by sheep or goats, or a sound similar to it. —*verb.* To make the noise or cry made by sheep or goats. **bleated, bleating.**

blimp

bleed *verb.* 1. To lose blood: If you cut your finger, it will *bleed.* 2. To feel sympathy or pity for: My heart *bleeds* for all war victims. 3. (Slang) To demand large sums of money from (someone): Blackmailers *bleed* their victims. **bled, bleeding.**

blem·ish (BLEM-ish) *noun.* A spot or mark which spoils the appearance of something: The bruise was a *blemish* on the otherwise perfect apple. **blemishes.** —*verb.* To spoil, spot, or mar: Ginny's absence *blemished* her perfect attendance record. **blemished, blemishing.**

blender

blend *verb.* 1. To mix for a new or different result: *Blend* the blue and yellow paint to make green. 2. To flow together in a pleasant way: The flowers in the garden *blend* so well that you can't tell where one color begins and another ends. **blended** or **blent, blending.** —*noun.* 1. A mixture: A milk shake is a *blend* of ice cream, flavored syrup, and milk. 2. A word which is formed from the combination of other words: The word "brunch" is a *blend* to describe a meal that takes the place of breakfast and lunch.

blend·er (BLEN-dər) *noun.* 1. A person or machine that mixes things. 2. A special kitchen tool with blades to mix food.

bless *verb.* 1. To make holy: The bishop *blessed* the new chapel. 2. To provide with a benefit, protection, or good fortune. 3. To wish good fortune to. **blessed** or **blest, blessing.**

bless·ed (BLESS-id) Also **blest** *adjective.* 1. Fortunate; gifted; happy: That woman is *blessed;* she has good health, prosperity, and a fine family. 2. Holy; sacred. —**blessedly** *adverb.*

bless·ing (BLESS-ing) *noun.* 1. A prayer or ritual offered to make something holy: The bishop led the *blessing* of the new chapel. 2. A prayer of praise. 3. A benefit or fortunate occurrence: Good health is a great *blessing.* 4. A wish for success or happiness; approval: I got Dad's *blessing* for my plan to travel.

blight *noun.* 1. A disease which causes injury or destruction of plants. 2. Any condition, such as slums or smog, which harms the environment.

blimp *noun.* A small nonrigid dirigible or lighter-than-air craft.

blind (BLYND) *adjective.* 1. Not able to see. 2. Having no exit: A dead-end street is a *blind* alley. 3. Refusing to understand: Mary insists on a new dress and is *blind* to the fact that we can't afford it. **blinder, blindest.** —*verb.* To make unable to see: The sun on the beach *blinded* us. **blinded, blinding.** —*noun.* A shutter or shade which shuts out light. —**blindly** *adverb.*

blind·fold (BLYND-fohld) *noun.* A cloth covering for the eyes which prevents seeing. —*verb.* To cover the eyes with a cloth. **blindfolded, blindfolding.**

blind·ness (BLYND-niss) *noun.* Lack of sight.

blink (BLINGK) *verb.* 1. To shut and open the eyes rapidly. 2. Shine unsteadily: The harbor lights *blinked* through the mist. **blinked, blinking.**

bliss *noun.* Happiness: We were in a state of *bliss* with the new baby.

bliss·ful (BLISS-fəl) *adjective.* Completely happy, full of joy. —**blissfully** *adverb.*

blis·ter (BLISS-tər) *noun.* 1. A raised swelling on the skin enclosing a watery substance. 2. A pocket of air on the surface of something: The house had *blisters* where the paint was peeling. —*verb.* To cause blisters. **blistered, blistering.**

blithe (BLYTH) *adjective.* Gay; carefree: John's *blithe* acceptance of trouble makes him a happy boy. **blither, blithest.** —**blithely** *adverb.*

blitz (BLITS) *noun.* A complete, all-out attack, particularly one that is sudden. **blitzes.** —*verb.* To attack suddenly and with great force. **blitzed, blitzing.**

bliz·zard (BLIZ-ərd) *noun.* A heavy snowstorm with strong, cold winds.

bloat (BLOHT) *verb.* 1. To cause to swell up with liquid or gas: The cattle were *bloated* after drinking too much water. 2. To puff up (with vanity): Jane was *bloated* with pride about her new dress. **bloated, bloating.**

blob *noun.* A small, formless drop or wad: When Jim finished the job, there was not a *blob* of paint on the floor. —*verb.* To cause or make a blob. **blobbed, blobbing.**

block (BLOK) *noun.* 1. A solid piece of wood, stone, or other material usually with straight sides: The baby plays with wooden *blocks.* 2. An area of land surrounded by streets. 3. The distance along a street from one crossing to the next. —*verb.* To prevent action or be in the way of: Tom *blocked* Jim's pass. **blocked, blocking.** —**block out.** To sketch or make an outline of: The architect *blocked out* the basic plan for the new building.

block·ade (blok-AYD) *noun.* 1. The closing off of an area by unfriendly forces to prevent supplies reaching the area: A *blockade* forced the city to surrender after food ran out. 2. An obstruction: All cars had to stop for inspection at the police *blockade.* **blockades.** —*verb.* To set up an obstruction: The bandits *blockaded* the road with logs. **blockaded, blockading.**

block and tackle. A system used for lifting heavy objects and made of a series of pulleys and ropes.

block·house (BLOK-howss) *noun.* 1. A fort with small openings for shooting or observation. 2. The control building at a missile site. **blockhouses.**

blond *noun, masculine.* Also **blonde** *noun, feminine.* A person with light hair, fair skin, and, usually, blue eyes. —*adjective.* Light in color. **blonder, blondest.**

blood (BLUHD) *noun.* 1. The liquid pumped by the heart through the veins and arteries of man and other animals: *Blood* carries oxygen to and waste material from all parts of the body. 2. Anything essential to the health or welfare of a living thing or an organization. 3. Spirit; temper; passion: The news made his *blood* boil. 4. Ancestry; family history: Politics has been in their *blood* for years. —**in cold blood.** Deliberately; with cruelty; mercilessly.

blood bank. A place where blood or blood plasma is collected, stored, and given out: My father gave a pint of blood to the *blood bank.*

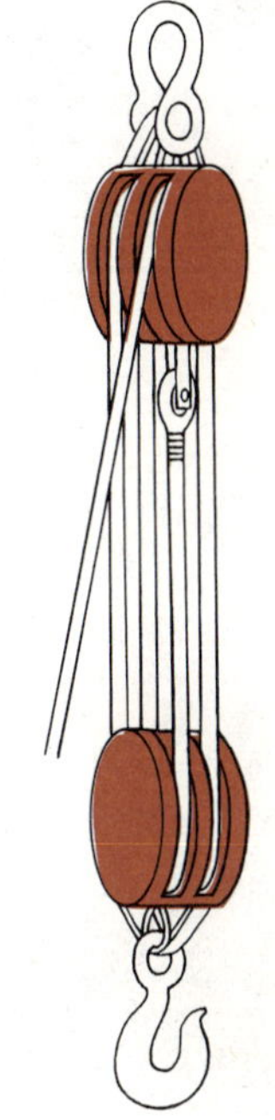

block and tackle

blockhouse

bloodhound

blowtorch

blood·cur·dling (BLUHD-kerd-ling) *adjective.* Awful, terrifying.

blood·hound (BLUHD-hownd) *noun.* 1. A dog with drooping ears, often used for tracking because of its sharp sense of smell. 2. A person who pursues or traces; a detective.

blood pressure. The pressure of the blood against the inside of the veins and arteries: *Blood pressure* is kept up by the pumping action of the heart.

blood·shed (BLUHD-shed) *noun.* Killing; the shedding of blood.

blood·thirst·y (BLUHD-ther-stee) *adjective.* Thirsting for violence or shedding of blood.

blood vessel. Any tube which carries blood through the body: An artery, vein, or capillary is a *blood vessel.*

bloom *noun.* The flower or blossom of a plant: Marigolds have yellow *blooms.* —*verb.* 1. To flower or blossom: Our roses *bloom* in June. 2. To flourish. **bloomed, blooming.**

blos·som (BLOSS-əm) *noun.* A flower or bloom of a plant, usually a fruit tree: Washington, D.C., is famous for its cherry *blossoms.* —*verb.* 1. To flower: The apple orchard *blossoms* soon. 2. To flourish: Mary *blossomed* into a beautiful girl. **blossomed, blossoming.**

blot *noun.* A small spot: Bill left a *blot* of ink on the paper when he dropped his pen. —*verb.* 1. To soak up: When the baby spills his milk, Mother *blots* it up with paper towels. 2. To darken or hide: The clouds *blot* out the sun. **blotted, blotting.**

blotch (BLOCH) *noun.* 1. A large spot: When Joe dropped the brush, he left a *blotch* of paint on the floor. 2. A redness of the skin: The rash caused Jane to break out in *blotches.* **blotches.** —*verb.* To cause or make a blotch. **blotched, blotching.**

blot·ter (BLOT-ər) *noun.* A soft paper used to soak up ink.

blouse (BLOWSS) *noun.* A garment worn on the upper part of the body; a shirt. **blouses.**

blow (BLOH) *verb.* 1. To make or let out a current of air, especially from the mouth: *Blow* out the candle. 2. To push, propel, or move by a current of air: The breeze is *blowing* papers across the lawn. 3. To move rapidly; rush: The winds can *blow* fiercely during a storm. 4. To explode: When the dynamite *blows,* the bridge will collapse. 5. (Slang) To waste; squander: Tom usually *blows* all his allowance on candy. 6. (Slang) To leave; go away: Let's *blow;* I want to go home. 7. (Slang) To mishandle or fail: You're going to *blow* the test unless you study. **blew, blown, blowing.** —*noun.* 1. A hard knock; a hit: He gave the nail a final *blow* with the hammer. 2. A sudden shock or misfortune. 3. A storm or gale: It is unsafe to go sailing; a *blow* is expected. —**blow a fuse.** (Slang) To get very angry, become enraged: Molly's mother *blew a fuse* when she saw the ink on the rug. —**blow one's stack.** (Slang) To show one's anger, to lose control of one's temper: The teacher *blew his stack* at the noisy class. —**blow one's top.** (Slang) To lose control of one's temper, to get violently angry. —**blow over.** To pass by; die out: The excitement over the robbery *blew over* by the following week. —**blow up.** 1. To explode or to destroy by causing an explosion. 2. To inflate; fill with air: The child *blew up* the balloon. 3. To enlarge (a photograph). 4. To lose one's temper: Harry *blew up* when he was insulted. —**come to blows.** To fight; begin to strike one another: The boys *came to blows* during their argument.

blow·torch (BLOH-torch) *noun.* A gas burner that produces a very hot flame: Plumbers use a *blowtorch* to melt metal. **blowtorches.**

blow·up (BLOH-up) *noun.* 1. An explosion. 2. A show of temper. 3. An enlargement of a photograph.

BLT (Slang) Bacon, lettuce, and tomato sandwich: Give me a *BLT* on toast. **BLT's.**

blub·ber (BLUHB-ər) *noun.* 1. Whale fat used to produce oil. 2. Extra fat on a person: Tom has a roll of *blubber* around his middle from eating too much. *—verb.* To weep loudly like a small child: Jane was too old to *blubber* about losing a doll. **blubbered, blubbering.**

blue (BLOO) *noun* (Also *adjective*). The color of a clear sky. *—adjective.* Sad or depressed: Sue was *blue* when her friend moved away. **bluer, bluest.**

blue·bell (BLOO-bel) *noun.* Any of several plants which bear blue flowers shaped like bells.

blue·ber·ry (BLOO-behr-ee) *noun.* A small, dark-blue, edible berry or the plant on which it grows. **blueberries.**

blue·bird (BLOO-berd) *noun.* A small bird with blue feathers, related to the robin and thrush.

Blue Bird. The youngest level of Camp Fire Girls.

blue·grass (BLOO-grass) *noun.* Any grass with bluish-green blades. **bluegrasses.**

blue jay *noun.* A crested blue and gray bird that lives in North America.

blue·print (BLOO-print) *noun.* 1. A photograph, usually taken of plans or diagrams, in which white lines are printed on a blue background. 2. Any detailed plan or diagram. *—verb.* To make a plan or blueprint. **blueprinted, blueprinting.**

blue ribbon. A ribbon of blue awarded for first place; the top award in a contest: Uncle Jed's bull won a *blue ribbon* at the fair.

blues (BLOOZ) *noun, plural.* 1. The state of being sad, depressed: Joe has the *blues* every Monday morning. 2. A type of jazz music.

bluff (BLUHF) *verb.* 1. To pretend to have the advantage or to have knowledge: Tom tried to *bluff* his way through the test; he failed. 2. To trick; to fool: Mary *bluffed* us; she isn't really going to Spain. **bluffed, bluffing.** *—noun.* 1. A high, steep bank with straight sides. 2. The act of tricking or fooling. *—adjective.* Having a warm, outgoing, or blunt nature.

blun·der (BLUHN-dər) *noun.* A foolish mistake: Jane made a *blunder;* she put salt on her cereal instead of sugar. *—verb.* 1. To move awkwardly: Joe entered the room and *blundered* into a chair. 2. To make a stupid mistake. 3. To say something stupid. **blundered, blundering.**

blunt (BLUHNT) *adjective.* 1. Dull; not sharp or pointed: The knife is *blunt;* it will not cut the steak. 2. Outspoken; not thinking about other people's feelings: Alex was *blunt* when he called Tom a liar. **blunter, bluntest.** *—verb.* To make dull: Bill *blunted* the arrow by shooting at a stone wall. **blunted, blunting.** **—bluntly** *adverb.*

blur (BLER) *verb.* 1. To smear: A spot of water *blurred* Mary's ink drawing. 2. To make vague in outline: The photo was *blurred* because the camera moved. 3. To dim or darken: Fog *blurred* the lighthouse beam. **blurred, blurring.** *—noun.* 1. A smear or blot. 2. Vague state of mind or sight: My mind was a *blur;* I couldn't remember what happened.

bluebells

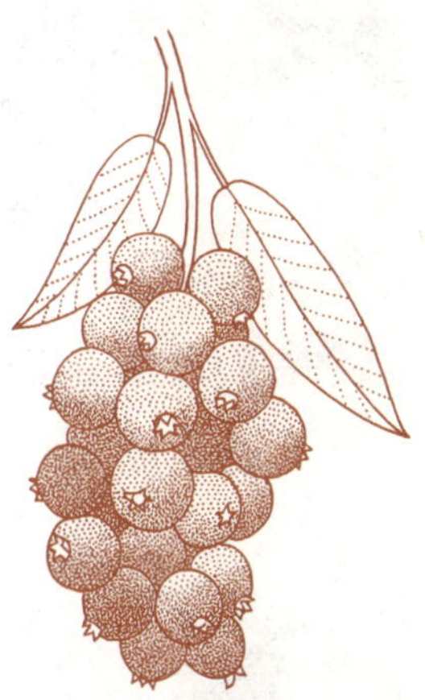
blueberries

blue jay

boa

boar

bobcat

bobsled

blurb (BLERB) *noun.* (Informal) A short statement, usually advertising something: There was a *blurb* in the newspaper about our school dance.

blurt (BLERT) *verb.* To speak suddenly without thinking: Tom *blurted* out that there was to be a surprise party. **blurted, blurting.**

blush (BLUHSH) *verb.* To turn red in the face because of embarrassment: Sally *blushed* when she was caught in her curlers. **blushed, blushing.** *—noun.* A sudden redness of the face: The excitement caused a *blush* to redden Ann's cheeks. **blushes.**

blus·ter (BLUHSS-tər) *verb.* 1. To blow or storm noisily: The wind *blustered* through the ship's rigging. 2. To talk noisily and angrily without regard to the truth: When Bill lost, he *blustered* that he had been cheated. **blustered, blustering.** *—noun.* 1. A loud, violent wind. 2. Empty, loud talk: He is all *bluster;* he never says anything worthwhile.

Blvd. *abbreviation.* Boulevard.

bo·a (BOH-ə) *noun.* 1. A large nonpoisonous snake of the tropics that squeezes its prey to death and then may swallow it. 2. A long scarf made of feathers.

boar (BOR) *noun.* 1. A wild hog or pig. 2. The male domesticated hog or pig.

board (BORD) *noun.* 1. A long, flat piece of wood; a plank. 2. A flat piece of wood or other material used for a special purpose: The *board* for our Monopoly game is missing. 3. Food or meals, especially ones provided for pay: He pays $30 each week for room and *board.* 4. A table on which food is served. 5. A committee; a council: The *board* voted on several important issues. *—verb.* 1. To cover with boards: Before the storm we *boarded* up the windows. 2. To provide or receive food for pay: I *board* at Mrs. Brown's home. 3. To get on a plane, ship, train, or other transport: He *boarded* the bus at Main Street. **boarded, boarding. —on board.** On or inside a ship, train, plane, or other transport.

boarding school. A school at which one lives for the school term.

boast (BOHST) *verb.* 1. To brag or speak too well of oneself. 2. To have something to be proud of: The museum *boasts* a new gallery. **boasted, boasting.** *—noun.* A bragging claim.

boat (BOHT) *noun.* A small, usually open, vessel for traveling on water. *—verb.* To travel by water: We *boated* on the river. **boated, boating. —in the same boat.** Having the same problems.

boat·house (BOHT-howss) *noun.* A house or shed for storing boats. **boathouses.**

boat·ing (BOH-ting) *noun.* Riding or traveling by boat, especially as a hobby or pastime.

boat·swain (BOH-sn) *noun.* A ship's petty officer who directs the work of sailors on deck.

bob *verb.* To move up and down with a quick, jerky motion: The children *bobbed* for apples. **bobbed, bobbing** *—noun.* 1. A cork or float for a fishing line. 2. A short haircut.

bob·bin (BOB-in) *noun.* A spool used to hold thread: Mother taught me how to thread the *bobbin* for the sewing machine.

bobby pin. A narrow metal clip used to hold hair in place.

bob·cat (BOB-kat) *noun.* A wildcat or lynx, living in North America, about three times as big as a house cat.

bob·o·link (BOB-ə-lingk) *noun.* A mostly black and white bird named for its song.

bob·sled (BOB-sled) *noun.* A racing sled which has a brake and a means of steering. *—verb.* To ride or steer a bobsled. **bobsledded, bobsledding.**

bob·white (bob-HWIGHT) *noun.* A reddish-brown bird of the quail family, sometimes called a partridge, named for its song.

bod·y (BOD-ee) *noun.* 1. The whole physical make-up of man or animal as opposed to the mind or spirit: Tom trains his mind with lessons and his *body* with exercise. 2. The torso or trunk of a human or an animal frame, excluding the arms, legs, and head. 3. The main part of anything: The *body* of the car was smashed. 4. A mass: *body* of water. 5. A dead person or animal. **bodies.**

bod·y·guard (BOD-ee-gahrd) *noun.* A person or persons whose job it is to guard another: The President is protected by his *bodyguard* of Secret Service men.

bog (BAWG) *noun.* 1. A swampy area. 2. A soft, muddy field with few trees but much grass and water. *—verb.* 1. To sink into or become caught in. 2. To slow (down); meet with difficulty: We were *bogged* down with homework. **bogged, bogging.**

bo·gey (BOH-gee) Also **bogy** or **bogie** *noun.* 1. An evil spirit; a goblin. 2. A score of one stroke more than par for a hole of golf. **bogeys.** *—verb.* To score a bogey. **bogeyed, bogeying.**

boil *verb.* 1. To bubble and turn into gas when heated: When we turned up the heat, the water *boiled* so hard it spilled down the sides of the pan. 2. To be angry: When Paul discovered his bat was missing, he *boiled* with rage. **boiled, boiling.** *—noun.* A painful swelling of the skin filled with pus and having a hard center.

boil·er (BOI-lər) *noun.* 1. A container, usually metal, in which liquids are boiled; a steam cooker. 2. A strong, closed tank in which water is heated into steam for use in an engine or heating system. 3. A tank in which water is heated and stored.

bois·ter·ous (BOI-stər-əss) *adjective.* Loud, noisy, and rough. **—boisterously** *adverb.*

bold (BOHLD) *adjective.* 1. Having courage, not afraid. 2. Striking or outstanding: a *bold* sign. 3. Shameless, unreserved. **bolder, boldest. —boldly** *adverb.* **—boldness** *noun.*

bo·le·ro (boh-LAIR-oh) *noun.* 1. A short jacket without fastenings. 2. A Spanish dance or the music for this dance. **boleros.**

boll (BOHL) *noun.* The pod containing the seed of cotton or flax.

bo·lo·gna (bə-LOH-nə or bə-LOH-nee) *noun. See* **baloney.**

bolt (BOHLT) *verb.* 1. To move suddenly: The horse *bolted* and ran away. 2. To eat rapidly without chewing: Mary *bolted* her food and ended up with a stomachache. 3. To fasten with a metal bar or lock. **bolted, bolting.** *—noun.* 1. A bar which slides into a fastener on a door; the moving part of a lock. 2. A threaded metal pin with a head and a removable nut, used to fasten things together. 3. A flash of lightning.

bomb (BOM) *noun.* 1. A container filled with explosives which blows up when it hits something or when a timer sets off the fuse. 2. (Slang) A failure: The picnic was a *bomb* because we left the food at home. 3. (Football slang) A very long forward pass. *—verb.* 1. To use a bomb. 2. (Slang) To fail. **bombed, bombing.**

bom·bard (bom-BAHRD) *verb.* 1. To attack with bombs or cannon shots. 2. To attack repeatedly: *bombard* a teacher with questions. **bombarded, bombarding. —bombardment** *noun.*

bo·nan·za (bə-NAN-zə) *noun.* 1. A rich mine containing a mineral such as gold or silver. 2. Any large and sudden increase in wealth; the source of such an increase.

bobwhite

bolt

bond *noun.* 1. Any means that binds or joins one thing to another. 2. An understanding tie or unity: There was a *bond* between Sally and Jane because they both liked poetry. 3. A promise or contract, particularly one which involves money. 4. Money put up to gain release from jail until time for trial. 5. A certificate issued by the government or a private business company as a means of borrowing money.

bond·age (BON-dij) *noun.* Slavery; lack of freedom.

bone (BOHN) *noun.* 1. One section or part of a skeleton. 2. Ivory or other materials resembling bone. 3. The deepest point: His insult cut me to the *bone.* **bones.** —*verb.* 1. To remove the bones from (a piece of meat). 2. (Slang) To study hard, apply oneself: The student *boned* up for his exams. **boned, boning.**

bon·er (BOH-nər) *noun.* (Slang) A mistake: He made a real *boner* when he tried to guess her weight.

bookmobile

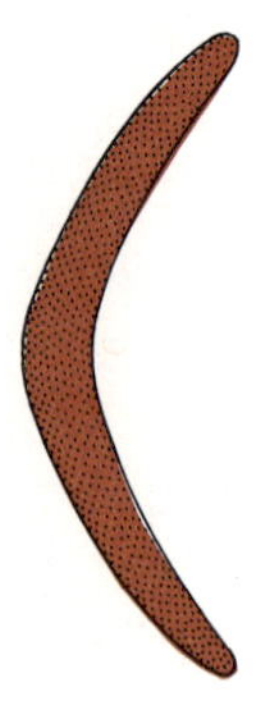

boomerang

bon·fire (BON-fighr) *noun.* A fire built outdoors: We toasted marshmallows over the *bonfire.* **bonfires.**

bong *verb.* To ring with a deep sound: The clock *bonged* 12. **bonged, bonging.** —*noun.* A ringing sound deep in tone.

bo·ni·to (bə-NEE-toh) Also **bonita** *noun.* A food and game fish which is related to and looks like the tuna. —**bonitos** or **bonito** *plural.*

bon·net (BON-it) *noun.* A hat that is tied under the chin with strings and has a brim that fits closely around the face: *Bonnets* are worn by babies.

bo·nus (BOH-nəss) *noun.* Extra money given as a gift beyond a salary: Some companies give their employees a Christmas *bonus.* **bonuses.**

boo *noun.* A sound made to frighten someone or to express disapproval. **boos.** —*verb.* To sound the word "boo." **booed, booing.**

boob tube. (Slang) A television set.

boo·by (BOO-bee) *noun.* 1. A stupid person. 2. A large sea bird found in warmer climates. **boobies.**

book (BUK) *noun.* 1. A series of printed pages bound within two covers. 2. A story, essay, or any group of writings, paintings, or other works of art gathered in a binding. —*verb.* To record, process, or take information from: The policeman *booked* the suspect at headquarters. **booked, booking.**

book·case (BUK-kayss) *noun.* A set of shelves used for holding books. **bookcases.**

book·keep·er (BUK-keep-ər) *noun.* A person who keeps track of the money paid to or spent by a business.

book·let (BUK-lit) *noun.* A thin book usually with paper covers.

book·mo·bile (BUK-moh-beel) *noun.* A bus or van equipped as a traveling library. **bookmobiles.**

book·rack (BUK-rak) *noun.* A shelf or small rack for books or magazines.

boom *noun.* 1. A long, deep hollow sound: The soldiers could hear the *boom* of the cannons. 2. A period of wealth and growth: The town had a *boom* when gold was discovered nearby. 3. A long, straight pole extending from a mast of a boat to hold the bottom of a sail. 4. The long arm of a crane or derrick. —*verb.* 1. To make a long, deep, hollow sound. 2. To increase in size, wealth, and activity. **boomed, booming.**

boo·mer·ang (BOO-mə-rang) *noun.* A flat, almost L-shaped wooden stick that, when thrown, returns to the thrower. —*verb.* To have unwanted or unexpected effects: Our practical joke *boomeranged* when Mother got angry and sent us to our rooms. **boomeranged, boomeranging.**

boost *verb.* 1. To lift or push from below or behind: Bill *boosted* Tom up the tree. 2. To improve or make better: Going to the movies *boosted* the boys' spirits. **boosted, boosting.** —*noun.* 1. An upward push. 2. An increase or raise: Dad received a *boost* in his salary.

boost·er (BOO-stər) *noun.* 1. Anything that increases power, strength, or success. 2. An extra amount of vaccine, as a *booster* shot. 3. A rocket that gives extra power to aircraft or spacecraft. 4. (Sports) A fan.

boot *noun.* 1. A shoe made for heavy wear or protection, at least ankle high but usually higher. 2. (Plural) Rubbers or outside shoes. 3. (Slang) A dismissal notice, a request to leave: The boss gave me the *boot.* —*verb.* 1. To kick or stomp. 2. To get rid of: The farmer *booted* out the vicious dog. **booted, booting.**

booth *noun.* 1. A small, closed area: Jim called from the corner telephone *booth.* 2. An eating area closed in on three sides and having two benches and a table: *Booths* lined the restaurant wall. 3. A small, covered stand for selling or showing off goods: We visited the *booths* at the fair. —**booths** (BOOTHZ) *plural.*

boo·ty (BOO-tee) *noun.* Goods stolen by an armed force: The pirates set fire to the town after they had searched the houses for *booty.*

booze (BOOZ) *noun.* (Slang) Alcoholic liquor.

bor·der (BOR-dər) *noun.* 1. The edge or rim of anything: Grass grows to the *border* of the pond. 2. The line which separates political divisions or private property: We were stopped for inspection when we crossed the *border* of Mexico. 3. A decorative edging: There was a *border* of lace on the hem of Jane's dress. —*verb.* To have a common boundary: Mexico *borders* the United States. **bordered, bordering.** —**border on.** To come close to, approach: Whispering during a test *borders on* cheating.

bore (BOR) *noun.* A dull and uninteresting person or thing: The movie was a *bore.* **bores.** —*verb.* 1. To make a hole (through or in) by drilling: We *bored* holes in the wood for the bolts. 2. To tire with dullness: He said the same thing so many times that he *bored* us. **bored, boring.**

bore·dom (BOR-dəm) *noun.* The state or condition of being bored or uninterested.

born *adjective.* 1. Brought into being. 2. Having a talent from birth: He is a *born* clown. —*verb. See* **bear.**

bor·ough (BER-oh) *noun.* A self-governing town or village.

bor·row (BOR-oh) *verb.* 1. To get the loan or temporary possession of, by permission of the owner: Jim *borrowed* a quarter from his sister until Saturday. 2. To take or use as one's own: His ideas were *borrowed,* not original. **borrowed, borrowing.**

bo's'n (BOH-sn) *noun.* Boatswain.

bos·om (BUZ-əm) *noun.* The breast of a woman; the chest of any human being. —*adjective.* Dearly loved: Sally is my *bosom* pal.

boss (BAWSS) *noun.* 1. The person who supervises other workers. 2. The top person in a political organization. **bosses.** —*verb.* 1. To direct or control: When Tom's father was sick, his assistant *bossed* the job. 2. To control in a disagreeable way: The bully *bossed* all the little boys. **bossed, bossing.**

bossy (BAW-see) *adjective.* Commanding in a very unpleasant way: Jim is *bossy;* he tells everyone what to do. **bossier, bossiest.** —*noun.* A cow. —**bossily** *adverb.*

boots

bot·a·nist (BOT-n-ist) *noun.* A scientist who studies plants.

bot·a·ny (BOT-n-ee) *noun.* A branch of biology consisting of the study of plants.

both (BOHTH) *adjective.* The two: *Both* girls like sewing. *—pronoun.* The one and the other: *Both* were good football players. *—conjunction.* Taken together: *Both* reading and writing are fun.

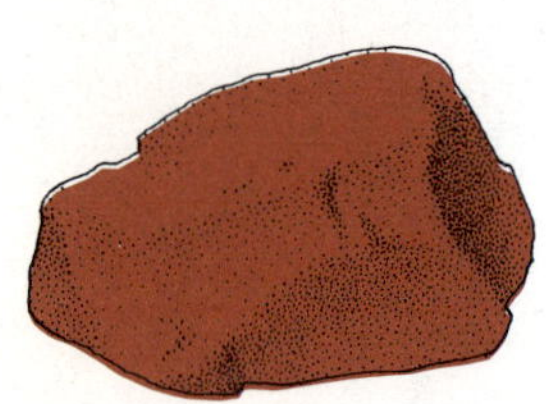
boulder

both·er (BOTH-ər) *noun.* A trouble or nuisance: Mary's nagging is a *bother.* *—verb.* 1. To trouble or upset: "I am a Bear of Very Little Brain, and long words *Bother* me." (A. A. Milne). 2. To take the trouble: Don't *bother* doing the dishes. **bothered, bothering.**

bot·tle (BOT-l) *noun.* A container, made of glass, metal, or plastic, usually with no handles and a narrow opening at the top. **bottles.** *—verb.* To put liquid into a container for storage or preservation. **bottled, bottling.**

bot·tle·neck (BOT-l-nek) *noun.* 1. The top part of a bottle, usually narrow. 2. Anything that slows or hinders movement: There was a *bottleneck* on the highway; one lane was being repaved.

bouquet

bot·tom (BOT-əm) *noun.* 1. The lowest part: The cards are in the *bottom* of the drawer. 2. The underside of an object: Who punched the hole in the *bottom* of my lunch box? 3. The base or root: At the *bottom* of Tom's bad mood was his fear of the test. *—adjective.* Lowest: John tripped on the *bottom* step.

bough (BOW) *noun.* A branch of a tree: The apple *bough* broke from the weight of the children's swing.

bought (BAWT) *verb. See* **buy.**

bouil·lon (BUL-yon) *noun.* A clear broth which is made from chicken, beef, or vegetables.

boul·der (BOHL-dər) *noun.* A large, rounded, smooth rock.

boul·e·vard (BUL-ə-vahrd) *noun.* A broad avenue.

bounce (BOWNSS) *verb.* 1. To spring back after hitting something: The ball *bounced* from the wall. 2. To make bounce: They took turns *bouncing* the ball. 3. To bound or spring: Jane *bounced* with joy. **bounced, bouncing.** *—noun.* A bound or jump: The ball made a *bounce* from the floor to the ceiling.

bound (BOWND) *adjective.* 1. Tied or fastened: The *bound* dog pulled at his leash. 2. Obliged, required: Jim is *bound* to repay the debt. 3. Determined: I'm *bound* to win this game! 4. Going toward: Jim is *bound* for home. *—verb.* 1. To leap or spring: Tess *bounded* for the telephone. 2. To limit or form the boundary of: Lake Erie *bounds* Ohio on the north. **bounded, bounding.** *—noun, usually plural.* A limit: His pride in his little sister knew no *bounds.*

bound·a·ry (BOWN-dree or BOWN-də-ree) *noun.* A line that limits or separates: The Rio Grande forms part of the *boundary* between Mexico and the United States. **boundaries.**

boun·ty (BOWN-tee) *noun.* 1. A reward: There was a *bounty* for capturing the killer. 2. Generosity: Dad in his *bounty* gave us an increase in our allowance. **bounties.** **—bountiful** *adjective.* **—bountifully** *adverb.*

bou·quet (boo-KAY) *noun.* 1. A bunch of flowers. 2. A pleasant odor: The *bouquet* of Beth's perfume remained in the room.

bout (BOWT) *noun.* 1. A contest between two people: Johnny was the winner in the wrestling *bout.* 2. A period of time: During his *bout* of illness, Paul read nothing but comic books.

[1]**bow** *verb.* 1. To bend the body or head downward in respect, greeting, agreement, or submission: The actress *bowed* to the clapping audience. 2. To give in or submit: Tom *bowed* to his father's wishes and stayed at home. 3. To overburden: Janet was *bowed* down with troubles. **bowed, bowing.** —*noun.* 1. A bending forward of the body as a sign of courtesy. 2. The front part of a ship.

[2]**bow** (BOH) *noun.* 1. A knot with fancy loops in it. 2. A weapon for shooting arrows. 3. A rod strung with horsehair used in playing stringed instruments: Jack used his *bow* on the violin with great skill.

bow·el (BOW-əl) *noun.* 1. Intestine. 2. (Usually plural) The deepest part of anything: The lava erupted from the *bowels* of the earth.

bowl (BOHL) *noun.* 1. A rounded dish: Sally passed a *bowl* of fruit. 2. A sports arena in the shape of a bowl, as the Rose *Bowl.* —*verb.* 1. To play a game by rolling a ball down a lane in an attempt to knock down wooden pins. 2. To move smoothly and rapidly: We *bowled* along the deserted highway. **bowled, bowling.**

bow·leg·ged (BOH-leg-id) *adjective.* Having legs that curve outward at the knees.

bow·sprit (BOW-sprit) *noun.* A pole or spar attached to the stem of a ship and used to support rigging.

[1]**box** (BOKS) *noun.* 1. A container, usually rectangular: Paul keeps his toys in that *box.* 2. A private section seating several people in a theater or a grandstand: We watched the ball game from a *box.* 3. A slap with the hand, as a *box* on the ears. 4. (Baseball) The location assigned to the batter, pitcher, or a coach: the pitcher's *box.* **boxes.**

[2]**box** (BOKS) *verb.* To fight with fists as a sport, usually wearing gloves: The fighters *boxed* for ten rounds. **boxed, boxing.**

box·car (BOKS-kahr) *noun.* A closed freight car on a train: Food and machinery are shipped in *boxcars* to protect them from wind and rain.

box·er (BOK-sər) *noun.* 1. A fighter; one who fights with his fists as a sport. 2. A kind of dog with short, brownish hair and a squared jaw.

box·ing (BOK-sing) *noun.* A sport in which men fight each other with padded gloves on their fists.

boy (BOI) *noun.* A male child.

boy·cott (BOI-kot) *verb.* To refuse to deal with someone or some group in order to gain some end: Our neighborhood is *boycotting* the local candy store until the owners clean it up. **boycotted, boycotting.** —*noun.* The act of refusing to deal with a person or organization.

boy·hood (BOI-hud) *noun.* The time spent as a boy.

boy·ish (BOI-ish) *adjective.* Acting or looking like a boy: Sally's short haircut makes her look *boyish.* —**boyishly** *adverb.*

Boy Scout. A boy who belongs to the Boy Scouts of America, a group organized to develop character.

bra (BRAH) *noun.* A brassiere.

brace (BRAYSS) *noun.* 1. An object that holds something together or in its place: Book ends are *braces* that keep books upright. 2. A device used to correct or support a part of the body: Tony must use an ankle *brace* when he plays basketball. 3. A pair or twosome: The farmer bought a *brace* of geese. 4. (Math) Either of the following symbols { } used to make groupings clear when parentheses, ( ), and square brackets, [ ], have already been used. **braces.** —*verb.* To support or strengthen: Paul *braced* the door with his shoulder to keep the dog out. **braced, bracing.**

boxer

boxing

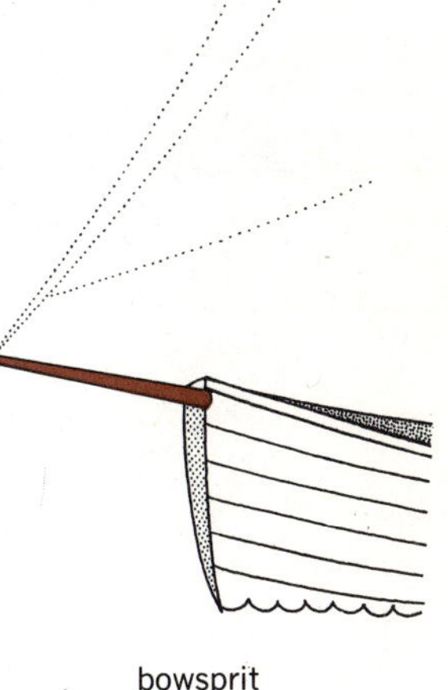
bowsprit

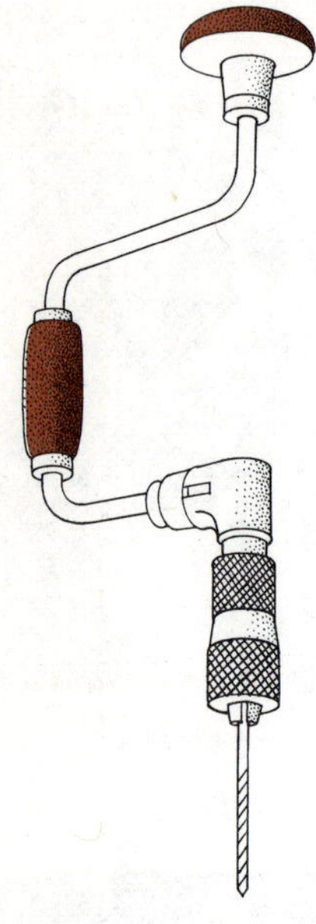
brace and bit

brace and bit. A boring device divided into two parts; the brace, or handle, which holds and turns the bit; and the bit, or sharp pointed drill, which bores into wood or metal.

brace·let (BRAYSS-lit) *noun.* A piece of jewelry or an ornament worn around the wrist or arm.

brack·et (BRAK-it) *noun.* 1. An L-shaped support made of metal, wood, or stone: John made bookshelves by nailing *brackets* on the wall and placing boards on them. 2. One of the following printed signs [ ] used to enclose words or numbers. 3. A group, division, or class: Many Americans are in the middle-income *bracket.* —*verb.* 1. To support with a bracket. 2. In writing, to place within brackets. 3. To place within a group or class. **bracketed, bracketing.**

brack·ish (BRAK-ish) *adjective.* 1. Containing salt; having a salty taste: It is unpleasant to drink *brackish* water. 2. Bad tasting.

brag *verb.* To boast; praise oneself or one's own achievements or possessions. **bragged, bragging.**

brag·gart (BRAG-ərt) *noun.* One who boasts.

braid (BRAYD) *verb.* 1. To weave or intertwine three or more strips of cloth, hair, rope, or other material. 2. To trim or decorate with braid. **braided, braiding.** —*noun.* A strip formed by the interweaving of three or more strands.

Braille (BRAYL) Also **braille** *noun.* A system of writing created for the blind in which raised dots on a page represent letters and numbers which may be "read" by passing the fingers over them.

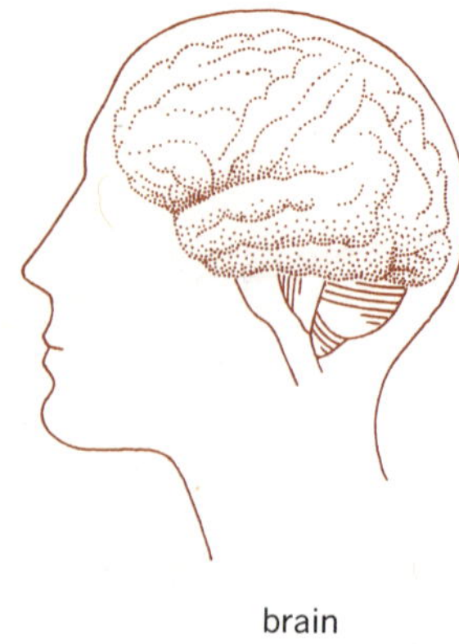
brain

brain (BRAYN) *noun.* 1. A cluster of nerve cells in the head that controls physical and mental activity. 2. (Slang) A smart person. —*verb.* To hit the skull: The animal was *brained* by the falling tree. **brained, braining.**

brain storm. A sudden, unusual idea.

brain trust. A group of people with special skills or knowledge who give advice, often on government matters.

brain·wash (BRAYN-wosh) *verb.* To pressure or mislead someone into feeling or thinking a certain way: Sue had *brainwashed* her little brother into thinking that she was his boss. **brainwashed, brainwashing.**

braise (BRAYZ) *verb.* To simmer meat and/or vegetables slowly in a covered pan after browning in fat. **braised, braising.**

brake (BRAYK) *noun.* 1. A device used to slow or stop a moving vehicle. 2. A thicket or dense growth of plants and bushes. 3. A fern. **brakes.** —*verb.* To stop, slow, or check: Tom *braked* the car to ten miles an hour. **braked, braking.**

bram·ble (BRAM-bəl) *noun.* A thorny, prickly shrub that grows close to the ground. **brambles.**

bran *noun.* The outer covering of grain, as wheat or rye, which is separated from the flour by grinding.

branch *noun.* 1. A part of a tree or bush which is an arm of the main trunk or stem. 2. A major section of an organization: There are three main *branches* of the United States government. 3. A local office of a company or an organization: A *branch* of the phone company is opening in our town. 4. A line or division of a family: The O'Malley *branch* of our family comes from Ireland. 5. A division or tributary of a river. **branches.** —*verb.* To divide; go in different directions: The hikers did not know which way to go, for the trail *branched* in two directions. **branched, branching.**

brand *verb.* 1. To mark with a hot iron as a means of identification: The cattle were *branded* with the sign of EZ Ranch. 2. To identify or reveal as bad or wrong: Tom's sticky fingers *branded* him as the jam thief. **branded, branding.** —*noun.* 1. A mark or symbol used as identification. 2. A particular type, quality, or make indicated by the name of the manufacturer; a trade name. 3. An iron used for branding. 4. A burning or partially burned piece of wood.

bran•dish (BRAN-dish) *verb.* To wave or fling around in a threatening way: Bill *brandished* his bat at the umpire. **brandished, brandishing.**

brand-new (BRAND-NOO or BRAND-NYOO) *adjective.* Entirely new, not yet used.

bran•dy (BRAN-dee) *noun.* A liquor made from the juice of various fruits such as peaches, apples, or apricots. **brandies.** —*verb.* To flavor or preserve with brandy. **brandied, brandying.**

brass *noun.* 1. A metal alloy mixing zinc and copper. 2. An ornament, utensil, or decoration made of brass. 3. A musical instrument having a cup-shaped mouthpiece and usually made of brass, as a trumpet or a French horn. 4. The section of the orchestra which is formed by brass instruments. 5. (Slang) High officials. 6. (Slang) Nerve, boldness. —**brass** *plural.*

bras•siere (brə-ZIHR) *noun.* A woman's undergarment worn to support the breasts. **brassieres.**

brat *noun.* An impolite or unruly child.

brave (BRAYV) *adjective.* Courageous or daring. **braver, bravest.** —*noun.* A warrior from a North American Indian tribe. **braves.** —*verb.* To face without fear: The men *braved* the blizzard in order to save the lost child. **braved, braving.** —**bravely** *adverb.*

brav•er•y (BRAY-və-ree or BRAYV-ree) *noun.* Courage; valor; a brave or daring action. **braveries.**

bra•vo (BRAH-voh) *noun.* A call used to show approval. —**bravos** or **bravoes** *plural.* —*interjection.* Well done! Hooray!

brawl *noun.* 1. A loud fight or dispute. 2. (Slang) A big, noisy party. —*verb.* To quarrel noisily. **brawled, brawling.**

brawn *noun.* Muscular strength: To be a good athlete, one must have brains and *brawn.*

brawny (BRAWN-ee) *adjective.* Strong, muscular. **brawnier, brawniest.**

bray *noun.* 1. The loud, grating sound made by a donkey. 2. A sound like that of a donkey. —*verb.* To make a sound like that of a donkey. **brayed, braying.**

bra•zen (BRAY-zən) *adjective.* Bold, shameless: The *brazen* shoplifter strolled past the store detective. —*verb.* To face without shame: When caught in his lie, the man decided to *brazen* it out and insist that he was misunderstood. **brazened, brazening.** —**brazenly** *adverb.*

breach (BREECH) *noun.* 1. A break or separation in a wall, a line of soldiers, or the like: The prisoners escaped through the *breach* in the wall. 2. A break (in friendship). 3. The breaking of a rule, a law, or a promise: To drive without a license is a *breach* of the law. **breaches.** —*verb.* 1. To break through or separate: The bomb *breached* the wall of the stockade. 2. To violate a law, a rule, or a promise. **breached, breaching.**

bread (BRED) *noun.* 1. Food made of flour and liquid, usually with some agent to make the dough rise. 2. Food in general: Man must toil to earn his *bread.* 3. (Slang) Money. —*verb.* In cooking, to coat with bread crumbs. **breaded, breading.**

breadth (BREDTH) *noun.* 1. Width; the span from side to side of an object. 2. Largeness of thought or of mind: Our art teacher has a wide *breadth* of interest and talent.

break (BRAYK) *verb.* 1. To damage something so that it can no longer be used: Don't *break* the window! 2. To split or crack: "Sticks and stones may *break* my bones . . . ." 3. To make known, make public: When should we *break* the news about our party? 4. To end, stop: Let's *break* off the meeting now. 5. To separate a part (from the whole): *Break* off a piece of the candy bar for me. 6. To train, make obedient: The cowboy could not *break* the stallion. 7. To lower in rank: Why did the captain *break* Corporal Jones to private? 8. To discover the meaning of (something): We must *break* the enemy's code. 9. To overcome, go beyond: Leo hopes to *break* the long-distance running record. 10. To violate (a law, a rule, or a promise). 11. To force one's way illegally. 12. To start to do something suddenly, as *break* into laughter. 13. To appear: We watched the sun *break* through the clouds. 14. To give up: The prisoner did not *break* under questioning. **broke, broken, breaking.** —*noun.* 1. A damage or an injury: There is a *break* in the water pipe. 2. An escape: There was a prison *break* this week. 3. An interruption of an action; a rest: Let's take a coffee *break*. 4. End of friendship or agreement: The *break* between the countries was a result of a boundary dispute. 5. (Slang) A fortunate chance: Many actors get their *break* when they are discovered by a talent scout. —**break in.** 1. To enter by force: The thieves *broke in* through the rear window. 2. To train for a job: The foreman *broke in* the new worker at the factory. 3. To use or wear until suitable or comfortable: It took several days to

breaker

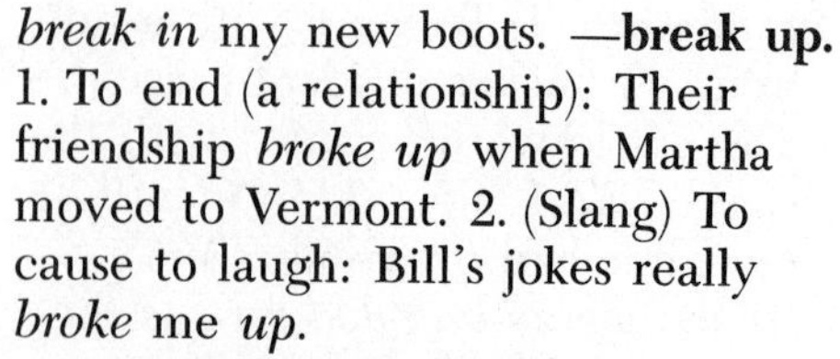

break in my new boots. —**break up.** 1. To end (a relationship): Their friendship *broke up* when Martha moved to Vermont. 2. (Slang) To cause to laugh: Bill's jokes really *broke* me *up*.

break·a·ble (BRAYK-ə-bəl) *adjective.* Able to be broken, fragile.

break·down (BRAYK-down) *noun.* 1. Collapse. 2. A failure to function. 3. An analysis: The president of the company asked for a *breakdown* of employee benefits.

break·er (BRAYK-er) *noun.* 1. A wave that crests (generally on the shore) and becomes foamy. 2. One who breaks (something).

break·fast (BREK-fəst) *noun.* The first meal of the day. —*verb.* To eat breakfast. **breakfasted, breakfasting.**

break·neck (BRAYK-nek) *adjective.* Dangerously fast: The racer came down the ski slope at *breakneck* speed.

break·through (BRAYK-throo) *noun.* 1. An important advance or discovery in a project, effort, or development: The doctors made a *breakthrough* in their efforts to find a cure for the disease. 2. A military advance through an enemy's lines.

break·wa·ter (BRAYK-waw-tər) *noun.* A wall or other barrier that protects a shore from the full force of waves.

breast (BREST) *noun.* 1. The upper front part of the body; the chest. 2. In female animals, the gland that produces milk. —*verb.* To face or meet, as in *breasting* the waves. **breasted, breasting.**

breast·bone (BREST-bohn) *noun.* A long flat bone at the front of the chest. **breastbones.**

breath (BRETH) *noun.* 1. Air taken in and out of the lungs. 2. The moisture or vapor carried out with air from the lungs: On a cold day you can see your *breath*. 3. Power, spirit, strength, life, or time: We'll save our *breath* for the hard work. 4. A rest or pause: Let me take a *breath* before we go on. 5. A slight breeze, a whiff, a whisper: Not a *breath* of air was stirring. **—in the same breath.** At the same time.

breathe (BREETH) *verb.* 1. To take air into the lungs and to let it out. 2. To live: Free men cannot *breathe* under a tyrant's rule. 3. To whisper: Don't *breathe* a word of this. 4. To take a rest, to pause: Give me a moment to *breathe.* 5. To give, instill: The leader's speech *breathed* new spirit into his followers. **breathed, breathing.**

breath·less (BRETH-ləss) *adjective.* 1. Out of breath: The boy ran until he was *breathless.* 2. Excited, scared: The little girl sat *breathless* watching the movie. 3. Dead, without life. **—breathlessly** *adverb.*

breath·tak·ing (BRETH-tayk-ing) *adjective.* Exciting, beautiful, awesome: The Grand Canyon is a *breathtaking* sight. **—breathtakingly** *adverb.*

breed *verb.* 1. To give birth to. 2. To cause plants or animals to reproduce. 3. To cause or produce: Slum conditions often *breed* crime. 4. To train or raise: The trainer *breeds* many thoroughbred horses. **bred, breeding.** *—noun.* A similar group or type: German shepherds and collies are dogs of different *breeds.*

breeze (BREEZ) *noun.* 1. A gentle wind. 2. (Informal) An easy job: Mary said that the math test was a *breeze.* *—verb.* To move quickly: Juan *breezed* along on his bike. **breezed, breezing.**

breeze·way (BREEZ-way) *noun.* A passageway between two buildings with a roof and sides that may either be open or have glass panels.

breez·y (BREE-zee) *adjective.* 1. Windy. 2. (Informal) Cheerful, lively: She has a *breezy* way of talking. **breezier, breeziest. —breezily** *adverb.*

brev·i·ty (BREV-ə-tee) *noun.* Shortness: The *brevity* of the speech surprised us.

brew (BROO) *verb.* 1. To make a drink such as tea or beer. 2. To bring about or produce: The girls are *brewing* a scheme. 3. To form or collect: The storm, which was *brewing* all day, broke suddenly. **brewed, brewing.** *—noun.* 1. The result or product of brewing. 2. A strange mixture: The witch's *brew* turned frogs into princes.

brew·er·y (BROO-ər-ee) *noun.* A place where beers and ales are brewed. **breweries.**

bri·ar (BRIGH-ər) Also **brier** *noun.* 1. A thorny bush or shrub. 2. A pipe made from briar: Samantha broke her father's favorite *briar.*

bribe (BRIGHB) *noun.* 1. A gift or payment given to encourage a wrong action. 2. A payment or gift given to persuade (someone or something): The dog needed a *bribe* before he would perform his tricks. **bribes.** *—verb.* To persuade or entice with a gift. **bribed, bribing.**

bric-a-brac (BRIK-ə-brak) *noun.* Small articles that are part of a collection or are used for decoration: Grandma's home is filled with *bric-a-brac* like Grandpa's bottle collection.

brick (BRIK) *noun.* 1. A rectangular block of clay that has been baked in the sun or in an oven: Building with *bricks* is expensive. 2. Anything in the shape of a brick: The *brick* of ice cream is still hard. *—verb.* To build or pave with bricks. **bricked, bricking.**

bride (BRIGHD) *noun.* A woman who has just been married or who is soon to be married. **brides.**

bride·groom (BRIGHD-groom) *noun.* A man who has just been married or is soon to be married.

brides·maid (BRIGHDZ-mayd) *noun.* A woman who attends the bride at a wedding ceremony.

bridegroom, bride, and bridesmaid

bridge

bridge (BRIJ) *noun.* 1. A structure that carries traffic over a river or a road. 2. The upper part of the nose bone. 3. The platform above the deck of a ship. 4. A card game. **bridges.** —*verb.* To make a bridge over. **bridged, bridging.**

bri·dle (BRIGHD-l) *noun.* 1. The part of a horse's harness used to guide or control the animal. 2. Anything that holds something back. **bridles.** —*verb.* 1. To put a bridle on. 2. To control or hold back: The man *bridled* his anger. 3. To react with resentment. **bridled, bridling.**

brief (BREEF) *adjective.* Short, to the point. **briefer, briefest.** —*noun.* 1. A short statement, a summary. 2. Notes or arguments regarding a case of law: The lawyer prepared his *brief* on the case. —*verb.* To instruct or inform: The President *briefed* the members of his cabinet. **briefed, briefing.** —**briefly** *adverb.*

briefcase

brief·case (BREEF-kayss) *noun.* A rectangular case used for carrying books or papers. **briefcases.**

brig *noun.* 1. A two-masted sailing vessel with square sails; a brigantine. 2. A ship's prison.

bri·gade (bri-GAYD) *noun.* 1. A large group of soldiers. 2. A group of people organized for a special purpose: a *brigade* of volunteer firemen. **brigades.**

brig·a·dier general (BRIG-ə-dihr). A military officer ranking above a colonel and below a major general.

brigantine

brig·an·tine (BRIG-ən-teen) *noun.* A two-masted sailing ship. **brigantines.**

bright *adjective.* 1. Shining with light. 2. Smart, clever. 3. Good or favorable: Children who study hard have *bright* prospects for the future. 4. Gay or happy: The *bright,* laughing group made their way to the beach. 5. Clear or strong: The *bright* red of Sally's dress made her seem to glow. **brighter, brightest.** —**brightly** *adverb.*

bright·en (BRIGHT-n) *verb.* 1. To add light to; make brighter. 2. To be made or become brighter or filled with more light: The sun came out, and the sky *brightened.* 3. To make cheerful or happy: The good news *brightened* my spirits. 4. To become cheerful or happy. **brightened, brightening.**

bright·ness (BRIGHT-niss) *noun.* 1. The state or quality of being bright; glare. 2. Intelligence.

bril·liance (BRIL-yənss) *noun.* 1. Strong shine or brightness: The *brilliance* of the diamond makes it stand out from other gems. 2. Great intelligence or talent.

bril·liant (BRIL-yənt) *adjective.* 1. Shiny, bright, glowing: The stars were *brilliant* last night. 2. Having great intelligence or talent. 3. Outstanding, excellent: The book is *brilliant;* it will be remembered for years. —**brilliantly** *adverb.*

brim *noun.* 1. The top rim of a container: The glass was filled to the *brim.* 2. The outer rim of a hat: The boys turned up the *brims* of their hats. —*verb.* To be full to the brim: The pitcher was *brimming* with fresh milk. **brimmed, brimming.**

brine (BRIGHN) *noun.* 1. Salty water. 2. The sea, ocean. 3. A salt-and-water solution used to preserve food.

bring *verb.* 1. To carry from one person or place to another: Everyone must *bring* sandwiches for the picnic. 2. To draw to or to attract: The girl's perfume seemed to *bring* a swarm of mosquitoes. 3. To make come to mind: The pictures *bring* back fond memories. 4. To make happen: Drug use often *brings* illness and death. 5. To persuade or convince: A study of smoking will *bring* you to the conclusion that smoking is bad for your health. 6. To sell for, get: Antique cars *bring* a good price on today's market. **brought, bringing.**

brink *noun.* 1. The edge of something: The sled teetered on the *brink* of the cliff. 2. The furthest edge or point, often connected with danger: The countries were on the *brink* of war.

brisk *adjective.* 1. Swift, active: The boys went for a *brisk* walk in the woods. 2. Cool, sharp: Autumn brings *brisk* weather. **brisker, briskest.** —**briskly** *adverb.*

bris·tle (BRISS-l) *noun.* A short, stiff hair like that of a hog. **bristles.** —*verb.* 1. To stand up like a bristle: The hair on the dog *bristled* in fear. 2. To show anger: The girl *bristled* when she was sent to the principal's office. 3. To be filled or covered with bristle-like things: The trail *bristled* with pine needles. **bristled, bristling.**

britch·es (BRICH-əz) *noun, plural.* Knee-length pants or trousers: The little boy's *britches* were covered with patches.

brit·tle (BRIT-l) *adjective.* Stiff; easily broken: The wooden model was so *brittle* that it snapped in George's hand.

broach (BROHCH) *verb.* To speak of for the first time: Johnny dared not *broach* the subject of his poor grades. **broached, broaching.** —*noun.* *See* **brooch.**

broad (BRAWD) *adjective.* 1. Very wide. 2. Having a large area: Before them was a *broad* expanse of wild flowers. 3. Open, clear: The robbery occurred in *broad* daylight. 4. Liberal, not narrow: The man's *broad* political views often got him into arguments. 5. General or chief: The *broad* meaning of the speech was that freedom should be for all men. **broader, broadest.** —**broadly** *adverb.*

broad·cast (BRAWD-kast) *verb.* 1. To put on the air over radio or television. 2. To announce, speak widely of: Please do not *broadcast* what I told you. **broadcast** or **broadcasted, broadcasting.** —*noun.* A program on radio or television.

broad·en (BRAWD-n) *verb.* 1. To make wider: They will *broaden* the narrow country lane. 2. To make more liberal or free: We feel that Jack's going to college will *broaden* his views. **broadened, broadening.**

broad-mind·ed (BRAWD-mighn-did) *adjective.* Open to new ideas; having respect for the views of others; liberal. —**broad-mindedly** *adverb.* —**broad-mindedness** *noun.*

broc·co·li (BROK-ə-lee) *noun.* A plant whose green stalks and flowers are eaten as a vegetable.

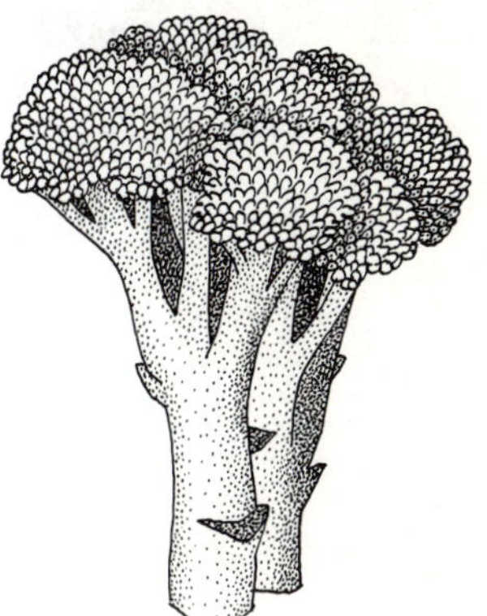
broccoli

broil *verb.* 1. To cook directly over or under a source of heat. 2. To be made or to make very hot: I am going to *broil* in this sun! **broiled, broiling.**

broke (BROHK) *adjective.* (Slang) Without money: I can't go to the movies because I am *broke.*

bro·ken-down (BROH-kən-DOWN) *adjective.* Not working; out of order: Tom bought a *broken-down* car and rebuilt it.

bro·ken·heart·ed (BROH-kən-HAHR-tid) *adjective.* Very sad: When Lassie died, Tim was *brokenhearted.* —**brokenheartedly** *adverb.*

broken play. *See* **busted play.**

bro·ker (BROH-kər) *noun.* A person who gets paid for buying and/or selling property for another person.

bron·chi·al (BRONG-kee-əl) *adjective.* Referring to the two branches, or tubes, of the windpipe that lead to the lungs: Lisa coughed a lot when she had *bronchial* pneumonia.

bronco

bron·chi·tis (brong-KIGH-təss) *noun.* Inflammation of the bronchial tubes.

bron·co (BRONG-koh) Also **broncho** *noun.* A wild or semiwild horse of western North America: In the West, the training of horses is often called *bronco* busting. **broncos.**

bron·to·saur (BRAHN-tə-sor) Also **brontosaurus** *noun.* A huge dinosaur that lived long ago in North America.

brontosaur

bronze

bronze (BRONZ) *noun.* 1. An alloy made of copper and tin. 2. A statue or figure made of bronze: The beautiful *bronze* was done by Rodin, the famous French sculptor. 3. (Also *adjective*) The color of bronze, brownish gold. *—verb.* 1. To cover with bronze: My mother had the children's baby shoes *bronzed.* 2. To make the color of bronze: The sun *bronzed* our skin. **bronzed, bronzing.**

brooch (BROHCH or BROOCH) Also **broach** *noun.* An ornamental pin or clasp. **brooches.**

brood *noun.* 1. A group born of the same mother at the same time: The "Ugly Duckling" was very different from the rest of the *brood.* 2. The children in one family: The woman hurried her *brood* into the car just as the storm broke. *—verb.* 1. To sit on or hatch. 2. To think about sadly; be moody: Henry was *brooding* about his final exams. **brooded, brooding.**

brook (BRUK) *noun.* A small stream of fresh water. *—verb.* To put up with, to bear: The author said he would *brook* no interference with his work. **brooked, brooking.**

broom

broom *noun.* 1. A long-handled brush for sweeping. 2. A small, yellow-flowered bush.

broom·stick (BROOM-stik) *noun.* The handle of a broom.

broth *noun.* 1. A soup made from water in which meat, fowl, and/or vegetables have been boiled. 2. The water in which meat or vegetables have been boiled.

broth·er (BRUTH-ər) *noun.* 1. A male who is born of the same father and mother as another child: Uncle Roger is Mother's *brother.* 2. One who shares a common ancestry or purpose with another. 3. A man or boy who belongs to the same club, organization, or profession as another: John is rooming with two of his fraternity *brothers.* 4. A member of a religious order.

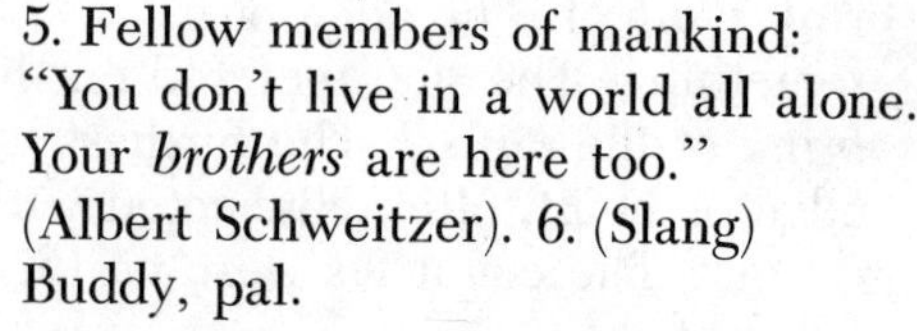
5. Fellow members of mankind: "You don't live in a world all alone. Your *brothers* are here too." (Albert Schweitzer). 6. (Slang) Buddy, pal.

brother-in-law (BRUTH-ər-in-law) *noun.* 1. The brother of a person's husband or wife. 2. The husband of a person's sister.—**brothers-in-law** *plural.*

broth·er·ly (BRUTH-ər-lee) *adjective.* 1. In a manner of or like a brother. 2. In a friendly or fond manner.

brow *noun.* 1. The ridge above the eye; the eyebrow. 2. The forehead. 3. The rim or edge of a high place: The car suddenly appeared over the *brow* of the hill.

brow·beat (BROW-beet) *verb.* To threaten or bully with words or actions; intimidate. **browbeat** or **browbeaten, browbeating.**

brown *noun* (and *adjective*). The color of chocolate, mud, or coffee without milk: the rich *brown* of a chocolate cake. **browner, brownest.** *—verb.* To heat something until it turns brown: Mother is *browning* the lamb chops in the frying pan. **browned, browning.**

brown·ie (BROW-nee) *noun.* 1. A fairy tale character; an elf or fairy who helps people secretly. 2. A small chocolate cake bar, usually with nuts. 3. [Capital B] A member of the youngest division of the Girl Scouts. **brownies.**

brown·stone (BROWN-stohn) *noun.* 1. Sandstone of reddish-brown color used as a building material. 2. A building constructed of this stone: In New York City, many of the old *brownstones* are being restored. **brownstones.**

browse (BROWZ) *verb.* 1. To look through; look here and there: I just love to *browse* through the books in the library. 2. To feed or eat: The deer can be seen *browsing* in the pasture at dusk. **browsed, browsing.**

bruise (BROOZ) *verb.* 1. To cause a painful dark spot on the flesh by hitting or pressing without breaking the skin. 2. To hurt or insult: The mean remark *bruised* Joan's feelings. **bruised, bruising.** —*noun.* A painful darkened spot on the skin that is the result of a fall or of being hit. **bruises.**

brunch *noun.* A meal that is a combination of breakfast and lunch; a late-morning meal. **brunches.** —*verb.* To eat such a meal. **brunched, brunching.**

bru·nette (broo-NET) *noun, feminine* Also **brunet** *noun, masculine.* A person with brown eyes, hair, or skin. **brunettes.** —*adjective.* Having dark eyes, hair, or skin.

brunt *noun.* The main impact, jolt, or weight: A strong car bumper will take the *brunt* of some collisions.

brush *noun.* 1. An object made of stiff hair or hair-like bristles that are set in a handle; used to arrange hair, clean, or paint. 2. The act of brushing. 3. A brief contact: John had a *brush* with the school guard at the rally. 4. Something that looks like a brush. 5. A thick growth of bushes or small trees. 6. A pile of broken or cut branches; shrubs. 7. The tail of a fox or similar animal. **brushes.** —*verb.* 1. To use a brush. 2. To come in contact with briefly and lightly: My nearsighted friend *brushed* past without recognizing me. **brushed, brushing.**

Brus·sels sprouts (BRUHSS-lz SPROWTS) *noun.* 1. A green plant of the cabbage family. 2. The small heads of this plant that are used as a vegetable.

bru·tal (BROOT-l) *adjective.* Cruel, mean, savage. —**brutally** *adverb.*

brute (BROOT) *noun.* 1. An animal, a beast. 2. A person who acts without humanity, like an animal. **brutes.** —*adjective.* 1. In the manner of an animal; without human intelligence. 2. Cruel, inhuman.

bub·ble (BUHB-əl) *noun.* 1. A glob of air or gas trapped in a liquid or a solid: The *bubble* in the glass made it unsalable. 2. A dream; something that doesn't last: Their *bubble* broke when they ran out of money. 3. The sound of bubbling. **bubbles.** —*verb.* 1. To make or give off bubbles. 2. To blow up bubble gum. 3. To boil: The witches' brew *bubbled* over the fire. 4. To be happy or excited: The little girl *bubbled* with joy when she saw her new doll. **bubbled, bubbling.**

bubble gum. Gum that can be chewed and blown into bubbles.

buc·ca·neer (buhk-ə-NIHR) *noun.* A pirate: *Buccaneers* often raided ships carrying gold and jewels.

buck (BUHK) *noun.* 1. A male animal, especially a deer or an antelope. 2. (Slang) An American dollar. —*verb.* 1. To rear up suddenly: The bronco *bucked* until it finally threw the cowboy to the ground. 2. To oppose; go against: If John *bucks* the team captain, he's in trouble. **bucked, bucking.** —**pass the buck.** To pass the blame or responsibility to someone else.

buck·et (BUHK-it) *noun.* 1. A metal, plastic, or wooden pail. 2. The shovel of a digging machine that scoops up the load. 3. A bucketful.

buck·le (BUHK-əl) *noun.* 1. A fastener that connects two loose ends of a belt or strap. 2. An ornament that looks like a buckle. **buckles.** —*verb.* 1. To put together by means of a buckle: "*Buckle* up for safety" is a slogan used to encourage the use of seat belts. 2. To bend or give way: The pavement sometimes *buckles* on very hot days. **buckled, buckling.**

buck·shot (BUHK-shot) *noun.* A large pellet of lead used in shotguns. —**buckshot** *plural.*

buck·skin (BUHK-skin) *noun.* 1. The skin of a male deer or sheep. 2. Leather made from buckskin.

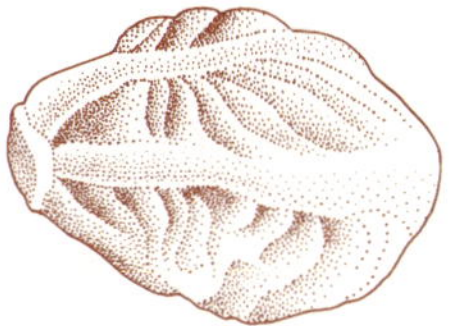
Brussels sprout

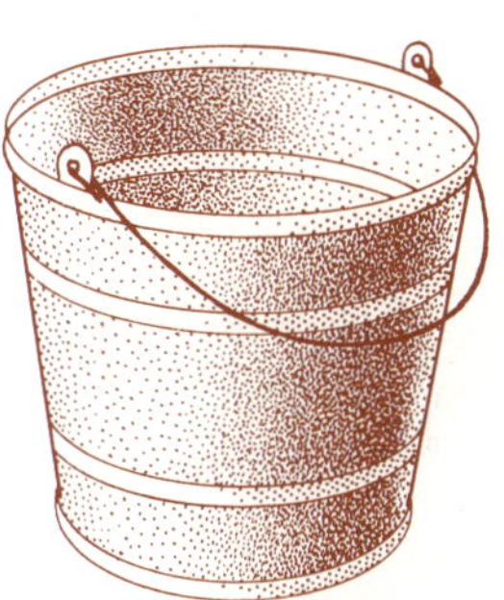
bucket

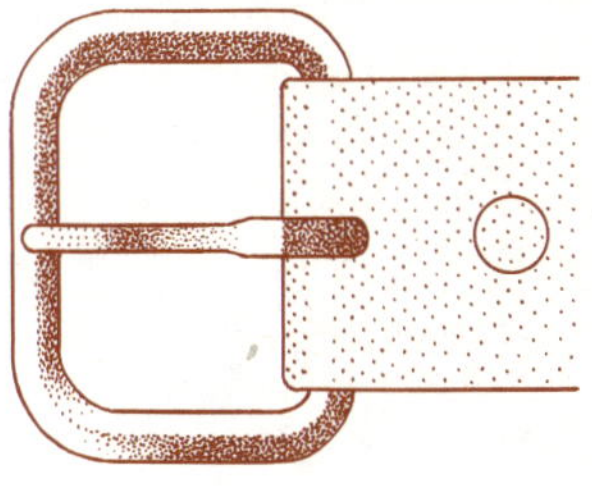
buckle

buggy

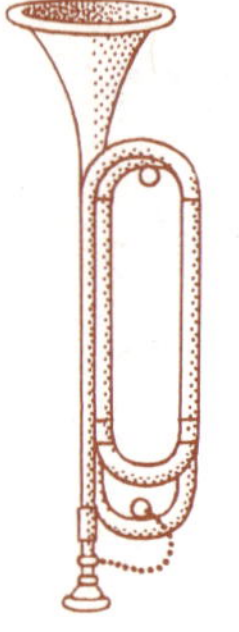
bugle

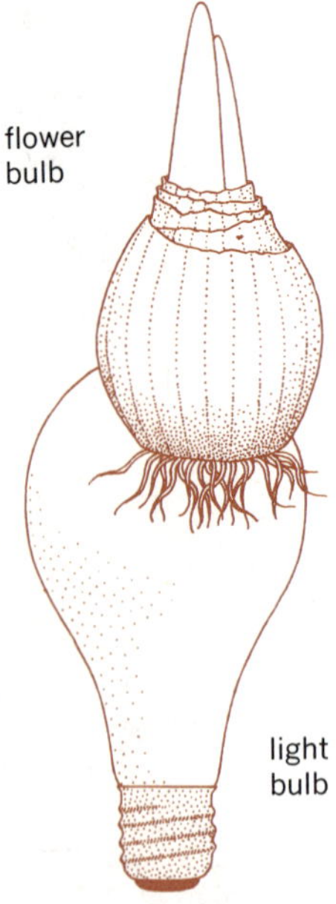

buck·wheat (BUHK-hweet) *noun.* A plant that produces seeds used to feed animals and to make flour.

bud (BUHD) *noun.* 1. The very beginning of a flower, a leaf, or a branch; a partly opened flower. 2. (Slang) Short for "buddy." —*verb.* To develop new leaves, branches, or flowers. **budded, budding.**

bud·dy (BUHD-ee) *noun.* 1. A friend or pal. 2. An informal manner of address: Hi, *buddy!* What's new? **buddies.**

budge (BUHDJ) *verb.* 1. To move a little bit: The boys could not *budge* the heavy door. 2. To change an opinion or a decision: The teacher would not *budge* from her decision to give a final exam. **budged, budging.**

bud·get (BUHJ-it) *noun.* 1. An outline of expected income and expenses. 2. The amount of money available for a given purpose or in a given time: I can never stay within my *budget.* —*verb.* To make an outline or plan of income and expenses. **budgeted, budgeting.**

bue·nos dí·as (BWAY-noss DEE-ahss) A Spanish greeting meaning *good day* or *good morning.*

buff (BUHF) *verb.* To clean by rubbing. **buffed, buffing.** —*noun.* 1. A thick leather of a yellow tone. 2. (Also *adjective*) A yellowish or tan color. 3. A person who is devoted to a particular sport, hobby, or other interest: Sara is a real tennis *buff.*

buf·fa·lo (BUHF-ə-loh) *noun.* A wild ox-like animal; the bison. —**buffaloes, buffalos, or buffalo** *plural.*

[1]**buf·fet** (BUHF-it) *verb.* To batter or push against: The winds and rough seas *buffeted* the small boat. **buffeted, buffeting.**

[2]**buf·fet** (bə-FAY) *noun.* 1. An informal meal at which guests help themselves. 2. A piece of dining room furniture used to hold linens, china, or silverware.

buf·foon (bə-FOON) *noun.* A clown.

bug (BUHG) *noun.* 1. An insect or something that resembles an insect. 2. (Informal) An illness, particularly a virus: There is a *bug* going around the class. 3. (Informal) A defect: My father tried to get the *bugs* out of his new car. 4. (Slang) A hidden device used to listen to another's conversations. —*verb.* (Slang) 1. To install a hidden listening device. 2. To tease or annoy: The word "ain't" *bugs* the teacher. **bugged, bugging.**

bug·gy (BUHG-ee) *noun.* 1. A horse-drawn carriage. 2. A baby carriage. **buggies.** —*adjective.* 1. Filled with bugs. 2. (Slang) Crazy. **buggier, buggiest.**

bu·gle (BYOO-gəl) *noun.* A brass musical instrument shorter than a trumpet and without valves or keys. **bugles.**

build (BILD) *verb.* 1. To make by putting things together. 2. To increase; develop: Jerry *built* his paper route by giving good service. **built, building.** —*noun.* Figure or shape: If Jimmy got more exercise, he would have a good *build.*

build·ing (BILD-ing) *noun.* 1. A structure such as a house, church, barn, or school. 2. The art or business of putting up structures.

bulb (BUHLB) *noun.* 1. A round stem or bud from which plants grow. 2. An electric light.

bulge (BUHLJ) *noun.* A part that sticks out: The gun made a *bulge* in the man's pocket. **bulges.** —*verb.* To stick out. **bulged, bulging.**

bulk (BUHLK) *noun.* 1. Size; great size: Goliath was a man of *bulk.* 2. The greatest part: The *bulk* of the work was done by Ethel. 3. Loose, not packaged.

bulk·y (BUHLK-ee) *adjective.* Of large or inconvenient size. **bulkier, bulkiest.**

bull (BUL) *noun.* 1. A male animal of certain species; for example, cattle, elephant, whale, or moose. 2. One with the strength of a bull: Only a *bull* like Alex could move that boulder. 3. (Slang) Lies, nonsense.

bull·dog (BUL-dawg) *noun.* A stocky, short-haired dog known for its courage. *—verb.* To flip over an animal, especially a steer, by grabbing its horns and twisting its neck. **bulldogged, bulldogging.**

bull·doz·er (BUL-doh-zər) *noun.* A heavy tractor with a large steel blade mounted in front used to move or clear earth and rocks.

bul·let (BUL-ət) *noun.* 1. A piece of lead or other metal that is fired from a gun. 2. A cartridge.

bul·le·tin (BUL-ət-n) *noun.* 1. A short account of the latest news: A *bulletin* on TV announced the end of the war. 2. A brief paper or magazine regularly issued by an organization.

bulletin board. A sheet of material, often of cork, on which written announcements, letters, and notices are fastened: The teacher tacked a list of grades on the *bulletin board.*

bull·finch (BUL-finch) *noun.* A small songbird found in Europe. **bullfinches.**

bull·frog (BUL-frawg) *noun.* A large frog with an especially loud croak.

bull·head·ed (BUL-hed-əd) *adjective.* Stubborn, wanting one's own way.

bul·lion (BUL-yən) *noun.* Gold or silver, especially when formed into bars.

bul·lock (BUL-ək) *noun.* A young bull or ox.

bull's eye. Also **bull's-eye** (BULZ-igh) 1. The center of a target. 2. A shot, as with an arrow or bullet, that strikes the center of a target. 3. Anything that achieves its goal.

bul·ly (BUL-ee) *noun.* A person who tries to frighten those smaller or weaker than himself. **bullies.** *—verb.* To try to frighten those who are smaller or weaker. **bullied, bullying.**

bul·wark (BUL-wərk) *noun.* 1. A wall or barrier used as a defense against an enemy force: The soldiers fired from behind their *bulwark.* 2. Anything that serves as a defense or safeguard: Hard work and careful planning are *bulwarks* against failure. 3. (*Usually plural*) The parts of a ship's sides that extend above the main deck.

bum (BUHM) *noun.* A person who chooses not to work, a tramp. *—verb.* (Slang) 1. To beg, ask for something free: He *bummed* a stick of gum from his friend. 2. To loaf: He *bummed* around during the summer. 3. To hitchhike: Keith *bummed* his way to the lake. **bummed, bumming.** *—adjective.* (Slang) 1. Poor in quality: My father was angry with the salesman who sold him a *bum* car. 2. False, wrong: He gave him *bum* information about the sale.

bum·ble·bee (BUHM-bəl-bee) *noun.* A large black and yellow bee that makes a buzzing noise in flight. **bumblebees.**

bum·mer (BUHM-ər) *noun.* (Slang) A letdown, a disappointment: That movie was a *bummer;* it was really very boring.

bump (BUHMP) *noun.* 1. A blow, sudden push, or jolt: We felt a *bump* when the car hit the curb. 2. A swelling or lump, especially one caused by a blow: The blow left a *bump* on his head. *—verb.* To give a sudden push or jolt. **bumped, bumping.**

bump·er (BUHM-pər) *noun.* A metal bar or similar device used to protect a car, boat, or other vehicle from the damage of collisions. *—adjective.* Especially large or successful: The farmers were delighted by their *bumper* crop.

bull

bulldogs

bumblebee

bullfrog

buoy

bun (BUHN) *noun.* 1. A small roll, sometimes sweetened. 2. Hair worn in a coil or knot.

bunch (BUHNCH) *noun.* 1. A cluster of similar things that grow or are gathered together: She bought a *bunch* of bananas. 2. (Informal) A group or gathering: A *bunch* of friends met at the party. **bunches.** —*verb.* To cluster; group (together): The cattle *bunched* together in the field. **bunched, bunching.**

bun•dle (BUHND-l) *noun.* 1. A number of things tied together: The *bundle* of newspapers is in the corner. 2. A package: The woman carried two *bundles* from the store. **bundles.** —*verb.* To gather or tie together; to package. **bundled, bundling.**

bun•ga•low (BUHNG-gə-loh) *noun.* A one-story house, usually small.

bun•gle (BUHNG-gəl) *verb.* To do something badly or in a clumsy manner; to ruin: Frank *bungled* the job; he spilled the paint and broke a window. **bungled, bungling.**

bunk (BUHNK) *noun.* 1. A narrow bed, usually attached to a wall: I'll take the top *bunk.* 2. (Slang) Insincere or silly talk: That's *bunk;* you don't mean a word you've said. —*verb.* 1. To sleep in, as in a bed or place: He *bunks* in the old cabin. 2. To share a room with: My brother *bunks* with Ed Walsh at college. **bunked, bunking.**

bunk•house (BUHNK-howss) *noun.* A building with beds for several people: Twelve boys slept in one *bunkhouse* at camp. **bunkhouses.**

bun•ny (BUHN-ee) *noun.* A child's term for a rabbit. **bunnies.**

bunt (BUHNT) *verb.* To hit softly, especially in baseball. **bunted, bunting.** —*noun.* A soft or short hit in baseball.

buoy (BOO-ee or BOI) *noun.* 1. A float anchored in water to mark a channel or to warn ships of danger. 2. A life preserver. —*verb.* 1. To keep afloat: The sailor was *buoyed* by his life jacket. 2. To enliven or encourage: The good news about vacation *buoyed* our spirits. **buoyed, buoying.**

buoy•an•cy (BOI-ən-see) *noun.* 1. The ability to float. 2. The upward force on an object in a fluid: *Buoyancy* kept the bottle bobbing on the surface. 3. Lightness of spirit, cheerfulness: Tom's *buoyancy* made his classmates forget their own disappointment.—**buoy•ant** (BOI-ənt) *adjective.*

bur (BER) Also **burr** *noun.* 1. The prickly seedcase of some plants or trees: The *burs* from the chestnut tree are all over our yard. 2. Anything that acts like a bur.

bur•den (BERD-n) *noun.* 1. A load, usually heavy: The boys soon tired of the *burden* of their backpacks. 2. Anything that causes difficulty or hardship: Charles found his stuttering a great *burden.* —*verb.* To cause difficulty or suffering for: It is selfish to *burden* parents with unnecessary expenses. **burdened, burdening.**

bur•den•some (BERD-n-səm) *adjective.* Hard to carry or endure; causing difficulty or hardship: A long paper route can prove *burdensome* to a boy with many homework assignments.

bur•eau (BYUR-oh) *noun.* 1. A chest of drawers for storing clothes. 2. A business office that performs a special duty: We asked for directions at the travel *bureau.* 3. A department of government: My uncle was an agent of the Federal *Bureau* of Investigation.

bu•reauc•ra•cy (byu-ROK-rə-see) *noun.* 1. Government bureaus and departments, staffed mostly with appointed officials. 2. A government in which officials tend to follow rigid rules and routines without exceptions. **bureaucracies.**

bur·gess (BER-jiss) *noun.* In colonial times, a member of the lawmaking body in Maryland or Virginia. **burgesses.**

bur·glar (BER-glər) *noun.* A person who breaks into a building to steal.

bur·glar·y (BER-glə-ree) *noun.* The crime of breaking into a building to steal. **burglaries.**

bur·i·al (BEHR-ee-əl) *noun.* Placing a body in a grave or tomb.

bur·lap (BER-lap) *noun.* A coarse fabric often used for bags.

bur·ly (BER-lee) *adjective.* Husky; strong: The *burly* workmen lifted the piano onto the stage. **burlier, burliest.**

burn (BERN) *verb.* 1. To be on fire. 2. To set on fire; destroy by fire: The spy *burned* the secret message. 3. To injure or damage by fire, heat, the sun's rays, chemicals, or other means: The child *burned* his hand on the hot stove. 4. To give off light: The night light *burned* until morning. 5. To cause to feel hot: The strong pepper *burns* my tongue. 6. To give off heat: The stove in the cabin *burned* warmly. 7. To feel strong or sudden emotion: She *burned* with anger. **burned, burning.** —*noun.* 1. An injury caused by fire or other means. 2. (Aerospace) Thrust produced by a single firing of a rocket.

bur·ner (BER-nər) *noun.* 1. The part of a stove that produces heat. 2. A stove, furnace, or other heating device.

bur·nish (BER-nish) *verb.* To polish, to make smooth by rubbing. **burnished, burnishing.**

bur·noose (ber-NOOSS) *noun.* A long hooded cloak: *Burnooses* are worn by the Arabs. **burnooses.**

burr (BER) *noun.* 1. A quality or manner of speech in which the "r" sound is pronounced more than once. 2. *See* **bur.**

bur·ro (BER-oh) *noun.* A donkey; a small pack animal. **burros.**

bur·row (BER-oh) *noun.* A hole or tunnel in the ground, especially one serving as an animal's dwelling. —*verb.* To dig a tunnel or hole in the ground. **burrowed, burrowing.**

burst (BERST) *verb.* 1. To break or open suddenly; explode. 2. To cause to break open or explode. 3. To express or display feelings suddenly: The girl *burst* into tears. 4. To enter or depart with suddenness or force: The policeman *burst* into the room. 5. To be extremely full. **burst, bursting.** —*noun.* 1. A breaking or opening forth: The *burst* of dynamite destroyed the shack. 2. A sudden display or spurt of activity or feeling: He finished the race with a *burst* of speed. 3. A group of shots: The soldiers were surprised by the *burst* of fire.

bur·y (BEHR-ee) *verb.* 1. To put something underground; to place a dead body into a grave or tomb. 2. To cover, especially to hide or conceal by covering: He *buried* the coins in the bottom of the drawer. 3. To involve deeply: Before the test, Mark *buried* himself in study. **buried, burying.**

bus (BUHSS) *noun.* A large motor vehicle with many seats for passengers. **buses** or **busses.** —*verb.* To move or travel by bus. **bused** or **bussed, busing** or **bussing.**

bush *noun.* 1. A shrub; a low, treelike plant with many branches. **bushes.** 2. A wild, wooded region: The hunters entered the *bush* in search of game. —**bush** *plural.*

bush·el (BUSH-əl) *noun.* 1. A unit of dry measure equal to 32 quarts or 4 pecks. 2. A container that holds a bushel.

bush·y (BUSH-ee) *adjective.* Growing thickly; resembling a bush in thickness or texture: Tim has dark, *bushy* hair. **bushier, bushiest.**

bus

burnoose

busi·ness (BIZ-nəss) *noun.* 1. An occupation; a trade: His *business* is plumbing. 2. Selling; commerce: The store opens for *business* at eight o'clock. 3. A place or organization for trade or commerce: Three new *businesses* rented space in the shopping center. 4. Personal concerns or activities: Mind your own *business;* don't worry about his. **businesses.**

bust (BUHST) *noun.* 1. A sculpture of a person's head and shoulders. 2. A person's chest; a woman's bosom. 3. (Slang) A failure; a waste of time: We left the party early; it was a *bust.* —*verb.* (Slang) 1. To break; burst: Tony *busted* the window. 2. To punch: He threatened to *bust* me in the nose. 3. To arrest: The crooks were *busted* by two policemen. **busted, busting.**

busted play Also **broken play.** (Football) A play that doesn't follow the quarterback's original plan: Our team made 15 yards on a *busted play;* even though the halfback missed a lateral, the fullback got the ball and ran it out.

bus·tle (BUHSS-l) *verb.* To work or hurry busily or noisily; to hustle: The waitress *bustled* about the crowded restaurant. **bustled, bustling.** —*noun.* Noisy activity.

bus·y (BIZ-ee) *adjective.* 1. Active; working; involved: The teacher was *busy* correcting papers. 2. Full of activity or bustle: The store was *busy* before the holiday. 3. In use; occupied: The phone was *busy.* **busier, busiest.** —*verb.* To make or keep active or occupied: Mother *busied* herself with her mending. **busied, busying.** —**busily** *adverb.* —**busyness** *noun.*

bus·y·bod·y (BIZ-ee-bod-ee) *noun.* Someone who interferes in other people's affairs; a meddler. **busybodies.**

buttercup

but (BUHT) *conjunction.* 1. Yet; still: Ann was tired, *but* she continued. 2. Except that; unless: It never rains *but* it pours. 3. On the other hand: Jim is short, *but* his brother is tall. 4. Other than: Ted does nothing *but* sleep all morning. —*adverb.* Only: I would have done the dishes had Mother *but* waited. —*preposition.* Except: No one came *but* Judy.

butch·er (BUCH-ər) *noun.* 1. A person who sells meat. 2. A person who kills animals and prepares their meat for sale. 3. Someone who kills without feeling. —*verb.* 1. To kill animals or prepare or cut up meat for sale. 2. To kill people or animals brutally or cruelly: The hunter *butchered* the seal pups. 3. To ruin; spoil: He *butchered* the plumbing job by breaking a pipe. **butchered, butchering.**

butt (BUHT) *noun.* 1. The handle or thick end of something: He held the *butt* of the pistol. 2. The stub of a cigarette or cigar. 3. An object of joking or ridicule: Why is Joel always the *butt* of Jim's jokes? 4. A blow from the head of a person or animal. —*verb.* 1. To hit with the head or with horns: The goat *butted* the farmer. 2. To place end to end: He *butted* the bricks in a neat row. **butted, butting.**

butte (BYOOT) *noun.* A steep hill, usually with flattened top. **buttes.**

but·ter (BUHT-ər) *noun.* 1. A soft yellow-colored food made by churning or whipping cream. 2. Any of a number of foods or substances, like peanut butter, that are similar to butter. —*verb.* To spread with butter. **buttered, buttering.**

but·ter·cup (BUHT-ər-kuhp) *noun.* 1. A small yellow flower shaped like a cup. 2. The plant on which this flower grows.

but·ter·fing·ers (BUHT-ər-fing-gerz) *noun.* A clumsy person; one who always drops things: The first baseman is a real *butterfingers;* he often drops the ball.

but·ter·fly (BUHT-ər-fligh) *noun.* 1. An insect with four wings, usually brightly colored. 2. (Slang) A person who cannot concentrate on one thing for very long. **butterflies.**

but·ter·milk (BUHT-ər-milk) *noun.* The liquid that remains after butter has been made from cream.

but·ter·nut (BUHT-ər-nuht) *noun.* An oily walnut grown in America; the tree on which it grows.

but·ter·scotch (BUHT-ər-skoch) *noun.* A syrup, sauce, or candy made by melting butter and brown sugar.

but·tock (BUHT-ək) *noun.* The rounded area at the back of the hip.

but·ton (BUHT-n) *noun.* 1. A small disk sewed on clothing to fasten through a matching hole. 2. A small disk sewed or pinned to clothing for decoration or for show: The students were wearing peace *buttons.* 3. A small knob or disk which acts as a control for such things as a bell or elevator. *—verb.* To close or to fasten with a button. **buttoned, buttoning.**

but·ton·hole (BUHT-n-hohl) *noun.* A slit or opening through which a button is passed. **buttonholes.** *—verb.* 1. To make a buttonhole. 2. To corner or trap in order to talk to: The reporters *buttonholed* the mayor in the hallway. **buttonholed, buttonholing.**

but·tress (BUHT-riss) *noun.* Something that supports or strengthens, especially a prop that gives strength or support to a wall. **buttresses.** *—verb.* To prop; strengthen or support. **buttressed, buttressing.**

bux·om (BUHK-səm) *adjective.* Plump; full bosomed.

buy (BIGH) *verb.* To purchase; get in exchange for money: I will *buy* the book for five dollars. **bought, buying.** *—noun.* (Informal) A bargain: The dress was a real *buy.*

buzz (BUHZ) *noun.* 1. The humming noise made by bees and other insects. 2. The murmur of several voices: *buzz* of conversation. **buzzes.** *—verb.* 1. To make a humming noise. 2. To push a button or buzzer: He *buzzed* for his secretary to come in. 3. To fly an airplane very low or close to something. **buzzed, buzzing.**

buz·zard (BUHZ-ərd) *noun.* 1. Any of several types of vulture or other birds of prey. 2. (Informal) An unpleasant or grouchy old person.

buz·zer (BUHZ-ər) *noun.* An electric signaling device such as a doorbell.

by (BIGH) *preposition.* 1. Near; close to: Let's sit *by* the fire. 2. Through the means of: Kim arrived *by* train. 3. During: George slept *by* day and worked *by* night. 4. Not later than: Mother will be here *by* noon. 5. Through the work of: The painting is *by* Rubens. 6. According to a certain schedule: My dad is paid *by* the week. 7. Following: Al became lonelier day *by* day. 8. To the amount of: We won the game *by* six points. *—adverb.* 1. Past; beyond: The train sped *by.* 2. Nearby; near: standing *by.*

by and by. After a while; soon.

by·gone (BIGH-gawn) *adjective.* Past; former: These ornaments are from a *bygone* day. *—noun.* That which is over or past. **bygones.**

by·law (BIGH-law) *noun.* A secondary law or rule made by an organization or group to apply to its own members or functions.

by·line (BIGH-lighn) *noun.* A line of print at the head of an article in a newspaper or magazine giving the name of the writer. **bylines.**

by-prod·uct (BIGH-prod-əkt) *noun.* A product made during the manufacture of another product.

butterfly

butternut

buzzard

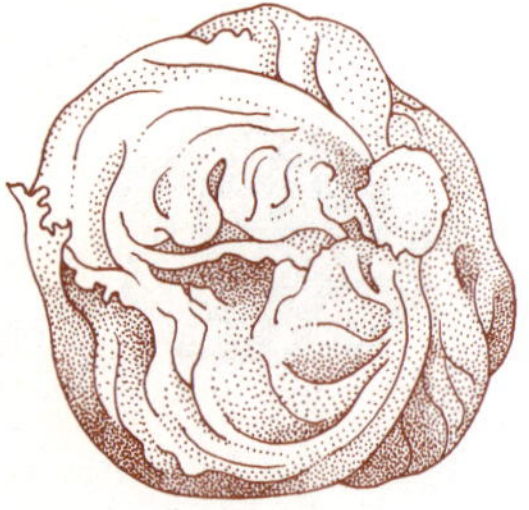
cabbage

cable car

caboose

C, c (SEE) *noun.* The third letter of the English alphabet.

C *abbreviation* 1. Centigrade. 2. Celsius.

cab (KAB) *noun.* 1. A taxi; an automobile with driver for hire, usually for short trips. 2. A horse-drawn carriage. 3. The driver's part of a truck, train, or other vehicle.

cab·bage (KAB-ij) *noun.* A common green-white or red vegetable with thick leaves which grow together in a tight ball or head. **cabbages.**

cab·in (KAB-in) *noun.* 1. A small plain house: Lincoln lived in a log *cabin.* 2. A room on a ship. 3. A section or space on an aircraft.

cab·i·net (KAB-ə-nit) *noun.* 1. A piece of furniture with shelves and doors used to store or display things. 2. [Usually capital C] A group of high officials who serve as advisers to the head of a government.

ca·ble (KAY-bəl) *noun.* 1. A strong, heavy rope, often made of metal. 2. A covered or insulated bundle of wires used to carry electric current. 3. A telegraph message sent by underwater cable; a cablegram. **cables.** —*verb.* To send a message by underwater cable. **cabled, cabling.**

cable car. A car that is towed by a moving cable, either along the ground or through the air.

ca·ble·gram (KAY-bəl-gram) *noun.* A message sent by underwater cable.

cable television Also **cable TV.** A system for transmitting television broadcasts by cable directly to each television set.

ca·boose (kə-BOOSS) *noun.* A railroad car, usually the last one on a freight train, in which trainmen have a place for shelter and rest. **cabooses.**

ca·ca·o (kə-KAH-oh or kə-KAY-oh) *noun.* 1. The seeds or beans from which chocolate and cocoa are made. 2. The tropical tree on which such seeds grow. **cacaos.**

cache (KASH) *noun.* Hidden treasure or supplies. **caches.** —*verb.* To put in a hiding place. **cached, caching.**

cack·le (KAK-əl) *noun.* 1. A high-pitched, stuttering noise made by a hen. 2. Any similar sound. **cackles** —*verb.* 1. To make a noise like a hen. 2. To laugh or chatter in a noisy or high-pitched manner. **cackled, cackling.**

cac·tus (KAK-təss) *noun.* A plant, found in dry, hot places, that has a fleshy stem and needles or spines instead of leaves. —**cactuses** or **cacti** (KAK-tigh) *plural.*

cad (KAD) *noun.* A man who acts in a rude or ungentlemanly way.

cad·die (KAD-ee) Also **caddy** *noun.* A person hired to help a golfer by carrying his clubs and performing other services. **caddies.** —*verb.* To serve as a caddie. **caddied, caddying.**

ca·det (kə-DET) *noun.* 1. A young man or boy enrolled at a military school. 2. A person preparing to become a military officer.

ca·fé (ka-FAY) *noun.* A small restaurant; a place for food, drinks, or entertainment. **cafés.**

caf·e·te·ri·a (kaf-ə-TIHR-ee-ə) *noun.* An eating place in which customers select food at a counter and carry it to tables. **cafeterias.**

caf·feine (kaf-EEN) *noun.* A substance that tends to cause wakefulness; found in coffee, tea, cola, and certain medicines.

cage (KAYJ) *noun.* 1. A place closed off by bars or wire in which birds or animals are kept. 2. Anything that looks or is used like an animal cage: a batter's *cage.* **cages.** *—verb.* To put in a cage. **caged, caging.**

cake (KAYK) *noun.* 1. A baked dessert made from flour, sugar, and other ingredients. 2. Any small, flattened form of food: pan*cake* or fish*cake.* 3. A molded shape of any substance: a *cake* of soap. **cakes.** *—verb.* To harden. **caked, caking.**

ca·lam·i·ty (kə-LAM-ə-tee) *noun.* Bad fortune or disaster: **calamities.**

cal·cite (KAL-sight) *noun.* A common mineral found in substances such as limestone and chalk.

cal·ci·um (KAL-see-əm) *noun.* A mineral found in chalk, marble, bone, and in such foods as milk and green vegetables.

cal·cu·late (KAL-kyə-layt) *verb.* 1. To use mathematics to arrive at an answer or result. 2. To figure out or estimate: Mother *calculated* she had enough food for two extra guests. 3. To arrange or intend: Jim's apology was *calculated* to win Father's forgiveness. **calculated, calculating.** **—calculation** (kal-kyə-LAY-shən) *noun.*

cal·cu·lus (KAL-kyə-ləss) *noun.* A system of higher, or advanced, mathematics. **—calculi** (KAL-kyə-lee) or **calculuses** *plural.*

cal·en·dar (KAL-ən-dər) *noun.* 1. A table or list of months, weeks, and days of a year or years. 2. A list or schedule of things to be done.

calf (KAF) *noun.* 1. A young cow or bull, or the young of similar four-legged mammals. 2. The soft leather that comes from a young cow or bull. 3. The fleshy back part of the leg between the knee and the ankle. **—calves** (KAVZ) *plural.*

cal·i·co (KAL-i-koh) *noun.* A coarse cloth, usually printed in bright colors. **—calicoes** or **calicos** *plural.* *—adjective.* Spotted: a *calico* cat.

Cal·i·for·nia (kal-ə-FORN-yə) *noun.* A Pacific state in the United States, 31st to join the Union (1850). **—Calif.** *abbreviation.* Also **CA** for Zip Codes.

California
★capital: Sacramento

ca·liph (KAY-lif) *noun.* A Moslem religious or political leader.

call (KAWL) *verb.* 1. To shout; speak loudly. 2. To name: They *called* the baby Marie. 3. To summon, invite, or command. 4. To telephone. 5. To visit. 6. To stop: The game was *called* because of rain. **called, calling.** *—noun.* 1. A shout. 2. An invitation or command. 3. A visit. 4. The cry of an animal: The hunter heard the *call* of the geese. **—call off.** 1. To cancel. 2. To keep back; restrain: *call off* a dog.

cal·lous (KAL-əss) *adjective.* 1. Hardened; toughened. 2. Without caring. **—callously** *adverb.*

cal·lus (KAL-əss) *noun.* A hardened place on the skin. **calluses.**

calm (KAHM) *noun.* Stillness; quiet; freedom from noise or bustle. *—adjective.* Still; quiet; free from noise or bustle. **calmer, calmest.** *—verb.* To make still, quiet, or relaxed. **calmed, calming.** **—calmly** *adverb.*

cal·o·rie (KAL-ə-ree) *noun.* 1. The amount of heat needed to raise the temperature of one gram of water one degree centigrade. 2. A unit for measuring the heat or energy released by food digested in the body. **calories.**

ca·lyx (KAY-liks) *noun.* The outer part of a flower. **calyxes.**

cam·el (KAM-əl) *noun.* A large animal with one or two humps on its back.

calf

camera

camper

canal

campus

cam·er·a (KAM-ər-ə or KAM-rə) *noun.* A device used for taking photographs, and making motion pictures or television pictures.

cam·ou·flage (KAM-ə-flahzh) *noun.* A hiding or disguising of anything; coloring that blends with the landscape: The fur of the arctic fox turns white in winter as *camouflage.* **camouflages.** *—verb.* To disguise or hide by painting or covering. **camouflaged, camouflaging.**

camp (KAMP) *noun.* 1. A place where soldiers or other groups of people live in tents or other temporary shelter. 2. A place where a person can go for rest and recreation. 3. A group of supporters: He is a member of the senator's *camp.* 4. Any matter or style that is oddly humorous, silly, or outlandish. *—verb.* To live in or set up a camp. **camped, camping.**

cam·paign (kam-PAYN) *noun.* 1. A series of military actions aimed at a special target. 2. Any series of actions organized for a specific purpose: a political *campaign.* *—verb.* To take part in a campaign. **campaigned, campaigning.**

camp·er (KAM-pər) *noun.* 1. A person who camps. 2. A vehicle designed to provide shelter while camping.

cam·phor (KAM-fər) *noun.* A substance with a strong, sharp smell, used in making medicines and products for protecting clothing from moths.

cam·pus (KAM-pəss) *noun.* The yards and buildings of a college or school. **campuses.**

can (KAN) *noun.* 1. A metal container. 2. The amount held by such a container: She poured a *can* of soup into the pot. *—helping verb.* To be capable or able to: I *can* lift that rock. **could.** *—verb.* 1. To preserve by sealing in an airtight jar or container. 2. (Slang) To dismiss (someone) from a job. **canned, canning.**

ca·nal (kə-NAL) *noun.* 1. A man-made waterway built to allow passage of ships and boats. 2. A ditch which supplies water to an area. 3. A tube, or duct, in the body of a human or animal.

ca·nar·y (kə-NAIR-ee) *noun.* A yellow songbird. **canaries.**

can·cel (KAN-sl) *verb.* 1. To put an end to; withdraw. 2. To cross out; mark so that a thing cannot be reused: The stamp on the letter was *canceled* at the post office. **canceled, canceling.** **—cancellation** (kan-sə-LAY-shən) *noun.*

can·cer (KAN-sər) *noun.* 1. A disease that spreads through the body destroying healthy tissue; a very harmful growth or tumor. 2. Any evil that spreads and causes great harm: Hatred is a *cancer* that can ruin the lives of men. **—cancerous** *adjective.*

Can·cer (KAN-sər) The fourth sign of the zodiac, also called the "Crab." The time of this sign is from June 22 through July 22.

can·did (KAN-did) *adjective.* Frank; honest; saying what one thinks. **—candidly** *adverb.*

can·di·date (KAN-də-dayt) *noun.* A person who runs or is considered for an office or position. **candidates.**

can·dle (KAN-dl) *noun.* A piece of wax or tallow with a wick running through its length which provides light when burned. **candles.** *—verb.* To check the freshness of (eggs) by viewing (them) in front of a candle or similar light. **candled, candling.**

can·dle·light (KAN-dl-light) *noun.* The glow of a candle.

can·dle·stick (KAN-dl-stik) *noun.* A holder for one or more candles.

can·dor (KAN-dər) *noun.* Frankness; honesty.

can·dy (KAN-dee) *noun.* Sweets made from sugar, usually with other ingredients such as chocolate, nuts, and flavoring. **candies.** *—verb.* To cover or cook with sugar or syrup. **candied, candying.**

cane (KAYN) *noun.* 1. A strong stick used for support when walking. 2. Any of several types of slender, jointed plant stems. 3. A plant having such stems. **canes.** —*verb.* 1. To beat with a cane or stick. 2. To weave with cane. **caned, caning.**

ca·nine (KAY-nighn) *noun.* 1. A dog. 2. One of the four pointed teeth, also called "eyeteeth," next to the incisors. **canines.**

can·ner·y (KAN-ər-ee) *noun.* A factory where foods are canned and prepared for shipment. **canneries.**

can·ni·bal (KAN-ə-bəl) *noun.* 1. A human who eats other human flesh. 2. An animal that eats other members of its own kind.

can·non (KAN-ən) *noun.* A large, mounted gun. —**cannons** or **cannon** *plural.*

can·not (KAN-ot or kə-NOT) *verb.* Can not.

can·ny (KAN-ee) *adjective.* Careful or shrewd. **cannier, canniest.**

ca·noe (kə-NOO) *noun.* A light, slender boat moved and steered by paddles. **canoes.** —*verb.* To travel by canoe. **canoed, canoeing.**

can·on (KAN-ən) *noun.* 1. A law, especially a church law. 2. A standard by which something is judged: the *canons* of good literature. 3. A clergyman serving in a cathedral.

can·on·ize (KAN-ə-nighz) *verb.* 1. To declare formally that a dead person is a saint. 2. To treat or regard as holy or glorious. **canonized, canonizing.**

can·o·py (KAN-ə-pee) *noun.* 1. A roof-like covering over a place or object, like a bed, altar, or throne. 2. Any covering that provides shade or shelter. **canopies.**

can't (KANT) *contraction.* A shortened form of *cannot.*

can·ta·loupe (KAN-tə-lohp) *noun.* A juicy melon with a rough skin and orange flesh. **cantaloupes.**

can·tank·er·ous (kan-TANG-kər-əss) *adjective.* Quarrelsome; easily irritated or annoyed: Children dislike *cantankerous* people.

can·teen (kan-TEEN) *noun.* 1. A small container for carrying water, especially on hikes. 2. A place where one can buy food and drink or enjoy entertainment.

can·ter (KAN-tər) *verb.* To ride at a pace between a trot and a gallop. **cantered, cantering.** —*noun.* A pace between a trot and a gallop.

can·tor (KAN-tər) *noun.* A singer of hymns or religious music, especially a person who sings or chants during a Jewish religious service.

can·vas (KAN-vəss) *noun.* 1. A coarse, heavy cloth used in making tents, awnings, and sails. 2. A piece of cloth on which a painting is made. **canvases.**

can·vass (KAN-vəss) *verb.* To visit or telephone people to gather information, seek support, or sell something: The students *canvassed* the town to sell tickets to the school play. **canvassed, canvassing.**

can·yon (KAN-yən) *noun.* A deep river gorge or other valley with steep sides: Grand *Canyon.*

cap (KAP) *noun.* 1. A hat with no brim or a short visor, often worn to indicate one's rank or position. 2. A cover or top for a container or opening: the *cap* of a toothpaste tube. 3. A small explosive. —*verb.* 1. To put a cover or top on. 2. To equal; surpass or outdo. 3. To put the finishing touch on: A burst of ten skyrockets *capped* the Fourth of July celebration. **capped, capping.**

ca·pa·bil·i·ty (kay-pə-BIL-ə-tee) *noun.* Ability; the capacity for a quality or action: He has the *capability* to become a fine athlete. **capabilities.**

canteen

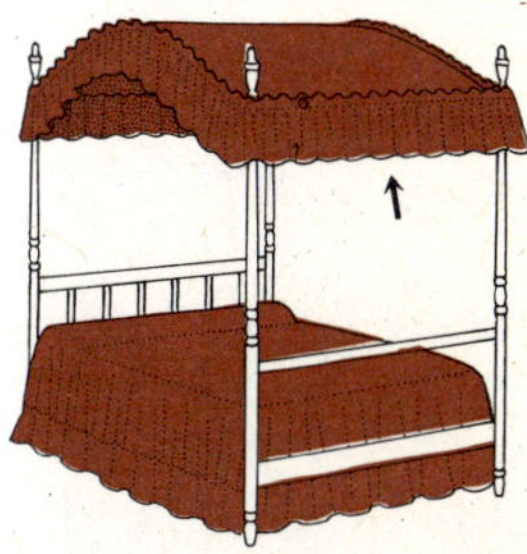

canopy

canyon

ca·pa·ble (KAY-pə-bəl) *adjective.* Able; having ability or capacity; competent. —**capably** *adverb.*

ca·pac·i·ty (kə-PASS-ə-tee) *noun.* 1. The amount that can be held by something, like a room, vehicle, or container: The *capacity* of that jar is 30 ounces. 2. Ability; capability. 3. Position; role: The doctor spoke in his *capacity* as chairman of the committee. **capacities.**

Capricorn

cape (KAYP) *noun.* 1. A sleeveless garment worn around the shoulders. 2. A piece of land that stretches out into a body of water. **capes.**

ca·per (KAY-pər) *verb.* To jump or prance about in a joyful or playful way. **capered, capering.** —*noun.* 1. A joyful or playful leap or jump. 2. A trick; a daring or exciting activity. 3. A green plant bud or berry used for flavoring.

capstan

cap·il·lar·y (KAP-ə-lehr-ee) *noun.* One of many very small blood vessels that join arteries to veins. **capillaries.**

cap·i·tal (KAP-ə-tl) *noun.* 1. The city in which the center of government for a state or nation is located. 2. Money or property owned by a person or organization. 3. A letter written or printed in larger size and different form than a small letter: The first word of a sentence begins with a *capital.* —*adjective.* 1. Major; most important. 2. Punishable by death: Kidnapping is a *capital* crime in many places. 3. Excellent.

cap·i·tal·ism (KAP-ət-l-iz-əm) *noun.* A system of economy in which property, the control of production, and the trading of goods are, in most instances, under private ownership or operation.

cap·i·tal·ize (KAP-ət-l-ighz) *verb.* 1. To make a letter or letters capitals: All the letters in the traffic sign were *capitalized.* 2. To use for one's advantage or benefit. **capitalized, capitalizing.**

cap·i·tol (KAP-ət-l) *noun.* 1. [Capital C] The building in Washington, D.C., in which Congress conducts business. 2. [Sometimes capital C] The building in which lawmakers of a state conduct business.

ca·price (kə-PREESS) *noun.* Fickleness; a sudden, unexpected change of mind. —**capricious** (kə-PRISH-əss) *adjective.*

Cap·ri·corn (KAP-ri-korn) *noun.* The tenth sign of the zodiac, also called the "Goat." The time of this sign is from December 22 through January 19.

cap·size (KAP-sighz) *verb.* To overturn or upset, especially a boat. **capsized, capsizing.**

cap·stan (KAP-stən) *noun.* A device used on ships for pulling in rope, cable, or chain.

cap·sule (KAP-sl) *noun.* 1. A case or container, especially a small one that is filled with medicine and dissolves after being swallowed. 2. A sealed compartment in a spacecraft. **capsules.**

cap·tain (KAP-tən) *noun.* 1. The man in charge of a ship or plane. 2. An army officer who ranks above a lieutenant and below a major. 3. A naval officer who ranks above a commander and below an admiral. 4. The head or leader of a team. 5. A leader, superior, or officer in any field. —*verb.* To lead or act as the head of: Jim *captained* his team. **captained, captaining.**

cap·tion (KAP-shən) *noun.* 1. A title, description, or explanation accompanying a picture or cartoon. 2. A heading for a document or other written matter.

cap·ti·vate (KAP-tə-vayt) *verb.* To fascinate; charm; gain the attention of: We were *captivated* by the show. **captivated, captivating.**

cap·tive (KAP-tiv) *noun.* A prisoner; one who is held against his will. **captives.** —*adjective.* Held as a prisoner; forced to remain in a particular place.

cap·tiv·i·ty (kap-TIV-ə-tee) *noun.* The state of being a captive or prisoner. **captivities.**

cap·tor (KAP-tər) *noun.* A person who captures another.

cap·ture (KAP-chər) *verb.* 1. To seize by force or surprise, as an animal, city, or weapon. 2. To fascinate; hold: The novel *captured* Jane's imagination. **captured, capturing.** —*noun.* The act of capturing or seizing: The *capture* of the fort was a great victory. **captures.**

car (KAHR) *noun.* 1. An automobile. 2. Any of a variety of vehicles on wheels: The trolley *car* waited at the railroad crossing for the freight *cars* to pass. 3. An enclosure bearing passengers: an elevator *car.*

car·a·mel (KA-rə-məl or KAHR-məl) *noun.* 1. A chewy candy flavored with burnt sugar. 2. Burnt sugar used for flavoring or coloring.

car·at (KA-rət) *noun.* 1. A unit of measure for the weight of a precious stone: The diamond weighed five *carats.* 2. *See* **karat.**

car·a·van (KA-rə-van) *noun.* 1. A group of people, such as merchants or settlers, traveling together. 2. A covered vehicle; a van.

car·bine (KAHR-bighn) *noun.* A type of rifle, usually lightweight. **carbines.**

car·bo·hy·drate (kahr-boh-HIGH-drayt) *noun.* A chemical compound made up of carbon, hydrogen, and oxygen; found in sugar, starches, and other foods. **carbohydrates.**

car·bon (KAHR-bən) *noun.* 1. A common chemical element present in all living things and found in large quantities in substances like coal and oil. 2. A sheet of carbon paper.

car·bon·ate (KAHR-bə-nayt) *noun.* One of the forms of carbon. —*verb.* To fill with carbon dioxide gas. **carbonated, carbonating.**

carbon copy. A copy of a letter or drawing made by inserting carbon paper between two sheets of paper.

car·bon di·ox·ide (KAHR-bən digh-OK-sighd). An odorless gas that is a combination of carbon and oxygen.

car·bon mon·ox·ide (KARH-bən mo-NOK-sighd). An odorless, poisonous gas, found in the exhaust from cars and other gas engines.

carbon paper. A thin sheet of coated paper inserted between two sheets of writing paper to make on the bottom sheet a copy of whatever is written on the top sheet.

car·bu·re·tor (KAHR-bə-ray-tər) *noun.* A mechanical device that combines air with fuel to make a mixture that will burn in an engine.

car·cass (KAHR-kəss) *noun.* 1. The body of any dead animal. 2. The bare framework of a body or structure. **carcasses.**

card (KAHRD) *noun.* 1. A rectangular piece of heavy printed paper used in games such as bridge. 2. A piece of printed paper or cardboard used for a variety of purposes, such as advertising or identification: social security *cards.* 3. (Informal) A very funny or odd person. —*verb.* To comb or straighten out the fibers of certain materials. **carded, carding.**

card·board (KAHRD-bord) *noun.* A stiff paper product used to make boxes and similar items.

car·di·gan (KAHR-di-gən) *noun.* A collarless sweater or jacket that buttons or zips down the front.

car·di·nal (KAHRD-n-l or KAHRD-nl) *noun.* 1. A crested, bright-red American songbird. 2. A high-ranking clergyman of the Roman Catholic Church. 3. (Also *adjective*) A bright-red color. —*adjective.* Main; major; of great importance. —**cardinally** *adverb.*

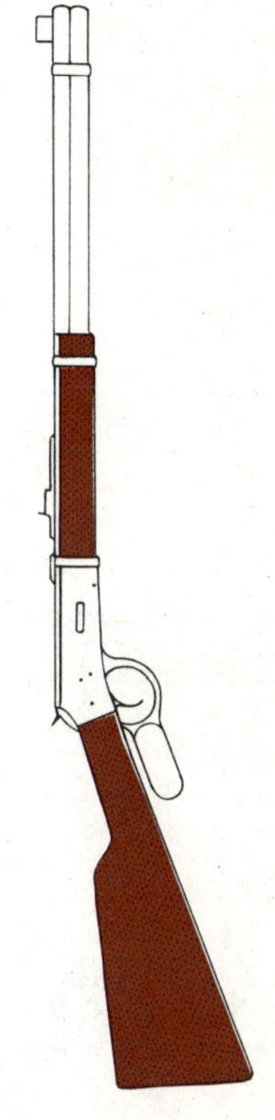

carbine

cardinal

caribou

carousel

carp

cardinal number. Any number that tells how many but not in what order the number comes: Three and seven are *cardinal numbers;* third and seventh are not.

care (KAIR) *noun.* 1. Worry; concern: Dad doesn't always share his *cares* and troubles with the family. 2. Watchfulness; attention: You should use *care* when lighting a fire. 3. Protection; charge; custody: The sick girl was placed under the *care* of the school nurse. **cares** —*verb.* 1. To be concerned about or interested in. 2. To desire or want: I don't *care* to go to the movies. **cared, caring.**

ca·reer (kə-RIHR) *noun.* 1. An occupation; a job or life's work. 2. A person's progress or passage through life or a part of his life: George Washington's *career* was a fascinating and successful one.

care·free (KAIR-free) *adjective.* Without care or worry; cheerful.

care·ful (KAIR-fəl) *adjective.* 1. Attentive; cautious: Ginny was *careful* in carrying the baby. 2. Done with care or accuracy: Ray did a *careful* job of painting his model plane. —**carefully** *adverb.*

care·less (KAYR-liss) *adjective.* 1. Inattentive; not watchful or cautious. 2. Done without care or accuracy: The lazy student did a *careless* job on his project. —**carelessly** *adverb.*

ca·ress (kə-RESS) *noun.* A gentle embrace, touch, or kiss indicating love or affection. **caresses.** —*verb.* To embrace, stroke, or touch gently. **caressed, caressing.**

care·tak·er (KAIR-tay-kər) *noun.* A person who takes care of a place, or thing; a watchman.

car·fare (KAHR-fair) *noun.* The money needed to ride on a bus or other public transportation. **carfares.**

car·go (KAHR-goh) *noun.* Goods or freight carried by a ship, airplane, or other type of transport. —**cargoes** or **cargos** *plural.*

car·hop (KAHR-hop) *noun.* A waitress or waiter at a drive-in restaurant.

car·i·bou (KA-rə-boo) *noun.* A large North American reindeer. —**caribou** or **caribous** *plural.*

car·il·lon (KA-rə-lon or kə-RIL-yən) *noun.* A set of bells, usually in a church or tower, on which melodies are played.

car·nage (KAHR-nij) *noun.* Slaughter; widespread killing or bloodshed.

car·na·tion (kahr-NAY-shən) *noun.* 1. A fragrant flower with fringed petals. 2. A pink or light-red color.

car·ni·val (KAHR-nə-vəl) *noun.* 1. A show or entertainment including games, rides, and exhibits, or a traveling group that puts on a show of this kind. 2. An occasion or period of celebration: Mardi Gras is the last *carnival* before Easter.

car·niv·or·ous (kahr-NIV-ər-əss) *adjective.* Meat-eating; feeding on flesh: The lion is *carnivorous.*

car·ol (KA-rəl) *noun.* A joyful song or hymn, especially a Christmas song. —*verb.* To sing a joyful song or hymn, especially a Christmas song. **caroled, caroling.**

car·ou·sel (ka-rə-SEL) Also **carrousel** *noun.* A merry-go-round.

carp (KAHRP) *noun.* A large, freshwater fish. —**carp** or **carps** *plural.* —*verb.* To complain unfairly; criticize. **carped, carping.**

car·pen·ter (KAHR-pən-tər) *noun.* A workman who builds or repairs things or buildings made of wood. —**carpentry** *noun.*

car·pet (KAHR-pit) *noun.* 1. A thick fabric used to cover a floor; a rug. 2. Anything resembling a rug in appearance: a *carpet* of snow. —*verb.* To cover, especially with a rug: The workmen *carpeted* the stairway. **carpeted, carpeting.**

car·port (KAHR-port) *noun.* A roofed

shelter for an automobile, usually extending from a house and having three sides open.

car·riage (KA-rij) *noun.* 1. A vehicle for carrying people, usually drawn by a horse. 2. Posture; bearing; a way of holding oneself erect. 3. A moving machine part that acts as a support for some other part: the typewriter's *carriage.* **carriages.**

car·ri·er (KA-ree-ər) *noun.* 1. An aircraft carrier; a naval ship with a deck designed for aircraft to take off and land. 2. A person, animal, or thing that spreads disease. 3. A person, thing, or group that carries or transports.

car·ri·on (KA-ree-ən) *noun.* The rotting or decayed flesh of a dead body.

car·rot (KA-rət) *noun.* 1. An edible orange-colored root. 2. The plant that grows with such a root.

car·ry (KA-ree) *verb.* 1. To transport; take from one place to another. 2. To transmit; act as a conductor for: The wires *carried* the electricity. 3. To hold or support: The woman *carried* her child in her arms. 4. To go over a distance: Randy's shouts *carried* across the lake. 5. To win or gain the support of: The man running for governor *carried* the largest city in the state. 6. To keep on hand. **carried, carrying.** —**carry out.** To complete.

carsick (KAHR-sik) *adjective.* Feeling ill as the result of the motion of an automobile.

cart (KAHRT) *noun.* Any wagon for moving freight or carrying passengers. *—verb.* To carry, especially in a wagon. **carted, carting.**

car·ti·lage (KAHR-tə-lij or KAHRT-lij) *noun.* A tough, flexible substance that forms part of the bodies of man and animals; gristle.

car·ton (KAHRT-n) *noun.* A box made of cardboard.

car·toon (kahr-TOON) *noun.* 1. A drawing or sketch intended to amuse or to present an idea about politics and other current events. 2. A comic strip or panel. 3. A short, funny motion picture.

car·tridge (KAHR-trij) *noun.* 1. A small cylinder or case that contains gunpowder and usually a bullet or pellets. 2. Any small container, especially one inserted into a mechanical device: a *cartridge* of film. **cartridges.**

cart·wheel (KAHRT-hweel) *noun.* 1. The wheel of a cart or wagon. 2. A handspring done sideways with arms and legs extended so as to suggest a wheel in motion.

carve (KAHRV) *verb.* 1. To slice; cut into slices. 2. To form or decorate by cutting: The artist *carved* a statue of marble. **carved, carving.**

cas·cade (kass-KAYD) *noun.* 1. A small waterfall or series of waterfalls. 2. Anything resembling a waterfall in appearance. **cascades.** *—verb.* To fall in a shower; pour down. **cascaded, cascading.**

case (KAYSS) *noun.* 1. A protective covering: Jim put his glasses in a leather *case.* 2. A box or container: The books were packed in a wooden *case.* 3. A physical condition: Barbara has a *case* of the mumps. 4. A situation, example, or occurrence: Their dispute was a *case* of misunderstanding. 5. An affair that requires examination or judgment: The detective solved the murder *case.* 6. An argument or position: The lawyer presented her *case* to the jury. 7. (Grammar) A form that shows the use of a word or its relationship to other words in a sentence: The subject of a sentence is in the nominative *case.* **cases.** *—verb.* 1. To pack in a container; enclose. 2. (Slang) To look over; examine; The thieves *cased* the store before they robbed it. **cased, casing.**

carrot

cartwheel

cascade

cashew

castle

casserole

cat

case·ment (KAYSS-mənt) *noun.* A window or window frame that opens on hinges.

cash (KASH) *noun.* Money; currency; bills and coins. *—verb.* To give or receive money in exchange for a check, bond, or other certificate. **cashed, cashing.**

cash·ew (KASH-oo) *noun.* An edible nut or the tropical tree on which it grows.

cash·ier (ka-SHIHR) *noun.* A person whose job it is to handle money in a bank, office, or store. *—verb.* To fire or dismiss, especially in disgrace. **cashiered, cashiering.**

cash·mere (KAZH-mihr or KASH-mihr) *noun.* A fine, soft wool or woolen fabric.

cask (KASK) *noun.* A barrel, made in various sizes and used especially for holding liquids.

cas·ket (KASS-kit) *noun.* 1. A coffin. 2. A small chest or container, often used to hold jewelry.

cas·se·role (KASS-ə-rohl) *noun.* 1. A dish, usually with a cover, in which foods are baked. 2. Food baked and served in a deep dish. **casseroles.**

cas·sette (ka-SET) *noun.* A cartridge-like case for sound tape or camera film. **cassettes.**

cast (KAST) *verb.* 1. To throw or toss. 2. To form or shape in a mold: The artist *cast* the figure in bronze. 3. To direct; send; point: The lighthouse *cast* its beam across the bay. 4. To record (a ballot): Dad *cast* a vote for the new candidate. 5. To select (a performer) for a play or movie. **cast, casting.** *—noun.* 1. A hard covering worn (on part of the body) to protect a damaged bone. 2. A group of performers (in a play or movie). 3. A toss from a fishing rod of a line with lure or bait. 4. Something formed in a mold: a bronze *cast* of President Kennedy.

caste (KAST) *noun.* Any of the Hindu social classes into which the people of India were traditionally divided. **castes.**

cas·ter (KASS-tər) Also **castor** *noun.* One of a set of small wheels attached to the bottom of furniture to make movement easier.

cas·ti·gate (KASS-tə-gayt) *verb.* To criticize or scold severely; punish. **castigated, castigating.**

cas·tle (KASS-l) *noun.* 1. A large building or group of buildings, usually with towers, constructed in medieval times as a fortification against attack. 2. A palace or an impressive residence that resembles a medieval castle. 3. One of the pieces in the game of chess; a rook. **castles.** *—verb.* (Chess) To move the king two squares toward the rook and, in the same move, the rook to the square next past the king. **castled, castling.**

castor oil. A vegetable oil used as a laxative or lubricant.

ca·su·al (KAZH-oo-əl) *adjective.* 1. Not careful or serious; careless. 2. Informal, relaxed; easygoing. 3. Occurring by chance or accident: They became good friends after a *casual* meeting at school. —**casually** *adverb.*

cas·u·al·ty (KAZH-oo-əl-tee) *noun.* 1. A severe accident or misfortune. 2. A person hurt or killed, or something destroyed in an accident or misfortune. 3. A soldier or sailor who suffers injury or death in war. **casualties.**

cat (KAT) *noun.* 1. A small, smooth-furred animal commonly kept as a pet. 2. A meat-eating mammal of the cat family including lions, leopards, and tigers. 3. (Slang) A sharp or dapper person.

cat·a·log (KAT-l-awg) Also **catalogue** *noun.* 1. A list or file, often in alphabetical order, indicating names or showing what is contained or available: The librarian looked for the title in the card *catalog.* 2. A book or booklet providing names, or listing or picturing things that are available. —*verb.* To arrange a list of names or things that are available. **cataloged, cataloging.**

cat·a·pult (KAT-ə-puhlt) *noun.* 1. A machine used in ancient warfare for hurling boulders, stones, or arrows. 2. A powerful machine used to launch planes from the deck of an aircraft carrier or other ship. —*verb.* To hurl as though from a catapult. **catapulted, catapulting.**

cat·a·ract (KAT-ə-rakt) *noun.* 1. A large or high waterfall. 2. A downpour; a flood. 3. A condition of the eye in which the lens becomes clouded, causing partial or complete blindness.

ca·tas·tro·phe (kə-TASS-trə-fee) *noun.* A sudden, severe, or widespread calamity or misfortune: The tornado was a *catastrophe* to the town, destroying many homes. **catastrophes.** —**catastrophic** (kat-ə-STROF-ik) *adjective.*

cat·bird (KAT-berd) *noun.* A gray songbird of North America that makes a sound like a cat.

catch (KACH) *verb.* 1. To capture or seize. 2. To trap or hook: Dad tried to *catch* the mole that was digging through our yard. 3. To grasp; hold on to: The shortstop couldn't *catch* the fly ball. 4. To reach in time to get on: Did Dad *catch* the plane? 5. To surprise or find in an act or condition: The teacher often *catches* Ralph sleeping in class. 6. To get (an infection or sickness). 7. (Informal) Hear; understand: I didn't *catch* the teacher's explanation. **caught, catching.** —*noun.* 1. The act of catching. 2. An amount taken, trapped, or hooked: Tom brought home a big *catch* of trout. 3. A game of throwing and catching a ball. 4. A fastener: Mother opened the *catch* on the cupboard door. 5. (Informal) A special condition or requirement; a loophole: The boat is inexpensive, but there's a *catch*—delivery takes three months. **catches.** —**catch on.** (Informal) 1. To understand; grasp; learn. 2. To become popular or stylish. —**catch up.** 1. To overtake; come up to or even with: The football player will *catch up* with the ball carrier and tackle him. 2. To regain a position; come even with what is expected or needed: The student tried to *catch up* on his history assignments before the exam. 3. To interest or involve: The fans were *caught up* in the excitement of the basketball game.

catapult

catch·er (KACH-ər) *noun.* A baseball player who squats behind home plate to catch the pitcher's throws.

cat·e·chism (KAT-ə-kiz-əm) *noun.* 1. A book of instruction about religion written in the form of questions and answers. 2. Instructions in the beliefs or principles of a religion.

cat·e·gor·y (KAT-ə-gor-ee) *noun.* A division, type, or class in a listing or system: That section of the library contains two *categories* of books, novels and biographies. **categories.**

catbird

ca·ter (KAY-tər) *verb.* 1. To supply food, and often servers and equipment, for a dinner, banquet, or similar affair. 2. To supply anything that pleases or satisfies: Mother *catered* to Mimi's every whim. **catered, catering.**

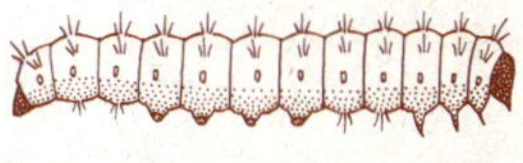
caterpillar

cat·er·pil·lar (KAT-ər-pil-ər) *noun.* A wormlike creature that is actually the larva of a butterfly, moth, or other insect.

cat·fish (KAT-fish) *noun.* Any of several types of scaleless fish having whisker-like feelers near the mouth. —**catfish** or **catfishes** *plural.*

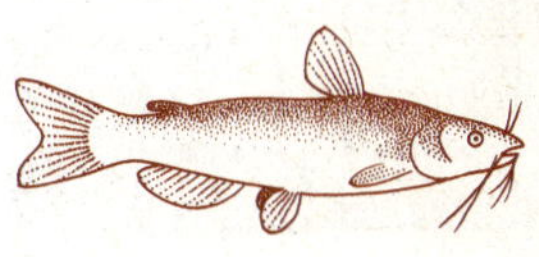
catfish

cattail

cauliflower

cavern

ca·the·dral (kə-THEE-drəl) *noun.* 1. A large or especially important church. 2. The main church in a bishop's area of authority.

cath·ode (KATH-ohd) *noun.* In a battery or other source of electrical current, the electrode or terminal with a negative electrical charge.

cath·o·lic (KATH-lik or KATH-ə-lik) *adjective.* 1. [Capital C] Of or descended from the original, united Christian church: *Catholic* churches today include the Roman Catholic, Eastern Orthodox, and Anglican churches. 2. Widespread; tolerant; involving or including all: Olga has very *catholic* interests in music; she likes opera, jazz, and popular music. *—noun.* [Capital C] A member of a Catholic church.

cat·nip (KAT-nip) *noun.* A plant of the mint family that has an odor that cats like.

cat·sup (KECH-əp, KACH-əp, or KAT-səp) Also **ketchup** *noun.* A thick sauce for hot dogs, hamburgers, and other foods, usually made from tomatoes and spices.

cat·tail (KAT-tayl) *noun.* Any of several types of reeds or marsh plants, often with long furry spikes or clusters at the ends of their stems.

cat·tle (KAT-l) *noun, plural.* Animals such as cows, bulls, or oxen.

cat·walk (KAT-wawk) *noun.* A narrow passageway, usually for workmen, on or connected to a bridge, ship, or other structure.

Cau·ca·sian (kaw-KAY-zhən) *noun.* A member of a race with skin tone that ranges from white to brown.

caught (KAWT) *verb. See* **catch.**

cau·li·flow·er (KAW-li-flow-ər) *noun.* A plant whose white flower center is used as a vegetable.

cause (KAWZ) *noun.* 1. Something that produces (an effect) or makes (a thing) happen: Not studying for his exams was the *cause* of Gene's failure. 2. A special purpose or idea pursued by a person or a group: Aid to education is a worthy *cause.* **causes.** *—verb.* To produce (an effect) or make (a thing) happen. **caused, causing.**

cause·way (KAWZ-way) *noun.* 1. A road built above a marsh or other wet area. 2. A highway.

cau·tion (KAW-shən) *noun.* 1. Care about one's safety or welfare; watchfulness. 2. A warning. *—verb.* To warn. **cautioned, cautioning.**

cau·tious (KAW-shəss) *adjective.* Careful; watchful. **—cautiously** *adverb.*

cav·al·cade (KAV-əl-kayd) *noun.* A procession, parade, or ceremony, especially one involving riders on horseback. **cavalcades.**

cav·al·ry (KAV-əl-ree) *noun.* 1. Horse-borne soldiers. 2. In modern warfare, units equipped with tanks, helicopters, or other armored vehicles: the air *cavalry.*

cave (KAYV) *noun.* A hollow space under the ground or in the side of a hill or mountain. **caves. —cave in.** To collapse; fall in.

cave man. A member of one of the races of savages who lived in caves in prehistoric times.

cav·ern (KAV-ərn) *noun.* A large cave. **—cavernous** *adjective.*

cav·i·ar (KAV-ee-ahr) *noun.* Fish eggs eaten as a food delicacy.

cav·i·ty (KAV-ə-tee) *noun.* 1. A hole; a hollow area. 2. A hole in a tooth caused by decay. **cavities.**

ca·vort (kə-VORT) *verb.* To prance about; to caper. **cavorted, cavorting.**

cay (KEE) *noun.* A reef or small island.

c.c. *abbreviation.* 1. Carbon copy. 2. Cubic centimeter.

cease (SEESS) *verb.* To stop; end. **ceased, ceasing.**

cease-fire (SEESS-FIGHR) *noun.* A period during which armed conflict is stopped; a truce.

cease•less (SEESS-liss) *adjective.* Without stopping or ending. —**ceaselessly** *adverb.*

ce•dar (SEE-dər) *noun.* 1. A type of evergreen tree. 2. The wood from this tree.

cede (SEED) *verb.* To yield; give over to another. **ceded, ceding.**

ceil•ing (SEE-ling) *noun.* 1. The overhead part of a room. 2. The upper limit; a maximum: The government put a *ceiling* on the price of steel. 3. The greatest height an aircraft can reach considering cloud cover or other conditions.

cel•e•brate (SEL-ə-brayt) *verb.* 1. To have a party or festive affair. 2. To honor happily: We *celebrated* Dad's birthday with a party. 3. To conduct (a religious service). **celebrated, celebrating.**

cel•e•brat•ed (SEL-ə-brayt-id) *adjective.* Famous; honored.

cel•e•bra•tion (sel-ə-BRAY-shən) *noun.* A festivity, a merry occasion; a religious service or ritual.

ce•leb•ri•ty (sə-LEB-rə-tee) *noun.* 1. A well-known or honored person. 2. Fame; popularity. **celebrities.**

cel•er•y (SEL-ər-ee) *noun.* A plant with crisp stalks used as a vegetable.

celestial navigation. (sə-LESS-chəl nav-ə-GAY-shən). Determining the course and position of a vessel, aircraft, or spacecraft by reference to sun, stars, or planets.

cell (SEL) *noun.* 1. A small room, especially one where a prisoner is confined. 2. One of the very small units that make up the living tissue of plants and animals. 3. A small hollow or cavity, usually one of many others in some object: *cells* in a honeycomb. 4. A device or structure that gives off electricity through the action of chemicals: *cells* of an automobile battery. —**cellular** *adjective.*

cel•lar (SEL-ər) *noun.* An underground room or area often used for storage; a room or area beneath a dwelling.

cel•list (CHEL-ist) *noun.* A musician who plays a cello.

cel•lo (CHEL-oh) Also **violoncello** (VEE-ə-lən-CHEL-oh) *noun.* A large, stringed musical instrument. **cellos.**

cel•lo•phane (SEL-ə-fayn) *noun.* A thin transparent material used for wrapping.

cel•lu•lose (SEL-yə-lohss) *noun.* A substance found in plants and important in the manufacture of paper and many other products.

Cel•si•us (SEL-see-əss or SEL-shəss) *adjective.* The new name for the temperature scale formerly called "centigrade."

ce•ment (si-MENT) *noun.* 1. A substance made from clay and limestone and mixed with sand and water, commonly used in paving, bricklaying, and other building processes. 2. A sticky substance that joins things together when it hardens. —*verb.* 1. To pave or build with cement. 2. To fasten together with a sticky substance; to glue. **cemented, cementing.**

cem•e•tery (SEM-ə-tehr-ee) *noun.* A place for burial; a graveyard. **cemeteries.**

cen•sor (SEN-sər) *noun.* A person whose job it is to examine movies, letters, books, or other works in order to remove any parts considered harmful or unsuitable. —*verb.* To remove harmful or unsuitable parts of a work. **censored, censoring.**

cedar

cello

cemetery

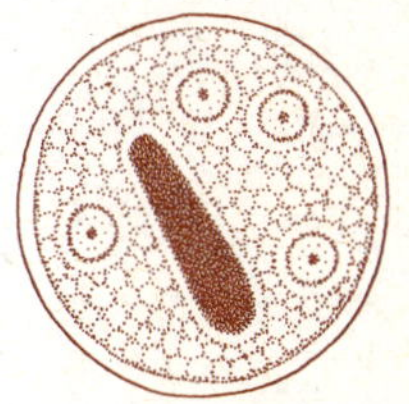

cell

cen·sor·ship (SEN-sər-ship) *noun.* The act of removing objectionable parts of a work.

cen·sure (SEN-shər) *noun.* Strong disapproval; blame; hostile criticism. —*verb.* To blame; express disapproval of. **censured, censuring.**

cen·sus (SEN-səss) *noun.* An official survey made to count the number of people living in an area and to gather information about them. **censuses.**

cent (SENT) *noun.* A penny; in the U.S. a coin worth $\frac{1}{100}$ of a dollar.

centaur

cen·taur (SEN-tor) *noun.* A creature in Greek myth that had the head, chest, and arms of a man and the body and legs of a horse.

cen·ten·ni·al (sen-TEN-ee-əl) *noun.* A 100th anniversary: The United States had its *centennial* in 1876.

cen·ter (SEN-tər) *noun.* 1. A point within a circle or sphere that is the same distance from all other points; a midpoint: A hub is at the *center* of a wheel. 2. The part, section, or point that is in the middle: The actor stood at the *center* of the stage. 3. A person or thing that is a cause of attention or concern: The pretty girl was the *center* of attention at the dance. 4. A place that is a main area for an activity: New York is a *center* for fashion. 5. A player's position in certain sports. —*verb.* 1. To place in the middle. 2. To direct (one's main efforts or interests): The army *centered* its attack near the bridge. **centered, centering.**

center of gravity. The point in an object at which its weight seems to be centered: A body will balance perfectly if supported at its *center of gravity.*

cen·ti- *prefix.* Indicates a hundredth: *centi*grade, *centi*gram.

cen·ti·grade (SEN-tə-grayd) *adjective.* Related to a system of measuring heat in which the freezing point of pure water is 0 degrees and the boiling point of pure water is 100 degrees. *See* **Celsius.**

cen·ti·meter (SEN-tə-mee-tər) Also **centimetre** *noun.* A unit of measure of distance that equals .3937 inch or .01 meter.

cen·ti·pede (SEN-tə-peed) *noun.* Any of various wormlike creatures with many pairs of legs. **centipedes.**

cen·tral (SEN-trəl) *adjective.* 1. At or near the center. 2. Main; principal: the *central* idea of a speech. —**centrally** *adverb.*

Central America. The area of North America that lies between Mexico and South America.

central nervous system. The main part of the nervous system, made up of the spinal cord and the brain.

cen·trif·u·gal (sen-TRIF-yə-gəl) *adjective.* Tending to move or be drawn away from an axis or center of rotation: If you whirl a stone at the end of a string, it is *centrifugal* force that pulls the string straight.

cen·tri·fuge (SEN-trə-fyooj) *noun.* A machine that spins rapidly to separate one substance from another. **centrifuges.**

cen·trip·e·tal (sen-TRIP-ət-l) *adjective.* Moving or being drawn toward a center of rotation, or spinning: Gravity is one kind of *centripetal* force.

cen·tu·ry (SEN-chə-ree) *noun.* A period of 100 years. **centuries.**

ce·ram·ics (sə-RAM-iks) *noun, plural.* 1. (*Used with a singular verb.*) The art or process of making pottery, porcelain, or similar products from clay. 2. Pottery, porcelain, or similar products made in this manner.

ce·re·al (SIHR-ee-əl) *noun.* 1. Any of various types of grain, like wheat, rice, and oats, or the plants or grasses bearing such grain. 2. A type of food made from grain.

cer·e·bel·lum (sehr-ə-BEL-əm) *noun.* A round section of the brain that is involved with balance and muscle movement. —**cerebellums** or **cerebella** *plural.*

ce·re·bral (sə-REE-brəl or SEHR-ə-brəl) *adjective.* 1. Of or related to the brain. 2. Appealing to or related to the intellect or mind.

ce·re·brum (sə-REE-brəm or SEHR-ə-brəm) *noun.* The section of the brain involved in the voluntary movement of muscles and in the organization of mental activities. —**cerebrums** or **cerebra** (sə-REE-brə) *plural.*

cer·e·mo·ni·al (sehr-ə-MOH-nee-əl) *adjective.* Of or related to ceremony; formal; stately. —**ceremonially** *adverb.*

cer·e·mo·ny (SEHR-ə-moh-nee) *noun.* 1. A formal occasion or a ritual, or the observances required by such a ritual. 2. Formal behavior; a polite manner of acting. **ceremonies.** —**ceremonious** *adjective.*

cer·tain (SERT-n) *adjective.* 1. Positive; sure. 2. Reliable; established. 3. Sure to happen. 4. Some; particular: Tim dislikes *certain* foods. —**certainly** *adverb.*

cer·tain·ty (SERT-n-tee) *noun.* 1. The state of being positive or sure. 2. That which is true, definite, or sure. **certainties.**

cer·tif·i·cate (sər-TIF-i-kit) *noun.* An official written statement or a document that gives proof of a condition, quality, or fact: a birth *certificate.* **certificates.**

cer·ti·fy (SER-tə-figh) *verb.* To issue a certificate or make or write a statement that something is true or proper. **certified, certifying.**

ces·sa·tion (se-SAY-shən) *noun.* A stop or end; a ceasing.

cess·pool (SESS-pool) *noun.* A covered pit into which sewage drains.

chafe (CHAYF) *verb.* 1. To rub; cause soreness or irritation by rubbing. 2. To be angry or very annoyed. 3. To make (someone) angry. **chafed, chafing.**

chaff (CHAF) *noun.* 1. Outer parts of grain that are separated from the seeds during threshing. 2. Anything worthless or of little value.

cha·grin (shə-GRIN) *noun.* A feeling of shame or disappointment.

chain (CHAYN) *noun.* 1. A series of connected links, usually of metal, used especially for hauling or binding. 2. (Plural) Bonds or captivity. 3. Any series of similar or connected objects or incidents: a *chain* of mountains. 4. A group or number of similar stores or businesses: a *chain* of restaurants throughout Texas. —*verb.* To connect or fasten with a chain. **chained, chaining.**

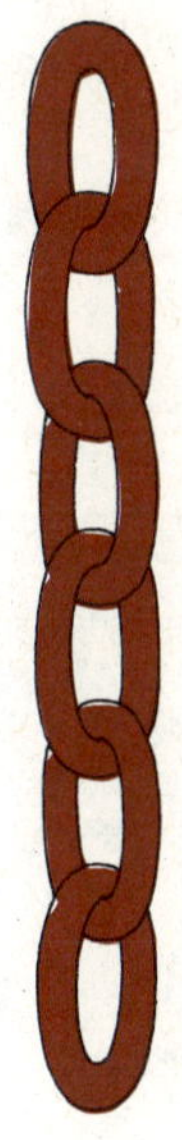

chain

chain reaction. Any series of events or actions in which each action results from one before it and causes another after it.

chain store. One of a number of similar stores operated by a single company or organization.

chair *noun.* 1. A seat with four legs, a back, and sometimes arms. 2. A position of authority or honor, or the person holding such a position. 3. A chairman: The *chair* announced a brief recess. —*verb.* To act as chairman. **chaired, chairing.**

chair·man (CHAIR-mən) *noun.* A person who runs a meeting or heads a committee. —**chairmen** *plural.*

cha·let (sha-LAY) *noun.* A house built in Swiss mountain style.

chal·ice (CHAL-iss) *noun.* A cup, especially one used for wine at Communion services. **chalices.**

chalk (CHAWK) *noun.* 1. A type of soft, white limestone. 2. A piece of white limestone or a substance like it used for writing or drawing,

chalice

chameleon

chandelier

especially on a blackboard. —*verb.* To mark, draw, or write on with chalk. **chalked, chalking.** —**chalk up.** To win or earn.

chal·lenge (CHAL-ənj) *noun.* 1. An offer to take part in a fight or contest: a *challenge* to a chess game. 2. A questioning; a demand for evidence or proof. **challenges.** —*verb.* 1. To offer to engage in a contest of any type. 2. To question the correctness of or to demand evidence for. **challenged, challenging.**

cham·ber (CHAYM-bər) *noun.* 1. A room, especially a bedroom. 2. A judge's office. 3. A meeting hall: the senate *chamber.* 4. A body of lawmakers or some other special council or committee: the *Chamber* of Commerce. 5. An enclosed space: the *chamber* of a rifle.

cha·me·leon (kə-MEEL-yən) *noun.* 1. A lizard whose skin changes color to blend in with its surroundings. 2. A changeable, unreliable, or inconstant person.

cham·ois (SHAM-ee) *noun.* 1. A small antelope that resembles a goat. 2. The soft leather of the chamois. —**chamois** (SHAM-eez) *plural.*

champ *noun.* (Informal) A champion. —*verb.* To chew noisily; to munch. **champed, champing.**

cham·pi·on (CHAM-pee-ən) *noun.* 1. A person who beats all others in a contest or competition. 2. One who fights for or supports a belief, person, or cause. —*verb.* To fight for or support (a belief, person, or cause). **championed, championing.**

cham·pi·on·ship (CHAM-pee-ən-ship) *noun.* The honor or state of being champion.

chance (CHANSS) *noun.* 1. Luck, fortune. 2. An opportunity: a *chance* to go to college. 3. Possibility: a *chance* that it may rain. 4. A risk or gamble. 5. A ticket or share in a raffle or lottery. **chances.** —*adjective.* Accidental: The meeting of the two friends was a *chance* occurrence. —*verb.* 1. To do or occur by accident: They *chanced* to meet. 2. To risk or gamble. **chanced, chancing.**

chan·cel·lor (CHAN-səl-ər or CHAN-slər) *noun.* 1. A high official in a government, court, church, or university. 2. In some countries, the prime minister or leader of a government.

chan·de·lier (shan-də-LIHR) *noun.* A lighting fixture that hangs from a ceiling.

change (CHAYNJ) *verb.* 1. To alter; rearrange: The actor *changed* his appearance with a wig and a false beard. 2. To replace or switch: Jim *changed* from his good clothes to his old ones. 3. To go from one thing to another: The traveler *changed* planes in Chicago. 4. To exchange money: Joel *changed* his quarter for two dimes and a nickel. **changed, changing.** —*noun.* 1. A variation or alteration: We noticed a *change* in Tina's behavior. 2. A different condition, thing, or circumstance: The sunshine was a pleasant *change* from the rainy weather. 3. Coins or money returned when a larger sum than is needed is given in payment. **changes.**

change·a·ble (CHAYN-jə-bəl) *adjective.* Able or likely to change or alter. —**changeably** *adverb.*

chan·nel (CHAN-l) *noun.* 1. The deepest part or passage in a harbor or waterway. 2. A strait; a waterway between two larger bodies of water: the English *Channel.* 3. The bed or bottom of a river, stream, or other waterway. 4. Any means of passing, conducting, or communicating. 5. A television or radio broadcast band; a station. —*verb.* 1. To direct: He *channeled* his energies into helping the poor. 2. To make a channel. **channeled, channeling.**

chant *noun.* A song in which several words or syllables are sung on the same note, used especially in religious services. *—verb.* 1. To sing. 2. To pray or speak with a steady or unchanging tone of voice. **chanted, chanting.**

Cha·nu·kah (HAH-nə-kə) Also **Hanukkah** or **Hanukah** *noun.* A Jewish holiday celebrated in memory of the Maccabees' victory over the Syrians, also called the "Feast of Lights."

cha·os (KAY-OSS) *noun.* Extreme confusion or disorder: When the teacher returned to the classroom, she found it in a state of *chaos.*

cha·ot·ic (kay-OT-ik) *adjective.* Very confused or disorderly. —**chaotically** *adverb.*

chap *verb.* To make rough or cracked, as skin: The cold wind *chapped* Joan's hands and face. **chapped, chapping.** *—noun.* (Informal) A fellow; a boy or man.

chap·el (CHAP-əl) *noun.* 1. A small building for worship. 2. A separate room for worship within a larger church or other building.

chap·er·on (SHAP-ə-rohn) Also **chaperone** *noun.* An adult who accompanies or watches over a gathering of young people to be sure that proper behavior is maintained. *—verb.* To act as a chaperon. **chaperoned, chaperoning.**

chap·lain (CHAP-lin) *noun.* A clergyman assigned to serve a particular group, especially a military or naval unit.

chaps (CHAPS or SHAPS) *noun, plural.* Seatless leather pants worn over regular trousers to protect the legs; worn particularly by cowboys.

chap·ter (CHAP-tər) *noun.* 1. A main section or division of a book. 2. A local branch or unit of an organization: There is a *chapter* of the Red Cross in our city.

char·ac·ter (KA-rik-tər) *noun.* 1. A person's individual manner of thinking and acting; the qualities of a person or thing that make it different from another: A good sense of humor and a deep respect for others are part of Jane's *character.* 2. A person in a novel, play, or other work: Billy Bones is a *character* in *Treasure Island.* 3. Moral or spiritual quality; moral strength: It takes *character* to overcome temptation. 4. A type or kind; a distinctive manner; a characteristic: The tourist noticed the unusual *character* of the sunsets in that area. 5. A single letter, number, comma, or other mark used in writing, typing, or printing. 6. (Informal) An odd or unusual person.

char·ac·ter·is·tic (ka-rik-tə-RISS-tic) *noun.* A distinctive manner or quality; a trait; a feature: Playfulness is a *characteristic* of puppies. *—adjective.* Distinctive; typical. —**characteristically** *adverb.*

char·ac·ter·i·za·tion (ka-rik-tər-ə-ZAY-shən) *noun.* A portrayal; a presentation, as through writing or acting, of a person's characteristics: The author's *characterization* of Lincoln was one of the book's outstanding features.

char·ac·ter·ize (KA-rik-tə-righz) *verb.* 1. To be typical or characteristic of: Gentleness *characterized* the old woman. 2. To outline or describe the characteristics or features of (someone or something). **characterized, characterizing.**

cha·rades (shə-RAYDZ) *noun, plural in form but used with a singular verb.* A game in which one person pantomimes a word or expression and others try to guess what it is.

char·coal (CHAHR-kohl) *noun.* A black substance, used especially for fuel, made by partly burning wood in an oven where little air is present.

chapel

chaps

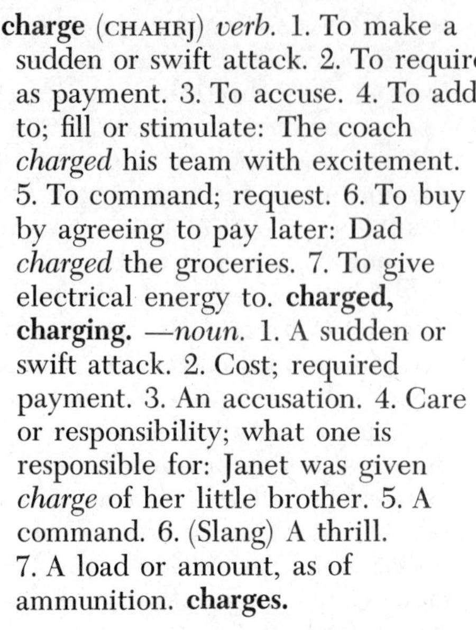

charge (CHAHRJ) *verb.* 1. To make a sudden or swift attack. 2. To require as payment. 3. To accuse. 4. To add to; fill or stimulate: The coach *charged* his team with excitement. 5. To command; request. 6. To buy by agreeing to pay later: Dad *charged* the groceries. 7. To give electrical energy to. **charged, charging.** —*noun.* 1. A sudden or swift attack. 2. Cost; required payment. 3. An accusation. 4. Care or responsibility; what one is responsible for: Janet was given *charge* of her little brother. 5. A command. 6. (Slang) A thrill. 7. A load or amount, as of ammunition. **charges.**

chariot

charg·er (CHAHR-jər) *noun.* 1. A horse trained to be ridden in battle. 2. A device for restoring energy to a storage battery.

char·i·ot (CHA-ree-ət) *noun.* A light, two-wheeled wagon drawn by one or more horses, used in ancient times for warfare, travel, or racing.

cha·ris·ma (kə-RIZ-mə) *noun.* Dynamic appeal or power, as of a magnetic leader.

char·i·ta·ble (CHA-ri-tə-bəl) *adjective.* 1. Kind; generous. 2. Related to an institution or process for giving aid or assistance. —**charitably** *adverb.*

char·i·ty (CHA-rə-tee) *noun.* 1. Generosity; a willingness to give aid or assistance. 2. Love or tolerance for others. 3. An institution or process for giving aid or assistance. **charities.**

charm (CHAHRM) *noun.* 1. Appeal; a pleasing or attractive quality: the *charm* of country life. 2. An object, action, or expression that is supposed to have a magic effect. 3. A trinket worn on a bracelet, necklace, or similar item. —*verb.* 1. To have a pleasing effect. 2. To use magic on. **charmed, charming.**

charm·ing (CHAHR-ming) *adjective.* Having charm; pleasing. —**charmingly** *adverb.*

chart (CHAHRT) *noun.* 1. A map, especially one used by sailors. 2. A list of information, diagrams, graphs, or similar material. —*verb.* 1. To make a map or a list of information or statistics. 2. To plan, especially to plan the course to be taken by a ship or plane. **charted, charting.**

char·ter (CHAHR-tər) *noun.* An official document setting forth the purpose, nature, and functions of an organization: the United Nations *charter.* —*verb.* 1. To grant or give a charter. 2. To hire: The school *chartered* two buses for the class trip. **chartered, chartering.**

chase (CHAYSS) *verb.* 1. To pursue; try to catch: The dog *chased* the squirrel. 2. To drive or scare away: The guard *chased* the children from the railroad tracks. **chased, chasing.** —*noun.* A pursuit; the act of trying to catch. **chases.**

chasm (KAZ-əm) *noun.* 1. A deep gap in the earth: The earthquake opened a *chasm* across the field. 2. Any gap, opening, or difference, as between opinions or ideas.

chas·sis (SHASS-ee or CHASS-ee) *noun.* 1. The supporting framework of an automobile, including the wheels and machinery. 2. The framework or the part that supports the body of any vehicle or other machine. —**chassis** (SHASS-eez) *plural.*

chaste (CHAYST) *adjective.* 1. Virtuous; pure. 2. Modest; refined; decent. 3. Simple in appearance; free from decoration. —**chastely** *adverb.*

chas·ten (CHAY-sn) *verb.* 1. To punish in order to correct or improve: The father *chastened* his son in the hope of changing his wild behavior. 2. To restrain, lessen; overcome: Life in the army *chastened* the young man's recklessness. **chasten, chastening.**

chas·tise (chass-TIGHZ) *verb.* To punish severely; to discipline or chasten. **chastised, chastising.**

chat *noun.* A relaxed or casual conversation. *—verb.* To talk in a casual way. **chatted, chatting.**

cha·teau (sha-TOH) *noun.* 1. A French castle. 2. An estate or country house, especially one in France. —**chateaux** (sha-TOHZ) *plural.*

chat·ter (CHAT-ər) *noun.* 1. Rapid talk, usually light or silly. 2. A rapid repetition of short noises, as from an animal or bird: a monkey's *chatter.* *—verb.* 1. To talk fast, especially in a light or silly conversation. 2. To make a series of short noises, like those made by an animal or bird. 3. To click together rapidly: The cold weather made Bob's teeth *chatter.* **chattered, chattering.**

chat·ty (CHAT-ee) *adjective.* Talkative; full of chatter. **chattier, chattiest.** —**chattily** *adverb.*

chauf·feur (SHOH-fər) *noun.* A person whose job it is to drive an automobile for someone else. *—verb.* To drive (others) in a car. **chauffeured, chauffering.**

cheap (CHEEP) *adjective.* 1. Low in price; inexpensive. 2. Inferior; low in quality. 3. Selfish; stingy. **cheaper, cheapest.** —**cheaply** *adverb.*

cheap·en (CHEE-pən) *verb.* To lower in price, value, or quality: The bright green paint on the house *cheapened* its appearance. **cheapened, cheapening.**

cheat (CHEET) *verb.* 1. To deceive or swindle; keep from someone what should be his. 2. To break the rules. **cheated, cheating.** *—noun.* 1. A fraud or swindle; a dishonest act. 2. A person who deceives, swindles, or breaks the rules.

check (CHEK) *noun.* 1. An examination or investigation. 2. A stopping or restraint: The rain was a *check* on our plans. 3. A bill in a restaurant, tavern, or similar place. 4. A financial form, often handwritten and always signed by hand, that serves as money. 5. A mark made to indicate that something has been examined, preferred, or corrected. 6. A pattern of squares or one of such squares: The tablecloth had red and white *checks.* *—verb.* 1. To examine or investigate. 2. To stop, restrain, or interfere with. 3. To indicate with a mark: The teacher *checked* the mistakes with a red pencil. 4. To store or keep temporarily: The customer *checked* his hat and coat. **checked, checking.**

chateau

check·er·board (CHEK-ər-bord) *noun.* A board or surface divided into 64 squares, usually alternating red and black, and used in playing checkers and chess.

check·ers (CHEK-ərz) *noun, plural in form but used with a singular verb.* A game played by two persons each of whom moves 12 disks about on a checkerboard.

check·mate (CHEK-mayt) Also **mate** *noun.* In the game of chess, a situation in which an opponent's king cannot escape capture, thereby ending the game. **checkmates.**

checkerboard

cheek *noun.* 1. The part of the face on either side of the nose. 2. Boldness; nerve; impudence.

cheep *noun.* A chirp or call like that made by a young bird. *—verb.* To chirp. **cheeped, cheeping.**

cheer (CHIHR) *noun.* 1. A shout or yell showing welcome, approval, or encouragement. 2. Happiness; joy. 3. Spirit; attitude: Be of good *cheer;* things are bound to get better. *—verb.* 1. To welcome, show gratitude, or encourage with shouts. 2. To cause happiness or joy. **cheered, cheering.**

cheer·ful (CHIHR-fəl) *adjective.* 1. Happy; full of cheer. 2. Bright and pleasant. —**cheerfully** *adverb.*

cheerleaders

cheetah

chef

chess

cheer·lead·er (CHIRH-lee-dər) *noun.* A person who directs the cheers at a sports event.

cheese (CHEEZ) *noun.* A solid food made from the milk of cows, goats or other animals. **cheeses.**

cheese·burg·er (CHEEZ-ber-gər) *noun.* A sandwich made of cooked ground beef and melted cheese.

cheese·cloth (CHEEZ-klawth) *noun.* A light, loosely woven cotton cloth.

chee·tah (CHEE-tə) *noun.* A large, very swift cat that resembles a leopard, found in Asia and Africa.

chef (SHEF) *noun.* A cook, especially one in charge of a restaurant's kitchen.

chem·i·cal (KEM-i-kəl) *adjective.* Of or related to chemistry. —*noun.* Any substance that results from or is used in the processes of chemistry. —**chemically** *adverb.*

chemical change. The change in a substance when its atoms join with or separate from atoms of another substance: When food is digested in the stomach, this is a *chemical change;* when water boils, this is not a *chemical change.* Also called "chemical reaction."

chem·ist (KEM-ist) *noun.* A person whose field of study or work is chemistry.

chem·is·try (KEM-iss-tree) *noun.* The science that is concerned with the make-up of substances, their characteristics, and the processes by which substances combine or are changed.

cher·ish (CHEHR-ish) *verb.* 1. To regard with love and devotion: Mother *cherishes* her family. 2. To hold in mind: *cherish* a dream. **cherished, cherishing.**

cher·ry (CHEHR-ee) *noun.* 1. Small, round fruit having a single, smooth pit. 2. The tree on which cherries grow. 3. (Also *adjective*) A bright-red color. **cherries.**

cher·ub (CHEHR-əb) *noun.* 1. An angel, usually pictured as a handsome child with wings. 2. A good-looking or well-behaved child. —**cherubs** or **cherubim** (CHER-ə-bim) *plural.*

chess *noun.* A game played by two people, each of whom moves 16 small figures about on a chessboard.

chest *noun.* 1. A box with a lid used for storing or carrying things. 2. The part of the body protected by the ribs; the front part of the body from neck to abdomen. 3. A piece of furniture, usually having drawers, used for storage; a bureau.

chest·nut (CHESS-nut) *noun.* 1. A nut with a prickly outer covering. 2. The tree on which chestnuts grow; the wood of such a tree. 3. (Also *adjective*) A reddish-brown color. 4. (Informal) A trite or overused expression, joke, or tale.

chew (CHOO) *verb.* 1. To bite or grind with the teeth. 2. To cut, break, or damage, as by tearing or shredding. **chewed, chewing.** —**chewy** *adjective.*

chewing gum. A sweetened combination of chicle and other substances that is pleasant to chew.

chic (SHEEK) *adjective.* Stylish or graceful; showing good taste.

Chi·can·o (chi-KON-oh) *noun.* An American of Mexican descent.

chick (CHIK) *noun.* 1. A young chicken or other young bird. 2. A child. 3. (Slang) A girl.

chick·a·dee (CHIK-ə-dee) *noun.* A small bird with black, white, and gray feathers. **chickadees.**

chick·en (CHIK-ən) *noun.* A bird or fowl, usually tame; hen or rooster. —*adjective.* (Slang) Timid or cowardly.

chicken pox. A childhood disease that causes a rash to appear on the skin.

chic·le (CHIK-əl) Also **chicle gum** *noun.* A gumlike substance taken from a tropical tree and used in making chewing gum.

chide (CHIGHD) *verb.* To scold, express disapproval. **chided, chiding.**

chief (CHEEF) *noun.* The head or leader of a group or organization. *—adjective.* Most important or highest in rank or position. **—chiefly** *adverb.*

chief·tain (CHEEF-tən) *noun.* The leader or head of a group or tribe.

chif·fon (shi-FON) *noun.* A thin cloth of silk, nylon, or similar material. *—adjective.* Having a light, frothy, or airy texture: Mother baked a lemon *chiffon* pie.

chig·ger (CHIG-ər) *noun.* A small insect whose larva attaches itself to the skin and causes itching.

Chi·hua·hua (chi-WAH-wah) *noun.* A tiny dog first bred in Mexico.

child (CHYLD) *noun.* 1. A young boy or girl. 2. A son or daughter. 3. An infant. **—children** (CHIL-drən) *plural.*

child·birth (CHYLD-berth) *noun.* The process of giving birth to a child.

child·hood (CHYLD-hud) *noun.* The state or period of being a child.

child·ish (CHYL-dish) *adjective.* Of or like a child; immature. **—childishly** *adverb.*

child's play. Something that can be done very easily.

chil·i (CHIL-ee) *noun.* 1. A pod that is dried and ground to make a hot pepper seasoning. 2. The plant on which this pod grows. 3. A hot pepper sauce. 4. Also **chili con carne.** A spicy food made from hot red pepper and meat, usually with beans added. **chilies.**

chill (CHIL) *noun.* 1. Mild coldness: a *chill* in the air. 2. A sudden feeling of cold through one's body: I had *chills* and a headache. *—verb.* 1. To cool; make mildly cold. 2. To cause disappointment; depress or displease. **chilled, chilling.** *—adjective.* Also **chilly.** 1. Mildly cold. 2. Unfriendly or displeased in manner. **—chillingly** *adverb.*

chime (CHIGHM) *noun.* 1. A bell or set of bells played by striking with one or more small hammers; sometimes played automatically. 2. The sound made by a chime or bell. **chimes.** *—verb.* To make such a sound. **chimed, chiming.**

chim·ney (CHIM-nee) *noun.* 1. A pipe or other structure through which smoke and fumes from a fire, stove, or furnace rise; a flue. 2. A glass cylinder or tube placed around the flame in a lantern or lamp.

chimp *noun.* (Informal) A chimpanzee.

chim·pan·zee (chim-pan-ZEE or chim-PAN-zee) *noun.* An ape found in Africa, larger than a monkey and smaller than a gorilla. **chimpanzees.**

chin *noun.* The front part of the lower jaw, beneath the lips. *—verb.* To raise oneself so that the chin is even with a bar from which one is hanging. **chinned, chinning.**

chi·na (CHIGH-nə) *noun.* A special type of porcelain or white, baked clay; the dishes and similar items made from this material.

chip *noun.* 1. A small piece, bit, or slice: The camper cut *chips* of wood to start his fire. 2. A cut or break in something where a piece is missing: The *chip* in the vase spoiled its appearance. 3. A token or disk used in playing games. *—verb.* 1. To break or slice off a piece or bit. 2. To be chipped or broken easily: The fine glasses will *chip* if they are treated roughly. **chipped, chipping. —chip in.** To share the cost or work. **—chip off the old block.** A person who is like one of his parents, especially a son who resembles his father.

chickens

Chihuahua

chimpanzee

chipmunk

choir

chopsticks

chip·munk (CHIP-muhngk) *noun.* A small squirrel-like striped rodent found in North America.

chirp (CHERP) *verb.* To make a short, sharp sound, like that of some insects and birds. **chirped, chirping.** —*noun.* A short, sharp sound.

chis·el (CHIZ-l) *noun.* A sharp tool used for chipping, shaving, or cutting stone, metal, or wood. —*verb.* 1. To cut with a chisel or other sharp tool. 2. (Slang) To swindle or cheat; get dishonestly. **chiseled, chiseling.** —**chiseler** *noun.*

chit·ter·lings (CHIT-linz) Also **chit·lins** or **chitlings** *noun, plural.* The small intestines of hogs, a "soul" food usually boiled and/or fried.

chiv·al·ry (SHIV-əl-ree) *noun.* 1. A system of conduct that stressed courage, honor, and courtesy to women, observed by knights in medieval times. 2. Courtesy; gallant and honorable behavior. **chivalries.** —**chivalrous** (SHIV-əl-rəss) *adjective.*

chlo·rine (KLOR-een) *noun.* A dangerously poisonous gas with a strong, unpleasant odor, used in making bleaches, purifying water, and other processes.

chlo·ro·form (KLOR-ə-form) *noun.* A colorless liquid used to cause unconsciousness. —*verb.* To make unconscious with chloroform. **chloroformed, chloroforming.**

chlo·ro·phyll (KLOR-ə-fil) Also **chlo·ro·phyl** *noun.* The green substance that enables plants to use sunlight to make food.

choc·o·late (CHOK-lit or CHOK-ə-lit) *noun.* 1. A candy, drink, or other food made from the roasted seeds or beans of the cacao plant. 2. (Also *adjective*) A dark-brown color. **chocolates.**

choice (CHOISS) *noun.* 1. Selection: The red dress was Joan's *choice* for the party. 2. A number or variety from which to select: a wide *choice* of magazines. **choices.** —*adjective.* Of the best quality; excellent: *choice* fruits and vegetables. **choicer, choicest.**

choir (KWIGHR) *noun.* 1. A group or organization of singers, especially one that sings for church services. 2. The part of a church provided for singers; a choir loft.

choke (CHOHK) *verb.* 1. To keep from breathing by blocking or squeezing the windpipe or throat; strangle. 2. To block or clog: Leaves *choked* the drainpipe. 3. To keep from growing or developing, as a plant, idea, or discussion: Weeds *choked* the young flowers. 4. To keep from showing; restrain: The little boy *choked* back his tears. **choked, choking.** —*noun.* A device that regulates the flow of air to a gasoline engine. **chokes.**

chol·er·a (KOL-ər-ə) *noun.* A serious disease, often fatal, that affects the stomach and intestines.

choose (CHOOZ) *verb.* To select; decide. **chose** (CHOHZ), **chosen** (CHOH-zən), **choosing.**

choos·y (CHOO-zee) *adjective.* (Informal) Fussy; hard to please. **choosier, choosiest.**

chop *verb.* 1. To cut, as with an ax or hatchet. 2. To cut into small pieces: Mother *chopped* up the celery. **chopped, chopping.** —*noun.* 1. A blow, especially with an ax or similar tool. 2. A cut or piece of meat: lamb *chops.* 3. (Plural) The jaws or the flesh between the jaws: The lion licked his *chops.*

chop·stick (CHOP-stik) *noun.* One of two narrow sticks held in one hand and used by Orientals to bring food to the mouth.

chord (KORD) *noun.* 1. A combination of musical tones made in harmony. 2. A feeling or emotion: The bitter remark struck a sensitive *chord.* 3. (Geometry) A straight line that joins two points on an arc.

chore (CHOR) *noun.* 1. An odd job or task. 2. A burden or difficulty: Studying is a *chore* for some students. **chores.**

cho·rus (KOR-əss) *noun.* 1. A group or organization of singers, a choir. 2. A song for a group of singers. 3. The part of certain songs that is repeated; a refrain. 4. A mixture or blending of voices or sounds: a *chorus* of cheers. **choruses.**

chow *noun.* 1. (Also **chow chow**) A dog, originally bred in China, of medium size having a thick coat of fur. 2. (Slang) Food.

chow·der (CHOW-dər) *noun.* A stew, usually made with fish or clams.

chris·ten (KRISS-n) *verb.* 1. To baptize as a Christian. 2. To give a name to, especially to a ship during a launching ceremony. **christened, christening.** —**christening** *noun.*

Christian (KRISS-chən) *noun* (and *adjective*). One who believes in Jesus Christ or follows a religion based on his teachings.

Christ·mas (KRISS-məss) *noun.* 1. A Christian holiday, occurring on December 25, that celebrates the birth of Jesus Christ. 2. A legal holiday, December 25, in the United States and other countries.

chro·mi·um (KROH-mee-əm) *noun.* A hard metal used in plating and in making alloys.

chro·mo·some (KROH-mə-sohm) *noun.* A part of the nucleus of plant and animal cells that transmits genetic traits from parent to offspring. **chromosomes.**

chron·ic (KRON-ik) *adjective.* 1. Lasting for a long time: a *chronic* illness. 2. Continual; habitual: a *chronic* complainer. —**chronically** *adverb.*

chron·i·cle (KRON-i-kəl) *noun.* A record of events listed in the order in which they occurred. **chronicles.** —*verb.* To write a history of events. **chronicled, chronicling.**

chron·o·log·i·cal (kron-ə-LOJ-i-kəl) Also **chronologic** *adjective.* Arranged in the order of occurrence: *chronological* order. —**chronologically** *adverb.*

chro·nom·e·ter (krə-NOM-ə-tər) *noun.* A very precise clock, watch, or other timepiece.

chrys·a·lis (KRISS-ə-liss) *noun.* 1. The stage of an insect's development when it is in a hard case or cocoon; the pupa stage. 2. An insect's cocoon. —**chrysalises** or **chrysalides** (kri-SAL-ə-deez) *plural.*

chry·san·the·mum (kri-SAN-thə-məm) *noun.* A large late-blooming flower, or the plant on which it grows.

chub·by (CHUHB-ee) *adjective.* Round and plump. **chubbier, chubbiest.**

chuck (CHUHK) *verb.* 1. To throw; hurl. 2. To pat; tap playfully: Grandpa *chucked* Bobby under his chin. 3. (Informal) To get rid of; throw away. **chucked, chucking.** —*noun.* 1. A throw or toss. 2. A pat or playful tap. 3. A shoulder cut or section of beef.

chuck·le (CHUHK-əl) *verb.* To laugh softly; laugh to oneself. **chuckled, chuckling.** —*noun.* A low laugh. **chuckles.**

chug (CHUHG) *verb.* To move with a repeated, deep, loud sound: The old tugboat *chugged* up the river. **chugged, chugging.** —*noun.* One of a series of dull, abrupt sounds.

chum (CHUHM) *noun.* A close friend; a buddy. —*verb.* To be friends. **chummed, chumming.**

chunk (CHUHNGK) *noun.* A thick piece or section.

church (CHERCH) *noun.* 1. A building for public worship. 2. [Capital C] A division or group of Christians: the Baptist *Church.* 3. A religious service: We were late for *church.* 4. [Capital C] Christianity; all Christians or Christian groups thought of together. **churches.**

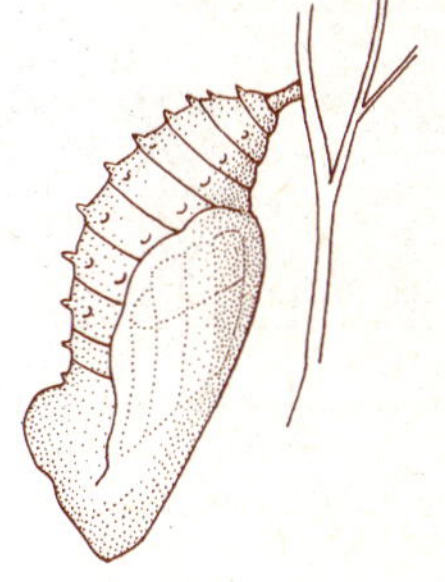

chrysalis

chrysanthemum

church

cicada

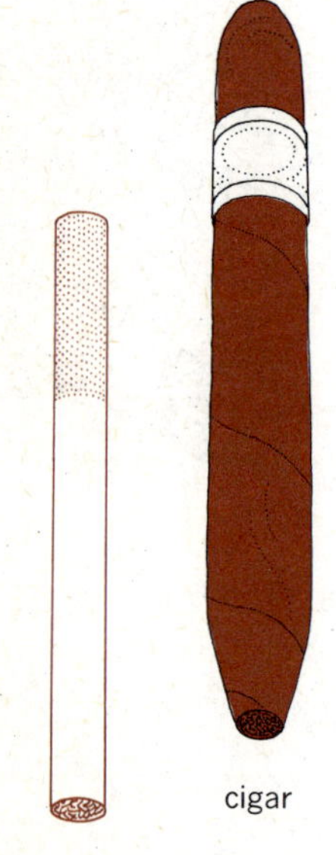
cigarette

cigar

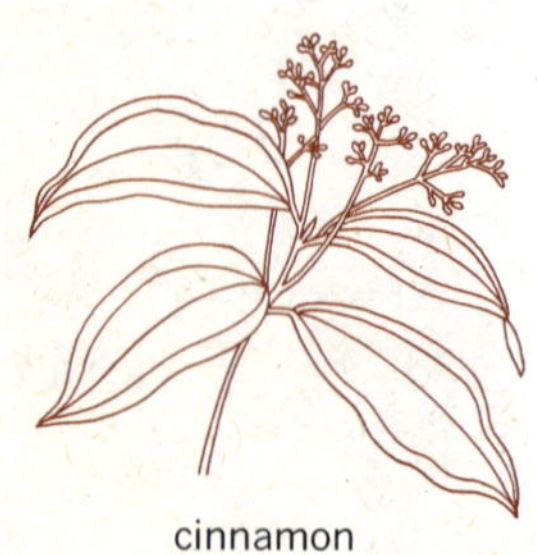
cinnamon

churn (CHERN) *verb.* 1. To stir up or cause to tumble and foam: The ship's propellers *churned* the water. 2. To make butter by stirring or whipping milk or cream. **churned, churning.** —*noun.* A device or container in which milk or cream is whipped or stirred into butter.

chute (SHOOT) *noun.* 1. A slope or channel down which things may flow, slide, or be rolled. 2. (Informal) A parachute. **chutes.**

ci·ca·da (si-KAY-də) *noun.* A large insect, the male of which is able to make a loud, long, high-pitched sound; a locust. —**cicadas** or **cicadae** (si-KAY-dee) *plural.*

-cide *suffix.* Indicating killing or a killer: infant*icide,* pesti*cide.*

ci·der (SIGH-dər) *noun.* A juice that is pressed out of apples, used as a sweet drink and for making vinegar.

ci·gar (si-GAHR) *noun.* Shredded tobacco rolled in a tobacco leaf for smoking.

cig·a·rette (sig-ə-RET) Also **cigaret** *noun.* Shredded tobacco held in a roll of thin paper for smoking. **cigarettes.**

cinch (SINCH) *noun.* 1. A strap that holds a pack or saddle in place. 2. (Slang) Something that is easy to do, or a person sure or able to do something. **cinches.** —*verb.* 1. To strap on. 2. (Slang) To make sure of; get a firm hold on: *cinch* the victory. **cinched, cinching.**

cin·der (SIN-dər) *noun.* A small, burned or partly burned piece of any hard fuel: When the coal fire burned out, only *cinders* were left.

cin·e·ma (SIN-ə-mə) *noun.* 1. A motion picture. 2. A theater for showing motion pictures. **cinemas.**

cin·na·mon (SIN-ə-mən) *noun.* 1. A reddish-brown spice made from the bark of a tree found in the East Indies; such a tree or its bark. 2. (Also *adjective*) A reddish-brown color.

ci·pher (SIGH-fər) *noun.* 1. A secret code; a special language used for sending a message. 2. A key or instruction for sending or understanding a code: The spy destroyed the *cipher.* 3. A zero; 0. —*verb.* 1. To do or work with arithmetic. 2. To write or put into coded form. **ciphered, ciphering.**

cir·cle (SER-kəl) *noun.* 1. A closed curve every point of which is the same distance from a point in the center; the area within such a curve. 2. A ring; a circular object or motion: The cowboy twirled his rope in a *circle.* 3. A group of people with a common interest or friendship: a *circle* of friends. **circles.** —*verb.* 1. To enclose in a circle: The ring *circled* her finger. 2. To go around: The plane *circled* the airport. **circled, circling.**

cir·cuit (SER-kit) *noun.* 1. The process of going around something: The ship's *circuit* of the island took three hours. 2. A path, line, or system of wires through which electricity flows. 3. A route taken or a pattern of places visited as part of a journey, tour, or business trip.

circuit breaker. A device that shuts off electric current when a circuit is dangerously overloaded.

cir·cu·lar (SER-kyə-lər) *adjective.* 1. Like or having the shape of a circle. 2. Moving in a circle: the *circular* movements of a hawk. —*noun.* A printed notice or advertisement distributed in large numbers.

cir·cu·late (SER-kyə-layt) *verb.* 1. To move (oneself or an object) around: Irene *circulated* the photos among her best friends. 2. To move through a circuit or in a circle: Blood *circulates* through the veins and arteries. **circulated, circulating.**

cir·cu·la·tion (ser-kyə-LAY-shən) *noun.* 1. Any act or process of circulating. 2. The passage of the blood through the heart, veins, and arteries of the body. 3. The number of magazines or other publications ordinarily sold by a company.

cir·cu·la·tory (SER-kyə-lə-tor-ee) *adjective.* Of or related to circulation, especially of blood.

circum- *prefix.* Indicating around or all about: *circum*navigate.

cir·cum·cise (SER-kəm-sighz) *verb.* To cut away a small covering of flesh from the penis, often as part of a religious ceremony. **circumcised, circumcising.**

cir·cum·fer·ence (sər-KUHM-fər-enss) *noun.* 1. The border or line that forms the edge of a circle or certain other areas. 2. The distance around a circle. **circumferences.**

cir·cum·scribe (ser-kəm-SKRIGHB) *verb.* 1. To draw a line or circle about something. 2. To restrict or limit: The activities of the students were *circumscribed* by strict new orders from the principal. **circumscribed, circumscribing.**

cir·cum·spect (SER-kəm-spekt) *adjective.* Watchful or cautious about all details; careful. —**circumspectly** *adverb.*

cir·cum·stance (SER-kəm-stanss) *noun.* A condition or occurrence that influences some act or event. **circumstances.**

cir·cus (SER-kəss) *noun.* A colorful show put on by a traveling group of clowns, acrobats, and other performers. **circuses.**

cir·rus (SIHR-əss) *noun.* A cloud formation, typically of high altitude with long, filmy white streaks. —**cirri** (SIHR-igh) *plural.*

cis·tern (SISS-tərn) *noun.* A tank or large container for storing water.

cit·a·del (SIT-ə-dl) *noun.* A fort, especially one protecting a city.

cite (SIGHT) *verb.* 1. To quote: *cite* a poem. 2. To use or refer to as an example. 3. To issue a statement praising someone for excellent accomplishments. **cited, citing.** —**citation** (sigh-TAY-shən) *noun.*

cit·i·zen (SIT-ə-zn) *noun.* 1. A person who by birth or choice is a member of a nation from which he receives certain rights and to which he owes loyalty. 2. A resident of a town, state, or county.

cit·i·zen·ship (SIT-ə-zn-ship) *noun.* 1. The state of being a citizen. 2. The rights and obligations of a citizen, or the manner in which one observes them: Voting is an act of good *citizenship.*

cit·rus (SIT-rəss) Also **citrous** *adjective.* Designating oranges, grapefruit, lemons, and similar fruit having thick rind and juicy flesh; the trees on which these fruits grow. —*noun.* A citrus tree or fruit. —**citruses** or **citrus** *plural.*

cit·y (SIT-ee) *noun.* 1. A large and important town. 2. All those who live in a large town. **cities.**

civ·et (SIV-it) *noun.* A flesh-eating catlike mammal; a civet cat.

civ·ic (SIV-ik) *adjective.* 1. Of or related to a city or town: *civic* problems. 2. Of or related to citizens or citizenship: Voting is a *civic* duty.

civ·il (SIV-əl) *adjective.* 1. Of or related to citizens or a society of citizens: *civil* war. 2. Polite; well-mannered; civilized. 3. Related to the usual concerns of citizens rather than to military or church concerns: *civil* law. —**civilly** *adverb.* —**civil liberties.** The freedom that a person possesses to use his rights as a citizen or resident. —**civil rights.** The rights or guarantees of personal freedom granted by the U.S. Constitution, especially by the Bill of Rights. —**civil war.** 1. A war between two factions or sides within the same country. 2. [Capital C and W] The war fought in the U.S., 1861–65, between North and South.

civet

cirrus

ci·vil·ian (sə-VIL-yən) *noun.* A person who is not a member of the armed forces.

civ·i·li·za·tion (siv-ə-lə-ZAY-shən) *noun.* 1. A condition of society that includes a high degree of development in agriculture, reading and writing, law, and art. 2. A people or nation having a highly developed society: the Inca *civilization.* 3. The process of becoming civilized.

civ·i·lize (SIV-ə-lighz) *verb.* To instruct in or help to bring about the conditions of civilization: The Romans helped to *civilize* many peoples. **civilized, civilizing.**

civil service. 1. Government operations or services not including lawmaking or judicial functions or activities of the armed forces: Tax collectors are members of the *civil service.* 2. A system for hiring people for government jobs according to merit.

claim (KLAYM) *verb.* 1. To seek a right; demand. 2. To contend, say, or hold to be true: John *claimed* that he could run faster than Bill. 3. To absorb or require: Homework *claimed* most of my time on Sunday evening. **claimed, claiming.** *—noun.* 1. A demand or that which is sought: a *claim* for insurance payment. 2. Something said to be true. 3. A piece of land that a person marks off or takes as rightfully his.

clair·voy·ance (klair-VOI-ənss) *noun.* The ability claimed by some to be able to see or perceive things far beyond their physical vision. **—clairvoyant** *adjective.*

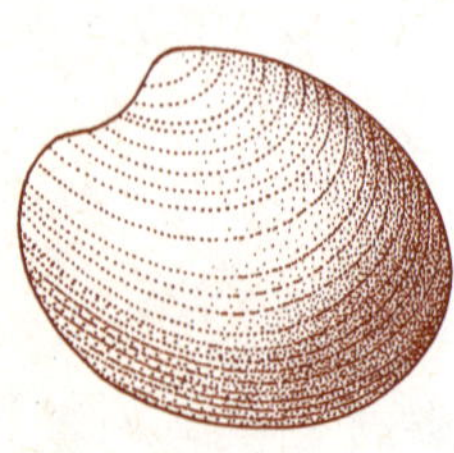
clam

clam (KLAM) *noun.* A common shellfish eaten raw or in various cooked dishes. *—verb.* To dig for clams. **clammed, clamming.**

clam·bake (KLAM-bayk) *noun.* A picnic at which clams and other foods are cooked and served.

clam·ber (KLAM-ər) *verb.* To climb, especially with difficulty, using both feet and hands: The soldiers *clambered* up the steep slope. **clambered, clambering.**

clam·my (KLAM-ee) *adjective.* Cold and sticky or damp: The walls of the deep cave were very *clammy.* **clammier, clammiest.**

clam·or (KLAM-ər) *noun.* 1. An uproar; a loud sound of shouting and confusion. 2. A loud demand or expression of protest: the workers' *clamor* for higher wages. *—verb.* To make an uproar or loud demand. **clamored, clamoring.**

clamp (KLAMP) *noun.* A device used to hold two or more things together. *—verb.* To fasten or hold together, especially with a mechanical device. **clamped, clamping. —clamp down.** (Informal) To become stricter: The teacher *clamped down* on the noisy class.

clan (KLAN) *noun.* 1. A group of relatives or related families. 2. A group of people with a common interest or bond.

clang (KLANG) *noun.* A sudden, sharp ringing sound, like that made by striking a bell. *—verb.* To make such a sound. **clanked, clanking.**

clank (KLANGK) *noun.* A short metallic sound. *—verb.* To make such a sound. **clanked, clanking.**

clap (KLAP) *verb.* 1. To make a sudden, sharp noise by slapping two objects together, especially the hands. 2. To give a light slap in a friendly way: When Tom won the race, his father *clapped* him on the shoulder. **clapped, clapping.** *—noun.* 1. A sudden, loud noise. 2. A slap or sudden blow.

clar·i·fy (KLA-rə-figh) *verb.* 1. To make understandable: *Clarify* the instructions. 2. To make clear or unclouded; purify: Passing water through a filter can *clarify* it. **clarified, clarifying.**

clar·i·net (kla-rə-NET) *noun.* Musical instrument of the woodwind family.

clar·i·ty (KLA-rə-tee) *noun.* 1. Clearness in expression or understanding: We admired the *clarity* of the teacher's explanation. 2. Clearness in quality or appearance.

clash (KLASH) *noun.* 1. A conflict, as of ideas or opinions. 2. A battle or collision. 3. A loud noise, usually metallic, caused by striking or colliding: A *clash* of cymbals ended the concert. **clashes.** *—verb.* 1. To conflict: Jim's desire to leave the party *clashed* with Tom's wish to stay. 2. To collide or to do battle with. 3. To make a loud noise, usually metallic, by striking. **clashed, clashing.**

clasp (KLASP) *noun.* 1. A holding or fastening device: The *clasp* on Mother's pocketbook is broken. 2. An embrace; hug. 3. A grip; a hold. *—verb.* 1. To fasten. 2. To embrace. 3. To grasp; hold or grip. **clasped, clasping.**

class (KLASS) *noun.* 1. A group of similar persons or things; a type; a classification: Mammals belong to one *class* of animals and reptiles to another. 2. A grade, level, or quality: The entertainment was of the highest *class.* 3. A level of society: Noblemen belonged to the upper *class.* 4. A group of students who take the same course; the course taken. 5. A group of students who graduate together. 6. (Informal) High style or quality: The actor has real *class.* **classes.** *—verb.* To classify; list or regard as a type or as similar. **classed, classing.**

clas·sic (KLASS-ik) *noun.* Art of lasting value or interest, especially of ancient Greece or Rome: The *Odyssey,* by the Greek poet Homer, is a *classic.* *—adjective.* 1. Also **classical.** Related to art, music, literature of lasting value or interest. 2. Having characteristics that make something an excellent representative of its class: The New England town meeting is a *classic* example of democracy. 3. Famous; excellent; highly regarded: The singer's performance was a *classic* one. **—classically** *adverb.*

clas·si·fi·ca·tion (klass-ə-fi-KAY-shən) *noun.* A class, category, or type; arrangement according to class.

clas·si·fy (KLASS-ə-figh) *verb.* 1. To arrange according to classes, groups, or similar types: Whales, dogs, and humans are *classified* as mammals. 2. To declare something to be secret or available only to a few: *classify* information. **classified, classifying.**

class·mate (KLASS-mayt) *noun.* A member of the same class or year in school. **classmates.**

class·room (KLASS-room) *noun.* A room where a class is taught.

clat·ter (KLAT-ər) *noun.* A series of sudden, hard sounds; disturbance; confusion: "When out on the lawn there arose such a *clatter,* I sprang from the bed to see what was the matter." (C. C. Moore). *—verb.* To make a clatter or move making such sounds: The train *clattered* along the tracks. **clattered, clattering.**

clause (KLAWZ) *noun.* 1. A group of words having a subject and predicate and forming part of a sentence. 2. A particular section or provision in a document: a *clause* in a contract. **clauses.**

claw (KLAW) *noun.* A sharp, sometimes curved nail on the foot of a bird or animal, or the foot itself. *—verb.* To scratch, rip, or dig with claws or hands. **clawed, clawing.**

clay (KLAY) *noun.* 1. Any natural material that is capable of being molded when wet and dried hard and firm under heat; used to make bricks, tiles, and pottery. 2. Moist soil; mud.

clarinet

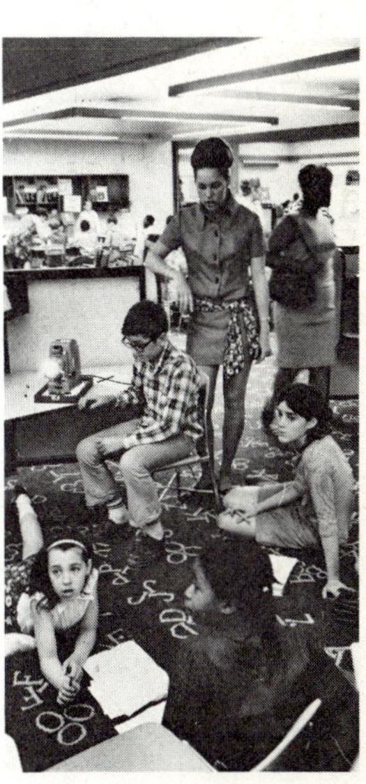
classroom

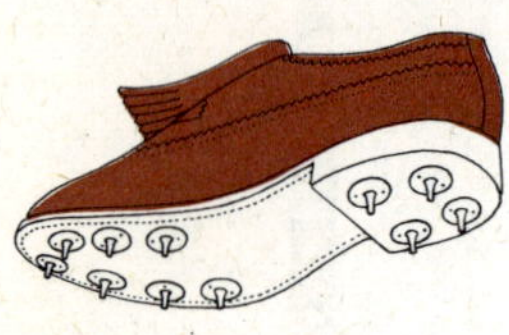
cleat

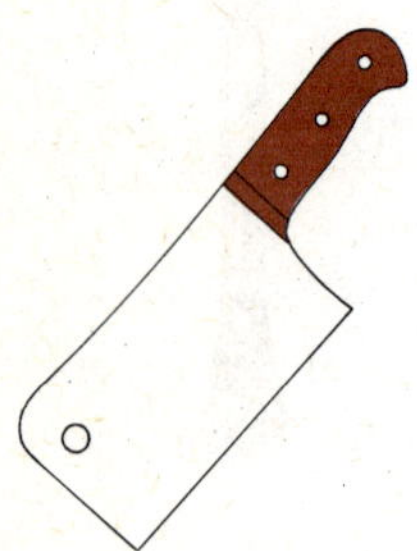
cleaver

clef

clean (KLEEN) *adjective.* 1. Free from dirt or stain. 2. Wholesome; pure; proper: A good person has a *clean* mind and heart. 3. Neat; simple; well-formed: The boys admired the *clean* shape of the new sailboat. 4. Complete: The robber made a *clean* getaway. **cleaner, cleanest.** —*adverb.* (Informal) Completely. —*verb.* To make clean or free from soil; cleanse; tidy up. **cleaned, cleaning.** —**cleanliness** *noun.*

clean-cut (KLEEN-kuht) *adjective.* 1. Trim; well-formed. 2. Neat and clean.

cleanse (KLENZ) *verb.* To make clean or pure. **cleansed, cleansing.**

cleans·er (KLENZ-ər) *noun.* A substance used for cleaning or scouring.

clear (KLIHR) *adjective.* 1. Easily seen through: The window was *clear.* 2. Understandable; obvious: It is *clear* what goes up must come down. 3. Easily seen or heard; sharp or precise. 4. Not cloudy. **clearer, clearest.** —*adverb.* (Informal) Completely; all the way: The ball was hit *clear* over the roof. —*verb.* 1. To make tidy. 2. To make an open space by removing trees from: Soldiers *cleared* a landing area in the jungle. 3. To cause to be free or empty: The police *cleared* the street of traffic. 4. To go over or past: The high jumper *cleared* six feet. 5. To prove not guilty or involved: The accused man was *cleared* of the crime. 6. To make a profit of: The committee *cleared* $50 from the cake sale. **cleared, clearing.** —**clearly** *adverb.* —**clear out.** Leave, depart. —**clear up.** 1. Solve or answer. 2. Change from stormy weather to fair. —**in the clear.** Free, untroubled.

clear-cut (klihr-KUHT) *adjective.* Clear; precise; easy to understand.

clear·ing (KLIHR-ing) *noun.* A section of land, especially one in a wooded area, free of trees and shrubs.

cleat (KLEET) *noun.* 1. A strip or piece of metal, wood, or other hard material fastened to a surface to provide strength, support, or traction: Some snow tires have metal *cleats* to grip the road. 2. A simple metal or wooden object on which a rope or line can be tied.

cleav·age (KLEE-vij) *noun.* A cleft or open space; a split.

[1]**cleave** (KLEEV) *verb.* To split, cut open, or divide. **cleft** or **cleaved** or **clove, cleaving.**

[2]**cleave** (KLEEV) *verb.* 1. To cling (to) or hold fast. 2. To hold or be faithful (to), as ideas or principles. **cleaved, cleaving.**

cleav·er (KLEE-vər) *noun.* A heavy cutting tool with a broad blade used by butchers to chop meat.

clef (KLEF) *noun.* A mark or symbol used in writing music to indicate the pitch of notes on a staff.

cleft (KLEFT) *noun.* A split; space; cleavage. —*adjective.* Split; separated; divided.

clem·en·cy (KLEM-ən-see) *noun.* 1. Mercy; leniency. 2. Mildness: the *clemency* of weather.

clench (KLENCH) *verb.* 1. To close or shut tightly: *Clench* your fists. 2. To grip or hold tightly. **clenched, clenching.** —*noun.* A tight grip or hold. **clenches.**

cler·gy (KLER-jee) *noun.* Persons such as ministers, priests, and rabbis ordained to perform religious service. **clergies.**

cler·gy·man (KLER-jee-mən) *noun.* A man who is part of the clergy. —**clergymen** *plural.*

cler·i·cal (KLEHR-i-kəl) *adjective.* 1. Related to clerks or the work done by a clerk: The secretary did filing and other *clerical* work. 2. Related to clergymen.

clerk (KLERK) *noun.* 1. A person who sells things or helps customers in a shop or market. 2. A person whose work is filing, making records, handling mail, and doing similar tasks. —*verb.* To work as a clerk. **clerked, clerking.**

clev·er (KLEV-ər) *adjective.* 1. Bright; intelligent; quick-witted. 2. Skillful; inventive: The entertainer did several *clever* card tricks. **cleverer, cleverest.** —**cleverly** *adverb.*

cli·ché (klee-SHAY) *noun.* A phrase that has lost its effectiveness through too much use: "Busy as a bee" is a *cliché.* **clichés.**

click (KLIK) *noun.* A short, sharp sound, usually metallic: Dave heard a *click* when the lock snapped shut. —*verb.* 1. To make a short, sharp sound, usually metallic. 2. (Slang) To get along well: Pete and Jim really *clicked.* **clicked, clicking.**

cli·ent (KLIGH-ənt) *noun.* 1. A person, group, or organization represented by a lawyer, accountant, or other professional person. 2. A customer.

cliff (KLIF) *noun.* A high, very steep wall or slope of rock or earth.

cli·mate (KLIGH-mit) *noun.* 1. The usual weather conditions of an area. 2. An area thought of in terms of its usual weather conditions: Polar bears live in very cold *climates.* 3. An atmosphere; a general attitude or feeling: a *climate* of joy throughout the school. **climates.**

cli·max (KLIGH-maks) *noun.* The point of greatest interest, importance, or excitement: the *climax* of the movie. **climaxes.** —*verb.* 1. To reach the point of greatest interest. 2. To bring to an end: A visit to the Grand Canyon *climaxed* our vacation. **climaxed, climaxing.**

climb (KLIGHM) *verb.* 1. To move, especially upward, using both hands and feet: The monkey *climbed* all over the tree. 2. To move upward; ascend. 3. To increase. 4. To grow over or upward: The roses have *climbed* the garden wall. **climbed, climbing.** —*noun.* 1. The act of climbing. 2. Growth; increase.

clinch (KLINCH) *verb.* 1. To make final; settle definitely: A touchdown *clinched* the victory. 2. To hold on to; put one's arms about, especially in boxing. 3. To fasten, as with nails or screws. 4. To bend or hammer down the end of a nail that projects through a surface. **clinched, clinching.**

cling (KLING) *verb.* 1. To stick or hold; remain close: Bob's wet shirt *clings* to his back. 2. To be faithful; adhere: My sister *clings* to her belief in fairies. **clung** (KLUHNG), **clinging.**

clin·ic (KLIN-ik) *noun.* 1. A section of a hospital, a private building, or other place where patients receive medical attention. 2. A meeting or course designed to consider or study a special problem or procedure.

clink (KLINGK) *noun.* 1. A short, sharp sound, like that made by striking a piece of metal or glass. 2. (Slang) A jail. —*verb.* To make a short, sharp sound. **clinked, clinking.**

clink·er (KLING-kər) *noun.* 1. A mass of material fused or melted together, as a lump of burned coals. 2. A type of hard brick, often used for paving. 3. (Slang) A mistake.

clip (KLIP) *verb.* 1. To fasten; attach: *clip* papers together. 2. To cut off; cut out; shorten: *clip* branches from a shrub. 3. (Slang) To overcharge or cheat. 4. (Informal) To hit or punch quickly. **clipped, clipping.** —*noun.* 1. An act of clipping. 2. A fastener: a paper *clip.* 3. (Informal) A quick punch. 4. (Informal) A pace or rate of movement: a very fast *clip.*

clip·per (KLIP-ər) *noun.* 1. (Usually plural) An instrument used for clipping or cutting. 2. A large 19th century sailing vessel famed for its speed.

clipper

clique (KLEEK or KLIK) *noun.* A close group of friends or associates often unfriendly to outsiders. **cliques.**

clock

clock

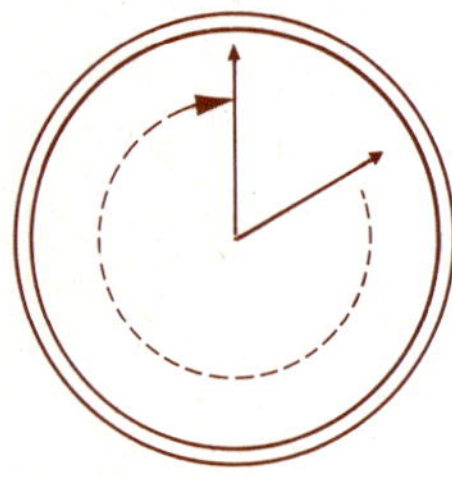
clockwise

club
(definition 5)

cloak (KLOHK) *noun.* 1. A loose-fitting outer garment. 2. That which covers or hides: a *cloak* of darkness. —*verb.* To cover or hide. **cloaked, cloaking.**

clock (KLOK) *noun.* A device, often large or stationary, for showing the time. —*verb.* To note the speed of a person, animal, or thing; to time. **clocked, clocking.**

clock·wise (KLOK-wighz) *adjective* or *adverb.* In the same direction that the hands on a clock move.

clod (KLOD) *noun.* 1. A lump of dirt or earth. 2. A dull or stupid person.

clod·hop·per (KLOD-hop-ər) *noun.* 1. A stupid, clumsy, or awkward country fellow. 2. (Plural) Any high, thick-soled, laced shoes.

clog (KLOG) *verb.* To block; obstruct: The drain pipe was *clogged* with leaves. **clogged, clogging.** —*noun.* A heavy shoe or sandal, often with a wooden sole.

clois·ter (KLOISS-tər) *noun.* 1. A convent or monastery. 2. A covered walk, often around a courtyard, with a wall on one side and a row of pillars on the other.

close (KLOHZ) *verb.* 1. To shut. 2. To finish; end. 3. To block; prevent passage; fill up: A fallen tree *closed* the main road. 4. To stop or conclude business or activity: The ski area is *closed* for the summer. 5. To move nearer; come together: The hounds *closed* rapidly on the fleeing fox. **closed, closing.** —*noun.* An end; conclusion. —(KLOHSS) *adjective.* 1. Near; nearby. 2. Having little space; crowded: *close* quarters. 3. Nearly the same in appearance, quality, or result: Purple is *close* to violet in color. 4. Especially dear or valued: Bob is Tom's *closest* friend. 5. Stingy: The old man is *close* with his money. 6. Stuffy; humid: The room became *close* when the air conditioner broke down. **closer, closest.** —**closely** *adverb.*

closed circuit. 1. An electrical system in which current can pass from one point to another without stop. 2. A television system that transmits to a limited number of receivers.

clos·et (KLOZ-it) *noun.* A small room, nook, or cupboard used for storing things. —*verb.* To shut up or enclose in a room, especially for a conference or meeting. **closeted, closeting.**

clot (KLOT) *noun.* A small lump or mass, especially of thickened blood. —*verb.* To form into a lump or mass; harden: The blood *clotted.* **clotted, clotting.**

cloth (KLAWTH) *noun.* 1. Fabric, usually woven. 2. A piece of fabric for a special purpose, as a wash*cloth* or dust*cloth.*

clothe (KLOHTH) *verb.* 1. To dress; put on: Jim *clothed* himself in a sweater and jeans. 2. To provide with clothing. 3. To cover: The valley was *clothed* with darkness. **clothed** or **clad, clothing.**

clothes (KLOHZ) *noun, plural.* Garments; apparel; dress.

clothes·pin (KLOHZ-pin) *noun.* A clip or fastener, usually of wood, used to hold laundry on a clothesline.

clothing (KLOTH-ing) *noun.* Garments; apparel; dress.

cloud (KLOWD) *noun.* 1. A layer or mass of vapor or mist in the sky. 2. Any mass, as of dust, steam, or insects: a *cloud* of dust. 3. An atmosphere or attitude, especially a discouraging one: a *cloud* of regret. —*verb.* 1. To become covered or filled with clouds. 2. To darken or make hard to see through: A layer of dust *clouded* the window. 3. To discourage or make unpleasant: The bad news *clouded* our spirits. **clouded, clouding.**

cloud·burst (KLOWD-berst) *noun.* A sudden downpour of rain.

cloud·y (KLOW-dee) *adjective.* 1. Covered or filled with clouds.

2. Darkened; confused; not easily seen through: *cloudy* water. 3. Gloomy. **cloudier, cloudiest.**

clout (KLOWT) *noun.* 1. (Informal) A blow or smack. 2. (Slang) Influence; power: The principal has plenty of *clout.* —*verb.* (Informal) To hit or strike: The batter *clouted* a home run. **clouted, clouting.**

clove (KLOHV) *noun.* 1. A spice or the tree from which it comes. 2. A section or piece of a plant bulb: a *clove* of garlic. **cloves.**

clo·ver (KLOH-vər) *noun.* A low, green plant with small flowers and leaves usually divided into three rounded parts, grown especially as feed for animals.

clo·ver·leaf (KLOH-vər-leef) *noun.* A highway intersection resembling a four-leaf clover. **cloverleaves.**

clown (KLOWN) *noun.* 1. A person, usually wearing funny clothes and make-up, whose job is to entertain people by odd or amusing behavior. 2. A foolish or silly person. —*verb.* To act in a foolish or silly manner. **clowned, clowning.**

club (KLUHB) *noun.* 1. A heavy stick used as a weapon. 2. A stick used to hit balls: golf *clubs.* 3. An organized group of people sharing the same interests: a *club* for stamp collectors. 4. A building or meeting place for a club or organization. 5. A playing card. —*verb.* To hit (a person or thing) very hard with a club. **clubbed, clubbing.**

club·house (KLUHB-howss) *noun.* A building or meeting place for a club. **clubhouses.**

cluck (KLUHK) *noun.* 1. A noise like a hen calling her chicks. 2. (Informal) A dull or stupid person. —*verb.* To make a sound like a hen. **clucked, clucking.**

clue (KLOO) Also **clew** *noun.* Anything that helps to solve a mystery; a hint. **clues.** —*verb.* To inform or tell. **clued, cluing.**

clump (KLUHMP) *noun.* 1. A solid mass; a lump: a *clump* of mud. 2. A group of things close together: a *clump* of shrubs. 3. A dull thud; the sound of heavy footsteps. —*verb.* To walk with loud, heavy footsteps. **clumped, clumping.**

clum·sy (KLUHM-zee) *adjective.* 1. Awkward; not graceful. 2. Poorly or awkwardly made: The home-made cart was a *clumsy* thing. **clumsier, clumsiest.** —**clumsily** *adverb.*

clung (KLUNG) *verb.* See **cling.**

clus·ter (KLUHSS-tər) *noun.* A group of similar or related things close together: a *cluster* of tents. —*verb.* To gather or grow in a group or bunch: The bees *clustered* around the hive. **clustered, clustering.**

clutch (KLUHCH) *verb.* 1. To grip or hold tightly. 2. To snatch or catch hold of: The drowning sailor *clutched* at pieces of driftwood. **clutched, clutching.** —*noun.* 1. A grip or grasp. 2. A device that connects or disconnects an engine from what it turns. 3. (Slang) A tight spot; a difficult situation: Depend on Jim in a *clutch.* **clutches.**

clut·ter (KLUHT-ər) *noun.* A messy, untidy state. —*verb.* To create disorder. **cluttered, cluttering.**

co. *abbreviation.* 1. Company. 2. County.

c/o *abbreviation.* Care of.

co- *prefix.* Indicates with or together with: *co*-author and *co*-education.

coach (KOHCH) *noun.* 1. A large, enclosed carriage; a stagecoach. 2. A passenger car on a train. 3. A bus. 4. A person who teaches or trains others, especially in athletics. **coaches.** —*verb.* To teach or train in some special skill or procedure. **coached, coaching.**

co·ag·u·late (koh-AG-yə-layt) *verb.* To thicken; to clot. **coagulated, coagulating.**

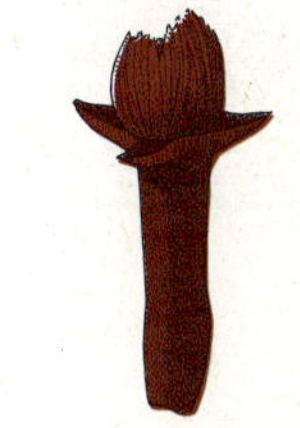
clove

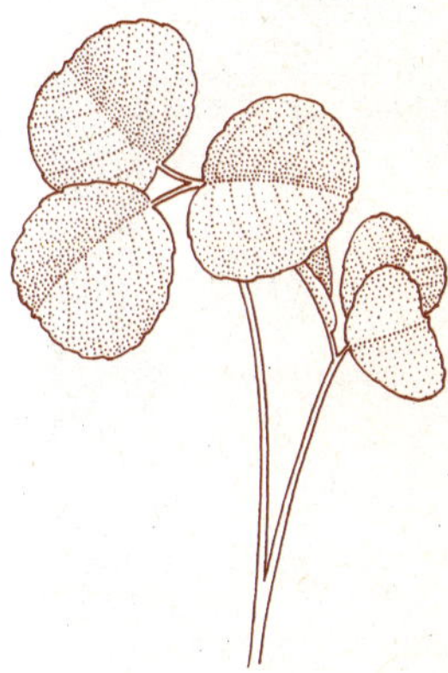
clover

clown

coal (KOHL) *noun.* 1. A hard, black mineral that is used as fuel; a piece of this material. 2. A glowing or burned piece of wood, coal, or other hard fuel; an ember.

co·a·li·tion (koh-ə-LISH-ən) *noun.* A coming together of various groups, often temporarily, out of necessity or for a particular purpose: The new committee is a *coalition* of student groups.

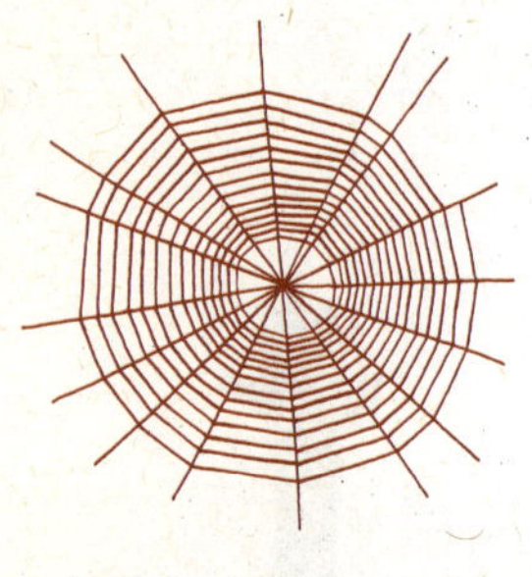
cobweb

coarse (KORSS) *adjective.* 1. Harsh; heavy; rough to the touch. 2. Inferior; low in quality. 3. Vulgar; crude; rough in manner: *coarse* speech. 4. Made up of large particles: *coarse* salt. **coarser, coarsest.** —**coarsely** *adverb.*

coast (KOHST) *noun.* Land that borders a body of water; a seashore. —*verb.* 1. To roll or slide down a slope or incline. 2. To continue moving after power, as from an engine, has been shut off. **coasted, coasting.**

cockatoo

Coast Guard. A naval service of the U.S. that protects ships and passengers, enforces naval laws, and guards against smuggling and other illegal acts along the coast.

coast·line (KOHST-lighn) *noun.* The border or edge where land meets the sea; the outline of a coast or seashore. **coastlines.**

coat (KOHT) *noun.* 1. An outer garment with sleeves, usually worn in cold or rainy weather. 2. A film or layer that covers something: a new *coat* of paint. 3. An outer covering grown by an animal or plant, such as fur, feathers, or bark. —*verb.* To cover or apply a coat or layer to: Leo *coated* the roof with tar. **coated, coating.**

coat·ing (KOH-ting) *noun.* A layer that covers or forms a surface: The candies had a *coating* of chocolate.

cocker spaniel

coat of arms. An emblem or shield having the special markings of a noble family.

coat of mail. A garment or covering of metal rings or disks, worn to protect a medieval warrior.

coax (KOHKS) *verb.* To tempt or influence with pleasing words or actions: *Coax* Tim to join our team. **coaxed, coaxing.**

coaxial cable. A cable used to send TV, telephone, and telegraph signals.

cob (KOB) *noun.* 1. The center part of an ear of corn beneath the kernels. 2. A short, sturdy horse.

co·balt (KOH-bawlt) *noun.* A hard, silver-white metal.

cob·bler (KOB-lər) *noun.* 1. A person who repairs shoes. 2. A fruit pie with a rich crust on top.

co·bra (KOH-brə) *noun.* A poisonous snake found in Asia and Africa.

cob·web (KOB-web) *noun.* The web or net spun by a spider, or a single strand of such a web.

coc·cus (KOK-əss) *noun.* 1. Any one of many round bacteria. 2. A part of certain fruits. —**cocci** (KOK-sigh) *plural.*

coch·le·a (KOK-lee-ə) *noun.* A spiral-shaped part of the inner ear in man and other animals. —**cochleae** (KOK-lee-ee) *plural.*

cock (KOK) *noun.* 1. A male chicken; any male bird. 2. A faucet or tap for controlling the flow of a liquid or gas. 3. An inclined or tilted position, as of one's head or hat. —*verb.* 1. To prepare a gun for firing by drawing back its hammer. 2. To place, wear, or hold in a tilted position: The bird *cocked* its head to one side. **cocked, cocking.**

cock·a·too (KOK-ə-too) *noun.* A parrot found in Australia, having bright fancy feathers. **cockatoos.**

cocker spaniel. A dog with droopy ears and long silky hair.

cock·eyed (KOK-ighd) *adjective.* 1. Having crossed eyes or a squinting eye. 2. (Slang) Out of order; confused; foolish.

cock·le (KOK-əl) *noun.* 1. A small shellfish or its shell. 2. A weed, especially one bearing burs. 3. A small boat. **cockles.**

cock·ney (KOK-nee) *noun.* [Often capital C] A person who was born and lives in the East End of London, England; the speech used by such persons.

cock·pit (KOK-pit) *noun.* 1. The section of an airplane that contains the controls and the pilot's seat. 2. An area on a small sailboat or other vessel, where steering is done.

cock·roach (KOK-rohch) *noun.* An insect pest, found especially in kitchens and other places where food is kept. **cockroaches.**

cock·tail (KOK-tayl) *noun.* 1. A drink made with liquor. 2. A small portion of food, such as shrimp, clams, or cheese, served before a main meal.

cock·y (KOK-ee) *adjective.* (Informal) Very confident; conceited; flippant. **cockier, cockiest.** —**cockily** *adverb.*

co·co (KOH-koh) *noun.* A coconut palm or its fruit, a coconut. **cocos.**

co·coa (KOH-koh) *noun.* 1. A powder made from the roasted seed or beans of the cacao tree. 2. A drink made by mixing cocoa powder with water or milk. 3. (Also *adjective*) A brown-red color.

co·co·nut (KOH-kə-nuht) *noun.* 1. The large, round, brown fruit of the coconut palm, having a hard shell with an edible, white lining and containing a milky liquid that may be drunk. 2. The white lining, or meat, of a coconut.

co·coon (kə-KOON) *noun.* A silky case or covering spun by some insects when they are in the larval or early stage of their development.

C.O.D. *abbreviation.* 1. Cash on delivery. 2. Collect on delivery.

cod (KOD) *noun.* A food fish found in North Atlantic waters; codfish. —**cod** or **cods** *plural.*

cod·dle (KOD-l) *verb.* 1. To pamper; treat very gently or easily. 2. To cook in water that is hot but not boiling. **coddled, coddling.**

code (KOHD) *noun.* 1. A system of signals used to send messages by telegraph, flags, or other means. 2. A system used to keep a message known only to those who know the system. 3. A collection of laws, rules, or principles used to govern or guide: a *code* of traffic laws. **codes.** —*verb.* To change or put into a secret form or code. **coded, coding.**

cod·fish (KOD-fish) *noun. See* **cod.** —**codfish** or **codfishes** *plural.*

codg·er (KOJ-ər) *noun.* (Informal) An odd or strange old man.

co-ed (KOH-ed) Also **coed** *noun.* A female student at a school or college attended by both males and females.

co-ed·u·ca·tion (koh-ej-uh-KAY-shən) *noun.* The education of both males and females at the same school or college. —**co-educational** *adjective.*

coe·la·canth (SEE-lə-kanth) *noun.* A fish regarded as extinct until 1938, when a living species was found off the coast of Africa.

co·erce (koh-ERSS) *verb.* To force or compel. **coerced, coercing.**

co·ex·is·tence (koh-ig-ZISS-tənss) *noun.* 1. The act of living together or at the same time. 2. The act of getting along peacefully with another person, group, or country in spite of differences of opinion.

cof·fee (KAW-fee) *noun.* 1. A seed or bean used to make a beverage; the tropical shrub on which such seeds grow. 2. The beverage made from this bean. 3. (Also *adjective*) A brown color. **coffees.** —**coffee break.** A short time taken out from work to enjoy coffee, tea, or snacks.

coffee table. A low table, usually placed in front of a sofa.

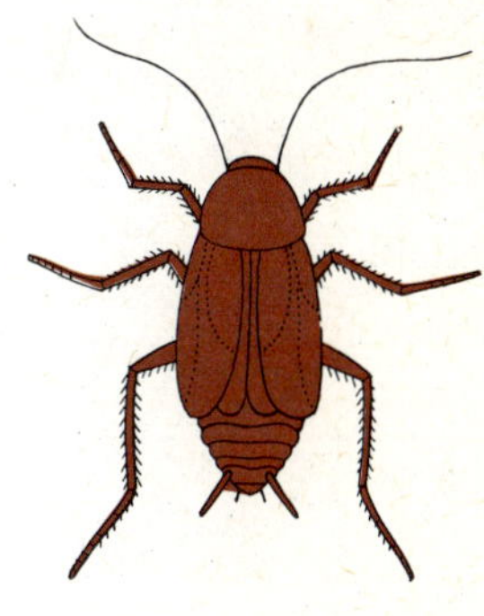
cockroach

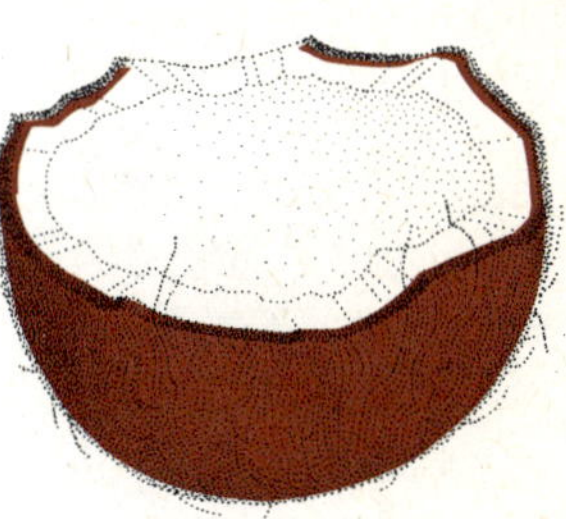
coconut

cocoon

cod

coffin

cof·fin (KAW-fən) *noun.* A box or chest in which a dead person is buried; a casket.

cog (KOG) *noun.* 1. A cogwheel. 2. A tooth on the edge of a cogwheel. 3. A person who performs a function, usually minor, in a large business or organization.

cog·wheel (KOG-hweel) *noun.* A wheel with a toothed or notched edge, used with other wheels to turn parts in a machine.

co·her·ent (koh-HIHR-ənt) *adjective.* 1. Orderly; making sense; logical. 2. Sticking or holding together. —**coherently** *adverb.*

co·he·sion (koh-HEE-zhən) *noun.* The process or state of sticking together: The *cohesion* of glue and paper holds a stamp on an envelope. —**cohere** (koh-HEER) *verb.*

co·hort (KOH-hort) *noun.* 1. A group or band, especially of soldiers. 2. (Informal) A friend or associate.

coil (KOIL) *noun.* 1. A series of loops into which a wire, rope, or similar item is wound; a spiral. 2. A single loop in a spiral. 3. A spiral of wire used for carrying electric current. —*verb.* To wind (something) into a series of loops. **coiled, coiling.**

coin

coin (KOIN) *noun.* A disk or piece of metal issued by a government for use as money. —*verb.* 1. To make metal money; to mint. 2. To make up or invent, as a word or an expression: Who *coined* the phrase "Better late than never"? **coined, coining.**

coin·age (KOI-nij) *noun.* The making of coins or the coins made.

coliseum

co·in·cide (KOH-in-sighd) *verb.* 1. To be in agreement; be similar or the same: Bob's plans *coincide* with mine. 2. To take the same position or occur at the same time. **coincided, coinciding.**

co·in·ci·dence (koh-IN-sə-dənss) *noun.* An unusual or accidental similarity; unrelated circumstances which seem to be related.

coke (KOHK) *noun.* 1. A hard substance used for fuel in industry, made from coal that has been baked. 2. [Capital C] A trademark for Coca-Cola.

cold (KOHLD) *adjective.* 1. Having a low temperature. 2. Not friendly or cheerful; without spirit. **colder, coldest.** —*noun.* 1. A low temperature. 2. A mild sickness, usually causing sneezing or coughing. —**coldly** *adverb.* —**coldness** *noun.*

cold-blood·ed (KOHLD-bluhd-id) *adjective.* 1. Related to animals whose body temperature changes with changes in the temperature around them: Fish and reptiles are *cold-blooded* animals. 2. Without feeling; without mercy; cruel. —**cold-bloodedly** *adverb.*

cold front. The front edge of a cold air mass that meets and replaces warmer air.

cold war. Tension between nations; a conflict that is carried on by economic and political means rather than by open warfare.

cole·slaw (KOHL-slaw) Also **cole slaw** *noun.* A salad made with sliced or shredded raw cabbage.

col·ic (KOL-ik) *noun.* A painful condition of the intestines or lower abdomen, generally caused by gas.

col·i·se·um (kol-ə-SEE-əm) Also **colosseum** *noun.* A stadium or large building for sporting events or other entertainment.

col·lab·o·rate (kə-LAB-ə-rayt) *verb.* 1. To work together with another person or group, especially on a work of art or science. 2. To assist or cooperate (with an enemy). **collaborated, collaborating.**

col·lapse (kə-LAPS) *verb.* 1. To fall down or cave in; fold up: the building *collapsed* during the earthquake. 2. To fail in plans, health, or well-being. **collapsed, collapsing.** —*noun.* A falling in; destruction; failure or breakdown.

col·laps·i·ble (kə-LAPS-ə-bəl) *adjective.* Able to be folded or made smaller, as for easier carrying or storage: Our new cot is *collapsible.*

col·lar (KOL-ər) *noun.* 1. The part of a shirt, coat, or other garment that goes around the neck. 2. A band, usually of leather, that goes around the neck of a dog, cat, or other animal. 3. Anything that resembles a collar in appearance or use. —*verb.* To grab; seize by the collar; capture. **collared, collaring.**

col·lar·bone (KOL-ər-bohn) *noun.* A bone that connects the breastbone to the shoulder blade. **collarbones.**

col·lard (KOL-ərd) *noun.* A green vegetable that is similar to cabbage and kale.

col·league (KOL-eeg) *noun.* A fellow worker; an associate in a business or profession. **colleagues.**

col·lect (kə-LEKT) *verb.* 1. To group or come together: The campers *collected* around the fire. 2. To gather; keep for a hobby: Jim *collects* stamps. 3. To gather or receive payment or a contribution: The conductor *collected* money for each ticket that he sold. 4. To bring under control: The angry man finally *collected* himself enough to speak calmly. **collected, collecting.** —*adjective* or *adverb.* With payment made by the person receiving a telegram, phone call, or package: Jane called her home *collect* because she had no money. —**collector** *noun.*

col·lec·tion (kə-LEK-shən) *noun.* 1. A group of things collected as a hobby. 2. The process of collecting money or other things. 3. A pile or gathering of anything collected.

col·lec·tive (kə-LEK-tiv) *adjective.* Total; relating to a group of people or things as a whole: The *collective* voting strength of our class won the election for John.

col·lege (KOL-ij) *noun.* A school of higher education beyond the level of high school. **colleges.**

col·lide (kə-LIGHD) *verb.* 1. To crash directly into. 2. To differ; disagree. **collided, colliding.**

col·lie (KOL-ee) *noun.* A large, long-haired dog, sometimes used for herding sheep. **collies.**

col·li·sion (kə-LIZH-ən) *noun.* 1. A direct crashing together: The *collision* of the two cars injured both drivers. 2. A conflict or disagreement.

col·lo·qui·al·ism (kə-LOH-kwee-əl-iz-əm) *noun.* An informal word or expression: "Gripe" is a *colloquialism* meaning "to complain." —**colloquial** (kə-LOH-kwee-əl) *adjective.* —**colloquially** *adverb.*

co·logne (kə-LOHN) *noun.* A fragrant or scented liquid used like perfume. **colognes.**

co·lon (KOH-lən) *noun.* 1. A punctuation mark (:) used to precede lists of items, to follow the salutation of a letter, and to introduce quotations. 2. A part of the large intestine.

colo·nel (KERN-l) *noun.* A military officer ranking just below brigadier general.

co·lo·ni·al (kə-LOH-nee-əl) *adjective.* 1. Of or related to a dependent territory: *colonial* times. 2. [Often capital C] Of or related to the 13 British colonies that became the United States.

collie

collard

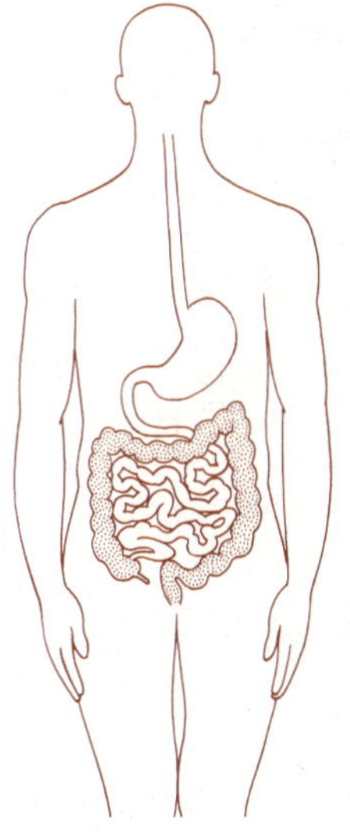
colon (definition 2)

col·o·nist (KOL-ə-nist) *noun.* A member of a colony, especially one who helps to found a colony.

col·o·ni·za·tion (kol-ə-nə-ZAY-shən) *noun.* The settling of a colony.

col·o·nize (KOL-ə-nighz) *verb.* To found or establish a colony. **colonized, colonizing.**

col·o·ny (KOL-ə-nee) *noun.* 1. People who move from their own country to settle in another land. 2. The land settled by such people; a territory governed by a faraway nation. 3. A group of people having common nationality, background, or interests. 4. [Capital C] One of the thirteen British colonies that became the United States. 5. A group of the same kind of animals or plants that live or grow together: a *colony* of wasps. **colonies.**

columbine

color (KUHL-ər) *noun.* 1. Red, blue, yellow, or any other hue that reflects from a surface when light hits it. 2. Paint, dye, or anything else that adds color. 3. The hue or shade of one's complexion. *—verb.* 1. To apply a color to an object, as with paint, crayon, or dye. 2. To misrepresent; make something appear different than it is. 3. To blush. **colored, coloring.**

Colorado
★capital: Denver

Col·o·ra·do (kol-ə-RAH-doh) *noun.* A state in western United States, 38th to join the Union (1876). **—Colo.** *abbreviation.* Also **CO** for Zip Codes.

col·or·a·tion (kuhl-ə-RAY-shən) *noun.* The color or combination of colors that something has.

col·or·blind (KUHL-ər-blynd) *adjective.* Not having the ability to tell one color from another. **—colorblindness** *noun.*

col·or·ful (KUHL-ər-fəl) *adjective.* 1. Having many colors; bright with varied hues. 2. Varied; vivid; interesting. **—colorfully** *adverb.*

col·or·ing (KUHL-ər-ing) *noun.* 1. The color or colors of a person or thing. 2. Something that adds color.

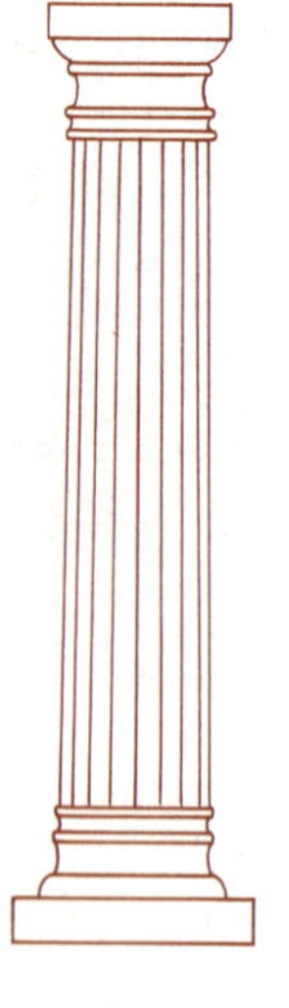

column

col·or·less (KUHL-ər-liss) *adjective.* 1. Without color; dull; drab. 2. Lacking excitement or interest.

co·los·sal (kə-LOSS-l) *adjective.* Huge; spectacular. **—colossally** *adverb.*

colour. British form of **color.**

colt (KOHLT) *noun.* A young male horse; a young donkey, mule, or similar animal.

col·um·bine (KOL-əm-bighn) *noun.* A plant with colorful flowers.

Columbus Day. A legal holiday in the United States celebrated on the Monday nearest October 12, in honor of Columbus' landing on the shores of America.

col·umn (KOL-əm) *noun.* 1. An upright shaft used for support or decoration in a structure; a pillar. 2. Anything resembling a pillar or column: a *column* of dust. 3. An up-and-down series of typed or printed lines on a page: The pages of this dictionary are printed in two *columns.* 4. Any line of things one behind or below the other, as a list of numbers or a row of soldiers. 5. An article that appears in a newspaper or other publication on a regular basis.

col·um·nist (KOL-əm-nist) *noun.* One who writes signed articles that appear on a regular basis in a newspaper.

com- *prefix.* With or together; *com*pile and *com*press.

co·ma (KOH-mə) *noun.* A long period of unconsciousness caused by sickness, poisoning, or injury.

comb (KOHM) *noun.* 1. A device with a row of teeth or prongs, used to arrange or clean the hair. 2. Any device used to clean, untangle, or arrange fibers, hair, or fur. 3. A crest or outgrowth on the head of a rooster or other bird. 4. A honeycomb. *—verb.* 1. To untangle, clean, or arrange with a comb or similar device. 2. To search or look through thoroughly: Dave *combed* the library to find information for his report. **combed, combing.**

com·bat (KOM-bat) *noun.* 1. Armed conflict; battle: The soldier was wounded in *combat.* 2. A struggle or conflict of any kind. —(kəm-BAT) *verb.* 1. To fight or struggle against. 2. To engage in armed conflict. **combated, combating.**

com·bat·ant (kəm-BAT-ənt) *noun.* A person or group involved in a fight or struggle. —*adjective.* Fighting.

com·bi·na·tion (kom-bə-NAY-shən) *noun.* 1. Something formed by the blending or joining of other things. 2. The numbers or letters that must be dialed to open certain locks.

com·bine (kəm-BIGHN) *verb.* To join together; unite; blend. **combined, combining.** —(KOM-bighn) *noun.* 1. An organization of persons joined together for a special purpose. 2. A machine for harvesting and threshing grain. **combines.**

com·bus·ti·ble (kəm-BUHSS-tə-bəl) *adjective.* Able to catch fire or to be burned.

com·bus·tion (kəm-BUHSS-chən) *noun.* The act or process of catching fire or burning.

come (KUHM) *verb.* 1. To move closer; approach. 2. To arrive at; reach: Please *come* to a decision. 3. To happen; take place: The party will *come* after the game. 4. To be from or part of: James *comes* from a small town in Michigan. 5. To extend or reach: The boots *come* to his knees. 6. To total; add up: The bill for lunch *comes* to $1.65. 7. To occur as part of a series: March *comes* before April. **came** (KAYM), **coming.** —**come about.** To happen. —**come across** or **come upon.** To meet; find. —**come by.** To get (something). —**come to.** To recover one's senses.

come·back (KUHM-bak) *noun.* 1. The regaining of a former state or position: The shortstop made a great *comeback* after his injury. 2. A clever answer or response.

co·me·di·an (kə-MEE-dee-ən) *noun, masculine.* Also **comedienne** (kə-mee-dee-EN) *noun, feminine.* 1. A person who acts in a comedy. 2. An entertainer or other person who amuses others with jokes and amusing actions.

com·e·dy (KOM-ə-dee) *noun.* 1. An entertainment form, as a play or movie, dealing with amusing events. 2. An amusing or entertaining event or situation. **comedies.**

come-on (KUHM-on) *noun.* An attraction or enticement.

com·et (KOM-it) *noun.* A heavenly body with a bright head and, when near the sun, a long, cloudy tail.

com·fort (KUHM-fərt) *noun.* 1. Relaxation, ease, peace, or freedom from worry or pain. 2. That which comforts: The little boy's toy bear was a *comfort* to him. —*verb.* To soothe; relieve from pain or sorrow. **comforted, comforting.**

com·fort·a·ble (KUHM-fər-tə-bəl) *adjective.* 1. Providing a pleasant or relaxed feeling. 2. Being in a state of comfort: The princess was not *comfortable* sleeping on the pea. 3. (Informal) Enough to give satisfaction, comfort, or pleasure: Uncle George makes a *comfortable* living. —**comfortably** *adverb.*

com·ic (KOM-ik) *noun.* 1. A comedian; an amusing person. 2. (Usually plural) Comic strips or books. —*adjective.* Also **comical.** Amusing; humorous; funny. —**comically** *adverb.*

comic book. A booklet or magazine containing entertaining stories presented in a set of drawings.

comic strip. A set of drawings that presents an entertaining story.

colt

comet

com·ma (KOM-ə) *noun.* A mark (,) used in writing to separate thoughts or parts of a sentence. **commas.**

com·mand (kə-MAND) *verb.* 1. To give an order; direct. 2. To control; be in charge of. 3. To have available: The wealthy man *commands* a large fortune. 4. To earn, deserve, or merit: Pat's courage *commands* respect. 5. To be in a place to overlook, influence, or control: The castle *commanded* a view of the valley. **commanded, commanding.** —*noun.* 1. An order. 2. Control; possession of authority. 3. Ability to use; understanding; grasp: a *command* of English. 4. A position of authority or the persons and facilities under one's authority, especially in a military situation: The general's *command* included 80 pilots.

command module

com·mand·er (kə-MAN-dər) *noun.* 1. A person who orders, commands, or has charge. 2. The officer in charge of a military unit. 3. A naval officer ranking above a lieutenant commander and below a captain.

commander in chief. [Often capital C] The commander with the highest authority over the armed forces of a nation: In the United States, the President is the *Commander in Chief* of the armed forces. —**commanders in chief** *plural.*

com·mand·ment (kə-MAND-mənt) *noun.* 1. A command or order. 2. [Usually capital C] One of the Ten Commandments.

command module. The part of a spacecraft that contains the controls and in which the astronauts live.

com·man·do (kə-MAN-doh) *noun.* A soldier specially trained for making surprise raids on enemy territory. **commandos** or **commandoes.**

com·mem·o·rate (kə-MEM-ə-rayt) *verb.* 1. To honor the memory of someone or something by a service or ceremony. 2. To serve as a reminder of someone or something: The bronze plaque *commemorates* the founding of our city. **commemorated, commemorating.**

com·mence (kə-MENSS) *verb.* To start; begin: The parade *commenced* at 11 o'clock. **commenced, commencing.**

com·mence·ment (kə-MENSS-mənt) *noun.* 1. A start or beginning. 2. A ceremony at which diplomas are awarded at a school or college; a graduation day or ceremony.

com·mend (kə-MEND) *verb.* 1. To praise: The student was *commended* for his excellent work. 2. To give over to the care of someone else; entrust: The man *commended* his son to the doctor's care. 3. To recommend or refer to as worthy of praise or regard. **commended, commending.** —**commendation** (kom-ən-DAY-shən) *noun.*

com·ment (KOM-ent) *noun.* A remark; statement. —*verb.* To make a remark, statement, or observation. **commented, commenting.**

com·men·tar·y (KOM-ən-tehr-ee) *noun.* A series of comments or notes; an explanation or evaluation: The school newspaper printed the principal's *commentary* on student behavior. **commentaries.**

com·men·ta·tor (KOM-ən-tay-tər) *noun.* A person who presents a commentary, especially on television or in the newspapers.

com·merce (KOM-ərss) *noun.* Extensive business or trade between peoples or places; widespread buying and selling.

com·mer·cial (kə-MER-shəl) *adjective.* Of or related to business, trade, or profit. —*noun.* An announcement or presentation on radio or television designed to sell a product. —**commercially** *adverb.*

com·mis·sar·y (KOM-ə-sehr-ee) *noun.* 1. A store or office that sells food and supplies in an institution such as a military camp. 2. A dining room or cafeteria in an institution such as a factory or office building. **commissaries.**

com·mis·sion (kə-MISH-ən) *noun.* 1. A group of people appointed or joined together for a special purpose: a *commission* to study taxes. 2. A duty, power, job, or obligation: My dad has a *commission* to paint a portrait. 3. A percentage of money from a sale given to the salesman. 4. A document that shows or authorizes rank for a military officer, or such a rank. 5. An act; a doing of something: *commission* of crime. —*verb.* 1. To give or assign powers, privileges, duties, or rank. 2. To place (a ship) into service. **commissioned, commissioning.** **—out of commission.** Not functioning or operating.

com·mis·sion·er (kə-MISH-ən-ər) *noun.* 1. An official who has charge of a government department: the police *commissioner.* 2. A member of a commission.

com·mit (kə-MIT) *verb.* 1. To do, usually something evil: *commit* a crime. 2. To give over to the care or authority of another person or of an institution; assign; entrust. 3. To put away, store, or preserve: Jane *committed* the phone number to memory. 4. To pledge or promise; obligate: Dad *committed* himself to coach the boys' baseball team. **committed, committing.** **—commitment** *noun.*

com·mit·tee (kə-MIT-ee) *noun.* A group of people selected or joined together for a special purpose: A *committee* was elected to plan our class trip. **committees.**

com·mo·di·ous (kə-MOH-dee-əss) *adjective.* Having much room; spacious. **—commodiously** *adverb.*

com·mod·i·ty (kə-MOD-ə-tee) *noun.* Something that is bought and sold: Wheat and corn are important *commodities.* **commodities.**

com·mon (KOM-ən) *adjective.* 1. Of all people in general; related to the public: a law for the *common* good. 2. Shared, possessed, or used by all members of a group or type: a *common* playground. 3. Widespread; well-known. 4. Lacking special qualities; ordinary; average. 5. Coarse; crude; vulgar: *common* language. 6. Without special position or rank: *common* seamen. **commoner, commonest.** —*noun.* A public plot of land, as a park or village green, usually in the center of town. **—commonly** *adverb.*

common noun. A noun that names a general rather than a particular person, place, or thing: *Common nouns* can be modified by articles such as "the" or "an." *See* **proper noun.**

com·mon·place (KOM-ən-playss) *adjective.* Ordinary; common; usual. —*noun.* An ordinary or trite remark. **commonplaces.**

common sense. Good judgment; the ability to think or act in a practical manner: Ann has enough *common sense* not to try drugs.

com·mon·wealth (KOM-ən-welth) *noun.* 1. A nation ruled by all its citizens. 2. The citizens of a nation or special union or group of nations. 3. A union or group of nations: Canada belongs to the British *Commonwealth* of Nations. 4. The official name of some U.S. states: the *Commonwealth* of Massa-chusetts.

com·mo·tion (kə-MOH-shən) *noun.* A confused disturbance; turmoil.

com·mun·al (kə-MYOON-l) *adjective.* Of or related to a community or an organization of people.

com·mune (KOM-yoon) *noun.* A small or specially organized community of people, usually people having similar interests or goals. **communes.** —(kə-MYOON) *verb.* To communicate or talk with in an intimate or private manner. **communed, communing.**

com·mu·ni·ca·ble (kə-MYOO-ni-kə-bəl) *adjective.* Able to be communicated, passed on, or spread, as a sickness or idea: Measles is a *communicable* disease. —**communicably** *adverb.*

com·mu·ni·cate (kə-MYOO-nə-kayt) *verb.* 1. To make (something) known; transmit; convey: Joe *communicated* the family's change in plans to his cousin. 2. To exchange thoughts or feelings. **communicated, communicating.**

com·mu·ni·ca·tion (kə-MYOO-nə-KAY-shən) *noun.* 1. An exchange of ideas in speaking or writing. 2. A message: The detective's *communication* contained a description of the criminal. 3. (Plural) The various means of spreading news and information, such as the press, radio, and television.

com·mun·ion (kə-MYOON-yən) *noun.* 1. A gathering or organization of people with similar ideas, goals, or religious beliefs. 2. A sharing of ideas or feelings. 3. [Capital C] The Christian sacrament that honors Jesus Christ's Last Supper.

com·mu·nism (KOM-yə-niz-əm) *noun.* A social or political system that includes the belief that all property and the means of production should be owned and controlled by the state acting in behalf of all the people.

com·mu·nist (KOM-yə-nist) *noun.* 1. A person who supports communism. 2. [Capital C] A member of the Communist party; a member of a specific political movement that supports the ideas of communism. —**communist** or **communistic** *adjective.*

com·mu·ni·ty (kə-MYOO-nə-tee) *noun.* 1. A group of people living in a particular area or town: The settlers formed a *community* in the valley. 2. Any group that lives together with similar interests, goals, or beliefs: a *community* of nuns. 3. The public or society in general. 4. Plants or animals living in the same area under the same conditions. **communities.**

com·mute (kə-MYOOT) *verb.* 1. To travel on a regular basis between one's home and job, especially to a city or town and back. 2. To exchange, as a prison sentence or a punishment, for something less: The governor *commuted* the prisoner's sentence from 30 to 15 years. 3. To change or transform. **commuted, commuting.**

com·mut·er (kə-MYOO-tər) *noun.* A person who travels on a regular basis between his home and job.

com·pact (kəm-PAKT or KOM-pakt) *adjective.* 1. Packed or constructed firmly or solidly; without unnecessary space or material: A cigar is a *compact* roll of tobacco. 2. To the point; without unnecessary words. —*verb.* To pack or construct firmly or solidly. **compacted, compacting.** —(KOM-pakt) *noun.* 1. A small case containing face powder or other cosmetics, often carried in a woman's purse. 2. An agreement or contract. —**compactly** *adverb.*

com·pan·ion (kəm-PAN-yən) *noun.* 1. A person who accompanies, lives with, or shares the activities of another; a comrade. 2. A thing that matches or accompanies something else, as in appearance or taste; part of a set: I have lost the *companion* to this mitten. —**companionable** (kəm-PAN-yə-nə-bəl) *adjective.* —**companionably** *adverb.*

com·pa·ny (KUHM-pə-nee) *noun.* 1. Association; fellowship: Don enjoys the *company* of his close friends. 2. A business firm. 3. Guests or visitors. 4. People joined together for a particular purpose, as for entertainment or protection: a *company* of dancers. 5. The crew of a ship or a unit of soldiers. **companies.** —**part company.** To separate from another person or persons.

com·pa·ra·ble (KOM-pər-ə-bəl) *adjective.* Able to be compared: A horse and a mule are *comparable* in size. —**comparably** *adverb.*

com·par·a·tive (kəm-PA-rə-tiv) *adjective.* 1. Relative; in comparison with something else. 2. (Grammar) Relating to the middle degree of an adjective or adverb: "Better" is the *comparative* degree of "good." —**comparatively** *adverb.*

com·pare (kəm-PAIR) *verb.* To study or show similarities and differences between things: The teacher *compared* the American Revolution and the French Revolution. **compared, comparing.** —**beyond compare.** Without equal: Roses are *beyond compare* for beauty.

com·par·i·son (kəm-PA-rə-sən) *noun.* 1. A showing of similarities and differences: Ralph's *comparison* of Europe and America was very interesting. 2. (Grammar) The change in an adjective or adverb to show positive, comparative, or superlative degree.

com·part·ment (kəm-PAHRT-mənt) *noun.* One of the spaces into which a larger space is divided: The desk drawer had *compartments* for holding paper and envelopes.

com·pass (KUHM-pəss or KOM-pəss) *noun.* 1. An instrument that shows direction by means of a needle that points to the North. 2. An instrument with two legs joined at one end, used for drawing circles and measuring distance. 3. A boundary or limit; range or extent: Baking a cake is not within the *compass* of Jim's talents. **compasses.**

com·pas·sion (kəm-PASH-ən) *noun.* Pity; sympathy: Pete showed *compassion* for the hungry dog by giving it half of his sandwich.

com·pas·sion·ate (kəm-PASH-ən-it) *adjective.* Showing pity; sympathetic. —**compassionately** *adverb.*

com·pat·i·ble (kəm-PAT-ə-bəl) *adjective.* In agreement; showing harmony; able to get along well together: The two girls are very *compatible.* —**compatibly** *adverb.*

com·pel (kəm-PEL) *verb.* To force or oblige; overpower: The storm *compelled* us to seek shelter. **compelled, compelling.**

com·pen·sate (KOM-pən-sayt) *verb.* 1. To make up; be a balance: Hard work *compensated* for his lack of talent. 2. To pay or reward; provide with something equal: Mother was *compensated* for her damaged car. **compensated, compensating.** —**compensation** (kom-pən-SAY-shən) *noun.*

com·pete (kəm-PEET) *verb.* To take part in a contest; strive or vie: The runners *competed* against one another. **competed, competing.** —**competitor** (kəm-PET-ə-tər) *noun.*

com·pe·tent (KOM-pə-tənt) *adjective.* Having skills or ability: a *competent* cook. —**competently** *adverb.*

com·pe·ti·tion (kom-pə-TISH-ən) *noun.* 1. A contest: The *competition* in the high jump began at two o'clock. 2. A rivalry; a striving against: Bob and Joan are in *competition* for the class presidency. 3. A rival or competitor. —**competitive** (kom-PET-ə-tihv) *adjective.* **competitively** *adverb.*

com·pile (kəm-PIGHL) *verb.* 1. To collect into a list or record: The librarian *compiled* titles of books on outer space. 2. To make or form by gathering together materials from various sources: Eleanor *compiled* a book of her favorite poems. **compiled, compiling.**

com·pla·cen·cy (kəm-PLAY-sn-see) Also **complacence** (kəm-PLAY-snss) *noun.* 1. A feeling of satisfaction, peace, or contentment. 2. Annoying self-confidence; smugness. —**complacent** *adjective.* —**complacently** *adverb.*

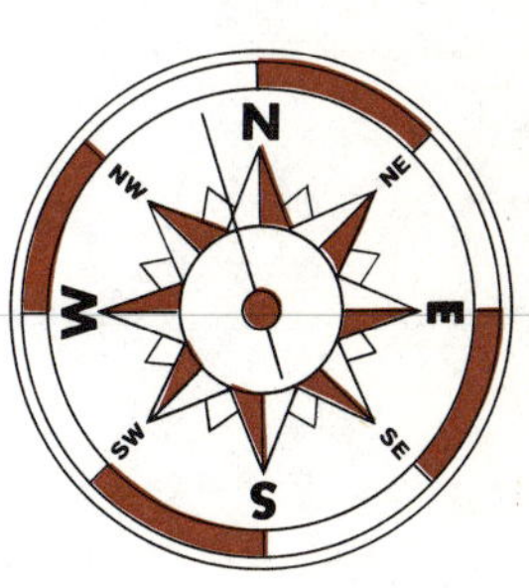

compass

com•plain (kəm-PLAYN) *verb.* 1. To speak out about what troubles or bothers (one); find fault: The students *complained* about the rainy weather. 2. To make a charge or protest: The citizen *complained* to the police about the damage to his property. **complained, complaining.**

com•plaint (kəm-PLAYNT) *noun.* 1. An expression of annoyance, discomfort, or displeasure. 2. A formal charge or protest. 3. A sickness or disorder.

com•ple•ment (KOM-plə-mənt) *noun.* 1. That which completes or makes entire: A pretty necklace was a beautiful *complement* to Aunt Beth's dress. 2. The amount or number required to make complete or full: The eight golf balls that Dad added to my four were the *complement* needed to make a dozen. 3. The number of persons required to make up a particular group, as a ship's crew. —*verb.* To make full or complete. **complemented, complementing.**

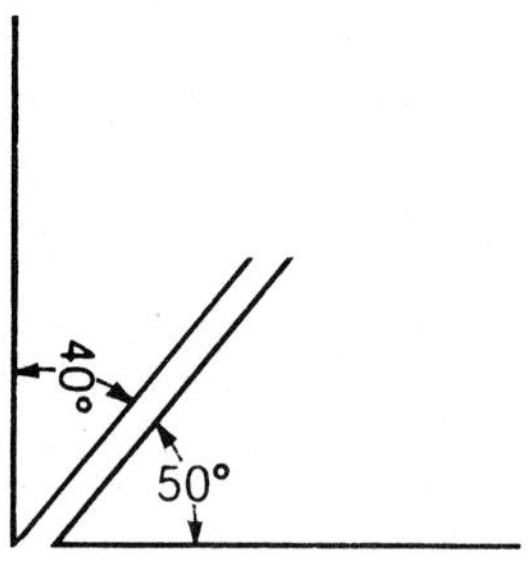

complementary angle. One of two angles that together make a right angle or 90 degrees.

complementary angles

com•plete (kəm-PLEET) *verb.* 1. To finish. 2. To make whole or entire: The valuable stamp *completed* Ron's collection. **completed, completing.** —*adjective.* 1. Entire; having all parts: a *complete* set of golf clubs. 2. Full; perfect: *complete* relaxation. 3. Finished. —**completely** *adverb.* **completion** (kəm-PLEE-shən) *noun.*

com•plex (kəm-PLEKS) *adjective.* 1. Having many parts: A television is a *complex* machine. 2. Complicated; involved: The *complex* instructions for filling out the application confused us. —(KOM-pleks) *noun.* 1. Something made up of many or intricate parts: A radio is a *complex* of wires, tubes, and other devices. 2. An idea or attitude that has a strong effect on one's behavior: Leo has a *complex* about his appearance; he worries that he is too fat. 3. A group of buildings serving closely related purposes: The medical *complex* includes a hospital and quarters for the staff. **complexes.** —**complexly** *adverb.*

complex fraction. A fraction in which one or both of the numbers above or below the line are, or contain, a fraction or fractions. Also called "compound fraction."

com•plex•ion (kəm-PLEK-shən) *noun.* 1. The condition of the skin, especially the skin of the face, in terms of color, clearness, and smoothness. 2. The nature or character of a situation: The *complexion* of the discussion changed when the two men became very angry.

com•plex•i•ty (kəm-PLEK-sə-tee) *noun.* A state of being intricate or involved; complication: The *complexity* of the arithmetic problem puzzled us. **complexities.**

complex sentence. A sentence composed of two or more clauses of which one is the main clause and the other or others are dependent clauses: When it is three o'clock (dependent clause), we will go home (main clause).

com•pli•cate (KOM-pli-kayt) *verb.* To make or become confused or involved: The flat tire *complicated* our plans for the trip. **complicated complicating.**

com•pli•ca•tion (kom-plə-KAY-shən) *noun.* 1. A situation that is intricate or involved; a problem. 2. A disease or disorder which attacks an already sick person: Elaine's bad cold was a *complication* that slowed her recovery from measles.

com•pli•ment (KOM-plə-mənt) *noun.* Praise; a statement of approval or admiration. —(KOM-plə-ment) *verb.* To express praise or admiration. **complimented, complimenting.**

com·pli·men·ta·ry (kom-plə-MEN-tə-ree or kom-plə-MEN-tree) *adjective.* 1. Expressing a compliment. 2. Given free of charge: *complimentary* tickets.

com·ply (kəm-PLIGH) *verb.* To consent; respond as desired. **complied, complying.**

com·po·nent (kəm-POH-nənt) *noun.* A part or ingredient of something: A picture tube is one *component* of a television set.

com·pose (kəm-POHZ) *verb.* 1. To form or make up: Concrete is *composed* of cement and sand or gravel. 2. To write a song, poem, or other work. 3. To calm or bring under control. **composed, composing.**

com·posed (kəm-POHZD) *adjective.* Calm; under control. —**composedly** (kəm-PO-zid-lee) *adverb.*

com·pos·er (kəm-POH-zər) *noun.* One who composes, especially a person who writes music.

com·pos·ite (kəm-POZ-it) *noun.* Something formed from several different ingredients: The statue is a *composite* of metal and stone. **composites.** —*adjective.* Composed of several different parts or ingredients.

composite number. A number formed by multiplying two or more whole numbers, each greater than one.

com·po·si·tion (kom-pə-ZISH-ən) *noun.* 1. An original song, poem, or other work. 2. A short written work done as an exercise by students. 3. The make-up or parts of something: The *composition* of a cake includes flour, sugar, and eggs. 4. The act or process of putting together or constructing.

com·pound (KOM-pownd) *noun.* 1. A mixture formed by combining two or more parts or elements. 2. An enclosed area for a particular group of buildings or people: a prison *compound.* —*adjective.* Having two or more parts or ingredients. —(kom-POWND) *verb.* 1. To mix; to form by combining various parts or ingredients. 2. To complicate, add to, or increase. **compounded, compounding.**

compound sentence. A sentence with two or more independent clauses usually joined by a linking word such as *and* or *but.*

com·pre·hend (kom-pri-HEND) *verb.* To understand; grasp: The student did not *comprehend* what he was supposed to do. **comprehended, comprehending.** —**comprehension** (kom-pri-HEN-shən) *noun.*

com·pre·hen·sive (kom-pri-HEN-siv) *adjective.* Including many things: The book gave a *comprehensive* study of the discovery of America. —**comprehensively** *adverb.*

com·press (kəm-PRESS) *verb.* To press together; make tighter or more compact. **compressed, compressing.** —(KOM-press) *noun.* A pad of folded cloth used to apply heat to the body or otherwise relieve pain. **compresses.** —**compression** *noun.*

com·prise (kəm-PRIGHZ) *verb.* To include; consist of. **comprised, comprising.**

com·pro·mise (KOM-prə-mighz) *verb.* 1. To settle an argument by having both sides change their demands to some degree. 2. To place in danger or under suspicion. **compromised, compromising.** —*noun.* A settlement of a dispute achieved by both sides lessening their demands to some degree. **compromises.**

com·pul·sion (kəm-PUHL-shən) *noun.* 1. Force; an act or state of being forced. 2. An impulse or desire that makes or urges a person to do something he really doesn't want to do: Some unfortunate people have a *compulsion* to steal. —**compulsive** (kəm-PUHL-siv) *adjective.* —**compulsively** *adverb.*

com·pul·so·ry (kəm-PUHL-sə-ree) *adjective.* 1. Required; necessary: Attendance at the meeting is *compulsory;* all must be present. 2. Using force or compulsion. —**compulsorily** *adverb.*

com·pute (kəm-PYOOT) *verb.* To use mathematics to arrive at an answer; calculate. **computed, computing.** —**computation** (kom-pyoo-TAY-shən) *noun.*

computer

com·put·er (kəm-PYOO-tər) *noun.* An electronic machine that can perform complex calculations with extreme speed and can store, relate, and reproduce large amounts of information.

com·rade (KOM-rad) *noun.* A close friend or companion. **comrades.**

con (KON) *noun.* 1. A reason, person, or vote against something that must be judged or decided: The committee examined the pros and the *cons* of the issue. 2. A member of a group in opposition to or disagreement with something. 3. (Slang) A convict. 4. (Slang) A swindle, trick, or fraud. —*adverb.* Against. —*verb.* 1. To study, learn, or memorize: The soldiers *conned* their lists of duties. 2. (Slang) To swindle, trick, or cheat. **conned, conning.**

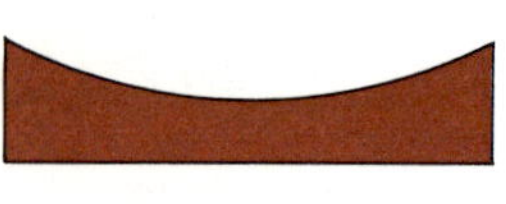
concave

con·cave (kon-KAYV) *adjective.* Hollow and curved like the inside of part of a sphere or circle: Our salad bowls are *concave* dishes.

con·ceal (kən-SEEL) *verb.* 1. To hide; keep out of sight: George *concealed* his money behind a row of books. 2. To keep secret: Bob *concealed* his failure from his parents. **concealed, concealing.** —**concealment** *noun.*

con·cede (kən-SEED) *verb.* 1. To admit or recognize to be true: Ralph *conceded* that Bill was a faster runner. 2. To give or grant as a right: The court *conceded* the man the right to build a store on his property. **conceded, conceding.**

con·ceit (kən-SEET) *noun.* 1. A vain or too-high opinion of one's own ability, attractiveness, or importance. 2. A whim or imaginary notion.

con·ceit·ed (kən-SEE-tid) *adjective.* Vain; showing too high an opinion of oneself. —**conceitedly** *adverb.*

con·ceiv·a·ble (kən-SEE-və-bəl) *adjective.* Able to be imagined or believed. —**conceivably** *adverb.*

con·ceive (kən-SEEV) *verb.* 1. To form in one's mind; make up: The boys *conceived* a plan to build a tree house. 2. To understand or imagine; have a clear idea of: It is hard to *conceive* limitless outer space. 3. To become pregnant. **conceived, conceiving.**

con·cen·trate (KON-sən-trayt) *verb.* 1. To fix one's attention upon something: Mary turned off TV so she could *concentrate* on her homework. 2. To focus, or draw toward one center. 3. To make more powerful: The company *concentrated* the soap powder so that it could clean very soiled clothing. **concentrated, concentrating.** —*noun.* Something that has been made more powerful or effective. **concentrates.**

con·cen·tra·tion (kon-sən-TRAY-shən) *noun.* 1. Undivided attention: To understand the instructions requires *concentration.* 2. The act or process of concentrating.

concentration camp. A prison camp in which captured soldiers, political prisoners, and others may be confined.

con·cept (KON-sept) *noun.* A notion, thought, or idea.

con·cep·tion (kən-SEP-shən) *noun.* 1. The act or process of conceiving; imagining, understanding, or bringing to mind. 2. A concept or idea: His *conception* of friendship differs from Harold's. 3. The beginning of the development of a child or offspring (in a female).

con·cern (kən-SERN) *noun.* 1. That which is of interest to someone: Improving his swimming style is an important *concern* of Mark's. 2. Anxiety or worry. —*verb.* 1. To have a relation to: The telephone call *concerned* Dad's election to the committee. 2. To be a cause of interest or worry to. **concerned, concerning.**

con·cern·ing (kən-SER-ning) *preposition.* About; with regard to.

con·cert (KON-sert) *noun.* 1. A musical performance. 2. Harmony; cooperation.

con·cer·ti·na (kon-sər-TEE-nə) *noun.* A small musical instrument like an accordion. **concertinas.**

con·cer·to (kən-CHEHR-toh) *noun.* A musical composition for an orchestra with leading parts for one or more instruments. **concertos.**

con·ces·sion (kən-SESH-ən) *noun.* 1. An admission; a recognition of the truth: Bob's *concession* that Jim was right ended the argument. 2. A granting or yielding. 3. That which is granted or yielded. 4. An independent service or business operated within a larger place: Mr. Johnson operates the car rental *concession* at the airport.

conch (KONGK or KONCH) *noun.* A large, spiral seashell. —**conchs** or **conches** *plural.*

con·cil·i·ate (kən-SIL-ee-ayt) *verb.* 1. To win over; please or satisfy. 2. To make up to; overcome bad feeling. **conciliated, conciliating.** —**conciliatory** *adjective.*

con·cise (kən-SIGHSS) *adjective.* To the point; having much meaning without unnecessary words or detail. —**concisely** *adverb.*

con·clude (kən-KLOOD) *verb.* 1. To finish; to end. 2. To come to a conclusion; figure out. 3. To settle or arrange: The agreement was *concluded* in a friendly manner. **concluded, concluding.**

con·clu·sion (kən-KLOO-zhən) *noun.* 1. The end or final part of something. 2. That which is concluded or figured out: Dad came to the *conclusion* that we couldn't afford a new car. 3. A result or outcome.

con·clu·sive (kən-KLOO-siv) *adjective.* Definite; settling or decisive: The *conclusive* evidence caused the jury to find the man guilty. —**conclusively** *adverb.*

con·coct (kən-KOKT) *verb.* 1. To make by mixing ingredients: Dad *concocted* a stew out of meat and vegetables. 2. To make up; to plan: The boy *concocted* a scheme to avoid doing his homework. **concocted, concocting.**

con·cord (KON-kord) *noun.* 1. Harmony; agreement. 2. Peace between peoples or nations.

con·crete (KON-kreet) *noun.* A building material made by mixing cement with water and sand or gravel. —*verb.* To put down concrete. **concreted, concreting.** —(kon-KREET) *adjective.* Solid, real; able to be observed by the senses. —**concretely** *adverb.*

con·cur (kən-KER) *verb.* 1. To agree. 2. To happen at the same time. 3. To act or work together; cooperate. **concurred, concurring.**

con·cus·sion (kən-KUHSH-ən) *noun.* 1. A sudden, violent shock or quake. 2. A brain injury caused by a blow.

con·demn (kən-DEM) *verb.* 1. To declare guilty or assign a punishment: The British *condemned* Nathan Hale to death by hanging. 2. To disapprove of strongly; find fault with. 3. To declare unsafe. **condemned, condemning.**

con·dem·na·tion (kon-dem-NAY-shən) *noun.* 1. The act of condemning or the state of being condemned. 2. Strong disapproval or severe criticism: The committee was shocked by the doctor's *condemnation* of the city's health program.

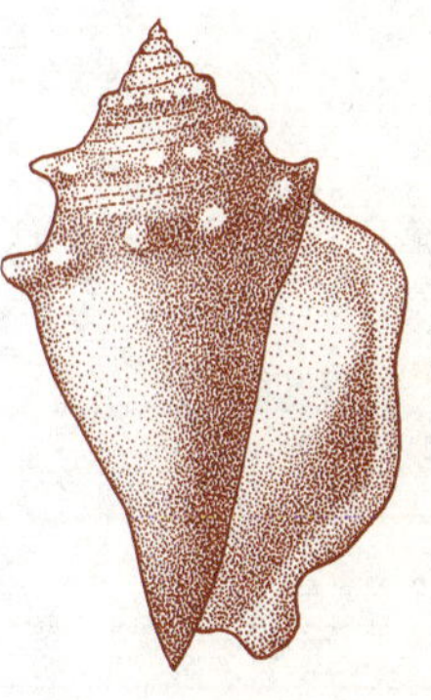

conch

con·den·sa·tion (kon-dən-SAY-shən) *noun.* 1. The act of making more compact or changing to a denser form. 2. That which results from condensing, as a liquid from a gas. 3. A story, book, or other work that is a shortened form of a longer work.

condor

con·dense (kən-DENSS) *verb.* 1. To make more compact. 2. To say or write in fewer words. 3. To change to a denser form, as a gas to a liquid. **condensed, condensing.**

con·den·ser (kən-DEN-sər) *noun.* A device that makes something denser or more compact, as one that changes a gas to a liquid.

con·de·scend (kon-di-SEND) *verb.* 1. To come down to the level of persons of lower rank or lesser ability: The governor *condescended* to visit the homes of the poor. 2. To show feelings of superiority to others. **condescended, condescending.**

conductor

con·di·tion (kən-DISH-ən) *noun.* 1. A state or situation: The automobile is in excellent *condition.* 2. What something depends on for completion or success: Studying is one *condition* for success in school. 3. Rank; position in society. *—verb.* 1. To train or make used to: The dogs were *conditioned* to respond to the man's whistle. 2. To put into a good state or into good working order: The mechanic *conditioned* the automobile engine. 3. To approve subject to specific requirements. **conditioned, conditioning.**

con·di·tion·al (kən-DISH-ən-l) *adjective.* Subject to a condition or requirement: The secretary's job is *conditional;* she must prove that she can type well. **—conditionally** *adverb.*

con·di·tion·ing (kən-DISH-ən-ing) *noun.* 1. A getting used to. 2. The training of a body to adjust to special conditions, such as learning to ice-skate. 3. A special training, as when a bird is trained to peck at one color and not another.

con·do·min·i·um (kon-də-MIN-ee-əm) *noun.* An apartment building or group of dwellings in which each unit is under individual ownership.

con·done (kən-DOHN) *verb.* To overlook, pardon, or forgive something improper or unlawful. **condoned, condoning.**

con·dor (KON-dor) *noun.* A large vulture found in South America and parts of California.

con·duct (KON-duhkt) *noun.* 1. Behavior; manner of acting: The student was praised for his good *conduct.* 2. Management or control, as of a business. —(kən-DUHKT) *verb.* 1. To behave: The children *conducted* themselves well at the party. 2. To manage or control: The teacher *conducted* the assembly from the stage. 3. To escort; serve as a guide to. 4. To carry or transmit: *conduct* electricity. 5. To lead or direct (an orchestra or band). **conducted, conducting.**

con·duc·tor (kən-DUHK-tər) *noun.* 1. A person who collects fares or sells tickets on a train, bus, or other means of transportation. 2. A person who leads an orchestra or band. 3. A material or thing that carries or transmits such forms of energy as electricity, sound, or heat.

cone (KOHN) *noun.* 1. A solid figure that rises to a point at one end from a rounded base at the other. 2. A cone-shaped, cracker-like holder for scoops of ice cream. 3. A scaly seed-bearing mass or pod that grows on evergreen trees. **cones.**

con·fec·tion (kən-FEK-shən) *noun.* A sweet food, such as candy or icing.

con·fed·er·a·cy (kən-FED-ər-ə-see) *noun.* 1. An organization of people, groups, or nations united for a special purpose: The three nations formed a *confederacy* for improving trade. 2. [Capital C] The organization of 11 states of the South that seceded from the U.S. in 1860–61. **confederacies.**

con·fed·er·ate (kən-FED-ər-it) *noun.* 1. An ally, helper, or companion. 2. [Capital C] A southerner loyal to the Confederacy. **confederates.**

con·fed·er·a·tion (kən-fed-ə-RAY-shən) *noun.* An alliance or union.

con·fer (kən-FER) *verb.* 1. To talk over; discuss; compare ideas. 2. To grant; give; present: *confer* an award. **conferred, conferring.**

con·fer·ence (KON-fər-ənss) *noun.* 1. A meeting or discussion organized for a particular purpose. 2. A league or association, as for colleges, businesses, or teams. **conferences.**

con·fess (kən-FESS) *verb.* 1. To admit or reveal, as a fault, sin, or crime: The man *confessed* that he had taken the money. 2. To tell one's sins to God or to a priest. **confessed, confessing.**

con·fes·sion (kən-FESH-ən) *noun.* 1. An act of confessing; an admitting or revelation. 2. That which is confessed or revealed. 3. An act of religion in which one tells his sins to God or to a priest.

con·fet·ti (kən-FET-ee) *noun, plural in form but used with a singular verb.* Bits of colored paper thrown during celebrations as a sign of joy or festivity.

con·fide (kən-FIGHD) *verb.* 1. (Used with *in*) To discuss something personal; to reveal as a secret: Kathy *confided* in her father that she was worried about her grades. 2. To have trust or confidence in. 3. To entrust to the care of another. **confided, confiding.**

con·fi·dence (KON-fə-dənss) *noun.* 1. Strong trust; faith in a person or thing: Our teacher had *confidence* that the class would win the spelling bee. 2. Strong trust in one's own abilities. 3. Something that is revealed or confided: The close friends shared *confidences* during their visit. **confidences.**

con·fi·dent (KON-fə-dənt) *adjective.* 1. Sure; certain: Jack is *confident* that our school will win the game. 2. Having faith in one's own abilities. —**confidently** *adverb.*

con·fi·den·tial (kon-fə-DEN-shəl) *adjective.* Secret; private. —**confidentially** *adverb.*

con·fine (kən-FIGHN) *verb.* 1. To limit; restrict: The principal *confined* his comments to school matters. 2. To keep physically restricted; shut up or imprison. **confined, confining.**

con·firm (kən-FERM) *verb.* 1. To show to be true; make certain: Our teacher *confirmed* the report that school will be closed tomorrow. 2. To strengthen: Her trust in Bob's ability was *confirmed* by his victory. 3. To ratify; approve formally: The agreement was *confirmed* by the signing of a contract. 4. To admit to full membership in a religion. **confirmed, confirming.**

con·fir·ma·tion (kon-fər-MAY-shən). *noun.* 1. An act or rite of confirming. 2. Proof or information that confirms: The birth certificate gave *confirmation* of the boy's age. 3. A religious ceremony by which a person is admitted to full membership in a church or religion.

con·firmed (kən-FERMD) *adjective.* Established or settled, as in a habit or condition: a *confirmed* bachelor. —**confirmedly** *adverb.*

con·fis·cate (KON-fiss-kayt) *verb.* 1. To take away, especially through one's authority: The guard *confiscated* the file and saw from the convict. 2. To seize for public use, especially as a penalty. **confiscated, confiscating.**

con·fla·gra·tion (kon-flə-GRAY-shən) *noun.* A large or widespread and destructive fire.

Confederate flag

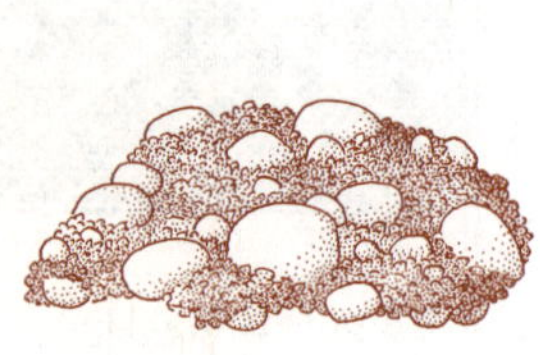
conglomerate

con·flict (KON-flikt) *noun.* 1. A fight or battle. 2. Opposition or disagreement, as of plans or attitudes. —(kən-FLIKT) *verb.* To be in opposition or disagreement. **conflicted, conflicting.**

con·form (kən-FORM) *verb.* 1. To act in agreement with rules, laws, or standards: The students *conformed* to the school regulations regarding attendance. 2. To be or make suitable or similar: The frame *conformed* to the size and shape of the picture. **conformed, conforming.** —**conformity** *noun.*

con·found (kən-FOWND or kon-FOWND) *verb.* 1. To confuse, amaze, or bewilder: The magician *confounded* us with his clever tricks. 2. To frustrate, thwart, or overcome: The general *confounded* the enemy with his daring raids. **confounded, confounding.**

con·front (kən-FRUHNT) *verb.* 1. To meet face to face; to encounter. 2. To face with defiance or hostility: The two boys *confronted* each other armed with snowballs. **confronted, confronting.**

con·fuse (kən-FYOOZ) *verb.* 1. To bewilder; perplex. 2. To mistake for another; fail to see a difference. **confused, confusing.**

con·fu·sion (kən-FYOO-zhən) *noun.* 1. Bewilderment; a state of being confused. 2. A mistaking of one thing for another. 3. Disorder; a mix-up: The traffic accident caused *confusion* among the cars.

con·geal (kən-JEEL) *verb.* To thicken or harden; coagulate: After a few minutes the paste began to *congeal.* **congealed, congealing.**

con·gen·ial (kən-JEEN-yəl) *adjective.* 1. Able to get along well; having similar likes and dislikes. 2. Pleasant; agreeable; suitable: The family moved from the unpleasant neighborhood to a more *congenial* one. —**congenially** *adverb.*

conifer

con·ges·tion (kən-JESS-chən) *noun.* An overcrowding; a clogging or stopping up.

con·glom·er·ate (kən-GLOM-ə-rit) *noun.* 1. A collection of different types of things. 2. (Geology) A rock made up of several stones or pebbles. **conglomerates.** —(kən-GLOM-ə-rayt) *verb.* 1. To gather in a group or mass. 2. To be gathered or formed into a mass. **conglomerated, conglomerating.**

con·grat·u·late (kən-GRACH-oo-layt) *verb.* To express good wishes, admiration, or happiness over another's success or good fortune. **congratulated, congratulating.** —**congratulation** (kən-grach-oo-LAY-shən) *noun.*

con·gre·gate (KONG-grə-gayt) *verb.* To gather together; assemble. **congregated, congregating.**

con·gre·ga·tion (kong-grə-GAY-shən) *noun.* 1. The act of assembling. 2. A gathering of people or things. 3. A group of people assembled for religious worship.

con·gress (KONG-griss) *noun.* 1. The lawmaking body of a government. 2. [Capital C] The lawmaking body of the U.S. Government, consisting of the Senate and the House of Representatives. 3. An assembly or meeting of any group of officials for a particular purpose. **congresses.**

con·gress·man (KONG-griss-mən) *noun.* A man who is a member of Congress. —**congressmen** *plural.*

con·ic (KON-ik) Also **conical** (KON-i-kəl) *adjective.* Having the form of a cone. A dunce cap is *conic* in shape. —**conically** *adverb.*

con·i·fer (KON-ə-fər) *noun.* A cone-bearing tree, such as a pine, cedar, or spruce. —**coniferous** (koh-NIF-ər-əss) *adjective.*

conj. *abbreviation.* 1. Conjunction. 2. Conjugation.

con·jec·ture (kən-JEK-chər) *noun.* A guess or opinion, often based on limited evidence. **conjectures.** —*verb.* To guess or form an opinion. **conjectured, conjecturing.**

con·ju·ga·tion (kon-ju-GAY-shən or kon-jə-GAY-shən) *noun.* (Grammar) 1. A listing of all the forms of a verb in its different tenses and persons. 2. A group of verbs that form their various persons and tenses in the same or in a similar way.

con·junc·tion (kən-JUHNGK-shən) *noun.* 1. A connecting word that joins words, phrases, or clauses, such as *and, or, because.* 2. A combination; a joining together: Dad went fishing in *conjunction* with a business trip.

con·jure (KON-jər) *verb.* To call forth a spirit; practice magic. **conjured, conjuring.**

con·nect (kə-NEKT) *verb.* 1. To join together. 2. To associate mentally; think of things as being related to one another. 3. To be associated (with). **connected, connecting.**

Con·nect·i·cut (kə-NET-ə-kət) *noun.* A New England state of the United States, fifth to ratify the Constitution (1788). —**Conn.** *abbreviation.* Also **CT** for Zip Codes.

con·nec·tion (kə-NEK-shən) *noun.* 1. That which joins or connects. 2. An association or relationship, as with a club or business. 3. A relationship of things or ideas. 4. A telephone contact or hookup.

conning tower. 1. The part of a submarine raised above the main deck, used as an entrance and exit and for observation. 2. The armored area on the deck of a warship that serves as the center of controls.

con·quer (KONG-kər) *verb.* 1. To put down by force; defeat: The English fleet *conquered* the Spanish Armada in 1588. 2. To control or overcome by any means. **conquered, conquering.**

con·quer·or (KONG-kər-ər) *noun.* A person who conquers; a victor or winner.

con·quest (KON-kwest) *noun.* 1. The act of overcoming or the state of being overcome. 2. That which is conquered or overcome. 3. A person who surrenders his affection or admiration to another.

con·science (KON-shənss) *noun.* The inclination or sense within a person that helps him to know what is right and wrong and that leads him to act properly. **consciences.**

con·sci·en·tious (kon-shee-EN-shəss) *adjective.* 1. Inclined to follow one's conscience or to do what is right. 2. Very careful; attentive to obligations or requirements: Marie was *conscientious* about answering all her mail promptly. —**conscientiously** *adverb.*

conscientious objector. A person who objects to war or military service for reasons of religion or conscience.

con·scious (KON-shəss) *adjective.* 1. In a state of being awake or able to think and feel. 2. Aware; having knowledge of. 3. Deliberate; intentional; with determination: a *conscious* effort. —**consciously** *adverb.*

con·scious·ness (KON-shəss-niss) *noun.* 1. The state of being conscious or awake. 2. Awareness. 3. All of one's thoughts and feelings considered together.

con·se·crate (KON-sə-krayt) *verb.* To dedicate or devote to a holy or special purpose. **consecrated, consecrating.**

con·sec·u·tive (kən-SEK-yə-tiv) *adjective.* Following one after the other: It rained five *consecutive* days. —**consecutively** *adverb.*

con·sen·sus (kən-SEN-səss) *noun.* 1. A generally held opinion: It was the *consensus* of the citizens that the mayor did a good job. 2. Agreement; accord.

Connecticut
★ capital: Hartford

conning tower

con·sent (kən-SENT) *noun.* Permission; agreement. —*verb.* To give permission; approve. **consented, consenting.**

con·se·quence (KON-sə-kwenss) *noun.* 1. A result or effect: His success was a *consequence* of his hard work. 2. Importance; significance: The matter that they discussed was of little *consequence.* **consequences.**

con·se·quent (KON-sə-kwent) *adjective.* Resulting; following as a result or effect: The athlete's failure to practice and his *consequent* defeat taught him a hard lesson. —**consequently** *adverb.*

con·ser·va·tion (kon-ser-VAY-shən) *noun.* Care, protection, or saving (of something): *Conservation* of our wilderness areas is important.

con·ser·va·tism (kən-SER-və-tiz-əm) *noun.* The beliefs of a conservative.

con·ser·va·tive (kən-SER-və-tiv) *adjective.* 1. Tending to avoid extremes, as in dress or customs. 2. Favoring the present state of things and resisting change. 3. Tending to protect; cautious. —*noun.* A person who is conservative or moderate. **conservatives.** —**conservatively** *adverb.*

con·serve (kən-SERV) *verb.* To preserve; keep safe; save. **conserved, conserving.** —(KON-serv) *noun.* A type of jam made of two or more fruits. **conserves.**

con·sid·er (kən-SID-ər) *verb.* 1. To think about; to study. 2. To think of or believe to be: Some people *consider* Jim a better athlete than Harry. 3. To take into account; remember: The team did very well if you *consider* that they had little time to practice. 4. To respect; be careful of: *Consider* the rights of others. **considered, considering.**

con·sid·er·a·ble (kən-SID-ər-ə-bəl) *adjective.* 1. Important; significant. 2. Large; great; much. —**considerably** *adverb.*

con·sid·er·ate (kən-SID-ər-ət) *adjective.* Respectful; kind. —**considerately** *adverb.*

con·sid·er·a·tion (kən-sid-ə-RAY-shən) *noun.* 1. The act of studying or considering: The mayor gave careful *consideration* to the committee's request. 2. Respect for the rights and feelings of others. 3. Something that should be taken into account or studied: Comfort and appearance are *considerations* in choosing a pair of shoes.

con·sign (kən-SIGHN) *verb.* 1. To give over; entrust: The sick old man was *consigned* to the care of a hospital. 2. To send or deliver, as items for sale: The company *consigned* a shipment of books to the store in Chicago. **consigned, consigning.**

con·sist (kən-SIST) *verb.* To be made up (of): The room's furnishings *consisted* of a table, four chairs, and a cabinet. **consisted, consisting.**

con·sis·ten·cy (kən-SISS-tən-see) *noun.* 1. The quality of thickness or firmness of a substance: Oil has a heavier *consistency* than water. 2. The state of being consistent. **consistencies.**

con·sis·tent (kən-SISS-tənt) *adjective.* 1. Following the same course (of thought or action): The teacher was *consistent* about assigning homework; every day she gave us four problems to do. 2. In harmony or agreement: Being overweight is not *consistent* with doing well in sports. —**consistently** *adverb.*

con·so·la·tion (kon-sə-LAY-shən) *noun.* 1. Comfort; relief; the state of being consoled. 2. A person or thing that gives comfort.

con·sole (kən-SOHL) *verb.* To give comfort, relief, or encouragement. **consoled, consoling.** —(KON-sohl) *noun.* 1. The area on an organ that contains the keyboard, pedals, and other controls. 2. A cabinet (as of a television or hi-fi) that stands on the floor. **consoles.**

con·sol·i·date (kən-SOL-ə-dayt) *verb.* 1. To combine or join together. 2. To strengthen or make secure: The businessman *consolidated* his excellent financial position by spending and investing his money wisely. **consolidated, consolidating.**

con·som·mé (kon-sə-MAY) *noun.* A clear broth made from meat stock. **consommés.**

con·so·nant (KON-sə-nənt) *noun.* Any letter of the alphabet other than *a, e, i, o, u* or, sometimes, *y.* —*adjective.* In harmony or agreement. —**consonantly** *adverb.*

con·sort (kən-SORT) *verb.* To associate or to be friendly with. **consorted, consorting.** —(KON-sort) *noun.* 1. A companion or escort. 2. A husband or wife, especially of a queen or king.

con·spic·u·ous (kən-SPIK-yoo-əss) *adjective.* 1. Standing out; obvious. 2. Remarkable; worthy of attention. —**conspicuously** *adverb.*

con·spir·a·cy (kən-SPIHR-ə-see) *noun.* 1. A secret plan to do something, usually evil or unlawful. 2. The group of persons involved in such a secret plan. **conspiracies.**

con·spir·a·tor (kən-SPIHR-ə-tər) *noun.* A person who plots or is part of a conspiracy.

con·spire (kən-SPIGHR) *verb.* 1. To plan secretly or plot with others to do something, usually evil or unlawful. 2. To work together toward the same goal. **conspired, conspiring.**

con·sta·ble (KON-stə-bəl) *noun.* A person whose job is to maintain law and order; a policeman, usually in rural areas. **constables.**

con·stant (KON-stənt) *adjective.* 1. Not stopping; continual. 2. Faithful; loyal: David was *constant* in his friendship with Jonathan. 3. Not changing; regular. —*noun.* Something that does not change. —**constantly** *adverb.*

con·stel·la·tion (kon-stə-LAY-shən) *noun.* A group or formation of stars.

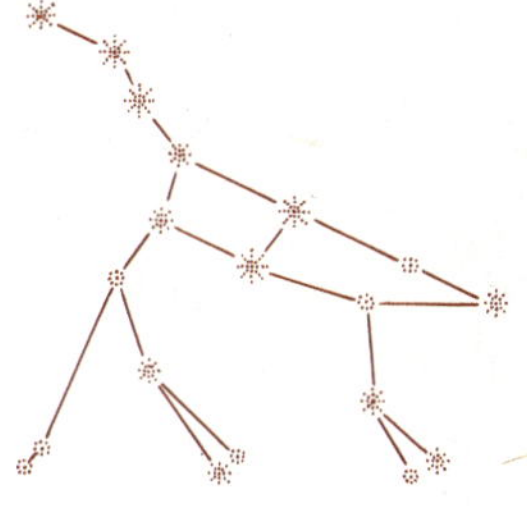

constellation

con·ster·na·tion (kon-stər-NAY-shən) *noun.* Great amazement or alarm.

con·sti·pa·tion (kon-sti-PAY-shən) *noun.* A condition in which the passage of waste material from the body is difficult or delayed.

con·stit·u·ent (kən-STICH-oo-ənt) *noun.* 1. A part of something: Copper and tin are *constituents* of bronze. 2. One represented by an elected official; a citizen or resident of a particular area.

con·sti·tute (KON-stə-toot or KON-stə-tyoot) *verb.* 1. To form or make up: Nine players *constitute* a baseball team. 2. To establish, as by a law or one's authority: *constitute* a committee. 3. To name; designate. **constituted, constituting.**

con·sti·tu·tion (kon-stə-TOO-shən or kon-stə-TYOO-shən) *noun.* 1. The structure or make-up of something. 2. A person's physical make-up or the condition of his health. 3. The basic laws by which a nation or organization is governed or a document containing such laws. 4. [Capital C] The set of basic laws by which the United States is governed or the written document containing these laws.

Constitution

con·sti·tu·tion·al (kon-stə-TOO-shən-l or kon-stə-TYOO-shən-l) *adjective.* 1. Of or related to the constitution or make-up of a person or thing. 2. Related to or in accordance with the constitution or basic laws of a nation or organization. —*noun.* A walk taken for good health or exercise. —**constitutionally** *adverb.*

con·straint (kən-STRAYNT) *noun.* 1. Force or obligation. 2. An uneasiness or holding back of one's real feelings: Our visitor talked with *constraint* until he began to feel at ease with us. 3. That which compels or confines.

con·strict (kən-STRIKT) *verb.* To bind; squeeze; make smaller. **constricted, constricting.**

con·struct (kən-STRUHKT) *verb.* To build; form; establish: The workers *constructed* a new bridge across the river. **constructed, constructing.**

con·struc·tion (kən-STRUHK-shən) *noun.* 1. The act or process of constructing. 2. The manner in which something is arranged or put together: The new office building is an example of modern *construction.* 3. The arrangement of words in a sentence. 4. A building.

con·struc·tive (kən-STRUHK-tiv) *adjective.* Tending to aid, develop, or improve. —**constructively** *adverb.*

con·strue (kən-STROO) *verb.* To find the meaning of, analyze, or explain: We *construed* Helen's remark to mean that she was disappointed. **construed, construing.**

con·sul (KON-sl) *noun.* A government official living in a foreign land, whose job is to look after the interests of his country and his fellow citizens.

con·sult (kən-SUHLT) *verb.* 1. To look up or ask for facts or advice, as from a book or person. 2. To think about or have regard for. **consulted, consulting.** —**consultation** (kon-sl-TAY-shən) *noun.*

con·sult·ant (kən-SUHL-tənt) *noun.* A person who advises others in a professional way.

con·sume (kən-SOOM or kən-SYOOM) *verb.* 1. To use up; to spend or waste: Mary's homework *consumed* an hour of her time. 2. To eat or drink up. 3. To destroy. 4. To fill up or take up the attention of: The athlete was *consumed* with the desire to become a champion. **consumed, consuming.**

con·sum·er (kən-SOOM-ər or kən-SYOOM-ər) *noun.* 1. A person who uses or consumes something. 2. One who buys and uses products: The mayor appointed a committee to protect *consumers* from poorly made or dangerous products.

con·sump·tion (kən-SUHMP-shən) *noun.* 1. The act or process of consuming. 2. The amount of something that is used up or taken in: The *consumption* of bread at our house is about two loaves each week. 3. A disease that affects the lungs; tuberculosis.

con·sump·tive (kən-SUHMP-tiv) *noun.* 1. A person afflicted with a disease that causes a destruction of tissue. 2. A person who has tuberculosis. —*adjective.* 1. Having a tendency to eat away; harmful or destructive. 2. Referring to a disease that wastes or destroys. —**consumptively** *adverb.*

cont. *abbreviation.* 1. Continue or continued. 2. Contraction. 3. Contents.

con·tact (KON-takt) *verb.* 1. To touch or come together. 2. (Informal) To get in touch with; communicate with. **contacted, contacting.** —*noun.* 1. A touching or coming together. 2. (Slang) A friend or acquaintance, especially one who can do you a favor.

contact lens. A small clear eyeglass worn directly on the eyeball.

con·ta·gion (kən-TAY-jən) *noun.* 1. The spreading of a disease by contact with the disease itself or with something infected by the disease. 2. A disease spread in this way. 3. A sudden spreading or wave, as of attitudes or emotions.

con·ta·gious (kən-TAY-jəss) *adjective.* 1. Able to be spread by direct contact: Chicken pox is a *contagious* disease. 2. Tending to spread or catch on, as an attitude or emotion: Polly's enthusiasm was *contagious.* —**contagiously** *adverb.*

con·tain (kən-TAYN) *verb.* 1. To hold or be able to hold: A pint bottle *contains* two cups. 2. To include:

The cake *contains* milk, butter, and flour. 3. To hold back; control: The woman could not *contain* her grief when her child was injured. 4. To restrict; to limit; prevent from making progress: The soldiers *contained* the enemy troops within the area of the valley. **contained, containing.**

con·tain·er (kən-TAYN-ər) *noun.* Something, such as a box or jar, used to hold or contain things.

con·tam·i·nate (kən-TAM-ə-nayt) *verb.* To spoil or make bad or harmful; corrupt. **contaminated, contaminating.**

con·tem·plate (KON-təm-playt) *verb.* 1. To look at or think about with deep attention; study: The artist *contemplated* the beautiful painting at the museum. 2. To intend or plan. **contemplated, contemplating.** —**contemplation** *noun.*

con·tem·po·rar·y (kən-TEM-pə-rehr-ee) *adjective.* 1. Belonging to, happening during, or living at the same period of time: Balboa and DeSoto were *contemporary* Spanish explorers. 2. Of or related to the present time: The governors were meeting to discuss *contemporary* problems. —*noun.* A person of about the same age as another. **contemporaries.** —**contemporarily** (kən-tem-pə-REHR-ə-lee) *adverb.*

con·tempt (kən-TEMPT) *noun.* 1. An attitude or feeling of scorn; a despising. 2. An act of disrespect or a lack of cooperation in a court of law.

con·tempt·i·ble (kən-TEMP-tə-bəl) *adjective.* Worthy of contempt or scorn. —**contemptibly** *adverb.*

con·temp·tu·ous (kən-TEMP-choo-əss) *adjective.* Showing contempt or scorn. —**contemptuously** *adverb.*

con·tend (kən-TEND) *verb.* 1. To fight against; put up with; struggle. 2. To state or declare (something) to be true. **contended, contending.**

[1]**con·tent** (KON-tent) *noun.* 1. The meaning or message of a work, as a speech or novel. 2. (Usually plural) That which fills or is contained by some other thing: What were the *contents* of the surprise package? 3. The amount that can be put into something; the capacity. 4. (Usually plural) The individual things that make a whole: table of *contents.*

[2]**con·tent** (kən-TENT) *adjective.* Happy or satisfied with things as they are. —*verb.* To make happy or content. **contented, contenting.** —*noun.* Happiness; satisfaction.

con·tent·ed (kən-TEN-tid) *adjective.* Satisfied; pleased. —**contentedly** *adverb.*

con·ten·tion (kən-TEN-shən) *noun.* 1. Strife; arguing; struggle. 2. That which a person argues for or declares to be true.

con·tent·ment (kən-TENT-mənt) *noun.* Satisfaction; a feeling of ease or well-being.

con·test (KON-test) *noun.* 1. A game in which two or more people strive for victory; a competition. 2. An argument; a struggle or conflict: The *contest* between the two countries for control of the island lasted for months. —(kən-TEST) *verb.* To dispute or argue about; struggle for. **contested, contesting.**

con·test·ant (kən-TESS-tənt) *noun.* A person involved in a game, conflict, or dispute; one who contests.

con·text (KON-tekst) *noun.* The section of a speech or written work in which a word occurs, usually influencing the way in which the word is understood.

con·ti·nent (KON-tə-nənt) *noun.* 1. One of the seven major masses of land areas on earth. 2. [Capital C] The mainland of Europe; Europe not including the British Isles. —*adjective.* Having control over one's desires or passions; chaste. —**continently** *adverb.*

con·ti·nen·tal (kon-tə-NENT-l) *adjective.* 1. Of or related to a continent. 2. [Usually capital C] Of or related to mainland Europe or the people living there. 3. [Capital C] Of or related to the original 13 American colonies or the people living there at the time of the Revolution. —*noun.* [Capital C] A soldier in the army of the original 13 American colonies during the American Revolution.

Continental Divide. A ridge formed by the Rocky Mountains separating rivers that flow east from those that flow west.

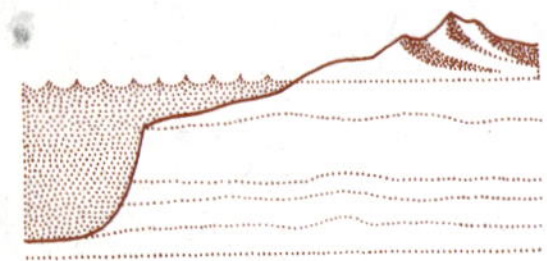
continental shelf

continental shelf. The underwater edge of a continent that extends from the shoreline to a point where the ocean floor drops sharply under very deep water.

con·tin·gent (kən-TIN-jənt) *adjective.* Relying upon some future or unknown condition: The town's safety was *contingent* upon the arrival of the army. —*noun.* A group or number of persons representing an organization, area, or country.

con·tin·u·al (kən-TIN-yoo-əl) *adjective.* 1. Without stopping; repeating at regular intervals: The *continual* dripping of the faucet kept me awake all night. 2. Often repeated; frequent: The student's *continual* interruptions annoyed his classmates. —**continually** *adverb.*

con·tin·u·ance (kən-TIN-yoo-ənss) *noun.* A continuing or repeating. **continuances.**

con·tin·ue (kən-TIN-yoo) *verb.* 1. To go on; keep doing. 2. To go on for a long time: The Colonists' dissatisfaction with Britain's rule *continued* until they achieved their independence. **continued, continuing.** —**continuation** (kən-tin-yoo-AY-shən) *noun.*

con·ti·nu·i·ty (kon-tə-NOO-ə-tee or kon-tə-NYOO-ə-tee) *noun.* Regular progress from one part to the next without interruption or distraction. **continuities.**

con·tin·u·ous (kən-TIN-yoo-əss) *adjective.* Without stopping; uninterrupted. —**continuously** *adverb.*

con·tour (KON-tur) *noun.* The outline of a figure, area, or thing: The *contour* of Italy resembles a boot.

con·tra- *prefix.* Indicates opposition to; the opposite: *contra*dict.

con·tra·band (KON-trə-band) *noun.* Anything imported or exported in violation of the law.

con·tract (KON-trakt) *noun.* A formal agreement involving two or more persons and binding them to some specific obligations. —(kən-TRAKT) *verb.* 1. To make or become smaller or tighter; reduce; shrink. 2. To make a formal agreement to meet some specific obligations. 3. To get or acquire, as a disease. **contracted, contracting.**

con·trac·tion (kən-TRAK-shən) *noun.* A shortened form of one or more words, usually involving the substitution of an apostrophe for one or more letters: "Don't" is a *contraction* for "do not."

con·trac·tor (KON-trak-tər) *noun.* A person who agrees to supply something or to perform a service in exchange for payment, especially such a person in the building trades.

con·tra·dict (kon-trə-DIKT) verb. 1. To state the opposite of something already stated: The witness *contradicted* the story of the accused man. 2. To be contrary or opposed to. **contradicted, contradicting.**

con·tra·dic·tion (kon-trə-DIK-shən) *noun.* 1. A statement that is the opposite of something already stated. 2. A denial of a charge or statement. 3. The condition or state of being opposed to something. —**contradictory** (kon-trə-DIK-tə-ree) *adjective.*

con·tral·to (kən-TRAL-toh) *noun.* 1. A female voice of the lowest range. 2. A female singer having a voice of the lowest range. **contraltos.**

con·tra·ry (KON-trehr-ee) *noun.* The opposite: I thought that Tom beat Bob in the race, but the *contrary* was true. —*adjective.* 1. Completely different; opposite. 2. (kon-TRAIR-ee) Inclined to have an opposite viewpoint; tending to argue. —**contrarily** *adverb.*

con·trast (KON-trast) *noun.* 1. A great difference between things that are compared: The *contrast* between the weight of lead and wood was easily seen. 2. A showing of differences or dissimilarities. —(kən-TRAST) *verb.* 1. To compare things in order to show differences between them. 2. To show or exhibit differences: Kathy's green skirt *contrasted* with her red blouse. **contrasted, contrasting.**

con·trib·ute (kən-TRIB-yoot) *verb.* 1. To give or donate money, goods, or services. 2. To write an article, poem, or other work for a newspaper, magazine, or other publication. 3. To add to; affect: Hard work and exercise *contributed* to Randy's great strength. **contributed, contributing.** —**contributor** *noun.*

con·tri·bu·tion (kon-trə-BYOO-shən) *noun.* 1. That which is contributed or donated: Mother's *contribution* to the party was a cake. 2. The act or process of contributing or donating.

con·trite (kən-TRIGHT or KON-tright) *adjective.* Having or showing sorrow or regret. —**contritely** *adverb.* —**contrition** (kən-TRISH-ən) *noun.*

con·triv·ance (kən-TRIGH-vənss) *noun.* A gadget or a device: A pencil sharpener is a useful *contrivance.* **contrivances.**

con·trive (kən-TRIGHV) *verb.* 1. To invent or design. 2. To plot or scheme, often for evil purposes. **contrived, contriving.**

con·trol (kən-TROHL) *verb.* 1. To command, direct, or regulate: The librarian *controls* the amount of money spent on books. 2. To keep in check; hold back; to limit: It is hard to *control* my temper during an argument. **controlled, controlling.** —*noun.* 1. Rule; command: The soldiers are under the *control* of the major. 2. The power to keep in check or regulate: Dad lost *control* of the car on the slippery road. 3. A device for regulating a machine.

control experiment. An experiment that tests a step at a time by keeping all conditions the same except for one detail that differs from another.

control tower. A tower at an airport from which takeoffs and landings of planes are controlled or regulated.

control tower

con·tro·ver·sial (kon-trə-VER-shəl) *adjective.* Causing disagreement. —**controversially** *adverb.*

con·tro·ver·sy (KON-trə-ver-see) *noun.* Disagreement; an argument or debate. **controversies.**

co·nun·drum (kə-NUHN-drəm) *noun.* 1. A riddle or puzzle whose answer is a pun: "How is a nose like a rotten fish?" "They both smell." 2. A difficult problem or mystery.

con·va·lesce (kon-və-LESS) *verb.* To begin to get back one's health after an illness; get better. **convalesced, convalescing.** —**convalescence** (kon-və-LESS-ənss) *noun.*

con·va·les·cent (kon-və-LESS-ənt) *noun.* A person who is convalescing.

con·vec·tion (kən-VEK-shən) *noun.* The transmitting of heat by movement of heated gases or liquids.

convection current. A flow of matter in a gas or liquid caused by temperature differences, the warmer material rising.

con·vene (kən-VEEN) *verb.* 1. To come together for a meeting. 2. To call together for a meeting. **convened, convening.**

con·ven·ience (kən-VEEN-yənss) *noun.* Comfort; ease; assistance. **conveniences.**

con·ven·ient (kən-VEEN-yənt) *adjective.* Easy to use or do; providing comfort or assistance. Nearby; close to: The house is *convenient* to stores and schools. —**conveniently** *adverb.*

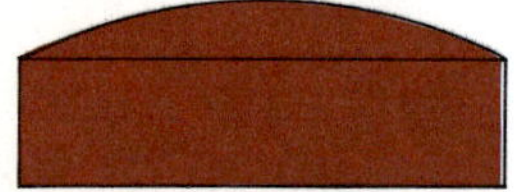

convex

con·vent (KON-vent) *noun.* 1. A group of nuns living and working together under religious vows. 2. The building in which such nuns live.

con·ven·tion (kən-VEN-shən) *noun.* 1. A meeting, usually of members of a special group, to discuss or decide on a special matter. 2. A traditional manner of doing something; a custom: Saluting is a *convention* in the armed forces. 3. An agreement about some issue; especially among a number of nations.

conveyor belt

con·ven·tion·al (kən-VEN-shən-l) *adjective.* Established; usual; not original. —**conventionally** *adverb.*

con·verge (kən-VERJ) *verb.* To come together at one place: The police cars *converged* from all directions at the scene of the robbery. **converged, converging.**

con·ver·sa·tion (kon-vər-SAY-shən) *noun.* Talking, especially in an informal way.

con·verse (kən-VERSS) *verb.* To talk with, especially in casual fashion. **conversed, conversing.**

convict

con·vert (kən-VERT) *verb.* 1. To change (one thing into another): The carpenter *converted* the barn into a fine home. 2. To change from one belief to another, especially with regard to religious beliefs. **converted, converting.** —(KON-vert) *noun.* One who has changed his beliefs. —**conversion** (kən-VER-zhən) *noun.*

con·vert·i·ble (kən-VER-tə-bəl) *noun.* 1. An automobile with a top that folds back. 2. A couch or sofa that converts into a bed. **convertibles.**

con·vex (kon-VEKS) *adjective.* Curved outward like the outer side of a ball. —**convexly** *adverb.*

con·vey (kən-VAY) *verb.* 1. To transport or carry. 2. To make known, communicate. **conveyed, conveying.**

con·vey·ance (kən-VAY-ənss) *noun.* Something that transports or carries, as a bus or car. **conveyances.**

conveyor belt. A wide, continuous belt, connected with moving wheels or rollers, used to carry things from one place to another in such places as farms and factories.

con·vict (kən-VIKT) *verb.* To find or declare a person guilty of a crime. **convicted, convicting.** —(KON-vikt) *noun.* A person who serves a prison term for a crime.

con·vic·tion (kən-VIK-shən) *noun.* 1. A finding or declaring guilty. 2. A strong belief.

con·vince (kən-VINSS) *verb.* To persuade; make a person sure of something. **convinced, convincing.**

con·viv·i·al (kən-VIV-ee-əl) *adjective.* Friendly, happy. —**convivially** *adverb.*

con·voy (KON-voi) *noun.* Something or someone that goes along with and protects: The destroyer acted as a *convoy* for the troop ship. —*verb.* (KON-voi or kən-VOI) To go along with and guard; to escort. **convoyed, convoying.**

con·vulse (kən-VUHLSS) *verb.* 1. To shake or disturb forcefully. 2. To cause uncontrolled tightening of the muscles. **convulsed, convulsing.**

con·vul·sion (kən-VUHL-shən) *noun.* Any severe involuntary tightening of the muscles. —**convulsive** *adjective.*

coo (KOO) *verb.* To make a low, soft sound like that made by a dove or pigeon. **cooed, cooing.**

cook (KUK) *verb.* To make food ready for eating, as by baking or frying. **cooked, cooking.** —*noun.* One who prepares food for eating.

cook·book (KUK-buk) *noun.* A book of recipes and cooking directions.

cook·y (KUK-ee) Also **cookie** *noun.* A small, flat biscuit or cake. **cookies.**

cool (KOOL) *adjective.* 1. Chilly; slightly cold. 2. Causing or permitting little heat: *cool* clothing. 3. Not enthusiastic; unfriendly. 4. Calm, not upset. 5. (Slang) Worthy of admiration; excellent of its kind: *cool* music. **cooler, coolest.** —*verb.* To reduce the temperature of; to become cool. **cooled, cooling.** —**cool it.** (Slang) Don't be excited.

coop (KOOP) *noun.* A small cage or pen in which chickens or other animals are kept. —*verb.* To confine in a small cage or pen; limit to a small area. **cooped, cooping.**

co·op·er·ate (koh-OP-ər-ayt) *verb.* To work or get along well together. **cooperated, cooperating.**

co·op·er·a·tion (koh-op-ər-AY-shən) *noun.* Working well together.

[1]**co-op·er·a·tive** (koh-OP-rə-tiv) Also **co-op** (koh-OP or KOH-op) *noun.* A building, store, or organization owned or operated by a group of people to gain more benefits, especially in the form of lower prices, than one person could get on his own. **co-operatives.**

[2]**co·op·er·a·tive** (koh-OP-rə-tiv or koh-op-ə-RAY-tiv) *adjective.* Inclined to work or get along well with others. —**cooperatively** *adverb.*

co·or·di·nate (koh-OR-də-nayt) *verb.* To make work together smoothly. **coordinated, coordinating.** —**coordination** (koh-or-də-NAY-shən) *noun.*

co·or·di·nates (koh-OR-də-nayts) *noun, plural.* The numbers on the bottom and the sides of a graph used to locate a point on the graph.

cop (KOP) *noun.* (Slang) A policeman. —*verb.* (Slang) 1. To seize; win: The team *copped* first prize. 2. To steal; to take illegally. **copped, copping.**

cope (KOHP) *verb.* To struggle or deal with in the hope of being successful. **coped, coping.**

co·pi·lot (KOH-pigh-lət) *noun.* A pilot who helps the chief pilot on an aircraft.

co·pi·ous (KOH-pee-əss) *adjective.* Plentiful; more than is needed. —**copiously** *adverb.*

cop out. (Slang) To give up; refuse; make up an excuse.

cop·per (KOP-ər) *noun.* 1. A reddish-colored metal, used especially as a conductor of heat and electricity. 2. (Slang) A policeman.

cop·per·head (KOP-ər-hed) *noun.* A poisonous reddish-brown snake found in North America.

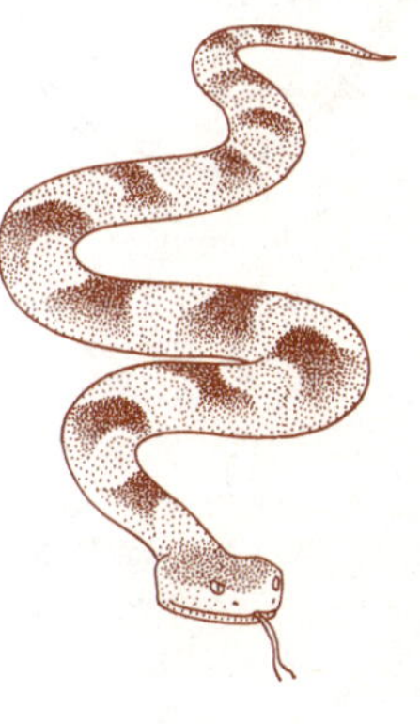

copperhead

cop·ra (KOHP-rə) *noun.* The dried inside part of a coconut (the meat) from which coconut oil is made.

copse (KOPS) *noun.* A group of small trees growing close together. **copses.**

cop·ter (KOP-tər) *noun.* (Informal) A helicopter.

cop·y (KOP-ee) *noun.* 1. Something made just like something else. 2. One of many issues of a book, magazine, or other publication. **copies.** —*verb.* 1. To duplicate. 2. To imitate. **copied, copying.**

cop·y·right (KOP-ee-right) *noun.* The legal right to be the only publisher or owner of a book, poem, picture, or other work. —*verb.* 1. To obtain the legal right to exclusive publication and sale of a book, poem, picture, or other work. 2. To protect by copyright. **copyrighted, copyrighting.**

coral

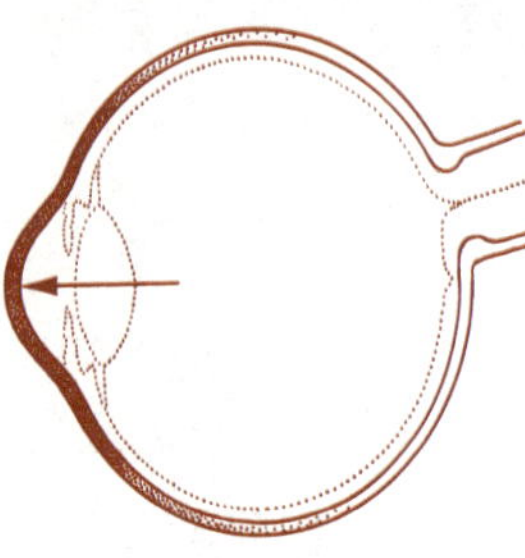
cornea

cormorant

cor·al (KOR-əl) *noun.* 1. A hard, often colorful, substance formed in the ocean from many skeletons of tiny saltwater animals. 2. (Also *adjective*) A reddish or pink color.

coral reef. An ocean reef or ridge made up of coral.

cord (KORD) *noun.* 1. A heavy string or twine. 2. An electric wire or wires covered with rubber or some other insulating material. 3. A stack of wood logs four feet wide, four feet high, and eight feet long.

cor·dial (KOR-jəl) *adjective.* Very friendly and warm. —*noun.* An alcoholic drink. —**cordially** *adverb.*

cor·du·roy (KOR-də-roi) *noun.* A heavy, ribbed cotton cloth.

core (KOR) *noun.* 1. The center part of an apple or other fruit. 2. The center: the *core* of the earth. 3. The basic or most important part of something. **cores.** —*verb.* To remove the core of an apple or other fruit. **cored, coring.**

cork (KORK) *noun.* 1. A lightweight, tough bark that grows on certain kinds of oak trees. 2. A piece of cork or similar material, often used to stop up the opening of a bottle. —*verb.* To stop up the opening of a bottle with a cork. **corked, corking.**

cork·screw (KORK-skroo) *noun.* A device used to remove corks from the tops of bottles. —*adjective.* Resembling a corkscrew in shape; spiral; twisted, as *corkscrew* curls.

cor·mo·rant (KOR-mər-ənt) *noun.* A large sea bird with a hooked bill.

corn (KORN) *noun.* 1. A common grain, usually yellow or white, used for cereal and other foods. 2. The plant on which such grain grows. 3. A growth of toughened skin, especially on a toe. —*verb.* To preserve food with salt or salt water. **corned, corning.**

corn bread. A bread or cake made from cornmeal.

corn·cob (KORN-kob) *noun.* The core or center part of an ear of corn.

cor·ne·a (KOR-nee-ə) *noun.* The transparent outer layer or covering of the eyeball. **corneas.**

cor·ner (KOR-nər) *noun.* 1. The spot where two streets or sidewalks meet. 2. The place where two surfaces or lines come together: Chairs were placed in each *corner* of the room. 3. A distant or remote area: Explorers have traveled to all *corners* of the earth. 4. A place or position from which there is no escape. —*verb.* To force into a position from which there is no escape: Detectives *cornered* the robber in the basement of the store. **cornered, cornering.** —**cut corners.** (Informal) To do something in a careless or quick way.

cor·net (kor-NET) *noun.* A musical brass instrument that looks like a short trumpet.

cor·nice (KOR-niss) *noun.* A heavy molding, often decorated, along the top of a wall or other structure. **cornices.**

corn·meal (KORN-MEEL) Also **corn meal.** Meal or coarse flour made from corn.

corn·starch (KORN-stahrch) *noun.* A starchy flour used in cooking to make certain foods thicker.

cor·nu·co·pi·a (kor-nə-KOH-pee-ə) *noun.* The horn of plenty—a symbol of a rich harvest in which foods are pictured overflowing from a cone-shaped horn. **cornucopias.**

corn·y (KOR-nee) *adjective.* (Slang) Silly or dull because of being crude, old-fashioned, or overused. **cornier, corniest.**

co·rol·la (kə-ROL-ə) *noun.* The petals of a flower. **corollas.**

cor·o·nar·y (KOR-ə-nehr-ee) *adjective.* Of or related to the heart and the blood vessels around it: The doctor gave the patient a complete *coronary* examination. —*noun.* (Informal) A severe heart attack. **coronaries.**

cor·o·na·tion (kor-ə-NAY-shən) *noun.* A ceremony at which a king or queen is crowned.

cor·o·ner (KOR-ə-nər) *noun.* A public official whose job is to find out the cause of death when someone dies from unknown or unnatural causes.

cor·o·net (kor-ə-NET) *noun.* 1. A small crown. 2. A decorated hat or headband.

corp. *abbreviation.* Corporation.

cor·po·ral (KOR-pə-rəl) *noun.* (U.S.) A soldier ranking above a private and below a sergeant. —*adjective.* Of or related to the body: *corporal* punishment.

cor·po·ra·tion (kor-pə-RAY-shən) *noun.* A group of persons united usually for business purposes to obtain certain legal rights distinct from the rights of the members as individuals.

corps (KOR) *noun.* 1. A group of persons organized for a special purpose: The police organized a *corps* of volunteers to search for the missing child. 2. A special unit in the armed forces: the Signal *Corps.* —**corps** (KORZ) *plural.*

corpse (KORPS) *noun.* A dead body, usually a human body. **corpses.**

cor·pu·lent (KOR-pyə-lənt) *adjective.* Fat, fleshy. —**corpulence** *noun.*

cor·pus·cle (KOR-pəss-l) *noun.* 1. A red or white cell found in the blood. 2. Any small rounded particle. **corpuscles.**

cor·ral (kə-RAL) *noun.* An enclosed place for keeping horses or other livestock. —*verb.* 1. To enclose in a pen or other small area. 2. To capture. **corralled, corralling.**

cor·rect (kə-REKT) *verb.* 1. To point out or remove mistakes. 2. To change or reform, often by punishment. **corrected, correcting.** —*adjective.* 1. Without errors; right. 2. Proper; well-mannered. —**correctly** *adverb.*

cor·rec·tion (kə-REK-shən) *noun.* 1. A correcting; a pointing out or removing of errors. 2. Reform; punishment. 3. A change from wrong to right.

cor·re·spond (kor-ə-SPOND) *verb.* 1. To exchange letters with someone. 2. To be in harmony or agreement with something else. 3. To be similar to. **corresponded, corresponding.**

cor·re·spon·dence (kor-ə-SPON-dənss) *noun.* 1. A set or series of letters exchanged by two or more persons. 2. Harmony or agreement. 3. Similarity. **correspondences.**

cor·re·spon·dent (kor-ə-SPON-dənt) *noun.* 1. One of two or more persons who exchange letters. 2. A person whose job it is to supply news from a certain place to a newspaper, television network, or other publisher of information.

cor·ri·dor (KOR-i-dər) *noun.* A hall or passageway, usually with rooms on one or both sides.

cor·rode (kə-ROHD) *verb.* To wear away slowly or rust. **corroded, corroding.** —**corrosive** *adjective.*

cor·ru·gate (KOR-ə-gayt) *verb.* To form into even folds or ridges: *corrugated* cardboard. **corrugated, corrugating.**

cor·rupt (kə-RUHPT) *adjective.* Dishonest; evil. —*verb.* To spoil or make evil: Bad companions *corrupted* Pinnochio. **corrupted, corrupting.** —**corruptly** *adverb.* —**corruption** (kə-RUHP-shən) *noun.*

cor·sage (kor-SAHZH) *noun.* A small bunch of flowers that can be pinned to a woman's dress. **corsages.**

cor·set (KOR-sit) *noun.* A woman's tight-fitting undergarment.

cos·met·ic (koz-MET-ik) *noun.* A coloring, powder, or other product used to make a person appear more attractive: My older sister carries lipstick, powder, and other *cosmetics* in her purse.

coronet

corral

corsage

cosmonaut

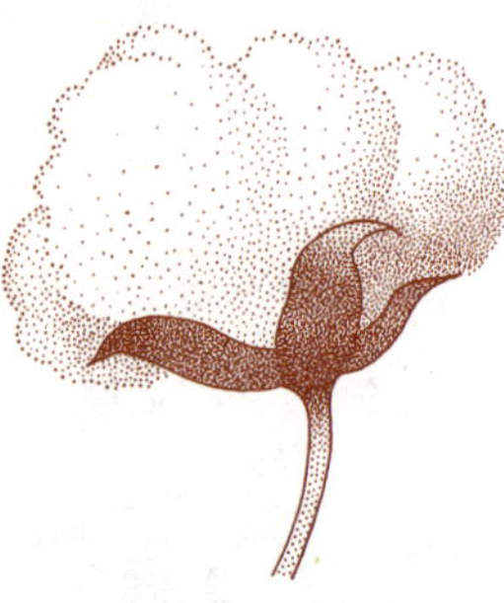
cotton

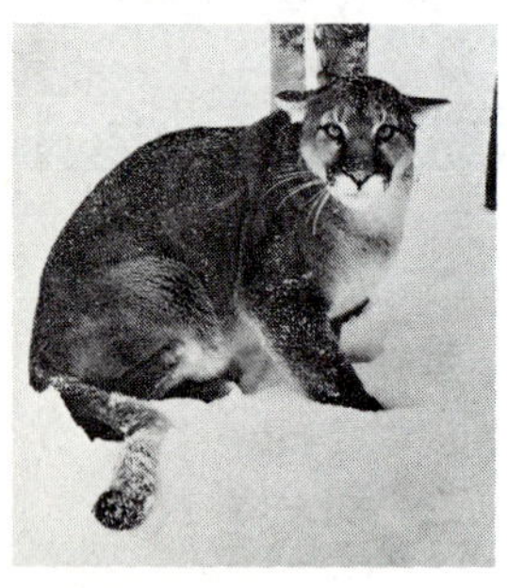
cougar

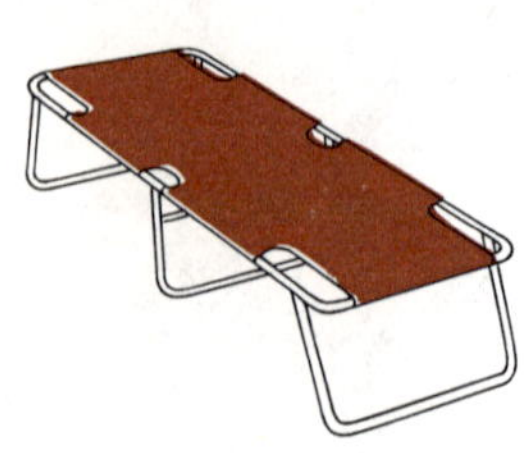
cot

cos·mic (KOZ-mik) Also **cosmical** *adjective.* 1. Of or related to the universe. 2. Immense; huge; boundless. —**cosmically** *adverb.*

cosmic ray. A very powerful ray or stream of energy that comes toward earth from outer space.

cos·mo·naut (KOZ-mə-nawt) *noun.* A crew member or pilot of a Russian spaceship; a Russian astronaut.

cos·mos (KOZ-məss) *noun.* 1. The world or universe. 2. A tall plant with bright, pretty flowers. —**cosmos** or **cosmoses** *plural.*

cost (KAWST) *noun.* 1. Price, value, or amount spent or asked. 2. What is used or lost to make an effort or gain; a sacrifice: Brave deeds are done by men who do not worry about the *cost.* —*verb.* To have a certain price, value, or amount. **cost, costing.**

cost·ly (KAWST-lee) *adjective.* 1. Expensive; highly priced. 2. Requiring much effort or sacrifice. **costlier, costliest.**

cos·tume (KOSS-toom or KOSS-tyoom) *noun.* 1. A fancy, strange, or funny outfit of clothing worn for special occasions. 2. The clothes worn by actors on stage. 3. The particular clothing of a place or time. **costumes.** —*verb.* To dress in or supply with a costume. **costumed, costuming.**

co·sy (KOH-zee) *adjective. See* **cozy.**

cot (KOT) *noun.* A lightweight, narrow bed.

cote (KOHT) *noun.* A shelter for sheep or birds. **cotes.**

cot·tage (KOT-ij) *noun.* A small house. **cottages.**

cottage cheese. A soft white cheese made from milk curds.

cotter pin (KOT-ər PIN) A slotted or split metal pin or wedge that, after being pushed through a hole, is spread apart to increase its holding power.

cot·ton (KOT-n) *noun.* 1. A plant, grown in warm climates, whose seeds are surrounded by fluffy white fibers. 2. Cotton fibers or thread made from them. 3. Fabric woven from cotton thread.

cotton gin. A machine that separates the seeds from the cotton fibers.

cot·ton·tail (KOT-n-tayl) *noun.* An American wild rabbit that has a fluffy white tail.

cot·ton·wood (KOT-n-wud) *noun.* 1. A poplar tree that has white cotton-like tufts on its seeds. 2. The wood of this tree.

couch (KOWCH) *noun.* 1. A padded or stuffed seat that is long enough to lie on. 2. A bed or place of rest. **couches.** —*verb.* To arrange (words, sentences, or speech) according to a special style or form: He *couched* his words carefully so as not to appear worried. **couched, couching.**

cou·gar (KOO-gər) *noun.* A large golden-brown wild cat found in North America and South America.

cough (KAWF) *verb.* To force air out of the lungs with a quick, deep-sounding noise. **coughed, coughing.** —*noun.* 1. The sound of coughing; the act of coughing. 2. A sickness that causes coughing. —**cough up.** (Slang) To pay money.

could (KUD) *verb. See* **can.**

could·n't (KUD-ənt) *contraction.* A shortened form of *could not.*

coun·cil (KOWN-sl) *noun.* 1. A group of people who meet to discuss problems or give advice. 2. A law-making body in some towns.

coun·cil·or (KOWN-sl-ər) *noun.* A member of a council.

coun·sel (KOWN-sl) *noun.* 1. Advice or opinion: My father gave me good *counsel* when he suggested I start my homework early. 2. The act of exchanging ideas or opinions. 3. A lawyer; legal adviser. —*verb.* 1. To give advice. 2. To recommend that something be done. **counseled** or **counselled, counseling** or **counselling.**

coun·sel·or (KOWN-sl-ər) Also **counsellor** *noun.* 1. One who gives advice. 2. A lawyer. 3. A person who works with children at a camp.

count (KOWNT) *verb.* 1. To go over (a list, collection, or group) one by one in order to find the total number: When I can't sleep, I *count* the stars. 2. To name the numerals in order: "When angry, *count* ten before you speak; if very angry [*count* to] a hundred." (Thomas Jefferson). 3. To add: *Count* up your test scores. 4. Add in: Don't forget to *count* yourself when you figure how many want to play. 5. To have value; be considered: How you act in class will *count* toward your mark. **counted, counting.** —*noun.* 1. Total number. 2. The act of counting. 3. (Law) A charge of lawbreaking: The man was arrested and charged with five *counts* of burglary. 4. A European nobleman. **—count on.** To rely on. **—count out.** To exclude.

count·down (KOWNT-down) *noun.* 1. The careful and exact marking off of the time just before the launching of a spaceship, as 10, 9, 8, 7, 6, 5, 4, 3, 2, 1—BLAST OFF! 2. Any count of this kind.

coun·te·nance (KOWN-tə-nənss) *noun.* The face; the expression or appearance of a face. —*verb.* To tolerate; approve of; allow: The teacher will not *countenance* any talking in study hall. **countenanced, countenancing.**

coun·ter (KOWN-tər) *noun.* 1. A table on which things are displayed for examination or sale in a store. 2. The shelf or divider across which business is done and money is exchanged in a bank, post office, or other place of business. 3. A narrow, built-in table-like shelf on which food is served in a restaurant or kitchen. 4. Any dial, board, or other device used to keep score, record numbers, or total numbers. 5. A chip, disk, or other small piece used in a game for play or adding score. —*verb.* 1. To act against; oppose; face with an opposite idea or movement. 2. To offer a different opinion or view; weaken or check by opposing. **countered, countering.**

coun·ter- *prefix.* Indicates the opposite or reverse: *counter*act; *counter*clockwise.

coun·ter·act (kown-tər-AKT) *verb.* To act in such a way as to stop or reverse: In order to *counteract* her own nervousness the new teacher told a joke. **counteracted, counteracting. —counteraction** *noun.* **—counteractive** *adjective.*

coun·ter·clock·wise (kown-tər-KLOK-wighz) *adjective* or *adverb.* Opposite to the direction of the hands of a clock: In order to open a jar, turn the cover *counterclockwise.*

counterclockwise

coun·ter·feit (KOWN-tər-fit) *noun.* 1. Illegal duplicate or copy; a fake meant to be accepted as the real thing. 2. Anything presented as real for the purpose of fooling. —*verb.* 1. To copy or imitate (usually money or bonds) with the purpose of passing the copy or imitation as the real thing. 2. To pretend. **counterfeited, counterfeiting.**

coun·ter·part (KOWN-tər-pahrt) *noun.* 1. A copy; duplicate: I see my *counterpart* in the mirror. 2. A perfect match; equal in appearance, action, or effect; that which goes with or fits together with: John is good at telling funny stories, and Harry is his *counterpart* when it comes to scary ones.

coun·ter·sign (KOWN-tər-sighn) *noun.* A prearranged signal, special word, or sign used to pass a guard post.

count·ess (KOWN-tiss) *noun.* 1. The wife or widow of a count (European) or earl (British). 2. A woman who, on her own, is entitled to the rank of count or earl. **countesses.**

counting numbers. The numbers that are used to count something, as 1, 2, 3, 4, 5, 6, . . . and so on, not including fractions or decimal numbers.

count·less (KOWNT-liss) *adjective.* More than anyone can or will count; innumerable.

coun·try (KUHN-tree) *noun.* 1. A person's nation; homeland; place of birth. 2. Any nation. 3. The citizens or people of a nation. 4. Farming area; rural area: "One day in the *country* is worth a month in town." (C. Rosetti). 5. Unused land: There's still a lot of wide open *country* in the West. **countries.**

coun·try·man (KUHN-tree-mən) *noun.* A person from the same country as another person. **—countrymen** *plural.*

coun·try·side (KUHN-tree-sighd) *noun.* 1. A section of the country; farmlands; scenic area. 2. The people of a section of the country. **countrysides.**

coun·ty (KOWN-tee) *noun.* (U.S.) A governmental division of a state. **counties.**

coup·le (KUHP-əl) *noun.* 1. Two together; a pair: Form a line in *couples.* 2. A man and woman who are married, engaged, dating, or dancing together. 3. (Informal) More than one; a few. **couples.** *—verb.* 1. To join together: The train crew *coupled* the engine to the freight cars. 2. To pair off; match up. **coupled, coupling.**

coup·let (KUHP-lit) *noun.* Two rhyming lines of verse, one after the other: "Avoid the chicken-pox and such,/ And don't fall out of windows much." (Edward Anthony).

coup·ling (KUHP-ling) *noun.* 1. Act of pairing or joining together. 2. Any mechanical device used for joining things together, as the *coupling* between railroad cars.

cou·pon (KOO-pon or KYOO-pon) *noun.* A stamp, ticket, advertisement, or other piece of printed paper that entitles the holder to something.

cour·age (KER-ij) *noun.* Braveness when faced with something frightening or dangerous. **—have the courage of one's convictions.** To act according to what you believe in the face of opposition.

cou·ra·geous (kə-RAY-jəss) *adjective.* Brave; not showing fear. **—courageously** *adverb.*

cou·ri·er (KOOR-ee-ər or KER-ee-ər) *noun.* A person who carries official or secret messages, as a government *courier.*

course (KORSS) *noun* 1. A planned program of study: My brother is taking a college *course* because he wants to go to law school. 2. Any specific part of such a program: Beginning algebra is easy, but the second *course* is hard. 3. A path, route, or channel that is followed: The ship's *course* was changed to avoid the hurricane. 4. A particular way or direction through time: "When in the *course* of human events . . . ." (Declaration of Independence). 5. The regular or customary way. 6. One part of a meal. **courses.** *—verb* 1. To hunt or chase with dogs. 2. To run swiftly, follow a path or channel; surge: The blood *coursed* through his veins. **coursed, coursing.**

court (KORT) *noun.* 1. An open place enclosed, in whole or part, by a building or wall. 2. An area laid out for the playing of tennis, basketball, or other sports. 3. The place where a king or other ruler lives or governs. 4. The people who serve, advise, or live with a king or ruler:

The *court* greeted the emperor with curtsies and bows. 5. (Law) The place where trials are held and legal questions are settled. 6. Judges or a judge hearing and deciding a legal action: The *court* ruled in favor of the defendant. —*verb.* 1. To try to win the affection of someone. 2. To take part in the social customs or practices leading to engagement or marriage. 3. To flatter for purposes of gain. 4. To act in a way that invites or brings on (something): John knew he was *courting* danger when he climbed onto the roof. **courted, courting.**

cour•te•ous (KER-tee-əss) *adjective.* Very polite; well-mannered; considerate of others. —**courteously** *adverb.*

cour•te•sy (KER-tə-see) *noun.* 1. Politeness; kind and thoughtful behavior. 2. A polite or considerate act: Mary's work at the hospital kept her busy but she never forgot the small *courtesies* that made the patients happy. 3. Favor; honor. **courtesies.**

court•house (KORT-howss) *noun.* A building where courts of law hold their sessions. **courthouses.**

court•i•er (KOR-tee-ər) *noun.* 1. A person who serves in a royal court. 2. One who seeks favor in a court.

court•ly (KORT-lee) *adjective.* 1. Polite and gracious; elegant: Grandfather delighted my friends with his *courtly* manners. 2. Of or suitable to a royal court. **courtlier, courtliest.**

court-martial (KORT-mahr-shəl) *noun.* A military or naval court that acts on cases involving military laws. —**courts-martial** *plural.* —*verb.* To bring (a serviceman) to trial in a military or naval court. **court-martialed, court-martialing.**

court•ship (KORT-ship) *noun.* The time of courting a woman before engagement or marriage.

court•yard (KORT-yahrd) *noun.* An enclosed area in or near a large building.

cou•sin (KUHZ-ən) *noun.* The son or daughter of one's uncle or aunt.

cove (KOHV) *noun.* A small harbor or bay, often hidden. **coves.**

cove

cov•er (KUHV-ər) *verb.* 1. To put something over or on in order to protect, shelter, or hide. 2. To extend over; to blanket: The leaves *cover* the grass. 3. To dress; put on clothes for warmth or protection. 4. (Military) To support advancing troops with firing from the rear. 5. To aim at with a gun or other weapon. 6. To include; take into account; work through: We *covered* the first part of the book page by page. 7. To meet a payment; have enough money to pay. 8. To report the news of (a particular area or field): The reporter *covered* Washington for many years. 9. To travel over. 10. To protect or guard: Bill *covers* right field well. **covered, covering.** —*noun.* 1. Anything that covers, as a lid, a hat, a blanket, a book jacket. 2. An envelope; a stamped envelope. 3. Woods; brush; undergrowth or the like: ground *cover.* 4. Hiding place; place of shelter: run for *cover.* 5. Something that limits visibility: cloud *cover.* 6. (Military) Protection provided by guns or airplanes. —**cover up.** To protect someone from punishment. —**under cover.** Acting secretly.

covered wagon. A large, heavy four-wheeled wagon with a canvas top.

covered wagon

cov•er•ing (KUHV-ər-ing) *noun.* Something put on (as a lid or hat), laid over (as a blanket), or wrapped around (as a book jacket), to protect, keep warm, keep in, keep clean, or hide.

cov•er•let (KUHV-ər-lit) *noun.* A bed cover; a bedspread.

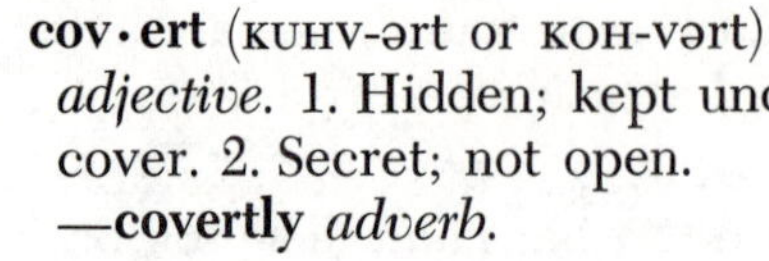

coyote

cov·ert (KUHV-ərt or KOH-vərt) *adjective.* 1. Hidden; kept under cover. 2. Secret; not open. —**covertly** *adverb.*

cov·et (KUHV-it) *verb.* 1. To want or wish for jealously what belongs to another person. 2. To wish for strongly or greedily: Even though I have a good collection, I *covet* every rare stamp I see. **coveted, coveting.** —**covetous** (KUHV-ə-təss) *adjective.* —**covetously** *adverb.*

cov·ey (KUHV-ee) *noun.* 1. A small flock of partridges or other birds. 2. A small group.

[1]**cow** (KOW) *noun.* 1. The female of cattle. 2. The female of the elephant, whale, and certain other animal families.

[2]**cow** (KOW) *verb.* To frighten by threatening: The fourth-grade bully *cowed* the second-grade boys. **cowed, cowing.**

cow·ard (KOW-ərd) *noun.* A person who has no courage or who is overly fearful.

cowbird

cow·ard·ice (KOW-ər-diss) *noun.* Strong fear; lack of courage: His *cowardice* kept him from diving off the low board.

cow·ard·ly (KOW-ərd-lee) *adjective* and *adverb.* Without courage; not brave: "'Do you think Oz could give me courage?' asked the *Cowardly* Lion." (Frank L. Baum).

cow·bird (KOW-berd) *noun.* A kind of blackbird of North America.

cowboy

cow·boy (KOW-boi) Also **cowhand** *noun.* 1. A man who herds cattle on a ranch. 2. (Slang) A reckless operator of an automobile or motorcycle.

cow·er (KOW-ər) *verb.* To crouch or bow fearfully: When I shook the newspaper at the puppy, he *cowered* in the corner. **cowered, cowering.**

cow·hide (KOW-highd) *noun.* 1. The skin of a cow. 2. The leather made from it.

cowl (KOWL) *noun.* 1. A hooded robe or cape worn by monks or the hood itself. 2. Any hood-shaped covering, as of an automobile engine.

cow·pea (KOW-pee) *noun.* 1. A pod-bearing vine. 2. The edible seed of this plant. **cowpeas.**

cow·punch·er (KOW-puhn-chər) *noun.* A cowboy.

cow·slip (KOW-slip) *noun.* 1. (United States) A wild plant with bright yellow flowers that grows in swamps, as a marsh marigold. 2. (England) An early spring plant with yellow flowers; a primrose.

cox·swain (KOK-sən) Also **cock·swain** *noun.* The person who steers a boat.

coy (KOI) *adjective.* 1. Acting shy; pretending to be bashful. 2. Shy; bashful; modest. **coyer, coyest.** —**coyly** *adverb.* —**coyness** *noun.*

coy·o·te (kigh-OH-tee or KIGH-oht) *noun.* A small, wild wolf of western North America with thick light brown fur and bushy tail. **coyotes.**

co·zy (KOH-zee) Also **cosy.** *adjective.* Warm and snug; very comfortable. **cozier, coziest.** —*noun.* A cloth covering, usually padded, put over a teapot to keep the tea warm. **cozies.** —**cozily** *adverb.*

crab (KRAB) *noun.* 1. A crustacean, or shell-covered animal, with eight legs, eyes on stalks, and a short flattened body. 2. (Zodiac) [Capital C] The sign for Cancer. 3. A person who is grouchy, cross, bad-tempered, quick to find fault. —*verb.* 1. To complain; find fault. 2. To fish for or catch crabs. **crabbed, crabbing.** —**crabby** *adjective.*

crab apple. 1. A small apple with a sour taste grown especially for making jams and jellies. 2. The tree on which these apples grow.

crab·grass (KRAB-grass) *noun.* Common type of grass that is considered a weed.

crack (KRAK) *noun.* 1. A narrow split; a break. 2. A short, witty, or nasty remark. 3. A sharp, sudden noise. 4. A slap; hard, sudden blow. 5. A break in the voice. 6. (Informal) A try; a chance: I'll take a *crack* at pitching in the next game. —*adjective.* Sharp; first-rate; the best; well-trained. —*verb.* 1. To break sharply and quickly: *crack* eggs. 2. To make a sharp, sudden noise, as the sound of snapping, breaking. 3. To make a crack; break without separating: He tried to smash the brick with a hammer, but all he did was *crack* it. 4. (Slang) To get into; open; work at: *crack* a book; *crack* a safe. 5. To lose control of oneself; to lose one's mind; to give in: He *cracked* under the strain of too much work. 6. (Music) To lose voice tone, volume, or control; break off, especially in singing high notes. 7. (Informal) To speak in a joking or rude way: *cracking* wise. 8. To distill oil. **cracked, cracking.** —**crack down.** To get strict; enforce rules or laws.

crack·er (KRAK-ər) *noun.* 1. A flat, crisp biscuit: Grandfather always crumbles *crackers* into his soup. 2. A firecracker. 3. A paper party favor in the shape of a roll that explodes or pops when both ends are pulled.

crack·le (KRAK-əl) *verb.* To make sudden, sharp, snapping sounds: The fire *crackled* whenever a dry log was put on it. **crackled, crackling.** —*noun.* A sudden, sharp sound.

crack·up (KRAK-uhp) *noun.* 1. A crash; a smashup; a collision: Speeding is the cause of most automobile *crackups.* 2. A mental or physical breakdown in health.

cra·dle (KRAYD-l) *noun.* 1. A small bed, most often on rockers, for a baby: 2. The place or location where something (a plan, idea, movement) is started and kept alive: Faneuil Hall in Boston is called the "*cradle* of American liberty." 3. Any structure that looks or works like a baby's cradle, such as the framework on which a ship sits while being built or repaired. 4. A low, flat piece of wood or metal on wheels that a mechanic lies on when working under a car. 5. A type of machine on rockers used by miners to sift gold particles from sand and rocks. **cradles.** —*verb.* 1. To rock or put in a cradle or cradle-like device. 2. To hold or rock in one's arms; shelter. **cradled, cradling.**

craft (KRAFT) *noun.* 1. Work involving skill and training: The *craft* of making shoes by hand is nearly forgotten because machines can do the work faster. 2. Work done by hand on various materials such as wood, metal, glass; a hobby: I took arts and *crafts* at camp. 3. Clever, sly, tricky behavior: He used all his *craft* to convince us he was not lying. 4. The members of a trade or a trade association. 5. A boat or airplane.

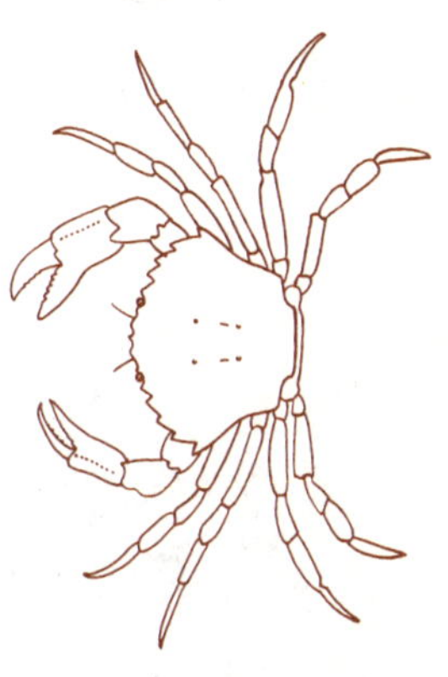
crab

crafts·man (KRAFTS-mən) *noun.* A worker trained in an occupation or industry: Silversmiths and jewelry makers are *craftsmen.* —**craftsmen** *plural.*

craft·y (KRAF-tee) *adjective.* Cleverly underhanded; sly; sneaky; deceitful. **craftier, craftiest.** —**craftily** *adverb.*

crag (KRAG) *noun.* A rough, uneven rock that sticks out from its surroundings.

cram (KRAM) *verb.* 1. To jam; stuff; force (in): We were *crammed* into the bus. 2. (Informal) To study or memorize for a test; try to learn many things at one time. **crammed, cramming.**

cramp (KRAMP) *noun.* 1. A pain in a muscle caused by an involuntary contraction. 2. (Usually plural) Sharp pain in the abdomen or stomach. —*verb.* 1. To cause a cramp. 2. To confine; hold in; hold back; squeeze in; to limit. **cramped, cramping.** —**cramp one's style.** (Slang) To keep from appearing at or doing one's best.

crampon

cranberry

crane

crater

cram•pon (KRAM-pən) Also, **crampoon** (kram-POON) *noun.* (Usually plural) A metal device with spikes on the bottom worn on a shoe or boot to prevent slipping on stone or ice.

cran•ber•ry (KRAN-behr-ee) *noun.* 1. A sour, red berry of an evergreen plant that grows in bogs. 2. The plant on which these berries grow. 3. (Also *adjective*) A deep red color. **cranberries.**

crane (KRAYN) *noun.* 1. A machine with a long, swinging arm for lifting, moving, or lowering heavy weights such as machinery or concrete blocks. 2. A metal bar or rod for holding a kettle or pot over an open fire. 3. A long-legged, long-necked wading bird, like the heron. **cranes.** *—verb.* To stretch: We *craned* our necks to see over the crowd. **craned, craning.**

cra•ni•um (KRAY-nee-əm) *noun.* 1. The skull of any creature with a backbone. 2. The part of the skull that contains the brain. **—craniums** or **crania** (KRAY-nee-ə) *plural.*

crank (KRANGK) *noun.* 1. The handle to or the part of a shaft that is turned to start motion. 2. (Informal) A crabby or ill-natured person. 3. (Informal) A person with strange, foolish, or crazy ideas. *—verb.* 1. To turn (a crank); make a circular motion: Really *crank* your arm around if you want power behind your throw. 2. (Informal) To do easily as routine: Fred can *crank* out a paper for English without even trying. **cranked, cranking.**

cran•ky (KRANG-kee) *adjective.* Crabby; in a bad mood, easily bothered; irritable. **crankier, crankiest.** **—crankily** *adverb.*

cran•ny (KRAN-ee) *noun.* A crack or small crevice as in a rock or wall. **crannies.**

crash (KRASH) *verb.* 1. To move with loud noise: Billy *crashed* through the woods thinking a bear was chasing him. 2. To run (into); collide: Anthony *crashed* into the wall because he was going too fast to make the corner. 3. To fall suddenly with loud noise: The milk bottle *crashed* onto the sidewalk. **crashed, crashing.** *—noun.* 1. A loud sound, as the *crash* of thunder; the *crash* of cymbals. 2. One thing or person bumping or running into another; a collision; an accident. 3. A sudden falling off of business. **crashes.** *—adjective.* Hurried or rushed: We had a *crash* course in Spanish before going to Mexico.

crash helmet. A hard head covering with thick padding inside.

crash pad. 1. A pad or padding within a vehicle, such as a spaceship, tank, or car, to protect passengers in case of rough going or a crash. 2. (Slang) A place for temporary lodging.

crate (KRAYT) *noun.* 1. A box, usually wooden, used to pack, transport, or store objects such as furniture, glass, or fruit. 2. (Slang) A vehicle that is old, in bad repair, or run-down. **crates.** *—verb.* To pack or put into a box. **crated, crating.**

cra•ter (KRAY-tər) *noun.* 1. The hollowed-out, cup-like opening at the top of a volcano. 2. Any cup-like depression formed naturally or by the impact of a large object such as a meteor or bomb.

crave (KRAYV) *verb.* 1. To long for, desire: When Polly is on a diet, she begins to *crave* candy bars. 2. To beg, ask for. **craved, craving.**

crawl (KRAWL) *verb.* 1. To move slowly on one's hands and knees. 2. To advance at a slow pace: Our cars *crawled* behind the heavy traffic. 3. To creep, as by the extending of parts of a vine outward. 4. To be filled or overrun: The dirty picnic table *crawled* with ants. **crawled, crawling.** —*noun.* 1. The act of crawling. 2. A swimming stroke in which the arms move one after the other out of and through the water while the feet kick.

cray·fish (KRAY-fish) Also **crawfish** *noun.* 1. A fish that is similar to a lobster but smaller in size. 2. A small, spiny lobster. —**crayfish** or **crayfishes** *plural.*

cray·on (KRAY-ən or KRAY-on) *noun.* A colored pencil or stick made of clay, wax, chalk, or other marking material, used for coloring, drawing, or writing. —*verb.* To draw with crayons. **crayoned, crayoning.**

craze (KRAYZ) *noun.* A passing fad or fashion. **crazes.** —*verb.* To make or become insane. **crazed, crazing.**

cra·zy (KRAY-zee) *adjective.* 1. Insane, mad. 2. (Informal) Not the usual thing; impractical: Dennis had the *crazy* idea of painting his bedroom purple with red spots. 3. (Informal) Impatient, enthusiastic, eager: Sal is *crazy* to try his new bike. **crazier, craziest.** —**crazily** *adverb.*

creak (KREEK) *verb.* To make a squeaking sound. **creaked, creaking.** —*noun.* A squeaking sound.

cream (KREEM) *noun.* 1. The heavier, richer part of milk, which contains most of the butterfat. 2. A medication, salve, or lotion: My sister puts a *cream* on her face to keep her skin soft. 3. [Usually plural] A kind of candy. 4. Liquid that is thick like cream or made from milk or cream: *cream* of tomato soup. 5. The top or best part: the *cream* of the crop. 6. (Also *adjective*) A color that is white with a yellow tint. —*verb.* 1. To add cream or a sauce containing cream to something. 2. To mash, beat, or stir something so that it is the thickness of cream. 3. To apply a lotion. 4. (Slang) To defeat badly. 5. To skim off cream. **creamed, creaming.**

crease (KREESS) *noun.* 1. A fold, line, ridge, or wrinkle: The old man's face was lined with *creases* of age. 2. The fold pressed into clothing. **creases.** —*verb.* 1. To make a fold or ridge. 2. To graze or wound slightly. **creased, creasing.**

cre·ate (kree-AYT) *verb.* 1. To make; bring something into being that had not existed before: "In the beginning God *created* the heavens and the earth." (Genesis). 2. To think of or have an idea for, as a piece of music, a painting, or a story. 3. To be the cause of: Jack *creates* problems wherever he goes. **created, creating.**

cre·a·tion (kree-AY-shən) *noun.* 1. The act of creating, of making or causing to be. 2. A thing that is or has been made. 3. The universe; the world. 4. [Capital C] God's bringing the universe into existence. 5. A product of the imagination, of the mind: Tom Sawyer was a *creation* of Mark Twain.

cre·a·tive (kree-AY-tiv) *adjective.* 1. Having the power to make or create. 2. Coming from imagination or original thought: *creative* writing. —**creatively** *adverb.* —**creativity** (kree-ay-TIV-ət-ee) *noun.*

cre·a·tor (kree-AY-tər) *noun.* 1. One who creates. 2. [Capital C] God.

crea·ture (KREE-chər) *noun.* 1. Any living thing, particularly an animal. 2. Man: That beggar is a poor *creature.* 3. Something made up or created: The ghost in the attic is only a *creature* of Teddy's imagination. **creatures.**

cre·den·tial (kri-DEN-shəl) *noun.* (Usually plural) Proof of authority, rights, or office.

cred·i·ble (KRED-ə-bəl) *adjective.* Reasonable; able to be believed: Sam gave a *credible* explanation of his low grade on the test. —**credibly** *adverb.*

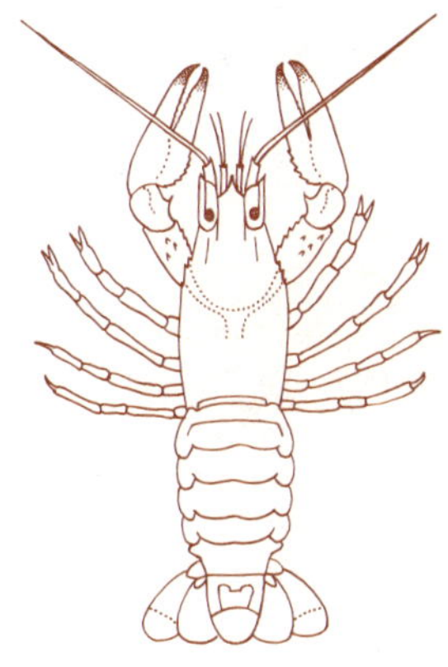

crayfish

cred·it (KRED-it) *noun.* 1. Honor, recognition, or praise for some deed, quality, or accomplishment. 2. A source of honor or praise: Mary Lou is a *credit* to her Girl Scout troop. 3. Belief in a person's promise to pay a debt: Mother bought her coat on *credit.* 4. Extra money in an account: Dad overpaid the telephone company last month, so he has a *credit* of $17 in his favor. —*verb.* 1. To trust, believe, or accept. 2. To acknowledge or add an amount: When Bill returned the coat, the clerk *credited* $50 to his account. 3. To have confidence in someone. **credited, crediting.**

cred·it·a·ble (KRED-it-ə-bəl) *adjective.* Deserving or bringing credit, praise, or honor: Joe played a *creditable* game of football today; he scored three touchdowns. —**creditability** (kred-it-ə-BIL-ə-tee) *noun.* —**creditably** *adverb.*

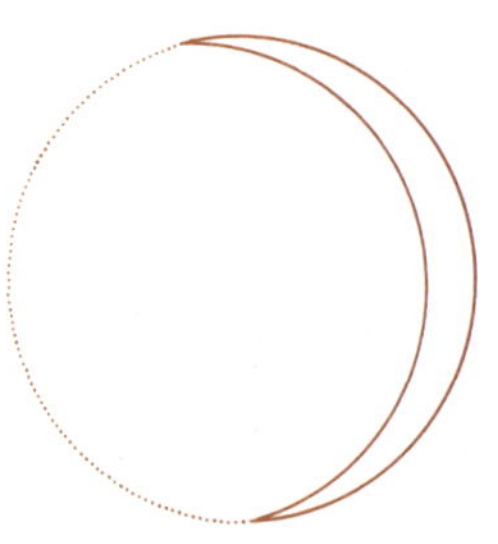
crescent

credit card. A card issued by a store or other business that allows a person to delay payment for goods or services.

cred·i·tor (KRED-ə-tər) *noun.* A person who is owed money or goods.

cred·u·lous (KREJ-u-ləss) *adjective.* Willing to believe someone or something without good reason. —**credulously** *adverb.*

creed (KREED) *noun.* 1. A statement or system of religious belief. 2. General belief or opinion: It is an American *creed* that all men are created equal.

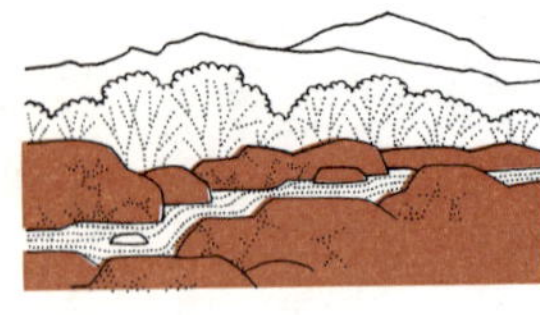
creek

creek (KREEK or KRIK) *noun.* 1. A path of water smaller than a river; a stream. 2. An inlet or bay of small size. —**up the creek.** (Slang) In trouble or difficulty.

creep (KREEP) *verb.* 1. To move slowly and quietly. 2. To move with the body touching or almost touching the ground. 3. To move slowly without much progress: The bus *creeps* along the snow-covered road. 4. To grow along the ground or other surface: The ivy *creeps* over the walls of the old house. 5. To have a sensation as of something creeping on the skin. **crept, creeping.** —*noun.* 1. The act of creeping. 2. (Slang) A dull, strange, or odd person. 3. (Geology) The slow downhill movement of dirt, sand, rocks, or gravel.

cre·mate (KREE-mayt) *verb.* To burn (a dead body) to ashes. **cremated, cremating.**

cre·ole (KREE-ohl) *noun.* [Capital C] 1. A person descended from the original French or Spanish settlers of Louisiana. 2. A black descendant of a line native to the Western Hemisphere, not of African origin. —*adjective.* 1. Relating to Creoles. 2. Cooked in a sauce made with tomatoes, peppers, and spices.

crept (KREPT) *verb. See* **creep.**

cres·cent (KRESS-ənt) *noun.* 1. The shape of the moon when it is less than a quarter full. 2. Anything of this shape. —*adjective.* 1. Having a shape like a new moon. 2. Growing, getting bigger.

cress (KRESS) *noun.* A plant of the mustard family used in salads or as a garnish.

crest (KREST) *noun.* 1. A growth of bone, skin, hair, or feathers on the head of an animal. 2. A decorative seal or part of a coat of arms. 3. The top or head of anything: the *crest* of a wave. —*verb.* To come to a head or form a crest. **crested, cresting.**

crest·fall·en (KREST-faw-lən) *adjective.* Downhearted, discouraged.

cre·vasse (krə-VASS) *noun.* A deep cut in the earth's surface or in the surface of a glacier. **crevasses.**

crev·ice (KREV-iss) *noun.* A crack, an opening. **crevices.** —**creviced** *adjective.*

crew (KROO) *noun.* 1. A group of people who do the same work or who work together: a ship's *crew;* a clean-up *crew.* 2. A group or bunch. 3. (Sports) Racing in long, narrow boats called shells.

crew cut. A man's closely cut hair style.

crib (KRIB) *noun.* 1. A baby's or a child's bed having closed sides. 2. A cattle stall. 3. A feeding container for animals; a manger. 4. (Informal) A means of cheating, as a list of answers or a translation. *—verb.* 1. To place or put in a crib. 2. (Informal) To steal work; use another's writing as one's own. 3. (Informal) To cheat with a crib; use an answer sheet or a translation. **cribbed, cribbing.**

crick·et (KRIK-it) *noun.* 1. A hopping or jumping insect that makes a chirping noise by rubbing its front wings together. 2. A game in which two teams of 11 members each score points by batting balls and running to one of two wickets, or goals. 3. Fair play; sportsmanship.

cricket

crime (KRIGHM) *noun.* 1. An act that is against the law. 2. Repeated acts of lawbreaking: a life of *crime.* 3. (Informal) A shame; a stupid or foolish act. **crimes.**

crim·i·nal (KRIM-ən-l) *noun.* A person who commits an act against the law. *—adjective.* 1. Of or referring to crime. 2. Terrible; shameful. **—criminally** *adverb.*

crim·son (KRIMZ-n) *noun* (and *adjective*). A bright shade of red. *—verb.* To make or become crimson. **crimsoned, crimsoning.**

cringe (KRINJ) *verb.* To shrink back, cower in fear or in slave-like obedience. **cringed, cringing.**

crin·kle (KRING-kəl) *verb.* 1. To fold as in a wrinkle: The old man's face *crinkled* when he smiled. 2. To make slight, rustling sounds. **crinkled, crinkling.** *—noun.* 1. A wrinkle or fold. 2. A crinkling sound; a crackle. **crinkles. —crinkly** *adjective.*

crip·ple (KRIP-əl) *verb.* To lame; disable; hurt so that something does not work properly. **crippled, crippling.** *—noun.* A person or animal that is lame or disabled. **cripples. —crippling** *adjective.*

cri·sis (KRIGH-siss) *noun.* 1. A turning point, often troubling, at which future events are determined: Our biggest family *crisis* came the year Dad lost his job. 2. The point at which the outcome of a story or series of events is determined. 3. The most intense state of a disease, after which a person either gets better or dies. **—crises** (KRIGH-seez) *plural.*

crisp (KRISP) *adjective.* 1. Brittle; hard, but easily broken. 2. Fresh; firm: *crisp* lettuce. 3. Quick and decided in manner. 4. Clean. 5. Refreshing. 6. In small, stiff curls. **crisper, crispest.** *—verb.* 1. To make or be made crisp. 2. To curl. **crisped, crisping. —crisply** *adverb.*

criss·cross (KRISS-krawss) *verb.* To mark with or form by crossed lines: The rabbits left prints that *crisscrossed* the new snow. **crisscrossed, crisscrossing.** *—adverb.* In a crisscrossed way. *—noun.* A mark or pattern of crossed lines. *—adjective.* Having many crossed lines.

crit·ic (KRIT-ik) *noun.* 1. A person, generally an expert on a subject, who judges, reviews, or gives his opinion on something. 2. A person who is likely to give harsh or rash judgments without enough reason: Pete is the class *critic;* he seldom approves anything we do.

crit·i·cal (KRIT-i-kəl) *adjective.* 1. Referring to a time of crisis, danger, or peril: The Revolution was a *critical* period in American history. 2. Likely to give harsh or rash judgments, as a *critical* person. 3. Referring to skilled judgment: The doctor gave a *critical* opinion of Johnny's illness. **—critically** *adverb.*

crit·i·cism (KRIT-ə-siz-əm) *noun.* 1. The act of judging or testing something, particularly a performance, a piece of writing, or a work of art: The newspaper's *criticism* of the new play was favorable. 2. The act of making an unfair or rash judgment.

crit·i·cize (KRIT-ə-sighz) *verb.* 1. To judge or test. 2. To find fault or blame. **criticized, criticizing.**

croak (KROHK) *verb.* 1. To make a sound like a frog; make a low sound from the throat. 2. (Slang) To die. **croaked, croaking.** —*noun.* A low, harsh sound.

cro·chet (kroh-SHAY) *verb.* To make a fabric by looping thread or yarn with a hooked needle. **crocheted, crocheting.** —*noun.* Needlework done with a hooked needle.

crock (KROK) *noun.* A pot, jar, or other container made of baked clay.

crock·er·y (KROK-ə-ree) *noun.* Dishes, jars, pots, or other containers made of baked clay.

croc·o·dile (KROK-ə-dighl) *noun.* A large lizard-like reptile with a thick-skinned body, long powerful tail, and long pointed snout. **crocodiles.** *See* illustration at **alligator.**

cro·cus (KROH-kəss) *noun.* A small plant with a single colorful flower that blooms in early spring. **crocuses.**

crone (KROHN) *noun.* An old woman. **crones.**

cro·ny (KROH-nee) *noun.* A pal; a friend. **cronies.**

crook (KRUK) *noun.* 1. (Informal) A thief; a dishonest person. 2. A bent or hooked pole. 3. A bend or hook in something: *crook* in the path.

crook·ed (KRUK-id) *adjective.* 1. Bent, curved, or twisted; not straight. 2. Not honest. —**crookedly** *adverb.*

croon (KROON) *verb.* To sing or hum in a low, pleasant, comforting way. **crooned, crooning.**

croquet

crocodile

crocus

crop (KROP) *noun.* 1. The vegetables, fruits, grains, or other growing things that a farmer plants and cares for. 2. The harvest of a particular season or plant: corn *crop.* 3. Any large supply: a *crop* of ideas. 4. A riding whip. 5. A short hair style. —*verb.* To cut off all or part of something. **cropped, cropping.** —**crop up.** To happen suddenly.

cro·quet (kroh-KAY) *noun.* An outdoor game played with wooden balls that are knocked with mallets through a series of wire wickets.

cro·quette (kroh-KET) *noun.* A small patty of minced meat, poultry, or fish rolled in bread crumbs and fried in fat. **croquettes.**

cross (KRAWSS) *noun.* 1. A shape (+) formed by one vertical line cutting across the middle of a horizontal line. 2. Anything in the shape of a cross. 3. A wooden structure on which people were put to death in ancient times. 4. [Capital C] The cross on which Jesus was crucified. 5. A mixture: My dog is a *cross* between a cocker spaniel and a bulldog. 6. (Boxing) A punch that is thrown across and over the opponent's punch. **crosses.** —*verb.* 1. To mark with a cross. 2. (Religion) To make the sign of the cross by moving the hand to forehead, heart, left shoulder, right shoulder. 3. To draw lines across: John always forgets to *cross* his "t's." 4. To go or pass across: Don't *cross* the street until the light turns green. 5. (Informal) To go against; oppose. 6. (Biology) To mix breeds of animals or types of plants. 7. To meet; intersect: The two main avenues *cross* in the center of town. **crossed, crossing.** —*adjective.* In a bad mood; angry. **crosser, crossest.** —**crossly** *adverb.*

cross·bar (KRAWSS-bahr) *noun.* A bar parallel to the floor used in gymnastics.

cross·bones (KRAWSS-bohnz) *noun, plural.* Two bones lying across each other as a sign of danger or death.

cross·bow (KRAWSS-boh) *noun.* An old-fashioned weapon used to shoot arrows from a bow mounted crosswise on a wooden handle.

cross-country (KRAWSS-KUHN-tree) *adjective.* Across open country, not on a road: a *cross-country* race.

cross-examine (krawss-ig-ZAM-in) *verb.* To ask questions about something already explained; examine closely. **cross-examined, cross-examining.**

cross-eyed (KRAWSS-ighd) *adjective.* Having either one eye or both eyes turning toward the nose.

cross-pol·li·nate (krawss-POL-ə-nayt) *verb.* To transfer pollen from one plant to another. **cross-pollinated, cross-pollinating.**

cross-reference (KRAWSS-REF-ər-ənss or KRAWSS-REF-rənss) *noun.* A suggestion to look in another part of a book for more information on a subject. **cross-references.**

cross·road (KRAWSS-rohd) *noun.* 1. A road that connects or crosses a main road or any other road. 2. (Plural) The place where roads cross. 3. (Plural) A time or place of decision.

cross section. 1. The surface exposed by cutting something across: The *cross section* of an apple shows its seeds and its core. 2. A sample; a representative section or group.

cross·walk (KRAWSS-wawk) *noun.* A marked lane in which people may walk to cross the street.

cross·ways (KRAWSS-wayz) Also **crosswise** *adverb.* Across, diagonally.

crossword puzzle. A word puzzle in which words must be guessed from clues and fitted across or down in a pattern of small squares.

crotch (KROCH) *noun.* The place where two things, as legs or branches, fork from the body or trunk. **crotches.**

crouch (KROWCH) *verb.* 1. To stoop or bend low to the ground. 2. To stoop or cringe in fear. **crouched, crouching.** —*noun.* The act or position of stooping low. **crouches.**

croup (KROOP) *noun.* A childhood disease that causes hard breathing and a harsh cough.

crow (KROH) *noun.* 1. A large, black bird with shiny feathers and a loud call. 2. A shrill cry or call: The rooster's *crow* wakes us every morning. —*verb.* 1. To make the sound of a rooster. 2. (Informal) To brag of one's own achievements or possessions. 3. To make a sound of happiness. **crowed, crowing.**

crow·bar (KROH-bahr) *noun.* A strong metal bar used for prying or lifting.

crowd (KROWD) *noun.* 1. A group of many people or objects: There was a *crowd* of 500 people at the baseball game. 2. A group of friends or associates: Our *crowd* likes to play baseball after school. 3. People considered as a whole: We vacation in the woods, far from the *crowd.* —*verb.* 1. To push or cram. 2. To come together in large numbers. **crowded, crowding.**

crown (KROWN) *noun.* 1. The top part of anything, as a head or a hat. 2. An elaborate headdress worn by royalty. 3. A championship: My favorite boxer won the heavyweight *crown.* —*verb.* 1. To place a crown on; give honor or power to. 2. To bestow an award or a title: She was *crowned* Miss America this year. 3. To reach or be at the top: A cherry *crowned* the ice-cream soda. 4. (Slang) To hit over the head. **crowned, crowning.**

crow's-nest (KROHZ-nest) *noun.* A high platform used for a lookout, particularly on a ship: The sailor in the *crow's-nest* yelled, "Land ho!"

crossbones

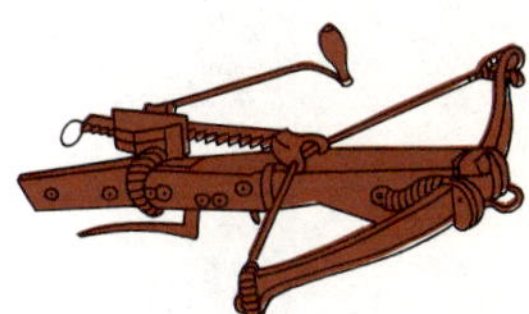
crossbow

crown

crow's-nest

crucifix

cru·cial (KROO-shəl) *adjective.* 1. Trying, difficult. 2. Of importance; decisive: It was the *crucial* point of the game; our team had to score the run or it would lose. —**crucially** *adverb.*

cru·ci·ble (KROO-sə-bəl) *noun.* A heat-resistant pot used to melt metals. **crucibles.**

cru·ci·fix (KROO-sə-fiks) *noun.* A religious object showing Jesus on the cross. **crucifixes.**

cru·ci·fix·ion (kroo-sə-FIK-shən) *noun.* 1. The act of putting to death on a cross. 2. [Capital C] The death of Jesus on the cross or a picture of it.

cru·ci·fy (KROO-sə-figh) *verb.* 1. To kill by nailing or tying to a cross. 2. To treat in a cruel manner. **crucified, crucifying.**

crude (KROOD) *adjective.* 1. In a natural, raw state, as *crude* oil. 2. Unrefined; vulgar: *crude* manners. 3. Rough, unfinished. **cruder, crudest.** —**crudely** *adverb.*

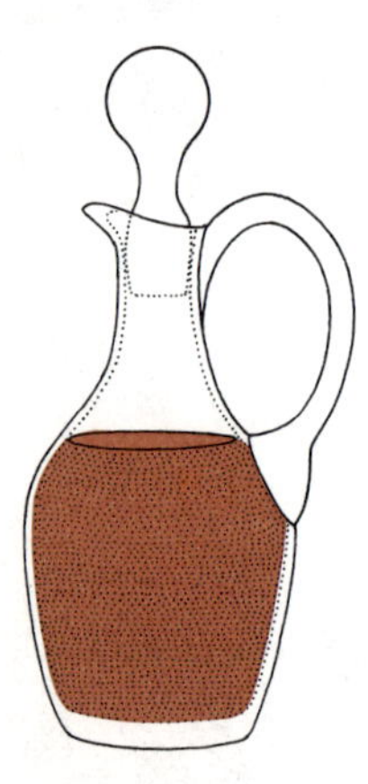
cruet

cru·el (KROO-əl) *adjective.* Harsh, mean; without mercy or pity. **crueler, cruelest.** —**cruelly** *adverb.*

cru·el·ty (KROO-əl-tee) *noun.* Meanness, harshness. **cruelties.**

cru·et (KROO-it) *noun.* A glass bottle used to hold liquids such as vinegar.

cruise (KROOZ) *verb.* 1. To sail from place to place for pleasure or in search of something. 2. To move smoothly, but not at top speed: The car *cruised* at 40 miles per hour. **cruised, cruising.** —*noun.* A pleasure trip in a ship. **cruises.**

cruis·er (KROO-zər) *noun.* 1. A large warship that can travel at high speeds for long distances. 2. A pleasure boat on which people can eat and sleep. 3. A police patrol car.

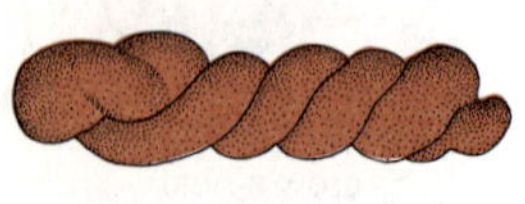
cruller

crul·ler (KRUHL-ər) *noun.* Sweet dough shaped in a long twist and fried in deep fat like a doughnut.

crumb (KRUHM) *noun.* 1. A small flake or piece of baked goods. 2. A tiny piece or scrap of anything: *crumbs* of information. —*verb.* To break up into very small pieces. **crumbed, crumbing.**

crum·ble (KRUHM-bəl) *verb.* To break up into small pieces; fall apart. **crumbled, crumbling.**

crum·ple (KRUHM-pəl) *verb.* 1. To press together into wrinkles: Joan *crumpled* the paper into a ball. 2. To fall down or give way. **crumpled, crumpling.**

crunch (KRUHNCH) *verb.* 1. To chew (something) noisily. 2. To crush. **crunched, crunching.** —*noun.* The sound of loud chewing. **crunches.**

cru·sade (kroo-SAYD) *noun.* 1. [Often capital C] A military journey made by Christians in the 11th through 13th centuries to recapture the Holy Land from the Moslems. 2. Any fight for a good cause or against wrongs: *crusade* against pollution. **crusades.** —*verb.* To work for a crusade. **crusaded, crusading.**

cru·sad·er (kroo-SAYD-ər) *noun.* 1. [Often capital C] A person of the 11th, 12th, or 13th centuries who took part in a religious march to recapture the Holy Land. 2. A person who works enthusiastically to support a cause: Sally is a *crusader* against litterbugs.

crush (KRUHSH) *verb.* 1. To break or wrinkle by pressing or squeezing: He *crushed* his hat when he sat on it. 2. To break into bits by grinding or mashing. 3. To overcome, subdue. **crushed, crushing.** —*noun.* 1. A crowd (of people) in the same area: There is always a *crush* of people in the locker room after the game. 2. (Informal) A temporary love for someone. **crushes.**

crust (KRUHST) *noun.* 1. The outer part of some baked products, as bread or pie. 2. The end slice of bread. 3. Any hard outer covering: a *crust* of ice. —*verb.* To cover with a crust. **crusted, crusting.**

crus·ta·cean (kruh-STAY-shən) *noun.* A creature that has no backbone and a hard outer shell, and lives in the water: Lobsters and shrimp are *crustaceans.*

crutch (KRUHCH) *noun.* 1. A support that fits under the arm to aid in walking, particularly when one leg is injured. 2. Something that supports in any way. **crutches.**

crux (KRUHKS or KRUKS) *noun.* 1. A critical or decisive point: the *crux* of a problem. 2. A baffling problem. **cruxes.**

cry (KRIGH) *verb.* 1. To sob; shed tears. 2. To make a loud sound or call. **cried, crying.** *—noun.* 1. A loud shout or call. 2. An animal's call or sound. 3. A fit of sobbing. **cries.** **—a far cry.** 1. A long way (from). 2. Very different, not at all the same.

cry·o·bi·ol·o·gy (krigh-oh-bigh-OL-ə-jee) *noun.* The study of the effects of low temperature and freezing on plants and animals.

cry·o·gen·ics (krigh-oh-JEN-iks) *noun.* The science that studies the effects of very low temperatures.

crys·tal (KRISS-tl) *noun.* 1. A type of glass that is clear and shiny. 2. A clear quartz. 3. The glass or plastic cover for the face of a watch. 4. A regularly shaped solid with many definite planes. *—adjective.* 1. Made of crystal. 2. Clear: *crystal* water.

crys·tal·line (KRISS-tl-in) *adjective.* 1. Made of crystal. 2. Clear as crystal.

crys·tal·lize (KRISS-tl-ighz) *verb.* 1. To form into crystals. 2. To fall into definite form: Joyce's plans for camp didn't *crystallize* until May. **crystallized, crystallizing.**

CST *abbreviation.* Central Standard Time.

cub (KUHB) *noun.* 1. A baby animal in such families as those of the bear or lion. 2. Any young person.

cube (KYOOB) *noun.* 1. A solid with six square sides that are all the same size. 2. Anything in the shape of a cube, as an ice *cube.* 3. (Math) The same number multiplied by itself twice: Eight is the *cube* of two (2 × 2 × 2). **cubes.** *—verb.* 1. To multiply a quantity or number by itself twice. 2. To form or cut into cubes. **cubed, cubing.**

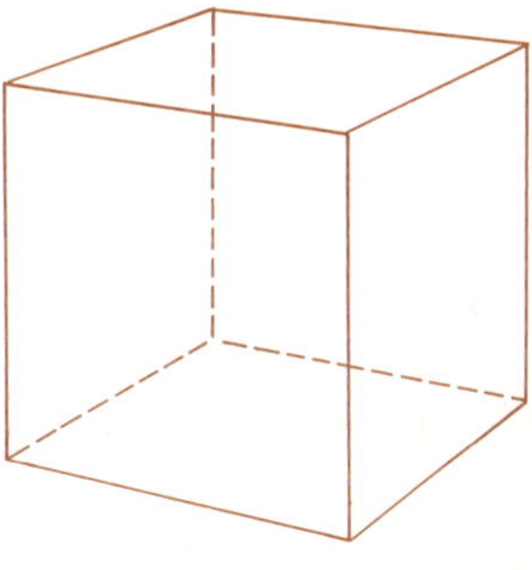
cube

cu·bic (KYOO-bik) *adjective.* 1. Of or related to a cube in form or shape. 2. Three-dimensional; having width, height, and length. 3. Describing the volume of a cube in terms of the length of any edge: *cubic* inch.

Cub Scout. A member of a junior division of the Boy Scouts.

cuck·oo (KOO-koo or KUK-oo) *noun.* A gray bird with a peculiar whistling call, native to Europe. **cuckoos.** *—adjective.* (Slang) Crazy, silly.

cuckoo

cu·cum·ber (KYOO-kuhm-bər) *noun.* A long fruit, green on the outside and white inside. **—cool as a cucumber.** Calm.

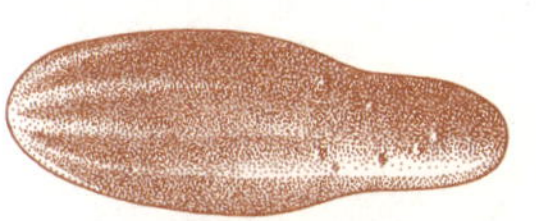
cucumber

cud (KUHD) *noun.* Food that is brought back from the first stomach of animals such as cows, deer, and goats to be chewed again.

cud·dle (KUHD-l) *verb.* 1. To hug gently. 2. To snuggle up to. **cuddled, cuddling.** **—cuddly** *adjective.*

cudg·el (KUHJ-əl) *verb.* To hit or strike with a heavy stick or club. **cudgeled, cudgeling.** *—noun.* A short, heavy stick or club.

cue (KYOO) *noun.* 1. A long, thin stick used to hit balls in billiards or pool. 2. (Theater) Any signal that tells an actor when to start his lines or actions. 3. A signal or hint. **cues.** *—verb.* To give a cue to. **cued, cuing.**

cuff (KUHF) *noun.* 1. The fold or turned-up part at the bottom of a pants leg. 2. A band at the wrist of a sleeve. 3. A blow with the hand; a slap. *—verb.* To hit or strike with the hand. **cuffed, cuffing.**

cu·li·nar·y (KYOOL-ə-nehr-ee or KUHL-ə-nehr-ee) *adjective.* Referring to kitchens or cooking.

cull (KUHL) *verb.* 1. To separate; pick one or a few from a group: *Cull* out the rotten apples; if you don't, the whole basket will rot. 2. To bring together in a group. **culled, culling.**

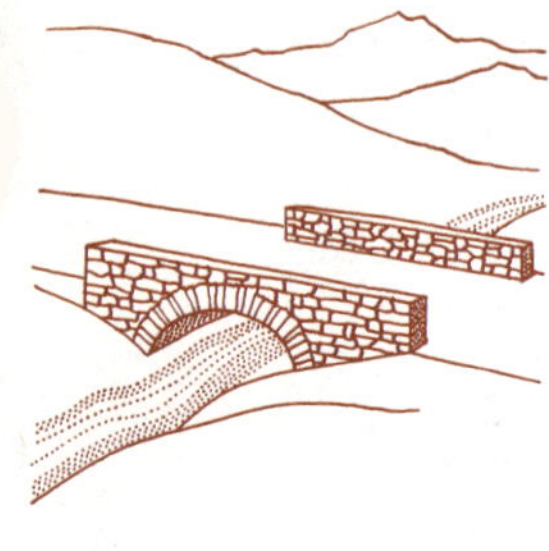
culvert

cul·mi·nate (KUHL-mə-nayt) *verb.* To attain the highest or most decisive point: Our science studies this year *culminated* in an exhibit of science projects. **culminated, culminating.**

cul·pa·ble (KUHL-pə-bəl) *adjective.* Guilty; deserving blame. —**culpably** *adverb.*

cul·prit (KUHL-prit) *noun.* One guilty of or charged with a crime.

cumulus

cul·ti·vate (KUHL-tə-vayt) *verb.* 1. To make land ready for crops, using various methods such as enriching the soil, plowing, or irrigating. 2. To care for in order to aid the growing process, as plants. 3. To study or practice for improvement or knowledge: Jack *cultivated* his fast ball and finally made the team. 4. To seek the friendship or good will of. **cultivated, cultivating.**

cul·ti·va·tion (kuhl-tə-VAY-shən) *noun.* 1. The act or process of tending or aiding the growth of something: *Cultivation* of land generally results in bigger and better crops. 2. Refinement, culture, social graces.

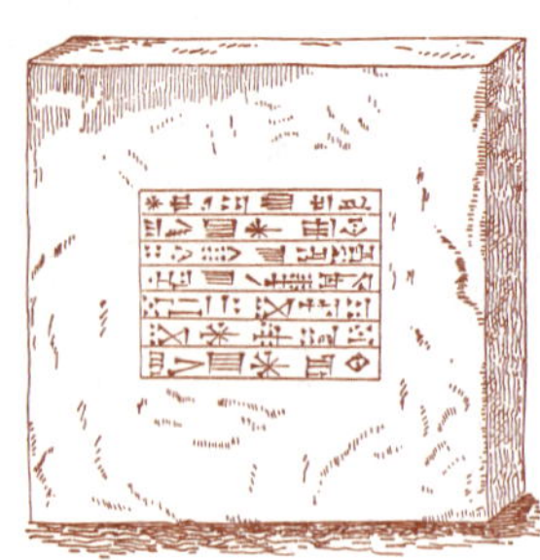
cuneiform

cul·ti·va·tor (KUHL-tə-vay-tər) *noun.* 1. One who cultivates. 2. A gardening tool or farm machine used to loosen soil and uproot weeds.

cul·ture (KUHL-chər) *noun.* 1. The result of being well-educated and refined. 2. The development of a group of tiny organisms for the purpose of scientific study: The scientist developed a *culture* of bacteria in the hope of finding a vaccine against flu. 3. The manner of living, the social behavior, or the artistic products of a particular group of people: The "blues" is a type of music developed by the black *culture.* 4. The caring for, tending, or developing of something: Soil *culture* usually leads to increased production. **cultures.** —**cultural** (KUHL-chər-əl) *adjective.* —**culturally** *adverb.*

cul·vert (KUHL-vərt) *noun.* A pipe or drain that goes under a road or some other passageway.

cum·ber·some (KUHM-bər-səm) *adjective.* Hard to handle; large or clumsy: The big package was a *cumbersome* load for the little girl.

cu·mu·la·tive (KYOOM-yə-lay-tiv or KYOOM-yə-lə-tiv) *adjective.* 1. Getting larger through additions: A snowball's increase in size as it rolls down a hill is a *cumulative* increase. 2. Obtained by or resulting from additions. 3. (Math) Forming a total by the addition of new material of the same kind.

cu·mu·lus (KYOOM-yə-ləss) *noun.* A white fluffy cloud that looks like a mound of whipped cream. —**cumuli** (KYOOM-yə-ligh) *plural.*

cu·ne·i·form (KYOO-nee-ə-form or kyoo-NEE-ə-form) *noun.* A type of ancient writing in which the characters had a wedge (or solid triangular) shape.

cun·ning (KUHN-ing) *adjective.* 1. Clever; showing inventiveness. 2. Crafty; sly. —*noun.* 1. Cleverness; inventiveness. 2. Craft; slyness. —**cunningly** *adverb.*

cup (KUHP) *noun.* 1. A rounded container, usually with a handle on one side, used for drinking. 2. A unit of measure that equals 16 tablespoons, 8 ounces, or one-half pint. 3. A cupful. 4. Anything that looks like a cup.

cup·board (KUHB-ərd) A cabinet or closet used to store food, dishes, or other items.

cup·cake (KUHP-kayk) *noun.* A small cup-shaped cake. **cupcakes.**

cup·ful (KUHP-ful) *noun.* The amount that can be put or poured into a cup.

cu·pid (KYOO-pid) *noun.* 1. [Capital C] In Roman myth, the god of love. 2. The figure of a winged baby boy that is used to represent love.

cu·pid·i·ty (kyoo-PID-ə-tee) *noun.* Greed; overpowering desire.

cu·po·la (KYOO-pə-lə) *noun.* A dome-like addition to a roof. **cupolas.**

cur (KER) *noun.* 1. A dog of mixed breed; a mongrel. 2. A person who is disagreeable or cowardly.

cur·a·ble (KYUR-ə-bəl) *adjective.* Able to be made well or healthy. —**curably** *adverb.*

cu·rate (KYUR-it) *noun.* A clergyman who is the assistant to a rector or a vicar. **curates.**

cu·ra·tor (kyu-RAY-tər) *noun.* A person in charge of a collection or exhibit, as in a museum or library.

curb (KERB) *noun.* 1. That which holds back, as a *curb* on the appetite. 2. A cement strip or other paved edging of a street. —*verb.* To hold back. **curbed, curbing.**

curd (KERD) *noun.* (Often plural) The lumpy part of soured milk that is used to make cheese.

cur·dle (KERD-l) *verb.* To turn into curds; get thick and lumpy. **curdled, curdling.**

cure (KYUR) *verb.* 1. To make well; heal. 2. To free from; get rid of. 3. To put (something) through a preserving, aging, or finishing process. **cured, curing.** —*noun.* Something that makes one well. **cures.**

cur·few (KER-fyoo) *noun.* 1. A set time when people must be off the streets, announced in ancient times by the ringing of a bell. 2. (Informal) A time set by parents, schools, or others when children must be home.

cu·ri·os·i·ty (kyur-ee-oss-ə-tee) *noun.* 1. A wish to know or learn about something. 2. Anything that is unusual or strange and, therefore, creates interest. **curiosities.**

cu·ri·ous (KYUR-ee-əss) *adjective.* 1. Desiring to know or learn: Jane is *curious* about wild horses and has read several books about them. 2. Odd; peculiar. —**curiously** *adverb.*

curl (KERL) *noun.* 1. A coil of hair. 2. Anything that is coiled in shape. —*verb.* 1. To make coils. 2. To roll up in a curve. **curled, curling.**

curl·y (KER-lee) *adjective.* Having or forming many curls: Jill has *curly* hair. **curlier, curliest.**

cur·rant (KER-ənt) *noun.* 1. A small round fruit that has a sour taste. 2. The thorny plant on which such fruit grows. 3. A small, sweet raisin.

currant

cur·ren·cy (KER-ən-see) *noun.* 1. Money issued by a country and in present use. 2. Popular use or acceptance: Although "ain't" has *currency,* it is not used by educated speakers. **currencies.**

cur·rent (KER-ənt) *noun.* 1. A steady flow: The river *current* carried Jo's hat downstream. 2. Electricity flowing through a wire. —*adjective.* 1. Happening now: *current* events. 2. Prevalent or in general use. —**currently** *adverb.*

cur·ric·u·lum (kə-RIK-yə-ləm) *noun.* 1. All the courses of study available in a school or other institution of learning. 2. The courses for a particular study or class: Each elementary grade has a different *curriculum.* —**curricula** (kə-RIK-yə-lə) or **curriculums** *plural.*

cur·ry (KER-ee) *verb.* To brush and clean a horse with a comb with metal teeth. **curried, currying.** —*noun.* A seasoning for food or a sauce made from this seasoning. **curries.** —**to curry favor.** To try to please by flattery.

curse (KERSS) *verb.* 1. To swear or use unacceptable language. 2. To call upon God to bring down evil upon others. 3. To bring misfortune upon: She is *cursed* by lameness. **cursed, cursing.** —*noun.* 1. Something that causes trouble or difficulties: Her slow reading is a *curse* to her. 2. A word used when swearing. **curses.**

curt (KERT) *adjective.* Short or brief; rude: Polly's reply to the invitation was a *curt* "no." —**curtly** *adverb.*

cur·tail (kər-TAYL) *verb.* To cut off or shorten: Bill's play hours were *curtailed* because he had too much work to do. **curtailed, curtailing.**

cur·tain (KERT-n) *noun.* 1. Any piece of material hung in a window or door as decoration or protection from sun or viewers. 2. A piece of cloth that conceals the stage from the audience.

curt·sy (KERT-see) *noun.* A woman's greeting or sign of respect made by bending the knees and bowing the body. **curtsies.** —*verb.* To make a curtsy. **curtsied, curtsying.**

cur·va·ture (KER-və-chur) *noun.* A bending or curving of a line or body.

curve (KERV) *noun.* 1. A line that continues to bend without any straight parts. 2. That which is curved: They couldn't see beyond the *curve* in the road. 3. (Baseball) A ball that is pitched so that it changes direction as it comes near the batter. **curves.** —*verb.* To bend in the shape of a curve: The garden *curved* along the driveway. **curved, curving.**

curved line. (Math) On a graph, a line that curves to show changes in quantity or other values.

cush·ion (KUSH-ən) *noun.* 1. A pad or pillow used on a piece of furniture to make it more comfortable. 2. Anything that is soft or makes a soft place. —*verb.* 1. To furnish with a cushion: Mother *cushioned* the armchair. 2. To soften a shock or blow. **cushioned, cushioning.**

cus·tard (KUHSS-tərd) *noun.* A boiled or baked mixture of eggs, milk, and flavoring that is served as a dessert.

cus·to·di·an (kuhss-TOH-dee-ən) *noun.* A person whose job it is to take care of or guard something: The *custodian* of the school made sure everyone had left before he locked up.

cus·to·dy (KUHSS-tə-dee) *noun.* 1. The state of being guarded or cared for: The money was put in the *custody* of the court. 2. Guardianship over (a person). **custodies.** —**in custody.** In jail or in the care of the police.

cus·tom (KUHSS-təm) *noun.* 1. An everyday habit: It is Father's *custom* to read the paper before dinner. 2. Something that has been done by a group of people for so long that it is considered bad manners not to do it: When you do not follow the *customs* of a foreign country, people may think you are rude. 3. (Plural) Taxes paid for goods brought in from a foreign country; the place where travelers' luggage is inspected for such goods.

cus·tom·ar·y (KUHSS-tə-mehr-ee) *adjective.* Usual: It is *customary* to exchange gifts at Christmas. —**customarily** *adverb.*

cus·tom·er (KUHSS-təm-ər) *noun.* A person who buys something.

cut (KUHT) *verb.* 1. To make an opening in; remove or separate into parts: Father *cut* into the turkey, *cut* the leg off, and *cut* the second joint into pieces. 2. To make shorter or trim. 3. To take the shortest way: Jim *cut* across the grass. 4. To make less in amount or price. 5. To divide into two parts: Kate *cut* the cards. 6. To snub. 7. To have (teeth) come through the gums. **cut, cutting.** —*noun.* 1. A place that has been sliced into: There was a *cut* on Bill's arm. 2. A piece that has been cut off: a *cut* of meat. 3. A snub or remark meant to hurt. 4. The way something is cut; fashion: the *cut* of a suit. —**cut and dried.** Fixed, certain, set by rules or habit.

cute (KYOOT) *adjective.* 1. Charmingly dainty or pretty: All the babies were *cute.* 2. Shrewd or clever in an unpleasant way: She didn't like his *cute* tricks. **cuter, cutest.** —**cutely** *adverb.*

cu·ti·cle (KYOO-ti-kəl) *noun.* The thick skin around a fingernail or toenail. **cuticles.**

cut·lass (KUHT-ləss) *noun.* A short, heavy sword with a curving blade. **cutlasses.**

cut·ler·y (KUHT-lehr-ee) *noun.* 1. Sharp instruments used for cutting, such as knives and scissors. 2. The knives, forks, and spoons used for serving and eating food.

cut·let (KUHT-lit) *noun.* 1. A thin slice of veal or lamb that is broiled or fried. 2. Ground meat or fish shaped into a flat patty and fried.

cut-rate (KUHT-rayt) *adjective.* Sold at discount or lower price.

cut·ter (KUHT-ər) *noun.* 1. A tool or machine for cutting: Meg collects cookie *cutters.* 2. A person who cuts special things: Amy's father is a diamond *cutter.* 3. A small motorboat used for police and rescue work by the U.S. Coast Guard. 4. A sailboat with one mast. 5. A small boat to carry passengers and supplies between shore and a ship.

cut·ting (KUHT-ing) *noun.* 1. Something cut off. 2. A piece of a plant used to grow a new plant. —*adjective.* 1. Hurting another's feelings: Ann's *cutting* remarks annoyed Sue. 2. Cold and chilling. —**cuttingly** *adverb.*

cut·worm (KUHT-werm) *noun.* Any of several caterpillars that cut off the stems of young plants near the ground and thereby destroy them.

-cy *suffix.* Indicates a state, condition, office, or rank: Presiden*cy*, bankrupt*cy*. **-cies.**

cy·a·nide (SIGH-ə-nighd) *noun.* Either of two deadly poisons—sodium *cyanide* or potassium *cyanide.* **cyanides.**

cy·cle (SIGH-kəl) *noun.* 1. A period of time in which repeating events are completed: The seasons follow each other in a *cycle* to complete the year. 2. A series of stories about a person or happening. **cycles.** —*verb.* 1. To ride a bicycle or motorcycle. 2. To move in a cycle. **cycled, cycling.**

cy·clist (SIGH-klist) Also **cycler** (SIGH-klər) *noun.* A person who rides a bicycle or a motorcycle.

cy·clone (SIGH-klohn) *noun.* A storm with violent winds blowing in a circular direction around a moving low-pressure spot. **cyclones.**

cy·clo·tron (SIGH-klə-tron) *noun.* A device that speeds up electrified particles to the point where they can bombard and split the nucleus of an atom.

cyl·in·der (SIL-ən-dər) *noun.* A long hollow or solid body with round sides and parallel ends. Mother's rolling pin is a *cylinder.*

cy·lin·dri·cal (sə-LIN-dri-kəl) *adjective.* Having the shape of a cylinder. —**cylindrically** *adverb.*

cym·bal (SIM-bəl) *noun.* One of a pair of metal musical instruments that are struck together to produce a ringing sound.

cyn·ic (SIN-ik) *noun.* A person who believes that people do things only for their own benefit.

cy·press (SIGH-prəss) *noun.* An evergreen tree valued for its wood, which is used in house siding and shingles. **cypresses.**

cyst (SIST) *noun.* A sac that grows abnormally in the body and fills with fatty tissue, gas, or liquid.

czar (ZAHR) Also **tsar, tzar** *noun.* 1. An emperor, especially a Russian emperor. 2. A person having great authority.

cyclone

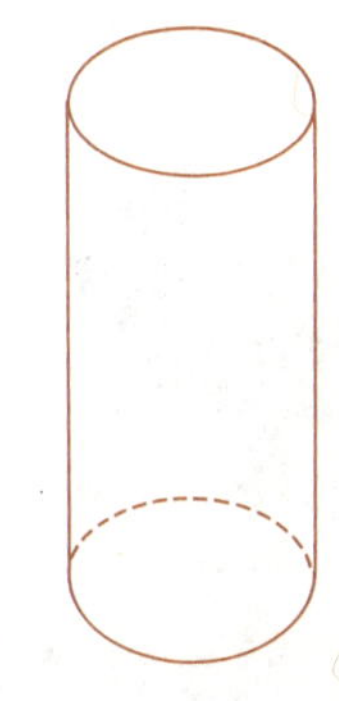
cylinder

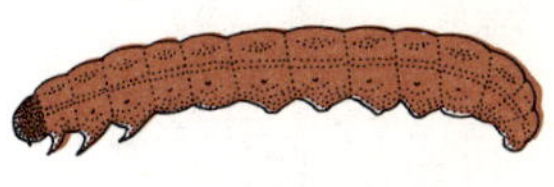
cutworm

cypress

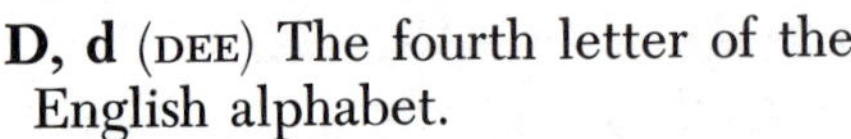

D, d (DEE) The fourth letter of the English alphabet.

d. *abbreviation.* 1. Died. 2. Date.

dab *verb.* To pat or stroke gently: He *dabbed* paint on the picture. **dabbed, dabbing.** *—noun.* 1. A small amount of something. 2. A light stroke or pat.

dachshund

dachs·hund (DAHKS-hunt) *noun.* A small dog with a long body and very short legs.

Da·cron (DAY-kron) *noun.* Trademark for man-made, washable material that does not wrinkle easily.

Dalmatian

dad·dy (DAD-ee) Also **dad** *noun.* (Informal) Father. **daddies.**

daddy longlegs. A spider-like creature with a small body and very long legs. **—daddy longlegs** *plural.*

daf·fo·dil (DAF-ə-dil) *noun.* 1. A plant with a yellow flower and long, narrow leaves. 2. (Also *adjective*) A bright yellow color.

daft *adjective.* 1. Silly, stupid. 2. Crazy, insane. **dafter, daftest.**

dag·ger (DAG-ər) *noun.* A short, sharp, knife-like weapon.

dahl·ia (DAL-yə) *noun.* 1. A plant with bright, large, colorful flowers. 2. The flower of this plant. **dahlias.**

dai·ly (DAY-lee) *adjective.* Happening every day. *—noun.* A newspaper published every day. **dailies.** *—adverb.* Happening every day.

dain·ty (DAYN-tee) *adjective.* 1. Small, pretty, delicate: Mother gave me a *dainty* lace handkerchief to take to school. 2. Particular, fussy: She has *dainty* manners. **daintier, daintiest.** **—daintily** *adverb.*

dair·y (DAIR-ee) *noun.* 1. A farm where milk and milk products, such as butter and cream, are produced. 2. A store that sells milk products. 3. A room or building where milk products are kept. **dairies.**

da·is (DAY-iss) *noun.* A raised platform in a room: the *dais* in the auditorium. **—daises** (DAY-i-siz) *plural.*

dai·sy (DAY-zee) *noun.* 1. A flower with a yellow center and white petals. 2. The plant on which this flower grows. **daisies.**

dale (DAYL) *noun.* A valley: over hill and *dale.* **dales.**

dal·ly (DAL-ee) *verb.* 1. To linger, loiter: Don't *dally* here; move on. 2. To treat lightly; toy (with): Don *dallied* with the rope, twisting it into knots. **dallied, dallying.**

Dal·ma·tian (dal-MAY-shən) *noun.* A short-haired white dog with black or dark-brown spots.

dam *noun.* 1. A wall or barrier that blocks the flow of water. 2. Mother of a four-legged animal. *—verb.* To hold back. **dammed, damming.**

dam·age (DAM-ij) *verb.* To hurt, injure: The heavy crate fell on the bananas and *damaged* them. **damaged, damaging.** *—noun.* 1. Harm, injury: A violent earthquake did much *damage* to our city. 2. (Plural) Money paid to someone to make up for harm done: The man who caused the accident was sued for *damages.* **damages.**

dame (DAYM) *noun.* 1. A woman, especially an older woman. 2. [Capital D] A British title of honor for women. 3. (Slang) Girl, woman. **dames.**

damn (DAM) *verb.* 1. To condemn, doom, convict. 2. To say something is wrong or bad: Father *damned* the book, which he said was full of lies. 3. To condemn to hell. **damned, damning.**

damp *adjective.* Wet, moist: The grass was *damp* after the shower. **damper, dampest.** —*noun.* Moisture, wetness: They wore sweaters in the cave because the *damp* made them chilly. —**damply** *adverb.*

dam•pen (DAM-pən) *verb.* 1. To wet; moisten: She *dampened* the cloth and washed her face. 2. To depress; reduce: The bad news *dampened* their spirits. **dampened, dampening.**

damp•er (DAM-pər) *noun.* 1. Someone or something that discourages or stops: The snowstorm put a *damper* on their plans to attend the basketball game. 2. Part of a fireplace or stove that controls the draft.

dam•sel (DAM-zl) *noun.* An unmarried girl or woman.

dance (DANSS) *noun.* 1. Certain movements or steps, usually done to music: The minuet, the polka, and the waltz are all *dances.* 2. A gathering for the purpose of dancing. **dances.** —*verb.* 1. To move one's body to a certain musical beat or in a certain pattern: The children love to *dance.* 2. To move lightly, quickly: Mary's fingers *danced* over the piano keys. 3. To run, leap excitedly: The baby *danced* with joy when he was given the teddy bear. **danced, dancing.**

dan•de•li•on (DAN-də-ligh-ən) *noun.* A common weed with notched leaves and yellow, feathery flowers.

dan•druff (DAN-drəf) *noun.* White flakes of dead skin that form on the scalp.

dan•dy (DAN-dee) *noun.* 1. A man who is fussy about his clothes and appearance. 2. (Informal) A person or thing that is outstanding. **dandies.** —*adjective.* (Informal) Excellent; very good. **dandier, dandiest.**

dan•ger (DAYN-jər) *noun.* 1. Unsafe condition; peril; risk: The small boat was in *danger* of capsizing in the high waves. 2. Something that can hurt or injure: Columbus faced many *dangers* when he crossed the ocean.

dan•ger•ous (DAYN-jər-əss) *adjective.* Risky, unsafe: Diving off cliffs into the water is a *dangerous* sport. —**dangerously** *adverb.*

dan•gle (DANG-gəl) *verb.* 1. To swing or hang loosely: A broken wire *dangled* from the telephone pole. 2. To hold (something) so that it hangs loosely. **dangled, dangling.**

dap•per (DAP-ər) *adjective.* Smartly dressed, neat in appearance.

dap•pled (DAP-əld) *adjective.* Spotted, marked with different colors: The *dappled* horse was spotted with brown and white.

dare (DAIR) *verb.* 1. To be brave enough to try or to do (usually something dangerous or difficult): I wouldn't *dare* talk back to my father. 2. To challenge someone to do something dangerous or difficult: Tommy *dared* me to let my frog loose in class. **dared, daring.** —*noun.* A challenge. **dares.**

dare•dev•il (DAIR-dev-əl) *noun.* One who dares to do dangerous stunts; a reckless person: The *daredevil* dove from a 50-foot board into 4 feet of water. —*adjective.* Daring, bold.

dar•ing (DAIR-ing) *adjective.* Without fear, brave: a *daring* acrobat. —*noun.* Fearless courage. —**daringly** *adverb.*

dark (DAHRK) *adjective.* 1. Not lighted: It was a *dark* night because the moon was hidden behind clouds. 2. Not light in color: *dark* blue. 3. Gloomy, depressing: The outlook for winning the game was *dark* when our best player got hurt. **darker, darkest.** —*noun.* Nighttime, darkness: I am not afraid to go out in the *dark* alone. —**darkly** *adverb.* —**in the dark.** Ignorant; not aware.

dark•en (DAHR-kən) *verb.* To block out light; make or become darker. **darkened, darkening.**

dam

dandelion

dark·ness (DAHRK-nəss) *noun.* 1. A state of being without light. 2. Ignorance, a state of not knowing.

dar·ling (DAHR-ling) *noun.* 1. Someone who is dearly loved. 2. A pet name used to show affection and love. —*adjective.* 1. Beloved: my *darling* little sister. 2. (Informal) Nice, lovely: a *darling* bracelet.

darn (DAHRN) *verb.* To mend by sewing rows of stitches back and forth: Grandma *darns* the holes in our socks. **darned, darning.** —*noun.* The part of a garment that has been darned.

dart

dart (DAHRT) *noun.* 1. A short, pointed object, usually having a feathered end, thrown at a target or used as a weapon. 2. A quick, sudden movement. 3. (Plural) A game in which players take turns throwing darts at a target. —*verb.* 1. To move quickly or suddenly; to race: The little girl *darted* out from between the parked cars. 2. To send or give out quickly or suddenly: Father *darted* a warning glance at the whining child. **darted, darting.**

dash *verb.* 1. To dart, race: Mother had to *dash* to the store before it closed. 2. To break by throwing: The baby *dashed* his toy to the floor, breaking it into several pieces. 3. To hit, crash: The high winds from the storm *dashed* the boat against the dock. 4. To splash: When Susan fainted, Mother *dashed* water into her face. 5. To ruin, put an end to: The thunderstorm *dashed* our hopes of going to a baseball game. **dashed, dashing.** —*noun.* 1. A short run or race. 2. A mark (—) used to show a pause or break in a sentence. 3. A tiny bit, a dab. 4. Liveliness; spirit: Jokes added *dash* to John's story. 5. (Radio) The long signal that, in various combinations with the short signal (dot), makes up the Morse code. **dashes.**

dash·board (DASH-bord) *noun.* The instrument panel in a car or truck.

da·ta (DAY-tə or DAH-tə) *noun, plural in form but sometimes used with a singular verb.* Information; facts: Ray spent many hours gathering *data* for his science project. —**datum** (DAY-təm or DAT-əm) *singular.*

data processing. 1. The analysis or storage of facts by a computer. 2. Getting material ready to be handled by a computer.

date (DAYT) *noun.* 1. The sweet fruit of some palm trees. 2. The day, month, and year (or just the year) when something happened or will occur. 3. (Informal) An agreement to meet, especially between male and female. 4. (Informal) The person whom one goes out with. —*verb.* 1. To put a date on. 2. To belong to a certain era: Jack's car *dates* back to the 1960's. 3. (Informal) To go out with. **dated, dating.**

daub (DAWB) *verb.* 1. To apply (a soft blob of something): Janie *daubed* lotion over the doll's face. 2. To paint in an untrained manner: John *daubed* with finger paint all day, creating a mess. **daubed, daubing.** —*noun.* A soft blob.

daugh·ter (DAW-tər) *noun.* A female offspring.

daughter-in-law (DAW-tər-in-law) *noun.* The wife of a person's son. —**daughters-in-law** *plural.*

daunt (DAWNT) *verb.* To frighten or discourage. **daunted, daunting.**

daunt·less (DAWNT-liss) *adjective.* Fearless, unafraid. —**dauntlessly** *adverb.*

daw·dle (DAWD-l) *verb.* To waste time; linger: He *dawdled* on his way home from the playground. **dawdled, dawdling.**

dawn *noun.* 1. The time of day when the sun first rises; daybreak: ". . . by the *dawn's* early light. . . ." (Francis Scott Key). 2. The beginning of anything: The orbiting of the first satellite was the *dawn* of the Space Age. —*verb.* 1. To begin;

grow light: The first day of our vacation *dawned* warm and sunny. 2. To first become clear or be realized: It *dawned* on her that the party is tonight. **dawned, dawning.**

day *noun.* 1. The 24-hour period during which the earth completes one full turn on its axis. 2. The period of light from sunrise to sunset. 3. Period of glory or importance: Our *day* will come; we'll have the best team in town. 4. A certain time in the past: in my grandfather's *day.*

day·break (DAY-brayk) *noun.* Dawn: *Daybreak* comes when light first appears.

day·dream (DAY-dreem) *verb.* To dream while awake, to wish: During history class, Anne *daydreamed* about her trip to Florida. **daydreamed, daydreaming.** —*noun.* Dreamlike thinking; nice thoughts.

day·light (DAY-light) *noun.* 1. Light from the sun: I was awakened by the *daylight* shining in my window. 2. Daytime: Let's play hide-and-seek while it's still *daylight.* 3. Dawn.

daylight-saving time. A time system used from late spring to early fall whereby clocks are set ahead an hour or more so that the extra hours of light come at the end of the day.

Day of Atonement. *See* **Yom Kippur.**

day·time (DAY-tighm) *noun.* The time between sunrise and sunset; the day.

daze (DAYZ) *noun.* A blurry, confused state of mind: Glen was in a *daze* after he fell off his bike. —*verb.* 1. To confuse, to shock: We were *dazed* by the news of the crash. 2. To stun, as with a blow: The ball hit John on the head and *dazed* him for a moment. **dazed, dazing.**

daz·zle (DAZ-l) *verb.* 1. To impress: The power of the huge waterfall *dazzled* us. 2. To overpower or confuse (usually by light): The brilliant firecrackers *dazzled* the children. **dazzled, dazzling.**

D.C. *abbreviation.* District of Columbia.

dc *Abbreviation.* Direct current.

D.D.S. *Abbreviation.* Doctor of Dental Surgery.

DDT. A poisonous substance used to kill insects.

de- *prefix.* 1. Undoing: *de*code. 2. Removal: *de*capitate. 3. Away from: *de*part. 4. Bring down: *de*grade. 5. Reduce: *de*flate.

dea·con (DEE-kən) *noun.* A church official, assistant to the minister.

dead (DED) *adjective.* 1. No longer living. 2. Unexciting, dull, quiet: a *dead* party. 3. Out of order, not working properly: The telephone was *dead.* 4. Exact: The dart hit the target in the *dead* center. 5. (Informal) Completely exhausted; tired or weary. —*adverb.* (Informal) 1. Completely: *dead* wrong. 2. Directly: The zoo is *dead* ahead. —*noun.* 1. The time of the most extreme darkness or coldness: the *dead* of night. 2. People who have died.

dead·en (DED-n) *verb.* To make dull, lessen: *deaden* a pain. **deadened, deadening.**

dead end. 1. A street or alley that is closed off at one end. 2. Any point beyond which one cannot go: Sally reached a *dead end* in her essay; she could think of nothing more to write.

dead letter. A letter improperly addressed that cannot be delivered or returned to the sender.

dead·line (DED-lighn) *noun.* A time limit applied to a job, assignment, or other deed: The *deadline* for handing in our art projects is next Wednesday. **deadlines.**

dead·lock (DED-lok) *noun.* The point beyond which it is impossible to progress, a standstill: When our club's voting came to a *deadlock,* the president's vote broke the tie. —*verb.* To bring to a standstill. **deadlocked, deadlocking.**

dead·ly (DED-lee) *adjective.* 1. Death-like: *deadly* pale. 2. Evil, harmful: a *deadly* poison. 3. Filled with hate or violence: *deadly* enemies. **deadlier, deadliest.**

deaf (DEF) *adjective.* 1. Unable to hear well, or to hear at all. 2. Unwilling to hear: Debbie was *deaf* to her mother's warnings. **deafer, deafest.** —**deafly** *adverb.*

deaf·ness (DEF-nəss) *noun.* Condition of not being able to hear.

deal (DEEL) *noun.* 1. An agreement: Tom made a *deal* with Harry to trade baseball bats. 2. An amount, portion: Grandma gave us a great *deal* of candy. —*verb.* 1. (Used with *with*) To tell or relate: The story *deals* with two lost children. 2. To distribute among a group: The librarian will *deal* out new books to our class tomorrow. 3. To trade; buy and sell: We *deal* with a grocery store on Main Street. 4. To handle by acting toward (a person) in a certain way: The baby sitter knows how to *deal* with children. 5. To give out playing cards for a game. **dealt, dealing.**

dean (DEEN) *noun.* 1. The head of a department or a group in a school or university: She is the *dean* of women. 2. The head of a group of churches or a priest in charge of a cathedral. 3. An elder, respected member of a group: He is the *dean* of American writers.

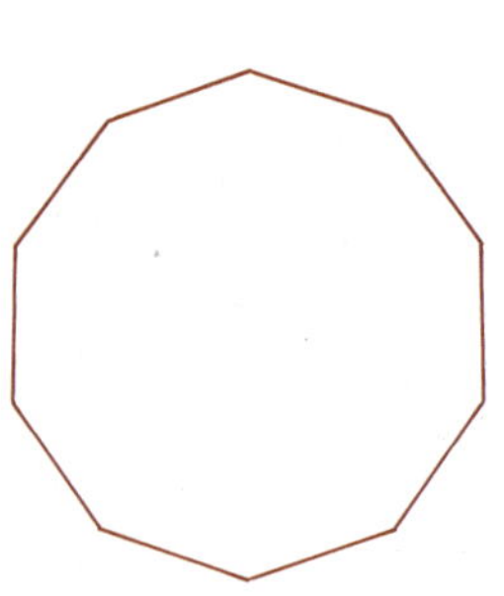

decagon

dear (DIHR) *adjective.* 1. Expensive, high-priced: We are growing our own tomatoes because they are so *dear* at the store. 2. Darling, beloved. **dearer, dearest.** —*noun.* A person who is loved very much. —**dearly** *adverb.*

dearth (DERTH) *noun.* Lack, scarcity: There is a *dearth* of food in some countries, such as India.

death (DETH) *noun.* 1. Dying, the end of life. 2. The end of anything: His laziness was the *death* of his career.

de·base (di-BAYSS) *verb.* To spoil, lower in worth: The beauty of the land was *debased* by litter. **debased, debasing.**

de·bate (di-BAYT) *verb.* 1. To argue, especially in a formal manner. 2. To consider carefully: He *debated* whether he should go to the party or do his homework. **debated, debating.** —*noun.* An argument, usually formal, in a public place: Our team won the *debate* on the question: "Should School Last All Year?" **debates.**

de·bris (də-BREE or day-BREE) *noun.* Litter, rubbish, waste.

debt (DET) *noun.* Something that is owed: I owe Joan 50 cents; I must pay the *debt.*

debt·or (DET-ər) *noun.* A person who owes something to another; one who is in debt.

de·but (di-BYOO or DAY-byoo) *noun.* 1. A coming out, a first public appearance: The *debut* of the new movie will be in New York City next week. 2. A party given to introduce a girl formally to society.

dec- *prefix.* Also **deca-** or **deka-** Indicates ten: *dec*ade, *dec*agon.

de·cade (DEK-ayd) *noun.* Ten years: From 1970 to 1980 is a *decade.* 2. A group of ten. **decades.**

dec·a·gon (DEK-ə-gon) *noun.* (Geometry) A ten-sided form.

de·cal (DEE-KAL) Also **de·cal·co·ma·ni·a** (dee-kal-kə-MAY-nee-ə) *noun.* A piece of specially prepared paper with a picture or form that can be transferred to certain surfaces.

de·cap·i·tate (di-KAP-ə-tayt) *verb.* To cut off the head of. **decapitated, decapitating.**

de·cay (di-KAY) *verb.* To rot, become bad: Food *decays* if not properly refrigerated. **decayed, decaying.** —*noun.* Rottenness, something gone bad: The dentist drilled Jimmy's tooth because he saw signs of *decay.*

de·cease (di-SEESS) *verb.* To die, stop living. **deceased, deceasing.** —*noun.* Death.

de·ceased (di-SEEST) *adjective.* Dead. My *deceased* uncle used to play the piano. —*noun.* A dead person.

de·ceit (di-SEET) *noun.* 1. A trick or lie. 2. The act of tricking or lying.

de·ceive (di-SEEV) *verb.* To trick, mislead: "Nature never *deceives* us; it is always we who *deceive* ourselves." (Rousseau). **deceived, deceiving.**

De·cem·ber (di-SEM-bər) *noun.* The twelfth month of the year: There are 31 days in *December.* —**Dec.** *abbreviation.*

de·cen·cy (DEE-sən-see) *noun.* Goodness, rightness, a state of being proper and courteous.

de·cent (DEE-sənt) *adjective.* 1. Right, proper: *decent* table manners. 2. Fairly good: *decent* grades. 3. Generous, friendly. —**decently** *adverb.*

de·cep·tion (di-SEP-shən) *noun.* A trick; a lie; something that deceives.

deci- *prefix.* Indicates one-tenth: *deci*gram.

de·ci·bel (DESS-i-bəl) *noun.* Unit used to measure the loudness of a sound or to compare the loudness of two sounds.

de·cide (di-SIGHD) *verb.* 1. To make up one's mind, conclude: We *decided* to play kickball during recess. 2. To settle a dispute; pronounce a victory: The winner of the boxing match was *decided* by the referee. **decided, deciding.**

de·cid·u·ous (di-SIJ-oo-əss) *adjective.* Shedding leaves during a certain season: Oak trees are *deciduous;* pine trees are not.

dec·i·mal (DESS-ə-məl) *adjective.* Based on or having to do with ten. —*noun.* Also **decimal fraction.** A fraction that has a denominator of 10, 100, 1,000 or any power of 10: The fraction 4/10 can be written as the *decimal* .4.

decimal point. A dot used at the left of a decimal fraction to show that its denominator is a power of ten: If you put a *decimal point* before 3, it becomes .3 or 3/10.

dec·i·me·ter (DESS-ə-mee-tər) *noun.* A unit of measure equal to one-tenth of a meter.

de·ci·pher (di-SIGH-fər) *verb.* 1. To unscramble, make sense of: *decipher* messy handwriting. 2. To translate from a code. **deciphered, deciphering.**

de·ci·sion (di-SIZH-ən) *noun.* 1. A conclusion, judgment: The *decision* has been made that we will not have school today. 2. A legal judgment: a judge's *decision.*

de·ci·sive (di-SIGH-siv) *adjective.* 1. Certain, definite, clear-cut: Our football team scored a *decisive* victory, 24–3. 2. Able to solve a question or dispute: a *decisive* battle. —**decisively** *adverb.*

deck (DEK) *noun.* 1. A floor, usually on a boat, which may be open or closed in by walls and a roof. 2. A pack of playing cards. —*verb.* (Slang) 1. To knock down: The boxer *decked* his opponent with a left hook. 2. (Often used with *out*) To dress in fine or fancy clothes: On the night of the dance, John was *decked* out in a tuxedo. **decked, decking.** —**clear the decks** or **hit the deck.** To get ready for a job or any action. —**on deck.** (Informal) Ready or waiting.

dec·la·ra·tion (dek-lə-RAY-shən) *noun.* 1. A formal public statement: The *Declaration* of Independence made clear the wishes of American Colonists. 2. The act of declaring: Mary's *declaration* that she would not go to school angered Mother.

de·clar·a·tive (di-KLAIR-ə-tiv) Also **de·clar·a·to·ry** (di-KLAIR-ə-tor-ee) *adjective.* Presenting a statement: A *declarative* sentence is one that states or explains something.

de·clare (di-KLAIR) *verb.* 1. To announce publicly and officially: The President *declared* that Thanksgiving Day would be a national holiday. 2. To state firmly. **declared, declaring.**

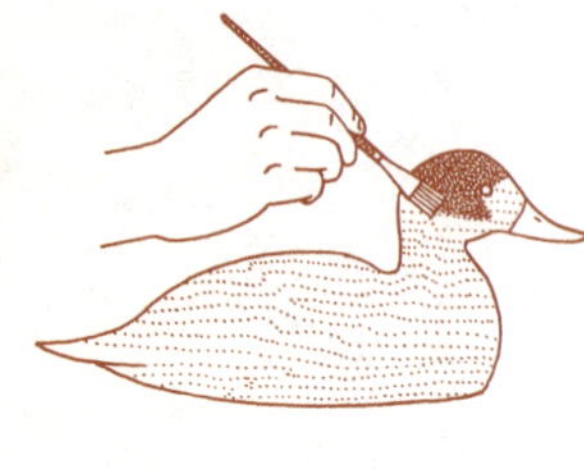
decoy

de·clen·sion (di-KLEN-shən) *noun.* 1. A listing of nouns, pronouns, or adjectives showing the different endings that tell how a word is related to other words in a sentence. 2. A class of nouns, pronouns, or adjectives that all have the same or similar endings.

dec·li·na·tion (dek-lə-NAY-shən) *noun.* 1. A downhill slope: The *declination* of that ramp is very steep. 2. A refusal.

de·cline (di-KLIGHN) *verb.* 1. To fail, become poorer: Her health *declined* during the cold winter months. 2. To refuse; turn down: Jim *declined* a second piece of pie. 3. To slope downward. 4. (Grammar) To show the different cases of a noun, adjective, or pronoun. **declined, declining.** —*noun.* 1. A downhill slant. 2. A lessening: There is a *decline* in the sale of soap this month. **declines.**

de·cliv·i·ty (di-KLIV-ə-tee) *noun.* A downward slant. **declivities.**

de·code (dee-KOHD) *verb.* To translate a code into understandable language. **decoded, decoding.**

de·com·pose (dee-kəm-POHZ) *verb.* 1. To rot, waste away. 2. To fall apart; disintegrate. **decomposed, decomposing. —decomposition** (dee-kom-pə-ZISH-ən) *noun.*

dec·o·rate (DEK-ə-rayt) *verb.* 1. To adorn, make prettier or brighter. 2. To present a medal or an award, especially to a soldier. **decorated, decorating.**

dec·o·ra·tion (dek-ə-RAY-shən) *noun.* 1. Something used to decorate or adorn: Christmas *decorations.* 2. The action of decorating. 3. A medal; an award.

dec·o·ra·tive (DEK-ər-ə-tiv) *adjective.* Pretty, pleasing to the eye.

de·co·rum (di-KOR-əm) *noun.* Politeness, fitness, or properness in behavior or appearance.

de·coy (DEE-koi or di-KOI) *noun.* 1. A real or imitation bird or animal used by hunters to attract game into their hunting area. 2. Anything that leads something or somebody into a trap. —*verb* (di-KOI). To lead into a trap. **decoyed, decoying.**

de·crease (di-KREESS) *verb.* 1. To lessen: You must *decrease* the amount of candy you eat. 2. To become smaller. **decreased, decreasing.** —(DEE-kreess) *noun.* A lessening. **decreases.**

de·cree (di-KREE) *noun.* An official proclamation or order. **decrees.** —*verb.* To proclaim; make an official order. **decreed, decreeing.**

de·crep·it (di-KREP-it) *adjective.* Old, run-down, worn: a *decrepit* car.

ded·i·cate (DED-ə-kayt) *verb.* 1. To say or write that a creative work is in honor of (a person): The book was *dedicated* to his wife. 2. To set aside for a special purpose. 3. To devote: She will *dedicate* her life to helping the poor. **dedicated, dedicating.**

ded·i·ca·tion (ded-ə-KAY-shən) *noun.* 1. Devotion: Ruth is known for her *dedication* to art. 2. An act or deed done in someone's honor: Our board of education announced the *dedication* of a new school in honor of the mayor. 3. An honorary statement at the beginning of a book, piece of music, or the like: the *dedication* at the front of a yearbook.

de·duct (di-DUHKT) *verb.* To subtract: Father *deducted* money from my allowance for several weeks to pay for the window I had broken. **deducted, deducting.**

de·duct·i·ble (di-DUHK-tə-bəl) *adjective.* Able to be deducted: The cost of the insurance was *deductible* from the income tax.

de·duc·tion (di-DUHK-shən) *noun.* 1. A subtraction; an amount taken away: The clerk made a *deduction* of $10 from our bill because the chair was scratched. 2. Arriving at an answer or solution to a problem by logical use of facts: Sherlock Holmes solved many crimes by his brilliant *deductions.*

deed *noun.* 1. Something that is done or performed: His many kind *deeds* have made him a respected and loved person. 2. A written paper or document that shows a sale of property. —*verb.* To transfer ownership of (property) to another person: He will *deed* the house and land to his son. **deeded, deeding.**

deep *adjective.* 1. Having a depth below the surface: The water is ten feet *deep* here. 2. From the front to the rear: The crowd stood four *deep* to watch the parade. 3. Complex, hard to understand. 4. Low in tone or sound: Our teacher has a *deep* voice. 5. Serious: Martin feels a *deep* love for his puppy. 6. Heavy, solid: Suzie awoke from a *deep* sleep. 7. Dark or brilliant: The sky was a *deep* blue. **deeper, deepest.** —*noun.* 1. The middle: the *deep* of winter. 2. Any very deep place, especially in the ocean. —**deeply** *adverb.* —**the deep.** The sea: The ships sailed out into *the deep.*

deep-root·ed (DEEP-ROO-tid) *adjective.* 1. Having long roots. 2. Firmly fixed: We can't change Grandma's *deep-rooted* idea that fresh air is harmful in her bedroom at night.

deer (DIHR) *noun.* A graceful, swift, brownish, four-footed wild animal. —**deer** *plural.*

de·face (di-FAYSS) *verb.* To ruin or spoil the appearance of something: He was arrested because he *defaced* the American flag. **defaced, defacing.**

de·feat (di-FEET) *verb.* 1. To conquer; be victorious over in war: We *defeated* England in the Revolutionary War. 2. To beat, win a game against. 3. To frustrate, to block: Pat's visit *defeated* Ted's plan to finish reading the book. **defeated, defeating.** —*noun.* 1. The act of winning over. 2. The state of being defeated.

[1]**de·fect** (DEE-fekt or di-FEKT) *noun.* A fault, a weakness.

[2]**de·fect** (di-FEKT) *verb.* To leave a cause or country to join another: The Cuban soccer player *defected* to the United States. **defected, defecting.** —**defector** *noun.*

de·fec·tive (di-FEK-tiv) *adjective.* Having a flaw; not working properly. —**defectively** *adverb.*

defence. British form of **defense.**

de·fend (di-FEND) *verb.* 1. To fight for; protect: The army will *defend* our country. 2. In an argument, to stand up for (one's point of view). **defended, defending.**

de·fen·dant (di-FEN-dənt) *noun.* (Law) The object of a court action.

de·fense (di-FENSS) *noun.* 1. Protection: He came to the *defense* of the smallest boy. 2. Something that protects or defends: I'll use snowballs as a *defense* against a sneak attack. 3. A speech that argues for a cause or a person: The lawyer made a strong *defense* for his client. 4. (Sports) A group of players that tries to stop the opponents from scoring.

de·fen·sive (di-FEN-siv) *adjective.* 1. Protective: The knight wore a *defensive* suit of armor. 2. Defending oneself: Jay was very *defensive* around the older boys. —*noun.* A state of defense: He is always on the *defensive* about his old car. —**defensively** *adverb.*

de·fer (di-FER) *verb.* 1. To put off until a later time. 2. To give in (to); submit (to); I *defer* to your better judgment. **deferred, deferring.** —**deferment** *noun.*

def·er·ence (DEF-ər-ənss) *noun.* Polite acceptance of another's views or wishes.

de·fi·ance (di-FIGH-ənss) *noun.* 1. Resistance to force: They fought in *defiance* of the army. 2. Refusal to accept or comply with: He shows *defiance* toward every rule.

de·fi·ant (di-FIGH-ənt) *adjective.* Showing opposition; unwilling to obey. —**defiantly** *adverb.*

de·fi·cien·cy (di-FISH-ən-see) *noun.* 1. A lack, inadequacy, or insufficiency: Improper eating can result in vitamin *deficiency.* 2. The amount needed or lacking. There is a ten-dollar *deficiency* in her checking account. **deficiencies.** —**deficient** (di-FISH-ənt) *adjective.* —**deficiently** *adverb.*

deficiency disease. An illness caused by the lack of a substance needed by the body: Columbus' men came down with scurvy, a *deficiency disease* caused by a lack of Vitamin C.

de·file (di-FIGHL) *verb.* To spoil, harm, ruin: She *defiled* his good name by telling lies about him. **defiled, defiling.**

de·fine (di-FIGHN) *verb.* 1. To give or tell the meaning of: Ted *defined* the word for the teacher. 2. To describe: He clearly *defined* how to make a model airplane. 3. To make clear the outline or form of: The mountains were sharply *defined* against the stormy sky. **defined, defining.**

def·i·nite (DEF-ə-nit) *adjective.* 1. Certain, without doubt: The trip is *definite;* we will leave today. 2. Exact, accurate: Howard told us that 2:15 was the *definite* arrival time of his plane. —**definitely** *adverb.*

def·i·ni·tion (def-ə-NISH-ən) *noun.* 1. The meaning of a word or phrase. 2. The act of giving the meaning or making something clear.

de·flate (di-FLAYT) *verb.* 1. To lower or make smaller by taking the air or gas from: A slow leak *deflated* my bike tire. 2. To lower or depress: Our hopes for having a picnic were *deflated* by the bad weather. **deflated, deflating.**

de·flect (di-FLEKT) *verb.* To turn away, bend to one side: The shield *deflected* the arrow and saved the knight's life. **deflected, deflecting.**

de·for·es·ta·tion (dee-for-iss-TAY-shən) *noun.* Destroying the trees in an area, as a forest or woodland.

de·form (di-FORM) *verb.* To ruin or spoil the shape of; disfigure. **deformed, deforming.** —**deformity** (di-FOR-mə-tee) *noun.*

de·fraud (di-FRAWD) *verb.* To cheat; take rights or money away through trickery: The dishonest salesman *defrauded* my parents; they paid him but never received the magazines. **defrauded, defrauding.**

de·frost (dee-FRAWST) *verb.* 1. To remove the frost and ice from, as to *defrost* a refrigerator. 2. To thaw, or raise the temperature from a frozen state: *defrost* the meat. **defrosted, defrosting.**

deft *adjective.* Nimble, skillful: Her *deft* fingers quickly opened the secret lock. **defter, deftest.** —**deftly** *adverb.*

de·fy (di-FIGH) *verb.* 1. To boldly refuse to obey; resist: He *defied* the teacher's rule and chewed gum anyway. 2. To be unconquerable by, able to resist: A hurricane *defies* man's attempts to control it. 3. To dare, challenge: We *defy* you to throw the first snowball. **defied, defying.**

de·gen·er·ate (di-JEN-ə-rayt) *verb.* To lose value or quality: Our serious conversation *degenerated* into a series of corny jokes. —(di-JEN-ər-it) *noun.* A person whose morals, values, or behavior are unacceptable to society. **degenerates.**

degenerative disease. A disease that gets worse as time goes by.

de·grade (di-GRAYD) *verb.* 1. To lower moral character of; debase: The man *degraded* himself by stealing from his employer. 2. To subject to disgrace or dishonor: The soldier's cowardice *degraded* him in the eyes of his friends. 3. To lower in rank or demote. **degraded, degrading.**

de·gree (di-GREE) *noun.* 1. One step or stage of development. 2. Scope or amount: murder in the second *degree.* 3. (Grammar) One of the three forms of an adjective or adverb: "Bigger" is the comparative *degree* of "big." 4. A unit of measure for an angle: 90 *degrees* in a right angle. 5. A unit of measure on a thermometer. 6. A certificate awarded after completion of a course of study. **degrees.** —**by degrees.** Gradually; step by step.

de·hu·mid·i·fy (dee-hyoo-MID-ə-figh) *verb.* To remove moisture or dampness; to dry. **dehumidified, dehumidifying.**

de·hy·drate (dee-HIGH-drayt) *verb.* 1. To lose water: Jay is *dehydrated* by heavy exercise. 2. To remove water; dry out. **dehydrated, dehydrating.**

deign (DAYN) *verb.* To stoop or lower oneself (to do something): Because he was such a snob, he did not *deign* to be seen with the newsboy. **deigned, deigning.**

de·i·ty (DEE-ə-tee) *noun.* 1. A god or goddess: Apollo was considered a *deity* by the Greeks. 2. [Capital D] God. **deities.**

de·jec·tion (di-JEK-shən) *noun.* Low spirits, discouragement, unhappiness. —**dejected** *adjective.*

dek- or **deka-** *prefix. See* **dec-.**

Del·a·ware (DEL-ə-wair) *noun.* An Atlantic coast state of the United States, first to ratify the Constitution (1787). —**Del.** *abbreviation.* Also **DE** for Zip Codes.

de·lay (di-LAY) *noun.* A setback or postponement. —*verb.* To hold up or put off until a later time. **delayed, delaying.**

del·e·gate (DEL-ə-gayt) *verb.* To assign a certain position, power, or duty (to someone): We *delegated* the choice of a dance band to Gerald. **delegated, delegating.** —(DEL-ə-gayt or DEL-ə-gət) *noun.* One chosen to represent a group: Jeff is the *delegate* from our school to the music conference. **delegates.**

del·e·ga·tion (del-ə-GAY-shən) *noun.* 1. A group of persons appointed or elected to represent others. 2. The act of delegating.

de·lete (di-LEET) *verb.* To cross out or erase a word or words. **deleted, deleting.**

de·lib·er·ate (di-LIB-ər-it) *adjective.* 1. Done on purpose, intentional: a *deliberate* lie. 2. Slow-acting and cautious: a *deliberate* man. —(di-LIB-ər-ayt) *verb.* To think about seriously, to consider. **deliberated, deliberating.** —**deliberately** *adverb.*

del·i·ca·cy (DEL-i-kə-see) *noun.* 1. A rare, expensive food. 2. Fineness in texture, workmanship, or beauty: The *delicacy* of the old vase makes it a treasure. 3. Tactfulness; extreme sensitivity to others' feelings. 4. A state of being weak or easily broken. 5. Extreme skillfulness or accuracy. **delicacies.**

del·i·cate (DEL-i-kit) *adjective.* 1. Beautifully fine, light, or airy: The bride wore a dress of *delicate* white lace. 2. Frail; sickly: *delicate* health. 3. Broken easily; fragile: Eggs are *delicate.* 4. Sensitive; careful of the feelings or needs of others. 5. Responding quickly or accurately: Electric typewriters are *delicate;* they respond to the lightest touch. 6. Needing care or caution: a *delicate* operation. —**delicately** *adverb.*

Delaware
★capital: Dover

delta

del·i·ca·tes·sen (del-i-kə-TESS-n) *noun.* A store that specializes in selling foods already cooked.

de·li·cious (di-LISH-əss) *adjective.* Tasting or smelling very good. —**deliciously** *adverb.*

de·light (di-LIGHT) *verb.* 1. To please very much: The new puppy *delighted* the baby and made him laugh. 2. To take pleasure: Jack *delights* in swimming. **delighted, delighting.** —*noun.* 1. Happiness, pleasure, enjoyment. 2. Something that gives pleasure or enjoyment.

de·light·ful (di-LIGHT-fəl) *adjective.* Wonderfully pleasing: We had a *delightful* time at the amusement park. —**delightfully** *adverb.*

de·lin·quen·cy (di-LING-kwən-see) *noun.* 1. Failure, neglect of duty: Failing to return the library books is a *delinquency.* 2. An offense, a crime: Juvenile *delinquency* means improper or criminal behavior by young people. **delinquencies.** —**delinquent** *adjective.*

de·lir·i·ous (di-LIHR-ee-əss) *adjective.* 1. Hysterical, not making sense (as often happens with a high fever). 2. Violently excited: The children were *delirious* with joy on Christmas morning. —**deliriously** *adverb.*

de·lir·i·um (di-LIHR-ee-əm) *noun.* A confused state of great excitement or hysteria. —**deliriums** or **deliria** (di-LIHR-ee-ə) *plural.*

de·liv·er (di-LIV-ər) *verb.* 1. To bring or carry: *deliver* a letter. 2. To distribute to a certain set place: The mailman *delivers* mail to our house. 3. To say or read aloud. 4. To assist in the birth process. 5. To give birth. 6. To set free or save: "*Deliver* us from evil." (Lord's Prayer) **delivered, delivering.**

de·liv·er·y (di-LIV-ə-ree) *noun.* 1. The act of delivering or bringing. 2. Something that is delivered or brought: The mailman's *delivery* included three letters. 3. A giving up, surrender: *delivery* of a prisoner. 4. The manner in which one says and does something: *delivery* of a speech. 5. The birth of a baby. 6. A setting free, release. 7. The act and manner of throwing a ball: a pitcher's smooth *delivery.* **deliveries.**

dell (DEL) *noun.* A small valley.

del·ta (DEL-tə) *noun.* A low plain formed at the mouth of a river by deposits of soil. **deltas.**

de·lude (di-LOOD) *verb.* To fool, trick: Don't try to *delude* me into thinking all your work is finished. **delude, deluding.**

del·uge (DEL-yooj) *noun.* 1. A heavy downpour of rain: We should carry an umbrella if we go out in this *deluge.* 2. Any kind of flood or overflow: A *deluge* of questions began after the teacher finished the lesson. **deluges.** —*verb.* To overpower like a flood: The radio station was *deluged* with requests for the new song. **deluged, deluging.**

de·lu·sion (di-LOO-zhən) *noun.* 1. An untruth, false belief: Although she is very pretty, Mary is under the *delusion* that she is ugly. 2. Any deluding or tricking.

delve (DELV) *verb.* To study by searching thoroughly: He *delved* into the problem by reading several books. **delved, delving.**

Dem. *abbreviation.* Democrat or Democratic.

de·mag·net·ize (dee-MAG-nə-tighz) *verb.* To remove the ability of certain substances to attract other substances by magnetism. **demagnetized, demagnetizing.**

de·mand (di-MAND) *verb.* 1. To order, insist on: I *demand* my money back. 2. To need, make necessary: Writing *demands* a great deal of concentration. **demanded, demanding.** —*noun.* 1. An order, something that is demanded: The union sends its *demands* to the mayor. 2. Requests, needs. —**in demand.** Popular, wanted by the public.

de·mean (di-MEEN) *verb.* To lower the quality of: He *demeans* himself by being so sloppy. **demeaned, demeaning.**

de·mean·or (di-MEE-nər) *noun.* Behavior; deportment.

de·ment·ed (di-MEN-tid) *adjective.* Crazy, mad, insane.

de·mer·it (di-MEHR-it) *noun.* A mark given for misconduct.

demi- *prefix.* Half or less: A *demi*tasse is a very small coffee cup.

de·moc·ra·cy (di-MOK-rə-see) *noun.* A country or system of government controlled by the people, who elect representatives to vote on laws and carry them out: The United States is a *democracy.* **democracies.**

dem·o·crat (DEM-ə-krat) *noun.* 1. A member of a democracy or a democratic government. 2. One who believes in equal rights for all. 3. [Capital D] A member of the Democratic political party.

dem·o·crat·ic (dem-ə-KRAT-ik) *adjective.* 1. Relating to democracy. 2. [Capital D] Relating to one of the major U.S. political parties.

de·mol·ish (di-MOL-ish) *verb.* To completely ruin, destroy, tear down. **demolished, demolishing.**

de·mon (DEE-mən) *noun.* 1. A bad or evil spirit; a devil. 2. An evil person. 3. A hard-working person.

dem·on·strate (DEM-ən-strayt) *verb.* 1. To show; explain with example: The teacher *demonstrated* how to model with the clay. 2. To give proof or facts to support something: *Demonstrate* your desire to go to the beach by helping me pack. 3. To come together to show feelings or views on something. **demonstrated, demonstrating.** —**demonstration** (dem-ən-STRAY-shən) *noun.*

de·mor·al·ize (di-MOR-ə-lighz) *verb.* 1. To take away the spirit, courage, or morale of: Our football players *demoralized* their smaller and weaker opponents. 2. To corrupt, lower the morals of. **demoralized, demoralizing.**

de·mote (di-MOHT) *verb.* To move down in rank. **demoted, demoting.**

de·mure (di-MYOOR) *adjective.* 1. Proper, soft-spoken, shy: a *demure* young lady. 2. Pretending to be shy or modest. **demurer, demurest.** —**demurely** *adverb.*

den *noun.* 1. Any secluded place or room. 2. A cave or other shelter used by animals as a home.

de·ni·al (di-NIGH-əl) *noun.* 1. A refusal to do or believe something. 2. A refusal to recognize: The New Testament tells of Peter's *denial* of Jesus Christ. 3. Saying that something is untrue: Dad believed my *denial* of having broken the window.

den·im (DEN-əm) *noun.* A heavy-duty cotton material, usually used to make dungarees and other work or play clothes.

den mother. A woman who is in charge of a Cub Scout den.

de·nom·i·na·tion (di-nom-ə-NAY-shən) *noun.* 1. A religious group: She is a member of the Roman Catholic *denomination.* 2. A name or designation for a group of things: U.S. paper money comes in *denominations* of one, five, ten, twenty dollars, and higher.

de·nom·i·na·tor (di-NOM-ə-nay-tər) *noun.* 1. The bottom number on a fraction that tells how many parts the numerator (the number above) is being divided into: In the fraction $2/3$, 3 is the *denominator.* 2. A common bond, something that is held in common: All the students were united by one *denominator*—the desire to win the game.

de·note (di-NOHT) *verb.* 1. To show, make clear: The bitter cold wind *denotes* that winter is almost here. 2. To indicate specifically: The word "rain" *denotes* drops of water falling to earth. **denoted, denoting.**

de·nounce (di-NOWNSS) *verb.* 1. To declare something to be wrong or evil: The coach *denounced* smoking as harmful for his players. 2. To accuse formally, as in court. **denounced, denouncing.**

dense (DENSS) *adjective.* 1. Thick, crowded: The child became lost in the *dense* forest. 2. (Informal) Stupid, slow-witted: One of the reasons that she is so *dense* is that she doesn't listen well. **denser, densest. —densely** *adverb.*

den·si·ty (DEN-sə-tee) *noun.* 1. Amount of objects in a certain space: population *density.* 2. The state of being dense, crowded, or thickly filled. 3. Stupidity; slowness in understanding. 4. (Physics) The mass or weight of anything in a given volume: The *density* of water is one gram per cubic centimeter. **densities.**

dent *noun.* A hollow in a surface, as that made by a blow: The ball put a *dent* in the car. *—verb.* 1. To make a dent or hollow in something. 2. To become dented. **dented, denting. —make a dent on.** 1. To make a start on (a task). 2. To make an impression on.

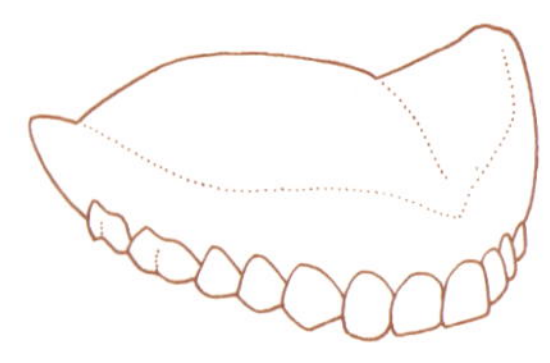

denture

den·tal (DEN-tl) *adjective.* Related to teeth or to the work of a dentist.

dental floss. A thin, strong, waxed thread used to clean between the teeth.

den·ti·frice (DEN-tə-friss) *noun.* Any powder or paste used for cleaning the teeth. **dentifrices.**

den·tist (DEN-tist) *noun.* A doctor who specializes in treating and caring for the teeth and gums.

den·ture (DEN-chər) *noun.* A set of false teeth to replace teeth that have been removed or lost. **dentures.**

de·ny (di-NIGH) *verb.* 1. To refuse to admit; say that something is not true. 2. To refuse to recognize. 3. To refuse to give; withold from: *deny* permission. **denied, denying.**

de·o·dor·ant (dee-OH-dər-ənt) *noun.* 1. Something used to get rid of or stop an unpleasant odor or smell. 2. A substance used to cover perspiration odor.

de·o·dor·ize (dee-OH-də-righz) *verb.* To get rid of or stop an unpleasant odor. **deodorized, deodorizing.**

de·part (di-PAHRT) *verb.* 1. To leave, go away from. 2. To die. 3. To go in a different course: She *departed* from tradition by wearing shorts to school. **departed, departing.**

de·part·ment (di-PAHRT-mənt) *noun.* A certain division or distinct part of a store, college, business, or other system: the clothing *department,* the English *department.*

de·par·ture (di-PAHR-chər) *noun.* 1. A going away: *departure* for Europe. 2. A veering from the expected way. **departures.**

de·pend (di-PEND) *verb.* 1. To trust, have confidence in. 2. To be decided by: Whether we go or not *depends* on Mother. 3. To rely for support or help. **depended, depending.**

de·pend·a·ble (di-PEN-də-bəl) *adjective.* Trustworthy, reliable; able to be depended upon. **—dependability** (di-pen-də-BIL-ə-tee) *noun.* **—dependably** *adverb.*

de·pen·dence (di-PEN-dənss) *noun.* 1. A reliance on for support: My brother now has a job and has ended his *dependence* on Dad. 2. A need: It is sad that he has such a *dependence* on drugs.

de·pen·dent (di-PEN-dənt) *adjective.* 1. Relying on or needing (something or someone else): A *dependent* clause is one that cannot stand alone but acts as a noun or as a modifier within a sentence. 2. Below in rank, class, or authority.

de·pict (di-PIKT) *verb.* To portray or represent by way of a picture or words. **depicted, depicting.**

de·plete (di-PLEET) *verb.* To finish or use up completely. **depleted, depleting. —depletion** *noun.*

de·plor·a·ble (di-PLOR-ə-bəl) *adjective.* To be regretted; a *deplorable* situation: **—deplorably** *adverb.*

de·plore (di-PLOR) *verb.* To regret; feel sad about. **deplored, deploring.**

de·port (di-PORT) *verb.* 1. To force out or banish from a certain country or place: The criminal was *deported* from the country. 2. To conduct oneself or behave in a certain manner: The old lady *deports* herself with great dignity. **deported, deporting.**

de·port·ment (di-PORT-mənt) *noun.* Manner of carrying or conducting oneself: Jane's *deportment* is calmer than that of her nervous cousin.

de·pose (di-POHZ) *verb.* 1. To dethrone (a king); remove (a high official) from a position. 2. To say under oath. **deposed, deposing.**

de·pos·it (di-POZ-it) *verb.* 1. To lay or put down: He *deposited* his book on the counter. 2. To put or place for safekeeping: *deposit* money at the bank. 3. To lay down by a natural process: A river *deposits* soil at its mouth. 4. To give money as a payment on something: My parents *deposited* a down payment on our new boat. **deposited, depositing.** *—noun.* 1. Something that is laid or put down, particularly by nature, as in an underground supply of minerals: coal *deposit.* 2. Money put in a bank. 3. Part of a payment.

de·pot (DEE-poh) *noun.* 1. A bus or train station. 2. A military warehouse or assembly station.

de·pre·ci·ate (di-PREE-shee-ayt) *verb.* 1. Lessen in value: Because a car *depreciates,* its trade-in value is considerably less than what was paid for it. 2. To make seem less important or of little value; downgrade. **depreciated, depreciating.**

de·press (di-PRESS) *verb.* 1. To make unhappy, lower the spirits of: The gloomy weather *depressed* her. 2. To decrease or lessen in activity or intensity: Lack of money has *depressed* new building in our town. 3. To press down on: *depress* a typewriter key. **depressed, depressing.**

de·pres·sion (di-PRESH-ən) *noun.* 1. Unhappiness, gloom: Jack was in a state of *depression* after he failed the test. 2. A hollow place, a dent: There was a *depression* in the sand where he dropped the rock. 3. A pressing down or a lowering. 4. [Often capital D] A time when business is bad or slows down.

dep·ri·va·tion (dep-rə-VAY-shən) *noun.* 1. State of poverty, need; state of being deprived: The *deprivation* of many people living in slums is tragic. 2. Act of depriving or taking away (from).

de·prive (di-PRIGHV) *verb.* To keep from: Dad *deprived* me of my bicycle for three weeks. **deprived, depriving.**

depth *noun.* 1. Deepness: The *depth* of the water is ten feet. 2. Seriousness, quality of being complex or having great knowledge, feeling, or the like: She is not a simple person; she has a lot of *depth.* 3. Quality of being very strong, deep, or intense: *depth* of a color, *depth* of a voice, *depth* of winter. 4. (Plural) A state of low moral character. 5. (Plural) The innermost or deepest part: the *depths* of the ocean.

depth charge. An underwater explosive device: *Depth charges* are used against submarines.

dep·u·tize (DEP-yə-tighz) *verb.* To install in the position of deputy: Marshal Dillon *deputized* Sam and told him to lead the posse. **deputized, deputizing.**

dep·u·ty (DEP-yoo-tee or DEP-yə-tee) *noun.* 1. An appointed assistant or official representative. 2. One who is appointed or elected to replace another official. **deputies.**

de·rail (dee-RAYL) *verb.* To cause to come off the rails or the tracks. **derailed, derailing.**

de·range (di-RAYNJ) *verb.* 1. To confuse or disturb the order or arrangement of. 2. To cause to go insane or mad. **deranged, deranging.**

derby

der·by (DER-bee) *noun.* 1. A meet or race of some kind: a soapbox *derby.* 2. A type of round and stiff felt hat. **derbies.**

der·e·lict (DEHR-ə-likt) *adjective.* Having been deserted: *derelict* ship. —*noun.* Someone or something that has been forsaken or abandoned.

de·ride (di-RIGHD) *verb.* To insult, make fun of. **derided, deriding.** —**derision** (di-RIZH-ən) *noun.*

de·ri·sive (di-RIGH-siv) *adjective.* Scornful, mocking: His *derisive* laughter when the girl sang off-key was unkind. —**derisively** *adverb.*

der·i·va·tion (dehr-ə-VAY-shən) *noun.* 1. Origin; beginning. 2. The source of a word: The *derivation* of "beef" is from the Old French "boef."

de·rive (di-RIGHV) *verb.* 1. To get from a certain source: Steel is *derived* from iron. 2. To obtain (as a conclusion) from reasoning or studying: They *derived* the answer to the difficult math problem by using the proper formula. 3. To start or originate: The river *derives* from many streams. **derived, deriving.**

de·rog·a·to·ry (di-ROG-ə-tor-ee) *adjective.* Insulting; making seem less important; downgrading.

derrick

der·rick (DEHR-ik) *noun.* 1. A tall crane used to lift heavy objects. 2. A high structure over an oil well that holds drilling equipment.

de·sal·i·ni·za·tion (dee-sal-ə-nə-ZAY-shən) *noun.* The process of removing salt from sea water.

de·scend (di-SEND) *verb.* 1. To move downward: The rain *descended* upon us. 2. To decline or slope downward. 3. To dive or swoop down (upon) in an attack: The eagle *descended* on its prey. 4. To come from, originate from (something or someone) in the past. **descended, descending.**

de·scend·ant (di-SEN-dənt) *noun.* 1. An offspring: The princess is a *descendant* of the king. 2. Something that owes its characteristics to an earlier related form: The piano is a *descendant* of the harpsichord.

de·scend·ent (di-SEN-dənt) Also **descendant** *adjective.* In a state of downward motion.

de·scent (di-SENT) *noun.* 1. The act of coming down or descending: He made a quick *descent* from the ladder. 2. A way downward: The *descent* from the mountain was by way of a steep path. 3. The family or place from which one originates.

descent stage. The period of time during which a spaceship or rocket re-enters the atmosphere and returns to the surface of the earth: Friction with the air in the *descent stage* heats the rocket enough to melt parts of its heat shield.

de·scribe (di-SKRIGHB) *verb.* 1. To write or tell about; picture in words: She *described* the beautiful lake to the class. 2. To draw or represent the outline of: She *described* a figure eight on the ice. **described, describing.** —**descriptive** (di-SKRIP-tiv) *adjective.*

de·scrip·tion (di-SKRIP-shən) *noun.* 1. A detailed account: His *description* of the delicious meal made us hungry. 2. Any act of describing. 3. Kind, type, variety: On her birthday, Mary received presents of every *description.*

de·seg·re·gate (dee-SEG-rə-gayt) To stop separation of people by race, as in schools or neighborhoods.

desegregated, desegregating. —**desegregation** (dee-seg-rə-GAY-shən) *noun.*

[1]**de·sert** (di-ZERT) *verb.* 1. To leave behind, forsake. 2. To leave the army without permission and with no plan to return. **deserted, deserting.** —*noun.* (Usually plural) Something deserved, either reward or punishment: The lazy grasshopper got its just *deserts.*

[2]**de·sert** (DEZ-ərt) *noun.* A dry, usually sandy region where there are few people, animals, or plants because of lack of water.

de·sert·er (di-ZERT-ər) *noun.* 1. In the military, one who leaves without permission. 2. Anyone who deserts someone or something, who fails or quits when needed.

de·serve (di-ZERV) *verb.* To be worthy of. **deserved, deserving.**

de·sign (di-ZIGHN) *verb.* 1. To plan the structure or arrangement of: She *designed* her own little doll house. 2. To intend for a certain use: The lounge was *designed* for relaxation and rest. **designed, designing.** —*noun.* 1. The drawing or plan of a structure or project: The architect gave the mayor his *design* for the school. 2. An artistic pattern, consisting of an arrangement of lines, colors, or forms. 3. Intention, purpose. —**designer** *noun.*

des·ig·nate (DEZ-ig-nayt) *verb.* 1. To appoint, choose: The players *designated* Eric captain. 2. To show or mark: The players are *designated* by the numbers on their uniforms. 3. To specify. 4. To name or call: Very large eggs are *designated* "jumbo." **designated, designating.**

de·sir·a·ble (di-ZIGHR-ə-bəl) *adjective.* 1. Pleasing, beautiful, enjoyable. 2. Worth being recommended or advised: *desirable* manners. —**desirably** *adverb.*

de·sire (di-ZIGHR) *verb.* To long for, to wish: Mother *desires* a new washing machine. **desired, desiring.** —*noun.* 1. A longing, a wish: I have a *desire* to be a doctor. 2. Something that is wanted: My *desire* is a room of my own. **desires.**

de·sist (di-ZIST) *verb.* To stop; cease. **desisted, desisting.**

desk *noun.* A table for working or studying, usually equipped with drawers or shelves for supplies.

des·o·late (DESS-ə-lit) *adjective.* 1. Lonely, not inhabited: The town was *desolate;* there was no sign of life. 2. Unhappy, gloomy: I was *desolate* when my best friend moved away. 3. Destroyed; devastated. —(DESS-ə-layt) *verb.* 1. To destroy, wipe out: An atomic war would *desolate* the earth. 2. To make sad: The rainy day *desolated* me. 3. To forsake, abandon. **desolated, desolating.** —**desolately** *adverb.*

de·spair (di-SPAIR) *verb.* To give up, lose hope: She *despaired* of her chances of passing the exam. **despaired, despairing.** —*noun.* 1. Hopelessness: I tried not to show my *despair* when Dad lost his job. 2. Someone or something causing hopelessness: My brother's messy room was Mother's *despair.*

des·per·ate (DESS-pər-it) *adjective.* 1. Stopping at nothing because of great despair or boldness: The *desperate* student tried to cheat on the exam. 2. Causing loss of hope; dangerous: The mountain climber is in *desperate* trouble. —**desperately** *adverb.*

des·per·a·tion (dess-pə-RAY-shən) *noun.* A state of despair; complete hopelessness.

de·spise (di-SPIGHZ) *verb.* To dislike, to hate, feel disgust for: John *despised* Tim for his dishonesty. **despised, despising.**

[2]desert

de·spite (di-SPIGHT) *preposition.* In spite of, regardless of: *Despite* my fear, I jumped off the high diving board.

de·spoil (di-SPOIL) *verb.* To rob, ruin, or destroy: Litterbugs *despoil* the park. **despoiled, despoiling.**

de·spond·ent (di-SPON-dənt) *adjective.* Unhappy, listless, discouraged. —**despondently** *adverb.*

des·pot (DESS-pət) *noun.* A tyrant; a ruler or leader who shares his power with no one and follows no wishes except his own.

des·sert (di-ZERT) *noun.* A sweet dish served after the main meal.

des·ti·na·tion (dess-tə-NAY-shən) *noun.* The place to which someone or something is going: Mars may be the *destination* of future space travelers.

des·tine (DESS-tin) *verb.* To set apart, appoint, or intend, sometimes almost as if by fortune or chance: Why was Washington *destined* to be known as "the Father of His Country"? **destined, destining.**

des·tin·y (DESS-tə-nee) *noun.* 1. Something that is sure to happen; fate: My *destiny* is always to lose at games. 2. The force that seems to cause things to happen. **destinies.**

des·ti·tute (DESS-tə-toot or DESS-tə-tyoot) *adjective.* 1. Desperately poor, poverty-stricken. 2. Lacking; without: The mean old man was *destitute* of friends. —**destitution** (des-tə-TYOO-shən) *noun.*

de·stroy (di-STROI) *verb.* To ruin completely, lay waste: Fire *destroyed* the house next door. **destroyed, destroying.**

destroyer

de·stroy·er (di-STROI-ər) *noun.* 1. A fast, fairly small warship. 2. Someone or something that destroys.

de·struc·tion (di-STRUHK-shən) *noun.* 1. Complete ruin, condition of being destroyed: Each year, fire causes much *destruction* of our forests. 2. The act of ruining or destroying. —**destructive** *adjective.* —**destructively** *adverb.*

de·tach (di-TACH) *verb.* 1. To separate; unfasten: *Detach* the sheet of paper from the notebook. 2. To send away (troops or ships) on a certain task: The general *detached* four battalions to encircle the enemy. **detached, detaching.**

de·tach·ment (di-TACH-mənt) *noun.* 1. Keeping oneself apart from others mentally or emotionally: There was an air of *detachment* about her; she did not want to join us. 2. The act of separating: We watched the *detachment* of the caboose from the train. 3. A group of soldiers or ships assigned to a certain job.

de·tail (di-TAYL or DEE-tayl) *noun.* 1. One small part of a whole: Getting paper plates was one *detail* we overlooked in planning the school picnic. 2. Many or all of the small parts of something: Mary's ability to concentrate on *detail* makes her a good planner. 3. (Military) A duty; the people picked for this duty: kitchen *detail.* —*verb.* 1. To give a complete account; report on all occurrences. 2. (Military) To assign to a duty. **detailed, detailing.**

de·tain (di-TAYN) *verb.* To hold back or make wait; stop from going: I hate to *detain* you, but I'm not ready yet. **detained, detaining.**

de·tect (di-TEKT) *verb.* To find, discover: Bill *detected* a fault in the TV. **detected, detecting.**

de·tec·tive (di-TEK-tiv) *noun.* One whose job it is to solve crimes and discover secret facts, often working with or for the police. **detectives.**

de·ter (di-TER) *verb.* To cause to stop or turn back: The "No Trespassing" sign *deterred* the hikers from entering the woods. **deterred, deterring.** —**deterrent** *noun* and *adjective.*

de·ter·gent (di-TER-jənt) *noun.* A soap substitute used for washing or cleaning.

de·ter·mine (di-TER-min) *verb.* 1. To decide, come to a conclusion: Mother finally *determined* what to serve at her dinner party. 2. To control, to guide: "The direction in which education starts a man will *determine* his future life." (Plato). 3. To pinpoint, to find out. **determined, determining.** —**determination** *noun.*

de·test (di-TEST) *verb.* To hate, dislike very much. **detested, detesting.**

de·test·a·ble (di-TEST-ə-bəl) *adjective.* Offensive; horrid: *detestable* manners. —**detestably** *adverb.*

de·throne (dee-THROHN) *verb.* To remove a king from his throne. **dethroned, dethroning.**

de·tour (DEE-toor) *verb.* To bypass; avoid a block on a main road by using another route. **detoured, detouring.** —*noun.* 1. The route used when a main road has been blocked. 2. Any turning away from the direct or main way.

de·tract (di-TRAKT) *verb.* To take away: Dick's dirty shoes *detract* from his appearance. **detracted, detracting.**

dev·as·tate (DEV-əss-tayt) *verb.* To completely wipe out or ruin: The tornado *devastated* the ranch. **devastated, devastating.** —**devastation** (dev-əss-TAY-shən) *noun.*

de·vel·op (di-VEL-əp) *verb.* 1. To improve or build up: *develop* one's health. 2. To work out in detail: *develop* a bulletin board display. 3. To grow: A child *develops* rapidly. 4. (Photography) To treat an exposed film or paper to make a picture visible. 5. To happen: Whatever *develops,* we will stick by you. 6. To come to be known; come to light. **developed, developing.**

de·vel·op·ment (di-VEL-əp-mənt) *noun.* 1. Something that has happened: What is the latest *development* in the football game? 2. Growth; progress or improvement: The *development* of cooking skill takes time and practice. 3. A group of houses or buildings designed and built by the same company. 4. The processing of photographic film to produce a picture.

de·vi·ate (DEE-vee-ayt) *verb.* To turn away or depart from a normal path or standard: She *deviated* from her usual routine by doing the grocery shopping a day early. **deviated, deviating.** —**deviation** *noun.*

de·vice (di-VIGHSS) *noun.* 1. An object or machine with a specific working purpose: A speedometer is a *device* that shows how fast a car is moving. 2. A plan or program to accomplish something: We used free balloons as a *device* to get more customers to the school fair. **devices.**

dev·il (DEV-əl) *noun.* 1. [Usually capital D] The spirit of evil; Satan. 2. One who is evil or cruel. 3. (Informal) A mischievous, playful person: This little boy is a *devil;* he is always playing pranks. —*verb.* (Informal) 1. To bother, pester, or tease. 2. To prepare food with hot or spicy flavorings: to *devil* eggs; *devil* ham. **deviled** or **devilled, deviling** or **devilling.**

dev·il·ish (DEV-əl-ish or DEV-lish) *adjective.* 1. Like a devil; cruel, evil. 2. Mischievous: a *devilish* puppy. —**devilishly** *adverb.*

devil's-food cake. A rich chocolate cake.

de·vise (di-VIGHZ) *verb.* 1. To plan; invent; think up: Terry *devised* an easy way to clean the erasers. 2. (Law) To leave property to someone in a will. **devised, devising.**

de·void (di-VOID) *adjective.* Lacking; not possessing: *devoid* of feelings.

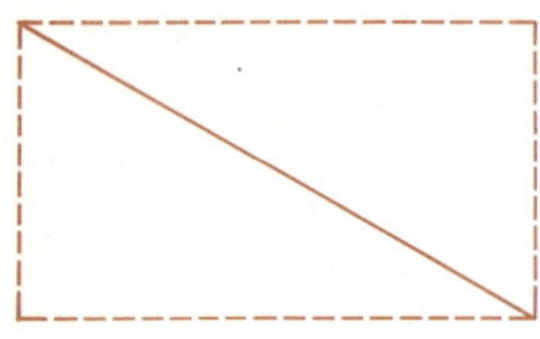
diagonal

de·vote (di-VOHT) *verb.* 1. To dedicate, give completely: Bob *devotes* Saturday to his piano practice. 2. To set aside for a certain purpose: One entire cabinet was *devoted* to a display of dolls from all nations. **devoted, devoting. —devoted to.** Very fond of.

de·vo·tion (di-VOH-shən) *noun.* 1. Deep love, loyalty: George Washington was known for his *devotion* to his country. 2. (Plural) A special prayer or worship service: The pastor led us in morning *devotions.*

de·vour (di-VOWR) *verb.* 1. To eat in a greedy way. 2. To consume or destroy: The fire *devoured* the forest. 3. To take in eagerly through the senses: My uncle *devours* books. **devoured, devouring.**

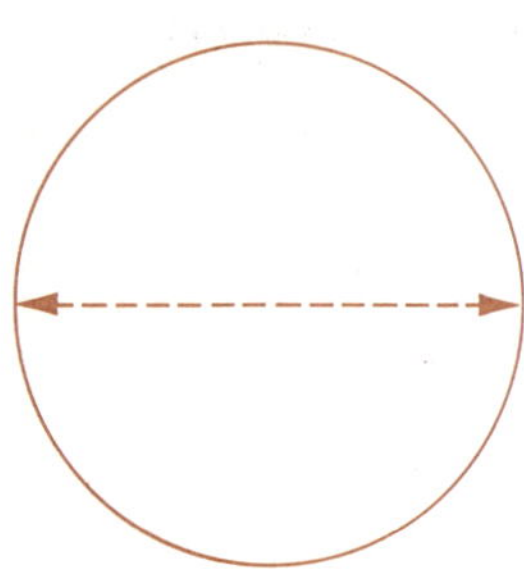
diameter

de·vout (di-VOWT) *adjective.* 1. Deeply religious. 2. Sincere, earnest: It is my *devout* wish that you succeed. **—devoutly** *adverb.*

dew (DOO or DYOO) *noun.* Small drops of water which form on outdoor objects at night.

dex·ter·i·ty (dek-STEHR-ə-tee) *noun.* Skill, ease of movement: He handles the ball with *dexterity.*

dia- *prefix.* Through or across: *dia*meter, *dia*gonal.

di·a·be·tes (digh-ə-BEE-tiss or digh-ə-BEE-teez) *noun.* A disease in which the body cannot absorb sugar normally.

diamond (definition 3)

di·a·bol·ic (digh-ə-BOL-ik) Also **diabolical** *adjective.* Devilish, cruel: The wolf had a *diabolic* plan to eat Little Red Riding Hood. **—diabolically** *adverb.*

di·ag·nose (digh-əg-NOHSS or digh-əg-NOHZ) *verb.* 1. To determine by examination of a sick person why he is ill. 2. To analyze any situation: When the clock stopped, Dad *diagnosed* the trouble as a dead battery. **diagnosed, diagnosing.**

di·ag·o·nal (digh-AG-ə-nl) *adjective.* Slanting: Dad's tie has *diagonal* red stripes. *—noun.* A slanting line drawn from one corner to the opposite corner of a square or other similar figure. **—diagonally** *adverb.*

di·a·gram (DIGH-ə-gram) *noun.* 1. A drawing made to show the various parts of an object and their relation to each other: Look at the *diagram* before you try to put the model airplane together. 2. A plan or chart: You will need a *diagram* of the new school in order to find your room. *—verb.* To explain by making an outline or drawing. **diagramed** or **diagrammed, diagraming** or **diagramming.**

di·al (DIGH-əl) *noun.* 1. The face of a clock or watch. 2. The face of a device that has marks over which a pointer moves to show amount, speed, direction, or other measures. 3. The control used to tune in radio stations or TV channels. 4. The disk on a telephone. *—verb.* To use a dial, as on a telephone or TV set. **dialed** or **dialled, dialing** or **dialling.**

di·a·lect (DIGH-ə-lekt) *noun.* A way of speaking that is used by people who live in the same region or have a common background: In the *dialect* of Texas, "y'all" is often used for "you all."

di·a·logue (DIGH-ə-log) Also **dialog** *noun.* 1. Conversation between two or more people: Pete and Mike had a lively *dialogue.* 2. Conversation between or among characters in a play or book. 3. Exchange of ideas: The difference in age made *dialogue* difficult between father and son. **dialogues.**

di·am·e·ter (digh-AM-ə-tər) *noun.* 1. A straight line through the center of a circle or a sphere from one side to the other or the length of such a line: The *diameter* cuts the circle into two equal parts. 2. The thickness of something round.

dia·mond (DIGH-mənd or DIGH-ə-mənd) *noun.* 1. A very hard stone, precious for its color and form. 2. A figure having four equal angled sides. 3. A playing card which bears such a figure. 4. A baseball field.

di·a·per (DIGH-ə-pər or DIGH-pər) *noun.* A folded cloth used to cover the lower part of a baby's torso. —*verb.* To put a diaper on (a baby). **diapered, diapering.**

di·a·phragm (DIGH-ə-fram) *noun.* 1. A large muscle that separates the chest from the abdomen: The *diaphragm* is used in breathing. 2. Any thin piece that divides or separates. 3. A thin disk that vibrates: Telephones, phonographs, and microphones have *diaphragms.*

di·ar·rhe·a (digh-ə-REE-ə) Also **diarrhoea** *noun.* A condition of the intestines that causes a person to have frequent and loose bowel movements.

di·a·ry (DIGH-ə-ree) *noun.* 1. A person's own written record of the things he does each day. 2. The book in which a daily record is written: Lulu writes in her *diary* every night. **diaries.**

di·a·tom (DIGH-ə-tom or DIGH-at-əm) *noun.* A tiny brown or gold water plant made up of only one cell: *Diatoms* are found in both salt and fresh water.

dice (DIGHSS) *noun, plural.* Small cubes with from one to six dots on each side, used in playing games of chance. —**die** *singular.* —*verb.* To cut into small cubes: *dice* vegetables. **diced, dicing.**

dic·tate (DIK-tayt) *verb.* 1. To say or read something aloud so that another person can write it down word for word. 2. To command or order: My conscience *dictates* that I tell the truth. **dictated, dictating.** —*noun.* An order or command: a *dictate* of the court. **dictates.**

dic·ta·tion (dik-TAY-shən) *noun.* 1. The giving of commands or orders: The angry boy did not like his father's stern *dictation.* 2. Words that have been dictated.

dic·ta·tor (DIK-tay-tər) *noun.* A ruler who has complete power: A *dictator* takes orders from no one.

dic·ta·to·ri·al (dik-tə-TOR-ee-əl) *adjective.* Like a dictator, overbearing. —**dictatorially** *adverb.*

dic·ta·tor·ship (dik-TAY-tər-ship) *noun.* 1. The office held by a dictator. 2. A state ruled by a dictator.

dic·tion (DIK-shən) *noun.* 1. Way of pronouncing words: Radio announcers must have good *diction.* 2. Choice and use of words; manner of expression: Churchill's books show excellent *diction.*

dic·tion·ar·y (DIK-shə-nehr-ee) *noun.* 1. A book listing words in alphabetical order, giving their meanings and usually pronunciations and other information about them. 2. A book listing the words of one language with meanings given in a second language: a Spanish-English *dictionary.* **dictionaries.**

did *verb. See* **do.**

did·n't (DID-ənt) *contraction.* A shortened form of *did not.*

die (DIGH) *verb.* 1. To stop living. 2. To lose force, fade away: "To let friendship *die* away by . . . silence is certainly not wise." (S. Johnson). 3. (Slang) To want something very much: She is *dying* to go to the show. **died, dying.** —*noun.* 1. A device used in shaping, cutting, or printing on various materials. 2. One of a pair of dice. —**the die is cast.** A decision has been made and cannot be changed.

die-hard (DIGH-hahrd) Also **diehard** *noun.* One who does not give up easily or is stubborn about changing.

die·sel engine (DEE-zl). An oil-burning engine in which fuel is ignited by heat of compressed air.

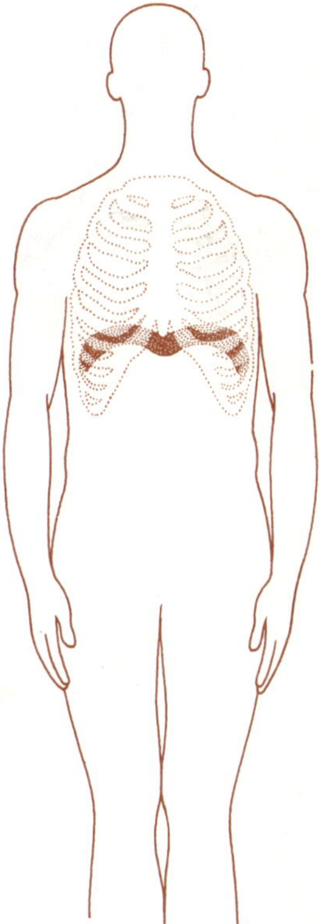
diaphragm

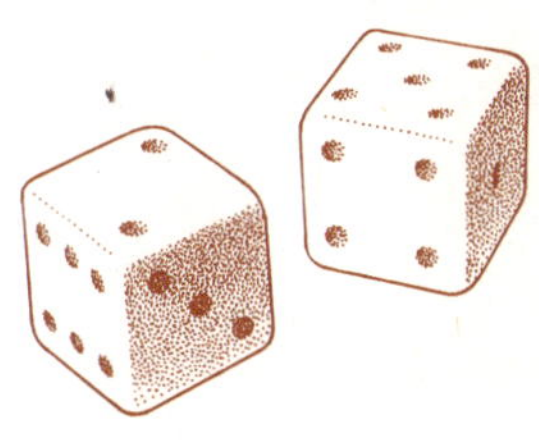
dice

[1]**di·et** (DIGH-ət) *noun.* 1. The things a person habitually eats and drinks each day: Your *diet* should include milk. 2. A plan of eating followed for special reasons: Some *diets* help you lose weight. 3. Anything done regularly: A *diet* of comic books will not improve your grades. —*verb.* To limit the amount or type of food eaten. **dieted, dieting.**

[2]**Di·et** (DIGH-ət) *noun.* A lawmaking body: the *Diet* of Japan.

di·e·ti·tian (digh-ə-TISH-ən) Also **dietician** *noun.* One whose job is to plan meals and prepare foods in a healthful way.

dif·fer (DIF-ər) *verb.* 1. To be unlike: Jane *differs* from her twin by having more freckles. 2. To disagree. **differed, differing.**

dif·fer·ence (DIF-ər-ənss, or DIF-rənss) *noun.* 1. The way or amount in which things are not alike: There is a great *difference* in size between a mouse and an elephant. 2. Disagreement, argument. 3. The amount by which quantities differ: The *difference* between five and ten is five. **differences.**

dif·fer·ent (DIF-ə-rənt or DIF-rənt) *adjective.* 1. Unlike; separate, not the same. 2. Unusual, out of the ordinary. —**differently** *adverb.*

dif·fer·en·ti·ate (dif-ə-REN-shee-ayt) *verb.* 1. To tell or show that things are not alike: *differentiate* between a mouse and a rat. 2. To serve to distinguish: The zebra's stripes *differentiate* it from the horse. **differentiated, differentiating.**

dif·fi·cult (DIF-i-kuhlt) *adjective.* 1. Not easy, hard to do or understand. 2. Hard to manage or get along with. —**difficultly** *adverb.*

dif·fi·cul·ty (DIF-i-kuhl-tee) *noun.* 1. Trouble, hardship. 2. The cause of trouble: The *difficulty* was a flat tire. 3. Something not easy to understand, solve, or do. 4. A disagreement. **difficulties.**

dif·fi·dent (DIF-ə-dənt) *adjective.* Shy, not sure of oneself. —**diffidence** *noun.* —**diffidently** *adverb.*

dif·frac·tion (di-FRAK-shən) *noun.* The bending of light rays when they pass close to an opaque object: *Diffraction* results in the formation of a series of light and dark bands.

dif·fuse (di-FYOOZ) *verb.* To spread out; cause to scatter or go away: Fresh winds finally *diffused* the smog. **diffused, diffusing.** —(di-FYOOSS) *adjective.* 1. Spread out or scattered. 2. Long-winded, having too many words: The lady gave a *diffuse* speech. —**diffusely** *adverb.* —**diffusion** (di-FYOO-zhən) *noun.*

dig *verb.* 1. To turn over earth by using a tool, hands, or claws. 2. To bring out by moving the earth away: A farmer *digs* potatoes. 3. To make a hole in the ground. 4. To go through something: He *digs* in the drawer for a pencil. 5. To search for information: The police are *digging* for clues. 6. (Slang) To enjoy or understand: Dad *digs* my record collection as much as I do. **dug, digging.** —*noun.* 1. A quick poke or thrust: The fighter received a *dig* in the ribs. 2. (Informal) A nasty remark. —**dig in.** To work hard.

di·gest (digh-JEST or di-JEST) *verb.* 1. To change into a form that can be used by the body: Milk *digests* easily. 2. To read and understand: *Digest* the directions before you start to work. **digested, digesting.** —(DIGH-jest) *noun.* A short form of a longer work: I did not read the book, but I read a *digest* of it.

di·gest·i·ble (digh-JESS-tə-bəl or di-JESS-tə-bəl) *adjective.* Able to be changed into a form that can be used by the body: Not all foods are *digestible* by babies.

di·ges·tion (digh-JESS-chən or di-JESS-chən) *noun.* 1. The process by which food is made useful to the body. 2. The ability to digest.

di·ges·tive (digh-JESS-tiv) *adjective.* Having to do with the changing of foods into a form that can be used by the body.

digestive system. The parts of the body that are concerned with breaking down food into a form that can be used by the body for energy and growth.

dig·it (DIJ-it) *noun.* 1. Any of the single figures 0, 1, 2, 3, 4, 5, 6, 7, 8, 9.: Our telephone number has seven *digits.* 2. A finger or toe.

dig·i·tal com·put·er (DIJ-ə-tl kəm-PYOO-tər). An electronic machine that solves mathematical problems by using numbers, usually just 0 and 1: Essentially a counting device, a *digital computer's* great speed makes it able to do in seconds what a man would take years to figure.

dig·ni·fy (DIG-nə-figh) *verb.* To honor or give dignity to: The mayor *dignified* our school assembly by his presence. **dignified, dignifying.**

dig·ni·tar·y (DIG-nə-tehr-ee) *noun.* One of high rank: The President and other *dignitaries* sat at the speakers' table. **dignitaries.**

dig·ni·ty (DIG-nə-tee) *noun.* 1. Noble bearing; a calm outward appearance. 2. True worth: the *dignity* of man. 3. A high office or position: the *dignity* of the Supreme Court. 4. A sense of self-worth.

dike (DIGHK) *noun.* A bank or dam used to hold back water. **dikes.** —*verb.* To protect by building dams or banks: The men *diked* the town against the flood. **diked, diking.**

di·lap·i·dat·ed (di-LAP-ə-day-tid) *adjective.* Run-down, worn-out: Jim bought a *dilapidated* car that he planned to use for parts.

di·late (digh-LAYT or DIGH-layt) *verb.* 1. To make larger: The boy *dilated* the balloon by blowing air into it. 2. To become larger: The pupils of the eyes *dilate* in the dark. **dilated, dilating.**

dil·i·gence (DIL-ə-jənss) *noun.* Earnest effort, attention to duty. —**diligent** *adjective.* —**diligently** *adverb.*

dill *noun.* A kind of plant having flavorful seeds and leaves that are used for seasoning.

dil·ly-dal·ly (DIL-ee-DAL-ee) *verb.* To waste time, delay: Don't *dilly-dally* on the way home from school. **dilly-dallied, dilly-dallying.**

di·lute (di-LOOT) *verb.* 1. To make weaker or thinner by adding water or other liquid. 2. To cut down the strength or value of by adding something that is not necessary: Lincoln's Gettysburg Address was not *diluted* by needless words. **diluted, diluting.** —*adjective.* Weak, thin: She gave the cat a *dilute* mixture of milk and water.

dim *adjective.* 1. Faint, not bright: The light was so *dim* we could hardly see each other. 2. Hazy, not clear: He has a *dim* memory of his childhood. 3. Gloomy, unpleasant: The old man takes a *dim* view of teen-agers who have long hair. **dimmer, dimmest.** —*verb.* 1. To make fainter: He *dimmed* the lights for the oncoming car. 2. To grow fainter or less bright. **dimmed, dimming.** —**dimly** *adverb.*

dime (DIGHM) *noun.* A U.S. or Canadian coin worth ten cents.

di·men·sion (di-MEN-shən) *noun.* 1. A measurement of length, width, or height: This block of wood has three *dimensions:* It is 15 inches long, 10 inches wide, and 6 inches high. 2. (Plural) Size, importance: a school fair of major *dimensions.*

di·min·ish (di-MIN-ish) *verb.* 1. To cut down or make smaller: The cloud *diminished* the light of the moon. 2. To taper: The cone *diminishes* to a point. 3. To fade away. **diminished, diminishing.**

dike

dinghy

di·min·u·tive (di-MIN-yə-tiv) *adjective.* 1. Small, tiny: The "Borrowers" in Mary Norton's books are *diminutive* people. 2. Expressing smallness. *—noun.* A word formed by adding a suffix that expresses smallness: The words "piglet" and "lambkin" are *diminutives.* **diminutives. —diminutively** *adverb.*

dim·ple (DIM-pəl) *noun.* A small dent or hollow place in the skin of the cheeks or chin. **dimples.** *—verb.* To form or show dimples. **dimpled, dimpling.**

din *noun.* A continuing loud noise: The *din* of the traffic kept me awake. *—verb.* 1. To make a loud noise. 2. To repeat many times: Mother *dinned* into us the value of saving money. **dinned, dinning.**

dine (DIGHN) *verb.* To eat dinner. **dined, dining.**

din·er (DIGH-nər) *noun.* 1. One who is eating dinner. 2. A railroad car in which food is served. 3. A small restaurant.

di·nette (digh-NET) *noun.* A small area, usually in a recessed part of a room, used for eating meals. **dinettes.**

ding-dong (DING-dawng or DING-dong) *noun.* Sound made by a bell. *—adjective.* Like the back-and-forth motion of a ringing bell: The fighters had a *ding-dong* battle.

din·ghy (DING-ee) Also **dingy** or **dingey** *noun.* A small rowboat. **—dinghies** *plural.*

din·gy (DIN-jee) *adjective.* Dull, dirty, covered with grime. **dingier, dingiest.**

dining room. The room in which meals are eaten.

din·ner (DIN-ər) *noun.* 1. The main meal of the day. 2. A party at which dinner is served.

din·ner·time (DIN-ər-tighm) *noun.* The hour when the main meal of the day is eaten.

di·no·saur (DIGH-nə-sor) *noun.* One of a group of long-tailed reptiles that lived on the earth millions of years ago.

dint *noun.* Power, force: He finished the race by *dint* of real effort.

di·o·cese (DIGH-ə-siss or DIGH-ə-seess) *noun.* The area in the charge of a bishop of a church. **dioceses.**

dip *verb.* 1. To put into a liquid and take out quickly: *Dip* your toe in the water. 2. To remove with the hand, spoon, or other container: *Dip* the water out of the boat. 3. To lower and raise again: He *dipped* the flag in salute. 4. To slope downward and then upward: The road *dips* here. 5. To read parts of: He *dipped* into the book. **dipped, dipping.** *—noun.* 1. A short swim: They took a *dip* in the ocean. 2. The amount that one spoon or container will hold: He gave me three *dips* of ice cream. 3. The liquid or mixture into which something is put and removed: Sheep *dip* is used to kill ticks. 4. A low place: a *dip* in the road. 5. A cream-like mixture: cheese *dip.*

diph·the·ri·a (dif-THIHR-ee-ə or dip-THIHR-ee-ə) *noun.* A serious disease of the throat that can be passed from one person to another.

diph·thong (DIF-thong or DIP-thong) *noun.* The sound of two vowels pronounced as one: *Diphthongs* are found in such words as "oil," "aisle," and "out."

di·plo·ma (di-PLOH-mə) *noun.* A paper stating that a student has successfully finished a course of study.

di·plo·ma·cy (di-PLOH-mə-see) *noun.* 1. The art or skill of handling relationships between nations. 2. Skill in dealing with other people so that they do not become angry: The teacher used *diplomacy* to prevent the quarrel between the two boys.

dip·lo·mat (DIP-lə-mat) *noun.* 1. One who represents his government in relations with other countries. 2. One who is skillful in dealing with others: Mother is a *diplomat* in keeping peace in our family.

dip·lo·mat·ic (dip-lə-MAT-ik) *adjective.* 1. Having the ability to deal skillfully with others. 2. Referring to the conduct of dealings between nations. —**diplomatically** *adverb.*

dip·per (DIP-ər) *noun.* 1. A container used for removing liquid. 2. [Capital D] A star formation: The Big *Dipper.*

Dip·ter·a (DIP-tər-ə) *noun.* An order of insects that have one pair of rounded wings: The housefly is one of the *Diptera.*

dire (DIGHR) *adjective.* 1. Terrible, dreadful: *dire* news. 2. Extreme, great: *dire* need. **direr, direst.** —**direly** *adverb.*

di·rect (də-REKT) *adjective.* 1. Straight; with few or no turns: Jim took the most *direct* route to school. 2. Honest, straightforward: I want a *direct* answer about whether you were cheating. 3. Having an unbroken family line: The prince is a *direct* descendant of King George. 4. Exact: He read a *direct* quote from the President. 5. Without anything or anyone in between: The teacher was in *direct* contact with our parents. —*verb.* 1. To point or show the way. 2. To be in charge of: He *directs* the camp. 3. To address by writing or speaking: *Direct* your question to the manager. 4. To lead or conduct: He *directs* the band. 5. To guide actors in a play or movie. 6. To order or tell (to do something). **directed, directing.**

direct current. A flow of electricity moving in only one direction.

di·rec·tion (də-REK-shən) *noun.* 1. The act of advising, guiding, or commanding: Students work under the teacher's *direction.* 2. The conducting of a group of musicians: The band was under the *direction* of John Philip Sousa. 3. A line or course followed relative to points on the compass: In what *direction* are you going? 4. (Plural) Instructions: Follow the *directions* on the bottle.

di·rect·ly (də-REKT-lee) *adverb.* 1. At once or soon: We will go *directly.* 2. In a straight line. 3. Without stopping: I came *directly* home.

direct object. The word or words in a sentence that show the person or thing that is acted on by the verb: In the sentence "He hit the ball," "ball" is the *direct object. See* **indirect object.**

di·rec·tor (də-REK-tər) *noun.* 1. One who gives orders or manages: In 1924, J. Edgar Hoover became *director* of the FBI. 2. Leader of a band or orchestra. 3. One of a group of persons who manages a business: He was a member of the board of *directors* of a large department store. 4. One who gives instructions to actors.

di·rec·to·ry (də-REK-tə-ree) *noun.* An alphabetical list giving names, addresses, and other information about a group of people: Our name and number are listed in the telephone *directory.* **directories.**

dire·ful (DIGHR-fəl) *adjective.* Dreadful, gloomy: We saw the *direful* results of the forest fire that had destroyed acres of trees. —**direfully** *adverb.*

dirge (DERJ) *noun.* Slow, solemn music played or sung at funeral services. **dirges.**

dir·i·gi·ble (DIHR-ə-jə-bəl) *noun.* A lighter-than-air airship that can be steered. **dirigibles.**

dirigible

dirk (DERK) *noun.* A kind of dagger.

dirt (DERT) *noun.* 1. Earth or soil. 2. Anything that soils or makes something unclean. 3. (Slang) Cruel gossip.

dirk

dirt·y (DER-tee) *adjective.* 1. Soiled, not clean. 2. Bad, foul: He used *dirty* words. 3. Unfair, not following the rules. **dirtier, dirtiest.** —*verb.* To soil. **dirtied, dirtying.** —**dirtily** *adverb.*

dis- *prefix.* Indicates: 1. Not: *dis*like. 2. Away or apart from: *dis*appear. 3. The opposite of: *dis*belief.

dis·a·bil·i·ty (diss-ə-BIL-ə-tee) *noun.* 1. The state of being unable to do something. 2. A handicap: My sprained ankle is a *disability.* **disabilities.**

dis·a·ble (diss-AY-bəl) *verb.* To damage or cripple: The train wreck *disabled* the engine. **disabled, disabling.**

dis·ad·van·tage (diss-əd-VAN-tij) *noun.* 1. Anything that makes success unlikely. 2. Handicap: A short boy has a *disadvantage* in playing basketball. 3. Harm or loss; The sun in my eyes worked to my *disadvantage.* **disadvantages.** —*verb.* To put in a poor or unfavorable position. **disadvantaged, disadvantaging.** —**disadvantageous** (diss-ad-vən-TAY-jəss) *adjective.*

dis·a·gree (diss-ə-GREE) *verb.* 1. To be different: Your answer *disagrees* with mine. 2. To argue, have a different opinion. 3. To have unpleasant results: The new soap *disagrees* with my skin, causing a rash. **disagreed, disagreeing.**

dis·a·gree·a·ble (diss-ə-GREE-ə-bəl) *adjective.* 1. Unpleasant. 2. Ill-tempered. —**disagreeably** *adverb.*

dis·a·gree·ment (diss-ə-GREE-mənt) *noun.* 1. A failure to agree; a difference of opinion. 2. An argument.

dis·ap·pear (diss-ə-PIHR) *verb.* 1. To go out of sight. 2. To die out, cease to be. **disappeared, disappearing.**

dis·ap·pear·ance (diss-ə-PIHR-ənss) *noun.* 1. A sudden absence. 2. A dying out: The automobile led to the *disappearance* of most horse-drawn buggies.

dis·ap·point (diss-ə-POINT) *verb.* To fail to meet a person's expectations. **disappointed, disappointing.**

dis·ap·point·ment (diss-ə-POINT-mənt) *noun.* Unhappiness, sadness because of (someone's or something's) unexpected failure to please.

dis·ap·prov·al (diss-ə-PROO-vəl) *noun.* Disfavor, objection, refusal to accept.

dis·ap·prove (diss-ə-PROOV) *verb.* 1. To object to, or to have a poor opinion of: Tom Sawyer's aunt *disapproved* of his swimming in the river. 2. To turn down, vote against: The voters *disapproved* the new tax. **disapproved, disapproving.** —**disapproving** *adjective.* —**disapprovingly** *adverb.*

dis·arm (diss-AHRM) *verb.* 1. To take away another's guns or other weapons. 2. To give up weapons: The nations of the world should agree to *disarm* to help the cause of peace. 3. To win over in a friendly way. **disarmed, disarming.** —**disarming** *adjective.* —**disarmingly** *adverb.*

dis·ar·ma·ment (diss-AHR-mə-mənt) *noun.* The act of giving up weapons or reducing the amount of weapons.

dis·ar·range (diss-ə-RAYNJ) *verb.* To mix up, put out of order. **disarranged, disarranging.**

dis·as·ter (di-ZASS-tər) *noun.* An event that causes widespread damage or suffering.

dis·as·trous (di-ZASS-truhss) *adjective.* Very bad, causing great damage or suffering. —**disastrously** *adverb.*

dis·band (diss-BAND) *verb.* To break up an organized group of people: The ski team has *disbanded* for the season. **disbanded, disbanding.**

dis·be·lief (diss-bə-LEEF) *noun.* A failure or refusal to believe.

dis·burse (dis-BERSS) *verb.* To pay out: The club treasurer *disburses* the money. **disbursed, disbursing.**

dis·burse·ment (dis-BERSS-mənt) *noun.* 1. The paying out of money. 2. The money paid out.

disc (DISK) Also **disk** *noun.* 1. Any round, thin object. 2. A phonograph record.

dis·card (diss-KAHRD) *verb.* 1. To throw away. 2. In a card game, to play an unwanted card or one that is of a different suit than the one led. **discarded, discarding.** —(DISS-kahrd) *noun.* The thing that is thrown away or the card that is played.

dis·cern (di-ZERN or di-SERN) *verb.* To see (something) that is difficult to make out: I *discerned* a shape in the dark waters. **discerned, discerning.** —**discernment** *noun.*

dis·charge (diss-CHAHRJ) *verb.* 1. To unload: *discharge* passengers. 2. To set free, release: *discharge* from the hospital. 3. To fire or dismiss. 4. To shoot or go off: His gun *discharged* by accident. 5. To pour forth, to flow: The octopus *discharges* a black liquid. 6. To pay off: He *discharged* all his debts. 7. To deliver electric current: Using the car lights causes the battery to *discharge.* 8. To perform (a duty). **discharged, discharging.** —(DISS-chahrj) *noun.* 1. An unloading or release. 2. A dismissal or the paper that states the dismissal has taken place: He has been given his *discharge* from the army. 3. A firing of a gun or cannon. 4. A flowing or pouring forth. 5. A flow of electric current. 6. Performance (of duty). **discharges.**

dis·ci·ple (di-SIGH-pəl) *noun.* 1. A student or follower who accepts and helps spread the teachings of a leader. 2. A follower of Jesus Christ, particularly one of the 12 Apostles. **disciples.**

dis·ci·pline (DISS-ə-plin) *noun.* 1. Training. 2. The behavior resulting from strict training: The class has good *discipline.* 3. Punishment. 4. A set of rules followed by an organization. 5. A field of study: Astronomy is one of the *disciplines* of science. **disciplines.** —*verb.* 1. To train. 2. To punish or force to behave in a certain way. **disciplined, disciplining.**

disc jockey. A radio announcer who presents a program of talk and records.

dis·claim (diss-KLAYM) *verb.* To deny: He *disclaimed* any knowledge of the crime. **disclaimed, disclaiming.**

dis·close (diss-KLOHZ) *verb.* 1. To uncover; make visible. 2. To tell or make known: We will never *disclose* our secret. **disclosed, disclosing.** —**disclosure** *noun.*

dis·col·or (diss-KUHL-ər) *verb.* To change or spoil the color of. **discolored, discoloring.**

dis·com·fort (diss-KUHM-fərt) *noun.* An uncomfortable feeling. —*verb.* To disturb or make uneasy. **discomforted, discomforting.**

dis·con·cert (diss-kən-SERT) *verb.* To confuse or upset: The noise *disconcerted* me. **disconcerted, disconcerting.**

dis·con·nect (diss-kə-NEKT) *verb.* To unfasten or take apart, cut off: The telephone company *disconnected* our telephone when we moved to a new house. **disconnected, disconnecting.**

dis·con·tent (diss-kən-TENT) *noun.* Unhappiness, sadness, lack of satisfaction. —**discontented** *adjective.* —**discontentedly** *adverb.*

dis·con·tin·ue (diss-kən-TIN-yoo) *verb.* 1. To cut off, put an end to: He *discontinued* his newspaper subscription because he was going on vacation. 2. To quit, to stop. **discontinued, discontinuing.**

dis·cord (DISS-kord) *noun.* 1. Disagreement among persons or groups. 2. An unpleasant noise. 3. Musical notes that lack harmony.

dis·count (DISS-kownt or diss-KOWNT) *verb.* 1. To reduce or subtract in advance, as in price. 2. To doubt or question the truth of: Everyone *discounted* the boy's story that a wolf was coming. **discounted, discounting.** —(DISS-kownt) *noun.* A reduction in price: The campus store gives students a *discount* on gym clothes. —*adjective.* Selling at less than regular prices.

dis·cour·age (diss-KER-ij) *verb.* 1. To take away hope, cause to lose confidence. 2. To try to persuade (a person) not to do something: Cinderella's stepsisters tried to *discourage* her from trying on the slipper. **discouraged, discouraging.** —**discouragement** *noun.* —**discouraging** *adjective.* —**discouragingly** *adverb.*

dis·course (diss-KORSS) *verb.* 1. To have a conversation. 2. To speak or write about a subject. **discoursed, discoursing.** —(DISS-korss) *noun.* 1. Conversation. 2. Spoken or written thoughts on a subject: He gave us a *discourse* on the high cost of living. **discourses.**

dis·cour·te·ous (diss-KER-tee-əss) *adjective.* Rude, lacking good manners. —**discourteously** *adverb.*

dis·cov·er (diss-KUHV-ər) *verb.* 1. To find or learn something for the first time. 2. To learn something by studying. **discovered, discovering.**

dis·cov·er·y (diss-KUHV-ər-ee) *noun.* 1. The act of finding, seeing, or learning something for the first time. 2. The thing or fact that is found: The wheel was one of man's great *discoveries.* **discoveries.**

dis·cred·it (diss-KRED-it) *verb.* 1. To disgrace. 2. To fail to believe, to doubt: The police *discredit* the man's story. 3. To cause disbelief in: The evidence *discredited* the thief's claims of innocence. **discredited, discrediting.** —*noun.* 1. Disgrace. 2. Loss of trust; doubt.

dis·creet (diss-KREET) *adjective.* Showing good judgment, careful in word and action. —**discreetly** *adverb.*

dis·cre·tion (diss-KRESH-ən) *noun.* 1. Care in making decisions. 2. Judgment; freedom of choice or action: The campers were allowed to use their own *discretion* about swimming in the river.

dis·crim·i·nate (diss-KRIM-ə-nayt) *verb.* 1. To distinguish, see small differences: The expert can *discriminate* between natural and man-made diamonds. 2. To show unfair favor for one thing, person, or group over all others. **discriminated, discriminating.**

dis·crim·i·na·tion (diss-krim-ə-NAY-shən) *noun.* 1. The ability to notice small differences: It takes *discrimination* to find the queen bee in the hive. 2. An act of unfairly favoring persons or groups: If we do not allow children of all races to join our club, we are practicing *discrimination.* 3. The ability to make a wise judgment; good taste.

dis·cus (DISS-kəss) *noun.* In athletic contests, a flat, circular object that is hurled as far as a competitor can throw. —**discuses** or **disci** (DISS-igh) *plural.*

dis·cuss (diss-KUHSS) *verb.* To speak or write about; talk over. **discussed, discussing.**

dis·cus·sion (diss-KUHSH-ən) *noun.* The act of talking about something: The class had a *discussion* about the coming elections.

dis·dain (diss-DAYN) *verb.* To look down at something or somebody: The movie star *disdained* cotton sheets and slept only on satin. **disdained, disdaining.** —*noun.* A feeling that one is better than someone else: Why should a fifth grader look at fourth graders with such *disdain?* —**disdainful** *adjective.* —**disdainfully** *adverb.*

dis·ease (di-ZEEZ) *noun.* An illness or loss of health: Chicken pox is a children's *disease.* **diseases.**

dis·em·bark (diss-im-BAHRK) *verb.* To come off or go ashore from a ship or boat. **disembarked, disembarking.**

dis·em·bod·y (diss-im-BOD-ee) *verb.* To free the soul or spirit from the human body: The friendly ghost said it was *disembodied* 300 years ago. **disembodied, disembodying.**

dis·fa·vor (diss-FAY-vər) *noun.* 1. A feeling of dislike, a lack of approval. 2. The state of being out of favor or disliked: Our cat is in *disfavor* because he ate the canary.

dis·fig·ure (diss-FIG-yər) *verb.* To mar or spoil the appearance of: The vandals *disfigured* the painting in the museum. **disfigured, disfiguring.**

dis·grace (diss-GRAYSS) *noun.* 1. A feeling of shame. 2. Something that causes shame. **disgraces.** —*verb.* To bring shame, embarrass. **disgraced, disgracing.**

dis·grace·ful (diss-GRAYSS-fəl) *adjective.* Shameful. —**disgracefully** *adverb.*

dis·guise (diss-GIGHZ) *verb.* 1. To change so as to appear to be something else: The robbers *disguised* themselves as window washers. 2. To hide or conceal: Tim tried to *disguise* the fact that he had broken a lamp. **disguised, disguising.** —*noun.* A make-up or costume used to change one's appearance. **disguises.**

dis·gust (diss-GUHST) *noun.* A strong feeling of dislike, a sickening feeling. —*verb.* To cause a strong distaste: Litter in the streets *disgusts* us. **disgusted, disgusting.**

dish *noun.* 1. A shallow, open container used to hold and serve food. 2. The amount of food contained in a dish: We each had a *dish* of ice cream. 3. Food prepared in a special way: Bean soup is his favorite *dish.* **dishes.** —*verb.* To serve from one container into another: He *dished* the potatoes onto our plates. **dished, dishing.** —**dish it out.** (Slang) To abuse with words or blows.

dish·cloth (DISH-klawth) *noun.* Any cloth used in washing dishes.

dis·heart·en (diss-HAHRT-n) *verb.* To discourage, take away hope: He *disheartened* us with the bad news. **disheartened, disheartening.**

di·shev·eled (di-SHEV-əld) *adjective.* Mussed up, untidy.

dis·hon·est (diss-ON-ist) *adjective.* Not to be trusted, not truthful. —**dishonestly** *adverb.* —**dishonesty** *noun.*

dis·hon·or (diss-ON-ər) *verb.* To disgrace, treat rudely: He *dishonored* the flag by stepping on it. **dishonored, dishonoring.** —*noun.* Shame or disgrace.

dis·hon·or·a·ble (diss-ON-ər-ə-bəl) *adjective.* Shameful, not to be trusted. —**dishonorably** *adverb.*

dish·pan (DISH-pan) *noun.* Container in which dishes and other kitchen equipment are washed.

dis·il·lu·sion (diss-i-LOO-zhən) *verb.* To disenchant; take beliefs or hopes away from: Tom thought he could make the baseball team until the coach *disillusioned* him. **disillusioned, disillusioning.** —*noun.* Also **disillusionment.** The realization that something unpleasant is true.

dis·in·fect (diss-in-FEKT) *verb.* To clean by killing disease germs. **disinfected, disinfecting.**

dis·in·fec·tant (diss-in-FEK-tənt) *noun.* A substance used to kill germs.

dis·in·te·grate (diss-IN-tə-grayt) *verb.* To come apart, separate into pieces: The airplane *disintegrated* when it crashed. **disintegrated, disintegrating.** —**disintegration** (diss-in-tə-GRAY-shən) *noun.*

dis·in·ter·est·ed (diss-IN-tri-stid or diss-IN-tə-ress-tid) *adjective.* Not on one side or another; not involved: The boys asked a *disinterested* teacher to settle their argument. —**disinterestedly** *adverb.*

disk Also **disc** *noun.* An object that is thin, flat, and round. —*verb.* To break up and level out plowed ground with a disk harrow. **disked, disking.**

dis·like (diss-LIGHK) *verb.* To be against, feel unpleasantly toward. **disliked, disliking.** —*noun.* A feeling of distaste: He has a *dislike* of fighting. **dislikes.**

dis·lo·cate (DISS-loh-kayt or diss-LOH-kayt) *verb.* 1. To put out of place: The boy *dislocated* his shoulder when he fell. 2. To put out of order; upset: Our plans to go hiking were *dislocated* by the bad weather. **dislocated, dislocating.** —**dislocation** *noun.*

dis·lodge (diss-LOJ) *verb.* 1. To force out of place: He used a stick to *dislodge* the heavy rock. 2. To cause to move from a shelter or hiding place: Fire *dislodged* the bear from his cave. **dislodged, dislodging.**

dis·loy·al (diss-LOI-əl) *adjective.* Unfaithful, false, not true. —**disloyally** *adverb.* —**disloyalty** *noun.*

dis·mal (DIZ-məl) *adjective.* 1. Gloomy, sad, dreary. 2. Downhearted; miserable: Her sad story made us feel *dismal.* 3. Poor, inadequate: Joe's composition is a *dismal* example of writing. 4. Hopeless: His chances of winning were *dismal.* —**dismally** *adverb.*

dis·man·tle (diss-MANT-l) *verb.* 1. To take apart piece by piece. 2. To remove furniture and equipment. **dismantled, dismantling.**

dis·may (diss-MAY) *verb.* To alarm or cause fear: **dismayed, dismaying.** —*noun.* Loss of courage, a troubled feeling.

dis·miss (diss-MISS) *verb.* 1. To send away or allow to leave: She *dismissed* the class at three o'clock. 2. To discharge from a job. 3. To put out of one's thoughts: I decided that the idea was foolish and *dismissed* it. **dismissed, dismissing.** —**dismissal** (diss-MISS-l) *noun.*

dis·mount (diss-MOWNT) *verb.* 1. To get off or down from something. 2. To remove from a setting or support. **dismounted, dismounting.**

dis·o·be·di·ence (diss-ə-BEE-dee-ənss) *noun.* Failure to obey orders.

dis·o·bey (diss-ə-BAY) *verb.* To fail to obey, refuse to follow orders, misbehave. **disobeyed, disobeying.**

dis·or·der (diss-OR-dər) *noun.* 1. Confusion, lack of neatness. 2. A riot or public disturbance: The police were called to put an end to the *disorder.* 3. Sickness or poor health: The doctor treated him for a stomach *disorder.*

dis·or·der·ly (diss-OR-dər-lee) *adjective.* 1. Messy, out of order: Mother scolded us for our *disorderly* appearance. 2. Unruly, not well-behaved: *disorderly* conduct.

dis·or·gan·ize (diss-OR-gə-nighz) *verb.* To cause disorder, break up the system or arrangement: Twin babies soon *disorganized* our household. **disorganized, disorganizing.**

dis·own (diss-OHN) *verb.* To refuse to recognize as one's own, turn out: The angry father has *disowned* his son. **disowned, disowning.**

dis·par·age (diss-PA-rij) *verb.* To run down, belittle: He *disparaged* my efforts to play basketball. **disparaged, disparaging.** —**disparaging** *adjective.* —**disparagingly** *adverb.*

dis·patch (diss-PACH) *noun.* 1. A message. 2. Haste, speed: The doctor came with *dispatch.* 3. A news story from a reporter in a distant place. **dispatches.** —*verb.* 1. To send off promptly: He *dispatched* a runner to the fort. 2. To finish quickly: The hungry boy *dispatched* five of the cookies. 3. To put to death. **dispatched, dispatching.**

dis·pel (diss-PEL) *verb.* To scatter or drive away: The sun *dispelled* the clouds. **dispelled, dispelling.**

dis·pense (diss-PENSS) *verb.* 1. To pass out or distribute: The coin machine *dispenses* candy and chewing gum. 2. To make up and give out medicine. 3. To apply or be in charge of: The judge *dispenses* justice according to the law. **dispensed, dispensing. —dispenser** *noun.* **—dispense with.** To do without.

dis·perse (diss-PERSS) *verb.* 1. To scatter or break up: The police *dispersed* the crowd. 2. To spread around, distribute: One sneeze *disperses* many cold germs. **dispersed, dispersing.**

dis·place (diss-PLAYSS) *verb.* 1. To move (something) out of position. 2. To put in a new thing for an old one; replace. 3. To drive one from his homeland: The rabbi's family was *displaced* during World War II. **displaced, displacing.**

dis·play (diss-PLAY) *verb.* 1. To show, demonstrate: Members of the art class *displayed* their paintings. 2. To reveal, uncover: She *displayed* her grief by crying. **displayed, displaying.** *—noun.* A show or exhibition: *display* of Christmas lights.

dis·please (diss-PLEEZ) *verb.* To annoy or cause an unpleasant feeling in. **displeased, displeasing.**

dis·pleas·ure (diss-PLEZH-ər) *noun.* Unhappiness, a feeling of dislike.

dis·pos·al (diss-POH-zl) *noun.* 1. The act of removing or getting rid of: The town needs a new method of trash *disposal.* 2. Arrangement: The manager directed the *disposal* of furniture in the new store. **—at one's disposal.** At one's service.

dis·pose (diss-POHZ) *verb.* 1. To place or arrange: The gardener *disposed* the flowers in a bed near the house. 2. To incline or make willing: Your actions do not *dispose* me to trust you. **disposed, disposing. —dispose of.** To get rid of; part with.

dis·posed (diss-POHZD) *adjective.* Willing; likely or ready (to).

dis·po·si·tion (diss-pə-ZISH-ən) *noun.* 1. Placement; arrangement. 2. The power to use or manage as one wishes: All the boats were at the captain's *disposition.* 3. Basic or general nature: The boy has a pleasant *disposition.*

dis·prove (diss-PROOV) *verb.* To show to be untrue or false. **disproved, disproving.**

dis·pute (diss-PYOOT) *noun.* An argument or quarrel. **disputes.** *—verb.* 1. To argue. 2. To question: We *disputed* Russia's right to have ships in our fishing grounds. 3. To contest or fight: Our football team was losing but they *disputed* every inch that the other team gained. **disputed, disputing.**

dis·qual·i·fy (diss-KWOL-ə-figh) *verb.* 1. To keep out or exclude (one who does not meet a special test or requirement): Being younger than 35 *disqualifies* a man from becoming U.S. President. 2. To break a rule and thereby become unfit: The skier *disqualified* himself by starting downhill before the signal was given. **disqualified, disqualifying.**

dis·qui·et (diss-KWIGH-it) *verb.* To cause worry; make uneasy. **disquieted, disquieting.** *—noun.* Disturbance, lack of peace.

dis·re·gard (diss-ri-GAHRD) *verb.* To pay no attention to or to fail to notice. **disregarded, disregarding.** *—noun.* A lack of care, attention, or regard.

dis·re·pair (diss-ri-PAIR) *noun.* The condition of needing repairs.

dis·rep·u·ta·ble (diss-REP-yə-tə-bəl) *adjective.* 1. Disgraceful, not well regarded by others: The thief had some *disreputable* friends. 2. Having a bad appearance: a *disreputable* coat. —**disreputably** *adverb.*

dis·re·spect (diss-ri-SPEKT) *noun.* Rudeness, lack of consideration for others. —**disrespectful** *adjective.* —**disrespectfully** *adverb.*

dis·robe (diss-ROHB) *verb.* To undress, take off one's clothes. **disrobed, disrobing.**

dis·rupt (diss-RUHPT) *verb.* To break up, upset the order of: The fire drill *disrupted* the class. **disrupted, disrupting.** —**disruption** *noun.* —**disruptive** *adjective.*

dis·sat·is·fac·tion (diss-sat-iss-FAK-shən) *noun.* Lack of happiness; discontent.

dis·sat·is·fy (diss-SAT-iss-figh) *verb.* To fail to please, disappoint. **dissatisfied, dissatisfying.**

dis·sect (di-SEKT or DIGH-sekt) *verb.* 1. To cut apart in order to study the inside: The science class is *dissecting* a frog. 2. To examine or study carefully. **dissected, dissecting.**

dis·sen·sion (di-SEN-shən) *noun.* Angry disagreement, difference of opinion; discord, strife.

dis·sent (di-SENT) *verb.* To disagree, have a different opinion: Six judges voted for the measure; three *dissented.* **dissented, dissenting.** —*noun.* A difference of opinion: There was *dissent* in the class regarding the new rules.

dis·ser·vice (diss-SER-viss) *noun.* A damaging act, an injury: To help another student cheat is to do him a *disservice.* **disservices.**

dis·sim·i·lar (diss-SIM-ə-lər) *adjective.* Unlike, different. —**dissimilarity** (di-sim-ə-LA-rə-tee) *noun.* —**dissimilarly** *adverb.*

dis·si·pate (DISS-ə-payt) *verb.* 1. To scatter, make disappear: The bright sun *dissipated* the fog. 2. To waste or spend foolishly: He has *dissipated* the fortune his father left him. **dissipated, dissipating.** —**dissipation** (diss-ə-PAY-shən) *noun.*

dis·so·lute (DISS-ə-loot) *adjective.* Not morally strong, showing poor conduct. —**dissolutely** *adverb.*

dis·solve (di-ZOLV) *verb.* 1. To break up and become part of a liquid: The sugar *dissolved* in the hot tea. 2. To change from a solid to a liquid: The ice cream *dissolved* into a sticky puddle. 3. To break up or come to an end: The crossing guard program *dissolved* at the end of the school year. **dissolved, dissolving.**

dis·so·nance (DISS-ə-nənss) *noun.* 1. A harsh or disagreeable sound; a lack of harmony. 2. A disagreement. **dissonances.**

dis·suade (di-SWAYD) *verb.* To advise against; turn one (from doing something): Dad *dissuaded* me from going sailing today. **dissuaded, dissuading.**

dis·tance (DISS-tənss) *noun.* The interval or space between two points or times: The *distance* between the bases is 90 feet. —**keep one's distance.** To be unfriendly; to stay away from.

dis·tant (DISS-tənt) *adjective.* 1. Far away in time, space, or relationship, as a *distant* country or a *distant* relative. 2. Cool or unfriendly: We tried to make friends with the new boy but he remained *distant.* —**distantly** *adverb.*

dis·taste (diss-TAYST) *noun.* A dislike, a failure to enjoy. **distastes.**

dis·taste·ful (diss-TAYST-fəl) *adjective.* Unpleasant, not to one's liking. —**distastefully** *adverb.*

dis·tem·per (diss-TEM-pər) *noun.* An easily caught, sometimes fatal animal disease, often affecting dogs and cats.

dis·tend (diss-TEND) *verb.* To become larger or cause to become larger; swell: The croaking frog *distends* its body when it is frightened. **distended, distending.**

dis·till (diss-TIL) *verb.* To heat a mixture so that one substance escapes as a gas which can be cooled to a liquid. **distilled, distilling.**

dis·til·la·tion (diss-tə-LAY-shən) *noun.* 1. A way of separating a mixture by heating. *See* **distill.** 2. The liquid collected through distilling.

dis·tinct (diss-TINGKT) *adjective.* 1. Not alike, different. 2. Clear, sharp, definite: The blue jay has *distinct* markings. —**distinctly** *adverb.*

dis·tinc·tion (diss-TINGK-shən) *noun.* 1. A way in which things differ: Sometimes it is hard to find a *distinction* between fact and fiction. 2. The act of finding a difference or keeping separate: Our school welcomes all races without *distinction.* 3. Importance, fine character: The judge is a man of *distinction.* 4. Special honor: Ted graduated with *distinction.*

dis·tinc·tive (diss-TINGK-tiv) *adjective.* Showing a difference; characteristic: Vanilla has a *distinctive* flavor. —**distinctively** *adverb.*

dis·tin·guish (diss-TING-gwish) *verb.* 1. To be able to tell the difference; recognize: He can *distinguish* clams from oysters. 2. To set apart or identify: A comet can be *distinguished* by its long tail. 3. Recognize by using one or more of the senses: I *distinguished* the smell of smoke in the air. 4. To make famous: Longfellow *distinguished* himself as a poet. **distinguished, distinguishing.**

dis·tort (diss-TORT) *verb.* 1. To change from its natural shape: The wind *distorts* the shapes of trees near the shore. 2. To change the meaning of: The mayor said the newspaper *distorted* his words. **distorted, distorting.** —**distortion** *noun.*

dis·tract (diss-TRAKT) *verb.* 1. To cause to turn one's attention away: The noise *distracted* me from my work. 2. To mix up or confuse: Her grief *distracted* her so much that she forgot her duties. **distracted, distracting.**

dis·trac·tion (diss-TRAK-shən) *noun.* 1. The act of having one's attention turned away: Stopping to mow the grass was a *distraction* from Tom's studies. 2. Anything that draws one's attention; an amusement: Watching television is my favorite *distraction.* 3. Madness; a confused mental state: I am almost driven to *distraction* when he plays his new drums.

dis·tress (diss-TRESS) *noun.* 1. Danger, trouble. 2. Worry or pain. 3. Hardship, need of money. **distresses.** —*verb.* To worry or cause pain; to trouble: The outbreak of war *distressed* the nation. **distressed, distressing.**

dis·trib·ute (diss-TRIB-yoot) *verb.* 1. To give out, deal out: He *distributed* books to all who needed them. 2. To scatter or spread out: Snakes are *distributed* throughout the world. **distributed, distributing.**

dis·tri·bu·tion (diss-trə-BYOO-shən) *noun.* 1. The act of giving out or dividing: The *distribution* of prizes took place during a school assembly. 2. The pattern or arrangement in which an amount is given out: the *distribution* of rainfall.

dis·trib·u·tive (diss-TRIB-yə-tiv or diss-TRIB-yoo-tiv) *noun.* (Grammar) A word that refers to members of a group individually or singly, such as *each, either, every,* or *none.* —*adjective.* Equal or having the same effect: The *distributive* law of mathematics makes it possible for elements of a set to be arranged in more than one way.

dis·trib·u·tor (diss-TRIB-yə-tər) *noun.* 1. A person or organization that gives out or sells items or goods. 2. Part of an engine: The *distributor* sends electric current to the spark plugs.

dis·trict (DISS-trikt) *noun.* 1. An area with definite limits set up for a special purpose: school *district.* 2. A general area: business *district.*

District of Columbia. The Federal District, formerly a part of Maryland, where the U.S. Capital is located.

dis·trust (diss-TRUHST) *noun.* Suspicion, lack of belief. —*verb.* To suspect, doubt. **distrusted, distrusting.** —**distrustful** *adjective.*

dis·turb (diss-TERB) *verb.* 1. To upset or mix up: Don't *disturb* the chess pieces. 2. To cause to worry; upset. 3. To interfere with, bother, or arouse. **disturbed, disturbing.**

dis·turb·ance (diss-TER-bənss) *noun.* 1. Noise or confusion. 2. Interruption. 3. Something that interrupts.

ditch (DICH) *noun.* A long, narrow opening or trench dug in the ground: A drainage *ditch* bordered the road. **ditches.** —*verb.* 1. To dig a trench or channel. 2. To put into a ditch. 3. To land a disabled plane on the water. 4. (Slang) To get rid of (an unwanted person or thing). **ditched, ditching.**

dit·ty (DIT-ee) *noun.* A little poem or simple song. **ditties.**

di·van (DIGH-van or di-VAN) *noun.* A couch or sofa, usually without back or arms.

dive (DIGHV) *verb.* 1. To go head first into the water. 2. To go underwater: The submarine crew prepared to *dive.* 3. To nose down steeply as in an airplane losing power. 4. To go quickly into anything, such as a job or other activity: He *dives* into his work as if he likes it. **dived** or **dove, diving.** —*noun.* 1. The act of going head first into something. 2. (Slang) A restaurant or gathering place with a bad reputation. **dives.**

diving bell

di·verse (də-VERSS or DIGH-verss) *adjective.* Distinct, different, unlike: "The wind blows from *diverse* points." (Dante). —**diversely** *adverb.*

di·ver·si·ty (də-VER-sə-tee) *noun.* 1. Difference. 2. Variety: The flower garden displayed a *diversity* of colors. **diversities.**

di·vert (də-VERT) *verb.* 1. To draw or turn away from a course or direction: The road block *diverted* the traffic. 2. To entertain or amuse. **diverted, diverting.** —**diversion** (də-VER-zhən) *noun.*

di·vide (də-VIGHD) *verb.* 1. To cut up or separate into parts. 2. To cause to take sides: The town council was *divided* on the subject of increased taxes. 3. To separate into equal parts by arithmetic: If you *divide* six by three the answer is two. 4. To separate one thing from another: A high fence *divides* our yard from theirs. 5. To branch or fork, as a road. **divided, dividing.** —*noun.* A point or line that separates: the Continental *Divide.*

div·i·dend (DIV-ə-dend) *noun.* 1. In an arithmetic problem, the number that is to be divided. 2. A share of the profits in a business that is distributed to the owners.

di·vid·er (də-VIGH-dər) *noun.* 1. Something that divides. 2. A screen or part of a wall: There is a room *divider* between the two beds. 3. (Plural) A measuring instrument similar to a compass: The boys used *dividers* in the mechanical drawing class.

di·vine (də-VIGHN) *adjective* 1. From God, or of God: The minister read the *divine* word from the Bible. 2. Godlike, holy: "To err is human, to forgive *divine.*" (Alexander Pope). 3. Excellent; superhuman. 4. (Slang) Very good, fine: —*noun.* A minister or priest. **divines.** —*verb.* To guess or predict the future. **divined, divining.** —**divinely** *adverb.*

diving bell. A bell-shaped vessel used to protect underwater workers and to supply them with air under pressure.

diving suit. A heavy, waterproof suit worn by underwater workers who receive air through tubes attached to the helmet.

di·vin·i·ty (də-VIN-ə-tee) *noun.* 1. The state or act of being godlike. 2. [Capital D] God. 3. Any god or goddess: The Greeks worshiped many *divinities.* 4. The study of religion. 5. A kind of fudge-like candy. **divinities.**

di·vis·i·ble (də-VIZ-ə-bəl) *adjective.* 1. Capable of being separated into parts. 2. (Math) Able to be divided evenly by a certain number without a remainder: Six is *divisible* by two.

di·vi·sion (də-VIZH-ən) *noun.* 1. The act of separating into parts. 2. One of the parts that has been separated. 3. (Math) The process of finding out how many times one number is contained in another. 4. A difference of opinion. 5. A large military unit containing several regiments. 6. Something that serves as a boundary or border. 7. One part of an organization or government. 8. The process by which some living things increase.

di·vi·sor (də-VIGH-zər) *noun.* The number or quantity by which another number is to be divided.

di·vorce (də-VORSS) *noun.* 1. The ending of a marriage by law. 2. The separation of two things that have been closely related. **divorces.** —*verb.* 1. To end a marriage by law. 2. To separate. **divorced, divorcing.**

di·vulge (də-VUHLJ) *verb.* To tell or make public. **divulged, divulging.**

diz·zi·ness (DIZ-ee-nəss) *noun.* The feeling that one is spinning around; confusion.

diz·zy (DIZ-ee) *adjective.* 1. Having a feeling of spinning; confused. 2. Causing a confused, mixed-up feeling: We saw the city from the *dizzy* heights of the Empire State Building. 3. (Slang) Foolish, silly. **dizzier, dizziest.** —*verb.* To give a feeling of confusion. **dizzied, dizzying.** —**dizzily** *adverb.*

DNA *noun.* A substance found in the cells of all living things: *DNA* carries the traits that are passed down from parent to offspring.

[1]**do** (DOO) *verb.* 1. To perform; carry out: As a scout, Janice pledged to *do* her duty to God and her country. 2. To finish: I will *do* my homework before dinner. 3. To act towards or treat. 4. To fix or arrange: How will you *do* your hair for the party? 5. To travel or go a distance: My brother has to *do* five miles each day on his paper route. 6. To be enough for; serve: Two apples for each of us will *do* nicely. 7. Used as a helping verb: a. To ask a question: *Do* you like ice cream? b. With "not" to form a negative statement: I *do* not like lima beans. c. To add strength to what is said: I *do* want to go on the picnic. 8. Used to fill in for another verb that is already used in a sentence: Gliders seem to fly as birds *do.* **did, done, doing.**

[2]**do** (DOH) *noun.* (Music) A sound used in singing to identify the first tone of a scale.

Do·ber·man pin·scher (DOH-bər-mən PIN-shər). A large black, short-haired dog, originally bred in Germany.

doc·ile (DOSS-l) *adjective.* Tame; easy to handle. —**docilely** *adverb.*

dock (DOK) *noun.* 1. A pier, a platform built over the water as a landing place for ships and boats. 2. The water between two piers. 3. A platform at which trucks or trains are loaded and unloaded. 4. A place where ships are repaired: The ship is in a dry *dock.* 5. A common kind of weed with small green or red flowers and smooth, red-veined leaves. 6. The solid part of an animal's tail. 7. The place in a courtroom where the prisoner stands or sits. —*verb.* 1. To come or

diving suit

Doberman pinscher

bring to a pier or loading platform. 2. To cut off the end of an animal's tail: Boxer dogs usually have their tails *docked* when they are puppies. 3. To hold back or keep part of: The boss *docks* our wages when we are late. **docked, docking.**

doc·tor (DOK-tər) *noun.* 1. A person trained and licensed in the art of healing. 2. A person who holds the highest degree awarded by a college or university. —*verb.* 1. To give medical treatment to. 2. To add something to (food or drink). 3. To falsify (a record or statement). **doctored, doctoring.**

doc·tor·ate (DOK-tər-it) *noun.* A university degree given to students who have earned the rank of doctor. **doctorates.**

doc·trine (DOK-trin) *noun.* A belief or principle. **doctrines.**

doc·u·ment (DOK-yə-mənt or DOK-yoo-mənt) *noun.* 1. A written or printed paper that proves information to be true: Birth certificates, deeds, and diplomas are all *documents.* 2. Any object that is used as proof. —*verb.* 1. To supply an official paper. 2. To support (a statement) by presenting proof: He *documented* his story with pictures of flying saucers. **documented, documenting.**

dodge (DOJ) *verb.* 1. To move quickly out of the way. 2. To avoid through a trick: The burglar *dodged* the police by climbing out the window. **dodged, dodging.** —*noun.* 1. A quick movement. 2. A sly trick. **dodges.**

dodo

do·do (DOH-doh) *noun.* 1. An extinct bird. 2. Someone or something that is out-of-date. 3. (Slang) A dull or slow person: dumb as a *dodo.* —**dodoes** or **dodos** *plural.*

doe (DOH) *noun.* The female of certain animals such as the deer. —**does** or **doe** *plural.*

does (DUHZ) *verb. See* **do.**

doesn't (DUHZ-nt) *verb.* A shortened form of the words *does not.*

doff *verb.* To take off, especially one's hat. **doffed, doffing.**

dog *noun.* 1. A four-legged animal often kept as a household pet or trained for hunting or herding. 2. (Plural, slang) Feet. 3. (Slang) Fellow or chap: He's a gay old *dog.* 4. (Slang) Something no one wants: Our old car is a *dog.* —*verb.* To follow closely, like a dog. **dogged, dogging.** —**go to the dogs.** To go to ruin. —**put on the dog.** Pretend to be wealthy or in fashion.

dog days. Days in July and August, often hot or humid and named for Sirius, the Dog Star, which rises and sets with the sun during this period.

dog-ear (DOG-ihr) Also **dog's-ear** *noun.* The turned-down corner of a page of a book. —*verb.* To turn down the corner of a page. **dog-eared, dog-earing.** —**dog-eared** *adjective.* Having dog-ears; worn-out or shabby.

dog·ged (DOG-id) *adjective.* Stubborn; determined; refusing to give up. —**doggedly** *adverb.*

dog·house (DOG-howss) *noun.* A small shelter for a dog. **doghouses.** —**in the doghouse.** (Slang) Out of favor, in trouble.

do·gie (DOH-gee) Also **do·gy** *noun.* A stray or motherless calf. **dogies.**

dog·ma (DOG-mə) *noun.* 1. A belief or statement accepted as absolute truth. 2. A set of beliefs that relate to one particular religion or church. —**dogmas** or **dogmata** (DOG-mə-tə) *plural.*

dog·mat·ic (dog-MAT-ik) *adjective.* 1. Having to do with dogma or nature of dogma. 2. Holding an opinion without regard for facts or new discoveries; opinionated. —**dogmatically** *adverb.*

dog·trot (DOG-traht) *noun.* A slow steady run like that of a dog.

—*verb.* To run at an easy, steady pace. **dogtrotted, dogtrotting.**

dog·wood (DOG-wud) *noun.* A flowering tree found in Eastern North America.

doi·ly (DOI-lee) *noun.* A small mat often trimmed with lace or needle-work, used to protect or decorate furniture. **doilies.**

do·ings (DOO-ingz) *noun, plural.* Events, happenings, acts.

dol·drums (DOHL-drəmz or DOL-drəmz) *noun, plural.* 1. A sad, low state of mind, without spirit: After we lost the game, our team was in the *doldrums.* 2. A calm part of the ocean near the Equator.

dole (DOHL) *verb.* 1. To give (out) money, food, or other items to the needy. 2. To pass (out) anything in small amounts. **doled, doling** —*noun.* 1. The act of passing out or receiving items. 2. Such items themselves. 3. (British) The money paid by the government to those without jobs.

dole·ful (DOHL-fəl) *adjective.* Sorrowful, unhappy. —**dolefully** *adverb.*

doll *noun.* 1. A small figure shaped like a person, often like a baby, and used as a plaything. 2. (Slang) A pretty child or woman. —*verb.* Also **doll up.** (Slang) To dress up. **dolled, dolling.**

dol·lar (DOL-ər) *noun.* A basic unit of money in the United States, Canada, and other countries: The U.S. *dollar* ($) is worth 100 cents.

dol·phin (DOL-fin) *noun.* An air-breathing sea animal, sometimes called a porpoise, related to the whale.

dolt (DOHLT) *noun.* A stupid or slow-witted person.

-dom *suffix.* Indicates: 1. The position or area ruled by: king*dom.* 2. A condition or state of being: free*dom.*

do·main (doh-MAYN) *noun.* 1. The land or area over which one has control: The kitchen is Mother's *domain.* 2. A region ruled by a king or government. 3. A branch of study: the *domain* of science.

dome (DOHM) *noun.* 1. A roof shaped like half a ball or nearly so: The Capitol in Washington has a large *dome.* 2. Any shape similar to half a ball. 3. (Slang) The head. **domes.** —*verb.* To shape or cover like a dome. **domed, doming.**

dome

do·mes·tic (də-MESS-tik) *adjective.* 1. Relating to the home or family life. 2. Relating to one's own country rather than a foreign country: The President is concerned with *domestic* affairs. 3. Tame, not wild. —*noun.* A person hired to do housework. —**domestically** *adverb.*

do·mes·ti·cate (də-MESS-tə-kayt) *verb.* 1. To train to live with and serve man; to tame. 2. To make to feel happy and comfortable at home or with family life: The new bride *domesticated* the cowboy. **domesticated, domesticating.**

dom·i·cile (DOM-ə-sil or DOM-ə-sighl) *noun.* A home, a place to live. **domiciles.** —*verb.* To place in a home. **domiciled, domiciling.**

dom·i·nate (DOM-ə-nayt) *verb.* 1. To control, govern, or be most important: Gene *dominated* the conversation by doing most of the talking. 2. To rise high above; be in a commanding position: The Statue of Liberty *dominates* New York harbor. **dominated, dominating.** —**dominance** (DOM-ə-nənss) *noun.* —**dominant** *adjective.* —**dominantly** *adverb.*

do·min·ion (də-MIN-yən) *noun.* 1. The right or power of ruling: The king had *dominion* over all the people in his kingdom. 2. The area over which a ruler has power: Napoleon tried to increase his *dominions* by war. 3. A self-governing territory of the British Commonwealth.

dolphin

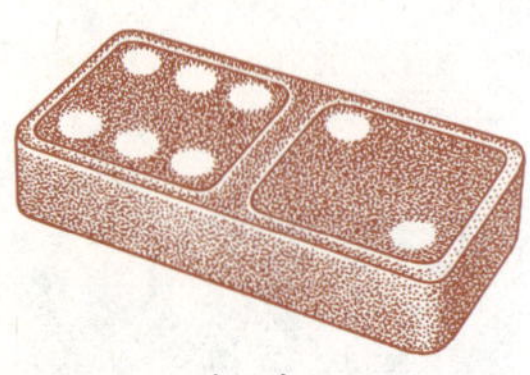
domino

donkey

dormer

dom·i·no (DOM-ə-noh) *noun.* 1. One of a set of black, oblong pieces of plastic, wood, or bone used in playing a game. 2. A hooded robe worn by certain clergymen, sometimes with a mask. —**dominoes** or **dominos** *plural.*

don *verb.* To put on: He *donned* his best clothes. **donned, donning.** —*noun.* 1. A Spanish gentleman. 2. A tutor or advanced student at a British university.

do·nate (DOH-nayt) *verb.* To give; contribute. **donated, donating.**

do·na·tion (doh-NAY-shən) *noun.* A gift made to a cause.

done (DUHN) *verb. See* **do.**

don·key (DONG-kee or DUHNG-kee) *noun.* 1. A tame animal of the ass family. 2. A stupid or stubborn person.

do·nor (DOH-nər) *noun.* 1. One who gives something. 2. One who gives blood or a part of the body for another.

don't (DOHNT) *contraction.* A shortened form of the words *do not.*

doo·dle (DOOD-l) *verb.* To draw or scribble, often while thinking about something else. **doodled, doodling.** —*noun.* A scribble or drawing. **doodles.**

doom *noun.* 1. Fate, usually evil or harmful. 2. A sad or tragic outcome; ruin. —*verb.* To mark for a bad end: Joan of Arc was *doomed* by her enemies. **doomed, dooming.**

door (DOR) *noun.* 1. A panel for closing an entrance to a room or building by swinging on hinges or sliding shut. 2. The doorway or opening in the wall of a building.

door·step (DOR-step) *noun.* 1. A step or block between an outside door and the ground. 2. The area in front of an outside door.

door·way (DOR-way) *noun.* 1. An opening or entrance to a room or building that is closed by a door. 2. A means of reaching a goal: Using study time wisely is the *doorway* to good grades.

dope (DOHP) *noun.* 1. Drugs, especially narcotics. 2. (Slang) Glue, such as is used on model airplanes. 3. (Slang) A stupid or dull person, or someone who acts that way. 4. The varnish used on canvas airplane wings. 5. (Slang) Information, data, facts. —*verb.* To put on drugs or to give narcotic drugs to. **doped, doping.**

dor·mant (DOR-mənt) *adjective.* 1. Sleeping, inactive, quiet; hibernating. 2. In a state of no growth, as is true of many trees in winter.

dor·mer (DOR-mər) *noun.* 1. A window set in a peak, or gable, of a roof. 2. The peak in which this window is set.

dor·mi·to·ry (DOR-mə-tor-ee) *noun.* 1. A large room with many beds. 2. A building with a number of rooms for sleeping and living, especially for students. **dormitories.**

dor·mouse (DOR-mowss) *noun.* A small rodent or mouse which looks like a squirrel. —**dormice** *plural.*

dor·sal (DOR-sl) *adjective.* Near or on the back: a *dorsal* fin on a fish.

do·ry (DOR-ee) *noun.* A small fishing boat with high curved sides and a flat bottom. **dories.**

dose (DOHSS) *noun.* A measured amount of something, especially medicine; the amount of medicine to be taken at any one given time. —*verb.* To give a measured amount of medicine to. **dosed, dosing.**

dot *noun.* 1. A tiny round mark. 2. A small round circle of color. 3. (Radio) The short signal that, in various combinations with the long signal (dash), makes up the Morse Code. —*verb.* 1. To mark, stain, or print small round marks on something: Be sure to *dot* your "i's." 2. To cover with dots or as with dots: The forest rangers *dotted* the snowy hills with bales of hay for the deer. **dotted, dotting.** **—on the dot.** (Slang) Exactly on time.

dote (DOHT) *verb.* 1. To be overly loving and fond. 2. To be childish in old age. **doted, doting.**

dou·ble (DUHB-əl) *verb.* 1. To add or increase by the same amount; make twice as much. 2. To fold up or in half: The camper *doubled* his blanket to stay warm. **doubled, doubling.** *—noun.* 1. A hit in a baseball or softball game by which the batter reaches second base. 2. Something that is twice as much or twice as many. 3. The same thing; two things just alike: The actor watched his *double* fill in on the last scene. 4. (Plural) A tennis game in which two people play on each side. **doubles.** *—adjective.* 1. Twice as much or twice as many: We all had a *double* scoop of ice cream. 2. Having two; paired: That knife has a *double* edge. 3. Made for two: Our house has a *double* garage for our two cars. **—doubly** *adverb.* **—double back.** To retrace one's steps; go back on the same path or road. **—double up.** 1. To put two of something or someone where one is supposed to be: After the game, Bill and Mary *doubled up* on Bill's bike to get home. 2. To tuck; fold the knees up against the chest. **—on the double.** (Informal) Quickly, twice as fast as usual.

double bass. The deepest sounding member of the string instrument family. **double basses.**

double boiler. Two pans that fit together so that water boiled in the lower pan warms the food placed in the upper pan.

dou·ble-cross (DUHB-əl-KROSS) *verb.* (Informal) To betray, do one thing after promising another; cheat or trick: Sam *double-crossed* the club by spending its money on his dog. **double-crossed, double-crossing.** *—noun.* The act of cheating; a betrayal. **double-crosses.**

dou·ble-deal·ing (DUHB-əl-DEEL-ing) *adjective.* Pretending to do one thing while really doing the opposite. *—noun.* Trickery, cheating, pretense.

dou·ble-head·er (DUHB-əl-HED-ər) *noun.* Two games, such as baseball, played one right after another by the same teams on the same day or evening.

dou·ble-joint·ed (DUHB-əl-JOIN-tid) *adjective.* Having a finger or toe or other joint that bends at abnormal angles.

double play. (Baseball) A play in which two players are put out.

double talk. 1. Fancy talk used to hide or avoid the truth. 2. Talk without meaning or sense.

dou·bloon (duh-BLOON) *noun.* An old Spanish gold coin.

doubt (DOWT) *verb.* To waver back and forth; be unsure, not certain; to question and wonder about: I *doubted* if the circus clown could walk the tightrope. **doubted, doubting.** *—noun.* The condition of being unsure, uncertain, lacking in conviction; a questioning: A slight *doubt* entered my mind after I had given the answer. **—doubtful** *adjective.* **—doubtfully** *adverb.*

doubt·less (DOWT-ləss) Also **doubtlessly** *adverb.* Without a doubt, surely, without question, certainly.

dough (DOH) *noun.* 1. A soft, sticky mass of flour, liquid, and other ingredients that is baked into bread or pastry. 2. (Slang) Money.

dough·nut (DOH-nət) *noun.* A small, round cake made of sweet dough and fried in deep fat.

dour (DUR or DOWR) *adjective.* 1. Severe, stern: a *dour* look. 2. Sullen or gloomy: *dour* old hound. **—dourly** *adverb.*

dormouse

double boiler

doughnut

douse (DOWSS) *verb.* 1. To throw liquid over something; soak or drench. 2. To stick or thrust something into water. 3. Put out, as a light or a fire. **doused, dousing.**

dove

[1]**dove** (DUHV) *noun.* 1. A bird of the pigeon family: The *dove* is often pictured as a symbol of peace. 2. (Informal) A person who is against war. **doves.**

[2]**dove** (DOHV) *verb. See* **dive.**

dow·dy (DOW-dee) *adjective.* Not well-dressed; not in fashion; shabby: *dowdy* old dress. **dowdier, dowdiest.**

dow·el (DOW-əl) *noun.* A rod or peg of wood, metal, or other material that fits into matched holes to hold two objects together.

down *adverb.* 1. Toward the ground; lower: The baby cried when he fell *down.* 2. Toward a lesser or smaller amount: The price of eggs has gone *down.* 3. To a quieter state; not so loud: Turn *down* the radio. 4. In part payment: Jim put $10 *down* on a new bike. 5. In writing: Mary Ann took *down* her homework. 6. Full; completely: The truck was loaded *down* with boxes. —*adjective.* 1. Going toward the ground: The *down* elevator was stuck. 2. Ill; not happy: I felt *down* all day. —*verb.* 1. To swallow at once, quickly: He *downed* a glass of water. 2. To put or knock something toward the ground: The hunter *downed* four ducks. **downed, downing.** —*noun.* 1. (Football) One of four plays allowed for a team to advance the ball ten yards. 2. Illness or bad luck: Everyone has ups and *downs.* 3. Soft feathers, especially goose or duck: My pillow is filled with *down.* —*preposition.* To, through, into, along, among, or toward: I sailed my boat *down* the river. —**down and out.** Without money, friends, or health.

down·cast (DOWN-kast) *adjective.* 1. Looking downward: *downcast* eyes. 2. Sad; discouraged.

down·fall (DOWN-fawl) *noun.* 1. Ruin or collapse, as the *downfall* of an empire. 2. A sudden and heavy rain or snow. —**downfallen** *adjective.*

down·grade (DOWN-grayd) *noun.* A slope, a drop in the land. **downgrades.** —*verb.* To point out only the bad things. **downgraded, downgrading.**

down·heart·ed (DOWN-HAHR-tid) *adjective.* Dejected, sad, depressed. —**downheartedly** *adverb.*

down·hill (DOWN-HIL) *adjective.* 1. From a high point to a low point; downward: The school had a *downhill* race. 2. (Slang) Easy: The test was *downhill* all the way. —*adverb.* Downwards on a slope.

down payment. The first payment on goods paid for in installments.

down·pour (DOWN-por) *noun.* A sudden and heavy rainfall.

down·right (DOWN-right) *adverb.* (Informal) Really, very, completely: Her gift was *downright* kind. —*adjective.* Complete, plain, or simple: a *downright* liar.

down·stairs (DOWN-STAIRZ) *noun, plural in form but used with a singular verb.* A lower floor or floors. —*adjective.* Situated on a lower floor: I helped mother by cleaning the *downstairs* rooms. —*adverb.* At or towards a lower floor.

down·stream (DOWN-streem) *adjective.* In the direction of the flow of a river. —(DOWN-STREEM) *adverb.* At or toward (the mouth of a river).

down·town (DOWN-TOWN) *noun.* The lower part of a town or its business and shopping section. —*adjective.* Concerning or located in the lower part of town or the business section. —*adverb.* At or to the business section.

down·ward (DOWN-wərd) Also **downwards** *adverb.* Down; toward the ground; to a lower level. —*adjective.* Going to a lower place.

down·y (DOWN-ee) *adjective.* 1. Like goose or duck feathers; covered or made of down. 2. Soft, fluffy. **downier, downiest.**

dow·ry (DOWR-ee) *noun.* The money or goods that a man gets from the woman he marries. **dowries.**

doze (DOHZ) *verb.* To snooze, sleep briefly, to nap. **dozed, dozing.** —*noun.* A nap, snooze, or light sleep. **dozes.**

doz·en (DUHZ-ən) *noun* (and *adjective*). A unit or group of 12.

Dr. *abbreviation.* 1. Doctor. 2. Drive.

drab *adjective.* 1. Dull, unappealing: a *drab* look. 2. Of a light brown color. **drabber, drabbest.** —*noun.* A dull light-brown or olive-brown color. —**drably** *adverb.*

draft *noun.* 1. A strong movement of air: a *draft* from the open window. 2. A drawing or plan of something to be built or written: *draft* of house plans. 3. A damper on a chimney. 4. The selection of men to serve in the armed forces. —*verb.* 1. To take someone into military service. 2. To make a drawing, outline, or plan of something. **drafted, drafting.**

draft·ee (draf-TEE) *noun.* A young man drafted to serve in the armed forces. **draftees.**

draft·y (DRAF-tee) *adjective.* Letting in or having drafts. **draftier, draftiest.**

drag *noun.* 1. Anything that holds back or has to be pulled along. 2. (Slang) A boring place or experience; a slow, dull activity. —*verb.* 1. To pull (something) along behind; haul: Jimmy *dragged* his sled up the hill. 2. To move along slowly: The winter afternoon seemed to *drag.* 3. To grapple or search in water with hooks, magnets, or other devices. **dragged, dragging.**

drag·gle (DRAG-əl) *verb.* 1. To be or be made wet and dirty by dragging in mud or water. 2. To trail behind, lag. **draggled, draggling.**

drag·net (DRAG-net) *noun.* 1. A net that is pulled through the water or along the ground to catch something. 2. A way of catching people wanted by the police.

drag·on (DRAG-ən) *noun.* In legend and folklore, a huge beast shaped like a snake, with wings and claws on its scaly body: *Dragons* were said to breathe fire and smoke.

drag·on·fly (DRAG-ən-fligh) *noun.* An insect with a slender body and two pairs of long, narrow, almost clear wings. **dragonflies.**

dragonfly

dra·goon (drə-GOON or dra-GOON) *noun.* A heavily armed soldier who fought on horseback in the 16th and 17th centuries. —*verb.* To force (someone) to do something. **dragooned, dragooning.**

drain (DRAYN) *verb.* 1. To cause to flow off slowly; empty: He *drained* the water from the car radiator. 2. To use up: "Tobacco *drains* your purse, burns your clothes and makes a chimney of your nose." (A. C. Doyle). 3. To flow (into): The Mississippi River *drains* into the Gulf of Mexico. **drained, draining.** —*noun.* 1. A pipe used to carry off water or other liquid. 2. Something that slowly uses up strength or resources: Taking care of the sick child was a *drain* on the mother.

drain·age (DRAY-nij) *noun.* 1. The act or way of drawing off a liquid. 2. The liquid drawn off. 3. A series or system of pipes or channels used for draining.

drake (DRAYK) *noun.* A male duck. **drakes.**

dra·ma (DRAH-mə or DRAM-ə) *noun.* 1. A story or poem written to be acted out on the stage; a play. 2. The art of writing or presenting plays. 3. An exciting or moving experience in real life.

dra·mat·ic (drə-MAT-ik) *adjective.* 1. Of or relating to the theater or a

drawbridge

play: a *dramatic* skit. 2. Exciting, moving. —**dramatically** *adverb.*

dra·mat·ics (drə-MAT-iks) *noun, plural in form but used with a singular verb.* The art of acting and presenting plays.

dram·a·tist (DRAM-ə-tist or DRAH-mə-tist) *noun.* One who writes plays.

dram·a·tize (DRAM-ə-tighz or DRAH-mə-tighz) *verb.* 1. To put into the form of a play or drama: Many of Charles Dickens' books have been *dramatized* in movies and on TV. 2. To present in an unusual or dramatic way. **dramatized, dramatizing.**

drank (DRANGK) *verb. See* **drink.**

drape (DRAYP) *verb.* 1. To place or hang in loose folds. 2. To fall in loose folds: Satin *drapes* well. 3. To place oneself limply: He *draped* himself over the chair. **draped, draping.** —*noun.* 1. Cloth hanging in loose folds, as curtains: A red *drape* hung at the window. 2. The way in which a piece of cloth hangs: I don't like the *drape* of her skirt. **drapes.**

drap·er·y (DRAY-pər-ee) *noun.* 1. Cloth or clothing hanging in loose folds. 2. (Plural) Heavy curtains. **draperies.**

dras·tic (DRASS-tik) *adjective.* Serious, extreme. —**drastically** *adverb.*

draw *verb.* 1. To make a picture or outline as with a pencil or pen. 2. To pull along: The engine *draws* the train. 3. To take out; move in some direction: That cowboy *draws* his gun quickly. 4. To attract: The honey *draws* ants. 5. To describe. 6. To use part of (with *on*): The old man must *draw* on his life savings. 7. To pull in: I could scarcely *draw* my breath. 8. To displace: The ship *draws* 30 feet of water. **drew, drawn, drawing.** —*noun.* 1. The act of bringing forth: The gunman was quick on the *draw.* 2. A tie: The contest ended in a *draw.* 3. A gully or natural drainage ditch.

draw·back (DRAW-bak) *noun.* A handicap, something that acts against one: It is a *drawback* that our team does not have a good place to practice.

draw·bridge (DRAW-brij) *noun.* A bridge that can be raised or moved to one side to allow the passage of ships. **drawbridges.**

draw·er (DROR) *noun.* 1. A boxlike part of a piece of furniture that slides in and out and is used to hold clothes and other objects. 2. (Plural) Underpants.

drawing room. 1. A formal room where guests are received and entertained. 2. A private room on a railroad car.

drawl *verb.* To lengthen words in speaking by prolonging vowels; speak slowly. **drawled, drawling.** —*noun.* A way of speaking in which prolonged vowels make words sound longer: The lady spoke in a Southern *drawl.*

dread (DRED) *verb.* To fear or worry greatly, usually about something that is going to happen. **dreaded, dreading.** —*noun.* A fear or worry.

dread·ful (DRED-fəl) *adjective.* Terrible, unpleasant. —**dreadfully** *adverb.*

dream (DREEM) *noun.* 1. A series of thoughts or scenes that pass through the mind of a sleeping person. 2. A wishful thought; an ambition: It is Roger's *dream* to become an astronaut. 3. Anything beautiful or pleasant. —*verb.* 1. To have a series of ideas or pictures while sleeping. 2. To think wishfully; long for: She *dreams* of becoming an actress. **dreamed** or **dreamt, dreaming.**

drear·y (DRIHR-ee) *adjective.* Dull, sad, gloomy. **drearier, dreariest.** —*adverb.* **drearily.**

dredge (DREJ) *noun.* 1. A machine used to scoop or scrape sand or mud from the bottom of a body of water. 2. A kind of net used for gathering shellfish. **dredges.** —*verb.* 1. To scrape underwater areas with a dredge. 2. To catch fish by using a special net. 3. To coat a piece of food with flour before cooking. **dredged, dredging.**

dregs (DREGZ) *noun, plural.* 1. Small bits of solid matter that settle to the bottom of a container of liquid: coffee *dregs.* 2. The worthless part.

drench *verb.* To soak, make very wet. **drenched, drenching.**

dress *noun.* 1. An outer garment worn by women. **dresses.** 2. Clothing in general. —*verb.* 1. To put on clothing: "In winter I get up at night/ And *dress* by yellow candle-light." (Stevenson). 2. To comb and arrange (hair). 3. To put on formal clothes. 4. To prepare for use: The farmer's wife *dressed* the turkey. 5. To put medicine and a bandage on. 6. To decorate, as a store window. **dressed, dressing.** —*adjective.* Formal, best: *dress* shoes. —**dress up.** To wear good clothes.

dress·ing (DRESS-ing) *noun.* 1. A sauce for salads and other foods. 2. A mixture used to stuff chicken, fish, or meat. 3. A bandage.

dress·mak·er (DRESS-may-kər) *noun.* A person who makes clothing for girls and women.

drew (DROO) *verb. See* **draw.**

drib·ble (DRIB-əl) *noun.* 1. A drip or trickle. 2. A small amount. 3. A way of controlling a ball by bouncing it or giving it short kicks: The *dribble* is used in basketball and in soccer. **dribbles.** —*verb.* 1. To fall or let fall in drops. 2. To allow a liquid in the mouth to run down the chin. 3. To control a ball by bouncing it rapidly or giving it quick, short kicks. **dribbled, dribbling.**

dried (DRIGHD) *verb. See* **dry.**

dri·er (DRIGH-ər) Also **dryer** (which see) *noun.* A substance added to paint or ink so that it will dry faster.

drift *verb.* 1. To float or be carried along by wind or water. 2. To wander from place to place without a set goal or purpose. 3. To pile up from the force of wind or water: During the storm, snow *drifted* across the road. **drifted, drifting.** —*noun.* 1. The act of being carried along by a stream of water or air. 2. A pile of material carried or left by the wind or water: *drifts* of snow. 3. Meaning: I failed to get the *drift* of his message.

drift·wood (DRIFT-wud) *noun.* Wood floating in the water or washed up on the shore.

drill (DRIL) *noun.* 1. A tool with a sharp point and cutting edge that is turned to make holes in hard materials: Our dentist uses a small *drill.* 2. Repeated practice: The school had a fire *drill* today. 3. Military training in such exercises as marching and gun handling. —*verb.* 1. To make holes by boring. 2. To go over something again and again. 3. To train in military skills. **drilled, drilling.**

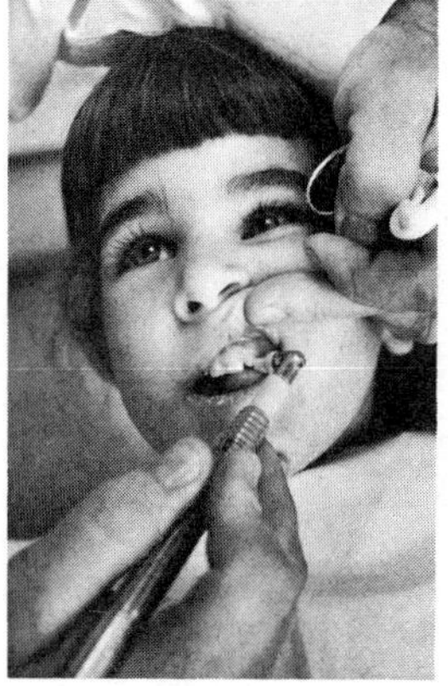

drill

drink *verb.* 1. To take liquid into the mouth and swallow it. 2. To soak up: "The thirsty earth soaks up the rain,/ And *drinks,* and gapes for drink again." (Cowley). 3. To take in eagerly through the senses: *drink* in knowledge. 4. To drink alcoholic liquids. **drank, drunk, drinking.** —*noun.* 1. Any liquid that one drinks. 2. An amount of liquid: a *drink* of water. 3. (Slang) A body of water: The sailor fell into the *drink.*

drip *verb.* To fall or let fall in drops. **dripped, dripping.** —*noun.* 1. Continual dropping; trickling: There was a steady *drip* through the leak in the roof. 2. The sound made by a liquid falling drop by drop. 3. (Slang) A dull person.

drip-dry (DRIP-DRIGH) *adjective.* Made of a cloth that dries without wrinkling (when smoothly hung).

drive (DRIGHV) *verb.* 1. To control the movement of a car, truck, or other vehicle. 2. To supply power to: The engine *drives* the train. 3. To go by car rather than by another form of transportation. 4. To force to go forward, overwork. 5. To pound into place: A hammer is used to *drive* nails into wood. 6. To hit, as a ball. **drove, driven, driving.** —*noun.* 1. Power or control: four-wheel *drive.* 2. A ride in a car. 3. Any organized effort: a *drive* to raise money for the hospital. 4. A road or street. 5. A cattle roundup. 6. A strong urge within a person.

drive-in (DRIGHV-in) *noun.* A place of business that allows customers or patrons to be served in their cars.

driv·er (DRIGH-vər) *noun.* 1. One who controls the movement of a machine or animal. 2. A person who forces others to work. 3. A golf club with a wooden head used in making long shots from the tee.

drive·way (DRIGHV-way) *noun.* A road from a street to a garage or private parking place.

driz·zle (DRIZ-l) *verb.* To rain lightly in fine drops. **drizzled, drizzling.** —*noun.* A gentle rain. **drizzles.**

droll (DROHL) *adjective.* Amusing, oddly funny: "His *droll* little mouth was drawn up like a bow." (C. C. Moore). **droller, drollest.**

dromedary

drom·e·dar·y (DROM-ə-dehr-ee) *noun.* A camel having one hump, often used as a beast of burden. **dromedaries.**

drone (DROHN) *noun.* 1. A male bee that does not work, makes no honey, and cannot sting. 2. A lazy person. 3. An aircraft operated by remote control. 4. A humming noise. **drones.** —*verb.* 1. To make a humming or buzzing noise. 2. To talk on and on in a dull way: "The minister gave out his text and *droned* along." (Twain). **droned, droning.**

drool *verb.* To let water run from the mouth. **drooled, drooling.**

droop *verb.* 1. To sag or bend downward: The branches *drooped* under the weight of the apples. 2. To become tired or sad; become wilted. **drooped, drooping.**

drop *noun* 1. A small bead of liquid in a rounded shape. 2. Anything shaped like a drop: cough *drop.* 3. The act of falling or the distance fallen: It was a short *drop* from the low roof to the ground. 4. A sudden loss or decrease: There was a sharp *drop* in temperature. 5. Something made to be lowered, as a stage curtain. 6. Something landed by parachute. —*verb.* 1. To fall or let fall. 2. To move down: Our team has *dropped* to fourth place. 3. To stop or put aside: We *dropped* the argument. 4. To leave out. **dropped, dropping. —a drop in the bucket.** A very small amount. **—drop a note.** To send off a short letter. **—drop back** or **drop behind.** To slow down or fail to keep up. **—drop in.** To pay an informal visit. **—drop out.** To stop taking part.

drop·out (DROP-owt) *noun.* One who leaves school before graduating.

drought (DROWT) Also **drouth** (DROWTH) *noun.* A long dry spell.

drove (DROHV) *noun.* 1. A flock or herd of animals. 2. A large group of people. **droves.** —*verb. See* **drive.**

drown *verb.* 1. To die by being kept underwater. 2. To kill in such a manner. 3. To overcome: The sound of the radio was *drowned* by the baby's crying. **drowned, drowning.**

drowse (DROWZ) *verb.* To nap; be half-asleep. **drowsed, drowsing.**

drow·sy (DROW-zee) *adjective.* Sleepy; ready for a nap. **drowsier, drowsiest. —drowsily** *adverb.*

drudge (DRUHJ) *noun.* One who does hard or dull work: "A writer of dictionaries [is] a harmless *drudge.*" (Samuel Johnson). **drudges.**

drudg·er·y (DRUHJ-ə-ree) *noun.* Hard, unpleasant, or dull work.

drug (DRUHG) *noun.* 1. A medicine or a substance in medicine used to cure illness or reduce pain. 2. Any of various habit-forming narcotics: Almost all *drugs* are dangerous to use without the advice of a doctor. *—verb.* 1. To give medicine to. 2. To add a harmful substance or poison to (food or drink). **drugged, drugging.**

drug·gist (DRUHG-ist) *noun.* A person who prepares or sells drugs for medicinal purposes.

drug·store (DRUHG-stor) Also **drug store** *noun.* A place where medicine is prepared and sold: Today's *drugstores* sell many other goods besides medicine. **drugstores.**

drum (DRUHM) *noun.* 1. A hollow musical instrument covered with a thin layer of skin on one or both ends and played by beating with sticks or with hands. 2. The sound made by such an instrument. 3. Something shaped like a drum: We use an oil *drum* for a trash can. *—verb.* 1. To play the drum. 2. To mark rhythm on any object by rapping or thumping: Pete is *drumming* on his desk. **drummed, drumming. —drum into.** To make clear to by repeating many times. **—drum up.** To stir up (interest or business).

drum major. *Feminine* **drum majorette.** The leader of a marching band.

drum·mer (DRUHM-ər) *noun.* A drum player.

drum·stick (DRUHM-stik) *noun.* 1. The lower part of the leg of a chicken, turkey, goose, or any other fowl. 2. A stick used to beat a drum.

drunk·ard (DRUHNG-kərd) *noun.* A person who regularly drinks too much alcoholic liquor.

drunk·en (DRUHNG-kən) *adjective.* 1. Having had too much alcoholic liquor. 2. Resulting from intoxication: *drunken* behavior. **—drunkenly** *adverb.*

dry (DRIGH) *verb.* To make not wet: When they get home, they will *dry* themselves with a towel and their clothes by the fire. **dried, drying.** *—adjective.* 1. Not wet or moist: The clothes are *dry.* 2. Having little or no rain: The *dry* spell worried the farmers. 3. Having little or no water: The well went *dry* last summer. 4. Ceasing to give milk: The cow is *dry.* 5. Thirsty: Jim was *dry* after the race. 6. Above water: We reached *dry* land safely. 7. Uninteresting: The book treated the subject in a *dry,* factual, and boring way. 8. Amusing in a detached and biting way: Nan was afraid of her brother's *dry* humor. **drier, driest. —dryly** *adverb.* **—dry up.** 1. To run out of ideas. 2. (Slang) To be quiet or stop talking. **—not dry behind the ears.** Young or lacking in experience.

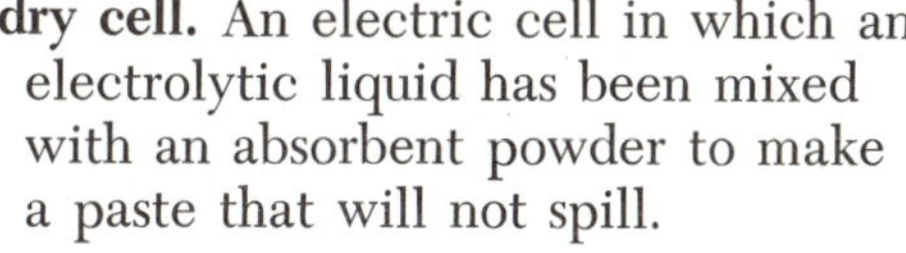

dry cell. An electric cell in which an electrolytic liquid has been mixed with an absorbent powder to make a paste that will not spill.

dry-clean (DRIGH-KLEEN) *verb.* To clean clothing or fabrics with chemical solutions. **dry-cleaned, dry-cleaning. —dry cleaning** *noun.*

dry·er (DRIGH-ər) *noun.* A machine that removes wetness by heat, usually combined with spinning or tumbling.

dry goods. Any kind of clothing, textiles, or related items.

Dry Ice. *trademark.* A cooling agent made of carbon dioxide that has been frozen solid.

DST *abbreviation.* Daylight Saving Time.

du·al (DOO-əl) *adjective.* 1. Having two parts or duplicate sets: Airliners have *dual* controls, one for the pilot and one for the co-pilot. 2. Having two aspects: The story of Dr. Jekyll and Mr. Hyde is a study of a *dual* personality. **—dually** *adverb.*

drum majorette

drummer

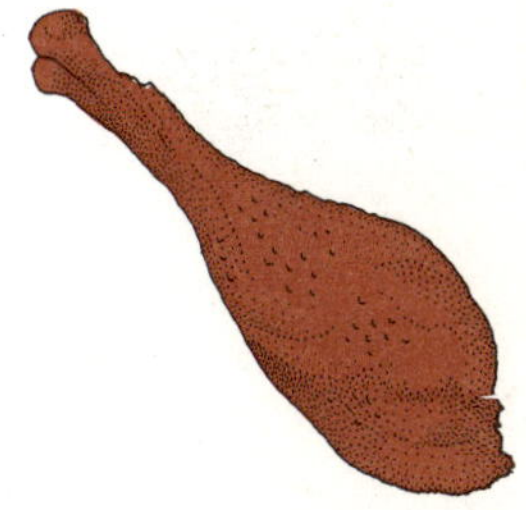

drumstick

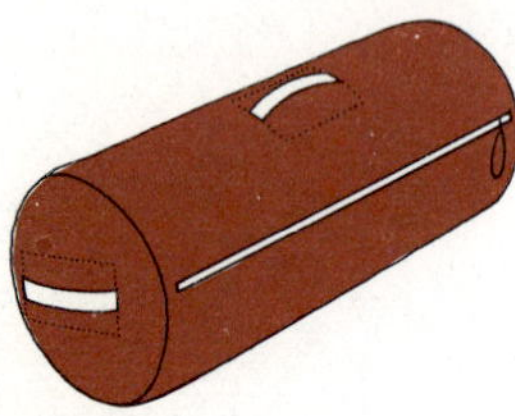
duffel bag

dub (DUHB) *verb.* 1. To give a nickname to: They *dubbed* Jack "Freckles" for one obvious reason. 2. To make a knight by touching lightly on the shoulder with a sword. 3. To add new or different sounds to a record or film: English dialogue was *dubbed* into the sound track of the French movie. **dubbed, dubbing.**

du·bi·ous (DOO-bee-əss or DYOO-bee-əss) *adjective.* 1. Doubtful, uncertain, or undecided. 2. Questionable as to quality or goodness: *dubious* behavior. —**dubiously** *adverb.*

duck

duch·ess (DUHCH-əss) *noun.* 1. The wife or widow of a duke. 2. A woman who has the land or rights of a duke. **duchesses.**

duck (DUHK) *noun.* 1. Any of several kinds of domesticated or wild waterfowl with webbed feet, short legs, and a flat bill. 2. The meat from this fowl. —*verb.* 1. To plunge or bob quickly in and out of water like a duck: We *ducked* for apples. 2. To avoid being hit by dodging: The batter *ducked* a wild pitch. 3. To move in a hurry in order not to be seen: The thieves *ducked* into an alley. 4. To lower (the head or body) suddenly. **ducked, ducking.**

duck·bill (DUHK-bil) *noun.* An egg-laying mammal with a bill like a duck's. *See* **platypus.**

duck·ling (DUHK-ling) *noun.* A young or baby duck.

duct (DUHKT) *noun.* 1. A tube or pipe for carrying liquids or wires. 2. A tube or vessel that carries fluids in the body.

dud (DUHD) *noun.* (Informal) 1. A bomb that does not explode when it should. 2. A failure: Bill was a *dud* when it came to sports.

dude (DOOD or DYOOD) *noun.* 1. A man who is a fancy dresser and overcareful about his clothes. 2. An Easterner or city dweller on a Western ranch. **dudes.**

duf·fel bag (DUHF-əl BAG). A large canvas container used to carry the clothes and equipment of campers or servicemen.

due (DOO or DYOO) *adjective.* 1. Owed as a debt: He is *due* five dollars for mowing the lawn. 2. Owed as a right: The children gave *due* obedience to the teacher. 3. Expected: A letter from June is *due* any day. 4. Fair or just: They received *due* punishment for breaking the window. —*noun.* (Plural) Fees paid for club membership. **dues.** —*adverb.* Directly: The school is *due* east of here. —**due to.** Because of or owing to: Cy's lateness was *due to* the traffic. —**in due course.** At an appropriate time: Dessert will be served *in due course.*

du·el (DOO-əl or DYOO-əl) *noun.* 1. A fight between two persons using weapons agreed upon in advance. 2. Any competition or debate between two persons or groups: a *duel* between sisters as to which does the dishes. —*verb.* To fight a duel. **dueled, dueling.**

du·et (doo-ET or dyoo-ET) *noun.* 1. A musical piece written for two voices or instruments. 2. Two people singing a duet.

dug (DUHG) *verb. See* **dig.**

dug·out (DUHG-owt) *noun.* 1. The shelter where baseball players sit when not on the field. 2. A boat made by hollowing out a log. 3. A hole or trench dug into the ground or the side of a hill for protection.

duke (DOOK or DYOOK) *noun.* 1. A royal hereditary office just below the rank of prince. 2. A nobleman of this rank. **dukes.**

dull (DUHL) *adjective.* 1. Not sharp: a *dull* pencil. 2. Not bright or shining. 3. Not colorful: *dull* green. 4. Stupid or slow: Sue's wits were *dull* because she didn't get enough sleep. 5. Not interesting: Ann found peeling potatoes a *dull* job. **duller,**

dullest. —*verb.* To make or become dull. **dulled, dulling.** —**dully** *adverb.*

dul·lard (DUHL-ərd) *noun.* A person who is or seems to be stupid.

dull·ness (DUHL-nəss) *noun.* A lack of brightness, sharpness, interest, liveliness, or intelligence.

du·ly (DOO-lee or DYOO-lee) *adverb.* Properly; at the right time.

dumb (DUHM) *adjective.* 1. Unable to speak: The *dumb* boy communicated by sign language. 2. Silent or refusing to speak. 3. (Informal) Stupid; not very bright or alert. **dumber, dumbest.** —**dumbly** *adverb.*

dumb·bell (DUHM-bel) *noun.* 1. A short bar with heavy weights on each end, used for lifting exercises. 2. (Slang) A stupid person.

dumb·found (DUHM-fownd) Also **dumfound** *verb.* To cause to be unable to speak because of astonishment or amazement. **dumbfounded, dumbfounding.**

dum·my (DUHM-ee) *noun.* 1. A figure made to imitate a person and used for such things as displaying clothes; a copy of the real thing. 2. A stupid or silent person. 3. In the game of bridge, the player who turns up his cards for his partner to play, or the cards that are turned up. **dummies.**

dump (DUHMP) *verb.* 1. To throw down from a truck or open container: The truck *dumped* the gravel in our driveway. 2. (Slang) To get rid of in an impolite or quick way: Tim *dumped* Fred as a friend without any explanation. **dumped, dumping.** —*noun.* 1. A place where garbage is taken: The town *dump* is filling up with bottles and cans. 2. A place for storage: an ammunition *dump.* 3. (Slang) A place that is badly kept: The whole neighborhood considered the run-down house a *dump.* —**in the dumps.** Depressed or unhappy.

dump·ling (DUHMP-ling) *noun.* 1. A small ball of dough cooked and served with a soup or stew. 2. A piece of dough or pastry containing fruit.

dump·y (DUHMP-ee) *adjective.* Short and fat. **dumpier, dumpiest.** —**dumpily** *adverb.*

dun (DUHN) *verb.* To ask for payment. **dunned, dunning.** —*noun.* A demand for payment.

dunce (DUHNSS) *noun.* A slow learner; a dull person. **dunces.**

dune (DOON or DYOON) *noun.* A hill of sand formed by the wind. **dunes.**

dune buggy. A small car with special tires and gearshift for driving on sand. **dune buggies.**

dun·ga·ree (duhng-gə-REE) *noun.* 1. A strong blue denim cloth. 2. (Plural) Trousers made of this cloth; also called "blue jeans" and "Levis." **dungarees.**

dun·geon (DUHN-jən) *noun.* A dark jail or cell, usually underground.

dunk (DUHNK) *verb.* To dip something into liquid. **dunked, dunking.**

dupe (DOOP or DYOOP) *noun.* A person who is easily tricked. **dupes.** —*verb.* To trick. **duped, duping.**

du·plex (DOO-pleks or DYOO-pleks) *noun.* A two-family house or apartment. **duplexes.**

du·pli·cate (DOO-pli-kət or DYOO-pli-kət) *noun.* An exact copy: Maggie used the office copying machine to make a *duplicate* of her letter. **duplicates.** —*adjective.* Copied exactly: Bill ordered *duplicate* prints of his snapshots. —(DOO-pli-kayt or DYOO-pli-kayt) *verb.* To make an exact copy. **duplicated, duplicating.**

du·ra·ble (DUR-ə-bəl or DYUR-ə-bəl) *adjective.* Lasting, even with much use: Babies grow out of clothes so quickly they do not need anything *durable.* —**durability** (dur-ə-BIL-ə-tee) *noun.* —durably *adverb.*

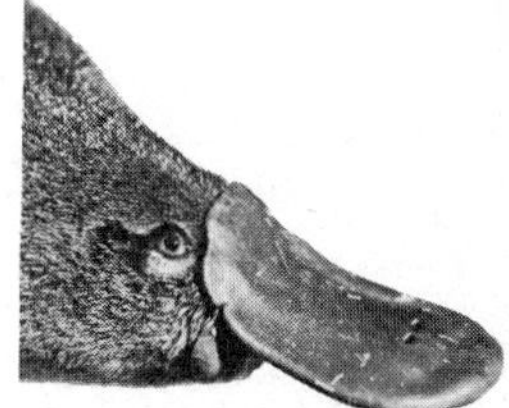

duckbill

dune buggy

du·ra·tion (du-RAY-shən or dyu-RAY-shən) *noun.* The length of time during which something goes on: After a laughing spell, Jill was quiet for the *duration* of the class.

dur·ing (DUR-ing or DYUR-ing) *preposition.* 1. Through the entire time of: I often catch cold *during* the winter. 2. At some point in a period of time: Father had a phone call *during* dinner.

dusk (DUHSK) *noun.* 1. Twilight just before dark. 2. Gloom: No sun filtered into the *dusk* of the forest.

dusk·y (DUHSK-ee) *adjective.* 1. Partly dark: a *dusky* room. 2. Somewhat dark in color. 3. Gloomy; shadowy. **duskier, duskiest.**

dust (DUHST) *noun.* Fine particles of dirt or other substances: flour *dust.* —*verb.* 1. To clean the dust from. 2. To shake on (something in powder form): Abbie *dusted* the tops of her cookies with sugar. **dusted, dusting.**

dustpan

dust·pan (DUHST-pan) *noun.* A flat shovel-like pan into which dust is swept from the floor.

dust·y (DUHST-ee) *adjective.* 1. Covered with dust: Her hands were *dusty* with flour. 2. Being like dust in color; grayish: Her *dusty* brown dress was drab. 3. Being powdery or like dust. **dustier, dustiest.**

du·ti·ful (DOO-ti-fəl or DYOO-ti-fəl) *adjective.* Obedient; doing what one is supposed to do: Ann was *dutiful* and followed the teacher's instructions. —**dutifully** *adverb.*

du·ty (DOO-tee or DYOO-tee) *noun.* 1. Something that one must do: It was Jane's *duty* to keep her room clean. 2. Something that a person feels he ought to do: Tom felt it was his *duty* to tell the truth. 3. A tax charged for bringing in goods bought in another country: Father paid *duty* on the Swiss watch he bought Mother. **duties.**

dwarf (DWORF) *noun.* 1. A person, animal, or plant that has not grown to normal height. 2. Tiny creatures in fairy tales: Snow White lived with seven *dwarfs.* —**dwarfs** or **dwarves** *plural.* —*verb.* To make seem small: The captain of the basketball team *dwarfed* us all. **dwarfed, dwarfing.**

dwell (DWEL) *verb.* 1. To live, stay, abide: We *dwell* in an old farmhouse. 2. To keep talking or thinking (with *on*): Why must Sue *dwell* on her faults so often? **dwelled** or **dwelt, dwelling.**

dwell·ing (DWEL-ing) *noun.* A place to live.

dwin·dle (DWIN-dl) *verb.* To become less and less: Their money *dwindled* as they bought more and more things at the drugstore. **dwindled, dwindling.**

dye (DIGH) *noun.* A substance dissolved in water and used to color cloth and other materials: *dyes* for Easter eggs. **dyes.** —*verb.* To color by using dyes. **dyed, dyeing.**

dy·nam·ic (digh-NAM-ik) *adjective.* Having power and force: a *dynamic* personality. —**dynamically** *adverb.*

dy·na·mite (DIGH-nə-might) *noun.* A powerful explosive often used in construction work. —*verb.* To blow up or blast with dynamite. **dynamited, dynamiting.**

dy·na·mo (DIGH-nə-moh) *noun.* 1. A machine that produces electricity by changing mechanical energy into electric energy. 2. (Slang) A person who is full of energy: Jack is a *dynamo* when it comes to work. **dynamos.**

dy·nas·ty (DIGH-nəss-tee) *noun.* 1. A line of rulers belonging to the same family. 2. The length of time a country is ruled by such a family. **dynasties.**

dys·en·ter·y (DISS-ən-tehr-ee) *noun.* A disease of the intestinal tract characterized by fever and diarrhea.

E, e (EE) *noun.* The fifth letter of the English alphabet.

E. *abbreviation.* 1. East, eastern. 2. English. 3. Earth.

each (EECH) *adjective.* Every person or object in a group considered one by one: *Each* child had a glass of milk with dinner. *—pronoun.* Each person, each one. *—adverb.* For each.

each other. One another (of two or more persons): They told *each other* all their secrets.

ea·ger (EE-gər) *adjective.* Having a great desire or wanting something. **—eagerly** *adverb.* **—eagerness** *noun.*

eager beaver. *See* **beaver.**

ea·gle (EE-gəl) *noun.* A large, powerful bird of prey. **eagles.**

-ean *suffix.* Indicates coming from or referring to: Europ*ean*.

ear (IHR) *noun.* 1. The organ of hearing (especially the outer part) one of which is located on either side of the head. 2. The ability to hear keenly: Jane has a good *ear* and can tell each member of the family by his footsteps. 3. The cluster of grain on certain plants such as corn and wheat. 4. Attention: "Friends, Romans, countrymen, lend me your *ears.*" (Shakespeare). **—be all ears.** To pay sharp attention or listen carefully to something: The children will *be all ears* when they learn that they are going to the movies. **—fall on deaf ears.** To be unheeded or ignored. **—play by ear.** To play an instrument without reading the music.

ear·ache (IHR-ayk) *noun.* A pain located in the ear. **earaches.**

ear·drum (IHR-druhm) *noun.* The membrane between the inner and outer ear which vibrates when sound strikes it.

earl (ERL) *noun.* The British title for a nobleman who ranks above a viscount and below a marquis.

ear·ly (ER-lee) *adjective.* 1. Near the start of a period of time or events: The *early* hours of the morning are the quietest. 2. Soon or near at hand: I am expecting an *early* reply to my letter. **earlier, earliest.** *—adverb.* Happening before a set time: The train arrived one minute *early.*

earn (ERN) *verb.* 1. To gain (pay) for one's work. 2. To win or deserve (through effort): Jane *earned* praise for her good report card. **earned, earning.**

earn·est (ER-nist) *adjective.* 1. Meaning what one says: Joe was *earnest* when he said he would be home on time. 2. Applying oneself with determination: Mary is an *earnest* piano player and practices every day. 3. Important or serious. **—earnestly** *adverb.* **—in earnest.** With or having definite intention: Bill is *in earnest* in his desire to make the team.

ear·phone (IHR-fohn) *noun.* Part of a telephone, radio, or television set that is held or attached to the ear for listening. **earphones.**

ear·ring (IHR-ring) *noun.* A piece of jewelry worn on the ear lobe.

earring

ear·shot (IHR-shot) *noun.* The distance in which a sound can be heard: Dave was within *earshot* of the explosion.

earth (ERTH) *noun.* 1. [Capital E] The planet on which man lives. 2. Soil

earthworm

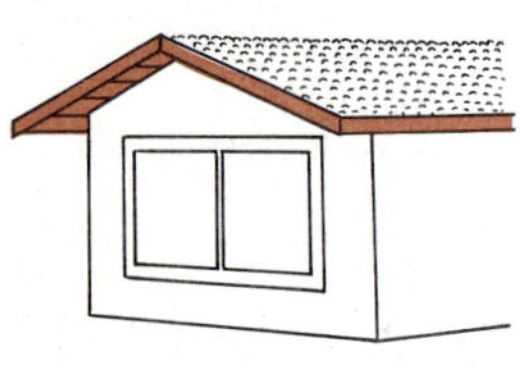
eaves

easel

or dirt: We turned the *earth* in the garden before planting. 3. That part of the earth's surface which is not water; land. —**down to earth.** Sensible or plain. —**run to earth.** To track down something: Sue will *run* the lies *to earth* and find out who started them.

earth·en (ERTH-ən) *adjective.* Made of earth, dirt, or clay.

earth·en·ware (ERTH-ən-wair) *noun* (and *adjective*). Any article made of baked clay.

earth·ly (ERTH-lee) *adjective.* 1. Concerning the earth or physical matters: In church, Tom changes his thoughts from *earthly* to spiritual matters. 2. Possible, sensible, or practical: Jim's silly idea was of no *earthly* use to us.

earth·quake (ERTH-kwayk) *noun.* Shock waves in the ground caused by volcanoes and shifts in the earth's rocky crust. **earthquakes.**

earth·worm (ERTH-werm) *noun.* A worm that lives in soil and is found in most gardens and lawns.

ear·wig (IHR-wig) *noun.* A small, harmless insect with two sharp claw-like arms.

ease (EEZ) *noun.* 1. Freedom from worry, pain, or difficulties. 2. Not having to work too hard to do something: Jim swims with *ease.* —*verb.* 1. To free from trouble or pain. 2. To make less tight: *Ease* the collar around the dog's neck. 3. To move slowly and carefully: They must *ease* the pane of glass into place. **eased, easing.**

ea·sel (EE-zl) *noun.* An upright frame used to hold an artist's painting in place while he is working on it or to show it after he has finished it.

eas·i·ly (EE-zə-lee) *adverb.* 1. Without trouble or difficulty. 2. Surely and without doubt: Jane is *easily* the best pupil in her class. 3. Probably or possibly: I could *easily* have been mistaken.

east (EEST) *noun.* 1. The direction in which the sun rises. 2. [Capital E] That part of the United States which lies along the Atlantic coast. 3. [Usually capital E] The countries of the East; Asia; the Orient. —*adjective.* At or from the east. —*adverb.* To or toward the east.

Eas·ter (EE-stər) *noun.* A Christian festival to honor the Resurrection of Jesus Christ.

east·ern (EE-stərn) *adjective.* 1. Toward or from the east. 2. [Usually capital E] Referring to the countries of Asia.

east·ward (EEST-wərd) *adverb.* Toward the east. —*adjective.* Toward or in the east.

eas·y (EE-zee) *adjective.* 1. Simple and not difficult to do, get, or learn. 2. Free from care, difficulty, and pain. 3. Comfortable and pleased. 4. Not strict or demanding: *easy* rules. **easier, easiest.** —**take it easy.** To relax or slow down.

easy chair A padded armchair.

eas·y·go·ing (EE-zee-GOH-ing) *adjective.* Relaxed; not rushed.

eat (EET) *verb.* 1. To chew and swallow. 2. To take a meal: We will *eat* soon. 3. To destroy or ruin as if by eating. 4. To make smaller or use (up). **ate, eaten, eating.** —**eat one's words.** To take back a statement.

eaves (EEVZ) *noun, plural.* The lower edges of a roof which hang out from a building.

eaves·drop (EEVZ-drahp) *verb.* To listen to a conversation without the speakers' knowing you can hear. **eavesdropped, eavesdropping.**

ebb (EB) *verb.* 1. To fall or flow back: The tide will *ebb* at seven tonight. 2. To lose strength: Jim felt his anger *ebb.* **ebbed, ebbing.** —*noun.* 1. The falling or flowing back of water to the sea. 2. A weakening.

eb·on·y (EB-ə-nee) *noun.* The dark, hard, heavy wood from the center of the ebony tree of Asia and Africa. —*adjective.* 1. Made of ebony. 2. Like ebony; dark, black.

ec·cen·tric (ek-SEN-trik) *adjective.* Behaving in an odd and queer manner or not as other people do. —*noun.* A person who behaves strangely. —**eccentrically** *adverb.*

ec·cle·si·as·ti·cal (ih-klee-zee-ASS-ti-kəl) *adjective.* Referring to religion or church.

ech·o (EK-oh) *noun.* A sound that is reflected from a hard surface. **echoes.** —*verb.* 1. To sound back: The cliff *echoed* Paul's voice. 2. To repeat or sound like: Stop *echoing* your brother and tell the truth. **echoed, echoing.**

echo sounder. An instrument that bounces sound waves off the bottom of a large body of water to tell how deep it is.

e·clipse (ih-KLIPS) *noun.* 1. The hiding or blocking of one heavenly body by another. 2. A blocking or dimming of light. **eclipses.** —*verb.* 1. To darken or conceal: The moon *eclipsed* the sun. 2. To completely outdo (others) so that they seem in the shade: The star *eclipses* the other actors. **eclipsed, eclipsing.**

e·clip·tic (ih-KLIP-tik) *noun.* The apparent circular path of the sun in the heavens during the year.

e·col·o·gist (ih-KOL-ə-jist) *noun.* A person who studies the science of ecology.

e·col·o·gy (ih-KOL-ə-jee) *noun.* The science of the relationship of living things to each other and to their surroundings. —**ecological** (ee-kə-LOJ-i-kəl) *adjective.* —**ecologically** *adverb.*

e·co·nom·ic (ee-kə-NOM-ik or ek-ə-NOM-ik) *adjective.* Pertaining to the study or management of labor, money, and goods: Capitalism is the *economic* system of the United States.

e·co·nom·i·cal (ee-kə-NOM-i-kəl or ek-ə-NOM-i-kəl) *adjective.* Not wasting; using carefully. —**economically** *adverb.*

e·co·nom·ics (ee-kə-NOM-iks or ek-ə-NOM-iks) *noun, plural in form but used with a singular verb.* The science of wealth and how it is made, shared, and used.

e·con·o·mize (ih-KON-ə-mighz) *verb.* To use money sparingly: Mother *economizes* by buying clothes for us only when they are on sale. **economized, economizing.**

e·con·o·my (ih-KON-ə-mee) *noun.* 1. Thrift and care in the use of money or other things. 2. Money management. 3. The working of a country's economic system: The American *economy* is one of the President's concerns. **economies.**

eco·sys·tem (EEK-oh-siss-təm) *noun.* Everything involved with life in a given area—animals, plants, geography, climate, and weather.

ec·sta·sy (EK-stə-see) *noun.* A state of great or intense joy. **ecstasies.**

ec·stat·ic (ek-STAT-ik) *adjective.* Referring to the state of ecstasy or great joy. —**ecstatically** *adverb.*

ec·to·derm (EK-tə-derm) *noun.* 1. The outer germ layer of the animal embryo from which the skin, teeth, nervous system, eyes, and ears are formed. 2. The outer layer of cells in some simple, many-celled animals.

-ed *suffix.* Indicates the past tense of regular verbs: walk*ed.*

ed·dy (ED-ee) *noun.* A current of wind or water whirling in a circle: An *eddy* of water swept the leaves around the pool. **eddies.** —*verb.* To move in such a current. **eddied, eddying.**

edge (EJ) *noun.* 1. The place where something begins or ends: The *edge* of the blanket was torn. 2. The cutting side of an instrument or tool: The *edge* of the ax was dull.

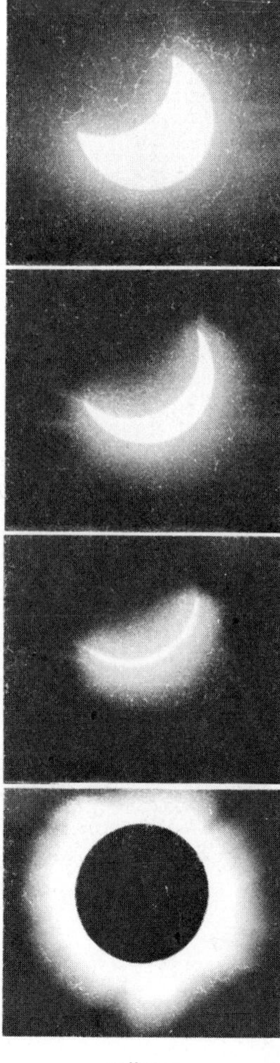

eclipse

3. An advantage: Bill has an *edge* over Jim at tennis; he is a better player. **edges.** —*verb.* 1. To put a border on: Father *edged* the lawn with flowers. 2. To move sideways: Jim *edged* his way through the crack. 3. To move slowly and carefully: Mary tried to *edge* out of the room without being seen. **edged, edging.** —**on edge.** Jumpy and easily angered.

edge·wise (EJ-wighz) or **edge·ways** (EJ-wayz) *adverb.* Having the edge forward. —**get a word in edgewise.** To say something to interrupt an overly talkative speaker.

edg·y (EJ-ee) *adjective.* Jumpy or nervous. **edgier, edgiest.**

ed·i·ble (ED-ə-bəl) *adjective.* Safe to eat.

e·dict (EE-dikt) *noun.* A decree, law, or order given publicly by an official or person of authority.

ed·i·fice (ED-ə-fiss) *noun.* A building, usually a large, impressive one. **edifices.**

ed·it (ED-it) *verb.* 1. To make (someone else's writing) ready for publication by correcting or making changes: A paper is *edited* for grammar and spelling before it is published. 2. To be in charge of a publication and decide its policy: My father *edits* the town newspaper. **edited, editing.**

e·di·tion (ih-DISH-ən) *noun.* All the copies of any printed matter that are printed at about the same time: The late *edition* of the newspaper carried changes in an earlier story about the fire.

ed·i·tor (ED-ə-tər) *noun.* 1. A person who checks and corrects written copy before it is printed in a book, magazine, or newspaper. 2. A person who directs writers and editors or who sets the ideas and rules for an entire magazine or other work.

ed·i·to·ri·al (ed-ə-TOR-ee-əl) *noun.* A comment on current events written by the editors or owners of a newspaper or magazine. —*adjective.* Having to do with editing: My mother does *editorial* work at home. —**editorially** *adverb.*

ed·u·cate (EJ-oo-kayt) *verb.* To train or teach. **educated, educating.**

ed·u·ca·tion (ej-oo-KAY-shən) *noun.* 1. Instruction; teaching. 2. Knowledge gained from study or instruction. —**educational** *adjective.* —**educationally** *adverb.*

-ee *suffix.* Indicates: 1. One who receives something: pay*ee.* 2. One to whom something is done: employ*ee.*

-eer *suffix.* Indicates doing or managing something: auction*eer;* election*eer.*

ee·rie (IHR-ee) Also **eery** *adjective.* Causing fear; strange or weird. **eerier, eeriest.**

ef·face (ih-FAYSS) *verb.* 1. To wipe out or erase. 2. To hide in a shy manner; to stay in the background. **effaced, effacing.**

ef·fect (ə-FEKT) *noun.* A result: The *effect* of so much rain was a flood. —*verb.* To make happen; bring about: The rain will *effect* a change in the temperature. **effected, effecting.** —**in effect.** In use or active: The rules have been *in effect* since last week.

ef·fec·tive (ə-FEK-tiv) *adjective.* 1. Producing a wanted result or happening: The red danger flag was *effective* in keeping the children off the ice. 2. In use: The law became *effective* at midnight. 3. Causing a good impression: The singer gave an *effective* performance. —**effectively** *adverb.* —**effectiveness** *noun.*

ef·fec·tu·al (ə-FEK-choo-əl) *adjective.* Producing or able to produce wanted results. —**effectually** *adverb.*

ef·fi·ca·cy (EF-ə-kə-see) *noun.* The power of producing a wanted result.

ef·fi·cien·cy (ih-FISH-ən-see) *noun.* The ability to produce with the least possible waste: The car's *efficiency* increased after the motor was tuned up.

ef·fi·cient (ih-FISH-ənt) *adjective.* Producing or doing with the least amount of wasted energy: The *efficient* housekeeper finishes her work quickly but does a good job. —**efficiently** *adverb.*

ef·fort (EF-ərt) *noun.* Exertion required to do something either mentally or physically: Tom made an *effort* to remember.

e.g. *abbreviation.* (From the Latin *exempli gratia*) For example.

egg (EG) *noun.* 1. The cell and surrounding material laid by female birds, reptiles, fish, and insects from which the young are produced. 2. (Slang) A person: He's a good *egg.* —**egg on.** To urge; goad: Paul always has to *egg* Jim *on* to fight.

egg·plant (EG-plant) *noun.* A large purple fruit grown in warm climates and eaten as a vegetable.

egg·shell (EG-shel) *noun.* 1. The thin breakable shell covering some eggs. 2. (Also *adjective*) A pale yellow color.

e·go (EE-goh) *noun.* 1. Awareness of oneself; one's opinion of oneself: The teacher's constant criticism hurt Sam's *ego.* 2. Conceit: You can see Sally has a big *ego* because she's always saying, "I, I, I." 3. (Psychiatry) The part of the mind that makes decisions. **egos.**

e·gret (EE-gret) *noun.* A bird of the heron family that has silky white plumes during its breeding season.

ei·der (IGH-dər) *noun.* Any of several large sea ducks usually found on northern coasts.

ei·der·down (IGH-dər-down) *noun.* 1. The soft feathers, or down, of an eider duck used for stuffing pillows and quilts. 2. A quilt stuffed with eiderdown.

eight (AYT) *noun* (and *adjective*). The cardinal number after seven and before nine; 8.

eight·een (ay-TEEN) *noun* (and *adjective*). The cardinal number after 17 and before 19; 18.

eighteenth (ay-TEENTH) *adjective.* Coming next after 17th; 18th. —*noun.* One of 18 equal parts.

eighth (AYTTH) *adjective.* Coming next after seventh; 8th. —*noun.* One of eight equal parts.

eight·i·eth (AY-tee-ith) *adjective.* Coming next after 79th; 80th. —*noun.* One of 80 equal parts.

eight·y (AYT-ee) *noun* (and *adjective*). The cardinal number after 79 and before 81; 80.

ei·ther (EE-thər or IGH-thər) *adjective.* 1. Each of two: *Either* end of the garden is shady. 2. One or the other as an alternative: *Either* coat is warm enough. —*pronoun.* One or the other: The books are the same; take *either.* —*conjunction.* (Used with *or*) Emphasizes a choice: *Either* he eats his dinner *or* he goes to bed. —*adverb.* Equally so: My sister wasn't invited to the party so I didn't go *either.*

e·ject (ih-JEKT) *verb.* 1. To throw out or oust: The teacher *ejected* Joe from the class for talking. 2. To leave (a plane) in an emergency: The pilot *ejected* from the crashing plane and landed safely. **ejected, ejecting.**

eke (EEK) *verb.* (Used with *out*) To piece together or collect in little bits; work hard in order to get along: He will have to *eke* out his allowance with extra jobs to get the money for a guitar. **eked, eking.**

e·lab·or·ate (ih-LAB-ər-it) *adjective.* Done with great care and attention to complicated detail: Her filmy

egg

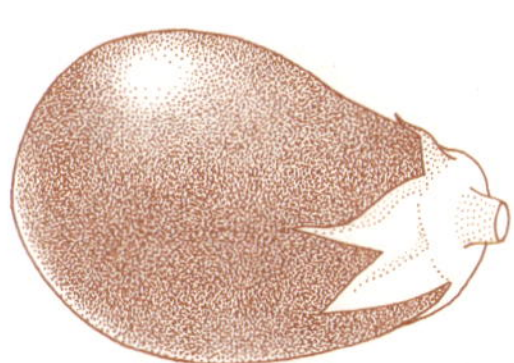
eggplant

egret

scarf was the last touch to her *elaborate* costume. —(ee-LAB-ə-rayt) *verb.* 1. To work out to the last detail: The architect *elaborated* his drawings for the new house. 2. To give further detail: Paul's mother insisted that he *elaborate* on his plans. **elaborated, elaborating.** —**elaborately** *adverb.*

e•lapse (ih-LAPS) *verb.* To glide or slip by, in the way time passes: They enjoyed themselves so much that they didn't realize how much time had *elapsed.* **elapsed, elapsing.**

e•las•tic (ih-LASS-tik) *noun.* Any material such as tape with rubber sewn in or a rubber band that is intended to stretch and then snap back into place. —*adjective.* Flexible and able to adjust to situations: An extra week of time makes a vacation trip *elastic* enough to allow for minor changes in plans.

e•late (ih-LAYT) *verb.* To lift to high spirits: Her good grades *elated* Tess. **elated, elating.** —**elatedly** *adverb.*

e•la•tion (ih-LAY-shən) *noun.* High spirits: The team's *elation* increased after the second touchdown.

el•bow (EL-boh) *noun.* 1. The joint between the upper and lower arm; the outer part of this joint. 2. A bent piece of metal used as a joint between two pipes. 3. Any curve that resembles a bent elbow: You'll see the house when you come around the *elbow* in the road. —*verb.* To jostle or push with the elbows. **elbowed, elbowing.** —**elbow grease.** Hard physical work or effort.

el•der (EL-dər) *noun.* 1. An older person. 2. A senior member or an officer of a church. —*adjective.* The older one of two.

el•der•ly (EL-dər-lee) *adjective.* Somewhat old.

e•lect (ih-LEKT or ee-LEKT) *verb.* 1. To choose by vote: The class *elected* officers for the school term. 2. To make one's own choice: Among the chores to be done, Sally *elected* to do the dishes. **elected, electing.**

e•lec•tion (ih-LEK-shən or ee-LEK-shən) *noun.* 1. Choosing between two or more people, usually by vote: The *election* was close; Jim won by only two votes. 2. The act or process of voting: Presidential *elections* are held every four years.

e•lec•tive (ih-LEK-tiv) *adjective.* 1. Able to be chosen by vote. 2. Filled by voting: Pete ran for *elective* office. —*noun.* A school course that is not required but may be chosen by pupils. **electives.**

e•lec•tor (ih-LEK-tər) *noun.* A member of the Electoral College, which formally elects the President of the United States.

electr- *prefix. See* **electro-.**

e•lec•tric (ih-LEK-trik) *adjective.* 1. Having to do with or run by electricity. 2. Thrilling and exciting: Sue has an *electric* personality and sparks up the dullest moments.

e•lec•tri•cal (ih-LEK-tri-kəl) *adjective.* 1. Electric. 2. Relating to electricity as a science: Ted's older brother is studying to be an *electrical* engineer. —**electrically** *adverb.*

electric eye. An electronic device that operates as a switch when the beam of light activating it is broken by the passage of a person or object; also called "photoelectric cell."

e•lec•tri•cian (ih-lek-TRISH-ən) *noun.* A man who earns his living by installing and repairing electric wiring, motors, and other equipment.

e•lec•tric•i•ty (ih-lek-TRISS-ə-tee) *noun.* Energy in the form of moving electrons: *Electricity* can easily be sent over wires and then converted to other forms of energy such as heat (electric heater), light (bulb), motion (electric motor), or radiation (radio transmitter).

e·lec·tri·fy (ih-LEK-trə-figh) *verb.* 1. To equip with electricity: Father hopes he will be able to *electrify* his hunting cabin next year. 2. To charge with electricity. 3. To thrill or shock suddenly. **electrified, electrifying. —electrification** (ih-lek-trə-fə-KAY-shən) *noun.*

electro- Also **electr-** *prefix.* Indicates having to do with electricity: *electro*cute, *electro*magnet.

e·lec·tro·cute (ih-LEK-trə-kyoot) *verb.* To kill by electric shock. **electrocuted, electrocuting. —electrocution** (ih-lek-trə-KYOO-shən) *noun.*

e·lec·trode (ih-LEK-trohd) *noun.* The point or part, usually made of metal, through which an electric current goes into or out of such things as batteries, cells, and vacuum tubes. **electrodes.**

e·lec·trol·y·sis (ih-lek-TROL-ə-siss) *noun.* A process by which a compound in solution is decomposed or dissolved into separate parts by conducting an electric current through the solution.

e·lec·tro·lyte (ih-LEK-trə-light) *noun.* A liquid that conducts electricity and in which electrolysis can take place. **—electrolytic** (ih-lek-trə-LIT-ik) *adjective.*

e·lec·tro·mag·net (ih-lek-troh-MAG-nit) *noun.* A magnet created by passing an electric current through an insulated wire coiled around a bar of soft iron.**—electromagnetic** (ih-lek-tro-mag-NET-ik) *adjective.*

electromagnetic wave. An energy wave in space that carries light, heat, radio, x-rays, or gamma rays.

e·lec·tro·mo·tive force (ih-lek-troh-MOH-tive FORSS) Also **EMF.** The force (measured in volts) that makes an electric current move.

e·lec·tron (ih-LEK-tron) *noun.* The smallest existing particle with a negative electric charge: *Electrons* form the outer ring of an atom.

e·lec·tron·ic (ih-lek-TRON-ik) *adjective.* 1. Having to do with electrons or electronics. 2. Operating by the movement of electrons: The radio is an *electronic* device. **—electronically** *adverb.*

e·lec·tron·ics (ih-lek-TRON-iks) *noun, plural in form but used with a singular verb.* 1. The science that studies how electrons move: We have better TV sets today because of new discoveries in *electronics.* 2. The industry that deals with electronic devices.

electron microscope. A device to magnify objects many hundreds of thousands of times.

electron tube. A glass or metal tube in which electrons or other charged particles are made to move in a controlled fashion: In TV, *electron tubes* produce the picture.

e·lec·tro·scope (ih-LEK-trə-skohp) *noun.* A device for detecting or measuring small electrical charges and indicating whether they are positive or negative. **electroscopes.**

el·e·gance (EL-ə-gənss) *noun.* Refined grace and taste combined with richness and simplicity. **—elegant** *adjective.* **—elegantly** *adverb.*

el·e·gy (EL-ə-jee) *noun.* A poem expressing sorrow and honor for the dead. **elegies.**

el·e·ment (EL-ə-mənt) *noun.* 1. One of more than 100 simple substances that cannot be chemically broken down and of which all matter is composed: Gold, silver, and lead are *elements.* 2. Any of the simplest parts that go to make the whole: Meat, milk, and vegetables are *elements* of a well-balanced meal. 3. (Plural) The forces that make bad weather: Jack put on his raincoat and went out to face the *elements.* **—in one's element.** Doing something that one does best and enjoys most: Jim is *in his element* on water skis.

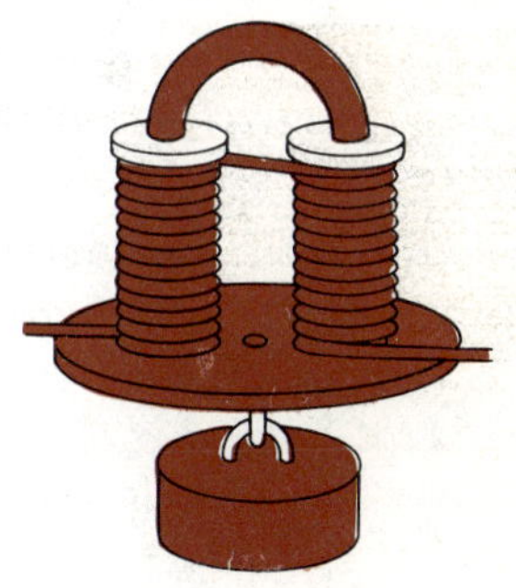

electromagnet

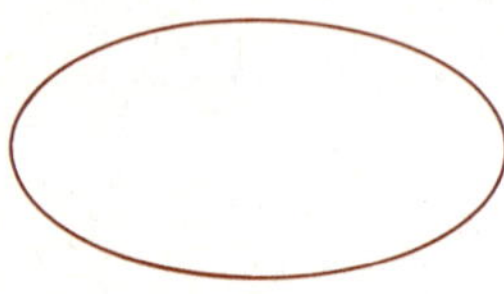

ellipse

elephant

elk

el·e·men·ta·ry (el-ə-MEN-tə-ree or el-ə-MEN-tree) *adjective.* First and simplest: *elementary* school. —**elementarily** (el-ə-men-TEHR-ə-lee) *adverb.*

el·e·phant (EL-ə-fənt) *noun.* A large animal of Africa and Asia with two ivory tusks and a very long trunk.

el·e·vate (EL-ə-vayt) *verb.* 1. To raise up: The crowd *elevated* the hero to their shoulders. 2. To move to a higher position; promote: The company *elevated* Jim's father to the presidency. **elevated, elevating.**

el·e·va·tion (el-ə-VAY-shən) *noun.* 1. A raised spot or place. 2. The altitude or height above sea level. 3. Any act of raising up.

el·e·va·tor (EL-ə-vay-tər) *noun.* 1. A cage or compartment used for moving people or goods up and down in a building. 2. A tall building used for storing grain.

e·lev·en (ih-LEV-ən) *noun* and *adjective.* The cardinal number after ten and before twelve; 11.

e·lev·enth (ih-LEV-ənth) *adjective.* Coming next after tenth; 11th. —*noun.* One of eleven equal parts.

elf *noun.* A tiny creature of fairy tales noted for the mischief he makes. —**elves** *plural.* —**elfin, elfish** *adjective.*

e·lic·it (ih-LISS-it) *verb.* To draw out or reveal a truth: The policeman *elicited* information about the accident from people who saw it. **elicited, eliciting.**

el·i·gi·ble (EL-ə-jə-bəl) *adjective.* Being fit or qualified for selection: Students with good grades will be *eligible* for class offices.

e·lim·i·nate (ih-LIM-ə-nayt or ee-LIM-ə-nayt) *verb.* To get rid of. **eliminated, eliminating.** —**elimination** (ih-lim-i-NAY-shən) *noun.*

elk *noun.* A large deer of northern Europe and Asia with antlers resembling those of a moose. —**elks** or **elk** *plural.*

el·lipse (ih-LIPS) *noun.* A closed geometrical curve longer in one direction than the other: Planets move around the sun in curves that are *ellipses.* **ellipses.**

el·lip·sis (ih-LIP-siss) *noun.* 1. The omission of a sentence part (without changing the meaning of the sentence): "Go to school" is an *ellipsis* for "You go to school." 2. A sign (. . . or * * *) used to show the omission of a word or words. —**ellipses** (ih-LIP-seez) *plural.*

el·lip·soid (ih-LIP-soid) *noun.* The solid or three-dimensional equivalent of an ellipse.

el·lip·tic (ih-LIP-tik) Also **elliptical** (ih-LIP-ti-kəl) *adjective.* 1. Referring to or shaped like an ellipse. 2. (Grammar) Having a word or words missing, having an ellipsis.

elm *noun.* A large, hardwood shade tree.

e·lon·gate (ih-LAWNG-gayt or ee-LAWNG-gayt) *verb.* To make longer, stretch out, or extend. **elongated, elongating.** —**elongation** (ee-lawng-GAY-shən) *noun.*

e·lope (ih-LOHP) *verb.* To run away to be married in secret. **eloped, eloping.**

el·o·quence (EL-ə-kwənss) *noun.* A way of speaking persuasively and gracefully with force, emotion, and sincerity.

el·o·quent (EL-ə-kwənt) *adjective.* 1. Having eloquence, appeal, or persuasion in expressing one's thoughts. 2. Showing much feeling. —**eloquently** *adverb.*

else (ELSS) *adjective.* 1. In addition: What *else* should we add to the shopping list? 2. Other or different: I don't like lamb. Couldn't we have something *else* for dinner? —*adverb.* 1. Differently; in another way: Let's think how *else* to arrange the furniture. 2. Otherwise: Turn down the radio, or *else* you'll wake the baby.

else·where (ELSS-hwair) *adverb.* In, at, or to another place.

e·lude (ih-LOOD) *verb.* 1. To escape or avoid by clever means. 2. To puzzle; be beyond (one's) understanding. **eluded, eluding.**

e·lu·sive (ih-LOO-siv) *adjective.* Difficult to hold on to or grasp: an *elusive* dream.—**elusively** *adverb.*

em- *prefix.* A form of *en-* used before *b, p,* and sometimes *m. See* **en-.**

e·man·ci·pate (ih-MAN-sə-payt) *verb.* To set free from slavery or any strict control. **emancipated, emancipating.** —**emancipation** (ih-man-sə-PAY-shən) *noun.*

Emancipation Proclamation. President Lincoln's announcement that on January 1, 1863, all slaves (in Confederate States still at war with the Union) would be free men.

em·balm (em-BAHM) *verb.* To preserve a dead body from decay by chemicals. **embalmed, embalming.**

em·bank·ment (em-BANGK-mənt) *noun.* A wall built to hold back water or support a roadway.

em·bar·go (em-BAHR-goh) *noun.* 1. A government order that prevents some ships from leaving or entering its ports. 2. Any government order that prevents trade. **embargoes.**

em·bark (em-BAHRK) *verb.* 1. To go aboard ship for a voyage. 2. To start out in a new business or venture. **embarked, embarking.**

em·bar·rass (em-BA-rəss) *verb.* To make ashamed, confused, or shy. **embarrassed, embarrassing.** —**embarrassment** *noun.*

em·bas·sy (EM-bə-see) *noun.* The official headquarters of a government in a foreign country where the ambassador works and lives.

em·bed (em-BED) *verb.* 1. To set or enclose firmly (in surrounding matter): The seashell was *embedded* in the sand. 2. To be fixed (in anything): Today's lesson is *embedded* in his mind. **embedded, embedding.**

em·ber (EM-bər) *noun.* A piece of wood, charcoal, or coal still glowing in the ashes of a fire.

em·bez·zle (em-BEZ-l) *verb.* To steal from others money that has been left in one's care. **embezzled, embezzling.** —**embezzlement** *noun.*

em·bit·ter (em-BIT-ər) *verb.* To make bitter. **embittered, embittering.**

em·blem (EM-bləm) *noun.* A symbol or sign standing for an idea or a thing: The *emblem* of the United States is the bald eagle.

em·body (em-BOD-ee) *verb.* To give body or expression to (an idea): The Bill of Rights *embodies* the ideals of our country. **embodied, embodying.**

em·boss (em-BAWSS) *verb.* 1. To create a raised design in the surface of a material for purposes of decoration. 2. To decorate and ornament with a raised design. **embossed, embossing.**

em·brace (em-BRAYSS) *verb.* 1. To hug or hold in the arms. 2. To take up eagerly: Mother *embraced* the fight against pollution. 3. To include: The school recreation program *embraces* many different sports and activities. **embraced, embracing.** —*noun.* A hug. **embraces.**

em·broi·der (em-BROI-dər) *verb.* 1. To decorate with fancy stitches. 2. To exaggerate with made-up details: Susan *embroidered* her story. **embroidered, embroidering.**

em·broi·der·y (em-BROI-də-ree) *noun.* 1. The art of fancy needlework. 2. A decoration made by such needlework. **embroideries.**

em·bry·o (EM-bree-oh) *noun.* 1. The beginning form of growth of animal life, before birth. 2. A plant before it has sprouted out of the seed. 3. Something that has not yet developed: Our plan is still in *embryo.* **embryos.** —**embryonic** *adjective.*

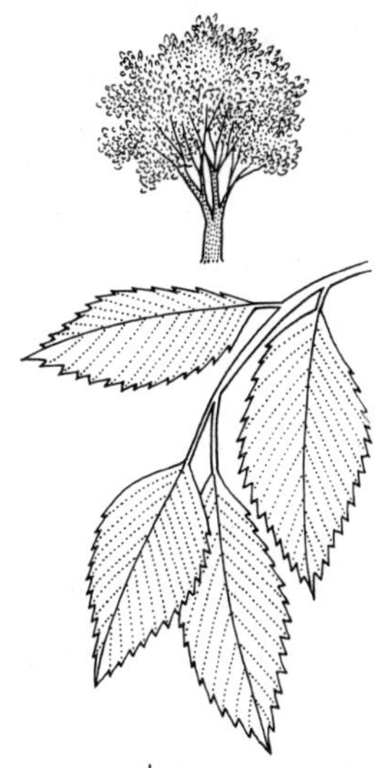
elm

em·bry·ol·o·gy (em-bree-OL-ə-jee) *noun.* The study of the embryo.

em·er·ald (EM-ər-əld or EM-rəld) *noun.* 1. A precious, bright green gem. 2. (Also *adjective*) A bright green color.

e·merge (ih-MERJ) *verb.* 1. To come out: The huge ship suddenly *emerged* from the fog. 2. To become known: The story of his narrow escape *emerged* several days later. **emerged, emerging.**

e·mer·gen·cy (ih-MER-jən-see) *noun.* A sudden and unexpected situation that must be taken care of immediately. **emergencies.**

e·mer·gent (ih-MER-jənt) *adjective.* Beginning or coming into being; becoming important or recognized: *emergent* nations.

em·er·y (EM-ə-ree or EM-ree) *noun.* A hard mineral that is used in powdered form for polishing and grinding.

-emia *suffix.* Indicates blood: an*emia.*

em·i·grant (EM-i-grənt) *noun.* A person who moves out of his own country to live in another.

em·i·grate (EM-i-grayt) *verb.* To move out of one country to another. **emigrated, emigrating.**

em·i·nence (EM-ə-nənss) *noun.* 1. A position above others in fame or rank; greatness. 2. A high spot such as a hill or mountain. **eminences.**

em·i·nent (EM-ə-nənt) *adjective.* Distinguished above others; very famous. —**eminently** *adverb.*

em·is·sar·y (EM-ə-sehr-ee) *noun.* A person sent as an agent. **emissaries.**

e·mit (ih-MIT) *verb.* To send out, give forth: The fire *emitted* more smoke than warmth. **emitted, emitting.**

e·mo·tion (ih-MOH-shən) *noun.* Any kind of feeling: Love, hate, anger, fear, and joy are *emotions.*

e·mo·tion·al (ih-MOH-shən-l) *adjective.* Relating to any strong feeling or emotion. —**emotionally** *adverb.*

em·per·or (EM-pər-ər) *noun.* The ruler of an empire.

em·pha·sis (EM-fə-siss) *noun.* 1. Stress on the importance of an idea or subject: That school puts *emphasis* on athletics. 2. A stress in language: *Emphasis* on the correct syllable aids our pronunciation. —**emphases** (EM-fə-seez) *plural.*

em·pha·size (EM-fə-sighz) *verb.* To stress. **emphasized, emphasizing.**

em·phat·ic (em-FAT-ik) *adjective.* With emphasis, force, or positiveness. —**emphatically** *adverb.*

em·phy·se·ma (em-fə-SEE-mə) *noun.* A disease that results in the wasting away of lung tissue, causing difficulty in breathing.

em·pire (EM-pighr) *noun.* A group of countries or states under a single government. **empires.**

em·ploy (em-PLOI) *verb.* 1. To hire and pay for work. 2. To use (as a tool): *employ* a power saw. **employed, employing.** —*noun.* Service for pay: She is no longer in their *employ.*

em·ploy·ee (em-PLOI-ee or em-ploi-EE) *noun.* A person who is paid to work for someone else.

em·ploy·er (em-PLOI-er) *noun.* A person or company that hires and directs workers.

em·ploy·ment (em-PLOI-mənt) *noun.* 1. Putting to work or having a job. 2. A person's occupation: His *employment* is teaching. 3. Use of (a tool or instrument): *Employment* of tools will make the job easier.

em·press (EM-priss) *noun.* 1. The wife of an emperor. 2. A woman ruler of an empire. **empresses.**

emp·ty (EMP-tee) *verb.* 1. To remove everything from: *Empty* that box and we'll use it. 2. To flow out: The Nile *empties* into the Mediterranean. **emptied, emptying.** —*adjective.* With nothing in it; vacant: The apartment has been *empty* since they moved out.

emptier, emptiest. —**emptily** *adverb.* —**emptiness** *noun.*

emp·ty-hand·ed (emp-tee-HAN-did) *adjective.* Having or bringing nothing: We arrived at the birthday party *empty-handed.*

empty set. (Math) A set or collection containing no elements, numbers, or rules, represented by a pair of braces, { }, or by the symbol ∅.

e·mu (EE-myoo) Also **emeu** *noun.* A large bird of Australia.

em·u·late (EM-yə-layt) *verb.* To try to equal or better: Amy *emulated* the most popular girl in the class. **emulated, emulating.**

e·mul·sion (ih-MUHL-shən) *noun.* A mixture of liquids in which tiny drops of one liquid hang in the other but do not dissolve: The suspension of milk fats in homogenized milk is an *emulsion.*

en- *prefix.* Indicates: 1. Putting on or into: *en*throne. 2. In or into: *en*close. 3. To make: *en*able.

-en *suffix.* Indicates: 1. The past participle of many verbs: shak*en.* 2. Gaining or giving: height*en.* 3. Made of: wood*en.* 4. To become or cause to be: redd*en.*

en·a·ble (en-AY-bəl) *verb.* To make able or possible: Mother's dishwasher *enables* us all to relax after dinner. **enabled, enabling.**

en·act (en-AKT) *verb.* 1. To make into law: Congress *enacted* the bill that provided money for the new dam. 2. To play (the part of): Billy *enacts* the part of an old man in our school play. **enacted, enacting.**

en·a·mel (ih-NAM-əl) *noun.* 1. A glasslike substance that is baked onto something to make a hard surface: Mother has some pans coated with *enamel.* 2. A paint with a hard, shiny surface. 3. The hard substance that covers teeth. —*verb.* To cover with enamel. **enameled** or **enamelled, enameling** or **enamelling.**

-ence Also **-ency** *suffix.* Indicates condition, quality, or act: depend*ence,* excell*ence.*

en·chant (en-CHANT) *verb.* 1. To cast a spell over by magic. 2. To delight or charm. **enchanted, enchanting.**

en·chant·ing (en-CHAN-ting) *adjective.* Having the power to delight or charm. —**enchantingly** *adverb.*

en·chant·ment (en-CHANT-mənt) *noun.* 1. Something enchanting or delightful. 2. Use of magic or spells.

en·chant·ress (en-CHAN-triss) *noun.* 1. A woman who casts spells; a witch. 2. A charming woman. **enchantresses.**

en·chi·la·da (en-chə-LAH-də) *noun.* A popular Mexican dish consisting of a rolled, stuffed tortilla covered with a chili-flavored tomato sauce.

en·cir·cle (en-SER-kəl or in-SER-kəl) *verb.* To form a ring around or move around in a circle. The children *encircled* the May Pole. **encircled, encircling.**

en·close (en-KLOHZ) *verb.* 1. To close in or surround. 2. To include with a letter or parcel: She *enclosed* photographs. **enclosed, enclosing.**

en·clo·sure (en-KLOH-zhər) *noun.* 1. A fenced-in space. 2. A wall or fence that closes in something. 3. Something enclosed with a letter or parcel. **enclosures.**

en·com·pass (en-KUHM-pəss) *verb.* To surround, encircle, or include. **encompassed, encompassing.**

en·core (AHNG-kor or AHN-kor) *noun.* A repeated or additional performance, usually by demand of the audience: The crowd clapped for an *encore.* **encores.** —*interjection.* Again! Once more!

en·coun·ter (en-KOWN-tər) *noun.* 1. An unexpected meeting. 2. An unpleasant meeting: Mother had an *encounter* with our neighbors when their cat ate our canary. 3. A battle. —*verb.* To meet: Sue *encountered* many difficulties. **encountered, encountering.**

emu

enchilada

en·cour·age (en-KER-ij) *verb.* 1. To give hope or confidence to. 2. To help; to support: Cold weather *encourages* the sale of warm clothing. **encouraged, encouraging.**

en·cour·age·ment (en-KER-ij-mənt) *noun.* Something that urges a person on: Tom was given a new bike as *encouragement* to continue his paper route.

en·croach (en-KROHCH) *verb.* 1. To trespass. 2. To go beyond ordinary limits: The water in the ditch *encroached* on the road. **encroached, encroaching.**

en·crust (en-KRUHST) *verb.* To cover with a layer: The bottom of the boat was *encrusted* with barnacles. **encrusted, encrusting.**

en·cum·ber (en-KUHM-bər) *verb.* 1. To overburden: Joe was *encumbered* with too much equipment for hiking. 2. To block or impede: The driveway was so *encumbered* with bicycles that Father could not park the car. **encumbered, encumbering.**

-ency *suffix. See* **-ence.**

en·cy·clo·pe·di·a (en-sigh-klə-PEE-dee-ə) Also **encyclopaedia** *noun.* A book or set of books that gives many facts about all branches of knowledge, usually in separate articles arranged alphabetically.

end *noun.* 1. The last part. 2. Where something stops; edge. 3. The aim or purpose: Bill's *end* in working was to earn money for college. 4. (Football) One of two players at either side of the forward line. —*verb.* To finish. **ended, ending.**

en·dan·ger (en-DAYN-jər) *verb.* To put in peril or danger: Tess *endangered* her life by swimming out too far. **endangered, endangering.**

en·dear (en-DIHR) *verb.* To make loved or valued: Sally's kindness *endeared* her to everyone. **endeared, endearing. —endearment** *noun.*

en·deav·or (en-DEV-ər) *noun.* An attempt or effort. —*verb.* To make an effort: Jill *endeavored* to finish the dress she was making. **endeavored, endeavoring.**

end·ing (EN-ding) *noun.* The last part.

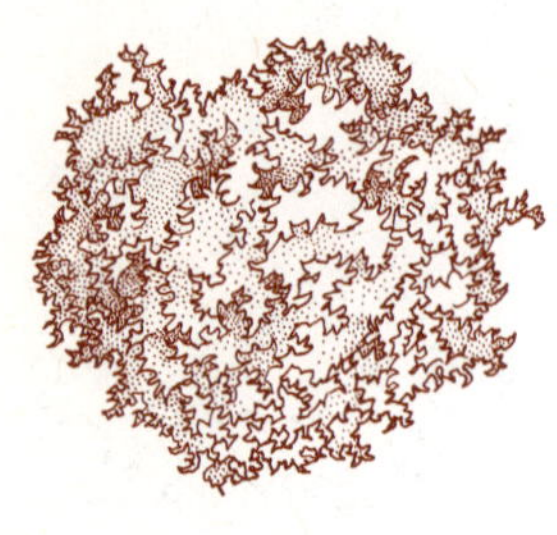

endive

en·dive (EN-dighv) *noun.* Either of two plants used in salads, with ragged, curly, or broad leaves.

end·less (END-liss) *adjective.* Having no end; going on forever. **—endlessly** *adverb.*

en·do·crine gland (EN-də-krin). Any of several glands that send secretions directly into the blood.

en·do·derm (EN-doh-derm) *noun.* The inner germ layer of the animal embryo from which the linings of some internal organs, such as the lungs and the intestines, are formed.

en·dorse (en-DORSS) *verb.* 1. To approve. 2. To sign one's name on the back of (a check). **endorsed, endorsing.**

en·dorse·ment (en-DORSS-mənt) *noun.* 1. Approval. 2. A signature on the back of a check.

en·dow (en-DOW) *verb.* 1. To give money or property or provide a source of income: Hospitals, universities, and museums are usually *endowed.* 2. To provide with a quality or thing: She was *endowed* with musical talent. **endowed, endowing. —endowment** *noun.*

en·dur·ance (en-DUR-ənss or en-DYUR-ənss) *noun.* 1. The ability to last a long time. 2. The ability to withstand pain or hardship: It takes great *endurance* to be a long-distance runner.

en·dure (en-DUR or en-DYUR) *verb.* 1. To last: Shakespeare's works have *endured* for centuries. 2. To stand, bear, or undergo: *endure* pain. **endured, enduring.**

en·e·ma (EN-ə-mə) *noun.* Liquid inserted into the rectum to clean out the bowels.

en·e·my (EN-ə-mee) *noun.* 1. A foe; not a friend. 2. Anything that does harm: Vanity was Sue's *enemy.* **enemies.**

en·er·get·ic (en-ər-JET-ik) *adjective.* Having great energy or enthusiasm; active. —**energetically** *adverb.*

en·er·gy (EN-ər-jee) *noun.* 1. Strength and vigor: Tom works off excess *energy* chopping wood. 2. (Science) The capacity of some forces to do work: Electricity is a form of *energy.* **energies.**

en·fold (en-FOHLD) *verb.* 1. To fold or shut in: The snow *enfolded* the town in a blanket of white. 2. To embrace. **enfolded, enfolding.**

en·force (en-FORSS) *verb.* To put into force or demand obedience to: The police *enforce* the laws. **enforced, enforcing.**

en·force·ment (en-FORSS-mənt) *noun.* The act of putting into force or compelling.

Eng. *abbreviation.* English or England.

en·gage (en-GAYJ) *verb.* 1. To agree to marry. 2. To occupy or keep busy: Phil was *engaged* in sorting his stamps. 3. To enter (into conflict): The troops were *engaged* in a bloody battle. 4. To hire: The owner of the apple orchard *engages* many men to pick apples. **engaged, engaging.**

en·gage·ment (en-GAYJ-mənt) *noun.* 1. An agreement to marry. 2. A date or appointment. 3. A battle.

en·gen·der (en-JEN-dər) *verb.* To bring forth or produce: Friendliness *engenders* harmony. **engendered, engendering.**

en·gine (EN-jən) *noun.* 1. A machine that changes energy into power: An automobile *engine* burns gasoline. 2. The machine used to pull trains. **engines.**

en·gi·neer (en-jə-NIHR) *noun.* 1. A person whose job is some type of engineering. 2. A person who runs an engine. —*verb.* To manage or plan: Terry *engineered* the school dance. **engineered, engineering.**

en·gi·neer·ing (en-jə-NIHR-ing) *noun.* The science dealing with the planning, building, and operation of machines, bridges, roads, or other constructions or equipment.

en·grave (en-GRAYV) *verb.* 1. To cut in: The store *engraved* Dad's initials on his new wrist watch. 2. To cut a design or letters on wood, metal, or other material for reproduction by printing. 3. To make a lasting impression: The night of the party is *engraved* in my memory. **engraved, engraving.**

en·grav·ing (en-GRAYV-ing) *noun.* 1. The art of cutting in a design on wood or metal for printing. 2. A picture or design from an engraved plate.

en·gross (en-GROHSS) *verb.* To take a person's full attention. **engrossed, engrossing.**

en·gulf (en-GUHLF) *verb.* To swallow up or cover: A wave *engulfed* our sand castle. **engulfed, engulfing.**

en·hance (en-HANSS) *verb.* To make better; add to: The ribbon in Inge's hair *enhanced* her looks. **enhanced, enhancing.** —**enhancement** *noun.*

e·nig·ma (ih-NIG-mə) *noun.* A problem or person that is hard to understand; a puzzle.

en·joy (en-JOI) *verb.* 1. To take pleasure in. 2. To have the benefit of: Our family *enjoys* the use of our neighbor's boat. **enjoyed, enjoying.** —**enjoyment** *noun.*

en·large (en-LAHRJ) *verb.* To make larger. **enlarged, enlarging.**

en·large·ment (en-LAHRJ-mənt) *noun.* 1. Making larger: The board of directors voted on *enlargement* of the museum. 2. Anything made larger or blown up: Shirley had *enlargements* made of her best photographs.

en·light·en (en-LIGHT-n) *verb.* To inform; give light or knowledge to. **enlightened, enlightening.**

en·list (en-LIST) *verb.* 1. To join: Joe *enlisted* in the Navy after finishing college. 2. To get the support or help of: Mother *enlisted* her neighbor's help in moving the furniture. **enlisted, enlisting.**

en·liven (en-LIGH-vən) *verb.* To make lively or cheerful. **enlivened, enlivening.**

e·nor·mous (ih-NOR-məss) *adjective.* Huge; very large; vast in size or number. —**enormously** *adverb.*

e·nough (ih-NUHF) *adjective.* Sufficient; as much as is needed: There's *enough* soup for everyone. —*adverb.* As much or as well as necessary: Lee played the clarinet well *enough* to join the band. —*noun.* The amount desired: George pushed back his plate and said, "I've had *enough.*"

en·rage (en-RAYJ) *verb.* To put in a rage. **enraged, enraging.**

en·rich (en-RICH) *verb.* To make richer. **enriched, enriching.**

en·roll (en-ROHL) Also **enrol** *verb.* 1. To become part of (with *in*): Martin *enrolled* in an art class. 2. To register on a list: Father *enrolled* as a voter. **enrolled, enrolling.**

en route (ahn ROOT). On the way: They must be *en route* to Hawaii by now.

en·shrine (en-SHRIGHN) *verb.* To cherish; hold (something) sacred: Americans *enshrine* the memory of Lincoln in their hearts. **enshrined, enshrining.**

en·sign (EN-sən) *noun.* 1. The lowest ranking officer in the U.S. Navy. 2. A flag or banner.

en·slave (en-SLAYV) *verb.* 1. To make a slave of. 2. To come under the influence of: Dad was *enslaved* by his smoking habit. **enslaved, enslaving.** —**enslavement** *noun.*

en·snare (en-SNAIR) *verb.* 1. To catch in a snare or trap. 2. To involve in troubles: The new mayor was *ensnared* by the city's problems. **ensnared, ensnaring.**

en·sue (en-SOO) *verb.* To follow as a result: When the treaty was signed, peace *ensued* between the two countries. **ensued, ensuing.**

en·sure (en-SHUR) *See* **insure.**

-ent *suffix.* 1. An ending used to form adjectives: depend*ent.* 2. An ending used to form nouns of power or action: ag*ent.*

en·tan·gle (en-TANG-gəl) *verb.* 1. To catch or twist up: The puppy was *entangled* in the bushes. 2. To involve, as in trouble: He was *entangled* in debts. **entangled, entangling.**

en·tan·gle·ment (en-TANG-gəl-mənt) *noun.* 1. Being entangled. 2. A trap or difficult situation.

en·ter (EN-tər) *verb.* 1. To go or come into: Sue *entered* the room. 2. To join: Sam *entered* the science club. 3. To cause to join: Marie's parents *entered* her in ballet classes. 4. To list or record: Joe *enters* all his expenses in an account book. **entered, entering.**

en·ter·prise (EN-tər-prighz) *noun.* 1. Energy and daring: Explorers of the Arctic had great *enterprise.* 2. A business undertaking. 3. A difficult or challenging project. **enterprises.**

en·ter·tain (en-tər-TAYN) *verb.* 1. To amuse. 2. To have as guests: Our class will *entertain* the second graders on Halloween. 3. To consider: June would never *entertain* such a notion. **entertained, entertaining.**

en·ter·tain·ment (en-tər-TAYN-mənt) *noun.* 1. Something that pleases, interests, or diverts. 2. Pleasure or amusement: A good hostess plans carefully for the *entertainment* of her friends.

en·thrall (en-THRAWL) *verb.* To charm, hold spellbound. **enthralled, enthralling.**

en·throne (en-THROHN) *verb.* 1. To place on a throne. 2. To exalt as if on a throne: Shakespeare is *enthroned* as the greatest English playwright. **enthroned, enthroning.**

en·thu·si·asm (en-THOO-zee-az-əm) *noun.* Eager excitement.

en·thu·si·as·tic (en-thoo-zee-ASS-tik) *adjective.* Being excited; eager: The boys were *enthusiastic* about sports. **—enthusiastically** *adverb.*

en·tice (en-TYSS) *verb.* To lure or attract. **enticed, enticing. —enticement** *noun.*

en·tire (en-TIGHR) *adjective.* Complete: George spent the *entire* day fishing. **—entirely** *adverb.*

en·ti·tle (en-TIGH-tl) *verb.* 1. To give a right: If we finish our chores, we're *entitled* to watch TV. 2. To give a title to. **entitled, entitling.**

en·ti·ty (EN-tə-tee) *noun.* Something that exists, especially as an independent unit.

[1]**en·trance** (EN-trənss) *noun.* 1. A door, opening, or place to enter. 2. An entering: The teacher's *entrance* caused immediate silence.

[2]**en·trance** (en-TRANSS) *verb.* To delight; enchant. **entranced, entrancing.**

en·treat (en-TREET) *verb.* To plead or implore. **entreated, entreating.**

en·treat·y (en-TREET-ee) *noun.* A plea or request.

en·trust (en-TRUHST) *verb.* To give (something or someone) to another for care: The coach *entrusted* the baseball equipment to us. **entrusted, entrusting.**

en·try (EN-tree) *noun.* 1. A hallway or vestibule through which one enters a building or house: 2. Entering: At the *entry* of the judge, everyone stood up. 3. A contestant: Jack was an *entry* in the potato bag race. 4. Something entered in a book or ledger: a daily *entry* in a diary. **entries.**

en·twine (en-TWIGHN) *verb.* To twist or weave together: Their fingers *entwined.* **entwined, entwining.**

e·nu·mer·ate (ih-NOO-mə-rayt or ih-NYOO-mə-rayt) *verb.* To number or list: Phil *enumerated* everything that had gone wrong. **enumerated, enumerating. —enumeration** (ih-noo-mə-RAY-shən or ih-nyoo-mə-RAY-shən) *noun.*

e·nun·ci·ate (ih-NUHN-see-ayt) *verb.* 1. To speak or pronounce clearly. 2. To announce. **enunciated, enunciating.**

e·nun·ci·a·tion (ih-nuhn-see-AY-shən) *noun.* 1. Clear pronunciation: The actor's *enunciation* was flawless. 2. An announcement.

en·vel·op (en-VEL-əp) *verb.* To wrap or surround: A huge fur collar *enveloped* Amy's face. **enveloped, enveloping.**

en·vel·ope (EN-və-lohp or ON-və-lohp) *noun.* A folded paper cover with a gummed flap in which to mail letters or papers. **envelopes.**

en·vi·ous (EN-vee-əss) *adjective.* Jealous. **—enviously** *adverb.*

en·vi·ron·ment (en-VIGH-rən-mənt) *noun.* The surroundings or conditions that affect a person or thing: The *environment* of a slum can harm a child's development. **—environmental** (en-vigh-rən-MENT-l) *adjective.*

en·voy (EN-voy or ON-voy) *noun.* 1. A minister or diplomat ranking just below an ambassador. 2. A person sent on a mission or errand: The President sent an *envoy* to China for private discussions.

en·vy (EN-vee) *verb.* To be jealous of: Sally *envied* her brother because he had new ice skates. **envied, envying.** *—noun.* 1. Jealousy. 2. A person or thing that causes jealousy.

en·zyme (EN-zighm) *noun.* Any of several substances secreted by plant and animal cells that create a chemical change in another substance: Digestion is dependent on *enzymes.* **enzymes.**

e·o·hip·pus (ee-oh-HIP-əss) *noun.* A small extinct prehistoric ancestor of the horse. **eohippuses.**

e·on (EE-on or EE-ən) *noun.* A very long time.

epi- *prefix.* Indicates on, upon, over, above, outside, or beside: *epi*dermis.

ep·ic (EP-ik) *noun.* A long poem in story form that recounts in a noble style the deeds of its hero. —*adjective.* Referring to a grand historical event: Custer's Last Stand climaxed an *epic* battle with the Sioux.

ep·i·dem·ic (ep-ə-DEM-ik) *noun.* 1. The fast spread of a disease through a population: We are vaccinated against smallpox to avoid *epidemics.* 2. Anything that is unusually widespread: There was an *epidemic* of folk music among the students.

ep·i·der·mis (ep-ə-DER-miss) *noun.* The outer layer of skin. **epidermises.**

ep·i·sode (EP-ə-sohd) *noun.* One or more of a series of happenings; part of a long series of events or of a long story: The argument was the only unpleasant *episode* of the entire vacation. **episodes.**

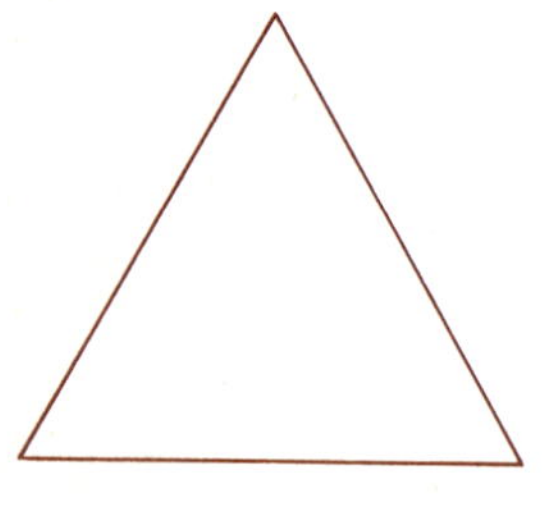

equilateral triangle

e·pis·tle (ih-PISS-l) *noun.* 1. A formal letter. 2. [Capital E] A letter in the New Testament written to the followers of Jesus by one of the apostles. **epistles.**

ep·och (EP-ək) *noun.* 1. The beginning of a new era: Man's first moon-walk opened a new *epoch* in space exploration. 2. A period of time noted for outstanding developments: The Renaissance was an *epoch* during which the arts flourished.

e·qual (EE-kwəl) *noun.* The same in quality or quantity: The two boys were *equals* on the playing field. —*verb.* 1. To be of the same quality or quantity: Sixteen ounces *equal* one pound. 2. To make or produce the same: The foundation promised to *equal* the contributions received by the school. **equaled** or **equalled; equaling** or **equalling.** —*adjective.* 1. Having the same quality or quantity: of *equal* weight. 2. Having sufficient strength or ability: Alice is *equal* to preparing dinner without help. —**equally** *adverb.*

e·qual·i·ty (ih-KWOL-ə-tee) *noun.* The same in quantity or quality: Jerry's idea of *equality* was having the same rules for everyone.

e·qual·ize (EE-kwə-lighz) *verb.* To make equal. **equalized, equalizing.**

e·qua·tion (ee-KWAY-zhən) *noun.* (Math) A mathematical expression of equality between two amounts: $5-1=4$ is an *equation.*

e·qua·tor (ee-KWAY-tər) *noun.* An imaginary circle on the earth halfway between the North and South Poles marking the dividing line between the Northern and Southern Hemispheres.

e·ques·tri·an (ih-KWESS-tree-ən) *noun.* A horseback rider.

e·qui·lat·er·al (ee-kwə-LAT-ər-əl) *adjective.* Having all sides equal.

equilateral triangle. A triangle with three equal sides and three equal angles of 60 degrees each.

e·qui·lib·ri·um (ee-kwə-LIB-ree-əm) *noun.* 1. Physical balance: Jerry tried walking the fence rail but lost his *equilibrium* and fell off. 2. Mental balance or neutrality.

e·qui·nox (EE-kwə-noks) *noun.* The time when the sun crosses the equator and the length of the day and the night are about equal: *Equinoxes* occur about March 21 and September 22. **equinoxes.**

e·quip (ee-KWIP) *verb.* To provide, furnish, or fit out: The Scouts were *equipped* with bedrolls and knapsacks for the overnight hike. **equipped, equipping.**

e·quip·ment (ih-KWIP-mənt) *noun.* Things needed for a particular use: Mother has a lot of kitchen *equipment,* including a blender, a toaster, and a can opener.

e·quiv·a·lence (ih-KWIV-ə-lənss) Also **equivalency** (ih-KWIV-ə-lən-see) *noun.* The state of being equivalent or equal in value. **equivalences** or **equivalencies.**

e·quiv·a·lent (ih-KWIV-ə-lənt) *adjective.* Equal or identical in amount or quantity: One mile is *equivalent* to 5,280 feet. —**equivalently** *adverb.*

equivalent sets. (Math) Two sets whose elements represent a one-to-one correspondence indicated by the sign ~.

-er *suffix.* Indicates: 1. Someone who does or is involved in a particular job: carpent*er;* build*er.* 2. The comparative degree of adjectives and adverbs: bright*er,* fast*er.*

er·a (IHR-ə) *noun.* 1. An important period in history: The 20th century has been an *era* of material progress. 2. A period of time starting from an important date: The Christian *era* began with the birth of Jesus.

e·rad·i·cate (ih-RAD-i-kayt) *verb.* To destroy or abolish. **eradicated, eradicating.**

e·rase (ih-RAYSS) *verb.* To rub out: The teacher *erased* the writing on the chalkboard. **erased, erasing.**

e·ras·er (ih-RAY-sər) *noun.* Anything used to rub out unwanted marks.

e·ra·sure (ih-RAY-shər) *noun.* Something that has been rubbed out or the place where it has been rubbed out: **erasures.**

e·rect (ih-REKT) *verb.* To build. **erected, erecting.** —*adjective.* Straight: The soldier stood *erect* before the reviewing officers. —**erectly** *adverb.*

er·mine (ER-min) *noun.* 1. A member of the weasel family whose fur is brown in summer and turns white in winter. 2. The white fur of this animal, used as decorative trim on clothing or for capes and coats. —**ermines** or **ermine** *plural.*

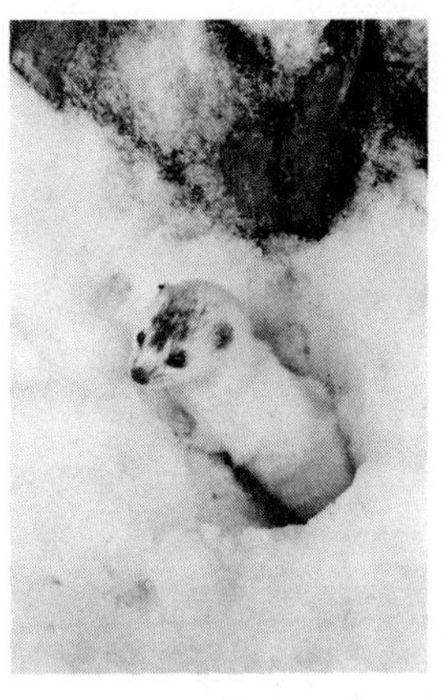
ermine

e·rode (ih-ROHD) *verb.* To eat away slowly and steadily: Rain and wind have *eroded* the soil. **eroded, eroding.**

e·ro·sion (ih-ROH-zhən) *noun.* A wearing away: The Grand Canyon is the result of millions of years of *erosion* by the Colorado River.

err (ER or EHR) *verb.* 1. To make a mistake. 2. To sin; do wrong: "To *err* is human, to forgive divine." (Pope). **erred, erring.**

er·rand (EHR-ənd) *noun.* A trip to take a message or get a particular thing.

er·rant (EHR-ənt) *adjective.* 1. Off the regular course, mistaken: *errant* behavior. 2. Wandering, roaming: Don Quixote thought he was a knight *errant;* he roamed the countryside chasing make-believe giants. —**errantly** *adverb.*

er·rat·ic (ih-RAT-ik) *adjective.* 1. Strange; different; odd. 2. Wandering; of no set pattern; not dependable: Jack's speech became *erratic* after he fell on his head. —**erratically** *adverb.*

er·ro·ne·ous (ih-ROH-nee-əss) *adjective.* Wrong; not correct; mistaken. —**erroneously** *adverb.*

er·ror (EHR-ər) *noun.* 1. A mistake, usually in words or actions. 2. State of being wrong or mistaken: He was in *error* when he thought he had not passed the test. 3. (Baseball) A bad play that helps the other team stay at bat or advance on base.

e·rupt (ih-RUHPT) *verb.* 1. To break out or burst forth as lava and hot ash do from a volcano. 2. To break out in a rash. **erupted, erupting.**

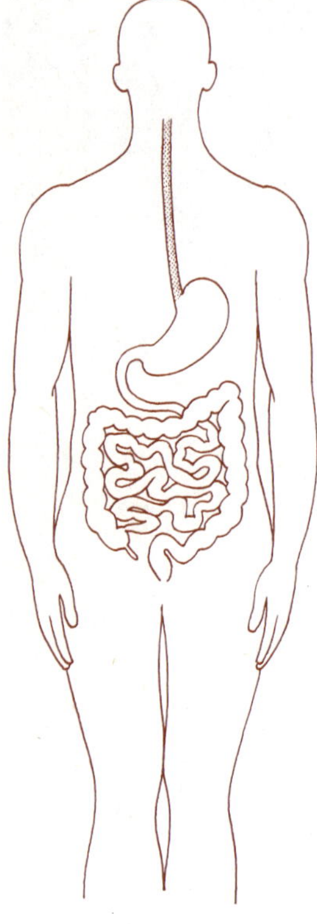
esophagus

escalator

e·rup·tion (ih-RUHP-shən) *noun.* 1. A bursting out or throwing forth: There was an *eruption* of lava from the volcano. 2. A rash; breaking out in a rash: An *eruption* on the body is a symptom of measles.

-ery *suffix.* Indicates: 1. The place where something is done: bak*ery*. 2. A collection of things: scen*ery*. 3. An act or work of: robb*ery*. 4. Condition or quality of: green*ery*. 5. A place for: nunn*ery*.

-es *suffix.* Used to form the plural of words ending in *s, sh, ch,* or *x*: kiss*es*, wish*es*, church*es*, fox*es*.

es·ca·late (ESS-kə-layt) *verb.* To make or become larger or more intense. **escalated, escalating.**

es·ca·la·tor (ESS-kə-lay-tər) *noun.* Stairs that move so that people can go up or down without walking.

es·ca·pade (ESS-kə-payd) *noun.* A daring, wild, or thoughtless prank; a break from routine. **escapades.**

es·cape (eh-SKAYP or ih-SKAYP) *verb.* 1. To get away; get out; get free: The prisoner *escaped* three times but was always caught. 2. To avoid; keep free from: Allen was the only one to *escape* the measles. 3. To leak out: The gas *escaped* from the balloon. **escaped, escaping.** —*noun.* 1. The act of getting away. 2. A way of escaping: *Escape* from the mountain was blocked by heavy snow. **escapes.** —*adjective.* Allowing (one) to get out: *escape* hatch of a jet fighter plane.

escape velocity. The rate of speed at which an object must travel in order to overcome the force of gravity.

es·ca·role (ESS-kə-rohl) *noun.* A plant with a broad frilled leaf that is used in salads.

es·cort (ESS-kort) *noun.* 1. A person or group that guides, protects, or honors. 2. A man who accompanies a woman. —(ess-KORT) *verb.* To take, accompany, guide, or protect. **escorted, escorting.**

Es·ki·mo (ESS-kə-moh) *noun.* One of a people who live in the Arctic regions of North America.

e·soph·a·gus (ih-SOF-ə-gəss) *noun.* The tube that connects the mouth to the stomach. —**esophagi** (ih-SOF-ə-jigh) *plural.*

ESP *abbreviation.* Extrasensory perception.

es·pe·cial (eh-SPESH-əl or ih-SPESH-əl) *adjective.* 1. Special; unusual. 2. Particular: Pay *especial* attention to the way he holds his guitar. —**especially** *adverb.*

es·pi·o·nage (ESS-pee-ə-nahzh) *noun.* The work of spies; spying.

es·py (eh-SPIGH or ih-SPIGH) *verb.* To see far away; catch a glimpse of. **espied, espying.**

-ess *suffix.* Indicating female; host*ess*, govern*ess*.

[1]**es·say** (ESS-ay) *noun.* A short piece of writing on a particular subject that gives the thoughts and feelings of the writer.

[2]**es·say** (ESS-ay or eh-SAY) *noun.* An attempt: His *essay* at robbing the store was a failure. —(eh-SAY) *verb.* To attempt. **essayed, essaying.**

es·sence (ESS-ənss) *noun.* 1. The basic or important part of a thing: The *essence* of chocolate is cocoa. 2. An extract: Concentrated orange juice is the *essence* of the juice of an orange. 3. A perfume. **essences.**

es·sen·tial (ə-SEN-shəl) *adjective.* Basic; absolutely necessary. —*noun.* A necessary element: Water is an *essential* of life. —**essentially** *adverb.*

E.S.T. *abbreviation.* Eastern Standard Time.

-est *suffix.* Indicating the superlative degree of adjectives: bigg*est*.

es·tab·lish (eh-STAB-lish or ih-STAB-lish) *verb.* 1. To set up in a firm, definite, or permanent way; settle. 2. To prove. **established, establishing.**

es·tab·lish·ment (eh-STAB-lish-mənt or ih-STAB-lish-mənt) *noun.* 1. Act of establishing. 2. A business, government, church, or other organization set up for a definite purpose. 3. [Usually capital E] The people in power; those who make the rules.

es·tate (eh-STAYT) *noun.* 1. A large piece of land with a house and other buildings. 2. The property and possessions of a person. **estates.**

es·teem (eh-STEEM or ih-STEEM) *verb.* 1. To think of as good or valuable. 2. To consider: I *esteemed* it an honor to receive the award for writing the best poem. **esteemed, esteeming.** —*noun.* Respect; high regard.

es·thet·ic (ess-THET-ik) Also **aesthetic** *adjective.* 1. Referring to the nature of what is beautiful. 2. Responding to what is beautiful; having a love of beauty in art or nature. —**esthetically** *adverb.*

es·ti·mate (ESS-tə-mayt) *verb.* To make a guess of size, age, value, or the like based on some facts or knowledge: I *estimate* his age as six or seven because his two front teeth are missing. **estimated, estimating.** —(ESS-tə-mit) *noun.* 1. A guess based on some knowledge: The repairman gave Dad an *estimate* of the cost of fixing our television. 2. An opinion: Ray gave us his *estimate* of the TV program.

es·ti·ma·tion (ess-tə-MAY-shən) *noun.* 1. Opinion or feeling about something: In my *estimation* it is more fun to play a game than to watch others play. 2. The act of making a guess; an estimate.

etc. *abbreviation.* Et cetera.

et cet·er·a (et SET-ər-ə) (Latin). And the like; and so forth.

etch (ECH) *verb.* To use acid to make designs or pictures on metal or glass. **etched, etching.**

e·ter·nal (ih-TER-nl) *adjective.* 1. Lasting forever; having no beginning and no end. 2. Nonstop; continual. 3. Not changing; always the same: *eternal* truth. —**eternally** *adverb.*

e·ter·ni·ty (ih-TER-nə-tee) *noun.* 1. Never-ending time. 2. Time that seems never-ending: Waiting for recess seemed an *eternity.* 3. Time after death. **eternities.**

-eth *suffix.* 1. A form of *-th* used after a vowel: twenti*eth*, thirti*eth.* 2. A present tense verb ending that is no longer used in everyday language: "Speech finely framed delight*eth* the ears." (II Maccabees 15:39)

e·ther (EE-thər) *noun.* 1. A colorless fluid whose fumes can be used to make a person unconscious. 2. (Poetry) The sky; the heavens above.

e·the·re·al (ih-THIHR-ee-əl) *adjective.* 1. Extremely delicate; light; airy. 2. Heavenly; atmospheric: "The spacious firmament on high,/ With all the *ethereal* sky." (Joseph Addison). —**ethereally** *adverb.*

eth·i·cal (ETH-i-kəl) *adjective.* 1. Relating to what is right or wrong in behavior: moral. 2. Pertaining to what is acceptable in a profession or occupation: Doctors and lawyers do not consider it *ethical* to advertise. —**ethically** *adverb.*

eth·ics (ETH-iks) *noun, plural.* 1. A set of rules for what is right and what is wrong. 2. A set of rules for a particular group, profession, or occupation.

eth·nic (ETH-nik) Also **ethnical** *adjective.* Of or about a group of people related by race or nationality: The Chicanos are a major *ethnic* group in the American Southwest. —**ethnically** *adverb.*

et·i·quette (ET-ə-ket or ET-ə-kit) *noun.* The widely accepted rules of good manners among people.

-ette *suffix.* Indicating: 1. Female: usher*ette.* 2. Small: kitchen*ette.* 3. Imitation: leather*ette.*

eucalyptus

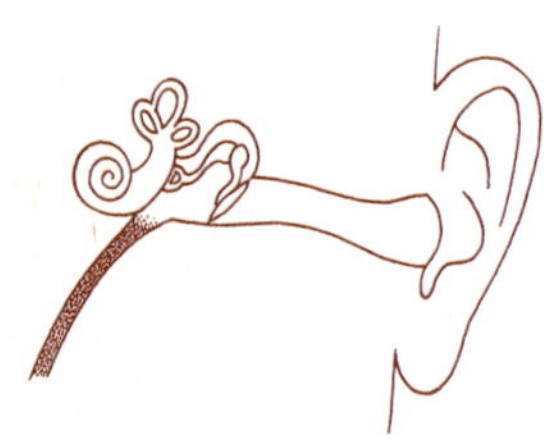
Eustachian tube

e·tude (AY-tood or AY-tyood) *noun.* (French) A musical piece intended for practice and exercise on some instrument: piano *etudes.* **etudes.**

et·y·mol·o·gy (et-ə-MOL-ə-jee) *noun.* The study of word origins and development, with special attention to how meanings and spellings change.

eu·ca·lyp·tus (yoo-kə-LIP-təss) *noun.* A tall tree, originally from Australia, valued for its wood and for the oil from its leaves. —**eucalyptuses** or **eucalypti** (yoo-kə-LIP-tigh) *plural.*

Eu·sta·chian tube (yoo-STAY-shən). A thin tube going from the middle ear to the throat in the region of the tonsils.

e·vac·u·ate (ih-VAK-yoo-ayt) *verb.* 1. To clear out of; leave: The farmers will *evacuate* their homes before the flood arrives. 2. To take out; remove: *evacuate* troops. 3. To empty. **evacuated, evacuating.** —**evacuation** (ih-vac-yoo-AY-shən) *noun.*

e·vade (ih-VAYD) *verb.* To avoid (something) by using tricks; to dodge: Bill *evaded* the teacher's question. **evaded, evading.**

e·val·u·ate (ih-VAL-yoo-ayt) *verb.* To figure out the cost, worth, or value. **evaluated, evaluating.** —**evaluation** (ih-val-yoo-AY-shən) *noun.*

e·van·ge·list (ih-VAN-jə-list) *noun.* 1. A minister, especially one who travels and preaches the gospel zealously. 2. [Capital E] Any of the authors of the four Gospels of the Bible: Matthew, Mark, Luke, or John.

e·vap·o·rate (ih-VAP-ə-rayt) *verb.* 1. To change from a solid or liquid into a gas or vapor: The water in the creek *evaporates* during the hot summer months. 2. To go away; disappear: His fear of the dark *evaporated* when Tim decided to try sleeping without a light on. **evaporated, evaporating.**

e·vap·o·ra·tion (ih-vap-ə-RAY-shən) *noun.* Act or condition of evaporating, of turning into a gas or vapor.

e·va·sion (ih-VAY-zhən) *noun.* 1. Act of evading; avoiding responsibility, obligation, or truth. 2. Use of some trick to avoid trouble or work.

e·va·sive (ih-VAY-siv) *adjective.* Trying to evade; not direct or exact: His answer was so *evasive* that I couldn't decide if he meant "Yes" or "No." —**evasively** *adverb.*

eve (EEV) *noun.* 1. [Usually capital E] The night before a holiday: Christmas *Eve,* New Year's *Eve.* 2. The time before any event: He could hardly sleep on the *eve* of the track meet. **eves.**

e·ven (EE-vən) *adjective.* 1. Level; smooth; flat. 2. Of equal measure; regular; unchanging: Dennis lets his horse run at an *even* pace. 3. On the same level; on a par: John is a year older than I but our heights are *even.* 4. (Math) Divisible by two: The numbers 2, 4, 6, 8, 10 are *even* numbers. —*adverb.* 1. Still; more so: I like that book *even* better than the first one. 2. Despite: *Even* with his head start, I beat him. —*verb.* To make equal or level: Don's touchdown *evened* the score of the game. **evened, evening.** —**evenly** *adverb.* —**even if** or **even though.** Although: *Even if* we fix the flat tire, we can't get to the movies on time.

eve·ning (EEV-ning) *noun.* The period of day between afternoon and night.

evening star. A planet, usually Venus, seen in the west early in the night.

even number. Any number that can be divided by two: Numbers such as 2, 4, 6, and 8 are *even* numbers.

e·vent (ih-VENT) *noun.* 1. A special happening. 2. Each of the parts of a sports program: There were 12 *events* at the track meet. —**in any event.** Whatever happens. —**in the event that.** In case; if.

e·vent·ful (ih-VENT-fəl) *adjective.* 1. Full of special happenings: The day of the school fair is an *eventful* time for everyone. 2. Having important results. —**eventfully** *adverb.*

e·ven·tide (EE-vən-tighd) *noun.* Night; evening: used mostly in poetry.

e·ven·tu·al (ih-VEN-choo-əl) *adjective.* Happening at last; final; in the end: After the long illness, his *eventual* recovery made everybody happy. —**eventually** *adverb.*

ev·er (EV-ər) *adverb.* 1. Always; at all times: A policeman is *ever* ready to help people in trouble. 2. Constantly: He has collected stamps *ever* since he was a child. 3. At any time: Have you *ever* been to Boston? 4. In any way: How will I *ever* explain why I was late?

ev·er·green (EV-ər-green) *noun.* A tree, shrub, or other plant whose foliage stays green all through the year.

ev·er·last·ing (ev-ər-LAST-ing) *adjective.* 1. Without end; lasting forever. 2. Going on too long: The audience was tired of the speaker's *everlasting* talk.

ev·er·more (ev-ər-MOR) *adverb.* Forever; from now on; always.

eve·ry (EV-ree) *adjective.* 1. Each: Please pick up *every* scrap of paper on the floor. 2. All possible: Firemen make *every* attempt to rescue people from a burning building.

eve·ry·bod·y (EV-ree-bod-ee) *pronoun.* Each individual person; every person; all: *Everybody* is going to the assembly.

eve·ry·day (EV-ree-day) *adjective.* 1. Of each day; daily: Doing the dishes is an *everyday* chore. 2. Typical of an ordinary day of the week; not special: A turkey dinner, with all the trimmings, is not an *everyday* meal.

eve·ry·one (EV-ree-wuhn) *pronoun.* Each of the people; every person.

eve·ry·thing (EV-ree-thing) *pronoun.* 1. Each single thing; all things: Will *everything* fit in the suitcase? 2. Something of great importance: My going to college means *everything* to my parents.

eve·ry·where (EV-ree-hwair) *adverb.* In each and every place; in all places.

e·vict (ih-VIKT) *verb.* To remove someone by law from a house, building, or land. **evicted, evicting.**

ev·i·dence (EV-ə-dənss) *noun.* 1. Something that shows what is so or what is not: The lawyer showed the jury a photograph as part of the *evidence.* 2. Proof. —*verb.* To prove; make very clear; show plainly. **evidenced, evidencing.**

ev·i·dent (EV-ə-dənt) *adjective.* Plain to see; easy to understand; obvious. —**evidently** (ev-ə-DENT-ly) *adverb.*

e·vil (EE-vəl) *adjective.* Wrong; bad; wicked: Stealing is an *evil* act. —*noun.* 1. Something bad, wrong: "The *evil* that men do lives after them. . . ." (Shakespeare). 2. Anything causing harm: ". . . I will fear no *evil.* . . ." (Psalms 23:4). —**evilly** *adverb.*

e·voke (ih-VOHK) *verb.* To bring forth; produce: The mention of the mountains *evoked* a happy memory of the summer he had spent there. **evoked, evoking.**

ev·o·lu·tion (ev-ə-LOO-shən) *noun.* 1. A gradual, continuing development: The *evolution* of the jumbo jets from the Wright brothers' simple airplane happened in less than a century. 2. A scientific theory that all living things gradually grew from earlier, simpler forms of life.

e·volve (ih-VOLV) *verb.* To develop gradually; change in form slowly: The Colonists' plan for independence *evolved* after many years of British rule. **evolved, evolving.**

ewe (YOO) *noun.* A female sheep.

ex- *prefix.* Indicates: 1. Before; once; at one time; former: *ex*-president. 2. From; out of; beyond: *ex*press, *ex*hale.

ex·act (eg-ZAKT) *adjective.* Completely correct; right. —*verb.* To force; to demand: If you break a law, the court can *exact* a fine from you. **exacted, exacting.** —**exactly** *adverb.*

ex·act·ing (eg-ZAK-ting) *adjective.* 1. Not easy to satisfy; strict; demanding much. 2. Needing great care or effort: Building model cars is an *exacting* hobby. —**exactingly** *adverb.*

ex·ag·ger·ate (eg-ZAJ-ə-rayt) *verb.* To add to the truth; make larger, worse, or better than it really is: I think Ralph *exaggerated* when he said he ate fourteen hot dogs for supper. **exaggerated, exaggerating.** —**exaggeratedly** *adverb.*

ex·ag·ger·a·tion (eg-zaj-ə-RAY-shən) *noun.* An addition to the truth; overstatement: To say that you would rather starve than eat green peas is an *exaggeration.*

ex·alt (eg-ZAWLT) *verb.* 1. To fill with happiness; make proud: He was more than just happy; he was *exalted.* 2. To raise up or promote to a high office. 3. To honor; to praise; to worship. **exalted, exalting.**

ex·am (eg-ZAM) *noun.* (Informal) Short for *examination;* a test.

ex·am·i·na·tion (eg-zam-ə-NAY-shən) *noun.* 1. A test of knowledge or ability. 2. The act of looking over carefully: All students must have a physical *examination* before starting school.

ex·am·ine (eg-ZAM-in) *verb.* 1. To look over with great care; inspect closely. 2. To test the knowledge, skill, or ability of; to question. **examined, examining.**

ex·am·ple (eg-ZAM-pəl) *noun.* 1. Something that shows what similar things are like; a sample: Recycling paper is an *example* of good ecological practice. 2. Something to be copied or imitated; a pattern: Older children are often asked to set a good *example* for younger ones. 3. Something used as a warning to others: The teacher made an *example* of the noisy boy by sending him out in the hall. **examples.**

ex·as·per·ate (eg-ZASS-pə-rayt) *verb.* To make angry; annoy; irritate. **exasperated, exasperating.**

ex·ca·vate (EKS-kə-vayt) *verb.* 1. To make a hole; dig; scoop out: We must *excavate* the ground before the building can be started. 2. To uncover; dig out: Schliemann *excavated* the ancient Greek city of Troy. **excavated, excavating.**

ex·ca·va·tion (EKS-kə-VAY-shən) *noun.* 1. The act of digging or scooping out: Many people watched the *excavation* for the new school's basement. 2. The hole made by excavating: The workmen told the boy to stay away from the edge of the *excavation.*

ex·ceed (ek-SEED) *verb.* 1. To go beyond (what) is necessary or allowed: The driver *exceeded* the speed limit. 2. To be greater than: "A man's reach should *exceed* his grasp, or what's a heaven for?" (R. Browning). 3. To be better than or superior to: The girl's ability to play the piano *exceeded* her brother's. **exceeded, exceeding.** —**exceedingly** *adverb.*

ex·cel (ek-SEL) *verb.* 1. To be very good; be superior in. 2. To outdo; be better than: He *excels* his teammates in the 50-yard dash. **excelled, excelling.**

ex·cel·lence (EK-sə-lənss) *noun.* State of being outstanding or better: Jane received an award of *excellence* for her baking.

ex·cel·lent (EK-sə-lənt) *adjective.* Extremely good; of first quality. —**excellently** *adverb.*

ex·cept (ek-SEPT) *preposition.* All but; excluding: Everyone is going on the field trip *except* Phyllis.

ex·cep·tion (ek-SEP-shən) *noun.* 1. A leaving out or failure to include: Tom did all his chores with the *exception* of sweeping the porch. 2. The thing not included: Mary's grades were excellent with one *exception.* 3. Something different from a general rule: The spelling of "seize" is an *exception* to the rule of "i" before "e." —**take exception.** To object; resent.

ex·cep·tion·al (ek-SEP-shən-l) *adjective.* 1. Not usual; out of the ordinary. 2. Outstanding; superior. —**exceptionally** *adverb.*

ex·cess (ek-SESS or EK-sess) *noun.* More than needed or allowed. **excesses.** —*adjective.* Over a set limit; extra.

ex·ces·sive (ek-SESS-iv) *adjective.* More than proper or necessary; too much. —**excessively** *adverb.*

ex·change (eks-CHAYNJ) *verb.* To give or take one thing in return for another; trade. **exchanged, exchanging.** —*noun.* 1. The act of giving or taking one thing in return for another. 2. A place for buying and selling certain items, such as stocks, livestock, grain, vegetables, or fruit: Many farmers sell their products at an agricultural *exchange.* 3. A telephone company facility serving a given area. **exchanges.**

ex·cit·a·ble (ek-SIGH-tə-bəl) *adjective.* Easily aroused or excited: Don't go near the hornets' nest; they are very *excitable.* —**excitably** *adverb.*

ex·cite (ek-SIGHT) *verb.* 1. To move to strong feeling; stir up; arouse. 2. To call into action; cause to act: Don't *excite* the dogs! They'll bark all night. **excited, exciting.**

ex·cite·ment (ek-SIGHT-mənt) *noun.* 1. State or condition of being aroused. 2. Anything that excites.

ex·claim (eks-KLAYM) *verb.* To speak out suddenly and loudly. **exclaimed, exclaiming.**

ex·cla·ma·tion (eks-klə-MAY-shən) *noun.* Something said suddenly and loud, usually caused by strong feeling: Oh!, Hey!, Ouch!, and Look! are all *exclamations.*

exclamation point. Also **exclamation mark.** A sign of punctuation (!) put after a word, phrase, or sentence used as an exclamation: Hurrah!

ex·clam·a·to·ry (eks-KLAM-ə-tor-ee) *adjective.* Having, using, or referring to an exclamation: *exclamatory* sentences.

ex·clude (eks-KLOOD) *verb.* To keep out; shut out; to bar: The Constitution of the United States of America *excludes* persons under 35 from serving as President. **excluded, excluding.**

ex·clu·sion (eks-KLOO-zhən) *noun.* 1. The act of keeping out or barring someone or something: the *exclusion* of cameramen from a courtroom. 2. The state of being kept out.

ex·clu·sive (eks-KLOO-siv) *adjective.* 1. Tending to exclude or shut out. 2. Not shared with anyone else: Mrs. Park gave me the *exclusive* right to the job of mowing her yard. 3. Uninterrupted or complete: Dad's tax return has his *exclusive* attention tonight. 4. Limited to certain people: Richard's family lives in an *exclusive* apartment house; only rich people can afford to live in it. —**exclusive of.** Not counting: The school day lasts six hours, *exclusive of* the lunch period. —**exclusively** *adverb.*

ex·crete (ek-SKREET) *verb.* To pass waste matter from the body. **excreted, excreting.**

ex·cre·tion (ek-SKREE-shən) *noun.* 1. Act of passing waste matter from the body. 2. The waste matter that is passed from the body. —**excretory** (EKS-krə-tor-ee) *adjective.*

stock exchange

ex·cur·sion (ek-SKER-zhən) *noun.* 1. A short trip, usually for fun. 2. A journey at a lower than usual fare: The airline offers weekend *excursions* to Bermuda.

ex·cus·a·ble (ek-SKYOOZ-ə-bəl) *adjective.* Capable of being pardoned; permitted: It is *excusable* to miss a club meeting because of a dentist's appointment. —**excusably** *adverb.*

ex·cuse (ek-SKYOOSS) *noun.* The reason given for something done; apology. **excuses.** —(ek-SKYOOZ) *verb.* 1. To pardon; forgive; overlook. 2. To dismiss; allow to leave: The teacher *excused* us at three o'clock. 3. To free from what is owed or due: If you are ill, you will be *excused* from your work. **excused, excusing.**

ex·e·cute (EK-si-kyoot) *verb.* 1. To do; perform; carry out (a job, task, or duty). 2. To enforce; put into action: The governor of a state must *execute* its laws. 3. To punish by death in a lawful manner. 4. To make or perform according to a plan: The famous statue of Lincoln in Washington was *executed* by the sculptor Daniel Chester French. **executed, executing.**

ex·e·cu·tion (ek-si-KYOO-shən) *noun.* 1. Doing; performing; carrying out of a job, task, or duty. 2. Enforcement; putting into action: The President is charged with the *execution* of the nation's laws. 3. Act of putting to death as ordered by law.

ex·ec·u·tive (eg-ZEK-yə-tiv) *noun.* A person in charge of running all or part of a business, or organization; a manager. **executives.** —*adjective.* 1. Able to run or direct things: Because of his *executive* ability, Roger was elected president of the student council. 2. Having to do with the enforcement of laws: The President, his cabinet, and the federal agencies make up the *executive* branch of government.

ex·em·pli·fy (eg-ZEM-plə-figh) *verb.* To serve or act as an example of. **exemplified, exemplifying.**

ex·empt (eg-ZEMPT) *verb.* To excuse or release (someone) from what is due or owed: The Army *exempted* my brother from service because of a knee injury. **exempted, exempting.** —*adjective.* Not responsible; freed: Our church is *exempt* from paying city taxes.

ex·emp·tion (eg-ZEMP-shən) *noun.* Freedom from some duty, rule, or payment: a tax *exemption.*

ex·er·cise (EK-sər-sighz) *verb.* 1. To move or use the different parts of the body: He *exercises* for ten minutes every day to keep in shape. 2. To use; act on: A good citizen *exercises* his right to vote. **exercised, exercising.** —*noun.* 1. Use of the body or the mind: Dad gets his *exercise* by walking to work. 2. Practice: You must finish your violin *exercises* before you go out to play. 3. Putting into use: With a great *exercise* of will power she refused dessert. 4. (Plural) Ceremony; performance: If it rains, the graduation *exercises* will be held indoors. **exercises.**

ex·ert (eg-ZERT) *verb.* To apply; use: The runner *exerted* every effort to win the race. **exerted, exerting.**

ex·er·tion (eg-ZER-shən) *noun.* 1. Strong effort; hard work: Jim was tired after the *exertion* of mowing the grass. 2. Making use of: With extra *exertion* of authority, the teacher got the class to settle down.

ex·hale (eks-HAYL) *verb.* 1. To breathe out. *See* **inhale.** 2. To pass off, as steam, smoke, or gas: In winter, outdoor pipes often *exhale* clouds of water vapor. **exhaled, exhaling.**

ex·haust (eg-ZAWST) *noun.* 1. The gases given off by an engine. 2. A device attached to an engine through which escaping gas passes. —*verb.* 1. To tire; wear out. 2. To use up; to empty: The cookie supply is *exhausted;* we'll have to bake more. **exhausted, exhausting.**

ex·haus·tion (eg-ZAWSS-chən) *noun.* 1. State of being very tired or worn out: It took him several hours to recover from his *exhaustion* after the long hike. 2. Act of using up: The *exhaustion* of the water supply will mean trouble for everyone.

exhaust pipe. A metal tube or pipe which carries vapor and waste material from an engine or motor.

exhaust velocity. The speed at which a rocket is traveling when exhaust gases begin to leave the nozzles of its engines.

ex·hib·it (eg-ZIB-it) *verb.* 1. To display; show; put on view. 2. To reveal or indicate: Your work *exhibits* a real talent for math. **exhibited, exhibiting.** —*noun.* 1. A presentation, showing, or display. 2. What is shown or displayed. 3. A thing or document entered as evidence in court.

ex·hi·bi·tion (ek-sə-BISH-ən) *noun.* 1. A public display. 2. A fair, usually lasting several days, at which machinery, hobbies, painting, or the like are shown.

ex·hil·a·rate (eg-ZIL-ə-rayt) *verb.* To enliven; make happy or excited. **exhilarated, exhilarating.** —**exhilaration** (eg-zil-ə-RAY-shən) *noun.*

ex·hort (eg-ZORT) *verb.* To urge; encourage; advise strongly: The coach *exhorted* each player to do his best. **exhorted, exhorting.**

ex·ile (EG-zighl or EK-sighl) *noun.* 1. A long separation from home or country. 2. A person who is sent from his home or country (usually not willingly). **exiles.** —*verb.* To banish or expel a person from his native country. **exiled, exiling.**

ex·ist (eg-ZIST) *verb.* 1. To be real or alive: Dinosaurs do not *exist* anymore, but we know that they once did. 2. To continue living: The farmers can barely *exist* on the sandy, rocky soil. **existed, existing.**

ex·ist·ence (eg-ZISS-tənss) *noun.* 1. Having being; existing: The *existence* of life on other planets has not yet been proved. 2. State of being real or actual: Do you believe in the *existence* of ghosts? 3. Way of life: Daredevil drivers have an exciting *existence.*

ex·it (EG-zit or EK-sit) *noun.* 1. A door or a passage out of a building. 2. The act of leaving or going out; departure. 3. A stage direction to show when or where an actor is to go offstage. —*verb.* To leave; go out. **exited, exiting.**

ex·o·dus (EK-sə-dəss) *noun.* 1. Departure; a leaving or going away, used of a large group of people: After Labor Day there is an *exodus* of people from the beaches. 2. [Capital E] The departure of the Jews from Egypt. **exoduses.**

ex officio (EKS-ə-FISH-ee-oh) (Latin) Because of the official position one holds: The president of the student council is a member, *ex officio,* of every council committee.

ex·or·bi·tant (eg-ZOR-bə-tənt) *adjective.* Not reasonable; too much: One dollar is an *exorbitant* price for an ice-cream soda. —**exorbitantly** *adverb.*

ex·o·skel·e·ton (ek-soh-SKEL-ə-tən) *noun.* The hard outside covering of some fishes and animals, such as the shells of lobsters and shrimp or the covering of grasshoppers.

ex·o·sphere (EK-soh-sfihr) *noun.* The outermost layer of the atmosphere of the earth.

ex·ot·ic (eg-ZOT-ik) *adjective.* 1. From a foreign country; not native: Papaya is an *exotic* fruit to Americans. 2. (Slang) Unusual; very colorful; strange: The girl wore an *exotic* dress made of blue feathers. —**exotically** *adverb.*

ex·pand (ek-SPAND) *verb.* 1. To grow larger or bigger. 2. To spread out; stretch; swell: The eagle *expanded* its wings and soared above the mountain. 3. To go into more detail, develop more: The teacher wants me to *expand* my book report. **expanded, expanding.**

ex·panse (ek-SPANSS) *noun.* A widely spread out area: Most deserts are vast *expanses* of sand. **expanses.**

ex·pan·sion (ek-SPAN-shən) *noun.* 1. The act of spreading out or getting larger, as in size or shape: An increased number of students makes the *expansion* of the school necessary. 2. The part that results from such enlargement.

ex·pect (ek-SPEKT) *verb.* 1. To wait for; look forward to (something) with good reason to believe it will happen. 2. To anticipate as right or due: The government *expects* every citizen to pay his taxes. 3. To suppose; believe. **expected, expecting.**

ex·pec·ta·tion (ek-spek-TAY-shən) *noun.* 1. A looking forward to: The little girl waited in excited *expectation* for the gift Santa Claus would bring. 2. Something looked forward to: The raise in his allowance was more than his *expectation.*

ex·pec·to·rate (ek-SPEK-tə-rayt) *verb.* To spit. **expectorated, expectorating.**

ex·pec·to·ra·tion (ek-spek-tə-RAY-shən) *noun.* 1. Clearing of the throat by spitting or coughing. 2. The matter cleared from the throat.

ex·pe·di·ent (ek-SPEE-dee-ənt) *adjective.* 1. Desirable; suitable for a particular purpose: Sometimes it is more *expedient* to listen than to talk. 2. Useful for one's purpose; to one's advantage: Martin found it *expedient* to stay quiet when his father asked who broke the window. —*noun.* A way to get a wanted result: Lying to avoid getting in trouble is not a good *expedient.*

ex·pe·dite (EK-spə-dight) *verb.* To assist or speed up the process of (something). **expedited, expediting.**

ex·pe·di·tion (ek-spə-DISH-ən) *noun.* 1. A journey or voyage taken for a special reason, such as exploration, warfare, adventure, or scientific purposes. 2. The persons, means of transportation, and equipment collected for such a journey: Columbus' first *expedition* sailed in three ships. 3. Quickness; speediness; promptness: Mark did his chores with *expedition* so that he could watch the football game.

ex·pel (ek-SPEL) *verb.* 1. To force out; drive away: The army *expelled* the enemy soldiers who were invading their country. 2. To send away; put out; exclude: The boy was *expelled* from school. **expelled, expelling.**

ex·pend (ek-SPEND) *verb.* 1. To use up; exhaust: The cheerleaders *expended* all their energy yelling for the baseball team. 2. To spend; pay out: The club *expended* its treasury on refreshments for the party. **expended, expending.**

ex·pend·i·ture (ek-SPEN-di-chər) *noun.* 1. Act of using up or exhausting: *expenditure* of time and work. 2. Cost; amount spent; expense: *expenditure* for food. **expenditures.**

ex·pense (ek-SPENSS) *noun.* Cost; amount charged; fee to be paid. **expenses.**

ex·pen·sive (ek-SPEN-siv) *adjective.* Very costly; high in price. —**expensively** *adverb.*

ex·pe·ri·ence (ek-SPIHR-ee-ənss) *noun.* 1. Any situation, event, or happening that a person has or meets in life. 2. Information; knowledge; skill learned by doing something. **experiences.** —*verb.* To have happen to one; meet with; feel; know by doing or seeing: Alice *experienced* great happiness when she was chosen to go to Japan. **experienced, experiencing.**

ex·per·i·ment (ek-SPEHR-ə-mənt) *noun.* A project or test to prove or discover something; a trial to gain information: Isaac Newton made several *experiments* to prove the law of gravity. —*verb.* To carry out tests: We *experimented* by mixing peanut butter and bacon. **experimented, experimenting.**

ex·per·i·men·tal (ek-spehr-ə-MEN-tl) *adjective.* As a test; not yet proved: The Wright Brothers' first plane was *experimental.* —**experimentally** *adverb.*

ex·pert (EK-spərt) *noun.* A person who knows a lot about a particular subject. —*adjective.* Highly skilled or trained: Only *expert* drivers can qualify for the Indianapolis 500. —**expertly** *adverb.*

ex·pi·ra·tion (ek-spə-RAY-shən) *noun.* 1. Giving out; coming to an end: the *expiration* of the school year. 2. The act of breathing out.

ex·pire (ek-SPIGHR) *verb.* 1. To come to an end: Your membership *expired* last month. 2. To die. 3. To die out: The campers sang songs and watched the fire *expire.* 4. To breathe out. **expired, expiring.**

ex·plain (ek-SPLAYN) *verb.* 1. To tell the meaning of: I can't *explain* the poem but I like it. 2. To make clear or understandable: If you'll *explain* how this machine works, I think I can run it. 3. To give a reason for: He *explained* that the lights went out because the storm had brought down several power lines. **explained, explaining.** —**explainable** *adjective.*

ex·pla·na·tion (ek-splə-NAY-shən) *noun.* 1. Act of explaining; what is said or written that explains: Bill's *explanation* of the way a car works was very clear. 2. Meaning, reason.

ex·plan·a·to·ry (ek-SPLAN-ə-tor-ee) *adjective.* Making understandable: *Explanatory* drawings made the science lesson clear.

ex·plic·it (ek-SPLISS-it) *adjective.* Clear; exact; to the point: The directions for the game were *explicit.* —**explicitly** *adverb.*

ex·plode (ek-SPLOHD) *verb.* 1. To blow up; come apart suddenly because of heat or other chemical force. 2. To cause to blow up. 3. To lose control of emotions: The audience *exploded* with laughter. 4. (Phonics) To give full sound to a consonant: The "p" in "put" is *exploded.* **exploded, exploding.**

ex·ploit (EKS-ploit) *noun.* An adventure; a deed of daring; a brave act. —(eks-PLOIT) *verb.* 1. To use to the utmost: Bill *exploited* his athletic ability to make the team. 2. To use selfishly or unfairly: Slaves were *exploited* by plantation owners. **exploited, exploiting.**

ex·plo·ra·tion (ek-splə-RAY-shən) *noun.* 1. The act of investigating strange places. 2. Careful examination; detailed search: The dentist's *exploration* of my mouth seemed to take forever.

ex·plore (ek-SPLOR) *verb.* 1. To journey to little-known or unknown places to find out about them. 2. To search carefully; examine closely: I found the baby *exploring* everything in Mother's pocketbook. **explored, exploring.**

ex·plor·er (ek-SPLOR-ər) *noun.* One who travels to faraway or unknown places in search of knowledge or admiration.

ex·plo·sion (ek-SPLOH-zhən) *noun.* 1. The act of exploding. 2. The noise made by an explosion. 3. A sudden and loud burst of noise, such as laughter or yelling.

ex·plo·sive (ek-SPLOH-siv) *noun.* Dynamite; TNT, or anything else that can be exploded. **explosives.** —*adjective.* Like an explosion; a loud, sudden, bursting forth: Her *explosive* laughter made everyone jump. —**explosively** *adverb.*

ex·po·nent (ek-SPOH-nənt) *noun.* 1. One who explains or presents specific ideas or viewpoints: The *exponent* of the longer school year had many good arguments. 2. A type; symbol; representative: Dan'l Boone is an *exponent* of the rugged individual. 3. (Algebra) The number or symbol placed to the right and slightly above another number or symbol (the base) showing the power to which the base is to be raised: 4^2 is four to the second power, or sixteen; ^{2} is the *exponent.*

ex·port (ek-SPORT or EK-sport) *verb.* To send goods to other countries for sale. **exported, exporting.** —(EK-sport) *noun.* 1. Something sold to another country. 2. The business or act of exporting: Hawaii raises pineapple for *export.* —*adjective.* Of or about things exported or about exporting itself: All the *export* items had to be carefully packed.

ex·pose (ek-SPOHZ) *verb.* 1. To reveal; uncover; open: We *exposed* some worms when we turned over the rock. 2. To leave open to the effects of sun, wind, or rain. 3. To tell or reveal something that was secret or unknown. 4. (Photography) To allow light to act on (sensitized film or paper): I *exposed* the film too long and all the pictures were spoiled. **exposed, exposing.**

ex·po·sé (ek-spoh-ZAY) *noun.* 1. The revealing of damaging facts: The *exposé* on the candidate's campaign spending led to his defeat. 2. A statement of the facts. **exposés.**

ex·po·si·tion (ek-spə-ZISH-ən) *noun.* 1. A big show or display of art, machinery, or other goods. 2. An explanation in detail.

ex·po·sure (ek-SPOH-zhər) *noun.* 1. Giving out secret or hidden information; a showing of what was hidden or covered. 2. Lack of shelter or protection: Too much *exposure* to the sun can cause dizziness. 3. Position in relationship to sun (or wind): A northern *exposure* makes a room cooler and darker. 4. (Photography) A section of film sufficient for one picture: This roll of film contains 12 *exposures.* 5. (Photography) Allowing light to strike sensitized paper or film. **exposures.**

ex·pound (ek-SPOWND) *verb.* To explain in detail or at great length. **expounded, expounding.**

ex·press (eks-PRESS) *verb.* 1. To put into words: Jack *expressed* the ideas of the group so well that no one had to add another word. 2. To show (feeling) by movement, tone of voice, appearance: His words were friendly, but his voice *expressed* nervousness. **expressed, expressing.** —*adjective.* 1. Very definite; to the point: Dad's *express* order was for me to do the dishes at once. 2. Speedy or nonstop: *express* train, *express* flight, *express* elevator. 3. Referring to anything related to such travel or shipping: The *express* office called to say our package had arrived. —*noun.* 1. A train or bus that travels from point to point with few or no stops. 2. A quick, direct, or special way of sending goods or money: We sent the gift *express* because it was too large for parcel post. **expresses.**

ex·pres·sion (eks-PRESH-ən) *noun.* 1. Act of expressing: an *expression* of opinion. 2. Show of emotion on the face: His *expression* showed how sad he was. 3. Words of explanation: I know how I feel but I can't give it *expression.* 4. The act of showing or representing feeling: An actor must be a master of *expression.* 5. A special word or words: "23 skidoo" was a popular *expression* around 1900. 6. (Math) A symbol or a combination of symbols that represent an amount or operation.

ex·pres·sive (eks-PRESS-iv) *adjective.*

1. Able to express: To a musician, a melody is more *expressive* than words. 2. Full of emotion and meaning: His speech was brief but *expressive.* —**expressively** *adverb.*

ex·press·way (eks-PRESS-way) *noun.* A main highway, usually divided, for fast and direct travel.

ex·pul·sion (eks-PUHL-shən) *noun.* The act of throwing out; forcing out.

ex·qui·site (EKS-kwi-zit) *adjective.* 1. Of fine, delicate beauty, as an *exquisite* face or flower. 2. Perfectly formed; skillfully made. 3. Intense, acute, particular: *exquisite* pleasure. 4. Special and refined: *exquisite* manners. —**exquisitely** *adverb.*

ex·tend (ek-STEND) *verb.* 1. To stretch out to full length: *Extend* your arms overhead to see if you can touch the ceiling. 2. To draw out in a single direction: Please *extend* the right-hand margin to the edge of the paper. 3. To spread out; reach: The line at the theater *extended* around the corner. 4. To increase in length or time: The homeroom period will be *extended* an additional ten minutes this morning. 5. To make larger or greater. 6. To offer; give: The guidance counselor *extends* help to students with problems. **extended, extending.**

ex·ten·sion (ek-STEN-shən) *noun.* 1. The act of spreading out; increasing; becoming larger or greater. 2. An addition: My father built an *extension* on our summer cottage. 3. More time in which to do something: Because Harry was ill, he got a three-week *extension* to finish his science project. 4. An added telephone using the same line as the main telephone.

ex·ten·sive (ek-STEN-siv) *adjective.* 1. Broad; wide or spread out over a big area: The tundra is an *extensive* area of arctic wasteland. 2. Far-reaching; long-range: The *extensive* research of Jonas Salk and many other scientists led to a vaccine for polio. —**extensively** *adverb.*

ex·tent (ek-STENT) *noun.* 1. How far something reaches in length, width, or area. 2. Full measure; all the way; extreme length: I will even go to the *extent* of paying for your ticket if you will go with me to the movies.

ex·te·ri·or (ek-STIHR-ee-ər) *noun* (and *adjective*). 1. Outside; outer surface, area, or part. 2. Outward appearance.

ex·ter·mi·nate (ek-STER-mə-nayt) *verb.* To wipe out; get rid of by killing; eliminate completely. **exterminated, exterminating.** —**extermination** (ek-ster-mə-NAY-shən) *noun.*

ex·ter·mi·na·tor (ek-STER-mə-nay-tər) *noun.* One who exterminates, particularly someone whose job is ridding buildings of such pests as rats or insects.

ex·ter·nal (ek-STER-nl) *adjective.* 1. Outer; on or from the outside. 2. For the outside: The medicine is for *external* use only; don't drink it. —*noun.* (Plural) Visible or obvious qualities or factors: Melinda is too concerned with *externals;* she judges people by their clothes. —**externally** *adverb.*

ex·tinct (ek-STINGKT) *adjective.* 1. Having died out completely: If we are not careful of our environment, man may become as *extinct* as the dinosaur. 2. Burned out; dead: Volcanoes that appear to be *extinct* sometimes erupt.

ex·tinc·tion (ek-STINGK-shən) *noun.* 1. The act of putting out: The *extinction* of the forest fire brought cheers from the tired fire fighters. 2. The condition of being extinct.

ex·tin·guish (ek-STING-gwish) *verb.* 1. To put out (fire); snuff out (candle); shut off (lights). 2. To cut off; put an end to. **extinguished, extinguishing.**

expressway

extinguisher

ex·tin·guish·er (ek-STING-gwish-ər) *noun.* A portable device used to put out fires.

ex·tol (ek-STOHL) *verb.* To praise greatly. **extolled, extolling.**

ex·tra (EKS-trə) *adjective.* 1. More than what is needed, usual, or expected; added. 2. Special; better. —*noun.* 1. Something more. 2. Added cost: Dessert comes with the meal in the restaurant but milk is *extra.* 3. Something that is unscheduled or out of the ordinary: a newspaper *extra.* 4. A person who appears in a crowd scene in a movie. —*adverb.* More than the usual or expected amount: High-test gasoline costs *extra.*

extra- Also **extro-** *prefix.* Indicates more, outside, greater: *extra*sensory, *extra*vagant. Often used with hyphen to emphasize or form a new word: *extra*-special, *extra*-strength.

ex·tract (ek-STRAKT) *verb.* 1. To pull or draw out: A dentist *extracts* teeth. 2. To take out the essence or juice by pressure or distilling as oil from coconuts, peanuts, olives, or other foods. **extracted, extracting.** —(EKS-trakt) *noun.* That which is extracted: vanilla *extract.*

ex·trac·tion (ek-STRAK-shən) *noun.* 1. The act of pulling out: Sometimes the *extraction* of a bad tooth is necessary. 2. National origin or family background: Chopin was of Polish *extraction* but lived in France most of his life.

ex·traor·di·nar·y (ek-STROR-də-nair-ee) *adjective.* More than ordinary; unusual; special. —**extraordinarily** *adverb.*

extrasensory perception (ek-strə-SEN-sə-ree pər-SEP-shən). The ability to know things without using the eyes, ears, or other physical senses: To know about something before it happens or when it happens far away is an example of *extrasensory perception.* Also called "ESP."

ex·trav·a·gance (ek-STRAV-ə-gənss) *noun.* Too much; waste; usually referring to excessive price: Putting on all the lights in the house is an *extravagance.* **extravagances.** —**extravagant** *adjective.* —**extravagantly** *adverb.*

ex·treme (ek-STREEM) *adjective.* 1. Greater than the ordinary or the usual: *Extreme* care should be used when working with electricity. 2. Farthest from a given point or spot: The lost child was found in an *extreme* north section of the forest. 3. Final; last: Sentencing a man to die is the *extreme* punishment under law. 4. Going beyond what is thought to be proper or right: Janice's *extreme* clothes made people stare at her. —*noun.* 1. One of two things as different from the other as it can be; opposites: the *extremes* of hot and cold. 2. The first and last things in a group: The letters A and Z are the *extremes* in the alphabet. 3. Anything that goes beyond what is usual. **extremes.** —**extremely** *adverb.* —**go to extremes.** Carry things too far.

ex·trem·ist (ek-STREEM-ist) *noun.* One who goes to extremes or who has or supports extreme ideas.

ex·trem·i·ty (ek-STREM-ə-tee) *noun.* 1. The far end; the tip. 2. (Plural) The hands or feet. 3. The worst possible condition; great danger or pain. 4. An action which is extreme or extraordinary. **extremities.**

ex·tri·cate (EKS-trə-kayt) *verb.* To untangle; free; loosen: The fly could not *extricate* itself from the spider's web. **extricated, extricating.**

ex·ult (eg-ZUHLT) *verb.* To show or feel great joy (followed by *in, at, over*); feel triumphant. **exulted, exulting.** —**exultation** (eg-zuhl-TAY-shən) *noun.*

ex·ult·ant (eg-ZUHL-tənt) *adjective.* Exulting; being extremely joyous. —**exultantly** *adverb.*

eye (IGH) *noun.* 1. The part of the body, located in the head, through which humans and animals see; the organ of sight. 2. The part of the eye that has color; the iris: I have green *eyes.* 3. The area around the eye: He got a black *eye* in a fight. 4. Ability to see something in a special way; appreciation: Baseball scouts have an *eye* for young men with talent. 5. Brief look; glance: Before he began his talk, the speaker hurriedly cast an *eye* over the audience. 6. Aim or intention; regard: an *eye* on the future. 7. (Plural) Judgment or opinion: In the *eyes* of most doctors, smoking is dangerous to health. 8. The center of influence, power, or the like. 9. Anything that looks like or resembles an eye: the *eye* of a needle. 10. Center of a hurricane or a tropical storm. 11. A loop or ring into which a hook fits: Dressmakers often use hooks and *eyes,* instead of buttons, to fasten clothes. **eyes.** —*verb.* 1. To look at; to view. 2. To watch closely; observe with attention: The guard carefully *eyed* each identification badge before letting anyone pass through the gates. **eyed, eying** or **eyeing.** —**be all eyes.** To give complete attention. —**catch one's eye.** To get a person's attention. —**give** (someone) **the eye.** To look at admiringly. —**have an eye for.** To be good at finding, recognizing, or selecting: Mary *has an eye for* bargains; she finds pretty clothes that have been marked down. —**keep an eye on.** To watch closely. —**make eyes at.** To flirt with. —**see eye to eye.** To be in complete agreement with; think alike.

eye·ball (IGH-bawl) *noun.* The eye itself without the lid, lashes, or other surrounding parts. —**eyeball to eyeball.** (Slang) Face to face.

eye·brow (IGH-brow) *noun.* The curved line of hair over the eye or the bony arch on which this hair grows.

eye·glass (IGH-glass) *noun.* 1. (Plural) A pair of lenses to help correct poor vision. 2. Any lens in an instrument to which the eye is put. 3. (Rare) A hand-held telescope used by seamen or explorers. **eyeglasses.**

eye·lash (IGH-lash) *noun.* 1. One of the hairs on the rim of the eyelid. 2. (Plural) The fringe of hairs on the rims of the eyelids. **eyelashes.**

eye·let (IGH-lət) *noun.* 1. A small hole, usually placed at the edge of a cloth, through which a lace or string is drawn. 2. A small metal ring placed around such a hole to give greater strength. 3. A small hole (in cloth) that has been decorated with embroidery.

eye·lid (IGH-lid) *noun.* The piece of skin that moves to cover the eye.

eye·piece (IGH-peess) *noun.* The lens or lenses of an optical instrument, such as a telescope or microscope, to which the eye is put for seeing images. **eyepieces.**

eye·sight (IGH-sight) *noun.* 1. Vision; sight; power of seeing: Eyeglasses will improve poor *eyesight.* 2. The area that can be seen by the eye; the range of one's vision: Stay within *eyesight* of the lifeguard.

eye·sore (IGH-sor) *noun.* Any unattractive object; something unpleasant to look at: Junkyards along the major highways are *eyesores* to travelers. **eyesores.**

eye·strain (IGH-strayn) *noun.* A feeling in the eyes of mild pain or discomfort caused by their overuse, incorrect use, or some physical fault.

eye·tooth (IGH-tooth) *noun.* One of the two pointed canine teeth in the upper jaw, lying below the eye. —**eyeteeth** (IGH-teeth) *plural.* —**cut one's eyeteeth.** To get understanding through age and experience. —**give one's eyeteeth for.** To want something very much.

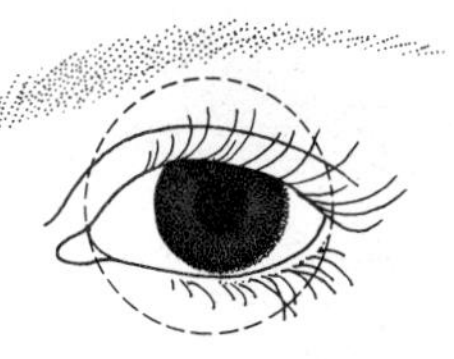
eye

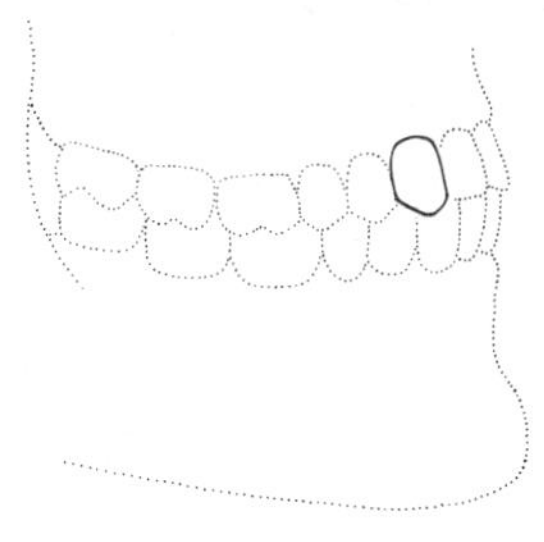
eyetooth

F, f (EF) *noun.* The sixth letter of the English alphabet.

F *abbreviation.* Fahrenheit.

f. *abbreviation.* Female; feminine.

fa (FAH) *noun.* The fourth note up in any major or minor scale in singing.

fa·ble (FAY-bəl) *noun.* 1. A short story, often with animals as characters, that teaches a lesson. 2. A legend or myth. 3. A lie. **fables.**

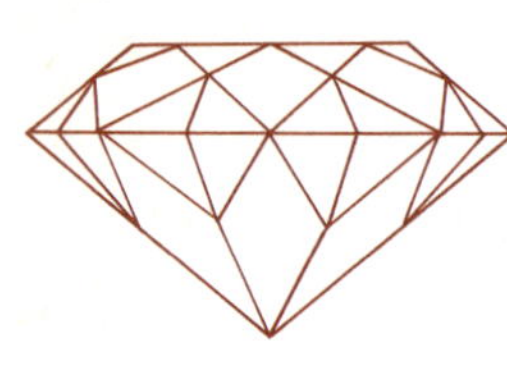

facets

fab·ric (FAB-rik) *noun.* 1. Cloth; woven or knitted material. 2. Basic structure; framework: The Constitution is the *fabric* of our government.

fab·u·lous (FAB-yə-ləss) *adjective.* 1. Almost impossible to believe; incredible. 2. Occurring only in fables or stories; not based on truth. 3. (Informal) Extremely enjoyable; wonderful. —**fabulously** *adverb.*

fa·cade (fə-SAHD) Also **façade** *noun.* 1. The front view or face of a building. 2. Outward appearance: a happy *façade.* **facades.**

face (FAYSS) *noun.* 1. The front of the head from the forehead to the chin and from ear to ear. 2. An insulting, funny, or twisted look on the face: When the teacher wasn't looking, the boy made a *face* at her. 3. The dial of a clock, watch, or similar device. 4. The front side; surface: The *face* of the building was covered with ivy. 5. Reputation: He tried to save *face* by denying that he had broken the window. 6. A side of a crystal, prism, or rock. 7. (Geometry) A side of a solid. —*verb.* 1. To stand opposite; look toward: *Face* the audience when you speak. 2. To have the front towards: The school *faces* a park. 3. To meet head on: Father *faced* a difficult problem. 4. To put a layer of one kind of material on another: The brick house was *faced* with tile. 5. To turn to a different direction: The sergeant ordered the soldiers to *face* left. **faced, facing.** —**on the face of it.** Apparently: *On the face of it,* there is no answer to your question. —**to one's face.** Directly; one to another: He told me *to my face* I was wrong.

fac·et (FASS-it) *noun.* 1. One of the small, polished surfaces of a jewel. 2. View; phase; aspect: One harmful *facet* of modern life is pollution.

fa·cial (FAY-shəl) *adjective.* Of, for, or about the face. —*noun.* A beauty treatment for the face.

fa·cil·i·tate (fə-SIL-ə-tayt) *verb.* To make easier: Taking the bus *facilitates* our getting to school. **facilitated, facilitating.**

fa·cil·i·ty (fə-SIL-ə-tee) *noun.* 1. Ease; lack of difficulty or inconvenience: Marsha does her homework with *facility.* 2. (Often plural) Conveniences; advantages: Dishwashers and freezers are welcome *facilities* for housekeeping. 3. A seemingly effortless manner: Harry plays the piano with such *facility* because he practices for two hours every day. **facilities.**

fact (FAKT) *noun.* 1. Anything that has happened or been done; anything that is really true; truth. 2. (Law) Any deed, act, thought, or event that has actually happened: That the defendant hit the boy is a matter of *fact;* whether he is guilty of a crime is a question of law. —**in fact.** Indeed; really: I will not stay here; *in fact,* I am leaving immediately.

fac·tion (FAK-shən) *noun.* A small group, within a larger one, that is formed because of mutual discontent or dissatisfaction.

fac·tor (FAK-tər) *noun.* 1. One part or element in a situation; one aspect of several that helps to achieve a result: One *factor* leading to the Revolutionary War was unfair taxation. 2. (Math) A number that, when multiplied with another number or numbers, results in a product: The numbers 5 and 3 are *factors* of the product 15. *—verb.* (Math) To find the factors of a number. **factored, factoring.**

fac·to·ry (FAK-tə-ree) *noun.* A building or group of buildings in which things are made. **factories.**

fac·tu·al (FAK-choo-əl) *adjective.* Having to do with facts; actual: a *factual* report. —**factually** *adverb.*

fac·ul·ty (FAK-əl-tee) *noun.* 1. The ability to do a certain thing; talent. 2. An ability of the mind: Memory, reason, and thought are human *faculties.* 3. One of the natural abilities of the body, such as taste. 4. The teachers and administrators of a school, college, or university. **faculties.**

fad *noun.* Something that is popular for a short time. —**faddish** *adjective.*

fade (FAYD) *verb.* 1. To lose or cause to lose brightness or color; become pale. 2. To become stale, weak, or less fresh. 3. To die away slowly; disappear gradually. **faded, fading.**

Fahr·en·heit (FAHR-ən-hight) *adjective.* Referring to a scale of measuring temperature in which the freezing point of pure water is 32° and the boiling point is 212°.

fail (FAYL) *verb.* 1. To be unsuccessful. 2. To do unsatisfactory work, as in school. 3. To omit; to neglect: Tom *failed* to arrive on time. 4. To be of little or no help; disappoint. 5. To become weak; grow less healthy. 6. To be unable to pay one's debts; go bankrupt. 7. To refuse to pass a student. 8. To be lacking: The military supplies *failed* at Valley Forge. **failed, failing.** —**without fail.** For certain.

fail·ure (FAYL-yər) *noun.* 1. Act of failing. 2. Omission; act of neglect. 3. Falling short, not being enough: *failure* of the wheat crop. 4. Growing less strong or active: *failure* of pulse. 5. Bankruptcy; inability to pay debts. 6. An unsuccessful person, thing, or event. **failures.**

faint (FAYNT) *verb.* To become unconscious, usually for a short time; swoon. **fainted, fainting.** *—noun.* State of being unconscious, usually for a short time; a swoon. *—adjective.* 1. Feeling dizzy; ready to swoon. 2. Dim; not bright, clear, or strong: A *faint* light came through the purple drapes. 3. Half-hearted; without enthusiasm: The cafeteria clean-up committee received *faint* cooperation from the students. 4. Shy; not bold: "*Faint* heart ne'er won fair lady!" (Cervantes). **fainter, faintest.** —**faintly** *adverb.*

faint-heart·ed (FAYNT-hahr-tid) *adjective.* Not brave; timid. **faint-heartedly** *adverb.*

fair *adjective.* 1. Treating everyone alike; not favoring one or the other. 2. Proper; according to the rules. 3. Good but not outstanding. 4. Bright and clear; sunny: *fair* weather. 5. Light-colored (of a person); blond. 6. Beautiful; attractive; lovely. **fairer, fairest.** *—noun.* 1. A show of farm animals and products entered in competition for prizes. 2. An exhibit of manufactured products (machines, tools, or equipment). 3. An exhibit and sale of products, often for charity, as a book *fair.* —**fair** or **fairly** *adverb.* —**fair and square.** (Informal) Just; honest: Our teacher is *fair and square;* she doesn't play favorites.

falcon

fair·ground (FAIR-grownd) Also **fairgrounds** *noun.* A location where fairs, carnivals, and similar activities take place.

fairy (FAIR-ee) *noun.* A tiny make-believe creature who can help or hurt humans at will. **fairies.**

fair·y·land (FAIR-ee-land) *noun.* 1. In stories, the place where fairies live. 2. An enchanting and beautiful place: The sun on the snow made a *fairyland* of our backyard.

faith (FAYTH) *noun.* 1. A strong belief or trust in someone or something: Parents usually have *faith* in their children. 2. A religion; religious belief: Cathy is of the Christian *faith;* Sam is of the Jewish *faith.* 3. A belief in a Supreme Being or God. 4. Any belief which cannot be proved. —**good faith.** Honesty; sincerity. —**keep the faith.** (Informal) Be true to an ideal or cause.

faith·ful (FAYTH-fəl) *adjective.* 1. Loyal; reliable: Robinson Crusoe had a *faithful* friend in Friday. 2. Accurate; true to the original: Mark gave a *faithful* account of the class trip. —*noun.* 1. People who believe in a specific religion: "O Come, All Ye *Faithful.*" 2. People loyal to a group: Only the *faithful* came to the meeting that stormy night. —**faithfully** *adverb.*

faith·less (FAYTH-liss) *adjective.* 1. Disloyal: Gossiping about a friend is a *faithless* act. 2. Unreliable; not trustworthy. 3. Lacking faith in a religion or a leader. —**faithlessly** *adverb.*

fake (FAYK) *verb.* 1. To pretend to have (a condition): Jean *faked* a headache to escape the test. 2. To copy and try to pass off as original or genuine: Dishonest artists *fake* paintings of great artists and sell them for high prices. **faked, faking.** —*noun.* 1. Anything made to seem other than what it is; a fraud; forgery. 2. A person who fakes.

fal·con (FAL-kən or FAWL-kən) *noun.* 1. A small bird, related to the hawk, that hunts and kills other animals for food. 2. A hawk trained to hunt other birds and small animals.

fall (FAWL) *verb.* 1. To drop freely: Leaves *fall* in the autumn. 2. To drop suddenly from a standing position: Tie your shoelaces or you will *fall.* 3. To fail, be defeated: The government will *fall* if the army *falls.* 4. To be wounded or killed. 5. To collapse: The shed will *fall* if the wind continues to blow. 6. To hang down: Ann's hair *falls* to her waist. 7. To come about; occur: Halloween *falls* on a Friday this year. 8. To be less in amount or value: During the night the temperature *falls* 10 degrees. 9. To lose liveliness: Did you see his face *fall* when the teacher said she overheard his remark? 10. To slope downward. 11. To give in to temptation. 12. To come to rest: Her eyes always seem to *fall* on her neighbor's paper during a test. **fell** (FEL), **fallen, falling.** —*noun.* 1. A sudden drop from a standing position. 2. The amount that comes down within a given period: The weather bureau measures the *fall* of rain. 3. The distance anything drops. 4. (Usually plural) A waterfall. 5. Autumn. 6. A downward slope. 7. A surrender: the *fall* of Germany at the end of World War II. 8. A lessening in value or amount. 9. A giving in to temptation: "In Adam's *fall,* we sinned all." (*New England Primer*). 10. A loss of power or high position. —**fall asleep.** To go to sleep. —**fall for.** (Informal) 1. To be tricked by. 2. To be attracted to; come to love. —**fall in with.** To become part of (a group). —**fall out.** 1. To end a friendship. 2. (Military) To leave one's place in a line: The sergeant ordered the work detail to *fall out.* —**fall short.** To be less than needed or desired. —**fall through.** To fail to happen.

fal·la·cy (FAL-ə-see) *noun.* 1. A false idea or belief: Men once believed in the *fallacy* of a flat earth. 2. Unsound reasoning: The argument that all men out of work are lazy is a *fallacy;* some may be too sick to work. **fallacies.**

falling star. A piece of material from outer space that burns when it enters the earth's atmosphere; a meteor.

fall·out (FAWL-owt) *noun.* 1. The extremely fine, often radioactive, particles of material in the air after an atomic explosion. 2. The fall of this material to the earth.

false (FAWLSS) *adjective.* 1. Untrue; incorrect. 2. Not loyal: a *false* friend. 3. Not genuine; artificial: *false* teeth. —**falsely** *adverb.*

false·hood (FAWLSS-hud) *noun.* 1. A lie. 2. The act of telling lies: No one will believe Mark because of his reputation for *falsehood.*

fal·si·fy (FAWL-sə-figh) *verb.* 1. To make a statement that is not true. 2. To change (an official paper or document) in order to make something appear to be what it is not: The boy *falsified* his test grade by changing it from an F to an A. **falsified, falsifying.** —**falsification** *noun.*

fal·ter (FAWL-tər) *verb.* 1. To move unsteadily; to stumble. 2. To talk in a broken manner; to stammer. 3. To hesitate. **faltered, faltering.**

fame (FAYM) *noun.* The state of being known far and wide, especially of having a good reputation: Columbus gained his *fame* by discovering the New World.

fa·mil·iar (fə-MIL-yər) *adjective.* 1. Well-known; common; met with or seen every day. 2. Having great knowledge of; understanding thoroughly: Please be *familiar* with chapter three; I will test you on it Friday. 3. Informal; friendly. —**familiarly** *adverb*

fam·i·ly (FAM-ə-lee or FAM-lee) *noun.* 1. Parents and their children. 2. All the children of the same parents: Mother and Father raised a *family* of five. 3. All close relatives; kin. 4. The descendants of a common ancestor: The Roosevelt *family* is well-known in American politics. 5. Any group of plants or animals that are related: The onion is a member of the lily *family.* **families.**

family room. A room of a house set aside for playing, watching TV, or similar activities; a playroom.

fam·ine (FAM-ən) *noun.* 1. A shortage of food; a period of widespread hunger. 2. An extreme lack or great shortage of anything. **famines.**

fam·ish (FAM-ish) *verb.* To be or make extremely or painfully hungry; starve. **famished, famishing.** —**famished** *adjective.*

fa·mous (FAY-məss) *adjective.* Known far and wide: Paul Revere's ride is a *famous* event. —**famously** *adverb.*

[1]**fan** *noun.* 1. A small device made of paper, silk, or wood and waved with the hand to produce a breeze. 2. A machine used to cool or circulate air. —*verb.* 1. To stir up the air; cool by moving air; blow upon: Mother *fanned* the air in the kitchen to get rid of the smoke. 2. To spread out in the shape of a fan. 3. (Baseball) To strike out the player at bat; be struck out by the pitcher. **fanned, fanning.**

[1]fan

[2]**fan** *noun.* Anyone keenly interested in or greatly enthusiastic about a particular subject or famous person.

fa·nat·ic (fə-NAT-ik) *noun.* Someone who goes to unreasonable extremes in beliefs, feelings, and actions about a given subject: Bonnie is such a *fanatic* about neatness that she will not hand in a paper with an erasure on it. —*adjective.* Also **fanatical.** Overly enthusiastic; extremely unreasonable. —**fanatically** *adverb.*

fan·ci·ful (FAN-si-fəl) *adjective.* 1. Imaginary; created by fancy: Aesop's fables are *fanciful* stories. 2. Having or showing imagination: Mother admired the children's *fanciful* drawings. —**fancifully** *adverb.* —**fancifulness** *noun.*

fan·cy (FAN-see) *noun.* 1. The ability to make mental pictures; imagination. 2. Mental picture or image: Mickey Mouse and Donald Duck were *fancies* of Walt Disney. 3. A whim; preference: My sister has a *fancy* for clanging bracelets. **fancies.** —*adjective.* 1. Of the highest quality: *Fancy* fruits and vegetables cost more than ordinary ones. 2. Elaborate: Mother makes a *fancy* dinner on holidays. **fancier, fanciest.** —*verb.* 1. To imagine: Can you *fancy* yourself as an astronaut? 2. To think something without being sure of it: I *fancy* that my father will let me go, but I will have to ask to make certain. 3. To like; be fond of: Aunt Jennie *fancies* tall flowers in her garden. **fancied, fancying.** —*interjection.* A term used to show slight surprise, usually used with *that: Fancy* that!

fang *noun.* A sharp, pointed tooth of an animal, especially the hollow tooth through which a snake shoots poison or the long tooth used for attacking and tearing by meat-eating animals.

fan·tas·tic (fan-TASS-tik) Also **fantastical** *adjective.* 1. Very strange or odd, as in size, shape, color: The art class made *fantastic* animals out of papier-mâché. 2. Highly imaginative: Mark told a *fantastic* tale of seeing pirates burying treasure chests. 3. (Slang) Marvelous; extremely pleasant. —**fantastically** *adverb.*

fan·ta·sy (FAN-tə-see) *noun.* 1. Wild imagination: Using his *fantasy,* the child drew all sorts of never-before-seen animals. 2. A mental picture; a daydream. **fantasies.**

far (FAHR) *adjective.* 1. Distant; remote: a *far* country; the *Far* East. 2. Of two things, the one more distant: the *far* side of the moon. —*adverb.* 1. At a distance; a long way. 2. Very much; considerably: This is *far* more money than I need. 3. To a specific distance in space or time: I will go only this *far* with you. **farther, farthest** (for space that can be measured: one mile *farther;* the *farthest* city). Also **further, furthest** (for quantities that can't be measured exactly: *further* consideration; *furthest* from my mind). —**far and away.** By a large margin: Jim is *far and away* a better skater than Tom. —**far and wide.** All around, all over: The news of the robbery spread *far and wide* by nightfall. —**by far.** By a wide margin: Mother's cookies are better *by far* than the ones bought in the store. —**so far, so good.** Good up to the present time.

far·a·way (FAHR-ə-way) *adjective.* 1. A long way off; remote. 2. Dreamlike; lost in thought: Peggy sat with a *faraway* look on her face, not hearing the noise in the room.

farce (FAHRSS) *noun.* 1. A ridiculous pretense. 2. (Theater) A comedy that is made up of exaggerated or ridiculous events. **farces.**

fare (FAIR) *noun.* 1. The amount of money charged a passenger on a bus, train, airplane, or boat. 2. The person who pays to ride on a bus, train, airplane, or boat: The taxi driver had only two *fares* today. 3. Food and drink: restaurant *fare.* **fares.** —*verb.* To get along (in a particular way): Our team *fared* well. **fared, faring.**

fare·well (fair-WEL) *interjection.* Good-by; may everything go well with you. —*noun.* Words spoken when leaving another, wishing him good luck. —*adjective.* Final; parting: Mary gave Grandmother a *farewell* kiss.

far-fetched (FAHR-FECHT) *adjective.* Not very likely; hard to believe.

farm (FAHRM) *noun.* 1. A section of land used for growing crops or raising animals. 2. A baseball team in a minor league. —*verb.* 1. To use land for growing crops or raising animals. 2. To till the soil: Land that is not *farmed* will go to weeds. 3. To give out (work) to another person: Because he is so busy, the contractor *farms* out the plumbing jobs in the houses he builds. **farmed, farming.**

farm·er (FAHR-mər) *noun.* One who operates or works on a farm.

far-off (FAHR-AWF or FAHR-AHF) *adjective.* At a great distance in space or time; faraway: Marco Polo traveled from Italy to *far-off* China.

far-out (FAHR-OWT) *adjective.* (Informal) Very unusual or out of the ordinary.

far-sight·ed (FAHR-SIGH-tid) *adjective.* 1. Able to see things in the distance better than those close at hand: Father is *far-sighted* and needs glasses for reading. 2. Able to think about things in the future with good judgment: Tom was *far-sighted* to wear his rubbers since it looked like rain. —**far-sightedly** *adverb.* —**far-sightedness** *noun.*

far·ther (FAHR-thər) *adjective* and *adverb.* See **far.**

far·thest (FAHR-thist) *adjective* and *adverb.* See **far.**

fas·ci·nate (FASS-ə-nayt) *verb.* 1. To hold the interest of (someone); captivate or charm. 2. To awe or make powerless: The car headlights so *fascinated* the deer that it was unable to run. **fascinated, fascinating.**

fas·ci·na·tion (fass-ə-NAY-shən) *noun.* Very strong attraction: Baseball holds a *fascination* for many boys.

fas·cism (FASH-iz-əm) *noun.* 1. A system of government (often ruled by a dictator) in which the state has complete power over business, labor, and individuals. 2. [Capital F] The Italian government under Mussolini from 1922 until 1943.

fash·ion (FASH-ən) *noun.* 1. A style or custom of the day: In Grandma's day it was the *fashion* to go for a Sunday stroll. 2. The manner in which a thing is done or made. —*verb.* To form, make, or shape: Sue *fashioned* her Halloween costume from odds and ends of old clothes. **fashioned, fashioning.** —**after a fashion.** Fairly well; not too badly: Bill can ski *after a fashion.*

fash·ion·a·ble (FASH-ən-ə-bəl) *adjective.* Stylish; in current use. —**fashionably** *adverb.*

fast *adjective.* 1. Quick or swift. 2. Ahead of the actual time: Jane's watch was five minutes *fast.* 3. Firm or secure: Tom and Joe remained *fast* friends even after Tom moved to another town. 4. Firmly set: If the colors in cloth are *fast,* they will not run when washed. **faster, fastest.** —*adverb.* 1. Quickly or swiftly. 2. Firmly or securely. 3. Deeply: *fast* asleep. —*verb.* To go without food. **fasted, fasting.** —*noun.* The act or time of going without food.

fas·ten (FASS-n) *verb.* 1. To lock or close; make secure. 2. To attach: The teacher *fastened* the drawings to the school bulletin board. 3. To fix or direct with attention: All eyes were *fastened* on the huge birthday cake. **fastened, fastening.**

fas·ten·ing (FASS-n-ing) *noun.* A device used to secure something.

fas·tid·i·ous (fa-STID-ee-əss) *adjective.* 1. Very careful of details. 2. Hard to please; overcritical: a *fastidious* eater. —**fastidiously** *adverb.*

fat *noun.* A greasy substance that develops in the tissues of animals and in the seeds of plants. —*adjective.* 1. Overly plump. 2. Full or abundant. **fatter, fattest.**

farm

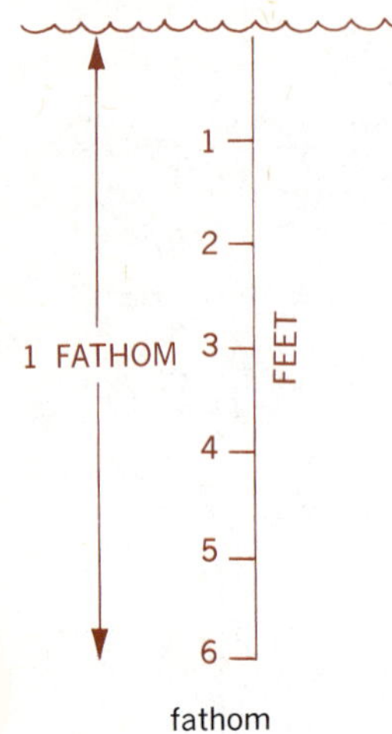

fathom

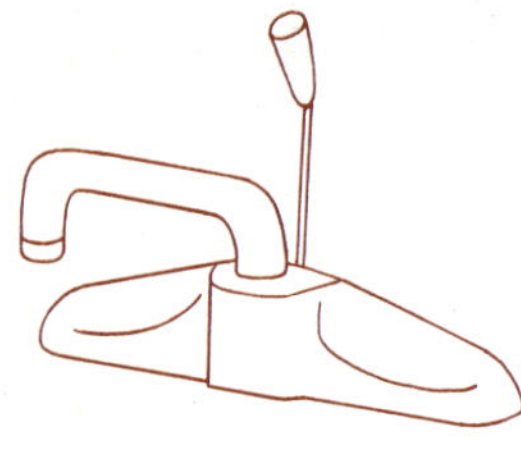
faucet

faun

fa·tal (FAYT-l) *adjective.* 1. Causing death: a *fatal* accident. 2. Causing ruin: The fire was *fatal* to our lumber business. 3. Determining a result: The *fatal* day will come when we must take the math test. —**fatally** *adverb.*

fa·tal·i·ty (fay-TAL-ə-tee) *noun.* A death resulting from an accident or other occurrence. **fatalities.**

fate (FAYT) *noun.* 1. A force believed to determine the course of all happenings: John believed *fate* would bring him wealth, but Bill believed in hard work. 2. Unavoidable result or outcome: It was Jim's *fate* to be elected captain.

fate·ful (FAYT-fəl) *adjective.* 1. Controlled by fate. 2. Determining an important event: The *fateful* decision of the jury would decide his whole future. 3. Causing death or disaster. —**fatefully** *adverb.*

fa·ther (FAH-thər) *noun.* 1. The male parent of a child. 2. [Capital F] God: "Our *Father* Who art in Heaven." (Lord's Prayer). 3. A priest. 4. A male ancestor. 5. A person who founds or starts something. 6. (Plural) Influential or important men; leaders: the town *fathers.* —*verb.* 1. To care for another as one's own child. 2. To create or originate: Alexander Graham Bell *fathered* the telephone. **fathered, fathering.**

father-in-law. The father of one's wife or husband. —**fathers-in-law** *plural.*

fa·ther·land (FAH-thər-land) *noun.* The country where one was born or from which one's family came.

fa·ther·ly (FAH-thər-lee) *adjective.* Typical of or acting like a father: The teacher gave Tom some *fatherly* advice.

fa·thom (FATH-əm) *noun.* A measure of length of six feet, usually applied to the depth of water: "Full *fathom* five thy father lies." (Shakespeare). —*verb.* 1. To measure the depth of water. 2. To get to the bottom of or understand: Mom couldn't *fathom* the dog's strange behavior. **fathomed, fathoming.**

fa·tigue (fə-TEEG) *noun.* 1. Weariness; exhaustion: By the end of the hard day *fatigue* overcame her. 2. (Plural) Clothes used by soldiers for hard physical work. **fatigues.** —*verb.* To make exhausted, tired, or weary. **fatigued, fatiguing.**

fat·ten (FAT-n) *verb.* 1. To make or become fat. 2. To increase or enlarge the size or amount of. **fattened, fattening.**

fau·cet (FAW-sit) *noun.* A device that controls the flow of liquid from a pipe, as a water *faucet.*

fault (FAWLT) *noun.* 1. A weakness or imperfection: "Every man has his *fault.* . . ." (Shakespeare). 2. A mistake. 3. Responsibility for something that goes wrong. 4. (Geology) A break in the earth's crust, with the rock formation on one side of the break being pushed out of place. —**at fault.** Deserving blame; guilty: Elaine didn't water her plant and was *at fault* when it died. —**find fault.** To look for and complain about faults.

fault·less (FAWLT-liss) *adjective.* Without a fault; perfect. —**faultlessly** *adverb.*

faul·ty (FAWL-tee) *adjective.* Having imperfections. —**faultily** *adverb.*

faun (FAWN) *noun.* In Greek and Roman legend, a god of the countryside who looked partly like a man but had the horns, ears, tail, and sometimes legs of a goat.

fau·na (FAW-nə) *noun.* The animal life of a particular area or time: the *fauna* of Africa. —**faunas** or **faunae** (FAW-nee) *plural.*

fa·vor (FAY-vər) *noun.* 1. An act of kindness. 2. Liking or good will: Our teacher showed us her *favor* by smiling. 3. A small gift: There was a *favor* beside each child's plate. —*verb.* 1. To oblige; show kindness to. 2. To prefer: The family *favored* the mountains for their vacation. 3. To show more preference to than is fair: Bill gets away with anything because the teacher *favors* him. 4. To look like or resemble: Jill *favors* her father's side of the family. **favored, favoring.** **—in one's favor.** To one's advantage.

fa·vor·a·ble (FAY-vər-ə-bəl or FAYV-rə-bəl) *adjective.* 1. Showing approval: Our teacher was *favorable* to our picnic plans. 2. Helpful; probably good: We decided to go to the beach if the weather was *favorable.* **—favorably** *adverb.*

fa·vor·ite (FAY-vər-it or FAYV-rit) *noun.* 1. Any thing or person that one likes best. 2. A contestant or team seen as most likely to win.

[1]**fawn** *noun.* 1. A deer during its first year. 2. (Also *adjective*) A yellowish or reddish brown.

[2]**fawn** *verb.* 1. To show affection or fondness. 2. To bow and scrape for favors. **fawned, fawning.**

FBI *abbreviation.* Federal Bureau of Investigation.

fear (FIHR) *noun.* The emotion of being afraid or frightened. *—verb.* 1. To be afraid of or frightened. 2. To be worried. **feared, fearing.**

fear·ful (FIHR-fəl) *adjective.* 1. Frightening, dreadful, horrible. 2. Feeling fear or being scared: Maria was *fearful* of being lost in the woods. 3. Being worried or uneasy. **—fearfully** *adverb.*

fear·less (FIHR-liss) *adjective.* Without fear of anything; brave. **—fearlessly** *adverb.*

fea·si·ble (FEE-zə-bəl) *adjective.* Capable of being carried out or being successful: Our plan to have a ball team became *feasible* when we were given a bat and ball. **—feasibility** *noun.* **—feasibly** *adverb.*

feast (FEEST) *noun.* 1. A fancy meal with much to eat, usually attended by many people. 2. A religious holiday, usually in memory of a particular person or event: March 17 is the *feast* of St. Patrick. *—verb.* 1. To feed well; entertain at a feast. 2. To eat at a feast. 3. To enjoy or take pleasure in: We *feasted* our eyes on the delicious birthday cake. **feasted, feasting.**

feat (FEET) *noun.* An outstanding act or achievement requiring skill, strength, or courage.

feath·er (FETH-ər) *noun.* 1. One of the light growths that cover birds. 2. Anything like a feather. 3. Type or kind: "Birds of a *feather* will gather together." (R. Burton). *—verb.* 1. To grow or cover with feathers. 2. To dress or decorate. 3. To cut hair by thinning and tapering. **feathered, feathering.** **—a feather in one's cap.** Unusual honor or distinction: Scoring the winning touchdown was *a feather in* Bill's *cap.* **—feather one's nest.** To put aside or collect money, usually unfairly.

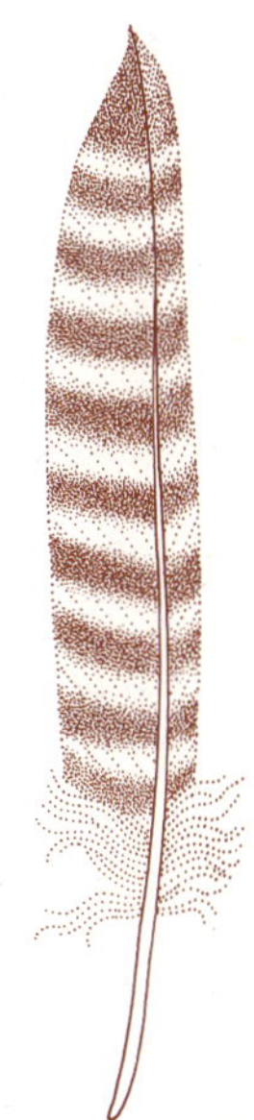

feather

feath·er·y (FETH-ər-ee) *adjective.* 1. Like feathers in shape or lightness. 2. Covered with feathers.

fea·ture (FEE-chər) *noun.* 1. A part of the face, such as the eyes, ears, or nose. 2. An outstanding part, aspect, or quality: Paul's best *feature* is his honesty. 3. The main movie or movies: a double *feature.* *—verb.* To display or emphasize. **featured, featuring.**

[1]fawn

Feb·ru·ar·y (FEB-roo-ehr-ee or FEB-yoo-ehr-ee) *noun.* The second month of the year: February usually has 28 days, but in leap years (years that have 366 days) it has 29. **—Feb.** *abbreviation.*

fed *verb.* *See* **feed.**

fed·er·al (FED-ər-əl) *adjective.* 1. Of or referring to a government made up of self-governing states or political units that recognize a central authority. 2. Of or referring to the central authority of such a government: *federal* law. 3. [Capital F] Of or referring to the central government of the U.S. **—federally** *adverb.*

fed·er·al·ism (FED-ər-ə-liz-əm) *noun.* The idea or the system of government made up of individual, self-governing states that recognize a central authority.

fed·er·a·tion (fed-ə-RAY-shən) *noun.* 1. A league of nations or states formed by mutual agreement for protection or other purposes with each having the power to govern its own affairs. 2. An association of groups or clubs pursuing similar goals: the *Federation* of Women's Clubs.

fee *noun.* A sum of money charged for services: doctor's *fee.* **fees.**

fee·ble (FEE-bəl) *adjective.* Weak: Tess was *feeble* after being sick. **feebler, feeblest.** —**feebly** *adverb.*

fee·ble-mind·ed (fee-bəl-MIGHN-did) *adjective.* Having less than normal intelligence.

feed *verb.* 1. To provide food for or to. 2. To give energy or strength to: Don't *feed* his anger by continuing to misbehave. 3. To eat: The horses *feed* in the pasture. **fed, feeding.** —*noun.* Food for animals: The baby chicks have a *feed* of mash. —**be fed up.** To be discouraged, angered; lose patience.

feel *verb.* 1. To examine or learn through the sense of touch: Father *felt* the paint to see if it was dry. 2. To have or experience emotion: Jill *feels* sad when she sees stray dogs. 3. To believe or think: The teacher *feels* sure the pageant will be a success. 4. To be aware of (a sensation): Father *feels* a pain in his shoulder when he moves his arm. 5. To search by touching: Jane *felt* for the light switch in the dark room. 6. To produce sensation: Snow *feels* cold when we touch it. **felt, feeling.**

feel·er (FEE-lər) *noun.* 1. One of an insect's antennae or an animal's whiskers that is used to feel with. 2. A cautious question or statement made in an effort to find out how others feel: Bill put out a *feeler* to see if he had a chance of using the family car.

feel·ing (FEE-ling) *noun.* 1. An emotion: The whole family had a happy *feeling* about the vacation plans. 2. A sensation or awareness: She had a *feeling* of coldness from the wind. 3. An opinion: Mother had a *feeling* that Father would be late for dinner. 4. Sympathy; tenderness. 5. (Plural) Sensitivity about oneself: You hurt my *feelings.*

feet *noun. See* **foot.**

feign (FAYN) *verb.* To pretend: Jim *feigned* sickness. **feigned, feigning.**

feint (FAYNT) *noun.* 1. A pretense intended to deceive: The quarterback made a *feint* of passing the ball but ran with it instead. —*verb.* To make a feint. **feinted, feinting.**

feld·spar (FELD-spahr or FEL-spahr) *noun.* A common mineral forming part of crystalline rocks and used in making porcelain and glass.

fe·line (FEE-lighn) *noun.* A member of the cat family: A jaguar is a *feline.* **felines.**

fell (FEL) *verb.* To cut down: *fell* a tree. **felled, felling.** *See also* **fall.**

fel·low (FEL-oh) *noun.* 1. A man or a boy. 2. A person of the same rank or position; an equal: They were *fellows* in the same boat. 3. Either of two things that match; the mate. —*adjective.* Being in the same group: They were *fellow* classmates.

fel·low·ship (FEL-oh-ship) *noun.* 1. Comradeship or friendliness. 2. A scholarship or grant of money for advanced study.

fel·o·ny (FEL-ə-nee) *noun.* A serious crime. **felonies.**

felt *noun.* A smooth cloth made of pressed wool, hair, or fur. —*verb. See* **feel.**

fe·male (FEE-mayl) *noun.* A woman or girl; any animal that can bear young. —*adjective.* 1. Pertaining to women or girls. 2. Relating to the sex that bears young or produces eggs: *Female* cattle are called cows.

fem·i·nine (FEM-ə-nin) *adjective.* 1. Pertaining to the female sex. 2. Having qualities that are thought to be womanly.

fen *noun.* A swamp or marsh.

fence (FENSS) *noun.* 1. A structure of wood, metal, or other material used to separate or enclose areas. 2. A person who buys and sells stolen goods. —*verb.* 1. To build a fence around: Bill's father *fenced* in the hogs. 2. To fight with swords. 3. To buy and sell stolen goods. **fenced, fencing.** —**on the fence.** (Informal) Undecided; not yet having chosen.

fenc·ing (FEN-sing) *noun.* 1. The art or sport of fighting with swords. 2. Any material, such as wood or wire, used to build a fence.

fend·er (FEN-dər) *noun.* 1. The curved metal guard placed over the wheel of a car or other vehicle to prevent splashing. 2. A guard placed in front of a fireplace to keep coals or burning logs from falling out.

fer·ment (fər-MENT) *verb.* To cause or undergo a gradual chemical change, such as the changing of sugar to alcohol: The cider *fermented* and became vinegar. **fermented, fermenting.** —(FER-ment) *noun.* 1. A substance, such as yeast, that causes fermentation. 2. A state of excited activity or trouble.

fer·men·ta·tion (fer-men-TAY-shən) *noun.* Any of a number of gradual chemical changes caused by enzymes: The process of *fermentation* is used to make cheese, wine, and vinegar.

fern *noun.* A flowerless leafy plant with roots and stems: *Ferns* reproduce by spores.

fe·ro·cious (fə-ROH-shəss) *adjective.* Savage and fierce. —**ferociously** *adverb.* —**ferocity** (fə-ROSS-ə-tee) *noun.*

fer·ret (FEHR-it) *noun.* 1. A yellowish-brown weasel of Western United States that hunts prairie dogs. 2. A polecat of Europe related to the weasel and trained to hunt rabbits, rats, and mice. —*verb.* 1. To hunt or track down with a ferret. 2. (Used with *out*) To search for and find. **ferreted, ferreting.**

fer·ry (FEHR-ee) *noun.* 1. A boat that carries people, cargo, and cars over water, usually back and forth over a short distance; a ferryboat. 2. The dock or place where a ferryboat is loaded. 3. Any means of regular transportation back and forth over short distances. **ferries.** —*verb.* 1. To carry from one place to another, either over water or through the air. 2. To ride on a ferry. **ferried, ferrying.**

fer·tile (FERT-l) *adjective.* 1. Producing abundantly: The *fertile* apple tree bore bushels of fruit. 2. Rich; fruitful: *fertile* soil. 3. Inventive: a *fertile* mind. —**fertilely** *adverb.* —**fertility** (fər-TIL-ə-tee) *noun.*

fer·ti·lize (FERT-l-ighz) *verb.* 1. To make (soil) able to produce more by adding organic or chemical material to it. 2. (Of a male cell) To unite with a female cell, causing or starting biological reproduction. **fertilized, fertilizing.** —**fertilization** (fert-l-ə-ZAY-shən) *noun.*

fer·ti·liz·er (FERT-l-igh-zər) *noun.* Manure, a chemical compound, or anything spread on or worked into the soil to make it produce more richly.

fer·vent (FER-vənt) *adjective.* Having great warmth, strong emotion, or passion. —**fervently** *adverb.*

fer·vor (FER-vər) *noun.* Strong feeling or great warmth; ardor, passion.

fes·ter (FESS-tər) *verb.* 1. To form, fill with, or emit pus. 2. To cause irritation. **festered, festering.**

fes·ti·val (FESS-tə-vəl) *noun.* 1. A special occasion or time marked by feasting, celebration, and rejoicing. 2. A group of related events, exhibits, entertainments: an arts and crafts *festival;* a film *festival.*

fes·tive (FESS-tiv) *adjective.* Happy or joyous. —**festively** *adverb.*

fence

ferret

fencing

fes·tiv·i·ty (fess-TIV-ə-tee) *noun.* 1. A joyous party or festive occasion. 2. The joyousness and happiness of a festival or party. 3. (Plural) The whole course of a party: The *festivities* were marked by song and laughter. **festivities.**

fez

fes·toon (fess-TOON) *noun.* A rope of leaves, flowers, or other decorative material hung in a loop. —*verb.* To decorate with festoons. **festooned, festooning.**

fetch (FECH) *verb.* 1. To go and get: *fetch* a pail of water. 2. (Informal) Get (a price). **fetched, fetching.**

fetch·ing (FECH-ing) *adjective.* (Informal) Attractive; charming. —**fetchingly** *adverb.*

fete (FAYT) Also **fête** *noun.* A festival or grand party. —*verb.* To honor with entertainment. **feted, feting.**

fet·ter (FET-ər) *noun.* (Often plural) 1. A chain or shackle used to make movement of the feet difficult. 2. Something which holds one back. —*verb.* 1. To put fetters on. 2. To hold back or restrain: His progress was *fettered* by his ignorance. **fettered, fettering.**

fe·tus (FEE-təss) Also **foetus** *noun.* An unborn but partially developed offspring. **fetuses.**

feud (FYOOD) *noun.* A bitter, long-standing quarrel. —*verb.* To carry on a feud. **feuded, feuding.**

feu·dal·ism (FYOOD-l-iz-əm) *noun.* The political and economic organization in Europe during the Middle Ages whereby lords received their land (fief) from a king and protected the serfs, or farmers, who worked the land. —**feudal** *adjective.* —**feudally** *adverb.*

fe·ver (FEE-vər) *noun.* 1. A higher than usual body temperature, generally caused by sickness. 2. Any disease that causes a rise in temperature: a tropical *fever.* 3. An excited condition. —**feverish** *adjective.* —**feverishly** *adverb.*

few (FYOO) *adjective.* Made up of a small number. **fewer, fewest.** —*noun.* A small number.

fez *noun.* A man's hat of Turkish origin, usually made of red felt. —**fezzes** (FEZ-iz) *plural.*

fi·an·cé (fee-ahn-SAY or fee-AHN-say) *noun.* A man engaged to marry.

fi·an·cée (fee-ahn-SAY or fee-AHN-say) *noun.* A woman engaged to marry.

fi·as·co (fee-ASS-koh) *noun.* A complete and utter failure. —**fiascoes** or **fiascos** *plural.*

fib *noun.* A lie about an unimportant thing: The movie actress told a *fib* about her age. —*verb.* To tell a fib. **fibbed, fibbing.** —**fibber** *noun.*

fi·ber (FIGH-bər) *noun.* 1. A long, thin piece of a substance; a strand: Threads in cloth are *fibers.* 2. Inner strength; character: Abraham Lincoln had strong moral *fiber.*

fick·le (FIK-əl) *adjective.* Changing or inconstant; not dependable.

fic·tion (FIK-shən) *noun.* 1. A story or novel in which the events are made up by the author. 2. Something made up to deceive or impress: It is pure *fiction* that Jack's uncle is an astronaut. —**fictional** *adjective.* —**fictionally** *adverb.*

fic·ti·tious (fik-TISH-əss) *adjective.* Like fiction; not real or true. —**fictitiously** *adverb.*

fid·dle (FID-l) *noun.* (Informal) A violin. —*verb.* 1. To play a violin. 2. To behave in an aimless and restless fashion. **fiddled, fiddling.**

fi·del·i·ty (fi-DEL-ə-tee or figh-DEL-ə-tee) *noun.* 1. Faithfulness or loyalty. 2. Truthfulness; accuracy.

fidg·et (FIJ-it) *verb.* To move restlessly and nervously. **fidgeted, fidgeting.** —**fidgety** *adjective.*

fief (FEEF) *noun.* A feudal estate.

field (FEELD) *noun.* 1. Flat, open land, such as a meadow or a place for growing crops. 2. A place, generally large and flat, reserved for a special purpose: a football *field.* 3. Scope or extent: *field* of vision. 4. An area of study or activity: the *field* of education. 5. (Plural) A broad region with mineral resources: the oil *fields* of the Near East. 6. The place of a battle. 7. A background or area on which something is shown: On the U.S. flag, white stars are set on a *field* of blue. —*verb.* 1. (Sports) To catch or capture (a ball). 2. To be able to meet (a challenge, question, or verbal attack): Steve *fielded* all his opponents' objections. **fielded, fielding.**

field trip. A trip by a group to see something firsthand.

fiend (FEEND) *noun.* 1. A demon: Pagans believed that *fiends* could torment them. 2. An evil, cruel person. 3. A person consumed or controlled by any interest: The dope *fiend* stole to get drugs. —**fiendish** *adjective.* —**fiendishly** *adverb.*

fierce (FIHRSS) *adjective.* 1. Savage or wild. 2. Violent or strong: a *fierce* scolding. **fiercer, fiercest.** —**fiercely** *adverb.*

fier·y (FIGHR-ee) *adjective.* 1. Made of or having fire. 2. Like fire in color: *fiery* red hair. 3. Easily excited: a *fiery* temper. 4. Extremely hot. 5. (Of foods or drinks) Giving a burning sensation: The highly spiced food was *fiery.* **fierier, fieriest.** —**fierily** *adverb.*

fi·es·ta (fee-ESS-tə) *noun.* A religious holiday in Spanish-speaking countries.

fife (FIGHF) *noun.* An instrument that looks like and is played like a flute.

fif·teen (fif-TEEN) *noun* (and *adjective*). The cardinal number after 14 and before 16; 15.

fif·teenth (fif-TEENTH) *adjective.* Coming after 14th; 15th. —*noun.* One of 15 equal parts.

fifth *adjective.* Coming next after fourth; 5th. —*noun.* 1. One of five equal parts. 2. An amount equal to one-fifth of a gallon or four-fifths of a quart.

fif·ti·eth (FIF-tee-ith) *adjective.* Coming next after 49th; 50th. —*noun.* One of 50 equal parts.

fif·ty (FIF-tee) *noun* (and *adjective*). The cardinal number after 49 and before 51; 50. **fifties.**

fif·ty-fif·ty *adverb* and *adjective.* (Informal) Having two equal parts or equal advantages; divided evenly.

fig *noun.* 1. A small, sweet fruit. 2. The tree on which this fruit grows.

fig. *abbreviation.* 1. Figure. 2. Figurative.

fight *verb.* 1. To oppose with violence or armed force. 2. To quarrel; argue. 3. To struggle: The Alaskan settlers had to *fight* against cold and hunger. **fought, fighting.** —*noun.* 1. A violent physical struggle; an armed conflict. 2. A quarrel.

fig·ur·a·tive (FIG-yər-ə-tiv) *adjective.* Having a meaning other than what would be usually understood: When Dad says that Jim is a chip off the old block, he is using a *figurative* expression. —**figuratively** *adverb.*

fig·ure (FIG-yər) *noun.* 1. The shape of a person's body. 2. A symbol representing a number: "2" and "8" are *figures.* 3. A form; shape: The hunter saw a huge *figure* lumbering through the darkened forest. 4. A person (usually well-known): Stonewall Jackson was a famous *figure* of the Civil War. 5. A drawing, design, or illustration. 6. An amount of money: Dad cannot afford to buy the house at the *figure* asked by the owner. **figures.** —*verb.* 1. To use arithmetic. 2. To have a special role: The heroic soldier *figured* in the capture of the enemy town. 3. (Informal) To reason out something; arrive at a conclusion. **figured, figuring.**

fife

figurehead

file

fig·ure·head (FIG-yər-hed) *noun.* 1. A person having little real power or authority although he has a special title or position. 2. A carved figure once commonly attached to the bow of a sailing ship.

figure of speech. A phrase or expression in which words are used in an unusual way in order to make an idea or image stronger or more dramatic. *See* **metaphor** and **simile.**

fil·a·ment (FIL-ə-mənt) *noun.* A very slender thread of metal or other material: A metal *filament* glows in a light bulb.

filch *verb.* To steal, especially small amounts. **filched, filching.**

file (FIGHL) *verb.* 1. To arrange or put in special order: Our teacher *files* our reports in her desk. 2. To move in a line: The students *filed* out of the school during the fire drill. 3. To record or register: The robbery victim *filed* a complaint at the police station. 4. To grind down or make smooth with a roughened tool: Mary *filed* her fingernails before painting them. **filed, filing.** —*noun.* 1. A cabinet or special place for keeping correspondence or other items in order. 2. An orderly arrangement of papers, letters, or other items. 3. A line of persons or things: a *file* of soldiers. 4. A roughened tool made of metal or other material used to grind down or smooth out surfaces. **files.**

fi·let (fi-LAY or FIL-ay) Also **fillet** *noun.* A cut of meat or fish from which the bones have been removed. —*verb.* To remove the bones from a cut of meat or fish. **fileted, fileting.**

fil·i·al (FIL-ee-əl) *adjective.* Appropriate for a son or daughter: Will's courtesy toward his parents was a sign of his *filial* respect. —**filially** *adverb.*

fil·i·bus·ter (FIL-ə-buhss-tər) *noun.* A lengthy speech or other delaying tactic planned to prevent the passage of a bill or law. —*verb.* To try to prevent the passage of a bill or law by making a lengthy speech or using other means of delay. **filibustered, filibustering.**

fill (FIL) *verb.* 1. To put the greatest amount possible into: The clerk *filled* the container with ice cream. 2. To become full: The glass *filled* with water. 3. To take up all the room in: The students *filled* the gym. 4. To seal or close up: The painter *filled* all the cracks in the plaster before starting to paint. 5. To take over or meet a need for: James *fills* the position of class secretary. **filled, filling** —*noun.* 1. That which makes something full: The workmen used gravel as *fill* to close up the old well. 2. The largest amount that is desired or that can be tolerated: Jill has had her *fill* of her brother's teasing.

fil·let (fi-LAY or FIL-ay) *See* **filet.**

fil·ling (FIL-ing) *noun.* Any material that fills or is used to fill.

fil·ly (FIL-ee) *noun.* A young female horse. **fillies.**

film *noun.* 1. A thin covering or surface: The workman coated the machine with a *film* of grease. 2. A material that reacts to light and is used for taking photographs. 3. A motion picture. —*verb.* To make a motion picture. **filmed, filming.**

film·strip (FILM-strip) *noun.* A strip of photographic film that contains a series of still pictures that can be shown on a screen one at a time.

film·y (FIL-mee) *adjective.* 1. Covered with a film; not clear. 2. Very thin or light: a *filmy* gown. **filmier, filmiest.** —**filmily** *adverb.*

fil·ter (FIL-tər) *noun.* 1. A device or substance used to strain out bits of solid matter from a gas or liquid: Mother emptied lint from the *filter* on the washing machine. 2. A device for adjusting or refining sound, light, gases, or the like. —*verb.* 1. To pass through a device used to strain out particles of solid matter. 2. To move through a screen: The sunlight *filtered* through the thin drapes. **filtered, filtering.**

filth *noun.* 1. Very foul or dirty matter: We cleaned up the *filth* left in the park by careless campers. 2. Indecent talk or material.

filth·y (FIL-thee) *adjective.* 1. Very foul or dirty. 2. Indecent or obscene. **filthier, filthiest.** —**filthily** *adverb.*

fil·tra·tion (fil-TRAY-shən) *noun.* A process used to filter out impurities from a substance.

fin *noun.* 1. A thin winglike or bladelike part of the body of a fish or certain other animals. 2. Any part or structure that resembles the fin of a fish: The rocket's *fins* helped to keep it moving straight. 3. (Slang) A five-dollar bill.

fi·nal (FIGH-nl) *adjective.* 1. Last: The audience left after the *final* melody had been played. 2. Decisive; not to be changed: The principal's decision is *final;* nothing can change it. —*noun.* 1. The last examination of a course of study: Jim passed his chemistry *final* at college. 2. (Usually plural) The last in a series of competitions: Our team is going to play in the *finals* of the basketball tournament. —**finally** *adverb.*

fi·na·le (fi-NAL-ee) *noun.* The last part of a performance, especially of a musical composition.

fi·nance (fi-NANSS or FIGH-nanss) *noun.* 1. The science or process of managing money. 2. (Plural) Savings; funds. **finances.** —*verb.* To supply funds for. **financed, financing.**

fi·nan·cial (fi-NAN-shəl) *adjective.* Of or related to money or the management of funds. —**financially** *adverb.*

fin·an·cier (fin-ən-SIHR or figh-nan-SIHR) *noun.* A person whose job involves the skillful handling of money.

finch *noun.* A small short-billed songbird. **finches.**

find (FYND) *verb.* 1. To come across: Milly seems to *find* friends wherever she goes. 2. To locate by looking for: If you look carefully, you will *find* your glove. 3. To learn: Jane will *find* that her grades will improve if she studies. 4. To decide; declare: The judge said, "I *find* you guilty." **found** (FOWND), **finding.** —*noun.* Something that is discovered.

fine (FIGHN) *adjective.* 1. Delicate; thin; not coarse: a *fine* wire. 2. Of excellent quality. 3. Good of its kind; pleasant: a *fine* meal; *fine* weather. 4. Sensitive; refined: Janet has *fine* tastes in art and music. 5. (Informal) In good health. **finer, finest.** —*noun.* An amount of money paid as a punishment for a wrongful action. —*verb.* To punish for a wrongful act by requiring payment of money. **fined, fining.** —**finely** *adverb.*

fine art. Painting, sculpture, music, and other types of art created for beauty rather than for usefulness.

fin·er·y (FIGH-nə-ree) *noun.* Fine or fancy clothes and accessories. **fineries.**

fin·ger (FING-gər) *noun.* 1. One of the extensions, or digits, on the hand other than the thumb. 2. Something that looks like a finger: a *finger* of flame, a *finger* of a glove. —*verb.* 1. To touch or handle lightly: Mary *fingered* the pretty necklace before she put it in the box. 2. (Slang) To name or tell about: The informer *fingered* the man as the thief. **fingered, fingering.** —**point the finger at.** To blame. —**keep one's fingers crossed.** To hope or trust to luck that what is desired will happen. —**lift a finger.** To help out, even slightly. —**put one's finger on.** To locate accurately.

fin·ger·nail (FING-gər-nayl) *noun.* The thin, hard covering on the top of the finger.

finger paint. Paint applied with the fingers to damp paper.

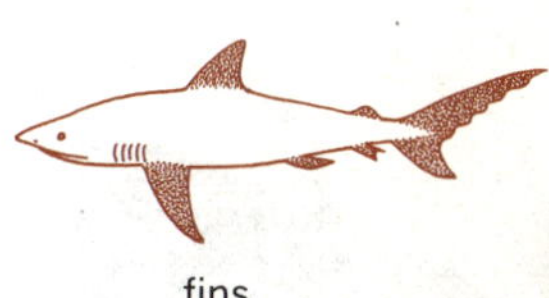
fins

finch

fingerprint

fire escape

fire engine

fin·ger·print (FING-gər-print) *noun.* The mark left by the small lines or ridges on the tip of the finger; often an impression of these lines taken in ink for identification purposes. —*verb.* To make an impression of the lines of the fingertip, usually by inking the fingers and pressing them on a clean surface, such as paper. **fingerprinted, fingerprinting.**

fin·ish (FIN-ish) *verb.* 1. To complete; come to the end of: The runners *finished* the race in record time. 2. To use up: The hungry boys *finished* the cookies and milk. 3. To apply a special surface or coating to: The carpenter *finished* the table with a smooth layer of varnish. **finished, finishing.** —*noun.* 1. End. 2. A surface or coating. **finishes.**

fi·nite (FIGH-night) *adjective.* Having definite limits; having a beginning and an end.

finite set. Any set that contains a countable number of elements: The total of the teams in a football league makes a *finite set.*

fir (FER) *noun.* Any of several types of evergreen trees; the wood from this tree.

fire (FIGHR) *noun.* 1. Burning that results in flames, light, and heat. 2. The discharging or firing of weapons. 3. Excitement; passion. —*verb.* 1. To ignite; set on fire. 2. To discharge from a position; get rid of. 3. To discharge a weapon. 4. To excite or make active: The pep rally *fired* the students' school spirit. **fired, firing.** —**hang fire.** To be put off or delayed. —**under fire.** 1. Receiving an enemy attack of bullets, rockets, or other weapons. 2. Subject to criticisms or accusations.

fire·crack·er (FIGHR-krak-ər) *noun.* A small explosive device made of paper and gunpowder, set off to make noise at celebrations.

fire drill. A practice session to prepare people to do the proper things in case of fire.

fire engine. A large vehicle containing equipment for fighting fires, usually with a means to pump or spray water.

fire escape. Metal steps or ladders attached to the outside of a building for use as an escape route in case of fire.

fire extinguisher. A small portable tank containing chemicals that can be sprayed on a fire in an emergency.

fire fighter. A person who combats fires; a fireman.

fire·fly (FIGHR-fligh) *noun.* A small beetle whose body gives off a glow at night; a lightning bug. **fireflies.**

fire·man (FIGHR-mən) *noun.* 1. A person who combats fires; a fire fighter. 2. A person whose job it is to tend the fire in a furnace. —**firemen** *plural.*

fire·place (FIGHR-playss) *noun.* A small structure, usually of brick or stone, in which a fire can be built.

fire·plug (FIGHR-pluhg) *noun.* A stationary water pipe to which hoses are attached and from which water is drawn in case of fire; a hydrant.

fire·proof (FIGHR-proof) *adjective.* Not able to burn or catch on fire. —*verb.* To make a place or thing safe from fire. **fireproofed, fireproofing.**

fire·side (FIGHR-sighd) *noun.* The area around a fire or fireplace; a hearth.

fire tower. A tower, especially in a forest area, from which observers can keep a watch for fires.

fire warden. A person whose job is to direct the prevention or fighting of fires in a particular area.

fire·wood (FIGHR-wud) *noun.* Wood cut to be used as fuel.

fire·works (FIGHR-werks) *noun, plural.* Any of a number of devices, such as skyrockets, cherry bombs, and firecrackers, that make loud noises or burn colorfully and are often used at celebrations.

firm (FERM) *adjective.* 1. Solid; not easily moved, crushed, or divided: The fresh melons have a *firm* rind. 2. Positive; strong: *firm* opinion. 3. Reliable; steady: *firm* friends. **firmer, firmest.** —*noun.* A business company. —**firmly** *adverb.*

fir·ma·ment (FER-mə-mənt) *noun.* The sky; the heavens.

first (FERST) *adjective.* 1. Being, happening, or coming before all others. 2. Coming before second; 1st. —*noun.* 1. The one that comes before all others: John was *first* in line. 2. The start; the beginning: I liked Milly from the *first.* 3. The winner: My sister was *first* in the baking contest. —*adverb.* 1. For the first time: I *first* came here when I was a baby. 2. Before all others: That boy ranks *first* in his class. 3. Instead; preferably: I won't eat the lima beans. I'll go to my room *first.* —**at first.** At the start.

first aid. Emergency treatment given to a sick or injured person in the absence of professional medical help.

first·hand (FERST-HAND) *adjective* or *adverb.* Direct; from the source: The reporter's account was not a rumor; it was *firsthand* information received from the mayor.

first-rate (FERST-RAYT) *adjective.* Of the finest quality; excellent.

firth (FERTH) *noun.* (Scottish) An inlet from the sea, usually long and narrow.

fish *noun.* 1. A cold-blooded animal that lives in the water, has a backbone and (usually) protective scales on its skin, swims by means of fins, and breathes through gills. 2. The flesh of fish which is eaten as food. —**fish** or **fishes** *plural.* —*verb.* 1. To catch or try to catch fish. 2. To look for something by feeling around: She *fished* in her bag for her comb. 3. To pull (out something): She *fished* her comb out of her bag. 4. To try to get or find out something indirectly: She *fished* for an invitation to the party by saying how much she wanted to meet new people. **fished, fishing.**

fish·er·man (FISH-ər-mən) *noun.* One who fishes, for fun or to earn a living. —**fishermen** *plural.*

fish·ery (FISH-ə-ree) *noun.* A place for raising fish; a hatchery. **fisheries.**

fish·hook (FISH-huk) *noun.* A barbed hook used to catch fish.

fish·y (FISH-ee) *adjective.* 1. Smelling or tasting like a fish. 2. Cold or dull: The man had *fishy* eyes. 3. (Informal) Suspicious; highly improbable. **fishier, fishiest.** —**fishily** *adverb.*

fis·sion (FISH-ən) *noun.* Any dividing or splitting into parts: Nuclear *fission* releases energy.

fis·sure (FISH-ər) *noun.* An opening or crack: A tree grew out of the *fissure* in the rock. **fissures.**

fist *noun.* A firmly closed hand, with the fingernails touching the palm.

fit *noun.* 1. A sudden, violent attack of illness: Our cat had a *fit* but recovered quickly. 2. A sudden but short mood or outburst: A *fit* of depression followed his *fit* of anger. —*verb.* 1. To be the correct size for: The clown had big hats and small hats but none that *fit* him. 2. To be correct or suitable to: Happy music *fits* a party. 3. To adjust: The dress was too large for Mary so her Mother *fitted* it. 4. To make parts go together properly: Joe had trouble *fitting* the airplane model together. 5. (Used with *up* or *out*) To make ready for: The campers were *fitted* out with knapsacks. **fit** or **fitted, fitting.** —*adjective.* 1. Healthy: After a long illness, Joe is finally *fit* again. 2. Right or proper: Bad language is not *fit* for anyone to use. 3. Suited or qualified: John's training is such that he is *fit* for the job. **fitter, fittest.** —**fitly** *adverb.*

fit·ful (FIT-fəl) *adjective.* Irregular; not steady. —**fitfully** *adverb.*

fireworks

fishhook

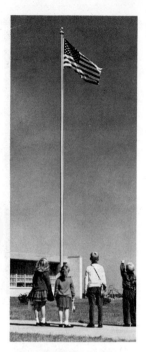

flagpole

flamingos

fjord

fit·ting (FIT-ing) *adjective.* Correct, proper, or suitable. —*noun.* 1. Trying on clothes to have them altered to fit properly. 2. A small part or piece of equipment for a machine or device. 3. (Plural) Fixtures or accessories. —**fittingly** *adverb.*

five (FIGHV) *noun* (and *adjective*). The cardinal number after four and before six; 5.

fix (FIKS) *verb.* 1. To repair. 2. To make secure or firm: Jim *fixed* the tent stakes firmly in the ground. 3. Prepare, arrange, or set right: Regina *fixed* her collar so that it lay flat. 4. To set or establish: Mother *fixed* six o'clock as the dinner hour. 5. To direct or concentrate: Joe *fixed* his eyes on the clock. 6. To place directly or to pinpoint: *fix* responsibility. **fixed, fixing.** —*noun.* 1. (Slang) A difficult situation or position. 2. (Slang) An injection of a narcotic, especially heroin, directly into a vein. **fixes.**

fixed star. A star at such a great distance from the earth that it seems not to move.

fix·ture (FIKS-chər) *noun.* An object that is permanently installed: The *fixtures* in our kitchen include the sink and dishwasher. **fixtures.**

fizz (FIZ) *verb.* To make a hissing sound. **fizzed, fizzing.** —*noun.* A hissing sound. **fizzes.**

fiz·zle (FIZ-l) *verb.* 1. To make a fizzing sound. 2. (Informal) To die out after a good start: The project *fizzled* because of lack of interest. **fizzled, fizzling.**

fjord (FYORD) Also **fiord** *noun.* A long, narrow, and deep arm of the sea running inland between high cliffs.

flab·ber·gast (FLAB-ər-gast) *verb.* (Informal) To astonish or dumbfound; surprise greatly. **flabbergasted, flabbergasting.**

flag *noun.* A piece of cloth, usually rectangular and varying in color and design, used as a symbol for a country or cause, for signaling, to give information, and for other purposes. —*verb.* 1. To signal: The construction worker *flagged* traffic to a stop. 2. To droop or grow weak: Joe's spirits *flagged* when he lost the race. **flagged, flagging.**

flag·pole (FLAG-pohl) *noun.* A pole from which a flag is hung.

flail (FLAYL) *noun.* A device used for threshing consisting of a swinging short stick attached to a long wooden handle. —*verb.* 1. To hit with a flail or as if with a flail: Sue *flailed* at the snake with a stick. 2. To wave (something) about like a flail. **flailed, flailing.**

flair *noun.* A natural talent or awareness: a *flair* for cooking.

flake (FLAYK) *noun.* A small, flat, thin piece: A *flake* of paint fell from the ceiling. —*verb.* To come off in flakes. **flaked, flaking.** —**flaky** *adjective.*

flam·boy·ant (flam-BOI-ənt) *adjective.* Highly colorful, brilliant, and showy. —**flamboyantly** *adverb.*

flame (FLAYM) *noun.* A flickering red or yellow tongue of burning gas that rises above a fire. —*verb.* 1. To blaze. 2. To resemble a flame in brilliance: The house *flamed* with light. **flamed, flaming.**

fla·min·go (flə-MING-goh) *noun.* A large tropical wading bird with pink to red plumage. —**flamingos** or **flamingoes** *plural.*

flam·ma·ble (FLAM-ə-bəl) *adjective.* Easily set on fire; inflammable. —**flammably** *adverb.*

flank (FLANGK) *noun.* 1. The side of a human or four-legged animal between the ribs and the hip. 2. Either side of a military formation: The left *flank* of the army bore the brunt of the attack. —*verb.* 1. To be at the side of: A meadow *flanked* the house. 2. To go around the side of (an army). **flanked, flanking.**

flan·nel (FLAN-l) *noun.* A soft woolen fabric.

flap *noun.* 1. A hanging piece that serves as protection: Jane sealed the *flap* of the envelope. 2. A fluttering movement or sound: They heard a *flap* of wings. 3. (Slang) State of being upset or disturbed: Paul was in a *flap* when he lost his notebook. —*verb.* 1. To move up and down: The birds *flapped* their wings and took off. 2. To move or make (something) move in a fluttering way: The flag *flapped* in the breeze. **flapped, flapping.**

flap·jack (FLAP-jak) *noun.* A pancake.

flare (FLAIR) *noun.* 1. A brief, bright burst of light. 2. A short spurt of emotion or activity. 3. An outward bell-like curving: Her skirt had a graceful *flare.* 4. A bright flamelike light used as a signal. —*verb.* 1. To burst briefly into flame. 2. To have a burst or spurt of emotion or activity. 3. To curve outwardly. **flared, flaring.**

flash *noun.* 1. A sudden, brief, bright light: A *flash* of lightning lit up the town. 2. An extremely short time: The dog knocked over the table and was out the door in a *flash.* 3. A brief, sudden feeling: With a *flash* of memory she recalled the incident. 4. A short announcement of important news: The program was interrupted for a news *flash.* 5. A device used to produce a fast, bright light for indoor photography. **flashes.** —*verb.* 1. To light briefly: He promised to *flash* the headlights as a signal. 2. To move with great speed or be seen for only a moment. 3. To sparkle: The water *flashed* with light. **flashed, flashing.**

flash flood. A sudden, raging flood occurring after heavy rains.

flash·light (FLASH-light) *noun.* A small, hand-held electric light operated by batteries.

flash·y (FLASH-ee) *adjective.* 1. Briefly flashing. 2. Showy or gaudy. **flashier, flashiest.** —**flashily** *adverb.*

flask *noun.* A small glass, metal, or plastic bottle with a narrow neck, with or without a cap.

flat *adjective.* 1. Smooth; even: The *flat* land stretched to the horizon. 2. Stretched out full length: George woke up *flat* on the floor. 3. Shallow or low: We need a *flat* box to grow seedlings in. 4. Without flavor: The stew tasted *flat* because Mary forgot to add salt. 5. Positive and absolute: The answer to Will's request for a motorcycle was a *flat* no. 6. Unchanging or exact: There was a *flat* rate for renting the mower. 7. With no air, as a *flat* tire. 8. (Music) Off-key. 9. Without expression: a *flat* tone of voice. **flatter, flattest.** —*noun.* 1. An apartment on one floor. 2. (Music) A note one-half step lower than a given tone; the sign (♭) that indicates a half tone. —*verb.* To make or become flat. **flatted, flatting. flat** or **flatly** *adverb.*

flatboat

flat·boat (FLAT-boht) *noun.* A barge or boat with a flat bottom used on rivers and canals to carry goods.

flatcar

flat·car (FLAT-kahr) *noun.* A railroad car that has neither sides nor roof.

flat·fish (FLAT-fish) *noun.* Any of a variety of fishes that have both eyes on one side of a flat body. —**flatfish** or **flatfishes** *plural.*

flat·i·ron (FLAT-igh-ərn) *noun.* An iron with a smooth, flat surface, which is heated on a stove and used for pressing clothes.

flatiron

flat-out (FLAT-OWT) *adverb.* (Informal) Directly or obviously: Say what you want to say *flat-out.*

flat·ten (FLAT-n) *verb.* To make or become flat: Joan *flattened* the can with her foot. **flattened, flattening.**

flat·ter (FLAT-ər) *verb.* 1. To praise too highly, usually in the hope of gaining favor. 2. To show as better than is true: She thought the portrait *flattered* her. **flattered, flattering.** —**flattery** *noun.*

flaunt (FLAWNT) *verb.* To show off; to exhibit in an exaggerated fashion. **flaunted, flaunting.**

flau·tist (FLAW-tist) *noun. See* **flutist.**

fla·vor (FLAY-vər) *noun.* Taste: Tim hates the *flavor* of tomato sauce. *—verb.* To season: Mother used spices to *flavor* the casserole. **flavored, flavoring.**

fla·vor·ing (FLAY-vər-ing) *noun.* Anything added to food or drink to give it a distinct taste.

flaw *noun.* A defect or fault in a thing or a person. *—verb.* To make or become defective.

flaw·less (FLAW-liss) *adjective.* Without a flaw; perfect. **—flawlessly** *adverb.*

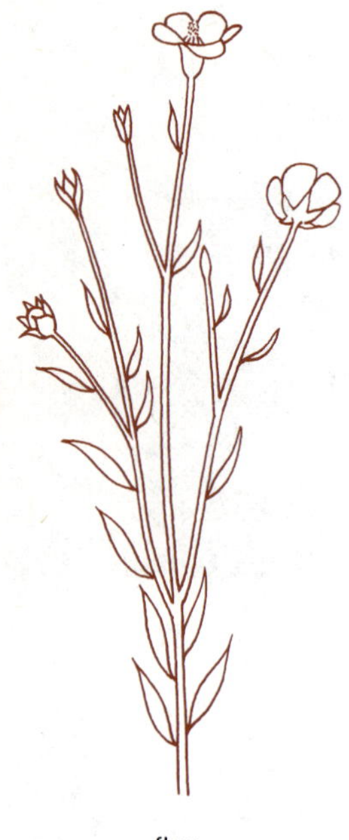
flax

flax (FLAKS) *noun.* 1. A tall, slender plant with blue flowers. 2. The threadlike parts of the stem of the flax plant from which linen thread is made.

flay *verb.* 1. To skin. 2. To criticize in a cruel, severe way: She *flayed* him with her tongue. **flayed, flaying.**

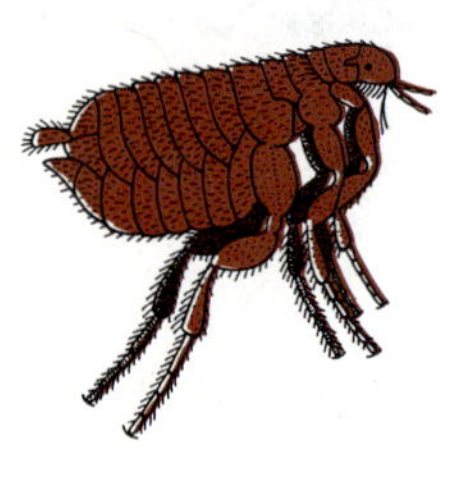
flea

flea (FLEE) *noun.* A tiny jumping insect that feeds on the blood of animals and humans.

fleck (FLEK) *noun.* A small spot or flake: There was a *fleck* of dandruff on his collar. *—verb.* To spot or fleck. **flecked, flecking.**

fled (FLED) *verb. See* **flee.**

fledg·ling (FLEJ-ling) *noun.* 1. A young bird. 2. A young person without experience.

flee *verb.* To leave quickly or run away. **fled, fleeing.**

fleece (FLEESS) *noun.* The woolly coat of a sheep. *—verb.* 1. To cut off the fleece of sheep. 2. To rob by trickery. **fleeced, fleecing.**

fleec·y (FLEESS-ee) *adjective.* Soft and white like fleece. **fleecier, fleeciest.**

fleet *noun.* 1. A group of ships under a single command, as the United States Fifth *Fleet.* 2. Any group of boats sailing together. 3. A group of trucks or other vehicles. *—adjective.* Swift or fast-moving. **fleeter, fleetest. —fleetly** *adverb.*

flesh *noun.* 1. The soft part of a body as opposed to bone. 2. Meat as food. 3. The soft part of a plant, as of a fruit. 4. The body, considered in relation to the soul. 5. Close relatives; kin. **—in the flesh.** Actually there in person.

flew (FLOO) *verb. See* **fly.**

flex (FLEKS) *verb.* To bend or contract: *flex* an arm; *flex* a muscle. **flexed, flexing.**

flex·i·ble (FLEK-sə-bəl) *adjective.* 1. Easily bent; possible to bend without breaking: Plastic straws are *flexible.* 2. Easy to change or adjust: Our club rules are *flexible;* we change them every day. 3. Willing to be influenced: Mrs. Brown is *flexible* about class projects. **—flexibility** *noun.* **—flexibly** *adverb.*

flick (FLIK) *noun.* 1. A quick, light snapping blow or tap: a *flick* of a whip; a *flick* of the fingers. 2. The sound of a flick. 3. (Slang) A motion picture. *—verb.* 1. To tap or hit lightly with a snapping motion. 2. To remove (something) with a flick: *Flick* the crumbs off your lap. 3. To move (something) with a snapping or jerking motion: *Flick* off the light switch. **flicked, flicking.**

[1]**flick·er** (FLIK-ər) *verb.* To burn or shine unevenly; to make an unsteady flame or light. **flickered, flickering.** *—noun.* 1. An unsteady flame or light. 2. A fluttering or quivering. 3. A flickering sensation: a *flicker* of pain. 4. A quick flash; a brief glow: a *flicker* of surprise.

[2]**flick·er** (FLIK-ər) *noun.* A kind of North American woodpecker with red and yellow markings.

fli·er (FLIGH-ər) Also **flyer** *noun.* 1. A person who pilots an airplane. 2. A wild or reckless action. 3. (Informal) A printed leaflet or advertisement.

flight *noun.* 1. Act of flying. 2. The distance, time, or course covered by flying: It is a fairly long *flight* to London. 3. A flying group: A *flight* of jets roared over the house. 4. A trip on an airplane. 5. A scheduled airplane trip: *Flight* 207 will land in ten minutes. 6. Techniques of flying an airplane: My brother is studying the principles of *flight.* 7. Running away: The frightened boys stumbled in their *flight.* 8. A going beyond or above ordinary limits: a *flight* of fancy. 9. A series of stairsteps connecting one floor to another.

flight·y (FLIGH-tee) *adjective.* Impulsive; unsettled.

flim·sy (FLIM-zee) *adjective.* 1. Not sturdy; thin or weak. 2. Insufficient; not clearly thought out: a *flimsy* argument; a *flimsy* excuse. **flimsier, flimsiest.** —**flimsily** *adverb.*

flinch *verb.* 1. To shrink away from what is dangerous, frightening, difficult, or the like. 2. To twitch with pain or in fear of pain; wince. **flinched, flinching.** —*noun.* Act of flinching. **flinches.**

fling *verb.* To throw forcefully or enthusiastically: *fling* a dart; *fling* oneself into a job. **flung, flinging.** —*noun.* (Informal) 1. A trial; temporary or brief involvement: I had a *fling* at surfing two summers ago. 2. A native dance of Scotland: the Highland *fling.* 3. A brief period of pursuing only fun and pleasure.

flint *noun.* 1. A hard, dull-colored stone. 2. A piece of this stone used for making sparks by friction, as in a lighter. 3. Anything hard or stubborn: His eyes turned to *flint.*

flint·lock (FLINT-lok) *noun.* 1. An old-fashioned device on a gun in which a piece of flint strikes against steel, causing sparks that ignite the gunpowder. 2. A gun with a flintlock.

flip *verb.* 1. To throw (an object) lightly or quickly into the air so that it turns over: *flip* a coin. 2. (Slang) To go wild over something; be enthusiastic; go to extremes emotionally. **flipped, flipping.** —*noun.* A drink made of liquor, sugar, egg, and spices. —*adjective.* (Informal) Saucy; not serious; flippant.

flip·pant (FLIP-ənt) *adjective.* Saucy; disrespectful; lightly joking in a serious situation. —**flippancy** *noun.* —**flippantly** *adverb.*

flip·per (FLIP-ər) *noun.* 1. A flat, broad fin used for swimming by such animals as seals and whales. 2. (Usually plural) Rubber devices for the feet in the shape of fins, used for swimming fast.

flirt (FLERT) *verb.* 1. To play at love; talk, gesture, or act playfully as if desiring affection. 2. To play, toy, or fool (with something): A race driver *flirts* with danger every day. **flirted, flirting.** —*noun.* A person who flirts.

flit *verb.* 1. To move quickly and lightly; skim. 2. To go quickly: The days of vacation seem to *flit* by. **flitted, flitting.**

float (FLOHT) *verb.* 1. To stay on the surface of a liquid or in the air: Oil *floats* on water; clouds *float* in the sky. 2. To move easily and slowly; drift. 3. To move or wander without plan, effort, or restriction: He *floated* around the room looking at the pictures. 4. To cause something to float. 5. (Business) Make arrangements for; start; organize: *float* a loan. **floated, floating.** —*noun.* 1. Anything used to keep things or persons afloat: When Bob's canoe turned over, he used it as a *float* until help came. 2. A decorated platform on wheels pulled in a parade. 3. A milk shake with ice cream floating atop.

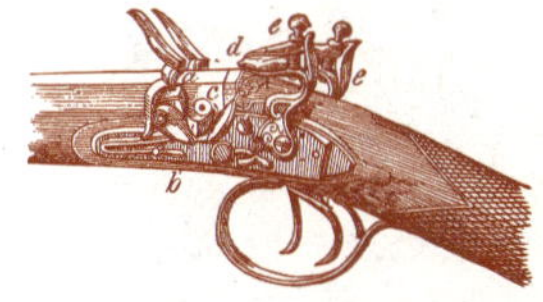
flintlock

[1]**flock** (FLOK) *noun.* 1. A group of birds, sheep, or goats who feed, eat, or stay together. 2. A large group of people, particularly members of a church. —*verb.* To go in a crowd; come together. **flocked, flocking.**

Florida
★capital: Tallahassee

[2]**flock** (FLOK) *noun.* 1. A fluffy bit, as of wool or hair. 2. Such bits of materials used for stuffing upholstery, mattresses, or the like. 3. Powdered wool or other material used to decorate wallpaper. *—verb.* 1. To stuff (something) with flock. 2. To decorate or cover with flock. **flocked, flocking.**

floe (FLOH) *noun.* 1. A big sheet of floating ice. 2. A piece of such a sheet of ice. **floes.**

flog *verb.* To hit or whip repeatedly as with a stick. **flogged, flogging.**

flood (FLUHD) *noun.* 1. An overflowing rush of water. 2. A gush or great stream of anything: The *flood* of light blinded me for a minute. 3. The coming in of the tide; flood-tide. *—verb.* 1. To overflow; wash over or cover with water or other liquid. 2. To give a great deal; overwhelm: When George was sick, his friends *flooded* him with get-well cards. **flooded, flooding.**

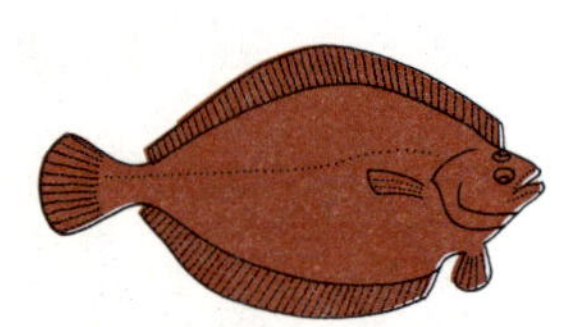

[2]flounder

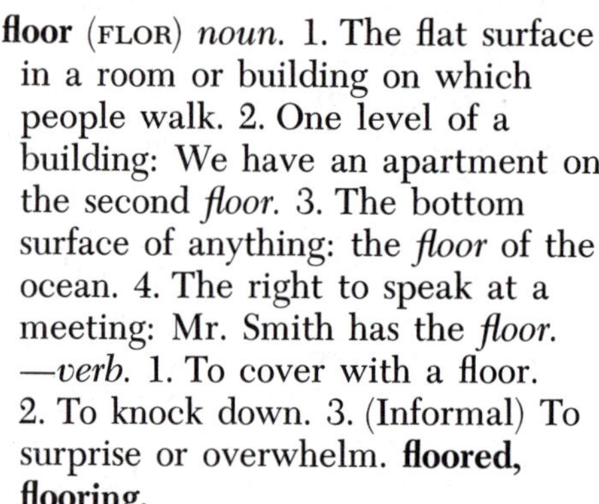

floor (FLOR) *noun.* 1. The flat surface in a room or building on which people walk. 2. One level of a building: We have an apartment on the second *floor.* 3. The bottom surface of anything: the *floor* of the ocean. 4. The right to speak at a meeting: Mr. Smith has the *floor.* *—verb.* 1. To cover with a floor. 2. To knock down. 3. (Informal) To surprise or overwhelm. **floored, flooring.**

flop *verb.* 1. To fall or go down suddenly and clumsily. 2. (Informal) To fail or do very poorly: Our bake sale *flopped;* we made no money. 3. To flap; make a flopping sound. 4. Move clumsily; flap in an awkward way: The wounded bird *flopped* around. **flopped, flopping.** *—noun.* 1. The act or sound of flopping. 2. (Informal) A failure: The play was a *flop.*

flor·a (FLOR-ə) *noun.* Plants in general, especially those of a certain season, area, or time. —**floras** or **florae** (FLOR-ee) *plural.*

flo·ral (FLOR-əl) *adjective.* Of, about, or like flowers: *floral* wallpaper.

Flor·i·da (FLOR-ə-də) *noun.* A state on the south Atlantic coast of the United States, 27th to join the Union (1845). —**Fla.** *abbreviation.* Also **FL** for Zip Codes.

flo·rist (FLOR-ist) *noun.* One whose business is growing or selling flowers and plants.

floss (FLAWSS) *noun.* 1. Untwisted silk fibers used in weaving or embroidery. 2. Any silky thread, such as dental *floss.*

flot·sam (FLOT-səm) *noun.* Any part of the wreckage of a ship that is found floating. *See* **jetsam.**

[1]**floun·der** (FLOWN-dər) *verb.* 1. To struggle in a clumsy way; lose balance or control. 2. To speak or act awkwardly. **floundered, floundering.**

[2]**floun·der** *noun.* Any of various flatfishes used widely for food.

flour (FLOWR) *noun.* 1. Finely ground and sifted grain meal, especially that used to make bread. 2. Any finely ground soft powder. *—verb.* To sprinkle or coat with flour. **floured, flouring.**

flour·ish (FLER-ish) *verb.* 1. To grow well or abundantly. 2. To be successful; develop fully. 3. To make wide, sweeping movements, as with a sword or a flag. **flourished, flourishing.** *—noun.* 1. Any dramatic, sweeping movement. 2. Any fancy or showy display or performance. 3. A fancy or special addition or decoration. 4. A special or showy passage of music. **flourishes.**

flout (FLOWT) *verb.* To scorn, insult, or scoff at; ignore or treat with disrespect. **flouted, flouting.**

flow (FLOH) *verb.* 1. To move along in a stream: The blood *flows* in your veins even when you're sleeping. 2. To come or go in a smooth, steady way: People *flowed* in and out of the store all day long. 3. To hang long and loosely: Sharon's hair *flows* prettily when she loosens her braids. 4. To rise and come forward: The tide *flows* in and ebbs away. **flowed, flowing.** —*noun.* 1. The speed or direction of flow: Weathermen measure the *flow* of the wind. 2. The rate at which liquid flows: The *flow* of water at the reservoir has to be increased in the summer. 3. Anything that flows; a stream. 4. Any movement or action that is like a stream. 5. The rise of the tide.

flow·er (FLOW-ər) *noun.* 1. The blossom of a plant; the part of a seed plant that contains the reproductive organs and their covers. 2. A flowering plant. 3. Full bloom. 4. The best or most beautiful part or time of anything: My grandfather says childhood is the *flower* of life. —*verb.* 1. To form flowers; to bloom. 2. To come into full development; reach the peak or best time. **flowered, flowering.**

flow·er·y (FLOW-ə-ree) *adjective.* 1. Having many flowers; covered with flowers. 2. Fancy or overelaborate: His vocabulary is too *flowery.* 3. Decorated with flower-like designs.

flown (FLOHN) *verb. See* **¹fly.**

flu (FLOO) *noun.* (Informal) Influenza.

fluc·tu·ate (FLUHK-choo-ayt) *verb.* 1. To change frequently; vary continually: Temperatures, prices, and moods are things that often *fluctuate.* 2. To move in waves or like waves. **fluctuated, fluctuating.** —**fluctuation** (fluhk-choo-AY-shən) *noun.*

flue (FLOO) *noun.* 1. The channel in a chimney through which smoke passes. 2. Any pipe or similar passageway for air, gas, or the like, such as a pipe that carries hot air in a heating system. **flues.**

fluent (FLOO-ənt) *adjective.* 1. Smooth and easy flowing: He speaks *fluent* Spanish. 2. Able to speak or write with ease. —**fluently** *adverb.*

fluff (FLUHF) *noun.* 1. Light, downy bits, as *fluffs* of cotton. 2. A mass of down; something soft or fluffy. 3. (Slang) An error or omission in speech, as in a play. —*verb.* 1. To make or become fluffy; puff out: *Fluff* your pillows when you make the bed. 2. (Slang) To make an error in speech. **fluffed, fluffing.**

fluff·y (FLUHF-ee) *adjective.* Made of fluff; covered with fluff; like fluff: *fluffy* mittens. **fluffier, fluffiest.**

flu·id (FLOO-id) *noun.* A liquid; anything that can flow. —*adjective.* 1. Liquid; flowing. 2. Of or about fluids. 3. Changeable; not firm or stiff: The dancer's movements were *fluid* and graceful. —**fluidly** *adverb.*

flung (FLUHNG) *verb. See* **fling.**

flunk (FLUHNGK) *verb.* (Informal) 1. To fail a test or course. 2. To give (a student) a mark that represents a failure: Mr. Brown *flunked* me in social studies. **flunked, flunking.** —**flunk out.** To drop out (of school or class) because of poor work.

flu·o·res·cent (floo-ər-ESS-nt or flur-ESS-nt) *adjective.* Able to produce light as a result of exposure to light waves, friction, or other stimulation: *Fluorescent* lights are coated inside with powders that give off light when an electrical charge is sent through the mercury vapors inside the tube.

flu·or·i·date (FLUR-ə-dayt) *verb.* To treat with fluoride. **fluoridated, fluoridating.**

flu·o·ride (FLUR-ighd) *noun.* (Chemistry) A compound of fluorine and another element: *Fluoride* is used to protect teeth from decay. **fluorides.**

flu·o·rine (FLUR-een) *noun.* A pale yellow gas that has many industrial applications.

flur·ry (FLER-ee) *noun.* 1. A quick puff of wind. 2. A brief snowfall. 3. A hubbub; a nervous burst of confusion or excitement. **flurries.**

fly

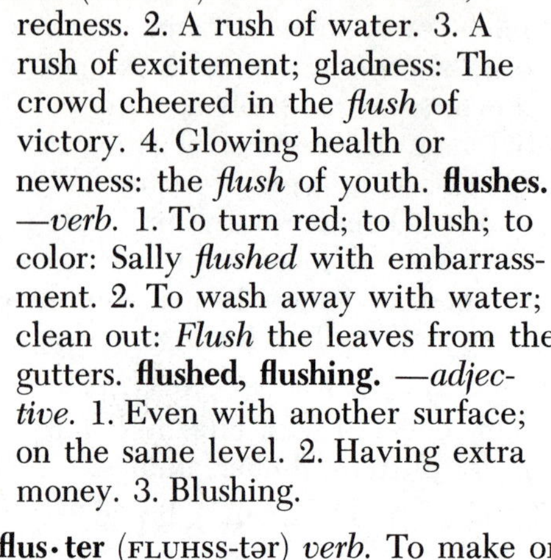

flush (FLUHSH) *noun.* 1. A blush; redness. 2. A rush of water. 3. A rush of excitement; gladness: The crowd cheered in the *flush* of victory. 4. Glowing health or newness: the *flush* of youth. **flushes.** —*verb.* 1. To turn red; to blush; to color: Sally *flushed* with embarrassment. 2. To wash away with water; clean out: *Flush* the leaves from the gutters. **flushed, flushing.** —*adjective.* 1. Even with another surface; on the same level. 2. Having extra money. 3. Blushing.

flus·ter (FLUHSS-tər) *verb.* To make or become confused or nervous. **flustered, flustering.** —*noun.* State of confusion; nervousness.

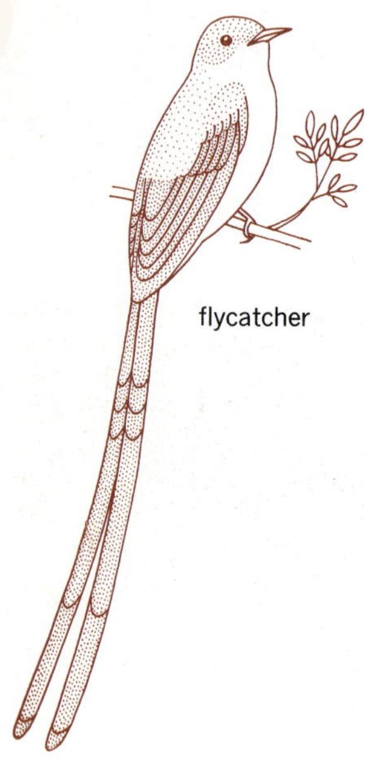
flycatcher

flute (FLOOT) *noun.* (Music) 1. A high-pitched wind instrument in the form of a tube with keys or finger holes. 2. An organ stop having wide flue pipes and making a flutelike sound. 3. (Architecture) A rounded indentation. 4. A pleat, ruffle, or groove in any material: Collars with *flutes* were worn in Shakespeare's time. **flutes.** —*verb.* 1. To play or make a sound like a flute. 2. To form flutes. **fluted, fluting.** —**flutelike** or **fluted** *adjective.*

flut·ist (FLOO-tist) Also **flautist** (FLAW-tist) *noun.* A flute player.

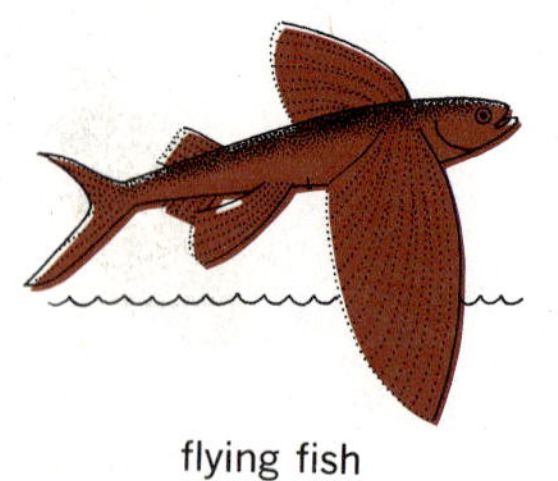
flying fish

flut·ter (FLUHT-ər) *verb.* 1. To wave or move lightly but rapidly: The clean clothes *fluttered* on the line. 2. To flap wings quickly, as a bird in landing. 3. To move in a quick, nervous way: Mom *fluttered* about doing last-minute things before the company came. **fluttered, fluttering.** —*noun.* 1. A fast, unsteady heartbeat. 2. A fluttering movement: "There was a considerable *flutter* when Brer Rabbit struck the bushes." (J. C. Harris). 3. A state of nervous excitement. —**fluttery** *adjective.* —**flutter kick.** (Swimming) A fluttering movement of the hands or feet.

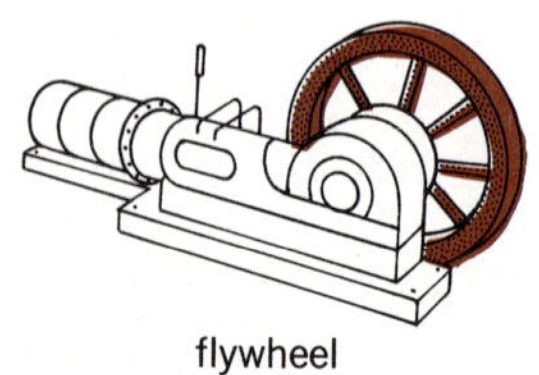
flywheel

[1]**fly** (FLIGH) *verb.* 1. To move through the air on wings as an insect, bird, or airplane. 2. To be carried or cause to be carried through the air by wind: My kite was *flying* high. 3. To move or flutter in the wind: Our flag won't *fly* on the moon because there is no wind. 4. To travel by plane or other aircraft. 5. To steer or pilot an airplane. 6. To move in a rush: Martin must *fly* down the street to catch the bus. 7. To run away. 8. (Baseball) To hit a fly ball. 9. To react abruptly or violently: *fly* into a rage. **flew, flied, flown, flying.** —*noun.* 1. A strip of fabric sewn on men's trousers to cover buttons or a zipper. 2. A tent flap or door. 3. (Baseball) A ball hit high into the air. **flies.** —**fly off the handle.** To get angry. —**let fly.** To let out or give forth forcefully.

[2]**fly** (FLIGH) *noun.* 1. Any of a variety of insects with wings (usually a single pair), such as a firefly, dragonfly, gnat, and, especially, a housefly. 2. A fishhook decorated to look like an insect. **flies.**

fly·catch·er (FLIGH-kach-ər) *noun.* A small bird that eats flying insects.

flying fish. A tropical fish with winglike side fins that enable it to glide over the water and briefly through the air.

flying saucer. A saucer-shaped flying object that some people have reported seeing, and that some think comes from outer space.

fly·pa·per (FLIGH-pay-pər) *noun.* A sticky paper used to trap flies.

fly·wheel (FLIGH-hweel) *noun.* A heavy wheel that steadies the speed of a machine.

foal (FOHL) *noun.* A newborn or very young horse, mule, or similar animal. —*verb.* To give birth to a horse, mule, or similar animal. **foaled, foaling.**

foam (FOHM) *noun.* A froth or light, bubbly substance: The soft drink had *foam* on top when it was first poured. —*verb.* To form a froth or light, bubbly substance. **foamed, foaming.**

focal length. The distance from a lens to its main focus, the image it forms on a screen or in an eyepiece.

fo·cus (FOH-kəss) *noun.* 1. The point at which rays of light (heat, sound, etc.) meet after being bent by passing through a lens. 2. The point at which something must be placed so that it can be clearly viewed through a lens. —**focuses** or **foci** (FOH-sigh) *plural.* —*verb.* 1. To adjust (a lens or other equipment) to get a clear view or picture. 2. To concentrate. **focused, focusing.**

fod·der (FOD-ər) *noun.* Food given to cattle and other livestock.

foe (FOH) *noun.* An enemy or opponent: France and Germany were *foes* during World Wars I and II. **foes.**

foe·tus (FEE-təss) *noun. See* **fetus.**

fog (FOG) *noun.* 1. A heavy mist that settles close to the level of the ground or water. 2. A state of confusion: He is in a *fog.* —*verb.* To cover with mist. **fogged, fogging.** —**fog·gy** (FAW-gee or FOG-ee) *adjective.* **foggier, foggiest.** —**foggily** *adverb.*

fog·horn (FOG-horn) *noun.* A horn sounded by ships or lighthouses as a warning during times of foggy weather.

fo·gy (FOH-gee) Also **fogey** *noun.* A person whose ideas and attitudes are old-fashioned. **fogies** or **fogeys.**

foil *noun.* 1. A very thin sheet of metal, as aluminum *foil.* 2. A slender sword used in fencing. 3. A person whose character contrasts with that of another. —*verb.* To keep from succeeding; prevent: The crooks' attempt to rob the bank was *foiled* by the police. **foiled, foiling.**

fold (FOHLD) *verb.* 1. To bend (something) over one or more times. 2. To cradle in or draw close with one's arms. 3. (Informal) To fail, as in competition or business. **folded, folding.** —*noun.* 1. A pleat or ridge of folded material. 2. A pen for sheep or other livestock.

fold·er (FOHL-dər) *noun.* 1. A folded piece of cardboard, plastic, or other material designed as a cover for sheets of paper. 2. A booklet formed of folded sheets of paper.

fo·li·age (FOH-lee-ij) *noun.* All of the leaves of the plants in an area.

folk (FOHK) *noun.* 1. (Usually plural) People in a group: The old *folks* sat talking. 2. (Informal; usually plural) Family; relatives. 3. An ethnic group or nation of people. —**folk** or **folks** *plural.* —*adjective.* Of or related to the common people of an area: *folk* melodies.

folk dance. A dance developed by the people common to an area.

folk·lore (FOHK-lor) *noun.* The customs, beliefs, and rituals long observed by the common people.

folk music. The music developed by the people of an area.

folk song. A song originating with the people of a region.

fol·low (FOL-oh) *verb.* 1. To move behind; come after: Jim walked toward the barn, and his dog *followed* him. 2. To come after in time: Disappointment *followed* the team's defeat. 3. To pursue; to trail: The detective *followed* the suspect from town to town. 4. To obey; heed: Students should *follow* the instructions of their teachers. 5. To go along: The hikers *followed* the woods road. 6. To keep in sight: The spectators *followed* the racing car's movements until it was out of sight. 7. To pay attention to; understand: The students could not *follow* the teacher's explanation. **followed, following.** —**follow up.** To complete something begun before.

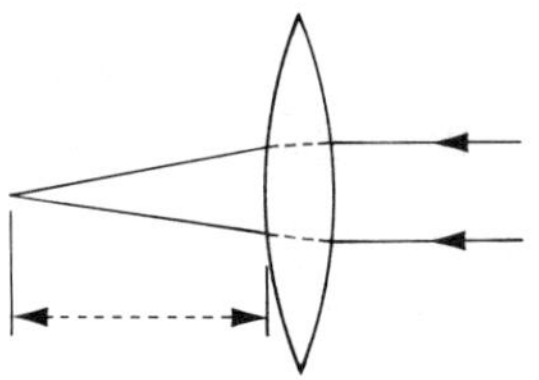

focal length

folk dance

fol·low·ing (FOL-oh-ing) *noun.* A group of supporters: The star quarterback has a large *following* of fans. —*adjective.* Coming after; next: On his birthday Otto ate too much; on the *following* day he was sick.

fol·ly (FOL-ee) *noun.* 1. Foolishness; lack of common sense: It would be *folly* for me not to study for the exam. 2. A foolish or disastrous act: People once thought the purchase of Alaska was a *folly.* **follies.**

fond *adjective.* 1. Having warm or loving feelings. 2. Having special interest in; liking: Jane is *fond* of classical music. 3. Treasured; most desired: *fond* hopes. **fonder, fondest.** —**fondly** *adverb.*

fon·dle (FOND-l) *verb.* To stroke; caress: The little girl *fondled* her pet kitten. **fondled, fondling.**

fond·ness (FOND-niss) *noun.* 1. Warm or loving feelings. 2. Special interest or liking.

fon·due (fon-DOO) *noun.* A thick, hot food, usually made from cheese and served with bread or toast. **fondues.**

football

food *noun.* 1. Anything consumed as nutrition by a plant or animal: Meat, bread, and milk are important *foods* for human beings. 2. Anything that supplies energy or activity: *food* for discussion.

food stamps. Stamps issued by a government agency that can be exchanged for food items by people who are in need.

food·stuff (FOOD-stuhf) *noun.* Any substance eaten in order to satisfy hunger; a food product.

fool *noun.* 1. A person who shows an extreme lack of good sense: Only a *fool* would go sailing during a hurricane. 2. A clown; jester: The king's *fool* made the court roar with laughter. —*verb.* 1. To tease; act in jest: The boys meant no harm; they were just *fooling* you. 2. To deceive; to trick: The robber *fooled* the police. **fooled, fooling.**

fool·har·dy (FOOL-hahr-dee) *adjective.* Bold to a dangerous degree.

fool·ish (FOOL-ish) *adjective.* Silly; showing a lack of good sense: The *foolish* man wasted all of his money by gambling. —**foolishly** *adverb.* —**foolishness** *noun.*

foot (FUT) *noun.* 1. The part of the body that extends from the end of the leg, and on which one walks. 2. Something that looks like or is in the position of the foot (or end): the *foot* of a bed; the *foot* of a mountain. 3. A low or inferior position: the *foot* of the line; the *foot* of the class. 4. A unit of measure equal to 12 inches or $\frac{1}{3}$ yard. 5. The part of a sock or stocking that covers the foot. 6. (Poetry) A unit consisting of a stressed or an unstressed syllable or syllables. —**feet** *plural.* —*verb.* (Slang) Pay: Dad will *foot* the bill. **footed, footing.** —**put one's best foot forward.** To show or use one's best qualities. —**put one's foot down.** To stop or forbid unwanted actions. —**put one's foot in one's mouth.** To make an embarrassingly tactless statement.

foot·ball (FUT-bawl) *noun.* 1. An oval ball, usually made of leather, used in the game of football. 2. A game played by two teams of 11 players each on a large, rectangular field.

foot·hill (FUT-hil) *noun.* A low hill near a mountain or a range of mountains.

foot·hold (FUT-hohld) *noun.* 1. A solid place that can support a person's foot. 2. A good start or a position that promises progress: The team's fourth victory gave it a *foothold* in its efforts to win the championship.

foot·lights (FUT-lights) (Plural) *noun.* Lights on or below floor level at the front of a stage.

foot·note (FUT-noht) *noun.* A note at the bottom of a page that provides extra information about something written on that page. **footnotes.**

foot·path (FUT-path) *noun.* A path

designed for people to walk along.

foot·print (FUT-print) *noun.* The mark or impression made by a person's foot, as in sand or mud.

foot·sore (FUT-sor) *adjective.* Having tender or painful feet: The boys were *footsore* after the hike.

foot·step (FUT-step) *noun.* 1. A single step or the distance covered by a single step. 2. The sound made by a person's step.

foot·stool (FUT-stool) *noun.* A low stool on which a person may rest his feet.

for *preposition.* 1. To be owned, used or enjoyed by: Dad bought a new bicycle *for* my brother. 2. Intended to gain possession of: Jim earned money *for* new skates. 3. Toward: Janet headed *for* the exit. 4. In place of: Tom traded his penknife *for* a new baseball. 5. The distance of: The hikers walked *for* eight miles. 6. During the time of: The students studied *for* 20 minutes. 7. Because of: The driver was arrested *for* speeding. 8. In favor or support of: Our mayor is *for* lower taxes. 9. In relation to or regarding: Jim is tall *for* his age. *—conjunction.* Because.

for·age (FOR-ij) *verb.* 1. To seek after or make a raid for food: The army *foraged* through the countryside looking for livestock. 2. To search through: Mother *foraged* through our attic for old clothes to give away. **foraged, foraging.** *—noun.* 1. Grain or other food for animals. 2. A search for food or other items. **forages.**

for·ay (FOR-ay) *noun.* 1. A raid to loot or rob an area. 2. Any beginning effort: our *foray* into space. *—verb.* To raid or loot. **forayed, foraying.**

for·bear (FOR-bair) *verb.* 1. To restrain; keep oneself from doing. 2. To be patient. **forbore, forborne, forbearing.**

for·bid (fər-BID) *verb.* To make a rule against; prevent: Mother said, "I *forbid* you to leave the house today." **forbade** or **forbad, forbidden** or **forbid, forbidding.**

for·bid·ding (fər-BID-ing) *adjective.* Having a discouraging or frightening appearance.

force (FORSS) *noun.* 1. Power; might: It took great *force* to lift the heavy crate. 2. Violence: The robber used *force* to take the money from the messenger. 3. Persuasion; power to convince: The *force* of Tom's argument made us agree with him. 4. A unit of soldiers or other armed men. 5. A group organized for a special task: a *force* of fire fighters. **forces.** *—verb.* 1. To bring about by physical power. 2. To break open or into: The thief entered the building by *forcing* a lock. 3. To require that something be done or accepted: The increase in taxes was *forced* upon us by higher prices. **forced, forcing.**

force·ful (FORSS-fəl) *adjective.* Having power; impressive: a *forceful* warning against smoking. **—forcefully** *adverb.*

for·ceps (FOR-səps) *noun, plural.* Small tongs, used especially by doctors and dentists, for holding or pulling.

for·ci·ble (FOR-sə-bəl) *adjective.* 1. Done by force: The thieves made a *forcible* entry into the factory. 2. Forceful. **—forcibly** *adverb.*

ford *noun.* A shallow area where a river or stream can be crossed by walking or riding through the water. *—verb.* To cross a river or stream by walking or riding through the water. **forded, fording.**

fore (FOR) *adverb* and *adjective.* At or toward the front; forward. *—noun.* The front or first part, as of a ship. *—interjection.* A warning given by golfers to indicate that a ball is about to be hit.

fore and aft. Extending along the length of a ship; from bow to stern.

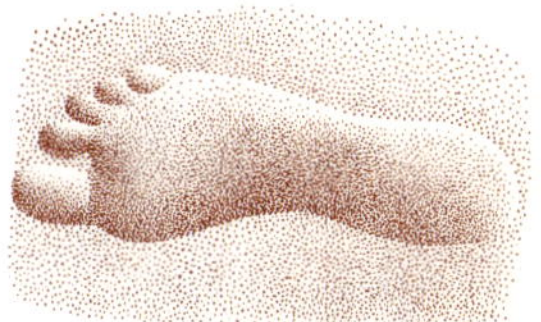
footprint

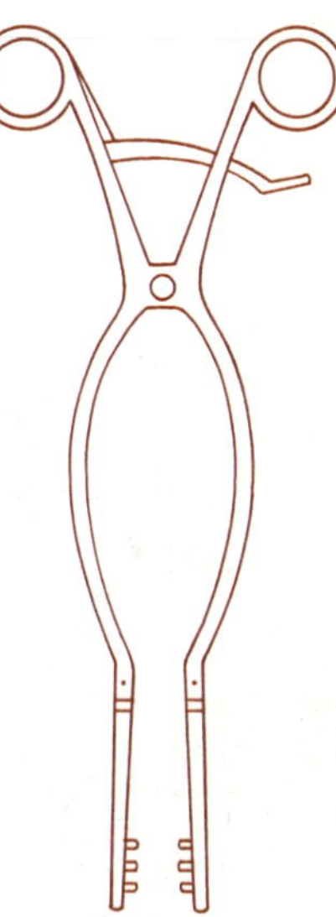
forceps

fore·arm (FOR-ahrm) *noun.* The part of the arm from the wrist to the elbow. *—verb.* To prepare or arm ahead for battle or some confrontation. **forearmed, forearming.**

fore·bear (FOR-bair) Also **forbear** *noun.* An ancestor.

fore·bod·ing (for-BOH-ding) *noun.* A strong feeling or indication that something bad is going to happen.

fore·cast (FOR-kast) *verb.* To predict; indicate beforehand. **forecast** or **forecasted, forecasting.** *—noun.* A prediction.

fore·deck (FOR-dek) *noun.* The front section of a ship's deck.

fore·fa·ther (FOR-fah-t̲h̲ər) *noun.* An ancestor.

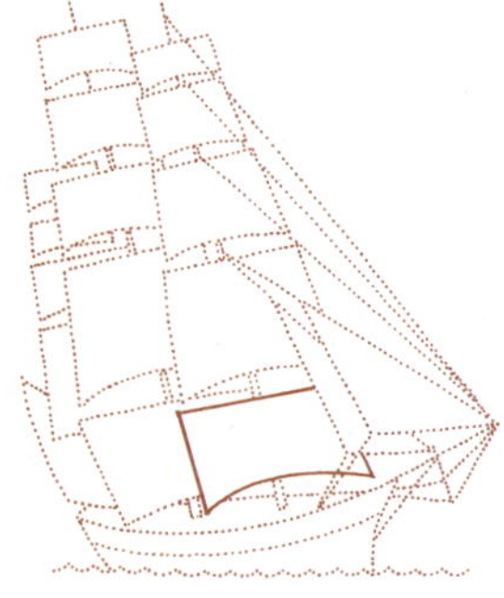

foresail

fore·fin·ger (FOR-fing-gər) *noun.* The finger next to the thumb, also called the index finger.

fore·foot (FOR-fut) *noun.* One of the two front feet of a four-legged animal. *—***forefeet** *plural.*

fore·front (FOR-fruhnt) *noun.* 1. The part of something that is farthest forward. 2. The most important or advanced position: The king was in the *forefront* of the battle.

fore·go (FOR-goh) To go before in place or time. **foregone, foregoing.**

fore·go·ing (for-GOH-ing or FOR-goh-ing) *adjective.* Going before; previous.

forest ranger

fore·gone (FOR-gawn) *adjective.* Already known or settled: It is a *foregone* conclusion that we will win.

fore·ground (FOR-grownd) *noun.* The part of a picture or scene that seems to be closest to the person looking at it.

fore·head (FOR-id or FOR-hed) *noun.* The section of the face between the hairline and the eyebrows.

for·eign (FOR-in) *adjective.* 1. Away from one's homeland: *foreign* countries. 2. Of or from another country: He is learning a *foreign* language. 3. Out of place; not belonging: The diner found some *foreign* matter in his coffee. 4. With other countries: *foreign* trade.

foreign aid. Money, food, or other items sent to help another country.

for·eign·er (FOR-ə-nər) *noun.* A person who is living or visiting in a country that is not his own: The Germans are *foreigners* in our country; we are *foreigners* in theirs.

foreign policy. The plan of action followed toward other countries: Our Secretary of State is concerned with the country's *foreign policy.*

fore·man (FOR-mən) *noun.* 1. A workman who is in charge of other workers. 2. The chairman of a jury. *—***foremen** *plural.*

fore·mast (FOR-məst) *noun.* The first mast; the mast nearest the front or bow of a ship.

fore·most (FOR-mohst) *adjective.* First; most important. *—adverb.* In the first or front order.

fore·noon (FOR-noon) *noun.* 1. The daylight hours before noon. 2. Late morning.

fore·sail (FOR-sl or FOR-sayl) *noun.* The lowest sail on the first mast of a sailing vessel having more than one mast.

fore·see (for-SEE) *verb.* To expect, know something before it happens. **foresaw, foreseeing.**

fore·sight (FOR-sight) *noun.* 1. The act of looking ahead. 2. Thoughtful preparation for the future: The ant scolded the grasshopper for lack of *foresight.*

for·est (FOR-ist) *noun.* Woodlands; trees and other plants growing close together.

for·est·er (FOR-i-stər) *noun.* A person whose job is to care for the growing things, as plants and trees, in a forest.

forest ranger. A worker who patrols and guards a woods or park area.

for·est·ry (FOR-i-stree) *noun.* The

science of growing and caring for trees and wooded areas.

fore•tell (for-TEL) *verb.* To tell what will happen in the future: Cold winds *foretell* the coming of winter. **foretold, foretelling.**

fore•thought (FOR-thawt) *noun.* 1. The act of thinking ahead. 2. Thoughtful readiness for the future.

for•ev•er (for-EV-ər or fər-EV-ər) *adverb.* 1. For all time; always. 2. Constantly; without stopping.

for•ev•er•more (for-ev-ər-MOR or fər-ev-ər-MOR) *adverb.* Always, forever.

fore•word (FOR-werd) *noun.* Preface; introduction: The *foreword* to a book is often written by someone other than the author of the book.

for•feit (FOR-fit) *verb.* To lose because of a fault or error: Our team had to *forfeit* the baseball game because we had only eight players. **forfeited, forfeiting.** —*noun.* 1. Something given up as a fine or penalty. 2. (Plural) A game in which players turn in articles, then do stunts to get them back.

forge (FORJ) *noun.* 1. A furnace or open fireplace where metals are heated and then hammered into shape. 2. A building containing equipment for heating and shaping metal. **forges.** —*verb.* 1. To shape (metal) by heating and pounding: The village blacksmith *forged* shoes for horses. 2. To make or create: Representatives from the two companies *forged* a contract. 3. To push on: It is time to *forge* ahead. 4. To make a false copy of something, especially to sign another's name. **forged, forging.**

for•ger•y (FOR-jər-ee) *noun.* 1. The act of imitating anything, as a signature or a painting, to mislead people. 2. The imitation produced in this manner: The painting was a *forgery.* **forgeries.**

for•get (fər-GET or for-GET) *verb.* 1. To be unable to think of something that one once knew. 2. To neglect or fail to remember or do something: Don't *forget* to vote. 3. To put out of mind on purpose: We tried to pay him, but he said to *forget* the bill. 4. To leave behind by mistake. **forgot, forgetting.**

for•get•ful (fər-GET-fəl or for-GET-fəl) *adjective.* Neglecting to remember; having a poor memory.

for•get-me-not (fər-GET-mee-not or for-GET-mee-not) *noun.* A low-growing plant with small blue flowers. **forget-me-nots.**

for•give (fər-GIV or for-GIV) *verb.* 1. To pardon; excuse (one) for doing wrong. 2. To cancel a debt. **forgave, forgiving.** —**forgiveness** *noun.*

for•go (for-GOH) Also **forego** *verb.* To give up; do without: to *forgo* dessert. **forwent, forgone, forgoing.**

for•got (for-GOT) *verb.* *See* **forget.**

fork *noun.* 1. A utensil with two or more sharp points (prongs) used for handling food in the kitchen or at the table. 2. A long-handled farm tool with several prongs used for digging and lifting; a pitchfork. 3. Anything shaped like a fork, such as a tree branch or a road that divides into parts. 4. One part of such a division: The left *fork* is the way to Bob's house. —*verb.* 1. To pick up with a fork. 2. To divide into the shape of a fork: The tree trunk *forks* into two big branches. **forked, forking.** —**fork over.** (Slang) To pay; hand over.

for•lorn (for-LORN) *adjective.* 1. Sad; hopeless. 2. Left alone; neglected. —**forlornly** *adverb.*

form *noun.* 1. Shape or outline: The cloud has the *form* of an elephant. 2. Kind; type: Steam and ice are two *forms* of water. 3. The body, not including the head: Helen of Troy was fair of face and fair of *form.* 4. Arrangement: The play was written in the *form* of a poem. 5. Manners: It is good *form* to say "Please" and "Thank you."

forget-me-not

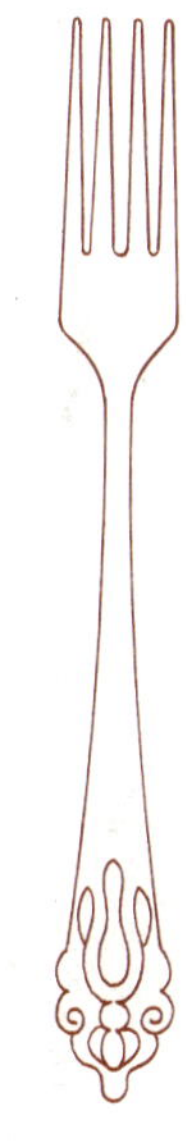

fork

paper containing blanks to be filled in: We completed the order *forms.* 7. Method; way of doing something: The Olympic judges rated the *form* of the divers. 8. Physical condition: The tennis player was in top *form.* 9. A mold: The machine pours chocolate into *forms* to cool. *—verb.* 1. To shape or make: He *formed* the dough into loaves. 2. To organize: *form* a chess club. 3. To develop: *form* a habit. **formed, forming.**

for·mal (FOR-məl) *adjective.* 1. Following set rules and customs: They were married in a *formal* ceremony. 2. Very proper; not relaxed: He greeted us in a *formal* way. 3. Suitable to wear to a ceremony or a special event: The guests wore *formal* clothes. *—noun.* 1. A social event where special dress is required. 2. An evening dress. **—formally** *adverb.*

fort

for·mal·i·ty (for-MAL-ə-tee) *noun.* 1. An established way of doing something: In some countries it is a *formality* to take off one's shoes before entering the house. 2. The act of behaving in a formal way. **formalities.**

for·ma·tion (for-MAY-shən) *noun.* 1. The act of shaping or organizing: The *formation* of the United Nations took place in 1945. 2. Something that has been shaped by nature: The Natural Bridge in Virginia is an interesting *formation.* 3. An arrangement of persons or equipment: The planes flew in *formation.*

for·mer (FOR-mər) *adjective.* Past, at a previous time: Our principal is a *former* teacher. *—noun.* The first of two: When the choice is play or work, he prefers the *former.* *See* **latter.** **—formerly** *adverb.*

for·mu·la (FOR-myə-lə) *noun.* 1. A statement written in symbols and figures: *Formulas* are used in mathematics and chemistry. 2. A recipe or prescription. 3. Words that express a belief or a truth: Franklin's *formula* for success was "Early to bed and early to rise. . . ." 4. A mixture including milk or a substitute for milk that is fed to infants. **—formulas** or **formulae** (FOR-myə-lee) *plural.*

for·mu·late (FOR-myə-layt) *verb.* 1. To invent. 2. To write as a formula. 3. To put together in a definite and orderly way: We *formulated* all our ideas for the school dance into a set plan. **formulated, formulating.**

for·sake (for-SAYK) *verb.* To leave behind or give up entirely: The little boy would never *forsake* his pet dog. **forsook, forsaken, forsaking.**

for·syth·i·a (for-SITH-ee-ə) *noun.* A bush with bright yellow flowers that bloom early in the spring.

fort *noun.* A stronghold; a place with strong walls and guns for defense against an enemy.

forth *adverb.* 1. Ahead; forward in either time or direction: "Go *forth* and teach all nations." (New Testament). 2. Into sight or view: The policeman ordered the burglar to come *forth.* **—and so forth.** More of the same.

forth·com·ing (forth-KUHM-ing) *adjective.* 1. Approaching; soon to appear: The children waited impatiently for the *forthcoming* holiday. 2. Ready at once: Food was *forthcoming* for the hungry hikers.

forth·right (FORTH-right) *adjective.* Direct; honest: My grandfather makes *forthright* remarks; he says what he thinks. **—forthrightly** *adverb.*

forth·with (forth-WITH) *adverb.* At once; without waiting.

for·ti·eth (FOR-tee-ith) *adjective.* Coming next after 39th; 40th. *—noun.* One of 40 equal parts.

for·ti·fi·ca·tion (for-tə-fi-KAY-shən) *noun.* 1. The act of making stronger. 2. A place with strong defenses, such as a fort. 3. A wall or shield.

for·ti·fy (FOR-tə-figh) *verb.* 1. To make stronger. 2. To add military strength. 3. To encourage or give strength: The hot soup *fortified* us against the cold. 4. To add a substance to: The milk is *fortified* with vitamin D. **fortified, fortifying.**

for·ti·tude (FOR-tə-tood or FOR-tə-tyood) *noun.* Moral strength, helping one to face pain or danger with courage.

fort·night (FORT-night or FORT-nit) *noun.* Two weeks; 14 days and nights. —**fortnightly** *adjective* and *adverb.*

for·tress (FOR-triss) *noun.* 1. A fort; a place built to be defended. 2. Any protection or safe place: "A mighty *fortress* is our God." (Luther). **fortresses.**

for·tu·nate (FOR-chə-nit) *adjective.* Lucky: It was *fortunate* that the woodsman came to Little Red Riding Hood's rescue. —*noun.* Those who have good luck: "It is the *fortunate* who should praise fortune." (Goethe). —**fortunately** *adverb.*

for·tune (FOR-chən) *noun.* 1. Wealth; a large sum of money: The movie star made a *fortune* but spent it before he died. 2. Good luck. 3. Fate; anything that happens by chance: "He that waits upon *fortune* is never sure of a dinner." (Benjamin Franklin). **fortunes.**

for·tune·tell·ing (FOR-chən-tel-ing) *noun* and *adjective.* Predicting the future.

for·tune·tell·er (FOR-chən-tel-ər) *noun.* One who claims to predict the future.

for·ty (FOR-tee) *noun* (and *adjective*). The cardinal number after 39 and before 41; 40. **forties.**

for·um (FOR-əm) *noun.* 1. A place where public meetings are held. 2. A discussion. 3. The central public square of an old Roman city.

for·ward (FOR-wərd) *adjective.* 1. At or toward the front: We entered through the *forward* door of the plane. 2. Eager, bold: The *forward* book salesman put his foot in the door. 3. Advanced, up-to-date: The old lady is *forward* in her thinking. 4. Toward the opponent's goal: He threw a *forward* pass. —*adverb.* Also **forwards.** 1. Ahead, toward the front or the future: "Look *forward* and not back." (E. E. Hale). 2. Into sight: Please come *forward;* I can't see you. —*verb.* 1. To send on: Please *forward* the mail to our new address. 2. To help or promote: He *forwarded* our cause by giving us money. **forwarded, forwarding.** —*noun.* A position or player on the first line of play in such sports as hockey, soccer, and basketball.

for·wards (FOR-wərdz) *adverb. See* **forward.**

fos·sil (FOSS-l) *noun.* The remains or the imprint of a plant or animal.

fos·ter (FAWSS-tər) *verb.* 1. To feed and care for. 2. To support and encourage: He *fosters* the cause of peace. 3. To hold fast to in one's mind: Terry *fostered* a hope of becoming a geologist. **fostered, fostering.** —*adjective.* Having or sharing in family life though not actually related by birth: *foster* child.

fought (FAWT) *verb. See* **fight.**

foul (FOWL) *adjective.* 1. Dirty, unpleasant to the senses: Burning garbage gives off a *foul* smell. 2. Bad, obscene: He uses *foul* language. 3. Against the rules. 4. Relating to a line that limits a sports playing area: The bowler's foot slid beyond the *foul* line. **fouler, foulest.** —*verb.* 1. To make dirty: Smoke *fouls* the air. 2. To tangle or mix up. 3. To break a rule: The basketball center *fouled* five times. 4. To hit a baseball outside the base lines. **fouled, fouling.** —*noun.* 1. A ball hit outside the base lines. 2. Breaking a rule in any sport. —**foul** or **foully** *adverb.* —**foul up.** Mix up, cause confusion.

fortress

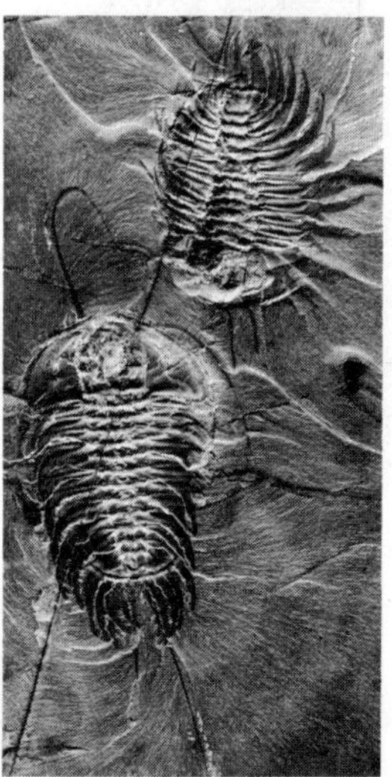

fossil

fox

fountain

[1]**found** (FOWND) *verb.* 1. To start or set up (something), as a government, college, or other institution. 2. To lay a base for or have a base. **founded, founding.**

[2]**found** (FOWND) *verb. See* **find.**

foun·da·tion (fown-DAY-shən) *noun.* 1. The base or ground on which something is founded: The *foundation* of their friendship is trust. 2. The lowest part of a building, set in or on the ground. 3. The act of founding a government or other institution. 4. An organization that handles money given for particular charities or projects. 5. A woman's undergarment.

[1]**found·er** (FOWN-dər) *noun.* 1. A person who founds, sets up, or establishes. 2. A person who makes metal castings.

[2]**found·er** (FOWN-dər) *verb.* 1. To fill with water and to sink: The ship *foundered* after hitting an iceberg. 2. To collapse or sink down, as an old building. 3. To fail completely. 4. To go lame; stumble. **foundered, foundering.**

found·ling (FOWND-ling) *noun.* A baby or child abandoned by unknown parents.

found·ry (FOWN-dree) *noun.* A factory where metal is melted down and poured into molds. **foundries.**

foun·tain (FOWNT-n) *noun.* 1. A spring of water bubbling out of the ground, often the source of a stream. 2. The starting place of something. 3. A man-made outlet for drinking water. 4. A structure of water outlets and pools used for decoration. 5. A container or reservoir for water or other liquids.

fountain pen. A writing instrument with a tube for holding ink.

four (FOR) *noun* (and *adjective*). The cardinal number after three and before five; 4.

four·score (FOR-skor) *adjective.* Eighty; 80; four times twenty.

four·teen (for-TEEN) *noun* (and *adjective*). The cardinal number after 13 and before 15; 14.

four·teenth (for-TEENTH) *adjective.* Coming next after 13th; 14th. —*noun.* One of 14 equal parts.

fourth (FORTH) *adjective.* Coming next after three; 4th. —*noun.* One of four equal sections.

fowl *noun.* 1. A farm bird, especially a chicken. 2. Older, less tender chicken or rooster used for soup or stew. 3. The meat of a farm bird as food. 4. Any bird, but most commonly, those raised or hunted for food. **fowl** or **fowls** *plural.* —*verb.* To hunt for or shoot game birds. **fowled, fowling.**

fox (FOKS) *noun.* 1. A wild, bushy-tailed, meat-eating member of the dog family, smaller than a wolf. 2. A clever, sly, or sneaky person. **foxes** or **fox** *plural.* —*verb.* (Informal) 1. To trick or fool. 2. To act in a clever way. **foxed, foxing.**

fox·y (FOK-see) *adjective.* Deceitful; sly; crafty; foxlike. **foxier, foxiest.**

foy·er (FOI-ər or FOI-ay) *noun.* 1. A large waiting room or lobby in a public building, as in a theater or hotel. 2. An entrance hall or area in a house or building.

Fr. *abbreviation.* 1. Father (priest). 2. France; French.

fra·cas (FRAY-kəss) *noun.* A noisy fight; a brawl. **fracases.**

frac·tion (FRAK-shən) *noun.* 1. (Math) A part of a unit or whole number: $\frac{1}{2}$, $\frac{1}{3}$, $\frac{1}{4}$. 2. A part of anything: I understood only a *fraction* of what he said. 3. A bit of something; a piece broken off. —**fractional** *adjective.* —**fractionally** *adverb.*

frac·ture (FRAK-chər) *noun.* 1. A break in a bone. 2. The way in which a bone is broken. 3. Any crack or break, as a fracture in a rock. **fractures.** —*verb.* 1. To break or crack. 2. (Slang) To cause amusement or amazement; dumbfound. **fractured, fracturing.**

frag·ile (FRAJ-əl or FRAJ-ighl) *adjective.* Easily broken or damaged.

frag·ment (FRAG-mənt) *noun.* 1. A small part or bit (of something): John cut his foot on a *fragment* of glass. 2. An unfinished part or piece of something: A *fragment* of a new play was found on the author's desk.

fra·grance (FRAY-grənss) *noun.* 1. A pleasant odor: The blooming roses filled the yard with *fragrance.* 2. Perfume, cologne, or toilet water. —**fragrant** *adjective.*

frail (FRAYL) *adjective.* 1. Weak; not in good health. 2. Easily broken: The branch was too *frail* to swing on. 3. Easily overcome: Mary's will power was too *frail* to make her refuse cake. —**frailty** *noun.*

frame (FRAYM) *noun.* 1. The enclosing or supporting edge of a picture, door, or window. 2. The parts of a structure that hold everything up or together: the *frame* of a house. 3. The (human) body; skeleton. 4. A special condition: *frame* of mind. 5. (Informal) An inning in baseball. 6. (Bowling) The box on the score sheet in which each player's score is recorded after each turn. 7. (Pool) The triangular holder used to set up the balls at the beginning of play. 8. One picture in a strip of film. **frames.** —*verb.* 1. To make a frame; begin construction. 2. To put a frame on or around: *frame* a picture. 3. To organize, outline, or set up (a plan, a story, the wording of a law). 4. (Slang) To make (an innocent person) seem guilty by distorting evidence. **framed, framing.**

frame·work (FRAYM-werk) *noun.* 1. A structure of joined parts. 2. An outline; a plan for organization: The Constitution is the *framework* of our government.

franc (FRANGK) *noun.* The unit of money in several countries, especially France, Belgium, and Switzerland.

frank (FRANGK) *adjective.* 1. Honest and open in speech; forthright. 2. Without cover, disguise, or hidden motive: a *frank* evaluation. **franker, frankest.** —*noun.* 1. The privilege of sending mail without postage. 2. A mark or signature on a letter or package which shows the use of this privilege. 3. (Informal) A frankfurter. —*verb.* To send without postage: Senators and Congressmen are allowed to *frank* their mail. **franked, franking.**

frank·furt·er (FRANGK-fər-tər) *noun.* A sausage usually made of beef or pork; a hot dog; a weiner.

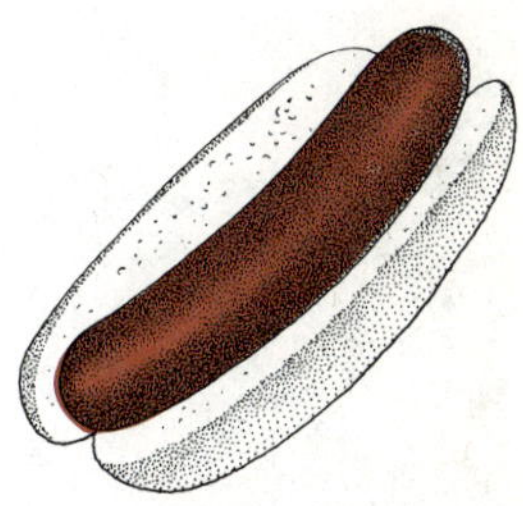

frankfurter

frank·in·cense (FRANGK-in-senss) *noun.* A dried, sweet-smelling substance that gives off a perfume when burned.

fran·tic (FRAN-tik) *adjective.* Greatly excited; wild with anger, pain, fear, sadness, or excitement. —**frantically** *adverb.*

fra·ter·nal (frə-TER-nl) *adjective.* 1. Brotherly; like a brother. 2. Referring to a group of men joined in a common interest: My uncle belongs to the Elks, a *fraternal* organization.

fra·ter·ni·ty (frə-TER-nə-tee) *noun.* 1. A social organization for male students. (*See* **sorority**). 2. A group of people joined in a common interest as if they were brothers. 3. Any group related by a common interest, profession, or other activity, as the legal *fraternity* (lawyers). 4. The condition of being brothers; brotherhood. **fraternities.**

fraud (FRAWD) *noun.* 1. Deception; trickery; dishonest practice: Exposing *fraud* is the job of the Better Business Bureau. 2. Any trick or deception. 3. A cheat; a deceiver.

fraud·u·lent (FRAWJ-ə-lənt) *adjective.* 1. Deceitful; cheating; using fraud. 2. Received through fraud. —**fraudulence, fraudulency** *noun.* —**fraudulently** *adverb.*

fraught (FRAWT) *adjective.* Filled: *fraught* with danger.

freeway

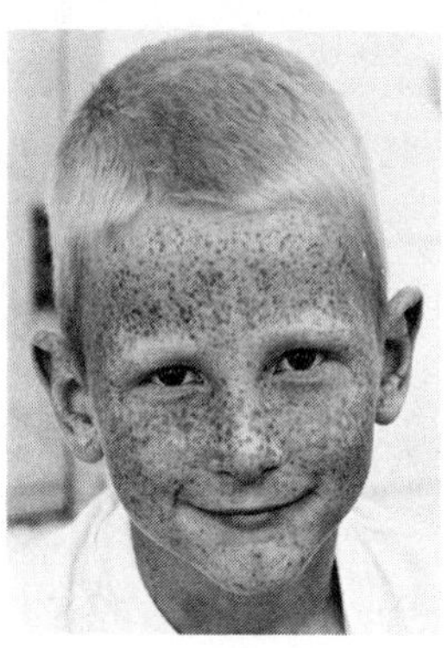
freckles

freight trains

[1]**fray** *noun.* A fight; an argument; a brawl.

[2]**fray** *verb.* To wear thin at the edges; unravel. **frayed, fraying.**

freak (FREEK) *noun.* 1. A strange, out-of-the-ordinary person, animal, plant, or thing. 2. (Slang) A keen fan; a person who is very fond of a particular thing: Harry is a cheese *freak;* he eats it at every meal. —*adjective.* Not normal; far from what is expected: a *freak* accident. —**freak out** (Slang) To completely lose mental or physical control, often while under the influence of drugs.

freak·y (FREE-kee) *adjective.* Strange; like a freak; seeming or behaving in a way that is not normal. **freakier, freakiest.** —**freakily** *adverb.*

freck·le (FREK-əl) *noun.* A small brown spot on the skin. **freckles.** —*verb.* To cause or develop freckles: I *freckle* easily. **freckled, freckling.**

free *adjective.* 1. Self-ruling; in charge of oneself; not under slavery or foreign rule. 2. Having or giving the privileges of liberty; enjoying the rights of a citizen: *free* government, *free* country, a *free* people. 3. Loose and spontaneous: *free* dancing, *free* play, *free* association (of thought). 4. Beyond or above; safe from: *free* from criticism. 5. Not stingy; using (money, time) without plan or thought: *free* spender. 6. Without cost: There will be *free* balloons for everyone. 7. Not under fixed rules or prices: *free* port. 8. Not following established rules or forms: *free* verse. 9. Not held, stopped, or blocked: *free* throw. 10. Not in use: The phone is never *free* at my house. **freer, freest.** —*verb.* 1. To make free; release; loosen. 2. To rid or clear of. **freed, freeing.** —*adverb.* 1. With no charge or cost. 2. (Also **freely**) In an unrestricted way.

free·dom (FREE-dəm) *noun.* 1. State of being free; liberty. 2. The right to act as one pleases. 3. Ease of moving or acting: Her full skirt gave her *freedom* to run. 4. Behavior that is overly frank or friendly.

free·hand (FREE-hand) *adjective.* Drawn by hand without the aid of measurements and instruments.

free·man (FREE-mən) *noun.* A person who can enjoy all the rights of a citizen. —**freemen** *plural.*

free verse. Poetry that does not follow the regular forms, such as rhyme, meter, and stanza.

free·way (FREE-way) *noun.* A toll-free superhighway.

freeze (FREEZ) *verb.* 1. To turn into ice; harden from liquid to solid through heat loss. 2. To harden because of cold: I hope my wet mittens won't *freeze.* 3. To become blocked with ice: Why did you let the garden hose *freeze?* 4. To be or to feel very cold. 5. To stiffen with fear, surprise, shock, as if frozen. **froze, frozen, freezing.** —*noun.* Act of freezing or condition of being frozen. **freezes.**

freez·er (FREEZ-ər) *noun.* 1. A storage chest for freezing food or keeping it frozen. 2. A machine for making ice cream.

freezing point. The temperature at which a liquid becomes solid through loss of heat: The *freezing point* of water is 32°F.

freight (FRAYT) *noun.* 1. Goods transported by train, plane, truck, or boat. 2. The cost of sending things by freight. —*verb.* To load or send cargo. **freighted, freighting.**

freight train. A train designed for carrying freight.

freight·er (FRAYT-ər) *noun.* A transport, usually a ship, that carries only goods or freight.

French fries. Potatoes cut in strips and fried in deep fat.

French toast. Bread soaked in a mixture of egg and milk and fried.

fren·zy (FREN-zee) *noun.* Wild mental excitement usually leading to feverish activity; brief loss of reason and control; unusual excitement. **frenzies.** —**frenzied** *adjective.*

fre·quen·cy (FREE-kwən-see) Also **frequence** (FREE-kwənss) *noun.* 1. The measure of how often something happens in a given time: The *frequency* (number of vibrations per second) of a sound wave determines its pitch. 2. The state of happening over and over regularly. **frequencies.**

frequency modulation Also **FM.** A static-free broadcasting system.

fre·quent (FREE-kwənt) *adjective.* Happening often and regularly. —(free-KWENT) *verb.* To visit regularly or often. **frequented, frequenting.** —**frequently** *adverb.*

fres·co (FRESS-koh) *noun.* 1. A painting done on wet plaster (walls or ceiling). 2. The method of painting on wet plaster. —**frescoes** or **frescos** *plural.* —*verb.* To paint on wet plaster. **frescoed, frescoing.**

fresh *adjective.* 1. Newly made or applied: *fresh* paint. 2. New; original: a *fresh* idea. 3. Newly added: a *fresh* supply of pencils. 4. Without salt: *fresh* water. 5. Clean; not stale, dirty, or worn: *fresh* clothing. 6. Not canned, pickled, or dried: *fresh* vegetables. 7. Lively; not tired. 8. (Slang) Rude; bold. 9. Inexperienced. 10. Having just arrived: *fresh* from college. **fresher, freshest.** —**freshly** *adverb.* —**freshness** *noun.*

fresh·en (FRESH-ən) *verb.* 1. To refresh. 2. To clean up and make oneself feel fresh. 3. To become less salty. **freshened, freshening.** —**freshener** *noun.*

fresh·et (FRESH-it) *noun.* 1. An abrupt overflowing of a stream caused by rain, melting snow, or ice. 2. A stream of fresh water that flows into the sea.

fresh·man (FRESH-mən) *noun.* 1. A first-year student in a high school or college. 2. A beginner; a newcomer: A newly elected senator is called a *freshman.* —**freshmen** *plural.*

fresh·wa·ter (FRESH-waw-tər or FRESH-wot-ər) *adjective.* From or referring to water that is not salt: *freshwater* fish.

[1]**fret** *verb.* 1. To worry or cause to worry; become irritated or upset. 2. To wear away; chew at; gnaw at; to rub. **fretted, fretting.** —*noun.* A worry or aggravation.

[2]**fret** Also **fretwork** *noun.* A decorative design of angles and straight lines. —*verb.* To decorate with fretwork. **fretted, fretting.**

[2]fret

[3]**fret** *noun.* A small ridge of metal, wood, or plastic set across the fingerboard of a stringed instrument such as a guitar.

fret·ful (FRET-fəl) *adjective.* Irritable; nervous: The *fretful* baby cried all night. —**fretfully** *adverb.*

fri·ar (FRIGH-ər) *noun.* A male member of any of several orders of the Roman Catholic Church.

fric·tion (FRIK-shən) *noun.* 1. A scraping or rubbing of one thing against another. 2. The power of one thing to resist a sliding movement of another: Without *friction,* the wheels of a car could not grip the road. 3. Arguments or quarrels: *Friction* with his boss made John give up his paper route.

Fri·day (FRIGH-dee or FRIGH-day) *noun.* The sixth day of the week. *Friday* is between Thursday and Saturday. —**Fri.** *abbreviation.*

friend (FREND) *noun.* 1. A person one knows and likes well. 2. An ally; the opposite of enemy: Our mayor is a *friend* to labor. 3. [Capital F] A member of the Society of Friends; a believer in the Quaker religion.

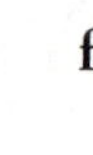

friend·ly (FREND-lee) *adjective.* Showing good will and liking; sweet, kind. **friendlier, friendliest.**

friend·ship (FREND-ship) *noun.* The feeling of warmth and kindness between people or nations.

frieze (FREEZ) *noun.* A decoration made of drawings or carvings that goes around the walls of a room or the outside of a building. **friezes.**

frigate

frig·ate (FRIG-it) *noun.* 1. A fast three-masted sailing vessel used in warfare during the 18th and 19th centuries. 2. A United States warship in the 5,000- to 7,000-ton class. **frigates.**

fright *noun.* 1. A sudden fear. 2. An ugly or ridiculous person or thing: Her messy hair was a *fright.*

fright·en (FRIGHT-n) *verb.* To scare or terrify. **frightened, frightening.**

frogmen

fright·ful (FRIGHT-fəl) *adjective.* 1. Shocking, terrible; making one afraid. 2. Ridiculous: Everyone laughed at her *frightful* wig. 3. (Informal) Very bad: The picnickers left the park a *frightful* mess. —**frightfully** *adverb.*

frig·id (FRIJ-id) *adjective.* 1. Extremely cold. 2. Unfriendly; without feeling or warmth. —**frigidly** *adverb.*

frill (FRIL) *noun.* 1. A ruffled, fluffy edging on clothing or curtains. 2. Something for show, without much use; a luxury: A bike without *frills* costs less. —**frilly** *adjective.*

fringe (FRINJ) *noun.* 1. A trimming of loose or bunched threads on the edge of clothing, curtains, tablecloths, and the like. 2. (Plural) Borders: People are moving to the *fringes* of big cities. **fringes.**

Frisbee

Fris·bee (FRIZ-bee) *trademark.* A plastic toy flung between players, shaped like a saucer and made in a variety of sizes and colors. **Frisbees.**

frisk *verb.* 1. To jump and skip about in a playful way. 2. (Slang) To search a person for hidden weapons. **frisked, frisking.**

frisk·y (FRISS-kee) *adjective.* Gay, playful, peppy. **friskier, friskiest.** —**friskily** *adverb.*

frit·ter (FRIT-ər) *noun.* A small fried batter-cake containing fruit, meat, or vegetable: corn *fritter.* —*verb.* (Used with *away*) To waste; use foolishly a little bit at a time. **frittered, frittering.**

friv·o·lous (FRIV-ə-ləss) *adjective.* Giddy; not responsible: In Aesop's fable, the *frivolous* grasshopper sang all summer while the ant worked. —**frivolously** *adverb.*

fro (FROH) *adverb.* Back from one place, usually in a repeated action: Shoppers hurried to and *fro.*

frock (FROK) *noun.* 1. A child's or woman's dress. 2. A robe worn by a monk, friar, or other clergyman.

frog (FRAWG) *noun.* 1. A small, smooth-skinned, tailless animal with webbed feet that lives both in water and on land. 2. An ornamental closing on a dress or coat. —**frog in the throat.** A slight hoarseness caused by mucus in the throat.

frog·man (FRAWG-man) *noun.* An underwater swimmer who wears skin-diving gear. —**frogmen** *plural.*

frol·ic (FROL-ik) *noun.* Gaiety, amusement; a playful trick: "A man cannot spend all this life in *frolic.*" (S. Johnson). —*verb.* To run about and play; have a good time. **frolicked, frolicking.**

from (FRUHM) *preposition.* 1. Starting or beginning at (a time or place): *from* New York to Chicago. 2. Compared to in position: far *from* home. 3. Compared to in kind or quality: Try to tell one twin *from* another. 4. Because of: tired *from* too much running. 5. Out of the possession or control of: Take the book *from* her. 6. Sent or given by: a letter *from* Mother.

frond *noun.* A large leaf, divided into many tiny sections, found in ferns and some palm trees.

front (FRUHNT) *noun.* 1. Part or side that faces forward; the important side: The *front* of a store faces the street. 2. The side or part that is at the beginning: The introduction is always at the *front* of a book. 3. The place or area ahead or before: A tall man sat down in *front* of me. 4. The edge of either cold or warm air that is moving into an area: A cold *front* is coming down from Canada. 5. Land facing a body of water: A house on the lake *front* is expensive. 6. A place or person used to hide real activities: A gangster had a florist shop as a *front.* 7. Appearance, manner: Whistling when you're afraid helps you to put up a brave *front.* 8. In a war, the area where the fighting is taking place. *—verb.* To be facing someone or something: The poorest part of the town *fronted* on the railroad tracks. **fronted, fronting.**

fron·tier (fruhn-TIHR) *noun.* 1. The edge of a country bordering on another country; boundary. 2. The edge of a country next to a wilderness or where people have not yet come to live: Alaska is our last *frontier.* 3. New areas of learning: Organ transplantation is one of the *frontiers* of medicine.

fron·tis·piece (FRUHN-tiss-peess) *noun.* A picture on the page that faces the title page of a book. **frontispieces.**

frost (FRAWST) *noun.* 1. Water from rain, dew, or vapor that has frozen into ice crystals on the ground, buildings, and other objects. 2. Weather in which the temperature is low enough to freeze water, soil, and plants. *—verb.* 1. To cover (a surface) with frost. 2. To cover with icing. **frosted, frosting.**

frost·bite (FRAWST-bight) *noun.* Damage to the tissues of the body by freezing; most often in the ears, nose, hands, or feet. *—verb.* To hurt a part of the body by freezing. **frostbit, frostbitten, frostbiting.**

frost·ed (FRAWSS-tid) *adjective.* 1. Coated with thick ice crystals: They drew pictures on the *frosted* windowpane. 2. Covered with icing. *—noun.* (Informal) A drink made of whipped cold milk and ice cream.

frost·ing (FRAWSS-ting) *noun.* 1. Icing on a cake. 2. A finish on glass or metal that looks like frost.

frost·y (FRAWSS-tee) *adjective.* 1. Cold enough to make frost. 2. Covered with frost. 3. Unfriendly. **frostier, frostiest.**

froth (FRAWTH) *noun.* 1. A mass of little bubbles or foam on top of a liquid. 2. Something silly and light, not to be taken seriously. *—verb.* To foam or make foam appear on the surface: The mad dog *frothed* at the mouth. **frothed, frothing.**

froth·y (FRAWTH-ee) adjective. 1. Filled with foam; with many small bubbles. 2. Gay, frivolous, unimportant. **frothier, frothiest.**

frown *noun.* An expression of displeasure or deep thought, usually shown by a wrinkled forehead and drawn-together eyebrows. *—verb.* 1. To crease the forehead in deep thought or in anger and disapproval. 2. To disapprove of something: Mother *frowns* on our eating candy. **frowned, frowning.**

froze (FROHZ) *verb. See* **freeze.**

fru·gal (FROO-gəl) *adjective.* 1. Thrifty, economical: "A penny saved is a penny earned," said the *frugal* man. 2. Cheap; costing little: a *frugal* dinner. **—frugally** *adverb.*

fruit (FROOT) *noun.* 1. The part of a plant that contains the seed, such as a nut, tomato, peach, or pea pod. 2. The seed-bearing part of a plant, usually soft and sweet, that is used as food. 3. Result of effort: Thomas Edison lived to see the *fruits* of his labor. **—fruit** or **fruits** *plural.* *—verb.* To bear fruit. **fruited, fruiting.**

fruit fly. A small fly that feeds on fruit while in the larva stage. **fruit flies.**

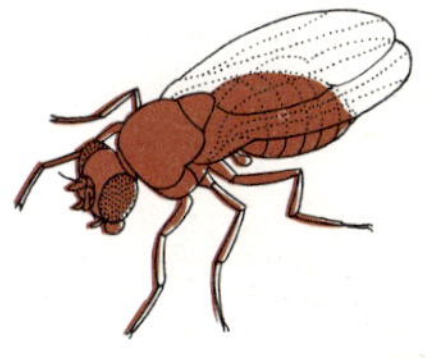
fruit fly

fruit·ful (FROOT-fəl) *adjective.* 1. Producing fruit. 2. Bringing good results: Our search for firewood was *fruitful.* —**fruitfully** *adverb.*

fruit·less (FROOT-liss) *adjective.* 1. Not bearing fruit. 2. Unsuccessful, unprofitable: All efforts to find the lost puppy were *fruitless.* —**fruitlessly** *adverb.*

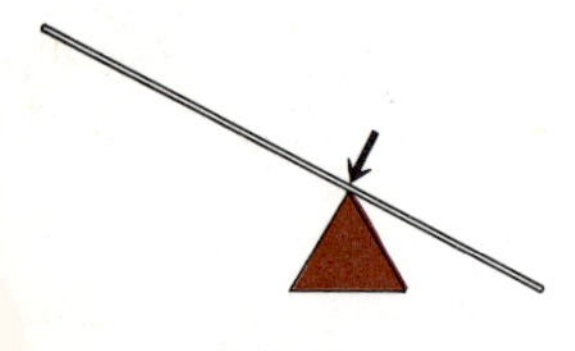
fulcrum

frus·trate (FRUHSS-trayt) *verb.* To prevent (someone) from achieving; to defeat: The wind died down and *frustrated* his plan to fly his kite. **frustrated, frustrating.** —**frustration** (fruhss-TRAY-shən) *noun.*

fry (FRIGH) *verb.* To cook in fat in a pan or on a griddle. **fried, frying.** —*noun.* 1. A fish that has just been hatched. 2. A picnic or outing where fried foods are served: The Rotary Club advertised its "Chicken *Fry.*" 3. (Plural) Something fried, such as potatoes. **fries.** —**small fry.** 1. Children. 2. Unimportant people.

ft. *abbreviation.* 1. Foot; feet. 2. Fort.

fudge (FUHJ) *noun.* 1. Soft candy made of butter, sugar, milk, and chocolate. 2. Silly talk; nonsense. —*verb.* To do something dishonestly or clumsily. **fudged, fudging.**

fu·el (FYOO-əl) *noun.* 1. A material such as coal, gas, oil, or wood that burns and produces heat or power. 2. Anything that increases a strong emotion: His harsh words were *fuel* to my anger. —*verb.* To give or take fuel: We waited an hour while the plane *fueled* up. **fueled** or **fuelled, fueling** or **fuelling.**

fu·gi·tive (FYOO-jə-tiv) *noun.* Someone who has run away or escaped, often from prison. **fugitives.** —*adjective.* 1. Fleeing. 2. Existing for only a short time. —**fugitively** *adverb.*

-ful *suffix.* 1. Filled with: beauti*ful.* 2. Having the character of: shame*ful.* 3. The quantity that would fill: tablespoon*ful.*

ful·crum (FUL-krəm) *noun.* A support on which a lever rests as it pushes or lifts something.

ful·fill (ful-FIL) Also **fulfil** *verb.* 1. To accomplish; to make something happen as promised or predicted: The principal *fulfilled* his promise of less homework. 2. To satisfy (needs or desires). **fulfilled, fulfilling.**

ful·fill·ment (ful-FIL-mənt) Also **fulfilment** *noun.* Completion; accomplishment; satisfaction.

full (FUL) *adjective.* 1. Containing as much as can be held: a *full* tank. 2. Steady, complete: a *full* hour of shoveling. 3. Round; plump: a *full* face. 4. With wide pleats or folds: *full* drapes. 5. Having eaten a great amount. **fuller, fullest.** —*adverb.* 1. Squarely, right on: He hit the thief *full* in the jaw. 2. Completely. 3. Very, extremely: You knew *full* well I didn't want you to stop.

full·back (FUL-bak) *noun.* Player in football, soccer, or hockey who stands farthest behind the front line.

full-fledged (FUL-FLEJD) *adjective.* 1. Entirely developed; mature. 2. Of full rank; completely qualified: a *full-fledged* lawyer.

full moon. The moon seen as a totally lighted disk.

ful·ly (FUL-ee) *adverb.* 1. Completely. 2. Satisfactorily.

fum·ble (FUHM-bəl) *verb.* 1. To search for something in a clumsy way: I *fumbled* in my pocket for the ticket. 2. To grope about blindly. 3. (Sports) To lose or drop a ball clumsily. **fumbled, fumbling.** —*noun.* A clumsy act. **fumbles.**

fume (FYOOM) *verb.* 1. To be very angry. 2. To send out unpleasant vapors, odors, gas, or smoke. **fumed, fuming.** —*noun.* Unpleasant smoke, vapors, gases, or odors. **fumes.**

fu·mi·gate (FYOO-mi-gayt) *verb.* To treat with a gas that will kill pests. **fumigated, fumigating.**

fun (FUHN) *noun.* Enjoyment; playfulness; joking. —**make fun of.** To tease; make (someone or something) appear ridiculous.

func·tion (FUHNGK-shən) *noun.* 1. The proper action or use of a person or thing: The *function* of an umpire is to rule on the plays of a game. 2. An important party or ceremony, either public or private: The biggest social *function* of the season was given by the Brown family. 3. (Mathematics) A quantity whose values depend upon another quantity. —*verb.* To operate or work: Our car *functions* well. **functioned, functioning.** —**functional** *adjective.* —**functionally** *adverb.*

fund (FUHND) *noun.* 1. Money collected and used for a special purpose: Each week our family added some money to the vacation *fund.* 2. A supply or abundance of something: The dictionary contains a *fund* of valuable information. 3. An organization that collects and uses money for a special purpose. —*verb.* To supply money or goods for a special purpose: The government *funded* the project to aid the poor. **funded, funding.**

fun·da·men·tal (fuhn-də-MENT-l) *adjective.* Basic; essential. —*noun.* Something basic or essential: Proper eating and sleeping habits are *fundamentals* of good health. —**fundamentally** *adverb.*

fu·ner·al (FYOO-nər-əl) *noun.* A ceremony in honor of a dead person followed by burial or cremation of the body.

fun·gus (FUHNG-gəss) *noun.* Any of several plants, such as mushrooms and molds, that do not have green color, leaves, or flowers. —**fungi** (FUHN-jigh) or **funguses** *plural.*

fun·nel (FUHN-l) *noun.* 1. A cone-shaped device with a tube at one end, used to pour liquids or powders into a narrow opening. 2. A chimney or smokestack as on a steamship or locomotive. —*verb.* To pour or go through a small opening or funnel: The nurse *funneled* cough syrup from a large bottle into several smaller ones. **funneled** or **funnelled, funneling** or **funnelling.**

fun·ny (FUHN-ee) *adjective.* 1. Entertaining; causing smiles or laughter. 2. Strange; odd: The hunter was puzzled by the *funny* footprints in the snow. **funnier, funniest.** —**funnies** *noun, plural.* Comic strips; cartoons.

fur (FER) *noun.* 1. The soft, hairy covering of many mammals: The bear's *fur* keeps him warm in winter. 2. A coat or other article of clothing made from fur.

fu·ri·ous (FYUR-ee-əss) *adjective.* 1. Very angry; enraged. 2. Wild, violent. —**furiously** *adverb.*

furl (FERL) *verb.* To roll up; fold: The marchers *furled* their banners after the parade. **furled, furling.**

fur·long (FER-lawng) *noun.* A unit of measure equal to $\frac{1}{8}$ of a mile.

fur·lough (FER-loh) *noun.* A period during which a soldier or other person is given a leave or vacation. —*verb.* To give a furlough to. **furloughed, furloughing.**

fur·nace (FER-niss) *noun.* A structure in which fuel is burned to heat a building or to bake or melt clay, metal, or some other substance. **furnaces.**

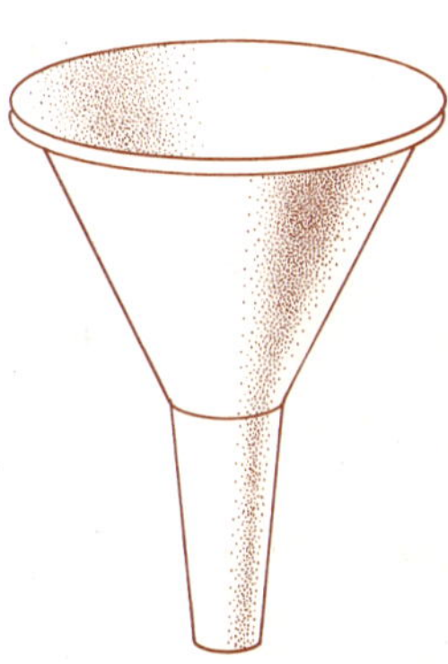
funnel

fur·nish (FER-nish) *verb.* 1. To supply (with furniture): We *furnished* our dining room with new maple furniture. 2. To supply: The school *furnished* a pen and pencil for each new student. **furnished, furnishing.**

fur·nish·ings (FER-nish-ingz) *noun, plural.* 1. The furniture, drapes, carpets, and other items with which a room is equipped. 2. The clothing and accessories that people wear: The store has a sale on jackets, belts, and other men's *furnishings.*

fur·ni·ture (FER-nə-chər) *noun.* Movable items, such as chairs, tables, desks, and beds, with which a room is equipped.

fur·ri·er (FER-ee-ər) *noun.* A person who makes or sells fur clothing.

fur·row (FER-oh) *noun.* 1. A shallow trench or cut in the earth, especially one made by a plow. 2. A deep wrinkle in the skin: The old man's face was lined with *furrows.* —*verb.* 1. To make furrows in. 2. To plow. **furrowed, furrowing.**

fur·ry (FER-ee) *adjective.* 1. Covered with or having fur: The beaver is a *furry* animal. 2. Like or related to fur: The blanket is made of a *furry* fabric. **furrier, furriest.**

fur·ther (FER-thər) *adjective* and *adverb. See* **far.** —*verb.* To assist; move forward: The large donation of money *furthered* the plans for a new hospital. **furthered, furthering.**

fur·ther·more (FER-thər-mor) *adverb.* In addition; besides: Irene wants to go to college; *furthermore,* she wants to become a doctor.

fur·ther·most (FER-thər-mohst) *adjective.* Most distant: The *furthermost* cabin is on the other side of the forest.

fur·thest (FER-thist) *adjective* and *adverb. See* **far.**

fu·ry (FYUR-ee) *noun.* 1. Extreme anger; rage. 2. Violent action: The *fury* of the storm caused great damage. 3. A person easily or often angered. **furies.**

fuse (FYOOZ) *noun.* 1. A wick used to set off an explosive. 2. A safety device used in an electric circuit to prevent overheating. **fuses.** —*verb.* 1. To melt or blend together with heat: The fire *fused* the plastic and metal parts of Tim's pen. 2. To unite. **fused, fusing.**

fu·se·lage (FYOO-sə-lahzh) *noun.* The body of an airplane to which the wings and tail are attached. **fuselages.**

fu·sion (FYOO-zhən) *noun.* 1. The act or process of melting or blending together: Intense heat caused the *fusion* of the two metals. 2. The combination of different things joined together. 3. A combining of atomic nuclei, releasing enormous energy.

fuss (FUHSS) *noun.* A commotion; excited activity: The passengers made a *fuss* when the bus stalled. **fusses.** —*verb.* 1. To make a commotion. 2. To be overly anxious or careful: Mother *fussed* over Janet's appearance. **fussed, fussing.**

fus·sy (FUHSS-ee) *adjective.* 1. Very careful about small details: Mother is so *fussy* that she dusts twice a day. 2. Tending to worry or become upset. **fussier, fussiest.** —**fussily** *adverb.*

fu·tile (FYOOT-l or FYOO-tighl) *adjective.* Useless; without success: The fireman's efforts to stop the raging fire were *futile.* —**futilely** *adverb.*

fu·ture (FYOO-chər) *noun.* 1. Time that has yet to come: The year 2050 is many years in the *future.* 2. The life or experiences that are yet to come for a person: Jim is planning for a prosperous *future* by saving some money each week. **futures.** —*adjective.* 1. Yet to come: *Future* discoveries in medicine may lead to better health for all. 2. (Grammar) Describing action that has not yet occurred: *future* tense.

fuzz (FUHZ) *noun.* 1. A mass or covering of a fine, light substance, usually hairs or fibers: The peach is covered with a light *fuzz.* 2. (Slang) The police.

fuzz·y (FUHZ-ee) *adjective.* 1. Like or covered with fuzz. 2. Blurred; not clear: The TV picture was *fuzzy* until Dad adjusted it. **fuzzier, fuzziest.** —**fuzzily** *adverb.*

-fy *suffix.* To make or become, as lique*fy.*

G, g (JEE) 1. The seventh letter of the English alphabet. 2. A symbol for the force of gravity.

g. *abbreviation.* 1. Gender. 2. Guide. 3. Gulf.

gab *verb.* (Informal) To talk a lot about trivial matters; to chatter. **gabbed, gabbing.** *—noun.* A lot of talk about very little.

gab·ble (GAB-əl) *verb.* To talk rapidly without making much sense; babble. **gabbled, gabbling.** *—noun.* Rapid talk without much meaning.

ga·ble (GAY-bəl) *noun.* The peak of the triangle formed by the sloping ends of a ridged roof on a building.

gad *verb.* To move restlessly; wander. **gadded, gadding.**

gad·a·bout (GAD-ə-bowt) *noun.* Someone who roams restlessly looking for fun.

gad·fly (GAD-fligh) *noun.* 1. A person who bothers or stirs up others, especially with constant criticism or demands. 2. A large fly that stings animals, especially cows and horses. **gadflies.**

gad·get (GAJ-it) *noun.* (Informal) A small device or tool made for a specific job.

gaff (GAF) *noun.* 1. A pole with a strong hook on the end, used to haul in large fish. 2. The pole supporting a fore-and-aft sail. *—verb.* To land or pull in with a gaff. **gaffed, gaffing. —stand the gaff.** (Slang) To take punishment or trouble without complaining.

gag *verb.* 1. To put something over or in someone's mouth to keep him from talking or crying out. 2. To forbid someone to speak out. 3. To be unable to swallow. **gagged, gagging.** *—noun.* 1. Anything stuffed in the mouth or covering it so as to prevent speech. 2. A rule, law, or act of terror to prevent free speech. 3. (Informal) A joke, a trick.

gai·e·ty (GAY-ə-tee) *noun.* 1. A feeling or condition of being gay, happy, merry. 2. Festivity or merrymaking. **gaieties.**

gai·ly (GAY-lee) *adverb.* 1. Merrily, happily; lightly, not seriously. 2. Brightly; in a showy manner.

gain (GAYN) *verb.* 1. To get; obtain; take possession of: Whoever wins the race will *gain* the silver cup. 2. To earn or receive as a benefit: By putting my money in the bank, I *gained* 50 cents interest. 3. To take or get as an addition: I *gained* three pounds during vacation. 4. To reach or get to: After climbing for hours, we finally *gained* the top of the mountain. **gained, gaining.** *—noun.* That which is achieved or won. **—gain on.** To move closer to: By continuing steadily, the tortoise finally *gained on* the hare.

gables

gain·ful (GAYN-fəl) *adjective.* Profitable, moneymaking; advantageous. **—gainfully** *adverb.*

gain·say (gayn-SAY) *verb.* To deny, speak against. **gainsaid, gainsaying.**

gait (GAYT) *noun.* 1. A way of moving, walking, or running. 2. Any of the steps taught to a horse.

ga·la (GAY-lə, GAL-ə, or GAH-lə) *adjective.* Festive, merry, gay. *—noun.* A celebration or festival.

gal·ax·y (GAL-ək-see) *noun.* 1. [Usually capital G] The Milky Way. 2. Any other such large group of stars. 3. A group of famous people or celebrities or an array of beautiful and brilliant things. **galaxies.**

galaxy

gale (GAYL) *noun.* 1. A strong wind. 2. A loud or emotional outburst, as a *gale* of laughter. **gales.**

gall (GAWL) *noun.* 1. A green, bitter fluid in animals, made by the liver and stored in the gallbladder. 2. Something bitter or unpleasant. 3. (Informal) Impolite boldness. 4. A sore on the skin of an animal caused by chafing or rubbing. 5. An irritation or annoyance. 6. A bare or worn spot, especially one caused by rubbing. 7. A tumor or growth on a plant caused by irritation: an oak *gall.* —*verb.* 1. (Informal) To make angry. 2. Make sore by rubbing. **galled, galling.**

gallows

gal·lant (GAL-ənt) *adjective.* 1. Brave, noble, courageous. 2. Courteous or polite to women. —(gə-LANT, gə-LAHNT, or GAL-ənt) *noun.* 1. A man with courage and nobility. 2. A man who is politely attentive to women. —**gallantly** *adverb.*

gal·lan·try (GAL-ən-tree) *noun.* 1. Noble behavior; dashing courage. 2. Extremely polite attention to women. **gallantries.**

galleon

gall·blad·der (GAWL-blad-ər) *noun.* A sac attached to the liver in which gall is stored.

gal·le·on (GAL-ee-ən) *noun.* A large Spanish sailing ship in use during the 15th and 16th centuries.

gal·ler·y (GAL-ə-ree) *noun.* 1. A room or building in which exhibits, art objects, or merchandise are displayed to the public. 2. A section of a fair or amusement park where one can play games on machines or shoot at moving objects. 3. The upper floor of a theater; the balcony. 4. The people who sit in the balcony. 5. A long narrow hall or walkway. **galleries.**

gal·ley (GAL-ee) *noun.* 1. A long narrow vessel having many rowers and one or two sails. 2. The kitchen area of a ship or airplane. 3. (Printing) A long steel tray to hold type that has been set.

gal·lon (GAL-ən) *noun.* A unit of liquid measure that equals 4 quarts, 8 pints, or 128 ounces.

gal·lop (GAL-əp) *verb.* 1. To ride (a horse) at a fairly fast gait. 2. To hurry; make rapid progress. **galloped, galloping.** —*noun.* 1. A horse's gait in which all four feet leave the ground in leaping movements. 2. Rapid movement.

gal·lows (GAL-ohz) *noun.* A wooden structure that has a crossbeam and a rope, used as a means of killing a person by hanging.

ga·losh·es (gə-LOSH-iz) *noun, plural.* Plastic or rubber outer shoes worn over other shoes to keep out water or snow.

gal·va·nize (GAL-və-nighz) *verb.* 1. To plate or cover with zinc by means of an electric current in a liquid. 2. To shock; startle; stimulate to action: Fear *galvanized* him. 3. To shock with an electric current. **galvanized, galvanizing.**

gam·ble (GAM-bəl) *verb.* 1. To wager or bet; take a chance at winning with the risk of loss. 2. To play a game based on chance and money, such as one with cards or dice. **gambled, gambling.** —*noun.* 1. A bet or wager. 2. An act involving both risk and opportunity. **gambles.**

gam·bler (GAM-blər) *noun.* Someone who plays games of chance for a living or as a hobby.

gam·bol (GAM-bəl) *verb.* To frolic about playfully. **gamboled, gamboling.** —*noun.* Frolic, play.

game (GAYM) *noun.* 1. A playful activity with or without rules. 2. A sport or other competition with specific rules, such as soccer or checkers. 3. The number of points needed for winning a game. 4. A toy, or group of objects made for playing with, such as a jigsaw puzzle. 5. (Slang) Any highly competitive business: the publishing *game;* the advertising *game.* 6. Any animal sought after by hunters, especially birds and fish; the meat of such animals eaten as food. —*adjective.* 1. (Slang) Ready; willing: Bill is always *game* for a party. 2. Bold, courageous.

game·cock (GAYM-kok) *noun.* A cock or rooster trained for cockfighting.

game plan. (Sports) A coach's plan, or strategy, as to how a particular game can best be played and won.

game warden. A warden or public official whose job is to see that game laws are obeyed.

gan·der (GAN-dər) *noun.* A male goose.

gang *noun.* 1. Any group of people, especially one gathered together for work or other special purpose: a *gang* of robbers; a railroad *gang.* 2. The people one plays or spends time with; friends and playmates. —*verb.* 1. To get together in a group for a common activity. 2. To put together, gather in a bunch. **ganged, ganging.** —**gang up on.** (Slang) To attack or oppose one or a few people with many.

gang·plank (GANG-plangk) *noun.* A movable board or ramp that is used for boarding or leaving a ship.

gan·grene (GANG-green or gang-GREEN) *noun.* The decay of a part of the body, caused by disease, injury, or poor blood supply. —**gangrenous** (GANG-grə-nəss) *adjective.*

gang·way (GANG-way) *noun.* 1. A gangplank. 2. A passageway or aisle. 3. A door or large hatch in the side of a ship. 4. A hanging walkway above machinery or a stage. —(GANG-WAY) *interjection.* (Slang) Make way!

gan·try (GAN-tree) *noun.* A cradle or platform for moving a crane boom, rocket, or other large object.

gaol (JAYL). British form of **jail.**

gap *noun.* 1. A space or hole. 2. A break, stoppage, or interruption. 3. A mountain pass or ravine.

gape (GAYP) *verb.* 1. To open the mouth wide. 2. To stare or gaze with the mouth open. 3. To become wide open. **gaped, gaping.**

ga·rage (gə-RAHZH) *noun.* 1. A building for parking one or more automobiles. 2. A repair shop for cars and other vehicles. **garages.**

garb (GAHRB) *noun.* 1. What one wears as clothing; clothes. 2. Style of dressing. —*verb.* To dress. **garbed, garbing.**

gar·bage (GAHR-bij) *noun.* 1. Uneaten food; waste matter. 2. (Informal) Waste or unwanted materials.

gar·ble (GAHR-bəl) *verb.* 1. To confuse or mix up: The static *garbled* the radio news report. 2. To change or mix up the sense of another's words deliberately. **garbled, garbling.**

gar·den (GAHRD-n) *noun.* A plot of ground where fruits, vegetables, or flowers are grown. —*verb.* 1. To work in a garden. 2. To grow things for food or for beauty. **gardened, gardening.** —**gardener** *noun.*

gar·de·ni·a (gahr-DEEN-yə) *noun.* A large sweet-smelling flower with waxy white or yellow petals.

gar·gle (GAHR-gəl) *verb.* To clean the mouth with a liquid by holding the head back and forcing air bubbles through the liquid to hold it at the back of the mouth. **gargled, gargling.**

gar·goyle (GAHR-goil) *noun.* A roof-gutter spout carved as a weird animal or human figure.

gar·land (GAHR-lənd) *noun.* A circle of woven flowers or plant leaves, used to decorate or honor the person or object on which it is placed. —*verb.* 1. To form or make into a garland. 2. To place a garland upon. **garlanded, garlanding.**

gar·lic (GAHR-lik) *noun.* 1. A strong-smelling onion-like plant. 2. The bulb of this plant, used to flavor food.

gar·ment (GAHR-mənt) *noun.* Anything worn as clothing.

gargoyle

gantry (with rocket)

gas mask

garter snake

gar·ner (GAHR-nər) *verb.* 1. To gather up, collect for storage; store up. 2. To acquire. **garnered, garnering.** —*noun.* A storage place for grain.

gar·net (GAHR-nit) *noun.* 1. A deep red gem. 2. A hard, glassy mineral of any color. 3. (Also *adjective*) A dark red color.

gar·nish (GAHR-nish) *verb.* 1. To add spice or decoration to (food). 2. To trim, adorn; make fancy. **garnished, garnishing.** —*noun.* 1. Something added to food for spice or color. 2. Trim, decoration. **garnishes.**

gar·ret (GA-rit) *noun.* The attic; the space or rooms just under the roof of a house or other building.

gar·ri·son (GA-ri-sən) *noun.* 1. A fort, a place where soldiers are stationed. 2. The soldiers assigned to a fort or a given area. —*verb.* To station troops in a particular place. **garrisoned, garrisoning.**

gar·ter (GAHR-tər) *noun.* An elastic band or a strap with a fastener used to keep up hose or stockings.

garter snake. A harmless common small snake found in North America, usually black or brown with three yellow stripes.

gas *noun.* 1. One of the three states in which matter exists; not a solid or liquid. 2. A substance that can expand without limit and has no set shape. 3. A gaseous substance used as an anesthetic. 4. Fumes that may be poisonous or irritating. 5. A gaseous mixture used as a fuel and for cooking. 6. Short for *gasoline.* 7. (Slang) An exciting event. —**gases** or **gasses** *plural.* —*verb.* 1. To poison by gas. 2. (Slang) To talk. **gassed, gassing.**

gas·e·ous (GASS-ee-əss, GASS-yəss, or GASH-əss) *adjective.* Existing as a gas, having vapors: Some of the *gaseous* elements are hydrogen, helium, oxygen, and nitrogen.

gash *verb.* To cut deeply; slash. **gashed, gashing.** —*noun.* A deep cut or wound; a tear. **gashes.**

gas·ket (GASS-kit) *noun.* A device, usually of asbestos, rubber, or metal, used to seal a joint to prevent seepage of air, steam, or fluid. —**blow a gasket.** (Slang) Let off steam; lose one's temper.

gas mask. A protection for the face with a filter that prevents breathing harmful gases.

gas·o·line (GASS-ə-leen or gass-ə-LEEN) *noun.* A highly flammable liquid made from crude petroleum, used chiefly as fuel for engines.

gasp *verb.* 1. To draw in breath suddenly, usually from fear or surprise. 2. To pant, breathe with difficulty. **gasped, gasping.** —*noun.* A sudden intake of breath, or the sound made by such an intake.

gas station. A place that sells gasoline for motor vehicles and usually provides other services for these vehicles.

gas·tric (GASS-trik) *adjective.* Of or referring to the stomach: *gastric* pain, *gastric* ulcers.

gate (GAYT) *noun.* 1. A door that allows passage through a wall or fence. 2. Anything that opens passage or gives access to: the *gate* to freedom; the *gate* to fame. 3. A structure controlling the flow of water, as in a canal. 4. The receipts or total number of tickets sold for an event. **gates.** —**give the gate to.** To get rid of or put out.

gath·er (GATH-ər) *verb.* 1. To collect; pick and join together. 2. To come (together), assemble. 3. To guess or infer: I *gather* she is right. 4. To gain a gradual increase in: He was *gathering* speed by the minute. 5. To summon up: He *gathered* his courage. 6. To pull fabric together with stitches to form puckering. 7. To swell and fester, as a boil. 8. To pull closer to or draw (around): I *gathered* my cape tightly about me to keep out the rain. **gathered, gathering.** —*noun.* (Usually plural) Tucks in cloth.

gath·er·ing (GATH-ər-ing) *noun.* A group of people; a meeting.

gau·cho (GOW-choh) *noun.* A cowboy or herdsman from the South American pampas. **gauchos.**

gaud·y (GAW-dee) *adjective.* Flashy; in poor taste. **gaudier, gaudiest.**

gauge (GAYJ) Also **gage** *noun.* 1. A standard measuring scale. 2. An instrument for measuring amounts: a gas *gauge.* **gauges.** —*verb.* 1. To measure, determine exactly: He *gauged* the amount of steam that escaped. 2. To judge or make an evaluation: I cannot *gauge* whether John is telling the truth or not. **gauged, gauging.**

gaunt (GAWNT) *adjective.* 1. Lean; thin and bony in appearance. 2. Bleak, barren, grim: The *gaunt* walls of the prison were no comfort to the condemned man. **gaunter, gauntest.**

gaunt·let (GAWNT-lit or GAHNT-lit) Also **gantlet** *noun.* 1. A knight's protective glove. 2. A long dress glove. —**run the gauntlet.** Be forced to run between two lines of men armed with clubs. —**throw down the gauntlet.** To challenge.

gauss (GOWSS) *noun.* A unit of measurement of the strength of a magnetic field. —**gauss** *plural.*

gauze (GAWZ) *noun.* 1. A thin, loosely woven fabric. 2. A thin, webbed cotton cloth used as a bandage.

gauzy (GAWZ-ee) *adjective.* Thin, wispy, filmy: "How handsome are your *gauzy* wings." (Mary Howitt). **gauzier, gauziest.**

gave (GAYV) *See* **give.**

gav·el (GAV-əl) *noun.* A wooden mallet or hammer used by presidents, judges, or others in charge of meetings to keep order or call for attention.

gawk (GAWK) *verb.* To stare in a stupid way. **gawked, gawking.** —*noun.* A foolish, awkward person. —**gawky** *adjective.*

gay *adjective.* 1. Cheerful, lighthearted. 2. Brightly colored; showy: Joan's blouse was *gay* with orange and red flowers. **gayer, gayest.** —**gaily** or **gayly** *adverb.*

gaze (GAYZ) *verb.* To look with fixed focus, to stare. **gazed, gazing.** —*noun.* A long, steady look; a stare. **gazes.**

ga·zelle (gə-ZEL) *noun.* A graceful antelope, small and swift, with spiraling horns, found in Africa and Asia. **gazelles.**

gaz·et·teer (gaz-ə-TIHR) *noun.* A dictionary of geographical names.

gear (GIHR) *noun.* 1. A notched wheel or mechanism that meshes with and moves a similar object. 2. Equipment, as tools or clothing needed to do something: The camper's *gear* includes a tent and sleeping bag. —*verb.* 1. To equip. 2. To adjust, adapt: The travelers *geared* their behavior to the countries they visited. **geared, gearing.** —**in gear.** 1. With its gears in position and ready to operate. 2. Ready to go. —**into high gear.** (Slang) Ready to do things quickly.

gear·shift (GIHR-shift) *noun.* A stick or mechanism for changing from one gear to another.

geese (GEESS) *See* **goose.**

Gei·ger count·er (GIGH-gər KOWN-tər) An electronic instrument for detecting and measuring radiation and radioactive substances.

gel·a·tin (JEL-ə-tən) Also **gelatine** *noun.* A jelly-like substance that comes from the bones and hoofs of animals and is used in foods, dyes, and photography.

gem (JEM) *noun.* 1. A precious stone or jewel, usually cut or polished. 2. Something highly valued.

Gem·i·ni (JEM-ə-nigh or JEM-ə-nee) *noun.* The third sign of the zodiac, also called the "Twins." The time of this sign is from May 21 through June 20.

gazelle

gavel

Gemini

gen·der (JEN-dər) *noun.* 1. (Grammar) Classification of a word as masculine, feminine, or neuter. 2. Sex, male or female, of an individual.

gene (JEEN) *noun.* Unit of heredity carried in the chromosomes of living cells: *Genes* determine the color of our eyes and other inherited characteristics. **genes.**

ge·ne·al·o·gy (jee-nee-AL-ə-jee) *noun.* 1. The study of ancestry and family relationships: *Genealogy* is used in legal matters and by individuals interested in tracing their family tree. 2. A record or list of one's descent from ancestors; family tree. **genealogies. —genealogical** (jee-nee-ə-LOJ-i-kəl) *adjective.*

gen·er·al (JEN-ər-əl) *noun.* An officer above a colonel in U.S. military rank: "Soldiers win battles and *generals* get the credit." (Napoleon). —*adjective.* 1. Widespread: "On all sides there seemed to be *general* rejoicing." (Hans Christian Andersen). 2. Concerning all, not local or special: The Constitution is concerned with the *general* welfare of all the people. 3. Usual, normal, common: A *general* custom for the British is to have tea in the late afternoon. 4. Most important in rank: the *general* manager of a store. **—generally** *adverb.* **—in general.** Usually, for the most part.

gen·er·al·i·ty (jən-ə-RAL-ə-tee) *noun.* 1. A broad, all-inclusive statement lacking specifics: She gave no details but described our course in *generalities.* 2. An observation or idea in general use: It is a *generality* that most little girls like to play with dolls. 3. The largest number; the main part. **generalities.**

gen·er·al·ize (JEN-ər-ə-lighz) *verb.* 1. To come to broad conclusions by inferring or forming ideas from definite facts: From the results of the poll, he *generalized* that the majority would vote for him. 2. To be general rather than specific: He *generalized* when he gave her the news, not telling her all the details. **generalized, generalizing.**

gen·er·al·i·za·tion (jen-ər-ə-lə-ZAY-shən) *noun:* A general statement or conclusion. "All *generalizations* are dangerous, even this one." (Dumas).

gen·er·ate (JEN-ə-rayt) *verb.* To bring into existence; produce: *generate* enthusiasm. **generated, generating.**

gen·er·a·tion (jen-ə-RAY-shən) *noun.* 1. One stage in a line of descent: Our fathers are of one *generation;* we are of another. 2. Contemporaries, people born at about the same time: "The torch has been passed to a new *generation* of Americans." (John F. Kennedy). 3. The average length of time between birth of parents and birth of their children: A *generation* is usually thought of as about 30 years. 4. The act of producing: the *generation* of electricity.

gen·er·a·tor (JEN-ə-ray-tər) *noun.* 1. A machine that produces or generates something: A dynamo is a *generator* that changes mechanical energy into electrical energy. 2. A person or thing that causes or generates.

gen·er·os·i·ty (jen-ə-ROSS-ə-tee) *noun.* 1. Willingness to give or share; unselfishness. 2. Abundance: Nature's *generosity.*

gen·er·ous (JEN-ər-əss) *adjective.* 1. Unselfish; willing to give or share. 2. Abundant; more than enough: She had a *generous* piece of pie. 3. Not bearing ill will or hard feelings: a *generous* gesture to the fallen foe. **—generously** *adverb.*

gen·e·sis (JEN-ə-siss) *noun.* 1. Birth, beginning, creation. 2. [Capital G] The first book of the Old Testament. **—geneses** (JEN-ə-seez) *plural.*

ge·net·ics (jə-NET-iks) *noun, plural in form but used with a singular verb.* The scientific study of heredity: *Genetics* is a branch of biology. **—genetic** *adjective.*

gen·ial (JEEN-yəl *or* JEE-nee-əl) *adjective.* 1. Cheerful, kindly. 2. Healthy; favorable for growth. —**geniality** *noun.* —**genially** *adverb.*

ge·nie (JEE-nee) *noun.* An imaginary creature with extraordinary powers: The *genie* allowed Aladdin to make three wishes. **genies.**

gen·i·tal (JEN-ə-təl) *adjective.* Of or referring to the production of young and to the organs involved in the production of young.

genitals (JEN-ə-təlz) *noun, plural.* The reproductive organs, especially those on the outside of the body.

gen·ius (JEEN-yəss) *noun.* 1. Superior intelligence; unusual creative ability: "*Genius* must be born and never can be taught." (Dryden). 2. A person who has this exceptional quality. 3. The particular character, quality, or spirit of a place, nation, person, or age: the American *genius* for invention. **geniuses.**

gen·tian (JEN-shən) *noun.* A plant with fringed, usually blue, flowers.

gen·tile (JEN-tighl) *noun.* [Usually capital G] 1. Anyone who is not a Jew. 2. Among Mormons, a non-Mormon. —*adjective.* [Often capital G] Christian as distinguished from Jewish.

gen·til·i·ty (jen-TIL-ə-tee) *noun.* 1. High status because of birth to an upper-class family. 2. Good breeding, politeness, good manners.

gen·tle (JEN-tl) *adjective.* 1. Soft, delicate, mild: She had a *gentle* voice. 2. Kind, considerate: The doctor was *gentle* when he broke the news. 3. Tame, docile. 4. Gradual, not sudden: We drove up a *gentle* incline. 5. Having manners acquired through social training. **gentler, gentlest.** —**gentleness** *noun.* —**gently** *adverb.*

gen·tle·man (JENT-l-mən) *noun.* 1. A man who is considerate and polite; a man of honor. 2. Formerly, someone born to wealth and high position. 3. Any man, often as a form of address: "God rest you merry, *gentlemen.*" (Christmas carol). **gentlemen.** —**gentlemanly** *adverb.* —**gentleman's agreement.** An agreement that is understood but not written down.

gen·u·ine (JEN-yoo-in) *adjective.* 1. Real, not phony or counterfeit. 2. Openly honest, sincere. —**genuinely** *adverb.* —**genuineness** *noun.*

ge·nus (JEE-nəss) *noun.* 1. A group of plants or animals; a category of classification in biology. 2. Any group with common or related qualities. —**genera** (JEN-ə-rə) *plural.*

geo- *prefix.* Indicates "the earth:" *geo*graphy, *geo*logy.

ge·ode (JEE-ohd) *noun.* (Geology) A hollow small stone lined inside with crystals. **geodes.**

ge·o·graph·ic (jee-ə-GRAF-ik) Also **geographical** *adjective.* 1. Having to do with geography. 2. Relating to the features of a region. —**geographically** *adverb.*

ge·og·ra·phy (jee-OG-rə-fee) *noun.* 1. The study of the natural features of the earth's surface, climate, resources, and inhabitants. 2. A book about this study. 3. The natural features of an area. **geographies.**

ge·o·log·ic (jee-ə-LOJ-ik) Also **geological** *adjective.* Having to do with geology. —**geologically** *adverb.*

gentian

ge·ol·o·gist (jee-OL-ə-jist) *noun.* A person whose field of study is geology.

ge·ol·o·gy (jee-OL-ə-jee) *noun.* The science of the history and structure of the earth's crust, particularly the study of rocks, minerals, and fossils.

ge·o·mag·net·ic (jee-oh-mag-NET-ik) *adjective.* Of or related to the earth's magnetic force. —**geomagnetically** *adverb.*

ge·o·met·ric (jee-ə-MET-rik) *adjective.* 1. Of or related to geometry. 2. Having a pattern or design consisting of geometric figures. —**geometrically** *adverb.*

Georgia
★capital: Atlanta

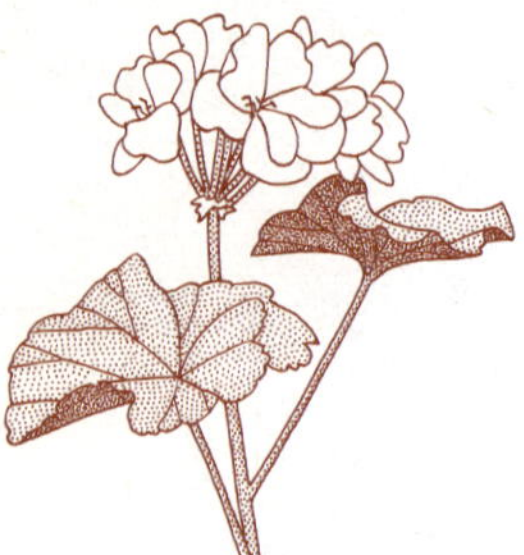
geranium

gerbil

ghost town

geometrical figure. Any one of a group of shapes dealt with in geometry, as circles, squares, triangles, polygons, cylinders, cubes, and polyhedrons.

ge·om·e·try (jee-OM-ə-tree) *noun.* (Math) The study of points, lines, surfaces, angles, and solids.

ge·o·phys·ics (jee-oh-FIZ-iks) *noun, plural in form but used with a singular verb.* The science concerned with the effect of winds, temperatures, and other natural agents on the earth.

Geor·gia (JOR-jə) *noun.* A south Atlantic state in the United States, fourth to ratify the Constitution (1788). —**Ga.** *abbreviation.* Also **GA** for Zip Codes.

geostationary orbit. A satellite orbit that lies 22,000 miles above the equator: Any satellite moving east in *geostationary orbit* will remain over the same spot on the earth.

ge·ra·ni·um (ji-RAY-nee-əm) *noun.* A plant with red, white, purple, or pink flowers.

ger·bil (JER-bil) *noun.* A small rodent that resembles a hamster and is widely popular as a pet.

germ (JERM) *noun.* 1. An extremely small plant or animal organism, especially one that causes disease. 2. The original or earliest stage in the development of a plant or animal; a seed. 3. The beginning of an idea or process: The sound of ocean waves was the *germ* for the songwriter's new melody.

German measles. A contagious disease, usually milder than ordinary measles, that causes a fever, rash, and throat irritation.

ger·mi·cide (JER-mə-sighd) *noun.* A substance used to destroy germs.

ger·mi·nate (JER-mə-nayt) *verb.* To start to develop or grow; to sprout: When planted, seeds *germinate;* shoots or stems appear through the soil. **germinated, germinating.**

ges·ture (JESS-chər) *noun.* 1. A motion of the hand or other part of the body that expresses a feeling or emphasizes something spoken: The boy shook his fist in a *gesture* of anger. 2. An action, often only for effect, performed as a sign or token of some attitude or feeling: The gentleman's offer to pay for our meal was a courteous *gesture.* **gestures.** —*verb.* To indicate or show (something) with a gesture. **gestured, gesturing.**

get *verb.* 1. To receive; obtain; acquire. 2. To earn or achieve. 3. To fetch or retrieve. 4. To do or prepare: *get* breakfast. 5. To persuade: Please *get* your brother to help with the chores. 6. To arrive; reach: We will *get* to school by eight o'clock. 7. (Informal) To understand: I don't *get* the point of your joke. 8. To kill or destroy: I'm going to *get* that fly. 9. (Slang) To bother or annoy. **got, got** or **gotten, getting.** —**get ahead.** To advance; succeed. —**get along.** 1. To be on friendly or cooperative terms. 2. To move on. 3. To grow old. —**get around.** 1. To move about; circulate. 2. To avoid. 3. To evade, as by flattery: Pat *gets around* her parents' anger by smiling sweetly. —**get at.** 1. To reach or grasp: The hunter's dogs tried to *get at* the raccoon. 2. To hint; suggest. 3. To understand; discover. —**get away with.** To do something, especially something wrong, without being caught or punished. —**get back at.** To take revenge on. —**get by.** To manage; be moderately successful. —**get even.** To take revenge on. —**get off.** 1. To come off or out of: *get off* a plane. 2. To begin; proceed: *get off* to a good start. 3. To send: *get off* a message. 4. To escape blame or punishment. —**get out of.** 1. To depart from; emerge. 2. To avoid; escape. —**get through.** 1. To survive or finish. 2. To make contact; communicate effectively: The teacher could not *get through* to the slow learner.

get·a·way (GET-a-way) *noun.* An escape or the act of escaping.

gey·ser (GIGH-zər) *noun.* A spring that from time to time erupts with sprays of hot water or steam.

ghast·ly (GAST-lee) *adjective.* 1. Horrible: The policeman described the shooting as a *ghastly* deed. 2. Like a corpse in appearance; very pale. 3. Very unpleasant. **ghastlier, ghastliest.**

ghet·to (GET-oh) *noun.* 1. A slum area of a city where people of one race or nationality reside. 2. A part of a European city in which Jews were confined. **ghettos.**

ghost (GOHST) *noun.* 1. The spirit of a dead person that, it is believed by some, is able to appear to or haunt the living. 2. A trace or very slight amount: The team does not have a *ghost* of a chance of winning. —**ghostly** (GOHST-lee) *adjective.* —**give up the ghost.** To die.

ghost town. A town, especially one in the American West, that has been deserted by its inhabitants.

ghost writer. A person who writes for another person for pay and allows that person to take credit for the work.

GI (JEE-IGH) *noun.* An enlisted man in the U.S. Army.

gi·ant (JIGH-ənt) *noun.* 1. An imaginary person of tremendous size and strength. 2. A person or thing of great size, ability, or importance: Shakespeare was a *giant* in the field of literature.

gib·bon (GIB-ən) *noun.* A slender long-armed ape found in Asia.

gibe (JIGHB) Also **jibe** *verb.* To make fun of; to taunt. **gibed, gibing.** —*noun.* A taunt; insult. **gibes.**

gib·let (JIB-lit) *noun.* (Usually plural) The heart, liver, or gizzard of fowl, often cooked separately and added to gravy or dressing.

gid·dy (GID-ee) *adjective.* 1. Silly; light-minded or foolish. 2. Tending to be or make dizzy. **giddier, giddiest.** —**giddily** *adverb.*

gift *noun.* 1. A present; something given to another. 2. A special talent: the *gift* of playing the piano well.

gif·ted (GIF-tid) *adjective.* Very skilled; of great natural ability.

gig *noun.* 1. A small horse-drawn carriage with two wheels. 2. A small boat.

gi·gan·tic (jigh-GAN-tik) *adjective.* Huge; enormous: The ship was battered by a *gigantic* wave. —**gigantically** *adverb.*

gig·gle (GIG-əl) *verb.* To laugh, especially in a silly manner. **giggled, giggling.** —*noun.* A laugh, especially a silly one. **giggles.**

gild *verb.* 1. To coat with a thin layer of gold. 2. To make something appear more attractive than it really is. **gilded** or **gilt, gilding.**

[1]**gill** (GIL) *noun.* The part of the body that permits fish and other animals to breathe in water.

[2]**gill** (JIL) A unit of liquid measure equal to four ounces.

gilt *noun.* A thin covering of gold. —*adjective.* Gilded; coated with a thin layer of gold.

gim·let (GIM-lit) *noun.* A small hand tool with a drill-like metal point, used for boring holes.

gim·mick (GIM-ik) *noun.* (Slang) 1. A tricky device. 2. A gadget.

[1]**gin** (JIN) *noun.* An alcoholic beverage made from grain and flavored with juniper berries.

[2]**gin** (JIN) *noun.* A machine used to separate seeds from cotton fiber. —*verb.* To separate the seeds from cotton. **ginned, ginning.**

gin·ger (JIN-jər) *noun.* 1. A fragrant spice made from the root of a tropical plant. 2. The plant or root of this spice. 3. (Informal) Pep; spirit: The students were full of *ginger* after the holiday.

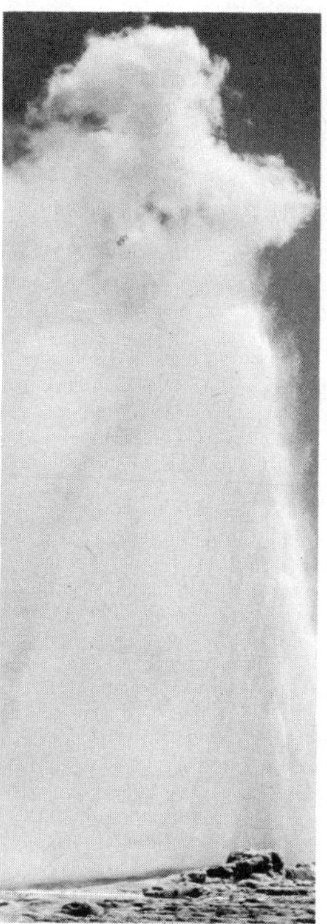

geyser

gibbon

giraffe

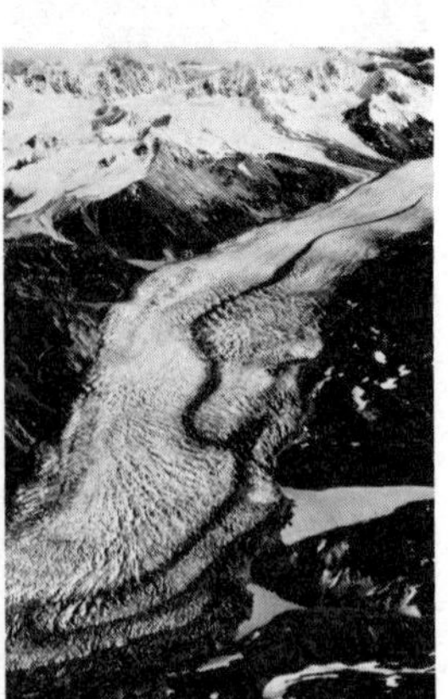

glacier

ginger ale. A sparkling soft drink flavored with ginger.

gin·ger·bread (JIN-jər-bred) *noun.* A brown cake flavored with ginger.

gin·ger·ly (JIN-jər-lee) *adverb.* Very carefully or cautiously.

gin·ger·snap (JIN-jər-snap) *noun.* A brown cookie flavored with ginger.

ging·ham (GING-əm) *noun.* A cotton fabric that is usually woven in checks, stripes, or plaids.

gipsy. British form of **gypsy.**

gi·raffe (ji-RAF) *noun.* A large spotted animal with long neck and legs, found in Africa. **giraffes.**

gird (GERD) *verb.* 1. To encircle or bind, as with a belt or sash. 2. To get ready for an activity: The men *girded* themselves for battle. 3. To surround. **girded** or **girt, girding.**

gird·er (GER-dər) *noun.* A large, strong metal or wooden beam used as a main support in a building or other structure.

gir·dle (GERD-l) *noun.* 1. An undergarment worn to make the figure appear slimmer or as a support for the waist and hips. 2. A belt or sash for the waist. 3. Anything that encircles or surrounds: A *girdle* of steel cable held the sides of the crate in place. **girdles.** —*verb.* 1. To fasten a belt or sash around the waist. 2. To encircle or surround. **girdled, girdling.**

girl (GERL) *noun.* 1. A female child. 2. A young woman. 3. (Informal) A sweetheart.

girl·hood (GERL-hud) *noun.* The period in a female's life between birth and womanhood: Grandmother told us stories of her *girlhood.*

Girl Scout. A girl who belongs to a worldwide group organized to encourage wholesome activities.

girth (GERTH) *noun.* 1. The distance around the middle of a person or thing. 2. A strap or belt that keeps a horse's saddle in place.

gist (JIST) *noun.* The main point or central idea: The *gist* of the teacher's talk was that she expected better behavior.

give (GIV) *verb.* 1. To donate; make a gift of. 2. To pay: The employer *gives* his workers $3 per hour. 3. To put in someone's possession; hand over. 4. To present; to exhibit: Tonight's paper *gives* a description of the explosion. 5. To yield or to collapse. 6. To cause. 7. To utter; to present: Our guest will *give* a short talk. 8. To result in: Good grades *give* a student great satisfaction. 9. To produce: Cows *give* milk. **gave, giving.** —**give in.** To yield; surrender: The army did not *give in* to the enemy. —**give out.** 1. To distribute: The teacher *gives out* the tests to her students. 2. To break down; become exhausted. —**give rise to.** To be the cause of. —**give up.** 1. To hand over. 2. To surrender. 3. To stop using. 4. To lose hope; stop trying. —**give way.** 1. To make room; to retreat: A driver should *give way* when he sees an approaching ambulance. 2. To collapse.

giv·en (GIV-ən) *adjective.* (Math) Accepted, assumed, or fixed at the start of a problem.

given name. A person's first name: Ralph Brown's *given name* is Ralph.

given set. (Math) The set assumed as a starting point before any operation; often an independent variable in set form.

giz·zard (GIZ-ərd) *noun.* A bird's second stomach that grinds up food.

gla·cial (GLAY-shəl) *adjective.* 1. Of or related to glaciers or large masses of ice. 2. Very cold.

gla·cier (GLAY-shər) *noun.* A large mass of ice, formed from snow, that moves slowly down mountain slopes.

glad *adjective.* 1. Happy; delighted. 2. Willing: She is always *glad* to help. 3. Causing pleasure. **gladder, gladdest.** —**gladly** *adverb.*

glad·den (GLAD-n) *verb.* To please; make happy: Our visit to Grandmother *gladdened* her greatly. **gladdened, gladdening.**

glade (GLAYD) *noun.* An open space in a forest. **glades.**

glad·i·a·tor (GLAD-ee-ay-tər) *noun.* A man who was forced or paid to fight in the arenas of ancient Rome.

glad·i·o·lus (glad-ee-OH-ləss) *noun.* A garden plant with long, blade-like leaves and handsome flowers that come in a variety of colors. —**gladioli** or **gladioluses** *plural.*

glam·our (GLAM-ər) *noun.* Magic or charm.

glam·our·ous (GLAM-ər-əss) *adjective.* Having glamour or charm. —**glamourously** *adverb.*

glance (GLANSS) *noun.* A fast look: Shirley was in a hurry and had only a *glance* at the Christmas display. **glances.** —*verb.* 1. To take a fast look. 2. (Used with *off*) To hit and bounce at an angle. **glanced, glancing.**

gland *noun.* An organ of the body that gives out substances that it extracts from the blood. —**glandular** *adjective.*

glare (GLAIR) *noun.* 1. An angry stare. 2. A strong, blinding light. **glares.** —*verb.* 1. To give an angry look. 2. To shine with a blinding quality: Police lights *glared* in the rioters' eyes. **glared, glaring.**

glass *noun.* 1. A hard, breakable substance that is usually transparent. 2. A drinking container made of glass. 3. The amount a glass will hold: Tess has a *glass* of orange juice every day. 4. A mirror. **glasses.** —*verb.* To surround or protect with glass. **glassed, glassing.**

glass blowing. The art of blowing melted glass into shapes.

glass·es (GLASS-iz) *noun, plural.* Spectacles or eyeglasses.

glass·ful (GLASS-ful) *noun.* The amount held in a glass. **glassfuls.**

glass·ware (GLASS-wair) *noun.* Objects made of glass, particularly ones designed to hold liquid.

glass·y (GLASS-ee) *adjective.* 1. Resembling glass: The ice on the sidewalk was *glassy.* 2. Having a vacant or expressionless stare. **glassier, glassiest.**

glaze (GLAYZ) *noun.* 1. A smooth, glossy finish: Jill chose a red *glaze* for the plate she made at camp. 2. A very thin coating of ice. **glazes.** —*verb.* 1. To make shiny or glossy: Ann *glazed* the cake. 2. To become shiny or glassy. **glazed, glazing.**

gleam (GLEEM) *noun.* A beam or flash of light: There was a *gleam* of light between the closed shutters. —*verb.* To shine: The silverware *gleamed* in the candlelight. **gleamed, gleaming.**

glean (GLEEN) *verb.* 1. To gather grain left by reapers. 2. To gather (information) little by little. **gleaned, gleaning.**

glee *noun.* Mirth, merriment, or joy: The children laughed with *glee* when Judy hit Punch.

glee club. A group formed for the purpose of singing together.

glee·ful (GLEE-fəl) *adjective.* Full of glee or mirth. —**gleefully** *adverb.*

glen *noun.* A narrow valley.

glib *adjective.* Easy, fluent, and usually insincere: A *glib* saleswoman tried to sell us a vacuum cleaner. **glibber, glibbest.** —**glibly** *adverb.*

glide (GLIGHD) *verb.* To move smoothly and without effort: The sea gulls *glided* over the water. **glided, gliding.**

glid·er (GLIGH-dər) *noun.* An aircraft that has no engine and remains in the air by gliding on air currents.

glim·mer (GLIM-ər) *noun.* 1. A faint, flickering light. 2. A faint indication (of something): We had only a *glimmer* of an idea about what was going on. —*verb.* To give out a faint or dim light. **glimmered, glimmering.**

gladiator

glass blowing

glider

glimpse (GLIMPS) *noun.* A brief or short look. **glimpses.** —*verb.* To get a brief or short look at. **glimpsed, glimpsing.**

glint *noun.* A short gleam or flash of light; a sparkle. —*verb.* To flash or sparkle. **glinted, glinting.**

glis·ten (GLISS-n) *verb.* To shine or sparkle. **glistened, glistening.**

glit·ter (GLIT-ər) *noun.* 1. A bright sparkling light. 2. A sparkling, showy presentation: There was a *glitter* about the entire musical. —*verb.* 1. To shine brightly. 2. To be showy or attractive, as in performance or appearance. **glittered, glittering.**

gloat (GLOHT) *verb.* To take mean pleasure and satisfaction: Tim *gloated* because his grades were higher than Jim's. **gloated, gloating.**

glob·al (GLOH-bəl) *adjective.* 1. Concerning the whole world: Pollution of the seas is a *global* problem. 2. Having the shape of a globe. —**globally** *adverb.*

globe

globe (GLOHB) *noun.* 1. A hollow sphere or ball with a map of the earth or the heavens on it. 2. The earth itself. 3. Any object shaped like a globe. **globes.**

glock·en·spiel (GLOK-ən-speel or GLAHK-ən-shpeel) *noun.* A musical instrument with metal bars arranged in a frame and played with two hammers.

gloom *noun.* 1. Darkness: Only the white furniture stood out in the *gloom* of the closed room. 2. Sadness or depression of spirit: A deep *gloom* overcame Phil when he thought of the end of vacation. —**gloomily** *adverb.* —**gloomy** *adjective.*

glo·ri·fi·ca·tion (glor-ə-fi-KAY-shən) *noun.* Glorifying or being glorified; worship or honor.

glo·ri·fy (GLOR-ə-figh) *verb.* 1. To praise, honor, or cover with glory. 2. To worship. **glorified, glorifying.**

glo·ri·ous (GLOR-ee-əss) *adjective.* 1. Deserving honor or fame: The *glorious* defenders of the city received medals for bravery. 2. Having magnificence and splendor: The inauguration ball was a *glorious* affair. 3. (Informal) Splendid or delightful: The children had a *glorious* time at the picnic. —**gloriously** *adverb.*

glo·ry (GLOR-ee) *noun.* 1. Great honor or fame. 2. Something that brings fame or honor. 3. A chief asset: For Mother, our house's *glory* is its formal garden. 4. Awesome magnificence and splendor: "Mine eyes have seen the *glory* of the coming of the Lord." (J. W. Howe). **glories.** —*verb.* To rejoice: They *gloried* in the beauty of the music. **gloried, glorying.** —**in (one's) glory.** Having great pride and satisfaction; doing one's best.

gloss (GLAWSS) *noun.* A shiny finish: The enamel paint in the kitchen has a clean, bright *gloss.* **glosses.** —*verb.* To put a gloss on. **glossed, glossing.** —**glossy** *adjective.* —**gloss over.** To make something seem all right by ignoring what is unacceptable.

glos·sa·ry (GLAWSS-ə-ree) *noun.* A list of special or difficult words with their meanings, usually found at the end of a book. **glossaries.**

glove (GLUHV) *noun.* 1. A covering for the hand that usually leaves the thumb and each finger separate. 2. A special padded glove, such as one made for boxing or baseball. **gloves.** —*verb.* To cover with a glove. **gloved, gloving.**

glow (GLOH) *noun.* 1. The light and color from something that is red-hot but without flames: The *glow* of the embers in the dying fire could still be seen. 2. A healthy appearance: There was a *glow* to his cheeks and eyes after the race. 3. A feeling of warmth: Tom felt a *glow* as he sipped the hot soup. —*verb.* 1. To shine warmly with heat: The molten steel *glowed* as it came from the furnaces. 2. To look or feel excited or eager. **glowed, glowing.**

glow·er (GLOW-ər) *verb.* To stare angrily with a scowl: Paul *glowered* at the teacher after being scolded. **glowered, glowering.** —*noun.* An angry, scowling stare.

glow·worm (GLOH-werm) *noun.* The glowing larva and wingless female of certain fireflies.

glu·cose (GLOO-kohss) *noun.* 1. A sugar found in plant and animal tissue. 2. A syrupy sugar mixture used for making candy and for other purposes, also known as "corn syrup."

glue (GLOO) *noun.* A sticky substance used to join wood and other materials together. **glues.** —*verb.* 1. To stick (together): Paul *glued* his airplane model together. 2. To hold in a fixed position: Jim's feet were *glued* to the floor in fear. **glued, gluing.**

glum (GLUHM) *adjective.* Gloomy and depressed; not happy: Tim is *glum* because the game was canceled. **glummer, glummest.** —**glumly** *adverb.*

glut (GLUHT) *noun.* 1. Too many goods of the same kind. 2. Any oversupply or excess. —*verb.* 1. To fill with or supply more than is needed; stuff. 2. To eat too much food; stuff oneself. **glutted, glutting.**

glu·ti·nous (GLOOT-n-əss) *adjective.* Sticky, like glue. —**glutinously** *adverb.*

glut·ton (GLUHT-n) *noun.* 1. A person who continually eats too much. 2. A person who can accomplish or accept a great amount: a *glutton* for work; a *glutton* for punishment.

gnarled (NAHRLD) *adjective.* Twisted and knotted.

gnash (NASH) *verb.* To grind (the teeth) together. **gnashed, gnashing.**

gnat (NAT) *noun.* Any of many small flying insects, especially one that bites.

gnaw (NAW) *verb.* 1. To bite and chew on. 2. To worry or give pain: The problem *gnawed* at him until his head ached. **gnawed, gnawing.**

gnome (NOHM) *noun.* 1. A mythical dwarflike creature of fables and myths who lives underground and guards precious treasures. 2. A shrunken old man. **gnomes.**

gnu (NOO or NYOO) *noun.* Any of several bearded and horned South African antelopes that are almost extinct; a wildebeest.

go (GOH) *verb.* 1. To move along: After a long wait, the traffic began to *go.* 2. To work or operate: The engine won't *go* in cold weather. 3. To depart, leave: The party was so nice no one wanted to *go.* 4. To belong or have a location: The pots *go* on the shelf. 5. To be used: All of Bill's money *goes* for movies. 6. To pass or disappear: Where did the time *go*? 7. To reach from one place or thing to another: The pipe *goes* from the pump to the house. 8. To proceed or move (to a place): Let's *go* to the movies. 9. To become: to *go* insane; to *go* hungry. 10. To be given: Her entire fortune was to *go* to a cat hospital. 11. To have a result: Jane hopes the test will *go* well. 12. To follow a certain pattern or sequence: How does the song *go*? 13. (Grammar) Used as a helping verb to express future action: I am *going* to sneeze. **went, gone, going.** —**go along.** To agree. —**go back on.** To change one's mind or refuse to recognize a previous agreement. —**go for.** (Informal) To be enthusiastic about. —**go in for.** To participate in. —**go in with.** To join as a partner. —**go through with.** To stay with (something) to the end. —**go together.** 1. Harmonize or agree. 2. To date (someone) steadily. —**let oneself go.** To relax and enjoy oneself. —**no go.** (Slang) Not acceptable or suitable. —**on the go.** Busy all the time.

glowworm

gnu

goblet

goalie

go-cart

goad (GOHD) *noun.* 1. A long pointed stick used to keep animals moving. 2. Anything used to prod or urge a person to act. —*verb.* To prod into action. **goaded, goading.**

goal (GOHL) *noun.* 1. A desired end; purpose, objective. 2. The place or structure that a ball or other object must pass through or over or must reach in order to score. 3. The score given for reaching the goal. 4. The place that is the end or finish of a race or trip.

goal·ie (GOHL-ee) *noun.* A goal-keeper. **goalies.**

goal·keep·er (GOHL-kee-pər) *noun.* The member of the team who protects the goal in certain games, such as hockey.

goat (GOHT) *noun.* 1. A grass-eating animal with horns, raised for milk and hides. 2. A scapegoat. —**get (one's) goat.** To make angry.

goat·ee (goh-TEE) *noun.* A short chin beard, often pointed. **goatees.**

goat·skin (GOHT-skin) *noun.* 1. The skin of a goat. 2. The leather made from goatskin, or something made from such leather, as a bag for wine.

gob·ble (GOB-əl) *verb.* 1. To gulp down; eat eagerly or too fast. 2. (Slang, usually used with *up*) To use or take quickly and eagerly: Leonard *gobbles* up all the ghost stories he can find in the library. 3. To make a noise like a turkey. **gobbled, gobbling.** —*noun.* The sound made by a male turkey or a sound like it.

gob·ble·dy·gook (GOB-əl-dee-guk) Also **gobbledegook** *noun.* (Informal) Speech or writing that is needlessly wordy and hard to understand.

gob·bler (GOB-lər) *noun.* A male turkey.

go-be·tween (GOH-bi-tween) *noun.* Someone who acts as a messenger or agent between two people or groups.

gob·let (GOB-lit) *noun.* A drinking glass shaped upon a narrow stem rising from a flat base.

gob·lin (GOB-lən) *noun.* A mischievous elf or ghost-like creature.

go-cart (GOH-kahrt) *noun.* 1. A small cart in which children sit and move themselves along by pushing with their feet. 2. A basket-like seat on casters in which babies learn to walk. 3. A motorized miniature car.

god *noun.* 1. [Capital G] The supreme being; the creator of the world; supernatural ruler. 2. A supernatural ruler according to a particular belief, myth, or religion: Neptune was the Roman *god* of the sea. 3. A statue or image of a god; an idol. 4. Any person or thing that is worshiped or adored.

god·child (GOD-chyld) *noun.* A child sponsored by an adult godparent in baptism or confirmation.

god·daught·er (GOD-daw-tər) *noun.* A female godchild.

god·dess (GOD-iss) *noun.* 1. A female god. 2. A very beautiful woman. 3. A woman who is worshiped or adored. **goddesses.**

god·fa·ther (GOD-fah-t͟hər) *noun.* A male godparent.

god·ly (GOD-lee) *adjective.* Living by God's laws; leading a good life; openly religious. **godlier, godliest.** —**godliness** *noun.*

god·moth·er (GOD-muht͟h-ər) *noun.* A female godparent.

god·par·ent (GOD-pair-ənt) *noun.* An adult who sponsors a child in baptism or confirmation.

god·send (GOD-send) *noun.* A lucky break; something unexpected but welcome: The holiday was a *godsend* because I didn't have my homework done.

god·son (GOD-suhn) *noun.* A male godchild.

go-get·ter (GOH-get-ər) *noun.* (Informal) A person who is aggressive; an eager worker: "He was the *go-getter* of the family, the one who was going to make them all rich again." (Disney).

gog·gle (GOG-əl) *verb.* To stare with eyes wide open: When he saw the huge sundae, he *goggled.* **goggled, goggling.**

gog·gles (GOG-əlz) *noun, plural.* Eyeglasses worn to protect the eyes; safety glasses.

go·ing (GOH-ing) *noun.* 1. A leaving: Mom cried at my first *going* to school. 2. The condition of roadways or walkways: The *going* was rough on the climb up the mountain. *—adjective.* Doing well; continuing to operate: a *going* business.

goi·ter (GOI-tər) Also **goitre** *noun.* An enlargement or swelling of the thyroid gland.

gold (GOHLD) *noun.* 1. A precious yellow metal easily shaped and rust free, used as a standard for money and in making jewelry. 2. Money or coins made of gold. 3. Riches. 4. Anything like gold in appearance, value, or worth: "New friends are silver; old friends are gold." (Old saying). 5. (Also *adjective*) A yellow-brown color.

gold·en (GOHL-dn) *adjective.* 1. Made of or having to do with gold. 2. Of the color of gold. 3. Of great value: Silence is *golden.*

gold·en·rod (GOHL-dn-rod) *noun.* A tall weed with yellow flowers.

golden rule. [Sometimes capital G, capital R] A teaching (Matthew 7:12) that one should treat others as one wants others to treat oneself.

gold·finch (GOHLD-finch) *noun.* A small yellow and black bird. **goldfinches.**

gold·fish (GOHLD-fish) *noun.* A small fish of gold or orange color. **—goldfish** *plural.*

gold·smith (GOHLD-smith) *noun.* One who makes or sells things of gold.

golf *noun.* An outdoor game in which players, using clubs, hit a small ball into each of 9 or 18 holes set far apart on a special course. *—verb.* To play golf. **golfed, golfing.**

golf course. An outdoor, grassy area on which golf is played.

gon·do·la (GON-də-lə) *noun.* 1. A flat-bottomed boat, especially one used on the canals of Venice, Italy. 2. A topless, flat-bottomed railroad freight car. 3. A car that hangs underneath a passenger balloon.

gone (GAWN) *adjective.* 1. Used up: The candy is *gone.* 2. (Informal) Deeply involved; very interested: Joan is *gone* on modern music. 3. Dead. 4. Lost, ruined: Many good fishing spots are *gone* because of pollution. *—verb. See* **go.**

gon·er (GAWN-ər) *noun.* 1. (Slang) Someone who is dying. 2. (Slang) A hopeless case; a sure loser.

good (GUD) *adjective.* 1. Honorable: *good* men and true. 2. Excellent; desirable: a *good* horse; my *good* shoes. 3. Well-behaved: The children were so *good.* 4. Above average; special: *good* marks; a *good* crop. 5. Entertaining; giving pleasure: *good* show; a *good* book. 6. Kind; considerate: He is *good* to me. 7. Right for the intended use; suitable: a *good* man for the job. 8. Worthy: a *good* cause. 9. Full; more rather than less: Take a *good* handful. 10. Helpful; beneficial: Exercise is *good* for you. **better, best.** *—noun.* 1. Anything that is worthwhile or useful. 2. Benefit: For the *good* of all the people. 3. (Plural) Merchandise; what is sold or traded: dry *goods.* *—interjection.* Expresses approval; satisfaction. **—as good as.** The same or almost the same as. **—for good.** Completely; finally. **—make good.** 1. Do well, succeed, reach a goal. 2. Complete a promise; pay a debt; make up for. **—to the good.** To one's profit; extra; for the best.

goat

gondola

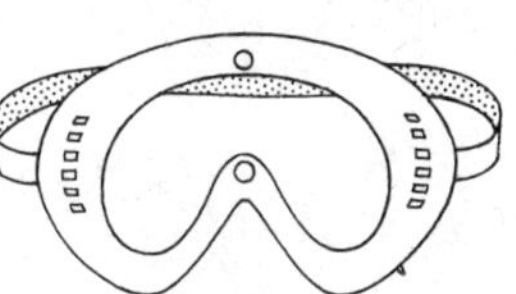
goggles

goldfinch

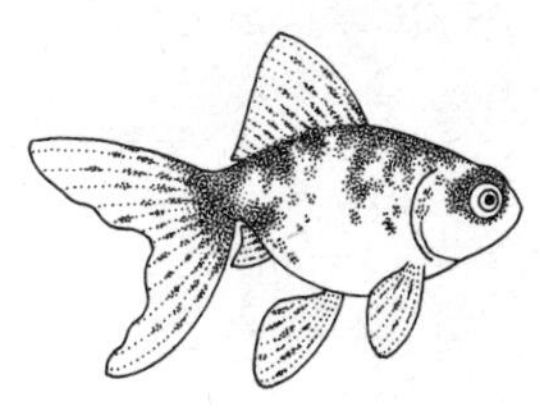
goldfish

gopher

gorilla

goose and goslings

good-by (gud-BIGH) Also **good-bye** *interjection.* Expresses parting; said to or by anyone who is leaving; a contraction for "God be with you." —*noun.* A farewell. —**good-bys** or **good-byes** *plural.*

good-heart·ed (GUD-HAHR-tid) *adjective.* Kind and loving; generous.

good-hu·mored (GUD-HYOO-mərd) *adjective.* Cheerful; jolly; good-natured.

good-na·tured (GUD-NAY-chərd) *adjective.* Basically kind, patient, friendly; not easily angered.

good·ness (GUD-niss) *noun.* 1. The state of being good. 2. Generosity, kindness, consideration. 3. The basic part of anything; best part; essence. —*interjection.* Expresses surprise: *Goodness!* You startled me!

good-tem·pered (GUD-TEM-pərd) *adjective.* Well-balanced; generally cheerful; not easily upset or angered.

good will Also **goodwill** (GUD-WIL). 1. Cheerful, friendly feeling. 2. The established reputation for reliability of a business.

good·y (GUD-ee) *noun.* (Informal) 1. Something delicious to eat, usually a sweet. 2. A joke or idea that is clever or unusual. 3. (Also **goody-goody**) A person who is sickeningly sweet. —**goodies** *plural.* —*interjection.* Expresses happiness: *Goody!* I won the prize!

goof *noun.* 1. (Informal) A mistake; an error. 2. (Slang) A stupid or foolish person. —*verb.* To err: I *goofed;* I forgot my lunch. **goofed, goofing.** —**goofy** *adjective.* —**goof off.** To waste time; be idle.

goo·gol (GOO-gol) *noun.* (Math) The number 1 followed by 100 zeros.

goon *noun.* (Slang) 1. A man hired to intimidate other people; a strike-breaker. 2. A stupid or silly person.

goose (GOOSS) *noun.* 1. A web-footed bird with a long neck: A *goose* honks; a duck quacks. 2. The female of this bird. (See **gander**). 3. The meat of a goose. 4. A foolish person. —**geese** (GEESS) *plural.* —**cook one's goose.** To get oneself into trouble.

goose·berry (GOOSS-behr-ee) *noun.* 1. A small, green fruit used in making pies, jams, and other foods. 2. The thorny bush on which this berry grows. —**gooseberries** *plural.*

goose flesh Also **goose pimples.** Small bumps on the skin caused by fear or cold.

go·pher (GOH-fər) *noun.* A ground squirrel common on the prairies.

[1]**gore** (GOR) *noun.* Thick blood, usually from a wound. —*verb.* To stick or wound with horns. **gored, goring.**

[2]**gore** (GOR) *noun.* A section of a skirt or sail that is wider at the bottom than at the top. —*verb.* To put or sew in a gore. **gored, goring.**

[1]**gorge** (GORJ) *noun.* A deep, narrow cut in the mountains, often with a river at the bottom. **gorges.**

[2]**gorge** (GORJ) *verb.* To eat fast and greedily. **gorged, gorging.** —*noun.* 1. The throat. 2. The act of eating greedily or excessively. 3. The contents of the stomach. **gorges.**

gor·geous (GOR-jəss) *adjective.* Very special or beautiful in appearance or coloring.

go·ril·la (gə-RIL-ə) *noun.* The largest member of the ape family, smaller but stronger than man: *Gorillas* are ground dwellers and are found in west equatorial Africa.

gor·y (GOR-ee) *adjective.* 1. Covered with blood. 2. Full of blood or killing: The *gory* movie gave Ted nightmares. **gorier, goriest.**

gosh *interjection.* Expresses: 1. Disbelief. 2. Surprise.

gos·ling (GOZ-ling) *noun.* A young goose.

gos·pel (GOSS-pəl) *noun.* 1. The teachings of Jesus Christ and his Apostles. 2. [Capital G] One of the four books of the New Testament written by the Apostles Matthew, Mark, Luke, and John. 3. Truth: My story may sound strange but it's the *gospel.*

gos·sa·mer (GOSS-ə-mər) *noun.* 1. A spider's web. 2. A fine, light fabric like a spider's web.

gos·sip (GOSS-əp) *noun.* 1. Useless, sometimes harmful, talk about others which may or may not be true. 2. Chatter; small talk. 3. (Also **gossiper**) A person who talks about other people, often thoughtlessly. *—verb.* 1. To talk thoughtlessly about other people. 2. To chat. **gossiped, gossiping.**

got *verb. See* **get.**

Goth·ic (GOTH-ik) *adjective.* [Capital G] Of or about a style of building in medieval Europe. *—noun.* 1. A language of early Germany. 2. A kind of printing type.

got·ten (GOT-n) *verb. See* **get.**

gouge (GOWJ) *noun.* 1. A tool with a curved blade used for digging into wood. 2. A hole or mark made by gouging. 3. (Informal) A cheating. 4. (Slang) A nasty remark. *—verb.* 1. To cut into with a digging motion; to dig with a gouge. 2. (Informal) To cheat or swindle. **gouged, gouging.**

gou·lash (GOO-lahsh) *noun.* 1. A stew made with meat, vegetables, and spiced with paprika. 2. (Slang) A stew-like mixture of things.

gourd (GORD) *noun.* A hard fruit, the shell of which, when dried, can be used as a bowl or cup.

gour·met (goor-MAY) *noun.* A lover of good food; an expert on food.

Gov. *abbreviation.* Governor.

gov·ern (GUHV-ərn) *verb.* 1. To lead or rule. 2. To control; to limit: *govern* a car's speed. 3. To guide, influence. **governed, governing.**

gov·ern·ess (GUHV-ər-niss) *noun.* A woman hired to teach children in a private home. **governesses.**

gov·ern·ment (GUHV-ərn-mənt) *noun.* 1. The process of controlling or ruling, as in a country or state. 2. The form of political control or rule: We prefer a democratic *government* to a dictatorship. 3. The people or offices in control of a political unit: He wrote to the city *government* for help. 4. The study of government. **—governmental** *adjective.* **—governmentally** *adverb.*

gov·er·nor (GUHV-ər-nər) *noun.* 1. The elected head of one of the states of the United States. 2. A person who governs. 3. A device that limits the speed of an engine or machine.

govt. *abbreviation.* Government.

gown *noun.* 1. A woman's dress, especially one worn for a special or formal occasion. 2. A garment worn for sleeping (night*gown*) or over one's nightclothes (dressing *gown*). 3. A loose robe worn by scholars, judges, or churchmen. *—verb.* To dress in a gown. **gowned, gowning.**

grab *verb.* 1. To take suddenly by force: The thief *grabbed* her purse. 2. To pick up in a hurry: He *grabbed* his books and headed for school. 3. (Slang) Appeal to: How does that *grab* you? **grabbed, grabbing.** *—noun.* 1. The act of taking hold suddenly. 2. The object taken. **—up for grabs.** (Informal) Ready to be taken by anyone.

grace (GRAYSS) *noun.* 1. Ease or beauty of form or movement: She skates with *grace.* 2. Favor, good will: Let's try to stay in Father's good *graces.* 3. A short prayer said at mealtime. 4. God's mercy or kindness. 5. Talent, skill. 6. Good taste, manners. 7. An extra period of time in which to pay a bill. 8. [Usually capital G] A title of respect used for royalty. **graces.** *—verb.* 1. To decorate; add charm to. 2. To honor or favor: The actress will *grace* us with her presence. **graced, gracing.**

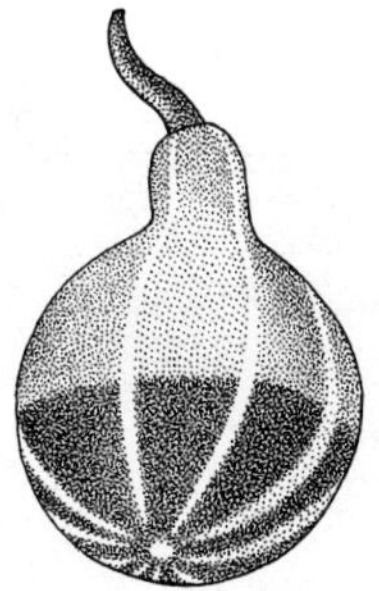
gourd

grace·ful (GRAYSS-fəl) *adjective.* 1. Showing beauty of form or motion. 2. Showing skill or courtesy. —**gracefully** *adverb.* —**gracefulness** *noun.*

grace·less (GRAYSS-liss) *adjective.* 1. Without skill or grace. 2. Lacking a sense of what is proper or right. —**gracelessly** *adverb.*

gra·ci·as (GRAH-see-ahss) *interjection.* A Spanish word meaning *thank you.*

gra·cious (GRAY-shəss) *adjective.* 1. Kind, having good manners: "If a man be *gracious* and courteous to strangers, it shows he is a citizen of the world." (Bacon). 2. Elegant, in good taste. —*interjection.* Indicates surprise or excitement. —**graciously** *adverb.* —**graciousness** *noun.*

grackle

grack·le (GRAK-əl) *noun.* A large blackbird with shiny feathers.

grade (GRAYD) *noun.* 1. A class level in school; the students in that level: The first *grade* goes to lunch first. 2. A rating by quality, appearance, or size: "Prime" is the best *grade* of meat. 3. A military or government rank: A Navy captain has the same *grade* as an Army colonel. 4. A mark given for school or college work. 5. A slope, as of a road or railroad: The engine pulled the train up the steep *grade.* **grades.** —*verb.* 1. To put into a class according to size, appearance, or quality. 2. To give a mark to (a student or his work). 3. To make level or smooth: The workman used a machine to *grade* the road. **graded, grading.** —**at grade.** On the same level. —**make the grade.** (Informal) To succeed. —**the grades.** Elementary school.

grade school. Elementary school, grades one through six or eight.

grad·u·al (GRAJ-oo-əl) *adjective.* Happening by very small degrees, a little at a time. —**gradually** *adverb.*

grad·u·ate (GRAJ-oo-ayt) *verb.* 1. To complete a course of study successfully. 2. To give diplomas to (students who complete a course). 3. To mark with figures for measuring: He *graduated* the bottle by painting red lines on the side. **graduated, graduating.** —(GRAJ-oo-it) *adjective.* 1. Relating to one who has a diploma. 2. Relating to courses beyond the usual four-year college course. —*noun.* One who has finished a course successfully.

grad·u·a·tion (graj-oo-AY-shən) *noun.* 1. The ceremony at which diplomas are given to students who have successfully completed a course. 2. The act of being graduated.

graf·fi·to (grə-FEE-toh) *noun.* A writing or drawing on a wall. —**graffiti** (grə-FEE-tee) *plural.*

[1]**graft** *verb.* 1. To place a small part of one plant in close contact with another so that the two unite and continue to grow as one. 2. To move tissue by surgery from one body or part of the body to another: Skin is often *grafted* on patients who have suffered burns. **grafted, grafting.** —*noun.* 1. The act or result of grafting. 2. The part of a plant used in a graft.

[2]**graft** *verb.* To get money unfairly or dishonestly because of one's position. **grafted, grafting.** —*noun.* Money made by dishonest means: The mayor was guilty of taking *graft.*

grain (GRAYN) *noun.* 1. A seed of a cereal plant such as corn, wheat, rice, or oats. 2. A collection of such plants or seeds: ". . . for amber waves of *grain.*" (K. L. Bates). 3. The arrangement of fibers in meat, wood, or cloth. 4. The arrangement of layers of rock. 5. A very small particle: *grains* of sand. 6. A very small unit of weight: 7,000 *grains* are equal to one pound. —*verb.* 1. To form into grains. 2. To make a design on something that imitates the grain of leather, wood, etc. **grained, graining.** —**against the grain.** Unpleasant, contrary to one's ideas or beliefs.

gram *noun.* A unit used to measure weight and mass in the metric system; one-thousandth of a kilogram.

-gram *suffix.* Indicating: 1. Something written or drawn: dia*gram.* 2. A weight in the metric system: kilo*gram.*

gram·mar (GRAM-ər) *noun.* 1. The study of the forms of words and the way they are arranged in sentences. 2. The application or use of this knowledge: The boy's *grammar* is poor. 3. A book that contains rules and examples for the study of words and sentences.

gram·mat·i·cal (grə-MAT-i-kəl) *adjective.* 1. In keeping with the rules of grammar. 2. Relating to grammar. —**grammatically** *adverb.*

gra·na·ry (GRAN-ə-ree or GRAY-nə-ree) *noun.* A building in which grain is stored. **granaries.**

grand *adjective.* 1. Great in size or value; outstanding. 2. Showing wealth. 3. Of higher rank than others in the same general rank: A *grand* duke outranks a duke. 4. Splendid, stately. 5. The most important: the *grand* staircase. 6. Pleasant, agreeable to all. 7. Complete: The bake sale brought into our treasury a *grand* total of $21.75. **grander, grandest.** —*noun.* (Slang) One thousand dollars. —**grandly** *adverb.*

grand- *prefix.* Indicates a relative more than one generation removed: *grand*father; *grand*child; *grand*aunt.

gran·deur (GRAN-jər or GRAN-jur) *noun.* The state of being large and impressive; greatness: the *grandeur* of the Pacific Ocean.

grand jury. A group, usually of 12 to 23 citizens, whose duty is to decide in secret whether an accused person should be tried in a court of law.

grand slam. 1. The winning of all the tricks in certain card games. 2. (Baseball) A home run with three men on base.

grand·stand (GRAND-stand) *noun.* Rows of seats, often covered with a roof, where people sit to watch races or other outdoor sports events. —*verb.* To perform in a showy way to win attention or approval. **grandstanded, grandstanding.**

grange (GRAYNJ) *noun.* 1. A farmhouse and nearby buildings. 2. [Usually capital G] An organization of farmers. **granges.**

gran·ite (GRAN-it) *noun.* A kind of very hard rock that often has a salt-and-pepper coloring and can be highly polished.

gran·ny (GRAN-ee) Also **grannie** *noun.* 1. A grandmother. 2. An old woman. **grannies.** —*adjective.* (Informal) Old-fashioned. —**granny boots.** High-laced shoes. —**granny dress.** An old-fashioned dress with a long skirt. —**granny glasses.** Eyeglasses with metal frames. —**granny hat.** A bonnet.

grant *verb.* 1. To give or allow: He *granted* us permission to swim in his pool. 2. To admit or agree: We *grant* that he is the tallest boy in the class. **granted, granting.** —*noun.* 1. The act of giving or allowing. 2. The thing given: The college was given a land *grant* by the government.

gran·ule (GRAN-yool) *noun.* A small grain; a very small particle. **granules.** —**granular** *adjective.* —**granulate** *verb.*

grape (GRAYP) *noun.* 1. A juicy, berry-like fruit that grows in bunches on a woody vine. **grapes.** 2. (Also *adjective*) Deep bluish-red; a dark purple color.

grape·fruit (GRAYP-froot) *noun.* The citrus fruit of an evergreen tree grown in warm climates. —**grapefruit** *plural.*

grape·vine (GRAYP-vighn) *noun.* 1. The woody vine on which grapes grow. 2. The spreading of news, rumors, or gossip from one person to another. **grapevines.**

grandstand

grapes

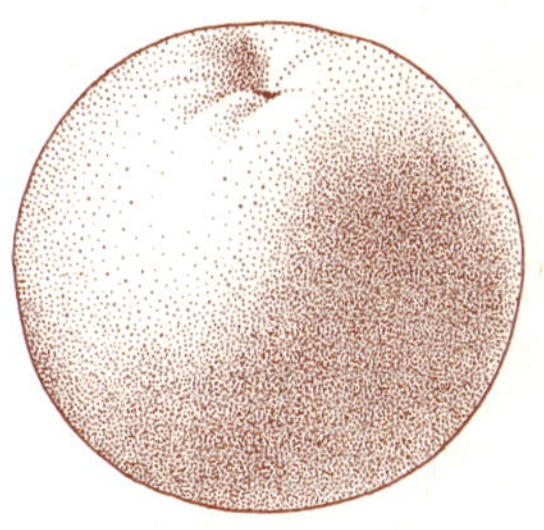
grapefruit

grasshopper

graph (GRAF) *noun.* A chart or drawing showing the relationship between two or more sets of figures. —*verb.* To make or use a graph. **graphed, graphing.**

-graph *suffix.* Indicating: 1. Something written or recorded so that it can be seen: auto*graph*, photo*graph*. 2. Equipment that makes a written record: seismo*graph*.

graph·ic (GRAF-ik) Also **graphical** *adjective.* 1. Like a picture; referring to something that is written, drawn, or painted: Printing is one of the *graphic* arts. 2. Shown by a graph: We have a *graphic* record of the rainfall for the year. 3. Very clear, full of detail: She gave us a *graphic* account of the fire. —**graphically** *adverb.*

graph·ite (GRAF-ight) *noun.* A soft form of carbon used in lead pencils, paints, lubricants, etc.: *Graphite* is used to lubricate machines.

-graphy *suffix.* Indicating: 1. A way of writing or recording: photo*graphy*. 2. The science of a particular field: oceano*graphy*.

grap·ple (GRAP-əl) *noun.* 1. A hooked tool for catching and holding on to something. 2. The act of using such a hooked tool. 3. A wrestling contest or hand-to-hand struggle. **grapples.** —*verb.* 1. To use a hook to catch or hold (something). 2. To wrestle or struggle. 3. To attempt to struggle with and understand (something): He is *grappling* with his homework. **grappled, grappling.**

grasp *verb.* 1. To hold tightly with the fingers. 2. To understand: Can you *grasp* the meaning of the poem? **grasped, grasping.** —*noun.* 1. The ability to reach and hold: The grapes were beyond the *grasp* of the fox. 2. Understanding, knowledge: He has a good *grasp* of mathematics. 3. Ownership, control: The company is in the *grasp* of a few businessmen.

grasping *adjective.* Greedy.

grass *noun.* 1. A large family of plants having narrow, blade-shaped leaves and hollow, jointed stems. 2. A member of this plant family: Bamboo is a *grass.* 3. An area or yard covered with grass: My brother is cutting the *grass.* 4. (Slang) Marijuana. **grasses.** —*verb.* To plant or grow grass; cover with grass. **grassed, grassing.**

grass·hop·per (GRASS-hop-ər) *noun.* A grass- or leaf-eating insect with very strong hind legs that it uses for jumping.

grass·land (GRASS-land) *noun.* An area covered with grass and other low-growing plants; a meadow.

grass·roots (GRASS-roots) *noun, plural.* 1. The ordinary people, generally those who are not involved in political activity. 2. Rural or farm areas or the people who live in these areas.

grass·y (GRASS-ee) *adjective.* 1. Covered with grass. 2. Like grass. **grassier, grassiest.**

grate (GRAYT) *verb.* 1. To cut into very fine pieces by scraping against a sharp edge; to shred. 2. To make an unpleasant, harsh scraping noise. **grated, grating.** —*noun.* 1. A metal framework: Some *grates* are used to hold fuel for burning; others cover openings in walls, sidewalks, or streets. 2. A fireplace. 3. A scraping noise. **grates.** —**grate on.** To annoy.

grate·ful (GRAYT-fəl) *adjective.* 1. Thankful. 2. Pleasantly welcome. —**gratefully** *adverb.*

grat·i·fi·ca·tion (grat-ə-fi-KAY-shən) *noun.* Pleasure, satisfaction.

grat·i·fy (GRAT-ə-figh) *verb.* 1. To give pleasure. 2. To satisfy. **gratified, gratifying.**

grat·ing (GRAYT-ing) *noun.* A framelike structure of parallel or crossed bars: *Gratings* over the windows keep children from falling out.

grat·i·tude (GRAT-ə-tood or GRAT-ə-tyood) *noun.* The state of being pleased or thankful.

[1]**grave** (GRAYV) *noun.* 1. A hole dug in the earth for a dead body. 2. A burial place; tomb. 3. Death. **graves.**

[2]**grave** (GRAYV) *adjective.* 1. Serious; thoughtful; dignified: a *grave* man. 2. Important: a *grave* problem. 3. Slow; solemn: *grave* music, a *grave* procession. **graver, gravest.** —**gravely** *adverb.*

grav·el (GRAV-əl) *noun.* Pebbles or small pieces of stone: Many walks and roads are made with *gravel.*

grave·stone (GRAYV-stohn) *noun.* A stone used to mark a grave and give birth and death dates of the person buried there; a tombstone.

grave·yard (GRAYV-yahrd) *noun.* A place for burying dead people; a cemetery.

grav·i·tate (GRAV-ə-tayt) *verb.* 1. To move or tend to move under the force of gravity. 2. To be attracted: People often *gravitate* to the scene of an accident. **gravitated, gravitating.**

grav·i·ta·tion (grav-ə-TAY-shən) *noun.* 1. The force that causes all bodies in the universe to tend to move towards one another; gravity. 2. Any tendency to be attracted: the *gravitation* of little children to a circus clown.

grav·i·ty (GRAV-ə-tee) *noun.* 1. Gravitational force, especially attraction of the earth for bodies on or near its surface: A body's weight is the force of *gravity* acting upon it. 2. Seriousness; importance: The *gravity* of the occasion kept everyone from laughing.

gra·vy (GRAY-vee) *noun.* 1. The juice that runs out of cooking meat. 2. A thickened sauce made from meat juices. 3. (Slang) Any extra, unearned, or unexpected profit. **gravies.**

gray Also **grey** *noun* (and *adjective*). A color between black and white; the color of the sky on a rainy day. —*adjective.* Not cheerful; gloomy.

graze (GRAYZ) *verb.* 1. To eat growing grass or other plants: Sheep *graze* in the meadow. 2. To put (animals) in a field or pasture to feed. 3. To barely touch; rub against or scrape lightly: The snowball *grazed* his ear. **grazed, grazing.** —*noun.* A light rubbing against; a scrape. **grazes.**

grease (GREESS) *noun.* 1. Animal fat used in cooking: Mother uses bacon *grease* for frying eggs. 2. Any thick, oily, or fatty substance; a lubricant: "The wheel that squeaks the loudest gets the *grease.*" (Proverb). —*verb.* To apply fat or oil to lubricate. **greased, greasing.**

greas·y (GREESS-ee or GREEZ-ee) *adjective.* 1. Covered with fat or oil: A mechanic's hands are often *greasy.* 2. Having a lot of grease: I don't like *greasy* hamburgers. 3. Oily to the touch; slippery.

great (GRAYT) *adjective.* 1. Large in size or amount; big: a *great* mob of people. 2. Of unusual intensity: *great* happiness. 3. Unusual in excellence and fame: *great* men, *great* books. 4. (Informal) Very good; expert: *great* at playing soccer. 5. (Informal) Very good; fine. **greater, greatest.** —*noun.* (Slang) A notable performer: Babe Ruth is one of the all-time *greats* of baseball. —**greatly** *adverb.*

great- *prefix.* Indicates one generation older or younger than a given relative: *great*-grandfather; *great*-grandchild; *great*-grandaunt.

greatest common factor. (Math) The largest number that will divide into another number without a fractional remainder.

greed *noun.* A selfish desire for more than one needs or deserves, especially money.

greed·y (GREED-ee) *adjective.* 1. Having a great desire for more than one has need for: *greedy* for money. 2. Having a great desire for food. **greedier, greediest.** —**greedily** *adverb.*

gravestone

greenhouse

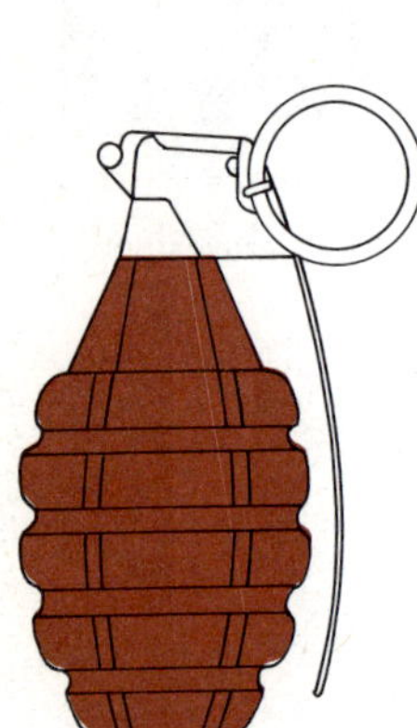
grenade

grenadiers

green *noun.* 1. (Also *adjective*) The color that can be made by combining blue and yellow; the color of grass, lettuce, or spinach. 2. (Plural) Leaves of plants eaten as food: turnip *greens,* dandelion *greens.* —*adjective.* 1. Covered or filled with green growing things, as grass. 2. Not ripe; not ready for eating: *Green* apples can make you sick. 3. Without training or experience. **greener, greenest.** —**green with envy.** Jealous.

green·horn (GREEN-horn) *noun.* (Informal) A person with little or no experience; a beginner, often one who is easy to fool or trick.

green·house (GREEN-howss) *noun.* A building, usually made of glass, in which plants are grown; a hothouse. **greenhouses.**

green thumb. The ability or talent to grow plants successfully.

greet *verb.* 1. To speak to or welcome. 2. To come before; meet: Flying pillows and feathers *greeted* Mother when she came into our room. **greeted, greeting.**

greet·ing (GREE-ting) *noun.* A sign of welcome.

gre·nade (grə-NAYD) *noun.* A small bomb thrown by hand or shot from a special rifle. **grenades.**

gren·a·dier (gren-ə-DIHR) *noun.* 1. At one time, a soldier who threw grenades. 2. A foot soldier in the British army who is a member of the Grenadier Guards.

grew (GROO) *verb.* See **grow.**

grey (GRAY) *noun.* See **gray.**

grey·hound (GRAY-hownd) *noun.* A large, slender, fast dog, used for hunting and racing.

grid *noun.* 1. A framework of crossed lines or bars; a grill or a grate. 2. (Electricity) A metal plate in a storage battery.

grid·dle (GRID-l) *noun.* A heavy, flat pan for cooking pancakes, bacon, eggs, and such. **griddles.**

grid·dle·cake (GRID-l-kayk) *noun.* A pancake; flapjack. **griddlecakes.**

grid·i·ron (GRID-igh-ərn) *noun.* 1. A cooking utensil with parallel bars for broiling food; a grill. 2. Any frame or pattern that resembles a gridiron. 3. A football field.

grief (GREEF) *noun.* 1. Great sorrow; mental pain or suffering. 2. Any cause of sorrow or suffering. —**come to grief.** To end badly; fail.

griev·ance (GREEV-ənss) *noun.* A cause of grief; a real or imagined wrong. **grievances.**

grieve (GREEV) *verb.* To feel or cause to feel great sorrow or sadness. **grieved, grieving.**

griev·ous (GREEV-əss) *adjective.* 1. Causing grief; sad. 2. Full of grief or sorrow. 3. Painful; severe. 4. Shocking; outrageous: a *grievous* mistake. —**grievously** *adverb.*

grill (GRIL) *noun.* 1. A cooking utensil with parallel bars for broiling food. 2. A dish of broiled food: The restaurant served a mixed *grill* of sausage, lamb chop, and bacon. 3. A dining room or restaurant that serves grilled dishes. —*verb.* 1. To cook on a grill; broil. 2. (Informal) To question (a person) closely for a long period of time. **grilled, grilling.**

grim *adjective.* 1. Harsh; savage: a *grim* punishment. 2. Not giving in; not easing up: *grim* determination. 3. Frightening; fierce: *grim* stories about war. 4. Appearing stern, hard, or fierce: a *grim* face. **grimmer, grimmest.** —**grimly** *adverb.*

gri·mace (gri-MAYSS or GRIM-iss) *noun.* A twisting of the face to show dislike; any expression on the face showing distaste or revulsion. **grimaces.** —*verb.* To twist the face to indicate disapproval. **grimaced, grimacing.**

grime (GRIGHM) *noun.* Dirt or soot rubbed into or on a surface: Use plenty of soap to remove the *grime* on your hands.

grim·y (GRIGHM-ee) *adjective.* Covered with grime; dirty. **grimier, grimiest.**

grin *verb.* To smile widely, showing the teeth. **grinned, grinning.** —*noun.* A wide smile.

grind (GRYND) *verb.* 1. To crush into little bits: *grind* wheat into flour. 2. To make sharp or smooth by rubbing against something hard: *grind* an axe. 3. To rub harshly; grate: *grind* one's teeth. 4. (Informal) To work hard. **ground, grinding.** —*noun.* 1. (Informal) Hard work. 2. (Slang) A student who studies hard.

grind·er (GRYND-ər) *noun.* 1. Anyone or anything that grinds: organ *grinder;* meat *grinder.* 2. A person or device that sharpens tools such as knives, axes, scissors, etc. 3. A molar; a back tooth. 4. (Slang) A sandwich in which meat, cheese, vegetables, and sauces are put between lengthwise slices of Italian or French bread or rolls; a submarine sandwich; sub; hero sandwich; hoagy or hoagie.

grind·stone (GRYND-stohn) *noun.* A revolving, round stone that is used to sharpen tools or to smooth and polish surfaces. **grindstones.**

grip *verb.* 1. To take firmly in one's hand; hold tightly. 2. To have control over; make a firm impression on: The possibility of going to Africa for a vacation *gripped* Jack's mind. **gripped, gripping.** —*noun.* 1. The act of taking and holding tightly; the act of grasping; a firm clasp. 2. Knowledge and understanding of a situation or subject: Mr. Davis has studied mathematics for many years and has a firm *grip* on the subject. 3. A small suitcase. 4. A handle. 5. A secret handshake used by members of certain clubs and organizations. 6. Any device that firmly holds two or more parts together, as on a machine.

gripe (GRIGHP) *verb.* (Informal) 1. To bother; annoy: It really *gripes* me to have to work on Saturday. 2. To complain constantly; carp. **griped, griping.**

grippe (GRIP) *noun.* Influenza; a contagious virus disease.

grist *noun.* 1. Grain that is to be ground into flour or meal. 2. The flour or meal that has been ground from grain.

gris·tle (GRISS-l) *noun.* A smooth, rubbery substance found in certain tissues of animals and humans that are connected to the skeleton; cartilage.

grit *noun.* 1. Very small, fine pieces of sand or stone. 2. Coarse sandstone. 3. Courage; daring: It took *grit* to stand up to the bully. —*verb.* To grind; to make a grinding sound: *grit* one's teeth. **gritted, gritting.**

grits *noun.* Coarsely ground kernels of corn; hominy grits.

grit·ty (GRIT-ee) *adjective.* 1. Sandy; resembling grit in touch or texture. 2. Courageous; brave. **grittier, grittiest.**

griz·zled (GRIZ-ld) *adjective.* 1. Having gray hair: a *grizzled* old man. 2. Gray or grayish in color.

griz·zly (GRIZ-lee) *adjective.* Grayish; gray; with gray hair. **grizzlier, grizzliest.**

grizzly bear Also **grizzly.** A large, wild bear of western North America, gray to grayish brown in color.

grizzly bear

groan (GROHN) *verb.* To make a low moaning sound because of pain, strain, sorrow, or disapproval: The class *groaned* when the test was announced. **groaned, groaning.** —*noun.* A low moaning sound.

gro·cer (GROH-sər) *noun.* The owner, manager, or clerk in a grocery.

gro·cer·y (GROH-sə-ree) *noun.* A store that sells food and household supplies. **groceries.**

gro·cer·ies (GROH-sə-reez) *noun, plural.* Supplies bought at a grocery.

grog·gy (GROG-ee) *adjective.* Dazed or wobbly. **groggier, groggiest.** —**groggily** *adverb.*

groin *noun.* The area where the thighs and the abdomen join.

groom *noun.* 1. A man who is about to be or has just been married; bridegroom. 2. A man or boy who takes care of horses. —*verb.* 1. To clean and care for (horses or other animals). 2. To take good care of one's person; keep clean and tidy. 3. To train, as for a certain job. **groomed, grooming.**

grosbeak

groove (GROOV) *noun.* 1. A narrow rut or channel in a surface: There was a *groove* on the cutting board in which to lay the knife. 2. A habit or settled routine. **grooves.** —*verb.* To make a groove in. **grooved, grooving.**

groov·y (GROO-vee) *adjective.* (Slang) Extremely pleasing; great. **groovier, grooviest.**

grope (GROHP) *verb.* 1. To feel about uncertainly with the hands: Walt *groped* his way to the light switch. 2. To search for a solution in a blind or uncertain fashion. **groped, groping.**

gros·beak (GROHSS-beek) *noun.* A large-billed bird of the finch family.

ground hog

gross (GROHSS) *adjective.* 1. Very fat; extremely large. 2. Coarse or vulgar: The man had *gross* table manners and chewed with his mouth open. 3. Thick: The *gross* jungle growth was almost impossible to cut through. 4. The total before anything has been taken out: My *gross* salary seems large until the taxes are deducted. 5. Extremely wrong or very bad: It was a *gross* error in judgment to allow the drunken man to drive. **grosser, grossest.** —*noun.* Twelve dozen; 144. —**grossly** *adverb.*

gro·tesque (groh-TESK) *adjective.* Odd or weird; ridiculous; outlandish: a *grotesque* look. —**grotesquely** *adverb.*

grot·to (GROT-oh) *noun.* 1. A cave. 2. A structure which looks like a cave. **grottoes** or **grottos.**

grouch (GROWCH) *noun.* 1. A person who is always complaining. 2. A complaint. **grouches.** —*verb.* To complain in a sulky way. **grouched, grouching.**

grouch·y (GROW-chee) *adjective.* Sulky and bad-humored. **grouchier, grouchiest.** —**grouchily** *adverb.*

[1]**ground** (GROWND) *noun.* 1. The earth's surface: The *ground* was covered with leaves. 2. A piece of land set aside for a special purpose: play*ground.* 3. (Plural) A reason or basis: *grounds* for being angry. 4. (Plural) The land around a building: school *grounds.* 5. (Plural) The grains of coffee left after the coffee has been made. —*verb.* 1. To run a ship or boat aground. 2. To connect (an electric wire) to the ground. 3. To require (an airplane) to stay on the ground. 4. (Slang) To deny (someone) all permission for social activities. **grounded, grounding.** —*adjective.* Of or on the ground: The office is on the *ground* floor. —**break ground.** 1. To dig into the earth to start a new building. 2. To start a new project. —**common ground.** A point on which two or more people agree. —**gain ground.** To improve or make progress. —**give ground.** To give way or retreat: Paul *gave ground* on some points in order to win others. —**stand one's ground:** To be firm and unyielding about one's position.

[2]**ground** (GROWND) *verb.* See **grind.**

ground·er (GROWND-ər) *noun.* (Baseball) A ball that hits the ground before being caught.

ground hog. *See* **woodchuck.**

ground-hog day (GROWND-hog DAY). A day, February 2, named for a legend that says if the ground hog comes out of his hole and sees his shadow on this day, there will be six more weeks of winter.

group (GROOP) *noun.* A collection of similar persons or things: A *group* of shoppers gathered around the display. *—verb.* 1. To put in a group: Sue *grouped* the yellow blocks. 2. To form a group. **grouped, grouping.**

group·er (GROO-pər) *noun.* A large fish of tropical waters.

grouse (GROWSS) *noun.* 1. A game bird of northern North America that somewhat resembles a hen and has feathered legs. 2. (Informal) A complaint. *—verb.* (Informal) To complain. **groused, grousing.**

grove (GROHV) *noun.* A cluster of trees; a small wooded area.

grov·el (GRUHV-əl) *verb.* To crawl or humble oneself before another: The slave *groveled* for mercy. **groveled, groveling.**

grow (GROH) *verb.* 1. To get bigger; expand; mature: My puppy will *grow* to be a large dog. 2. To become: The days *grow* hot early during summer. 3. To raise: Anne *grows* flowers for the house. 4. To be able to exist: Ferns *grow* in shady spots. **grew, grown, growing.**

growing season. The period of the year during which crops grow.

growl *verb.* 1. To make a deep rumbling sound in the throat: The watchdog *growled* when he heard us. 2. To speak in an angry or unpleasant manner. **growled, growling.** *—noun.* A deep, rumbling, threatening sound made in the throat.

grown (GROHN) *adjective.* Finished growing; fully developed: The woman had three *grown* children. *—verb. See* **grow.**

grown-up (GROHN-uhp) Also **grownup** *noun.* An adult. *—adjective.* 1. Fully grown or developed. 2. Having to do with adults.

growth (GROHTH) *noun.* 1. Additional size or maturity: Jane had one inch of *growth* in a year. 2. Increase: The *growth* of the boom town was amazing. 3. Anything that is grown: A *growth* of corn covered the fields.

grub (GRUHB) *noun.* 1. The larva of an insect, particularly of a beetle, that looks like a thick worm. 2. (Slang) Food. *—verb.* 1. To dig up from the ground by the roots: They *grubbed* the potatoes. 2. To work hard at a dull job for little money. 3. To dig. 4. (Slang) To get something by begging. **grubbed, grubbing.**

gru·el (GROO-əl) *noun.* A thin porridge made by boiling oatmeal or other meal in water or milk.

gru·el·ing (GROO-ə-ling) *adjective.* Difficult and tiring.

grue·some (GROO-səm) *adjective.* Ghastly or frightening; horrible, shocking. **—gruesomely** *adverb.*

gruff (GRUHF) *adjective.* 1. Harsh, rough, or unfriendly: Tim pretends to be *gruff* to hide his shyness. 2. Deep and tough; hoarse: a *gruff* voice. **—gruffly** *adverb.*

grum·ble (GRUHM-bəl) *verb.* 1. To mutter in protest; complain. 2. To make a low, rumbling noise. **grumbled, grumbling.** *—noun.* 1. A complaint. 2. A low, rumbling noise.

grump (GRUHMP) *noun.* A bad-tempered, complaining person.

grump·y (GRUHM-pee) *adjective.* Bad-tempered and cranky; irritable. **grumpier, grumpiest. —grumpiness** *noun.* **—grumpily** *adverb.*

grun·ion (GRUHN-yən) *noun.* A small fish of the West Coast that lays its eggs on the beaches.

grunt (GRUHNT) *noun.* 1. A short, deep, throaty sound, as that made by a hog. 2. (Slang) An ordinary foot-soldier; a GI. *—verb.* To make a deep, throaty sound, especially as an expression of disgust or strain. **grunted, grunting.**

grouper

grouse

guar·an·tee (ga-rən-TEE) *noun.* A promise to redo work or accept the return of goods if the original work or goods prove unsatisfactory. **guarantees.** —*verb.* 1. To assume responsibility for work done or goods sold: The company *guaranteed* our refrigerator for one year; if it needs repair during that time, there will be no charge. 2. To obtain security for: Theft insurance *guaranteed* him against loss if his car were stolen. 3. To promise. **guaranteed, guaranteeing.**

guar·an·ty (GA-rən-tee) *noun.* 1. Something that is put up as security to assure that a thing will be done: The bank held some of Father's stocks as a *guaranty* that he would repay the loan. 2. An agreement to take responsibility for another person's debt or duty if he fails to do so himself. **guaranties.**

guard (GAHRD) *verb.* 1. To watch over or protect from harm. 2. To watch over (to prevent something): They *guarded* the prisoners so none would escape. 3. To be very cautious or careful: Jill's mother *guards* against accidents by driving safely. **guarded, guarding.** —*noun.* 1. One that watches over or protects. 2. A person who watches over prisoners. 3. Any device that protects against injury. —**off guard.** Relaxed; not alert. —**on guard.** Alert and ready.

guard·ed (GAHR-did) *adjective.* 1. Protected or watched. 2. Very careful and cautious: *guarded* answers. —**guardedly** *adverb.*

guard·house (GAHRD-howss) *noun.* 1. A building or house used to house military guards. 2. A building used as a jail for minor offenses, as in the military.

guard·i·an (GAHR-dee-ən) *noun.* 1. A person who protects. 2. A person who is appointed to take care of a minor until he is old enough to assume legal responsibility. —**guardianship** *noun.*

guer·ril·la (gə-RIL-ə) Also **guerilla** *noun.* A member of a small, secret band of fighters who oppose their enemies with unexpected raids, sniper fire, and other tactics.

guess (GESS) *verb.* 1. To form an opinion without enough facts to be sure: Paul *guessed* the trunk held old letters. 2. To believe or suppose: Phil's mother *guessed* that his father would let him use the car. 3. To have a correct hunch or impression: I *guessed* where Roger was hiding. 4. (Often used with *at*) To predict: We *guessed* at the amount of money the drive would bring in. **guessed, guessing.** —*noun.* An opinion, answer, or prediction given without knowing all the facts. **guesses.**

guest (GEST) *noun.* 1. A visitor; one who receives hospitality in a home, a classroom, or a similar setting. 2. A customer in a restaurant, hotel, or other public place. 3. One who receives free services from some group or establishment.

guid·ance (GIGH-dənss) *noun.* Advice or counseling: Children receive *guidance* from teachers, parents, grandparents, and friends.

guide (GIGHD) *noun.* 1. A person who leads, directs, or shows the way: Father had a *guide* on his fishing trip in the mountains. 2. A book that gives directions. 3. Anything that shows the way: "The only *guide* to man is his conscience." (Churchill). —*verb.* 1. To lead or show the way. 2. To regulate or control; influence: The pilot *guided* the plane to a smooth landing. **guided, guiding.**

guided missile. A missile that can be steered in flight by remote control.

guild (GILD) *noun.* 1. A society of people in the same trade who unite to help or advance their common interests: actors' *guild.* 2. A union of craftsmen or merchants in the Middle Ages.

guile (GIGHL) *noun.* Deceit or craftiness. —**guileful** *adjective.* —**guilefully** *adverb.*

guil·lo·tine (GIL-ə-teen or GEE-ə-teen) *noun.* A machine used to execute people by cutting off their heads.

guilt (GILT) *noun.* 1. The fact of having done wrong. 2. A feeling of remorse for having done wrong.

guilt·y (GIL-tee) *adjective.* 1. (Often used with *of*) Responsible for some bad act or crime. 2. Aware that one has done wrong: Tom had a *guilty* look after telling a lie. —**guiltily** *adverb.*

guinea pig (GIN-ee PIG). 1. A small rodent kept as a pet and for laboratory experiments. 2. Anyone used for experimental purposes.

guise (GIGHZ) *noun.* 1. Outward appearance or dress: The wolf's *guise* made Little Red Riding Hood think he was her grandmother. 2. Pretense; false appearance: Tom Sawyer got the fence painted under the *guise* of making it seem like fun. **guises.**

gui·tar (gi-TAHR) *noun.* A musical instrument usually with six strings that are plucked or strummed.

gulch (GUHLCH) *noun.* A small valley or ravine. **gulches.**

gulf (GUHLF) *noun.* 1. A large inlet of saltwater; arm of an ocean or sea that is partly surrounded by land. 2. A deep, wide crack in the earth's surface. 3. A gap or separation: Their differing views on politics created a *gulf* between the men.

Gulf Stream. A warm ocean current that flows out of the Gulf of Mexico into the Atlantic, northeast along the coast of the United States, and then east to Europe.

gull (GUHL) *noun.* A water bird having webbed feet and a strong, hooked bill.

gul·li·ble (GUHL-ə-bəl) *adjective.* Easily deceived or tricked. —**gullibly** *adverb.*

gul·ly (GUHL-ee) *noun.* A deep ditch made by running water after heavy rains. **gullies.**

gulp (GUHLP) *verb.* 1. To swallow quickly or greedily: Jim *gulped* down his breakfast because he was late. 2. To swallow or gasp out of fear or nervousness. **gulped, gulping** —*noun.* A swallow or gasp.

gum (GUHM) *noun.* 1. A sticky juice from trees used for gluing things together; the tree from which it is obtained. 2. Chewing gum. 3. (Plural) The parts of the mouth in which teeth are embedded. —*verb.* To make sticky or sluggish: Tar *gummed* up the bottom of Tom's shoes. **gummed, gumming.** —**gummy** *adjective.*

gum·bo (GUHM-boh) *noun.* 1. A soup made from okra and other ingredients. 2. Okra. **gumbos.**

gum·drop (GUHM-drop) *noun.* A small candy made of a gumlike substance.

gump·tion (GUHMP-shən) *noun.* (Informal) Bold spirit; spunk: Only Jim had enough *gumption* to stand up to the bully.

gun (GUHN) *noun.* 1. A weapon that fires bullets, shells, or shot. 2. A device that resembles a pistol or other gun in appearance or function: spray *gun.* —*verb.* 1. To shoot: The hunter *gunned* down a large bear. 2. To speed up (as an engine): The racer *gunned* his car along the racetrack. **gunned, gunning.** —**jump the gun.** 1. To begin a race before the signal to start has been given. 2. To begin anything too soon. —**stick to one's guns.** To remain firm in one's actions or opinions.

gun·boat (GUHN-boht) *noun.* A small, armed vessel.

gun control. All the laws or methods used to insure that guns are sold and used for proper purposes.

gun·fire (GUHN-fighr) *noun.* The shooting of guns.

guillotine

guinea pigs

guitar

gull

gun·ner (GUHN-ər) *noun.* A person who operates or fires a gun, especially one trained to fire guns for military purposes.

gun·pow·der (GUHN-pow-dər) *noun.* An explosive powder that supplies the power for blasting, firing bullets, and fireworks.

gun·wale (GUHN-l) Also **gunnel** *noun.* The upper edge of the side of a ship or boat. **gunwales.**

gup·py (GUHP-ee) *noun.* A very small, colorful tropical fish. **guppies.**

gur·gle (GER-gəl) *verb.* 1. To flow with a deep, bubbling sound. 2. To make a sound like that made by water bubbling in a brook. **gurgled, gurgling.** —*noun.* A deep sound like that made by water bubbling in a brook. **gurgles.**

gush (GUHSH) *verb.* 1. To pour out suddenly and forcefully: Water *gushed* out when the fire hose broke. 2. To speak or act in an annoyingly emotional manner: When will Mary stop *gushing* so much about her family's new car? **gushed, gushing.** —*noun.* A sudden pouring out. —**gushy** *adjective.*

gypsy moth

gush·er (GUHSH-ər) *noun.* An oil well that supplies large quantities of oil.

gust (GUHST) *noun.* 1. A sudden and forceful rush of wind: A violent *gust* tipped over the small sailboat. 2. A sudden rush of emotion: Maria felt a *gust* of anger over the insult. —*verb.* To rush or flow suddenly, as a wind or strong feeling. **gusted, gusting.**

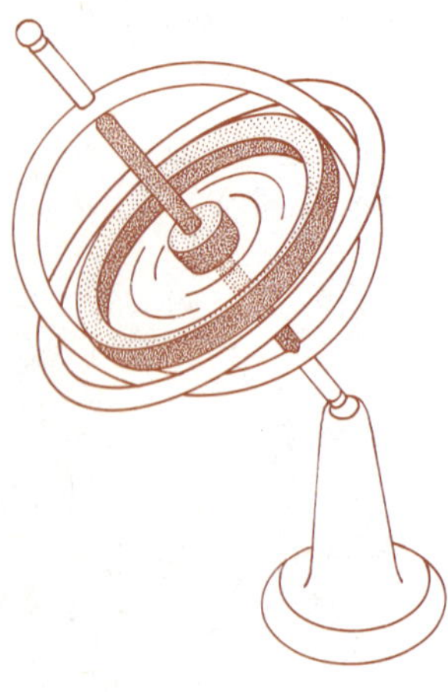

gyroscope

gust·y (GUHST-ee) *adjective.* Occurring in gusts, as with winds. **gustier, gustiest.** —**gustily** *adverb.*

gut (GUHT) *noun.* 1. The intestine; digestive tract. 2. A tough string made from the intestines of animals. 3. (Plural, slang) Courage; daring. —*verb.* 1. To destroy the interior of: Fire *gutted* the old factory. 2. To remove the internal organs of an animal. **gutted, gutting.**

gut·ter (GUHT-ər) *noun.* 1. A ditch or lowered section along a roadway for draining off water. 2. A metal structure attached along the bottom edge of a roof to drain off water. 3. A channel or groove.

gut·tur·al (GUHT-ər-əl) *adjective.* 1. Of or related to the throat. 2. Deep or harsh in sound: The sound of gargling is a *guttural* one. —**gutturally** *adverb.*

guy (GIGH) *noun.* 1. A rope or cable attached to something in order to strengthen or steady it. 2. (Informal) A fellow; male.

gym (JIM) *noun.* A gymnasium.

gym·na·si·um (jim-NAY-zee-əm) *noun.* A large room or building especially equipped for exercise and athletic performances.

gym·nas·tics (jim-NASS-tiks) *noun, plural.* Exercises done especially for developing strength and agility, usually with the aid of special equipment.

gyp (JIP) Also **gip** *verb.* (Informal) To cheat.—*noun.* An act of cheating.

gyp·sum (JIP-səm) *noun.* A soft, white mineral used in making plaster, fertilizer, and other products.

gyp·sy (JIP-see) Also **gipsy** *noun.* 1. [Capital G] One of a wandering race of people with dark skin and eyes who are found throughout the world. 2. A person who travels frequently or lives casually in the manner of the Gypsies. **gypsies.**

gypsy moth. A moth whose larva is very destructive to plant life.

gy·rate (JIGH-rayt) *verb.* To rotate or move in a circle; spin: The blades of the helicopter *gyrated* rapidly. **gyrated, gyrating.**

gy·ro·scope (JIGH-rə-skohp) *noun.* A device used to keep ships, planes, and the like steady or level. **gyroscopes.**

H, h (AYCH) *noun.* The eighth letter of the English alphabet.

ha (HAH) *interjection.* Used to express surprise or triumph.

hab·it (HAB-it) *noun.* 1. A usual or regular practice or action: Getting up early is one of Dad's *habits.* 2. A special outfit, such as that worn by some nuns.

hab·it·a·ble (HAB-ə-tə-bəl) *adjective.* Good enough to live in: Early man found caves *habitable.* —**habitably** *adverb.*

hab·i·tat (HAB-ə-tat) *noun.* The place where an animal or plant lives.

hab·i·ta·tion (hab-ə-TAY-shən) *noun.* 1. A home; dwelling place. 2. The process of dwelling in: The drafty old shack is not fit for *habitation.*

ha·bit·u·al (hə-BICH-oo-əl) *adjective.* Done out of habit; regular; customary: Tipping his hat was a *habitual* gesture for the old gentleman. —**habitually** *adverb.*

ha·ci·en·da (hah-see-EN-də) *noun.* In the Southwest or Latin America, a large ranch house.

[1]**hack** (HAK) *verb.* 1. To cut with rough strokes: The camper *hacked* the log with his hatchet. 2. To give repeated short coughs. 3. (Slang) To handle (a difficult situation). **hacked, hacking.**

[2]**hack** (HAK) *noun.* 1. A taxicab, carriage, or other vehicle available for hire. 2. A person hired to do a routine job, especially as a writer. 3. A repeated dry cough.

hack·saw (HAK-saw) *noun.* A saw with very hard, small teeth, used for cutting through metal.

had *verb. See* **have.**

had·dock (HAD-ək) *noun.* A small saltwater fish similar to the cod. —**haddock** or **haddocks** *plural.*

haddock

had·n't (HAD-nt) *contraction.* A shortened form of the words *had not.*

hag *noun.* 1. A gnarled or ugly old woman. 2. A witch.

hag·gard (HAG-ərd) *adjective.* Having a worn or exhausted appearance.

hai·ku (HIGH-koo) *noun.* A type of short, three-line poem especially popular in Japan. —**haiku** *plural.*

[1]**hail** (HAYL) *noun.* Small, round pieces of ice that fall from the sky like rain. —*verb.* To fall as hail from the sky. **hailed, hailing.**

[2]**hail** (HAYL) *noun.* A cry to attract attention: The taxi driver ignored our *hails.* —*verb.* 1. To greet or welcome. 2. To attract by calling out to. **hailed, hailing.** —*interjection.* A cry of praise or welcome.

hail·stone (HAYL-stohn) *noun.* A single piece of hail; a frozen raindrop. **hailstones.**

hair *noun.* 1. One of the many threadlike growths on the skin of mammals, including man. 2. All of these threadlike growths, especially those on the head of people: She washed her *hair.* 3. A very narrow margin or space: The first racer beat the second by a *hair.* —**get in one's hair.** To annoy or interfere with someone. —**split hairs.** To stress or complain about very minor details.

hair·cut (HAIR-kuht) *noun.* 1. A cutting or trimming of one's hair. 2. The style in which one has his hair cut.

hair·dres·ser (HAIR-dress-ər) *noun.* A person whose job is to cut and arrange hair.

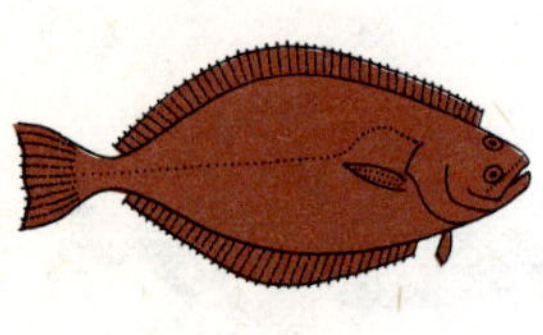
halibut

hair·pin (HAIR-pin) *noun.* A thin U-shaped pin used by women to keep their hair in place. —*adjective.* Doubled back; shaped like a hairpin: a *hairpin* curve in the road.

hair·y (HAIR-ee) *adjective.* 1. Covered with hair. 2. (Slang) Rugged; dangerous. **hairier, hairiest.**

hale (HAYL) *adjective.* Healthy; energetic: The athletes looked *hale* and hearty. **haler, halest.** —*verb.* To make (someone) come: I was *haled* into the principal's office. **haled, haling.**

half (HAF) *noun.* One of two equal or nearly equal parts of something: Four is *half* of eight. —**halves** (HAVZ) *plural.* —*adjective.* Being one of two equal or nearly equal parts: a *half* quart; a *half* pound. —*adverb.* Partly; in the amount of about one-half.

half·back (HAF-bak) *noun.* In football, one of two players positioned behind the forward line.

half brother. A brother related through either mother or father only.

half·heart·ed (HAF-HAHR-tid) *adjective.* Without much interest or enthusiasm. —**halfheartedly** *adverb.*

half-mast (HAF-MAST) *noun.* The mid-position of a pole or mast where a flag is flown as a signal of trouble or a sign of mourning.

half-moon (HAF-MOON) *noun.* The moon when only one-half of its disk is visible.

half-past (HAF-PAST) *adjective.* Thirty minutes after the hour.

half sister. A sister related through either mother or father only.

half tone. (Music) An interval equal to one half step or tone. Also called "semitone."

half·way (HAF-way) *adjective.* 1. At or about half of the way. 2. Partial; incomplete. —*adverb.* 1. To a middle position between two points: *halfway* around the world. 2. Half; partly: *halfway* finished.

half-wit (HAF-wit) *noun.* A stupid or foolish person.

hal·i·but (HAL-ə-bət) *noun.* A large saltwater food fish. —**halibut** or **halibuts** *plural.*

hall (HAWL) *noun.* 1. A passageway that connects rooms in a house or other building. 2. A large room or building used for large gatherings. 3. A room just inside the entrance of a house or other building. 4. A large building on an estate or campus. 5. A building that is used for public business: a town *hall.*

hal·low (HAL-oh) *verb.* To make or think of as holy: "*Hallowed* be Thy name." (Matthew 6:9). **hallowed, hallowing.**

Hal·low·een (hal-oh-EEN) Also **Hallowe'en** *noun.* October 31, the evening before All Saints' Day.

hal·lu·ci·na·tion (hə-loo-sn-AY-shən) *noun.* The seeing or otherwise sensing of things that are not real; a delusion.

ha·lo (HAY-loh) *noun.* 1. A ring of light often placed around the heads of saints and angels in works of art. 2. A ring of light seen around the moon or other heavenly body. —**halos** or **haloes** *plural.*

halt (HAWLT) *verb.* To bring to a stop. **halted, halting.** —*noun.* A stop.

hal·ter (HAWL-tər) *noun.* 1. A rope or strap fastened to the head of an animal, used to lead or control it. 2. A brief upper garment worn by women.

halt·ing (HAWLT-ing) *adjective.* Hesitant; uneven: The frightened woman told her story in a *halting* manner. —**haltingly** *adverb.*

halve (HAV) *verb.* 1. To divide into two equal parts. 2. To reduce by about half. **halved, halving.**

ham *noun.* 1. Meat, usually smoked, from the upper part of a hog's hind leg. 2. Part of the rear section of the body, from the knee to the buttock. 3. (Informal) An amateur radio operator. 4. (Slang) An actor who exaggerates speeches or actions. *—verb.* (Slang) To overact or exaggerate. **hammed, hamming.**

ham·burg·er (HAM-bər-gər) *noun.* 1. Ground or chopped beef. 2. A broiled or fried patty of this meat.

ham·let (HAM-lit) *noun.* A small town.

ham·mer (HAM-ər) *noun.* 1. A tool with a metal head and a handle, used for driving nails, bending metal, and for pounding or crushing. 2. Any of a number of devices, such as the hammer on a gun, that look or function like a hammer. *—verb.* 1. To drive, as a nail; pound; bend. 2. To exert repeated force or action: The football team *hammered* at the center of the opponents' line. **hammered, hammering.**

ham·mock (HAM-ək) *noun.* A bed or couch made of fabric and hung or supported by means of ropes or chains at each end.

ham·per (HAM-pər) *verb.* To interfere with (progress); hinder. **hampered, hampering.** *—noun.* A large covered basket.

ham·ster (HAM-stər) *noun.* A rodent that resembles a mouse and is sometimes kept as a pet.

hand *noun.* 1. The part of the body at the end of the arm. 2. One of the pointers on the face of a clock or other dial. 3. Handwriting: The old man wrote with a fine *hand.* 4. Applause: Let's give Jim a *hand* for scoring three touchdowns! 5. Help; aid: Mother asked us to give her a *hand* with the housework. 6. A person who does physical work: a hired *hand.* 7. (Cards) A player's cards; one round of a card game. 8. A member of a crew or a group. 9. (Plural) Keeping or control: in the *hands* of God. 10. A promise or agreement; handshake: Your *hand* is enough; there is no need to sign a contract. 11. Skill: Veronica decorated the Christmas tree with the *hand* of an artist. 12. Side: on my right *hand.* 13. A measurement, equal to four inches, generally used to measure the height of horses. *—verb.* To pass or give: *Hand* me the hammer. **handed, handing. —hand in hand.** Together. **—hands down.** Easily, without effort. **—on hand.** Ready, available.

hand·bag (HAND-bag) *noun.* 1. A pocketbook; purse. 2. A small piece of luggage.

hand·ball (HAND-bawl) *noun.* 1. A game in which two or four players compete by slapping a ball against a wall. 2. A small, hard rubber ball used in the game of handball.

hand·book (HAND-buk) *noun.* A book, usually small, that contains instructions, as for the operation of an automobile.

hand·cuff (HAND-kuhf or HAN-kuhf) *noun.* One of a pair of metal rings, joined by a chain, that can be fastened to the wrists of a person to restrict his movements. *—verb.* To put handcuffs on (a person). **handcuffed, handcuffing.**

hand·ful (HAND-ful or HAN-ful) *noun.* 1. As large an amount as one can hold in one hand. 2. A small number. 3. (Informal) A person or thing difficult to control.

hand·gun (HAND-guhn) *noun.* A small gun or pistol that may be held and fired with one hand.

hand·i·cap (HAN-dee-kap) *noun.* 1. A disadvantage or drawback, especially a physical one: Deafness is a severe *handicap.* 2. A scoring advantage or disadvantage given to sports contestants. *—verb.* To cause a disadvantage; hinder: A sore foot *handicapped* the runner. **handicapped, handicapping.**

hand·i·craft (HAN-dee-kraft) *noun.* A craft or work requiring skill with the hands.

hand·ker·chief (HANG-kər-chif) *noun.* A small square cloth used for wiping one's nose or face.

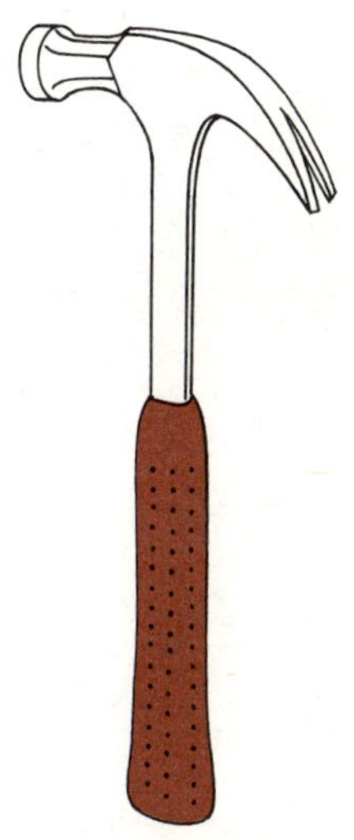
hammer

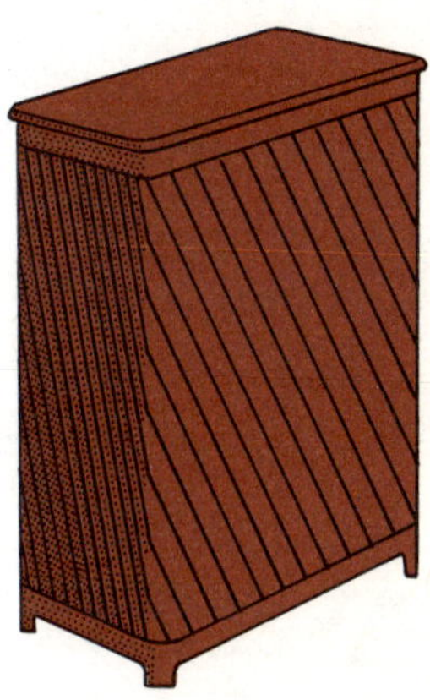
hamper

hamster

han·dle (HAN-dl) *noun.* 1. That part of an object that is intended to be held or turned. 2. (Slang) A person's name. **handles.** —*verb.* 1. To touch, move, or hold with the hands. 2. To manage or control: The coach *handled* his players strictly. 3. To react to being handled; respond: The automobile *handled* smoothly on the new highway. 4. To buy and sell; deal in. **handled, handling.**

han·dle·bar (HAN-dl-bahr) *noun.* (Usually plural) The curved metal bar by which a bicycle, motorcycle, or scooter is steered.

hand·rail (HAND-rayl) *noun.* A rail to be held by the hand as a support or guard, as on a stairway or balcony.

hand·shake (HAND-shayk or HAN-shayk) *noun.* The clasping of hands by two people, as in saying "hello."

hand·some (HAN-səm) *adjective.* 1. Good-looking (usually referring to a male). 2. Considerable or generous: The millionaire left a *handsome* estate to his heirs. **handsomer, handsomest.** —**handsomely** *adverb.* —**handsomeness** *noun.*

hand·writ·ing (HAND-right-ing) *noun.* Writing done with the hand.

hand·y (HAN-dee) *adjective.* 1. Skillful in the use of the hands: Joe is *handy* at fixing broken toys. 2. Easily reached: Mother keeps the first-aid kit in a *handy* place. 3. Useful or easy to use. **handier, handiest.** —**handily** *adverb.*

hang *verb.* 1. To fasten or be fastened from above: *hang* a chandelier. 2. To decorate: *hang* a tree with ornaments. 3. To let droop: When our dog *hangs* his tail, we know he's been bad. 4. To execute by fixing to the neck a rope on which the body suspends. 5. To be executed in this way. 6. To affix or put onto a wall: *hang* a painting, *hang* wallpaper. 7. To put (something) up so that it can move: *hang* a door. 8. To be unable to reach a decision (especially a jury). **hung** (or **hanged** for meanings 4 and 5) **hanging.** —*noun.* The right way of doing a thing: Jean got the *hang* of sewing at once. —**hang in.** (Slang) To refuse to quit or give up. —**hang out.** (Slang) To stay around a place.

hang·ar (HANG-ər) *noun.* A shed or building used for parking aircraft.

hang·er (HANG-ər) *noun.* 1. A device on which to place clothes so that they may be hung in a closet or on a hook. 2. Someone that hangs things: a paper*hanger.*

hang·nail (HANG-nayl) *noun.* A small strip of skin pulled loose at the side or base of the fingernail.

hang·o·ver (HANG-oh-vər) *noun.* 1. An illness or unpleasant physical state brought about by drinking too much alcoholic liquor. 2. Something held over from one time to another: Jan's fear of the dark is a *hangover* from her early childhood.

hang-up (HANG-uhp) *noun.* (Slang) 1. Something that restrains or irritates; a hindrance or handicap: Fear of being hurt is a *hang-up* that keeps Tim from playing football. 2. A fixation: Mary has a *hang-up* about saving bottles for recycling.

hank (HANGK) *noun.* A coil or loop, as of hair or yarn.

han·ker (HANG-kər) *verb.* To have a longing or great desire (usually followed by *for* or *after*): At camp Bill *hankered* for his mother's cooking. **hankered, hankering.**

Ha·nuk·kah (HAH-nə-kə) *noun. See* **Chanukah.**

hap·haz·ard (hap-HAZ-ərd) *adjective.* Happening by chance or accident; not planned. —**haphazardly** *adverb.*

hap·pen (HAP-ən) *verb.* 1. To take place. 2. To do a thing or take place by luck or chance: Paul claimed he just *happened* to see the Christmas presents. **happened, happening.** —**happen on.** To find by luck.

hap·pen·ing (HAP-ən-ing) *noun.* 1. Any event. 2. Some special unrehearsed occurrence or performance: a *happening* in honor of the coach.

hap·pi·ness (HAP-ee-niss) *noun.* Joy, content, glee; good fortune.

hap·py (HAP-ee) *adjective.* 1. Being or looking glad. 2. Lucky: It was a *happy* accident for them that they found their way home. 3. Fitting the occasion: Sue's gift was a *happy* choice. 4. Obsessed with: used in such combinations as trigger-*happy*, gadget-*happy*. **happier, happiest** —**happily** *adverb.*

har·ass (HA-rəss or hə-RASS) *verb.* 1. To irritate; to worry or disturb constantly: He was *harassed* by debts. 2. To wear out by constant attacks: The guerrillas *harassed* their enemies. **harassed, harassing.** —**harrassment** *noun.*

har·bor (HAHR-bər) *noun.* 1. A port or sheltered water. 2. Any shelter or place of safety. —*verb.* 1. To give shelter or protection to. 2. To hold in mind: *harbor* grudges. **harbored, harboring.**

hard (HAHRD) *adjective.* 1. Not soft; unyielding; firm. 2. Difficult to do or understand. 3. Stern; demanding: The teacher is a *hard* taskmaster. 4. Difficult to go through: Lack of fuel made it a *hard* winter. 5. Energetic and determined: Dave is a *hard* worker. 6. Containing dissolved minerals: *hard* water. 7. Physically or mentally tough, strong, or rugged. **harder, hardest.** —*adverb.* 1. Energetically. 2. In a solid state: We'll have to wait until the ice freezes *hard* before skating. 3. With determination: Jane tries *hard* to be neat. —**hardness** *noun.* —**hard and fast.** Exact, fixed: *hard and fast* rules. —**hard of hearing.** Unable to hear clearly. —**hard up.** Lacking money.

hard·boiled (HAHRD-BOILD) *adjective.* 1. Boiled until firm, as *hardboiled* eggs. 2. (Informal) Unfeeling: a *hardboiled* employer.

hard·en (HAHRD-n) *verb.* 1. To make or become hard or solid: When the bread *hardens,* we feed it to the pigeons. 2. To make or become unfeeling: *harden* one's heart. 3. To make strong or tough, mentally or physically. **hardened, hardening.**

hard hat. A helmet worn for protection by construction workers.

hard-hat *noun.* (Informal) 1. A construction worker. 2. A person with conservative political beliefs.

hard-hat area. The area in and around a building under construction closed to everyone except those wearing hard hats.

hard·head·ed (HAHRD-HED-id) *adjective.* 1. Practical. 2. Stubborn. —**hardheadedly** *adverb.*

hard·heart·ed (HAHRD-HAHR-tid) *adjective.* Lacking pity, sympathy, or other warm feelings. —**hardheartedly** *adverb.*

hard·ly (HAHRD-lee) *adverb.* Barely or only just: *hardly* enough money.

hard·ship (HAHRD-ship) *noun.* Extreme difficulty or misfortune.

hard·ware (HAHRD-wair) *noun.* Metal articles such as tools, nails, and screws.

hard·wood (HAHRD-wud) *noun.* The hard, dense wood of any tree with broad leaves that fall every year: Oak is a *hardwood;* pine is not.

har·dy (HAHR-dee) *adjective.* 1. Strong; able to stand difficulties. 2. Showing courage; bold. **hardier, hardiest.** —**hardily** *adverb.*

hare (HAIR) *noun.* Any of several mammals that look like rabbits but are larger and have longer ears and stronger hind legs. **hares.**

hare·brained (HAIR-BRAYND) *adjective.* Flighty or heedless: Sue is *harebrained;* her mind jumps from one subject to the next.

hark (HAHRK) *verb.* To listen with attention: *"Hark! hark!* the lark at heaven's gate sings." (Shakespeare). **harked, harking.**

harbor

harlequin

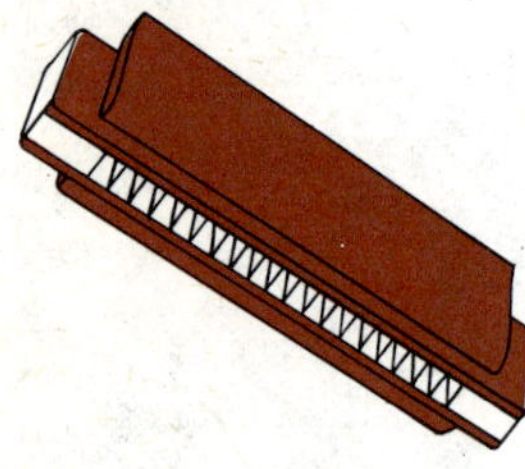
harmonica

harp

har·le·quin (HAHR-lə-kwən or HAHR-lə-kən) *noun.* [Capital H] A traditional clown of Italian comedy who wears a mask and multicolored tights. —*adjective.* Brightly colored: The *harlequin* cake sparkled with specks of pink peppermint.

harm (HAHRM) *verb.* To hurt or injure: Our dog barks a lot, but he has never *harmed* anyone. **harmed, harming.** —*noun.* Injury or damage.

harm·ful (HAHRM-fəl) *adjective.* Capable of causing damage or harm. —**harmfully** *adverb.*

harm·less (HAHRM-liss) *adjective.* Not capable of causing damage or harm. —**harmlessly** *adverb.*

har·mon·i·ca (hahr-MON-i-kə) *noun.* A small, flat, rectangular musical instrument with metal reeds, played by blowing or sucking in air. Also called "mouth organ."

har·mo·ni·ous (hahr-MOH-nee-əss) *adjective.* 1. Going together well in sound or appearance: *harmonious* colors. 2. Getting along well together. —**harmoniously** *adverb.*

har·mo·nize (HAHR-mə-nighz) *verb.* 1. To sing together so that the voices carrying the melody of a song blend with voices singing chord-like other parts. 2. To get along well together. **harmonized, harmonizing.**

har·mo·ny (HAHR-mə-nee) *noun.* 1. State of getting along well together. 2. Going well together in appearance or sound. 3. The study of musical chords and their structure. **harmonies.**

har·ness (HAHR-niss) *noun.* The leather gear used to strap a horse to whatever it is going to pull. **harnesses.** —*verb.* 1. To put a harness on. 2. To control and direct the power of: Man *harnesses* streams to produce electric power. **harnessed, harnessing.**

harp (HAHRP) *noun.* A large musical instrument with strings in a triangular frame, played by plucking the strings. —**harp on.** To continually nag or repeat.

har·poon (hahr-POON) *noun.* A barbed spear used for catching whales and large fish. —*verb.* To strike or kill with a harpoon. **harpooned, harpooning.**

harp·si·chord (HAHRP-si-kord) *noun.* A keyboard instrument that looks like a small grand piano but in which sound is produced by plucks on the strings rather than by hammers.

har·row (HA-roh) *noun.* A farm implement consisting of a heavy frame with upright teeth or disks that break up and smooth over plowed soil. —*verb.* 1. To use a harrow. 2. To torment or distress. **harrowed, harrowing.**

har·ry (HA-ree) *verb.* To raid, rob, or loot; harass. **harried, harrying.**

harsh (HAHRSH) *adjective.* 1. Cruel or unkind; demanding: He was a *harsh* master. 2. Unpleasant to the senses. **harsher, harshest.** —**harshly** *adverb.*

har·vest (HAHR-vist) *noun.* 1. Crop: a corn *harvest.* 2. The time when crops are gathered: *Harvest* was late this year. 3. The result of any behavior: Sue's welcome was the *harvest* of her good deeds. —*verb.* 1. To gather or reap crops. 2. To get (the results or benefits of something done). **harvested, harvesting.**

har·vest·er (HAHR-viss-tər) *noun.* A person or machine that gathers crops.

has (HAZ) *verb. See* **have.**

hash *noun.* 1. A dish made of leftover chopped meat and potatoes. 2. A mess or jumble. 3. (Informal) Hashish. **hashes.** —*verb.* 1. To chop into small pieces. 2. (Informal) To go over thoroughly; discuss. 3. (Informal) To mess things up. **hashed, hashing.**

hash·ish (HASH-eesh or HASH-ish) Also **hasheesh** (HAH-sheesh) *noun.* A narcotic made from a resin in the hemp plant.

has·n't (HAZ-nt) *contraction.* A shortened form of the words *has not.*

has·sle (HASS-l) *noun.* 1. (Informal) An argument or disagreement. 2. (Slang) Trouble; bother. **hassles.** —*verb.* (Informal) To argue or disagree. **hassled, hassling.**

has·sock (HASS-ək) *noun.* A hard stuffed cushion used as a footstool.

haste (HAYST) *noun.* 1. Quickness; fast action. 2. Careless rush.

has·ten (HAY-sən) *verb.* To hurry or cause to hurry; act quickly. **hastened, hastening.**

has·ty (HAYSS-tee) *adjective.* 1. Quick or hurried. 2. Done without care: *hasty* homework. 3. Easily aroused: a *hasty* temper. **hastier, hastiest.** —**hastily** *adverb.*

hat *noun.* A covering for the head, usually having a crown and brim. —**keep under one's hat.** To keep (a secret). —**pass the hat.** To take up a collection. —**take one's hat off to.** To salute or praise. —**toss one's hat into the ring.** To announce that one is running for public office.

[1]**hatch** (HACH) *verb.* 1. To break through and come out from an eggshell. 2. To cause (an egg or eggs) to produce young. 3. To think up or plot: *hatch* a plan. **hatched, hatching.**

[2]**hatch** (HACH) *noun.* An opening in the deck of a ship through which cargo is loaded. **hatches.**

hatch·er·y (HACH-ə-ree) *noun.* A place where eggs are hatched. **hatcheries.**

hatch·et (HACH-it) *noun.* A small ax with a short handle.

hate (HAYT) *noun.* 1. A strong feeling of dislike. 2. An object that is greatly disliked: Snakes are her pet *hate.* **hates.** —*verb.* To dislike strongly. **hated, hating.**

hate·ful (HAYT-fəl) *adjective.* 1. Full of ill will. 2. Deserving one's dislike: Teasing the cat is a *hateful* thing to do. —**hatefully** *adverb.*

ha·tred (HAY-trid) *noun.* A strong feeling of dislike; hate.

haugh·ty (HAW-tee) *adjective.* Proud, lordly. **haughtier, haughtiest.** —**haughtily** *adverb.*

haul (HAWL) *verb.* 1. To pull or drag. 2. To carry in a truck or wagon. **hauled, hauling.** —*noun.* 1. The act of pulling or dragging. 2. The distance over which something travels or is carried: a long *haul.* 3. Something taken: The burglars made quite a *haul.*

haunch (HAWNCH) *noun.* 1. The upper part of a leg, including the hip. 2. (Always plural) The hindquarters of an animal. **haunches.**

haunt (HAWNT) *verb.* 1. To return often. 2. To hang around. 3. To visit in ghostly form. **haunted, haunting.** —*noun.* 1. A place one visits often. 2. A ghost.

have (HAV) *verb.* 1. A helping verb used with the past participle: I *have* come home. 2. To own or possess. 3. To hold: I *have* a pencil in my hand. 4. To contain: How many windows does this room *have?* 5. To be forced. 6. To undergo: *have* the measles. 7. To think up: I *have* an idea. 8. To defeat or trick: "I *have* you now," said Joe as he won the checker game. 9. To give birth to: *have* kittens. 10. To take or accept: I'll *have* bacon and eggs. 11. To take part in: Let's *have* a parade! 12. To show or use (an emotion or quality): *Have* a heart! **had, having.** —*noun, plural.* Those who are not poor: "There are only two families in the world, the *Haves* and the Have-Nots." (Cervantes). —**have it out.** Settle it; get it over.

ha·ven (HAY-vən) *noun.* 1. A port for ships. 2. Any safe place.

harpoon

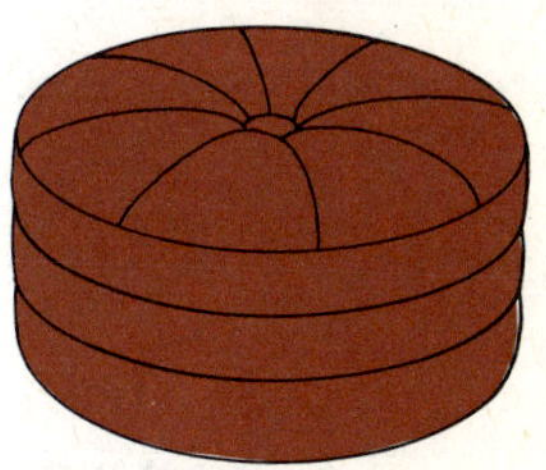

hassock

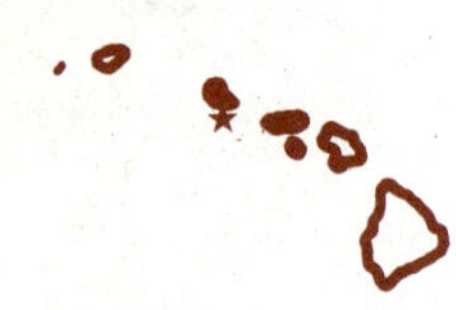

Hawaii
★capital: Honolulu

hawk

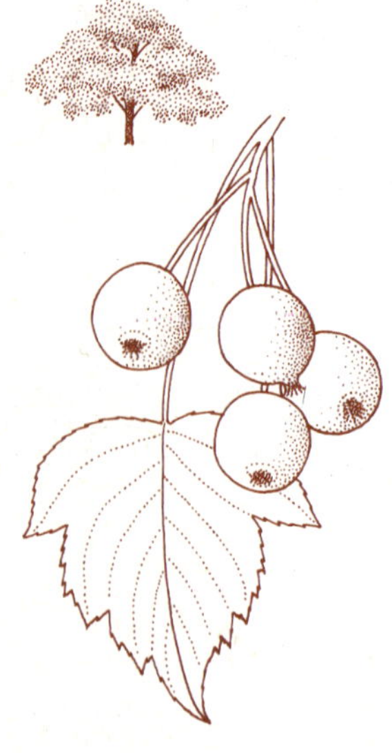

hawthorn

have·n't (HAV-ənt) *contraction.* A shortened form of the words *have not.*

hav·er·sack (HAV-ər-sak) *noun.* A bag worn on the back or shoulder.

hav·oc (HAV-ək) *noun.* Ruin, damage.

haw *noun.* 1. The hawthorn tree. 2. The hawthorn berry.

Ha·wai·i (hə-WIGH-ee or hə-WAH-yə) Also **Hawaiian Islands** *noun.* A state in Pacific United States, 50th to join the Union (1959). —**H.I.** *abbreviation.* Also **HI** for Zip Code.

[1]**hawk** *noun.* 1. A bird of prey with a curved bill and strong claws. 2. (Informal) A person who favors a warlike policy for his country.

[2]**hawk** *verb.* To sell goods by calling out the name of the product. **hawked, hawking.**

haw·ser (HAW-zər) *noun.* A heavy rope used to tow or dock a ship.

haw·thorn (HAW-thorn) *noun.* A small tree or shrub having many sharp thorns.

hay *noun.* Grass and other plants that are cut, dried, and stored for use as animal feed. —*verb.* To cut hay. **hayed, haying.** —**hit the hay.** (Slang) To go to bed; retire.

hay fever. An illness caused by a reaction to the pollen of certain plants such as ragweed.

hay·loft (HAY-lawft) *noun.* The upper floor of a barn, where hay is stored.

hay·mow (HAY-mow) *noun.* The part of a barn in which hay is stored.

hay·stack (HAY-stak) *noun.* A pile of hay.

hay·wire (HAY-wighr) *noun.* Wire used to fasten hay into bales. —*adjective.* 1. Makeshift, poorly put together. 2. (Informal) Crazy. —**go haywire.** Come apart, go to pieces.

haz·ard (HAZ-ərd) *noun.* 1. A danger. 2. A possible cause of accident. 3. An obstacle on a golf course, such as a sand trap. —*verb.* To risk or take a chance. **hazarded, hazarding.**

haz·ard·ous (HAZ-ər-dəss) *adjective.* 1. Dangerous. 2. Risky.

haze (HAYZ) *noun.* 1. Light smoke or mist in the air. 2. Confusion in the mind. —*verb.* To discomfort or embarrass by forcing (someone) to do silly tasks. **hazed, hazing.**

ha·zel (HAY-zl) *noun.* 1. A small nut with a smooth brown shell. 2. The shrub or small tree on which this nut grows. 3. (Also *adjective*) A light brown color.

ha·zel·nut (HAY-zl-nuht) *noun.* The nut of the hazel tree.

ha·zy (HAY-zee) *adjective.* 1. Misty, smoky. 2. Not clear, uncertain. **hazier, haziest.** —**hazily** *adverb.*

H-bomb (AYCH-bom) *noun. See* **hydrogen bomb.**

he (HEE) *pronoun.* 1. A male person who has just been mentioned or indicated. 2. Anyone, a person in general: "*He* laughs best who laughs last." (John Vanbrugh).

head (HED) *noun.* 1. The top part of the body containing (in man and some animals) the brain, eyes, ears, nose, and mouth. 2. The mind. 3. Control; calm: When Liz saw the mouse, she lost her *head.* 4. (Usually plural) The side of a coin that has the more important design; the opposite of tails. 5. The first position: at the *head* of the class. 6. Each member of a set or group: count *heads.* 7. The leader; the most important or powerful one. 8. A plant part that has leaves formed into a ball: a *head* of lettuce. 9. The part of something that is at the top: the *head* of a hammer. —*verb.* 1. To go toward: *head* home. 2. To be in charge of. **headed, heading.** —**head off.** To get in front of; to cut off. —**out of one's head.** Crazy; out of control. —**over one's head.** Beyond one's ability to do or understand.

head·ache (HED-ayk) *noun.* 1. A pain in the head. 2. (Informal) A problem. **headaches.**

head·band (HED-band) *noun.* A strip of material worn around the head.

head·dress (HED-dress) *noun.* Something worn on the head: The chief had a *headdress* made of eagle feathers. **headdresses.**

head·first (HED-ferst) Also **head·fore·most** (HED-FOR-mohst) *adverb.* With the head leading the rest of the body: He fell into the pool *headfirst.*

head·land (HED-lənd) *noun.* A point of land that extends out into water.

head·light (HED-light) *noun.* A bright light on the forward end of a vehicle such as a car or train.

head·line (HED-lighn) *noun.* A few words in large type that give the subject of a news story. **headlines.** *—verb.* 1. To be first in importance: The comedian will *headline* the program. 2. To write headlines for. **headlined, headlining.**

head·long (HED-lawng) *adjective* and *adverb.* 1. Headfirst. 2. Without thinking. 3. Very fast or forceful.

head·quar·ters (HED-kwor-tərz) *noun, plural in form but sometimes used with singular verb.* The main office.

head start. An early start before others, as in a race.

head·strong (HED-strawng) *adjective.* Stubborn, hard to handle.

head·wa·ters (HED-waw-tərz) *noun, plural.* The small streams that flow together to form a river.

head·way (HED-way) *noun.* 1. Forward motion; progress. 2. The open space in a doorway or under an arch.

heal (HEEL) *verb.* 1. To return to health: 2. To cure or help to become healthy. **healed, healing.**

health (HELTH) *noun.* 1. The state of being free from disease. 2. The general state of one's body: He asked about my *health.*

health·ful (HELTH-fəl) *adjective.* Wholesome, good for the body. —**healthfully** *adverb.*

health·y (HELTH-ee) *adjective.* 1. Well; in good health. 2. Good for the body. 3. Large or strong: a *healthy* serving of ice cream. **healthier, healthiest.**

heap (HEEP) *noun.* 1. Pile. 2. A large amount. *—verb.* To put into a pile. **heaped, heaping.**

hear (HIHR) *verb.* 1. To sense through the ear. 2. To pay attention. **heard, hearing.**

heard (HERD) *verb. See* **hear.**

hear·ing (HIHR-ing) *noun.* 1. The ability to sense sounds by ear. 2. A chance for all points of view to be presented: a Senate *hearing.*

hear·say (HIHR-say) *noun.* 1. Something heard from someone else. 2. Gossip. *—adjective.* Not reliable.

hearse (HERSS) *noun.* Car or other vehicle used to carry a dead person. **hearses.**

heart (HAHRT) *noun.* 1. The organ that pumps blood throughout the body. 2. Emotion or feeling toward others: a warm *heart,* a hard *heart.* 3. The center or most important part: the *heart* of a matter. 4. A heart-shaped figure; a playing card marked with a heart-shaped figure. —**take heart.** Have courage; cheer up. —**take to heart.** To take seriously or personally.

heart·ache (HAHRT-ayk) *noun.* Great sadness, unhappiness. **heartaches.**

heart·bro·ken (HAHRT-broh-kən) *adjective.* Deeply sad; overcome by sorrow. —**heartbrokenly** *adverb.*

heart·en (HAHRT-n) *verb.* To fill with hope and cheer; to encourage. **heartened, heartening.**

heart·felt (HAHRT-felt) *adjective.* Truly felt; sincere.

hearth (HAHRTH) *noun.* 1. The floor of a fireplace. 2. The fireside; home. 3. The lowest part of a blast furnace where melted metal collects.

headband

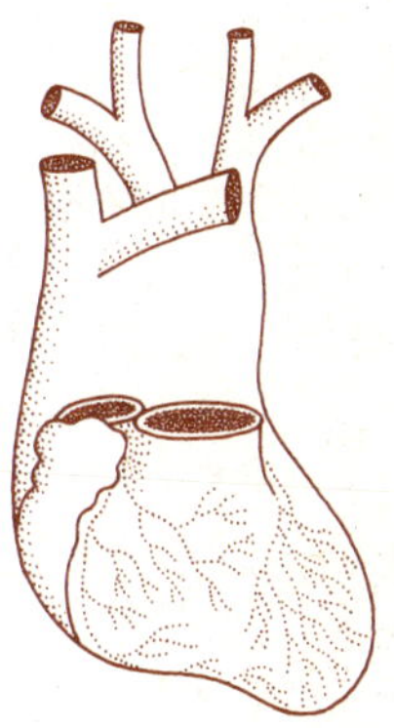

heart (definition 1)

heart (definition 4)

heart·less (HAHRT-liss) *adjective.* Cold and unfeeling. —**heartlessly** *adverb.*

hearts (HAHRTZ) *noun, plural in form but used with a singular verb.* A card game in which one must get all or none of the hearts in order to win.

heart·y (HAHR-tee) *adjective.* 1. Enthusiastic, cheerful, approving. 2. In large amounts; abundant. 3. In good health. **heartier, heartiest.** —**heartily** *adverb.* —**heartiness** *noun.*

heat (HEET) *noun.* 1. State of being hot. 2. The amount of hotness in an object or substance. 3. Extreme emotion, such as anger or excitement: the *heat* of an argument. 4. One of the trials in a race or contest. —*verb.* 1. To make or become hot, warm, or less cold. 2. To make excited or angry. **heated, heating.**

heat·er (HEET-ər) *noun.* Something that makes heat, such as a stove.

heath (HEETH) *noun.* 1. A wasteland with low bushes and few trees. 2. A small evergreen shrub.

hea·then (HEE-t͟hən) *noun.* 1. Someone who does not belong to the Christian, Jewish, or Moslem religions. 2. A pagan or person who worships many gods, no god, or a god different from the God of the Bible.

heath·er (HET͟H-ər) *noun.* A low evergreen shrub with small purple flowers.

heat shield. Covering on a spacecraft to protect it against heat on re-entry into the earth's atmosphere.

heave (HEEV) *verb.* 1. To lift with effort; to raise (something heavy): Help me *heave* this trunk. 2. To make (a sound) with a deep breath: *heave* a sigh of relief. 3. To go up and down in rhythm: Her chest *heaved* with sobs. 4. To pant for breath. 5. To gag or vomit. 6. To haul in a rope or cable with effort. **heaved, hove, heaving.**

heav·en (HEV-ən) *noun.* 1. In many religions, the place where the souls of the blessed dead go. 2. [Capital H] The place where God dwells. 3. A place or feeling of great pleasure. 4. (Plural) The space high above earth; the skies.

heav·en·ly (HEV-ən-lee) *adjective.* 1. Of or in the heavens or skies: The stars are *heavenly* bodies. 2. Sacred, blessed. 3. (Informal) Very delightful, beautiful.

heav·y (HEV-ee) *adjective.* 1. Having great weight. 2. Having greater weight than others of its kind: a *heavy* oil. 3. Of greater force, size, or amount than ordinary: *heavy* seas. 4. Bowed down (with weight): trees *heavy* with snow. 5. Dull, uninteresting, hard to understand: a *heavy* lecture. 6. Deep, serious: a *heavy* loss. 7. Difficult: a *heavy* job. 8. Very important: a *heavy* responsibility. 9. Gloomy: *heavy* clouds. **heavier, heaviest.** —**heavily** *adverb.*

heav·y·weight (HEV-ee-wayt) *noun.* 1. Someone above average in weight. 2. A wrestler or boxer who weighs more than 175 pounds.

He·brew (HEE-broo) *noun.* 1. A descendent of ancient tribes who lived in what is now Israel; a Jew. 2. The language of the ancient Jews.

heck·le (HEK-əl) *verb.* To annoy, embarrass, or disturb with many questions or insults. **heckled, heckling.** —**heckler** *noun.*

hec·tic (HEK-tik) *adjective.* Full of frantic activity and confusion. —**hectically** *adverb.*

he'd (HEED) *contraction.* A shortened form of *he had* or *he would.*

hedge (HEJ) *noun.* 1. A fence or boundary made of a row of bushes, shrubs, or trees planted close together. 2. A protection or defense against something: Water fluoridation is used as a *hedge* against tooth decay. **hedges.** —*verb.* 1. To plant a row of low shrubs or trees. 2. (Used with "in") To surround. 3. To avoid a definite answer. **hedged, hedging.**

hedge·hog (HEJ-hog) *noun.* 1. (Europe) A small insect-eating animal with spines on its back. 2. (United States) A porcupine.

heed *verb.* To take notice of, pay attention to. **heeded, heeding.** —*noun.* Attention; careful listening.

heed·less (HEED-liss) *adjective.* Not caring; not noticing. —**heedlessly** *adverb.*

heel *noun.* 1. The rear, underside part of the foot. 2. Anything like a heel or in the position of a heel: the *heel* of a shoe. 3. (Slang) An ungentlemanly man. —*verb.* 1. To put heels on. 2. To walk behind (a person's heel): You should teach your dog to *heel* on command. **heeled, heeling.** —**cool one's heels.** To wait. —**down at the heels.** Run-down; the worse for wear. —**well-heeled.** Wealthy.

heft *verb.* (Informal) 1. To raise, lift. 2. To try to decide weight by lifting and feeling: He *hefted* the suitcase before weighing it. **hefted, hefting.** —*noun.* Bigness, heaviness: books of great *heft.*

heft·y (HEFT-ee) *adjective.* (Informal) Heavy, strong, large: *hefty* wrestlers. **heftier, heftiest.**

height (HIGHT) *noun.* 1. Measurement of someone or something from bottom to top. 2. The fullest possible amount: the *height* of silliness. 3. Distance from ground or sea level upward; altitude.

height·en (HIGHT-n) *verb.* To make or become great or greater. **heightened, heightening.**

heir (AIR) *noun, usually masculine.* A person who inherits or expects to inherit property or a title after its owner dies.

heir·ess (AIR-iss) *noun.* A female heir. **heiresses.**

heir·loom (AIR-loom) *noun.* An object with special meaning or value handed down from one generation to another.

held *verb. See* **hold.**

hel·i·cop·ter (HEL-i-kop-tər) *noun.* A type of aircraft with large blades or propellers on top that enable it to move up and down as well as forward.

hel·i·port (HEL-ə-port) *noun.* A place for helicopters to land and take off.

he·li·um (HEE-lee-əm) *noun.* A very light odorless, colorless gas.

hell (HEL) *noun.* 1. In some religions, the place where damned souls are punished after death. 2. Any place, event, or feeling of pain, misery, suffering, or evil: "War is *hell.*" (General Sherman).

he'll (HEEL) *contraction.* A shortened form of the words *he will* or *he shall.*

hell·ish (HEL-ish) *adjective.* As if coming from hell; causing great suffering. —**hellishly** *adverb.*

hel·lo (hə-LOH) *interjection.* 1. A greeting. 2. Expression of surprise. —*noun.* A greeting. **hellos.**

helm *noun.* 1. A lever or wheel for controlling the rudder of a ship and steering it. 2. The highest position; the leadership.

hel·met (HEL-mit) *noun.* A protective covering for the head, usually made of metal, leather, or plastic.

help *verb.* 1. To make easier; assist. 2. To be of service. 3. To keep from: I can't *help* laughing. 4. To improve or cure. **helped, helping.** —*interjection.* Expresses fright, terror, a call for assistance. —*noun.* 1. Assistance. 2. A person or thing that helps. 3. Hired worker or workers. —**help oneself.** 1. To serve oneself with food or drink. 2. To take without asking.

help·er (HEL-pər) *noun.* Someone who helps; an assistant or aid.

help·ing (HEL-ping) *noun.* A portion of food served one person at a time.

help·less (HELP-liss) *adjective.* Not able to help oneself; without strength or power. —**helplessly** *adverb.* —**helplessness** *noun.*

hedgehog (definition 1)

helicopter

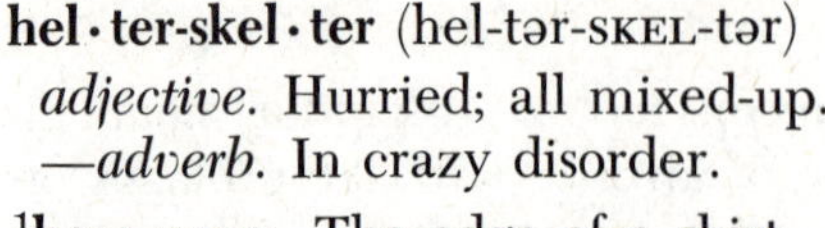

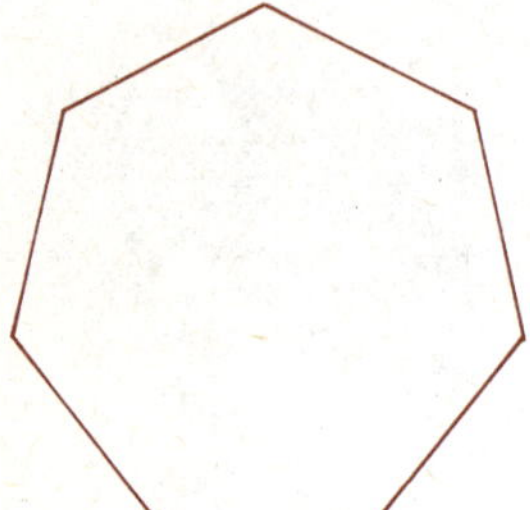
heptagon

hel·ter-skel·ter (hel-tər-SKEL-tər) *adjective.* Hurried; all mixed-up. —*adverb.* In crazy disorder.

[1]**hem** *noun.* The edge of a skirt, curtain, towel, etc. that has been folded over and sewed. —*verb.* To sew a hem. **hemmed, hemming.** —**hem in.** To surround; enclose.

[2]**hem** *noun.* Cough-like sound made to attract attention or express hesitation. —*verb.* To make such a sound. **hemmed, hemming.** —**hem and haw.** To speak with many pauses.

hem·i·sphere (HEM-ə-sfihr) *noun.* 1. Half of a sphere or globe. 2. [Often Capital H] One of the halves into which the earth is divided. **hemispheres.**

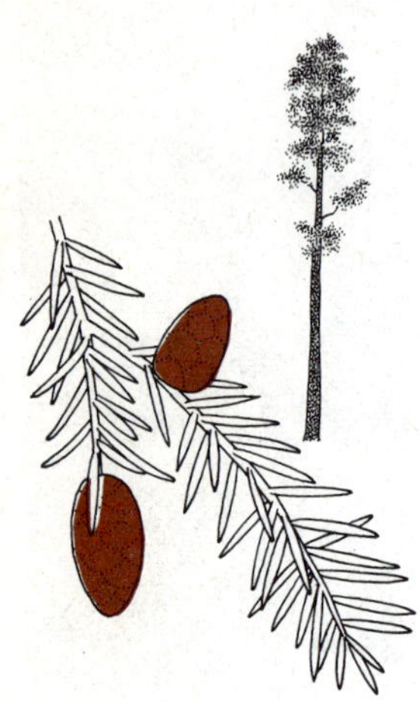
hemlock

hem·lock (HEM-lok) *noun.* 1. An evergreen tree, somewhat like the pine, with small needles and drooping branches. 2. A poisonous herb; the drink made from it.

he·mo·glo·bin (HEE-mə-gloh-bən) *noun.* Oxygen-carrying substance in red blood cells.

hem·or·rhage (HEM-ə-rij or HEM-rij) *noun.* A heavy flow of blood. **hemorrhages.** —*verb.* To lose a large amount of blood. **hemorrhaged, hemorrhaging.**

hemp *noun.* 1. A tall plant with strong, tough fibers. 2. Fibers used to make rope and heavy cloth. 3. A narcotic, such as hashish, which is made from the flowers and leaves of some kinds of hemp.

hen

hen *noun.* Any female bird, especially an adult female chicken or domestic fowl.

hence (HENSS) *adverb.* 1. From this time forward; from now. 2. As a consequence; therefore.

hence·forth (HENSS-forth) *adverb.* From this time on.

hen-pecked (HEN-pekt) Also **henpecked** *adjective.* (Informal) Constantly nagged, browbeaten, or dominated by a wife.

hep·ta·gon (HEP-tə-gon) *noun.* A figure that has seven sides and seven angles.

her *pronoun.* 1. A form of *she* used as the object of verbs or prepositions. 2. (Also *adjective*) Belonging to her.

her·ald (HEHR-əld) *noun.* 1. A person who announces or publicizes; in ancient times a royal messenger. 2. Something that comes before an event, a forerunner. —*verb.* To announce, proclaim: The falling leaves *herald* the coming of winter. **heralded, heralding.**

her·ald·ry (HEHR-əl-dree) *noun.* 1. The science of recording, designing, and tracing family coats of arms. 2. Pomp and ceremony.

herb (ERB) *noun.* 1. A plant whose stem is not woody and that lasts only one season. 2. Any of various plants used in medicine or cooking.

her·ba·ceous (her-BAY-shəss) *adjective.* Pertaining to herbs as distinguished from other plants.

her·biv·o·rous (her-BIV-ər-əss) *adjective.* Feeding on plants rather than on animals.

herd *noun.* A group of one type of animals that stay or are kept together: *herd* of cows. —*verb.* To gather, move, or form in a herd. **herded, herding.**

here (HIHR) *adverb.* 1. In or at this place. 2. To this place: Come *here.* 3. In this life, on earth: After the accident John exclaimed, "We are lucky to still be *here.*" —*noun.* This place. —**neither here nor there.** Having nothing to do with what is being discussed.

here·a·bout (HIHR-ə-bowt) Also **hereabouts** *adverb.* In the general area or neighborhood.

here·af·ter (hihr-AF-tər) *adverb.* 1. From this time forward. 2. In the life after death. —*noun.* 1. Life after death. 2. The future.

here·by (hihr-BIGH) *adverb.* By this act or means: The judge said, "I *hereby* sentence you to jail."

he·red·i·tar·y (hə-RED-ə-tehr-ee) *adjective.* 1. Passed on from parents to children; inborn: "Virtue is not *hereditary.*" (Thomas Paine). 2. Gained through inheritance: a *hereditary* title. 3. Coming from one's ancestors; traditional.

he·red·i·ty (hə-RED-ə-tee) *noun.* 1. The transmission of certain characteristics from parents to their children. 2. Qualities biologically acquired from one's parents. **heredities.**

her·e·sy (HEHR-ə-see) *noun.* 1. Any belief or opinion contrary to established religious belief. 2. A belief or opinion contrary to accepted beliefs in philosophy, politics, science, or morality. 3. Holding such an opposing opinion. **heresies.**

her·e·tic (HEHR-ə-tik) *noun.* One who holds a view contrary to established belief in religion, politics, or science, or to other accepted standards.

he·ret·i·cal (hə-RET-ə-kəl) *adjective.* Against established beliefs.

here·to·fore (HIHR-tə-for) *adverb.* Before this; up to this time.

here·up·on (HIHR-ə-pon) *adverb.* Instantly following this; at this point.

here·with (HIHR-with) *adverb.* Along with this; hereby.

her·i·tage (HEHR-ə-tij) *noun.* 1. An inheritance 2. Something other than property that is acquired or belongs to one because of one's birth: Your *heritage* includes the traditions of your country. **heritages.**

her·mit (HER-mit) *noun.* 1. A person who chooses to live alone. 2. A spiced cookie made with molasses.

her·ni·a (HER-nee-ə) *noun.* A sticking out or protrusion of a body part, as of an organ, through the wall that usually encloses it. —**hernias** or **herniae** (HER-nee-ee) *plural.*

he·ro (HIHR-oh) *noun.* 1. A boy or man who shows courage or is admired for his outstanding achievements. 2. The main male character in a poem, story, or play. 3. A kind of sandwich. *See* **grinder.**

he·ro·ic (hih-ROH-ik) *adjective.* 1. Having the qualities of a hero; courageous, daring, fearless. 2. Describing deeds of heroes as in a poem or story. —**heroically** *adverb.*

her·o·in (HEHR-oh-ən) *noun.* A very powerful habit-forming drug made from morphine.

her·o·ine (HEHR-oh-in) *noun.* 1. A girl or woman who shows courage or is admired for her outstanding achievements. 2. The main female character in a poem, story, or play. **heroines.**

her·o·ism (HEHR-oh-iz-əm) *noun.* Bravery; courageous conduct.

her·on (HEHR-ən) *noun.* A wading bird with long legs and a long neck.

her·ring (HEHR-ing) *noun.* A small fish, popular as food.

hers (HERZ) *pronoun.* Something that belongs to a female previously named: *Hers* was the best cake.

her·self (her-SELF) *pronoun.* A form of *she* used: 1. For emphasis: She did it *herself.* 2. When the subject and object of a verb are the same: Nancy dressed *herself.* 3. To describe a normal or usual state: She was worried and not *herself.*

he's (HEEZ) *contraction.* A shortened form of the words *he is* or *he has.*

hes·i·tant (HEZ-ə-tənt) *adjective.* Undecided; holding back; tending to hesitate. —**hesitantly** *adverb.*

hes·i·tate (HEZ-ə-tayt) *verb.* 1. To hold back because of fear; pause because of indecision: "He who *hesitates* is sometimes saved." (James Thurber). 2. To feel reluctant or unwilling. 3. To speak with pauses in between words. **hesitated, hesitating.** —**hesitation** (hez-ə-TAY-shən) *noun.*

heron

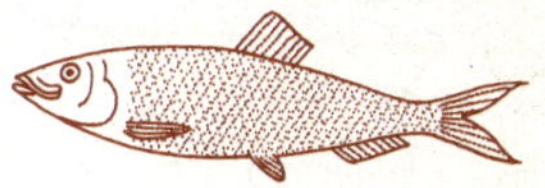

herring

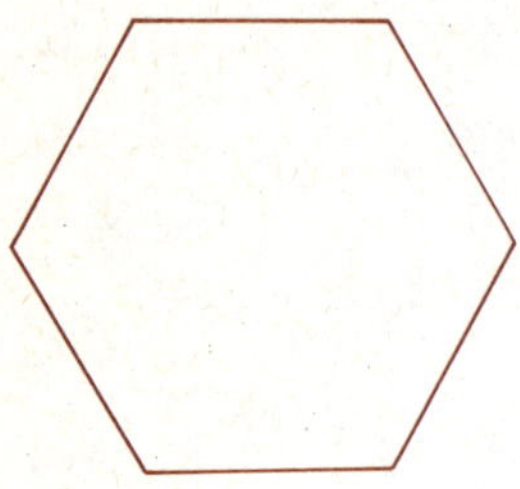

hexagon

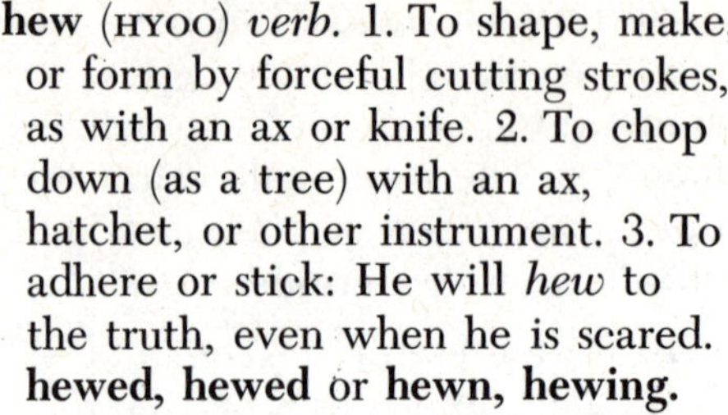

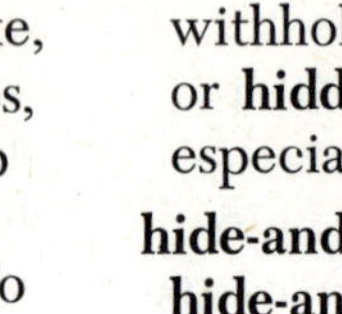

hew (HYOO) *verb.* 1. To shape, make, or form by forceful cutting strokes, as with an ax or knife. 2. To chop down (as a tree) with an ax, hatchet, or other instrument. 3. To adhere or stick: He will *hew* to the truth, even when he is scared. **hewed, hewed** or **hewn, hewing.**

hex (HEKS) *noun.* A curse, an evil spell, something that brings bad luck. **hexes.** —*verb.* To put a curse on (someone); cast an evil spell. **hexed, hexing.**

hex·a·gon (HEKS-ə-gon) *noun.* A figure having six sides and six angles.

hey (HAY) *interjection.* An exclamation that attracts attention or shows surprise, wonder, or pleasure.

hey·day (HAY-day) *noun.* The prime period of greatest popularity or success: in the *heyday* of his career.

hibachi

hi (HIGH) *interjection.* (Informal) Short for "hello."

hi·ba·chi (hi-BAH-chee) *noun.* A small charcoal-burning stove, originally from Japan.

hi·ber·nate (HIGH-bər-nayt) *verb.* 1. To sleep all winter: Bears *hibernate.* 2. To withdraw: She was so tired of company, she decided to *hibernate* for a while. **hibernated, hibernating.** —**hibernation** (high-bər-NAY-shən) *noun.*

hieroglyphics

hic·cup (HIK-uhp) Also **hiccough** *noun.* An abrupt noise caused by sudden spasms of muscles used in breathing. —*verb.* To make a hiccup. **hiccuped** or **hiccupped, hiccuping** or **hiccupping.**

hick·o·ry (HIK-ə-ree or HIK-ree) *noun.* A North American tree known for its smooth or shaggy bark, edible nuts, and valuable hardwood. **hickories.**

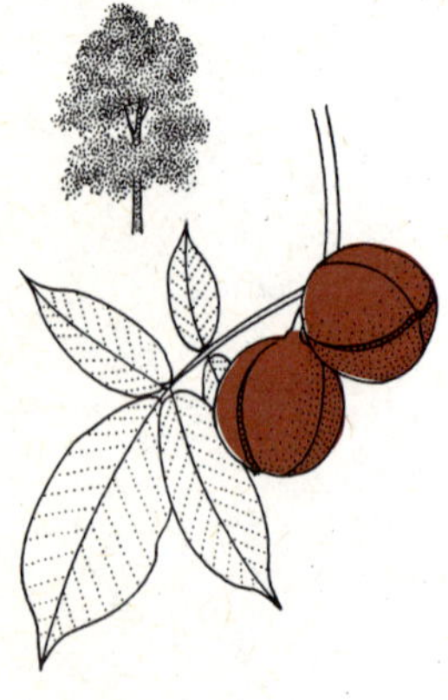

hickory

hid *verb. See* **hide.**

hid·den (HID-n) *adjective.* Concealed, out of sight. —*verb. See* **hide.**

hide (HIGHD) *verb.* 1. To conceal. 2. To cover up, to obstruct from view. 3. To keep secret, to withhold from knowledge. **hid, hid** or **hidden, hiding.** —*noun.* Skin, especially of an animal.

hide-and-seek (HIGHD-N-SEEK) Also **hide-and-go-seek** *noun.* A children's game in which one player looks for others who hide.

hid·e·ous (HID-ee-əss) *adjective.* Frightfully ugly; horrible to see; shocking. —**hideously** *adverb.*

hide·out (HIGHD-owt) *noun.* A place to hide.

hid·ing (HIGHD-ing) *noun.* A hard spanking.

hi·er·o·glyph·ic (high-ər-ə-GLIF-ik or high-rə-GLIF-ik) *adjective.* Describing a system of writing based on picture symbols. —*noun.* (Plural) 1. Ancient Egyptian writing using such symbols. 2. Any writing that is hard to read.

hi-fi (HIGH-figh) *noun* or *adjective.* Abbreviation for *high fidelity* in sound reproduction.

high *adjective.* 1. Tall; lofty. 2. Near the peak; at the fullest: *high* noon. 3. Shrill; in the upper range of the musical scale: a *high* note. 4. Greater than usual: *high* pressure; *high* prices. 5. Important: a man of *high* rank. 6. (Slang) Happy; excited: *high* spirits. 7. (Slang) Drunk. 8. (Slang) Under the influence of drugs. **higher, highest.** —*noun.* 1. (Automobiles) The gear that allows the greatest speed. 2. (Slang) The condition of being under the influence of alcohol or drugs. —**highly** *adverb.*

high·brow (HIGH-brow) *noun.* (Informal) 1. One who is or pretends to be interested in classical music, art, literature. 2. A snob.

high fidelity. The quality of faithful reproduction of sound by records, radio, and tapes.

high·hand·ed (HIGH-HAN-did) *adjective.* Bossy; overbearing. —**highhandedly** *adverb.*

high jump. (Sports) 1. An unassisted jump over a horizontal bar. 2. A contest to see who can jump the highest without touching the bar.

high·land (HIGH-lənd) *noun.* 1. An area of high ground; a cliff. 2. (Plural) The mountains of any region.

high·light (HIGH-light) *verb.* 1. To point out or emphasize: He *highlighted* the important parts of the chapter. 2. (Art) To brighten sections of a painting or photograph; to design a work of art so certain parts catch the light. **highlighted, highlighting.** —*noun.* 1. The most important or outstanding part. 2. (Art) A bright area in a picture or work of art.

high school. A school coming after elementary school; a secondary school that covers grades 9–12 or grades 7–12.

high-spir·it·ed (high-SPIHR-ə-tid) *adjective.* Lively; proud and bold. —**high-spiritedly** *adverb.*

high-strung (high-STRUHNG) *adjective.* Very nervous; sensitive; tense.

high tide. 1. The ocean tide at its greatest height, just before it begins to ebb. 2. The time of high tide.

high·way (HIGH-way) *noun.* 1. A main public road, often with more than two lanes. 2. A state or interstate road, rather than a town or city road.

high·way·man (HIGH-way-mən) *noun.* A roadside robber, especially one mounted on a horse. —**highwaymen** *plural.*

highway patrol. State policemen assigned to duty on the highways.

highway robbery. (Informal) Charges far greater than they should be.

hike (HIGHK) *noun.* 1. A long walking trip, especially in the country. 2. A raise; a going up: a *hike* in prices. 3. A tug or pull up. **hikes.** —*verb.* 1. To march or walk for a distance. 2. To raise, as prices. 3. To tug or pull (up). **hiked, hiking.**

hi·lar·i·ous (hi-LAIR-ee-əss) *adjective.* Very funny; extremely jolly or boisterous. —**hilariously** *adverb.*

hi·lar·i·ty (hi-LAIR-ə-tee) *noun.* Loud gaiety and laughter.

hill (HIL) *noun.* 1. A natural, noticeable rise in the land, more rounded and less high than a mountain. 2. A heap or mound of earth: an ant*hill.*

hill·ock (HIL-ək) *noun.* A small hill.

hill·side (HIL-sighd) *noun.* The side or sloping part of a hill. **hillsides.**

hill·top (HIL-top) *noun.* The highest part of a hill.

hilt *noun.* The handle of a sword or dagger. —**to the hilt.** Deeply; fully.

him *pronoun.* A form of *he* used as the object of verbs or prepositions.

him·self (him-SELF) *pronoun.* A form of *he* used: 1. For emphasis: He wrote it *himself.* 2. When the subject and object of a verb are the same: He taught *himself* to ride a bike. 3. To describe a normal or usual state: Ned didn't seem *himself* after the game.

[1]**hind** (HYND) *adjective.* At the back or rear: *hind* legs.

[2]**hind** (HYND) *noun.* A mature female red deer. —**hinds** or **hind** *plural.*

hin·der (HIN-dər) *verb.* To hold back; interrupt; prevent. **hindered, hindering.** —**hindrance** (HIN-drənss) *noun.*

hind·quar·ter (HYND-kwor-tər) *noun.* 1. The rear part of a side of beef, lamb, or similar meat. 2. (Always plural) The upper rear part of a four-legged animal.

hind·sight (HYND-sight) *noun.* An understanding of the causes of something after it has happened.

hinge (HINJ) *noun.* The movable jointed device by which a door, gate, or lid is joined to a frame. —*verb.* 1. To install or apply a hinge or hinges. 2. To depend (on). **hinged, hinging.**

hint *noun.* A suggestion or clue. —*verb.* To give a hint. **hinted, hinting.**

[1]hip *noun.* 1. The part of the body from the waist to the thigh. 2. The joint that connects the leg to the trunk of the body.

[2]hip *adjective.* (Slang) Understanding; knowing the latest styles and fads.

hip·pie (HIP-ee) Also **hippy** *noun.* A person who believes in doing whatever makes him feel happy, often in defiance of conventional standards. **hippies.**

hippopotamus

hip·po·pot·a·mus (hip-ə-POT-ə-məss) *noun.* A large plant-eating water animal with a thick hide; native to Africa. —**hippopotamuses** or **hippopotami** (hip-ə-POT-ə-migh) *plural.*

hire (HIGHR) *verb.* To employ someone for a paid job. **hired, hiring.**

his (HIZ) *pronoun.* 1. (Also *adjective*) Belonging to a male previously named: *his* bicycle. 2. Something that belongs to him: That pen is *his.*

hiss *verb.* 1. To make a long *s* sound like that made by a snake. 2. To show dissatisfaction by making such a sound. **hissed, hissing.** —*noun.* The act or sound of hissing. **hisses.**

his·to·ri·an (hiss-TOR-ee-ən) *noun.* A person who studies, writes, or teaches history.

his·tor·ic (hiss-TOR-ik) *adjective.* Of importance in history; history-making: the Pilgrims' *historic* landing at Plymouth Rock.

his·tor·i·cal (hiss-TOR-ə-kəl) *adjective.* Relating to or based on history, on events that are known to have really happened. —**historically** *adverb.*

historical fiction. Stories or novels based partly or largely on true events in history.

his·to·ry (HISS-tə-ree) *noun.* 1. Information or knowledge about the past. 2. A book or record of important events. 3. The past; what has happened. 4. A story. 5. A person's medical records. **histories.**

hit *verb.* 1. To slap or strike. 2. To bump into: The car *hit* the tree. 3. To reach with a throw or a shot: *hit* the target. 4. To find; come (upon) by chance: The girls *hit* upon a good name for their club. 5. To affect severely: The news *hit* Bill hard. **hit, hitting.** —*noun.* 1. A strike or collision. 2. (Baseball) A successful blow with a bat, enabling the batter to reach a base. 3. A book, play, or other entertainment that is very well-received.

hit-and-run (hit-n-RUHN) *adjective.* Leaving the scene of an accident of which one was the cause.

hitch (HICH) *verb.* 1. To tie or fasten with a hook, rope, belt, etc. 2. To attach (an animal) to a cart, sleigh, or wagon. 3. To pull or tug (up): *Hitch* up your socks. 4. To get caught (on): My sleeve *hitched* onto the doorknob. 5. To move in a clumsy way; hump along. 6. (Informal) To hitchhike. 7. (Slang) To join together; get married. **hitched, hitching.** —*noun.* 1. A knot; a joining. 2. A holding up; a block; a restriction. 3. A period of service in the armed forces. **hitches.**

hitch·hike (HICH-highk) *verb.* (Informal) To travel by begging rides from passing drivers. **hitchhiked, hitchhiking.**

hith·er (HI<u>TH</u>-ər) *adverb.* To or toward here: Come *hither.* —*adjective.* Nearer. —**hither and yon.** Here and there.

hith·er·to (hi<u>th</u>-ər-TOO) *adverb.* Before now; until now.

hit·ter (HIT-ər) *noun.* 1. (Baseball) The person at bat. 2. One who hits.

hive (HIGHV) *noun.* 1. A shelter for bees. 2. A community of bees. 3. A place where many people are milling about. **hives.**

hives (HIGHVZ) *noun, plural.* A disease of the skin that causes an outbreaking of welts that itch.

ho (HOH) *interjection.* A word shouted to gain attention.

hoa·gie (HOH-gee) *noun.* A type of sandwich. *See* **grinder.**

hoard (HORD) *noun.* A stored supply: The squirrel's *hoard* of nuts is almost gone. —*verb.* To store up for future use; save; collect; amass in a greedy way. **hoarded, hoarding.**

hoar·frost (HOR-frost) *noun.* Frozen dew on grass, leaves, and the like.

hoarse (HORSS) *adjective.* 1. Scratchy, weak, or harsh in sound. 2. Having a harsh, rasping voice. **hoarser, hoarsest.** —**hoarsely** *adverb.*

hoar·y (HOR-ee) *adjective.* 1. Ancient; old. 2. Covered with gray or white hair (resembling hoarfrost). **hoarier, hoariest.**

hoax (HOHX) *noun.* Something that tricks or deceives: The cake iced with shaving cream was a *hoax.* **hoaxes.** —*verb.* To cheat or mislead. **hoaxed, hoaxing.**

hob·ble (HOB-əl) *verb.* 1. To walk with a limp. 2. To chain or tie the legs of a horse or other animal so he can't run away. **hobbled, hobbling.** —*noun.* 1. A limping walk. 2. The rope or chain used to hobble a horse or other animal. **hobbles.**

hob·by (HOB-ee) *noun.* An activity followed for pleasure: Woodworking, stamp collecting, and embroidery are *hobbies.* **hobbies.**

hob·by·horse (HOB-ee-horss) Also **hobby horse** *noun.* 1. A toy horse on rockers, or sometimes a stick with a horse's head on one end. 2. A subject that a person talks or thinks about at great length: Getting and eating honey is Winnie-the-Pooh's *hobbyhorse.* **hobbyhorses.**

hob·gob·lin (HOB-gob-lən) *noun.* 1. A goblin or elf who plays tricks and causes trouble. 2. A ghost, spirit; anything that haunts one's mind and causes fear.

hob·nail (HOB-nayl) *noun.* A short nail with a large head fastened to the soles of certain boots and shoes for protection or traction.

ho·bo (HOH-boh) *noun.* A person who wanders from place to place begging or doing occasional odd jobs; a tramp. —**hoboes** or **hobos** *plural.*

hock·ey (HOK-ee) *noun.* 1. A game played on ice by two teams of skaters; ice hockey. 2. A similar game played on a field with a small ball; also called "field hockey."

hod *noun.* 1. A small tray attached to a long pole and carried on the shoulder of a builder, used for carrying bricks, stones, or prepared cement. 2. A scuttle.

hodge·podge (HOJ-poj) *noun.* A collection of assorted items; a jumble: My father can never find anything in his desk drawer because it's such a *hodgepodge.*

hoe (HOH) *noun.* A long-handled tool at the bottom of which is a flat blade, used to break up and loosen soil or cut weeds. **hoes.** —*verb.* To dig, break up, loosen soil, or weed with a hoe. **hoed, hoeing.**

hog *noun.* 1. A pig or sow, especially one that is fully grown and has been raised for food. 2. (Informal) A greedy, selfish, or unclean person; one who takes more than his share: a road *hog.* —*verb.* (Informal) To take more than one's share of. **hogged, hogging.**

ho·gan (HOH-gawn or HOH-gən) *noun.* A Navaho shelter built from logs and branches and covered with earth.

hogs·head (HOGZ-hed) *noun.* 1. A large barrel or cask that may hold from 63 gallons to 140 gallons. 2. A unit of liquid measure equal to 63 gallons.

hoist *verb.* To raise or lift up, usually with a rope and pulley or crane. **hoisted, hoisting.** —*noun.* 1. The act of raising or lifting up. 2. Any device used for raising up, such as a block and tackle, elevator, crane, or derrick.

hockey

hog

hobbyhorse

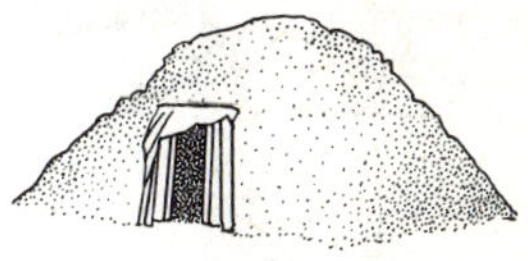

hogan

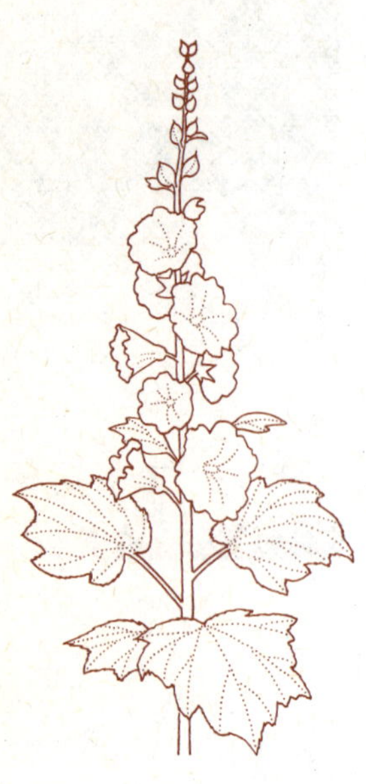
hollyhock

[1]**hold** (HOHLD) *verb.* 1. To take or keep, as in one's hand or arms: *Hold* my jacket. 2. To keep (in a certain state, condition, place): *Hold* the picture in place. 3. To support. 4. To have; conduct: *hold* a meeting. 5. To have control over: *hold* one's temper. 6. To keep back; detain: *Hold* the visitor. 7. To own; keep as one's own. 8. To contain. 9. To decide legally: Will the judge *hold* you guilty? 10. To be in force: The rule does not *hold* true in all cases. **held, holding.** —*noun.* 1. Act of holding; taking or keeping in one's hand. 2. Something by which to grasp a thing; handle. 3. Great influence (over someone). 4. (Music) A sign (𝄐) telling that a note should be given more time than it would ordinarily have. 5. (Aerospace) The period during which the steps in getting a rocket ready for firing are stopped for a time. —**hold forth.** 1. To talk at great length. 2. To offer. —**hold in.** To keep back or in; restrain. —**hold off.** 1. To keep at a distance. 2. To postpone; keep from acting on. —**hold on.** 1. To keep on; to continue with. 2. To stop: *Hold on,* you're going too fast. —**hold one's own.** To keep one's condition, position, or views against opposition or competition.

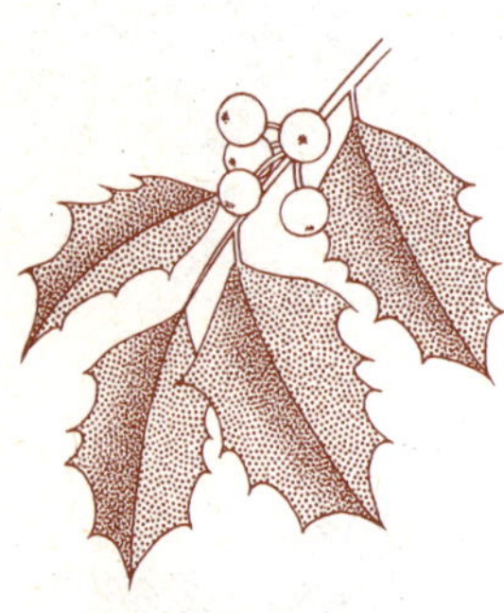
holly

[2]**hold** (HOHLD) *noun.* The area in a ship below deck for stowing cargo.

hold·out (HOHLD-owt) *noun.* (Informal) A person who refuses to agree or delays in signing a contract.

hold·o·ver (HOHLD-oh-vər) *noun.* 1. A person or thing still around from an earlier time or situation. 2. One who stays in an office longer than one term.

holster

hold·up (HOHLD-uhp) *noun.* 1. A robbery, especially with a weapon. 2. Any stopping or slowing up.

hole (HOHL) *noun.* 1. A hollow place in anything solid: *hole* in the road. 2. An open space through a surface: a *hole* in the paper. 3. A spot dug out by an animal for his home: rat *hole.* 4. A small, shabby residence. 5. (Golf) The cup-like opening in the ground into which the ball is hit. 6. Fault; error: an argument full of *holes.* 7. A deep pit; dungeon. **holes.** —**hole in the wall.** A small, usually inconvenient or unattractive place. —**hole up.** To keep oneself away from others; to hide.

hol·i·day (HOL-ə-day) *noun.* A day, set by law or religious custom, on which most schools and businesses are closed.

ho·li·ness (HOH-lee-niss) *noun.* 1. State of being holy; saintliness. 2. [Capital H] A title (used following *His* or *Your*) for the Pope.

hol·ler (HOL-ər) *verb.* (Slang) To shout; call out loudly. **hollered, hollering.**

hol·low (HOL-oh) *adjective.* 1. Not solid; having a hole on the inside: a *hollow* pipe. 2. Curved inward; concave: *hollow* cheeks. 3. Deep, muffled in sound. 4. Worthless or insincere: *hollow* praise. —*noun.* 1. An empty place; a hole. 2. An area which curves inward. 3. A valley: "The Legend of Sleepy *Hollow.*" —*verb.* To make hollow. **hollowed, hollowing.**

hol·ly (HOL-ee) *noun.* 1. An evergreen shrub or tree with prickly leaves and red berries. 2. The leaves and berries of such a plant. **hollies.**

hol·ly·hock (HOL-ee-hok) *noun.* 1. A tall garden plant with big showy flowers. 2. The flower of this plant.

hol·o·caust (HOL-ə-kawst or HOH-lə-kawst) *noun.* Massive destruction of life and property.

hol·ster (HOHL-stər) *noun.* A case or holder, usually leather, for a pistol.

ho·ly (HOH-lee) *adjective.* 1. Belonging to or coming from God; sacred; religious: *holy* Bible; *holy* water. 2. Saintly; devout: a *holy* person. 3. Worthy of deep respect or reverence: *holy* ground. **holier, holiest.**

hom·age (HOM-ij or OM-ij) *noun.* Respect; honor; praise.

hom·bre (OM-bray or OM-bree) *noun.* (Spanish) A man. **hombres.**

home (HOHM) *noun.* 1. The place in which one lives. 2. The place of one's birth; one's native country. 3. An institution for sick, disabled, or homeless persons: a *home* for the blind. 4. The place where a thing originates or is usually found: Kentucky is the *home* of thoroughbred horses. 5. (Baseball) Home plate. 6. The goal or object of many games. *—adverb.* As far as possible or intended: The remark struck *home.*

home·land (HOHM-land) *noun.* The country or place of one's birth; native land.

home·less (HOHM-liss) *adjective.* Without a home: *homeless* war victims.

home·like (HOHM-lighk) *adjective.* Like home; comfortable; warm and friendly.

home·ly (HOHM-lee) *adjective.* 1. Referring to or connected with the home. 2. Plain; natural. 3. Not pretty; ugly. **homelier, homeliest.**

home·mak·er (HOHM-may-kər) *noun.* 1. A housewife. 2. A person who provides and runs a home for others.

home plate. (Baseball) The spot at which a player stands to bat.

hom·er (HOH-mər) *noun.* (Baseball) *See* **home run.**

home·room (HOHM-room) *noun.* The schoolroom to which a student reports at the start of each day.

home run. (Baseball) A hit that enables the batter to run to all four bases and score a run.

home·sick (HOHM-sik) *adjective.* Unhappy at being away from home.

home·spun (HOHM-spuhn) *noun.* Cloth made at home or from yarn spun at home. *—adjective.* Simple, plain, not fancy: *homespun* humor.

home·stead (HOHM-sted) *noun.* 1. A house (and other buildings) and the land on which it stands, used as the home of its owner; a farm and its buildings. 2. Land given to a settler by the U.S. Government under the Homestead Act to be developed as a farm. *—verb.* To claim and settle on land, as under the Homestead Act. **homesteaded, homesteading.**

home·ward (HOHM-wərd) Also **homewards** (HOHM-wərdz) *adverb* (and *adjective*). In the direction of home; toward home.

home·work (HOHM-wərk) *noun.* 1. A school assignment to be done at home or outside of class. 2. Any work done at home for outside business. 3. Background work or study to prepare oneself: One must do one's *homework* to get the most from a museum tour.

home·y (HOH-mee) *adjective.* (Informal) Like home; simple and comfortable. **homier, homiest.**

hom·i·cide (HOM-ə-sighd) *noun.* The killing of one person by another person. **—homicidal** *adjective.*

hom·i·ny (HOM-ə-nee) *noun.* Whole kernels of corn that have been hulled, dried, and cooked in boiling water before eating. **—hominy grits.** *See* **grits.**

ho·mog·e·nize (hə-MOJ-ə-nighz) *verb.* To blend or mix together (all the parts of something): To *homogenize* milk is to blend the cream and milk so that they do not separate. **homogenized, homogenizing.**

hom·o·graph (HOM-ə-graf or HOH-mə-graf) *noun.* A word that is spelled the same as another word, but has a different meaning (and sometimes a different pronunciation): The noun "bear" and the verb "bear" are *homographs.*

hom·o·nym (HOM-ə-nim or HOH-mə-nim) *noun.* A word that sounds the same as another word (and is sometimes spelled the same) but has a different meaning: "To" and "two" are *homonyms.*

honeybee

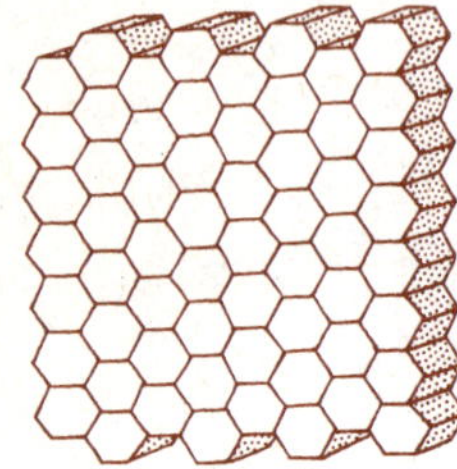
honeycomb

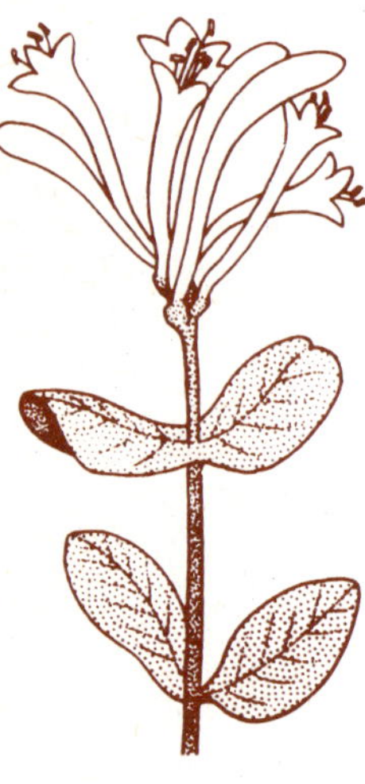
honeysuckle

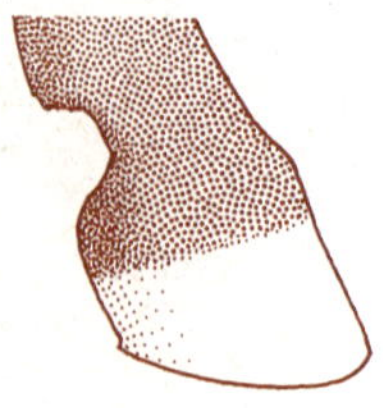
hoof

hom·o·phone (HOM-ə-fohn) *noun.* A word having the same sound as another but a different meaning and often a different spelling: "Right," "write," and "rite" are *homophones.*

Hon. *abbreviation.* Honorable.

hon·est (ON-ist) *adjective.* 1. Honorable; truthful; fair. 2. Sincere; open: an *honest* smile. 3. Genuine; pure: *honest* merchandise. —**honestly** *adverb.* —**honesty** *noun.*

hon·ey (HUHN-ee) *noun.* 1. A thick, sweet fluid made by bees from flower nectar. 2. The nectar, or sweet liquid, in flowers. 3. Sweetness. 4. Darling (used as a term of affection). **honeys.**

hon·ey·bee (HUHN-ee-bee) *noun.* A bee that makes honey. **honeybees.**

hon·ey·comb (HUHN-ee-kohm) *noun.* 1. A structure of wax rows of six-sided cells made by bees for storing honey, pollen, and eggs. 2. Any structure or pattern that resembles a bee's honeycomb. —*verb.* To fill with cells or holes: Small apartments now *honeycomb* the converted mansion. **honeycombed, honeycombing.**

hon·ey·moon (HUHN-ee-moon) *noun.* The period of time spent together by a newly married couple, usually in traveling or vacationing.

hon·ey·suck·le (HUN-ee-suhk-əl) *noun.* A climbing shrub or vine with sweet-smelling yellow, white, or pink flowers.

honk (HAWNGK or HONGK) *noun.* 1. The sound made by the wild goose. 2. A sound like that of a wild goose: the *honk* of a car horn. —*verb.* To make a honking sound. **honked, honking.**

hon·or (ON-ər) *noun.* 1. Good character or reputation: "Take *honor* from me and my life is done." (William Shakespeare). 2. Fame, glory: The victorious general enjoyed his *honor* very briefly. 3. A source or cause of praise: Be an *honor* to the school. 4. Great respect. 5. A special favor; privilege: I have the *honor* of introducing today's speaker. 6. [Capital H] A title of respect for a judge, mayor, and other officials: His *Honor,* the Mayor of New York City. 7. (Plural) Special recognition of a student whose work is much above average. 8. (Plural) An act or mark of respect: He was buried with military *honors.* —*verb.* 1. To respect greatly; show respect to. 2. To accept in payment: *honor* credit cards. **honored, honoring.**

hon·or·a·ble (ON-ər-ə-bəl) *adjective.* 1. Worthy of honor. 2. [Capital H] Due respect because of title or high position: the *Honorable* Justice Marshall. —**honorably** *adverb.*

honorable mention. A special recognition, usually in a contest, that an entry has merit even though it has won no prize.

hon·or·ar·y (ON-ə-rehr-ee) *adjective.* 1. Made or given as a mark of respect: an *honorary* degree. 2. Serving in a position without pay and without the usual duties of the position: an *honorary* chairman.

hood (HUD) *noun.* 1. A covering for the head and neck, often fastened to another garment such as a coat or cloak. 2. Anything that resembles or is used as a hood: a *hood* for a bird cage. 3. The part of an automobile that covers the engine. 4. (Slang) Hoodlum. —*verb.* To cover with a hood. **hooded, hooding.**

-hood *suffix.* Indicates: 1. A state of being: child*hood.* 2. Membership in a group: brother*hood.*

hood·lum (HUD-ləm) *noun.* 1. A gangster; one who commits small crimes. 2. A juvenile delinquent.

hoof (HUF or HOOF) *noun.* 1. The hard material that covers the foot of some animals such as the horse, cow, sheep, ox, and pig. 2. The foot itself of such an animal. —**hoofs** or **hooves** *plural.*

hook (HUK) *noun.* 1. A curved piece of metal or other firm material used for catching, dragging, or hanging up things. 2. A bent piece of metal with a sharp tip for catching fish; a fish*hook*. 3. Anything curved, bent, or shaped like a hook, as a curve in a road or river. 4. A long, narrow, curved strip of land that juts into a body of water: Sandy *Hook*. *—verb.* 1. To catch, drag, or hang up with a hook. 2. To catch (a fish). 3. To tie with hooks. 4. (Slang) To be addicted. **hooked, hooking. —by hook or by crook.** By any means, fair or foul. **—hook up.** To connect a machine to a source of power. **—on one's own hook.** By one's own self.

hooked (HUKT) *adjective.* 1. Shaped like a hook; having a hook. 2. Made with a hook: *hooked* rugs. 3. (Slang) Addicted, as to drugs.

hook·worm (HUK-werm) *noun.* 1. A blood-sucking worm that causes disease in man and other animals. 2. The disease itself.

hook·y (HUK-ee) *noun.* (Informal) Absence from school without a good excuse, generally used after the verb *play*.

hoop *noun.* 1. A circle of metal or wood used around barrels. 2. A large circular band used as a toy.

hoo·ray (HOO-ray) *interjection. See* **hurrah.**

hoot *noun.* 1. The cry of an owl. 2. A loud call or cry, generally used to show disapproval. *—verb.* To make a hooting or scornful sound. **hooted, hooting. —not give a hoot.** Not to care about.

[1]**hop** *verb.* 1. To move by making short jumps. 2. To move by making short jumps on one foot. 3. To get on: I *hopped* the bus. **hopped, hopping.** *—noun.* 1. A short jump. 2. (Informal) A dance. 3. A plane trip over a short distance.

[2]**hop** *noun.* 1. (Plural) Dried flowers used in the making of beer. 2. The vine on which these flowers grow.

hope (HOHP) *verb.* To wish or desire; yearn. **hoped, hoping.** *—noun.* 1. A wish or expectation that one feels will be fulfilled. 2. A person or thing in which one trusts. **hopes.**

hope·ful (HOHP-fəl) *adjective.* Wishful, desirous, or expectant. *—noun.* A person who would like to achieve something: a presidential *hopeful.* **—hopefully** *adverb.*

hope·less (HOHP-liss) *adjective.* 1. Without hope, in despair. 2. With no possibility of being cured. 3. Not able to be changed or improved: Our situation is *hopeless;* we can't win the game. **—hopelessly** *adverb.*

hop·per (HOP-ər) *noun.* A storage container that is filled from the top and emptied from the bottom: a coal *hopper.*

hop·scotch (HOP-skoch) *noun.* A game played by hopping within squares marked on the ground.

horde (HORD) *noun.* A large group; a mass: A *horde* of children swarmed in the playground at recess. **hordes.**

ho·ri·zon (hə-RIGH-zn) *noun.* 1. The line where the sky and the earth seem to meet. 2. (Usually plural) The scope of what one thinks, knows, and does: Ann's trip to Europe broadened her *horizons.*

hor·i·zon·tal (hor-ə-ZON-tl) *adjective.* Parallel to the horizon; flat: The floor of a room is *horizontal.* **—horizontally** *adverb.*

hor·mone (HOR-mohn) *noun.* A chemical substance that is made by one body organ and regulates or stimulates the action of other organs. **hormones.**

horn *noun.* 1. A hard, usually sharp, growth on the head of some animals. 2. A musical instrument. 3. A device that makes a warning noise: a bicycle *horn.* 4. A container made from or shaped like an animal horn.

horned toad Also **horned lizard.** A lizard that has hornlike growths on its head and bumpy scales over its body.

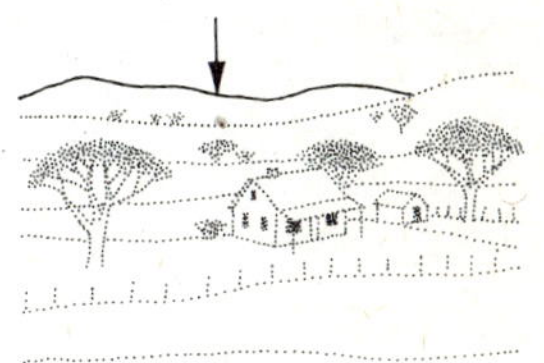

horizon

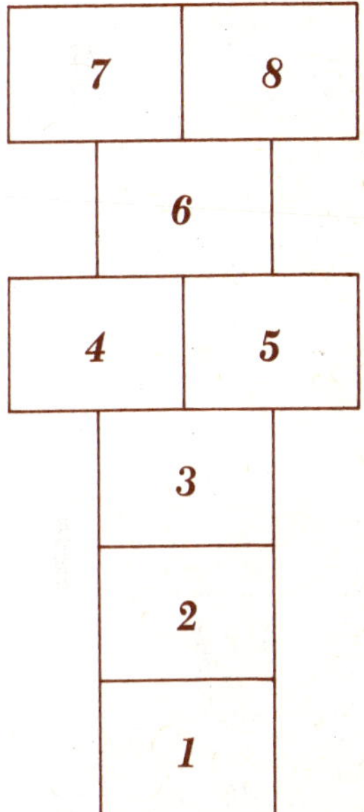

one form of hopscotch

horned toad

horses

hor·net (HOR-nit) *noun.* A wasp.

horn of plenty. A horn-shaped container filled to overflowing with flowers, fruit, and other foods as a sign of wealth and plenty.

horn·y (HOR-nee) *adjective.* 1. Hard, like an animal's horn. 2. Having horns, or something like horns.

hor·o·scope (HOR-ə-skohp) *noun.* (Astrology) A chart that shows the positions of the planets, the signs of the zodiac, and other data used to foretell the future.

hor·ri·ble (HOR-ə-bəl) *adjective.* 1. Terrifying; awful. 2. Unpleasant, disagreeable. —**horribly** *adverb.*

hor·rid (HOR-id) *adjective.* Horrible.

hor·ri·fy (HOR-ə-figh) *verb.* 1. To terrify; fill with horror. 2. To disgust; shock. **horrified, horrifying.**

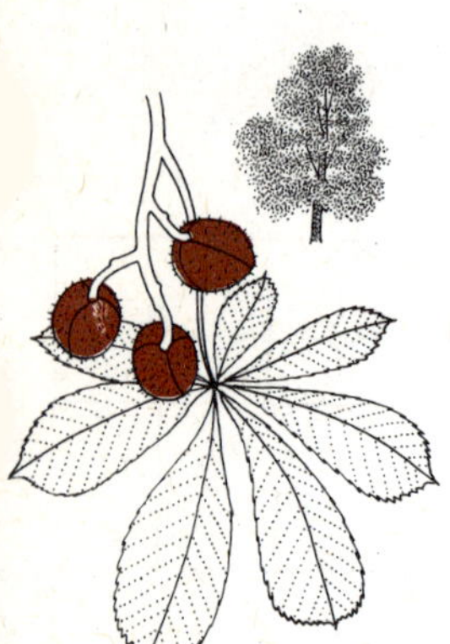
horse chestnut

hor·ror (HOR-ər) *noun.* 1. Terror; great fear. 2. Disgust; great dislike.

horse (HORSS) *noun.* 1. A large four-legged animal used for riding and for pulling loads. 2. Something that looks like a horse: a rocking *horse;* a sea *horse.* 3. (Slang) Heroin. **horses.** —**horse around.** To fool around; play tricks or pranks.

horse·back (HORSS-bak) *adverb.* On a horse's back.

horsefly

horse chestnut. 1. A brown shiny nut encased in a spiky bur. 2. The shade tree on which this nut grows.

horse·fly (HORSS-fligh) *noun.* A large fly that sucks blood. **horseflies.**

horse·play (HORSS-play) *noun.* Loud, rough joking or playing.

horse·pow·er (HORSS-pow-ər) *noun.* A unit used to measure power of an engine, equal to the power needed to move 33,000 pounds one foot in one minute.

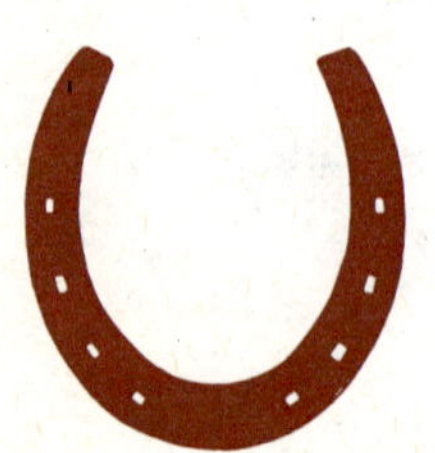
horseshoe

horse·shoe (HORSS-shoo) *noun.* 1. A U-shaped piece of iron nailed to a horse's hoof to protect it from injury. 2. Anything of this shape, particularly when used as a good luck piece. **horseshoes.**

horse·shoes (HORSS-shooz) *noun, plural in form but used with a singular verb.* A game in which players try to throw horseshoes over stakes in the ground.

hor·ti·cul·ture (HOR-tə-kuhl-chər) *noun.* The study or art of growing and caring for plants. —**horticultural** *adjective.*

ho·san·na (hoh-ZAN-ə) *interjection.* An expression of praise of God.

hose (HOHZ) *noun.* 1. A bendable tube, usually of rubber or plastic, through which liquids or gases can travel. 2. Stockings; socks. —**hoses** (Sense 1) and **hose** (Sense 2) *plural.* —*verb.* To wash or wet by means of a hose: Dad asked me to *hose* down the car. **hosed, hosing.**

ho·sier·y (HOH-zhə-ree) *noun.* Stockings, socks, or panty hose.

hos·pi·ta·ble (HOSS-pi-tə-bəl or hoss-PIT-ə-bəl) *adjective.* Friendly, warm, or generous with guests. —**hospitably** *adverb.*

hos·pi·tal (HOSS-pi-tl) *noun.* A place where trained people, such as doctors and nurses, take care of the sick and injured.

hos·pi·tal·i·ty (hoss-pi-TAL-ə-tee) *noun.* The state or act of being friendly and welcoming to guests.

hos·pi·tal·ize (HOSS-pi-tl-ighz) *verb.* To put (someone) into the hospital. **hospitalized, hospitalizing.**

host (HOHST) *noun.* 1. A man who invites and entertains guests. 2. An army: The enemy *host* descended on the city. 3. A large number. 4. [Often capital H] The blessed wafer or bread used in a Christian Communion Service. 5. An animal or plant on which another animal or plant relies for the support of its own life: A dog is often a *host* for many fleas. —*verb.* (Informal) To act as a host. **hosted, hosting.**

hos·tage (HOSS-tij) *noun.* A person who is held against his will until certain requirements are met: The bank robbers held the guard as *hostage* until they could get away.

hos·tel (HOSS-tl) *noun.* A place where travelers may stay for a low price.

host·ess (HOHSS-tiss) *noun.* A woman who invites and entertains guests. **hostesses.**

hos·tile (HOSS-tl) *adjective.* 1. Showing or having unfriendly or warlike feeling. 2. Referring to an enemy: The *hostile* forces were camped in the next town.

hos·til·i·ty (hoss-TIL-ə-tee) *noun.* 1. An unfriendly or warlike posture. 2. (Plural) Warfare. **hostilities.**

hot *adjective.* 1. Having great heat; the opposite of cold. 2. Warmer than is usual or comfortable. 3. Emotionally intense; fierce: a *hot* argument. 4. Fresh; recent: *hot* news. 5. Carrying electric current: a *hot* wire. 6. (Slang) Stolen: The policeman knew the car was *hot,* so he arrested the driver. 7. Having many or strong spices. **hotter, hottest.** —**hotly** *adverb.*

hot·bed (HOT-bed) *noun.* 1. A heated bed of earth, covered with glass, for growing plants. 2. Any place that makes things or activities grow fast: Lil's mind is a *hotbed* for wild schemes.

hot dog. A frankfurter; a sausage made of pork and/or beef.

ho·tel (hoh-TEL) *noun.* A building where guests pay for rooms and where meals are usually served.

hot·head·ed (HOT-HED-id) *adjective.* Having a quick temper.

hot·house (HOT-howss) *noun.* An enclosed heated place for growing plants; greenhouse.

hot pants. (Informal) Very short pants, usually worn by women.

hot rod. (Slang) A car, generally an old one, that has been changed or rebuilt to go fast.

hot war. A war in which actual fighting or combat has begun. *See* **cold war.**

hound (HOWND) *noun.* 1. A hunting dog. 2. A person who likes something very much: a food *hound.* —*verb.* To track, follow, or trail without stopping. **hounded, hounding.**

hour (OWR) *noun.* 1. A period of time that equals 60 minutes or $\frac{1}{24}$ of a day. 2. A time of day: What is the *hour?* 3. A particular time in the day set aside for something: story *hour.*

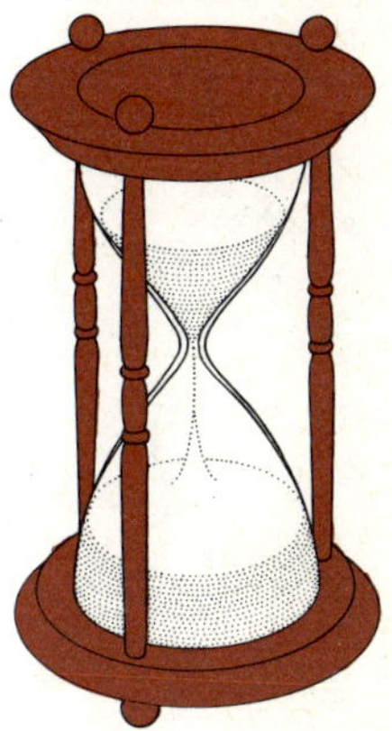

hourglass

hour·glass (OWR-glass) *noun.* A device used to measure the passing of time by the dropping of grains of sand from the upper section of a glass container to the bottom section. **hourglasses.**

hour·ly (OWR-lee) *adverb* and *adjective.* Each hour: The clock strikes *hourly.*

house (HOWSS) *noun.* 1. A place in which to live. 2. The people in a house: The whole *house* was awakened by the loud crash. 3. [Often capital H] Generations of a family, particularly of a noble one: the *House* of Bourbon. 4. A theater or the audience in a theater. 5. (Capital H) One part of a government legislature: the House of Representatives. —(HOWZ) *verb.* To lodge; provide living quarters for. **housed, housing.**

houseboat

house·boat (HOWSS-boht) *noun.* A barge or boat on which people can live.

house·fly (HOWSS-fligh) *noun.* A flying insect that often gets into houses. **houseflies.**

house·hold (HOWSS-hohld) *noun.* 1. All the people who live together in one house. 2. The place where they live.

house·keep·er (HOWSS-keep-ər) *noun.* A person whose job is taking care of a house, doing or directing others in jobs like cleaning or cooking.

house·keep·ing (HOWSS-keep-ing) *noun.* The charge and care of a home.

house·wife (HOWSS-wighf) *noun.* A married woman whose chief job is to take care of the home and family. —**housewives** (HOWSS-wighvz) *plural.*

house·work (HOWSS-werk) *noun.* The tasks that keep a home clean, neat, and pleasant to live in.

hous·ing (HOW-zing) *noun.* 1. Kind of houses: The *housing* in our area is new and attractive. 2. Shelter; the providing of houses: The government supplied *housing* for the victims of the flood. 3. A covering or frame that protects or supports a piece of machinery or other device.

Hovercraft

hov·el (HUHV-əl or HOV-əl) *noun.* A small, poorly constructed, and unpleasant dwelling; a hut.

hov·er (HUHV-ər or HOV-ər) *verb.* 1. To remain in or near one place in the air: The helicopter *hovered* over the scene of the accident. 2. To remain near one place; linger. 3. To be in a wavering or uncertain condition: The injured player *hovered* between life and death. **hovered, hovering.**

Hov·er·craft (HUHV-ər-kraft) *trademark.* A vehicle that can move over land or water upon a cushion of air supplied by powerful fans on the bottom of the vehicle. —**Hovercraft** *plural.*

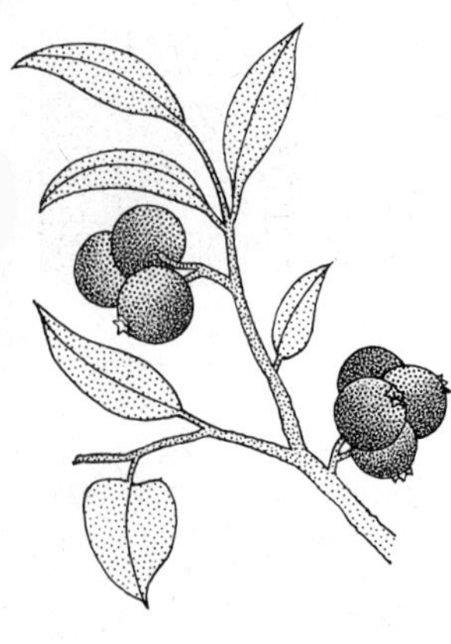

huckleberries

how *adverb.* 1. In what manner: *How* did the deer cross the river? 2. In what condition: *How* is your health? 3. To what extent: *How* long must we wait for the next bus? 4. For what purpose; why: *How* can you call George lazy?

how·ev·er (how-EV-ər) *conjunction.* Nevertheless; on the other hand. —*adverb.* 1. By whatever method: *However* you prepare the food, the dog will not eat it. 2. To whatever extent, amount, or degree: *However* fast you run, I'll run faster.

howl *verb.* 1. To make the long, sad cry sometimes made by wolves, dogs, and other animals. 2. To cry out in pain or grief. 3. To shout or roar. **howled, howling.** —*noun.* 1. A long, sad cry. 2. A loud cry caused by pain or grief.

hub (HUHB) *noun.* 1. The center part of a wheel. 2. A center of activity or interest: Washington is the *hub* of our nation's government.

hub·bub (HUHB-uhb) *noun.* An uproar; loud noise and confusion.

huck·le·ber·ry (HUHK-əl-behr-ee) *noun.* 1. A small, dark-blue berry similar to the blueberry. 2. The shrub on which this fruit grows. **huckleberries.**

huck·ster (HUHK-stər) *noun.* 1. A person who sells small items; peddler. 2. A person, especially a persuasive one, who advertises or sells a product.

hud·dle (HUHD-l) *verb.* To gather close together at one place. **huddled, huddling.** —*noun.* 1. A group gathered close together. 2. (Football) A group of players receiving signals. **huddles.**

hue (HYOO) *noun.* 1. A color: The bright *hues* of the sunset made the sky glorious. 2. A shade or tint of color: The curtains come in three different *hues* of green. **hues.** —**hue and cry.** A public uproar, outcry, or argument.

huff (HUHF) *verb.* To blow, puff: The wolf threatened to *huff* and puff and blow the house down. **huffed, huffing.** —*noun.* A state of anger or irritation: Dad is in a *huff* because of the bad news.

hug (HUHG) *verb.* 1. To hold close and tight with the arms; embrace. 2. To stay close to: The bus *hugged* the right side of the road during the storm. **hugged, hugging.** —*noun.* A close, tight hold with the arms; an embrace.

huge (HYOOJ) *adjective.* Extremely large; enormous: A skyscraper is a *huge* building. **huger, hugest.** —**hugely** *adverb.*

hulk (HUHLK) *noun.* 1. A very large, clumsy person or thing. 2. The frame or remains of a wrecked ship.

hulk·ing (HUHL-king) *adjective.* Very large and clumsy.

hull (HUHL) *noun.* 1. The main part of the body of a ship. 2. The outer covering of a seed, fruit, or nut. —*verb.* To remove the outer covering from (a seed or fruit). **hulled, hulling.**

hul·la·ba·loo (HUHL-ə-bə-loo or huhl-ə-bə-LOO) *noun.* An uproar; state of noisy confusion. **hullabaloos.**

hum (HUHM) *verb.* 1. To make a low, continuous noise similar to that made by a bee. 2. To sing while the lips are closed, without pronouncing the words. 3. To be busy or active. **hummed, humming.** —*noun.* A low, continuous noise like that made by a bee.

hu·man (HYOO-mən) *noun.* A person; human being. —*adjective.* Typical of or related to human beings: It is *human* to make mistakes.

human being. A man, woman, or child.

hu·mane (hyoo-MAYN) *adjective.* Kind; considerate. —**humanely** *adverb.*

humane society. [Often capitals H, S] An organization that encourages kindness toward animals.

hu·man·i·ty (hyoo-MAN-ə-tee) *noun.* 1. All human beings; mankind: An end of all warfare would be a blessing for *humanity.* 2. Human nature; the state of being human: "Nothing at bottom is real except *humanity.*" (Comte). 3. Kindness. 4. (Plural) The studies of literature, art, and history. **humanities.**

hum·ble (HUHM-bəl) *adjective.* 1. Unduly modest; not proud or conceited. 2. Low in importance; very simple or plain. **humbler, humblest.** —*verb.* To make less proud or lower in importance: The boastful tennis player was *humbled* by his defeat. **humbled, humbling.** —**humbly** *adverb.*

hum·bug (HUHM-buhg) *noun.* A trick; nonsense.

hum·drum (HUHM-druhm) *adjective.* Very dull; boring.

hu·mid (HYOO-mid) *adjective.* Containing much moisture (describing air); damp.

hu·mid·i·fi·er (hyoo-MID-ə-figh-ər) *noun.* A mechanical device that increases or regulates humidity.

hu·mid·i·ty (hyoo-MID-ə-tee) *noun.* 1. The amount of moisture in the air. 2. Dampness.

hu·mil·i·ate (hyoo-MIL-ee-ayt) *verb.* To cause to be less proud; greatly embarrass. **humiliated, humiliating.**

hu·mil·i·ty (hyoo-MIL-ə-tee) *noun.* The quality of being humble; modesty.

humming bird. A very small, brightly-colored bird with slender wings that make a humming sound during flight.

humming bird

hu·mor (HYOO-mər) *noun.* 1. A quality that causes or expresses laughter or mirth. 2. The ability to appreciate or express that which is laughable. 3. A mood or attitude: Pop's toothache has put him in a bad *humor.* —*verb.* To go along with someone's ideas or moods; oblige: The boys played very quietly in order to *humor* their old neighbor. **humored, humoring.**

hu·mor·ist (HYOO-mər-ist) *noun.* 1. A person well known for his ability to talk or write in an amusing manner. 2. A person with an especially good sense of humor.

hu·mor·ous (HYOO-mər-əss) *adjective.* Causing laughter or mirth; funny. —**humorously** *adverb.*

humour. British form of humor.

hump (HUHMP) *noun.* 1. A raised, round lump: A camel has a *hump* on its back. 2. A very low hill; a mound. —*verb.* To form into a round lump. **humped, humping.**

hump·back (HUHMP-bak) Also **hunchback** *noun.* A person with a hump on his back.

hu·mus (HYOO-məss) *noun.* A dark, fertile substance found in soil and formed by decaying plant and animal life.

hunch (HUHNCH) *verb.* To form into a hump; arch: The two cats *hunched* their backs and hissed at each other. **hunched, hunching.** *—noun.* 1. A guess or instinctive feeling: I have a *hunch* that our team will win tomorrow. 2. A hump; lump. **hunches.**

hurdle

hunch·back (HUHNCH-bak) Also **humpback** *noun.* A person with a hump on his back.

hun·dred (HUHN-drid) *noun* (and *adjective*). The cardinal number that comes after 99 and before 101; 100.

hun·dredth (HUN-dridth) *adjective.* Coming next after 99th; 100th. *—noun.* One of 100 equal parts.

hundred thousand. One hundred times one thousand; 100,000.

hung (HUHNG) *verb. See* **hang.**

hun·ger (HUHNG-gər) *noun.* 1. An unpleasant feeling caused by a lack of food. 2. A strong desire or need for food. 3. Any strong desire or need: Robert has a *hunger* for attention. *—verb.* 1. To feel a strong desire or need for food. 2. To feel any strong desire or need (for something). **hungered, hungering.**

hun·gry (HUHNG-gree) *adjective.* 1. Having a strong desire or need for food. 2. Having any strong desire: *hungry* for success. **hungrier, hungriest.** **—hungrily** *adverb.*

hunk (HUHNK) *noun.* A chunk or lump.

hunt (HUHNT) *verb.* 1. To seek or chase (animals) for food or sport. 2. To look for; to search. **hunted, hunting.** *—noun.* 1. A seeking for or chasing after animals for food or sport. 2. A search; quest.

hunt·er (HUHN-tər) *noun.* 1. A person who hunts. 2. A horse, dog, or other animal specially trained for hunting.

hur·dle (HER-dl) *noun.* 1. A bar or fencelike device over which a contestant must jump in certain races. 2. Any difficulty that is met; obstacle: Tom worried, for math was a real *hurdle.* **hurdles.** *—verb.* To jump over (a barrier). **hurdled, hurdling.**

hur·dy-gur·dy (HER-dee-GER-dee) *noun.* A mechanical device that makes music when a handle or crank is turned. **hurdy-gurdies.**

hurl (HERL) *verb.* To throw forcefully. **hurled, hurling.**

hur·rah (hu-RAH) Also **hurray** *interjection.* Expresses enthusiasm, excitement, or pleasure.

hur·ri·cane (HER-ə-kayn) *noun.* A severe storm that develops in tropical areas, with strong winds of more than 73 miles an hour. **hurricanes.**

hur·ry (HER-ee) *verb.* 1. To move quickly. 2. To urge to speed: Mother *hurried* Jan through her lunch. **hurried, hurrying.** *—noun.* Rush; haste: What's your *hurry?*

hurt (HERT) *verb.* 1. To cause pain or physical harm to. 2. To hinder: The bad weather *hurt* the runner's chances to set a record. 3. To offend; insult. **hurt, hurting.** *—noun.* Pain; injury; harm.

hurt·ful (HERT-ful) *adjective.* Harmful; causing pain or damage. **—hurtfully** *adverb.*

hur·tle (HER-tl) *verb.* To move or rush wildly and noisily: The freight train *hurtled* out of control down the steep slope. **hurtled, hurtling.**

hus·band (HUHZ-bənd) *noun.* The man to whom a woman is married. *—verb.* To manage carefully or thriftily: The woman *husbanded* her family's small savings. **husbanded, husbanding.**

hus·band·ry (HUHZ-bənd-ree) *noun.* 1. Farming. 2. Careful or thrifty management, as of a family's funds.

hush (HUHSH) *verb.* To make or become quiet. *—noun.* A period of quiet or calm. *—interjection.* Expresses a command or desire for silence.

hush puppy. A small, deep-fried cornmeal fritter, especially popular in the South. **hush puppies.**

husk (HUHSK) *noun.* The dry outer covering of some seeds, grains, or nuts. *—verb.* To remove the husk from. **husked, husking.**

[1]**husk·y** (HUHSS-kee) *adjective.* 1. Rough, raspy; hoarse: a *husky* voice. 2. Strong, big, or broad. **huskier, huskiest.**

[2]**hus·ky** *noun.* [Often capital H] An Eskimo dog; a short, strong dog often teamed with others to pull a snow sled. **huskies.**

hus·tle (HUHSS-l) *verb.* 1. To work or play with energy and zest. 2. To hurry or rush. 3. To move or be moved roughly; push or shove. **hustled, hustling.** *—noun.* Energy; spirit.

hut (HUHT) *noun.* A small, plain house of one room.

hutch (HUHCH) *noun.* 1. An enclosed pen for small animals. 2. A small hut. 3. A movable cupboard. **hutches.**

hy·a·cinth (HIGH-ə-sinth) *noun.* A plant with slender leaves and a spike of bell-shaped blossoms.

hy·brid (HIGH-brid) *noun.* 1. An offspring from two different varieties of plants or animals: The mule is a *hybrid* of the donkey and the horse. 2. Anything of mixed background or origin.

hy·dra (HIGH-drə) *noun.* A tiny water animal with a tube-like body; if cut in two, each half grows another half. —**hydras** or **hydrae** (HIGH-dree) *plural.*

hy·dran·ge·a (high-DRAYN-jee-ə or high-DRAYN-jə) *noun.* A shrub with large clumps of showy blue, white, or pink flowers.

hy·drant (HIGH-drənt) *noun.* A fireplug; a capped, upright section of water pipe with spouts and a valve.

hy·drau·lic (high-DRAW-lik) *adjective.* 1. Moved or operated by liquids which carry force from one piston to another: a *hydraulic* tractor. 2. Hardening under water: *hydraulic* mortar.

hy·drau·lics (high-DRAW-liks) *noun, plural in form but used with a singular verb.* The study and scientific application of how liquids act when moving or at rest.

hy·dro·e·lec·tric (high-droh-i-LEK-trik) *adjective.* Having to do with electricity produced by falling water.

hy·dro·gen (HIGH-drə-jən) *noun.* A clear gas with no smell that burns easily; the lightest of all chemical elements.

hydrogen bomb Also **H-bomb.** An extremely powerful bomb whose heat and explosive force come from the fusion of hydrogen atoms.

hy·drom·e·ter (high-DROM-ə-tər) *noun.* A device for measuring the specific gravity of a liquid.

hy·dro·pho·bia (high-drə-FOH-bee-ə) *noun.* 1. Rabies; a disease in animals. 2. A fear of water.

hy·dro·phone (HIGH-drə-fohn) *noun.* A device for detecting the direction and distance of sound waves carried by water. **hydrophones.**

hy·dro·plane (HIGH-drə-playn) *noun.* 1. A light motorboat with a flat bottom, built to plane or ski across the surface of the water. 2. A seaplane; an airplane that can land on or take off from water.

hy·dro·sphere (HIGH-drə-sfihr) *noun.* The layer of water covering the earth; all surface water.

hydrant

[2]huskies

hydrogen bomb

hyena

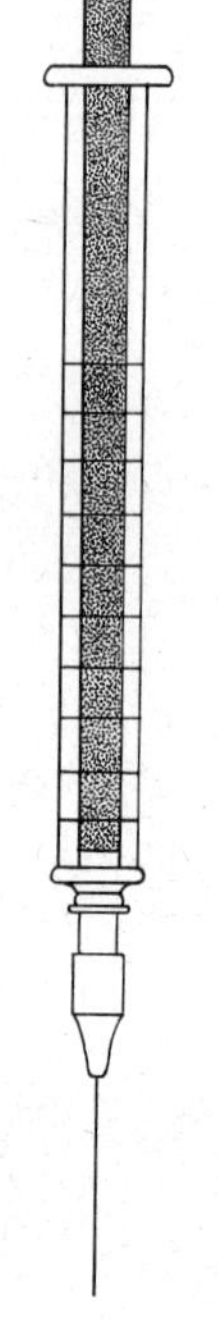
hypodermic

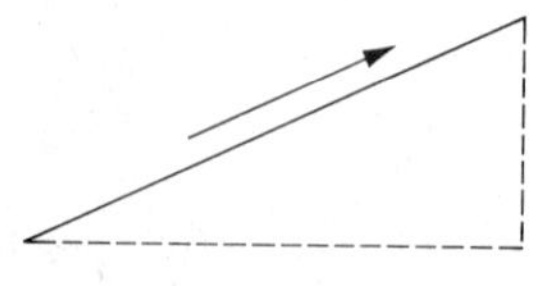
hypotenuse

hy·e·na (high-EE-nə) *noun.* A wild dog or wolf of Africa and Asia with a shrill, laugh-like bark.

hy·giene (HIGH-jeen) *noun.* 1. The science or study of health and how to maintain it. 2. The system or rules for keeping healthy.

hy·grom·e·ter (high-GROM-ə-tər) *noun.* A scientific device for measuring the amount of water vapor or moisture in the air.

hymn (HIM) *noun.* 1. A song in praise or honor of God. 2. Any song of praise. —*verb.* To sing a song of praise; glorify in a hymn. **hymned, hymning.**

hym·nal (HIM-nl) Also **hymnbook** *noun.* A book that contains a collection of hymns; a church songbook. —*adjective.* Of or from hymns.

hyper- *prefix.* Indicating more than usual; in great excess: *hyper*sensitive.

hy·phen (HIGH-fən) *noun.* A mark of punctuation (-) that connects the parts of a compound word, as in mother-in-law, or divides a word between syllables, as at the end of a line of type or writing.

hy·phen·ate (HIGH-fə-nayt) *verb.* To print or write a hyphen between word syllables or the parts of a compound word. **hyphenated, hyphenating.**

hyp·no·sis (hip-NOH-siss) *noun.* A sleeplike state induced by suggestion in which a person may be active and react easily to directions. —**hypnotic** *adjective.*

hyp·no·tism (HIP-nə-tiz-əm) *noun.* 1. The science or study of hypnosis. 2. The act of putting someone into a sleep-like state or trance.

hyp·no·tize (HIP-nə-tighz) *verb.* 1. To put (someone) into a sleep-like state. 2. To bewitch or fascinate. **hypnotized, hypnotizing.** —**hypnotist** *noun.*

hy·poc·ri·sy (hi-POK-rə-see) *noun.* 1. Pretense or falseness; saying one thing and doing another. 2. A claiming of virtues or beliefs which one does not have.

hyp·o·crite (HIP-ə-krit) *noun.* A pretender; one who professes beliefs and virtues that he does not have. **hypocrites.** —**hypocritical** (hip-ə-KRIT-ə-kəl) *adjective.* —**hypocritically** *adverb.*

hyp·o·der·mic (high-pə-DER-mik) *noun.* 1. A needle or syringe for forcing or injecting fluid into or under the skin. 2. The fluid or medicine injected by a syringe.

hy·pot·e·nuse (high-POT-n-ooss or high-POT-n-yooss) *noun.* The side opposite the right angle in a right-angled triangle. **hypotenuses.**

hy·poth·e·sis (high-POTH-ə-siss) *noun.* An unproven idea or theory accepted as true and used as a basis for more reasoning and study until a better theory is found. —**hypotheses** (high-POTH-ə-seez) *plural.*

hy·po·thet·i·cal (high-pə-THET-i-kəl) *adjective.* Not proven; uncertain. —**hypothetically** *adverb.*

hys·ter·ec·to·my (hiss-tə-REK-tə-mee) *noun.* Removal by surgery of part or all of the uterus. **hysterectomies.**

hys·ter·ia (hiss-TIHR-ee-ə) *noun.* 1. A wild fit of laughter or crying; a loss of emotional self-control. 2. A sickness or disturbance of the mind when one may be unable to move, see, or hear, and may suffer pains that have no visible cause.

hys·ter·i·cal (hiss-TEHR-ə-kəl) *adjective.* 1. Having hysteria. 2. Uncontrollably excited. 3. (Slang) Incredibly funny; provoking great mirth. —**hysterically** *adverb.*

hys·ter·ics (hiss-TEHR-iks) *noun. plural in form, but often used with a singular verb.* An outbreak of uncontrolled emotion; an attack of hysteria.

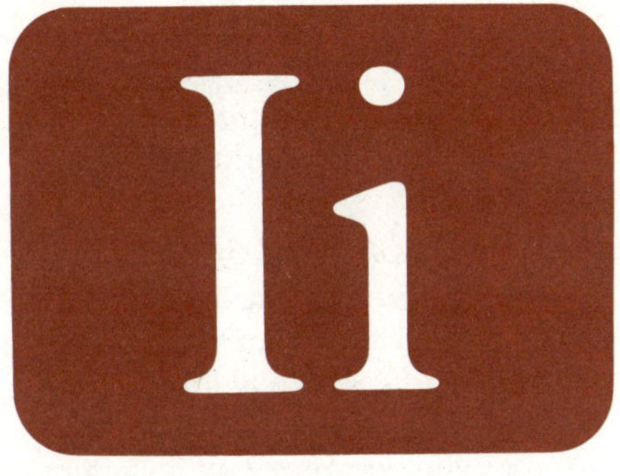

I, i (IGH) *noun.* The ninth letter of the English alphabet.

I (IGH) *pronoun.* A word used by a person in place of his own name: Robert said, "*I* am going now."

I. *abbreviation.* Island.

-ial *suffix.* Indicates: of; referring to; part of: professor*ial.*

i·am·bic (igh-AM-bik) *noun* (Also *adjective*). A metrical foot of verse made up of one unaccented syllable followed by an accented one: "The MOUSE/ran UP/the CLOCK"/contains three *iambics.*

iambic pen·tam·e·ter (pen-TAM-ə-tər) Verse written with five iambic feet to every line: John Keats used *iambic pentameter* in his sonnet, "When I Have Fears That I May Cease To Be."

-ian *suffix.* Indicates: of; part of; similar to: Paris*ian.*

i·bex (IGH-beks) *noun.* A wild goat of the mountains of Asia, Africa, and Europe; its long horns are ridged and curved backward. —**ibex** or **ibexes** *plural.*

i·bis (IGH-biss) *noun.* A wading bird with a long slender bill, found in warm regions. —**ibis** or **ibises** *plural.*

-ic *suffix.* Indicates: of; referring to; part of: satan*ic;* alcohol*ic.*

ice (IGHSS) *noun.* 1. Water made solid by freezing. 2. A frozen dessert, usually made with sweetened fruit juice. **ices.** —*verb.* 1. To cover (a cake) with frosting or icing. 2. To make cold with ice: The boys *iced* the fish they caught. **iced, icing.** —**on thin ice.** In a risky spot.

ice age. A period of coldness when glaciers covered a great deal of the earth's surface.

ice·berg (IGHSS-berg) *noun.* A mass of ice broken away from a glacier and floating in the ocean.

ice·box (IGHSS-boks) *noun.* 1. A box containing ice to cool food. 2. A refrigerator. **iceboxes.**

ice·break·er (IGHSS-bray-kər) *noun.* A ship with a reinforced bow, built to break a passage through ice.

ice cap. A wide-reaching, permanent cover of ice and snow.

ice cream. A frozen dessert made of milk or cream, sugar, flavoring, and sometimes eggs and fruit.

i·ci·cle (IGH-si-kəl) *noun.* A long, hanging piece of ice formed when dripping water is frozen. **icicles.**

ic·ing (IGH-sing) *noun.* A sweet cooked or uncooked mixture used to cover cookies and cakes; frosting.

i·con (IGH-kon) Also **ikon** or **eikon** *noun.* A symbol, especially a religious image or picture.

-ics *suffix.* Indicates: 1. The study or art of: ceram*ics.* 2. The act or the doing of: dramat*ics;* athlet*ics.*

i·cy (IGH-see) *adjective.* 1. Covered with ice; slippery. 2. Like ice in feeling: Joe's feet were *icy* with cold. 3. Very, very cold: an *icy* wind. 4. Cold in manner: an *icy* look. **icier, iciest.** —**icily** *adverb.*

I'd (IGHD) *contraction.* A shortened form of the words *I would, I had,* or *I should.*

I·da·ho (IGH-də-hoh) *noun.* A state in western United States, 43rd to join the Union (1890). —**Id.** *abbreviation.* Also **ID** for Zip Codes.

i·de·a (igh-DEE-ə) *noun.* 1. A thought or mental plan: Joe has an *idea* for our class skit. 2. An opinion or notion.

ibex

iceberg

ibis

Idaho
★capital: Boise

i·de·al (igh-DEE-əl or igh-DEEL) *noun.* A model of perfection to be imitated: Her teacher was Sally's *ideal.* —*adjective.* The best possible. —**ideally** *adverb.*

i·de·al·ism (igh-DEE-ə-liz-əm) *noun.* Thinking of the world and life as it should be, not as it is.

i·de·al·ist (igh-DEE-ə-list) *noun.* One whose thinking is affected more by ideas of perfection than by reality.

i·de·al·ize (igh-DEE-ə-lighz) *verb.* To believe to be perfect or ideal: Ed *idealizes* his brother. **idealized, idealizing.**

i·den·ti·cal (igh-DEN-ti-kəl) *adjective.* Exactly alike: The twins wear *identical* dresses. —**identically** *adverb.*

i·den·ti·fi·ca·tion (igh-den-tə-fi-KAY-shən) *noun.* Anything that is used to identify a person or thing: Dad uses his driver's license as *identification.*

i·den·ti·fy (igh-DEN-tə-figh) *verb.* 1. To establish (who someone is): The sentry asked the man to *identify* himself. 2. To recognize. **identified, identifying.**

i·den·ti·ty (igh-DEN-tə-tee) *noun.* 1. The individual characteristics which make one person different from another. 2. The state of being exactly the same. **identities.**

id·i·o·cy (ID-ee-ə-see) *noun.* 1. A state of abnormally low mental ability. 2. A stupid act: It was *idiocy* to go hiking in the snow without warm clothes. **idiocies.**

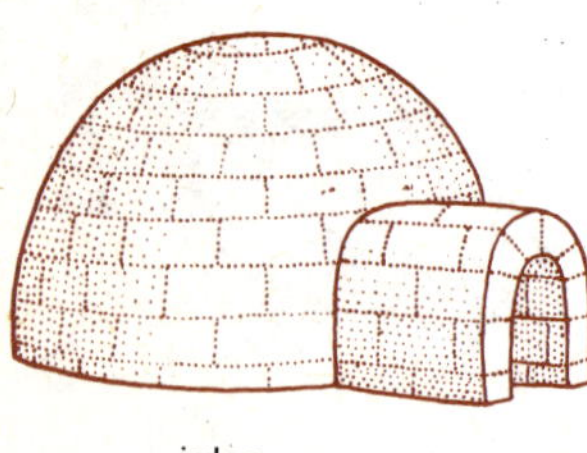
igloo

id·i·om (ID-ee-əm) *noun.* 1. The grammar or structure characteristic of a language. 2. An expression or phrase used within a given language to mean something different from the strict meaning of the words: "Stick to the ribs" is an *idiom* used in speaking of food that is filling. 3. Any manner of expression peculiar to a special region or group of people: Southern *idiom.*

id·i·ot (ID-ee-ət) *noun.* 1. A person born without the mental ability to learn even the simplest things. 2. One who does foolish things.

id·i·ot·ic (id-ee-OT-ik) *adjective.* Extremely foolish. —**idiotically** *adverb.*

i·dle (IGHD-l) *adjective.* 1. Not working or active: *Idle* hands make mischief. 2. Lazy or unwilling to work: The *idle* girl wouldn't help with the chores. 3. Useless: It is an *idle* thought because it will never happen. **idler, idlest.** —*verb.* 1. To do no work; waste time: Sue *idled* away the afternoon gazing out the window. 2. To run (a motor) when it is not in gear. **idled, idling.** —**idleness** *noun.* —**idly** *adverb.*

i·dler (IGHD-lər) *noun.* A person who does nothing or is idle.

i·dol (IGHD-l) *noun.* 1. An image made as an object of worship. 2. One who is very much loved.

i·dol·ize (IGHD-l-ighz) *verb.* To worship or love very much. **idolized, idolizing.**

i.e. *abbreviation.* (Latin) *Id est,* meaning *that is.*

if *conjunction.* 1. In the event that: *If* you drop the vase it will break. 2. On condition that: We will go on the picnic *if* it is sunny. 3. Whether: He wondered *if* it would rain.

ig·loo (IG-loo) *noun.* A house, usually built of hard snow and ice, used especially by Eskimos. **igloos.**

ig·ne·ous (IG-nee-əss) *adjective.* (Geology) Formed by great heat or from molten material: Volcanic rocks are *igneous* rocks.

ig·nite (ig-NIGHT) *verb.* 1. To set fire to: The Scouts *ignited* the kindling with a magnifying glass. 2. To catch fire: Dry hay *ignites* easily. **ignited, igniting.**

ig·ni·tion (ig-NISH-ən) *noun.* 1. A mechanism that makes a spark to set afire the fuel in an engine. 2. Setting or catching on fire.

ig·no·ble (ig-NOH-bəl) *adjective.* 1. Lacking honor or generosity;

mean. 2. Of low or common birth. —**ignobly** *adverb.*

ig·no·ra·mus (ig-nə-RAY-məss) *noun.* A person who knows nothing or is ignorant. **ignoramuses.**

ig·no·rant (IG-nər-ənt) *adjective.* Lacking knowledge. —**ignorance** *noun.* —**ignorantly** *adverb.*

ig·nore (ig-NOR) *verb.* To pay no attention to; disregard on purpose. **ignored, ignoring.**

i·gua·na (ih-GWAH-nə) *noun.* Any of several large lizards found in tropical America.

ill (IL) *adjective.* 1. Not healthy; sick. 2. Evil: ". . . the *ill* wind which blows no man to good." (Shakespeare). **worse, worst.** —*adverb.* Badly: *ill* done. **worse, worst.** —*noun.* A sickness; an evil.

ill. *abbreviation.* Illustrated; illustration.

I'll (IGHL) *contraction.* A shortened form of the words *I will* or *I shall: I'll* go when I am ready.

il·le·gal (ih-LEE-gəl) *adjective.* Against the law. —**illegally** *adverb.*

il·leg·i·ble (ih-LEJ-ə-bəl) *adjective.* Difficult or impossible to read: *illegible* writing. —**illegibly** *adverb.*

Il·li·nois (il-ə-NOI or il-ə-NOIZ) *noun.* A state in north central United States, 21st to join the Union (1818). —**Ill.** *abbreviation.* Also **IL** for Zip Codes.

il·lit·er·ate (ih-LIT-ər-it) *adjective.* 1. Unable to read or write. 2. Having little knowledge of the proper use of language: Tom's teacher said his paper was *illiterate.* —*noun.* A person who is unable to read or write. **illiterates.** —**illiterately** *adverb.*

ill-man·nered (IL-MAN-ərd) *adjective.* Having bad manners. —**ill-manneredly** *adverb.*

ill-na·tured (IL-NAY-chərd) *adjective.* Disagreeable or bad tempered.

ill·ness (IL-niss) *noun.* Sickness; poor health. **illnesses.**

il·log·i·cal (ih-LOJ-i-kəl) *adjective.* Not making any sense: *illogical* chatter. —**illogically** *adverb.*

ill-tem·pered (IL-TEM-pərd) *adjective.* Having a bad temper; disagreeable.

il·lu·mi·nate (ih-LOO-mə-nayt) *verb.* To light or become light: The sun *illuminated* the sky. **illuminated, illuminating.**

il·lu·mi·na·tion (ih-loo-mə-NAY-shən) *noun.* 1. Lighting or brightness. 2. Clarification; explanation.

illus. *abbreviation.* Illustrated; illustration.

il·lu·sion (ih-LOO-zhən) *noun.* 1. An appearance that seems to be real, but is not. 2. A false belief.

il·lus·trate (IL-ə-strayt or ih-LUHSS-trayt) *verb.* 1. To explain by stories, examples, and similar material: The story of Cinderella *illustrates* the virtues of modesty and obedience. 2. To provide with drawings or other material to decorate or make a text more understandable. **illustrated, illustrating.**

il·lus·tra·tion (il-əss-TRAY-shən) *noun.* 1. A picture, diagram, or the like that explains or decorates a text. 2. A story or example used as an explanation: Picking up nails with a magnet is an *illustration* of magnetism.

il·lus·tra·tor (ILL-əss-tray-tər) *noun.* A person who makes drawings or illustrates.

il·lus·tri·ous (ih-LUSS-tree-əss) *adjective.* Famous or well known.

ill will. Unfriendly feeling or dislike.

I'm (IGHM) *contraction.* A shortened form of the words *I am.*

im·age (IM-ij) *noun.* 1. A picture or statue. 2. Something seen through a lens or reflected as in a mirror. 3. A copy: She is the *image* of her mother. 4. Something seen in the mind only. **images.**

im·ag·i·na·ble (ih-MAJ-ə-nə-bəl) *adjective.* Capable of being pictured in the mind: the best vacation *imaginable.* —**imaginably** *adverb.*

iguana

Illinois
★capital: Springfield

im·ag·i·nar·y (ih-MAJ-ə-nehr-ee) *adjective.* Not real; existing only in the mind.

im·ag·i·na·tion (ih-MAJ-ə-nay-shən) *noun.* The ability or act of creating or inventing in one's mind. —**imaginative** *adjective.*

im·ag·ine (ih-MAJ-ən) *verb.* 1. To form a mental picture of. 2. To guess; think. **imagined, imagining.**

im·be·cile (IM-bə-sil) *noun.* A person of low intelligence. **imbeciles.** —*adjective.* Also **imbecilic.** Stupid.

im·bibe (im-BIGHB) *verb.* 1. To drink. 2. To take into the mind. **imbibed, imbibing.**

im·i·tate (IM-ə-tayt) *verb.* 1. To copy the actions or speech of another. 2. To look like: The markings on one kind of butterfly *imitate* a dead leaf. **imitated, imitating.**

im·i·ta·tion (im-ə-TAY-shən) *noun.* 1. The act of copying another's actions or speech: The actor does *imitations* of famous people. 2. An object made by copying: It is hard to tell which is the natural pearl and which is the *imitation.* —*adjective.* Fake; not what it appears to be: The coat is *imitation* fur.

im·mac·u·late (ih-MAK-yə-lit) *adjective.* 1. Clean, spotless. 2. Pure, having no faults. —**immaculately** *adverb.*

im·ma·ture (im-ə-TYOOR) *adjective.* 1. Young, not fully grown. 2. Behind in development. —**immaturely** *adverb.*

im·meas·ur·a·ble (ih-MEZH-ər-ə-bəl) *adjective.* Not capable of being measured; very great. —**immeasurably** *adverb.*

im·me·di·ate (ih-MEE-dee-it) *adjective.* Done at once; not delayed. 2. Closely related: Only members of the *immediate* family were present. 3. Most direct; nearest in time or space. —**immediately** *adverb.*

im·mense (ih-MENSS) *adjective.* Very large. —**immensely** *adverb.*

im·merse (ih-MERSS) *verb.* 1. To dip (something) into a liquid so that the whole is covered. 2. To baptize (a person) by placing in water. 3. To be completely occupied mentally: He is *immersed* in his work. **immersed, immersing.**

im·mi·grant (IM-i-grant) *noun.* A person who comes to one country from another to settle permanently.

im·mi·grate (IM-i-grayt) *verb.* To move into a country to live permanently. **immigrated, immigrating.** —**immigration** (im-i-GRAY-shən) *noun.*

im·mi·nent (IM-ə-nənt) *adjective.* About to happen: A thunderstorm is *imminent.* —**imminently** *adverb.*

im·mo·bile (ih-MOH-bəl) *adjective.* 1. Unable to move or be moved. 2. Motionless: His face was *immobile.* —**immobility** *noun.*

im·mo·bil·ize (ih-MOH-bə-lighz) *verb.* To stop or prevent movement of: Jamie's broken leg will *immobilize* him. **immobilized, immobilizing.**

im·mod·est (ih-MOD-ist) *adjective.* 1. Bold, not shy. 2. Unrestrained in behavior. —**immodestly** *adverb.*

im·mor·al (ih-MOR-əl) *adjective.* Outside the standards of good behavior; not decent or proper. —**immorally** *adverb.*

im·mor·tal (ih-MORT-l) *adjective.* Deathless; able to live forever. —*noun.* 1. One who lives forever. 2. A person with lasting fame. —**immortally** *adverb.*

im·mor·tal·i·ty (im-or-TAL-ə-tee) *noun.* 1. The state of living forever. 2. Lasting fame.

im·mov·a·ble (ih-MOO-və-bəl) *adjective.* Fixed in one position. —**immovably** *adverb.*

im·mune (ih-MYOON) *adjective.* 1. (Medicine) Protected by inoculation or by the body's resistance: Once you have had the mumps, you are usually *immune* to the disease. 2. Safe, free, unaffected.

im·mu·ni·ty (ih-MYOO-nə-tee) *noun.* 1. The ability to resist (a disease). 2. Freedom from a debt, penalty, or duty. **immunities.**

im·mu·nize (IM-yə-nighz) *verb.* To make (a person or animal) able to resist a disease. **immunized, immunizing.**

imp *noun.* 1. A small mischievous spirit. 2. A child who plays tricks or does not behave. —**imp·ish** (IMP-ish) *adjective.* —**impishly** *adverb.*

im·pact (IM-pakt) *noun.* 1. The coming together of two objects; a crash. 2. An effect.

im·pair (im-PAIR) *verb.* To lessen or damage. **impaired, impairing.**

im·pale (im-PAYL) *verb.* To poke through, spear, or pierce: *impale* a piece of paper on a spindle. **impaled, impaling.**

im·part (im-PAHRT) *verb.* 1. To give (a mood): The dim light *imparts* an air of mystery to the stage. 2. To make known. **imparted, imparting.**

im·par·tial (im-PAHR-shəl) *adjective.* Fair; favoring neither side. —**impartiality** (im-par-shee-AL-ə-tee) *noun.* —**impartially** *adverb.*

im·pass·a·ble (im-PASS-ə-bəl) *adjective.* Impossible to travel across or along: *impassable* roads.

im·pas·sioned (im-PASH-ənd) *adjective.* Dramatic; full of feeling.

im·pas·sive (im-PASS-iv) *adjective.* Without feeling; showing no emotion. —**impassively** *adverb.*

im·pa·tience (im-PAY-shənss) *noun.* A restless feeling; a dislike of waiting. —**im·pa·tient** (im-PAY-shənt) *adjective.* —**impatiently** *adverb.*

im·peach (im-PEECH) *verb.* To accuse (a person in public office) of failure to carry out duties properly: A President who is *impeached* must be tried by the U.S. Senate. **impeached, impeaching.** —**impeachment** *noun.*

im·pede (im-PEED) *verb.* To cause to go slow; get in the way. **impeded, impeding.**

im·ped·i·ment (im-PED-ə-mənt) *noun.* 1. Something that gets in the way. 2. A defect.

im·pel (im-PEL) *verb.* 1. To drive forward; push. 2. To force or cause. **impelled, impelling.**

im·pen·e·tra·ble (im-PEN-ə-trə-bəl) 1. Impossible to enter or break into. 2. Mysterious; not understandable.

im·per·a·tive (im-PEHR-ə-tiv) *adjective.* 1. Urgent; necessary: The doctor said an operation was *imperative.* 2. (Grammar) Expressing a command: "Man the lifeboats!" is an *imperative* sentence. —*noun.* The form of a verb used in a command. —**imperatively** *adverb.*

im·per·cep·ti·ble (im-pər-SEP-tə-bəl) Very slight; hard to notice: The snail's motion was *imperceptible.* —**imperceptibly** *adverb.*

im·per·fect (im-PER-fikt) *adjective.* 1. Not perfect. 2. Not complete: I have an *imperfect* knowledge of the game of chess. 3. (Grammar) Relating to a verb form: "Was running" is the *imperfect* tense of "run." —**imperfectly** *adverb.*

im·per·fec·tion (im-pər-FEK-shən) *noun.* 1. The state of being less than perfect. 2. A mistake or flaw: She found an *imperfection* in her new sweater.

im·pe·ri·al (im-PIHR-ee-əl) *adjective.* 1. Relating to an empire. 2. Royal.

im·pe·ri·al·ism (im-PIHR-ee-ə-liz-əm) *noun.* A national policy of establishing control over other countries, usually for economic reasons.

im·per·il (im-PEHR-əl) *verb.* To put in danger. **imperiled, imperiling.**

im·per·son·al (im-PER-sn-l) *adjective.* 1. (Grammar) Not referring to any particular person: An *impersonal* verb has "it" as a subject, as in "It is raining." 2. Not relating to a person; nonhuman: Nature is an *impersonal* force. 3. Without feeling or bias. —**impersonally** *adverb.*

im·per·son·ate (im-PER-sə-nayt) *verb.* To pretend to be (someone else): It is against the law to *impersonate* a policeman. **impersonated, impersonating.**

im·per·ti·nent (im-PER-tə-nənt) *adjective.* 1. Rude: an *impertinent* child. 2. Not pertinent or related. —**impertinence** *noun.* —**impertinently** *adverb.*

im·pet·u·ous (im-PECH-oo-əss) *adjective.* 1. Hasty, rash; acting without forethought or common sense. 2. Forceful; violent. —**impetuosity** (im-pech-oo-oss-ə-tee) *noun.* —**impetuously** *adverb.*

im·pe·tus (IM-pə-təss) *noun.* 1. The energy of motion; momentum: The ball rolled down the hill under its own *impetus.* 2. A motivating or rousing force; stimulation: Desire for a new bike was the *impetus* that made Tim work harder.

im·pinge (im-PINJ) *verb.* 1. To hit; come together with force. 2. To intrude: Imprisonment without trial *impinges* on the rights of a citizen. **impinged, impinging.**

im·ple·ment (IM-plə-mənt) *noun.* A tool or instrument: We keep the garden *implements* in the garage. —(IM-plə-ment) *verb.* To carry out or put into use: Our teacher plans to *implement* a new project on ecology next week. **implemented, implementing.**

im·pli·cate (IM-pli-kayt) *verb.* 1. To suggest or imply. 2. To involve; connect (particularly with a misdeed): Don't *implicate* me in your plan to play hooky. **implicated, implicating.**

im·plic·it (im-PLISS-it) *adjective.* 1. Understood but not spoken or written: My brother and I have an *implicit* agreement to protect each other. 2. Full; unquestioning: I have *implicit* faith in his honesty. —**implicitly** *adverb.*

im·plore (im-PLOR) *verb.* To beg urgently. **implored, imploring.**

im·ply (im-PLIGH) *verb.* To suggest or hint. **implied, implying.**

im·po·lite (im-pə-LIGHT) *adjective.* Rude; lacking good manners. —**impolitely** *adverb.* —**impoliteness** *noun.*

im·port (im-PORT or IM-port) *verb.* 1. To bring from a foreign country: The United States *imports* coffee from Colombia. 2. To mean; convey. **imported, importing** —(IM-port) *noun.* 1. Something that comes from another country. 2. Meaning: The *import* of the doctor's words was that Mary was seriously ill.

im·por·tance (im-POR-tənss) *noun.* The state of ranking high in value, weight, size, or influence; prominence or significance. —**important** *adjective.* —**importantly** *adverb.*

im·por·ta·tion (im-por-TAY-shən) *noun.* 1. The act of bringing in things from another country: the *importation* of foreign cars. 2. An import.

im·pose (im-POHZ) *verb.* 1. To put into force (a tax, punishment, or other duty): Before the Revolution, the British *imposed* many taxes on the Colonists. 2. To force one's wishes (on someone); take unfair advantage of: The uninvited guest *imposed* upon his host. **imposed, imposing.** —**imposition** (im-pə-ZISH-ən) *noun.*

im·pos·ing (im-POH-zing) *adjective.* Important; impressive in size or appearance.

im·pos·si·ble (im-POSS-ə-bəl) *adjective.* 1. Not likely to happen; not to be done; hopeless: "It is *impossible* to please all the world and one's father." (LaFontaine). 2. (Informal) Very unpleasant or hard to deal with: He was an *impossible* child. —**impossibility** (im-poss-ə-BIL-ə-tee) *noun.* —**impossibly** *adverb.*

im·pos·tor (im-POSS-tər) *noun.* One who pretends to be someone else.

im·po·tent (IM-pə-tənt) *adjective.* Incapable; lacking in power or strength. —**impotence** *noun.* —**impotently** *adverb.*

im·pound (im-POWND) *verb.* 1. To shut up or confine; particularly in a public enclosure such as a dog pound. 2. To take into legal custody. **impounded, impounding.**

im·pov·er·ish (im-POV-ər-ish) *verb.* 1. To make poor in goods, health, or spirit: Gambling has *impoverished* many people. 2. To take strength or richness from. **impoverished, impoverishing.** —**impoverishment** *noun.*

im·prac·ti·ca·ble (im-PRAK-ti-kə-bəl) *adjective.* Impossible; not capable of being put into practice.

im·prac·ti·cal (im-PRAK-ti-kəl) *adjective.* 1. Not useful or workable. 2. Unwise; lacking in common sense.

im·preg·na·ble (im-PREG-nə-bəl) *adjective.* Firm; unyielding; able to withstand attack.

im·press (im-PRESS) *verb.* 1. To win the respect of: His smart answers *impressed* the whole class. 2. To put (an idea) firmly in one's mind: She *impressed* on us the importance of the bicycle safety rules. 3. To stamp; leave a mark by pressing: For his birthday Rob got stationery *impressed* with his own name. 4. To take by force: In Colonial times the British *impressed* men into the navy. **impressed, impressing.** —(IM-press) *noun.* A mark made by pressing or stamping. **impresses.**

im·pres·sion (im-PRESH-ən) *noun.* 1. Imprint made by pressing: The FBI keeps files of fingerprint *impressions.* 2. A feeling: I got the *impression* he didn't like me. 3. An effect made on someone: Politeness makes a good *impression.*

im·pres·sive (im-PRESS-iv) *adjective.* Creating a strong feeling of respect or admiration: The blind boy's achievements were *impressive.* —**impressively** *adverb.*

im·print (IM-print) *noun.* 1. A mark made by pressing, printing, or stamping: We saw the *imprint* of bear paws on the trail. 2. An effect, as on the mind or feelings: A frightening show leaves its *imprint* on an audience. 3. A publisher's name and address printed on the title page of a book —(im-PRINT) *verb.* 1. To make (a mark) by pressing, stamping, or printing. 2. To impress, as on the mind: My grandfather's face is *imprinted* on my memory. **imprinted, imprinting.**

im·pris·on (im-PRIZ-n) *verb.* 1. To put into and keep locked in prison. 2. To lock up in any way: Modern zoos do not *imprison* animals in cages. **imprisoned, imprisoning.** —**imprisonment** *noun.*

im·prob·a·ble (im-PROB-ə-bəl) *adjective.* 1. Not likely to happen. 2. Not likely to be true or believable. —**improbability** *noun.* —**improbably** *adverb.*

im·prop·er (im-PROP-ər) *adjective.* Not correct or fitting; lacking good taste. —**improperly** *adverb.*

improper fraction. A fraction with the numerator equal to or greater than the denominator: $^{8}/_{5}$, $^{7}/_{3}$, and $^{15}/_{15}$ are *improper fractions.*

im·prove (im-PROOV) *verb.* 1. To make better: She should *improve* her grades. 2. To get better. **improved, improving.**

im·prove·ment (im-PROOV-mənt) *noun.* 1. A better state or condition. 2. An addition to or alteration of property that makes it more valuable.

im·pro·vise (IM-prə-vighz) *verb.* 1. To make up and perform (a skit, song, speech, etc.) without rehearsal or planning. 2. To make from whatever is on hand: The explorer *improvised* a shelter with branches. **improvised, improvising.**

im·pu·dence (IM-pyə-dənss) *noun.* Rude disrespect. —**impudent** *adjective.* —**impudently** *adverb.*

im·pulse (IM-puhlss) *noun.* 1. A sudden urge: I felt a strong *impulse* to run. 2. A thrust; a pushing with force. **impulses.**

im·pul·sive (im-PUHL-siv) *adjective.* 1. Acting suddenly without real thought; in the habit of acting by impulse: The *impulsive* children spent all their money on candy. 2. Having power, drive, force. —**impulsively** *adverb.*

im·pure (im-PYUR) *adjective.* 1. Not clean or wholesome: The water was *impure;* it had been used for washing. 2. Mixed with something else, often of less value: *impure* silver. 3. Not proper; not modest or decent. —**impurely** *adverb.* —**impurity** *noun.*

in *preposition.* 1. Within the limits of: *in* the house. 2. Covered or surrounded by: buried *in* the snow. 3. During or at the end of: They arrived *in* an hour. 4. Into: Come *in* the house. 5. Showing or feeling: *in* fear. 6. Employed by: *in* government. 7. With; by means of: painted *in* watercolor. 8. According to: *in* my mind. —*adverb.* 1. Inside (a place): Make him stay *in.* 2. Inside, coming from outside: Step *in.* —*adjective.* 1. Leading inward; inside: the *in* door. 2. (Informal) Fashionable; having influence: the *in* people. —*noun.* 1. (Informal) Power or influence (with): Dad has an *in* with the mayor. 2. (Plural) The people in power: the *ins.*

in- *prefix.* Indicates: 1. Not; not having; without: *in*attention. 2. In; within; into: *in*board. 3. Strong action: *in*flame. 4. An action that causes (something): *in*augurate.

in. *abbreviation.* Inch; inches.

in·a·bil·i·ty (in-ə-BIL-ə-tee) *noun.* Lack of ability, means, or power; the state of being unable.

in·ac·ces·si·ble (in-ak-SESS-ə-bəl) *adjective.* Not possible to reach or approach: The mountaintop was *inaccessible.*

in·ac·cu·rate (in-AK-yə-rit) *adjective.* Not correct; wrong or faulty: an *inaccurate* answer. —**inaccuracy** *noun.* —**inaccurately** *adverb.*

in·ac·tive (in-AK-tiv) *adjective.* Not active; idle. —**inactively** *adverb.* —**inactivity** *noun.*

in·ad·e·quate (in-AD-i-kwit) *adjective.* 1. Not enough: The amount of money was *inadequate.* 2. Not competent or good enough: *inadequate* typing. —**inadequacy** *noun.* —**inadequately** *adverb.*

in·ad·vis·a·ble (in-ad-VIGH-zə-bəl) *adjective.* 1. Not likely to be successful. 2. Not recommended.

in·al·ien·a·ble (in-AYL-yən-ə-bəl) *adjective.* Not to be taken from a person or given up by him: We have certain *inalienable* rights.

in·ane (in-AYN) *adjective.* Stupid or silly: His *inane* jokes made him unpopular. —**inanely** *adverb.*

in·an·i·mate (in-AN-ə-mit) *adjective.* 1. Not alive; lacking the qualities of growth or motion: Statues are *inanimate.* 2. Dull; not lively.

in·ap·pro·pri·ate (in-ə-PROH-pree-it) *adjective.* Not suitable or becoming: Her party dress was *inappropriate* for the picnic. —**inappropriately** *adverb.* —**inappropriateness** *noun.*

in·at·ten·tive (in-ə-TEN-tiv) *adjective.* Not paying attention; careless.

in·au·gu·rate (in-AW-gyə-rayt) *verb.* 1. To place in office, or install (an official) with a formal ceremony: George Washington was *inaugurated* in New York. 2. To begin or introduce: The teacher *inaugurated* a new rule. 3. To place in public use with a ceremony: The mayor *inaugurated* the new town hall. **inaugurated, inaugurating.** —**inauguration** (in-aw-gyə-RAY-shən) *noun.*

in-be·tween (IN-bi-tween) *noun.* One that comes in the middle of, or between, two things: the expert, the beginner, and the *in-between.*

in·board (IN-bord) *adjective* and *adverb.* Inside or toward the center of a ship or plane: *inboard* motor.

in·born (IN-born) *adjective.* Natural; present since birth: *inborn* charm.

inc. *abbreviation.* 1. [Capital I] Incorporated. 2. Including. 3. Increase.

in·can·des·cent (in-kən-DESS-ənt) *adjective.* 1. Hot enough to glow or give light. 2. Shining brightly; gleaming. —**incandescence** *noun.*

in·ca·pa·ble (in-KAY-pə-bəl) *adjective.* Not capable; without the power, skill, or other quality needed for a purpose: *incapable* of hitting a ball. —**incapability** (in-kay-pə-BIL-ə-tee) Also **incapableness** *noun.*

in·car·na·tion (in-kahr-NAY-shən) *noun.* 1. The coming into or taking on of human form. 2. [Capital I] God's taking on the human form of Jesus. 3. One who personifies a quality: Patty is the *incarnation* of honesty; she never tells a lie.

in·cen·di·ar·y (in-SEN-dee-ehr-ee) *adjective.* 1. Creating a fire: *incendiary* bombs. 2. Involving a fire set on purpose to damage or destroy property. 3. Arousing strong emotions such as resentment or hatred: *incendiary* writing.

in·cense (IN-senss) *noun.* 1. A substance such as gum or spices that gives a sweet or fragrant smell when burned. 2. A pleasing smell or perfume. **incenses.** —*verb.* (in-SENSS) To fill with anger: The lawyer's constant interruptions *incensed* the judge. **incensed, incensing.**

in·censed (in-SENST) *adjective.* Filled with anger.

in·cen·tive (in-SEN-tiv) *noun.* Something that makes one try harder: His mother's offer of a dog was the *incentive* that made Tim study more often. **incentives.**

in·cep·tion (in-SEP-shən) *noun.* The start or beginning: the *inception* of an idea.

in·ces·sant (in-SESS-nt) *adjective.* Not stopping; constant: *incessant* talking. —**incessantly** *adverb.*

inch *noun.* A unit, used to measure length, equal to $^1/_{12}$ of a foot. **inches.** —*verb.* To move slowly but steadily. **inched, inching.**

inch

in·ci·dent (IN-sə-dənt) *noun.* 1. A happening or event. 2. An event that is not very important.

in·ci·den·tal (in-sə-DENT-l) *adjective.* Of minor importance. —**incidental to.** Likely to be connected with: I don't like all the dishwashing *incidental to* a big family party.

in·ci·den·tal·ly (in-sə-DEN-tl-ee or in-sə-DENT-lee) *adverb.* 1. In addition to other matters: In her talk, the teacher spoke *incidentally* about tardiness. 2. By the way; in passing: *Incidentally,* how's your sister?

in·cin·er·a·tor (in-SIN-ə-ray-tər) *noun.* A furnace used for burning waste materials.

in·ci·sion (in-SIZH-ən) *noun.* A cut made by a doctor or the scar resulting from such a cut.

in·ci·sor (in-SIGH-zər) *noun.* A front tooth that has a sharp edge used for cutting.

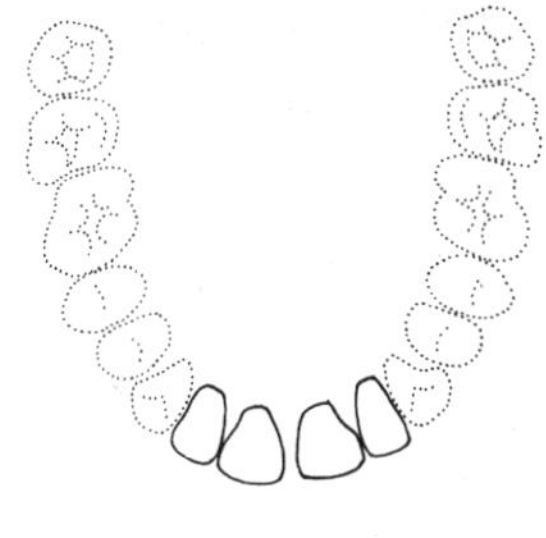

incisors

in·cite (in-SIGHT) *verb.* To urge or stir (to action): The stranger *incited* the mob to throw stones. **incited, inciting.**

in·clem·ent (in-KLEM-ənt) *adjective.* 1. Rough, bad, or stormy: *inclement* weather. 2. Showing no mercy.

in·cli·na·tion (in-klə-NAY-shən) *noun.* 1. A liking; a natural desire or leaning: an *inclination* for math. 2. A trend; that which is likely to happen: The city shows an *inclination* to grow. 3. A slope or slant.

in·cline (in-KLIGHN) *verb.* 1. To bend; slope; slant. 2. To tend; be likely or willing: Sally *inclines* to giggle too much. **inclined, inclining.** —(IN-klighn) *noun.* A slope or surface that slants. **inclines.**

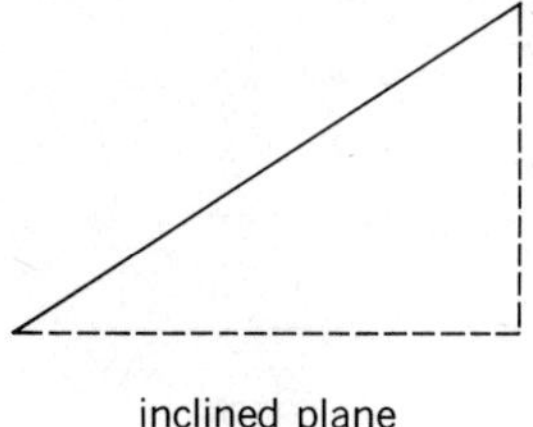
inclined plane

inclined plane. A simple machine which raises objects against the force of gravity by moving them along a wedge-shaped ramp: *Inclined planes* made of dirt were used to raise the big stones of the Egyptian pyramids.

in·close (in-KLOHZ) *verb. See* **enclose.**

in·clude (in-KLOOD) *verb.* To involve or contain, as part of a whole or among other things: Desserts on the menu *include* pie but not ice cream. **included, including.** —**inclusion** *noun.*

in·clu·sive (in-KLOO-siv) *adjective.* Considering everything; taking into account all that comes within given limits plus the limits as well: We did problems one to ten *inclusive,* or ten in all. —**inclusively** *adverb.*

in·cog·ni·to (in-KOG-nə-toh or in-kog-NEE-toh) *adjective* and *adverb.* With identity hidden; using a false name or disguise to escape notice.

in·come (IN-kuhm) *noun.* Money that is received or comes from earnings, profits, dividends, interest, or the like. **incomes.**

in·com·pa·ra·ble (in-KOM-pər-ə-bəl) *adjective.* Not capable of being equaled or surpassed: "How *incomparable* are the Emperor's new clothes." (Hans Christian Andersen). —**incomparably** *adverb.*

in·com·pe·tent (in-KOM-pə-tənt) *adjective.* Unable to do something; not capable. —**incompetence** *noun.* —**incompetently** *adverb.*

in·com·plete (in-kəm-PLEET) *adjective.* Not finished or complete. —**incompletely** *adverb.*

in·com·pre·hen·si·ble (in-kom-pri-HEN-sə-bəl) *adjective.* Not able to be understood; not clear: I find this math problem *incomprehensible.* —**incomprehensibly** *adverb.*

in·con·ceiv·a·ble (in-kən-SEE-və-bəl) *adjective.* Not to be imagined; incredible, unthinkable, unbelievable. —**inconceivably** *adverb.*

in·con·sid·er·ate (in-kən-SID-ər-it) *adjective.* Unthinking, unkind, —**inconsiderately** *adverb.*

in·con·sis·tent (in-kən-SISS-tənt) *adjective.* 1. Not reliable; uneven, lacking uniformity: My brother's low grade in English was *inconsistent* with his high grades in other subjects. 2. In disagreement or conflict; illogical: Joe's accounts of the evening were *inconsistent;* he told Dad he was studying, but he told me all about a movie he had seen on TV. —**inconsistently** *adverb.*

in·con·spic·u·ous (in-kən-SPIK-yoo-əss) *adjective.* Not attracting much attention: The street sign was so *inconspicuous* we had trouble finding the house. —**inconspicuously** *adverb.*

in·con·ven·ience (in-kən-VEEN-yənss) *noun.* Annoyance, bother; something that causes irksome discomfort or difficulty. —*verb.* To cause trouble or annoyance for. **inconvenienced, inconveniencing.** —**inconvenient** *adjective.* —**inconveniently** *adverb.*

in·cor·po·rate (in-KOR-pə-rayt) *verb.* 1. To unite or combine into one body; include: This report *incorporates* only textbook facts, not your own ideas. 2. To form into a corporation or legal entity. **incorporated, incorporating.**

in·cor·rect (in-kə-REKT) *adjective.* 1. Not right; inaccurate: *incorrect* answers. 2. Not appropriate or proper: *incorrect* manners. —**incorrectly** *adverb.*

in·crease (in-KREESS) *verb.* To gain, add, become greater or larger, grow, multiply. **increased, increasing.** —(IN-kreess) *noun.* 1. The amount of gain: He received a five-dollar *increase* in his weekly salary. 2. Growth: There was a noticeable *increase* in Joel's height this year. **increases.**

in·creas·ing·ly (in-KREESS-ing-lee) *adverb.* More and more: He became *increasingly* upset as the noise became louder.

in·cred·i·ble (in-KRED-ə-bəl) *adjective.* Not believable, seemingly impossible: *incredible* luck. —**incredibly** *adverb.*

in·cred·u·lous (in-KREJ-ə-ləss) *adjective.* Feeling or showing a great lack of belief; unsure: Did you see the *incredulous* look on Mother's face when I offered to do the dishes? —**incredulously** *adverb.*

in·cre·ment (IN-krə-mənt) *noun.* An additional amount; growth or expansion.

in·cu·bate (IN-kyə-bayt) *verb.* 1. To hatch eggs by means of artificial or body heat. 2. To keep in a warm place in order to aid growth. **incubated, incubating.** —**incubation** (in-kyoo-BAY-shən) *noun.*

in·cu·ba·tor (IN-kyə-bay-tər) *noun.* 1. Box-like, heated device used to hatch eggs. 2. Any similar device, such as one in which a very tiny baby may be kept if born too soon.

in·cur·a·ble (in-KYUR-ə-bəl) *adjective.* 1. Beyond cure or medical help; hopeless. 2. Not to be helped or modified: an *incurable* habit. —**incurably** *adverb.*

in·debt·ed (in-DET-id) *adjective.* Owing another money favors, or the like. —**indebtedness** *noun.*

in·de·cent (in-DEE-sənt) *adjective.* Not decent, proper, or modest; shameless. —**indecently** *adverb.*

in·deed (in-DEED) *adverb.* Truly, really; without question; in fact: "*Indeed,* unless the billboards fall, I'll never see a tree at all." (Ogden Nash). —*interjection.* Expresses surprise or disbelief.

in·def·i·nite (in-DEF-ə-nit) *adjective.* 1. Not clearly defined; vague; not specific. 2. Without limits or boundaries: An *indefinite* number of words can be used to make a sentence. 3. (Grammar) Not specifying: "An" is an *indefinite* article. —**indefinitely** *adverb.*

indefinite pronoun. A word that takes the place of a noun but does not tell about the noun it replaces: "Many" is an *indefinite pronoun.*

in·del·i·ble (in-DEL-ə-bəl) *adjective.* Not to be removed or washed away; permanent. —**indelibly** *adverb.*

in·dent (in-DENT) *verb.* 1. To cut notches (in). 2. To begin a printed line farther right than other lines of the text: *Indent* the first line of a paragraph. **indented, indenting.** —**indentation** (in-den-TAY-shən) or **indention** *noun.*

in·de·pend·ence (in-di-PEN-dənss) *noun.* Freedom, liberty, self-sufficiency; the state of being independent.

in·de·pend·ent (in-di-PEN-dənt) *adjective.* 1. Not under someone else's control; free. 2. Politically free; having self-government. 3. Having enough money to live without working: Her husband left her enough to be *independent.* 4. Not belonging to any particular political party: an *independent* voter. 5. Able to think and act for oneself; self-reliant: Mary was *independent* at an early age. —**independently** *adverb.*

in·de·scrib·a·ble (in-di-SKRIGH-bə-bəl) *adjective.* Impossible or difficult to put into words or describe fully: *indescribable* beauty. —**indescribably** *adverb.*

in·dex (IN-deks) *noun.* 1. The part of a book or other written work that is an alphabetical list of people, places, and topics mentioned in the work and the pages on which these references occur. 2. Any list or file used as a guide for reference: Our teacher keeps a card *index* of all our test grades. 3. That which acts as a sign or indication (of something): Some believe that a person's wealth is an *index* of his success. —**indexes** or **indices** (IN-də-seez) *plural.* —*verb.* To make or list in an index. **indexed, indexing.**

incubator

Indiana
★capital: Indianapolis

indigo

index finger. The finger that is next to the thumb; the forefinger.

In·di·an (IN-dee-ən) *noun.* 1. One of the people who were the first inhabitants of America. 2. An inhabitant of India.

In·di·an·a (in-dee-AN-ə) *noun.* A state in north central United States, 19th to join the Union (1816). —**Ind.** *abbreviation.* Also **IN** for Zip Codes.

in·di·cate (IN-di-kayt) *verb.* 1. To show, designate, point out: I *indicated* which piece of chicken I wanted. 2. To imply, be a sign of: A dark sky *indicates* an approaching storm. **indicated, indicating.** —**indication** (in-di-KAY-shən) *noun.*

in·dic·a·tive (in-DIK-ə-tiv) *adjective.* 1. Acting to point out: Those clouds are *indicative* of bad weather ahead. 2. (Grammar) Referring to or naming a mood of a verb that is used to express a fact: In the sentence "I am here," "am" is in the *indicative* mood.

in·di·ca·tor (IN-di-kay-tər) *noun.* 1. Something that points out or shows. 2. A device that measures or records how machinery is working.

in·dict (in-DIGHT) *verb.* 1. To charge with a crime; accuse. 2. (Law) To bring a formal charge of crime against, especially as a result of the findings of a grand jury. **indicted, indicting.**

in·dif·fer·ent (in-DIF-ər-ənt) *adjective.* 1. Impartial, neutral. 2. In-between, ordinary: C is an *indifferent* grade. —**indifference** *noun.* —**indifferently** *adverb.*

in·dig·e·nous (in-DIJ-ə-nəss) *adjective.* Native to an area: The orangutan is *indigenous* to Borneo. —**indigenously** *adverb.*

in·di·ges·tion (in-digh-JESS-chən or in-di-JESS-chən) *noun.* Stomach pain or discomfort after eating.

in·dig·na·tion (in-dig-NAY-shən) *noun.* An angry reaction to unjust acts. —**indignant** (in-DIG-nənt) *adjective.* —**indignantly** *adverb.*

in·di·go (IN-di-goh) *noun.* 1. Any of several blue plants used particularly in making dye. 2. (Also *adjective*) A deep blue-violet color. —**indigos** or **indigoes** *plural.*

in·di·rect (in-di-REKT) *adjective.* 1. Not direct; not taking the shortest route. 2. Not to the point; evasive. 3. Occurring as a side effect: Jim's knowledge of other lands is the *indirect* result of his keen interest in stamps. —**indirectly** *adverb.*

in·dis·pen·sa·ble (in-diss-PEN-sə-bəl) *adjective.* Absolutely necessary; essential: Food and water are *indispensable* for the life and growth of all animals. —**indispensably** *adverb.*

in·dis·posed (in-diss-POHZD) *adjective.* 1. Unwilling; not inclined. 2. Slightly ill; not feeling well.

in·dis·tinct (in-diss-TINGKT) *adjective.* Not clear; indefinite, dim, vague, hazy. —**indistinctly** *adverb.*

in·di·vid·u·al (in-də-VIJ-oo-əl) *adjective.* 1. Referring to a single person: *individual* rights. 2. Existing as one; alone, single: Each shoe was put in an *individual* compartment. 3. Showing or marked by a special characteristic or distinction. —*noun.* 1. One person or thing regarded as separate from others. 2. A self-reliant person. 3. One person in particular. —**individually** *adverb.*

in·di·vid·u·al·i·ty (in-də-vij-oo-AL-ə-tee) *noun.* The state or quality of being distinctive or different from others.

in·di·vis·i·ble (in-də-VIZ-ə-bəl) *adjective.* 1. Not able to be divided. 2. (Math) Not able to be divided exactly without leaving a remainder: Three is *indivisible* by two. —**indivisibly** *adverb.*

in·do·lent (IN-də-lənt) *adjective.* Lazy; usually or often idle. —**indolence** *noun.* —**indolently** *adverb.*

in·dom·i·ta·ble (in-DOM-ə-tə-bəl) *adjective.* Impossible to conquer or subdue. —**indomitably** *adverb.*

in·door (IN-dor) *adjective.* 1. Referring to the inside of a house or building. 2. Happening or existing inside a house or building.

in·doors (in-DORZ) *adverb.* In or into a house or other enclosed structure.

in·dorse (in-DORSS) *verb. See* **endorse.**

in·duce (in-DOOSS or in-DYOOSS) *verb.* 1. To cause to happen; to effect (something) or bring on: The accident *induced* a lawsuit. 2. To persuade or cause (someone to do something); to influence: I tried to *induce* her to stay. **induced, inducing.** —**inducement** *noun.*

in·duct (in-DUHKT) *verb.* 1. To summon into military service. 2. To install (in an office); to accept or admit as a member. **inducted, inducting.**

in·duc·tion (in-DUHK-shən) *noun.* 1. Any act of admitting into or of being admitted. 2. The formal ceremony by which a civilian becomes a member of the armed forces. 3. A process of thinking in which it is shown that what holds true for one (part, item, individual) holds true for all. 4. The process by which an electrical or magnetic conductor becomes charged.

in·dulge (in-DUHLJ) *verb.* 1. To allow wide freedom (of choice, behavior, or the like): Grandma *indulges* us whenever we visit her. 2. (Used with *in*) To take part without restraint: Mom diets all week so she can *indulge* in a big dinner on Sunday. **indulged, indulging.** —**in·dul·gence** (in-DUHL-jənss) *noun.*

in·dul·gent (in-DUHL-jənt) *adjective.* Excessively generous or lenient; liberal toward oneself or others. —**indulgently** *adverb.*

in·dus·tri·al (in-DUHSS-tree-əl) *adjective.* 1. Having to do with industry: *industrial* wastes. 2. Having many or well-developed industries or factories: an *industrial* city. —**industrially** *adverb.*

Industrial Revolution. The general changeover from the use of hand tools to the use of machinery in factories, starting in England around 1760 and spreading throughout the civilized world.

in·dus·tri·ous (in-DUHSS-tree-əss) *adjective.* Hard-working; busy. —**industriously** *adverb.*

in·dus·try (IN-duhss-tree) *noun.* 1. All manufacturers, workers, products; business: the *industry* of the nation. 2. A specific manufacturing group: the auto *industry.* 3. Steadiness; close attention. **industries.**

in·e·bri·ate (in-EE-bree-ayt) *verb.* To make intoxicated. **inebriated, inebriating.** —(in-EE-bree-it) *noun.* An intoxicated person. **inebriates.**

in·ed·i·ble (in-ED-ə-bəl) *adjective.* Not fit to eat: The steak was so tough it was *inedible.*

in·ef·fec·tive (in-i-FEK-tiv) *adjective.* Not getting or giving the desired result; useless. —**ineffectively** *adverb.* —**ineffectiveness** *noun.*

in·ef·fi·cient (in-i-FISH-ənt) *adjective.* 1. Wasteful of energy, time, money, or the like. 2. Not skillful; having little ability to produce. —**inefficiency** *noun.* —**inefficiently** *adverb.*

in·ept (in-EPT) *adjective.* 1. Not capable; clumsy: Sal is an *inept* painter. 2. Inappropriate; not proper or fitting. —**ineptly** *adverb.*

in·e·qual·i·ty (in-i-KWOL-ə-tee) *noun.* The state of being not equal. **inequalities.**

in·ert (in-ERT) *adjective.* 1. Lifeless; still; without motion or activity. 2. Having little or no chemical effect: Neon is an *inert* gas.

in·er·tia (in-ER-shə) *noun.* 1. The state or condition of not changing; resistance to change or activity. 2. (Physics) The property of matter that keeps it still or active until acted upon: The law of *inertia* is that a body in motion tends to stay in motion; a body at rest tends to stay at rest.

in·es·cap·a·ble (in-ə-SKAY-pə-bəl) *adjective.* Unavoidable; necessary. —**inescapably** *adverb.*

in·ev·i·ta·ble (in-EV-ə-tə-bəl) *adjective.* Not to be avoided; sure to happen: No matter how long summer seems, the start of school is *inevitable.* —*noun.* Something that is sure to come about: "There is no good in arguing with the *inevitable.*" (J. R. Lowell). —**inevitably** *adverb.*

in·ex·act (in-eg-ZAKT) *adjective.* Inaccurate; not precisely correct; not detailed: His map was *inexact.* —**inexactly** *adverb.*

in·ex·cus·a·ble (in-eks-KYOO-zə-bəl) *adjective.* Not to be forgiven; without reason or excuse. —**inexcusably** *adverb.*

in·ex·haust·i·ble (in-eg-ZAWSS-tə-bəl) *adjective.* 1. Untiring; full of energy. 2. Without the possibility of being used up: Our natural resources are not *inexhaustible.* —**inexhaustibly** *adverb.*

in·ex·pen·sive (in-eks-PEN-siv) *adjective.* Not costly; cheap. —**inexpensively** *adverb.*

in·ex·pe·ri·ence (in-eks-PIHR-ee-ənss) *noun.* The lack of knowledge or practice: He was not hired because of his *inexperience.* —**inexperienced** *adjective.*

in·fal·li·ble (in-FAL-ə-bəl) *adjective.* 1. Not capable of error: *infallible* memory. 2. Positive; sure; without the possibility of failure. —**infallibility** *noun.* —**infallibly** *adverb.*

in·fa·mous (IN-fə-məss) *adjective.* 1. Known to be bad or evil: an *infamous* criminal. 2. Causing or bringing on disgrace or shame. —**infamously** *adverb.*

in·fam·y (IN-fə-mee) *noun.* 1. A reputation for being evil: "December 7, 1941—a date which will live in *infamy.*" (F. D. Roosevelt). 2. A well-known, shocking, or brutal act or crime. **infamies.**

in·fan·cy (IN-fən-see) *noun.* 1. The early period of life; babyhood. 2. The first steps or beginning of anything: Space exploration is still in its *infancy.*

in·fant (IN-fənt) *noun.* 1. A baby. 2. A beginner.

in·fan·tile (IN-fən-tighl or IN-fən-til) *adjective.* 1. Of or about infants. 2. Like a baby; childish; not mature.

infantile paralysis. *See* poliomyelitis.

in·fan·try (IN-fən-tree) *noun.* 1. Soldiers trained to fight on foot. 2. A unit or regiment of foot soldiers.

in·fat·u·ate (in-FACH-oo-ayt) *verb.* To charm; hold fascinated. **infatuated, infatuating.**

in·fect (in-FEKT) *verb.* 1. To spread disease germs; cause to be sick. 2. To bring on a particular mood in: His enthusiasm *infected* the crowd. **infected, infecting.** —**infection** *noun.*

in·fec·tious (in-FEK-shəss) *adjective.* 1. Able to pass along disease or to contaminate. 2. Able to be passed on without direct contact: One can catch an *infectious* disease just by being near a sick person. 3. Easily spread or caught: Gertie's laugh is *infectious;* I laugh every time she does. —**infectiously** *adverb.*

in·fer (in-FER) *verb.* To figure out or understand on the basis of evidence: She *inferred* from his expression that he was sad. **inferred, inferring.**

in·fer·ence (IN-fər-ənss) *noun.* 1. The result of inferring; conclusion: Your *inference* is wrong: Bill was in the room, but he didn't spill the milk. 2. The act of inferring. **inferences.**

in·fe·ri·or (in-FIHR-ee-ər) *adjective.* 1. Less in value, importance, or quality: These apples are *inferior* to the others in taste. 2. Below in position: The vice president is *inferior* to the president. —*noun.* One who is below another in rank.

in·fe·ri·or·i·ty (in-fihr-ee-OR-ə-tee) *noun.* The condition or quality of being inferior. **inferiorities.**

in·fer·nal (in-FER-nl) *adjective.* 1. Of or about hell; hellish. 2. Extreme; great. —**infernally** *adverb.*

in·fest (in-FEST) *verb.* To invade or overrun harmfully or in a pesty way. **infested, infesting.**

in·fi·del (IN-fə-dl or IN-fə-del) *noun.* 1. One who does not believe in any religion. 2. One who is not a believer in a certain religion.

in·field (IN-feeld) *noun.* (Baseball) 1. The area bounded by the base lines and home plate; the diamond. 2. The three basemen and the shortstop.

in·fil·trate (in-FIL-trayt or IN-fil-trayt) *verb.* To enter by filtering into. **infiltrated, infiltrating.** —**infiltration** (in-fil-TRAY-shən) *noun.*

in·fi·nite (IN-fə-nit) *adjective.* 1. Beyond measure; very great: an *infinite* number of reasons. 2. Without limits: the *infinite* universe. —*noun.* Something that is boundless. —**infinitely** *adverb.*

infinite set. (Math) A set containing an infinite number of members.

in·fin·i·tive (in-FIN-ə-tiv) *noun.* (Usually preceded by *to*) A verb form used as a noun or modifier: "To see" is an *infinitive.*

in·firm (in-FERM) *adjective.* Not strong physically; weakened.

in·fir·ma·ry (in-FER-mə-ree) A place for taking care of minor illnesses; a small hospital. **infirmaries.**

in·fir·mi·ty (in-FER-mə-tee) *noun.* 1. A bodily weakness caused by illness, injury, or old age. 2. Any feeble condition. **infirmities.**

in·flame (in-FLAYM) *verb.* 1. To work up to a great degree of excitement or violence: The city was *inflamed* with anger during the riots. 2. To make red and sore. **inflamed, inflaming.** —**inflammation** *noun.*

in·flam·ma·ble (in-FLAM-ə-bəl) *adjective.* 1. Inclined to burn or burst into flame: Don't buy *inflammable* curtains. 2. Excitable; easily aroused. —**inflammably** *adverb.*

in·flate (in-FLAYT) *verb.* 1. To blow up or fill with air, as a balloon. 2. To cause a feeling of importance: *inflate* with pride. 3. To enlarge or expand beyond normal: *inflate* prices. **inflated, inflating.** —**inflation** *noun.*

in·flex·i·ble (in-FLEK-sə-bəl) *adjective.* 1. Not easily bent or moved. 2. Firm; stubborn: His *inflexible* attitude made arguing useless. —**inflexibly** *adverb.*

infield

in·flict (in-FLIKT) *verb.* To put upon; impose; cause (something unwanted or painful). **inflicted, inflicting.**

in·flu·ence (IN-floo-ənss) *noun.* 1. The power or ability to act on or affect others: "A teacher affects eternity; he can never tell where his *influence* stops." (H. B. Adams). 2. A person or thing that has such ability or power: Louisa is a good *influence* on her sister. **influences.** —*verb.* To have or use such ability or power. **influenced, influencing.**

in·flu·en·tial (in-floo-EN-shəl) *adjective.* Having great influence or importance. —**influentially** *adverb.*

in·flu·en·za (in-floo-EN-zə) *noun.* A contagious disease like a very bad cold but more serious.

in·form (in-FORM) *verb.* 1. To pass on knowledge or facts. 2. To reveal secrets. **informed, informing.**

in·for·mal (in-FOR-məl) *adjective.* 1. Not according to strict rules or social customs; relaxed and casual: an *informal* meeting. 2. Used in everyday talk: *informal* speech. —**informally** *adverb.*

in·for·ma·tion (in-fər-MAY-shən) *noun.* 1. Knowledge given or received; facts about a particular subject. 2. General knowledge.

in·fra-red (in-frə-RED) *adjective.* Referring to radiation that has a longer wavelength than the visible red rays in the spectrum: *Infra-red* rays are used to take nighttime photographs without flash bulbs.

in·fre·quent (in-FREE-kwənt) *adjective.* Not often; rare. —**infrequently** *adverb.*

in·fringe (in-FRINJ) *verb.* To trespass; cross over the boundaries of; violate (a contract, an agreement, or the rights of another): When Joe pushed in at the head of the line he *infringed* on the rights of all the rest of us. **infringed, infringing.**

in·fu·ri·ate (in-FYUR-ee-ayt) *verb.* To make very angry. **infuriated, infuriating.**

in·fuse (in-FYOOZ) *verb.* To fill (with); put (into); instill: She *infused* a love of music in her children. **infused, infusing.**

in·gen·ious (in-JEEN-yəss) *adjective.* Clever or inventive: an *ingenious* device. —**ingeniously** *adverb.*

in·ge·nu·i·ty (in-jə-NOO-ə-tee or in-jə-NYOO-ə-tee) *noun.* Great skill in inventing things, making up reasons, planning or designing; cleverness. **ingenuities.**

in·gen·u·ous (in-JEN-yoo-əss) *adjective.* 1. Open; frank: The boy gave an *ingenuous* answer, without any excuses or lies. 2. Natural; innocent. —**ingenuously** *adverb.*

in·got (ING-gət) *noun.* A block of metal hardened in a mold.

ingots

in·gra·ti·ate (in-GRAY-shee-ayt) *verb.* To bring oneself into the good favor of another: Sally *ingratiated* herself with her friend's mother by praising her cooking. **ingratiated, ingratiating.** —**ingratiatingly** *adverb.*

in·grat·i·tude (in-GRAT-ə-tood) *noun.* The quality or act of not being thankful or grateful.

in·gre·di·ent (in-GREE-dee-ənt) *noun.* A part of a mixture: Sugar is the main *ingredient* in candy.

in·hab·it (in-HAB-it) *verb.* To live in (a particular place or residence). **inhabited, inhabiting.**

in·hab·i·tant (in-HAB-ə-tənt) *noun.* A person or animal that lives in a particular place; a resident.

in·ha·la·tor (IN-hə-lay-tər) *noun.* A machine or other device to help one breathe in air, vapor, or medicinal fumes.

in·hale (in-HAYL) *verb.* 1. To breathe in. *See* **exhale.** 2. To take something into the lungs, especially tobacco smoke. **inhaled, inhaling.**

in·her·ent (in-HIHR-ənt or in-HEHR-ənt) *adjective.* Belonging naturally to; existing as an inseparable part of: *inherent* good humor. —**inherently** *adverb.*

in·her·it (in-HEHR-it) *verb.* 1. To receive (property, money, or other goods) as an heir. 2. To get traits, features, characteristics (from one's ancestors): Harold *inherited* his red hair from his great-grandmother. **inherited, inheriting.**

in·her·it·ance (in-HEHR-ə-tənss) *noun.* 1. The act or right of inheriting. 2. Anything that is or may be inherited, such as property or traits. **inheritances.**

in·hu·man (in-HYOO-mən) *adjective.* 1. Without human feelings; cruel. 2. Not human: Two-headed monsters were *inhuman* creatures. —**inhumanly** *adverb.*

in·i·tial (ih-NISH-əl) *adjective.* At the beginning; first: the *initial* chapters of a book. —*noun.* The first letter of a word; the first letter of a proper name: The *initials* U.N. stand for United Nations. —*verb.* To write the initials of. **initialed, initialing.** —**initially** *adverb.*

in·i·ti·ate (ih-NISH-ee-ayt) *verb.* 1. To begin; start: The school will *initiate* a hot lunch program. 2. To introduce or teach the basics of a subject. 3. To admit a person into a club, organization, or society, often by a secret ceremony. —**initiated,**

initiating. —**initiation** (ih-nish-ee-AY-shən) *noun.*

in·ject (in-JEKT) *verb.* 1. To force (a fluid, such as a medicine) under the skin and into the bloodstream by use of a needle: The doctor *injected* the vaccine into my arm. 2. To insert unexpectedly: to *inject* a funny remark into a serious talk. **injected, injecting.**

in·jec·tion (in-JEK-shən) *noun.* 1. The act of injecting. 2. The fluid injected, especially medicine: I got an *injection* to prevent poison ivy.

injection velocity. The speed at which a satellite must move to stay in its selected orbit: The farther from earth the orbit, the slower the *injection velocity.*

in·jure (IN-jər) *verb.* To damage; to hurt, to harm: Alice *injured* her arm in the fall. **injured, injuring.**

in·ju·ri·ous (in-JUR-ee-əss) *adjective.* Harmful; causing damage or hurt; wrongful. —**injuriously** *adverb.*

in·ju·ry (IN-jə-ree) *noun.* Any kind of harm done to a person or thing; damage. **injuries.**

in·jus·tice (in-JUHSS-tiss) *noun.* 1. Act of being unfair. 2. Any unfair action; unfairness. **injustices.**

ink (INGK) *noun.* 1. A fluid used in writing, printing, or drawing. 2. A dark fluid given off by octopuses and other animals when protecting themselves. —*verb.* To cover with ink; to use ink. **inked, inking.**

in·laid (IN-layd) *adjective.* Placed into the surface of an object for decoration or as a part of a design.

in·let (IN-let) *noun.* 1. A narrow stream of water running between two islands or into a coastline; a small bay. 2. An entrance.

in·mate (IN-mayt) *noun.* 1. A person kept in a prison, sanitarium, or hospital. 2. A person who lives in the same house with others; an occupant. **inmates.**

inn (IN) *noun.* 1. A house or small hotel that has rooms and often food for travelers. 2. A restaurant; a tavern.

in·ner (IN-ər) *adjective.* 1. Inside; placed far in: an *inner* closet. 2. More secret or private than usual: *inner* thoughts and feelings.

in·ning (IN-ing) *noun.* 1. (Baseball) The time during which each team has a turn at bat: Each *inning* has six outs, three to a side. 2. In some other games the time during which one team or side has a chance to score; a turn.

in·no·cence (IN-ə-sənss) *noun.* 1. State of being free from guilt, evil, or wrong. 2. State of being natural, open, and sincere. 3. Lack of experience. —**innocent** *adjective.* —**innocently** *adverb.*

in·no·vation (in-ə-VAY-shən) *noun.* 1. Anything new or different from the ordinary. 2. The act of making changes, of introducing new or different things or ways.

in·nu·mer·a·ble (ih-NOO-mər-ə-bəl) *adjective.* Countless; very great in number: *innumerable* grains of sand.

in·oc·u·late (ih-NOK-yə-layt) *verb.* To inject (into a person or animal) germs that cause a mild form of a disease and prevent a serious case of the disease. **inoculated, inoculating.** —**inoculation** *noun.*

in·of·fen·sive (in-ə-FEN-siv) *adjective.* Harmless; not causing disapproval or dislike. —**inoffensively** *adverb.*

in·or·gan·ic (in-or-GAN-ik) *adjective.* Not coming from animal or vegetable life; mineral.

in·quire (in-KWIGHR) *verb.* (Used with *into, about, after*) To get information by asking questions. **inquired, inquiring.**

in·quir·y (in-KWIGHR-ee or IN-kwə-ree) *noun.* 1. A question: Did you answer her *inquiry?* 2. The act of inquiring; questioning. 3. Investigation; a search for information. **inquiries.**

in·quis·i·tive (in-KWIZ-ə-tiv) *adjective.* 1. Curious; eager to know. 2. Too curious; prying; nosy. —**inquisitively** *adverb.*

in·sane (in-SAYN) *adjective.* 1. Not sane; mentally ill; crazy. 2. Completely senseless; very foolish: an *insane* idea. —**insanely** *adverb.*

in·san·i·ty (in-SAN-ə-tee) *noun.* 1. The condition of being insane; mental illness; craziness. 2. Extreme foolishness. **insanities.**

in·sa·tia·ble (in-SAY-shə-bəl) *adjective.* Not able to be satisfied; greedy: *insatiable* hunger. —**insatiably** *adverb.*

in·scribe (in-SKRIGHB) *verb.* 1. To write or engrave (letters, words, numbers) upon a surface: My identification bracelet is *inscribed* with my name and address. 2. To write a brief message in a book, on a photograph, etc. 3. To make a lasting impression, especially on the mind: The scene of the accident was *inscribed* on her memory. **inscribed, inscribing.** —**inscription** (in-SKRIP-shən) *noun.*

inscribed circle. The largest circle that can be drawn within any regular polygon.

in·sect (IN-sekt) *noun.* 1. A small animal whose body is divided into three parts, with six legs and, usually, four wings. 2. Any small animal with similar features, such as a spider.

in·sec·ti·cide (in-SEK-tə-sighd) *noun.* A poisonous substance made to kill insects. **insecticides.**

in·sen·si·tive (in-SEN-sə-tiv) *adjective.* Having little or no feeling or concern: *insensitive* to another's feelings; *insensitive* to pain.

in·sep·a·ra·ble (in-SEP-ə-rə-bəl) *adjective.* Always together; unable to get or keep apart: Roy and Bob were *inseparable* friends until they were sent to different schools. —**inseparably** *adverb.*

in·sert (in-SERT) *verb.* Place in; set in; put among: *insert* a letter into an envelope. **inserted, inserting.** —(IN-sert) *noun.* Anything placed in or set in: The newspaper had an advertising *insert* today. —**insertion** (in-SER-shən) *noun.*

in·side (in-SIGHD or IN-sighd) *noun.* 1. The part within; the interior: the *inside* of a building. 2. The inner side: the *inside* of the arm. 3. (Plural) The stomach; the inner organs of the body: He laughed until his *insides* hurt. —(in-SIGHD) *adverb* and *preposition.* Within; in; on the inner side: come *inside; inside* the school. —(IN-sighd) *adjective.* 1. On the inside; interior. 2. Known to few; secret: *inside* information.

in·sight (IN-sight) *noun.* The power or ability to look into people, situations, and things and have a clear understanding of them.

in·sig·ni·a (in-SIG-nee-ə) *noun, plural.* Marks and signs, such as medals, badges, and ribbons, that indicate an office or an honor: Stars are the *insignia* of generals in the army. —**insigne** (in-SIG-nee) *singular.*

in·sig·nif·i·cant (in-sig-NIF-i-kənt) *adjective.* Of little or no meaning or importance. —**insignificance** *noun.* —**insignificantly** *adverb.*

in·sin·cere (in-sin-SIHR) *adjective.* False; not in earnest. —**insincerely** *adverb.*

in·sin·u·ate (in-SIN-yoo-ayt) *verb.* 1. To hint slyly; suggest in an indirect way. 2. To make one's way into a situation by roundabout means: Jane *insinuated* herself into the club by always hanging around. **insinuated, insinuating.** —**insinuation** (in-sin-yoo-AY-shən) *noun.*

in·sist (in-SIST) *verb.* To be firm about a demand, condition, or wish; refuse to give in: Miss Clark *insists* that we write in ink. **insisted, insisting.** —**insistence** *noun.* —**insistent** *adjective.* —**insistently** *adverb.*

in·so·lent (IN-sə-lənt) *adjective.* Disrespectful; insulting; very rude. —**insolently** *adverb.*

in·sol·u·ble (in-SOL-yə-bəl) *adjective.* 1. Not able to be dissolved: Marble is *insoluble* in water. 2. Not able to be solved; unexplainable.

in·spect (in-SPEKT) *verb.* To examine closely. **inspected, inspecting.** —**inspection** *noun.*

in·spec·tor (in-SPEK-tər) *noun.* 1. A person whose job is to examine (something): an elevator *inspector.* 2. A police officer ranking just below chief.

in·spi·ra·tion (in-spə-RAY-shən) *noun.* 1. Something that influences the mind or emotions, especially so as to motivate or reassure. 2. The state of being inspired. 3. A creative idea or attitude. 4. The act of breathing in. —**inspirational** *adjective.*

in·spire (in-SPIGHR) *verb.* 1. To enliven or influence, as the mind or the emotions: Emily was *inspired* by the poet's work. 2. To breathe in. **inspired, inspiring.**

in·stall (in-STAWL) *verb.* 1. To fix in place for use: Dad *installed* the washing machine in the basement. 2. To put officially into office or in a position: The mayor *installed* the new judge. **installed, installing.** —**installation** (in-stə-LAY-shən) *noun.*

in·stall·ment (in-STAWL-mənt) Also **instalment** *noun.* 1. One of many partial payments made to cover a debt: Two more *installments* of two dollars and my bike will be paid for. 2. Anything that is given out or displayed in parts: the second *installment* of a TV series.

in·stance (IN-stənss) *noun.* 1. A sample; illustration: Tom's outburst today was an *instance* of his bad temper. 2. One part or point in many parts or points: We checked all the doors of the building and in only one *instance* had the janitor failed to lock the door. **instances.** —**for instance.** For example.

in·stant (IN-stənt) *noun.* 1. A very short space of time. 2. The exact time: At the *instant* of 12 o'clock, the coach turned into a pumpkin. —*adjective.* 1. Happening right away: *instant* action. 2. Immediate; of pressing need. 3. Made or gotten ready immediately: *instant* coffee. —**instantly** *adverb.*

in·stan·ta·ne·ous (in-stən-TAY-nee-əss) *adjective.* Happening immediately: an *instantaneous* broadcast of the men landing on the moon. —**instantaneously** *adverb.*

instant replay. A showing of a taped TV recording of an event or action right after it has taken place.

in·stead (in-STED) *adverb.* As a replacement: We can't go skating, so let's go to the movies *instead.*

in·step (IN-step) *noun.* The arched part of the foot between the ankle and the toes.

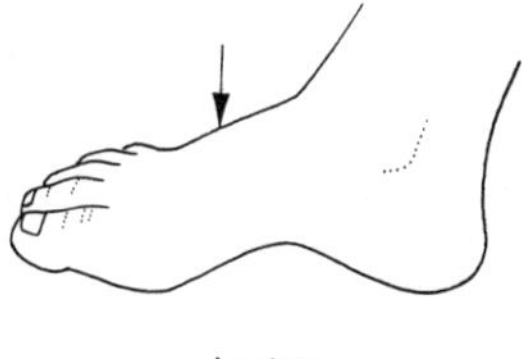
instep

in·sti·gate (IN-sti-gayt) *verb.* 1. To start (something): Mary *instigated* the surprise party for Jean. 2. To urge or spur on. **instigated, instigating.**

in·still (in-STIL) *verb.* To fill; infuse. **instilled, instilling.**

in·stinct (IN-stingkt) *noun.* 1. An inner force that moves one to action: *Instinct* guides animals to places where they can find food and water. 2. A natural inner trait: an artistic *instinct.*

in·stinc·tive (in-STINGK-tiv) *adjective.* Coming from a natural urge or force: My *instinctive* reaction was to duck when I saw the bird coming at me. —**instinctively** *adverb.*

in·sti·tu·tion (in-stə-TOO-shən or in-stə-TYOO-shən) *noun.* 1. The act of starting: *institution* of new rules. 2. Something done the same way many times: Having pancakes on Sunday is an *institution* in our family. 3. An organization set up for a particular purpose: a mental *institution.* —**institutional** *adjective.* —**institutionalize** *verb.*

in·struct (in-STRUHKT) *verb.* 1. To teach; cause to learn: Kathy *instructs* the first grade swimming class. 2. To guide, order, or direct. **instructed, instructing. —instructive** *adjective.* **—instructor** *noun.*

in·struc·tion (in-STRUHK-shən) *noun.* 1. Teaching: Maria has had dancing *instruction* since she was three years old. 2. (Plural) Directions: Tom followed Dad's *instructions* and was able to fix the flat tire.

in·stru·ment (IN-strə-mənt) *noun.* 1. A device used to do something: a musical *instrument,* a doctor's *instruments.* 2. Anything that is a means of doing (something): Good will among men is an *instrument* of peace. 3. A device used to measure or indicate (something): The gas gauge in a car is an *instrument* that shows how much fuel is left.

in·stru·men·tal (in-strə-MEN-tl) *adjective.* 1. Aiding the doing of (something): Ben Franklin's kite was *instrumental* in the discovery of some principles of electricity. 2. Of, for, or by musical instruments: The concert was *instrumental.* **—instrumentally** *adverb.*

in·suf·fi·cient (in-sə-FISH-ənt) *adjective.* Not enough: There was *insufficient* food. **—insufficiency** *noun.* **—insufficiently** *adverb.*

in·su·late (IN-sə-layt) *verb.* 1. To stop (heat, sound, or electricity) from going in or out of by covering with some material: Dad *insulated* the electric wire by wrapping it with tape. 2. To keep apart or alone. **insulated, insulating.**

in·su·la·tion (in-sə-LAY-shən) *noun.* A material that prevents the passage of heat, sound, or electricity.

in·su·lin (IN-sə-lən) *noun.* 1. A substance (hormone) made in the pancreas that regulates the level of sugar in the blood. 2. The same material from oxen or pigs used to treat diabetes in human beings.

in·sult (in-SUHLT) *verb.* To treat with meanness or contempt; be rude to. **insulted, insulting.** —(IN-suhlt) *noun.* A mean or rude act or remark.

in·sur·ance (in-SHUR-ənss) *noun.* 1. Protection against the results of some harm by means of a contract that is a promise to make up for loss or damage. 2. The amount that is promised for the damage or loss of what is insured.

in·sure (in-SHUR) Also (for meaning 2) **ensure** (en-SHUR) *verb.* 1. To make a contract that protects against loss or damage. 2. To make certain; guarantee: Ned wrote his name and address in the book to *insure* its return. **insured, insuring.**

in·sur·rec·tion (in-sə-REK-shən) *noun.* Rebellion against established powers.

in·tact (in-TAKT) *adjective.* 1. Whole; all together: The Monopoly game is *intact;* not one piece is missing. 2. Not damaged.

in·take (IN-tayk) *noun.* 1. An opening through which a liquid can enter a pipe or container. 2. The amount taken in. 3. The act of taking in.

in·tan·gi·ble (in-TAN-jə-bəl) *adjective.* 1. Not able to be heard, touched, smelled, or seen: A hug is tangible; love is *intangible.* 2. Not easily described or defined. **—intangibly** *adverb.*

in·te·ger (IN-tə-jər) *noun.* Any whole number, positive or negative, or zero; any number that is not a fraction.

in·te·grate (IN-tə-grayt) *verb.* 1. To bring together. 2. To form a whole. 3. To make available to all regardless of color or race. **integrated, integrating.**

in·te·gra·tion (in-tə-GRAY-shən) *noun.* 1. The act of bringing together or forming into a whole. 2. A system or situation in which all people have equal rights to the same facilities, such as housing and schools.

in·teg·ri·ty (in-TEG-rə-tee) *noun.* 1. Honor; honesty. 2. The state of being whole, complete, or sound.

in·tel·lect (IN-tə-lekt) *noun.* The ability to think and learn.

in·tel·lec·tu·al (in-tə-LEK-choo-əl) *adjective.* 1. Referring to the intellect. 2. Of importance to the mind rather than the emotions. 3. Possessing a great ability for thinking, learning, or knowing. —*noun.* One who has a great ability for thinking, reasoning, or knowing. —**intellectually** *adverb.*

in·tel·li·gence (in-TEL-ə-jənss) *noun.* 1. The ability to learn or understand, and to use what one has learned. 2. The ability to think and reason. 3. Information. 4. An organization that seeks and gathers information: Army *intelligence* reports that the truce has been broken. —**intelligent** *adjective.* —**intelligently** *adverb.*

in·tend (in-TEND) *verb.* 1. To mean, to plan: I did not *intend* to be late; I was delayed by traffic. 2. To have (a purpose) in mind. **intended, intending.** —**intent** (in-TENT) *noun.*

in·tense (in-TENSS) *adjective.* 1. Very great; severe: *intense* pain, *intense* cold. 2. Showing effort or strain: John always looks so *intense* when he studies. —**intensely** *adverb.*

in·ten·si·fy (in-TEN-sə-figh) *verb.* To increase to a great degree: The coldness of the day was *intensified* by a sharp wind. **intensified, intensifying.** —**intensification** (in-ten-sə-fi-KAY-shən) *noun.*

in·ten·si·ty (in-TEN-sə-tee) *noun.* 1. The state of being intense or severe: Mark could not hide the *intensity* of his anger. 2. The amount of strength, energy, or power (of something). **intensities.**

in·ten·sive (in-TEN-siv) *adjective.* Showing great effort; thorough: Ted gets good marks as a result of *intensive* study. —**intensively** *adverb.*

in·ten·tion (in-TEN-shən) *noun.* An idea, goal, or plan.

in·ten·tion·al (in-TEN-shən-l) *adjective.* Done knowingly; deliberate. —**intentionally** *adverb.*

inter- *prefix.* Indicates: 1. Between or in a group with: *inter*continental. 2. Jointly or together: *inter*lock.

in·ter (in-TER) *verb.* To bury. **interred, interring.**

in·ter·cede (in-tər-SEED) *verb.* 1. To speak for another; Pete asked me to *intercede* with Mother for her permission to go to the game. 2. To act as a judge or referee between: The teacher *interceded* when John and Bill began to argue. **interceded, interceding.**

in·ter·cept (in-tər-SEPT) *verb.* To stop or halt; cut off (the progress of): The policeman *intercepted* the robber at the bank door. **intercepted, intercepting.**

in·ter·change (IN-tər-CHAYNJ) *verb.* To place (one person, thing, or group) in the place of another. **interchanged, interchanging.** —*noun.* 1. A giving in return for something received: The *interchange* of ideas in class enabled the teacher to understand the students' problems. 2. An intersection of a highway that allows cars to move easily from one road to another. **interchanges.**

in·ter·change·a·ble (in-tər-CHAYN-jə-bəl) *adjective.* Able to change places with or to be used instead of something else: The words "disappear" and "vanish" are often *interchangeable.* —**interchangeably** *adverb.*

in·ter·com (IN-tər-kahm) *noun.* An electronic communications system for talking or signaling between different places.

in·ter·course (IN-tər-korss) *noun.* 1. Communication, as between people or countries. 2. Sexual relations.

in·ter·de·pen·dent (in-tər-di-PEN-dənt) *adjective.* Relying on one another. —**interdependently** *adverb.*

in·ter·est (IN-tər-ist) *noun.* 1. Concern or desire to know about: Dad has great *interest* in world affairs. 2. A share or part of: I have a 50-percent *interest* in the bike, since I paid half the cost. 3. (Often plural) Position, profit, or benefit: Bob is concerned only with his own *interests;* he never worries about anyone else. 4. The amount paid or earned as a fee for borrowing or lending money. —*verb.* To create concern or a desire to know about or participate: I wish I could *interest* you in skiing. **interested, interesting.**

in·ter·est·ing (IN-tər-iss-ting) *adjective.* Engaging the interest or attention: an *interesting* book. —**interestingly** *adverb.*

in·ter·fere (in-tər-FIHR) *verb.* 1. To be a block or snag: Dad says that watching TV *interferes* with my homework. 2. To mix in other people's business: Mildred, please don't *interfere* in this argument. 3. (Football) To block illegally an opposing player's attempt to catch a pass. **interfered, interfering.**

in·ter·fer·ence (in-tər-FIHR-ənss) *noun.* 1. The act of interfering. 2. Signals that jumble or distort radio and television broadcasts. 3. (Football) The protection by his teammates of the man carrying the ball. 4. (Football) Illegal blocking of a pass receiver. **interferences.**

in·te·ri·or (in-TIHR-ee-ər) *noun.* 1. Inner space, the inside. 2. The center part of a land area, as of an island, country, or continent. —*adjective.* 1. Located inside. 2. Removed from the edges or from the shore; inland.

in·ter·ject (in-tər-JEKT) *verb.* To put within or between: Freddie said, "May I *interject* a question?" **interjected, interjecting.**

in·ter·jec·tion (in-tər-JEK-shən) *noun.* 1. A cry or word spoken suddenly. 2. (Grammar) Words that are not part of a sentence, as *oh* or *hey.*

in·ter·lock (in-tər-LOK) *verb.* To join together tightly: The policemen *interlocked* arms to keep the crowd back. **interlocked, interlocking.**

in·ter·lude (IN-tər-lood) *noun.* 1. An event or space of time that comes between two major events: Summer vacation is a pleasant *interlude* between school terms. 2. A form of amusement between the acts of a play. 3. A short piece of music between longer pieces. **interludes.**

in·ter·me·di·ate (in-tər-MEE-dee-it) *adjective.* In a middle position; in between in time or distance: The *intermediate* years in many schools are the fourth, fifth and sixth grades. —**intermediately** *adverb.*

in·ter·mi·na·ble (in-TER-mə-nə-bəl) *adjective.* Endless; extremely long: The hike seemed *interminable* to the weary soldier. —**interminably** *adverb.*

in·ter·min·gle (in-tər-MING-gəl) *verb.* To mix together; blend. **intermingled, intermingling.**

in·ter·mis·sion (in-tər-MISH-ən) *noun.* A period of rest or inactivity between periods of activity: There was a 20-minute *intermission* between the halves of the game.

in·ter·mit·tent (in-tər-MIT-nt) *adjective.* Stopping and beginning again from time to time: The picnic was spoiled by *intermittent* rain showers. —**intermittently** *adverb.*

in·tern (IN-tərn) Also **interne** *noun.* An advanced student or graduate who works under supervision to advance in his chosen profession, especially in medicine. —*verb.* 1. To serve as an intern. 2. (in-TERN) To restrict or keep captive, as during time of war: The foreign scientist was *interned* until the end of the war. **interned, interning.**

in·ter·nal (in-TER-nl) *adjective.* 1. Related to the inside of the body: A stomach ache is an *internal* disorder. 2. Related to events or situations within a country: The American Civil War was an *internal* struggle. 3. Related to the inside of anything; inner. —**internally** *adverb.*

internal combustion. The burning of fuel within an engine to produce power.

internal wave. A wave deep down in the ocean, moving between two water masses of different temperature or density: An *internal wave* may have smashed the submarine *Thresher.*

in·ter·na·tion·al (in-tər-NASH-ən-l) *adjective.* Between or among nations: The six countries reached an *international* agreement on fishing rights. —**internationally** *adverb.*

in·ter·plan·e·tar·y (in-tər-PLAN-ə-tehr-ee) *adjective.* Between or among planets: Our space program involves *interplanetary* flights between Earth and Mars.

in·ter·pret (in-TER-prit) *verb.* 1. To explain or make clear: The teacher *interpreted* the difficult story for his students. 2. To translate: The guide for the American tourists *interpreted* the comments of the French shopkeeper. 3. To express an idea or feeling, as through music, dance, or art: The composer *interpreted* his joy in a beautiful song. **interpreted, interpreting.** —**interpreter** *noun.*

in·ter·pre·ta·tion (in-ter-prə-TAY-shən) *noun.* 1. An interpreting; making clear. 2. The expression of an idea or feeling, as through music, dance, or art.

in·ter·ra·cial (in-ter-RAY-shəl) *adjective.* Between or among different races. —**interracially** *adverb.*

in·ter·re·lat·ed (in-ter-ri-LAY-tid) *adjective.* Closely associated with one another: Smoke and fire are *interrelated.*

in·ter·ro·gate (in-TEHR-ə-gayt) *verb.* To question closely; examine. **interrogated, interrogating.**

in·ter·rog·a·tive (in-tə-ROG-ə-tiv) *adjective.* Asking a question: An *interrogative* sentence is one that asks a question. —*noun.* A word or sentence that asks a question: "Who" and "where" are *interrogatives.* —**interrogatively** *adverb.*

in·ter·rupt (in-tə-RUHPT) *verb.* 1. To cause a break or pause; to halt temporarily: The meeting was *interrupted* by a one-hour break for lunch. 2. To break in upon the speech or actions of another: It was rude of Ralph to *interrupt* our guest speaker. **interrupted, interrupting.**

in·ter·rup·tion (in-tə-RUHP-shən) *noun.* A break or halt in an activity: The fire drill caused a brief *interruption* of our class.

in·ter·sect (in-tər-SEKT) *verb.* 1. To cut across; divide: The new road *intersected* the golf course. 2. To cut across one another: A new traffic light was put in where the busy avenues *intersect.* **intersected, intersecting.**

in·ter·sec·tion (in-tər-SEK-shən) *noun.* 1. A place where two roads or other lines cross each other. 2. The process of intersecting.

in·ter·state (in-tər-STAYT) *adjective.* Between or among states. —*noun.* [Often capital I] A major highway running through several states.

in·ter·stel·lar (in-tər-STEL-ər) *adjective.* Between the stars: *Interstellar* space is not empty but contains a few molecules, atoms, charged particles, and dust.

in·ter·val (IN-tər-vəl) *noun.* 1. The time between two things or events: The planes left the airport at three-minute *intervals.* 2. The distance between objects or places: The lanterns were hung along the fence at *intervals* of 20 feet. 3. (Music) The difference in pitch between two notes or tones.

interstate highway

in·ter·ven·tion (in-tər-VEN-shən) *noun.* 1. An involvement; an attempt to help or offer assistance: The boy would have drowned except for the *intervention* of the lifeguard. 2. Interference in affairs of another nation or political group.

in·ter·view (IN-tər-vyoo) *noun.* 1. A meeting between persons for the purpose of obtaining information: During their *interview,* the mayor explained his plans to the newspaper reporter. 2. A writing or recording that contains the information gathered at an interview. —*verb.* To meet with someone for the purpose of obtaining information: The employer *interviewed* several people who applied for the new job. **interviewed, interviewing.**

in·tes·tine (in-TESS-tin) *noun.* (Usually plural) The lower tube-like section of the digestive canal, below the stomach; bowel. **intestines.**

in·ti·ma·cy (IN-tə-mə-see) *noun.* The state or condition of a close personal relationship; familiarity. **intimacies.**

[1]**in·ti·mate** (IN-tə-mit) *adjective.* 1. Very personal; private: Close friends share even their *intimate* secrets. 2. Very friendly; familiar: Joan and Barbara are *intimate* friends. —*noun.* A close personal friend. **intimates. —intimately** *adverb.*

[2]**in·ti·mate** (IN-tə-mayt) *verb.* To hint; suggest: Tim *intimated* that he wanted to leave the game early. **intimated, intimating.**

in·tim·i·date (in-TIM-ə-dayt) *verb.* To influence by threatening or frightening: The bully tried to *intimidate* the smaller boys. **intimidated, intimidating.**

in·to (IN-too) *preposition.* 1. Toward the inside of: The bee flew *into* the kitchen. 2. To the form or condition of: The tadpole turned *into* a frog. 3. Against: The car crashed *into* the stone wall.

in·tol·er·a·ble (in-TOL-ər-ə-bəl) *adjective.* Not to be endured or accepted; unbearable: The teacher found the outside noise *intolerable,* so she closed her door. **—intolerably** *adverb.*

in·tol·er·ance (in-TOL-ər-ənss) *noun.* 1. An unwillingness or inability to accept or consider the ideas or opinions of others. 2. The inability to adjust to or endure. **—intolerant** *adjective.* **—intolerantly** *adverb.*

in·tox·i·cate (in-TOK-sə-kayt) *verb.* 1. To make drunk: Too much liquor *intoxicates* people. 2. To make very excited or enthusiastic: The children were *intoxicated* by the delights of the circus. **intoxicated, intoxicating.**

in·tox·i·ca·tion (in-tok-sə-KAY-shən) *noun.* 1. Drunkenness. 2. Very great excitement or enthusiasm.

in·tra·ve·nous (in-trə-VEE-nəss) *adjective.* In or within a vein. **—intravenously** *adverb.*

in·trep·id (in-TREP-id) *adjective.* Fearless; courageous: The *intrepid* fireman ran into the burning building. **—intrepidly** *adverb.*

in·tri·cate (IN-trə-kit) *adjective.* 1. Very complicated: It took the students an hour to solve the *intricate* problem. 2. Having very many details or parts: The inside of a radio contains an *intricate* system of wires and other parts. **—intricately** *adverb.*

in·trigue (in-TREEG) *verb.* 1. To interest; greatly arouse the curiosity of: The child was *intrigued* by the music box. 2. To plot or plan secretly: The spies *intrigued* against the foreign government. **intrigued, intriguing.** —*noun.* (IN-treeg or in-TREEG) Secret plotting or planning. **intrigues.**

in·tro·duce (in-trə-DOOSS or in-trə-DYOOSS) *verb.* 1. To make known or acquaint, as one person to another: Sally *introduced* me to her cousin from Detroit. 2. To make (someone) aware of for the first time: Aunt Jane *introduced* Mother to a new way of making gravy. 3. Insert; include. 4. To begin; start off with: The minister *introduced* his sermon with a reading from the Bible. **introduced, introducing.**

in·tro·duc·tion (in-trə-DUHK-shən) *noun.* 1. An opening or beginning part of something; a preface: The *introduction* to the book followed the table of contents. 2. Act of being introduced: Martha was delighted by her *introduction* to my brother.

in·tro·duc·to·ry (in-trə-DUHK-tə-ree) *adjective.* Opening; beginning: The speaker's *introductory* remarks were funnier than what followed.

in·trude (in-TROOD) *verb.* To move or enter into without being invited or wanted: We were annoyed when our nosy neighbor *intruded* on our conversation. **intruded, intruding.**

in·tru·sion (in-TROO-zhən) *noun.* An intruding; an entering in where one is not welcome.

in·trust (in-TRUHST) Also **entrust** *verb.* To give over (to the care of); trust with: The woman *intrusted* her child to the care of a baby sitter. **intrusted, intrusting.**

in·un·date (IN-uhn-dayt) *verb.* To flood: The dam broke and water *inundated* the town. **inundated, inundating.** —**inundation** (in-uhn-DAY-shən) *noun.*

in·vade (in-VAYD) *verb.* 1. To enter into by force; take over: The army *invaded* the area west of the river. 2. To violate; interfere with: The campers did not want anyone to *invade* their privacy. **invaded, invading.**

[1]**in·va·lid** (IN-və-lid) *noun.* One who has a long-lasting illness.

[2]**in·val·id** (in-VAL-id) *adjective.* 1. Not legal. 2. False; incorrect.

in·val·u·a·ble (in-VAL-yoo-ə-bəl) *adjective.* Extremely valuable; beyond price: Our city's art museum owns several *invaluable* paintings. —**invaluably** *adverb.*

in·var·i·a·ble (in-VAIR-ee-ə-bəl) *adjective.* Never changing; always the same: Sally's *invariable* response to criticism is to cry. —**invariably** *adverb.*

in·va·sion (in-VAY-zhən) *noun.* 1. An entering with force; taking over: The army made an *invasion* of the enemy island. 2. Any intrusion or violation: Jack resented his sister's *invasion* of his room.

in·vent (in-VENT) *verb.* 1. To create or think up: Thomas Edison *invented* the phonograph. 2. To make up: Jim *invented* an excuse for being late. **invented, inventing.**

in·ven·tion (in-VEN-shən) *noun.* 1. The design and production of something new: The steamboat was an *invention* of the nineteenth century. 2. The ability to make up or produce something new: Ben Franklin was famous for his wisdom and *invention.* —**inventive** *adjective.* —**inventively** *adverb.*

in·ven·tor (in-VEN-tər) *noun.* A person who invents a new device.

in·ven·to·ry (IN-vən-tor-ee) *noun.* 1. A list of items on hand or in stock, as in a store or factory. 2. The items or stock on hand. **inventories.** —*verb.* To make a list of items that are on hand, **inventoried, inventorying.**

in·verse (in-VERSS or IN-verss) *adjective.* Reversed or opposite in value, position, or result: Snowfall and automobile traffic are in an *inverse* relationship; the more snow we have, the less traffic. —**inversely** *adverb.*

inverse operation. Any mathematical operation that is the reverse of another: Subtraction is the *inverse operation* of addition.

in·ver·sion (in-VER-zhən) *noun.* 1. Being in an inverse position or relationship. 2. A weather condition in which a high layer of warm air prevents air near the earth's surface from rising.

in·vert (in-VERT) *verb.* To reverse; turn upside down or backward: Tom *inverted* the hourglass after the sand had all run to the bottom. **inverted, inverting.**

in·ver·te·brate (in-VER-tə-brit or in-VER-tə-brayt) *noun.* An animal that does not have a backbone: A jellyfish is an *invertebrate.* **invertebrates.** *—adjective.* Without a backbone.

in·vest (in-VEST) *verb.* 1. To use (money) in order to earn a profit: Uncle James *invested* money in the new clothing company. 2. To give power or authority to: The company's new manager was *invested* with the power to hire and fire employees. **invested, investing.**

in·ves·ti·gate (in-VESS-tə-gayt) *verb.* To look into or examine closely: The police thoroughly *investigated* the bank robbery. **investigated, investigating. —investigation** *noun.*

in·ves·ti·ga·tor (in-VESS-tə-gay-tər) *noun.* A person who investigates.

in·vest·ment (in-VEST-mənt) *noun.* Use of money to earn a profit or the amount used for that purpose.

in·ves·tor (in-VESS-tər) *noun.* A person who invests.

in·vig·or·ate (in-VIG-ə-rayt) *verb.* To fill with liveliness or energy: The good food and fresh air *invigorated* the campers. **invigorated, invigorating.**

in·vin·ci·ble (in-VIN-sə-bəl) *adjective.* Not able to be overcome; unbeatable: The general thought his troops were *invincible* until they lost the battle. **—invincibly** *adverb.*

in·vis·i·ble (in-VIZ-ə-bəl) *adjective.* Not able to be seen; not visible: At night the man's black coat made him nearly *invisible.* **—invisibly** *adverb.*

in·vi·ta·tion (in-və-TAY-shən) *noun.* 1. A request to come to a place or to attend some event. 2. An attraction; lure: The feast presented an *invitation* to overeat.

in·vite (in-VIGHT) *verb.* 1. To request someone's presence at a place or event. 2. To lure. **invited, inviting.**

in·vit·ing (in-VIGHT-ing) *adjective.* Attractive; tempting: The cool pond looked *inviting.* **—invitingly** *adverb.*

in·voke (in-VOHK) *verb.* 1. To call on (a divine higher being) for help: The soldiers *invoked* God's help for a victory. 2. To point to as justification for. 3. To enforce (a law or regulation). 4. To call forth by spells or magic. **invoked, invoking.**

in·vol·un·tar·y (in-VOL-ən-tehr-ee) *adjective.* 1. Required; without choice: Their work was *involuntary* and therefore poor. 2. Not usually controlled by the will: Breathing is *involuntary.* **—involuntarily** *adverb.*

involuntary muscle. A muscle not controlled by will: *Involuntary muscles* control the alimentary canal and blood vessels.

in·volve (in-VOLV) *verb.* 1. To include: Baking *involves* measuring, mixing, and cooking. 2. To draw into a situation. 3. To occupy or absorb. **involved, involving.**

i·o·dine (IGH-ə-dighn or IGH-ə-din) *noun.* 1. An element of a gray-black color, often used in medicine. 2. A mixture of iodine and alcohol used to kill germs.

i·on (IGH-ən) *noun.* An electrified atom or molecule that has lost or gained electrons.

i·on·o·sphere (igh-ON-ə-sfihr) *noun.* The ionized or electrically conducting outer layers of the earth's atmosphere.

IOU (igh-oh-yoo) *noun.* (Informal) A written promise to repay (I owe you): I gave my brother an *IOU* for the dime I borrowed. —**IOU's** or **IOUs** *plural.*

I·o·wa (IGH-ə-wə) *noun.* A state in north central United States, 29th to join the Union in 1846. —**Ia.** *abbreviation.* Also **IA** for Zip Codes.

Iowa
★capital: Des Moines

i·rate (IGH-rayt or igh-RAYT) *adjective.* Very angry. —**irately** *adverb.*

i·ris (IGH-riss) *noun.* 1. A plant with decorative flowers that come in a variety of colors. 2. The colored part of the eye around the pupil.

irk (ERK) *verb.* To irritate or annoy. **irked, irking.**

irk·some (ERK-səm) *adjective.* Tedious or annoying. —**irksomely** *adverb.*

i·ron (IGH-ərn) *noun.* 1. A common, hard metal used in making steel, tools, machinery, and other things. 2. An appliance used to press clothes by hand. 3. (Plural) Chains or shackles. 4. A device made of iron or another hard metal, usually heated until very hot and used for such things as branding animals and curling hair. —*verb.* To press with an iron. **ironed, ironing.**

i·ro·ny (IGH-rə-nee) *noun.* 1. The use of words in speech or writing to express the opposite of what has actually been said: "Just what I wanted," said Joe with *irony,* as he unwrapped the doll. 2. The difference between what has happened and might be expected to happen: It was an *irony* that the happy occasion had an unhappy ending. **ironies.** —**ironic** (igh-RON-ik) *adjective.* —**ironically** *adverb.*

ir·ra·di·ate (ih-RAY-dee-ayt) *verb.* 1. To throw light on. 2. To treat with or expose to radiation. **irradiated, irradiating.**

ir·reg·u·lar (ih-REG-yə-lər) *adjective.* 1. Not in the usual order or way. 2. Not according to rule. 3. Varying from time to time. 4. Not straight or even: The hemline was *irregular.* —**irregularly** *adverb.* —**irregularity** (ih-reg-yə-LAR-ə-tee) *noun.*

irregular verb. A verb that does not form its past tense and past participle by adding *ed:* "Go" is an *irregular verb.*

ir·re·sis·ti·ble (ihr-i-ZISS-tə-bəl) *adjective.* Impossible to resist. —**irresistibly** *adverb.*

ir·re·spon·si·ble (ihr-i-SPON-sə-bəl) *adjective.* Lacking care or responsibility. —**irresponsibly** *adverb.*

ir·rev·er·ent (ih-REV-ər-ənt) *adjective.* Having or showing no reverence or respect: an *irreverent* act. —**irreverently** *adverb.* —**irreverence** *noun.*

ir·ri·gate (IHR-ə-gayt) *verb.* 1. To supply (land) with water either by using a system of canals, ditches, or pipes, or by sprinkling. 2. To wash out with water or medicine: *irrigate* a cut. **irrigated, irrigating.** —**irrigation** (ihr-i-GAY-shən) *noun.*

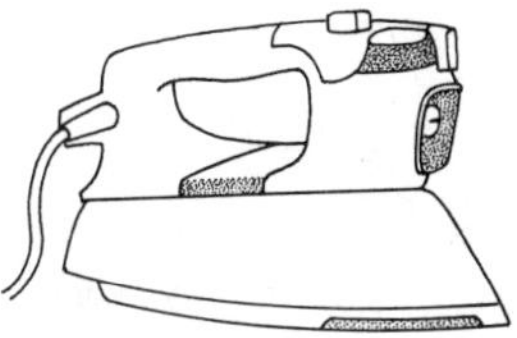

iron

ir·ri·ta·ble (IHR-ə-tə-bəl) *adjective.* 1. Easily annoyed or angered. 2. Unusually sensitive: *irritable* skin. —**irritably** *adverb.*

ir·ri·tate (IHR-ə-tayt) *verb.* 1. To annoy or anger: Phil *irritates* Mother by slamming doors. 2. To make sore. **irritated, irritating.** —**irritation** (ihr-ə-TAY-shən) *noun.*

is (IZ) *verb. See* **be.**

-ish suffix. Indicates: 1. Nationality: Turk*ish.* 2. Likeness to: mann*ish.* 3. Somewhat: brown*ish.*

Is·lam (ISS-ləm) *noun.* The religion of the Moslems.

is·land (IGH-lənd) *noun.* 1. A body of land, smaller than a continent, surrounded by water. 2. Anything that suggests an island: An *island* in the street separates lanes of traffic.

island

isle (IGHL) *noun.* An island, usually a small one. **isles.**

is·n't (IZ-nt) *contraction* A shortened form of the words *is not.*

i·so·bar (IGH-sə-bahr) *noun.* A line on a map connecting points that are equal in pressure: *Isobars* on the weather map separate areas with different barometric pressures.

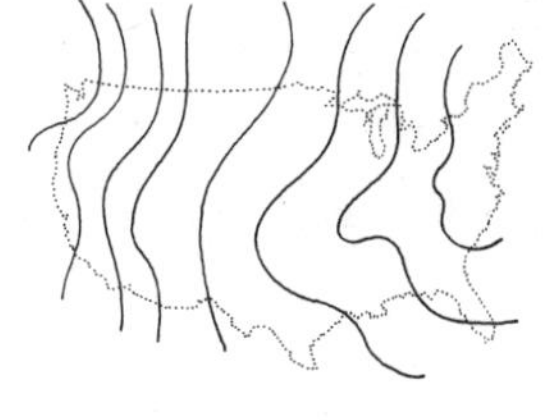

isobars

i·so·late (IGH-sə-layt) *verb.* To separate or keep apart: The people on the island were *isolated* from the mainland. **isolated, isolating.**

i·so·la·tion (igh-sə-LAY-shən) *noun.* Being isolated or separated: They enjoyed the *isolation* created by the heavy snows.

i·sos·ce·les (igh-soss-ə-leez) *adjective.* (Geometry) Describing a triangle that has two equal sides and two equal angles.

is·sue (ISH-oo) *noun.* 1. A single edition of a publication: the June *issue* of a magazine. 2. The point of a discussion or argument: The *issue* was whether Jane would be allowed to wear make-up. 3. A problem of public interest: The *issue* of welfare was widely debated by the voters. 4. Children or descendants. **issues.** —*verb.* 1. To publish: They *issued* the magazine monthly. 2. To come or go out: Steam *issues* from the kettle. **issued, issuing. —take issue.** To disagree.

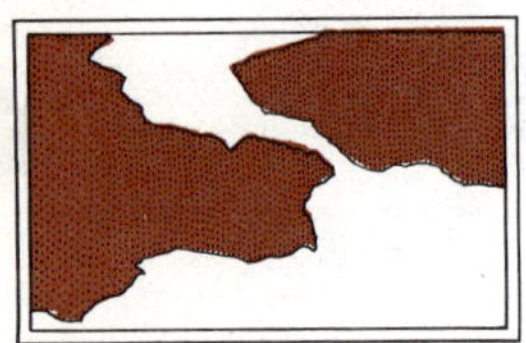

isthmus

isth·mus (ISS-məss) *noun.* A narrow strip of land connecting two larger bodies of land: The *Isthmus* of Panama connects North and South America. —**isthmuses** or **isthmi** (ISS-migh) *plural.*

it *pronoun.* 1. An animal, place, or thing previously named or indicated: The floor is splashed with water and *it* is wet. 2. An addition used to complete or fill out a sentence: *It* is sunny. 3. (Informal) Used to stand for something considered perfect: That swim was really *it!*

i·tal·ic (ih-TAL-ik or igh-TAL-ik) *adjective.* Printed in a type that slants to the right, used to set off a word or phrase for a particular reason: *This is italic type.*

i·tal·i·cize (ih-TAL-ə-sighz) *verb.* To print in italic type: Writers *italicize* words or phrases to give them emphasis or set them apart. **italicized, italicizing.**

itch (ICH) *noun.* 1. A prickling sensation of the skin that makes one want to scratch. 2. Any of various skin diseases that make one want to scratch. 3. A restless urge or feeling: Bill had an *itch* to do something exciting. **itches.** —*verb.* 1. To feel or cause a need to scratch: Sue's arms *itch* from poison ivy. 2. To feel a restless urge or desire: Tom *itched* to be on vacation. **itched, itching.**

i·tem (IGH-təm) *noun.* 1. A separate article or thing: Shoes, a dress, and a warm coat were *items* Sue needed to go to school. 2. A short piece of news: an *item* in the paper.

i·tem·ize (IGH-tə-mighz) *verb.* To set down in a list item by item: Father *itemizes* his expenses when he's on a business trip. **itemized, itemizing.**

it'll (IT-l) *contraction.* A shortened form of the words *it will* or *it shall.*

its *pronoun.* Belonging to it.

it's *contraction.* A shortened form of the words *it is* or *it has.*

it·self (it-SELF) *pronoun.* A form of *it* used: 1. For emphasis: The view *itself* is worth the climb. 2. When the object of a verb is the same as the subject: The dog scratches *itself.*

-ity *suffix.* Indicates state, quality, or amount: humid*ity;* fluid*ity.*

-ium *suffix.* (Chemistry) Used to form the names of elements: uran*ium.*

I've (IGHV) *contraction.* A shortened form of the words *I have.*

-ive *suffix.* Indicates: performing; tending to: declarat*ive;* sedat*ive.*

i·vo·ry (IGH-və-ree or IGHV-ree) *noun.* 1. The hard, whitish substance forming the tusks of elephants and some other animals such as the walrus. 2. (Also *adjective*) A yellowish white.

i·vy (IGH-vee) *noun.* A climbing green vine; also one that spreads out over the ground.

-ize *suffix.* Indicates: 1. To make or become: italic*ize.* 2. To make like: revolution*ize.* 3. To treat or think of as: glamor*ize.* 4. To make subject to: hypnot*ize.* 5. To change: sensit*ize.*

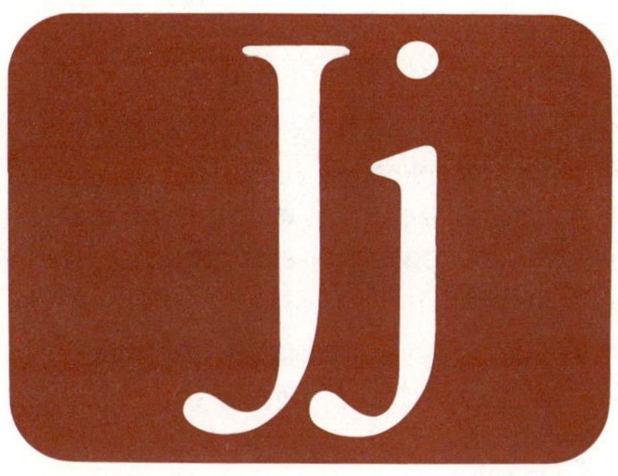

J, j (JAY) *noun.* The tenth letter in the English alphabet.

jab *verb.* To poke or stab. **jabbed, jabbing.** —*noun.* A quick poke.

jab·ber (JAB-ər) *verb.* 1. To talk rapidly; to chatter. 2. To make sounds with no meaning. **jabbered, jabbering.** —*noun.* Idle talk.

jack (JAK) *noun.* 1. A device used to lift up or push: We used a *jack* to lift the car. 2. A picture playing card between the ten and queen. 3. (Plural) A game played with a small ball and six-pointed metal pieces. 4. A jackstone, the metal piece used in playing the game of jacks. 5. A plug for electrical connections. —*verb.* To raise by using a lever or jack. **jacked, jacking.**

jack·al (JAK-əl or JAK-awl) *noun.* A doglike wild animal.

jack·ass (JAK-ass) *noun.* 1. A male donkey. 2. A fool. **jackasses.**

jack·et (JAK-it) *noun.* 1. A short coat. 2. Any protective covering: She cooked the potatoes in their *jackets.*

jack-in-the-box (JAK-in-thə-boks) *noun.* A toy in which a puppet springs out of a box when the lid is opened. —**jack-in-the-boxes** or **jacks-in-the-box** *plural.*

jack·knife (JAK-nighf) *noun.* 1. A folding knife carried in the pocket. 2. A dive in which the diver touches his feet with his hands and straightens out before entering the water. **jackknives.** —*verb.* To fold like a jackknife: The trailer-truck *jackknifed.* **jackknifed, jackknifing.**

jack-of-all-trades (jak-əv-AWL-traydz) *noun.* One who can do many kinds of jobs. **jacks-of-all-trades.**

jack-o'-lan·tern (JAK-ə-lan-tərn) *noun.* A Halloween lantern made by scooping out a pumpkin and carving a face into the shell.

jack·pot (JAK-pot) *noun.* 1. The first prize or reward. 2. All of the money bet in a game of chance. —**hit the jackpot.** (Informal) To have great success or luck.

jack rabbit. A large hare of western North America having long, strong hind legs and long ears.

jade (JAYD) *noun.* 1. A hard, pale green or white gemstone. 2. (Also *adjective*). A pale green color.

jag·ged (JAG-id) *adjective.* Rough; having sharp points.

jag·uar (JAG-wahr or JAG-yoo-ahr) *noun.* A large wildcat found in the jungles of South America.

jail (JAYL) *noun.* A prison; a building in which persons who have broken the law are locked up. —*verb.* To put in prison. **jailed, jailing.**

jail·er (JAYL-ər) Also **jailor** *noun.* The person in charge of a jail or prison.

ja·lop·y (jə-LOP-ee) Also **jaloppy** *noun.* (Informal) A beaten-up old car, truck, or airplane. **jalopies.**

jam *noun.* 1. A sweet, sticky spread made by cooking fruit and sugar. 2. Many things crowded close together: We were caught in a traffic *jam.* 3. Any bad situation. —*verb.* 1. To squeeze or push: *jam* onto the train. 2. To injure by squeezing or crushing. 3. To use or push suddenly: He *jammed* on the brakes. 4. To be put out of action by a sticking part: The gun *jammed* and he could not use it. 5. To keep a radio signal from being heard by broadcasting on the same wavelength. **jammed, jamming.** —**jam session.** A group of jazz musicians playing together informally.

jack-o'-lantern

jack rabbit

jaguar

jamb (JAM) *noun.* The up-and-down parts of a door or window frame.

jam·bo·ree (jam-bə-REE) *noun.* 1. A celebration. 2. A large gathering of people: Boy Scouts from many countries came to the *jamboree.* **jamborees.**

jan·gle (JANG-gəl) *noun.* 1. An unpleasant noise. 2. The sound of pieces of metal striking together. **jangles.** —*verb.* 1. To make such a sound. 2. To annoy. **jangled, jangling.**

jan·i·tor (JAN-ə-tər) *noun.* A person who cleans and takes care of a large building.

Jan·u·ar·y (JAN-yoo-ehr-ee) *noun.* The first month of the year: There are 31 days in *January.* —**Jan.** *abbreviation.*

jar (JAHR) *noun.* 1. A container made of glass or pottery. 2. The amount such a container holds: We ate three *jars* of pickles. 3. A sudden shake or jolt: The earthquake gave us quite a *jar.* 4. A harsh sound. —*verb.* 1. To shake up. 2. To make a harsh noise. **jarred, jarring.**

jar·gon (JAHR-gən) *noun.* 1. The special words and expressions used by people who have a common interest: The *jargon* of scientists is full of technical words. 2. A mixture of languages. 3. Any talk that is hard to understand; slang.

jaunt (JAWNT or JAHNT) *noun.* A short pleasure trip. —*verb.* To make such a trip. **jaunted, jaunting.**

jaun·ty (JAWN-tee or JAHN-tee) *adjective.* Gay, carefree. **jauntier, jauntiest.** —**jauntily** *adverb.*

jave·lin (JAV-lən or JAV-ə-lən) *noun.* 1. A lightweight spear, formerly used as a weapon. 2. A wooden spear thrown at field meets.

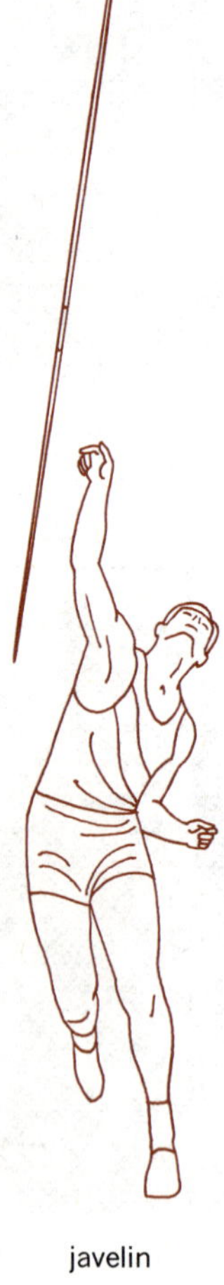
javelin

jaw *noun.* 1. Either of the two bony structures that form the mouth, hold the teeth, and open and close, as in talking and eating. 2. Something that performs a closing or grasping function: the *jaws* of a trap. —*verb.* (Slang) To talk or chat at length. **jawed, jawing.**

jay *noun.* A brightly colored bird related to the crow but smaller in size: a blue *jay.*

jay·walk (JAY-wawk) *verb.* To walk in the street without regard for traffic rules. **jaywalked, jaywalking.** —**jaywalker** *noun.*

jazz (JAZ) *noun.* 1. A kind of popular music first played by black musicians in the South: "If you have to ask what *jazz* is, you'll never know." (Louis Armstrong). 2. (Slang) Bragging talk.

jealous (JEL-əss) *adjective.* 1. Wanting all of another's love and attention: The *jealous* child watched his mother care for the new baby. 2. Unhappy over another's success or wealth: The losers were *jealous* when the prizes were presented. 3. Careful; watchful: He kept a *jealous* eye on his box of candy. —**jealously** *adverb.*

jeal·ous·y (JEL-əss-ee) *noun.* 1. A desire to have all the love and attention of another. 2. Envy; wanting what another has. **jealousies.**

jeans (JEENZ) *noun, plural.* Pants or overalls made of heavy cotton material, usually blue.

jeep *noun.* A small, sturdy car used in rough country: World War II soldiers gave the nickname *jeep* to their General Purpose (GP) vehicles.

jeer (JIHR) *verb.* 1. To make fun in a cruel way. 2. To shout unpleasant remarks. **jeered, jeering.** —*noun.* An unpleasant remark or shout.

jell (JEL) *verb.* 1. To change from a liquid into a soft solid: The dessert will *jell* as it cools. 2. (Informal) To take shape: Our plans for the evening have not yet *jelled.* **jelled, jelling.**

Jell-O (JEL-oh) *trademark.* A fruit-flavored gelatin used for salads and desserts.

jel·ly (JEL-ee) *noun.* 1. A sweet substance, soft but firm, usually made from fruit juice and sugar. 2. Any substance that is like jelly. **jellies.** *—verb.* To form or make into jelly. **jellied, jellying.**

jel·ly·fish (JEL-ee-fish) *noun.* 1. A sea animal with a soft bell-shaped body. 2. (Informal) A weak person. —**jellyfish** or **jellyfishes** *plural.*

jeop·ard·ize (JEP-ər-dighz) *verb.* To risk; put in danger. **jeopardized, jeopardizing.**

jeop·ard·y (JEP-ər-dee) *noun.* 1. Danger. 2. (Law) The chance that a person on trial will be found guilty. **jeopardies.**

jerk *verb.* 1. To move or be moved by a sudden motion: The dog *jerked* the rope from my hand. 2. To preserve (meat) by drying. **jerked, jerking.** *—noun.* 1. A jolt: The train stopped with a *jerk.* 2. A twitch. 3. (Slang) An annoying person.

jerk·y (JER-kee) *adjective.* Bumpy; full of jolts. **jerkier, jerkiest.** —**jerkily** *adverb.*

jer·sey (JER-zee) *noun.* 1. A soft knitted material often used for clothing. 2. A shirt made of such material. 3. [Capital J] A kind of dairy cattle.

jest *noun.* A joke, prank, or amusing remark. *—verb.* To make a joke or play a prank. **jested, jesting.**

jest·er (JESS-tər) *noun.* A clown.

jet *noun.* 1. A stream of liquid or gas forced through a small opening: A *jet* of water squirted from the drinking fountain. 2. The hole through which the liquid or gas moves. 3. An engine that moves forward as a reaction to heated gases escaping from the rear end. 4. An aircraft powered by a jet engine. 5. (Also *adjective*) A shiny black color. *—verb.* 1. To shoot forth 2. To travel by jet aircraft. **jetted, jetting.**

jet·port (JET-port) *noun.* An airfield from which jet aircraft operate.

jet·sam (JET-səm) *noun.* Things that are thrown overboard to lighten the load of a ship in trouble.

jet stream. A swift current of air found at high altitudes.

jet·ti·son (JET-i-sən) *verb.* To discard or throw out: The crew of the sinking ship *jettisoned* the cargo. **jettisoned, jettisoning.**

jet·ty (JET-ee) *noun.* 1. A structure built out into the water to protect a harbor, channel, or shoreline. 2. A wharf or pier. **jetties.**

Jew (JOO) *noun.* 1. A descendent of the ancient Hebrews. 2. A person whose religion is Judaism.

jew·el (JOO-əl) *noun.* 1. A gem; a valuable stone such as a ruby or diamond. 2. A piece of jewelry set with valuable stones. 3. A real or man-made stone used to replace a metal part in the works of a watch. 4. Anyone who is highly regarded.

jew·el·er (JOO-ə-lər) *noun.* A person who sells, makes, or repairs jewelry.

jew·el·ry (JOO-əl-ree or JOOL-ree) *noun.* 1. A collection of precious gems. 2. Adornments such as necklaces, bracelets, or earrings.

jib *noun.* A three-cornered sail set forward of the mast.

jibe (JIGHB) *verb.* 1. To shift the forward sail from one side to the other. 2. To agree. **jibed, jibing.**

jif·fy (JIF-ee) *noun.* An instant. —**in a jiffy.** In no time; right away.

jig *noun.* 1. A lively dance. 2. The music for such a dance. 3. A device to hold work and guide a cutting tool. *—verb.* To dance or play a jig. **jigged, jigging.** —**the jig is up.** That's the end of that.

jig·ger (JIG-ər) *noun.* A small measure for liquor.

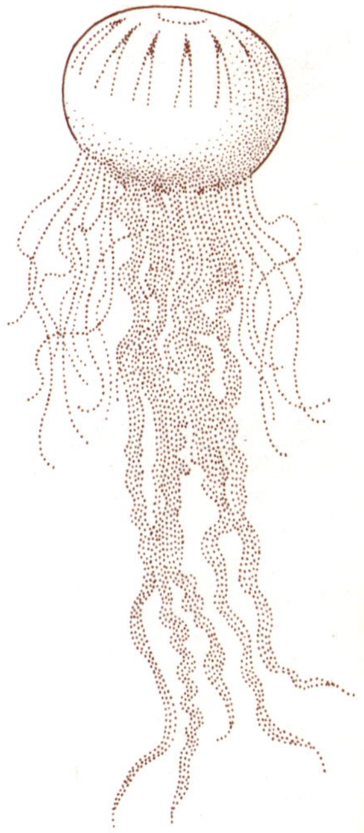

jellyfish

jigsaw puzzle

jockeys

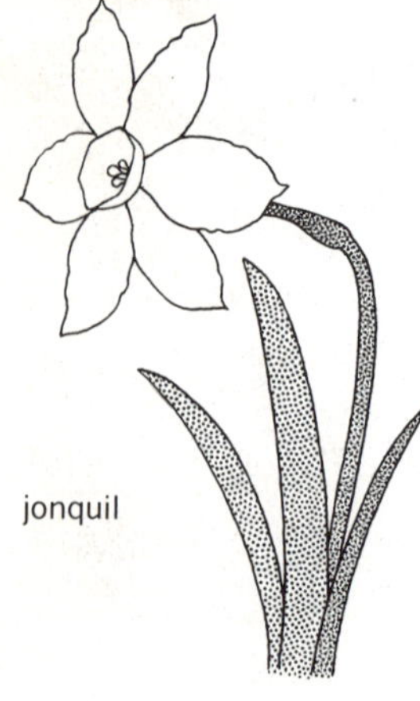
jonquil

jig·gle (JIG-əl) *verb.* To move loosely up and down: The pictures on the wall *jiggle* when the train goes by. **jiggled, jiggling.** —*noun.* A slight movement. **jiggles.**

jig·saw (JIG-saw) *noun.* A saw with a narrow vertical blade used to cut out curved or oddly shaped pieces.

jigsaw puzzle. A puzzle completed by fitting together a picture that has been cut into uneven and differently shaped pieces.

jin·gle (JING-gəl) *noun.* 1. A simple poem or short song. 2. The sound made by pieces of metal striking together. **jingles.** —*verb.* To make a tinkling sound. **jingled, jingling.**

jit·ters (JIT-ərz) *noun, plural.* A nervous feeling.

jit·ter·y (JIT-ər-ee) *adjective.* Nervous.

job *noun.* 1. Any activity which requires work. 2. Regular work for which one is paid. 3. A separate unit or definite amount of work: The piano tuner is paid by the *job,* not by the hour. —**on the job.** Wide-awake; alert.

jock·ey (JOK-ee) *noun.* One who rides race horses. —*verb.* 1. To ride a race horse. 2. To try to get into a good position: The boys *jockeyed* for the best position in the race. **jockeyed, jockeying.**

jog *verb.* 1. To move at a slow steady trot. 2. To arouse or give a slight push: Let me *jog* your memory. 3. To turn or bend: The road *jogs* to the right. **jogged, jogging.** —*noun.* 1. A steady trot. 2. A bend or turn. 3. A slight push.

jog·ging (JOG-ing) *noun.* A popular form of exercise in which a person trots each day to keep fit.

jog·gle (JOG-əl) *verb.* To bounce or shake; to jiggle. **joggled, joggling.**

join *verb.* 1. To connect or bring together: *join* two ropes. 2. To become a member. 3. To unite; come together. **joined, joining.**

joint *noun.* 1. The joining of two bones, especially where movement occurs, as the elbow *joint,* the knee *joint.* 2. The starting point of new growth in a plant, as where a branch joins the trunk. 3. The place where two parts are joined to form a unit, as a *joint* in a sink pipe. 4. (Slang) A marijuana cigarette. 5. (Informal) A hangout; an ordinary public restaurant or bar. —*adjective.* 1. Combined; together: The fifth and sixth grades will have a *joint* cake sale. 2. Shared; presented, owned, or used as if by one: *joint* bank account. —**jointly** *adverb.*

joist *noun.* A wooden, iron, or steel beam used to support flooring in a building or the laths in a ceiling.

joke (JOHK) *noun.* 1. Something written, said, or done to make people laugh. 2. A person or thing that is laughed at. **jokes.** —*verb.* To say or do things that are meant to be funny. **joked, joking.**

jok·er (JOHK-ər) *noun.* 1. A person who jokes and fools around. 2. An extra playing card used in some games.

jol·ly (JOL-ee) *adjective.* Happy; gay; joyous. **jollier, jolliest.**

jolt (JOHLT) *verb.* To shake (someone or something) suddenly; jerk. **jolted, jolting.** —*noun.* A sudden shake; a jerk; a shock: a *jolt* of electricity.

jon·quil (JONG-kwil) *noun.* A yellow or white flower that looks like a daffodil; a type of narcissus.

jos·tle (JOSS-l) *verb.* To move or push aside in a clumsy or rude way. **jostled, jostling.** —*noun.* The act of jostling or being jostled.

jot *noun.* A very small part of anything; a little bit: It's not worth a *jot.* —*verb.* To make a note of; write down quickly: Please *jot* down the number. **jotted, jotting.**

jounce (JOWNSS) *verb.* To bounce or jolt; move up and down. **jounced, jouncing.** —*noun.* An up-and-down movement; a bounce. **jounces.**

jour·nal (JER-nl) *noun.* 1. A daily record of events, conditions, or observations and ideas; a diary. 2. A newspaper or magazine.

jour·nal·ism (JER-nl-iz-əm) *noun.* The writing, editing, and operating of newspapers and magazines.

jour·nal·ist (JER-nl-ist) *noun.* One who writes or edits newspapers.

jour·ney (JER-nee) *noun.* A trip. —*verb.* To make a trip; travel. **journeyed, journeying.**

jo·vi·al (JOH-vee-əl) *adjective.* Joyous; merry. —**jovially** *adverb.*

joy (JOI) *noun.* 1. A feeling of great pleasure; happiness. 2. Whatever causes great pleasure.

joy·ful (JOI-fəl) *adjective.* 1. Full of joy or happy feeling: a *joyful* group. 2. Showing happiness and pleasure: a *joyful* look. 3. Able to cause joy: a *joyful* day. —**joyfully** *adverb.*

joy·ous (JOI-əss) *adjective.* Full of joy; joyful. —**joyously** *adverb.*

jr. Also **Jr.** *abbreviation.* Junior.

ju·bi·lant (JOO-bə-lənt) *adjective.* Feeling or showing great joy; filled with gladness. —**jubilantly** *adverb.*

ju·bi·lee (JOO-bə-lee or joo-bə-LEE) *noun.* 1. A special anniversary celebration, particularly for the 50th or 25th anniversary. 2. Celebration and rejoicing. **jubilees.**

Ju·da·ism (JOO-dee-iz-əm) *noun.* A religion started by the ancient Hebrews whose history and beliefs are recorded in the Old Testament.

judge (JUHJ) *noun.* 1. A legal officer in charge of a court; the person who decides points of law and justice. 2. A person who decides who wins in a contest, race, or other competition. 3. A person who is well qualified to evaluate: a good *judge* of men. —*verb.* 1. To decide guilt, innocence, or responsibility in a court of law. 2. To decide who the winner is in a contest or other competition. 3. To form an opinion. **judged, judging.**

judg·ment (JUHJ-mənt) Also **judgement** *noun.* 1. The act of judging. 2. A decision, as of a court case, contest, or race. 3. The talent or ability to decide or evaluate. 4. An opinion; a measure: He made a quick *judgment.*

ju·di·cial (joo-DISH-əl) *adjective.* 1. Of or about courts and the judgments of courts; of or about justice: a *judicial* decree. 2. Like a judge; fair. —**judicially** *adverb.*

ju·di·cious (joo-DISH-əss) *adjective.* Showing good judgment; thoughtful or sensible. —**judiciously** *adverb.*

ju·do (JOO-doh) *noun.* A type of Japanese wrestling that is a form of jujitsu. *See* **jujitsu.**

jug (JUHG) *noun.* A container with a handle and a spout or small opening, used for liquids.

jug·gle (JUHG-əl) *verb.* 1. To do tricks, as with balls, rings, or knives; by keeping various objects moving in the air at the same time. 2. To change or alter (records) so as to deceive: The treasurer *juggled* the club's books to hide the fact that he was using the money for himself. **juggled, juggling.** —**juggler** *noun.*

jug·u·lar (JUHG-yə-lər) *adjective.* Having to do with the throat or neck. —*noun.* One of the large veins in the neck.

juice (JOOSS) *noun.* 1. The liquid part of fruits, vegetables, or animals: orange *juice.* 2. (Slang) Electric current. **juices.** —**juicy** *adjective.*

ju·jit·su (joo-JIT-soo) *noun.* A Japanese way of wrestling.

Ju·ly (ju-LIGH or joo-LIGH) *noun.* The seventh month of the year: There are 31 days in *July.*

jum·ble (JUHM-bəl) *verb.* To mess together; mix up; confuse. **jumbled, jumbling.** —*noun.* A mess; muddle; confusion. **jumbles.**

jum·bo (JUHM-boh) *adjective.* Large; very big. —*noun.* A very large person, animal, or thing. **jumbos.**

judo

jugs

juggler

Jungle gym

juniper

junk

jump (JUHMP) *verb.* 1. To leap; to spring. 2. To cause to leap: *jump* a horse. 3. To move unexpectedly. 4. To increase suddenly (as in cost, amount, or number). 5. To skip; pass over. 6. To run off (the track). **jumped, jumping.** —*noun.* 1. A leap; a spring. 2. The distance passed over in a leap: a *jump* of five feet. 3. A sudden increase: a *jump* in prices. 4. A head start: get the *jump* on someone. 5. (Sports) A game or race in which a jump is involved. —**jumpy** *adjective.* —**jump the gun.** Move too soon.

jump·er (JUHMP-ər) *noun.* A dress without sleeves.

jump rope. 1. A rope used for skipping or play. 2. The game of using a jump rope.

jump suit. A coverall combining blouse and pants in one garment.

junc·tion (JUHNGK-shən) *noun.* 1. Act of joining or being joined; a union. 2. A place where two or more things join or meet. 3. A station where railroad lines meet.

June (JOON) *noun.* The sixth month of the year: There are 30 days in *June.*

jun·gle (JUHNG-gəl) *noun.* An area of wild land thickly covered with trees and other plants, usually found in hot climates. **jungles.**

Jungle gym *trademark.* A piece of playground equipment with ladders and connected climbing bars.

jun·ior (JOON-yər) *adjective.* 1. The younger (added to the name of a son with the same name as his father; often written as *Jr.*). 2. Of or about a newcomer: a *junior* senator. —*noun.* 1. A younger person. 2. A person with junior standing. 3. A student in the third year of high school or college.

ju·ni·per (JOO-nə-pər) *noun.* An evergreen tree or shrub with purple or blue-green berries.

[1]**junk** (JUHNGK) *noun.* 1. Any useless material which is thrown out; trash; rubbish; anything of little value. 2. (Slang) Narcotic drugs, especially heroin. —*verb.* To throw out as useless. **junked, junking.**

[2]**junk** (JUHNGK) *noun.* A flat-bottomed Chinese sailboat.

jun·ket (JUHNG-kit) *noun.* 1. An outing or trip. 2. A party or picnic.

junk·ie (JUHNG-kee) Also **junky** *noun.* (Slang) A drug addict, especially one who uses heroin. **junkies.**

Ju·pi·ter (JOO-pə-tər) *noun.* The largest planet, fifth from the sun.

ju·ror (JUR-ər or JUR-or) *noun.* A member of a jury.

ju·ry (JUR-ee) *noun.* 1. A group of people appointed by a court or judge to hear evidence in a lawsuit and give a verdict. 2. A group of people who choose the winner in a contest. **juries.**

just (JUHST) *adjective.* 1. Fair; in accord with what is right: a *just* man; a *just* price. 2. Deserved; right: a *just* reward. —*adverb.* 1. At the right time: *just* now; *just* in time. 2. Precisely: *just* right; *just* so. 3. A short while ago: He *just* left. 4. (Informal) No question; really: *just* great. —**just about.** Almost; nearly.

jus·tice (JUHSS-tiss) *noun.* 1. The quality of being just; fairness. 2. Lawful treatment. 3. A judge.

jus·ti·fi·a·ble (JUHSS-tə-figh-ə-bəl or juhss-tə-FIGH-ə-bəl) *adjective.* Explainable; able to be defended as just or fair. —**justifiably** *adverb.*

jus·ti·fy (JUHSS-tə-figh) *verb.* To show to be fair, just, or reasonable. **justified, justifying.** —**justification** (juhs-tə-fə-KAY-shən) *noun.*

jut (JUHT) *verb.* To project; stick out. **jutted, jutting.**

jute (JOOT) *noun.* 1. A fiber made from plants grown in India, used to make rope, cloth, and carpets. 2. The plant from which jute comes.

ju·ve·nile (JOO-və-nl or JOO-və-nighl) *adjective.* 1. Of, for, or about children: *juvenile* novels, *juvenile* styles. 2. Young.

K, k (KAY) *noun.* The 11th letter of the English alphabet.

kale (KAYL) *noun.* A leafy green vegetable; a variety of cabbage that does not grow in a head.

ka·lei·do·scope (kə-LIGH-də-skohp) *noun.* 1. A tube that contains mirrors and fragments of colored glass: As you look through a *kaleidoscope,* many beautiful patterns appear. 2. Any changing scene or pattern. **kaleidoscopes. —kaleidoscopic** (kə-ligh-də-SKOP-ik) *adjective.*

kan·ga·roo (kang-gə-ROO) *noun.* A large animal, native to Australia, with a long thick tail and powerful hind legs. **kangaroos.**

Kan·sas (KAN-zəss) *noun.* A state in north central United States, 34th to join the Union (1861). **—Kans.** *abbreviation.* Also **KS** for Zip Codes.

kar·at (KA-rət) Also **carat** *noun.* A unit of measure of the amount of gold in an object: Pure gold is 24-*karat*; a 14-*karat* gold ring has 14 parts pure gold to 10 parts of another metal.

ka·ra·te (kə-RAH-tee) *noun.* A system of self-defense developed in Japan.

ka·ty·did (KAY-tee-did) *noun.* A large green insect in the grasshopper family.

kay·ak (KIGH-ak) Also **kaiak** *noun.* 1. An Eskimo canoe with a skin cover on a light wooden frame and an opening in the middle for a person. 2. A lightweight canoe, usually made of canvas.

keel *noun.* 1. A ship's main line of support, a wooden or steel backbone that runs the length of the craft. 2. Any bottom base similar to a ship's keel. *—verb.* To capsize. **keeled, keeling. —keel over.** 1. To fall suddenly, as if in a faint. 2. To upset; turn upside down. **—on an even keel.** Balanced, steady, not upset.

keen *adjective.* 1. Sharp: a *keen* razor blade. 2. Shrewd; intelligent: a *keen* mind. 3. Eager; enthusiastic: Tommy was *keen* about going to the circus. 4. Very sensitive; acute: Despite her old age, she had very *keen* hearing. 5. Piercing; severe: a *keen* wind. 6. Strong: "A fresh *keen* outdoor smell, a smell that didn't belong to a house at all." (Untermeyer). 7. (Slang) Great; wonderful. **keener, keenest. —keenly** *adverb.* **—keenness** *noun.*

keep *verb.* 1. To have as one's own; possess: I shall *keep* the watch. 2. Hold back; detain: She *keeps* her dog locked up. 3. Save; store in a particular place: You may *keep* your suitcase in the closet. 4. To be preserved: Cheese *keeps* best in the refrigerator. 5. Be faithful to; fulfill: *Keep* the faith! 6. To associate with: I don't like the company she *keeps.* 7. Maintain or operate: *keep* house, *keep* a store. 8. Prevent: The snow will *keep* us from going. 9. Continue (an activity or direction): *keep* straight ahead; *keep* going. 10. To protect; guard: May God *keep* you. **kept, keeping.** *—noun.* 1. A living; room and board: John had to work hard to earn his *keep.* 2. The main tower or stronghold of a castle. **—keep at.** To persist. **—keep time.** 1. To record time correctly, as a watch or clock. 2. To mark or maintain the beat of music. **—keep your chin up.** Don't give up hope.

keep·er (KEEP-ər) *noun.* A person who keeps or guards something.

keep·sake (KEEP-sayk) *noun.* A token, memento, or remembrance. **keepsakes.**

kangaroos

Kansas
★capital: Topeka

katydid

kayak

Kentucky
★capital: Frankfort

keyboard

kettle

kettledrum

keg *noun.* A small barrel or cask used as a container.

kelp *noun.* 1. A brown coarse seaweed. 2. The ashes of this seaweed, a source of iodine.

ken·nel (KEN-l) *noun.* A place where dogs are bred, raised, or boarded. *—verb.* To board; place in a kennel for care. **kenneled, kenneling.**

Ken·tuck·y (kən-TUHK-ee) *noun.* A state in south central United States, 15th to join the Union (1792). **—Ky.** *abbreviation.* Also **KY** for Zip Codes.

kept *verb. See* **keep.**

ker·chief (KER-chif) *noun.* A piece of cloth used either as a head covering or around the neck as a scarf.

ker·nel (KER-nl) *noun.* 1. A grain or seed. 2. The inner part of a nut or fruit pit, usually edible. 3. The core or center of anything: the *kernel* of a story.

ker·o·sene (KER-ə-seen) Also **kerosine** *noun.* An oil that is used as a fuel in lamps, stoves, and jet aircraft.

ketch (KECH) *noun.* A small sailboat with two masts. **ketches.**

ketch·up (KECH-əp or KACH-əp) Also **catchup** and **catsup** *noun.* A tomato sauce flavored with spices.

ket·tle (KET-l) *noun.* 1. A heavy pot used for cooking foods or boiling liquids. 2. A teakettle. **kettles.**

ket·tle·drum (KET-l-druhm) *noun.* A large drum that has skin stretched tight over a hollow metal base.

[1]**key** (KEE) *noun.* 1. A metal object shaped to fit and open a lock. 2. A metal device for turning any bolt, nut, or mechanism: I need the *key* to tighten my skates. 3. A lever to be pressed, as on a piano or typewriter. 4. A guide; an important clue: The gun was the *key* to the solution of the crime. 5. (Music) A scale or system of related notes based on a particular note: He played the concerto in the *key* of B flat. 6. Something that controls something else: Healthful food is one *key* to good health. *—verb.* 1. To adjust to a particular thing; coordinate: The colors in her bedroom were *keyed* to match. 2. To provide information or an explanation. **keyed, keying. —key up.** To arouse; to exite.**—low key.** Quiet; not extreme or excited.

[2]**key** (KEE) *noun.* A small reef or island lying low and close to shore.

key·board (KEE-bord) *noun.* A row or set of keys, as on a piano or typewriter.

key·hole (KEE-hohl) *noun.* The opening in a lock for the key. **keyholes.**

key·stone (KEE-stohn) *noun.* 1. The central stone wedged in at the top of an arch. 2. The main or fundamental part of something. **keystones.**

khak·i (KAK-ee or KAH-kee) *noun.* 1. Heavy dull-olive cloth used for soldiers' uniforms. 2. (Plural) A soldier's uniform. 3. (Also *adjective*) A dull color of olive mixed with yellow and brown tones. **—khakis** *plural.*

kib·butz (ki-BUTS) *noun.* A collective community in Israel, usually agricultural. **—kibbutzim** (ki-but-SEEM) *plural.*

kib·butz·nik (ki-BUTS-nik) *noun.* An individual who lives and works on a kibbutz.

kick (KIK) *verb.* 1. To hit with the foot: John *kicked* the football down the field. 2. To move the legs and feet: "He lay on his back and *kicked* up his heels in delight." (Frank R. Stockton). 3. (Informal) To complain or grumble. **kicked, kicking.** *—noun.* 1. A blow struck with the foot. 2. (Informal) A complaint: He had no *kicks* about the service. 3. (Slang) A thrill; fun: I get a *kick* out of playing my father's old records.

kick·ball (KIK-bawl) *noun.* A game similar to baseball, except that the pitcher rolls the ball and the player kicks the ball.

kick·off (KIK-awf or KIK-of) *noun.* 1. (Football) A kick that begins play for each half or starts play again after one team has scored. 2. The starting step of something; first stage.

kick the can. A children's game somewhat like hide-and-seek but played with a can as goal.

kid *verb.* To tease; joke. **kidded, kidding.** —*noun.* 1. A young goat. 2. Very soft leather from the skin of a young goat. 3. (Informal) A child.

kid·nap (KID-nap) *verb.* To seize (a person) and hold in captivity, usually for ransom. **kidnaped** or **kidnapped, kidnaping** or **kidnapping.**

kid·ney (KID-nee) *noun.* One of a pair of bean-shaped organs in the body that separate waste matter from the blood and pass it out of the body through the bladder.

kidney bean. An edible reddish bean shaped like a kidney.

kill (KIL) *verb.* 1. To slay; cause death. 2. To destroy; finish. 3. To fritter away: *kill* an hour. **killed, killing.** —*noun.* The object killed.

kiln (KIL or KILN) *noun.* An oven or furnace for baking or hardening, usually used for clay products.

kilo- *prefix.* Indicates a thousand: *kilo*gram.

kil·o·gram (KIL-ə-grəm) *noun.* A unit, used to measure volume, equal to 1,000 grams, or 2.2046 pounds.

kil·o·me·ter (KIL-ə-mee-tər or ki-LOM-ə-tər) *noun.* A unit, used to measure length, equal to 1,000 meters, or .62137 of a mile.

kil·o·watt (KIL-ə-wat) *noun.* A unit of electrical power equal to 1,000 watts.

kilt *noun.* A pleated woolen skirt worn at knee length by Scotsmen.

ki·mo·no (kə-MOH-nə or kə-MOH-noh) *noun.* A long Japanese robe. **kimonos.**

kin *noun.* Family; relative —*adjective.* Of the same nature.

kind (KYND) *adjective.* Gentle; good; tender; good-natured. **kinder, kindest.** —*noun.* A class or special grouping: Meat is one *kind* of food.

kin·der·gar·ten (KIN-dər-gahrt-n) *noun.* A class for young children before the regular school grades.

kind·heart·ed (KYND-HAHR-tid) *adjective.* Showing sympathy.

kin·dle (KIND-l) *verb.* 1. To start (a fire). 2. To begin or arouse (feeling). **kindled, kindling.**

kin·dling (KIN-dling) *noun.* Small pieces of wood or other flammable material used to start a fire.

kind·ly (KYND-lee) *adverb.* In a gentle or cordial manner. —*adjective.* Kind; pleasant. **kindlier, kindliest.**

kind·ness (KYND-niss) *noun.* 1. A kind act or generous deed. 2. Sympathy; friendliness; tenderness. **kindnesses.**

kin·dred (KIN-drid) *noun.* Kin; relatives. —*adjective.* Similar; of the same nature.

ki·net·ic (ki-NET-ik) *adjective.* Concerning motion.

king *noun.* 1. A ruler; head of a kingdom or country. 2. Top person in any field. 3. A playing card.

king·dom (KING-dəm) *noun.* 1. Territory or country ruled by a king. 2. Any area ruled by someone. 3. One of three groupings in nature: animal, vegetable, or mineral.

king·fish·er (KING-fish-ər) *noun.* A crested bird, brilliantly colored.

king·ly (KING-lee) *adjective.* Regal; stately; fit for a king. **kinglier, kingliest.** —*adverb.* Regally; royally.

king of the mountain. A children's game where one player stands on top of a hill and the other players try to get him off.

kink (KINGK) *noun.* 1. A curl, twist, or spiral. 2. A cramp or soreness in a muscle. 3. An odd idea; a strange notion. —*verb.* To cause to twist or curl. **kinked, kinking.**

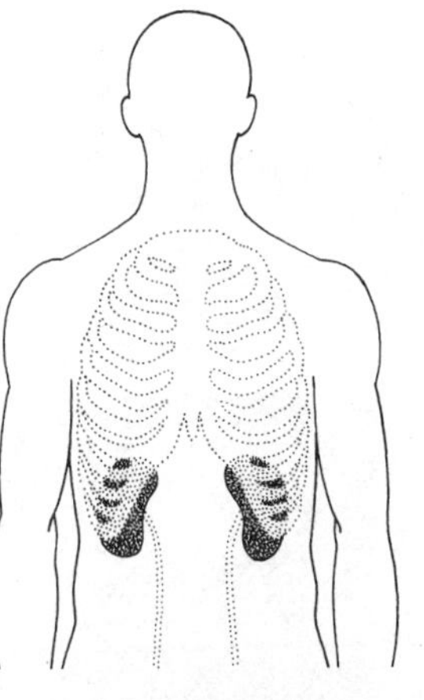
kidney

kilts

kimono

kink·y (KING-kee) *adjective.* 1. Very curly; with many short tight curls. 2. (Slang) Eccentric; behaving strangely. **kinkier, kinkiest.**

kins·man (KINZ-mən) *noun.* A male relative; kin. —**kinsmen** *plural.*

kiss *verb.* To press the lips against another's lips, face, or body as a greeting or sign of affection. **kissed, kissing.** —*noun.* 1. A touch from the lips. 2. A small candy. **kisses.**

kite

kit *noun.* A set of tools or other items for a special purpose; a container for these tools or objects.

kitch·en (KICH-ən) *noun.* A room or place where food is cooked.

kitch·en·ette (kich-ə-NET) *noun.* 1. A small kitchen. 2. A part of a room used as a kitchen. **kitchenettes.**

kite (KIGHT) *noun.* 1. A light frame covered with thin material, usually paper or plastic, tied to the end of a long string and flown in the wind. 2. A kind of hawk with long, pointed wings. **kites.** —**go fly a kite.** Go away, don't bother me.

kith and kin. Friends and relatives.

kit·ten (KIT-n) *noun.* A baby cat.

kitten

kit·ty (KIT-ee) *noun.* 1. A pet name for cat. 2. A collection of money or objects to which people contribute for a special purpose. **kitties.**

Kleen·ex (KLEE-neks) *trademark.* A soft paper tissue used as a handkerchief.

km. *abbreviation.* Kilometer.

kn. *abbreviation.* Knot.

knack (NAK) *noun.* Ability; talent; special skill.

knap·sack (NAP-sak) *noun.* A bag or pack, often of canvas, for carrying supplies on the back.

knave (NAYV) *noun.* A rascal or scoundrel. **knaves.**

knead (NEED) *verb.* 1. To prepare (dough or clay) for use by pressing, squeezing, and folding with the hands. 2. To squeeze or massage. **kneaded, kneading.**

knee (NEE) *noun.* The leg joint between the thigh and the calf. **knees.**

knee·cap (NEE-kap) *noun.* The flat, triangular bone located in front of the knee.

knee socks. Socks reaching up to the knee.

kneel (NEEL) *verb.* To bend or rest on one or both knees: *Kneel* before the king. **knelt** or **kneeled, kneeling.**

knell (NEL) *verb.* 1. To ring (a bell) slowly, as for a funeral. 2. To warn of or announce, usually something sad. **knelled, knelling.** —*noun.* 1. The slow, solemn ringing of a bell. 2. A warning or signal that the end has come: "The curfew tolls the *knell* of parting day." (Thomas Gray).

knelt (NELT) *verb. See* **kneel.**

knew (NOO or NYOO) *verb. See* **know.**

knick·er·bock·ers (NIK-ər-bok-ərz) *noun, plural.* Short, loose-fitting trousers gathered at the knee.

knick·ers (NIK-ərz) *noun, plural.* Knickerbockers.

knick·knack (NIK-nak) *noun.* A small article of little value, such as a souvenir or an ornament.

knife (NIGHF) *noun.* A tool with a handle and a thin blade (usually of metal) that has a sharp cutting edge. **knives.** —*verb.* To cut or stab, using a knife. **knifed, knifing.**

knight (NIGHT) *noun.* 1. A mounted soldier in the Middle Ages. 2. A title of honor in the British Empire, giving a man the right to use "Sir" before his name. 3. In the game of chess, a piece that usually has the shape of a horse's head. —*verb.* To give the rank of knight. **knighted, knighting.**

knight·hood (NIGHT-hud) *noun.* 1. The rank or profession of a knight. 2. The customs or character of a knight, such as courage, bravery, and chivalry. 3. The entire order or group of knights.

knit (NIT) *verb.* 1. To make a fabric by joining loops of thread or yarn by hand needles or machine. 2. To unite or grow close together: A broken bone *knits* quickly in a child. 3. To contract; draw together: The judge *knitted* his brows. **knit** or **knitted, knitting.**

knob (NOB) *noun.* 1. A handle, usually rounded, on a drawer or door, for opening or closing it. 2. A rounded part sticking out of something else: a gnarled *knob* on a tree trunk.

knock (NOK) *verb.* 1. To hit, strike, or rap: The messenger *knocked* on the door. 2. To strike and make fall: The dog *knocked* the vase from the table with his tail. 3. To make a repeated thumping or pounding sound: The motor won't *knock* if you use better gasoline. 4. To cause by hitting: The explosion *knocked* an opening in the wall. 5. (Informal) To criticize: People *knock* the things they don't understand. **knocked, knocking.** —*noun.* A hard blow or the sound made by it. —**don't knock it.** Do not criticize or judge harshly. —**knock it off.** To stop doing something: The captain told the noisy soldiers to *knock it off.*

knock·out (NOK-owt) *noun.* 1. A blow that makes a person unconscious. 2. (Boxing) A blow that knocks down a fighter who cannot then get up before the count of ten. 3. Something unusually impressive or attractive: Jane's new dress is a *knockout.*

knot (NOT) *noun.* 1. A fastening or tie made with a string, rope, etc.: A Boy Scout can tie many kinds of *knots.* 2. A close tie or bond: the marriage *knot.* 3. A difficulty or problem not easy to solve. 4. A hard lump on a tree trunk or a part of this lump in a wooden surface. 5. A small group of people or things: A *knot* of busybodies formed. 6. A unit of speed used by sailors and fliers; a nautical mile, equal to 6,076.1 feet, an hour. —*verb.* 1. To bind or tie with a knot. 2. To become tangled up. **knotted, knotting.**

knot·ty (NOT-ee) *adjective.* 1. Having knots: a *knotty* string. 2. Difficult or puzzling: a *knotty* question. **knottier, knottiest.**

know (NOH) *verb.* 1. To have clear in one's mind: I *know* when the sun goes down. 2. To be acquainted with: The newsboy *knows* the people on his route. 3. To recognize; be able to tell apart: He *knows* the different kinds of trees. **knew, known, knowing.** —**in the know.** Sharing secret or special information.

knowl·edge (NOL-ij) *noun.* 1. Information; understanding; what someone knows: You gain much *knowledge* by travel. 2. Awareness: I had no *knowledge* of Kevin's plans. 3. All that is known.

known (NOHN) *adjective.* Proved; already determined: the *known* facts in the case. —*noun.* The information that people have: We are always extending the borders of the *known.* —*verb.* See **know.**

knuck·le (NUHK-əl) *noun.* A joint of the finger or the area around the joint. **knuckles.** —*verb.* To press hard with the knuckles. **knuckled, knuckling.** —**knuckle down.** To do something seriously and with effort: You had better *knuckle down* to your studies. —**knuckle under.** To give in; to concede: John had to *knuckle under* to Dad's decision.

KO (KAY-OH) *verb.* (Slang) To knock out. **KO'd, KO'ing.**

ko·a·la (koh-AH-lə) *noun.* An animal of Australia that looks like a teddy bear and lives in trees.

ko·sher (KOH-shər) *adjective* 1. Prepared according to Jewish dietary laws; clean and fit to eat by religious Jews: *kosher* meat. 2. (Informal) Proper; correct: Bill's behavior was not *kosher;* he shouldn't have done that.

kt. *abbreviation.* 1. Karat; carat. 2. Knight.

ku·dos (KYOO-dohz) *noun.* Praise; acclaim. **kudoses.**

knots

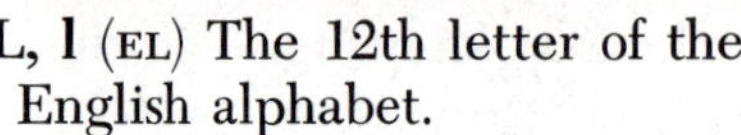

L, l (EL) The 12th letter of the English alphabet.

lace

la (LAH) *noun.* (Music) The sixth note in any standard major or minor scale of eight notes..

lab (LAB) *noun.* (Informal) A laboratory.

la·bel (LAY-bəl) *noun.* A paper slip or other tag that gives information about the article to which it is attached: The *label* on the bottle says that it contains poison. *—verb.* 1. To place a label on. 2. To name; classify: The dishonest student was *labeled* a cheater. **labeled** or **labelled, labeling** or **labelling.**

la·bor (LAY-bər) *noun.* 1. Work. 2. Workmen as a group: *Labor* is trying to gain increases in wages. 3. The process of giving birth. *—verb.* 1. To work. 2. To make progress slowly or with difficulty: Tim *labored* through deep snow. **labored, laboring.**

lab·o·ra·to·ry (LAB-ə-rə-tor-ee) *noun.* A room or building designed for scientific work. **laboratories.**

ladder

Labor Day. A legal holiday in the United States and Canada celebrated on the first Monday in September in honor of workers.

la·bor·er (LAY-bər-ər) *noun.* A worker, especially one whose work involves physical effort.

labour. British form of **labor.**

Lab·ra·dor re·triev·er (LAB-rə-dor ri-TREE-vər). A large dog with a thick, short-haired, black or brown coat.

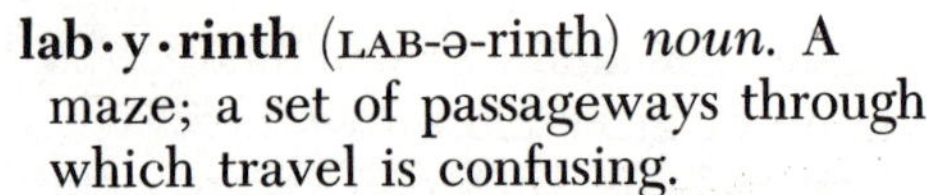

lab·y·rinth (LAB-ə-rinth) *noun.* A maze; a set of passageways through which travel is confusing.

lace (LAYSS) *noun.* 1. A fancy, finely woven fabric, usually used to trim clothing, household furnishings, and other items. 2. A cord used to fasten parts of clothing: shoe *laces.* **laces.** *—verb.* To fasten with laces. **laced, lacing.**

lac·er·ate (LASS-ə-rayt) *verb.* 1. To mangle; to tear: Broken glass *lacerated* the face of the accident victim. 2. To wound or hurt (the feelings). **lacerated, lacerating.** **—laceration** (lass-ə-RAY-shən) *noun.*

lack (LAK) *verb.* To be without; have very little: The sick child *lacks* energy. **lacked, lacking.** *—noun.* A shortage; absence.

lac·quer (LAK-ər) *noun.* A liquid, applied to wood and other materials, that leaves a hard, shiny surface when it dries. *—verb.* To cover with such a liquid. **lacquered, lacquering.**

lad *noun.* A boy; young man.

lad·der (LAD-ər) *noun.* A device used for climbing, consisting of rungs or steps spaced evenly between two upright supports.

lad·en (LAYD-n) *adjective.* Loaded; burdened, as with weight or grief.

la·dle (LAYD-l) *noun.* A spoon with a long handle and large bowl, used for serving soups and other liquids. **ladles.** *—verb.* To dish out with a ladle. **ladled, ladling.**

la·dy (LAY-dee) *noun.* 1. A woman, especially one who is polite and refined. 2. (British) [Capital L] A woman of noble rank. **ladies.**

la·dy·bug (LAY-dee-buhg) *noun.* A small, flying, red-colored beetle with black spots.

lag *verb.* To fall behind; move slowly: The racing car began to *lag* when it developed engine trouble. **lagged, lagging.** *—noun.* A falling behind.

la·goon (lə-GOON) *noun.* A shallow body of water separated from a larger body of water by a ring of land, especially of sand or coral.

laid (LAYD) *verb. See* [1]**lay.**

lain (LAYN) *verb. See* [2]**lie.**

lair *noun.* The living or resting place of a wild animal; den.

lake (LAYK) *noun.* A large body of water surrounded by land. **lakes.**

lamb (LAM) *noun.* 1. A young sheep. 2. The meat from a lamb.

lame (LAYM) *adjective.* 1. Crippled; unable to walk normally because of an injury or deformity. 2. Weak; unacceptable: a *lame* excuse. **lamer, lamest.** —*verb.* To make lame or crippled. **lamed, laming.** —**lamely** *adverb.* —**lameness** *noun.*

la·ment (lə-MENT) *verb.* 1. To express deep sorrow over; mourn. 2. To regret. **lamented, lamenting.** —*noun.* An expression of deep sorrow; dirge. —**lamentable** *adjective.* —**lamentably** *adverb.*

lam·i·nat·ed (LAM-ə-nay-təd) *adjective.* Formed or constructed in layers: Plywood is a *laminated* material.

lamp *noun.* 1. A device used for producing light by means of an electric bulb, oil and wick, or other method. 2. A device which gives off light or heat rays: a sun *lamp.*

lam·prey (LAM-pree) *noun.* A large-mouthed water animal that looks like an eel.

lance (LANSS) *noun.* A long, narrow, spear-like weapon with a pointed metal head. **lances.** —*verb.* 1. To cut or pierce with a lance. 2. To slice open, as in minor surgery: *lance* a boil. **lanced, lancing.**

land *noun.* 1. The solid part of the earth's surface. 2. A country or region: foreign *lands.* 3. Property; real estate: *Land* is expensive in this neighborhood. 4. Soil: fertile *land.* —*verb.* 1. To reach land after travel on water or in air: *land* at the airport. 2. To reach or arrive at a certain point: Falling rock *landed* on the roof. 3. To catch: The fisherman *landed* six trout. 4. (Informal) To obtain; achieve: My brother *landed* an excellent job. **landed, landing.**

land·ing (LAN-ding) *noun.* 1. The act or process of reaching land or going ashore. 2. A platform at the end of a flight of stairs.

land·la·dy (LAND-lay-dee) *noun.* A woman who rents houses, apartments, rooms, or other property to people. **landladies.**

land·lord (LAND-lord) *noun.* A man who rents houses, apartments, rooms, or other property to people.

land·lub·ber (LAND-luhb-ər) *noun.* A person who has little knowledge or experience of life at sea.

land·mark (LAND-mahrk) *noun.* 1. A famous building, monument, or other noticeable feature of an area: Pikes Peak is a well-known *landmark* in Colorado. 2. A very important event: The discovery of Salk vaccine was a *landmark* in man's battle against polio.

land·scape (LAND-skayp) *noun.* 1. A wide view of land: a beautiful *landscape.* 2. A picture showing a view of land, usually of a country area. **landscapes.** —*verb.* To make property more attractive by planting or rearranging trees, shrubs, and other plants. **landscaped, landscaping.**

land·slide (LAND-slighd) *noun.* 1. The sliding of a mass of earth and rocks down a mountain or hillside. 2. A great victory, especially in an election. **landslides.**

lane (LAYN) *noun.* 1. A narrow road; path. 2. A route over which planes or ships travel: shipping *lanes.* 3. A route or path used for runners or vehicles traveling in the same direction: The driver signaled that he was moving from the left *lane* to the right. **lanes.**

lambs

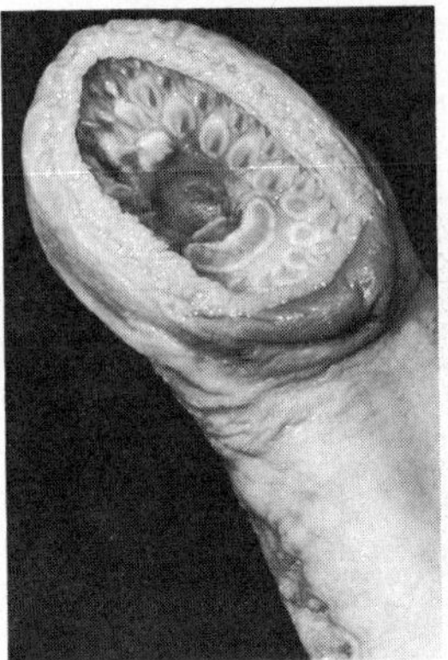

lamprey

landslide

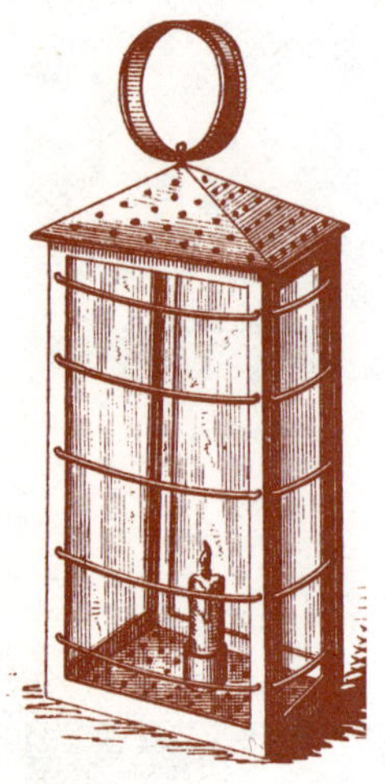
lantern

lark

lapels

lan·guage (LANG-gwij) *noun.* 1. Speech or writing by which humans communicate with one another. 2. Any set of signs or signals for communication: Many deaf persons use sign *language.* 3. The speech and writing common in a particular country: Portuguese is the major *language* spoken in Brazil. 4. The style of speech used by a particular person or group: We were amused by the clown's insulting *language.* **languages.**

lan·guid (LANG-gwid) *adjective.* Lacking liveliness, energy, or enthusiasm. —**languidly** *adverb.*

lan·guish (LANG-gwish) *verb.* To be without liveliness or energy: The patient *languished* for weeks after his fever was gone. **languished, languishing.**

lank (LANGK) *adjective.* 1. Slender; lean. 2. Long and straight, limp: *lank* hair. —**lankly** *adverb.*

lank·y (LANG-kee) *adjective.* Tall and thin, often to the point of lacking gracefulness. **lankier, lankiest.**

lan·tern (LAN-tərn) *noun.* A device, usually made of glass and metal, containing a flame or bulb and used to provide light.

lap *noun.* 1. The front part of a seated person from the waist to the knees. 2. A place or situation in which one remains or is cared for: The prince lived in the *lap* of luxury. 3. One run or trip around a racetrack. —*verb.* 1. To lick or draw up liquid with the tongue. 2. To wash easily against something: The waves *lapped* on the beach. 3. To overlap; place partly over (something else). **lapped, lapping.**

la·pel (lə-PEL) *noun.* A lower section of a coat or jacket collar that folds back against the garment.

lapse (LAPS) *verb.* 1. To decline; fall into a lower or worse condition or position: The sick man *lapsed* into a coma. 2. To become useless or ineffective: Uncle Jim's insurance policy *lapsed* when he forgot to make his payments. **lapsed, lapsing.** —*noun.* 1. A decline or fall to a lower or worse condition or position. 2. A minor fault or failure: a *lapse* of memory. 3. A passage of time: The rain started again after a *lapse* of just a few minutes. **lapses.**

lar·ce·ny (LAHR-sə-nee) *noun.* The crime of stealing; theft.

larch (LAHRCH) *noun.* A type of pine tree that loses its needles in the fall; the wood from this tree. **larches.**

lard (LAHRD) *noun.* Fat from hogs, melted down and made clear for cooking purposes. —*verb.* 1. To add lard to. 2. To add to in order to make richer or more appealing: The storyteller *larded* his tale with many exciting details. **larded, larding.**

lar·der (LAHR-dər) *noun.* 1. A storage area where food supplies are kept. 2. The food supplies themselves.

large (LAHRJ) *adjective.* 1. Big; of great size or amount. 2. Of great degree or importance: Commanding a naval ship is a *large* responsibility. **larger, largest.**

large·ly (LAHRJ-lee) *adverb.* Mostly; to a great degree.

lar·i·at (LA-ree-ət) *noun.* A lasso; a rope with a slip loop at the end for catching or holding horses, cattle, and other livestock.

lark (LAHRK) *noun.* 1. Any of several types of songbirds. 2. (Informal) Something done just for fun; a carefree adventure.

lark·spur (LAHRK-sper) *noun.* A plant having blue-colored flowers with green, spur-like growths beneath them.

lar·va (LAHR-və) *noun.* 1. The wormlike stage of an insect's life. 2. The young of any animal that goes through several stages before it becomes an adult: A tadpole is the *larva* of a frog. —**larvae** (LAHR-vee) *plural.* —**larval** *adjective.*

lar·yn·gi·tis (la-rən-JIGH-tiss) *noun.* An illness that affects the part of the throat known as the larynx.

lar·ynx (LA-ringks) *noun.* The part of the breathing system, located in the throat, that contains the vocal cords. —**larynges** (la-RIN-jeez) or **larynxes** *plural.*

la·sa·gna (lə-ZAHN-yə) *noun.* Wide flat noodles baked in tomato sauce with cheese and (usually) meat.

la·ser (LAY-zər) *noun.* A device that sends out a concentrated beam of light: The intense beam of the *laser* is used in delicate surgery, to carry telephone messages, and even to bore holes in metal.

lash *noun.* 1. The long string-like end of a whip. 2. A stroke of a whip. 3. An eyelash. **lashes.** —*verb.* 1. To strike with a whip. 2. To hit with force: High waves *lashed* the ship. 3. To scold or speak forcefully: Lincoln *lashed* out against slavery. 4. To tie with cord. **lashed, lashing.**

lass Also **las·sie** (LASS-ee) *noun.* A girl or young woman. **lasses.**

las·so (LASS-oh) *noun.* A long rope with a slip knot that forms a loop at one end used for catching cattle or horses. **lassos** or **lassoes.** *See* **lariat.** —*verb.* To capture with a lasso. **lassoed, lassoing.**

last *adjective.* 1. Final, at the end: the *last* day of the year. 2. Newest, most recent. —*adverb.* Also **lastly.** 1. At the end: I will go *last.* 2. Most recently. —*noun.* 1. The one remaining: He ate the *last* of the cookies. 2. A form on which shoes are made. —*verb.* To go on or continue: "My candle burns at both ends/ It cannot *last* the night. . . ." (Edna St. Vincent Millay). **lasted, lasting.** —**at last.** Finally.

last·ing (LASS-ting) *adjective.* Continuing, going on for a long time: The world needs *lasting* peace. —**lastingly** *adverb.*

latch (LACH) *noun.* A fastening or lock, often on a door or gate. **latches.** —*verb.* To close with a latch. **latched, latching.** —**latch onto.** To get and keep.

late (LAYT) *adverb.* 1. Not on time, tardily. 2. Near the end: The honor came *late* in life. —*adjective.* 1. Not on time. 2. No longer living: my *late* uncle. 3. Near the end: *late* teens. 4. Most recent: *late* news developments. **later, latest.**

late·ly (LAYT-lee) *adverb.* Recently.

la·tent (LAY-tənt) *adjective.* Hidden, but present: a *latent* desire.

lat·er·al (LAT-ər-əl) *adjective.* Of, on, or to the side. —**laterally** *adverb.* —**lateral pass.** A football pass to the side rather than toward the goal.

la·tex (LAY-teks) *noun.* 1. A milky liquid from plants such as the rubber tree. 2. A solution of this liquid used in paints and plastics. —**latices** (LAT-ə-seez) or **latexes** *plural.*

lath (LATH) *noun.* A narrow strip of wood or metal used (with others) to support other building material.

lathe (LAYTH) *noun.* A machine tool that holds and spins objects, such as pieces of wood or metal, so that a second tool may be used for cutting, grinding, or sanding. **lathes.** —*verb.* To use a lathe. **lathed, lathing.**

lath·er (LATH-ər) *noun.* 1. Suds made by mixing soap or detergent with water. 2. A light foam on a horse caused by sweat. —*verb.* To make, cover, or be covered by a lather. **lathered, lathering.**

Latin America. Mexico and other parts of South America, Central America, and the West Indies in which Spanish or Portuguese is the official language.

lat·i·tude (LAT-ə-tood or LAT-ə-tyood) *noun.* 1. (Geography) The distance north or south of the equator measured in degrees. 2. Space, freedom of choice. **latitudes.**

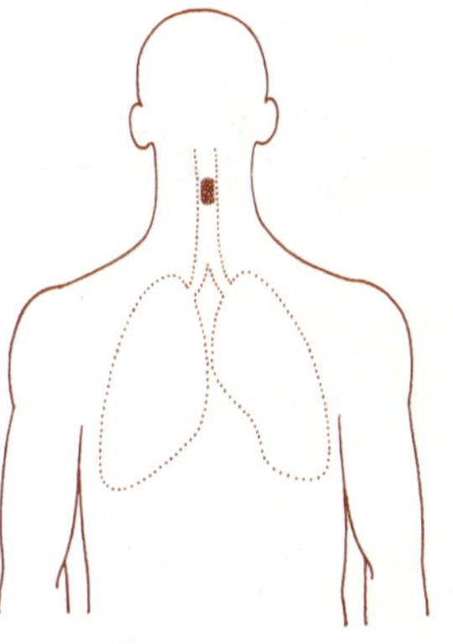
larynx

lasso

latitude

lattice

lat·ter (LAT-ər) *adjective.* 1. Toward the last: the *latter* pages of the book. 2. Designating the second of two things named: If the choice is between spinach and cake, I'll take the *latter.* *See* **former.**

lat·tice (LAT-iss) *noun.* 1. An open framework, often made of crossed wood or metal strips. 2. Anything formed like such a framework. 3. The arrangement of atoms in a crystal. **lattices.** —*verb.* To make a lattice. **latticed, latticing.**

laud (LAWD) *verb.* To praise or pay honor to. **lauded, lauding.**

laugh (LAF) *verb.* 1. To make a happy sound; to show amusement by making a wordless, vocal noise accompanied by a smile. 2. (Used with *at*) To make fun of someone: They *laughed* at Columbus when he said the world was round. **laughed, laughing.** —*noun.* 1. The act or sound of laughing. 2. (Informal) A joke.

laugh·a·ble (LAF-ə-bəl) *adjective.* Funny, amusing. —**laughably** *adverb.*

laugh·ter (LAF-tər) *noun.* The act or sound of laughing.

launching pad

launch (LAWNCH or LAHNCH) *verb.* 1. To fire, send off with force or power: *launch* a rocket. 2. To put into the water for the first time: *launch* a ship. 3. To begin something: The track team *launched* a drive for funds. **launched, launching.** —*noun.* 1. The act of launching (a rocket). 2. An open motorboat. **launches.**

launch pad or **launching pad.** The concrete base from which a rocket is fired.

laun·der (LAWN-dər or LAHN-dər) *verb.* To wash or to wash and iron (clothing or household articles). **laundered, laundering.**

Laun·dro·mat (LAWN-drə-mat) *trademark.* A business that has machines in which customers wash and dry their laundry.

laun·dry (LAWN-dree or LAHN-dree) *noun.* 1. Clothes and other articles that are to be washed or have been washed. 2. A place where clothes are laundered. **laundries.**

lau·rel (LOR-əl) *noun.* 1. A kind of evergreen tree or shrub. 2. The leaves from such a plant: The Greeks crowned the hero with a wreath of *laurel.* 3. (Usually plural) Honor or glory. —**rest on one's laurels.** To be content with past successes.

la·va (LAH-və or LAV-ə) *noun.* 1. The hot melted rock that flows from an active volcano. 2. Such rock after it has cooled.

lav·a·to·ry (LAV-ə-tor-ee) *noun.* A washroom. **lavatories.**

lav·en·der (LAV-ən-dər) *noun.* 1. A plant with pale purple blossoms and velvety leaves, grown for its fragrance. 2. The dried leaves and flowers of this plant, often used to make linens fragrant. —*noun* (Also *adjective*). A pale shade of purple or violet.

lav·ish (LAV-ish) *adjective.* Overly generous, extravagant. —*verb.* To give or spend freely: He *lavishes* large sums of money on his hobby. **lavished, lavishing.** —**lavishly** *adverb.*

law *noun.* 1. A rule. 2. A rule or all the rules made by a government body: In a democracy, the people who make *laws* are chosen by election. 3. Court decisions that may later be applied to other legal cases. 4. The study of such rules and decisions. 5. The work of a lawyer: the practice of *law.* 6. A principle of science: Boyle's *law* explains the behavior of gases.

law·ful (LAW-fəl) *adjective.* Legal; according to or allowed by law. —**lawfully** *adverb.*

law·less (LAW-liss) *adjective.* Not following legal rules; disobedient; out of control. —**lawlessly** *adverb.* —**lawlessness** *noun.*

law·mak·er (LAW-mayk-ər) *noun.* A person elected to make government rules; a legislator or member of Congress.

lawn *noun.* 1. Ground covered with grass, usually closely cut. 2. A kind of thin cotton or linen cloth.

lawn mower. A machine for cutting grass.

law·suit (LAW-soot) *noun.* The action of taking an argument or question to court to be decided by law.

law·yer (LAW-yər) *noun.* A person who is trained and authorized to give others advice about legal matters or represent them in court.

lax (LAKS) *adjective.* 1. Careless, forgetful: He is *lax* about doing his homework. 2. Loose; not tight or strict: *lax* rules. —**laxly** *adverb.* —**laxness** *noun.*

lax·a·tive (LAK-sə-tiv) *noun.* A medicine that causes bowel movements. **laxatives.**

[1]**lay** *verb.* 1. To put or place. 2. To spread or put in the proper location: The workmen will *lay* the carpet. 3. To settle: The rain will *lay* the dust. 4. To produce (eggs). 5. To make or put forth: *lay* plans for a program. **laid, laying.** *See* [2]**lie.** —**lay off.** To fire or dismiss (workers). —**lay to rest.** To bury (a person). —**lay waste.** To destroy.

[2]**lay** *noun.* A poem or song that tells a story: Macaulay wrote *lays* about the early Romans.

[3]**lay** *adjective.* 1. Relating to those who are not of the clergy; of the common man. 2. Of the common person, as distinct from one trained in law, medicine, or a particular profession: This medical textbook was written for doctors, not for *lay* readers.

lay·er (LAY-ər) *noun.* 1. A single thickness: The cake has three *layers.* 2. One that places or lays: brick*layer.* —*verb.* To put or make into layers. **layered, layering.**

lay·man (LAY-mən) *noun.* 1. A person who is not trained in a particular science or profession. 2. One who is not a clergyman. —**laymen** *plural.*

la·zy (LAY-zee) *adjective.* 1. Idle, not fond of work. 2. Slow-moving: a *lazy* river. **lazier, laziest.** —**lazily** *adverb.* —**laziness** *noun.*

leach (LEECH) *verb.* 1. To run water through (something) so as to dissolve and flush out certain parts. 2. To remove substances that dissolve when water runs through: Heavy rains *leach* valuable chemicals from the soil. **leached, leaching.** —*noun.* 1. The act of separating in this way. 2. The substance or liquid that is separated. **leaches.**

[1]**lead** (LEED) *verb.* 1. To go first or show the way to: "A little child shall *lead* them." (Isaiah 11:6). 2. To guide by using a rope or leash. 3. To go in a direction: This path *leads* to the river. 4. To direct or conduct: *lead* a band. 5. To live: She *leads* a busy life. **led, leading.** —*noun.* 1. The most important part: He plays the *lead* in the school play. 2. The distance that one is ahead of another: The winning swimmer has a *lead* of four feet. 3. A rope or leash used to control an animal. 4. The first play in a card game. 5. (Baseball) The start taken by a player running bases. 6. Useful information; a clue: The police are checking *leads* on the bank robbery.

[2]**lead** (LED) *noun.* 1. A soft heavy bluish-white metal. 2. Bullets. 3. Graphite or other marking material used in lead pencils. —*verb.* To cover, fill, or line with lead. **leaded, leading.**

lead·en (LED-n) *adjective.* 1. Made of lead. 2. Slow-moving; without energy or enthusiasm. 3. Sad or depressed, as though carrying a burden: *leaden* spirits. 4. Having the color of lead; dull or bluish gray. —**leadenly** *adverb.*

laurel

lead·er (LEED-ər) *noun.* 1. One who goes ahead or directs; the head; the person in charge. 2. The wire or cord that fastens a hook to a fish line.

lead·er·ship (LEED-ər-ship) *noun.* 1. Direction: Under Washington's *leadership* the Colonies won the war. 2. The ability to lead: The football captain was chosen for his *leadership.*

leaf (LEEF) *noun.* 1. A flat, usually green, growth on the stem of a plant: A *leaf* uses water, carbon dioxide, and sunlight to make food for the plant. 2. A single sheet of a book or magazine. 3. An extra board for a dining table or a hinged section of a table. 4. A very thin layer of metal: The dome of the Capitol is covered with gold *leaf.* —**leaves** (LEEVZ) *plural.* —*verb.* 1. To put forth leaves. 2. To turn over the pages of a book rapidly. **leafed, leafing.** —**turn over a new leaf.** To decide to do better.

lean-to

leapfrog

leaf·let (LEEF-lit) *noun.* 1. A small leaf of a plant. 2. A page of printed matter, usually folded.

leaf·y (LEE-fee) *adjective.* Having many leaves: Cabbage and lettuce are *leafy* vegetables.

league (LEEG) *noun.* 1. An organization made up of people or groups with a common interest. 2. (Sports) Teams or clubs that play against each other during a season. 3. (Rare) A measure of distance equal to about three miles: "20,000 *Leagues* Under the Sea." **leagues.**

leak (LEEK) *noun.* 1. An opening or crack that allows air, gas, or a liquid to flow through, usually by mistake: a *leak* in the roof. 2. The release of secret information or the source of such information. —*verb.* 1. To pass through a crack or hole: All the water *leaked* out of the fish tank. 2. To give out secret information: The secretary *leaked* the story to the newspapers. **leaked, leaking.**

leak·age (LEE-kij) *noun.* 1. The act of leaking. 2. The substance that leaks.

leak·y (LEE-kee) *adjective.* Having cracks or holes: Never go to sea in a *leaky* boat. **leakier, leakiest.**

lean (LEEN) *adjective.* Thin, skinny. **leaner, leanest.** —*noun.* Meat without fat: "Jack Sprat could eat no fat,/ His wife could eat no *lean.*" (Nursery rhyme). —*verb.* 1. To tilt or slant to one side: The Tower of Pisa *leans.* 2. To rely (on) for support or encouragement: The injured player *leaned* on his teammate. 3. To prefer: I *lean* toward water-color rather than oil painting. **leaned, leaning.**

lean-to (LEEN-too) *noun.* 1. A small shed, with one sloped roof, that is attached to a larger building. 2. A rough shelter made from branches or other covering slanted against supporting poles. **lean-tos.**

leap (LEEP) *verb.* To jump; hop; spring. **leaped** or **leapt, leaping.** —*noun.* A jump; a quick, light springing movement.

leap·frog (LEEP-frawg) *noun.* A game in which one player jumps over the backs of others who lean over.

leap year. A year with 366 days, in which February has 29 days instead of 28: Years whose number is divisible by 4 are *leap years* except century years (2000) which must be divisible by 400.

learn (LERN) *verb.* 1. To be taught; gain knowledge or skills: *learn* to walk. 2. To be informed; discover: She *learned* that her mother was ill. 3. To memorize. **learned** or **learnt, learning.**

learn·ed (LER-nid) *adjective.* Scholarly; having wide knowledge.

lease (LEESS) *verb.* To rent; hire: *lease* a car. **leased, leasing.** —*noun.* A written agreement whereby land or property is rented for a stated fee and a stated length of time. **leases.**

leash (LEESH) *noun.* A leather strap, chain, or long line used to lead or restrain a dog or other animal. **leashes.** —*verb.* 1. To put on a leash; tie up. 2. To control: *leash* one's temper. **leashed, leashing.**

least (LEEST) *adjective.* Smallest, minimum, slightest: not the *least* bit afraid. —*noun.* The smallest amount: What is the *least* you can spend for a decent dinner? —*adverb.* In the smallest degree. —**at least.** 1. Not less than: You should *at least* learn reading, writing, and arithmetic. 2. In any case; at any rate.

leath·er (LETH-ər) *noun.* The skin of an animal, tanned and processed for use in making such things as shoes, belts, and luggage.

leave (LEEV) *verb.* 1. To go away or depart from: She *leaves* home early each morning. 2. To withdraw from; quit; drop out of: It is a mistake to *leave* high school before graduating. 3. To let alone; allow to stay: *Leave* that door open. 4. To cause to remain behind: *leave* a book at home by mistake. 5. To arrange for money or property to go to someone else upon death: Grandmother is going to *leave* her jewelry to me. **left, leaving.** —*noun.* 1. Permission to do something. 2. Period of time during which one is away from a job. **leaves.**

lec·ture (LEK-chər) *noun.* 1. A talk about a particular subject; a speech. 2. A long scolding. **lectures.** —*verb.* 1. To give an informative talk. 2. To scold. **lectured, lecturing.**

lec·tur·er (LEK-chər-ər) *noun.* A person who delivers a lecture.

led *verb. See* [1]**lead.**

ledge (LEJ) *noun.* 1. A narrow shelf-like ridge of rock that juts out from a cliff. 2. Any flat shelf-like surface: a window *ledge.* **ledges.**

ledg·er (LEJ-ər) *noun.* A book for keeping accounts or money records.

lee *noun.* The sheltered side; the part protected from the wind.

leech *noun.* 1. A bloodsucking worm that lives in ponds and streams. 2. A person who clings to another for personal gain. **leeches.**

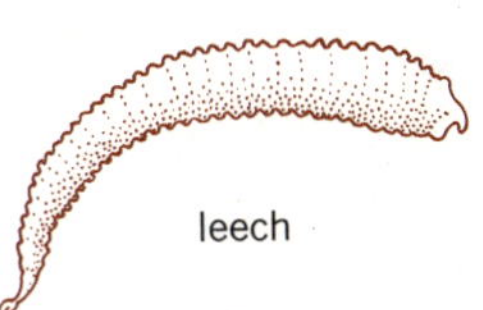
leech

leek *noun.* A plant similar to the onion, with a bulb-like root that is eaten as a vegetable.

leer (LIHR) *verb.* To give a sly, sidelong look showing evil intent. **leered, leering.** —*noun.* A sly look.

lee·ward (LEE-wərd or LOO-ərd) *adjective.* Away from the wind.

lee·way (LEE-way) *noun.* Room for change or freedom, as of time or spending: Having extra money gave us some *leeway* in selecting a gift.

left *adjective.* In a position or direction that is west when one faces north. —*adverb.* Toward or on the left: Turn *left.* —*noun.* 1. A direction or position on the left: She sat at my *left.* 2. A liberal or radical political position. —*verb. See* **leave.**

left-hand (LEFT-hand) *adjective.* Referring to the left side: Take the *left-hand* fork in the road.

left-hand·ed (LEFT-HAN-did) *adjective.* 1. Able to do things more easily with the left hand. 2. Clumsy, crude, or fumbling: A *left-handed* compliment is one that lacks sincere or honest praise.

left·o·ver (LEFT-oh-vər) *noun.* Something that remains; an unused or uneaten portion.

leg *noun.* 1. The part of the body (of man and some animals) that is used to hold up or move the rest of the body. 2. Anything that looks like or does the job of a leg: the *leg* of a chair. 3. Clothing that covers the leg: a pants *leg.* 4. (Geometry) A side of a right triangle other than the hypotenuse. —**leg it.** To walk fast or run. —**not have a leg to stand on.** To have no reasonable excuse or defense. —**shake a leg.** (Slang) Hurry!

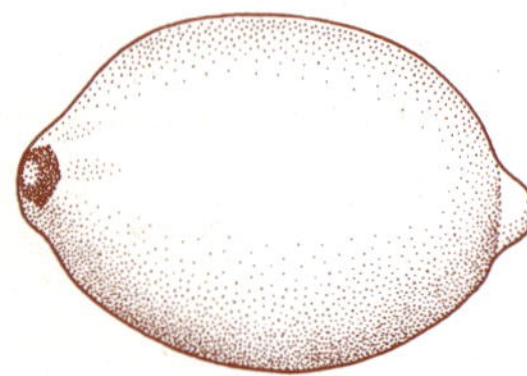

lemon

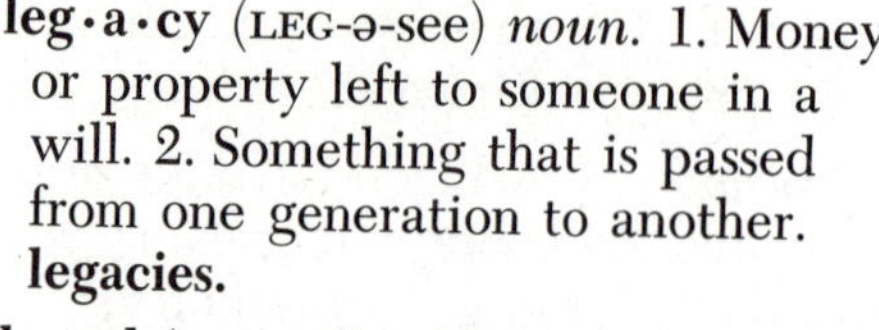

leg·a·cy (LEG-ə-see) *noun.* 1. Money or property left to someone in a will. 2. Something that is passed from one generation to another. **legacies.**

le·gal (LEE-gəl) *adjective.* 1. Lawful; allowed by law: He was driving within the *legal* speed limit. 2. Pertaining to the law: Lawyers belong to the *legal* profession. —**legality** (lee-GAL-ə-tee) *noun.* —**legally** *adverb.*

leg·end (LEJ-ənd) *noun.* 1. A story of the past that may or may not be true: The story of Robin Hood is a *legend.* 2. The writing on a coin, medal, building, statue, etc. 3. Text explaining an illustration or map.

leg·i·ble (LEJ-ə-bəl) *adjective.* Readable; clear: *legible* handwriting. —**legibly** *adverb.*

le·gion (LEE-jən) *noun.* 1. A military unit of ancient Rome. 2. An army unit. 3. A very large number of people.

leg·is·late (LEJ-iss-layt) *verb.* To create or pass laws. **legislated, legislating.**

leg·is·la·tion (lej-iss-LAY-shən) *noun.* 1. Lawmaking. 2. Laws that are passed.

leg·is·la·tive (LEJ-iss-lay-tiv) *adjective.* Relating to the power to make laws: Congress is the *legislative* branch of our government.

leg·is·la·tor (LEJ-iss-lay-tər) *noun.* A person who can make laws: Members of the Senate or House of Representatives are *legislators.*

leg·is·la·ture (LEJ-iss-lay-chər) *noun.* An official body of persons given the power to make laws in a state or nation. **legislatures.**

le·git·i·mate (lə-JIT-ə-mit) *adjective.* 1. Lawful; legal; allowed: He was the *legitimate* owner of the house. 2. Reasonable: a *legitimate* excuse. 3. Authentic; genuine: a *legitimate* diamond. 4. Born of parents who are married to each other. —**legitimately** *adverb.*

lemmings

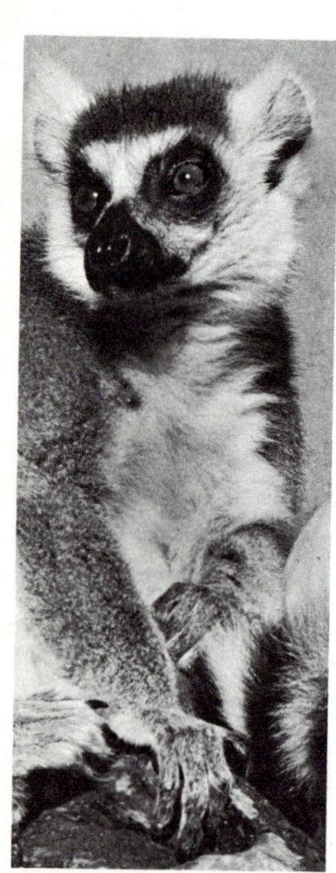

lemur

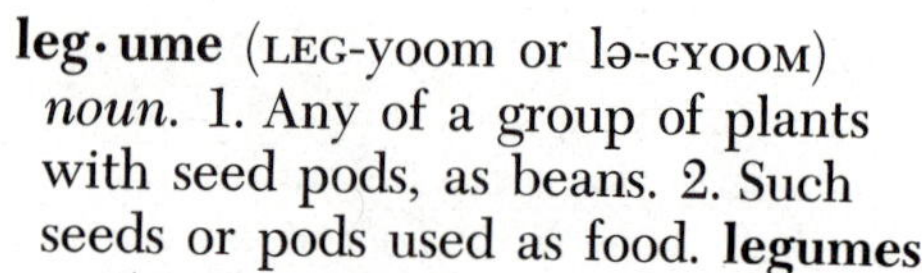

leg·ume (LEG-yoom or lə-GYOOM) *noun.* 1. Any of a group of plants with seed pods, as beans. 2. Such seeds or pods used as food. **legumes.**

lei·sure (LEE-zhər or LEZH-ər) *noun.* Spare time; freedom from work; time for recreation or relaxation.

lei·sure·ly (LEE-zhər-lee or LEZH-ər-lee) *adjective* and *adverb.* At an easy pace; not rushed.

lem·ming (LEM-ing) *noun.* A member of the rodent family, small and mouselike: *Lemmings* live in arctic regions and make periodic mass migrations, often ending in a suicidal march into the sea.

lem·on (LEM-ən) *noun.* 1. A yellow, oval citrus fruit with a sour taste. 2. The tree on which this fruit grows. 3. (Also *adjective*) A yellow color.

lem·on·ade (lem-ə-NAYD) *noun.* A drink made from lemon juice, water, and sugar.

le·mur (LEE-mər) *noun.* A big-eyed furry animal with a long tail, native of Africa.

lend *verb.* 1. To loan; permit (someone) to borrow for a period of time: Will you *lend* me your history book for tonight? 2. To give or offer: *lend* a helping hand. 3. To loan (money) for a price. **lent, lending.**

length (LENGKTH or LENGTH) *noun.* 1. Extent of something measured from end to end: The *length* of my ruler is 12 inches. 2. Duration: I spent the whole *length* of my vacation in Canada. 3. The longest side: The *length* of that table is twice its width. —**at length.** 1. Finally; at last. 2. Fully; in a detailed way. —**go to any length.** To act without any limitation to achieve a goal.

length·en (LENGK-thən or LENG-thən) *verb.* To make or become longer; extend. **lengthened, lengthening.**

length·wise (LENGKTH-wighz) *adverb* and *adjective.* In the direction of the longest side or part.

length·y (LENGH-thee or LENG-thee) *adjective.* Long; prolonged; too long. **lengthier, lengthiest.**

le·ni·ent (LEE-nee-ənt or LEEN-yənt) *adjective.* Not strict; gentle; merciful. —**leniency** or **lenience** *noun.* —**leniently** *adverb.*

lens (LENZ) *noun.* 1. A piece of glass or plastic that has been curved and shaped so that rays of light passing through it are brought closer together or sent wider apart. 2. A part of the eye that focuses light rays upon the retina to form an image. **lenses.**

Lent *noun.* A religious season of fasting and penitence lasting for the 40 weekdays before Easter.

len·til (LENT-l) *noun.* 1. A plant in the pea family whose small round seeds are used for food. 2. The edible seed of such a plant.

Le·o (LEE-oh) *noun.* The fifth sign of the zodiac, also called the "Lion." The time of this sign is from July 24 through August 23.

leop·ard (LEP-ərd) *noun.* A large wild spotted cat of Africa and Asia.

le·o·tard (LEE-ə-tahrd) *noun.* 1. A one-piece, tight-fitting outfit worn by dancers and acrobats. 2. (Plural) Tights.

lep·er (LEP-ər) *noun.* A person who has leprosy.

lep·i·dop·ter·an (lep-ə-DOP-tər-ən) *noun.* An insect that has four scaly wings; a butterfly or moth. —**lepidoptera** *plural.*

lep·re·chaun (LEP-rə-kawn) *noun.* An imaginary creature in Irish tales.

lep·ro·sy (LEP-rə-see) *noun.* A disease that causes sores and white scaly scabs and eventually eats away parts of the body.

less *adjective.* Smaller; not so much: "It takes *less* time to do a thing right than to explain why you did it wrong." (Longfellow). —*adverb.* Not so much: He talked *less* than I did. —*noun.* A smaller amount: John carried *less* than Tom. —*preposition.* Minus: He returned my marbles *less* the two I said he could keep.

-less *suffix.* Indicates a lack of: joy*less*; pain*less*.

less·en (LESS-n) *verb.* To make or become smaller. **lessened, lessening.**

less·er (LESS-ər) *adjective.* Smaller; inferior in size or quality.

les·son (LESS-n) *noun.* 1. An assignment to be learned or studied. 2. Anything learned: The accident taught Bob a *lesson.* 3. A unit of instruction: the first math *lesson.*

lest *conjunction.* For fear that: Be quiet *lest* you wake the children.

let *verb.* 1. To leave alone: *Let* it stay there. 2. To allow; to permit: *Let* me watch TV. 3. To rent; to lease: She had rooms to *let.* **let, letting.** —**let down.** To disappoint. —**let up.** To lessen or stop. —**let up on.** (Informal) To be easier (on); reduce pressure or demands.

Leo

-let *suffix.* Indicates: 1. Smallness (in size or importance): play*let*. 2. Worn on the body: ank*let*.

let·down (LET-down) *noun.* 1. A lessening or slowing down: Holiday excitement caused a *letdown* in class effort. 2. Disappointment: We found the movie a *letdown.*

le·thal (LEE-thəl) *adjective.* Causing death. —**lethally** *adverb.*

leth·ar·gy (LETH-ər-jee) *noun.* 1. Laziness; inaction. 2. The state of being tired or sleepy. —**lethargic** (lə-THAR-jik) *adjective.*

let's *contraction.* A shortened form of the words *let us.*

let·ter (LET-ər) *noun.* 1. A written note or message. 2. A symbol or mark used in writing to stand for a sound; an alphabet sign or character. —*verb.* To write, print, or draw letters. **lettered, lettering.**

let·ter·ing (LET-ər-ing) *noun.* 1. The act or process of printing, writing, or drawing letters. 2. A group of letters.

lettuce

Libra

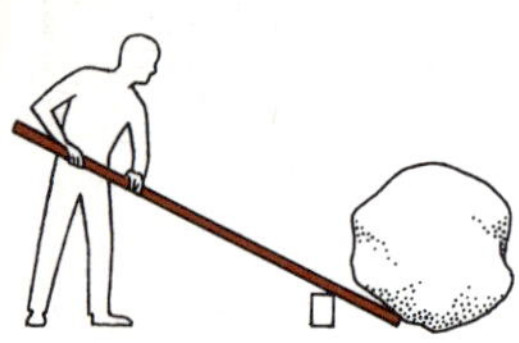
lever

library

let·tuce (LET-əss) *noun.* 1. A green plant whose crisp leaves are used in salads. 2. (Slang) Paper money.

lev·ee (LEV-ee) *noun.* 1. A mound or embankment built along a river to prevent flooding. 2. A pier or other place along a river bank where boats can land. **levees.**

lev·el (LEV-əl) *adjective.* 1. Not sloping; flat; even. 2. The same in position, height, or rank: The floodwater was *level* with our bottom porch step. *—noun.* 1. A position or rank: Dad was promoted to a new *level* of authority. 2. A height: The floodwaters rose to a dangerous *level.* 3. An instrument used to show whether a surface is horizontal. *—verb.* 1. To make even or flat: Dad *leveled* the table by shortening one leg. 2. To destroy or knock down completely: The huge bombs *leveled* the factory. 3. To direct or aim (at): The angry coach *leveled* his remarks at the quarterback. **leveled** or **levelled, leveling** or **levelling. —level with.** (Informal) To be open or honest with: *Level with* me on why you're angry.

lev·er (LEV-ər or LEE-vər) *noun.* A solid metal bar used as a tool to pry up or move heavy objects.

le·ver·age (LEV-ər-ij or LEE-vər-ij) *noun.* 1. The action or advantage provided by a lever in prying or lifting. 2. An advantage provided by one's position or influence.

lev·y (LEV-ee) *verb.* To establish or collect, as a fine or a tax. **levied, levying.** *—noun.* That which is levied. **levies.**

lex·i·con (LEK-si-kon) *noun.* A dictionary.

li·a·ble (LIGH-ə-bəl) *adjective.* 1. Likely (to happen): If you don't study, you are *liable* to fail. 2. Responsible under the law: Those who cause accidents are *liable* for the damages. **—liability** *noun.*

li·ar (LIGH-ər) *noun.* A person who does not tell the truth.

lib·er·al (LIB-ər-əl) *adjective.* 1. Plentiful; full: a *liberal* dose of cough syrup. 2. Generous: Bob was *liberal* with his time and effort. 3. Tolerant; not narrow in one's opinions: a *liberal* attitude. 4. Favoring individual freedom and reform, especially in politics. *—noun.* A person who favors new methods and ideas. **—liberally** *adverb.*

lib·er·ate (LIB-ə-rayt) *verb.* To release; set free. **liberated, liberating. —liberation** *noun.*

lib·er·ty (LIB-ər-tee) *noun.* 1. Freedom; the right to do as one wants: George Washington fought for his country's *liberty.* 2. A period of time granted for a sailor to go ashore. 3. (Often plural) Departure from accepted rules or behavior: Our guests took *liberties* in helping themselves to food. **liberties.**

Li·bra (LIGH-brə or LEE-brə) *noun.* The seventh sign of the zodiac, also called the "Balance." The time of this sign is from September 24 through October 23.

li·brar·i·an (ligh-BRAIR-ee-ən) *noun.* A person who runs or helps to run a library.

li·brar·y (LIGH-brehr-ee) *noun.* 1. A building or room where books, records, or similar items are kept. 2. A collection of books or other items: a record *library.* **libraries.**

li·cense (LIGH-snss) *noun.* 1. An official document or permit granting permission for some action or situation: a driver's *license.* 2. Official permission for some action or condition. 3. An abuse of freedom through excess: The riot was an example of *license.* **licenses.** *—verb.* To issue a license to; to permit. **licensed, licensing.**

li·chen (LIGH-kən) *noun.* A tiny plant that resembles moss and grows on trees and rocks.

lick (LIK) *verb.* 1. To move the tongue over; lap up. 2. To touch with a flickering movement: The flames *licked* at the edge of the log. 3. (Informal) To defeat; beat. **licked, licking.** —*noun.* 1. A movement of the tongue over something. 2. A block or deposit of salt for animals to lick, or a place where such salt can be found. 3. A small amount: My lazy brother didn't do a *lick* of homework. 4. A physical effort or activity, especially a blow or hit.

lic·o·rice (LIK-ər-iss or LIK-ər-ish) *noun.* 1. A chewy, black candy. 2. A plant whose root is used for flavoring.

lid *noun.* 1. A removable top or cover for a box, pot, or other container. 2. An eyelid.

[1]**lie** (LIGH) *noun.* A deliberate untruth; falsehood. **lies.** —*verb.* To tell a lie. **lied, lying.**

[2]**lie** (LIGH) *verb.* 1. To be or settle in a reclining or horizontal position: The baby *lies* in her crib. 2. To be in a certain condition or situation: The plates *lie* empty on the kitchen table. 3. To be in a certain place: Indiana *lies* next to Ohio. **lay, lain, lying.**

lieu·ten·ant (loo-TEN-ənt) *noun.* 1. One of two military ranks for army officers below the rank of captain. 2. One of two ranks for naval officers between the ranks of ensign and lieutenant commander. 3. A person who assists or acts in behalf of a superior.

life (LIGHF) *noun.* 1. The ability to grow and reproduce that ends with death. 2. The period during which a human being, plant, or animal is alive. 3. A human being: Many *lives* were lost in World War II. 4. Living things as a group: There is little plant *life* near the North Pole. 5. A manner of living: The explorer led an exciting *life.* 6. A work written about a person's life; a biography. 7. Spirit; enthusiasm: The pep talk gave us new *life.* —**lives** (LIGHVZ) *plural.*

life·boat (LIGHF-boht) *noun.* An open boat used to rescue passengers from a sinking ship.

life buoy. A device placed around a person's body to keep him afloat in the water; a life preserver.

life·guard (LIGHF-gahrd) *noun.* One who is paid to watch over swimmers at a pool or beach.

life·less (LIGHF-liss) *adjective.* 1. Without life; dead. 2. Without spirit; dull. —**lifelessly** *adverb.*

life·like (LIGHF-lighk) *adjective.* Having the appearance of being alive: The statue looked *lifelike.*

life·long (LIGHF-lawng) *adjective.* For the length of one's life: Mr. Gray was Grandfather's *lifelong* friend.

life preserver. A belt or jacket placed around a person's body to keep him afloat in the water; a life buoy.

life support system. The arrangement or system of devices that provides spacemen with air and other supplies necessary to maintain life.

life·time (LIGHF-tighm) *noun.* The period during which a person, plant, or animal is alive. **lifetimes.**

lift *verb.* 1. To raise to a higher place, rank, or position: The workman *lifted* the toolbox and placed it on the table. 2. To rise; go away: The fog *lifted.* 3. To end or cancel; call off: The ban on street parking was *lifted* after all the snow was removed. 4. (Slang) To steal. **lifted, lifting.** —*noun.* 1. A lifting; raising up. 2. A force that lifts or raises: The heavily loaded plane could not get enough *lift* to get off the ground. 3. A raising of one's spirits: The good news gave the weary soldiers a *lift.* 4. A ride: Dad gave his neighbor a *lift* into town. 5. (British) An elevator.

lift·off (LIFT-awf) *noun.* The first part, or launch, of a rocket flight.

lig·a·ment (LIG-ə-mənt) *noun.* A band of tough tissue that holds bones together or gives support to other parts of the body.

lifeboats

life preserver

[1]**light** *noun.* 1. A form of energy that permits us to see; illumination: There was enough *light* in the room for us to read. 2. A flame, bulb, or other source of illumination. 3. Daylight. 4. A flame, match, or other source of fire. 5. Knowledge or information: He shed more *light* on the subject. *—verb.* 1. To set fire to; ignite. 2. To turn on, as a lamp or other source of light. 3. To brighten; illuminate: Sunshine *lighted* the classroom. **lighted** or **lit, lighting.** *—adjective.* 1. Bright: The room was *light* and cheerful. 2. Pale: The girl wore a *light* blue dress. **lighter, lightest.** **—lightly** *adverb.*

[2]**light** *adjective.* 1. Not heavy: The box of feathers was *light.* 2. Less than usual in force, weight, or amount: a *light* rainfall. 3. Not difficult to do or bear: a *light* assignment. 4. Graceful; able to move easily. 5. Gay; not serious: The children laughed at the *light* opera. **lighter, lightest.** *—verb.* To land: The bird *lighted* on the rose bush. **lighted** or **lit, lighting. —lightly** *adverb.*

light·en (LIGHT-n) *verb.* 1. To make brighter. 2. To make less heavy or difficult: *lighten* a load. 3. To make more cheerful: The teacher's joke *lightened* our mood. **lightened, lightening.**

light·head·ed (LIGHT-HED-id) *adjective.* 1. Dizzy; faint. 2. Silly.

light·heart·ed (LIGHT-HAHR-tid) *adjective.* Cheerful; carefree.

light·house (LIGHT-howss) *noun.* A tower with a bright light at the top that serves as a signal to guide ships or warn of danger. **lighthouses.**

lighthouse

light·ness (LIGHT-niss) *noun.* 1. The condition of being light in weight. 2. Gaiety; freedom from seriousness.

light·ning (LIGHT-ning) *noun.* A discharge of electricity in the sky causing a flash of light and the sound of thunder.

lightning bug. A small beetle that gives off a glow at night; a firefly.

light·weight (LIGHT-wayt) *adjective.* Not weighing very much. *—noun.* A boxer or wrestler weighing between 127 and 135 pounds.

light-year. The distance that light travels in one year, nearly six trillion miles.

lik·a·ble (LIGH-kə-bəl) Also **likeable** *adjective.* Attractive; popular. **—likably** or **likeably** *adverb.*

[1]**like** (LIGHK) *verb.* 1. To enjoy; delight in: Sarah *likes* swimming. 2. To want or desire: I would *like* more cake. **liked, liking.** *—noun.* (Plural) The thing one favors or prefers: Mother knows my *likes* and dislikes in food. **likes.**

[2]**like** (LIGHK) *preposition.* 1. Comparable; similar to: Marty is *like* his father. 2. In the usual way of: That's just *like* Ray, to run off when there's trouble. 3. Willing to: I don't feel *like* going to the party. 4. As if there will be: It looks *like* snow. *—adjective.* Similar or the same. *—noun.* Things or people that are alike: In the attic we found clothes, furniture, and the *like.* **likes.**

-like *suffix.* Indicates similarity: child*like;* bird*like.*

like·li·hood (LIGHK-lee-hud) *noun.* Probability: There is little *likelihood* of snow on such a warm day.

like·ly (LIGHK-lee) *adjective.* 1. Probable; to be expected: a *likely* result. 2. Appropriate; suitable: The valley was a *likely* place to build a cabin. 3. Believable: This is not a very *likely* excuse. **likelier, likeliest.** *—adverb.* Probably.

lik·en (LIGH-kən) *verb.* To match or compare: Dad *likened* the clever salesman to a sly fox. **likened, likening.**

like·ness (LIGHK-niss) *noun.* 1. A resemblance; similarity: Jim bears a strong *likeness* to his older brother.

2. A drawing, picture, or other representation: This sketch is an excellent *likeness* of General Lee.

like·wise (LIGHK-wighz) *adverb.* 1. In the same manner: One monkey climbed up the tree, and a second one did *likewise.* 2. Also; too.

lik·ing (LIGH-king) *noun.* A state of caring for; fondness.

li·lac (LIGH-lək) *noun.* 1. A shrub that bears clusters of fragrant purple or white flowers. 2. (Also *adjective*). A pale purple color.

lilt *noun.* 1. A pleasant, lively melody. 2. A pleasant rhythm or quality of sound: the *lilt* of the child's laughter.

lil·y (LIL-ee) *noun.* A plant that has bell-shaped flowers in a variety of colors. **lilies.**

lily of the valley. 1. A bell-shaped, white, sweet-smelling flower. 2. The plant on which this flower grows.

lima bean (LIGH-mə been) 1. A flat, green seed that is eaten as a vegetable. 2. The plant on which this seed grows.

limb (LIM) *noun.* 1. A big branch of a tree. 2. One of the extensions of the body used for moving or holding, as the arms and legs. —**out on a limb.** In a difficult or awkward situation.

lim·ber (LIM-bər) *adjective.* Flexible; able to bend or twist easily: Rubber is a *limber* material. —*verb.* To make or become limber or flexible. **limbered, limbering.**

[1]**lime** (LIGHM) *noun.* 1. A green, sour-tasting fruit used for flavoring. 2. The tree on which this fruit grows. 3. (Also *adjective*) A yellow-green color. **limes.**

[2]**lime** (LIGHM) *noun.* A mineral used in making cement and mortar.

lim·er·ick (LIM-ər-ik) *noun.* A humorous poem of five lines.

lime·stone (LIGHM-stohn) *noun.* A rock often used for building purposes or for making lime.

lim·it (LIM-it) *noun.* 1. The greatest amount, distance, or degree allowed; a restriction: The speed *limit* on the highway is 60 miles per hour. 2. A boundary: A fence marked the *limit* of the farmer's property. —*verb.* To place a limit on. **limited, limiting.** —**limitation** (lim-ə-TAY-shən) *noun.*

lim·ou·sine (lim-ə-ZEEN or LIM-ə-zeen) *noun.* 1. A large, fancy automobile that is usually driven by a chauffeur. 2. A small bus used to transport people to and from airports. **limousines.**

[1]**limp** *verb.* To walk as though lame; hobble. **limped, limping.** —*noun.* A faltering step: walk with a *limp.*

[2]**limp** *adjective.* Not firm or rigid; drooping. **limper, limpest.** —**limply** *adverb.*

lin·den (LIN-dən) *noun.* A large tree with yellow-white flowers and heart-shaped leaves.

[1]**line** (LIGHN) *noun.* 1. A thin mark, such as the result of running a pencil across a sheet of paper. 2. Any thin mark; a wrinkle: *lines* on the face. 3. A length of string, rope, or wire: a fishing *line.* 4. A length of wire or pipe used to carry electricity, water, or gas. 5. A boundary or limit: the state *line.* 6. A row of people or things. 7. A row of printed or written words: The poem was 14 *lines* long. 8. A series of people or things following one after the other: The prince comes from a long *line* of royalty. 9. A particular interest or activity: Coin collecting is not my *line.* 10. A particular type of sales item: a *line* of soap products. 11. A system of transportation: There are several rail *lines* that provide service to Chicago. 12. (Football) The row of players positioned in front of the backfield. **lines.** —*verb.* 1. To make a thin mark on. 2. To form a border along. **lined, lining.** —**line up.** 1. To form into a row. 2. To organize.

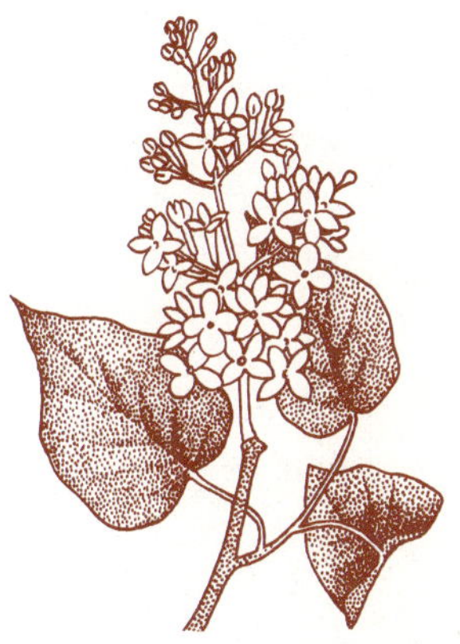

lilac

lilies of the valley

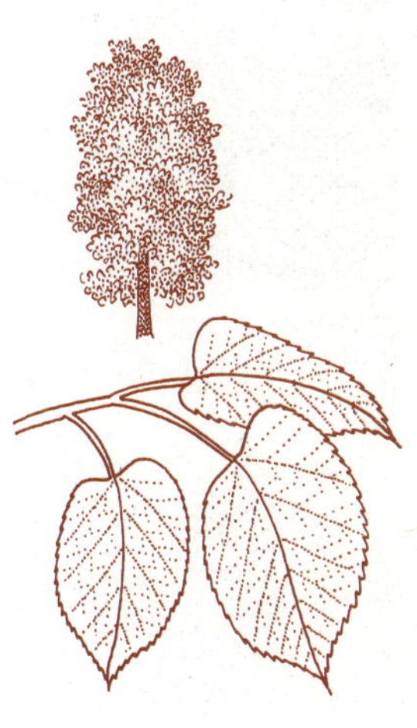

linden

lintel

lion

liner

linnet

[2]**line** *verb.* To cover the inside of something: The drawer was *lined* with paper. **lined, lining.**

lin·e·age (LIN-ee-ij) *noun.* Ancestry; line of descent: I come from African *lineage.*

lin·e·ar (LIN-ee-ər) *adjective.* Related to or resembling a line or lines.

linear measure. A system for measuring length: Feet, yards, and inches are units of *linear measure.*

lin·en (LIN-ən) *noun.* 1. Thread made from flax. 2. Cloth woven from this thread. 3. (Often plural) Goods made from such cloth, especially sheets, tablecloths, napkins, and the like.

line of force. The path which a charged particle will follow in an electrical or magnetic field.

line of symmetry. Any line that divides an organism or a geometrical figure into two identical parts.

lin·er (LIGH-nər) *noun.* 1. An airplane or a ship used for carrying passengers: an ocean *liner;* an air*liner.* 2. A piece of material placed inside or on the back of something: Mother always puts a plastic *liner* in my lunch box.

line segment. Any portion of a straight or curved line.

lin·ger (LING-gər) *verb.* To remain or stay for a while. **lingered, lingering.**

lin·ing (LIGH-ning) *noun.* A piece of material or a coating inside or on the back of something: My navy jacket has a red *lining.*

link (LINGK) *noun.* 1. Something that joins or connects. 2. One of the loops in a chain. 3. Anything that looks like or acts like a link in a chain: sausage *links.* —*verb.* To join or be joined: The policemen *linked* arms to keep the crowd back. **linked, linking.**

lin·net (LIN-it) *noun.* A small, brown song bird found in Europe, Africa, and Asia.

li·no·le·um (li-NOH-lee-əm) *noun.* A hard, long-lasting washable material formed into sheets and used as a covering, particularly on floors.

lin·seed (LIN-seed) *noun.* The seed of the flax plant.

linseed oil. A yellow oil pressed from the seeds of the flax plant, used in making ink, paint, linoleum, and other products.

lint *noun.* Fuzz or small bits of loose material or thread.

lin·tel (LINT-l) *noun.* A piece of material such as wood that forms the top part of a window or door and supports the wall above it.

li·on (LIGH-ən) *noun.* A large, golden-brown, meat-eating cat found in Africa and parts of Asia.

li·on·ess (LIGH-ə-niss) *noun.* A female lion. **lionesses.**

lip *noun.* 1. One of the two folds of flesh that surround the mouth. 2. Anything that resembles or acts like a lip: the *lip* of a pitcher. 3. (Slang) Impudent remarks.

lip-read (LIP-reed) *verb.* To understand (without hearing) another person's words by watching the movement of his lips and face. **lip-read, lip-reading.**

lip·stick (LIP·stik) *noun.* A small wax-like stick used to color lips.

liq·ue·fy (LIK-wə-figh) Also **liquify** *verb.* To make or become liquid. **liquefied, liquefying.**

liq·uid (LIK-wid) *noun.* A fluid, like water, that is able to flow and change into the shape of its container. —*adjective.* 1. Melted; fluid: Pour *liquid* butter over the popcorn. 2. Flowing smoothly and pleasantly: a *liquid* voice. 3. Easily changed into cash: *liquid* assets.

liquid measure. A system for measuring liquid quantities: Quarts are units of *liquid measure.*

liq·uor (LIK-ər) *noun.* 1. An alcoholic drink. 2. A liquid.

lisp *noun.* A speech defect that makes it difficult to pronounce words clearly, especially the sounds of *s* and *z.* —*verb.* To talk with a lisp. **lisped, lisping.**

[1]**list** *noun.* A series of names, as of items, persons, or events: a grocery *list.* —*verb.* To make a list or put on a list: Mary *listed* all the things she wanted for her birthday. **listed, listing.**

[2]**list** *verb.* To tip to the side: The boat *listed* after it hit the rock. **listed, listing.** —*noun.* A tipping to the side.

lis·ten (LISS-n) *verb.* To hear on purpose; pay attention. **listened, listening.**

list·less (LIST-liss) *adjective.* Having no energy or spirit: Very warm weather makes me *listless.* —**listlessly** *adverb.*

lit *verb.* See [1]**light.**

li·ter (LEE-tər) *noun.* A unit, in the metric system of measurement, equal to 1.056 liquid quarts.

lit·er·al (LIT-ər-əl) *adjective.* 1. Having the exact meaning of the word or words presented. 2. Word for word the same as someone has written or spoken: The reporter used a tape recorder to get a *literal* report of the interview. 3. Concerned only with facts; uninspired. —**literally** *adverb.*

lit·er·ar·y (LIT-ə-rehr-ee) *adjective.* Of or referring to literature.

lit·er·ate (LIT-ər-it) *adjective.* 1. Having the ability to read and write. 2. Having education; speaking or writing clearly or eloquently. —**literacy** *noun.*

lit·er·a·ture (LIT-ər-ə-chur) *noun.* 1. Written works highly regarded for their excellence. 2. The writings of a particular group or of a particular field: French *literature.* 3. Any written matter such as pamphlets and advertisements.

lithe (LYTH) *adjective.* Having the ability to move easily and gracefully. —**lithely** *adverb.*

lith·o·sphere (LITH-ə-sfihr) *noun.* The outer layer of the earth containing all the rocks but not including the oceans or the atmosphere.

lit·mus (LIT-məss) *noun.* A powder, made from certain plants, that is often used to find out if substances are acids or bases.

litmus paper. Paper that has been treated with litmus powder.

lit·ter (LIT-ər) *noun.* 1. Scattered objects, especially paper, cans, bottles, and other rubbish that has been carelessly discarded. 2. A stretcher for carrying the sick and injured. 3. The young born to an animal at one time: a *litter* of kittens. 4. A seat attached to long poles and carried on men's shoulders or the backs of animals. —*verb.* To throw away trash carelessly. **littered, littering.**

litter (definition 4)

lit·ter·bug (LIT-ər-buhg) *noun.* (Slang) One who litters.

lit·tle (LIT-l) *adjective.* 1. Small. 2. Lasting for a short time: a *little* while. 3. Not strong: a *little* push. 4. Not important: a *little* gift. 5. Mean or spiteful: a *little* person. **littler** or **less, littlest** or **least.** —*noun.* A small amount. —*adverb.* Not a lot; not much. **less, least.**

live (LIV) *verb.* 1. To exist; be alive: George Washington *lived* in the 18th century. 2. To make one's home (in): Pierre *lives* in France. 3. To conduct or spend: to *live* a life of crime. 4. To be remembered or used: The great works of art *live* long after their creators are dead. —(LIGHV) *adjective.* 1. Existing, alive. 2. Burning, afire: a *live* ash. 3. Able to be exploded: a *live* bomb. 4. Filled with energy: a *live* wire. —**liveliness** *noun.* —**lively** *adverb.*

live·li·hood (LIGHV-lee-hud) *noun.* The way someone earns a living.

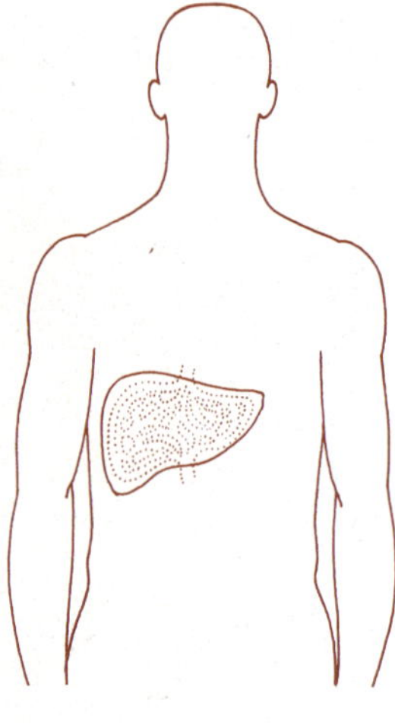
liver

lobster

llamas

live·long (LIV-lawng) *adjective.* Complete, whole: "I've been working on the railroad all the *livelong* day." (Old song).

liv·er (LIV-ər) *noun.* An organ in the body of man and certain animals that helps in the formation of blood and aids in the body's absorption of food.

live·stock (LIGHV-stok) *noun.* Farm animals such as cows, horses, pigs, or sheep.

liv·id (LIV-id) *adjective.* 1. Ashen; grayish: John turned *livid* when he saw the cars crash. 2. Very angry. 3. Black-and-blue, as from a bruise. —**lividly** *adverb.*

liv·ing (LIV-ing) *adjective.* 1. Alive. 2. Referring to all people alive. —*noun.* 1. The state of having life. 2. Self-support; livelihood: How does your dad make his *living*? 3. All those alive: Pray for all men, the *living* and the dead.

living room. The room in a home used for relaxation and entertainment of guests.

liz·ard (LIZ-ərd) *noun.* A reptile with four legs, a long tail, and a scaly body.

lla·ma (LAH-mə) *noun.* An animal of South America related to the camel, used to carry loads and as a source of wool.

LM Also **LEM** *abbreviation.* Lunar module.

load (LOHD) *noun.* 1. The amount that something can or does hold: This elevator will support a *load* of no more than 1,500 pounds. 2. Something that is carried: a *load* of groceries. 3. A burden (either physical or mental): a *load* off my mind. 4. (Informal, often plural) A lot: Jenny has *loads* of dolls. —*verb.* 1. To put a load in or on: The men *loaded* the truck with furniture. 2. To fill (with something): to *load* a camera. **loaded, loading.**

[1]**loaf** (LOHF) *noun.* A molded mass of food that has been formed into an oblong shape and baked: a *loaf* of bread. —**loaves** (LOHVZ) *plural.*

[2]**loaf** (LOHF) *verb.* To idle, waste time. **loafed, loafing.**

loafer (LOHF-ər) *noun.* 1. A person who idles or wastes time. 2. A soft slipper-like shoe.

loam (LOHM) *noun.* Rich soil made up of sand, fine earth (usually from a river or lake), decayed leaves, and clay.

loan (LOHN) *noun.* 1. Money given upon the promise of repayment. 2. Anything given (for short-term use) upon the promise that it will be returned. —*verb.* To lend. **loaned, loaning.**

loath (LOHTH) Also **loth** *adjective.* Not willing.

loathe (LOHTH) *verb.* To dislike intensely. **loathed, loathing.**

loath·ing (LOH-thing) *noun.* A strong dislike; distaste.

loath·some (LOHTH-səm or LOHTH-səm) *adjective.* Creating a feeling of strong dislike or distaste: The princess thought the dragon *loathsome.* —**loathsomely** *adverb.*

lob·by (LOB-ee) *noun.* 1. An entrance hall or waiting room. 2. A group of people who try to influence those who hold office or make laws. **lobbies.** —*verb.* To try to influence officeholders or lawmakers. **lobbied, lobbying.**

lobe (LOHB) *noun.* A rounded part that protrudes or is otherwise set apart: an ear*lobe*; a *lobe* of the brain. **lobes.**

lob·ster (LOB-stər) *noun.* An edible sea animal with ten legs (the front two having claws), a hard outer covering, and no backbone.

lo·cal (LOH-kəl) *adjective.* Referring to, situated in, serving, or limited to a small area: *local* newspaper. —*noun.* A train or bus that makes all the stops on a route. —**locally** *adverb.*

lo·cale (loh-KAL) *noun.* A place or area (in which something happened). **locales.**

lo·cal·i·ty (lo-KAL-ə-tee) *noun.* A particular area, place, or spot: There are no movie theaters in our *locality.* **localities.**

lo·cate (LOH-kayt) *verb.* 1. To find the place of: Dad couldn't *locate* the leak in the roof. 2. To put or place: Mr. Joseph will *locate* his store in the shopping center. **located, locating.**

lo·ca·tion (loh-KAY-shən) *noun.* 1. A place, a position: The store has moved to a new *location.* 2. The act of finding or locating. **—on location.** (Motion pictures) A place away from the movie studio: The film about Eskimos was made *on location* in Alaska.

lock (LOK) *noun.* 1. A device for fastening (something) securely. 2. A strand of hair. 3. An enclosed section of a canal used to raise or lower the water level and thus float boats up or down a slope. 4. The part of the gun that causes the explosion to take place. *—verb.* 1. To fasten securely as with a bolt or key. 2. To stick or become immovable: The drawbridge is *locked* in the open position. **locked, locking. —lock up.** 1. To lock all the doors and windows (of a house). 2. To put in jail.

lock·er (LOK-ər) *noun.* An enclosed storage place in a school or public place that can be fastened with a lock.

lock·et (LOK-it) *noun.* A small case in which something such as a picture can be carried; usually worn on a chain around the neck.

lock·jaw (LOK-jaw) *noun.* A disease that makes it difficult to open the mouth or swallow: *Lockjaw* is also called "tetanus."

lock·smith (LOK-smith) *noun.* One who makes or repairs locks.

lo·co·mo·tion (loh-kə-MOH-shən) *noun.* The act or method of moving from place to place: Bicycle riding is his favorite form of *locomotion.*

lo·co·mo·tive (loh-kə-MOH-tiv) *noun.* A railroad engine; a machine used to move trains on railroad tracks.

lo·cust (LOH-kəst) *noun.* 1. A plant-eating insect of the grasshopper family. 2. A hardwood tree of North America, with sweet-smelling white flowers.

lode (LOHD) *noun.* A layer or vein of metal ore. **lodes.**

lode·stone (LOHD-stohn) **Also loadstone** *noun.* 1. A rock containing iron that acts like a magnet. 2. Anything that attracts. **lodestones.**

lodge (LOJ) *verb.* 1. To stay or provide a place to stay. 2. To make or file: We *lodged* a protest over the poor service. 3. To stick or become fixed: His foot was *lodged* between the rocks. **lodged, lodging.** *—noun.* 1. A place to stay or live in. 2. A cabin or country house used by sportsmen. 3. A branch of a secret society, or the place where it meets. **lodges.**

lodg·er (LOJ-ər) *noun.* One who lives in a rented room.

loft (LAWFT) *noun.* 1. The upper floor of a barn or stable where hay is stored. 2. The upper story of a factory or warehouse. 3. An attic.

loft·y (LAWF-tee) *adjective.* 1. High: Switzerland has *lofty* mountains. 2. Noble: He has *lofty* ambitions. **loftier, loftiest. —loftily** *adverb.*

log (LAWG) *noun.* 1. A piece of rough wood, such as part of a fallen tree trunk or limb. 2. A daily record of a trip: They found the ship's *log* in the wreckage. *—verb.* 1. To cut down trees. 2. To keep a record. 3. To fly a plane or sail a ship (a certain time or distance): The pilot *logged* 800 hours. **logged, logging.**

log·ging (LAW-ging) *noun.* The cutting down of trees for use as lumber.

locomotive

locust

lock

longhorn

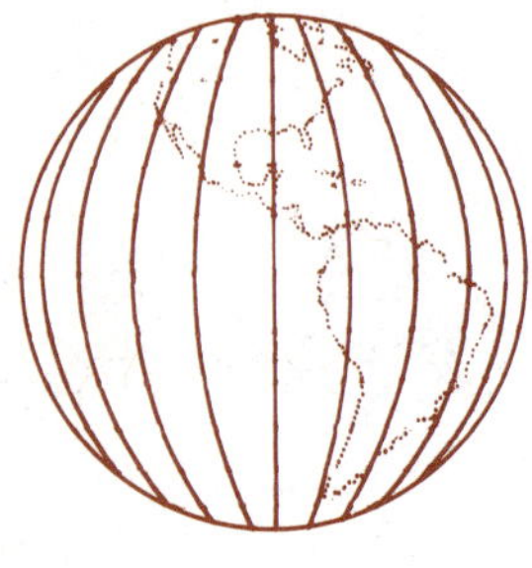
longitude

loon

log·ic (LOJ-ik) *noun.* 1. Careful, sensible thinking. 2. The science that deals with reasoning.

log·i·cal (LOJ-i-kəl) *adjective.* Reasonable; in keeping with what is known. —**logically** *adverb.*

loin *noun.* The part of a man or an animal between the hips and the lower ribs.

loi·ter (LOI-tər) *verb.* To waste time; stand around idly. **loitered, loitering.**

loll (LOL) *verb.* To lounge; relax: The boys were *lolling* on the front step. **lolled, lolling.**

lol·li·pop (LOL-ee-pop) Also **lollypop** *noun.* A sucker; a piece of candy on a stick.

lone (LOHN) *adjective.* Single; by oneself: a *lone* wolf.

lone·ly (LOHN-lee) *adjective.* 1. Without any companions: "I wandered *lonely* as a cloud." (Wordsworth). 2. Without friendly or close companions. 3. Deserted: The road was dark and *lonely.* **lonelier, loneliest.** —**loneliness** *noun.*

lone·some (LOHN-səm) *adjective.* 1. Sad at being by oneself. 2. Causing one to feel lonely. —**lonesomely** *adverb.*

long (LAWNG) *adjective.* 1. Not short; greater than most in length or time: a *long* nose; a *long* nap. 2. Of a set distance from end to end: How *long* is that stick? **longer, longest.** —*adverb.* Over or during a considerable time: The snow fell all day *long.* —*verb.* To wish or desire. **longed, longing.** —**before long.** Soon. —**so** (or **as**) **long as.** 1. On the condition that: You can go out, *so long as* you're home by 10:30. 2. Because of the fact that; since: *So long as* you're up, would you turn off the TV?

long·hand (LAWNG-hand) *noun.* Handwriting: The letter was not typed but written in *longhand.*

long·horn (LAWNG-horn) *noun.* A breed of cattle having long horns.

long·ing (LAWNG-ing) *noun.* A strong desire or wish.

lon·gi·tude (LON-jə-tood or LON-jə-tyood) *noun.* The distance, given in degrees, east or west from a line that runs from the North Pole to the South Pole and passes through Greenwich, England: Washington, D.C., is located at 77° west *longitude.* **longitudes.** —**longitudinal** *adjective.*

long-playing (LAWNG-PLAY-ing) Also **LP** *adjective.* Referring to a narrow-grooved phonograph record made to be played at a speed of $33\frac{1}{3}$ revolutions per minute.

long-wind·ed (LAWNG-WIN-did) *adjective.* Wordy; talking or writing too much.

look (LUK) *verb.* 1. To use the eyes for seeing; direct one's glance. 2. To appear to be: She *looks* sick. 3. To search (for). **looked, looking.** —*noun.* 1. The act of seeing. 2. Appearance: The cloth has the *look* of silk. 3. (Plural) Personal appearance: I don't like his *looks.* —**look after.** To take care of. —**look down on.** To regard as bad or of little value. —**look up.** To search for, as in a book: *Look up* the word in the dictionary.

looking glass. A mirror.

look·out (LUK-owt) *noun.* 1. A close watch: Be on the *lookout* for sharks. 2. A watchman. 3. A high place from which one has a good view.

[1]**loom** *noun.* A machine or frame on which cloth is woven.

[2]**loom** *verb.* To take form or appear in a magnified or strange way: A monster *loomed* out of the mist. **loomed, looming.**

loon *noun.* 1. A large bird that catches fish by diving into the water. 2. A foolish person.

loop *noun.* 1. The nearly oval shape formed when something such as a line, string, or wire curves and crosses over itself: Her handwriting has large *loops* on the "l's." 2. Anything similar to this in shape: He put a rope through the belt *loops* to hold up his jeans. *—verb.* To form or fasten with a loop. **looped, looping.**

loop·hole (LOOP-hohl) *noun.* 1. A small opening in a wall: The soldier fired his gun through the *loophole.* 2. A way of avoiding something; a *loophole* in an agreement. **loopholes.**

loose (LOOSS) *adjective.* 1. Not tight or secure: a *loose* tooth. 2. Not packaged: You can buy grass seed in packages or *loose* by the pound. 3. Not well-controlled; having poor habits or morals. **looser, loosest.** *—adverb.* Not tied up or enclosed: Dogs are not allowed to run *loose* in the city. *—verb.* To set free: "He hath *loosed* the fateful lightning of His terrible swift sword." (J. W. Howe). **loosed, loosing. —loosely** *adverb.*

loos·en (LOO-sən) *verb.* To untie or make looser: He *loosened* the rope around the dog's neck. **loosened, loosening.**

loot *noun.* 1. Stolen goods or money. 2. (Slang) Money made in an easy way. *—verb.* To steal from or cause damage to: The retreating soldiers *looted* homes along the way. **looted, looting.**

lope (LOHP) *verb.* To run gracefully with long strides. **loped, loping.** *—noun.* The act of moving in this manner.

lop·sid·ed (LOP-sigh-did) *adjective.* Having sides that do not match; heavier or larger on one side. **—lopsidedly** *adverb.*

lord *noun.* 1. A ruler or master. 2. A landholder during the Middle Ages. 3. (British) Title given to a nobleman. 4. [Capital L] God; Jesus Christ.

lore (LOR) *noun.* 1. History or legends. 2. A particular kind of knowledge: animal *lore.*

lose (LOOZ) *verb.* 1. To misplace; be unable to find. 2. To be unable to keep: *lose* your balance. 3. To fail to win: *lose* the game. 4. To be deprived of, as by death, accident, or destruction: The storm caused us to *lose* our maple tree. 5. To stray from: *lose* one's way. **lost, losing.**

los·er (LOOZ-ər) *noun.* 1. One who fails to win. 2. (Informal) A person who repeatedly fails.

loss (LAWSS) *noun.* 1. Something that is lost. 2. The harm suffered as a result of losing: His death was a *loss* to his family. **losses.**

lost (LAWST) *adjective.* 1. Misplaced, missing. 2. Ruined; damaged beyond repair: The boat is *lost;* it's sinking fast. 3. Missed; not taken advantage of: Grandpa regrets the *lost* chances of his youth. 4. Confused; needing help: I'm *lost;* I just can't do this math problem. *—verb. See* **lose.**

lot *noun.* 1. A piece of land with definite boundaries: All the *lots* on the street are the same size. 2. A number of persons or things taken as a whole: The stock was sold in *lots* of 100 shares. 3. An object drawn to decide by chance: The *lots* were slips of paper with numbers on them. 4. The result of deciding in such a way: It was my *lot* to go last. 5. Fate or fortune: "The policeman's *lot* is not a happy one." (W. S. Gilbert). **—a lot.** 1. (Informal) A large quantity or number: There is *a lot* of snow on the ground. 2. Much: He is *a lot* taller now.

lo·tion (LOH-shən) *noun.* A liquid, often containing medicine, to use on the skin.

lot·ter·y (LOT-ə-ree) *noun.* A method of awarding a prize: In a *lottery,* tickets are sold or passed out, and the winner is chosen when a matching ticket is drawn by lot. **lotteries.**

lo·tus (LOH-təss) *noun.* A water lily, a plant with large waxy blossoms. **lotuses.**

lotus

loud (LOWD) *adjective.* 1. Great in volume of sound; noisy. 2. Too strong or colorful: *loud* clothes. **louder, loudest.** —*adverb.* Also **loudly.** In a loud way: Don't talk so *loud.* —**loudness** *noun.*

loud·speak·er (LOWD-spee-kər) *noun.* A device to change electrical signals into amplified sounds that can be heard from a distance.

Louisiana
★capital: Baton Rouge

Lou·i·si·an·a (loo-ee-zee-AN-ə) A state in south central United States, 18th to join the Union (1812). —**La.** *abbreviation.* Also **LA** for Zip Codes.

lounge (LOWNJ) *verb.* To sit, stand, or move in a relaxed way. **lounged, lounging.** —*noun.* 1. A room or area with comfortable furniture for relaxing. 2. A couch. **lounges.**

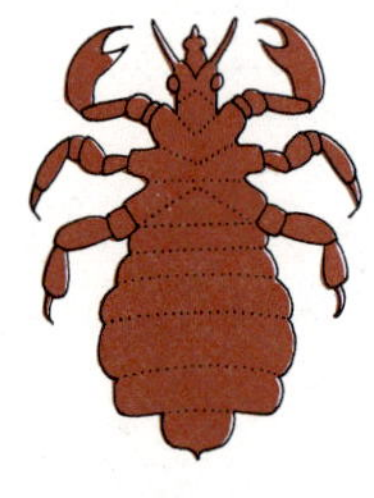

louse

louse (LOWSS) *noun.* 1. A tiny, wingless biting or sucking insect that lives on warm-blooded animals. 2. A wingless insect that lives on plants. 3. (Slang) A mean, unpleasant person. —**lice** (LIGHSS) *plural.* —**louse up.** (Slang) To spoil.

lous·y (LOW-zee) *adjective.* 1. Having lice. 2. (Slang) Poor or not good: We had a *lousy* time. **lousier, lousiest.**

lov·a·ble (LUHV-ə-bəl) *adjective.* Attracting love; endearing. —**lovably** *adverb.*

love (LUHV) *noun.* 1. A feeling of deep affection. 2. A strong attraction or liking for: Father has a *love* of good food. 3. A person who is loved: "Come live with me, and be my *love.*" (Marlowe). **loves.** —*verb.* 1. To have a deep, affectionate feeling for. 2. To have a strong liking for. **loved, loving.**

love·ly (LUHV-lee) *adjective.* Delightful; lovable; beautiful. **lovelier, loveliest.** —**loveliness** *noun.*

lov·er (LUHV-ər) *noun.* 1. A person in love with another person. 2. A person having a strong liking for something: a *lover* of good food.

[1]**low** (LOH) *adjective.* 1. Not tall: *low* table. 2. Close to the ground: They ducked under the *low* limb. 3. Mean or spiteful: a *low* trick. 4. Below normal in cost, degree, or standard: *low* price. 5. Depressed: Sally is *low* today. 6. Nearly out of: The storm caught them *low* on food. 7. Deep in the musical scale: The men sang the *low* notes. 8. Not loud: *low* music. **lower, lowest.** —*adverb.* In or to a low level, rank, degree, cost, or standard: Play the radio *low.* —*noun.* A lowest level: Jane's bowling score hit a new *low.*

[2]**low** (LOH) *verb.* To moo or make a sound like cattle. **lowed, lowing.** —*noun.* A moo.

low·er (LOH-ər) *verb.* 1. To let or pull down: *Lower* the shade. 2. To reduce: to *lower* prices. **lowered, lowering.** —*adjective.* Less high.

low·ly (LOH-lee) *adjective.* Unimportant or humble. **lowlier, lowliest.**

[1]**lox** (LOKS) *noun.* Salmon that has been preserved by smoking.

[2]**lox** (LOKS) *noun.* Liquid oxygen, used as fuel for rockets.

loy·al (LOI-əl) *adjective.* 1. Faithful to one's government or leader: a *loyal* citizen. 2. Steadfast in devotion to a person, idea, or thing: a *loyal* friend. —**loyally** *adverb.*

loy·al·ty (LOI-əl-tee) *noun.* Being faithful or loyal. **loyalties.**

LSD. A dangerous chemical (lysergic acid diethylamide) that, taken internally, can cause wild and frightening fantasies, sometimes resulting in senseless and dangerous actions. Also known as **acid.**

lu·bri·cant (LOO-bri-kənt) *noun.* An oil, grease, or other material used on moving parts of a machine to make them work smoothly.

lu·bri·cate (LOO-bri-kayt) *verb.* To

apply oil or grease to the moving parts of a machine. **lubricated, lubricating.** —**lubrication** *noun.*

lu·cid (LOO-sid) *adjective.* 1. Easy to understand: *lucid* instructions. 2. Sane: The court ruled the old man was *lucid* and knew what he was doing. **lucider, lucidest.** —**lucidly** *adverb.*

luck (LUHK) *noun.* Fortune, especially good fortune; chance: Tom won the game by *luck.*

luck·y (LUHK-ee) *adjective.* Having good fortune or luck: Jane was *lucky* not to catch cold after being in the storm. **luckier, luckiest.** —**luckily** *adverb.*

lu·di·crous (LOO-di-krəss) *adjective.* So ridiculous or absurd as to be laughable: The actions of the clown were *ludicrous.*

lug (LUHG) *verb.* To drag or pull with difficulty: Joe had to *lug* the garbage cans out. **lugged, lugging.**

lug·gage (LUHG-ij) *noun.* Baggage; suitcases.

luke·warm *adjective.* 1. Not hot and not cold. 2. Showing little enthusiasm or concern.

lull (LUHL) *verb.* To calm or soothe; quiet: We *lulled* the baby to sleep with songs. **lulled, lulling.** —*noun.* A period of calm or quiet: There was a *lull* in the storm.

lull·a·by (LUHL-ə-bigh) *noun.* A quiet song to put a baby to sleep. **lullabies.**

lum·ber (LUHM-bər) *noun.* Sawed timber ready for use; boards; planks. —*verb.* 1. To saw or cut timber to make it ready for use. 2. To move clumsily and noisily: The bear *lumbered* through the undergrowth. **lumbered, lumbering.**

lum·ber·jack (LUHM-bər-jak) *noun.* A person who cuts down trees and prepares logs for the mill.

lum·ber·man (LUHM-bər-mən) *noun.* 1. A lumberjack. 2. A person who buys or sells lumber. —**lumbermen** *plural.*

lu·mi·nous (LOO-mə-nəss) *adjective.* 1. Giving off light; bright: Jack could see only the dog's *luminous* eyes in the dark. 2. Clear; easy to understand. —**luminously** *adverb.*

lump (LUHMP) *noun.* 1. A mass of no special shape: *lump* of coal. 2. A swelling or bump: Joe had a *lump* on his head. 3. A cube, as of sugar. —*verb.* 1. To put together: The boys *lumped* their money to buy a bat. 2. To form lumps: The custard *lumped* because the oven was too hot. **lumped, lumping.**

lu·na·cy (LOO-nə-see) *noun.* 1. Insanity. 2. Foolishness: It was *lunacy* to go without a coat in the rain.

lu·nar (LOO-nər) *adjective.* Related to the moon: *lunar* eclipse.

lunar module. A self-contained unit that lands on the moon and is a part of a larger spacecraft.

lu·na·tic (LOO-nə-tik) *noun.* An insane person. —*adjective.* 1. Insane. 2. Very foolish or wild: *lunatic* behavior.

lunch (LUHNCH) *noun.* A light meal, usually in the middle of the day. **lunches.** —*verb.* To eat lunch. **lunched, lunching.**

lunch·eon (LUHN-chən) *noun.* 1. A lunch. 2. A party in the middle of the day at which a lunch is served.

lung (LUHNG) *noun.* Either of the pair of organs, found in the chest of man and animals, that take in air to supply the blood with oxygen and remove carbon dioxide from the blood.

lunge (LUHNJ) *noun.* A sudden forward movement: The bus started with a *lunge* and Jane almost fell. **lunges.** —*verb.* To move forward suddenly. **lunged, lunging.**

lumberjack

lunar module

lynx

lyre

lurch (LERCH) *verb.* To roll or stagger suddenly: The ship *lurched* in the heavy seas. **lurched, lurching.** —*noun.* A sudden stagger. **lurches.**

lure (LUR) *noun.* 1. Something that attracts or tempts: the *lure* of outdoors on the first warm day of spring. 2. A device used as bait for fish. **lures.** —*verb.* To attract with bait; tempt. **lured, luring.**

lu·rid (LUR-id) *adjective.* 1. Shocking or terrible: The details of the accident were *lurid.* 2. Glowing red; lighted up: a *lurid* sky. —**luridly** *adverb.*

lurk (LERK) *verb.* To hide or wait without being detected: "Danger *lurks* within." (Shakespeare). **lurked, lurking.**

lus·cious (LUHSH-əss) *adjective.* Delicious and sweet to taste or smell: *luscious* pear. —**lusciously** *adverb.*

[1]**lush** (LUHSH) *adjective.* 1. Having heavy green growth: *Lush* vegetation grew in the jungle. 2. Luxuriant: *lush* carpets. **lusher, lushest.**

[2]**lush** *noun.* (Slang) A person who habitually drinks too much. **lushes.**

lus·ter (LUHSS-tər) *noun.* 1. A gloss or shine: The car had a deep *luster* after Gene waxed it. 2. Brightness; brilliance: The diamond shone with a fiery *luster.*

lus·trous (LUHSS-trəss) *adjective.* Having a shining surface: *lustrous* pearl. —**lustrously** *adverb.*

lust·y (LUHSS-tee) *adjective.* Full of vigor and strength. **lustier, lustiest.** —**lustily** *adverb.*

lute (LOOT) *noun.* A stringed instrument played by plucking with the fingers. **lutes.**

lux·u·ri·ant (luhg-ZHUR-ee-ənt) *adjective.* 1. Growing thickly or lushly: The garden was *luxuriant* after the rains. 2. Richly made or decorated. —**luxuriance** *noun.* —**luxuriantly** *adverb.*

lux·u·ri·ous (luhg-ZHUR-ee-əss) *adjective.* 1. Having a love for luxury: *luxurious* tastes in clothes. 2. Having the qualities of luxury: a *luxurious* restaurant. —**luxuriously** *adverb.*

lux·u·ry (LUHG-zhə-ree or LUHK-shə-ree) *noun.* 1. Great ease and comfort; enjoyment of costly things. 2. Anything that provides such comfort, especially something that is nice to have but not absolutely necessary. **luxuries.**

-ly *suffix.* Indicates: 1. In a certain manner; sad*ly*, glad*ly*. 2. Having a resemblance to: man*ly*. 3. Occurring at certain intervals: year*ly*. 4. In, to, or from a certain direction: a souther*ly* wind. 5. In a certain place: third*ly*.

lye (LIGH) *noun.* A liquid or powder used in making soap and in cleaning. **lyes.**

ly·ing (LIGH-ing) *noun.* Telling an untruth or lie. —*verb. See* [1]**lie.**

lymph (LIMF) *noun.* A clear, yellowish liquid, made up mostly of white blood cells, that travels through body tissues to carry bacteria and other substances back to the bloodstream.

lynch (LINCH) *verb.* To execute, especially to hang, without giving a trial by law. **lynched, lynching.**

lynx (LINGKS) *noun.* Any of several wildcats of North America that have short tails and long legs. —**lynx** or **lynxes** *plural.*

lyre (LIGHR) *noun.* A harplike stringed instrument played especially in ancient times. **lyres.**

lyr·ic (LIHR-ik) *adjective.* Relating to poetry that expresses personal emotion and has a songlike quality. —*noun.* 1. A lyric poem. 2. (Plural) The words of a song.

lyr·i·cal (LIHR-ə-kəl) *adjective.* Songlike; emotional; excited. —**lyrically** *adverb.*

M, m (EM) The 13th letter of the English alphabet.

m. *abbreviation.* 1. Male. 2. Mile. 3. Meter. 4. [Capital M] Mach number.

Ma'am (MAM) *contraction.* A shortened form of the word *Madam.*

mac·ad·am (mə-KAD-əm) *noun.* Layers of broken stone, usually mixed with tar or asphalt, that are pressed down to make a smooth, solid road.

mac·a·ro·ni (mak-ə-ROH-nee) *noun.* 1. A food made of wheat flour paste that is formed into various shapes, dried, and boiled before being eaten. 2. (Rare) A dude; a dandy.

mac·a·roon (MAK-ə-ROON) *noun.* A sweet cooky made of sugar, egg white, and coconut or almond paste.

ma·chet·e (mə-SHET-ee or mə-CHET-ee) *noun.* A big heavy knife used for cutting (vines, sugar cane, etc.) and as a weapon.

ma·chine (mə-SHEEN) *noun.* 1. A device whose various parts connect or work together so as to do a special job: a washing *machine.* 2. Anything operated by a machine, as an airplane or automobile. 3. A device that applies force, often increasing the amount of force or changing the direction in which it is applied: The pulley, lever, and wheel are simple *machines.* 4. A living thing or one of its systems: man's digestive *machine.* 5. A group of people who control a political party, unit of government, or other organization. **machines.**

machine gun *noun.* An automatic gun that shoots numbers of bullets rapidly.

ma·chin·er·y (mə-SHEE-nər-ee) *noun.* 1. Machines: At five o'clock the factory workers turned off the *machinery.* 2. All of the parts of a machine. 3. Any working system: the *machinery* of government.

ma·chin·ist (mə-SHEE-nist) *noun.* 1. A person who runs a machine or makes or repairs machinery. 2. A person who works with machine tools.

Mach number (MAHK NUHM-bər) *noun.* The ratio of the speed of an object to the speed of sound: A rocket traveling at twice the speed of sound is traveling at *Mach* 2.

mack·er·el (MAK-ər-əl or MAK-rəl) *noun.* A food fish found in the sea. —**mackerel** or **mackerels** *plural.*

mackerel

mack·i·naw (MAK-ə-naw) *noun.* A short heavy coat of woolen material, usually with a plaid design.

mac·ra·mé (MAK-rə-may) *noun.* A material made by knotting cord or thread into a special design for use in trimming, decoration, belts, and the like.

ma·cron (MAY-kron) *noun.* A short line (¯), placed over a vowel to show that it has a long sound, as ō for the vowel sound in *home.*

mad *adjective.* 1. Insane; crazy. 2. Very excited or upset. 3. (Informal) Very enthusiastic: Bill is *mad* about collecting stamps. 4. Having rabies or hydrophobia. 5. (Informal) Very angry. **madder, maddest.** —**madly** *adverb.* —**madness** *noun.*

mad·am (MAD-əm) *noun.* 1. [Capital M] A polite term used in talking to or about a lady or woman of rank: *Madam* Chairman. 2. (Informal) The female head of a household. —**madams** or **mesdames** (may-DAHM) *plural.*

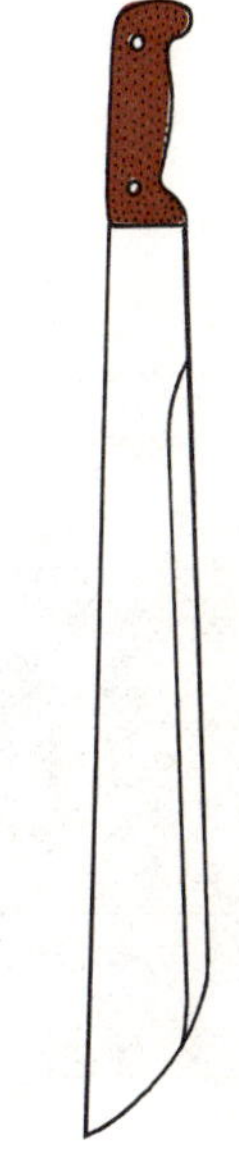
machete

MN

mad·cap (MAD-kap) *noun.* A person who does gay, wild, or reckless things without thinking. —*adjective.* Wild or reckless: a *madcap* idea.

made (MAYD) *See* **make.**

Mad·e·moi·selle (mad-mwah-ZEL) *noun.* The French word for *Miss.* —**Mesdemoiselles** (mayd-mwah-ZEL) *plural.*

mad·house (MAD-howss) *noun.* 1. (Rare) A place where mentally ill people are kept. 2. (Informal) A place full of disorder. **madhouses.**

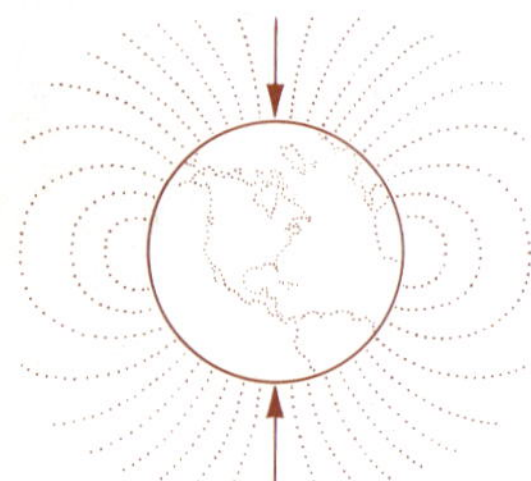

magnetic field of the earth

ma·dras (MAD-rəss or mə-DRASS) *noun.* A fine, woven cotton cloth, often with designs.

mag·a·zine (MAG-ə-zeen or mag-ə-ZEEN) *noun.* 1. A publication that appears at regular intervals and contains articles, pictures, and the like. 2. A place where ammunition and explosives are kept. 3. A metal container of cartridges, used in an automatic gun. 4. The place in a camera that holds film. **magazines.**

mag·got (MAG-ət) *noun.* An insect in an early form of its life, when it is soft and legless like a worm.

mag·ic (MAJ-ik) *noun.* 1. The art of making things seem to happen in a strange or mysterious way. 2. Something that is mysterious or full of charm. —**magical** *adjective.* —**magically** *adverb.*

ma·gi·cian (mə-JISH-ən) *noun.* 1. A person, like a witch or a fairy in a story, who does things by magic. 2. A person who does unusual or puzzling tricks to entertain others.

magic square

magic square. A square containing rows of numbers arranged so that the sum of the numbers in every horizontal, vertical, or diagonal row is exactly the same.

mag·is·trate (MAJ-is-trayt) *noun.* 1. An official who has the power to put laws into effect and see that they are obeyed. 2. A minor judge. **magistrates.**

mag·nan·i·mous (mag-NAN-ə-məss) *adjective.* Good, generous, or forgiving. —**magnanimously** *adverb.*

mag·nate (MAG-nayt) *noun.* A powerful person; a person who runs a big business. **magnates.**

mag·net (MAG-nit) *noun.* 1. An object, usually metal, with the force to draw to itself iron, steel, or certain other materials. 2. A thing or person that attracts.

mag·net·ic (mag-NET-ik) *adjective.* 1. Having the power of a magnet: a *magnetic* piece of steel. 2. Able to be magnetized. 3. Able to attract: a *magnetic* voice. —**magnetically** *adverb.*

magnetic field. The space around a magnet or an electrical conductor throughout which its magnetic attraction can be detected.

magnetic pole. 1. One of two points on a magnet at which its attracting force seems to be strongest. 2. One of the two regions of the earth to which a magnetic needle points from any spot on the globe: One *magnetic pole* is in the Arctic, the other in the Antarctic.

mag·net·ism (MAG-nə-tiz-əm) *noun.* 1. The power of a magnet. 2. The study or science of magnets and their effect. 3. The ability to charm or attract.

mag·net·ize (MAG-nə-tighz) *verb.* 1. To give the power of a magnet to. 2. To charm or attract like a magnet. **magnetized, magnetizing.**

mag·nif·i·cent (mag-NIF-ə-sənt) *adjective.* Very fine; splendid; wonderful in appearance: a *magnificent* mansion. —**magnificently** *adverb.* —**magnificence** *noun.*

mag·ni·fy (MAG-nə-figh) *verb.* 1. To make something look larger than it really is: This lens *magnifies* a fly ten times. 2. To exaggerate: make something seem more important than it is. —**magnified, magnifying.**

magnifying glass. A lens or glass that makes anything seen through it look bigger.

mag·ni·tude (MAG-nə-tood or MAG-nə-tyood) *noun.* 1. Greatness in size, position, importance: The *magnitude* of the problem frightens many people. 2. Degree of brightness of a star: a star of the first *magnitude.* **magnitudes.**

mag·no·lia (mag-NOHL-yə) *noun.* A shrub or tree that has large white, purple, or pink flowers.

mag·pie (MAG-pigh) *noun.* 1. A very noisy bird with a long tail and black-and-white feathers. 2. A person who chatters a great deal.

ma·hog·a·ny (mə-HOG-ə-nee) *noun.* 1. A tree of tropical America. 2. The dark, reddish-brown wood of this tree, often used to make fine furniture. 3. (Also *adjective*) A dark reddish-brown color.

maid (MAYD) *noun.* 1. A girl or woman who works as a servant. 2. A girl; an unmarried woman.

maid·en (MAYD-n) *noun.* A girl or young unmarried woman. —*adjective.* 1. Not married. 2. First; earliest: the airplane's *maiden* flight.

[1]**mail** (MAYL) *noun.* Letters, cards, and packages sent by a postal system. —*verb.* To send by the postal system. **mailed, mailing.**

[2]**mail** (MAYL) *noun.* A protective garment, made of linked pieces of metal and thus less rigid than suits of armor, worn in medieval times.

mail·box (MAYL-boks) *noun.* 1. A box into which mail is put for delivery by the postal service. 2. A box, as in a home or office, in which the mailman leaves the mail. **mailboxes.**

mail·man (MAYL-man) *noun.* One whose job is delivering mail. —**mailmen** *plural.*

mail order. An order sent by mail for goods that are usually also delivered by mail.

maim (MAYM) *verb.* To cripple or injure seriously. **maimed, maiming.**

main (MAYN) *adjective.* Chief; most important; leading: Jill has the *main* part in the play. —*noun.* 1. A big pipe that carries water, gas, electrical wire, etc. 2. (Rare) The open ocean: Pirates sailed the *main* long years ago. —**mainly** *adverb.*

Maine (MAYN) *noun.* A New England state of the United States, 23rd to join the Union (1820). —**Me.** *abbreviation.* Also **ME** for Zip Codes.

Maine
★capital: Augusta

main·land (MAYN-land) *noun.* The main part of a continent, not including peninsulas or nearby islands.

main·mast (MAYN-məst) *noun.* The tallest, most important mast on a ship.

magpie

main·sail (MAYN-sl) *noun.* The biggest sail on a ship.

main·spring (MAYN-spring) *noun.* 1. The most important spring of a watch, clock, or other mechanism. 2. A central reason or force.

main·stay (MAYN-stay) *noun.* 1. The rope that holds the mainmast in position. 2. The main support: Dad is the *mainstay* of our family.

main·stream (MAYN-streem) *noun.* The most popular or strongest trend: the *mainstream* of opinion.

main·tain (mayn-TAYN) *verb.* 1. To carry on or continue; keep: He *maintained* his grip on the oar. 2. To support: She *maintains* the children in comfort. 3. To declare to be true: The lawyer *maintains* they are guilty. 4. To defend against attack: The soldiers *maintained* their position under fire. **maintained, maintaining.**

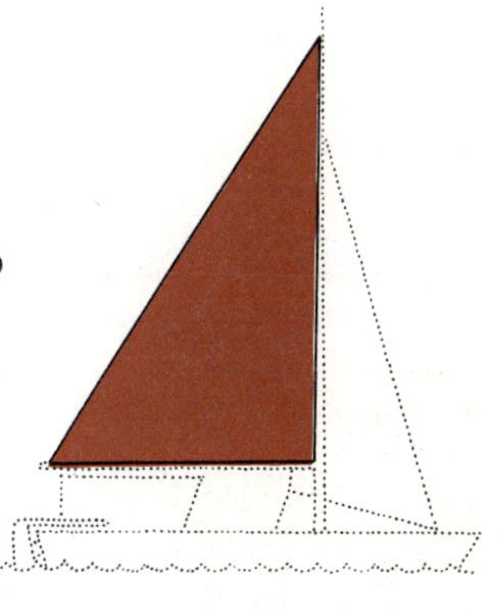

mainsail

main·te·nance (MAYN-tə-nənss) *noun.* 1. Support; upkeep: Her mother sends money for her *maintenance.* 2. Keeping up, maintaining, or continuing: the *maintenance* of order.

maize (MAYZ) *noun.* (British) Corn.

maj·es·ty (MAJ-iss-tee) *noun.* 1. Stateliness or great dignity. 2. The nobility, greatness, or power of a king or other rulers. 3. [Capital M] A title used for a king or other ruler: Make way for Her *Majesty* the Queen. **majesties. —majestic** (mə-JESS-tik) *adjective.* **—majestically** *adverb.*

ma·jor (MAY-jər) *noun.* 1. A military officer ranking just under a lieutenant colonel and just above a captain. 2. The main field of study of a student: a history *major.* —*verb.* To study as a main subject: *major* in science. **majored, majoring.** —*adjective.* 1. Greater; larger; more important: He spends the *major* part of the day studying. 2. (Music) Relating to one of two standard scales, or keys, the other one being *minor.*

major general. A U.S. military officer in the Army, Air Force, or Marine Corps who ranks just below a lieutenant general.

ma·jor·i·ty (mə-JOR-ə-tee) *noun.* 1. More than half; the greater number: A *majority* of the Scouts voted for the hike. 2. The number of votes by which one side is greater than the total of all the rest: If you get 40 votes and Mary gets 10, you win by a *majority* of 30 votes. 3. The legal age at which a person becomes an adult. **majorities.**

make (MAYK) *verb.* 1. To build, form, create: to *make* a boat. 2. To do; perform: *Make* an effort to do better. 3. To cause to be: The air conditioner *makes* us cool. 4. To meet the requirements of: She *makes* a fine mother. 5. To amount to; equal: Two nickels *make* a dime. 6. To gain or earn; acquire: *make* money, *make* friends. 7. To force or cause to: The dogcatcher *makes* us get a license for our dog. 8. To cause to succeed: Hard work *makes* many a man. 9. To understand: I can *make* nothing of this funny writing. 10. To travel at a speed of; reach: He *makes* ten miles an hour in heavy traffic. 11. To reach or arrive at: That ship always *makes* port on time. **made, making.** —*noun.* 1. Build, style; the way a thing is made: the *make* of a coat. 2. A kind or brand: a bicycle of a popular *make.* **makes. —make fast.** To attach firmly. **—make off with.** To steal. **—make up.** 1. To become friends again after a fight. 2. To put on cosmetics. 3. To create.

make-be·lieve (MAYK-bi-leev) *noun.* Something that is pretended, not real.

make·shift (MAYK-shift) *noun.* A thing used instead of the usual or proper thing: They used the cellar as a *makeshift* for a gym.

make-up (MAYK-uhp) *noun.* Also **makeup.** 1. The composition, arrangement, or construction (of something): the *make-up* of our government. 2. Colorings used to improve or change one's facial appearance; cosmetics. 3. A special examination or test given to a student who missed or failed an earlier one.

mal- *prefix.* Indicates bad or wrong: *mal*function.

mal·a·dy (MAL-ə-dee) *noun.* A sickness or disease. **maladies.**

ma·lar·i·a (mə-LAIR-ee-ə) *noun.* A tropical disease that causes attacks of fever, sweating, and chills.

male (MAYL) *noun.* One whose sex is masculine; an animal or person who can become a father. **males.**

mal·ice (MAL-iss) *noun.* Spite; ill will; the desire to hurt someone.

ma·li·cious (mə-LISH-əss) *adjective.* Showing ill will; full of malice: a *malicious* rumor. **—maliciously** *adverb.*

ma·lign (mə-LIGHN) *verb.* To speak badly of; spread evil rumors about. **maligned, maligning.** —*adjective.* 1. Evil. 2. Showing a desire to harm.

ma·lig·nant (mə-LIG-nənt) *adjective.* 1. Causing sickness or death. 2. Very evil or hateful. —**malignancy** *noun.*

mall (MAWL) *noun.* 1. A public walkway, usually shaded by trees. 2. A shop-lined street from which cars are barred. 3. The strip dividing lanes of traffic going in opposite directions.

mal·lard (MAL-ərd) *noun.* A type of wild duck with a green head and a white ring around the neck.

mal·le·a·ble (MAL-ee-ə-bəl) *adjective.* Capable of being hammered or pressed into various shapes.

mal·let (MAL-it) *noun.* A wooden hammer used for pounding or as a club in sports like croquet and polo.

mal·nu·tri·tion (mal-noo-TRISH-ən or mal-nyoo-TRISH-ən) *noun.* Inadequate diet or digestion, usually resulting in poor health.

mal·prac·tice (mal-PRAK-tiss) *noun.* Careless or improper actions or care, especially improper treatment by a doctor or a lawyer.

malt (MAWLT) *noun.* Grain, usually barley, that has been soaked in water until it has sprouted, used in making beer, ale, and liquor.

mal·treat (mal-TREET) *verb.* To treat harshly; to abuse. **maltreated, maltreating.** —**maltreatment** *noun.*

ma·ma (MAH-mə or mə-MAH) Also **mamma** *noun.* (Informal) Mother.

mam·mal (MAM-əl) *noun.* Any animal, including a human, that has a backbone and some hair and, in the female, feeds its young with breast or udder milk.

mam·moth (MAM-əth) *noun.* A type of huge elephant, no longer existing, that had a hairy body and very long, curved tusks. —*adjective.* Huge; gigantic: An aircraft carrier is a *mammoth* ship.

man *noun.* 1. An adult, male human. 2. A human being: *Man* is a warm-blooded animal. 3. Mankind; the human race: *Man* has been on earth for thousands of years. 4. A male servant: Robinson Crusoe's *man* Friday. —**men** *plural.* —*verb.* To supply with men, as for some function or activity: The captain *manned* his ship with experienced sailors. **manned, manning.**

man·age (MAN-ij) *verb.* 1. To supervise or direct. 2. To keep under control. 3. To succeed at something; survive: The soldiers *managed* to cross the desert. **managed, managing.** —**manageable** *adjective.* —**manageably** *adverb.*

man·age·ment (MAN-ij-mənt) *noun.* 1. Direction; control: *Management* of a large company requires hard work. 2. The persons who manage or direct something.

man·ag·er (MAN-ij-ər) *noun.* A person who manages, as a business.

man·date (MAN-dayt) *noun.* 1. An order or command: The mayors obeyed the governor's *mandate.* 2. The will or desire of citizens, made known to their representatives in government. **mandates.**

man·di·ble (MAN-də-bəl) *noun.* 1. Either part of the beak or jaws of birds, insects, or other animals. 2. The jaw, especially the lower jaw. **mandibles.**

man·do·lin (MAN-də-lin or man-də-LIN) *noun.* A stringed musical instrument with a bowl-shaped wooden body.

mane (MAYN) *noun.* The long, thick hair on the neck of a horse, lion, or other animal. **manes.**

ma·neu·ver (mə-NOO-vər or mə-NYOO-vər) Also **manoeuver** *noun.* 1. A planned and directed movement of troops and military equipment, as in battle or a training exercise. 2. A carefully planned trick or action. —*verb.* 1. To carry out some plan or action, as a military operation. 2. To plan carefully; to scheme: The ambitious student *maneuvered* to win the class election. **maneuvered, maneuvering.**

mallard

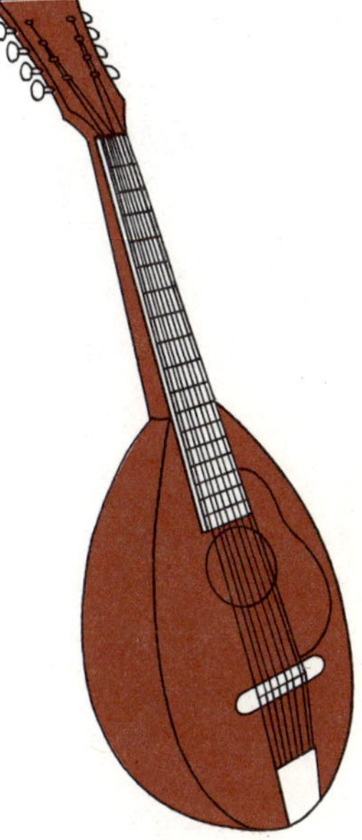
mandolin

mammoth

man·ga·nese (MANG-gə-neess) *noun.* A hard gray-white metal used in steel alloys.

man·ger (MAYN-jər) *noun.* A box in which hay or other feed is placed for farm animals to eat.

man·gle (MANG-gəl) *verb.* 1. To rip or shred badly: The explosion *mangled* the soldier's leg. 2. To do badly; to ruin: The nervous actor *mangled* his lines. **mangled, mangling.**

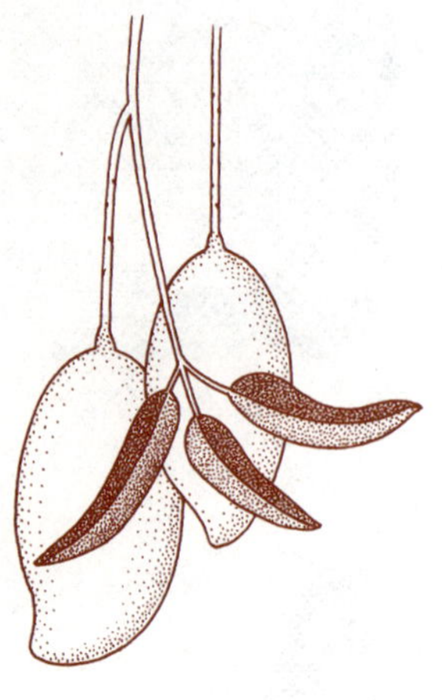
mangoes

man·go (MANG-goh) *noun.* 1. A juicy, yellow-red tropical fruit. 2. The tree on which this fruit grows. —**mangoes** or **mangos** *plural.*

man·hood (MAN-hud) *noun.* 1. The period or state of being a man. 2. Manliness; bravery. 3. Mankind.

ma·ni·a (MAY-nee-ə or MAYN-yə) *noun.* 1. A form of insanity involving extreme excitement. 2. An unusual or extreme attraction or enthusiasm: a *mania* for eating.

ma·ni·ac (MAY-nee-ak) *noun.* A madman; insane person.

man·i·cure (MAN-i-kyur) *noun.* The care of the hands and fingernails, as cleaning and cutting the nails. **manicures.** —*verb.* To care for the hands and fingernails. **manicured, manicuring.**

man·i·fest (MAN-ə-fest) *verb.* To reveal; show clearly. **manifested, manifesting.** —*adjective.* Obvious; very clear: The teacher's anger was *manifest.* —*noun.* A list of the cargo or passengers on a ship, plane, etc. —**manifestly** *adverb.*

man·i·fes·ta·tion (man-ə-fess-TAY-shən) *noun.* An example or demonstration: The old man's gift was a *manifestation* of his kindness.

man·i·fold (MAN-ə-fohld) *adjective.* 1. Many and varied: The duties of a policeman are *manifold.* 2. Having many forms or parts: The general developed a *manifold* plan to win the battle. —*noun.* A pipe having openings for several connections, as in an automobile engine.

ma·nip·u·late (mə-NIP-yə-layt) *verb.* 1. To handle or operate skillfully. 2. To manage or control, especially in an unfair manner: The selfish student *manipulated* his classmates so that they did his work for him. 3. To change or rearrange records for one's own financial gain. **manipulated, manipulating.** —**manipulation** (mə-nip-yə-LAY-shən) *noun.*

man·kind (MAN-KYND or MAN-kynd) *noun.* The human race; all men considered together.

man·ly (MAN-lee) *adjective.* 1. Having qualities expected of a man, such as courage, strength, and honesty. 2. Fit for a man: a *manly* sport. **manlier, manliest.** —**manliness** *noun.*

man·ner (MAN-ər) *noun.* 1. A way of doing or occurring: The wind swayed the branches in a gentle *manner.* 2. Style; habit; method: the sly *manner* of a fox. 3. (Plural) Style of actions or behavior: fine table *manners.* 4. Type; kind: What *manner* of plant is this?

man-of-war (man-ə-WOR) *noun.* A warship. —**men-of-war** *plural.*

man·or (MAN-ər) *noun.* 1. A large estate. 2. In the Middle Ages, the land on which a lord and those subject to him lived.

man·sion (MAN-shən) *noun.* A large, impressive house.

man·slaugh·ter (MAN-slaw-tər) *noun.* Murder, especially a killing that is not planned in advance.

man·tel (MANT-l) Also **mantelpiece** *noun.* The trim over or on either side of a fireplace, especially a shelf over a fireplace.

man·tle (MANT-l) *noun.* 1. A sleeveless cloak. 2. Anything that covers like a cloak or garment: a *mantle* of frost. **mantles.**

man·u·al (MAN-yoo-əl) *noun.* A book or booklet that gives instructions or explains how to use something: The *manual* for our automobile explains how to change a flat tire. *—adjective.* Done with or related to the hands: *manual* labor. **—manually** *adverb.*

man·u·fac·ture (man-yə-FAK-chər) *verb.* 1. To make or produce, especially by machinery: Dad's factory *manufactures* radios. 2. To make up; invent: The student *manufactured* a story to explain his missing homework. **manufactured, manufacturing.** *—noun.* The making or producing of things, especially by machinery.

man·u·fac·tur·er (man-yə-FAK-chər-ər) *noun.* A person or company that makes or produces things, especially by machinery.

ma·nure (mə-NUR or mə-NYUR) *noun.* The waste matter of animals, used to make soil more fertile.

man·u·script (MAN-yə-skript) *noun.* A book or paper written by hand or typed before being printed.

man·y (MEN-ee) *adjective.* Numerous; of a large number: *Many* bees live in that hive. **more, most.** *—pronoun.* A large number of people or things: *Many* said that they would attend the party. *—noun, singular in form but used with a plural verb.* A large number: *Many* of the boxes were empty.

map *noun.* A drawing or other representation of all or part of the earth's surface or the sky, showing countries, seas, cities, and other features. *—verb.* 1. To make a map or chart of. 2. (Often used with *out*) To plan: The teacher *mapped* out a weekly schedule. **mapped, mapping.**

ma·ple (MAY-pəl) *noun.* 1. A shade tree, one variety of which produces the sap used in making maple syrup. 2. The wood of the maple tree. **maples.**

mar (MAHR) *verb.* To damage; harm; spoil: The spilled ink *marred* the new desk. **marred, marring.**

mar·a·thon (MA-rə-thon) *noun.* 1. A foot race over a course of 26 miles, 385 yards. 2. Any very long contest.

mar·ble (MAHR-bəl) *noun.* 1. A hard stone, often colored, that is used in building and sculpture. 2. A small glass or stone ball used in children's games. 3. (Plural) A children's game played with small glass or stone balls. **marbles. —lose one's marbles.** (Slang) To lose one's senses; go mad.

march (MAHRCH) *verb.* 1. To walk with a regular step, as soldiers often do. 2. To move forward on foot: The farmer *marched* across his field. 3. To cause to move forward: The teacher *marched* the unruly student to the principal's office. **marched, marching.** *—noun.* 1. A movement forward: "The *march* of the human mind is slow." (E. Burke). 2. The distance traveled or time taken on a journey: a day's *march* from camp. 3. A piece of music suitable to accompany marchers. **marches.**

March (MAHRCH) *noun.* The third month of the year: There are 31 days in *March.* **—Mar.** *abbreviation.*

mare (MAIR) *noun.* A female horse, donkey, or similar animal. **mares.**

mar·ga·rine (MAHR-jə-rin) Also **margarin** *noun.* A substance made from vegetable oils and used as a substitute for butter; oleomargarine.

mar·gin (MAHR-jən) *noun.* 1. An edge or border: "Along the *margin* of the bay . . . ." (Wordsworth). 2. The blank space around words on a page. 3. An extra amount beyond what is needed or necessary.

mar·i·gold (MA-rə-gohld) *noun.* A flower, usually orange or yellow, or the plant on which it grows.

mar·i·jua·na (ma-rə-WAH-nə) Also **marihuana** *noun.* 1. The hemp plant. 2. The dried flower and leaves of this plant, smoked in cigarettes to bring about a temporary change in mood or outlook. (Also called "grass" and "pot.")

maple

marigold

marijuana

marionette

marmoset

ma·ri·na (mə-REE-nə) *noun.* A docking area where small boats can find shelter, fuel, and other services.

ma·rine (mə-REEN) *adjective.* 1. Related to the sea: Seaweed is a *marine* plant. 2. Related to the navy or to shipping: Barges serve as an important part of *marine* transportation. —*noun.* 1. A soldier assigned to duty on a ship. 2. [Capital M] A member of the U.S. Marine Corps. 3. Shipping and ships considered together: Japan has a huge merchant *marine.* **marines.**

mar·i·ner (MA-rə-nər) *noun.* A seaman or sailor.

mar·i·o·nette (ma-ree-ə-NET) *noun.* A puppet or doll-like figure moved by strings. **marionettes.**

mar·i·time (MA-rə-tighm) *adjective.* 1. Related to or near the sea: Deep-sea fishing is a *maritime* activity. 2. Related to shipping: *maritime* traffic.

mark (MAHRK) *noun.* 1. A spot, line, or similar impression made on a surface: The wet glass left a *mark* on the table. 2. A characteristic; typical quality: Patience is one *mark* of a good fisherman. 3. A grade, as in school. 4. A special symbol that indicates the make or other information about a product: A red star is the *mark* of that company's products. 5. A printed or written symbol: Periods and commas are common punctuation *marks.* —*verb.* 1. To make a spot, line, or similar impression on a surface. 2. To give a grade to. 3. To indicate visibly: Dad used a crayon to *mark* the capitals on a map of the U.S. 4. To provide a sign or marker for: A flag *marked* the end of the ski slope. 5. To notice; heed: Did you *mark* the sailor's warning? **marked, marking.** —**hit the mark.** To be accurate or appropriate: Jim *hit the mark* when he guessed that the lucky number was seven. —**make one's mark.** To suceed; establish a reputation.

marked (MAHRKT) *adjective.* Easily seen; obvious: There is a *marked* difference between summer and winter in the north. —**markedly** (MAHR-kid-lee) *adverb.*

mar·ket (MAHR-kit) *noun.* 1. A store, usually where just one kind of food is sold: vegetable *market.* 2. A gathering of people to buy and sell: The farmers bring their goods to *market* on Saturdays. 3. The place where such a gathering occurs. 4. A demand: There is always a *market* for mousetraps. 5. An area where goods can be sold: The United States is a *market* for many imported products. —*verb.* 1. To sell. 2. To shop; buy food: Sally often *markets* for her mother. **marketed, marketing.**

mar·ma·lade (MAHR-mə-layd) *noun.* A jamlike preserve made of oranges and other fruit. **marmalades.**

mar·mo·set (MAHR-mə-set) *noun.* A small monkey of South and Central America with soft thick fur and a long tail.

mar·mot (MAHR-mət) *noun.* Any of several animals like the woodchuck, having short legs and bushy tails.

[1]**ma·roon** (mə-ROON) *verb.* 1. To leave (someone) stranded, as on a deserted island from which there is little hope of escape. 2. To leave in a helpless position: We were *marooned* in a cabin for two days during the blizzard. **marooned, marooning.**

[2]**ma·roon** (mə-ROON) *noun* (and *adjective*). A dark, reddish-brown color.

mar·quis (mahr-KEE or MAHR-kwiss) Also (British) **marquess** (MAHR-kwiss) *noun.* A nobleman ranking below a duke and above an earl or count. —**marquis** or **marquises** *plural.*

mar·riage (MA-rij) *noun.* 1. The state of living together as husband and wife. 2. The wedding ceremony. 3. A joining: Opera is a *marriage* of music and drama. **marriages.**

mar·row (MA-roh) *noun.* 1. A soft substance, found in the hollow centers of most bones, that contains fat and developing red blood cells. 2. The innermost or best part.

mar·ry (MA-ree) *verb.* 1. To take as husband or wife. 2. To become husband and wife. 3. To join as husband and wife: The minister will *marry* Tom and Jane. **married, marrying.**

Mars (MAHRZ) *noun.* The planet that is fourth in distance from the sun.

marsh (MAHRSH) *noun.* A swamp or bog. **marshes.**

mar·shal (MAHR-shəl) *noun.* 1. A federal or city officer who carries out court orders. 2. The chief of a police or fire department. 3. In some foreign countries, the highest ranking officer. 4. A person in charge of the order of a parade. *—verb.* To gather and organize: Jim *marshaled* his facts for the test. **marshaled, marshaling.**

marsh·mal·low (MAHRSH-mal-oh or MAHRSH-mel-oh) *noun.* A soft, white candy rolled in powdered sugar.

mar·su·pi·al (mahr-soo-pee-əl) *noun.* A mammal, such as the kangaroo, with a pouch in which the newborn stay and nurse until they are strong enough to emerge.

mart (MAHRT) *noun.* A market or trade center.

mar·ten (MAHRT-n) *noun.* 1. A thin, meat-eating animal that is valued for its fine fur. 2. The fur from this animal.

mar·tial (MAHR-shəl) *adjective.* 1. Of or about war: *martial* music. 2. Warlike: a *martial* appearance. **—martially** *adverb.*

martial law. Rules or law enforced by military forces in times of war or civil disorder.

Mar·tian (MAHR-shən) *adjective.* Of or about the planet Mars. *—noun.* One who is supposed to live on Mars.

mar·tin (MAHRT-n) *noun.* An insect-eating bird related to the swallow.

mar·tyr (MAHR-tər) *noun.* 1. A person who chooses to die or suffer for a cause. 2. A person who pretends to suffer in order to attract attention or sympathy. *—verb.* To cause (a person) to die or suffer because of his beliefs. **martyred, martyring.**

mar·vel (MAHR-vəl) *noun.* Something that fills one with wonder or astonishment: Man's first voyage to the moon was a *marvel.* *—verb.* To be filled with wonder. **marveled, marveling.**

mar·vel·ous (MAHR-vəl-əss) Also **marvellous** *adjective.* 1. Wonderful; astonishing; unbelievable: "In all things of nature there is something . . . *marvelous.*" (Aristotle). 2. Of top quality or the best. **—marvelously** or **marvellously** *adverb.*

Mar·y·land (MAIR-ə-lənd) *noun.* A mid-Atlantic state in the United States, seventh to ratify the Constitution (1788). **—Md.** *abbreviation.* Also **MD** for Zip Codes.

mas·cot (MASS-kot) *noun.* An animal, person, or thing believed to bring good luck.

mas·cu·line (MASS-kyə-lin) *adjective.* Relating to men; male.

mash *noun.* 1. Any soft mass. 2. A mixture of ground grain and water used to feed livestock and poultry. **mashes.** *—verb.* To make into a soft mass by crushing or beating: *mash* potatoes. **mashed, mashing.**

mask (MASK) *noun.* 1. A covering worn on the face as a disguise or protection: Halloween *mask,* catcher's *mask.* 2. A copy of a person's face made of wax, clay or some other material. *—verb.* 1. To cover or conceal. 2. To put on a mask: The robbers *masked* themselves before entering the bank. 3. To disguise (one's intentions or feelings): Jane's good manners *masked* her dislike of the visitors. **masked, masking.**

marten

martins

Maryland
★capital: Annapolis

African tribal mask

ma·son (MAYSS-n) *noun.* A person who earns his living by building with stone or brick.

ma·son·ry (MAYSS-n-ree) *noun.* 1. The trade of a mason. 2. Anything built of stone or brick.

mas·quer·ade (mas-kər-AYD) *noun.* 1. A party or ball at which masks and costumes are worn. 2. A disguising of oneself or one's true feelings: Tess felt it was a *masquerade* to pretend she liked the party. **masquerades.** —*verb.* 1. To wear a mask or costume. 2. To disguise one's true feelings or identity. **masqueraded, masquerading.**

mass *noun.* 1. A shapeless lump: a *mass* of clay. 2. A large number of things considered as a whole: a *mass* of people. 3. The greater part or majority: The *mass* of the residents favors the new playground. 4. The amount of matter a body contains: Weight is a measure of an object's *mass.* **masses.** —*verb.* To group into or be in a mass. **massed, massing.**

Mass *noun.* The religious service of Holy Communion in the Roman Catholic and other churches.

Massachusetts
★capital: Boston

Mas·sa·chu·setts (mass-ə-CHOO-sits) *noun.* A New England state of the United States, sixth to ratify the Constitution (1788). —**Mass.** *abbreviation.* Also **MA** for Zip Codes.

mas·sa·cre (MASS-ə-kər) *noun.* 1. Violent killing, usually of large numbers. 2. (Informal) The loss of a game by a wide margin. **massacres.** —*verb.* 1. To kill violently. 2. (Informal) To overcome (in a game) by a very wide margin. **massacred, massacring.**

mas·sage (mə-SAHZH) *noun.* The rubbing and kneading of the body to relax muscles and increase blood circulation. **massages.** —*verb.* To give a massage to. **massaged, massaging.**

mas·sive (MASS-iv) *adjective.* Solid, large, or heavy. —**massively** *adverb.*

mass media *plural.* Newspapers, television, and other forms of public communication to a large number of people. —**mass medium** *singular.*

mass production. Making goods in large quantities, usually in factories with conveyor-belt assembly.

mass transit. Public transportation for large numbers of people.

mast *noun.* 1. A tall upright pole on a boat or ship to which the sail and rigging are attached. 2. Any upright pole.

mas·ter (MASS-tər) *noun.* 1. A person who rules or controls others, especially a ship's captain. 2. A highly skilled workman or craftsman. 3. A male teacher. 4. [Capital M] A title of respect for a boy too young to be called Mister. —*adjective.* 1. Most important; controlling all others: *master* switch, *master* plan. 2. Of the highest degree: *master* craftsman. —*verb.* 1. To control or overcome: It is difficult for a drug addict to *master* his habit. 2. To become skilled in: Sally is *mastering* Spanish. **mastered, mastering.**

mas·ter·ful (MASS-tər-fəl) *adjective.* 1. Liking power; bossy. 2. Expert; skillful: a *masterful* job. —**masterfully** *adverb.*

mas·ter·ly (MASS-tər-lee) *adjective.* Like a master; skillful: He played the piano with *masterly* ability.

master of ceremonies. The host for an entertainment program or for a formal occasion.

mas·ter·piece (MASS-tər-peess) *noun.* 1. A piece of work or art or an action that stands above others. 2. One's best or greatest work: Many think that *Hamlet* is Shakespeare's *masterpiece.*

mas·ter·y (MASS-tər-ee) *noun.* 1. Control, such as that of a master. 2. A skill or command of a field of knowledge: The Frenchman's *mastery* of English surprised us.

mast·head (MAST-hed) *noun.* 1. The top of the mast on a ship. 2. The listing in a periodical of the owners, staff, and related information.

mas·tiff (MASS-tif) *noun.* A large, strong dog with a tan-colored coat.

mas·to·don (MASS-tə-don) *noun.* A large animal, like the elephant, that lived thousands of years ago.

mat *noun.* 1. A small piece of material used as a floor covering or for wiping the feet: a door *mat.* 2. A small pad used to protect the surface of a table from heat or scratches. 3. A tangled growth: a *mat* of fur. 4. A thick pad, as for wrestling or tumbling on. *—verb.* To tangle. **matted, matting.**

mat·a·dor (MAT-ə-dor) *noun.* The chief bullfighter who lures the bull with his cape and makes the kill.

match (MACH) *noun.* 1. A small piece of wood, cardboard, or other material tipped with a substance that catches fire when scraped against a rough surface. 2. An equal (to another): A horse is no *match* for a car. 3. Suited to each other: Potatoes and gravy are a good *match.* 4. A contest: tennis *match.* 5. A marriage. 6. A person looked on as a possible spouse. **matches.** *—verb.* 1. To go well together: The rugs *match* the drapes. 2. To be alike or equal to. 3. To put in contest together: The golfers *matched* their skills in the playoff round. **matched, matching.**

match·less (MACH-liss) *adjective.* Having no equal.

mate (MAYT) *noun.* 1. One of a pair. 2. An officer of a merchant ship below a captain in rank. 3. A husband or wife. 4. A friend or companion: play*mate.* **mates.** *—verb.* 1. To marry. 2. To breed. **mated, mating.**

ma·te·ri·al (mə-TIHR-ee-əl) *noun.* 1. The substance out of which a thing is built or made: roofing *material.* 2. Fabric or cloth. *—adjective.* 1. Of or about the body and physical things: *material* possessions. 2. Standing out or important: a *material* witness. **—materially** *adverb.*

ma·ter·nal (mə-TERN-l) *adjective.* 1. Like a mother; motherly. 2. Related through or coming from the mother. **—maternally** *adverb.*

math *noun.* Mathematics.

math·e·mat·i·cal (math-ə-MAT-i-kəl) *adjective.* 1. Having to do with mathematics. 2. Exact: *mathematical* precision. **—mathematically** *adverb.*

math·e·ma·ti·cian (math-ə-mə-TISH-ən) *noun.* An expert in mathematics.

math·e·mat·ics (math-ə-MAT-iks) *noun, plural in form but used with a singular verb.* The study of numbers, measurements, and shapes.

mat·i·nee (MAT-n-ay) *noun.* An afternoon performance of a play, movie, or concert. **matinees.**

mat·ri·mo·ny (MAT-rə-moh-nee) *noun.* Marriage.

ma·trix (MAY-triks) *noun.* 1. Something within or from which another thing begins or develops: "Freedom of expression is the *matrix* . . . of nearly every other form of freedom." (B. N. Cardozo). 2. A mold or die. **—matrices** (MAY-trə-seez) or **matrixes** *plural.*

ma·tron (MAY-trən) *noun.* 1. A married woman, especially an older woman. 2. A woman in charge of an institution, as a school or prison.

mat·ter (MAT-er) *noun.* 1. What things are made of; what takes up space: The universe is made up of *matter.* 2. The substance or backbone of something written, printed, or thought: The book's subject *matter* is science. 3. Trouble: What is the *matter?* 4. An estimated amount or quantity: a *matter* of a few days. 5. Business or affair: a financial *matter.* *—verb.* To be important: Winning the contest *matters* to us. **mattered, mattering.**

mastiff

matador

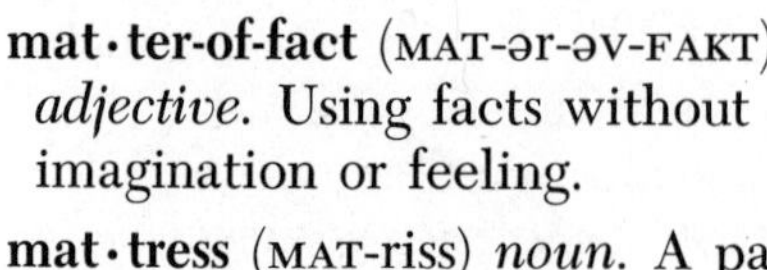

mat·ter-of-fact (MAT-ər-əv-FAKT) *adjective.* Using facts without imagination or feeling.

mat·tress (MAT-riss) *noun.* A pad, with or without springs, used to sleep on. —**mattresses** *plural.*

meadowlark

ma·ture (mə-TYUR or mə-CHUR) *adjective.* 1. Ripe, fully grown. 2. Well-developed physically, emotionally, or mentally, **maturer, maturest.** —*verb.* 1. To ripen, become fully developed. 2. To become due or payable: The bonds will *mature* next April. **matured, maturing.** —**maturely** *adverb.* —**maturity** (mə-TYUR-ə-tee or mə-CHUR-ə-tee) *noun.*

maul (MAWL) *noun.* A heavy hammer with a large head. —*verb.* To beat; treat roughly: The lion *mauled* its trainer. **mauled, mauling.**

mau·so·le·um (maw-sə-LEE-əm) *noun.* A tomb; a building that contains graves of the dead.

mauve (MOHV) *noun* (and *adjective*). A medium purple or violet color.

max·im (MAK-sim) *noun.* An old saying or proverb; a rule of conduct.

max·i·mum (MAK-sə-məm) *noun.* 1. The most; the greatest amount, number, or degree. 2. The upper limit: a *maximum* load. —**maximums** or **maxima** *plural.*

May *noun.* The fifth month of the year: There are 31 days in *May.*

may *verb.* 1. To be allowed or have permission: He *may* use my car. 2. A helping verb meaning to be likely or possible: I *may* go. **might.**

may·be (MAY-bee) *adverb.* Perhaps.

may·day (MAY-day) *noun.* A distress signal for ships and airplanes.

may·on·naise (may-ə-NAYZ) *noun.* A thick salad dressing made of olive oil, eggs, vinegar, and spices.

may·or (MAY-ər) *noun.* The elected head of a city or town government.

maze (MAYZ) *noun.* 1. A confusing arrangement of tunnels or passageways that makes it difficult to go directly from one point to another. 2. Confusion. **mazes.**

M.D. *abbreviation.* Doctor of Medicine.

me (MEE) *pronoun.* A form of *I* used as the object of verbs or prepositions: I asked Joe to give *me* back my ball.

mead·ow (MED-oh) *noun.* A grassy field; a field for raising hay.

mead·ow·lark (MED-oh-lahrk) *noun.* A North American bird noted for its song: The *meadowlark* has a yellow breast marked with a black V.

mea·ger (MEE-gər) Also **meagre** *adjective.* Scarce, poor, in a small amount: a *meager* supper.

meal (MEEL) *noun.* 1. Food eaten at a regular time: We eat three *meals* a day. 2. The amount of food eaten at one time. 3. Grain that has been coarsely ground: corn*meal.* 4. Any similar substance: bone *meal.*

meal·y (MEE-lee) *adjective.* Having the look or feel of coarsely ground grain. **mealier, mealiest.**

mean (MEEN) *adjective.* 1. Poor or low: Lincoln came from *mean* surroundings. 2. Cruel or unkind: The boy is *mean* to animals. 3. Midway between two extremes: The *mean* arithmetic grade in our class was 72. 4. Selfish: The old man is *mean* with his money. **meaner, meanest.** —*noun.* 1. The middle point between two extremes. 2. (Plural) Method: a *means* to raise the money. 3. (Plural) Wealth or income: Washington was a man of *means.* —*verb.* 1. To intend or have in mind: It is hard for her to say what she *means.* 2. To be defined as or be equal to: "Bon" *means* "good" in French. **meant, meaning.**

me·an·der (mee-AN-dər) *verb.* 1. To follow a winding route or path: The river *meanders* to the sea. 2. To wander with frequent changes in direction. **meandered, meandering.**

mean·ing (MEE-ning) *noun.* 1. A

definition or explanation: The word "board" has several *meanings.* 2. The thought in mind, intention: the *meaning* of poetry.

mean·time (MEEN-tighm) *noun.* The time between two events: Dinner won't be ready for an hour so let's watch TV in the *meantime.* —*adverb.* Meanwhile; at the same time: *Meantime,* help had arrived.

mean·while (MEEN-hwighl) *adverb.* During the same period: He went for help, but *meanwhile* the fire was spreading. —*noun.* Meantime.

mea·sles (MEE-zəlz) *noun, plural in form but sometimes used with a singular verb.* A contagious disease: *Measles* causes red spots on the skin.

meas·ure (MEZH-ər) *verb.* 1. To find the size, weight, or amount of, using an object of known size: He *measured* the rug with a yardstick. 2. To be of a certain size, weight, or amount: The room *measures* 10 by 14 feet. **measured, measuring.** —*noun.* 1. A device for determining size, weight, or quantity. 2. (Music) The rests and notes between two bars on a staff. 3. (Plural) Action: The city will take *measures* to speed up the flow of traffic. 4. A system of measure: liquid *measure,* linear *measure.* **measures.** —**beyond measure.** Limitless. —**measure up to.** To meet a standard; be what is expected or required.

meas·ure·ment (MEZH-ər-mənt) *noun.* 1. The information gained by measuring: The *measurements* of the room are 9 feet by 12 feet. 2. The act of measuring. 3. A system of determining amount or size: Metric *measurements* are used by most of the world's scientists.

meat (MEET) *noun.* 1. The flesh of animals used for food, generally not including fish and poultry. 2. Food in general: *meat* and drink. 3. The part of anything that is eaten: Coconut *meat* is used in candy. —**meaty** *adjective.* **meatier, meatiest.**

meat·ball (MEET-bawl) *noun.* 1. A mixture of ground meat and seasonings shaped into a small ball and cooked. 2. (Slang) A dull person.

meat·head (MEET-hed) *noun.* (Slang) A stupid person.

meat loaf. A mixture of ground meat and other ingredients shaped into a loaf and baked.

me·chan·ic (mi-KAN-ik) *noun.* One who builds and repairs machines or is skilled in using tools.

me·chan·i·cal (mi-KAN-i-kəl) *adjective.* 1. Relating to machinery; made or run by machine: *mechanical* toys. 2. Without liveliness or expression: Jill recited the poem in a *mechanical* way. —**mechanically** *adverb.*

me·chan·ics (mi-KAN-iks) *noun, plural in form but used with a singular verb.* 1. The branch of science that studies the action of forces and their effects on matter. 2. The design or operation of a machine: the *mechanics* of a car.

mech·a·nism (MEK-ə-niz-əm) *noun.* 1. A machine or the working parts of a machine. 2. Anything with parts that work together: the *mechanism* of an engine.

mech·a·nize (MEK-ə-nighz) *verb.* 1. To change over from human or animal labor to machine: The reaper *mechanized* the harvesting of wheat. 2. To put a machine into something; make mechanical: The boy *mechanized* his soapbox racer. **mechanized, mechanizing.**

med·al (MED-l) *noun.* A piece of metal stamped with words or a picture and used as an award.

medal

me·dal·lion (mə-DAL-yən) *noun.* 1. A large medal. 2. Anything that looks like a large medal.

med·dle (MED-l) *verb.* To interfere; become involved (in other people's affairs). **meddled, meddling.** —**meddler** *noun.*

med·dle·some (MED-l-səm) *adjective.* Nosy; concerned with others' affairs.

me·di·a (MEE-dee-ə) *noun. See* **medium** and **mass media.**

me·di·an (MEE-dee-ən) *adjective.* At or near the middle. *—noun.* The thing located at the middle: In the series 2, 7, 12 the *median* is 7.

me·di·ate (MEE-dee-ayt) *verb.* To act as a go-between in settling arguments or differences between persons or groups. **mediated, mediating.** —**mediation** *noun.*

med·ic (MED-ik) *noun.* (Informal) 1. A doctor. 2. (Military) A soldier assigned to the medical corps.

med·i·cal (MED-i-kəl) *adjective.* Related to the study or practice of medicine. —**medically** *adverb.*

medical center. A building or group of buildings where doctors have offices and give medical advice and treatment.

med·i·cate (MED-ə-kayt) *verb.* To treat with medicine: Mother *medicated* my cold with aspirin and nose drops. **medicated, medicating.** —**medication** (med-ə-KAY-shən) *noun.*

med·i·cine (MED-ə-sn) *noun.* 1. A substance used to treat an illness or injury. 2. The science concerned with the improvement of health and the care and treatment of diseases and injuries. **medicines.**

megaphone

me·di·e·val (mee-dee-EE-vəl or med-EE-vəl) Also **mediaeval** *adjective.* Like or belonging to the Middle Ages, the time between the 5th and 15th centuries.

me·di·o·cre (mee-dee-OH-kər) *adjective.* Ordinary; average.

med·i·tate (MED-ə-tayt) *verb.* 1. To think deeply (about a subject). 2. To intend or plan. **meditated, meditating.** —**meditation** (med-ə-TAY-shən) *noun.*

me·di·um (MEE-dee-əm) *adjective.* Average; in between: *medium* height. *—noun.* 1. A position halfway between two extremes. 2. A substance or agent that carries or relays something: Copper wire is a *medium* for carrying electricity. 3. Any means by which something is relayed or accomplished. 4. A method of communication: Newspapers are one *medium;* TV is another. 5. The substance in which a living thing is able to exist: The shrimp eggs hatched in a *medium* of salt water. 6. A person believed to be able to communicate with the dead. —**media** (MEE-dee-ə) or **mediums** (only form for sense 6) *plural.*

med·ley (MED-lee) *noun.* (Music) A group of songs combined in a single arrangement: The band played a *medley* of show tunes.

me·dul·la (mə-DUHL-ə) *noun.* The base of the brain. —**medullas** or **medullae** (mə-DUHL-ee) *plural.*

meek *adjective.* 1. Patient; gentle and peace-loving. 2. Weak; timid. **meeker, meekest.** —**meekly** *adverb.*

meet *verb.* 1. To come upon: We will *meet* a car coming the other way. 2. To join: The roads *meet* in the center of town. 3. To be introduced or come to know: I want you to *meet* my brother. 4. To come together: The council *meets* at seven o'clock. 5. To pay: He *meets* his bills on time. 6. To be present at a certain time: We will *meet* the train. **met, meeting.** *—noun.* An athletic meeting or contest.

meet·ing (MEET-ing) *noun.* 1. The coming together of a number of people. 2. The people thus gathered: The mayor spoke to the *meeting.*

meg·a·lop·o·lis (meg-ə-LOP-ə-liss) *noun.* A densely populated region that includes several cities and the built-up areas that surround them. **megalopolises.**

meg·a·phone (MEG-ə-fohn) *noun.* A cone-shaped device that directs and increases the loudness of the human voice: The cheerleader used a *megaphone.* **megaphones.**

mel·an·chol·y (MEL-ən-kol-ee) *adjective.* Gloomy, extremely sad. —*noun.* Sadness; tendency to be gloomy: "The sad companion, dull-eyed *melancholy.*" (Shakespeare).

mel·low (MEL-oh) *adjective.* 1. Fully ripe, mature: a *mellow* pear. 2. Seasoned, improved with age: a *mellow* wine. 3. Soft; not harsh: a *mellow* tone. **mellower, mellowest.** —*verb.* 1. To make or become mellow: "But fell like autumn fruit that *mellowed* long." (Dryden). 2. To age gracefully, make or become gentle: Grandfather has *mellowed.* **mellowed, mellowing.**

me·lo·di·ous (mə-LOH-dee-əss) *adjective.* 1. Musical, tuneful. 2. Pleasing to the ear: a *melodious* voice. —**melodiously** *adverb.*

mel·o·dra·ma (MEL-ə-drah-mə) *noun.* 1. A play that exaggerates suspense and emotion. 2. Any activity, speech, or event involving or creating exaggerated emotion. —**melodramatic** (mel-ə-drə-MAT-ik) *adjective.*

mel·o·dy (MEL-ə-dee) *noun.* A pleasing arrangement of notes forming a musical theme, tune, or song. **melodies.**

mel·on (MEL-ən) *noun.* A large, juicy fruit that has a hard rind and grows on a vine.

melt *verb.* 1. (Of a solid) To become liquid. 2. To dissolve. 3. To disappear slowly: The black clouds *melted* away. 4. To soften; make gentle: The lame boy *melted* the old man's heart. **melted, melting.**

melting point. The temperature at which a solid melts and becomes liquid.

mem·ber (MEM-bər) *noun.* 1. One who belongs to an organization or group. 2. Part of an animal or person, as a leg or arm.

mem·ber·ship (MEM-bər-ship) *noun.* 1. The state of being a member: He found his *membership* in the Cub Scouts very worthwhile. 2. The total number of members in a group.

mem·brane (MEM-brayn) *noun.* A thin layer of soft tissue lining or covering certain parts of a person, animal, or plant. **membranes.**

me·men·to (mə-MEN-toh) *noun.* A remembrance; a souvenir. —**mementos** or **mementoes** *plural.*

mem·o (MEM-oh) *noun.* A memorandum. **memos.**

mem·o·ra·ble (MEM-ər-ə-bəl) *adjective.* Remarkable, notable, unforgettable: a *memorable* happening.

mem·o·ran·dum (mem-ə-RAN-dəm) *noun.* 1. A brief note, usually written as a reminder. 2. A form of written report or informal communication often used in offices. —**memorandums** or **memoranda** (mem-ə-RAN-də) *plural.*

me·mo·ri·al (mə-MOR-ee-əl) *noun.* A statue, holiday, or other remembrance that honors the memory of a person or event.

Memorial Day. A holiday in the United States celebrated (in most states) on the last Monday in May to honor servicemen who gave their lives in war.

mem·o·rize (MEM-ə-righz) *verb.* To learn by heart; learn to recite exactly from memory. **memorized, memorizing.**

mem·o·ry (MEM-ər-ee) *noun.* 1. The ability to remember or power of remembering: "No man has a good enough *memory* to make a successful liar." (Lincoln). 2. A recollection; a remembrance. 3. All that one can remember. **memories.**

men *noun.* *See* **man.**

men·ace (MEN-iss) *verb.* To threaten; endanger. **menaced, menacing.** —*noun.* 1. A threat, danger, or hazard: Water pollution is a *menace* to our health. 2. A nuisance; a troublesome person.

melon
(cantaloupe)

me·nag·er·ie (mə-NAJ-ə-ree) *noun.* A place where many wild animals are kept, usually for exhibition; a collection of animals. **menageries.**

mend *verb.* 1. To repair or fix. 2. To improve; make or become better: She finally *mended* her ways. **mended, mending.** —*noun.* A place repaired: the *mend* in a dress.

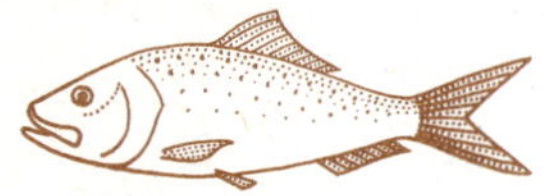
menhaden

men·ha·den (men-HAYD-n) *noun.* A fish of the herring family, used to make oil and fertilizer. —**menhaden** or **menhadens** *plural.*

me·ni·al (MEE-nee-əl) *adjective.* Pertaining to or fit for servants; low: *menial* chores. —*noun.* A servant. —**menially** *adverb.*

men·stru·a·tion (men-stroo-AY-shən) *noun.* A process in human females whereby blood and dead tissue are discharged from the uterus, generally occurring about once a month between the ages of about 12 and 50. —**menstrual** (MEN-stroo-əl) *adjective.*

-ment *suffix.* Indicates a result, act, condition, or means: detach*ment.*

men·tal (MENT-l) *adjective.* 1. Referring to the mind or intelligence. 2. Done in the mind: I did some *mental* arithmetic. —**mentally** *adverb.*

men·tal·i·ty (men-TAL-ə-tee) *noun.* Intelligence; mental ability.

mental telepathy. *See* **telepathy.**

men·tion (MEN-shən) *verb.* To refer to briefly. **mentioned, mentioning.** —*noun.* 1. A brief reference: He didn't get any *mention* in the paper, although he won the contest. 2. A citation for outstanding achievement: honorable *mention.*

men·u (MEN-yoo or MAYN-yoo) *noun.* 1. A list of the food available at a restaurant. 2. The food served at any meal: What's the *menu* for dinner tonight?

me·ow (mee-ow) *noun.* The cry of a cat. —*verb.* To make the sound of a cat. **meowed, meowing.**

mer·ce·na·ry (MER-sə-nehr-ee) *noun.* A soldier who is paid to serve in a foreign army. **mercenaries.** —*adjective.* Done only for pay; concerned only with money.

mer·chan·dise (MER-chən-dighz) *noun.* Goods or items bought and sold; wares.

mer·chant (MER-chənt) *noun.* One who buys and sells goods for profit; a storekeeper.

merchant marine. 1. All the ships of a country used in commerce. 2. The men employed on these ships.

mer·ci·ful (MER-si-fəl) *adjective.* Kindhearted, compassionate, forgiving. —**mercifully** *adverb.*

mer·ci·less (MER-si-liss) *adjective.* Cruel, without mercy, heartless. —**mercilessly** *adverb.*

mer·cu·ry (MER-kyə-ree) *noun.* 1. A heavy, silvery-white metal that is liquid at ordinary temperatures: *Mercury* is used in thermometers. 2. [Capital M] The smallest planet, closest in distance to the sun.

mer·cy (MER-see) *noun.* 1. Kindness; forgiveness; pity: "Surely goodness and *mercy* shall follow me all the days of my life. . . ." (Psalms 23:5). 2. Relief, aid of distress: a mission of *mercy.* 3. A fortunate circumstance: It was a *mercy* the firemen came so quickly. **mercies.** —*interjection.* My goodness! —**at the mercy of.** Unable to avoid; under the control of.

mere (MIHR) *adjective.* Just this; only; nothing more: a *mere* boy. **merest.** —**merely** *adverb.*

merge (MERJ) *verb.* To combine; join one or more things together to form one new whole. **merged, merging.** —**merger** *noun.*

me·rid·i·an (mə-RID-ee-ən) *noun.* 1. An imaginary circle around the earth passing through the North and South Poles; a longitudinal line. 2. The highest point; peak.

me·ringue (mə-RANG) *noun.* 1. A white topping for pie or pastry made by beating sugar and egg whites until stiff and then baking. 2. A shell made of meringue.

me·ri·no (mə-REE-noh) *noun.* 1. A breed of sheep having fine, soft wool. 2. The wool of such a sheep or cloth made from it. **merinos.**

mer·it (MEHR-it) *noun.* 1. Worth; excellence; value: The idea has *merit.* 2. (Plural) The actual facts or basic truth of a matter: The jury decided the case strictly on its *merits.* —*verb.* To deserve: She *merits* respect. **merited, meriting.**

mer·maid (MER-mayd) *noun.* In legend, a sea creature with the head and upper body of a woman, but the lower body of a fish.

mer·ry (MEHR-ee) *adjective.* Gay; lively; full of fun. **merrier, merriest.** —**merrily** *adverb.* —**merriment** (MEHR-i-mənt) *noun.*

merry-go-round (MEHR-ee-goh-rownd) *noun.* A large circle of life-size animal figures mounted on a platform that rotates, usually to the sound of music, and on which one rides for fun.

me·sa (MAY-sə) *noun.* A flat-topped hill with steep sides.

mesh *noun.* 1. The open spaces in a net or screen. 2. The framework of threads or wire that form a net or screening. **meshes.** —*verb.* To engage or interlock: The gears *meshed* perfectly. **meshed, meshing.**

mes·o·derm (MEZ-ə-derm) *noun.* The middle germ layer of an embryo: In mammals the *mesoderm* develops into the muscular, reproductive, and excretory systems.

mes·o·sphere (MEZ-ə-sfihr) *noun.* An atmospheric layer about 50 miles above the earth.

mess *noun.* 1. A state of disorder; jumble; confusion: His room was a *mess,* with clothes thrown all over. 2. Trouble; a problem situation. 3. A quantity of food: a *mess* of fish. 4. A group of persons, especially servicemen, who usually eat together; also the meal eaten by the group. **messes.** —*verb.* 1. To clutter; to litter; make untidy. 2. To interfere; meddle. 3. (Used with *up*) To make mistakes; spoil by errors. **messed, messing.**

mes·sage (MESS-ij) *noun.* 1. A note; a communication sent from one person or group to another. 2. Basic theme of a written or artistic work: "Please all, and you will please none," is Aesop's *message* in "The Man, the Boy, and the Donkey."

mes·sen·ger (MESS-ən-jər) *noun.* One who delivers a message.

mes·si·ah (mə-SIGH-ə) *noun.* 1. [Capital M] a. The leader expected in Biblical times to be king of the Jews. b. Jesus Christ. 2. Any leader accepted by people who expect him to save them.

mess·y (MESS-ee) *adjective.* Dirty; disorderly; untidy. **messier, messiest.**

met *verb.* See **meet.**

me·tab·o·lism (mə-TAB-ə-liz-əm) *noun.* The way in which food is taken in, changed, and used by animals and plants: *Metabolism* produces growth, body heat, energy, and waste products.

met·al (MET-l) *noun.* 1. A chemical element such as iron, gold, copper, or tin that is usually shiny and can conduct heat and electricity. 2. An alloy of these elements such as brass or bronze. 3. A person's character; mettle. —**metallic** *adjective.*

met·al·lur·gy (MET-l-er-jee) *noun.* The science or method of using and working with metals.

met·a·mor·phic (met-ə-MOR-fik) *adjective.* (Geology) Relating to any change caused by heat, pressure, or water: *metamorphic* rocks.

met·a·mor·pho·sis (met-ə-MOR-fə-siss) *noun.* 1. Change in the way a person or thing looks or acts. 2. A change in form. —**metamorphoses** (met-ə-MOR-fə-seez) *plural.*

merinos

mermaid

mesa

meteor

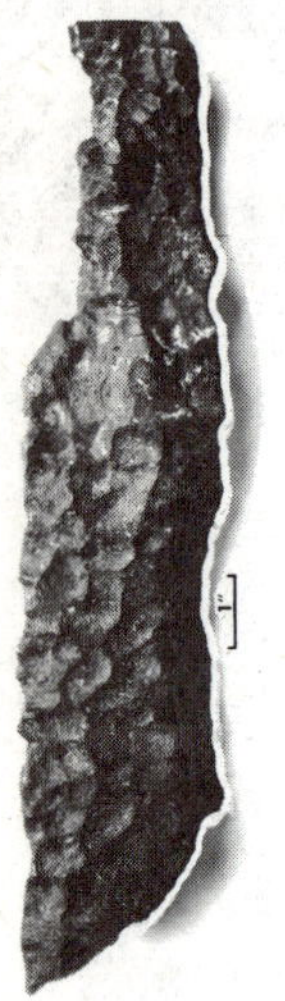
meteorite

Michigan
★capital: Lansing

met·a·phor (MET-ə-for) *noun.* A figure of speech that suggests similarity between two unlike things, as "Wind is a cat/ that prowls at night." (E. R. Fuller). *See* **simile.**

mete (MEET) *verb.* To give each his share; distribute. **meted, meting.**

me·te·or (MEE-tee-ər) *noun.* A shooting star; the glow from a meteoroid that ignites from friction upon entering the earth's atmosphere.

me·te·or·ic (mee-tee-OR-ik) *adjective.* Flashing; like a meteor; brilliant and swift at first and then disappearing. —**meteorically** *adverb.*

me·te·or·ite (MEE-tee-ə-right) *noun.* The stone or metal remains of a meteoroid that lands on earth without burning completely in the atmosphere. **meteorites.**

me·te·or·oid (MEE-tee-ə-roid) *noun.* One of the countless objects in outer space that we see as meteors if they burn in the earth's atmosphere.

me·te·or·ol·o·gist (mee-tee-ə-ROL-ə-jist) *noun.* A person who studies the atmosphere and is concerned with weather and weather predictions. —**meteorology** (mee-tee-ə-ROL-ə-jee) *noun.*

me·ter (MEE-tər) *noun.* 1. A unit of measure of length in the metric system that equals 39.37 inches. 2. The measured rhythm of poetry or music. 3. A device used to measure or record: a water *meter.*

meth·od (METH-əd) *noun.* 1. An orderly way of doing something: He had a *method* for getting his work done. 2. A certain way of doing something: one *method* of cooking. —**methodical** (mə-THOD-i-kəl) *adjective.* —**methodically** *adverb.*

met·ric (MET-rik) *adjective.* Pertaining to use of the metric system.

metric system. A system of weights and measures. *See page 457.*

met·ro·nome (MET-rə-nohm) *noun.* A device that can be set at different speeds to sound a beat for practicing music. **metronomes.**

me·trop·o·lis (mə-TROP-ə-liss) *noun.* 1. The most important city in a country, state, or region. 2. Any large, important city. **metropolises.**

met·ro·pol·i·tan (met-rə-POL-ə-tn) *adjective.* Of or about a large city.

met·tle (MET-l) *noun.* 1. Basic temperament or character: the *mettle* of a man. 2. Courage; bravery; spirit. —**on one's mettle.** Ready to do the best one can.

mew (MYOO) *noun.* The sound a cat makes. —*verb.* To meow; make the sound of a cat. **mewed, mewing.**

mez·za·nine (MEZ-ə-neen or mez-ə-NEEN) *noun.* A floor or story of a building midway between two regular floors. **mezzanines.**

mi (MEE) *noun.* The third note in any standard major or minor scale of eight notes.

mi. *abbreviation.* Mile.

mi·ca (MIGH-kə) *noun.* A mineral that has thin, partly clear layers.

mice (MIGHSS) *noun. See* **mouse.**

Mich·i·gan (MISH-i-gən) *noun.* A state in north central United States, 26th to join the Union (1837). —**Mich.** *abbreviation.* Also **MI** for Zip Codes.

mi·crobe (MIGH-krohb) *noun.* A germ; a tiny organism that carries disease. **microbes.**

mi·cro·film (MIGH-krə-film) *noun.* A film used to record and preserve printed materials in a reduced size.

mi·cro·or·gan·ism (migh-kroh-OR-gən-iz-əm) *noun.* A microscopic animal or plant form.

mi·cro·phone (MIGH-krə-fohn) *noun.* A device that changes sound waves into electrical current so that they can be made louder, recorded, or sent by radio and TV. **microphones.**

Metric System

Converting to the Metric System	Converting from the Metric System
LENGTH	
1 inch = 2.54 centimeters 1 foot = 0.3048 meter 1 yard = 0.9144 meter 1 rod = 5.0292 meters 1 mile = 1.609 kilometers	1 centimeter = 0.39 inch 1 meter = 39.37 inches, 3.28 feet, 1.094 yards, or 0.199 rod 1 kilometer = 0.62 mile
AREA	
1 square inch = 6.4516 square centimeters 1 square foot = 929.030 square centimeters 1 square yard = 0.836 square meter 1 acre = 4.047 square meters 1 square mile = 2.590 square kilometers	1 square centimeter = 0.155 square inch 1 square meter = 10.764 square feet or 1.196 square yards 1 square kilometer = 0.386 square mile
VOLUME	
1 cubic inch = 16.387 cubic centimeters 1 cubic foot = 0.028 cubic meter 1 cubic yard = 0.765 cubic meter	1 cubic centimeter = 0.061 cubic inch 1 cubic meter = 35.315 cubic feet or 1.308 cubic yards
CAPACITY	
1 fluid ounce = 29.573 milliliters 1 liquid pint = 0.473 liter 1 liquid quart = 0.946 liter 1 gallon = 3.785 liters	1 milliliter = 0.338 fluid ounce 1 liter = 2.113 liquid pints, 1.057 liquid quart, or 0.264 gallon
DRY MEASURE	
1 dry pint = 0.551 liter 1 dry quart = 1.101 liters 1 peck = 8.810 liters 1 bushel = 35.238 liters	1 liter = 1.816 dry pint, 0.908 dry quart, or 0.628 bushel
WEIGHT	
1 grain = 0.065 gram 1 avoirdupois ounce = 28.350 grams 1 pound = 0.454 kilogram 1 (short) hundredweight = 45.359 kilograms 1 (short) ton = 0.907 metric ton	1 gram = 15.432 grains or 0.035 avoirdupois ounce 1 kilogram = 2.205 pounds or 0.022 (short) hundredweight 1 metric ton = 1.102 (short) tons

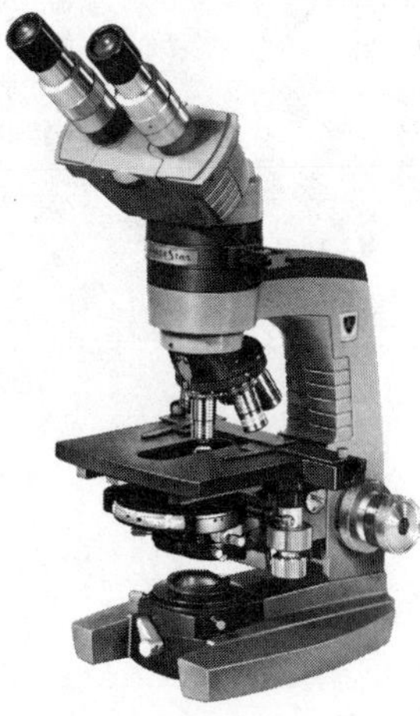
microscope

mi·cro·scope (MIGH-krə-skohp) *noun.* A device that makes small things appear larger, especially objects too small to be seen by the eye alone. **microscopes.**

mi·cro·scop·ic (migh-krə-SKOP-ik) *adjective.* 1. Too small to be seen without a microscope. 2. Tiny; very small: *microscopic* writing.

mid- *prefix.* Indicates the middle: *mid*way, *mid*section.

mid·dle (MID-l) *adjective.* 1. In the center; of equal distance from either end or side. 2. Medium; in between: a girl of *middle* height. —*noun.* 1. The center; the point or part that is of equal distance from all edges: in the *middle* of the room. 2. The waist.

middle age. The time of life between the ages of about 40 and about 60.

mid·dy (MID-ee) *noun.* 1. (Informal) A midshipman. 2. A loose blouse like a sailor's, usually worn by young children and girls. **middies.**

midge (MIJ) *noun.* A small insect, as a gnat or fly. **midges.**

midg·et (MIJ-it) *noun.* 1. A very small person. 2. Anything that is very small of its kind: *midget* cars.

midget football. A football league for boys between the ages of 9 and 13.

mid·night (MID-night) *noun.* Twelve o'clock at night; the middle of the night. —**burn the midnight oil.** To work or study late into the night.

midnight sun. The sun seen at midnight during summer in regions near the North and South Poles.

mid·point (MID-point) *noun.* A point at the center; the middle.

mid·ship·man (MID-ship-mən or mid-SHIP-mən) *noun.* A student at the United States Naval Academy or the United States Coast Guard Academy. —**midshipmen** *plural.*

midst *noun.* The middle; center part. —**in the midst of.** Among; surrounded by; during. —**in our midst.** Among us.

mid·way (MID-way) *adjective* and *adverb.* Halfway; in or at the middle part. —*noun.* The place at a carnival, circus, or fair where the rides, games, and other amusements are located.

mid·wife (MID-wighf) *noun.* A woman trained to assist at births. —**midwives** (MID-wyvz) *plural.*

mien (MEEN) *noun.* The way one looks or carries himself; one's manner: the serious *mien* of a judge.

[1]**might** *verb. See* **may.**

[2]**might** *noun.* Great strength or power: *Might* does not make right.

might·y (MIGH-tee) *adjective.* 1. Having great strength or power. 2. Huge; great in size: *mighty* redwood trees. **mightier, mightiest.** —*adverb.* (Informal) Very: I'm *mighty* happy to meet you.

mi·grant (MIGH-grənt) *noun.* 1. A person, animal, or bird that moves from one place to another. 2. A worker who travels in search of jobs, often to harvest crops.

mi·grate (MIGH-grayt) *verb.* 1. To move from one place to settle in another. 2. To move from one place to another as the seasons change. **migrated, migrating.**

mi·gra·tion (migh-GRAY-shən) *noun.* 1. The act of moving from one place to another. 2. A number or amount of persons or animals moving at the same time. —**migratory** (MIGH-grə-tor-ee) *adjective.*

mike (MIGHK) *noun.* (Informal) A microphone. **mikes.**

mild (MYLD) *adjective.* 1. Gentle; not harsh: *mild* manners. 2. Neither cold nor hot: a *mild* climate. 3. Not strong tasting; not sour or bitter: *mild* tea. **milder, mildest.** —**mildly** *adverb.* —**mildness** *noun.*

mil·dew (MIL-doo or MIL-dyoo) *noun.* A fungus that grows on plants or damp clothes, paper, etc. —*verb.* To become covered with mildew. **mildewed, mildewing.**

mile (MIGHL) *noun.* A unit used to measure length, equal to 5,280 feet. **miles.**

mile•age (MIGH-lij) *noun.* 1. The total number of miles traveled. 2. Money for automobile expenses.

mile•stone (MIGHL-stohn) *noun.* 1. A stone or marker by the side of a road that shows the distance in miles to a particular place. 2. An important event: a *milestone* in space exploration. **milestones.**

mil•i•tant (MIL-ə-tənt) *adjective.* Fighting hard in a war or for a cause: a *militant* worker for women's rights. —*noun.* One who is militant. —**militantly** *adverb.*

mil•i•tar•y (MIL-ə-tehr-ee) *adjective.* 1. Having to do with the army or war: *military* force. 2. Having to do with soldiers: a *military* life. —*noun.* The army; soldiers as a group.

mi•li•tia (mə-LISH-ə) *noun.* An army of citizens used in emergencies.

milk *noun.* 1. A white fluid produced by female mammals to feed their young. 2. Cow's milk. 3. Any fluid that looks like milk: coconut *milk.* —*verb.* To take milk from a mammal by hand or machine. **milked, milking.**

milk•man (MILK-man) *noun.* A person who sells or delivers milk. —**milkmen** *plural.*

milk•weed (MILK-weed) *noun.* Any of several types of plants having pods containing a white juice.

milk•y (MIL-kee) *adjective.* 1. Having or giving milk. 2. White in color. **milkier, milkiest.**

Milky Way. The galaxy in which our solar system is located, seen at night from earth as a misty band of stars.

[1]**mill** (MIL) *noun.* 1. A factory: a steel *mill.* 2. A building or machine for grinding grain: a flour *mill.* 3. A machine or device for grinding or crushing any material: a pepper *mill.* —*verb.* 1. To grind; crush: to *mill* grain into flour. 2. To cut grooves on the edge of (a coin). 3. To move aimlessly: We *milled* about the store. **milled, milling.**

[2]**mill** (MIL) *noun.* One-tenth of a cent.

mil•len•ni•um (mə-LEN-ee-əm) *noun.* 1. One thousand years. 2. A time when peace and complete happiness are expected. —**millenniums** or **millennia** (mə-LEN-ee-ə) *plural.*

mill•er (MIL-ər) *noun.* 1. A person who owns or runs a mill. 2. A machine for grinding grain. 3. A type of moth that looks as if it were covered with white flour.

mil•let (MIL-it) *noun.* Any of several kinds of grain used as food for animals.

mil•li•me•ter (MIL-ə-mee-tər) *noun.* A thousandth part of a meter.

mil•li•ner (MIL-ə-nər) *noun.* A person who makes or sells hats for women.

mil•lion (MIL-yən) *noun* (and *adjective*). The cardinal number after 999,999 and before 1,000,001; 1,000,000.

mil•lion•aire (mil-yə-NAIR) *noun.* A person with at least a million dollars. **millionaires.**

mil•lionth (MIL-yənth) *adjective.* Coming next after 999,999th; 1,000,000th. —*noun.* One of a million equal parts.

mil•li•pede (MIL-ə-peed) Also **millepede** *noun.* An insect with a wormlike body and many legs.

mill•stone (MIL-stohn) *noun.* 1. One of a pair of round stones used for grinding grain. 2. Anything used for grinding. **millstones.** —**a millstone about one's neck.** A heavy and unwanted burden or responsibility.

mim•e•o•graph (MIM-ee-ə-graf) *noun.* 1. A machine for making stencil copies of letters, advertisements, tests, announcements, etc. 2. A copy made on such a machine. —*verb.* To make copies with mimeograph. **mimeographed, mimeographing.**

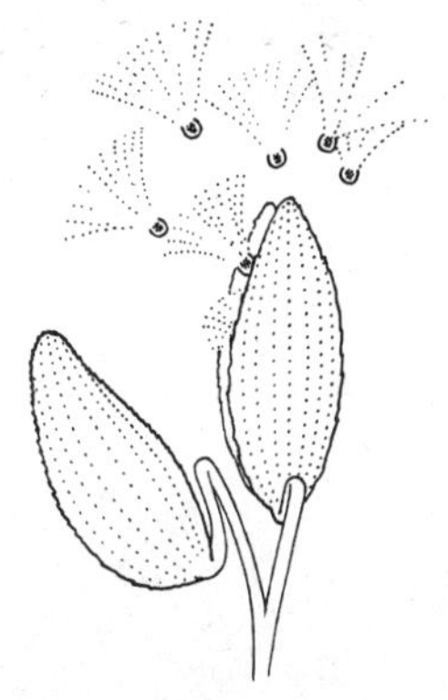
milkweed

Milky Way

mim·ic (MIM-ik) *verb.* 1. To ridicule by imitating. 2. To copy; do or be an imitation of: Sally can *mimic* a baby's cry perfectly. **mimicked, mimicking.** —*noun.* Any person or thing that imitates.

min. *abbreviation.* 1. Minute. 2. Minimum.

min·a·ret (min-ə-RET) *noun.* A high, thin tower on a Moslem temple.

minarets

mince (MINSS) *verb.* 1. To cut up into tiny pieces. 2. To walk with small, dainty steps. 3. To behave or speak in an overly polite way. **minced, mincing.**

mince·meat (MINSS-meet) *noun.* A mixture of finely chopped meat, apples, raisins, animal fat, spices, and flavorings used to make pies and similar desserts.

mind (MYND) *noun.* 1. The center of human awareness; the part of the brain that thinks, reasons, and remembers. 2. Memory: Put it out of your *mind.* 3. Opinion: Make up your *mind.* 4. A person of unusual intelligence: Benjamin Franklin was one of the great *minds* of American history. —*verb.* 1. To pay attention to; take notice of: *Mind* what I say. 2. To take care of: Charles has to *mind* his little brother. 3. To obey: You must *mind* the baby sitter. 4. To object to: Do you *mind* going to the store for me? **minded, minding. —bear in mind.** To remember. **—be of one mind.** To agree; hold the same opinion. **—give a piece of one's mind.** To give a scolding. **—have a mind to.** To be inclined to (do something). **—lose one's mind.** To become insane, go crazy. **—make up one's mind.** To decide.

minibike

mind·ful (MYND-fəl) *adjective.* Aware; paying attention; careful: Be *mindful* of the snow and ice.

[1]**mine** (MIGHN) *pronoun.* Something that belongs to oneself: That scarf is *mine.*

[2]**mine** (MIGHN) *noun.* 1. A large hole or tunnel made in the ground to get out mineral ores or other valuable materials: coal *mine,* salt *mine.* 2. A plentiful source of anything: My brother is a *mine* of misinformation. 3. A bomb placed in the water or just under the ground to destroy enemy ships or ground forces. **mines.** —*verb.* 1. To dig a mine. 2. To take ores and other materials out of the ground. 3. To plant or set out explosive mines: *mine* a field against enemy tanks. **mined, mining.**

min·er (MIGH-nər) *noun.* A person who works in a mine.

min·er·al (MIN-ər-əl) *noun.* A nonliving substance, such as rock or metal, that occurs in nature as part of neither animal nor plant life.

min·gle (MING-gəl) *verb.* 1. To mix; blend; combine. 2. To participate; associate with other persons: The children *mingled* together on the playground. **mingled, mingling.**

min·i·a·ture (MIN-ee-ə-chur or MIN-ə-chur) *noun.* 1. A very small painting or portrait. 2. A tiny copy of anything: I have a *miniature* racing car. **miniatures.**

min·i·bike (MIN-ee-bighk) *noun.* A motorcycle with a short wheelbase and small wheels. **minibikes.**

min·i·mum (MIN-ə-məm) *noun.* The least amount needed, possible, or allowed: We're packing a *minimum* of clothes for the weekend at Grandfather's farm. **—minimums** or **minima** (MIN-ə-mə) *plural.* —*adjective.* As low as possible; of the least allowed: *minimum* wages.

min·ing (MIGH-ning) *noun.* The business or occupation of taking metals, salt, coal, and other natural products out of the earth.

min·i·skirt (MIN-ee-skert) *noun.* A skirt no longer than midthigh; a skirt eight to ten inches above the knee.

min·is·ter (MIN-i-stər) *noun.* 1. A

clergyman; pastor. 2. An official in charge of a particular department of government. 3. A person, not as high in rank as an ambassador, who represents his government in another country. —*verb.* 1. To take care of or serve. 2. To act as a religious minister. **ministered, ministering.**

min·is·try (MIN-i-stree) *noun.* 1. The position, duties, and time in office of a minister. 2. Any one group of church or government ministers. 3. Any government department under the direction of a minister. 4. The building in which government ministers have their offices and sometimes live. **ministries.**

mink (MINGK) *noun.* 1. A weasel-like animal with webbed feet. 2. The fur of this animal.

Min·ne·so·ta (min-ə-SOH-tə) *noun.* A state in north central United States, 32nd to join the Union (1858). —**Minn.** *abbreviation.* Also **MN** for Zip Codes.

min·now (MIN-oh) *noun.* A small freshwater fish.

mi·nor (MIGH-nər) *adjective.* 1. Slight in importance, size, or degree: a *minor* accident. 2. (Music) Relating to one of two standard scales or keys, the other being *major.* —*noun.* One not yet the age to be recognized by law as an adult.

mi·nor·i·ty (mə-NOR-ə-tee or migh-NOR-ə-tee) *noun.* 1. Less than half of a whole group. 2. A group of people who are different in race, religion, or other ways from larger groups around them. 3. A political party that is smaller or less powerful than the party in power. 4. The time before coming of age legally. **minorities.**

min·strel (MIN-strəl) *noun.* 1. A musical performer in the Middle Ages. 2. Any musician or poet.

¹**mint** *noun.* 1. Any of several plants with fragrant leaves and a tangy flavor. 2. A mint-flavored candy.

²**mint** *noun.* 1. A place where coins are made. 2. A great deal, especially of money. —*verb.* 1. To make coins. **minted, minting.** —*adjective.* 1. Not used or cancelled: a *mint* stamp. 2. Fresh and new: *mint* condition.

min·u·end (MIN-yoo-end) *noun.* The number from which another number is subtracted: in 33 minus 11, 33 is the *minuend. See* **subtrahend.**

min·u·et (min-yoo-ET) *noun.* 1. A slow, formal dance from the 17th century. 2. Music written for, or in the rhythm of, this dance.

mi·nus (MIGH-nəss) *preposition.* 1. (Math) Less: Three *minus* two equals one. 2. (Informal) Not having; without: I am *minus* my mittens. —*adjective.* 1. (Math) Less than zero or part of a negative scale. 2. Lower or less than: I got a C *minus* on the test. —*noun.* 1. The sign (−). 2. An amount less than zero. **minuses.**

¹**min·ute** (MIN-it) *noun.* 1. Sixty seconds; 1/60th of an hour. 2. The distance traveled in a minute: We're only a *minute* away from school. 3. A short time: Wait a *minute.* 4. (Plural) The written summary of a meeting. 5. (Geometry) One of 60 equal parts in one degree of angular measurement. **minutes.** —*adjective.* Prepared very quickly: *minute* steak.

²**mi·nute** (migh-NOOT or migh-NYOOT) *adjective.* 1. Very small; tiny: a *minute* seed. 2. Exact; detailed: a *minute* explanation.

min·ute·man (MIN-it-man) *noun.* [Sometimes capital M] One of a group of volunteer soldiers who, before and during the American Revolution, were ready to fight at very short notice. —**minutemen** *plural.*

mir·a·cle (MIHR-ə-kəl) *noun.* 1. A strange and wonderful happening that seems to have a supernatural cause. 2. Any marvelous or wonderful event or thing. **miracles.**

minstrel

mink

Minnesota
★capital: St. Paul

minuteman

mi·rac·u·lous (mə-RAK-yə-ləss) *adjective.* 1. Of or about a miracle; supernatural. 2. Unexpected and wonderful: a *miraculous* victory. —**miraculously** *adverb.*

mi·rage (mi-RAHZH) *noun.* An optical illusion caused by heat waves that make distant objects seem near or make a flat surface look like a body of water. **mirages.**

mire (MIGHR) *noun.* A muddy, slushy swamp. **mires.** —*verb.* (Used mostly before *down*) 1. To stick or get stuck (in mud). 2. To experience trouble or delay: I got *mired* down in too many projects. **mired, miring.**

mir·ror (MIHR-ər) *noun.* 1. A glass with a coated backing that gives a reflection. 2. Anything that gives a reflection. —*verb.* To reflect or duplicate, as in a mirror. **mirrored, mirroring.**

mirth (MERTH) *noun.* Gleeful joy; feeling of amusement expressed in laughter. —**mirthful** *adjective.* —**mirthfully** *adverb.*

mis- *prefix.* Indicates: 1. In error: *mis*quote. 2. Wrong action: *mis*conduct. 3. Not suitable: *mis*fit.

mis·be·have (miss-bi-HAYV) *verb.* To be naughty; to behave badly. **misbehaved, misbehaving.** —**misbehavior** *noun.*

mis·cel·la·ne·ous (miss-l-AY-nee-əss) *adjective.* Made up of an assortment without apparent order or relationship: a *miscellaneous* collection.

mis·chief (MISS-chif) *noun.* 1. Annoying or harmful behavior; pranks that annoy: Halloween *mischief.* 2. A person who habitually plays jokes or causes trouble.

mis·chie·vous (MISS-chə-vəss) *adjective.* Full of naughtiness, often playful; troublesome; causing harm: *mischievous* children. —**mischievously** *adverb.*

mis·con·duct (miss-KON-duhkt) *noun.* Bad behavior; improper or illegal conduct.

mis·deed (miss-DEED) *noun.* An evil act.

mi·ser (MIGH-zər) *noun.* A person who hates to spend money.

mis·er·a·ble (MIZ-ər-ə-bəl or MIZ-rə-bəl) *adjective.* 1. Very unhappy. 2. Inadequate; causing misery: *miserable* conditions. 3. Bad; poorly done: a *miserable* lie. —**miserably** *adverb.*

mis·e·ry (MIZ-ər-ee) *noun.* 1. A state of great suffering or pain. 2. Great unhappiness caused by being deprived or poor. 3. A cause of worry or misfortune. **miseries.**

mis·fit (MISS-fit) *noun.* 1. A person who doesn't belong or can't adjust: Being in a new school can make one feel like a *misfit.* 2. Anything that does not fit correctly.

mis·for·tune (miss-FOR-chən) *noun.* 1. Bad luck. 2. Any accident or disaster. **misfortunes.**

mis·giv·ing (miss-GIV-ing) *noun.* A suspicious feeling; not knowing for sure; doubt.

mis·hap (MISS-hap) *noun.* 1. Misfortune. 2. An accident.

mis·judge (miss-JUHJ) *verb.* To judge incorrectly or unfairly. **misjudged, misjudging.**

mis·lay (miss-LAY) *verb.* To put in a place that is forgotten. **mislaid, mislaying.**

mis·lead (miss-LEED) *verb.* 1. To give the wrong idea; confuse or trick; lead (someone) into making a mistake. 2. To give incorrect or poor directions. **misled, misleading.**

mis·place (miss-PLAYSS) *verb.* To put in a wrong place; mislay or lose. **misplaced, misplacing.**

mis·pro·nounce (miss-prə-NOWNSS) *verb.* To use the wrong sounds or stress in saying a word. **mispronounced, mispronouncing.**

mis·quote (miss-KWOHT) *verb.* To repeat written or spoken words incorrectly. **misquoted, misquoting.**

mis·read (miss-REED) *verb.* 1. To misunderstand what is read. 2. To read incorrectly. **misread** (miss-RED) **misreading.**

mis·rep·re·sent (miss-rep-ri-ZENT) *verb.* To give an incorrect, improper, or false impression. **misrepresented, misrepresenting.**

[1]**miss** *verb.* 1. Not to make contact or connection with: *miss* a good pitch. 2. Not to understand or be aware of: Trudy *missed* the speaker's meaning. 3. Not to do or gain: Pete *missed* third place in the race by five seconds. 4. Not to go to: *miss* school. 5. To feel lonely for: Sally *misses* home when she is at camp. 6. To skip or leave out: Flo failed the test because she *missed* the two problems on the second page. 7. To find (something) gone or lost: I *missed* my purse when I got off the bus. **missed, missing.** —*noun.* A failure (to make contact, reach a goal, or locate): hits and *misses.*

[2]**miss** *noun.* 1. [Capital M] A title given an unmarried female. 2. A girl or single woman: These fashions are for the young *miss.* **misses.**

mis·shap·en (miss-SHAYP-ən) *adjective.* Badly out of shape; deformed.

mis·sile (MISS-l) *noun.* Something thrown, shot, or launched, as a bullet, arrow, or bomb. **missiles.**

miss·ing (MISS-ing) *adjective.* Lacking; lost; not present.

mis·sion (MISH-ən) *noun.* 1. A specific job or errand on which a person or group is sent. 2. The person or group of people sent to do such a job or errand. 3. The purpose, work, working place, or living place of people sent out to teach a religion. 4. A duty or purpose, especially one that a person chooses for himself: a *mission* in life.

mis·sion·ar·y (MISH-ə-nehr-ee) *noun.* A person sent to teach religion in a particular place, often a foreign land. **missionaries.**

Mission Control. The headquarters of the U.S. space travel program (National Aeronautics and Space Administration) through which contact is maintained between space travelers and Earth.

Mis·sis·sip·pi (miss-ə-SIP-ee) *noun.* A state in south central United States, 20th to join the Union (1817). —**Miss.** *abbreviation.* Also **MS** for Zip Codes.

Mississippi
★capital: Jackson

Mis·sou·ri (mi-ZUR-ee or mi-ZUR-ə) *noun.* A state in north central United States, 24th to join the Union (1821). —**Mo.** *abbreviation.* Also **MO** for Zip Codes.

Missouri
★capital: Jefferson City

mis·spell (miss-SPEL) *verb.* To spell incorrectly. **misspelled** or **misspelt, misspelling.**

mis·step (miss-STEP) *noun.* 1. A wrong step. 2. Improper choice of behavior; bad behavior.

mist *noun.* 1. A thin fog near the ground. 2. Anything that blurs the vision by washing over the eyes: a *mist* of tears. —*verb.* 1. To rain softly. 2. To blur; dim; fog over. **misted, misting.**

mis·take (mi-STAYK) *noun.* Making a wrong choice; doing, saying, or thinking (something) incorrectly. **mistakes.** —*verb.* 1. To take one person or thing for another: People often *mistake* me for my brother. 2. Not to understand; hold a wrong viewpoint or idea. **mistook, mistaken, mistaking.**

mis·tak·en (mi-STAY-kən) *adjective.* Wrong; in error: a *mistaken* idea. —**mistakenly** *adverb.*

Mis·ter (MISS-tər) *noun.* A form of address used before the name of a man or the name of the office he holds; usually abbreviated to *Mr.*

mis·tle·toe (MISS-l-toh) *noun.* An evergreen plant with small white berries.

mistletoe

mis·treat (miss-TREET) *verb.* To treat with cruelty or unkindness. **mistreated, mistreating.**

mis·tress (MISS-triss) *noun.* 1. A woman who owns or operates a household or other establishment. 2. [Capital M] In former times, a title often used in place of *Miss* or *Mrs.* 3. A woman who owns or controls: The dog came when his *mistress* called. **mistresses.**

mis·trust (miss-TRUHST) *verb.* To lack trust in; suspect: The sheriff *mistrusted* the stranger in town. **mistrusted, mistrusting.** —*noun.* A lack of trust; suspicion.

mist·y (MISS-tee) *adjective.* 1. Made hazy or clouded by mist: The steaming kettle made the kitchen windows *misty.* 2. Like or of mist. **mistier, mistiest.**

mis·un·der·stand·ing (miss-uhn-dər-STAN-ding) *noun.* 1. A state or condition of not understanding. 2. A quarrel; argument.

mis·use (miss-YOOZ) *verb.* 1. To use incorrectly. 2. To treat badly or cruelly. **misused, misusing.** —(miss-YOOSS) *noun.* Incorrect or harsh use: The *misuse* of one's talents can lead to failure in school. **misuses.**

mite (MIGHT) *noun.* 1. A very small thing or amount, as of money: Even the old beggar gave a *mite* to help the sick children. 2. A tiny animal that lives on certain plants and animals. **mites.**

mitt (MIT) *noun.* 1. A large, padded glove worn by baseball players. 2. A mitten. 3. (Slang) A hand.

mitten

mit·ten (MIT-n) *noun.* A piece of cold-weather clothing for the hand that covers the four fingers in one section and the thumb in another.

mix (MIKS) *verb.* 1. To blend or stir together: The artist *mixed* blue paint with yellow. 2. To combine or join together: Water will not *mix* with oil. 3. To make by blending or stirring together: Dad *mixed* a batch of pancakes. 4. To get along with; make friends: The shy boy did not *mix* with the others at the party. **mixed, mixing.** —*noun.* 1. A mixture; blend: Concrete is a *mix* of cement and sand or gravel. 2. A food product in which the ingredients are measured and mixed before packaging: cake *mix.* **mixes.**

mixed (MIKST) *adjective.* 1. Blended or combined: a *mixed* drink. 2. Formed from different parts or feelings: *mixed* candy; *mixed* emotions. 3. Composed of people of different race, nationality, or sex. 4. (Informal, generally followed by *up*) Confused.

mixed number. A whole number plus a fraction: 1⅝ and 3⅖ are *mixed* numbers.

mix·ture (MIKS-chər) *noun.* 1. A blend; a mix: Salad dressing is a *mixture* of oil, vinegar, and spices. 2. The process of mixing or blending. **mixtures.**

mix-up (MIKS-uhp) *noun.* A state of confusion or disorder.

moan (MOHN) *noun.* A long, low sound, as of pain or sorrow. —*verb.* 1. To utter a moan. 2. To complain. **moaned, moaning.**

moat (MOHT) *noun.* A deep, wide ditch, usually filled with water, surrounding a town or castle to protect it against enemy attack.

mob *noun.* 1. A large crowd, especially a disorderly or lawless one. 2. The masses of people in general. 3. A gang or organization of criminals. —*verb.* 1. To crowd around: We *mobbed* the football team after the game was won. 2. To attack or abuse in a mob: The sheriff was injured when the crowd *mobbed* him. **mobbed, mobbing.**

mo·bile (MOH-bəl) *adjective.* Able to move or be moved, especially with ease: Our TV stand has wheels on the bottom to make it *mobile.* —(MOH-beel) *noun.* A type of sculpture or decoration made of pieces of wood, metal, plastic, etc., suspended from a number of strings or wires and able to turn freely. —**mobility** (moh-BIL-ə-tee) *noun.*

mobile home. A home especially designed and equipped to allow it to be moved from place to place by towing with a car or truck.

moc·ca·sin (MOK-ə-sn) *noun.* 1. A soft leather shoe or slipper. 2. A poisonous snake of the U.S. South.

mo·cha (MOH-kə) *noun.* 1. A type of coffee. 2. A combination of coffee and chocolate flavors. 3. (Also *adjective*) A dark tan or yellow-brown color.

mock (MOK) *verb.* To make fun of; imitate; to copy. **mocked, mocking.** —*adjective.* Imitation; fake: The soldiers made a *mock* attack.

mock·er·y (MOK-ər-ee) *noun.* 1. A mocking; ridicule. 2. An outright fake: The unfair trial was a *mockery* of justice. **mockeries.**

mock·ing·bird (MOK-ing-berd) *noun.* A bird that can imitate the calls or songs of other birds.

mod *adjective.* (Slang) In style.

mode (MOHD) *noun.* 1. A manner or method: Flying is a popular *mode* of travel. 2. A fashion or custom: a current *mode.* **modes.**

mod·el (MOD-l) *noun.* 1. A small copy of a larger object: a *model* of an airplane. 2. Someone or something regarded as an example to be followed or imitated: General Eisenhower was a *model* of courage for his troops. 3. A type or style: Dad does not like this year's *model* of that automobile. 4. A person who wears clothes to display them for customers. 5. A person who poses for an artist or photographer. —*verb.* 1. To imitate or follow an example: Janet *modeled* herself after her favorite actress. 2. To shape, give form to: The artist *modeled* a lion's head in clay. 3. To wear clothes for display to customers. 4. To pose for an artist or photographer. **modeled, modeling.**

mod·er·ate (MOD-ər-it) *adjective.* Not extreme or excessive, as in degree, opinion, or actions: *moderate* prices. —*noun.* A person whose opinions are not extreme. **moderates.** —(MOD-ə-rayt) *verb.* To make or become milder: The hot weather was *moderated* by a gentle breeze. 2. To lead a discussion. **moderated, moderating.** —**moderately** *adverb.*

mod·er·a·tion (mod-ər-AY-shən) *noun.* An avoiding of extreme actions or behavior; mildness: Persons on diets must exercise *moderation* when eating.

mod·er·a·tor (MOD-ə-ray-tər) *noun.* A person who presides or rules (over a meeting): *moderator* of the panel discussion.

mod·ern (MOD-ərn) *adjective.* Related to the present time; up-to-date: Space travel is a *modern* activity. —*noun.* A person who is up-to-date.

mod·est (MOD-ist) *adjective.* 1. Not regarding oneself too highly or vainly; unassuming in behavior. 2. Decent; not vulgar or showy in one's dress or behavior. 3. Shy; not bold or rude. 4. Unpretentious in appearance: The family lived in a *modest* house. —**modestly** *adverb.*

mod·es·ty (MOD-iss-tee) *noun.* 1. The absence of vanity or pride: "He who obeys with *modesty* appears worthy of being some day a commander." (Cicero). 2. Decency; an absence of showiness in dress or behavior. 3. Shyness; bashfulness.

mod·i·fy (MOD-ə-figh) *verb.* 1. To change; rearrange: The automobile was *modified* so that it would ride more smoothly. 2. To make less extreme; make milder: When he had calmed down, Bill *modified* his harsh statement. 3. (Grammar) To change or limit the meaning of a word: An adjective is a word that *modifies* a noun or a pronoun. **modified, modifying.**

mod·u·late (MOJ-u-layt or MOD-yə-layt) *verb.* 1. To regulate or change; make more moderate. 2. To change the sound or tone of, as of music or the voice. **modulated, modulating.**

mobile home

moccasin

mockingbird

[2]mole

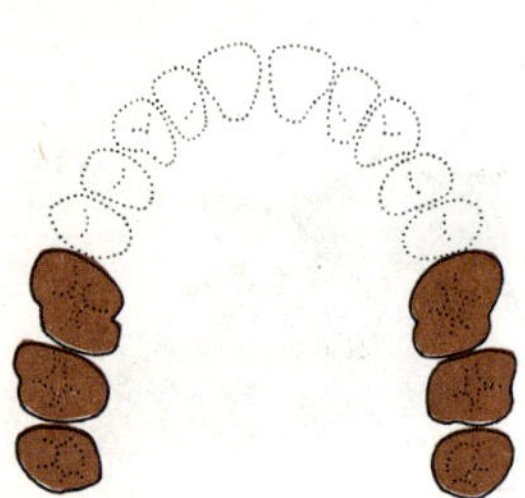
molars

mod·ule (MOJ-ool or MOD-yool) *noun.* 1. A standard or unit of measurement. 2. A self-contained unit or part of a spacecraft. **modules.**

mo·hair (MOH-hair) *noun.* The soft hair of an Asiatic goat or a fabric made of this hair.

moist *adjective.* Damp; lightly wet. **moister, moistest.** —**moistly** *adverb.*

mois·ten (MOISS-ən) *verb.* To make or become moist or damp: A stamp must be *moistened* before it will stick. **moistened, moistening.**

mois·ture (MOISS-chər) *noun.* Dampness; light wetness: My breathing caused *moisture* to form on the cold windowpane.

mo·lar (MOH-lər) *noun.* A wide tooth toward the back of the mouth, used for grinding food.

mo·las·ses (mə-LASS-iz) *noun.* A thick, dark syrup formed in making sugar.

[1]**mold** (MOHLD) *noun.* 1. A form or container in which metals, foods, or other materials can be shaped or hardened. 2. A thing or shape that is set or hardened in a mold: *molds* of clay. —*verb.* 1. To form or harden in a mold. 2. To develop or form: The boy's character was *molded* by years of training. **molded, molding.**

[2]**mold** (MOHLD) *noun.* A fuzzy fungus growth that sometimes develops on foods or other substances.

mold·er (MOHL-dər) *verb.* To decay; crumble slowly into dust: "John Brown's body lies a-*moldering* in the grave." (T. B. Bishop). **moldered, moldering.**

mold·ing (MOHL-ding) *noun.* 1. A strip of wood or other material that decorates or edges a surface, as a wall. 2. The act of shaping.

mold·y (MOHL-dee) *adjective.* 1. Covered with mold. 2. Stale; musty: The cave had a *moldy* smell. **moldier, moldiest.**

[1]**mole** (MOHL) *noun.* A small, usually dark spot on the skin. **moles.**

[2]**mole** (MOHL) *noun.* A small, furry animal that makes and lives in underground tunnels. **moles.**

mol·e·cule (MOL-ə-kyool) *noun.* A stable combination of atoms in a fixed pattern. 2. The smallest unit into which a substance can be divided and still keep all its characteristics. **molecules.**

mo·lest (mə-LEST) *verb.* To disturb or harass; to abuse: The tourist was upset when he was *molested* by a beggar. **molested, molesting.**

mol·lusk (MOL-əsk) Also **mollusc** *noun.* Any of a number of animals, like clams and snails, that have a soft body, usually protected by a shell.

molt (MOHLT) *verb.* To shed a coat of skin, feathers, or other covering that is soon replaced by a new coat. **molted, molting.**

mol·ten (MOHLT-n) *adjective.* Melted, usually by intense heat: The worker poured *molten* steel into a mold.

mo·ment (MOH-mənt) *noun.* 1. A very brief period of time; an instant: The busy salesman could talk with us for only a *moment.* 2. Importance: The day of the invasion was a time of great *moment.*

mo·men·tar·y (MOH-mən-tehr-ee) *adjective.* Lasting for only a moment or instant. —**momentarily** *adverb.*

mo·men·tous (moh-MEN-təss) *adjective.* Of very great importance: Choosing a new general was a *momentous* decision for the President. —**momentously** *adverb.*

mo·men·tum (moh-MEN-təm) *noun.* The force with which an object moves: The truck lost *momentum* when its engine failed. —**momenta** or **momentums** *plural.*

mon- *prefix. See* **mono-.**

mon·arch (MON-ərk) *noun.* A ruler, especially a royal one, as a king or queen.

mon·ar·chy (MON-ər-kee) *noun.* 1. A country ruled by a monarch. 2. A government headed by a monarch. **monarchies.**

mon·as·ter·y (MON-ə-stehr-ee) *noun.* A building in which monks live. **monasteries.**

Mon·day (MUHN-dee or MUHN-day) *noun.* The second day of the week: *Monday* is the day between Sunday and Tuesday. —**Mon.** *abbreviation.*

mon·e·tar·y (MON-ə-tehr-ee) *adjective.* Of or related to money or coinage: a *monetary* reward.

mon·ey (MUHN-ee) *noun.* 1. The paper notes or coins issued by a country to be used for buying and selling. 2. Wealth; property. —**moneys** or **monies** *plural.*

mon·goose (MONG-gooss) *noun.* A small animal of Africa and Asia that resembles a weasel and is a skillful hunter of snakes. **mongooses.**

mon·grel (MONG-grəl) *noun.* A dog or other animal or plant that is of mixed breed: Rex is a *mongrel;* he is part spaniel and part collie. —*adjective.* From any mixed beginnings or sources.

mon·i·tor (MON-ə-tər) *noun.* 1. A student who helps a teacher, as by keeping records or watching over other students. 2. A device, like a TV set, used to keep watch over some process: The store used a TV *monitor* to keep a watch for shoplifters. —*verb.* To watch over or check, especially with an electronic device: *monitor* on radar. **monitored, monitoring.**

monk (MUHNGK) *noun.* A man who leads a life of religious devotions within a monastery.

mon·key (MUHNG-kee) *noun.* Any of several mammals that somewhat resemble man, especially a small, long-tailed mammal that looks like a small ape. —*verb.* (Informal) To meddle, fool, or play (with). **monkeyed, monkeying.**

monkey business. (Slang) 1. Silly behavior. 2. Improper or suspicious conduct.

mono- *prefix.* Indicates: one; sole or single: *mono*rail.

mon·o·gram (MON-ə-gram) *noun.* A design that includes the initials of a person's name and is used on such objects as clothing, jewelry, and luggage.

mon·o·logue (MON-ə-lawg) Also **monolog** *noun.* 1. A long speech spoken by one individual. 2. A short play or other entertainment given by one person. **monologues.**

mon·o·nu·cle·o·sis (mon-oh-noo-klee-OH-siss) *noun.* An infectious disease, common among children and young adults, characterized by fever, swelling of the lymph glands, and general weakness. Also called "mono."

mon·o·plane (MON-ə-playn) *noun.* An airplane that has a single pair of wings. **monoplanes.**

mo·nop·o·ly (mə-NOP-ə-lee) *noun.* 1. Total possession or control of a product or service: My uncle's oil company has a *monopoly* in our town. 2. Exclusive possession of a thing such as a talent or quality: a *monopoly* on success. **monopolies.**

mon·o·rail (MON-ə-rayl) *noun.* 1. A railroad that operates on a single rail or track. 2. A single rail.

mon·o·syl·la·ble (MON-ə-sil-ə-bəl) *noun.* A word of only one syllable: "In," "out," "through" are *monosyllables.* **monosyllables.**

mon·o·tone (MON-ə-tohn) *noun.* Speech or sound of unchanging pitch.

mo·not·o·nous (mə-NOT-n-əss) *adjective.* 1. Unchanging; always the same: *monotonous* scenery. 2. Boring, dull, or tiring because of the lack of change: a *monotonous* speech. 3. Said in the same tone; using the same sound: a *monotonous* voice. —**monotonously** *adverb.* —**monotony** *noun.*

mongoose

monorail

monkeys

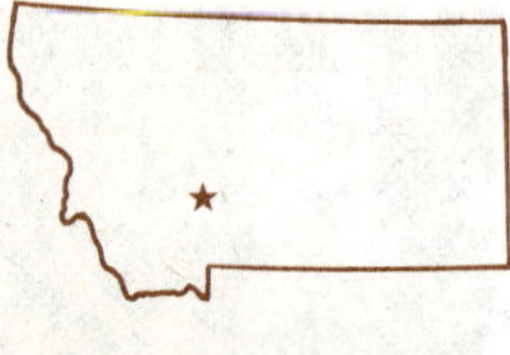

Montana
★capital: Helena

moon crater

moon buggy

mon·soon (mon-SOON) *noun.* 1. The southwest summer wind and the northeast winter wind in southern Asia. 2. The very heavy rainfall season caused by the southwest summer wind in southern Asia.

mon·ster (MON-stər) *noun.* 1. Any unnatural or extraordinarily unusual creature. 2. A plant or animal that is not normal in form; a freak. 3. An unusually cruel or wicked person. 4. A huge animal or thing.

mon·strous (MON-strəss) *adjective.* 1. Huge; very great in amount or size. 2. Horrible; very frightening. 3. Like a monster; greatly unnatural in shape or looks. **—monstrously** *adverb.*

Mon·tan·a (mon-TAN-ə) *noun.* A state in western United States, 41st to join the Union (1889). **—Mont.** *abbreviation.* Also **MT** for Zip Codes.

month (MUHNTH) *noun.* 1. One of the 12 divisions of the year. 2. A time period from a numbered day in one month to the same numbered day in the next month.

month·ly (MUHNTH-lee) *adjective.* 1. Happening once a month. 2. Received every month: a *monthly* salary. *—noun.* A newspaper, magazine, or other material published once a month. **monthlies.**

mon·u·ment (MON-yə-mənt) *noun.* 1. Something built in memory of a person or event, such as a building, tomb, or statue; a memorial. 2. Any structure or thing from an earlier period of time that is thought of as historically important. 3. An important and lasting example of something: Washington, D.C., is a *monument* of city planning.

mon·u·men·tal (mon-yə-MENT-l) *adjective.* 1. Of or like a monument. 2. Large or significant **—monumentally** *adverb.*

moo *noun.* The sound a cow makes. **moos.** *—verb.* To make the sound of a cow; to low. **mooed, mooing.**

[1]**mood** *noun.* 1. The way one feels or thinks at any particular time: in the *mood* for a party. 2. (Plural) Fits of sadness or depression: Cheer up Ann; she is in one of her *moods.*

[2]**mood** *noun.* Any of various verb forms that show whether a sentence is a statement or question (the indicative *mood*), a command (the imperative *mood*), or a wish (the subjunctive *mood*).

mood·y (MOOD-ee) *adjective.* 1. Sad; unhappy; having fits of gloominess. 2. Changing moods often. **moodier, moodiest. —moodily** *adverb.*

moon *noun.* 1. The heavenly body that goes around the earth every 28 days. 2. Any other body that goes around a planet; a natural satellite. 3. A lunar month of 28 days. *—verb.* To behave as if in a trance; to daydream; idle. **mooned, mooning.**

moon·beam (MOON-beem) *noun.* A ray of moonlight.

moon buggy. A four-wheeled vehicle used by astronauts for exploring on the moon.

moon crater. One of many holes or volcano-like openings on the moon's surface.

moon crevice. A split or crack in the moon's surface.

moon dust. The finely ground, powdery soil that covers the moon's surface.

moon·light (MOON-light) *noun.* The light of the moon. *—adjective.* By or with the light of the moon: a *moonlight* ride. *—verb.* To work at a second job while holding a main job. **moonlighted, moonlighting.**

moon man. An astronaut who has landed on the moon; a moon explorer.

moon mission. The total operation of a flight to the moon, involving many people, plans, and machines.

[1]**moor** (MUR) *noun.* An area of open wasteland, with peaty soil covered with heather.

[2]**moor** (MUR) *verb.* 1. To hold a ship in place with ropes, cables, anchors, etc. 2. To fix anything firmly in place. **moored, mooring.**

Moor (MUR) *noun.* A member of a Moslem people, descended from Arabs and now settled primarily in Northern Africa. —**Moorish** *adjective.*

moor·ing (MUR-ing) *noun.* 1. Equipment such as anchors and ropes used to moor a ship. 2. The place where a ship is moored.

moose (MOOSS) *noun.* A large North American animal of the deer family. —**moose** *plural.*

mop *noun.* 1. A tool for cleaning floors, made usually of rags, heavy string, or sponge fastened to a long handle. 2. A thick head of hair; bushy hair. —*verb.* 1. To use a mop. 2. To wipe: *mop* the forehead with a handkerchief. **mopped, mopping.**

mope (MOHP) *verb.* To be depressed; sulk. **moped, moping.** —*noun.* A person who mopes.

mo·raine (mə-RAYN) *noun.* A mass of stone, earth, and other material carried by a glacier and left at its sides or end.

mor·al (MOR-əl) *adjective.* 1. Concerned with what is right and wrong: *moral* questions. 2. Right; correct; good in conduct: a *moral* person. 3. Knowing the difference between right and wrong: Animals are not *moral* creatures. 4. Showing the difference between right and wrong; teaching good conduct: a *moral* book. 5. Almost the same (as): a *moral* victory. —*noun.* 1. The lesson or meaning of a fable, tale, or an experience: The *moral* of the tale is that you must work to eat. 2. (Plural) Behavior; one's nature in regard to right and wrong: the *morals* of a saint. —**morally** *adverb.*

mo·rale (mə-RAL) *noun.* The attitude that reflects the degree of enthusiasm, confidence, cheerfulness, or bravery: the *morale* of the team.

mo·ral·i·ty (mə-RAL-ə-tee) *noun.* 1. The right or wrong or good or evil of a thing. 2. Goodness; virtue: A liar has little *morality.* 3. A set of rules for what is right and wrong: a code of *morality.* **moralities.**

mor·al·ize (MOR-ə-lighz) *verb.* 1. To think, talk, or be concerned with what is right and wrong. 2. To explain the rightness or wrongness of a thing. **moralized, moralizing.**

mor·a·to·ri·um (mor-ə-TOR-ee-əm) *noun.* 1. A legal act that allows delay in repaying a debt. 2. The time during which debts may be delayed. 3. A delay of any action; the time covered by such a delay: a *moratorium* on war. —**moratoriums** or **moratoria** *plural.*

mo·rass (mə-RASS) *noun.* An area of low, soft, wet ground; a swamp; a bog. **morasses.**

mor·bid (MOR-bid) *adjective.* 1. Not healthy; unwholesome; very gloomy in outlook: *morbid* thoughts. 2. Diseased; caused by or like a disease. —**morbidly** *adverb.*

more (MOR) *adjective.* (Comparative form of **much** or **many.**) Greater in amount, degree, quantity, or number: *more* sugar, *more* players. *See* **most.** —*noun.* An additional or greater amount, quantity, or number: That is not enough money; we need *more.* —*adverb.* 1. To a greater degree or extent: *more* humorous, *more* slowly. 2. Again: Play it once *more.* —**more or less.** To some degree; somewhat.

more·o·ver (mor-OH-vər) *adverb.* Besides; also; further.

mo·res (MOR-ayz) *noun, plural.* The customs and moral habits of a group.

morgue (MORG) *noun.* 1. A place where dead bodies are kept for a time, particularly those that have not been identified. 2. (Journalism) A reference file of newspapers, clippings, and photographs. **morgues.**

moose

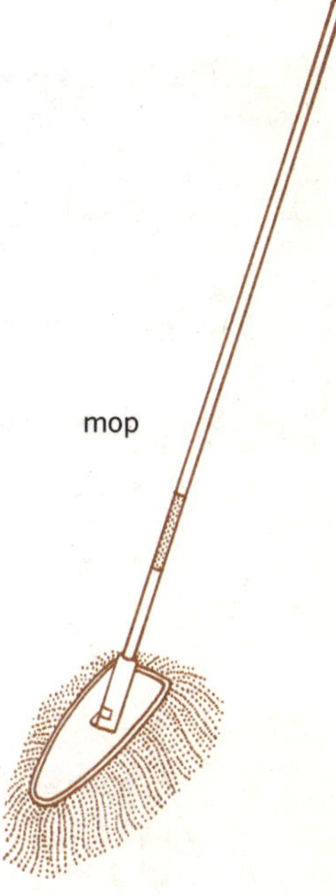
mop

mosaic

mosque

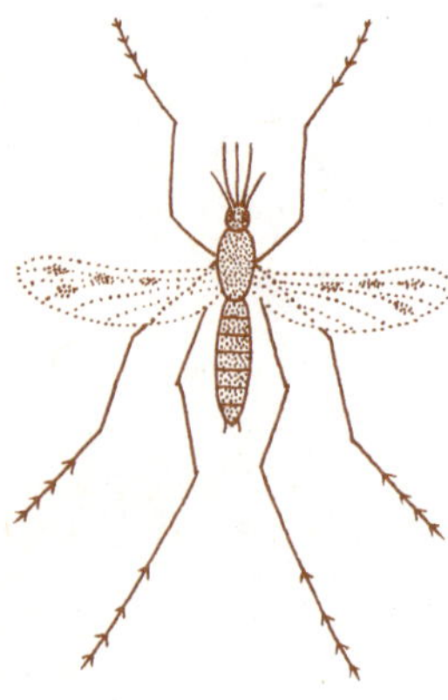
mosquito

morn *noun.* (Poetic) Morning.

morn·ing (MOR-ning) *noun.* The part of day between sunrise and noon or between midnight and noon.

morn·ing-glo·ry (MOR-ning-glor-ee) *noun.* 1. A flower of a fluted funnel shape that closes toward the end of the day. 2. The vine on which this flower grows. **morning-glories.**

mo·ron (MOR-on) *noun.* 1. An adult with the mentality of an 8- to 12-year-old child. 2. Any person with less than average intelligence.

mo·rose (mə-ROHSS) *adjective.* Very unhappy or gloomy; sulky.

mor·pheme (MOR-feem) *noun.* A unit of language that cannot be broken down into smaller parts: The *morphemes* in "onto" are "on" and "to." **morphemes.**

mor·phine (MOR-feen) *noun.* A drug used to cause sleep and lessen pain.

mor·row (MOR-oh) *noun.* (Rare) 1. Tomorrow. 2. Morning.

Morse code. A system of relaying messages by telegraph or light by the substitution of dots and dashes for letters and numbers.

mor·sel (MOR-sl) *noun.* A small piece or quantity.

mor·tal (MORT-l) *noun.* A human being: "What fools these *mortals* be!" (Shakespeare). *—adjective.* 1. Causing death; fatal: *mortal* disease. 2. Certain to die: *mortal* man. 3. Human: *mortal* flesh; *mortal* weakness. 4. Lasting until death: *mortal* enemy. 5. Causing the death of the soul or spirit: *mortal* sin. **—mortally** *adverb.*

mor·tar (MOR-tər) *noun.* 1. A material made of cement or lime mixed with sand and water that is used to hold bricks or stones together. 2. A bowl made of hard material in which drugs, spices, etc., are crushed into powder. *See* illustration at **pestle.** 3. A short cannon for firing explosives in a high arc or curve.

mort·gage (MOR-gij) *noun.* 1. Pledging of property, such as a house or land, as security that borrowed money will be paid back. 2. A document or paper that states the right or title to property, given to a lender. **mortgages.** *—verb.* To put property under a mortgage. **mortgaged, mortgaging.**

mor·ti·fy (MOR-tə-figh) *verb.* 1. To shame or make ashamed; embarrass: My error *mortified* me. 2. To control the desires of the body by pain, fasting, and discipline: *mortify* the flesh. **mortified, mortifying.**

mo·sa·ic (moh-ZAY-ik) *noun* (and *adjective*). 1. A design or picture made of small pieces of colored glass, stone, tile, wood, etc. 2. Anything that looks like a mosaic.

Mos·lem (MOZ-ləm) Also **Muslim** (MUHZ-ləm or MUZ-ləm) *noun.* One who believes in the Islamic religion.

mosque (MOSK) *noun.* A Moslem place of worship. **mosques.**

mos·qui·to (mə-SKEE-toh) *noun.* Any of several types of small insects, the female of which sucks blood. **—mosquitoes** or **mosquitos** *plural.*

moss (MAWSS) *noun.* Small green plant that grows in velvety clumps on damp ground, rocks, etc. **mosses.**

moss·y (MAWSS-ee) *adjective.* 1. Covered with moss. 2. Like moss in appearance or color.

most (MOHST) *adjective.* 1. The highest degree of *many,* indicating the largest number or amount. 2. The highest degree of *much,* indicating the largest amount, manner, or size. 3. In the largest number of cases: *Most* babies cry. *—noun.* 1. The biggest section or part: *Most* of the day was spent at the lake. 2. (Used with a plural verb) The largest number: *Most* of the girls have long hair. *—adverb.* 1. In the highest amount, span, or degree (Often used to form the superlative degree of some adjectives and adverbs): *most* polite; *most* happily. 2. Extremely: a *most* enjoyable day. 3. (Informal) Nearly, almost: *most* all of the children.

-most *suffix.* Used to form the superlative degree of some adjectives and adverbs: outer*most.*

mo·tel (moh-TEL) *noun.* A hotel on or near a main road that has rooms for travelers and a garage or parking spaces for their cars.

moth (MAWTH) *noun.* Any of several types of insects that look like butterflies but usually fly at night: Some *moths* lay eggs on cloth; their larvae then feed on the fabric. **—moths** (MAWTHZ or MAWTHSS) *plural.*

[1]**moth·er** (MUHTH-ər) *noun.* 1. A female parent. 2. A nun who is the leader of a convent or religious order for women. 3. A woman thought of as a mother or having the authority of a mother: den *mother.* 4. The source of anything: England was the *mother* of the American colonies. *—verb.* To care for; treat as a mother would: Our neighbor *mothers* all the children on the street. **mothered, mothering. —motherly** *adjective.*

[2]**moth·er** (MUHTH-ər) *noun.* A scum that forms on the surface of fermenting liquids as they turn sour.

moth·er·hood (MUTH-ər-hud) *noun.* The state of being a mother.

moth·er-in-law (MUTH-ər-in-law) *noun.* The mother of a person's wife or husband. **—mothers-in-law** *plural.*

moth·er-of-pearl (MUTH-ər-əv-perl) *noun.* A hard rainbow-colored material formed inside certain shells and used for buttons and jewelry.

mo·tion (MOH-shən) *noun.* 1. The act of moving; the changing of place or position: the *motion* of a train. 2. A movement of the body; a gesture. 3. A suggestion or proposal, offered during a meeting, that must be voted on. *—verb.* To show one's meaning by a gesture or movement: *motion* one's agreement. **motioned, motioning. —in motion.** Moving.

mo·tion·less (MOH-shən-liss) *adjective.* Not moving.

motion picture. A series of pictures shown on a screen in such rapid succession that people and objects seem to move.

mo·ti·vate (MOH-tə-vayt) *verb.* To give a motive to; give (a person or group) a desire to do something. **motivated, motivating.**

mo·tive (MOH-tiv) *noun.* A need or feeling that makes a person act: a *motive* for studying hard. **motives.**

mot·ley (MOT-lee) *adjective.* 1. Made up of many different parts or kinds: a *motley* collection. 2. Having many colors: a *motley* pattern. *—noun.* The costume of a clown.

mo·tor (MOH-tər) *noun.* 1. An engine that makes things go or work: an electric *motor.* 2. A car. *—verb.* To travel in a car. **motored, motoring.**

mo·tor·boat (MOH-tər-boht) *noun.* A small boat run by a gasoline motor.

mo·tor·cade (MOH-tər-kayd) *noun.* A parade of cars. **motorcades.**

mo·tor·car (MOH-tər-kahr) *noun.* An automobile; a car.

mo·tor·cy·cle (MOH-tər-sigh-kəl) *noun.* A two-wheeled vehicle that is run by a motor. **motorcycles.**

mo·tor·ist (MOH-tər-ist) *noun.* A person who drives or is a passenger in an automobile.

mo·tor·man (MOH-tər-mən) *noun.* 1. One who drives an electric train, subway, or streetcar. 2. One who runs a motor. **—motormen** *plural.*

mot·to (MOT-oh) *noun.* 1. A short sentence or phrase used to show what one believes in: The *motto* of the United States is "In God We Trust." 2. Any significant word, phrase, or sentence. **—mottoes** or **mottos** *plural.*

mound (MOWND) *noun.* 1. A hill or heap, as of soil, sand, stones. 2. (Baseball) The raised area on which the pitcher stands.

moth

motorboats

motorcycles

mountain goats

mountain lion

mouse

[1]**mount** (MOWNT) *verb.* 1. To climb up; climb on: *mount* the stairs; *mount* a horse. 2. To put into place: *mount* a cannon on the hill. 3. To attach to a backing or support: *mount* a picture. 4. To place in a setting: *mount* a jewel. 5. To grow in intensity: His anxiety *mounted.* **mounted, mounting.** —*noun.* A backing, board, or other support on which something is mounted.

[2]**mount** (MOWNT) *noun.* 1. (Poetic) A mountain; hill. 2. A riding horse.

moun·tain (MOWNT-n) *noun.* 1. A very high, steep land mass of earth and rock, higher than a hill. 2. A very high pile (of something).

moun·tain·eer (mownt-n-IHR) *noun.* 1. A person who lives on a mountain or in a mountain area. 2. A person who climbs mountains for sport.

mountain goat. A white, long-haired, black-horned antelope found in the Rocky Mountains.

mountain lion. A large wildcat of North and South America; a panther, cougar, puma.

moun·tain·ous (MOWNT-n-əss) 1. Referring to an area with many mountains. 2. Like a mountain; very high, steep, huge.

mountain range. Several mountains connected in a row; a line or chain of mountains.

mourn (MORN) *verb.* To feel or show sorrow (over a loss): *mourn* for the dead. **mourned, mourning.**

mourn·ful (MORN-fəl) *adjective.* Gloomy; sad; showing or causing sorrow. —**mournfully** *adverb.*

mourn·ing (MOR-ning) *noun.* 1. The act of showing or expressing sorrow. 2. The customs or clothing appropriate to grief for the dead.

mouse (MOWSS) *noun.* 1. A small rodent found in houses and fields. 2. (Informal) A shy or easily frightened person. —**mice** (MIGHSS) *plural.*

mouth (MOWTH) *noun.* 1. The opening in the body through which food and drink are taken in, and from which voice sounds come. 2. That which resembles or has the function of a mouth, as the *mouth* of a river. —*verb.* (MOW<u>TH</u>) To speak affectedly or pompously. **mouthed, mouthing.**

mouth·ful (MOWTH-ful) *noun.* 1. An amount that fills the mouth. 2. The amount in the mouth at one time. 3. (Slang) A long or complicated word or group of words.

mouth organ. *See* **harmonica.**

mouth·piece (MOWTH-peess) *noun.* 1. The part of a telephone, musical instrument, pipe, or the like that is held in or near the mouth. 2. The padding used by athletes, especially boxers, for protecting the teeth. 3. (Slang) A spokesman.

mouth·wash (MOWTH-wosh) *noun.* A liquid used to rinse the mouth and teeth, so as to prevent infection or sweeten breath. **mouthwashes.**

mov·a·ble (MOO-və-bəl) Also **moveable** *adjective.* 1. Able to be moved; not fastened down: *movable* furniture. 2. Changeable; varying in date from one year to another: Easter is a *movable* feast day.

move (MOOV) *verb.* 1. To change location or position. 2. To change the position of: He *moved* his desk to the other side of the room. 3. To change the place where one lives: We *moved* to a new town. 4. To put in motion: The water in the stream *moves* the small boat. 5. To stir emotionally; gain sympathy: His sad story *moved* everyone. 6. To act; make a choice or decision: Don't *move* until you hear from me. 7. To suggest; propose; make a motion: I *move* that the meeting be adjourned. **moved, moving.** —*noun.* 1. The act of moving. 2. An act done or a step taken to achieve a goal. 3. In a game, the actions a player makes during his turn. **moves.**

move·ment (MOOV-mənt) *noun.* 1. The act or way of moving. 2. A group of people united in an activity or plan with a particular goal: a clean air *movement.* 3. The part of a mechanism, as a watch, that causes and transfers motion. 4. The emptying of the bowels. 5. (Music) A principal part of a long composition.

mov·ie (MOOV-ee) *noun.* (Informal) A motion picture; a film. **movies.**

mov·ing (MOOV-ing) *adjective.* 1. In motion: a *moving* target. 2. Emotional; causing (one to feel) emotion, as of pity or sympathy.

moving picture. A motion picture; movie; a film.

[1]**mow** (MOH) *verb.* To cut (hay or grass) with a tool or machine. **mowed, mowing.**

[2]**mow** (MOW) *noun.* 1. The part of a barn where hay, straw, and grain are stored. 2. A pile of hay, straw, or grain.

mow·er (MOH-ər) *noun.* A person, machine, or device that cuts down grass, hay, weeds, and the like.

mpg Also **m.p.g.** *abbreviation.* Miles per gallon.

mph Also **m.p.h.** *abbreviation.* Miles per hour.

Mr. (MISS-tər) *noun.* An abbreviation of the title *Mister,* used before a name or another title: *Mr.* White.

Mrs. (MISS-iz) *noun.* A title or manner of addressing a married woman.

Ms. (MIZ) *noun.* A title or way of addressing both married and unmarried women.

ms *abbreviation.* Manuscript. —**mss** *plural.*

MST *abbreviation.* Mountain Standard Time.

mt. *abbreviation.* Mountain, mount.

mtn. *abbreviation.* Mountain.

much (MUHCH) *adjective.* In great amount or degree: There was too *much* fuss. **more, most.** —*noun.* 1. A great amount; a lot: We had *much* to talk about. 2. A thing of importance or concern: Her painting is not *much* to look at. —*adverb.* To a great degree: *much* larger; *much* smaller. **more, most.** —**make much of.** To treat as important.

mu·ci·lage (MYOO-sə-lij) *noun.* A sticky, gum-like material for holding things together; glue. **mucilages.**

muck (MUHK) *noun.* 1. A sticky kind of mud; filth. 2. Moist manure.

mu·cus (MYOO-kəss) *noun.* A sticky substance found in openings of the body such as the nose and throat. —**mucous** *adjective.*

mud *noun.* 1. Wet, soft, sticky earth. 2. (Informal) False and harmful charges: to throw *mud* at a political opponent.

mud·dle (MUHD-l) *verb.* To act in a confused or unplanned way: *muddle* through a problem. **muddled, muddling.** —*noun.* A mess; confusion. **muddles.**

mud·dy (MUHD-ee) *adjective.* 1. Covered with mud; containing mud: *muddy* boots; *muddy* water. 2. Not clear; not pure: *muddy* brown. 3. Confused; not easily understood: *muddy* thinking. **muddier, muddiest.** —*verb.* To make or become muddy. **muddied, muddying.**

muff (MUHF) *noun.* A heavy fabric or fur sewn into the form of a tube into which the hands are put to keep them warm. —*verb.* 1. To fail to catch a ball. 2. To handle in a clumsy way. **muffed, muffing.**

muf·fin (MUHF-in) *noun.* A small, round bread or cake, shaped like a cupcake, and usually eaten warm.

muf·fle (MUHF-əl) *verb.* 1. To wrap (as a scarf about the throat or face) to keep warm. 2. To wrap or cover so as to dull or stop a sound. **muffled, muffling.**

mug

muf·fler (MUF-lər) *noun.* 1. A heavy scarf for the neck. 2. Anything used to lessen sound: a car *muffler.*

mug (MUHG) *noun.* 1. A heavy drinking cup with a handle. 2. (Slang) The face; the mouth. —*verb.* 1. (Informal) To attack (a person), usually in order to rob. 2. (Informal) To make funny or ugly faces, usually in front of a camera. **mugged, mugging.**

mug·gy (MUG-ee) *adjective.* Hot and humid; damp: *muggy* weather. **muggier, muggiest.** —**mugginess** *noun.*

mul·ber·ry (MUHL-behr-ee) *noun.* 1. A tree with dark-colored berries whose leaves are used to feed silkworms. 2. The berry grown on these trees. 3. (Also *adjective*) A dark, purple-red color. **mulberries.**

mulch (MUHLCH) *noun.* A covering of dirt and dead vegetable matter used to cover and protect the roots of garden plants. **mulches.** —*verb.* To cover or spread over with mulch. **mulched, mulching.**

mule (MYOOL) *noun.* 1. An animal whose father is a donkey and whose mother is a horse. 2. A stubborn or stupid person. **mules.** —**mulish** (MYOOL-ish) *adjective.*

[1]**mull** (MUHL) *verb.* To think over; ponder. **mulled, mulling.**

[2]**mull** (MUHL) *verb.* To heat (a drink such as juice or cider), adding sugar and spice. **mulled, mulling.**

mul·let (MUHL-it) *noun.* Any one of several types of edible fish found in both salt and fresh water. —**mullets** or **mullet** *plural.*

multi- *prefix.* Indicates: 1. Many, much. 2. Two or more: *multi*colored.

mul·ti·ple (MUHL-tə-pəl) *adjective.* Having more than one part. —*noun.* (Math) A number into which another number can be divided with no remainder: 16 is a *multiple* of 4. **multiples.**

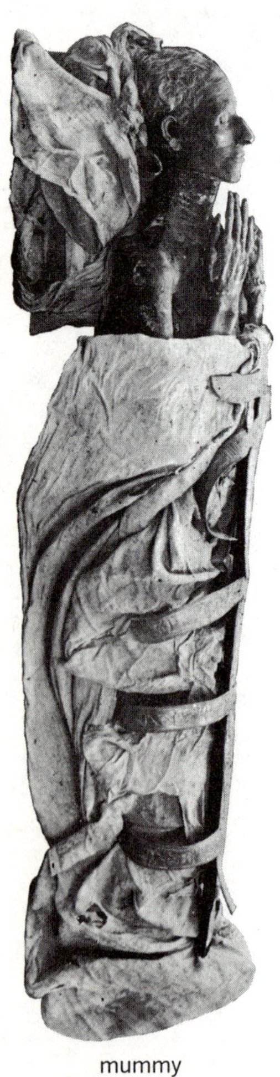
mummy

mul·ti·pli·cand (muhl-tə-pli-KAND) *noun.* (Math) A number that is multiplied by another: If ten is multiplied by seven, the *multiplicand* is ten.

mul·ti·pli·ca·tion (muhl-tə-pli-KAY-shən) *noun.* 1. The act of multiplying. 2. The condition of being multiplied. 3. (Math) Adding a number to itself a certain number of times: The *multiplication* of 12 by 3 is the same as adding 12 and 12 and 12.

multiplication table. A chart that shows the products of the process of multiplying, usually for the numbers 1 through 12.

mul·ti·pli·er (MUHL-tə-pligh-ər) *noun.* 1. The number by which another number is multiplied: If five is multiplied by two, two is the *multiplier.* 2. A person or thing that multiplies.

mul·ti·ply (MUHL-tə-pligh) *verb.* 1. To increase (a number or amount) a given number of times: If John *multiplies* five by three, he has increased five three times, making fifteen. 2. To increase in number: When people *multiply* too quickly, there is a population explosion. **multiplied, multiplying.**

mul·ti·tude (MUHL-tə-tood or MUHL-tə-tyood) *noun.* 1. A great number. 2. Crowd; throng: The Emperor spoke to the *multitude* that had come to hear him. **multitudes.**

mum (MUHM) *adjective.* Keeping silent; not telling: The girls were *mum* about the surprise. —*noun.* (Informal) A chrysanthemum.

mum·ble (MUHM-bəl) *verb.* To speak in a way that cannot be heard or understood, as with the mouth almost closed: The shy girl *mumbled* frequently. **mumbled, mumbling.** —*noun.* Mumbling, or the act of mumbling. **mumbles.**

mum·my (MUHM-ee) *noun.* The preserved body of a dead person. **mummies.**

mumps (MUHMPS) *noun, plural in form but used with a singular verb.* A contagious disease that causes certain glands in the neck to swell and makes it hard to swallow.

munch (MUHNCH) *verb.* To chew noisily and steadily. **munched, munching.**

mu·nic·i·pal (myoo-NISS-ə-pəl) *adjective.* Having to do with a city or town: *municipal* employees. —**municipally** *adverb.*

mu·nic·i·pal·i·ty (myoo-niss-ə-PAL-ə-tee) *noun.* A community, such as a city or town, that has its own government. **municipalities.**

mu·ni·tions (myoo-NISH-ənz) *noun, plural.* Weapons and ammunition used in warfare.

mur·der (MER-dər) *noun.* The unlawful killing of a person, especially when done on purpose. —*verb.* 1. To kill (a person) unlawfully. 2. (Informal) To ruin or do badly: She *murders* her lines in the play. **murdered, murdering.**

mur·der·er (MER-dər-ər) *noun.* A person who commits murder.

mur·der·ous (MER-dər-əss) *adjective.* 1. Able to murder: a *murderous* slash with a knife. 2. Deadly; bloody: a *murderous* fight. 3. (Informal) Extremely difficult or unpleasant: *murderous* heat. —**murderously** *adverb.*

murk (MERK) *noun.* Darkness or gloom: She could hardly see through the *murk* of the night. —**murk·y** (MER-kee) *adjective.* —**murkily** *adverb.*

mur·mur (MER-mər) *noun.* 1. A low, indistinct, flowing sound: A soft *murmur* of voices downstairs lulled Sally to sleep. 2. A barely audible complaint or protest. —*verb.* 1. To make a low, indistinct, flowing sound: Waves *murmured* in the distance. 2. To speak faintly: Elaine could only *murmur* her apology. 3. To grumble or complain in a low voice. **murmured, murmuring.**

mus·cle (MUHSS-l) *noun.* 1. Body tissue which can be tightened or relaxed to cause movement. 2. Physical strength. 3. Power or influence. **muscles.** —*verb.* (Used with *in*) To force one's way into something: In spite of the fact that he wasn't welcome, Phil *muscled* in on the party. **muscled, muscling.**

muscle system. A system of tissues, found in all animals except the lowest, that produces movement by contraction of the muscle cells.

mus·cu·lar (MUHSS-kyə-lər) *adjective.* 1. Having to do with muscles: *muscular* pain. 2. Having strong muscles: a *muscular* man.

[1]**muse** (MYOOZ) *verb.* To be lost in thought; ponder or think (about something). **mused, musing.**

[2]**muse** (MYOOZ) *noun.* 1. [Capital M] Any of the nine goddesses who in Greek mythology watched over the arts and sciences. 2. A spirit or power considered as a source of inspiration to artists. **muses.**

mu·se·um (myoo-ZEE-əm) *noun.* A building or part of a building where works of art or other objects of interest and value are kept for people to look at: a *museum* of science and industry.

mush (MUHSH) *noun.* 1. Boiled cornmeal. 2. Anything thick and soft: The spongy land next to the creek is a *mush* every spring. —*interjection.* Expresses a command by a sled driver for his dogs to speed up. —**mushy** *adjective.*

mush·room (MUHSH-room) *noun.* A fleshy fungus with an umbrella-shaped cap that springs up overnight in fields and woods: Some wild *mushrooms* are poisonous to eat. —*verb.* 1. To grow rapidly: Father thinks the new industry will make our town *mushroom.* 2. To become umbrella-shaped like a mushroom: The atomic cloud *mushroomed.* **mushroomed, mushrooming.**

mushrooms

mustangs

musk ox

muskrat

mu·sic (MYOO-zik) *noun.* 1. A pleasing arrangement of sounds made by musical instruments or singers. 2. The notes read by musicians to play a particular piece of music. 3. Any pleasing sound: ". . . the *music* of dancing waves. . . ." (S. E. Morison).

mu·si·cal (MYOO-zi-kəl) *adjective.* 1. Having to do with music: The piano is a *musical* instrument. 2. Having a pleasant sound: a *musical* voice. 3. Being accompanied by music: a *musical* comedy. 4. Fond of or skilled in music. *—noun.* A play with music and dance. **—musically** *adverb.*

mu·si·cian (myoo-ZISH-ən) *noun.* A skilled player of a musical instrument, a singer, or a composer, especially one who earns his living this way.

musk (MUHSK) *noun.* 1. A strong-smelling substance taken from a gland in the musk ox and used for making perfume. 2. The smell of musk. **—musky** *adjective.*

mus·ket (MUHSS-kit) *noun.* A gun fired from the shoulder, used before the invention of the rifle.

musk·mel·on (MUHSK-mel-ən) *noun.* A sweet, juicy melon with orange to reddish flesh; a cantaloupe.

musk ox. A large, shaggy mammal of northern North America and Greenland which looks like a cross between a sheep and an ox.

musk·rat (MUHSK-rat) *noun.* 1. A water animal of North America, somewhat like a large rat. 2. The fur of this animal. **—muskrat** or **muskrats** *plural.*

Mus·lim (MUHZ-ləm) *noun.* A Moslem.

mus·lin (MUHZ-lin) *noun.* A strong cotton cloth used for sheets, curtains, dresses, and other items.

muss (MUHSS) *verb.* To make untidy; rumple. **mussed, mussing.** *—noun.* A mess; disorder.

mus·sel (MUHSS-l) *noun.* A bluish-black shellfish, somewhat like a clam, which is found in both fresh and salt water.

must (MUHST) *verb.* Used as a helping verb to indicate: 1. Be obliged to: Children *must* go to school to learn. 2. Should: Laurie promised, so she *must* do it. 3. Certain to be: It's so late; my Mother *must* be worried. *—noun.* A requirement: This book is a *must* if you want to learn about horses.

mus·tache (MUHSS-tash or mə-STASH) *noun.* Hair grown on the upper lip.

mus·tang (MUHSS-tang) *noun.* A wild horse of the plains of North America.

mus·tard (MUHSS-tərd) *noun.* 1. A seed that is ground and mixed with liquids and herbs as flavoring for foods. 2. The plant on which this seed grows. 3. (Also *adjective*) A brownish-yellow color.

mus·ter (MUHSS-tər) *verb.* 1. To assemble; gather together; collect: "*Muster* the men for inspection," said the General. 2. To summon or gather: Lita is shy and has to *muster* up her courage whenever she meets strangers. **mustered, mustering.** *—noun.* A gathering or collection.

mustn't (MUHSS-nt) *contraction.* A short form of the words *must not.*

mus·ty (MUHSS-tee) *adjective.* 1. Having the smell or taste of mold; moldy: The old trunk was full of *musty* clothes. 2. Out-of-date; stale: *musty* ideas. **mustier, mustiest.**

mu·tant (MYOO-tənt) *noun.* An animal or plant that is changed in some way as a result of mutation.

mu·ta·tion (myoo-TAY-shən) *noun.* 1. A change in the inheritable character of a given animal or plant that makes it different from its parent and that it passes on to offspring. 2. Any change, as of shape or kind.

mute (MYOOT) *adjective.* 1. Not speaking; silent: The prisoner was *mute* in front of his questioners. 2. Unable to speak: The *mute* boy learned sign language so he could communicate. *—noun.* 1. A person who is unable to talk. 2. A device used on a musical instrument to soften its tone. *—verb.* To soften (the sound or color of something). **muted, muting.** —**mutely** *adverb.*

mu·ti·neer (myoot-n-IHR) *noun.* A person who is guilty of mutiny.

mu·ti·nous (MYOOT-n-əss) *adjective.* 1. Tending toward or being in a state of mutiny: *mutinous* troops. 2. Rebellious: The *mutinous* boy refused to obey.

mu·ti·ny (MYOOT-n-ee) *noun.* Open resistance to lawful authority, especially by crewmen or soldiers against their commanding officers. **mutinies.** *—verb.* To take part in a rebellion or mutiny. **mutinied, mutinying.**

mutt (MUHT) *noun.* (Slang) A dog of crossed breeding; mongrel.

mut·ter (MUHT-ər) *verb.* 1. To speak unclearly in a low voice. 2. To grumble or complain. **muttered, muttering.** *—noun.* A low, unclear remark, usually a complaint.

mut·ton (MUHT-n) *noun.* The meat of a grown sheep.

mu·tu·al (MYOO-choo-əl) *adjective.* 1. Given each to the other and taken each from the other in equal amounts: John and Henry had a *mutual* friendship. 2. Common to two or more: It was in the *mutual* interest of the children, parents, and teachers that the school remain open. —**mutually** *adverb.*

muz·zle (MUHZ-l) *noun.* 1. The snout of an animal such as a dog or cow. 2. A cage-like covering for a dog's jaws. 3. The mouth or front end of a gun. **muzzles.** *—verb.* 1. To put a muzzle on. 2. To silence. **muzzled, muzzling.**

my (MIGH) *pronoun* (and *adjective*). Belonging to oneself: I painted *my* bike. *—interjection.* Expresses surprise; happiness; discouragement: "Lions and tigers and bears, oh *my!*" (L. Frank Baum).

myr·tle (MERT-l) *noun.* 1. An evergreen shrub of Mediterranean lands having a pleasing smell, glossy leaves, pink or white flowers, and blue-black berries. 2. A creeping evergreen vine of Canada and the United States, having blue flowers; periwinkle.

my·self (migh-SELF) *pronoun.* A form of *I* used: 1. For emphasis: I did it *myself.* 2. When the subject and object of a verb are the same: I cut *myself.* 3. To describe a normal or usual state: I wasn't *myself* all week; the cold made me cranky.

mys·te·ri·ous (miss-TIHR-ee-əss) *adjective.* Difficult to explain or understand: *Mysterious* noises can be heard coming from our attic. —**mysteriously** *adverb.*

mys·ter·y (MISS-tər-ee) *noun.* 1. Something that is unknown, unexplained, or secret: They never did solve the *mystery* of the judge's disappearance. 2. A novel about a puzzling crime. **mysteries.**

mys·ti·fy (MISS-tə-figh) *verb.* To puzzle or bewilder: Paul's behavior *mystifies* his parents. **mystified, mystifying.**

myth (MITH) *noun.* 1. An old legend which used gods and heroes to explain the origin and history of man and nature. 2. Any made-up story or person: It was a *myth* that Phil had ever been a trapeze artist.

myth·i·cal (MITH-i-kəl) *adjective.* 1. Existing only in myth: *mythical* giants. 2. Invented or imaginary: His royal birth is *mythical.* —**mythically** *adverb.*

my·thol·o·gy (mi-THOL-ə-jee) *noun.* The myths of a people or country: Greek *mythology.* **mythologies.**

musket

N, n (EN) *noun.* The 14th letter of the English alphabet.

N., n. *abbreviation.* 1. Noun. 2. North; northern. 3. Number.

[1]**nag** *verb.* 1. To annoy with constant scolding; find fault with time after time. 2. To bother continually; make uneasy: Jim was *nagged* by doubt. **nagged, nagging.** —*noun.* A person who nags or finds fault constantly.

[2]**nag** *noun.* A horse, especially one that is very slow or worn-out.

nai·ad (NAY-əd or NIGH-əd) *noun.* In ancient stories, one of many nymphs or female spirits who lived in brooks or streams. —**naiades** (NAY-ə-deez) or **naiads** *plural.*

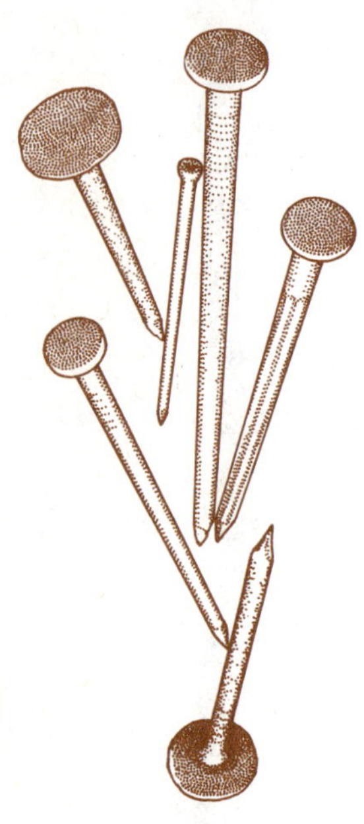

nails

nail (NAYL) *noun.* 1. A hard, slender piece of pointed metal, hammered into wood or other materials to fasten or hold together. 2. A fingernail or toenail. —*verb.* 1. To fasten or hold together with a nail or nails: The carpenter *nailed* the shelf to the wall. 2. (Slang) To catch, stop, or hit: The policeman *nailed* the driver for speeding. **nailed, nailing.** —**hit the nail on the head.** To figure out, say, or guess what is exactly correct.

na·ive (nah-EEV) Also **naïve** *adjective.* Simple or childlike in attitude; innocent: Only a *naive* person believes that all people are honest. —**naively** *adverb.*

na·ked (NAY-kid) *adjective.* 1. Having no clothes or other covering; bare. 2. Open; not hidden or avoided: the *naked* truth. —**nakedly** *adverb.* —**nakedness** *noun.*

name (NAYM) *noun.* 1. A word or words used to identify a person, place, or thing: My father's *name* is Edward. 2. A reputation; fame: Lying and cheating will give you a bad *name.* 3. (Informal) An important or well-known person: Many big *names* attended the senator's party. **names.** —*verb.* 1. To give a name to. 2. To mention the name of; identify: Can you *name* the countries of South America? 3. To select or appoint: The mayor *named* a new chief of police. **named, naming.** —*adjective.* (Informal) Well known for quality or popularity; famous: a *name* brand.

name·less (NAYM-liss) *adjective.* 1. Without a name. 2. Not known or identified: The money was given by a *nameless* donor. 3. Difficult to describe: A *nameless* feeling of dread filled the ship's crew. —**namelessly** *adverb.*

name·ly (NAYM-lee) *adverb.* That is to say; to be specific: Our team lacks just one thing, *namely,* talent.

name·sake (NAYM-sayk) *noun.* A person named after someone else.

[1]**nap** *noun.* A short sleep, especially during the day. —*verb.* To take a short sleep; doze: Barbara *napped* for an hour after school. **napped, napping.**

[2]**nap** *noun.* The short, soft threads or fibers on the surface of certain fabrics.

na·palm (NAY-pahm) *noun.* A jelly made of aluminum soap and gasoline used in bombs and flame throwers.

nape (NAYP) *noun.* The back of the neck. **napes.**

naph·tha (NAF-thə or NAP-thə) *noun.* A clear liquid made from petroleum and commonly used as a cleaning fluid or a fuel.

nap·kin (NAP-kin) *noun.* A piece of

cloth or paper used at meals to protect one's clothing or wipe one's fingers and mouth.

nar·cis·sus (nahr-SISS-əss) *noun.* A spring plant with long, slender leaves and yellow or white flowers. **narcissuses** or **narcissi** (nahr-SISS-igh or nahr-SISS-ee) *plural.*

nar·cot·ic (nahr-KOT-ik) *noun.* A drug that causes deep relaxation, sleepiness, or relief from pain, and that may become habit-forming.

nar·rate (NA-rayt) *verb.* 1. To tell a story. 2. To give an account of; describe. **narrated, narrating.** —**narrator** (NA-ray-tər) *noun.*

nar·ra·tive (NA-rə-tiv) *noun.* 1. A story. 2. The process of telling a story. **narratives.**

narrative poem. A poem that tells a story.

nar·row (NA-roh) *adjective.* 1. Not wide; slender: a *narrow* line. 2. Limited or restricted: a *narrow* attitude. 3. Close; without a wide difference or margin: The team won a *narrow* victory. **narrower, narrowest.** —*verb.* To become closer or more slender: The road *narrows* from four lanes to two. **narrowed, narrowing.** —**narrowly** *adverb.*

nar·row-mind·ed (NA-roh-MIGHN-did) *adjective.* Limited or restricted in attitude or outlook; not tolerant: *Narrow-minded* people think that ideas that differ from theirs are bad.

NASA (NASS-ə) *noun.* Acronym for National Aeronautics and Space Administration.

na·sal (NAYZ-l) *adjective.* 1. Of or related to the nose: *nasal* passages. 2. Related to or resembling sounds made through the nose: "M" is a *nasal* sound. —**nasally** *adverb.*

na·stur·tium (nə-STER-shəm) *noun.* A plant with handsome yellow or reddish flowers and a sharp scent.

nas·ty (NASS-tee) *adjective.* 1. Not decent or wholesome: *nasty* language. 2. Hard to get along with; very unfriendly. 3. Disgusting; filthy: The garbage dump had a *nasty* smell and appearance. 4. Very unpleasant, difficult to handle: A *nasty* wind turned over three sailboats. **nastier, nastiest.** —**nastily** *adverb.* —**nastiness** *noun.*

na·tion (NAY-shən) *noun.* 1. A group of people organized under the same government and usually living in the same area or country: Europe is made up of many different *nations.* 2. A tribe or group of people who have the same language and customs: The Mohawk Indians belong to the Iroquois *nation.*

na·tion·al (NASH-ən-l) *adjective.* Of or related to a nation: The deeds of the astronauts are a cause of *national* pride. —*noun.* A citizen of a nation: Three enemy *nationals* were arrested. —**nationally** *adverb.*

na·tion·al·ism (NASH-ən-l-iz-əm) *noun.* A spirit or movement that seeks to gain the greatest benefit or advantages for a particular nation or country.

na·tion·al·i·ty (nash-ə-NAL-ə-tee) *noun.* 1. The state of being part of a nation; citizenship: His *nationality* is French. 2. Existence as a separate nation or country. 3. A group of people organized under the same government and usually within the same country. **nationalities.**

na·tive (NAY-tiv) *adjective.* 1. Describing or denoting the place of one's birth: *native* land. 2. Natural; inborn: *native* ability in sports. 3. Coming from, grown, or made in a particular place: Kangaroos are *native* to Australia. 4. Of or related to the original inhabitants of a particular place: The explorers discovered a *native* village near the river. —*noun.* 1. A person born in a particular place: Jim is a *native* of Chicago. 2. One of the original inhabitants of a place: The *natives* were amazed at the sailing ships of the explorers. **natives.** —**natively** *adverb.*

na·tiv·i·ty (nə-TIV-ə-tee) *noun.* 1. Birth. 2. [Capital N] The birth of Christ; Christmas: The *Nativity* is celebrated on December 25.

nat·u·ral (NACH-er-əl) *adjective.* 1. Of or related to nature; not man-made: Sunsets and snowfalls are *natural* events. 2. Inborn, as part of a person's make-up: "The skilled poet is one who knows much by *natural* gift." (Pindar). 3. Logical; sensible: It was *natural* to expect the truck to stop when the gas ran out. 4. Free from falsity or pretension: The actor's performance was very *natural.* 5. (Music) Not changed by a sharp or flat.

nat·u·ral·ist (NACH-ər-ə-list) *noun.* A person who studies plants and animals.

nat·u·ral·ize (NACH-ər-ə-lighz) *verb.* 1. To grant citizenship to (a person of another nationality). 2. To adjust or make suitable to new conditions or surroundings: The horse was *naturalized* in America several centuries ago. **naturalized, naturalizing. —naturalization** (nach-ər-l-ə-ZAY-shən) *noun.*

nat·u·ral·ly (NACH-ər-ə-lee or NACH-rə-lee) *adverb.* 1. In a natural way: Pose for the picture *naturally.* 2. By or through an inborn talent; by or through nature: Tim is a *naturally* good athlete. 3. Of course; surely.

natural resources. Lumber, water, minerals, and other materials found in nature that are used by man.

na·ture (NAY-chər) *noun.* 1. The world, including all things not made by man. 2. The manner in which a person or thing ordinarily behaves, acts, or is: It is part of human *nature* to want to be liked by others. 3. Type; sort: What is the *nature* of their argument? 4. An area or condition free from man-made things or processes: We enjoyed getting out of the city and into closeness with *nature.*

naught (NAWT) Also **nought** *noun.* 1. Zero; 0. 2. Nothing: My efforts to find the keys came to *naught.*

naugh·ty (NAW-tee) *adjective.* 1. Misbehaving; full of mischief. 2. Not decent or wholesome. **naughtier, naughtiest. —naughtily** *adverb.*

nau·se·a (NAW-zee-ə) *noun.* 1. An uneasy feeling in the stomach, especially the feeling that one is going to vomit. 2. Deep disgust. **—nauseous** *adjective.*

nau·ti·cal (NAW-ti-kəl) *adjective.* Of or related to ships, sailors, or navigation: *nautical* charts. **—nautically** *adverb.*

nautical mile. A unit of length, used to measure air and sea distances, equal to about 6,076 feet.

na·val (NAY-vəl) *adjective.* Of or related to a navy, warships, or sailors.

na·vel (NAY-vəl) *noun.* The small scar in the center of a person's abdomen resulting from removal of the umbilical cord.

nav·i·ga·ble (NAV-ə-gə-bəl) *adjective.* 1. Having enough depth and width to allow the passage of ships or other vessels: The river is *navigable* as far as the waterfalls. 2. Able to be steered or navigated.

nav·i·gate (NAV-ə-gayt) *verb.* 1. To plan the position and course of a craft, especially a ship or airplane. 2. To sail or travel on, over, or across. **navigated, navigating.**

nav·i·ga·tion (nav-ə-GAY-shən) *noun.* 1. The process of navigating. 2. The process or science of planning the direction and location of a ship, airplane, or spacecraft.

nav·i·ga·tor (NAV-ə-gay-tər) *noun.* A person who navigates, especially one whose special job it is to plan the course that a ship, airplane, or spacecraft will take.

na·vy (NAY-vee) *noun.* 1. [Often capital N] All of a country's sailors, ships, and other equipment maintained for waging war at sea. 2. A fleet of ships, especially warships. 3. (Also *adjective*) A dark-blue color. **navies.**

navy beans. A variety of kidney beans rich in food value.

nay *adverb.* 1. (Rare) No: *Nay,* I will not go. 2. Not only that, but in addition: The queen was annoyed, *nay,* furious over the insult. —*noun.* A vote against, especially by voice.

neap tide (NEEP TIGHD). The tide in which there is the smallest difference between high and low tides.

near (NIHR) *adverb.* To or at a short distance or period of time: The pony raised his head when the child drew *near.* —*preposition.* Close to in distance, time, or degree: The football is *near* the goal line. —*adjective.* 1. Close to in distance, time, or degree. 2. Close to in friendship or relationship: Charles is a *near* friend of the family. **nearer, nearest.** —*verb.* To move close to; approach: The train *neared* the station. **neared, nearing.** —**nearness** *noun.*

near·by (NIHR-BIGH) *adjective* and *adverb.* Near; close at hand.

near·ly (NIHR-lee) *adverb.* Almost: The swimmer *nearly* drowned.

near·sight·ed (NIHR-sigh-tid) *adjective.* Not able to see distant objects clearly. —**nearsightedly** *adverb.*

neat (NEET) *adjective.* 1. Clean and well-kept: My sister's room is very *neat.* 2. Tending to keep oneself or one's possessions in a clean and orderly condition. 3. (Slang) Attractive: Bob bought a *neat* pair of skates. 4. Skillfully or cleverly done: The skier made several *neat* turns during the race. **neater, neatest.** —**neatness** *noun.* —**neatly** *adverb.*

Ne·bras·ka (nə-BRASS-kə) *noun.* A state in north central United States, 37th to join the Union (1867). —**Nebr.** *abbreviation.* Also **NB** for Zip Codes.

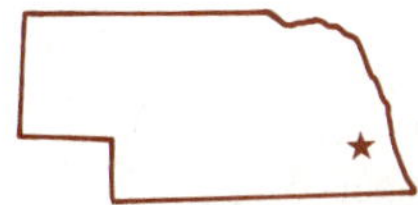

Nebraska
★capital: Lincoln

neb·u·la (NEB-yə-lə) *noun.* Hazy bright or dark patches, seen among the stars, that include dust clouds, glowing gases, star clusters, and distant galaxies. —**nebulae** (NEB-yə-lee) or **nebulas** *plural.*

nebula

nec·es·sar·y (NESS-ə-sehr-ee) *adjective.* 1. Needed; required. 2. Coming or following (as a result): Imprisonment is a *necessary* end of a life of crime. —**necessarily** *adverb.*

ne·ces·si·tate (nə-SESS-ə-tayt) *verb.* To make necessary. **necessitated, necessitating.**

ne·ces·si·ty (nə-SESS-ə-tee) *noun.* 1. The state of needing or being necessary: The *necessity* for sleep made us go to bed early. 2. Something that is necessary: Food and air are *necessities* of human life. **necessities.**

neck (NEK) *noun.* 1. The part of the body between the head and the shoulders or upper chest. 2. The part of a piece of clothing that fits around a person's neck. 3. A narrow section, as of land reaching out into a body of water. —*verb.* (Slang) To kiss and caress. **necked, necking.**

neck·er·chief (NEK-ər-chif) *noun.* A small scarf worn around one's neck.

neck·lace (NEK-liss) *noun.* An ornament, such as a string of pearls or a gold chain, worn around the neck. **necklaces.**

necklace

neck·tie (NEK-tigh) *noun.* A long, tapered piece of cloth worn under the collar of a man's shirt and tied in front. **neckties.**

nec·tar (NEK-tər) *noun.* 1. A sweet liquid produced by many flowers. 2. The unmixed juice of a fruit. 3. In ancient legends, a liquid drunk by the gods. 4. Any delicious liquid.

need *verb.* To want; lack; require: I *need* money for lunch. **needed, needing.** —*noun.* 1. Necessity: The sick man has a *need* for medical help. 2. Poverty, or lack of what is necessary: in his time of *need.* 3. (Plural) Things required for ordinary living: Our *needs* are very few. —**if need be.** If necessary.

need·ful (NEED-fəl) *adjective.* Necessary; needed.

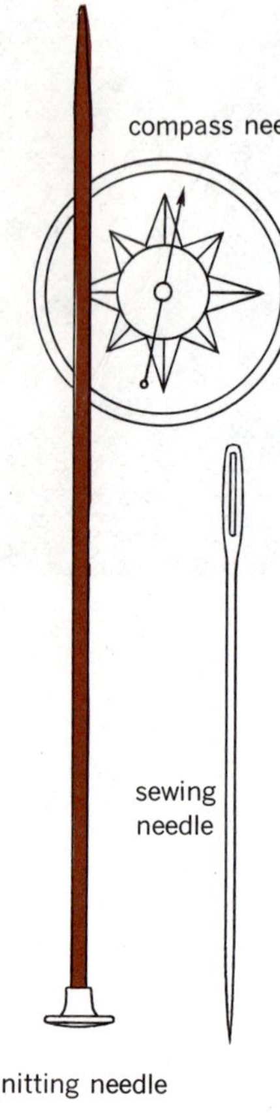

nee·dle (NEED-l) *noun.* 1. A thin steel instrument with a hole at one end and a point at the other, used for sewing. 2. A long, slender plastic or metal instrument used in knitting and crocheting. 3. A slender, hollow, sharp metal instrument with a hole near the end, used for giving injections to people or animals. 4. A narrow metal pointer on a compass, gauge, or dial. 5. A short, slender length of metal or other material that touches the grooves of a record when it is played. 6. A stiff, thin leaf, as on a pine or other evergreen tree. **needles.** —*verb.* 1. (Informal) To tease. 2. (Informal) To urge by teasing: The boys *needled* Jim into climbing the tree. **needled, needling.**

need·less (NEED-liss) *adjective.* Not necessary. —**needlessly** *adverb.*

nee·dle·work (NEED-l-werk) *noun.* Sewing, embroidery, or other work done with a needle.

needn't (NEED-nt) *contraction.* A shortened form of *need not.*

need·y (NEE-dee) *adjective.* In need of something; poor. **needier, neediest.**

ne'er (NAIR) *contraction.* A shortened form of the word *never.*

neg·a·tive (NEG-ə-tiv) *adjective.* 1. Expressing or saying *no:* When we asked to stay up late, Dad gave us a *negative* reply. 2. Not positive or encouraging: a *negative* view of life. 3. (Math) Related to a number less than zero: -3 and $-2/5$ are *negative* numbers. —*noun.* An exposed section of film on which dark areas of a picture show up light, and light areas dark. **negatives.** —**negatively** *adverb.*

neg·lect (ni-GLEKT) *verb.* 1. To give little or no attention to: ignore. 2. To fail to do; forget. **neglected, neglecting.** —*noun.* 1. The act of neglecting: *neglect* of duty. 2. A lack of care or attention. —**neglectful** *adjective.*

neg·li·gent (NEG-li-jənt) *adjective.* 1. Showing neglect; giving little or no attention to. 2. Careless.

ne·go·ti·ate (ni-GOH-shee-ayt) *verb.* 1. To try to reach an agreement; discuss: The workers *negotiated* for higher wages. 2. To reach an agreement; arrange: *negotiate* a new contract. 3. To move around, over, or through successfully: The skier *negotiated* a dangerous turn. **negotiated, negotiating.**

Ne·gro (NEE-groh) *noun.* One who belongs to any of the black races originally of Africa. **Negroes.**

neigh (NAY) *verb.* To make the long sound of a horse; to whinny. **neighed, neighing.** —*noun.* The sound of a horse; whinny.

neigh·bor (NAY-bər) *noun.* 1. A person who lives next door or nearby. 2. Someone or something that is located nearby: Washington and its *neighbor,* Oregon, are two states I have never visited. 3. One's fellow man.

neigh·bor·hood (NAY-bər-hud) *noun.* 1. The area in a community that has certain characteristics: Jim lives in a wealthy *neighborhood.* 2. A particular area or section, especially that in which one's home is located: We drove through several strange *neighborhoods* when we were lost. 3. The people of a particular area: Our *neighborhood* is made up of people of many nationalities. —**in the neighborhood of.** Nearly or almost.

neigh·bor·ly (NAY-bər-lee) *adjective.* Friendly and helpful, like the actions of a good neighbor.

nei·ther (NEE-thər or NIGH-thər) *adjective.* Not either: *Neither* shoe is wet. —*pronoun.* Not either one: *Neither* of the twins likes tennis. —*conjunction.* Nor: Dad does not smoke; *neither* does Mother.

neo- Also **Neo-** *prefix.* Indicates new or recent: *neo*logism.

ne·ol·o·gism (nee-OL-ə-jiz-əm) *noun.* A new word or a new meaning for an old word.

ne·on (NEE-on) *noun.* A gas that glows when electricity goes through it.

neph·ew (NEF-yoo) *noun.* The son of a person's brother or sister.

Nep·tune (NEP-toon or NEP-tyoon) *noun.* The planet eighth in distance from the sun.

nerve (NERV) *noun.* 1. A fiber or group of fibers that carries impulses between the brain and spinal cord and other parts of the body. 2. Courage; steadiness of will. 3. (Informal) Boldness; rudeness.

nerv·ous (NER-vəss) *adjective.* 1. Of or related to nerves: *nervous* system. 2. Restless; jittery: Lack of sleep made me *nervous* and cranky. 3. Fearful; tense: The soldier was *nervous* about the next battle. —**nervously** *adverb.*

nervous system. The system in man and animals that includes the nerves, brain, and spinal cord and that carries impulses or feelings and regulates body activities.

-ness *suffix.* Indicates a manner or state of being: happi*ness.*

nest *noun.* 1. A place or structure in which birds, insects, or other animals lay their eggs or raise their young. 2. A cozy, peaceful place. 3. A set of things that fit neatly one inside the other: a *nest* of mixing bowls. —*verb.* To build and live in a nest. **nested, nesting.**

nes·tle (NESS-l) *verb.* 1. To settle comfortably: "The children were *nestled* all snug in their beds. . . ." (C. C. Moore). 2. To be in a sheltered or protected location: The cabin *nestled* among rolling, green hills. 3. To hold close with pleasant feelings: Mary *nestled* the doll in her arms. **nestled, nestling.**

nest·ling (NEST-ling) *noun.* A bird that is too young to fly from its nest.

[1] **net** *noun.* 1. A fabric or cloth that is loosely woven and has large spaces between the threads or cords. 2. A device made of net fabric, used to trap fish, insects, or other animals. 3. A fine cloth of open weave. —*verb.* To catch in a net. **netted, netting.**

nets

[2] **net** *adjective.* Remaining after expenses, weights, or other factors have been subtracted: After subtracting expenses from the 100 dollars he had collected, the salesman made a *net* profit of 15 dollars. —*verb.* To earn or have left after expenses are subtracted: The salesman *netted* 15 dollars for his day's work. **netted, netting.**

net·tle (NET-l) *noun.* A plant with sharp growths that sting the skin when touched. **nettles.** —*verb.* To irritate; make angry. **nettled, nettling.**

net·work (NET-wərk) *noun.* 1. Any system of crossed or blended parts; a complex: a *network* of roads. 2. A group of radio or TV stations under a single control or cooperating with one another. 3. A net or fabric of open weave.

neu·ron (NOOR-on or NYOOR-on) *noun.* One of the many cells that make up the nerve tissue of the body.

neu·ter (NOO-tər or NYOO-tər) *adjective.* (Grammar) Related to a group of words that refer to things that are neither male nor female: "Workman" is a masculine noun, "waitress" is feminine, and "tree" is *neuter.*

nest

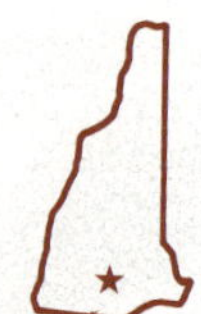
New Hampshire
★capital: Concord

New Jersey
★capital: Trenton

Nevada
★capital: Carson City

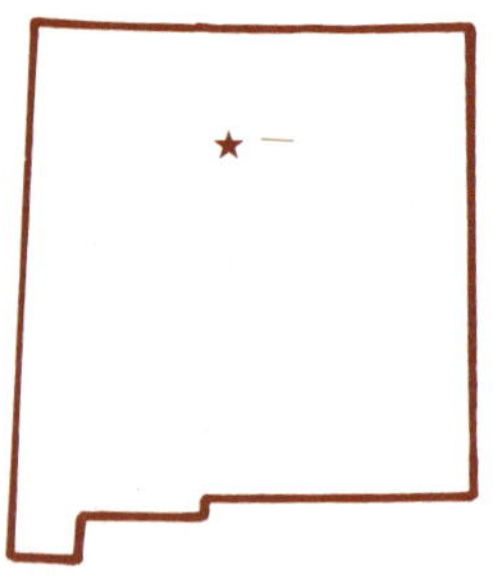
New Mexico
★capital: Sante Fe

neu·tral (NOO-trəl or NYOO-trəl) *adjective.* 1. Not favoring either side in an argument or war. 2. Having no definite qualities; indifferent: The quiet boy has a *neutral* personality. 3. Having little distinct color: It is best to wear a *neutral* blouse with a bright plaid skirt. —**neutrally** *adverb.*

neu·tral·ize (NOO-trə-lighz or NYOO-trə-lighz) *verb.* 1. To make ineffective: In the lengthy cross-country race, Jack's speed was *neutralized* by Bob's ability to run long distances. 2. To make chemically inactive: An acid will *neutralize* a base. **neutralized, neutralizing.**

neu·tron (NOO-tron or NYOO-tron) *noun.* An uncharged elementary particle, closely similar to the proton, found in all atomic nuclei except that of hydrogen.

Ne·vad·a (nə-VAD-ə or nə-VAH-da) *noun.* A state in western United States, 36th to join the Union (1864). —**Nev.** *abbreviation.* Also **NV** for Zip Codes.

nev·er (NEV-ər) *adverb.* 1. Not ever: George *never* told a lie. 2. Not at all; in no manner: That plan will *never* work.

nev·er·the·less (nev-ər-t͟hə-LESS) *adverb.* Yet; in spite of that: I love to eat; *nevertheless,* I must diet.

new (NOO or NYOO) *adjective.* 1. Made, used, thought of, or shown for the first time; different: The scientist invented a *new* type of engine. 2. Modern; recent: Mother likes the *new* methods of education followed at our school. 3. Not familiar with: Bob is *new* to the position of halfback. **newer, newest.** —*adverb.* Recently; freshly.

new·born (NOO-born or NYOO-born) *adjective.* Recently born.

new·com·er (NOO-kuhm-ər or NYOO-kuhm-ər) *noun.* One who has arrived recently: The principal welcomed the *newcomers* at a school assembly.

New England (NOO or NYOO ING-lənd) *noun.* The northeastern states of Connecticut, Massachusetts, Maine, New Hampshire, Rhode Island, and Vermont.

new·fan·gled (NOO-FANG-gəld or NYOO-FANG-gəld) *adjective.* Of a new type; novel: *newfangled* idea.

New Hamp·shire (NOO or NYOO HAMP-shər) *noun.* A New England state of the United States, ninth to ratify the Constitution (1788). —**N.H.** *abbreviation.* Also **NH** for Zip Codes.

New Jer·sey (NOO or NYOO JER-zee) *noun.* A state in middle Atlantic United States, third to ratify the Constitution (1787). —**N.J.** *abbreviation.* Also **NJ** for Zip Codes.

new·ly (NOO-lee or NYOO-lee) *adverb.* Recently; lately: The *newly* painted walls looked bright and cheerful.

New Mex·i·co (NOO or NYOO MEK-si-koh) *noun.* A state in western United States, 47th to join the Union (1912). —**N.Mex.** *abbreviation.* Also **NM** for Zip Codes.

new moon. 1. The time during which the moon travels between the earth and the sun and either can't be seen or can be seen only as a thin crescent just after sunset. 2. The thin crescent moon at the time of the new moon.

news (NOOZ or NYOOZ) *noun, plural in form but used with a singular verb.* 1. Information about recent events: The *news* about the war shocked the citizens. 2. New information: His marriage was *news* to me.

news·boy (NOOZ-boi or NYOOZ-boi) *noun.* A boy who delivers or sells newspapers.

news·cast (NOOZ-kast or NYOOZ-kast) *noun.* A program on radio or television that presents news.

news·man (NOOZ-man or NYOOZ-man) *noun.* A man who records or reports news for a newspaper or a radio or television program. —**newsmen** *plural.*

news•pa•per (NOOZ-pay-pər or NYOOZ-pay-pər) *noun.* A publication, usually sold daily or weekly, that contains news and other features.

news•reel (NOOZ-reel or NYOOZ-reel) *noun.* A short motion picture that presents current events.

news•stand (NOOZ-stand or NYOOZ-stand) *noun.* A booth at which newspapers, magazines, and other items are sold.

newt (NOOT or NYOOT) *noun.* Any of a variety of salamanders, or small, lizard-like animals, that live on land or in the water.

New Year's Day. A legal U.S. holiday celebrating the start of a new year on January 1.

New York (NOO or NYOO YORK) *noun.* A state in middle Atlantic United States, 11th to ratify the Constitution (1788). **—N.Y.** *abbreviation.* Also **NY** for Zip Codes.

next (NEKST) *adjective.* 1. Nearest: The *next* store is a mile away. 2. Following just after: The *next* bus will be here in five minutes. *—adverb.* 1. In the following time, place, or position: Bob arrived first, and Jim arrived *next.* 2. At the first time after this: When you *next* see Barbara, give her my greetings. **—next to.** Alongside of; beside.

n.g. *abbreviation.* No good.

nib•ble (NIB-əl) *verb.* 1. To eat or chew with quick, small bites. 2. To eat small amounts slowly: We *nibbled* at popcorn during the movie. **nibbled, nibbling.** *—noun.* A small bite or rapid series of small bites. **nibbles.**

nice (NIGHSS) *adjective.* 1. Pleasant. 2. Proper; respectable: Marie has *nice* table manners. 3. With a pleasing personality. **nicer, nicest. —nicely** *adverb.*

niche (NICH) *noun.* 1. A recess or open compartment in a wall, as for a statue or ornament. 2. A suitable position: Uncle Tom has found his *niche* as a salesman. **niches.**

nick (NIK) *noun.* A small cut or chip in an object. *—verb.* To make a small cut or chip: I *nicked* the table. **nicked, nicking.**

nick•el (NIK-əl) *noun.* 1. A coin equal to five cents. 2. A kind of hard metal that looks like silver and is often mixed with other metals to make alloys.

nick•name (NIK-naym) *noun.* 1. A name, often describing a characteristic, used in place of a person's real name: The thin boy's *nickname* was "Slim." 2. A shortened form of a first name: "Tim" is a *nickname* for "Timothy." **nicknames.**

nic•o•tine (NIK-ə-teen) *noun.* A poisonous substance contained in tobacco.

niece (NEESS) *noun.* The daughter of a person's brother or sister. **nieces.**

nif•ty (NIF-tee) *adjective.* (Slang) Stylish; attractive: a *nifty* new sportscar. **niftier, niftiest.**

nig•gard•ly (NIG-ərd-lee) *adjective* and *adverb.* 1. Stingy; not generous. 2. Inadequate; cheap.

night *noun.* The time of darkness between sunset and sunrise.

night•club (NIGHT-kluhb) *noun.* A place where adults find entertainment by dancing and watching performers.

night•fall (NIGHT-fawl) *noun.* The coming of darkness at end of day.

night•gown (NIGHT-gown) *noun.* A dress-like garment worn to bed.

night•in•gale (NIGHT-n-gayl) *noun.* A brown bird, found in Europe, that sings a beautiful song at night. **nightingales.**

night•ly (NIGHT-lee) *adjective* and *adverb.* 1. Occurring at night. 2. Occurring every night.

night•mare (NIGHT-mair) *noun.* 1. A horrible or frightening dream. 2. Something that is like a bad dream: Amelia thought the test was a *nightmare.* **nightmares. —nightmarish** *adjective.*

new moon

New York
★capital: Albany

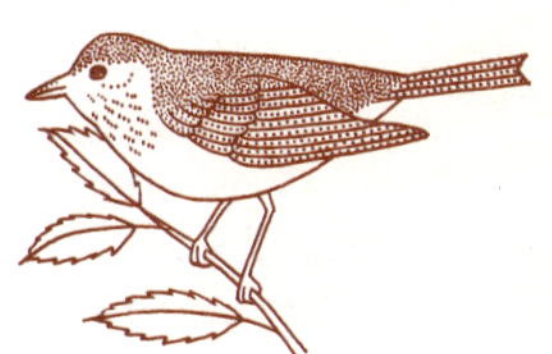

nightingale

nimbostratus

night·shade (NIGHT-shayd) *noun.* Any of several flowering plants that grow in tropical or temperate areas.

nim·ble (NIM-bəl) *adjective.* 1. Light and fast: "Jack be *nimble,* Jack be quick. . . ." (Nursery rhyme). 2. Clever, quick to learn. **nimbler, nimblest. —nimbly** *adverb.*

nim·bo·stra·tus (nim-boh-STRAY-təss or nim-boh-STRAT-əss) *noun.* A low gray or dark gray cloud from which rain, snow, or sleet falls.

nine (NIGHN) *noun* (and *adjective*). The cardinal number after eight and before ten; 9. **nines.**

nine·teen (NIGHN-TEEN) *noun* (and *adjective*). The cardinal number after 18 and before 20; 19.

nine·teenth (NIGHN-TEENTH) *adjective.* Coming next after 18th; 19th. *—noun.* One of 19 equal parts.

nine·ti·eth (NIGHN-tee-ith) *adjective.* Coming next after 89th; 90th. *—noun.* One of 90 equal parts.

nine·ty (NIGHN-tee) *noun* (and *adjective*). The cardinal number after 89 and before 91; 90. **nineties.**

ninth (NYNTH) *adjective.* Coming next after 8th; 9th. *—noun.* One of nine equal parts.

nip *verb.* 1. To pinch; to squeeze; to bite. 2. To cut or clip. 3. To cause a smarting or stinging feeling. 4. To take a small bit of an alcoholic drink. **nipped, nipping.** *—noun.* A squeeze; pinch; bite. 2. A tiny amount. 3. A smarting or stinging feeling: a *nip* in the air. 4. A short alcoholic drink. **—nip in the bud.** To stop the development (of) at the start: *nip* my protest *in the bud.* **—nip and tuck.** So close that the result (of a contest) is in doubt.

nip·ple (NIP-əl) *noun.* 1. The small, cone-shaped tip of the breast on mammals from which young can get milk. 2. The top of a baby bottle. 3. Anything that looks like or acts like a nipple. **nipples.**

ni·trate (NIGH-trayt) *noun.* One of various chemical compounds containing nitrogen and oxygen: *Nitrates* are used in fertilizers and explosives. **nitrates.**

ni·tro·gen (NIGH-trə-jən) *noun.* A colorless, odorless element that makes up about four-fifths of the air we breathe.

nit·ty-grit·ty (NIT-ee-GRIT-ee) *noun.* (Slang) The heart of a matter.

no (NOH) *adverb.* 1. The opposite of *yes.* 2. Not in any way or amount: Our house is *no* bigger than yours. *—noun.* A negative answer: Sue can never say *no.* *—adjective.* 1. None: We have *no* bananas. 2. Not in any way: I'm *no* artist.

no. *abbreviation.* 1. North; northern. 2. Number.

no·bil·i·ty (noh-BIL-ə-tee) *noun.* 1. Nobles as a class. 2. The noble rank. 3. Generosity; greatness of character. **nobilities.**

no·ble (NOH-bəl) *adjective.* 1. Born to high rank. 2. Of a generous or kind nature. 3. Splendid; impressive. **nobler, noblest.** *—noun.* One born to high rank. **nobles. —nobly** *adverb.*

no·ble·man (NOH-bəl-mən) *noun, masculine.* Also **noblewoman** (NOH-bəl-wum-ən) *noun, feminine.* A person born to high rank. **—noblemen** or **noblewomen** *plural.*

no·bod·y (NOH-bod-ee) *pronoun.* No one. *—noun.* A person without power or importance. **nobodies.**

noc·tur·nal (nok-TERN-l) *adjective.* 1. Referring to or happening at night. 2. Awake or active at night: The owl is a *nocturnal* animal. **—nocturnally** *adverb.*

nod *noun.* A bow of the head. *—verb.* 1. To move the head up and down: Frank *nodded* as he dozed in the chair. 2. To gesture with a motion of the head: Janice *nodded* hello as she rushed by. 3. To move in a swaying motion: The daisies *nodded* in the breeze. **nodded, nodding.**

nod·ule (NOJ-ool) *noun.* A rounded bump, lump, or knot. **nodules.**

nog·gin (NOG-in) *noun.* (Slang) The head.

noise (NOIZ) *noun.* 1. A sound or sounds, particularly when loud or annoying. 2. Cries, hubbub. **noises.** —*verb.* To spread news or rumor. **noised, noising.** —**noisy** *adjective.* —**noisily** *adverb.*

no·mad (NOH-mad) *noun.* A wanderer who has no settled home and travels in search of food and water, usually as part of a tribe. —**nomadic** *adjective.*

nom·i·nate (NOM-ə-nayt) *verb.* 1. To suggest formally (for a position): Pamela *nominated* Harry for class president. 2. To appoint (to or as): Winnie's father *nominated* my dad as his assistant on the project. **nominated, nominating.** —**nomination** (nom-ə-NAY-shən) *noun.*

nom·i·nee (nom-ə-NEE) *noun.* A person who is nominated. **nominees.**

non- *prefix.* Indicates not: *non*fiction.

non·cha·lant (non-shə-LAHNT) *adjective.* Showing lack of concern. —**nonchalance** (non-shə-LAHNSS) *noun.* —**nonchalantly** *adverb.*

non·con·duc·tor (non-kən-DUHK-tər) *noun.* A material that does not transmit heat or electricity.

non·con·form·ist (non-kən-FOR-mist) *noun.* A person who does not act and think like the majority of people.

non·de·script (non-di-SKRIPT) *adjective.* Having no remarkable or unusual quality; hard to describe: Sally's dress was *nondescript.*

none (NUHN) *pronoun.* No one; not any. —*adverb.* By no means; not at all: Help arrived *none* too soon.

non·fic·tion (non-FIK-shən) *noun.* Writing that presents or discusses facts; writing that is not fiction.

non·par·ti·san (non-PAHR-təz-n) *adjective.* Referring to a person or group that does not take sides in politics, games, or disputes.

non·por·ous (non-POR-əss) *adjective.* Without openings that allow the passage of gas or liquids.

non·sense (NON-senss or NON-sənss) *noun.* 1. That which has no sense or meaning. 2. Silliness. —*interjection.* Expresses: 1. Disbelief: *Nonsense!* It won't rain today. 2. Mild anger.

non·stop (NON-STOP) *adjective* and *adverb.* Not making any stops.

non·vi·o·lence (non-VIGH-ə-lənss) *noun.* A program based on the belief that goals can be reached without using force or violence. —**nonviolent** *adjective.*

noo·dle (NOOD-l) *noun.* 1. A long thin piece of dough that is first dried and then boiled for eating. 2. (Slang) A person's head. **noodles.**

nook (NUK) *noun.* 1. A small, quiet place. 2. A corner: A breakfast *nook.*

noon *noun.* The 12th hour of the day; midday.

noose (NOOSS) *noun.* A loop in the end of a rope that gets smaller when pulled. **nooses.**

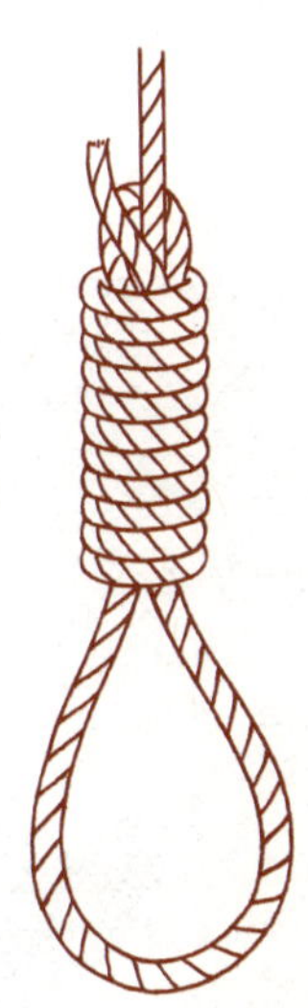
noose

nope (NOHP) *adverb.* (Slang) The opposite of *yes;* no.

nor *conjunction.* 1. (Used with neither) And not, also not: Neither Sally *nor* Suzy will go. 2. And not: Sally will not go; *nor* will Suzy.

nor'eas·ter (nor-EESS-tər) *noun.* A storm in which the wind blows from a northeast direction.

nor·mal (NOR-məl) *adjective.* 1. Usual, characteristic: Lenny was in his *normal* mood. 2. (Math) Forming a right angle. —*noun.* 1. That which is usual or average. 2. (Math) That which forms a right angle. —**normally** *adverb.*

north *noun.* 1. The opposite of south; the direction to the left when facing east. 2. [Often capital N] The arctic regions. 3. The northern section of an area or country. 4. (United States) [Capital N] The states above the Ohio River, Maryland, and Missouri.

North America. The continent in the Western Hemisphere extending north from Panama to the Arctic.

North Carolina
★capital: Raleigh

North Car·o·li·na (NORTH ka-rə-LIGH-nə) *noun.* A state in south Atlantic United States, 12th to ratify the Constitution (1789). —**N.C.** *abbreviation.* Also **NC** for Zip Codes.

North Dakota
★capital: Bismarck

North Da·ko·ta (NORTH də-KOH-tə) *noun.* A state in north central United States, 39th or 40th (with South Dakota) to join the Union (1889). —**N.Dak.** *abbreviation.* Also **ND** for Zip Codes.

north·east (north-EEST) *noun.* 1. The direction that is midway between north and east. 2. The northeast section of a region or country. —**northeastern** (north-EESS-tərn) *adjective. See* illustration at **compass.**

north·er·ly (NOR-thər-lee) *adjective.* Going to or from the north.

north·ern (NOR-thərn) *adjective.* Referring to the north.

northern lights. *See* **aurora borealis.**

northern lights

North Star. The star around which, in the Northern Hemisphere, all other stars seem to rotate.

north·west (north-WEST) *noun.* 1. The direction that is midway between north and west. 2. The northwest section of a region or country. —**northwestern** (north-WESS-tern) *adjective. See* illustration at **compass.**

nose (NOHZ) *noun.* 1. The part of the body near the middle of the face through which one smells and breathes air in and out. 2. A talent or ability to find, as though by smelling: Ray has a *nose* for trouble; he knows just when to run. 3. That which looks like a nose; the front part: the *nose* of a rocket. 4. The sense of smell: Grandma said, "I don't smell anything, but my *nose* isn't as good as it was." **noses.** —*verb.* 1. To pry or snoop for information. 2. To move (something) forward cautiously: The captain *nosed* the ship to the dock. 3. To sniff or touch with the nose: Prince *nosed* the piece of meat before he ate it. **nosed, nosing.** —**look down one's nose at.** To treat or look upon as inferior. —**turn one's nose up at.** To reject or refuse.

nose·bleed (NOHZ-bleed) *noun.* A flowing of blood from the nose.

nose cone. The front, cone-shaped part of a rocket or a missile.

nose dive. A sudden downward thrust or plunge, particularly of an aircraft.

nos·tril (NOSS-trəl) *noun.* One of the two openings of the nose.

nosy (NOH-zee) *adjective.* Prying into the affairs of others; snoopy.

not *adverb.* In no manner; in no amount: It will *not* rain today.

no·ta·ble (NOH-tə-bəl) *adjective.* Of importance or interest: The signing of the Declaration of Independence was a *notable* event in American history. —*noun.* A person of importance or interest. **notables.** —**notably** *adverb.*

no·ta·ry (NOH-tə-ree) *noun.* A notary public. **notaries.**

notary public. A person whose job is to witness the signing of papers, the taking of oaths, and other legal matters. —**notaries public** *plural.*

no·ta·tion (no-TAY-shən) *noun.* A brief note made as a reminder.

notch (NOCH) *noun.* 1. A V-shaped cut. 2. A narrow pass between mountains. **notches.** —*verb.* To make a V-shaped cut in. **notched, notching.**

note (NOHT) *noun.* 1. A short letter or message. 2. A brief jotting or word to serve as a reminder: Mother has a *note* of everyone's birthday on the calendar. 3. A brief explanation or additional information about something in the text of a book: Read the *note* at the bottom of the page. 4. (Music) a. A musical sound or tone. b. A written sign that shows the pitch and length of a tone. 5. Good reputation; distinction: Shirley's mother is a person of *note* in the community. 6. A signed agreement to pay back borrowed money. **notes.** —*verb.* 1. To write down as a reminder. 2. To observe, pay attention to, or notice: Mac's mother *noted* that his friend had good manners. **noted, noting.**

note·book (NOHT-buk) *noun.* A book in which notes are kept.

not·ed (NOHT-id) *adjective.* Well-known or famous: a *noted* celebrity. —**notedly** *adverb.*

note·wor·thy (NOHT-wer-thee) *adjective.* Worth being noticed; remarkable.

noth·ing (NUHTH-ing) *noun.* 1. Not a thing: There was *nothing* in Bill's bag. 2. Zero. 3. A matter of no importance or interest: There is *nothing* playing at the movies.

no·tice (NOH-tiss) *noun.* 1. Heed; attention: Ann took *notice* of the fine clothes in the shop window. 2. A written or printed announcement: a *notice* on the bulletin board. 3. A written or spoken statement that one plans to leave one's job or leased dwelling. 4. A review: The school play received a good *notice.* **notices.** —*verb.* To see or pay attention to. **noticed, noticing.** —**serve notice.** To give a warning.

no·tice·a·ble (NOH-tiss-ə-bəl) *adjective.* Easily apparent to the senses: There is a *noticeable* smell at the dump. —**noticeably** *adverb.*

no·ti·fy (NOH-tə-figh) *verb.* To let know or inform. **notified, notifying.**

no·tion (NOH-shən) *noun.* 1. A general idea: Martin had a *notion* about how the watch worked. 2. A view or theory: Burt had a *notion* that if he dug deep enough he would reach China. 3. A whim. 4. (Plural) Small items such as pins, thread, and ribbons.

no·to·ri·ous (noh-TOR-ee-əss) *adjective.* Well known for something bad: a *notorious* jewel thief. —**notoriously** *adverb.*

not·with·stand·ing (not-with-STAN-ding or not-with-STAN-ding) *preposition.* In spite of: Tess finished the book *notwithstanding* its length. —*adverb.* Nevertheless: It was cold, but Arthur decided to go swimming, *notwithstanding.*

nou·gat (NOO-gət) *noun.* A sweet made of sugar syrup and chopped nuts.

nought (NAWT) Also **naught** *noun.* Nothing; naught; zero, 0.

noun (NOWN) *noun.* A word used to name a person, place, thing, quality, or action: Words such as "Virginia," "city," "book," and "sweetness" are *nouns.*

nour·ish (NER-ish) *verb.* 1. To give (a living thing) the food it needs to stay alive and grow: Arabelle *nourishes* her African violet with plant food. 2. To support or foster. **nourished, nourishing.**

nour·ish·ment (NER-ish-mənt) *noun.* Food.

no·va (NOH-və) *noun.* A star that suddenly increases many times in brightness and then, over a period of weeks, months, or years, returns to its original appearance. —**novae** (NOH-vee) or **novas** *plural.*

nov·el (NOV-əl) *noun.* A book-length fictional story. —*adjective.* New or unusual.

nov·el·ty (NOV-əl-tee) *noun.* 1. Newness: the *novelty* of moon landings. 2. Anything new, unusual, or strange: Travel was a *novelty* to me. 3. (Plural) Small, inexpensive toys, games, or trinkets. **novelties.**

No·vem·ber (noh-VEM-bər) *noun.* The 11th month of the year: There are 30 days in *November.* —**Nov.** *abbreviation.*

nov·ice (NOV-iss) *noun.* 1. One who is new to something; a beginner. 2. A person in a religious order who has not yet taken final vows. **novices.**

now *adverb.* 1. At the present time. 2. Immediately: Do it *now;* why wait? 3. As things are: Marcia saved enough to buy a dress; *now* she can go to the dance. —*conjunction.* Since: *Now* that it is warm, we play outdoors at night. —*noun.* The present moment: *Now* is the time to eat.

now·a·days (NOW-ə-dayz) *adverb.* At the present time.

no·where (NOH-hwair) *adverb.* Not at, in, or to any place.

nox·ious (NOK-shəss) *adjective.* Poisonous or harmful. —**noxiously** *adverb.*

noz·zle (NOZ-l) *noun.* The tip on a hose or pipe through which a usually controlled amount of water or gas flows. **nozzles.**

nub (NUHB) *noun.* 1. A knob or lump. 2. The point: Jim rambled and never got to the *nub* of the story.

nu·cle·ar (NOO-klee-ər or NYOO-klee-ər) *adjective.* 1. Concerning or using the atomic nucleus: *nuclear* physics; *nuclear* energy. 2. Having or having to do with atomic or hydrogen bombs: *nuclear* war.

nuclear energy. Energy released from the nuclei of atoms, either by splitting of heavy nuclei or by fusion of light nuclei.

nuclear fission. The splitting apart of the nucleus of a heavy atom.

nuclear reactor. Any device capable of starting a controlled chain reaction.

nuclear reaction. Any process that releases energy by making certain changes in the nucleus of an atom.

nuclear reactor

nu·cle·us (NOO-klee-əss or NYOO-klee-əss) *noun.* 1. The central part or thing around which other parts are gathered or developed: The *nucleus* of the camp was the big building containing the kitchen and dining hall. 2. A beginning: The *nucleus* of his fortune was 500 dollars that he invested wisely. 3. The central mass of an atom. 4. The middle part of a plant or animal cell; essential to growth and reproduction. —**nuclei** (NOO-klee-igh) *plural.*

nude (NOOD or NYOOD) *adjective.* Without clothes; naked. —**nudity** *noun.*

nudge (NUHJ) *verb.* To push against lightly: Tess *nudged* her sister to wake her up. **nudged, nudging.** —*noun.* A light push. **nudges.**

nug·get (NUHG-it) *noun.* 1. A small lump: a *nugget* of gold. 2. A small, valuable part: a *nugget* of information.

nui·sance (NOO-sənss or NYOO-sənss) *noun.* A bothersome or annoying person, thing, or happening. **nuisances.**

null (NUHL) *adjective.* Having no value or meaning. —**null and void.** (Of an agreement or law) Invalid; canceled.

num·ber (NUHM-bər) *noun.* 1. The total: The *number* of children trying out for the band is 30. 2. A quantity, or many: A *number* of parents attended the school fair. 3. A numeral: 2, 4, 6, and 8 are *numbers.* 4. An identifying numeral: My apartment *number* is 13. 5. A single issue of a magazine. —*verb.* 1. To count: Tim *numbered* his reasons for wanting to take the job. 2. To total or amount to: The class *numbered* 30. 3. To include or list as one of a group: Ed *numbered* bird watching as one of his favorite hobbies. **numbered, numbering.** —**without number.** Too much or many to be counted.

num·ber·less (NUHM-bər-liss) *adjective.* Too much or many to be counted; of a great number.

numb·skull (NUHM-skuhl) Also **numskull** *noun.* A stupid person.

nu·mer·al (NOO-mər-əl or NYOO-mər-əl) *noun.* A word, figure, or letter used to stand for a number: Two, 2, and II are numerals.

nu·mer·a·tion (noo-mər-AY-shən or nyoo-mər-AY-shən) *noun.* The process of counting or giving numbers to something.

nu·mer·a·tor (NOO-mər-ay-tər or NYOO-mər-ay-tər) *noun.* The number appearing above the line in a fraction: In the fraction $\frac{5}{6}$, 5 is the *numerator.* See **denominator.**

nu·mer·i·cal (noo-MEHR-i-kəl or nyoo-MEHR-i-kəl) *adjective.* Pertaining to a number or numbers. —**numerically** *adverb.*

nu·mer·ous (NOO-mər-əss or NYOO-mər-əss) *adjective.* Many in number: Stan has *numerous* friends. —**numerously** *adverb.*

nun (NUHN) *noun.* A woman who belongs to a religious order and devotes her life to good works.

nup·tial (NUHP-chəl) *adjective.* Pertaining to a wedding: a *nuptial* ceremony. —*noun.* (Usually plural) A wedding ceremony: —**nuptially** *adverb.*

nurse (NERSS) *noun.* 1. A person trained to take care of the sick or feeble. 2. A person who takes care of the babies or children of others. **nurses.** —*verb.* 1. To take care of (a sick person or child). 2. To feed from the breast. 3. To take milk from the breast. 4. To be especially protective about: Sally *nursed* her plant through the winter. **nursed, nursing.**

nurs·er·y (NER-sər-ee or NERSS-ree) *noun.* 1. A special room in a house for the use of small children. 2. A place where small children are cared for during the day. 3. A place where flowers, bushes, and trees are grown for sale and replanting. **nurseries.**

nursery school. A school for very young children.

nur·ture (NER-chər) *verb.* 1. To nourish or care for. 2. To bring up or train. **nurtured, nurturing.** —*noun.* 1. Bringing up or training. 2. Nourishment or food.

nut (NUHT) *noun.* 1. A fruit with a hard shell enclosing a kernel that can usually be eaten. 2. The edible kernel found inside a shell. 3. A small piece of metal with a threaded hole that screws on a bolt to keep it tightly in place. 4. (Slang) A person who does odd or peculiar things.

nut·crack·er (NUHT-krak-ər) *noun.* A device used for cracking nutshells.

nut·meg (NUHT-meg) *noun.* 1. A hard, round, light brown seed that is ground and used as a flavoring in foods. 2. The tropical tree on which this seed grows. —*noun* (and *adjective*). A light brown color.

nu·tri·ent (NOO-tree-ənt or NYOO-tree-ənt) *noun.* A substance that is nourishing: A balanced diet provides every *nutrient* needed for growth and good health.

nu·tri·tion (noo-TRISH-ən or nyoo-TRISH-ən) *noun.* 1. The process of nourishing or being nourished: Good *nutrition* is necessary for growth. 2. The steps by which a living thing uses food for growth.

nu·tri·tious (noo-TRISH-əss or nyoo-TRISH-əss) *adjective.* Nourishing; good for the body as food: a *nutritious* meal. —**nutritiously** *adverb.*

nuz·zle (NUHZ-l) *verb.* To rub softly with the nose: The dog *nuzzled* Emily. **nuzzled, nuzzling.**

ny·lon (NIGH-lon) *noun.* 1. A strong synthetic material used to make clothing, parachutes, textiles, bristles, and other things. 2. (*Plural*) Stockings made of nylon.

nymph (NIMF) *noun.* A Greek or Roman goddess who was believed to dwell in the rivers, streams, forests, and hills of the countryside.

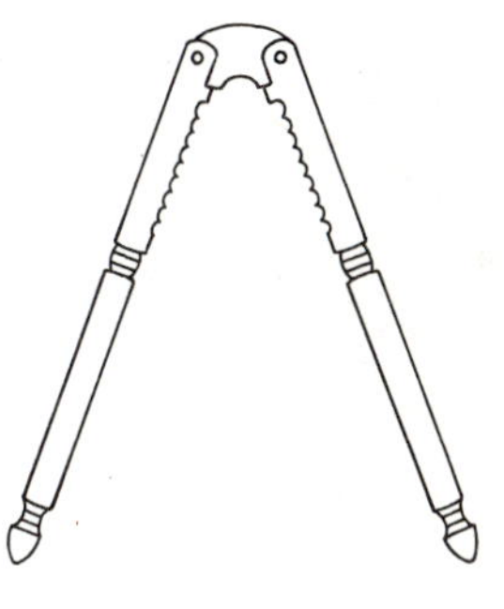

nutcracker

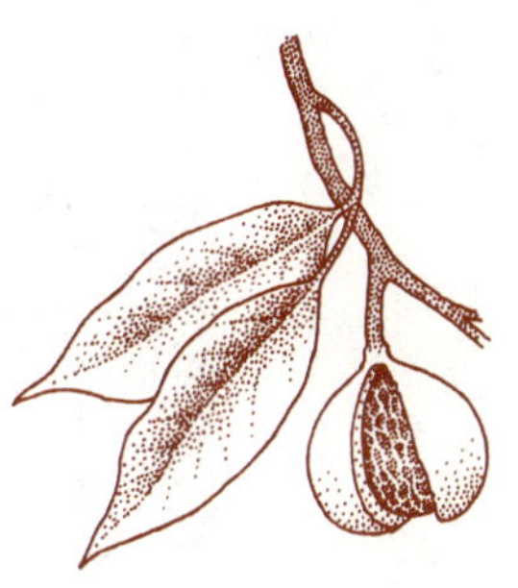

nutmeg

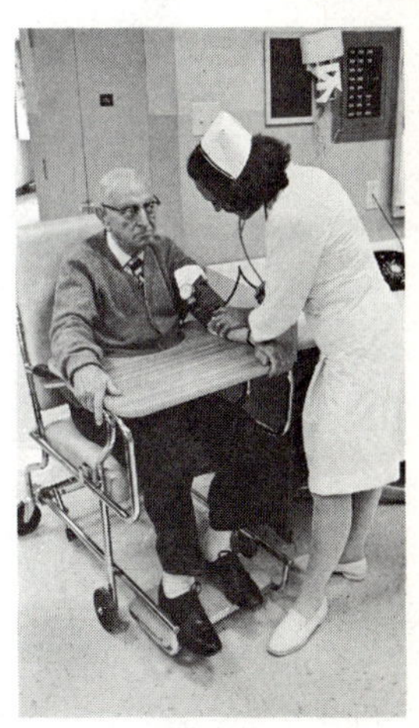

nurse

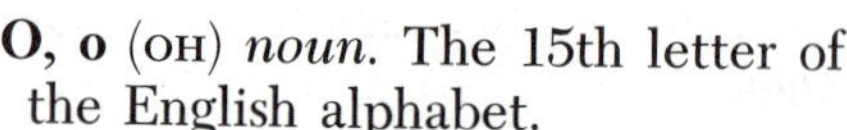

O, o (OH) *noun.* The 15th letter of the English alphabet.

oaf (OHF) *noun.* A clumsy or stupid person.

oak (OHK) *noun.* 1. A tree that has hard wood and large leaves and produces seeds called acorns. 2. The tough, hard wood of the oak. —**oaken** (OHK-ən) *adjective.*

oar (OR) *noun.* 1. A long pole, used to row a boat, with one flat end that pushes against the water. 2. One who rows. —**rest on one's oars.** To stop working and rest awhile.

oars·man (ORZ-mən) *noun.* A man who rows. —**oarsmen** *plural.*

o·a·sis (oh-AY-siss) *noun.* 1. A small fertile watering spot in the desert. 2. A refreshing place; a place to relax in: The park is an *oasis.* —**oases** (oh-AY-seez) *plural.*

oat (OHT) *noun.* 1. A cereal plant whose grain is used as food for men and animals. 2. (Usually plural) The grain of the oat plant. —**feel one's oats.** (Informal) To be very lively; feel or act important. —**sow one's wild oats.** To behave in a wild and unruly way when one is young.

oath (OHTH) *noun.* 1. A promise, made in God's name or the name of some holy or respected person or thing, to tell the truth or keep one's word. 2. A curse; the use of a religious word, such as "God," to show anger or irreverence.

oat·meal (OHT-meel) *noun.* 1. Ground or rolled oats; oats made into meal. 2. Hot cereal made from rolled oats.

o·be·di·ence (oh-BEE-dee-ənss) *noun.* Obeying; doing what one is told to do. —**obedient** *adjective.* —**obediently** *adverb.*

ob·e·lisk (OB-ə-lisk) *noun.* A tall four-sided pillar of stone that narrows to a pyramid shape on top.

o·bey (oh-BAY) *verb.* 1. To do what one is told: A good soldier *obeys.* 2. To follow the orders of: *Obey* the principal. **obeyed, obeying.**

ob·ject (OB-jikt or OB-jekt) *noun.* 1. A real thing; something one can see and touch. 2. A person or thing toward which one directs his attention, action, or feeling. 3. Something aimed at; a purpose or goal: The *object* of the sport is to develop your body. 4. (Grammar) A word (or phrase) that: (a) is affected by the action of a verb; (b) completes a prepositional phrase: In "Give the book to the librarian," "book" is the *object* of "give" and "the librarian" is the *object* of "to." —(əb-JEKT) *verb.* 1. (Usually followed by *to*) To dislike; disapprove: She *objects* to the boy's bad conduct. 2. To give as an argument or reason for not liking: The girl *objects* that the bus comes too late. **objected, objecting.**

ob·jec·tion (əb-JEK-shən) *noun.* 1. A reason for not liking something. 2. A feeling against: I have no *objection* to playing now.

ob·jec·tion·a·ble (əb-JEK-shən-ə-bəl) *adjective.* Not likable or pleasant. —**objectionably** *adverb.*

ob·jec·tive (əb-JEK-tiv) *noun.* A purpose or goal; something that one aims at: Our *objective* is to do better. —*adjective.* 1. Able to look at facts without being influenced by personal feelings: Can anybody be *objective* all the time? 2. Existing as a real thing outside the mind or feelings: Deeds are *objective,* but thoughts are not. 3. (Grammar) Relating to the object of a verb or preposition: the *objective* case. —**objectively** *adverb.*

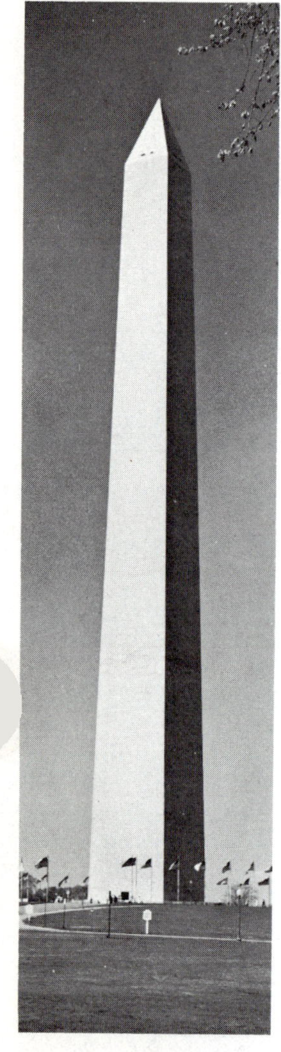

obelisk

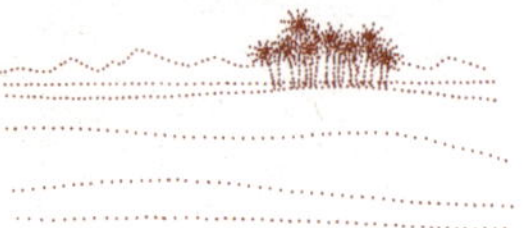

oasis

ob·li·gate (OB-lə-gayt) *verb.* To hold or bind by a duty or responsibility: We are *obligated* to repay our debts. **obligated, obligating.**

ob·li·ga·tion (ob-lə-GAY-shən) *noun.* 1. A duty or responsibility: I have an *obligation* to attend the meeting. 2. The state of being obligated or in debt or of owing thanks.

o·blige (ə-BLIGHJ) *verb.* 1. To force or compel: His good heart *obliges* him to share with others. 2. To feel that one owes something in return for a favor: We are *obliged* to her for her kindness. 3. To do a favor for: Will you please *oblige* me by opening the door? **obliged, obliging.**

o·blig·ing (ə-BLIGHJ-ing) *adjective.* Kind; helpful; willing or ready to do favors. —**obligingly** *adverb.*

ob·lique (oh-BLEEK or əb-LEEK) *adjective.* 1. Slanting or sloping; not straight up and down or level. 2. (Math) Describing an angle that is not a right angle. 3. Not open and straightforward: *oblique* answers to questions. —**obliquely** *adverb.*

ob·lit·er·ate (əb-LIT-ər-ayt) *verb.* To blot out; destroy; remove with no trace. **obliterated, obliterating.** —**obliteration** (əb-lit-ər-AY-shən) *noun.*

ob·liv·ion (əb-LIV-ee-ən) *noun.* The state of being completely forgotten: Some customs pass into *oblivion.*

ob·liv·i·ous (əb-LIV-ee-əss) *adjective.* Forgetting or not aware; not noticing: *oblivious* of efforts to help. —**obliviously** *adverb.*

ob·long (OB-lawng) *adjective.* In a rectangular shape; longer than it is wide. —*noun.* Any rectangle except a square.

ob·nox·ious (ob-NOK-shəss) *adjective.* Very displeasing or offensive; hateful or disgusting. —**obnoxiously** *adverb.*

o·boe (OH-boh) *noun.* A wooden wind instrument with a double reed in the mouthpiece. **oboes.**

ob·scene (ob-SEEN) *adjective.* Disgusting or indecent; shocking to a person's sense of modesty. —**obscenely** *adverb.*

ob·scure (ob-SKYUR) *adjective.* 1. Not clear; indistinct; hard to hear, see, or understand: an *obscure* idea. 2. Not easy to discover; out of the way: an *obscure* desert tribe. 3. Not well-known: an *obscure* writer of books for boys. —*verb.* To make obscure; hide from sight; make dark or dim: The clouds *obscure* the sun. **obscured, obscuring.** —**obscurely** *adverb.*

ob·scur·i·ty (ob-SKYUR-ə-tee) *noun.* 1. The state of being hard to hear, see, or understand. 2. The condition of being unknown: He is a great player in spite of his *obscurity.* 3. Darkness or dimness.

ob·serv·ance (əb-ZER-vənss) *noun.* 1. The act of keeping, obeying, or celebrating (holidays, customs, or laws): the *observance* of the Fourth of July. 2. The performing of an act or ceremony, as of a religion: Sunday morning *observances.* 3. Obeying or following: *observance* of the law. **observances.**

ob·serv·ant (əb-ZER-vənt) *adjective.* 1. Alert, watchful; quick to observe or notice: The *observant* player intercepted the pass. 2. Careful in obeying or following (a law, rule, or custom). —**observantly** *adverb.*

ob·ser·va·tion (ob-zər-VAY-shən) *noun.* 1. The act of seeing; the habit or power of noticing or observing: *observation* of the sky. 2. Being noticed or seen: The girl's tears escaped *observation.* 3. Seeing and noting something for a special purpose; a thing so seen and noted. 4. A remark or statement.

ob·serv·a·to·ry (əb-ZER-və-tor-ee) *noun.* A building with special equipment, such as telescopes, for observing the stars and planets, the weather, or other things in nature. **observatories.**

oboe

observatory

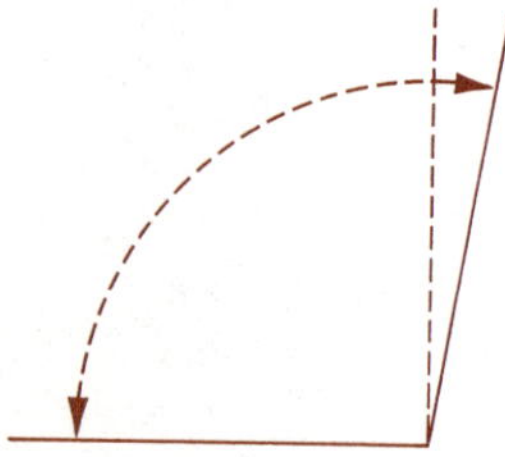
obtuse angle

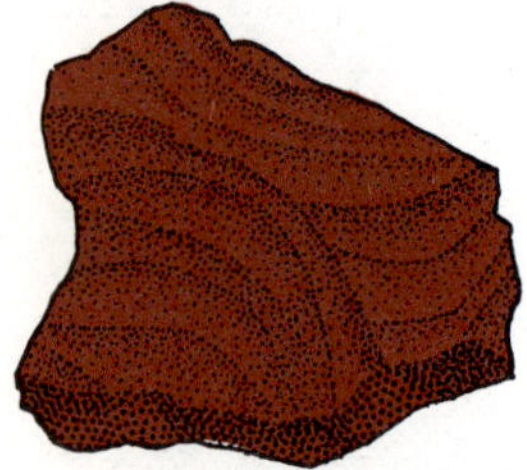
obsidian

ob·serve (əb-ZERV) *verb.* 1. To see or notice: The detective *observed* something curious in the dark hallway. 2. To study; examine for a special purpose: The doctor *observed* the sick man carefully. 3. To obey; be guided by; keep: *observe* the rules. 4. To celebrate; show respect for: We *observe* Thanksgiving with a feast. 5. To make a remark or comment. **observed, observing.**

ob·ses·sion (əb-SESH-ən or ob-SESH-ən) *noun.* An idea or feeling, usually unreasonable, that takes over one's thoughts: an *obsession* that he can rule the world.

ob·sid·i·an (ob-SID-een-ən) *noun.* A hard, glassy rock that is usually black and is formed by a volcano.

ob·so·lete (ob-sə-LEET or OB-sə-leet) *adjective.* Out-of-date; not used any longer: The automobile made the blacksmith *obsolete.*

ob·sta·cle (OB-stə-kəl) *noun.* A thing that stands in the way or halts progress. **obstacles.**

ob·sti·nate (OB-stə-nit) *adjective.* 1. Stubborn; pigheaded; unwilling to change one's mind or do what someone else wants: The *obstinate* dog won't obey. 2. Hard to treat, remove, or bring under control: an *obstinate* pain. —**obstinacy** *noun.* —**obstinately** *adverb.*

ob·struct (əb-STRUHKT or ob-STRUHKT) *verb.* 1. To block up or clog: The stalled car *obstructs* the street. 2. To be in the way of: *obstruct* the view. 3. To hold up, hinder, or make difficult. **obstructed, obstructing.** —**obstruction** *noun.*

ob·tain (əb-TAYN or ob-TAYN) *verb.* To get or acquire; come to possess: *obtain* a bicycle. **obtained, obtaining.**

ob·tain·a·ble (əb-TAYN-ə-bəl or ob-TAYN-ə-bəl) *adjective.* Possible to obtain or acquire: Passes are *obtainable* in the office.

ob·tuse (ob-TOOSS) *adjective.* 1. Stupid or dull; slow to understand: An *obtuse* child needs extra help in school. 2. Not sharp or pointed; blunt. —**obtusely** *adverb.*

obtuse angle. An angle of over 90 degrees; an angle greater than a right angle.

ob·vi·ous (OB-vee-əss) *adjective.* Clear; easy to notice or understand: *obvious* error. —**obviously** *adverb.*

oc·ca·sion (ə-KAY-zhən) *noun.* 1. A time: I saw her on a few *occasions.* 2. A special time or happening: New Year's Day is an *occasion.* 3. An opportunity: Take advantage of the *occasion.* 4. A reason: I never have any *occasion* to speak to him. **occasioned, occasioning.**

oc·ca·sion·al (ə-KAY-zhən-l) *adjective.* Happening once in a while. —**occasionally** *adverb.*

oc·cu·pant (OK-yə-pənt) *noun.* A person who occupies or possesses a place or a position, such as a home, office, post; a tenant.

oc·cu·pa·tion (ok-yə-PAY-shən) *noun.* 1. A job, profession, or kind of work; main activity: My *occupation* is teaching. 2. The state of being occupied; possession.

oc·cu·py (OK-yə-pigh) *verb.* 1. To fill or take up: The pictures *occupy* most of the wall. 2. To give one's time to: He *occupies* himself with baseball. 3. To be in (an office): The President *occupies* the position of chief executive. 4. To live in: We *occupy* the first house down the street. 5. (Military) To take possession of. **occupied, occupying.**

oc·cur (ə-KER) *verb.* 1. To take place or happen: The final defeat of the British army in America *occurred* in 1783. 2. To be found; appear or exist: This kind of storm *occurs* only in the tropics. 3. To suggest itself; come to a person's mind: An idea *occurs* to me. **occurred, occurring.**

oc·cur·rence (ə-KER-ənss) *noun.* 1. An event or happening; something that occurs. 2. The fact of existing or taking place. **occurrences.**

oc·ean (OH-shən) *noun.* 1. The large body of salt water that covers about three-fourths of the surface of the globe. 2. Any one of the main parts into which this body of water is divided, such as the Atlantic, Pacific, Arctic, Antarctic, and Indian oceans. 3. A great quantity, area, or expanse: an *ocean* of grass.

o·cean·og·ra·phy (oh-shə-NOG-rə-fee) *noun.* The science or study of the ocean and its plants and animals.

oc·e·lot (oss-ə-lot or OH-sə-lot) *noun.* A yellow or gray wildcat of medium size that has black spots. It is found in the southwestern United States and in Latin America.

o·cher or **o·chre** (OH-kər) *noun.* 1. A clay, usually yellow or red, that is used to add color to paint. 2. (Also *adjective*) Deep yellow.

o'clock (ə-KLOK) *adverb.* Of the clock: The expression "o'clock" indicates the hour, as in "It is three *o'clock.*"

oc·ta·gon (OK-tə-gon) *noun.* An eight-sided figure. —**octagonal** (ok-TAG-ə-nl) *adjective.* —**octagonally** *adverb.*

oc·tave (OK-tive) *noun.* (Music) 1. The interval between two notes, one of which is five whole tones and two half tones higher or lower than the other. 2. A series of eight notes or tones, of which the first is an octave higher or lower than the last. **octaves.**

Oc·to·ber (ok-TOH-bər) *noun.* The tenth month of the year: There are 31 days in *October.* —**Oct.** *abbreviation.*

oc·to·pus (OK-tə-pəss) *noun.* A sea animal that has a soft body and eight long arms covered with suckers. —**octopuses** or **octopi** (OK-tə-pigh) *plural.*

oc·u·list (OK-yə-list) *noun.* A doctor who examines and treats the eyes.

odd (OD) *adjective.* 1. Strange; not normal or usual: the tourists' *odd* behavior. 2. With a remainder of 1 when divided by 2: 5 and 9 are *odd* numbers. 3. With the other one of a pair missing: There is an *odd* shoe in the closet. 4. More or less; a little more than: There are 300 *odd* stamps in my collection. 5. Not regular; occasional: *odd* jobs. **odder, oddest.** —**oddly** *adverb.*

odd·i·ty (OD-ə-tee) *noun.* 1. Strangeness; state of being unusual: The *oddity* of the event puzzled the detectives. 2. A strange thing or person: The rock formations were *oddities.* **oddities.**

odds (ODZ) *noun, plural.* 1. The advantage that one contestant, side, or likelihood has against another: The *odds* are that we will not win the game. 2. The rate at which a bet may be placed on the result of a contest or event: If my team wins at 4–1 *odds,* I will win a dollar for the quarter that I bet. —**at odds.** Not in agreement. —**odds and ends.** Various unimportant items.

ode (OHD) *noun.* A poem of deep feeling and formal or dignified style. **odes.**

o·di·ous (OH-dee-əss) *adjective.* Hateful; revolting: I think that snakes and spiders are *odious.*

o·dom·e·ter (oh-DOM-ə-tər) *noun.* A device that indicates how far an automobile or other vehicle has traveled.

o·dor (OH-dər) *noun.* A scent or smell: the *odor* of flowers.

o'er (OR) *contraction.* Over (often used in poetry): *"O'er* the ramparts we watched. . . ." (F. S. Key).

of (UHV) *preposition.* 1. Coming from or because of: ringing *of* the bell; tired *of* running. 2. Ruling: King *of* England. 3. Belonging to: the roof *of* our house. 4. Made from; containing: a suit *of* wool. 5. Having: a man *of* charm. 6. About: to sing *of* love. 7. Called or named: the State *of* Ohio. 8. By: poems *of* Keats.

ocelot

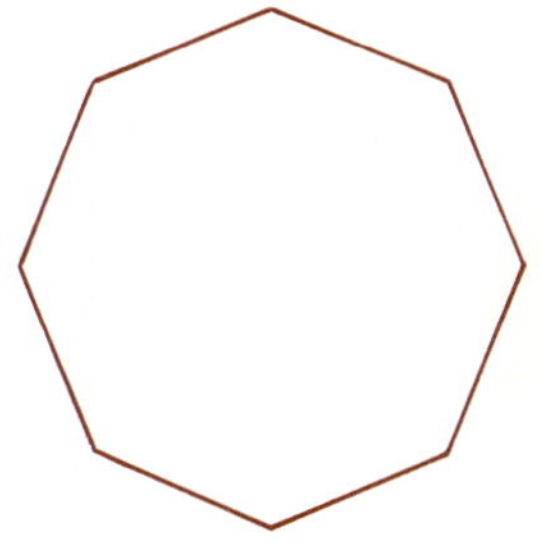
octagon

octopus

off *adverb.* 1. Away to another place or distant point: The ship sailed *off.* 2. So as to become disconnected: When the wind blew, the branch fell *off.* 3. Separated from oneself: Mother took *off* her ring. 4. In or to a non-operating condition: I turned *off* the lawn mower. 5. Away or free from regular work or duty: We had Thanksgiving *off.* —*preposition.* 1. Down from: The actor fell *off* the stage. 2. Away from: The boat was two miles *off* its course. 3. Not normal or usual with regard to: The runner is *off* his pace. 4. From the goods or nourishment of: The old man lived *off* the food that he begged. 5. Not on; free from: The sailor is *off* duty. —*adjective.* 1. Not normal or usual: The warm weather caused an *off* season for skiing. 2. Away: Jim is *off* on a trip. 3. Stopped; not operating: The machine is *off.* 4. Not on or connected: The boy's shoes were *off.*

of·fend (ə-FEND) *verb.* To insult; annoy: The speaker *offended* the audience. **offended, offending.**

[1]**of·fense** (ə-FENSS) *noun.* 1. The violation of a rule, regulation, or code; crime. 2. Harm or insult; annoyance: Jack did not mean to cause any *offense* by his comments.

[2]**of·fense** (OFF-enss) *noun.* 1. The act of attacking: The army is moving forward on the *offense.* 2. Those who are attacking or moving forward, especially those on a team who try to score.

of·fen·sive (ə-FEN-siv) *adjective.* 1. Causing annoyance or unpleasantness: an *offensive* smell. 2. Related to weapons, persons, or actions of attack: *offensive* weapons. —*noun.* The process of attacking. **offensives.** —**offensively** *adverb.*

of·fer (OFF-ər) *verb.* 1. To present for acceptance or taking: Jim *offered* me candy. 2. To volunteer: Uncle Ed *offered* to drive me home. 3. To present as an act of religion: *offer* prayers for the sick. 4. To present or suggest as payment: I *offered* three dollars for the two books. **offered, offering.** —*noun.* 1. An act of offering; a presenting or suggesting: an *offer* of help. 2. A proposal: the salesman's *offer.*

of·fer·ing (OFF-ər-ing) *noun.* Something offered; a donation, especially as an act of religious worship.

off·hand (OFF-HAND) *adjective* or *adverb.* Without preparation or planning; casual: *offhand* remarks.

of·fice (OFF-fiss) *noun.* 1. A central position of authority, as in a government or organization: the *office* of treasurer. 2. A room or place where business is carried on. 3. The people who work in an office. 4. (Plural) Effort; favor: Dad got his job through the *offices* of Mr. Jones. **offices.**

of·fi·cer (OFF-i-sər) *noun.* 1. A person who holds an office or position of authority; an official. 2. A person of any of several ranks who commands others in the armed forces: Captains, and admirals are *officers.* 3. A policeman.

of·fi·cial (ə-FISH-əl) *adjective.* 1. Related to an office or position of authority: *official* permission for a holiday. 2. Of an authorized or accepted type: our team's *official* colors. —*noun.* A person who holds an office or position of special authority: *officials* at a football game. —**officially** *adverb.*

of·fi·ci·ate (ə-FISH-ee-ayt) *verb.* 1. To perform the duties of an official: a new umpire *officiated.* 2. To perform the duties of a clergyman: A bishop will *officiate* Sunday. **officiated, officiating.**

off·shoot (OFF-shoot) *noun.* Something that branches or grows out (from something else).

off·shore (OFF-SHOR) *adjective* and *adverb.* Away from the shore.

off·side (OFF-SIGHD) *adjective.* (Sports)

Beyond the limits allowed for a player: an *offside* penalty.

off•spring (OFF-spring) *noun.* One's child or children. —**offspring** *plural.*

oft (OFFT) *adverb.* (Poetry) Often.

of•ten (AW-fən) *adverb.* Frequently; many times: It *often* rains here.

o•gre (OH-gər) *noun.* 1. An imaginary monster or giant in fairy tales. 2. A cruel or frightening person. **ogres.**

oh *interjection.* Expresses: 1. Surprise: *Oh!* I didn't expect you. 2. Fear: *Oh* don't harm me! 3. Discomfort; pain: *Oh!* It hurts. —**oh's** or **ohs** *plural.*

O•hi•o (oh-HIGH-oh) *noun.* A north central state of the United States, 17th to join the Union (1803). —**O.** *abbreviation.* **OH** for Zip Codes.

ohm *noun.* A unit used to measure electrical resistance.

-oid *suffix.* Indicates similarity: meteor*oid.*

oil *noun.* 1. Any of a variety of greasy substances, usually liquid, that come from mineral, animal, or vegetable sources, are lighter than water, easily burned, and often used for fuel or for cooking purposes: Kerosene is a type of *oil.* 2. (Often plural) Paint made by mixing coloring in oil. —*verb.* To apply oil to; lubricate. **oiled, oiling.**

oil•cloth (OIL-kloth) *noun.* A fabric waterproofed with oil and pigment.

oil well. A well drilled in the earth's surface to get crude oil (petroleum).

oil•y (OI-lee) *adjective.* 1. Of or like oil; greasy. 2. Smooth or polite in a suspicious or unpleasant way: an *oily* way of behaving. **oilier, oiliest.**

oint•ment (OINT-mənt) *noun.* An oily substance spread over the skin to make it soft or to cure an ailment.

O.K. (OH-KAY) Also **OK, okay** *noun.* (Informal) Consent. —**O.K.'s, OK's** or **okays** *plural.* —*verb.* To accept; consent to: Will you *O.K.* this order? **O.K.'d, OK'd,** or **okayed, O.K.'ing, OK'ing,** or **okaying.**

o•ka•pi (oh-KAH-pee) *noun.* An African animal like a giraffe but small and short-necked. —**okapi** or **okapis** *plural.*

O•kla•ho•ma (oh-klə-HOH-mə) *noun.* A south central state of the United States, 46th to join the Union (1907). —**Okla.** *abbreviation.* Also **OK** for Zip Codes.

o•kra (OH-krə) *noun.* 1. A green pod used as a vegetable, particularly in soups. 2. The plant it grows on.

old (OHLD) *adjective.* 1. Having lived or existed for many years; aged: an *old* man. 2. Not new or modern: an *old* joke. 3. Of age: My sister is 12 years *old.* 4. Used; worn-out: Jim replaced the *old* battery. 5. Of or related to aged people: *old* age. 6. Of an earlier time; former: This house is larger than our *old* one. 7. Of ancient times; long in the past: the *old* Roman Empire. **older** or **elder, oldest** or **eldest.**

old•en (OHL-dn) *adjective.* Long-ago; ancient: in *olden* days.

old-fash•ioned (OHLD-FASH-ənd) *adjective.* Of or related to old ideas, methods, or things; out-of-date.

old maid. 1. An unmarried woman, especially an older one. 2. (Informal) A very fussy or strictly proper person. 3. A child's card game.

o•le•o•mar•ga•rine (oh-lee-oh-MAHR-jə-rin) *noun.* A substance made from vegetable oils, used as a butter substitute. Also called "oleo" or "margarine."

ol•fac•to•ry (ol-FAK-tə-ree) *adjective.* Of or related to the sense of smell.

ol•ive (OL-iv) *noun.* 1. A small oval fruit eaten green or ripe, often pressed for its oil. 2. The tree on which it grows. 3. (Also *adjective*) A yellow-green color. **olives.**

om•e•let (OM-lit) Also **omelette** *noun.* A dish of eggs beaten and cooked with milk or water, and sometimes other ingredients.

okapi

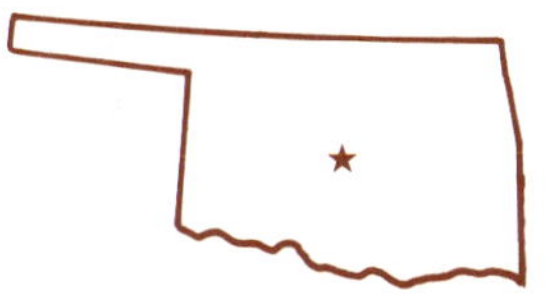
Oklahoma
★capital: Oklahoma City

Ohio
★capital: Columbus

oil wells

o·men (OH-mən) *noun.* An event or phenomenon that some people believe to be a sign telling something about the future.

om·i·nous (OM-ə-nəss) *adjective.* Suggesting something bad or difficult; threatening: an *ominous* sign. —**ominously** *adverb.*

o·mis·sion (oh-MISH-ən) *noun.* 1. An omitting or leaving out; oversight. 2. Something omitted or left out.

o·mit (oh-MIT) *verb.* 1. To leave out: If you *omit* the sugar, the cake won't taste good. 2. Overlook; fail to do. **omitted, omitting.**

om·nip·o·tent (om-NIP-ə-tənt) *adjective.* Having all power or authority; almighty: "Only God is *omnipotent,*" said the minister. —**omnipotence** *noun.* —**omnipotently** *adverb.*

on *preposition.* 1. Above and held up by: The lamp is *on* the table. 2. Against: leaning *on* the wall. 3. Supported or nourished by: The sailors lived *on* pork and beans. 4. About: a talk *on* history. 5. Covering or in contact with: boots *on* his feet. 6. In the direction of; toward: the house *on* my right. 7. Upon: Snow fell *on* the hills. 8. At (a certain time): We left home *on* Sunday. 9. Resulting from: Jack climbed the tree *on* a dare. 10. Active or busy with: Janet went *on* a hike. 11. At a cost to; paid by: The treat was *on* Dad. 12. Connected with as a member: *on* the swimming team. —*adverb.* 1. So as to cover: Harry put *on* his hat. 2. Forward: The soldiers marched *on.* 3. Toward an action or thing: The fans looked *on* when the players entered. 4. Continuously: The radio played *on* for hours. —*adjective.* 1. In operation; running: The motor is still *on.* 2. Being done; in action: The store was closed when the strike was *on.* 3. Planned: The game is still *on.*

onion

once (WUHNSS) *adverb.* 1. At a time in the past: Kings *once* ruled in France. 2. One time only: Take a pill *once* a day. —*conjunction.* Whenever; after: You will like the food *once* you have tried it. —*noun.* One time: Let me go this *once.* —**at once.** Immediately.

one (WUHN) *adjective.* 1. Single; without others: *one* man. 2. Some; any: *One* day he will return. 3. United; together: *one* in spirit. 4. Only; special: Spinach is the *one* food that I don't like. —*noun.* 1. The cardinal number after zero and before two; 1. Three subtracted from four equals *one.* 2. A single person or thing. —*pronoun.* A person or thing: You are the *one!*

one·self (wuhn-SELF) *pronoun.* Used: 1. When the subject and direct object of a sentence are the same: One can teach *oneself* to sew. 2. For emphasis: One must do certain things *oneself.*

one-sid·ed (WUHN-SIGH-did) *adjective.* 1. Not equal; with one side far superior to the other: a *one-sided* game. 2. Liking or favoring one side more than the other, especially unfairly: a *one-sided* opinion.

on·ion (UHN-yən) *noun.* 1. A plant bulb, usually with a sharp taste and smell, eaten as a vegetable. 2. The plant on which this bulb grows.

on·look·er (ON-luk-ər) *noun.* A person who looks or watches.

on·ly (OHN-lee) *adjective.* Alone of its kind or type: Rex is the *only* collie in the area. —*adverb.* 1. With no other reason than; solely: Bob smiled *only* to seem cheerful. 2. Just; merely: The book costs *only* 50 cents. —*conjunction.* But; except that: I'd go, *only* I have no money.

on·o·mat·o·poe·ia (on-ə-mat-ə-PEE-ə) *noun.* The use of a word or words that echo the sound described: Alfred Noyes used *onomatopoeia* in the verse: "Tlot-tlot . . . The horse-hoofs ringing clear. . . ."

on·rush (ON-ruhsh) *noun.* A powerful rush forward: an *onrush* of people.

on·set (ON-set) *noun.* 1. A beginning: the *onset* of winter. 2. An attack.

on·slaught (ON-slawt) *noun.* An attack of great force: The enemy's *onslaught* drove the army back.

on·to (ON-too) *preposition.* 1. To a place upon: The cat jumped *onto* the piano. 2. (Informal) Aware of: The sheriff was *onto* the plan.

on·ward (ON-wərd) Also **onwards** (ON-wərdz) *adverb* and *adjective.* Forward or ahead: "*Onward,* Christian soldiers. . . ." (Baring-Gould).

oo·dles (oo-dəlz) *noun, plural.* (Informal) Lots; a large amount: Bill found *oodles* of things to do.

ooze (ooz) *verb.* 1. To leak out gradually or slowly: Oil *oozed* from the pipe. 2. To slip (away): Jim's courage *oozed* away. **oozed, oozing.** —*noun.* 1. A slow leak. 2. Soft mud. —**oozy** *adjective.*

o·pal (OH-pəl) *noun.* A gem that shines with changing colors: Some *opals* are milky in color, others green and blue.

o·paque (oh-PAYK) *adjective.* 1. Not allowing light through; not transparent: Black paint on the panes made the window *opaque.* 2. Dull; dark; not reflecting light: The table had an *opaque* finish. 3. Hard to understand; not clear: an *opaque* explanation.

o·pen (OH-pən) *adjective.* 1. Not shut or closed: an *open* window. 2. Not covered, enclosed, protected, or restricted: an *open* bottle. 3. Still to be had: Jill was lucky there was a place *open.* 4. Without pretense or prejudice; willing to listen: an *open* mind. —*verb.* 1. To make or become unclosed: *Open* all the windows. 2. To expose or uncover: *open* a jar. 3. To unfold; spread out: The flowers *opened* after the rain. 4. To begin: *open* a business. 5. To separate: The waters *opened* for Moses and the Israelites escaping from Egypt. **opened, opening.** —**openly** *adverb.*

open-air (OH-pən-AIR) *adjective.* Outdoors: an *open-air* theater.

o·pen·ing (OH-pən-ing) *noun.* 1. A hole or open space: an *opening* in the clouds. 2. A chance; a job that has not yet been taken: an *opening* for a delivery boy. 3. A gap; pause: an *opening* in the conversation. 4. A beginning: the *opening* of a book. 5. The first showing of a business, entertainment, or exhibit.

open-minded (OH-pən-MIGHN-did) *adjective.* Having a mind open to new ideas; without prejudice.

op·er·a (OP-rə or OP-ər-ə) *noun.* A form of drama that combines a play with orchestral music so that lines are mostly sung.

op·er·ate (OP-ər-ayt) *verb.* 1. To run or manage: *operate* a power saw. 2. To function: *operate* without a hitch. 3. To bring about an effect. 4. To cut into the body for purposes of health: The doctor *operated* to remove Jim's tonsils. **operated, operating.**

op·er·a·tion (op-ər-AY-shən) *noun.* 1. Cutting into the body for purposes of health: a heart *operation.* 2. The act or process of working: The *operation* of a car requires attention. 3. The way a thing works: The *operation* of the machine is noiseless. 4. A military or naval action. —**operational** *adjective.* —**operationally** *adverb.*

op·er·a·tor (OP-ər-ay-tər) *noun.* 1. A person who runs or operates a machine or device: a telephone *operator.* 2. (Informal) A person who uses cunning or shrewd ways to get what he wants.

op·er·et·ta (op-ər-ET-ə) *noun.* A light and amusing opera with some spoken dialogue.

o·pin·ion (ə-PIN-yən) *noun.* 1. A belief, not necessarily based on knowledge. 2. An estimation or judgment of worth: a good *opinion* of Jose. 3. The judgment or advice of an expert: medical *opinion.*

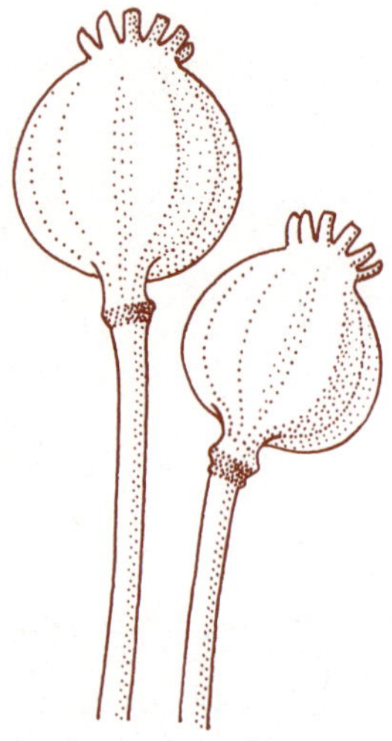
opium

opossums

orangutan

o·pin·ion·at·ed (ə-PIN-yə-nay-tid) *adjective.* Sticking to one's beliefs or opinions stubbornly.

o·pi·um (OH-pee-əm) *noun.* A drug derived from the opium poppy that lessens pain and causes sleep. Repeated use results in addiction.

o·pos·sum (ə-POSS-əm) *noun.* A small animal that carries its offspring in a pouch and pretends to be dead when cornered or captured. Also called "possum." —**opossum** or **opossums** *plural.*

op·po·nent (ə-POH-nənt) *noun.* One who is on the other side in a conflict, game, or debate.

op·por·tu·ni·ty (op-ər-TOO-nə-tee or op-ər-TYOO-nə-tee) *noun.* A favorable time or situation; a chance. **opportunities.**

op·pose (ə-POHZ) *verb.* To be against; resist: All those who *oppose* Jim's idea say "No." **opposed, opposing.**

op·po·site (OP-ə-zit) *noun.* Something that is completely different from something else: Night is the *opposite* of day. **opposites.** —*adjective.* 1. Facing: Lizzy's friend lives across the street in the *opposite* house. 2. Completely different; the reverse of each other: North is the *opposite* direction to South. —*preposition.* Across from: Place the couch *opposite* the fireplace.

op·po·si·tion (op-ə-ZISH-ən) *noun.* 1. The act or state of being against; resistance: strong *opposition.* 2. [Often capital O] A group opposing the main group or the political party in power.

op·press (ə-PRESS) *verb.* 1. To rule or put down unfairly. 2. To weigh heavily upon the emotions; depress: Tom was *oppressed* by his failure. —**oppressed, oppressing.** —**oppression** (ə-PRESH-ən) *noun.*

op·pres·sive (ə-PRESS-iv) *adjective.* 1. Unfairly burdensome or harsh: *oppressive* rules. 2. Hard for the mind or body to bear: *oppressive* weather. —**oppressively** *adverb.*

op·ti·cal (OP-ti-kəl) *adjective.* Having to do with vision or the eye: An *optical* illusion fools the eye.

op·ti·cian (op-TISH-ən) *noun.* A person who makes or sells eyeglasses or other optical aids.

optic nerve. The nerve that connects the eye to the brain.

op·ti·mism (OP-tə-miz-əm) *noun.* A tendency to think everything will turn out well. —**optimistic** (op-tə-MISS-tik) *adjective.* —**optimistically** *adverb.*

op·ti·mist (OP-tə-mist) *noun.* A believer in optimism.

op·tom·e·trist (op-TOM-ə-trist) *noun.* A person who examines eyes and fits them with corrective lenses.

or *conjunction.* Indicates: 1. A choice: The soup may be served hot *or* cold. 2. An explanation of the previous word: Tardiness, *or* lateness, is not acceptable.

-or *prefix.* Indicates: 1. A person or thing that does an action: cultivat*or.* 2. A state, manner, or act: pall*or.*

or·a·cle (OR-ə-kəl) *noun.* 1. A sacred place in ancient Greece or Rome where one could ask a god to foretell events. 2. The priest or priestess through whom the god answered the question. 3. The answer or prophecy made by the god. 4. A wise person from whom advice is asked. **oracles.**

o·ral (OR-əl) *adjective.* 1. Spoken: an *oral* report. 2. Relating to the mouth. —**orally** *adverb.*

or·ange (OR-inj) *noun.* 1. A sweet-tasting citrus fruit. 2. The tree on which this fruit grows. 3. (Also *adjective*) A reddish-yellow color.

o·rang·u·tan (oh-RANG-ə-tan or ə-RANG-ə-tan) Also **orangutang** *noun.* A large ape that has long arms and no tail and lives in trees in the forests of Borneo and Sumatra.

o·ra·tion (or-AY-shən) *noun.* A formal speech.

or·a·tor (OR-ə-tər) *noun.* 1. A person

who gives an oration. 2. A person skilled at public speaking.

orb *noun.* 1. A sphere or globe. 2. A heavenly body, as a star. 3. The eye.

or·bit (OR-bit) *noun.* 1. The path traveled by a heavenly body or a man-made satellite around another heavenly body. 2. An area of experience or influence: Cooking is out of my *orbit.* —*verb.* To travel around (a heavenly body) in an orbit. **orbited, orbiting.**

orbital velocity. The speed at which a body must move in order to stay in an orbit: The closer to a planet a satellite orbits the faster the *orbital velocity.*

or·chard (OR-chərd) *noun.* A piece of land on which fruit or nut trees are grown, or the trees themselves.

or·ches·tra (OR-kess-trə) *noun.* 1. A group of musicians who perform together. 2. The place just below the front of a stage, where musicians sit. 3. The main floor of a theater or the section in front of the musicians. **orchestras.**

or·chid (OR-kid) *noun.* 1. A tropical flower of unusual shape and color. 2. The plant on which this flower grows. 3. (Also *adjective*) A light purple color.

or·dain (or-DAYN) *verb.* 1. To decree by law or fate: "We, the people. . . do *ordain* and establish this Constitution. . . ." (U.S. Constitution). 2. To consecrate as a minister of God or give holy orders to. **ordained, ordaining.**

or·deal (or-DEEL) *noun.* A severely difficult and trying experience or test.

or·der (OR-dər) *noun.* 1. The way in which one thing follows another: numerical *order.* 2. A state where everything is correctly or neatly placed: The room was in good *order.* 3. A command: a doctor's *order.* 4. A request for something wanted: Mother phoned her *order* to the butcher. 5. A serving of food in a restaurant: an *order* of soup. 6. Proper conduct: The police maintain law and *order.* 7. A group of persons living under the same religious rules. —*verb.* 1. To command. 2. To ask that something be done. **ordered, ordering.**

or·der·ly (OR-dər-lee) *adjective.* 1. In order; neat or tidy. 2. Well-behaved or peaceful. —*noun.* 1. A soldier who waits on an officer. 2. A man who works in a hospital doing chores. **orderlies.**

or·di·nal (ORD-n-əl) *adjective.* Showing a place in a numbered series.

ordinal number. A number showing placement in a series: Fifth (5th) is an *ordinal number.*

or·di·nance (ORD-n-ənss) *noun.* A rule or law, often local. **ordinances.**

or·di·nar·i·ly (ord-n-EHR-ə-lee) *adverb.* Usually.

or·di·nary (ORD-n-ehr-ee) adjective. 1. Usual: My *ordinary* bedtime is nine o'clock. 2. Common, not special.

ord·nance (ORD-nənss) *noun.* 1. Military weapons and things connected with them. 2. Heavy weapons; artillery.

ore (OR) *noun.* Any natural material containing minerals from which metal can be extracted. **ores.**

Or·e·gon (OR-ə-gən or OR-ə-gon) *noun.* A Pacific state of the United States, 33rd to join the Union (1859) —**Oreg.** *abbreviation.* Also **OR** for Zip Codes.

or·gan (OR-gən) *noun.* 1. A musical instrument made up of a keyboard and pipes through which air is blown. 2. Any part of an organism that has a particular use: an *organ* of sight. 3. A means of action; a medium or instrument: an *organ* of justice. 4. A means of communication, especially a publication of a firm or organization: a house *organ.*

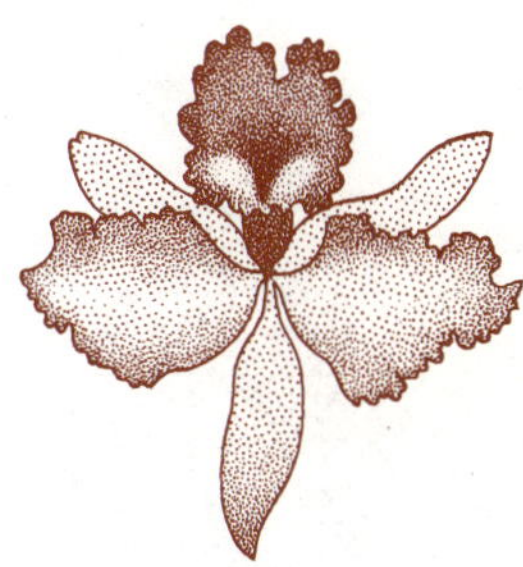

orchid

orchestra

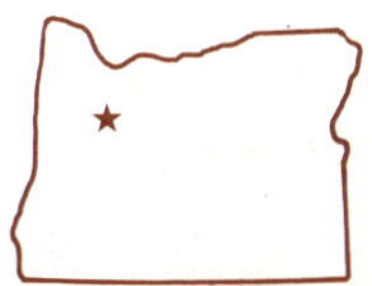

Oregon
★capital: Salem

or·gan·ic (or-GAN-ik) *adjective.* 1. Having to do with living organs or organisms. 2. Having interrelated parts that fit or work together to form a single unit: an *organic* whole. 3. (Chemistry) Having to do with carbon compounds.

or·gan·ism (OR-gə-niz-əm) *noun.* 1. Any living individual, animal, or plant. 2. That which is similar to an organism; a whole made up of parts, the workings of which affect each other: A family is a small social *organism.*

or·gan·ist (OR-gə-nist) *noun.* A person who plays an organ.

or·gan·i·za·tion (or-gən-ə-ZAY-shən) *noun.* 1. A group formed to accomplish a special purpose. 2. The state of being put together, planned, or organized: *Organization* makes the household run smoothly. —**organizational** *adjective.*

oriole

or·gan·ize (OR-gən-ighz) *verb.* 1. To put together or arrange in order. 2. To form a labor union or other group. **organized, organizing.**

o·ri·ent (OR-ee-ənt) *noun.* 1. The east. 2. [Capital O] The countries of eastern Asia: Thailand, China, and Japan are parts of the *Orient.* —*verb* (OR-ee-ent) 1. To place in a particular direction: Mother wants to *orient* the front of our new cabin to the south. 2. To get one's bearings; adjust to a position or new situation by noting related landmarks or facts: It didn't take the new pupil long to *orient* himself to the layout of our school. **oriented, orienting.**

or·i·gin (OR-ə-jin) *noun.* 1. The beginning or source: the *origin* of a river. 2. Ancestry or parentage.

o·rig·i·nal (ə-RIJ-ən-l) *adjective.* 1. The first: the *original* owner. 2. New; first of its kind: *original* menus. 3. Inventive or creative: Einstein had many *original* ideas. —*noun.* 1. The first form of something: The revision of my essay is better than the *original.* 2. A work of art or other unique item from which copies are made: The *original* of the U.S. Constitution is in the National Archives Building. —**originally** *adverb.*

o·rig·i·nal·i·ty (ə-rij-ə-NAL-ə-tee) *noun.* 1. The quality of being original, fresh, or new: the *originality* of a design. 2. The ability to think, do, or create in a new or original way: His composition shows his *originality.*

o·rig·i·nate (ə-RIJ-ə-nayt) *verb.* 1. To invent; create; make for the first time: I *originated* a new system. 2. To begin; come about; arise: The custom of shaking hands *originated* long ago. **originated, originating.**

o·ri·ole (OR-ee-ohl) *noun.* A songbird of America and Europe with black and yellow or orange feathers. **orioles.**

or·na·ment (OR-nə-mənt) *noun.* 1. A decoration; something that improves or adds beauty: Christmas tree *ornaments.* 2. A person who adds honor or beauty to a group, place, etc., by being part of it: Martha Washington was an *ornament* to Virginia society. —(OR-nə-ment) *verb.* To decorate; make more attractive; add ornaments to. **ornamented, ornamenting.**

or·na·men·tal (or-nə-MENT-l) *adjective.* Used as an ornament; adding beauty: an *ornamental* plant. —**ornamentally** *adverb.*

or·nate (or-NAYT) *adjective.* Very showy; having much decoration: The fancy French chairs looked *ornate.* —**ornately** *adverb.*

or·ner·y (OR-nə-ree) *adjective.* (Slang) Mean, bad-tempered; stubborn.

or·phan (OR-fən) *noun.* A child whose parents are dead. —*verb.* To make an orphan: The flood *orphaned* many children. **orphaned, orphaning.**

or·phan·age (OR-fə-nij) *noun.* A home where orphans are cared for.

or·tho·don·tist (or-thə-DON-tist) *noun.* A dentist who specializes in straightening the teeth, usually of young people.

or·tho·dox (OR-thə-doks) *adjective.* 1. Generally accepted; usual; proper in religion, morals, politics, etc. 2. Holding to strict or traditional beliefs in religion —**orthodoxly** *adverb.* —**orthodoxy** *noun.*

-ory *suffix.* Indicates: 1. A place for or means of: deposit*ory* 2. Doing the job of or having the effect of: inflammat*ory.*

os·cil·lo·scope (ə-SIL-ə-skohp) *noun.* An instrument that shows on a special screen a wave-like image representing an electric current. **oscilloscopes.**

-os·i·ty *suffix.* A word ending used to make adjectives ending in *-ous* and *-ose* into nouns, as "curious" into "curi*osity.*"

os·prey (oss-pree or oss-pray) *noun.* A large brown-and-white hawk that feeds on fish; a fish hawk.

os·tra·cize (oss-trə-sighz) *verb.* To bar, banish, or shut out; refuse to have any dealings with. **ostracized, ostracizing.**

os·trich (oss-trich or AWSS-trich) *noun.* A large, long-legged flightless bird, found especially in dry regions of Asia and Africa: An *ostrich* can run fast because of its powerful legs. —**ostriches** or **ostrich** *plural.*

o·ther (UTH-ər) *adjective.* 1. Different; not the same; another: I will give you some *other* toy. 2. More; additional: We have no *other* games to play. 3. Remaining: Tell Mary the *other* girls are late for the meeting. 4. Not this; the second of two: I live on this side of the street; Mary lives on the *other* side. —*pronoun.* 1. (Plural) More persons or things: Many *others* have color TV sets. 2. Not this one; the second one of two: I don't like this one; I prefer the *other.*

o·ther·wise (UHTH-ər-wighz) *adverb.* 1. In another way; differently: Many wanted slavery, but Lincoln felt *otherwise.* 2. In every other way: He's very sloppy, but *otherwise* he's a fine man. 3. Or else: He likes it; *otherwise* he'd make a face. —*adjective.* Different; anything else: John is always honest; he doesn't know how to be *otherwise.*

ot·ter (OT-ər) *noun.* 1. A furry water animal with a long tail and webbed feet: The *otter* has playful habits. 2. The thick, shiny fur of the otter, usually a dark brown color.

ouch (OWCH) *interjection.* A cry made when one feels sudden pain.

ought (AWT) A helping verb, used with *to,* expressing: 1. Duty: You *ought* to call. 2. Likeliness or probability: It *ought* to be cold.

ounce (OWNSS) *noun.* 1. A unit of weight: 16 *ounces* make one pound. 2. A liquid measure: 16 *ounces* make one pint. 3. Just a little: an *ounce* of courage. **ounces.**

our (OWR) *pronoun.* Belonging to oneself and one or more other persons: *Our* secret password is "ghost."

ours (OWRZ) *pronoun.* Something that belongs to oneself and one or more other persons: Ed's kite is flying but *ours* is stuck in a tree.

our·selves (OWR-selvz) *pronoun, plural.* A form of *we* used: 1. For emphasis: We will save the money *ourselves.* 2. When the subject and object of a verb are the same: We scared *ourselves.* 3. To describe a normal or usual state: We will be *ourselves* again after we have some lunch.

-ous *suffix.* Indicates fullness; likeness; possession: beaute*ous.*

oust (OWST) *verb.* To drive out; force to leave: *oust* the enemy. **ousted, ousting.** —**ouster** *noun.*

osprey

otter

ostrich

out (OWT) *adverb.* 1. Outward; from a place: pop *out* of a hole. 2. Away, as from a home: Dad went *out.* 3. To a non-burning state: The fire went *out.* 4. Plainly; aloud: Call *out* if you need help. 5. Omitted: leave *out* a word. 6. (Baseball) In such a way as to be retired from play: strike *out.* 7. Thoroughly; entirely: We are worn *out.* 8. From among others: Pick *out* a good book. 9. To other people: He rents *out* the top floor. —*adjective.* 1. Away; not at home, school, work, etc.: I will be *out* until ten. 2. Not lighted any more; not burning: The lamp is *out.* 3. Wrong; mistaken. 4. Known; published: The truth is *out* now. 5. Bare; exposed: *out* at elbows. 6. Having had a loss of: I am *out* 50 cents. 7. Not having: *out* of work. —*noun.* 1. A means of escape: I had no *out* when I was caught. 2. One not in political office. 3. (Baseball) A retiring or being retired from play. —*preposition.* Forward from; through: The canary flew *out* the window. —**out-and-out.** Thorough; complete.

out- *prefix.* Indicates: 1. A greater degree; a higher level: *out*distance. 2. An outer place: *out*doors.

outboard motor

outboard motor. A small gasoline motor attached to the outside of the stern, or back, of a boat.

out·break (OUT-brayk) *noun.* 1. A sudden breaking out; an outburst. 2. A disturbance or riot.

out·build·ing (OWT-bil-ding) *noun.* A building or shed not far from a main building or house.

out·burst (OWT-berst) *noun.* 1. A bursting forth: an *outburst* of applause. 2. A sudden show of powerful feeling: an *outburst* of anger.

out·cast (OWT-kast) *noun.* 1. One who has been cast out; one that others will have nothing to do with. 2. A wanderer without a home.

out·come (OWT-kuhm) *noun.* The result; the way a thing comes out.

out·cry (OWT-krigh) *noun.* A crying out; a sudden shout of protest or anger. **outcries.**

out·dis·tance (owt-DISS-tənss) *verb.* To leave far behind. **outdistanced, outdistancing.**

out·do (OWT-DOO) *verb.* To do something better than; be more effective than: I can't *outdo* my brother at chess. **outdid** (owt-DID), **outdone** (owt-DUHN), **outdoing.**

out·door (OWT-dor) *adjective.* Belonging, happening, or done out in the open or outside a building.

out·doors (owt-DORZ) *adverb.* Out-of-doors; not in a building or indoors; in or into the open air. —*noun.* The open air; the world outside.

out·er (OWT-ər) *adjective.* On the outside; closer to the outside; farther out: *outer* space.

out·er·most (OWT-ər-mohst) *adjective.* Farthest from the inside; farthest out: the *outermost* layer.

out·field (OWT-feeld) *noun.* (Baseball) 1. The part of the field that is beyond the diamond or infield. 2. The three outfield players.

out·field·er (OWT-feeld-ər) *noun.* (Baseball) A player whose position is in the outfield.

out·fit (OWT-fit) *noun.* 1. The clothing and/or equipment or supplies needed for some job or purpose: A rifle is part of a soldier's *outfit.* 2. A group of people who work together; a unit of the armed forces: Many soldiers in Uncle Stan's *outfit* were wounded. —*verb.* To provide (with an outfit): The hikers were *outfitted* with warm clothes. **outfitted, outfitting.**

out·go·ing (OWT-goh-ing) *adjective.* 1. Leaving; going out: an *outgoing* plane. 2. Warm and friendly; sociable: an *outgoing* person.

out·grow (owt-GROH) *verb.* 1. To grow too big for: Dave *outgrows* his clothing very fast. 2. To grow away from; lose as one grows older: She has *outgrown* her interest in collecting stamps. 3. To grow faster or bigger than: Mary is *outgrowing* all the boys in her class. **outgrew** (owt-GROO), **outgrown** (owt-GROHN), **outgrowing.**

out·growth (OWT-grohth) *noun.* 1. A natural result or development: The truce was an *outgrowth* of the peace talks. 2. That which grows out of or on something else; an offshoot: A wart is an *outgrowth.*

out·ing (OWT-ing) *noun.* A short outdoor trip for pleasure.

out·land·ish (owt-LAN-dish) *adjective.* Ridiculous; strange or unusual; not familiar. —**outlandishly** *adverb.*

out·last (owt-LAST) *verb.* To last longer than: My suit coat *outlasted* the pants. **outlasted, outlasting.**

out·law (OWT-law) *noun.* A bandit; one who has done things that are against the law. —*verb.* To declare or make unlawful; forbid: Should cigarettes be *outlawed?* **outlawed, outlawing.**

out·lay (OWT-lay) *noun.* The act of spending or laying out; the amount that is spent or paid: Our vacation plans call for an *outlay* of money.

out·let (OWT-let) *noun.* 1. A passage or other means for letting something out: the *outlet* of a sewage system. 2. A place where a power supply can be tapped: an electric *outlet* in a wall. 3. A place to sell goods; a store: The company needs more *outlets.* 4. A way to use or satisfy: an *outlet* in art.

out·line (OWT-lighn) *noun.* 1. A line that runs (or seems to run) along the edge of a thing and shows its shape: In the twilight I saw the *outline* of a house. 2. A drawing that shows only the outer line of a shape, without shading: Some cartoons are little more than *outlines.* 3. A general plan, sketch, or report that gives only the most important facts: Write an *outline* of the book. **outlines.** —*verb.* To make an outline. **outlined, outlining.**

out·live (owt-LIV) *verb.* To live or last longer than (others); survive. **outlived, outliving.**

out·look (OWT-luk) *noun.* 1. The view; what one sees when one looks out: I like the *outlook* from the porch. 2. What can be expected to happen: With our best player sick, the *outlook* for our team is not good. 3. Point of view; the way a person thinks.

out·ly·ing (OWT-ligh-ing) *adjective.* Far from the center or the main body; out-of-the-way: an *outlying* district.

out·mod·ed (owt-MOH-did) *adjective.* Out-of-date; not in fashion or general use any longer: an *outmoded* dress.

out·num·ber (owt-NUHM-bər) *verb.* To be more in number than: Girls *outnumber* boys in our class. **outnumbered, outnumbering.**

out-of-date (owt-əv-DAYT) *adjective.* Old-fashioned; not in general use.

out-of-doors (owt-əv-DORZ) *adverb and noun.* Outdoors.

out·post (OWT-pohst) *noun.* 1. A station or post placed some distance from a main body of troops to guard them and warn them in case of attack. 2. The troops stationed at such a place. 3. An outlying settlement; a frontier settlement.

out·rage (OWT-rayj) *noun.* 1. A cruel and violent act that shows no respect for the feelings or rights of others. 2. A feeling of anger caused by an insult or unjust act: The Indians showed their *outrage* by attacking the settlement. **outrages.** —*verb.* To offend greatly. **outraged, outraging.**

out·ra·geous (owt-RAY-jəss) *adjective.* 1. Shocking; very bad. 2. Doing great harm. —**outrageously** *adverb.*

out·rig·ger (OWT-rig-ər) *noun.* 1. A framework with a float on the end that is attached to a boat to keep it from turning over. 2. A boat with such a framework attached.

outrigger

out·right (OWT-right) *adjective.* 1. Total; complete: Only an *outright* fool turns down such a good chance. 2. Direct or straightforward: an *outright* insult. —*adverb.* 1. Entirely; completely; in one deal: We will buy the equipment *outright.* 2. Openly; without reserve: She cried *outright.* 3. On the spot; at once: The soldiers fired, killing many *outright.*

out·run (owt-RUHN) *verb.* 1. To run faster or farther than: I can *outrun* him by a mile. 2. To go beyond; leave behind; exceed: His desire to work *outruns* his strength. **outran, outrunning.**

out·set (OWT-set) *noun.* A start or beginning: From the *outset* our visit was a happy one.

out·side (owt-SIGHD or OWT-sighd) *noun.* The outer part or surface: The *outside* of the barn is made of wood. —*adjective.* 1. Outer or exterior: The *outside* surface of the house was made of brick. 2. Coming from another place: *Outside* experts came to study our city's problems. 3. Extreme; far-fetched: There is only an *outside* chance that it will rain. —*adverb.* On or to the outer part; outdoors. —*preposition.* 1. On or to the outer part of: She ran *outside* the house. 2. Except for: *Outside* of Jim, there are only girls in the group.

oval

out·sid·er (owt-SIGHD-ər) *noun.* A person who is not from a certain place or part of a certain group or organization.

out·skirts (OWT-skerts) *noun, plural.* The areas near the border or just outside a town or other place.

out·spo·ken (owt-SPOH-kən) *adjective.* Not reserved or shy in speaking out; very frank. —**outspokenly** *adverb.*

out·spread (OWT-spred) *adjective.* Spread out; in an opened position: The duck landed with *outspread* wings.

out·stand·ing (OWT-stan-ding or owt-STAN-ding) *adjective.* 1. Excellent; unusually capable: Glenn is an *outstanding* pitcher. 2. Unpaid: Uncle Ed has several *outstanding* debts. —**outstandingly** *adverb.*

out·strip (owt-STRIP) *verb.* 1. To do better than; exceed. 2. To run or go faster than; outrun: **outstripped, outstripping.**

out·ward (OWT-wərd) *adjective.* 1. Outer; related to the outside. 2. Going away or toward the outside: The *outward* voyage took us away from the port. 3. External; related to the way that things appear: The actor's *outward* appearance was calm. —*adverb.* Also **outwards, outwardly.** Toward or on the outside or outer part.

out·weigh (owt-WAY) *verb.* 1. To have more weight than: Otto *outweighs* Tim by 20 pounds. 2. To have more importance or significance than: The reasons for staying *outweighed* those for leaving. **outweighed, outweighing.**

out·wit (out-WIT) *verb.* To overcome by being shrewd or clever. **outwitted, outwitting.**

out·worn (OWT-worn) *adjective.* 1. Worn-out; shabby: Mother used our *outworn* clothes as cleaning rags. 2. Out-of-date; old-fashioned: *outworn* customs.

o·val (OH-vəl) *adjective.* Shaped like an egg: The racetrack is *oval* in design. —*noun.* Something that is egg-shaped. —**ovally** *adverb.*

o·va·ry (OH-və-ree) *noun.* 1. One of a pair of glands in females that produce eggs that may become offspring. 2. A plant part in which seeds are produced. **ovaries.**

o·va·tion (oh-VAY-shən) *noun.* An outburst of cheering and applause; a spirited welcome.

ov·en (UHV-ən) *noun.* A device or compartment in which foods or other items are baked or dried.

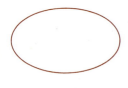

o·ver (OH-vər) *preposition.* 1. Above: A flag fluttered *over* the fort. 2. Above and beyond: The bird flew *over* the lake. 3. So as to cover. 4. To or at the other side; across: The soldiers crossed *over* the ocean. 5. Beyond and down from: The bowl fell *over* the edge of the table. 6. Throughout; in all areas of: The disease spread *over* the country. 7. During: *over* the years. 8. More than: *over* three dollars. 9. With regard to: We fought *over* the ball. 10. Higher in rank or importance than: A major is *over* a sergeant. —*adverb.* 1. Above and beyond: I heard a plane fly *over.* 2. From one side to the other: When the bridge opened, the train crossed *over.* 3. Beyond, as an edge or limit: The log near the waterfall soon drifted *over.* 4. Sideways or upside down: Turn the cards *over.* 5. In a manner that covers: The lake was frozen *over.* 6. From one person or thing to another: Hand it *over.* 7. Again: Do your homework *over.* 8. In addition: Is anything left *over?* 9. In all details: Think the problem *over* carefully. —*adjective.* 1. At an end; through: The party is *over.* 2. (Slang) Cooked on both sides.

over- *prefix.* Indicates higher or greater rank or amount: *over*eat.

o·ver·all (OH-vər-awl) *adjective.* Considering or including everything.

o·ver·alls (OH-vər-awlz) *noun, plural.* Work trousers of a coarse material, usually with a section that covers the chest, often worn over other clothes to protect them.

o·ver·bear·ing (oh-vər-BAIR-ing) *adjective.* Inclined to dominate or take charge; bossy.

o·ver·board (OH-vər-bord) *adverb.* Over the side of a ship into the water: The sailor fell *overboard.*

o·ver·cast (OH-vər-kast or oh-vər-KAST) *adjective.* Cloudy; gloomy.

o·ver·coat (OH-vər-koht) *noun.* A coat worn over indoor clothing.

o·ver·come (oh-vər-KUHM) *verb.* 1. To defeat; conquer. 2. To be successful or rise above some difficulty or problem: *overcome* a handicap. 3. To overwhelm; exhaust or make ill. **overcame, overcome, overcoming.**

o·ver·do (oh-vər-DOO) *verb.* 1. To do too much. 2. Exaggerate: He will believe your tall tale if you don't *overdo* it. 3. To cook too long. **overdid, overdone, overdoing.**

o·ver·dose (oh-ver-DOHSS) Also **overdosage** *noun.* Too large a dose or quantity, especially of medicine or drugs. **overdoses** or **overdosages.**

o·ver·due (oh-vər-DOO or oh-vər-DYOO) *adjective.* Beyond the scheduled time for arrival or payment: The train is *overdue.*

o·ver·eat (oh-vər-EET) *verb.* To eat too much. **overate, overeaten, overeating.**

o·ver·flow (oh-vər-FLOH) *verb.* To flow or pour over (the edge or rim): The coffee *overflowed* the rim of the cup. **overflowed, overflowing.** —(OH-vər-floh) *noun.* 1. An abundance or surplus: an *overflow* of grain. 2. Something that flows over: A saucer caught the *overflow* from the cup.

o·ver·grow (oh-vər-GROH or OH-vər-groh) *verb.* To cover or grow over, as with weeds or vines. **overgrew, overgrown, overgrowing.**

o·ver·hang (oh-vər-HANG) *verb.* To extend beyond; hang over: Maple branches *overhang* the shady path. **overhung, overhanging.** —(OH-vər-hang) *noun.* A part that extends beyond or hangs over: The *overhang* of the barn roof gave us shelter.

o·ver·haul (oh-vər-HAWL or OH-vər-hawl) *verb.* 1. To examine and repair: We found two loose wires when we *overhauled* our lawn mower. 2. To overtake; catch up with. **overhauled, overhauling.** —(OH-vər-hawl) *noun.* An examination and repair: Dad left our car at the garage for an *overhaul.*

o·ver·head (OH-vər-hed) *adjective* and (oh-vər-HED) *adverb.* Over or above the head. —(OH-vər-hed) *noun.* The expenses involved in running a store or business: Rent is part of a store's *overhead.*

o·ver·hear (oh-vər-HIHR) *verb.* To hear by chance: *overhear* a secret. **overheard, overhearing.**

o·ver·joyed (oh-vər-JOID) *adjective.* Delighted; filled with joy.

o·ver·lap (oh-vər-LAP) *verb.* To lie over the edge of; partially cover: The shingles *overlap* one another. **overlapped, overlapping.**

o·ver·lay (oh-vər-LAY) *verb.* To cover or spread over, as with a decorative coating: The steel watch was *overlaid* with silver. **overlaid, overlaying.** —(OH-vər-lay) *noun.* 1. A coating or cover, especially a decorative one. 2. A transparent cover or sheet containing sketches or other features, placed over an illustration such as a map or diagram to make additional information available.

o·ver·load (oh-vər-LOHD) *verb.* To load or fill too heavily or too much: The man *overloaded* his donkey with firewood. **overloaded, overloading.** —(OH-vər-lohd) *noun.* A load or amount that is too much.

o·ver·look (oh-vər-LUK) *verb.* 1. To ignore; fail to notice. 2. To have a view of from above; be over: The mountain cabin *overlooks* the valley below. 3. To excuse; pretend not to notice: We *overlooked* the insult.

o·ver·pass (OH-vər-pass) *noun.* A bridge or elevated section of roadway or railroad track that carries traffic over a second roadway or other obstacle.

overpasses

o·ver·pow·er (oh-vər-POW-ər) *verb.* To overcome; conquer. **overpowered, overpowering.**

o·ver·rate (oh-vər-RAYT) *verb.* To rate or rank too highly: The coach *overrated* his new runner. **overrated, overrating.**

o·ver·rule (oh-vər-ROOL) *verb.* 1. To rule or decide against: The judge *overruled* the decision to fire the policeman. 2. To show more power or influence than: The 20 men who voted for the law *overruled* the 12 who voted against it. **overruled, overruling.**

o·ver·run (oh-vər-RUHN) *verb.* 1. To spread or grow over, especially in a harmful manner; infest: *overrun* with weeds. 2. To conquer; overpower. **overran, overrun, overruning.**

o·ver·seas (oh-vər-SEEZ or OH-vər-seez) *adverb* and *adjective.* Across the sea; to or in a foreign place.

o·ver·see (oh-vər-SEE) *verb.* To watch over; manage. **oversaw, overseen overseeing.** —**overseer** (OH-vər-see-ər) *noun.*

o·ver·shad·ow (oh-vər-SHAD-oh) *verb.* To be more significant or important than: The news of the explosion *overshadowed* other news. **overshadowed, overshadowing.**

o·ver·shoe (OH-vər-shoo) *noun.* (Usually plural) Boots worn over shoes to protect the feet in cold or wet weather. **overshoes.**

o·ver·sight (OH-vər-sight) *noun.* An unintentional error.

o·ver·sleep (oh-vər-SLEEP) *verb.* To sleep longer than one should. **overslept, oversleeping.**

o·ver·state (oh-vər-STAYT) *verb.* To overstress; exaggerate. **overstated, overstating.** —**overstatement** *noun.*

o·ver·step (oh-vər-STEP) *verb.* To exceed; go beyond, as a right or limit. **overstepped, overstepping.**

o·ver·take (oh-vər-TAYK) *verb.* To catch up with. **overtook, overtaken, overtaking.**

o·ver·throw (oh-vər-THROH) *verb.* To defeat; put out of power: The rebels planned to *overthrow* the government. **overthrew, overthrown, overthrowing.** —(OH-vər-throh) *noun.* A bringing to an end; putting out of power.

o·ver·time (OH-vər-tighm) *noun.* 1. A period beyond a scheduled time or limit, as of work or a game: Our team won by two points in *overtime.* 2. Time worked beyond the usual limit. 3. Money paid for such work: The salesman made 20 dollars in *overtime.*

o·ver·tone (OH-vər-tohn) *noun.* 1. A suggestion or hint: The principal's comments had an *overtone* of humor. 2. (Music) A fainter tone produced with the main tone. **overtones.**

o·ver·ture (OH-vər-chur) *noun.* A piece of music that introduces a longer work, as an opera. **overtures.**

o·ver·turn (oh-vər-TERN) *verb.* 1. To turn over; upset: The violent storm *overturned* several sailboats. 2. To defeat; overthrow: The rebels *overturned* the government. **overturned, overturning.**

o·ver·weight (oh-ver-WAYT) *adjective.* Above the normal or permitted weight. —(OH-vər-wayt) *noun.* Weight that is above what is normal or healthy.

o·ver·whelm (oh-vər-HWELM) *verb.* 1. To overcome or defeat completely. 2. To cover completely: The rushing flood waters *overwhelmed* the farmland. **overwhelmed, overwhelming.**

o·vule (OH-vyool) *noun.* 1. A very small plant part that develops into a seed. 2. In female animals, a very small or undeveloped egg. **ovules.**

owe (OH) *verb.* 1. To have to pay; have a debt: I *owe* Bob 50 cents. 2. To be morally obliged to give: We *owe* respect to our parents. **owed, owing.** —**owing to.** Because of; due (to).

owl *noun.* A bird with a large head and eyes that are directed forward out of a flat face: The *owl* hunts at night.

own (OHN) *verb.* To possess or have. **owned, owning.** —*adjective.* Belonging to oneself: The boy has his *own* bike. —*noun.* That which belongs to oneself: The mother hen raised the duckling as if it were her *own.* —**own up.** To admit or confess.

own·er (OHN-ər) *noun.* The person to whom something belongs.

own·er·ship (OHN-ər-ship) *noun.* The state or condition of holding or possessing something: He had papers to prove his *ownership.*

ox (OKS) *noun.* 1. A large hoofed animal with two toes on each foot, a long tail, and horns. 2. A full-grown male member of the cattle family raised and trained to do work such as plowing. —**oxen** (OK-sən) *plural.*

ox·bow (OKS-boh) *noun.* 1. A curved U-shaped collar worn by a working ox. 2. A bend in a river shaped like such a collar.

ox·cart (OKS-kahrt) *noun.* A small wagon drawn by oxen.

ox·ford (OKS-fərd) *noun.* A low shoe that is laced and tied over the instep or front of the foot.

ox·i·da·tion (ok-sə-DAY-shən) *noun.* The process by which a substance combines with oxygen: Burning is rapid *oxidation.*

ox·ide (OK-sighd) *noun.* A compound formed when oxygen combines with another substance. **oxides.**

ox·i·dize (OK-sə-dighz) *verb.* To combine with oxygen. **oxidized, oxidizing.**

ox·y·gen (OK-si-jən) *noun.* A gas that has no color, odor, or taste and makes up about one-fifth of the air surrounding the earth.

oys·ter (OISS-tər) *noun.* A saltwater shellfish found in shallow parts of the ocean: The soft body of the *oyster* is protected by a hard two-part shell.

oz. *abbreviation.* Ounce.

o·zone (OH-zohn) *noun.* 1. A form of oxygen: *Ozone* is blue gas created when an electrical charge passes through ordinary oxygen. 2. (Informal) Fresh air.

oxen

oxcart

owl

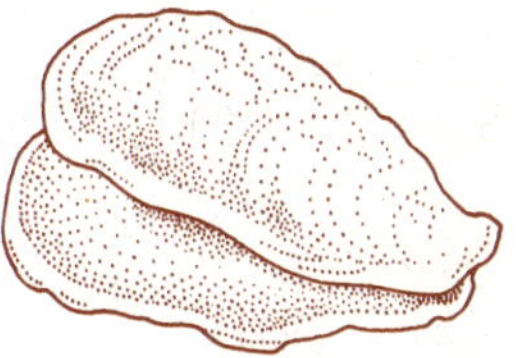
oyster

P, p (PEE) *noun.* The 16th letter of the English alphabet.

pa (PAH) *noun.* (Informal) Father; a short form of *papa.*

pace (PAYSS) *noun.* 1. One long step; a stride. 2. The distance covered by a pace: 20 *paces* from the house. 3. A rate of moving or of doing something: a very fast *pace.* 4. A certain gait of a horse in which both legs on one side are raised when those on the other side are lowered. **paces.** —*verb.* 1. To step or walk, especially back and forth: *pace* up and down the hall. 2. To measure by counting one's paces or steps: *pace* off the length of the room. **paced, pacing.** —**put through one's paces.** To have someone demonstrate his talents or ability. —**set the pace.** To establish a speed or standard for others to equal or exceed.

pace·mak·er (PAYSS-may-kər) *noun.* 1. A person who leads or sets the pace in a race. 2. A person who sets an example or is outstanding in any activity. 3. (Medicine) An electronic device used to regulate the heartbeat.

pa·cif·ic (pə-SIF-ik) *adjective.* 1. Making or encouraging peace. 2. Peaceful; tranquil.

pac·i·fist (PASS-ə-fist) *noun.* A person who is opposed to war or violence, especially one who refuses to fight in the armed forces.

pac·i·fy (PASS-ə-figh) *verb.* 1. To make peaceful; stop violence or war. 2. To calm; make quiet: Pacify the crying baby. **pacified, pacifying.** —**pacification** (pass-ə-fə-KAY-shən) *noun.*

pack (PAK) *noun.* 1. A tied bundle; a sack or other container for carrying things on the back. 2. A package containing a standard number of items: a *pack* of cards. 3. A group of animals; crowd: Wolves often travel in *packs.* 4. (Informal) A set, amount, or number (of things): Jim found a *pack* of magazines. 5. A large mass of ice and snow crushed together. —*verb.* 1. To fill a trunk, bundle, or other container. 2. To wrap or put into a bundle or package: Mother *packed* my lunch. 3. To crowd; cram: The fans *packed* the arena. 4. To press down; make more solid. 5. To fill in, as to prevent drafts or leaks: use clay to *pack* the holes. 6. (Informal) To carry: The man *packed* a gun. 7. (Informal) To have; be able to give: A mule *packs* a powerful kick. **packed, packing.** —**pack off.** To send (someone) away. —**send packing.** To send (someone) away in a hasty fashion.

pack·age (PAK-ij) *noun.* A bundle or box; a group of things wrapped together. **packages.** —*verb.* To wrap or form into a bundle, especially for selling. **packaged, packaging.**

pack·et (PAK-it) *noun.* 1. A small package. 2. A boat that carries passengers or goods on a regular schedule, usually on a river.

pact (PAKT) *noun.* An agreement; treaty.

pad *noun.* 1. A cushion; a mass of soft material used to protect or make comfortable. 2. The soft layer on the bottom of the feet of dogs and some other animals. 3. A number of sheets of paper fastened together along one edge; tablet. 4. The large, floating leaf of a water lily or other water plant. 5. The surface area from which a rocket is launched. 6. (Slang) A small apartment or room of one's own.

—verb. 1. To fill or cover with soft material. 2. To add unnecessary words to a speech or written work. 3. To add items dishonestly, as on a bill or expense account. 4. To walk quietly. **padded, padding.**

pad·dle (PAD-l) *noun.* 1. A short oar with a broad blade, used with both hands to move a canoe or boat through the water. 2. Anything shaped like this, often used for striking or beating: Ping-Pong *paddle.* 3. One of the boards of a paddle wheel. **paddles.** *—verb.* 1. To move (a canoe or boat) through water with a paddle. 2. To strike or spank with a paddle or similar object. 3. To splash or move about in the water by moving the hands and feet rapidly. **paddled, paddling.**

paddle wheel. A large wheel turned by steam or other power and fitted with paddles that move a boat through water.

pad·dock (PAD-ək) *noun.* 1. A fenced area close to a stable where horses graze or exercise. 2. A fenced area near a racetrack where horses are kept before a race.

pad·dy (PAD-ee) *noun.* An irrigated field for growing rice. **paddies.**

pad·lock (PAD-lok) *noun.* A lock, easily attached or removed, that has a curved bar that snaps shut over a chain or rod. *—verb.* To attach or lock with a padlock. **padlocked, padlocking.**

pa·gan (PAY-gən) *noun.* 1. A person who is not a Christian, Jew, or Moslem, especially one who has no religion. 2. One who worships more than one god, as in ancient Greece and Rome.

[1]**page** (PAYJ) *noun.* 1. One side or surface of a sheet of paper: A sheet of paper printed on both sides constitutes two *pages.* 2. A single sheet of paper in a book. **pages.** *—verb.* 1. To number the pages of. 2. To turn the pages: *page* through a book. **paged, paging.**

[2]**page** (PAYJ) *noun.* 1. An employee who runs errands, carries messages, and does similar jobs. 2. In former times, a young man who acted as a servant to a knight or other person of high rank. **pages.** *—verb.* To try to find someone by calling out his name, often over a public-address system. **paged, paging.**

pag·eant (PAJ-ənt) *noun.* 1. An exciting and colorful parade, show, or other entertainment. 2. A public drama or show that re-creates a historical event.

pa·go·da (pə-GOH-də) *noun.* A temple, common in Oriental countries, that is shaped like a tower of many tiers.

paid (PAYD) *verb. See* **pay.**

pail (PAYL) *noun.* 1. A container with a handle, used to hold and carry liquids; bucket. 2. A pailful.

pail·ful (PAYL-ful) *noun.* The amount that can be held in a pail.

pain (PAYN) *noun.* 1. The suffering or hurt that comes from injury, sickness, or misfortune. 2. (Plural) Great effort or care: take *pains* to do it right. 3. (Slang) A bother. *—verb.* To cause pain or suffering to. **pained, paining. —under pain of.** Faced with the penalty of. **—pain in the neck.** (Slang) A troublesome person or thing; a bother.

pains·tak·ing (PAYNZ-tayk-ing) *adjective.* Done with great effort or care; very careful. **—painstakingly** *adverb.*

paint (PAYNT) *noun.* A mixture of coloring matter and oil, water, or another liquid, used to cover a surface. *—verb.* 1. To cover with paint. 2. To make a picture with paints. 3. To represent (something) in a painting: The artist *painted* a seaside scene. 4. To describe in detail: *paint* an exciting story. 5. To cover or apply (something) as with paint: *paint* a cut with iodine. **painted, painting.**

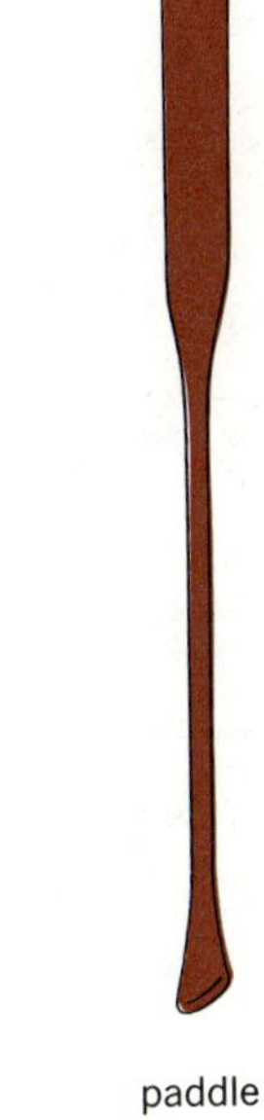

paddle

paddle wheel

pagoda

paint·er (PAYN-tər) *noun.* 1. A person who paints pictures; an artist. 2. A person whose job it is to paint walls, furniture, or such; a decorator.

paint·ing (PAYN-ting) *noun.* 1. A picture or work of art done in paints. 2. The process of applying paint, as to a wall. 3. The art of making pictures or similar painted works.

palette

pair *noun.* 1. A set of two items that have a single purpose or function: a *pair* of shoes. 2. A single thing having two similar parts: a *pair* of pants. 3. Two persons or animals thought of as a unit or set: Mr. and Mrs. Burns are a happy *pair.* —*verb.* 1. (Often used with *off*) To form a pair: The boys and girls *paired* off for the next dance. 2. To match something with another similar item: *Pair* the stocking with its mate. **paired, pairing.**

pa·ja·mas (pə-JAH-məz or pə-JAM-əz) *noun, plural.* A light, loosely fitting pair of pants and a top, worn for sleeping or lounging.

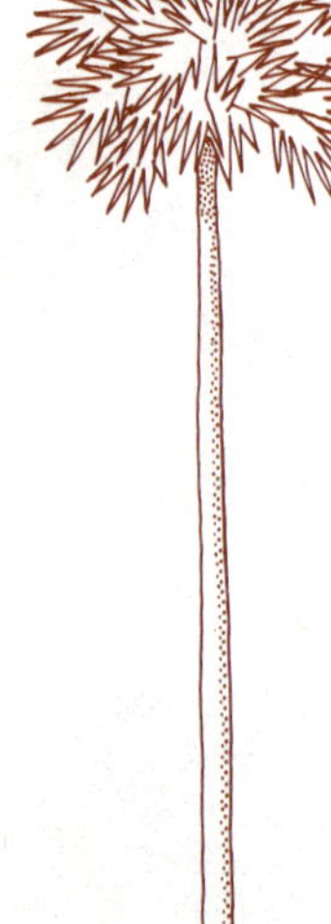

palm

pal *noun.* (Informal) A friend or companion; buddy. —*verb.* (Informal, used with *around*) To go about or do things with: *pal* around together. **palled, palling.**

pal·ace (PAL-iss) *noun.* 1. A building that is the official dwelling of a king or other person of high rank. 2. A large, handsome dwelling or other building; a mansion. **palaces.**

pal·at·a·ble (PAL-i-tə-bəl) *adjective.* Pleasant to taste; suitable for eating.

pal·ate (PAL-it) *noun.* 1. The roof of the mouth. 2. The sense of taste: Candy delights my *palate.* **palates.**

[1]**pale** (PAYL) *adjective.* 1. Having a whitish complexion or color. 2. Without intensity, depth, or brightness; as of light or color: a *pale* blue. **paler, palest.** —*verb.* To make or become pale or whitish: The woman *paled* at the bad news. **paled, paling.** —**palely** *adverb.*

[2]**pale** (PAYL) *noun.* A stake or fence post. **pales.** —**beyond the pale.** Outside the accepted boundaries of good taste or proper behavior.

pa·le·on·tol·o·gy (pay-lee-on-TOL-ə-jee) *noun.* The study of fossils and ancient forms of life.

pal·ette (PAL-it) *noun.* A thin board on which an artist lays out and mixes oil paints. **palettes.**

pal·i·sade (pal-ə-SAYD) *noun.* 1. A line or fence of pointed stakes that forms a defense or fortification. 2. (Plural) A row of steep cliffs.

[1]**pall** (PAWL) *noun.* 1. A cloth covering, especially one for a coffin. 2. A coffin. 3. A dark or depressing effect: The bad news cast a *pall* over the party.

[2]**pall** (PAWL) *verb.* To become dull or distasteful, especially because of excess: The delight of candy can *pall* if too much is eaten. **palled, palling.**

pal·let (PAL-it) *noun.* A narrow, hard bed or a straw mattress.

pal·lid (PAL-id) *adjective.* Pale; lacking color. —**pallidly** *adverb.*

pal·lor (PAL-ər) *noun.* Paleness; a lack of color.

[1]**palm** (PAHM) *noun.* 1. Any of a variety of tall, tropical trees with long, bare trunks and very large leaves or branches at the top. 2. A leaf or branch from a palm tree.

[2]**palm** (PAHM) *noun.* The surface of the inner part of the hand between the wrist and the bottom of the fingers. —*verb.* To hide something in or under the hand, as in a card trick. **palmed, palming.** —**palm off.** To sell or get rid of dishonestly.

pal·met·to (pal-MET-oh) *noun.* A small palm tree with large leaves shaped like fans. —**palmettos** or **palmettoes** *plural.*

Palm Sunday. The Sunday before Easter, when palm fronds are distributed to churchgoers in some Christian services.

pal·pi·tate (PAL-pə-tayt) *verb.* To beat or throb rapidly; tremble: Fear makes the heart *palpitate.* **palpitated, palpitating.** —**palpitation** (pal-pə-TAY-shən) *noun.*

pal·sy (PAWL-zee) *noun.* A disease or condition in which the body is affected by paralysis or the inability to feel or move.

pal·try (PAWL-tree) *adjective.* Very small; of little value or importance: a *paltry* amount. **paltrier, paltriest.**

pam·pas (PAM-pəz) *noun, plural.* Huge, grassy plains in the southern part of South America.

pam·per (PAM-pər) *verb.* To coddle; spoil: *pamper* a child. **pampered, pampering.**

pam·phlet (PAM-flit) *noun.* A paper-covered booklet or folder.

pan *noun.* 1. A wide metal vessel used for cooking. 2. Anything shaped like a pan. —*verb.* 1. (Informal) To criticize; complain about. 2. To wash gravel or earth in a pan to separate pieces of gold from it. **panned, panning.** —**pan out.** To turn out or finish, especially with good results.

pan·cake (PAN-kayk) *noun.* A thin, round cake fried on a pan or griddle. **pancakes.**

pan·cre·as (PANG-kree-əss) *noun.* A long gland near the stomach that produces insulin and gives off a fluid that aids in digestion. **pancreases.** —**pancreatic** (pang-kree-AT-ik) *adjective.*

pan·da (PAN-də) *noun.* 1. Also **giant panda.** A black and white Asian animal that resembles a bear. 2. Also **lesser panda.** A reddish-brown animal, found in India, that resembles a raccoon.

pane (PAYN) *noun.* A sheet of glass in a door or window. **panes.**

pan·el (PAN-l) *noun.* 1. A raised or recessed section of a surface, usually rectangular and often framed: the *panels* in a door. 2. A surface on which dials, switches, or similar devices are arranged: The instrument *panel* of an automobile is on the dashboard. 3. A group of persons selected or assembled to judge something or offer opinions: a *panel* of experts. 4. A long, narrow section of cloth, wood, or other material. —*verb.* To cover with wooden panels: The carpenter *paneled* the playroom. **paneled** or **panelled, paneling** or **panelling.**

pang *noun.* A brief but intense feeling of pain, physical or mental.

pan·ic (PAN-ik) *noun.* Sudden and powerful terror that often spreads rapidly to others: The loud explosion caused a *panic* in the auditorium. —*verb.* To cause or be affected by panic. **panicked, panicking.**

pan·o·ra·ma (pan-ə-RAM-ə) *noun.* 1. A sweeping, unbroken, wide view of a very large area. 2. A painting, photo, or other representation that shows such a view. —**panoramic** *adjective.*

pan·sy (PAN-zee) *noun.* A small flower, usually of several colors, or the plant on which it grows. **pansies.**

pant *verb.* 1. To breathe rapidly and heavily: The dog *panted* after his long run. 2. To speak or make voice sounds with short, quick breaths. **panted, panting.** —*noun.* A short, heavy breath; gasp.

pan·ther (PAN-thər) *noun.* A leopard, jaguar, or other large wild cat, especially a black, unspotted leopard.

pan·to·mime (PAN-tə-mighm) *noun.* 1. A play or entertainment in which actors use gestures and facial expressions but not words. 2. Gestures and facial expressions used instead of words to express meaning. **pantomimes.** —*verb.* To substitute gestures and facial expressions for words. **pantomimed, pantomiming.**

pansy

panda

panther

pan·try (PAN-tree) *noun.* A small room or closet where food and kitchen equipment are stored. **pantries.**

pants *noun, plural.* Any garment with a section for each leg, usually designed to cover the body from the waist to the ankles: Trousers and jeans are different kinds of *pants.*

pants suit. An outfit for a girl or woman made up of slacks and a jacket or blouse to be worn together.

pan·ty·hose (PAN-tee-HOHZ) *noun.* Stockings and underpants combined in a single knit piece.

parachute

pa·pa (PAH-pə or pə-PAH) *noun.* Father.

pa·paw (PAW-paw) Also **pawpaw** *noun.* 1. A soft yellow-green fruit. 2. The North American tree that bears this fruit.

pa·pa·ya (pə-PAH-yə) *noun.* 1. A large melon-like fruit. 2. The evergreen tree that grows in warm climates and bears this fruit.

pa·per (PAY-pər) *noun.* 1. A material made from wood pulp or rags and formed into very thin sheets. 2. A sheet of such material. 3. A newspaper. 4. Something written or printed on paper, such as a report or document. —*verb.* To cover with paper, especially wallpaper. **papered, papering.**

pa·pier-mâ·ché (pay-pər-mə-SHAY) *noun.* A mixture of wet paper and paste or glue that can be formed into figures that hold their shape when dry.

parade

pa·poose (pa-POOSS) *noun.* A baby or young child in North American Indian tribes. **papooses.**

pap·ri·ka (pap-REE-kə) A red powdered seasoning made by grinding dried sweet red peppers.

pa·py·rus (pə-PIGH-rəss) *noun.* 1. A tall grassy plant that grows in or near water in Egypt. 2. Paper made from the leaves of this plant. 3. A document written on papyrus. —**papyruses** or **papyri** (pə-PIGH-righ) *plural.*

par (PAHR) *noun.* 1. A standard, average, or set value: Tom's score was below *par.* 2. Equal level: My pay is on a *par* with yours. 3. (Golf) The standard number of strokes that good players are expected to score on each hole. —**up to par.** Up to standard.

par·a·ble (PA-rə-bəl) *noun.* A short, simple story told to point out a religious or moral lesson. **parables.**

pa·rab·o·la (pə-RAB-ə-lə) *noun.* (Geometry) The curve formed by cutting a cone by a plane parallel to its side.

par·a·chute (PA-rə-shoot) *noun.* A large umbrella-shaped device, made of silk or nylon and attached to a harness, used to slow the fall of a person or object from a great height, usually from an airplane. **parachutes.** —*verb.* To drop by parachute. **parachuted, parachuting.**

pa·rade (pə-RAYD) *noun.* 1. A colorful march or procession along a public street. 2. A formal display of military troops. 3. A showy display of persons or objects. **parades.** —*verb.* 1. To march or ride in formation. 2. To display in a showy way. **paraded, parading.**

par·a·dise (PA-rə-dighss) *noun.* 1. Heaven. 2. Any beautiful or perfect place. 3. A happy state of mind. 4. [Capital P] The Garden of Eden. **paradises.**

par·a·dox (PA-rə-doks) *noun.* 1. A statement that seems to disagree with itself: "He that loseth his life . . . shall find it," is a *paradox* from the Bible. 2. A person or substance that does not behave as expected. **paradoxes.** —**paradoxical** (pa-rə-DOKS-i-kəl) *adjective.*

par·af·fin (PA-rə-fin) *noun.* A waxy white or colorless substance often used to make candles.

par·a·graph (PA-rə-graf) *noun.* 1. A sentence or group of sentences that relate to one subject and are part of a longer written work. 2. The mark (¶) used to show where such a section of writing begins. 3. A short news item or story. *—verb.* To divide into paragraphs. **paragraphed, paragraphing.**

par·a·keet (PA-rə-keet) Also **parrakeet** *noun.* A small parrot with a long tail.

par·al·lel (PA-rə-lel) *adjective.* 1. Equally distant from each other at all points: *Parallel* lines never cross. 2. Alike, very similar: The twins have led *parallel* lives. *—noun.* 1. A line or surface that is at all points an equal distance from another given line or surface. 2. (Geography) One of the imaginary lines circling the earth used to indicate distance from the equator. 3. Likeness, similarity: There is a *parallel* between the voyage of Columbus and the astronauts' trip to the moon. *—verb.* 1. To move in a line that is parallel to: Our street *parallels* the railroad. 2. To be like: His story *parallels* my own. **paralleled** or **parallelled, paralleling** or **parallelling.**

par·al·lel·o·gram (pa-rə-LEL-ə-gram) *noun.* A four-sided figure whose opposite sides are parallel and equal in length.

pa·ral·y·sis (pə-RAL-ə-siss) *noun.* 1. The loss of ability to feel and move (a part of the body). 2. Stoppage or helplessness: The strike of dock workers brought *paralysis* to the shipping industry. **—paralyses** (pə-RAL-ə-seez) *plural.*

par·a·lyze (PA-rə-lighz) *verb.* 1. To cause to lose the ability to feel or move: The jellyfish stings and *paralyzes* its prey before eating it. 2. To bring to a stop. 3. To make helpless for a time: Fear *paralyzed* the child. **paralyzed, paralyzing.**

par·a·me·ci·um (pa-rə-MEE-shee-əm or pa-rə-MEE-see-əm) *noun.* A tiny one-celled animal that lives in water. **—paramecia** (pa-rə-MEE-shee-ə or pa-ra-MEE-see-ə) or **parameciums** *plural.*

par·a·mount (PA-rə-mownt) *adjective.* Most important, supreme: "My *paramount* object in this struggle is to save the Union." (Lincoln).

par·a·pet (PA-rə-pit or PA-rə-pet) *noun.* 1. A low wall or railing along the top of a building, bridge, or other structure. 2. A wall used to protect troops from enemy fire.

par·a·pher·na·li·a (pa-rə-fər-NAYL-yə) *noun, singular* or *plural.* 1. Personal belongings or property. 2. Equipment needed for a particular activity: The photographer gathered up his *paraphernalia.*

par·a·site (PA-rə-sight) *noun.* 1. A plant or animal that lives off another plant or animal without contributing anything in return. 2. A person who takes everything he can get without giving anything in return. **parasites. —parasitic** (pa-rə-SIT-ik) Also **parasitical** *adjective.*

par·a·sol (PA-rə-sol) *noun.* A kind of umbrella, usually carried as protection against the sun.

par·a·troop·er (PA-rə-troop-ər) *noun.* A soldier equipped and trained to make landings by parachute.

par·cel (PAHR-sl) *noun.* 1. A package. 2. A piece of land. 3. A pack of like things or people: a *parcel* of thieves. *—verb.* To divide into shares. **parceled, parceling.**

parcel post. Mail service for the delivery of packages.

parch (PAHRCH) *verb.* 1. To cook by dry heat. 2. To dry out or cause to dry out. **parched, parching.**

parch·ment (PAHRCH-mənt) *noun.* 1. The very thin skin of a sheep or goat prepared and used for writing paper. 2. Paper that looks like this material. 3. A document written on parchment.

parakeets

parasol

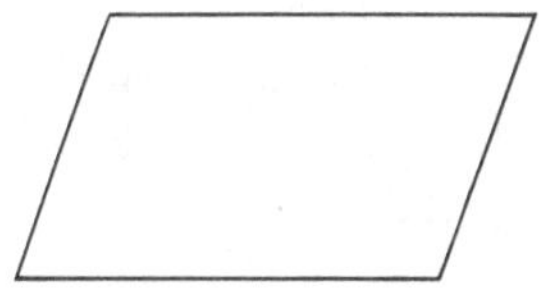

parallelogram

parrot

parsley

parkas

par·don (PAHRD-n) *verb.* 1. To forgive or excuse. 2. To free from punishment. **pardoned, pardoning.** —*noun.* Forgiveness.

pare (PAIR) *verb.* 1. To peel or remove the skin (from a fruit or vegetable). 2. To cut off a thin layer. 3. To make smaller by cutting. **pared, paring.**

par·ent (PAIR-ənt) *noun.* 1. A father or mother. 2. Any living thing that produces offspring. 3. The origin or beginning: "Fear is the *parent* of cruelty." (J. A. Froude). —**parental** (pə-RENT-l) *adjective.*

par·ent·age (PAIR-ən-tij) *noun.* One's parents, ancestry, or background.

pa·ren·the·sis (pə-REN-thə-siss) *noun.* One of the curved marks ( ) used to separate a word or group of words from the rest of written or printed material. —**parentheses** (pə-REN-thə-seez) *plural.* —**parenthetical** (pa-rən-THET-i-kəl) *adjective.* —**parenthetically** *adverb.*

par·fait (pahr-FAY) *noun.* A frozen dessert made of ice cream, fruit, syrup, and served in a tall glass.

par·ish (PA-rish) *noun.* 1. The people and area served by one church. 2. In Louisiana, a county or local division of government. **parishes.**

park (PAHRK) *noun.* 1. An open area set aside for public use, recreation, or the protection of animals. 2. A field where sports events are held: a ball *park.* 3. The lawn, gardens, and wooded areas around a large country house. —*verb.* 1. To steer a car or other vehicle into a space and leave it there for a time. 2. (Informal) To place: He *parked* his feet on the desk. **parked, parking.**

par·ka (PAHR-kə) *noun.* 1. A fur garment with a hood, worn by Eskimos. 2. A similar windproof garment made of cloth.

par·lia·ment (PAHR-lə-mənt) *noun.* 1. The lawmaking body in certain countries. 2. A meeting of high-ranking government officials. 3. [Capital P] The British lawmaking body. —**parliamentary** (pahr-lə-MEN-tə-ree) *adjective.*

parliamentary law. The widely accepted rules for conducting a meeting based on the procedure followed in the British Parliament.

par·lor (PAHR-lər) *noun.* 1. The room in a home where guests are entertained. 2. A public place used for a special purpose: a beauty *parlor.*

pa·ro·chi·al (pə-ROH-kee-əl) *adjective.* 1. Referring to a parish or the area served by a church: a *parochial* school. 2. Limited, not widespread or public: The meeting was of *parochial* interest. —**parochially** *adverb.*

par·rot (PA-rət) *noun.* A brightly colored bird with a hooked bill: *Parrots* can be taught to copy the sounds of human speech. —*verb.* To repeat words or actions of another without considering the meaning. **parroted, parroting.**

par·ry (PA-ree) *verb.* 1. To turn aside a blow or an attack: He *parried* every thrust of the sword. 2. To avoid (questions) cleverly: The mayor knew how to *parry* reporters' questions. **parried, parrying.**

pars·ley (PAHRSS-lee) *noun.* A plant with small bright green curly leaves, often used for seasoning.

pars·nip (PAHRSS-nip) *noun.* 1. A plant with a thick white root. 2. The root of this plant that is eaten as a vegetable.

par·son (PAHR-sən) *noun.* A minister or preacher.

par·son·age (PAHR-sə-nij) *noun.* The house that a church provides as a home for its minister. **parsonages.**

part (PAHRT) *noun.* 1. Some, but not all; a share. 2. One of the portions or sections into which a thing can be or is divided. 3. A piece for a machine: a *part* for an old car. 4. A role in a play. 5. A side in an argument. 6. (Music) The notes written for one voice or instrument: the soprano *part.* 7. (Often plural) Area or region. 8. A line on the head where hair is separated. —*verb.* 1. (Usually followed by *from*) To leave or go away. 2. To separate; divide: "A fool and his money are soon *parted.*" (Unknown author). 3. To comb the hair by separating it along a line on the head. **parted, parting. —for the most part.** Usually, generally. **—in part.** Partly, not entirely.

par·take (pahr-TAYK) *verb.* 1. To take, share, or receive. 2. To eat or drink. **partook, partaken, partaking.**

par·tial (PAHR-shəl) *adjective.* 1. Not all; part: *partial* payment. 2. Favoring one over another: A baseball umpire must not be *partial.* **—partiality** (pahr-shee-AL-ə-tee) *noun.* **—partially** *adverb.*

par·tic·i·pant (pahr-TISS-ə-pənt) *noun.* One who takes part.

par·tic·i·pate (pahr-TISS-ə-payt) *verb.* To take part, share (in): *participate* in the game. **participated, participating. —participation** (pahr-tiss-ə-PAY-shən) *noun.*

par·ti·ci·ple (PAHR-tə-sip-əl) *noun.* One of two verb forms (past *participle* and present *participle*) used either as an adjective or with a helping verb: In "The charming lady served tea," "charming" is a present *participle* used as an adjective. In "She looks dazed," "dazed" is a past *participle* used with a linking verb. **participles.**

par·ti·cle (PAHR-tə-kəl) *noun.* 1. A tiny bit or piece. 2. (Grammar) A single uninflected word or part of a word, such as *a* or *-wise.* **particles.**

par·tic·u·lar (pər-TIK-yə-lər) *adjective.* 1. Of or belonging to one person or group: Rugmaking is a *particular* skill of that Indian tribe. 2. One apart from all others: I do not like that *particular* necktie. 3. Careful, exact: She is a *particular* housekeeper. —*noun.* (Plural) Details: the *particulars* of a trip. **—in particular.** Especially.

par·tic·u·lar·ly (pər-TIK-yə-lər-lee) *adverb.* 1. Especially. 2. With emphasis on. 3. In a certain manner.

part·ing (PAHR-ting) *noun.* 1. The act of leaving or separating: "*Parting* is such sweet sorrow. . . ." (Shakespeare). 2. A division or separation: a *parting* of our paths. —*adjective.* Leaving: "Speed the *parting* guest." (A. Pope).

par·ti·san (PAHR-tə-zn) *noun.* 1. One who takes sides; a supporter or follower. 2. One of an armed band of civilians, not part of a regular army, that opposes occupying forces. —*adjective.* One-sided; favoring one idea, person, or party.

par·ti·tion (pahr-TISH-ən) *verb.* To divide into parts or sections: The egg carton is *partitioned* into small squares. **partitioned, partitioning.** —*noun.* 1. The act of dividing. 2. An object that forms a division; a wall.

part·ly (PAHRT-lee) *adverb.* Not entirely.

part·ner (PAHRT-nər) *noun.* 1. One who shares; an associate. 2. Wife or husband; spouse, mate. 3. In business, one who shares the profits and losses in a formal arrangement. 4. A companion in a dance. 5. One of a pair of players on the same side in a game or sport.

part·ner·ship (PAHRT-nər-ship) *noun.* The state of being a partner; a formal relationship of joint interest, usually in business.

part of speech. A word category determined by the function each word serves in a sentence: Nouns and verbs are *parts of speech.*

par·tridge (PAHR-trij) *noun.* Any of several plump game birds belonging to the same group as the grouse, pheasant, or quail. **partridges.**

partridge

passenger pigeon

par·ty (PAHR-tee) *noun.* 1. A gathering for a celebration or festive time: a birthday *party.* 2. A group; a body of people jointly participating in something: a *party* of six. 3. A political group: the Republican or Democratic *party.* 4. A person concerned or involved: the *party* who broke the window. **parties.**

pass *noun.* 1. Free ticket or written permit: a *pass* to a game. 2. A narrow path, a gap in or a way through a mountain range. 3. (Football) A toss or throw. 4. A state or situation: Tom's friendship for Bill came to a sad *pass.* 5. (Slang) A flirtatious gesture. **passes.** —*verb.* 1. To overtake and go beyond: Jim *passed* Bill in the race. 2. To move on, to proceed: "The wind is *passing* by." (C. Rossetti). 3. To run; go by; extend: The railroad tracks *pass* through the center of our town. 4. To deliver; hand over; to transfer: Please *pass* the rolls. 5. To get through; do well: He *passed* all his tests. 6. To vote approval: *pass* a law. 7. To spend (time): "And they *passed* the night in a crockery-jar." (E. Lear). 8. To come to an end: The summer *passed.* 9. To happen, take place: No one knew what *passed* that night. 10. In some card games, to make no bid. **passed, passing.** —**come to pass.** To happen, take place. —**pass away.** To die. —**pass for.** To be accepted for something one is not. —**pass up.** To give up an opportunity, let go by.

pas·sage (PASS-ij) *noun.* 1. A corridor or hallway; a means of passing through or around something. 2. A voyage; a going across. 3. A section or selection from a speech or from a written or musical work. 4. Affirmative vote on a bill: *Passage* of the bill was certain. **passages.**

pas·sage·way (PASS-ij-way) *noun.* A passage, corridor, opening, or lane by which one may pass.

pas·sen·ger (PASS-n-jər) *noun.* A traveler on any means of transportation such as a train, bus, or car.

passenger pigeon. A North American wild pigeon that is now extinct.

pas·ser-by (PASS-ər-bigh) *noun.* One who passes by, sometimes by chance. —**passers-by** *plural.*

pas·sion (PASH-ən) *noun.* 1. A powerful emotion, fervor, or strong feeling. 2. An outburst of emotion, rage, or fury. 3. Love, affection, desire. 4. Great enthusiasm, craze.

pas·sion·ate (PASH-ən-it) *adjective.* Having very strong feelings; enthusiastic; fervent. —**passionately** *adverb.*

pas·sive (PASS-iv) *adjective.* 1. Inactive; very patient or docile. 2. (Grammar) Indicating the voice of a verb whose action is received by the subject: In the sentence "He was caught," the verb is in the *passive* voice. —**passively** *adverb.*

Pass·o·ver (PASS-oh-vər) *noun.* [Capital P] A Jewish holiday commemorating the Jews' delivery from slavery in Egypt.

pass·port (PASS-port) *noun.* 1. An official document issued by a government that certifies identity and citizenship, often required for anyone traveling to a foreign country. 2. Anything that grants passage or admission.

pass·word (PASS-wərd) *noun.* A secret word or phrase that grants one admission to a restricted area or meeting.

past *adjective.* 1. Gone by, over. 2. Referring to time just gone by: this *past* month. 3. Having served earlier: a *past* president. 4. (Grammar) Expressing an action that has already happened: "Jumped" is the *past* tense of "jump." —*noun.* 1. An earlier time, time gone by. 2. Earlier background of an individual: She had an interesting *past.* —*adverb.* By, to and beyond: "Cars race fast, trucks bump *past.*" (Lois Lenski). —*preposition.* 1. Beyond in time, age, extent, or amount: The clock read five *past* three. 2. Beyond a place, by: I walked *past* the car.

pas·ta (PAHSS-tə) *noun.* A dough, made of flour, eggs, and water, that is dried and then cooked in boiling water.

paste (PAYST) *noun.* 1. A moist adhesive substance used to stick paper and other things together. 2. Any soft, moist, smooth substance: tooth*paste.* 3. A smooth dough used in baking. 4. A shiny hard glass used to make imitation gems. **pastes.** —*verb.* To make stick by using paste. **pasted, pasting.**

paste·board (PAYST-bord) *noun.* A firm, hard material made from sheets of paper pasted together.

pas·tel (pass-TEL) *noun.* 1. A crayon made from a paste of ground pigment, similar to colored chalk. 2. A picture drawn using this crayon. 3. A pale, soft shade: Light pink is a *pastel.*

pas·teur·ize (PASS-chər-ighz) *verb.* To destroy harmful germs by a heating process: *pasteurize* milk. **pasteur-ized, pasteurizing.** —*noun* **pasteur-ization** (pass-chər-ə-ZAY-shən).

pas·time (PASS-tighm) *noun.* A pleasant activity of recreation, amusement, or relaxation: Reading is my favorite *pastime.* **pastimes.**

pas·tor (PASS-tər) *noun.* A minister who has his own church or parish.

pas·tor·al (PASS-tər-əl) *adjective.* 1. Referring to shepherds or rural life. 2. Referring to simple and leisurely ways, as in country living. 3. Referring to a pastor or his responsibilities. —*noun.* A creative work that depicts rural life: Beethoven's Sixth Symphony is called "The *Pastoral.*"

pas·try (PAYSS-tree) *noun.* 1. A dough made from flour, water, and shortening that is used in pies, tarts, and other baked goods. 2. Foods made with this dough. 3. Any fancy baked confection. **pastries.**

pas·ture (PASS-chər) *noun.* 1. A grassy area of land used for grazing cattle; a meadow. 2. Grass and other plants eaten by cattle or sheep. **pastures.** —*verb.* 1. To put to pasture. 2. To graze or feed. **pastured, pasturing.**

PA system. Short form for "public-address system."

pat. *abbreviation.* Patent.

pat *noun.* 1. A light tap or stroke: a *pat* on the back. 2. The sound made by this tap. 3. A small lump: a *pat* of butter. —*verb.* To touch gently. **patted, patting.** —*adjective.* Just right, appropriate: a *pat* reply. —**have down pat.** To know thoroughly. —**stand pat.** To hold a position without wavering.

patch (PACH) *noun.* 1. A piece of material used to cover a worn area. 2. A small portion of land with something on it: a berry *patch.* 3. A small part of anything: *patches* of sunlight. 4. A small shield, usually black, worn over an injured eye. 5. A bandage on a wound. 6. An emblem or badge worn on a sleeve. **patches.** —*verb.* 1. To put a patch on. 2. To mend or repair, usually in a hurry. **patched, patching.** —**patch up.** To settle, as a quarrel.

pat·ent (PAT-nt) *noun.* 1. A legal document granting an inventor sole rights to his invention for a fixed period of time. 2. Something patented. —*adjective.* 1. (PAYT-nt) Plain, evident. 2. Protected by a patent. —*verb.* To secure a patent. **patented, patenting.**

patent leather. Very glossy leather.

pa·ter·nal (pə-TER-nl) *adjective.* Fatherly; on the father's side of the family. —**paternally** *adverb.*

path *noun.* 1. A narrow road or trail. 2. A way worn by footsteps: a *path* to our back door. 3. A route or course: the *path* of an arrow. 4. A direction or way of life.

pa·thet·ic (pə-THET-ik) *adjective.* Moving, sad, pitiful. —**pathetically** *adverb.*

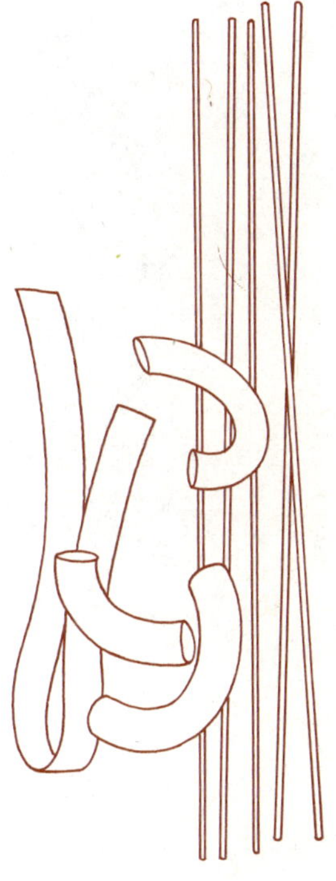
pasta

path·way (PATH-way) *noun.* A path.

pa·tience (PAY-shənss) *noun.* 1. Perseverance, endurance. 2. Tolerance.

pa·tient (PAY-shənt) *adjective.* 1. Calm, kind, tolerant. 2. Persevering: *patient* training. 3. Long-suffering, enduring, submissive: We have been *patient* too long with our enemies. —*noun.* One who is under a doctor's care. —**patiently** *adverb.*

pat·i·o (PAT-ee-oh or PAH-tee-oh) *noun.* A courtyard; a paved area adjoining a house. **patios.**

pa·tri·arch (PAY-tree-ahrk) *noun.* The father and male leader of a family, group, or tribe; also a highly respected elderly man.

pa·tri·ot (PAY-tree-ət) *noun.* A person who loves his country and supports it with loyalty, devotion, and enthusiasm.

pa·tri·ot·ic (pay-tree-OT-ik) *adjective.* Loyal, filled with fervor for and devotion to one's country. —**patriotically** *adverb.*

patriotism (PAY-tree-ə-tiz-əm) *noun.* Loyalty and devotion to one's country.

pa·trol (pə-TROHL) *noun.* 1. A person or group of persons moving about, watching or guarding an area, usually for security. 2. A military unit sent ahead to scout a situation. 3. Part of a troop in the Boy Scouts. —*verb.* To guard by walking a regular route and being alert for any threat to security; to be part of a patrol. **patrolled, patrolling.**

patrolman

pa·trol·man (pə-TROHL-mən) *noun.* A policeman or guard who watches over and patrols a given area. —**patrolmen** *plural.*

pa·tron (PAY-trən) *noun.* 1. A person who sponsors and supports another; a benefactor, usually in the field of the arts or learning. 2. A customer.

pa·tron·age (PAY-trən-ij or PAT-rən-ij) *noun.* 1. Support by a patron. 2. Regular business or trade from customers. 3. Customers or clients. 4. The power to give government jobs and contracts or favors and thereby reward political loyalty.

pa·tron·ize (PAY-trən-ighz or PAT-rən-ighz) *verb.* 1. To back, sponsor, finance, or support. 2. To deal with, to trade with: I like to *patronize* local stores. 3. To treat in a haughty or superior manner. **patronized, patronizing.**

[1]**pat·ter** (PAT-ər) *noun.* A series of quick, light sounds: the *patter* of raindrops. —*verb.* To make a series of such sounds. **pattered, pattering.**

[2]**pat·ter** (PAT-ər) *verb.* To talk rapidly and glibly. **pattered, pattering.** —*noun.* A fast line of talk, often by a professional entertainer.

pat·tern (PAT-ərn) *noun.* 1. A form or sample to follow: a dress *pattern.* 2. A model, an example. 3. A repeated design; an arrangement: The tablecloth had a checkerboard *pattern.* —*verb.* To follow an example: Please *pattern* your behavior after your brother's. **patterned, patterning.**

pat·ty (PAT-ee) *noun.* 1. A small, flat rounded portion of chopped or ground food, often meat or fish. 2. A small pie. **patties.**

paunch (PAWNCH or PAHNCH) *noun.* The abdomen, particulary if overlarge. **paunches.**

pau·per (PAW-pər) *noun.* An extremely poor person; one with no means of support who may be living on charity.

pause (PAWZ) *noun.* 1. A brief stop; a short rest; a hesitation. 2. A sign in music indicating that a note or rest is to be held. **pauses.** —*verb.* To hesitate. **paused, pausing.**

pave (PAYV) *verb.* To cover with a smooth firm surface; usually to cover a road with concrete or asphalt. **paved, paving.** —**pave the way.** To make easier; to prepare (for).

pave·ment (PAYV-mənt) *noun.* A paved or smooth surface, usually a sidewalk or road.

pa·vil·ion (pə-VIL-yən) *noun.* 1. An elaborate tent with a pointed or rounded top. 2. A small, light structure or low building with open sides seen at fairs or in parks. 3. An annex to a building.

pav·ing (PAYV-ing) *noun.* Pavement.

paw *noun.* The foot of a four-footed clawed animal, as a cat. —*verb.* 1. To strike, hit, or touch with a paw. 2. To handle in a rough manner. **pawed, pawing.**

[1]**pawn** *verb.* To leave (something) with a broker as security or pledge for money borrowed. **pawned, pawning.** —*noun.* The security or pledge left when money is borrowed.

[2]**pawn** *noun.* 1. In chess, one of the playing pieces of lowest value: The *pawn* moves straight forward along the row on which it starts. 2. A person who is used for someone else's selfish purpose.

pawn·shop (PAWN-shop) *noun.* A shop or place of business that loans money upon the receipt of personal property, which is held until repayment is made.

paw·paw (PAW-paw) *noun. See* **papaw.**

pay *verb.* 1. To give money or goods to, usually for work done, goods received, or services given: *pay* the storekeeper. 2. To give (an amount of money or goods) for what is received: *pay* ten cents for a newspaper. 3. To fulfill, as a debt or duty: *pay* one's debt to society. 4. To make up for: I must *pay* for my mistake. 5. To make a profit or be worth time or effort: The lemonade stand didn't *pay;* we lost money. 6. To give or make: *pay* attention. **paid, paying.** —*noun.* An amount received or given for work done; salary. —*adjective.* Requiring money to operate: a *pay* phone.

pay·ment (PAY-mənt) *noun.* 1. The amount paid. 2. The act of giving or paying.

pea (PEE) *noun.* 1. A round, green seed, found in pods, used as a vegetable. 2. The plant on which such pods grow.

peace (PEESS) *noun.* 1. Freedom from war, quarrels, or tension. 2. A treaty or pact to end fighting. 3. Calmness, quiet. —**hold one's peace.** To stop oneself from speaking, remain quiet. —**keep the peace.** To help maintain order and quiet.

peace·a·ble (PEE-sə-bəl) *adjective.* Tending to avoid trouble, arguments, and disorder. —**peaceably** *adverb.*

peace·ful (PEESS-fəl) *adjective.* 1. Free from fighting, arguments, or disorder; quiet, calm. 2. Referring to a time of peace. —**peacefully** *adverb.*

peach (PEECH) *noun.* 1. A yellow-pink, rounded, sweet fruit. 2. The tree on which this fruit grows. 3. (Also *adjective*) A yellow-pink color. **peaches.**

pea·cock (PEE-kok) *noun.* A large male bird with a colorful tail.

peacock

pea jacket. A heavy double-breasted wool jacket of a type often worn by sailors.

pea jacket

peak (PEEK) *noun.* 1. The highest point or level: the *peak* of a mountain; the *peak* of a career. 2. The part of a cap that extends forward to shade the eyes. —*verb.* To reach the highest point or level: Excitement *peaked* when we reached the fire. **peaked, peaking.**

peal (PEEL) *verb.* To ring: The bells *pealed* when the soldiers returned. **pealed, pealing.** —*noun.* 1. The ringing of bells. 2. A loud sound: a *peal* of laughter.

pea·nut (PEE-nuht) 1. A nut-like seed, found in brittle pods, that can be eaten. 2. The plant on which these seeds grow. 3. (Plural, informal) A small or unimportant amount: Joey bought his water gun for *peanuts.*

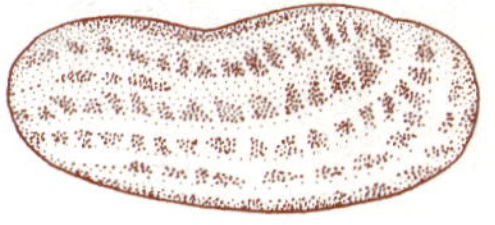

peanut

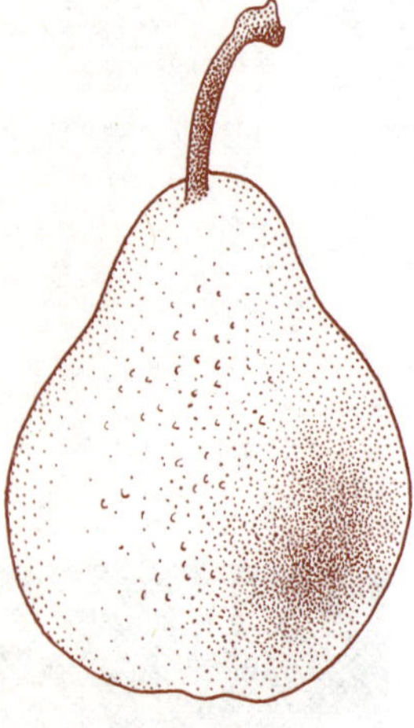
pear

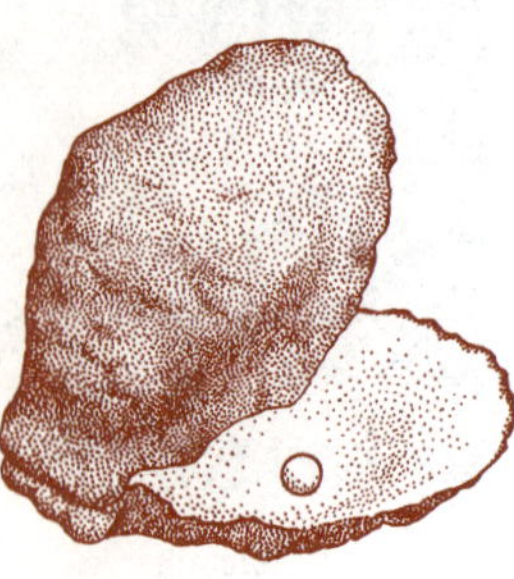
pearl

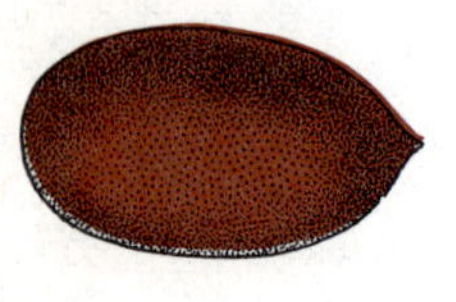
pecan

peccary

peanut butter. A food spread made from roasted and ground peanuts.

pear (PAIR) *noun.* 1. A sweet green or brown fruit that is wide and round at the bottom and narrow at the top. 2. The tree on which this fruit grows.

pearl (PERL) *noun.* A smooth creamy or pink-white gem found in some oysters.

peas·ant (PEZ-nt) *noun.* 1. In Europe or Asia, a small farmer or farm laborer. 2. A crude or ignorant person.

peas·ant·ry (PEZ-n-tree) *noun.* Peasants considered as a group.

peat (PEET) *noun.* A moss found in marshy areas and used as a fuel when dried.

peb·ble (PEB-əl) *noun.* A small, smooth stone. **pebbles.**

pe·can (pi-KAHN or pi-KAN) *noun.* 1. A tasty nut with a smooth, oval-shaped shell. 2. The tree on which this nut grows.

pec·ca·ry (PEK-ə-ree) *noun.* A wild animal similar to a pig and covered with long bristles. **peccaries.**

[1]**peck** (PEK) *verb.* 1. To hit or jab with a beak or something like a beak. 2. To pick up with a beak: a hen *pecking* corn. **pecked, pecking.** —*noun.* 1. A jab, as with a beak. 2. A quick kiss.

[2]**peck** (PEK) *noun.* 1. A unit of dry measure equal to eight quarts. 2. (Informal) A large amount: a *peck* of trouble.

pe·cu·liar (pi-KYOOL-yər) *adjective.* 1. Odd; strange: a *peculiar* look. 2. Belonging solely to; distinctive: A brown dress with beanie is a uniform *peculiar* to the Brownies. —**peculiarity** (pi-kyoo-lee-AIR-ə-tee) *noun.* —**peculiarly** *adverb.*

ped·al (PED-l) *noun.* A foot lever: a bicycle *pedal;* a piano *pedal.* —*verb.* 1. To use a pedal. 2. To propel a bicycle. **pedaled** or **pedalled, pedaling** or **pedalling.**

ped·dle (PED-l) *verb.* To move (merchandise) about in order to make sales, particularly door-to-door: to *peddle* magazines. **peddled, peddling.**

ped·dler (PED-lər) *noun.* One who moves from place to place in order to sell something.

ped·es·tal (PED-ə-stəl) *noun.* 1. A base, as for a statue. 2. A place of honor (in the mind): Wally puts his mother on a *pedestal.*

pe·des·tri·an (pə-DESS-tree-ən) *noun.* One who walks from place to place. —*adjective.* 1. Traveling on foot. 2. Ordinary or common; dull and uninteresting: a *pedestrian* lecture.

pe·di·a·tri·cian (pee-dee-ə-TRISH-ən) *noun.* A doctor who treats babies and children.

ped·i·gree (PED-ə-gree) *noun.* Ancestry, or a list of ancestors: My dog has no *pedigree;* he's a mutt. **pedigrees.**

pe·dom·e·ter (pi-DOM-ə-tər) *noun.* A device that records the number of footsteps a person takes and thereby the approximate distance he travels.

peek *verb.* To look quickly or secretly. **peeked, peeking.** —*noun.* A quick or secret look.

peel *verb.* 1. To take off the outside covering: *peel* a banana. 2. To come off in flakes or strips: The paint is *peeling.* **peeled, peeling.** —*noun.* An outside covering, as rind or skin. —**keep one's eyes peeled.** To be alert or watchful.

[1]**peep** *noun.* A little, shrill sound, like that of a bird. —*verb.* To make such a sound. **peeped, peeping.**

[2]**peep** *verb.* To look (at) quickly and in secret. **peeped, peeping.** —*noun.* 1. A quick, secret look. 2. The first appearance: the *peep* of dawn.

[1]**peer** (PIHR) *noun.* 1. An equal: The children in my class are my *peers;* my parents are not. 2. (British) A duke, earl, marquis, viscount, or baron.

[2]**peer** (PIHR) *verb.* 1. To look closely or intently. 2. To appear only in part: stars *peering* through the clouds. **peered, peering.**

peer·less (PIHR-liss) *adjective.* Having no equal: a *peerless* performance.

pee·vish (PEE-vish) *adjective.* Easily irritated. —**peevishly** *adverb.*

pee·wee (PEE-wee) *noun.* (Informal) Someone or something very small.

peg *noun.* 1. A round piece of wood or metal used to hang things from or hold objects together. 2. A degree or level: Melvin is just a *peg* above me in math. —*verb.* 1. To put a peg in. 2. To work without stopping: John *pegged* away until he finished. the job. **pegged, pegging.**

Pe·king·ese (pee-kə-NEEZ) *noun.* A small dog with long hair, a flat nose, and short legs.

pel·i·can (PEL-i-kən) *noun.* A large bird with a pouch under its beak.

pel·let (PEL-it) *noun.* 1. A small ball (of something). 2. A bullet.

pell-mell (PEL-MEL) Also **pell·mell** *adverb.* 1. In an upset or confused way. 2. In a confused hurry: Russ ran *pell-mell* into the policeman.

[1]**pelt** *noun.* The skin of an animal, particularly a hairy or furry one.

[2]**pelt** *verb.* 1. To hit again and again: The hail *pelted* us. 2. To throw things at. **pelted, pelting.**

pel·vis (PEL-viss) *noun.* A basin-like area enclosed by the hipbones at the lower end of the backbone. —**pelvic** *adjective.*

[1]**pen** *noun.* An instrument for writing or drawing in ink. —*verb.* To write with a pen. **penned, penning.**

[2]**pen** *noun.* A fenced-in area: Pigs are kept in *pens.* —*verb.* To put in a pen. **penned** or **pent, penning.**

pe·nal·ize (PEE-nə-lighz or PEN-ə-lighz) *verb.* To punish, fine; demand a forfeit: *penalize* a team. **penalized, penalizing.**

penal system. The laws and manner of dealing with punishment for crime.

pen·al·ty (PEN-l-tee) *noun.* A punishment given, a fine levied, or a forfeit required for a crime, offense, or other wrong action. **penalties.**

pence (PENSS) *noun.* (British) A plural of **penny.**

pen·cil (PEN-sl) *noun.* A thin rod of soft carbon, crayon, or other marking material enclosed in wood, plastic, or metal and used for marking. —*verb.* To write or draw with a pencil. **penciled** or **pencilled, penciling** or **pencilling.**

pen·dant (PEN-dənt) *noun.* An object that hangs from something else, particularly a piece of jewelry hanging from a chain.

pend·ing (PEN-ding) *adjective.* In discussion or work, but not settled or completed: patent *pending.* —*preposition.* Until; waiting for: We'll stay *pending* Dick's decision.

pen·du·lum (PEN-ju-ləm or PEN-dyə-ləm) *noun.* An object hung from a fixed point from which it can swing freely: the *pendulum* in a clock.

pen·e·trate (PEN-ə-trayt) *verb.* 1. To go or see through: a spear *penetrating* a shield. 2. To spread throughout. 3. To understand or figure out. **penetrated, penetrating.** —**penetration** (pen-ə-TRAY-shən) *noun.*

pen·guin (PEN-gwin) *noun.* A web-footed, white-breasted water bird, found in the cold areas of the Southern Hemisphere, that swims and dives but cannot fly.

pen·i·cil·lin (pen-ə-SIL-in) *noun.* A substance obtained from mold or chemicals and used in the treatment of infection and disease.

pen·in·su·la (pə-NIN-sə-lə) *noun.* An arm-like extension of land into a body of water.

pe·nis (PEE-niss) *noun.* A body organ of male mammals, used for sexual intercourse and the discharge of urine.

pelican

penguins

pen·i·tence (PEN-ə-tənss) *noun.* Sorrow for wrongdoing. —**penitent** *adjective.* —**penitently** *adverb.*

pen·i·ten·tia·ry (pen-ə-TEN-shə-ree) *noun.* A prison. **penitentiaries.**

peony

pen·knife (PEN-nighf) *noun.* A small knife with blades that fold into a case or handle. —**penknives** (PEN-nyvz) *plural.*

pen·man·ship (PEN-mən-ship) *noun.* The manner or art of handwriting.

pen name. A false name used by a writer: Lewis Carroll was the *pen name* of C. L. Dodgson, author of *Alice in Wonderland.*

pen·nant (PEN-ənt) *noun.* A flag or banner, usually long, narrow, and pointed at the end.

pen·ni·less (PEN-ee-liss or PEN-ə-liss) *adjective.* Without a penny; very poor. —**pennilessly** *adverb.*

Pennsylvania
★capital: Harrisburg

Penn·syl·va·nia (pen-səl-VAYN-yə or pen-səl-VAY-nee-ə) *noun.* A middle-Atlantic state in the United States, second to ratify the Constitution (1787). —**Pa.** *abbreviation.* Also **PA** for Zip Codes.

pen·ny (PEN-ee) *noun.* 1. A coin equal to one cent in the United States. 2. A coin of small value in various other countries. **pennies.**

pen pal. A person with whom one exchanges letters on a regular basis.

pen·sion (PEN-shən) *noun.* A regular payment, not salary, made on a fixed basis to a retired employee or one who cannot work because of injuries.

pen·sive (PEN-siv) *adjective.* Quietly thoughtful: "In vacant or in *pensive* mood." (Wordsworth). —**pensively** *adverb.*

pent *adjective.* Penned, confined: *pent* up in the house with mumps.

Pentagon

pen·ta·gon (PEN-tə-gon) *noun.* 1. A flat figure with five sides and five angles. 2. [Capital P] A five-sided building near Washington, D.C., used as headquarters for the U.S. Defense Department.

pent·house (PENT-howss) *noun.* An apartment on the roof of a building. **penthouses.**

pe·on (PEE-on or PEE-ən) *noun.* (Latin-American) A common laborer.

pe·o·ny (PEE-ə-nee) *noun.* A hardy plant with red, pink, or white flowers. **peonies.**

peo·ple (PEE-pəl) *noun, singular* and *plural, used with plural verb.* 1. Persons; human beings; men, women, and children: "Common-looking *people* are the best in the world." (Lincoln). 2. Persons of the same race, country, or culture: the German *people.* 3. The public, the persons who elect or are represented: "We, the *people* of the United States. . . ." (U.S. Constitution). 4. Persons under another's rule: The king ruled his *people.* 5. One's family, relations. —**people** or **peoples** *plural.* —*verb.* To populate, fill with people. **peopled, peopling.**

pep *noun.* (Informal) Energy, vigor, liveliness. —*verb.* (Informal, used with *up*) To give energy; make lively. **pepped, pepping.** —**peppy** *adjective.*

pep·per (PEP-ər) *noun.* 1. The small pungent berry of a tropical vine, used ground or whole as a hot, sharp seasoning for food. 2. A bell-shaped fruit of several different varieties varying in flavor from mild to hot and in color from red to green. —*verb.* To sprinkle with pepper. **peppered, peppering.**

pep·per·corn (PEP-ər-korn) *noun.* The dried berry of the pepper plant.

pep·per·mint (PEP-ər-mint) *noun.* 1. An herb with small purple or white flowers and fuzzy leaves that produce a fragrant oil. 2. The oil from this plant used as a flavoring. 3. A candy made with this flavoring.

pep pill. (Slang) A small pill or capsule that stimulates the body by acting on the central nervous system: *Pep pills* can be dangerous if taken without a prescription.

per *preposition.* 1. For each: one *per* person. 2. Through; by means of. 3. According to: *per* instructions.

per annum (AN-əm) Each year, annually.

per capita (KAP-ə-tə) For each individual: 50 dollars *per capita* for police protection.

per·ceive (per-SEEV) *verb.* 1. To see; observe; distinguish: "I *perceive* a young bird in this bush." (E. Lear). 2. To become aware of; understand; realize. **perceived, perceiving.**

per cent Also **per·cent** (pər-SENT). In, for, or out of each hundred; per hundred: ten *per cent* of the class.

per·cent·age (pər-SEN-tij) *noun.* 1. A rate or proportion based on one hundred: What *percentage* of increase do you expect? 2. Part; proportion: a large *percentage.*

per·cep·ti·ble (pər-SEP-tə-bəl) *adjective.* Visible, able to be perceived, noticeable. **—perceptibly** *adverb.*

per·cep·tion (pər-SEP-shən) *noun.* Knowledge gained through the senses; insight, intuition, or awareness.

[1]**perch** *noun.* 1. A place for a bird to sit. 2. A place to rest or sit. **perches.** *—verb.* To sit, rest, or alight on a particular place. **perched, perching.**

[2]**perch** *noun.* A small freshwater fish, valued as food. **—perch** or **perches** *plural.*

per·chance (pər-CHANSS) *adverb.* Perhaps, maybe, possibly.

per·co·late (PER-kə-layt) *verb.* 1. To drip or drain through small holes; to filter. 2. To make (coffee) by letting water boil through ground coffee. **percolated, percolating.**

per·cus·sion (pər-KUHSH-ən) *noun.* The hitting of one thing against another, as the ear being struck by sound waves.

percussion instrument. An instrument in which a musical tone is produced by hitting or striking.

per·en·ni·al (pər-EN-ee-əl) *adjective.* Lasting more than one year; continually recurring. *—noun.* A plant that survives from year to year. **—perennially** *adverb.*

per·fect (PER-fikt) *adjective.* 1. Having no faults, no flaws, no blemishes. 2. Having all parts. 3. Utter, absolute: a *perfect* stranger. 4. (Grammar) Verb tense showing completed action. —(pər-FEKT) *verb.* To make perfect: *perfect* a method. **perfected, perfecting. —perfectly** *adverb.*

per·fec·tion (pər-FEK-shən) *noun.* 1. The highest degree of excellence; the condition of being perfect. 2. A person or thing that is perfect. 3. A making complete or perfect.

per·fo·rate (PER-fə-rayt) *verb.* 1. To make holes by boring, piercing, or puncturing. 2. To make a line of holes (in paper or other material) to enable easy separating by tearing. **perforated, perforating. —perforation** (pər-fə-RAY-shən) *noun.*

per·form (pər-FORM) *verb.* 1. To accomplish, do, carry out. 2. To act before an audience. **performed, performing. —performer** *noun.*

per·form·ance (pər-FOR-mənss) *noun.* 1. The act of carrying out an action; a deed or feat: His *performance* in battle was outstanding. 2. A show before an audience. **performances.**

per·fume (PER-fyoom or pər-FYOOM) *noun.* 1. A fragrance, a pleasing odor. 2. A fragrant liquid used on the skin. **perfumes.**

[2]perch

perhaps (pər-HAPS) *adverb.* Maybe; possibly if not surely.

per·i·gee (PEHR-ə-jee) *noun.* The point in the orbit of the moon or a man-made satellite at which it is nearest to the earth.

per·il (PEHR-əl) *noun.* Danger; hazard; a threat of being harmed. **—perilous** (PEHR-ə-ləss) *adjective.*

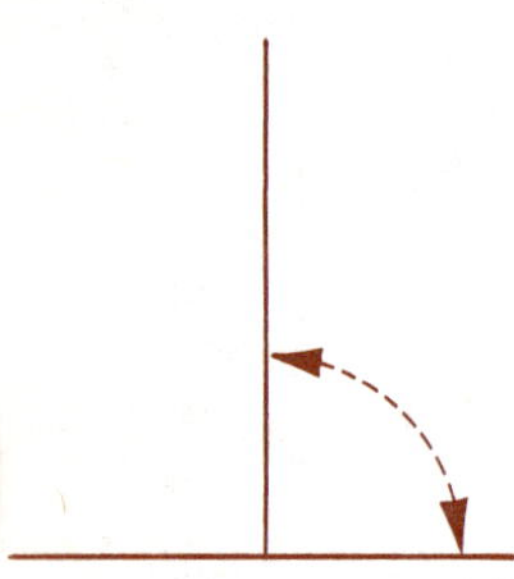
perpendicular

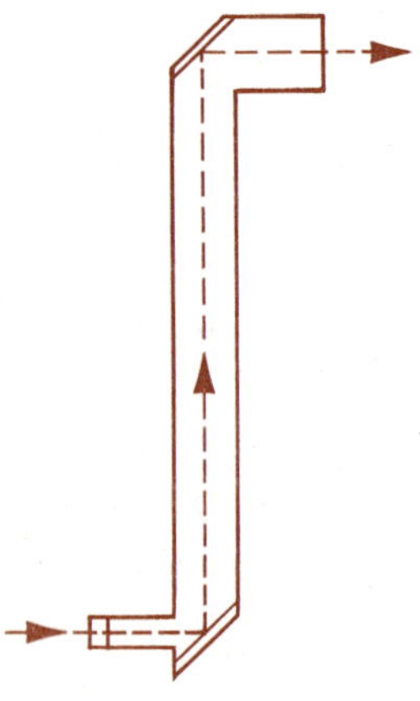
periscope

[1]periwinkle

pe·rim·e·ter (pə-RIM-ə-tər) *noun.* 1. The outer edge of an area: the *perimeter* of campgrounds. 2. (Math) The measurement around a surface or area: *perimeter* of a circle.

pe·ri·od (PIHR-ee-əd) *noun.* 1. A historical age or time: the Civil War *period.* 2. An interval of time marked by certain conditions or events: It was a *period* of great unrest in our country. 3. A dot (.) used as a punctuation mark at the end of sentences or after an abbreviation. 4. A division of time: the fourth *period* of the game.

pe·ri·od·ic (pihr-ee-OD-ik) *adjective.* 1. Happening now and then: *periodic* lapses of memory. 2. Happening at regular cycles or intervals: a *periodic* rise and fall of the tides.

pe·ri·od·i·cal (pihr-ee-OD-ə-kəl) *noun.* A magazine or other publication issued regularly.

periodic table. (Chemistry) A listing of the elements in related groups according to their atomic numbers.

per·i·scope (PEHR-ə-skohp) *noun.* An optical instrument with mirrors arranged so that one can see something not in a direct line of vision: A *periscope* enables those in a submerged submarine to see what happens on the surface. **periscopes.**

per·ish (PEHR-ish) *verb.* To die, especially in a violent or unusual manner. **perished, perishing.**

per·ish·a·ble (PEHR-ish-ə-bəl) *adjective.* Apt to become rotten or spoiled; easily destroyed.

[1]**per·i·win·kle** (PEHR-ee-wing-kəl) *noun.* An evergreen plant with trailing vines, shiny leaves, and blue, white, or purple flowers.

[2]**per·i·win·kle** (PEHR-ee-wing-kəl) *noun.* A small, edible snail with a thick cone-shaped shell. **periwinkles.**

per·ju·ry (PER-jer-ee) *noun.* The act of testifying falsely, of deliberately lying under oath.

perk *verb.* 1. To lift quickly; raise briskly: The dog *perked* his ears. 2. (Often used with *up*) To become lively, alert, or cheerful. **perked, perking.** —**perky** *adjective.*

per·ma·nent (PER-mə-nənt) *adjective.* Lasting; enduring; for all time. —**permanently** *adverb.*

per·me·ate (PER-mee-ayt) *verb.* To penetrate; pervade; to pass or seep through: The smell *permeated* the room. **permeated, permeating.**

per·mis·sion (pər-MISH-ən) *noun.* Consent; approval; authorization.

per·mit (pər-MIT) *verb.* 1. To allow; give consent; authorize. 2. To make possible: If conditions *permit,* we'll go tomorrow. **permitted, permitting.** —*noun.* (PER-mit) A formal written authorization; a license.

per·ni·cious (pər-NISH-əss) *adjective.* Destructive, harmful, damaging.

per·pen·dic·u·lar (pər-pən-DIK-yə-lər) *adjective.* 1. Upright; standing straight up. 2. Meeting another line at a right angle. —*noun.* A line or plane at right angles to another line or plane.

per·pe·trate (PER-pə-trayt) *verb.* To commit, as a crime; do (something) wrong; carry out (a prank or trick). **perpetrated, perpetrating.**

per·pet·u·al (pər-PECH-oo-əl) *adjective.* 1. Everlasting; continuing forever. 2. Constant; uninterrupted: *perpetual* barking. —**perpetually** *adverb.*

per·pet·u·ate (pər-PECH-oo-ayt) *verb.* To continue; make certain something lasts: *perpetuate* his memory. **perpetuated, perpetuating.**

per·plex (pər-PLEKS) *verb.* To puzzle, mystify, confuse. **perplexed, perplexing.** —**per·plex·i·ty** (pər-PLEK-sə-tee) *noun.*

per·se·cute (PER-sə-kyoot) *verb.* To be mean or oppressive to; cause injury or torment to, often without cause. **persecuted, persecuting.**

per•se•vere (per-sə-VIHR) *verb.* To keep on trying; not give up in spite of difficulties. **persevered, persevering.** —**perseverance** *noun.*

per•sim•mon (pər-SIM-ən) *noun.* 1. An orange-red fruit shaped like a plum. 2. The tree on which this fruit grows.

per•sist (pər-SIST) *verb.* 1. To keep at, continue (to do something): She *persisted* in biting her nails. 2. To endure or last: The heat wave *persisted* for two weeks. **persisted, persisting.** —**persistence** *noun.* —**persistent** *adjective.* —**persistently** *adverb.*

per•son (PER-sn) *noun.* 1. An individual; a human being; someone. 2. Someone's self or body: He took good care of his *person* by bathing often. 3. (Grammar) A form of pronouns and verbs indicating the speaker (first *person*), the person spoken to (second *person*), or the person or object spoken of (third *person*).

per•son•age (PER-sn-ij) *noun.* A person, especially an important person. **personages.**

per•son•al (PER-sn-l) *adjective.* 1. Private, individual: *personal* business; *personal* phone. 2. Done in person: a *personal* visit. 3. Of the body: *personal* tidiness. 4. Of, about, or against another person: Kate's *personal* remarks embarrassed me.

per•son•al•i•ty (per-sn-AL-ə-tee) *noun.* 1. The special qualities or traits that make an individual the way he is: a pleasant *personality.* 2. (Informal) A person of note: movie *personalities.* **personalities.**

per•son•al•ly (PER-sn-l-ee) *adverb.* 1. In person: I went *personally.* 2. As far as oneself is concerned: *Personally,* I prefer football to baseball. 3. As a person: While liking the mayor *personally,* my parents don't like his politics. 4. As though directed at oneself: Don't take his criticism *personally.*

per•son•i•fy (pər-SON-ə-figh) *verb.* 1. To think of or show as human (something that is not human). 2. To be a good example of: He *personifies* honesty. **personified, personifying.**

per•son•nel (per-sn-EL) *noun.* 1. (Used with a plural verb) The people employed by a business or organization. 2. (Used with a singular verb) The department of a business or organization that hires and directs relations with employees.

per•spec•tive (pər-SPEK-tiv) *noun.* 1. A way in which something is pictured on a flat surface (two dimensions) so as to give the appearance of distance or depth (three dimensions). 2. A point of view: Now that time has passed, we have a new *perspective* on the war. **perspectives.**

per•spire (pər-SPIGHR) *verb.* To sweat; give off salty moisture through the pores of the skin. **perspired, perspiring.** —**perspiration** (per-spə-RAY-shən) *noun.*

per•suade (pər-SWAYD) *verb.* To get (someone) to do something by arguing or coaxing. **persuaded, persuading.** —**persuasion** (pər-SWAY-zhən) *noun.*

per•sua•sive (pər-SWAY-siv) *adjective.* Having the ability to persuade. —**persuasively** *adverb.*

pert *adjective.* Saucy or impertinent; lively. —**pertly** *adverb.*

per•tain (pər-TAYN) *verb.* To have to do with; refer. **pertained, pertaining.**

per•ti•nent (PERT-n-ənt) *adjective.* Having to do with the matter at hand; to the point: Your remark is not *pertinent* to our discussion of cars. —**pertinently** *adverb.*

per•turb (pər-TERB) *verb.* To make uneasy. **perturbed, perturbing.**

pe•ruse (pə-ROOZ) *verb.* To read or look over carefully. **perused, perusing.**

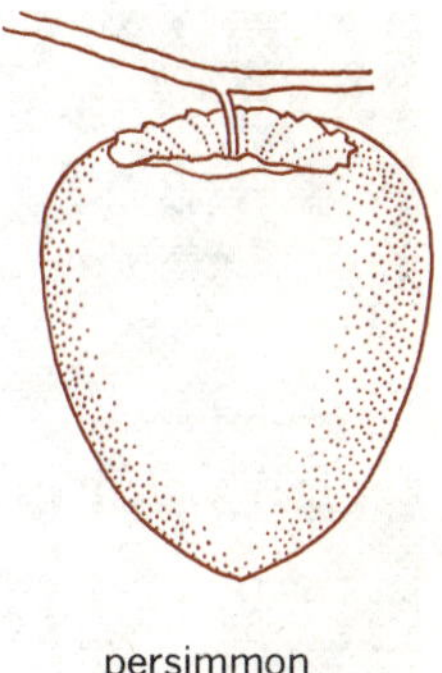
persimmon

petrel

pewee

pharaoh

per·vade (pər-VAYD) *verb.* To spread throughout: Happiness *pervades* their home. **pervaded, pervading.**

per·verse (pər-VERSS) *adjective.* 1. Contrary; stubborn: The *perverse* mule had to be dragged. 2. Evil; wicked. —**perversely** *adverb.*

pe·so (PAY-soh) *noun.* The basic unit of money in Mexico, many Latin American countries, and the Philippines. **pesos.**

pes·si·mism (PESS-ə-miz-əm) *noun.* A tendency to look at everything from the gloomy side.

pes·si·mist (PESS-ə-mist) *noun.* One who looks at everything from the gloomy side. —**pessimistic** (pess-ə-MISS-tik) *adjective.* —**pessimistically** *adverb.*

pest *noun.* 1. Any animal, insect, or plant that is harmful to crops or human beings. 2. A person who is a bother or nuisance.

pest·er (PESS-tər) *verb.* To annoy; bother. **pestered, pestering.**

pes·ti·cide (PESS-tə-sighd) *noun.* Any chemical substance used to kill insects or other pests. **pesticides.**

pes·ti·lence (PESS-tə-lənss) *noun.* Any disease that spreads quickly and usually causes death. **pestilences.**

pes·tle (PESS-l) *noun.* A straight hand tool with a rounded end used to crush something in a bowl called a mortar. **pestles.**

pet *noun.* 1. An animal kept for enjoyment or friendship. 2. A favorite. —*verb.* To pat or stroke. **petted, petting.**

pet·al (PET-l) *noun.* One of the outer parts of a flower, usually having bright color.

pet·i·ole (PET-ee-ohl) *noun.* 1. (Botany) A leafstalk. 2. (Zoology) The thin, stalklike connection between the abdomen and thorax in some insects. **petioles.**

pe·tite (pə-TEET) *adjective.* Small or trim: a *petite* girl.

pe·ti·tion (pə-TISH-ən) *noun.* A formal written request: Twelve neighbors have signed Mother's *petition* asking for a stop sign at the corner. —*verb.* To make a formal request. **petitioned, petitioning.**

pet·rel (PET-rəl) *noun.* Any of several small sea birds capable of flying long distances from land.

pet·ri·fy (PET-rə-figh) *verb.* 1. To turn into stone. 2. To paralyze with fear or some other strong emotion: Bill *petrifies* his friends with stories of ghosts. **petrified, petrifying.**

pe·tro·le·um (pə-TROH-lee-əm) *noun.* Oil as found in the ground before it is refined to make gasoline, kerosene, and other products.

pet·ti·coat (PET-ee-koht) *noun.* A woman's or girl's skirt worn under her outer garment.

pet·ty (PET-ee) *adjective.* 1. Small or insignificant: *petty* details. 2. Having a mean or narrow outlook. **pettier, pettiest.** —**pettily** *adverb.*

pet·u·lant (PECH-ə-lənt) *adjective.* Irritable or peevish for little or no reason. —**petulantly** *adverb.*

pe·tu·nia (pə-TOON-yə or pə-TYOON-yə) *noun.* A plant of the nightshade family that has funnel-shaped flowers of various colors.

pew (PYOO) *noun.* A backed bench used in churches to seat people.

pe·wee (PEE-wee) Also **peewee** *noun.* A small woodland bird of North America related to the phoebe and named for its call. **pewees.**

pew·ter (PYOO-tər) *noun.* 1. An alloy of tin, lead, and other metals having a silver-gray color. 2. Utensils made of pewter.

phan·tom (FAN-təm) *noun.* 1. A ghost. 2. Something that appears only in the imagination: The flying saucer was only a *phantom.* —*adjective.* Ghostlike; not real.

phar·aoh (FAIR-oh) *noun.* [Often capital P] A ruler of ancient Egypt.

Phar·i·see (FA-rə-see) *noun.* A member of an ancient Jewish sect that strictly followed and upheld its own laws and religious traditions. **Pharisees.**

phar·ma·cist (FAHR-mə-sist) *noun.* A druggist; a person who dispenses medicines.

phar·ma·cy (FAHR-mə-see) *noun.* 1. A place where medicines are sold; drugstore. 2. The profession of preparing and selling medicines.

phar·ynx (FA-ringks) *noun.* The part of the alimentary canal that begins at the nasal cavity and ends at the larynx. —**pharynges** (fə-RIN-jeez) or **pharynxes** *plural.*

phase (FAYZ) *noun.* 1. One of the steps in the development of anything: Learning to talk is one *phase* of early childhood. 2. One side or part of a matter: "Literature is a *phase* of life." (Marianne Moore). 3. The apparent shape of the moon or a planet at a particular time: The new moon is the first of five *phases* of the moon. **phases.**

pheas·ant (FEZ-nt) *noun.* A game bird, the male of which has a long tail and brilliant feathers.

phe·nom·e·nal (fə-NOM-ə-nl) *adjective.* Extraordinary: The runner had *phenomenal* endurance. —**phenomenally** *adverb.*

phe·nom·e·non (fə-NOM-ə-non) *noun.* 1. Any happening that can be detected by the senses and can be scientifically explained: Thunder is a *phenomenon* of nature. 2. An extraordinary or unusual person, thing, or occurrence. —**phenomena** (fə-NOM-ə-nə) or **phenomenons** (for 2) *plural.*

phil·an·throp·ic (fil-ən-THROP-ik) *adjective.* Tending to help mankind. —**philanthropically** *adverb.*

phi·lan·thro·pist (fə-LAN-thrə-pist) *noun.* A person who loves mankind and wants to further its welfare through works or gifts.

phi·los·o·pher (fə-LOSS-ə-fər) *noun.* 1. One who studies and loves wisdom and knowledge. 2. A person who lives his life according to a particular system of philosophy.

phi·los·o·phy (fə-LOSS-ə-fee) *noun.* 1. The study of the nature of mankind and of the universe. 2. A system of principles by which to live. 3. A calm and reasonable acceptance of life and what it brings. **philosophies.** —**philosophic** (fil-ə-SOF-ik) or **philosophical** *adjective.* —**philosophically** *adverb.*

phlox (FLOKS) *noun.* A garden plant with a long stem and many clusters of small bright blossoms. —**phloxes** or **phlox** *plural.*

phoe·be (FEE-bee) *noun.* A small woodland bird of North America related to the pewee. **phoebes.**

phone (FOHN) *noun.* A telephone. **phones.** —*verb.* To telephone. **phoned, phoning.**

pho·net·ic (fə-NET-ik) *adjective.* Representing the sounds of speech by a set of symbols or letters: *Phonetic* spelling is used in this dictionary to show pronunciations.

phon·ics (FON-iks) *noun, plural in form but used with a singular verb.* A system for teaching beginners how to read by sounding out words.

pho·no·graph (FOH-nə-graf) *noun.* An instrument that reproduces sound from records.

pho·ny (FOH-nee) *noun* (and *adjective*). (Informal) A person or thing that is not honest or real; a fake. **phonies.**

phos·phate (FOSS-fayt) *noun.* 1. A chemical salt that contains phosphorus. 2. A fertilizer that contains phosphate. **phosphates.**

phos·pho·rus (FOSS-fə-rəss) *noun.* A nonmetallic chemical element needed for plant and animal growth and used in fireworks and fertilizer. —**phosphorous** *adjective.*

phlox

phoebe

pheasant

piano

piccolo

piazza

pho·to (FOH-toh) *noun.* A photograph. **photos.**

pho·to·e·lec·tric cell *See* **electric eye.**

pho·to·graph (FOH-tə-graf) *noun.* A picture made with a camera. —*verb.* To make a photograph of. **photographed, photographing.** —**photographic** (foh-tə-GRAF-ik) *adjective.*

pho·tog·ra·pher (fə-TOG-rə-fər) *noun.* A person who takes pictures with a camera.

pho·tog·ra·phy (fə-TOG-rə-fee) *noun.* The art, science, or profession of taking pictures with a camera.

pho·ton (FOH-ton) *noun.* The smallest possible quantity of light energy or radiant energy.

Pho·to·stat (FOH-tə-stat) *trademark.* 1. A camera-like device that makes copies of printed material on a special paper. 2. A copy made by this device.

pho·to·syn·the·sis (foh-toh-SIN-thə-siss) *noun.* A process by which green plants use the energy of sunlight to make sugars and starches from carbon dioxide and water.

phrase (FRAYZ) *noun.* 1. A group of two or more words that go together or form one idea but are not a complete sentence: "In a car" is a *phrase.* 2. A distinctive way of speaking or writing: "Eight bells" is a sailor's *phrase.* 3. A short expression; a few words that express something very well: I can describe the house in a single *phrase.* 4. A section or a few measures of music. **phrases.** —*verb.* To write or say in a certain way. **phrased, phrasing.**

phys·ic (FIZ-ik) *noun.* A laxative; a medicine used to move the bowels.

phys·i·cal (FIZ-i-kəl) *adjective.* 1. Having to do with the body: a *physical* examination. 2. Having to do with things that can be seen, heard, felt, tasted, or smelled: the *physical* world. 3. Natural, or having to do with natural sciences such as physics or biology: a *physical* law. —*noun.* A medical examination. —**physically** *adverb.*

phy·si·cian (fi-ZISH-ən) *noun.* A doctor; one who is duly qualified to practice medicine.

phys·i·cist (FIZ-ə-sist) *noun.* An expert in the field of physics.

phys·ics (FIZ-iks) *noun, plural in form but used with a singular verb.* The science that deals with matter, energy, and motion.

phys·i·ol·o·gy (fiz-ee-OL-ə-jee) *noun.* The science that deals with how the parts or organs of living things work.

pi (PIGH) *noun.* (Math) A number equal to about 3.14, obtained when the distance around a circle (circumference) is divided by the distance across the circle (diameter): In math, the Greek letter π stands for *pi.*

pi·an·ist (pee-AN-ist or PEE-ə-nist) *noun.* A person who plays the piano, especially one with skill.

pi·an·o (pee-AN-oh) *noun.* A large musical instrument with a keyboard: When the keys of a *piano* are touched, they force special hammers to hit metal strings and thus produce musical sounds. **pianos.** —*adverb.* (Music) A direction to play music softly.

pi·az·za (pee-AZ-ə or pee-AHZ-ə) *noun.* 1. An open public square in an Italian city or town. 2. A long porch with columns along one or more sides.

pic·co·lo (PIK-ə-loh) *noun.* A small flute that makes sounds an octave higher than a regular flute. **piccolos.**

pick (PIK) *verb.* 1. To select or choose: *Pick* a card. 2. To gather or remove, usually with the fingers: *pick* apples off a tree. 3. To take small pieces from (with a pointed object or the fingers): *pick* your teeth. 4. To clean or make ready by taking away useless parts: *Pick* all the feathers from the turkey. 5. To start: *pick* a quarrel. 6. To open without a key: *pick* locks. 7. To steal something from: Arrest him; he *picked* my pocket. 8. To pluck the strings of a musical instrument. 9. To eat just a little: *pick* at one's food. **picked, picking.** —*noun.* 1. A pickax. 2. A choice or the act of choosing: Take your *pick* of candy. 3. The best one or ones: This black kitten is the *pick* of the litter. —**pick on.** To bully; annoy.

pick·ax or **pick·axe** (PIK-aks) *noun.* A heavy metal tool with a point at one or both ends and a long handle.

pick·er·el (PIK-ər-əl or PIK-rəl) *noun.* A large fresh-water fish with a long, narrow head.

pick·et (PIK-it) *noun.* 1. A stake or post driven into the ground, especially to make a fence. 2. A person who stands or marches outside a building as a method of protest, usually carrying a sign expressing a grievance. 3. A soldier or a small group of soldiers placed outside the main body of troops to warn them if the enemy comes. —*verb.* To act as a picket. **picketed, picketing.**

pick·le (PIK-əl) *noun.* 1. A fruit or vegetable, especially a cucumber, preserved in spices and vinegar or salt water. 2. The liquid used to preserve pickles. 3. (Slang) Trouble; a bad situation: If you get into a *pickle,* call for help. **pickles.** —*verb.* To preserve by placing in a pickle: She *pickled* tomatoes. **pickled, pickling.**

pick·pock·et (PIK-pok-it) *noun.* Someone who steals things from another's pocket.

pickup truck. A small light truck.

pic·nic (PIK-nik) *noun.* 1. An outing on which food is taken along and eaten out-of-doors. 2. (Slang) An enjoyable time: We had a *picnic* at the ball game. —*verb.* To go on a picnic. **picnicked, picnicking.**

pic·to·ri·al (pik-TOR-ee-əl) *adjective.* 1. Pertaining to or having pictures: the *pictorial* feature of a book. 2. Vivid; having word pictures: a *pictorial* poem. 3. Explaining something by means of pictures: *pictorial* charts.

pic·ture (PIK-chər) *noun.* 1. A photograph, drawing, or painting. 2. A scene: The playful kittens made a charming *picture.* 3. An idea: I have a *picture* of what you mean. 4. A description, especially a clear and vivid one: Sam's words gave us a vivid *picture* of the accident. 5. (Often plural) A motion picture. 6. The image on a television screen. 7. A very good example of: the *picture* of happiness. 8. The likeness; the image: He is the *picture* of his grandfather. **pictures.** —*verb.* 1. To imagine; see in the mind: Can you *picture* how I feel? 2. To show; make into a picture: Whistler *pictured* his mother in a chair. 3. To describe in words. **pictured, picturing.**

pic·tur·esque (pik-chər-ESK) *adjective.* 1. Like a picture; fit for a picture; beautiful or interesting: *picturesque* views. 2. Vivid; making a clear picture for the mind: a *picturesque* report of the trip.

picture window. A large window, usually placed so as to give an attractive view.

picture writing. 1. The art of writing with pictures instead of words; a piece of such writing: The Indians left examples of *picture writing* in the mountains of the Southwest. 2. The pictures themselves.

pie (PIGH) *noun.* 1. A food containing fruit, meat, or fish baked in a shell of dough. 2. Something that looks like a pie: a mud *pie.* **pies.** —**easy as pie.** Very easy.

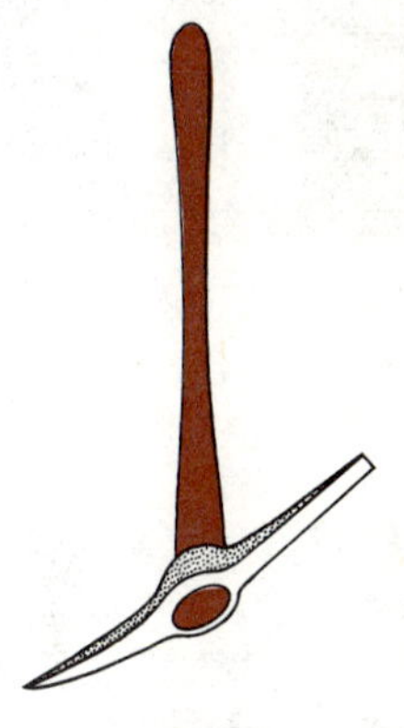
pickax

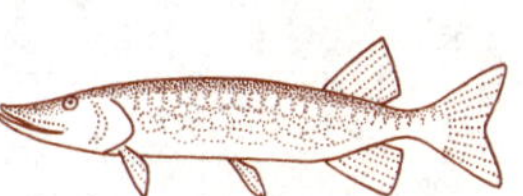
pickerel

pickup truck

pig

piglets

pigeons

piece (PEESS) *noun.* 1. A scrap, bit, or chunk; one of the parts that make up a thing: The dish fell and broke into a hundred *pieces.* 2. A single thing in a set or collection: Three *pieces* in the dessert set are cracked. 3. A limited part or quantity: a *piece* of land. 4. A particular length, size, or quantity; a complete unit. 5. A creative work, such as a play, statue, painting, or musical composition: *pieces* of art. 6. An example of something: Fighting is a *piece* of stupidity. 7. A coin: a twenty-five-cent *piece.* 8. A revolver, rifle, or cannon. **pieces.** —*verb.* 1. To make by joining pieces: She will *piece* together a Halloween costume for me. 2. To mend, patch, or complete by adding pieces: He *pieced* the model plane with scraps of balsa. **pieced, piecing.** —**give a person a piece of one's mind.** To scold someone; give someone a critical, blunt opinion. —**go to pieces.** To lose one's control; to break down.

piece·meal (PEESS-meel) *adverb.* 1. A little at a time; bit by bit; by degrees: I do my homework *piecemeal.* 2. In pieces or fragments; apart. —*adjective.* Made or done piece by piece: a *piecemeal* job.

pied (PIGHD) *adjective.* Having patches of two or more colors.

pier (PIHR) *noun.* 1. A structure built on posts out over water and used as a dock or a walk. 2. A support or pillar, as of a bridge or building.

pierce (PIHRSS) *verb.* 1. To go into or through; penetrate; stab: The nail *pierces* the board. 2. To make a hole through; bore through: The doctor *pierced* her ears for earrings. 3. To make a way through or into: Daniel Boone *pierced* the wilds of Kentucky. 4. To see through or understand: Her sharp eyes will *pierce* your disguise. 5. To touch emotionally; affect sharply: The baby's cry *pierces* him to the heart. **pierced, piercing.**

pi·e·ty (PIGH-ə-tee) *noun.* 1. Respect for God. 2. Faithful adherence to one's religion. 3. Regard or respect for one's parents or family. **pieties.**

pig *noun.* 1. A swine or hog; an animal with a broad snout and a fat body covered with bristles. 2. (Slang) A person who is greedy, selfish, or untidy. 3. An oblong piece of metal, such as iron or lead, of a standard size.

pi·geon (PIJ-ən) *noun.* 1. A bird with short legs and a plump body, similar to but larger than a dove. 2. (Slang) A naive person; one who is easily duped.

pigeon pea. 1. A woody shrub of the tropics, with yellow flowers and flat pods containing small nourishing peas. 2. The pea that grows on this shrub.

pigeon·toed (PIJ-ən-tohd) *adjective.* Having the toes turned in.

piggy bank. A coin bank shaped like a pig.

pig·head·ed (PIG-hed-id) *adjective.* Stubborn; not willing to concede.

pig·let (PIG-lit) *noun.* A baby pig.

pig·ment (PIG-mənt) *noun.* 1. A coloring matter; a powder that is mixed with a liquid to make paint, ink, or dyes. 2. Certain substances that appear in living cells and give them color: skin *pigment.*

pig·my (PIG-mee) *noun.* *See* **pygmy.**

pig·tail (PIG-tayl) *noun.* A braid of hair hanging down from the back of the head.

[1]**pike** (PIGHK) *noun.* A long slender fresh-water fish that is used for food. —**pike** or **pikes** *plural.*

[2]**pike** (PIGHK) *noun.* A weapon with a long wooden shaft and a sharp metal point, used by soldiers long ago. **pikes.**

[3]**pike** (PIGHK) *noun.* A road, especially one that allows people to travel directly from one place to another with little stopping; a turnpike. **pikes.**

[1]**pile** (PIGHL) *noun.* 1. A group of items stacked or heaped upon each other: a wood *pile.* 2. A mass or mound: a sand *pile.* 3. (Informal) A large amount: a *pile* of money. **piles.** —*verb.* 1. To stack or heap things, one upon the other. 2. To form a pile. **piled, piling.**

[2]**pile** (PIGHL) *noun.* A long heavy post of concrete or wood that helps to support a bridge, pier, etc. **piles.**

[3]**pile** (PIGHL) *noun.* 1. A soft, thick surface, as of a carpet or velvet, made of upright yarns that are looped or cut. 2. Down; fine soft hair, as on fur. **piles.**

pil·fer (PIL-fər) *verb.* To steal small amounts of money or things of little value. **pilfered, pilfering.**

pil·grim (PIL-grim) *noun.* 1. A religious person who makes a long trip to a holy place as an act of worship. 2. A traveler; a wanderer. 3. [Capital P] One of the English Puritans who settled in Massachusetts in 1620.

pil·grim·age (PIL-grə-mij) *noun.* 1. A trip to a holy place. 2. A trip to any place for a special purpose.

pill (PIL) *noun.* 1. A medicine in the form of a small ball that is usually swallowed whole. 2. Something unpleasant that has to be accepted: a bitter *pill* to swallow. 3. (Slang) An unpleasant person.

pil·lage (PIL-ij) *verb.* To take booty; rob or loot with violence. **pillaged, pillaging.** —*noun.* The act of robbing or looting violently.

pil·lar (PIL-ər) *noun.* 1. A column; a long upright support for a roof. 2. Any major support; a person who is considered a leading supporter of something: a *pillar* of the church.

pil·lo·ry (PIL-ə-ree) *noun.* 1. A wooden frame with holes in which a person's head and hands were locked as a form of public punishment. 2. Any public means used to ridicule a person. **pillories.** —*verb.* 1. To place a person in a pillory. 2. To hold up to abuse or ridicule by the public. **pilloried, pillorying.**

pil·low (PIL-oh) *noun.* A cushion; a case filled with soft material, used as a support for the head. —*verb.* 1. To lay or rest on as on a pillow. 2. To be a pillow for: His breast *pillowed* the sleeping kitten. **pillowed, pillowing.**

pil·low·case (PIL-oh-kayss) *noun.* A cloth cover placed over a pillow.

pi·lot (PIGH-lət) *noun.* 1. A person who steers a ship or airplane. 2. A leader or guide. —*verb.* To steer or guide. **piloted, piloting.**

pilot project. A project set up as a guide, for study or as an example.

pim·ple (PIM-pəl) *noun.* A small inflamed swelling of the skin, sometimes sore and containing pus.

pin *noun.* 1. A small piece of metal wire with a flat head at one end and a sharp point at the other, used to fasten things together. 2. A badge or emblem with a clasp to attach it to one's clothing: Our club has its own *pin.* 3. A brooch; an ornament with a pin, worn on the clothing. 4. A short rod or peg of wood or metal, used to hang things on or fasten them together. 5. A wooden club, shaped like a bottle, that is used in bowling. —*verb.* 1. To fasten or join as with a pin; put a pin through. 2. To hold fast in one place: He *pinned* Jim to the mat. **pinned, pinning.** —**on pins and needles.** Very anxious or jumpy. —**pin down.** To establish (details) as accurate. —**pin (something) on (a person).** To place the blame on someone.

pin·a·fore (PIN-ə-for) *noun.* 1. A garment without sleeves worn over a dress. 2. A sleeveless house dress. **pinafores.**

pin·cers (PIN-sərz) *noun.* 1. A tool with two jaws used to grip things. 2. The large claws of lobsters and crabs.

pillory

pinafore

pintos

pineapple

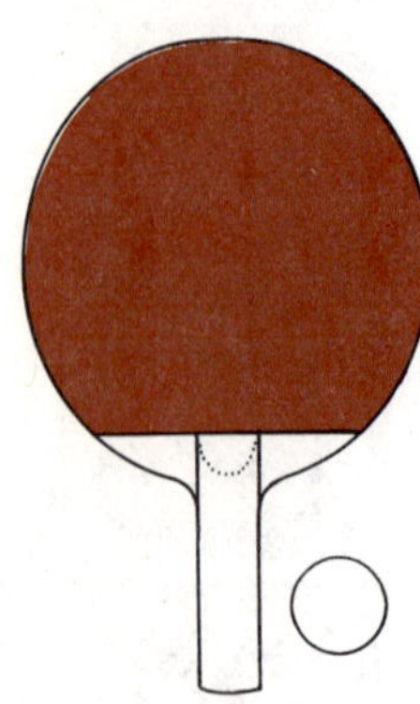
Ping-Pong

pinch *verb.* 1. To clasp and press (something) between two hard surfaces or between the ends of the thumb and a finger. 2. To press hard, so that it hurts: Tom's glasses *pinch* his nose. 3. To shrink; to cause to look thin: Their faces were *pinched* by the cold. 4. To nip or cut off: The gardener *pinched* off the buds. 5. (Slang) To arrest. 6. (Slang) To steal. 7. To be very thrifty: We *pinched* until we had enough money. **pinched, pinching.** —*noun.* 1. A nip or squeezing: a *pinch* on the cheek. 2. The amount that can be taken up between the ends of the thumb and a finger; a tiny amount: two *pinches* of sugar. 3. Pain, hardship, or pressure: the *pinch* of hunger. 4. (Slang) An arrest. 5. A difficult moment; an emergency: I can count on him in a *pinch.* **pinches.**

[1]**pine** (PIGHN) *noun.* 1. An evergreen tree that bears cones and needle-like leaves. 2. The wood of this tree. **pines.**

[2]**pine** (PIGHN) *verb.* 1. To mourn or long (for something). 2. (Used with *away*) To fade or die from sorrow or longing. **pined, pining.**

pine·ap·ple (PIGHN-ap-əl) *noun.* 1. A sweet, tropical fruit with a rough, brown covering and golden-yellow flesh inside. 2. The plant on which the pineapple grows. 3. (Slang) A hand explosive; grenade. **pineapples.**

Ping-Pong (PING-pawng) *trademark.* A game like lawn tennis, played on a table with paddles and a small, light ball. Also called "table tennis."

pink (PINGK) *noun.* 1. (Also *adjective*) A light shade of red. 2. Any of several flowers related to the carnation. —**in the pink.** In the best shape, condition, or health.

pink·eye (PINGK-igh) Also **pink eye** *noun.* A disease in which the membrane of the eyelid becomes irritated and sore.

pink·ie (PING-kee) Also **pinky** *noun.* (Informal) The little finger. **pinkies.**

pin·na·cle (PIN-ə-kəl) *noun.* 1. The peak of a mountain; any high pointed place. 2. The most important position. 3. A spire.

pin·point (PIN-point) *verb.* To locate and describe accurately: *pinpoint* the trouble in a motor. **pinpointed, pinpointing.**

pint (PYNT) *noun.* 1. A unit of liquid measure equal to 16 fluid ounces or one-half quart. 2. A unit of dry measure equal to 33.6 cubic inches or one-half quart.

pin·to (PIN-toh) *noun.* A spotted horse. —**pintos** or **pintoes** *plural.* —*adjective.* Spotted with white and another color.

pi·o·neer (pigh-ə-NIHR) *noun.* 1. One of the first persons to settle or enter a new territory. 2. One who is first to do something. —*verb.* To act as a pioneer. **pioneered, pioneering.**

pi·ous (PIGH-əss) *adjective.* Having or showing strong religious feelings.

pipe (PIGHP) *noun.* 1. A tube or hollow cylinder that carries fluids (water, oil, etc.) or gases. 2. A tube with a small bowl on one end, used for smoking tobacco. 3. Part of a musical instrument. 4. (Usually plural) A set of flutes or bagpipes. **pipes.** —*verb.* 1. To move or carry by means of pipes. 2. To play or signal on a pipe. **piped, piping.**

pipe·line (PIGHP-lighn) *noun.* 1. A long line of pipes through which oil, water, gas, or the like is moved. 2. (Informal) A source of information, usually secret. **pipelines.**

pi·ra·cy (PIGH-rə-see) *noun.* 1. Robbery at sea. 2. Stealing or using illegally another's ideas.

pi·rate (PIGH-rit) *noun.* 1. A person who commits robbery at sea. 2. One who uses another's ideas. —*verb.* To steal the ideas or work of others. **pirated, pirating.**

Pi·sces (PIGH-seez) *noun.* The 12th sign of the zodiac, also called the "Fish." The time of this sign is from February 20 through March 20.

pis·ta·chi·o (pi-STASH-ee-oh or pi-STAH-shee-oh) *noun.* 1. A sweet greenish nut. 2. The tree on which this nut grows. 3. (Also *adjective*) A yellow-green color. **pistachios.**

pis·til (PISS-til) *noun.* The part of a flower that holds the seeds.

pis·tol (PISS-tl) *noun.* A small gun that is held and fired in one hand.

pis·ton (PISS-tən) *noun.* A machine part made up of a solid cylinder that moves back and forth inside a tube under the pressure of a gas or fluid.

[1]**pit** *noun.* 1. A deep hole in the ground. 2. A depression in the surface of anything, as a scar from smallpox. 3. An area beside a track where racing cars are refueled and repaired. 4. The place in front of a stage where an orchestra sits. —*verb.* 1. To make pits or scars. 2. To set (one person, group, force against another); match: *pit* one against another. **pitted, pitting.**

[2]**pit** *noun.* The seed or stone in certain fruits such as peaches, cherries, and plums. —*verb.* To remove the seeds or stones from fruit. **pitted, pitting.**

[1]**pitch** (PICH) *noun.* 1. A black, sticky substance, made from tar or petroleum, used on roofs, streets, etc. 2. The sap of evergreen trees.

[2]**pitch** (PICH) *verb.* 1. To throw, fling, or toss. 2. (Baseball) To throw a ball to a batter. 3. To set up or put up: *pitch* a tent. 4. (Music) To set a musical key or tone: *Pitch* your voice a little lower. 5. To dip and rise, as the bow of a ship in heavy waves. 6. To fall suddenly forward with force. **pitched, pitching.** —*noun.* 1. (Baseball) The throw of the ball by a pitcher: a bad *pitch.* 2. A level, point, or degree: spirits are at a high *pitch.* 3. (Music) The highness or lowness of a tone.

pitch·blende (PITCH-blend) *noun.* The ore from which uranium and radium are obtained.

pitch·er (PICH-ər) *noun.* 1. (Baseball) The player who throws the ball to the batter. 2. A wide-mouthed container with a lip for pouring liquid.

pitcher plant. Any of several kinds of plants with pitcher-like leaves that store water and trap and digest insects.

pitch·fork (PICH-fork) *noun.* A long-handled fork used to lift and toss hay.

pit·e·ous (PIT-ee-əss) *adjective.* Worthy of pity; deserving pity.

pit·fall (PIT-fawl) *noun.* 1. A hidden or unexpected danger; a trap. 2. A concealed hole for trapping animals.

pith *noun.* 1. The spongy, central core of some plant stems. 2. The most important part; the central core: the *pith* of the story. —**pithy** *adjective.*

pit·i·a·ble (PIT-ee-ə-bəl) *adjective.* 1. Causing pity; worthy of pity. 2. Causing contempt along with pity: Stop that *pitiable* complaining.

pit·i·ful (PIT-i-fəl) *adjective.* 1. Worthy of pity; causing pity. 2. Causing contempt or scorn. —**pitifully** *adverb.*

pit·i·less (PIT-i-liss) *adjective.* Without pity; showing no mercy; cruel. —**pitilessly** *adverb.*

pi·tu·i·tar·y (pi-TOO-ə-tehr-ee or pi-TYOO-ə-tehr-ee) *noun.* A small, oval gland at the base of the brain.

pit·y (PIT-ee) *noun.* 1. A feeling of sorrow or sympathy for the unhappiness or pain of other people. 2. A reason for feeling sympathy or sorrow: It's a *pity* you can't come with us. —*verb.* To feel pity. **pitied, pitying.**

Pisces

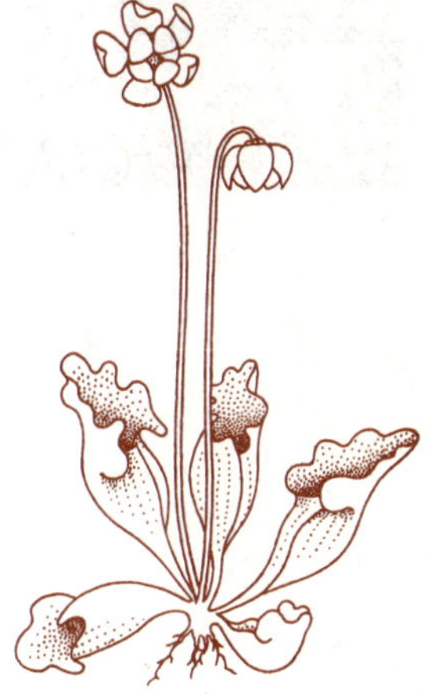
pitcher plant

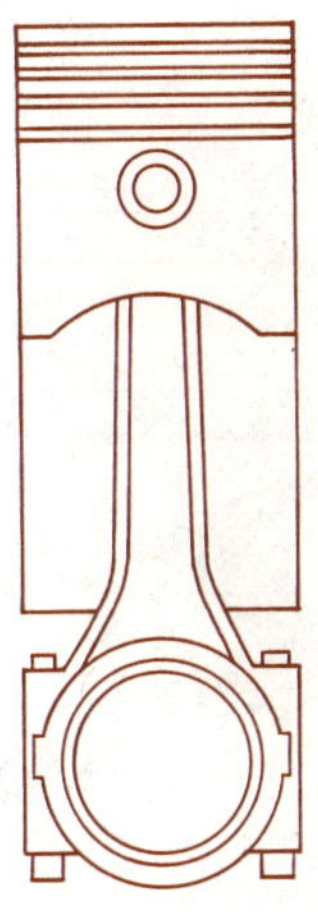
piston

piv·ot (PIV-ət) *noun.* 1. A pin, point, or shaft on which something turns. 2. A central idea or event which causes a turn in feeling, thinking, or direction. 3. Stepping around with one foot while keeping the other foot firmly on the floor. *—verb.* 1. To turn as on a pivot. 2. To mount on a pivot. **pivoted, pivoting.**

pix·y (PIK-see) Also **pixie** *noun.* A fairy or elf. **pixies.**

piz·za (PEET-sə) *noun.* An Italian dish consisting of a thin layer of dough covered with tomato sauce, spices, cheese, and toppings such as sausage, peppers, etc.

plaid

pk. *abbreviation.* 1. Park. 2. Pack. 3. Peak. 4. Peck.

pkg. *abbreviation.* Package.

pl. *abbreviation.* Plural.

Pl. *abbreviation.* Place (as part of a street name).

plac·ard (PLAK-ərd) *noun.* A poster or notice put in a public place.

place (PLAYSS) *noun.* 1. Any spot or location. 2. Where someone belongs, lives, or works: a *place* in the country. 3. A location or building used for a specific purpose: a *place* of business. 4. An occupied or assigned space, location, or position: "A *place* for everything, and everything in its *place.*" (Old saying). 5. Position in order or rank: third *place.* 6. A short street. 7. A table setting for one person. **places.** *—verb.* 1. To put in a particular spot, position, or location. 2. To identify by making a mental connection: I can't *place* her face. 3. To have a certain position in a race, league, contest, etc.: His team *placed* last. **placed, placing.**

place mat. A small mat on which a single table setting is arranged.

place value. The amount represented by any digit in a series of digits as determined by position in the series: In the number 213, the digit 2 has a *place value* of 200.

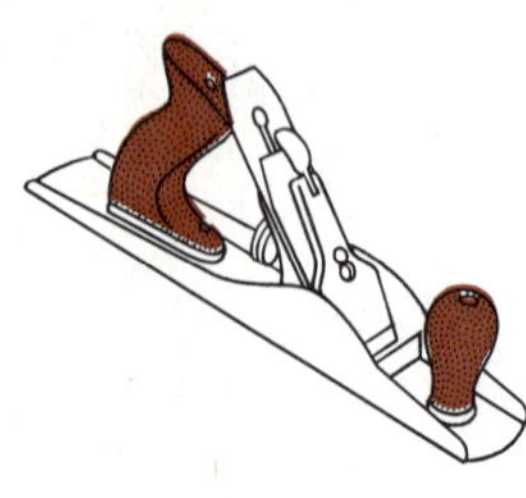

[1]plane

plac·id (PLASS-id) *adjective.* Peaceful; calm; quiet.

pla·gia·rize (PLAY-jə-righz) *verb.* To take the words, ideas, or creations of another person and use them as one's own work. **plagiarized, plagiarizing.** —**plagiarism** *noun.*

plague (PLAYG) *noun.* 1. A disease that spreads rapidly and kills many people. 2. Anything that causes great annoyance or trouble. **plagues.** *—verb.* 1. To overwhelm with suffering or trouble. 2. To annoy endlessly. **plagued, plaguing.**

plaid (PLAD) *noun.* 1. A pattern formed by crossing vertical and horizontal stripes. 2. Such a pattern worn by Scots to show membership in a particular family or clan.

plain (PLAYN) *noun.* A large, flat or nearly flat, area of land. *—adjective.* 1. Easily understood, heard, or seen. 2. Not decorated; simple. 3. Ordinary; not unusual. 4. Not beautiful; common: a *plain* face. 5. To the point; honest: *plain* talk. **plainer, plainest.** —**plainly** *adverb.*

plain-spo·ken (PLAYN-SPOH-kən) *adjective.* Frank; honest and simple in speech.

plain·tiff (PLAYN-tif) *noun.* A person who sues another in a court of law.

plain·tive (PLAYN-tiv) *adjective.* Expressing or showing sadness.

plait (PLAYT or PLAT) *noun.* 1. A braid. 2. A fold of cloth; a pleat. *—verb.* 1. To braid. 2. To fold into a pleat or pleats. **plaited, plaiting.**

plan *noun.* 1. The ideas for a way of getting something done. 2. A diagram or drawing showing how something is arranged: a floor *plan.* *—verb.* 1. To work out a way of getting something done. 2. To keep in mind; make arrangements for. **planned, planning.**

[1]**plane** (PLAYN) *noun.* A carpenter's tool used to make wood smooth. **planes.** *—verb.* To make smooth with a plane. **planed, planing.**

[2]**plane** (PLAYN) *noun.* 1. A flat, level surface. 2. A level or step in achieving or growing: a higher *plane* of thinking. 3. An airplane. **planes.** —*adjective.* (Geometry) Dealing with flat-surface figures, rather than solid figures.

plane figure. A figure or curve drawn on one plane.

plan·et (PLAN-ət) *noun.* A heavenly body that emits no light but is lighted by the sun, around which it orbits. —**planetary** *adjective.*

plan·e·tar·i·um (plan-ə-TAIR-ee-əm) *noun.* 1. A projector that shows, on a domed ceiling, a representation of the heavenly bodies and their movements. 2. A building that contains such a projector. —**planetariums** or **planetaria** (plan-ə-TAIR-ee-ə) *plural.*

plan·e·toid (PLAN-ə-toid) *noun.* A heavenly body that resembles a small planet; an asteroid.

plane tree. A tree with broad leaves; a sycamore tree.

plank (PLANGK) *noun.* 1. A long, thick wooden board. 2. Any one of the principles in a political platform.

plank·ton (PLANGK-tən) *noun.* Very tiny animals and vegetable matter that float in lakes and oceans.

plant *noun.* 1. Any living thing that is a member of the vegetable kingdom. 2. A vegetable, flower, etc., rather than a tree or shrub. 3. A factory; the buildings and equipment of a particular business or institution. 4. A place where energy or power is produced: a nuclear *plant.* 5. (Slang) A person or thing used secretly to gather information: He was an FBI *plant.* —*verb.* 1. To put into the ground for growing. 2. To set in place; to put down: *plant* one's feet firmly. 3. To establish: Columbus *planted* colonies of Spain in the New World. 4. (Slang) To hide, conceal, or place for the purpose of spying. **planted, planting.**

plan·ta·tion (plan-TAY-shən) *noun.* 1. A large farm or estate in the southern United States or the tropics. 2. A large area planted with trees or plants producing a special crop or product.

plant·er (PLAN-tər) *noun.* 1. An ornamental container for plants. 2. The owner or manager of a plantation.

plaque (PLAK) *noun.* A thin plate or marker on a surface, that decorates or gives information. **plaques.**

plas·ma (PLAZ-mə) *noun.* The liquid part of blood in which cells are suspended.

plas·ter (PLASS-tər) *noun.* A thick, sticky mixture which is spread on walls and ceilings where it dries to a hard surface. —*verb.* 1. To cover with plaster; to spread (anything) as if using plaster. 3. To cover fully or widely: The walls were *plastered* with pictures. **plastered, plastering.**

plas·tic (PLASS-tik) *noun.* Any of many synthetic materials that can be shaped into many forms, including fibers for clothing, containers for food, and packaging materials. —*adjective.* 1. Able to be molded or shaped. 2. Made of plastic. 3. (Slang) Phony; imitation: *plastic* hippie.

plate (PLAYT) *noun.* 1. A dish, almost flat, and usually round in shape. 2. A thin, flat piece or sheet of any hard material. 3. A thin layer. 4. (Baseball) The marker at which the batter stands. 5. A dish or basket used to take up collections. 6. The part of a denture which holds false teeth. 7. Dishes, candlesticks, forks, knives, or other utensils covered with silver or gold. 8. (Printing) An engraved or molded form which is used to make printed impressions. 9. (Photography) A sheet of metal, glass, or paper made sensitive to chemicals or light and used to reproduce pictures. **plates.** —*verb.* To coat with a thin layer, especially of metal. **plated, plating.**

planetarium

pla·teau (pla-TOH) *noun.* A large, flat area of land high above sea level. —**plateaus** or **plateaux** (pla-TOHZ) *plural.*

plat·form (PLAT-form) *noun.* 1. A flat structure, like a stage or stand, that is raised above the area around it. 2. A formal statement of the beliefs or plans of an official, political party, or other group.

plat·i·num (PLAT-ə-nəm) *noun.* A valuable gray or silver-colored metal, often used in jewelry.

pla·toon (plə-TOON) *noun.* 1. A small unit of soldiers. 2. In sports, a small group or unit: a *platoon* of football players.

plat·ter (PLAT-ər) *noun.* A large dish, often oval, commonly used for serving meat or fish at a meal.

platypus

plat·y·pus (PLAT-i-pəss) *noun.* A small mammal, found in Australia, that is an excellent swimmer, lays eggs, and has webbed feet and a beak that looks like a duck's bill; a duckbill. —**platypuses** or **platypi** (PLAT-i-pigh) *plural.*

plau·si·ble (PLAW-zə-bəl) *adjective.* Seeming to be true or reasonable: a *plausible* explanation.

play *verb.* 1. To take part in a game or other form of recreation: *play* checkers. 2. To do things just for fun: *play* outside before school. 3. To make music on an instrument: *play* the violin. 4. To cause to sound (as a radio or other device): *play* a record. 5. To take a role in a drama. 6. To compete against: Bob will *play* Ralph in tennis. 7. To move across lightly and rapidly: Moonlight *played* over the rippling water. 8. To fill a position, as in sports: *play* second base. 9. To make use of, as in sports: The coach *played* his second team. 10. To do, usually for fun: *play* a trick. 11. To bet on: *play* the horses. 12. To pretend: *play* dead. 13. To be shown or performed. 14. To do or act in a certain way: *play* fair. **played, playing.** —*noun.* 1. A drama; performance by actors. 2. Participation in games or other recreation: Children often like *play* more than study. 3. A move or action in a game: a running *play.* 4. Freedom or looseness of movement or action: I like the *play* in my fishing rod. 5. Jest: Tim wasn't serious; he made the comment in *play.* —**play-off.** A game or competition to break a tie or decide a winner.

play·er (PLAY-ər) *noun.* 1. A person who plays or performs an action, as in sports, music, or drama. 2. A device that plays: record *player.*

play·ful (PLAY-fəl) *adjective.* 1. Liking or full of play or fun. 2. Humorous; joking. —**playfully** *adverb.*

play·ground (PLAY-grownd) *noun.* A place, often next to a school, where one can take part in outdoor games or other forms of play.

play·house (PLAY-howss) *noun.* 1. A theater. 2. A very small house meant for children to play in. 3. A toy house; doll house. **playhouses.**

playing card. One of a set of cards, each with different markings, used in playing games.

play·mate (PLAY-mayt) *noun.* A person with whom one plays.

play·room (PLAY-room or PLAY-rum) *noun.* A room, often with special furniture or equipment, used for games or play.

play·thing (PLAY-thing) *noun.* A toy or other object with which one plays.

play·wright (PLAY-right) *noun.* A person who writes plays.

pla·za (PLAH-zə or PLAZ-ə) *noun.* A public square or other large, open area in a city or town.

plea (PLEE) *noun.* 1. A request; a call for help. 2. An excuse: The tardy student's *plea* was that his alarm clock had stopped. 3. (Law) An accused person's formal answer to charges against him.

plead (PLEED) *verb.* 1. To ask for in an urgent manner; beg. 2. To give as an excuse: The quarterback *pleaded* sickness as the reason for his poor play. 3. To argue for or against, as in a courtroom: *plead* a case. 4. To make a formal answer to legal charges. **pleaded** or **pled, pleading.**

pleas·ant (PLEZ-nt) *adjective.* Pleasing, delightful: *pleasant* weather. —**pleasantly** *adverb.*

please (PLEEZ) *verb.* 1. To cause pleasure or satisfaction. 2. To do or be what one wants: Do whatever you *please.* 3. To be willing to (used in polite requests): *Please* pass the butter. **pleased, pleasing.**

pleas·ing (PLEEZ-ing) *adjective.* Causing delight or satisfaction.

pleas·ure (PLEZH-ər) *noun.* 1. A feeling of delight or satisfaction. 2. That which gives delight or satisfaction: Swimming can be a *pleasure* on a hot day. 3. A wish or choice. **pleasures.**

pleat (PLEET) *noun.* A fold in a fabric, held in place by stitching or ironing. —*verb.* To fold into pleats. **pleated, pleating.**

pled *verb. See* **plead.**

pledge (PLEJ) *noun.* 1. A formal promise: "The *Pledge* of Allegiance to the Flag." 2. Something given as a sign of an agreement or promise: The prince gave the princess a ring as a *pledge* of his love. 3. One who goes through a trial period before gaining full membership, as in a club. **pledges.** —*verb.* To make a pledge. **pledged, pledging.**

plen·te·ous (PLEN-tee-əss) *adjective.* Plentiful. —**plenteously** *adverb.*

plen·ti·ful (PLEN-ti-fəl) *adjective.* Available in large numbers or amounts. —**plentifully** *adverb.*

plen·ty (PLEN-tee) *noun.* 1. A large number or amount. 2. A condition or situation in which there is an abundance: a time of *plenty.*

pli·a·ble (PLIGH-ə-bəl) *adjective.* 1. Easily bent or twisted; flexible: Rubber is a *pliable* material. 2. Easily influenced or changed: We can persuade Jim; he is *pliable.*

pli·ant (PLIGH-ənt) *adjective.* 1. Easily bent; pliable. 2. Easily influenced.

pli·ers (PLIGH-ərz) *noun, plural.* A tool, hinged somewhat like scissors, that is used to hold, twist, or cut small objects and wire.

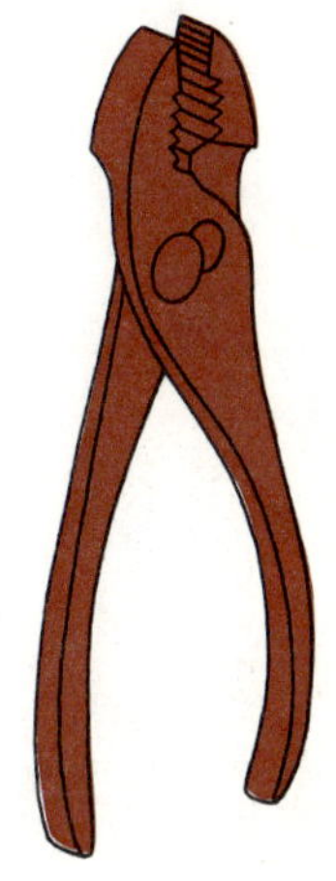
pliers

[1]**plight** *noun.* A state or situation that is difficult or dangerous.

[2]**plight** *verb.* To pledge or promise solemnly. **plighted, plighting.**

plod *verb.* 1. To walk in a heavy-footed manner: The soldiers *plodded* through the muddy field. 2. To work in a steady but slow manner. **plodded, plodding.**

plop *noun.* A sound like that made by a stone hitting still water. —*verb.* 1. To make such a noise. 2. To fall or drop in a relaxed or weary manner: Tom *plopped* into an easy chair. **plopped, plopping.**

plot *noun.* 1. A plan or scheme, usually for an evil purpose: The mutineers formed a *plot* to take over the ship. 2. A small section (of land): Mary Ann set aside a *plot* of land for her garden. 3. The series of actions that make up a story or play. —*verb.* 1. To make a plan or scheme, usually for an evil purpose. 2. To draw or diagram, as on a map: *plot* a course. **plotted, plotting.**

plow Also **plough** *noun.* 1. A tool or device, usually pulled by a tractor or horse, used to cut into and turn over soil. 2. A device used for pushing or lifting quantities, as of snow or earth. —*verb.* 1. To cut into and turn over soil with a plow. 2. To push aside or lift snow, dirt, or some other substance. 3. To move ahead by pushing through or aside what is in front: The boat *plowed* through the huge waves. 4. To do or accomplish with difficulty. **plowed, plowing.**

plow

plow·share (PLOW-shair) Also **plough-share** *noun.* The blade or cutting edge of a plow. **plowshares.**

pluck (PLUHK) *verb.* 1. To pick; pull off: *pluck* a rose. 2. To pick at; pull at and release quickly: Joel *plucked* the strings of his banjo. 3. To pull out: *pluck* feathers from a chicken. **plucked, plucking.** —*noun.* Courage; spirit.

pluck·y (PLUHK-ee) *adjective.* Brave, courageous; spirited. **pluckier, pluckiest.**

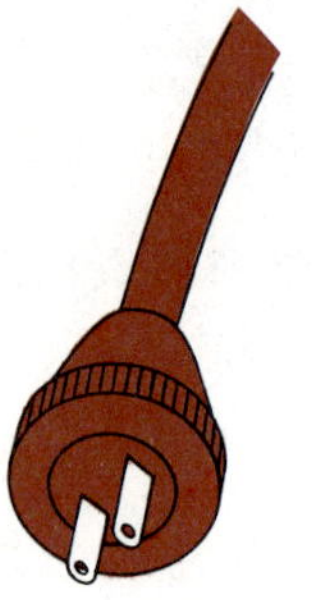
plug

plug (PLUHG) *noun.* 1. An electrical device with two metal prongs, used at the end of a cable to make an electrical connection. 2. Any object used to close up a hole or opening: the *plug* for a sink. 3. A fireplug; hydrant. 4. A piece of chewing tobacco. 5. (Informal) A mention or recommendation, especially on radio or television, for a product, person, or event. 6. (Slang) A worn-out horse. —*verb.* 1. (Informal) To work in a steady but slow or difficult manner; plod. 2. To connect an electrical plug to a socket: *plug* in a toaster. 3. To close up a hole or opening: *plug* a leak. 4. (Informal) To mention or recommend: The author *plugged* his new book on TV. 5. (Slang) To shoot (someone) with a gun. **plugged, plugging.**

plum

plum (PLUHM) *noun.* 1. A round smooth-skinned fruit with a large pit. 2. The tree on which this fruit grows. 3. Something good or desirable; prize: Uncle Ed's new job is quite a *plum.* —*noun* (and *adjective*). A bluish-red color.

plum·age (PLOOM-ij) *noun.* The feathers of a bird.

plumb (PLUHM) *noun.* A weight at the end of a line or string used to find the depth of water or to find out whether a wall or other upright surface is perpendicular. —*verb.* 1. To measure depth or test straightness with a plumb. 2. To investigate; look into. **plumbed, plumbing.** —*adjective.* 1. Vertical; straight up and down: a *plumb* wall. 2. (Also *adverb,* informal) Downright; completely: The wild horse is *plumb* dangerous.

plumb·er (PLUHM-ər) *noun.* A person whose job is installing or repairing pipes and other parts of a building's water or heating system.

plumb·ing (PLUHM-ing) *noun.* 1. Pipes and other elements of a building's water system. 2. The work done by a plumber.

plume (PLOOM) *noun.* 1. A large feather, sometimes worn as a decoration. 2. A figure or form that resembles a fluffy feather: *plume* of smoke. **plumes.** —*verb.* 1. To smooth or fluff feathers: The swan *plumed* its tail feathers. 2. To supply or decorate with plumes. **plumed, pluming.**

[1]**plump** (PLUHMP) *adjective.* Full or fattened in shape; chubby. —*verb.* To fluff up; make full: *plump* up pillows. **plumped, plumping.**

[2]**plump** (PLUHMP) *noun.* 1. A sudden, heavy fall. 2. The sound made by something hitting a surface heavily: The bag of sugar made a *plump* when it hit the table. —*verb.* To drop or fall suddenly and heavily. **plumped, plumping.**

plun·der (PLUHN-dər) *verb.* To rob; take by force. **plundered, plundering.** —*noun.* 1. Things that are stolen: The thieves hid their *plunder* in the cellar. 2. The act of robbing or taking by force.

plunge (PLUHNJ) *verb.* 1. To dive or rush into: *plunge* into a pool. 2. To thrust or push something quickly into: The cook *plunged* the lobster into boiling water. 3. To rush forward or downward: The car *plunged* down the steep hill when its brakes failed. 4. To do or act upon with energy: The children *plunged* into the game. **plunged, plunging.** —*noun.* A dive or sudden thrust forward or downward.

plu·ral (PLUR-əl) *noun.* (Grammar) The form of a word indicating that more than one person or thing is involved: "Hats" is the *plural* of "hat."

plus (PLUHSS) *preposition.* Added to: 6 *plus* 8 equals 14. —*noun.* 1. An amount greater than zero. 2. The symbol or mark (+) that is used to indicate addition. 3. An added or extra benefit or amount: Nora's tan was a *plus* from her trip.

plush (PLUHSH) Also **plushy** *adjective.* Elegant; luxurious: a *plush* hotel. **plusher, plushest.** —*noun.* A fabric similar to thick velvet.

Plu·to (PLOO-toh) *noun.* The planet ninth in distance from the sun.

plu·to·ni·um (ploo-TOH-nee-əm) *noun.* A radioactive chemical element used in producing nuclear energy.

[1]**ply** (PLIGH) *noun.* 1. One of two or more layers that form such things as plywood or fabric. 2. One of two or more strands twisted together to form a rope, yarn, or the like. **plies.**

[2]**ply** (PLIGH) *verb.* 1. To do (a job); apply (a skill or talent): *ply* a trade. 2. To supply; direct toward: *ply* with food. 3. To use, as a tool: *ply* an ax. 4. To travel over a route or between places on a regular basis: The ship *plied* the Atlantic Ocean. **plied, plying.**

ply·wood (PLIGH-wud) *noun.* A type of board or building material formed by gluing and pressing together several thin layers of wood.

p.m. *abbreviation.* Also **P.M.** (Latin) *Post meridiem,* used to indicate time between noon and midnight.

pneu·mat·ic (noo-MAT-ik or nyoo-MAT-ik) *adjective.* Related to, filled with, or run by air or gas: a *pneumatic* drill. —**pneumatically** *adverb.*

pneu·mo·nia (noo-MOHN-yə) *noun.* A disease that involves inflammation of the lungs.

P.O. *abbreviation.* Post Office.

[1]**poach** (POHCH) *verb.* To cook, especially unshelled eggs, by simmering in hot water or other liquid. **poached, poaching.**

[2]**poach** (POHCH) *verb.* 1. To trespass on private property, especially to hunt or fish. 2. To hunt or catch game or fish illegally. **poached, poaching.**

pock·et (POK-it) *noun.* 1. A carrying pouch sewn into or onto a garment. 2. A small vein or lode of ore in the earth. 3. A downward current (of air): air *pocket.* —*verb.* 1. To put in one's pocket. 2. To take dishonestly: The cashier shortchanged customers and *pocketed* the difference. **pocketed, pocketing.**

pocket billiards. *See* **pool.**

pock·et·book (POK-it-buk) *noun.* A woman's handbag; a purse.

pock·et·knife (POK-it-nighf) *noun.* A small knife with blades and sometimes other tools that fold into the handle. —**pocketknives** (POK-it-nighvz) *plural.*

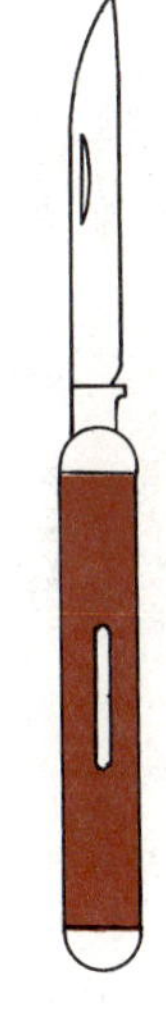

pocketknife

pod *noun.* A shell that contains the seeds of a plant: pea *pod.*

po·em (POH-əm) *noun.* A composition, frequently written in measured rhythm and in rhyme, intended to convey ideas or emotions.

po·et (POH-it) *noun.* A person who writes poems.

po·et·ry (POH-i-tree) *noun.* 1. A type of literature that uses rhyme, rhythm, or other special word patterns to express emotion or tell a story. 2. Any piece written in verse. —**poetic** (poh-ET-ik) or **poetical** *adjective.* —**poetically** *adverb.*

po·go stick (POH-goh). A stick-like toy, with footrests and a heavy spring at the bottom, on which one can hop.

poin·set·ti·a (poin-SET-ee-ə) *noun.* 1. A small yellow flower with red or white petal-like leaves. 2. The tropical shrub on which it grows.

poinsettia

poison ivy

polar bear

point *noun.* 1. A sharp end: the *point* of a pencil. 2. A narrow piece of land that extends into the sea. 3. A dot or period mark. 4. A spot or place: This is the *point* where we stopped for lunch. 5. A degree, stage, or condition where something happens: freezing *point.* 6. A use or purpose: Mother saw no *point* in buying something we didn't need. 7. The main idea: the *point* of a story. 8. A quality or trait: His one good *point* is that he is always honest. 9. A unit of scoring: Our team lost by only one *point.* —*verb.* 1. To aim: *Point* the hose at the flower bed. 2. To show the direction or position of: Amy *pointed* to the piece of chicken she wanted. 3. To bring to the attention of: Mother *pointed* out it was getting late. **pointed, pointing.** —**beside the point.** Having nothing to do with the question at hand. —**stretch a point.** To make an exception. —**point of view.** The way in which a thing is looked at: His *point of view* is a happy one.

point·blank (POINT-BLANGK) *adjective.* 1. Close; at close range, as of a gunshot. 2. Direct; blunt; to the point. —*adverb.* Closely; directly.

point·er (POIN-tər) *noun.* 1. A long, narrow stick used to point out things as on a chart or map. 2. The indicator on a scale, clock, or other measuring device. 3. A helpful hint on how to do something better. 4. A short-haired hunting dog trained to face in the direction of hidden game.

poise (POIZ) *verb.* To balance; hover: The acrobat *poised* on his hands before doing a somersault. **poised, poising.** —*noun.* A calm or easy manner.

poi·son (POI-zən) *noun.* 1. A substance that is harmful to the body and may cause death. 2. Anything that is harmful: Gossip is a *poison.* —*verb.* 1. To give poison to; put poison on or into. 2. To have a very bad effect on: Envy *poisons* the mind. **poisoned, poisoning.**

poison ivy. A shrub or vine with shiny, three-part leaves that can cause a rash if touched.

poison oak. Any of various shrubs that can cause a rash if touched.

poi·son·ous (POI-zən-əss) *adjective.* 1. Containing poison. 2. Characterized by ill will or malice: a *poisonous* look. —**poisonously** *adverb.*

poke (POHK) *verb.* 1. To jab or prod; push. 2. To dawdle. **poked, poking.** —*noun.* A jab. **pokes.** —**poke fun at.** To make fun of; tease.

pok·er (POH-kər) *noun.* 1. A metal rod for poking a fire. 2. A card game.

pok·ey (POH-kee) *noun.* (Slang) Jail.

pok·y (POH-kee) *adjective.* Slow: the *poky* puppy. **pokier, pokiest.**

po·lar (POH-lər) *adjective.* Having to do with the North or South Pole: *polar* regions; *polar* bear.

polar bear. A large white bear found in the Arctic or north polar regions.

po·lar·i·ty (poh-LA-rə-tee) *noun.* 1. The difference or split between such forces as magnetic poles. 2. Any difference or separation: Dad says there is a *polarity* between old-timers and the newcomers.

pole (POHL) *noun.* 1. A long rod of wood, metal, or other material: a fishing *pole.* 2. Either of the opposite ends of the axis around which the earth rotates: North *Pole,* South *Pole.* 3. Either of two places where opposite magnetic or electric forces are strongest. **poles.** —*verb.* To propel a boat with a pole. **poled, poling.**

pole·cat (POHL-kat) *noun.* 1. A small, brown, meat-eating animal of Europe noted for its bad smell when alarmed. 2. The skunk of North America.

pole·star (POHL-stahr) *noun.* The star

seen from Earth above the North Pole; the North Star.

pole vault. A contest in which the competitor pushes himself up and over a high crossbar with the aid of a pole.

po·lice (pə-LEESS) *noun, plural.* A department of government in charge of keeping law and order and preventing or detecting crimes. —*verb.* 1. To keep law and order in: *police* the streets. 2. To clean up: *police* the grounds after the picnic. **policed, policing.**

police force. The members of a police department.

po·lice·man (pə-LEESS-mən) *noun.* A male member of the police force. —**policemen** *plural.*

po·lice·wom·an (pə-LEESS-wum-ən) *noun.* A female member of the police force. —**policewomen** *plural.*

pol·i·cy (POL-ə-see) *noun.* 1. Principles determining action; a regular or usual way of handling things. 2. A written contract with an insurance company. **policies.**

po·li·o (POH-lee-oh) *noun.* A shortened form of the word *poliomyelitis.*

po·li·o·my·e·li·tis (poh-lee-oh-migh-ə-LIGH-tiss) *noun.* A disease that paralyzes legs, arms, or other body parts; also called "infantile paralysis" because it usually occurs in children.

pol·ish (POL-ish) *verb.* 1. To make or become smooth and shiny: *polish* the floor. 2. To improve or finish: *polish* a speech. **polished, polishing.** —*noun.* 1. A substance used to make something smooth and shiny: shoe *polish.* 2. Shininess: the *polish* of silver. 3. Skill and smoothness of performance. **polishes.**

po·lite (pə-LIGHT) *adjective.* Well-behaved and considerate; having good manners. **politer, politest.** —**politely** *adverb.*

po·lite·ness (pə-LIGHT-nəss) *noun.* Consideration and good manners.

po·lit·i·cal (pə-LIT-i-kəl) *adjective.* Referring to government or politics. —**politically** *adverb.*

pol·i·ti·cian (pol-ə-TISH-ən) *noun.* A person who holds or runs for government office, or who is influential in political party affairs.

pol·i·tics (POL-ə-tiks) *noun, plural in form but often used with a singular verb.* 1. The art or science of government. 2. The ways in which people try to control the machinery of government, for themselves or for others. 3. Political opinions. 4. Partisan or factional behavior within any group.

pol·ka (POHL-kə) *noun.* 1. A lively dance. 2. The music for this dance.

poll (POHL) *noun.* 1. The casting or recording of votes. 2. The number of votes cast. 3. (Usually plural) Voting places. 4. A canvassing of public opinion on an issue. —*verb.* 1. To cast (a vote). 2. To receive (votes). 3. To sample public opinion. **polled, polling.**

pol·len (POL-ən) *noun.* A fine dust that acts as the male seed in giving life to flowering plants.

pol·li·nate (POL-ə-nayt) *verb.* To give life to a flower by carrying pollen from the male stamen to the female pistil. **pollinated, pollinating.** —**pollination** (pol-ə-NAY-shən) *noun.*

pol·li·wog (POL-ee-wog) Also **pollywog** *noun.* A tadpole.

pol·lute (pə-LOOT) *verb.* To make impure or tainted. **polluted, polluting.** —**pollution** (pə-LOO-shən) *noun.*

po·lo (POH-loh) *noun.* A game played by men on horseback in which players try to drive a wooden ball through the opponent's goal with a wooden mallet. —**polo shirt.** A short-sleeved knitted pullover.

pol·ter·geist (POHL-tər-gyst) *noun.* A prankish ghost that makes its presence known by thumping and rapping.

pole vault

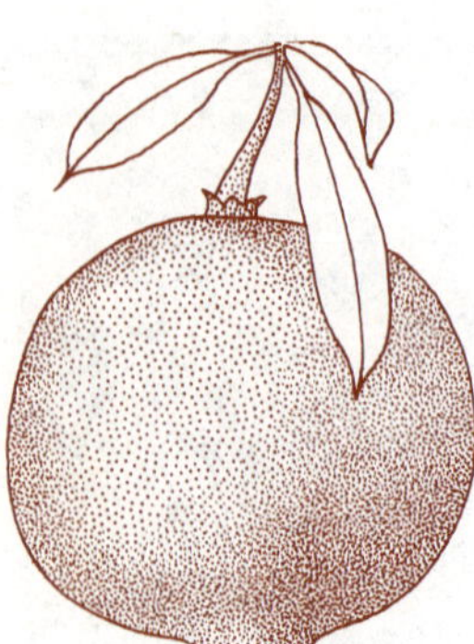
pomegranate

poly- *prefix.* Indicates two or more: *poly*gon.

pol·y·es·ter (pol-ee-ESS-tər) *noun.* Any of several man-made resins used in various forms as fibers, adhesives, and plastics.

pol·y·gon (POL-ee-gon) *noun.* A plane figure with at least three straight sides and usually five or more.

pol·yp (POL-ip) *noun.* A small water animal with a tube-like body and tentacles around the mouth.

pome·gran·ate (POM-gran-it) *noun.* 1. An acidic seedy fruit with red pulp and tough rind. 2. The shrub or small tree on which this fruit grows. **pomegranates.**

pony express

pom·mel (PUHM-əl) *noun.* 1. The knob on the front of a saddle. 2. The knob on the hilt of a sword. *—verb.* To pummel. **pommeled, pommeling.**

pomp *noun.* A display of magnificence, wealth, or splendor.

pom·pom (POM-pom) Also **pompon** *noun.* An ornamental ball of wool, feathers, or other decoration worn on clothing, often on hats.

pom·pous (POM-pəss) *adjective.* Exhibiting an exaggerated opinion of one's own importance: the *pompous* drum major. **—pompously** *adverb.*

poodle

pon·cho (PON-choh) *noun.* 1. A large wool cloak, with a slit in the center for the head, worn by South American Indians. 2. A raincoat of the same design. **ponchos.**

pond *noun.* A body of water smaller than a lake: a goldfish *pond.*

pon·der (PON-dər) *verb.* 1. To consider carefully. 2. To meditate: "Once upon a midnight dreary, while I *pondered,* weak and weary." (Poe). **pondered, pondering.**

pon·der·ous (PON-dər-əss) *adjective.* 1. Extremely heavy; clumsy. 2. Dull and heavy-going.

pon·iard (PON-yərd) *noun.* A dagger.

pon·toon (pon-TOON) *noun.* 1. A flat-bottomed boat used by the military in the construction of temporary bridges. 2. A float on a seaplane which permits taking off from and landing on water.

po·ny (POH-nee) *noun.* 1. Any of several breeds of small horses. 2. A translation of a foreign-language text or a synopsis of a text assigned for study. **ponies.**

pony express. Relay teams of men on swift ponies who carried mail in the American West (1860-1861).

pooch *noun.* (Slang) A dog. **pooches.**

poo·dle (POOD-l) *noun.* A curly-haired dog, originally raised as a hunter but now common as a house pet.

pool *noun.* 1. A small pond. 2. A man-made structure enclosing water: a swimming *pool.* 3. A game played on a table with balls and a stick for knocking the balls into pockets; also called "pocket billiards." 4. A combining for mutual benefit: a car *pool.* *—verb.* To put (money) into a common fund. **pooled, pooling.**

poor (PUR) *adjective.* 1. Having little or no money. 2. Lacking in quality: a *poor* book. 3. Worthy of pity: The *poor* man is crippled. **poorer, poorest. —poorly** *adverb.*

poor boy. A submarine sandwich. *See* **grinder.**

pop *verb.* 1. To make, or burst with, a quick, sharp sound: She *popped* her gum. 2. To go, come, or move quickly or unexpectedly: My friend likes to *pop* in for a visit. 3. To fly open: Her eyes *popped.* **popped, popping.** *—noun.* 1. A quick, sharp sound. 2. A carbonated soft drink: soda *pop.*

pop·corn (POP-korn) *noun.* A kind of corn that, when heated, bursts open into puffed kernels.

pope (POHP) *noun.* (Usually capital P) The head of the Roman Catholic Church, who is also the Bishop of Rome.

pop·lar (POP-lər) *noun.* 1. A tall, slender tree with triangular leaves. 2. The soft wood of this tree.

pop·py (POP-ee) *noun.* 1. A bright red, orange, or white flower. 2. The plant on which it grows. **poppies.**

pop·u·lace (POP-yə-liss) *noun.* 1. People in general; the masses. 2. All the people in a certain area.

pop·u·lar (POP-yə-lər) *adjective.* 1. Liked or respected by many: a *popular* person. 2. Held or believed by, or representing, most people: *popular* opinion. —**popularity** (pop-yə-LA-rə-tee) *noun.* —**popularly** *adverb.*

pop·u·late (POP-yə-layt) *verb.* 1. To people; provide residents for: Bobby *populated* his fort with toy soldiers. 2. To live or take up residence in. **populated, populating.**

pop·u·la·tion (pop-yə-LAY-shən) *noun.* The people who live in a particular area, such as a city or country: the *population* of Chicago.

pop·u·lous (POP-yə-ləss) *adjective.* Occupied by many people.

por·ce·lain (PORSS-lin or POR-sl-in) *noun.* 1. A white, glass-like material made of baked clay. 2. Anything made from this material.

porch *noun.* A platform or partly enclosed room attached to a house or other building. **porches.**

por·cu·pine (POR-kyə-pighn) *noun.* An animal of the rodent family with long, sharp quills covering its back.

[1]**pore** (POR) *noun.* An opening in a surface, as in the skin, that permits the passage of air and fluids. **pores.**

[2]**pore** *verb.* (Used with *over*) To look at, study, or think about with great care: *pore* over books. **pored, poring.**

pork *noun.* Meat from a pig.

po·rous (POR-əss) *adjective.* 1. Having pores. 2. Allowing the passage of gas or fluids: A sponge is *porous.*

por·poise (POR-pəss) *noun.* A sea animal that is of the whale family, but much smaller in size; a dolphin.

por·ridge (POR-ij) *noun.* Oatmeal or other cereal that is boiled and usually served with milk.

[1]**port** *noun.* 1. A harbor or a town that has a harbor. 2. The left side of a ship or airplane. 3. A porthole.

[2]**port** *noun.* A sweet wine, usually of a dark-red color.

port·a·ble (POR-tə-bəl) *adjective.* Able to be moved or carried.

port·age (POR-tij or por-TAHZH) *noun.* 1. The moving of a boat or goods overland from one body of water to another. 2. The route taken during such a move. **portages.** —*verb.* To move a boat or goods in this way. **portaged, portaging.**

por·tal (PORT-l) *noun.* A doorway or other entrance.

port·cul·lis (port-KUHL-iss) *noun.* Bars, usually of iron, set in a frame that hangs above an entrance and may be dropped to prevent entry. **portcullises.**

por·tend (por-TEND) *verb.* To be a sign or warning of. **portended, portending.**

por·tent (POR-tent) *noun.* 1. A sign or warning. 2. A wonderful, unusual, or amazing thing.

por·ter (POR-tər) *noun.* 1. One whose job is to carry luggage. 2. One who helps passengers on a railroad car.

port·hole (PORT-hohl) *noun.* A small, usually round, window on a boat, ship, or airplane.

por·ti·co (POR-ti-koh) *noun.* A roof, supported by columns, at the entrance of or around a building. **porticoes.**

por·tion (POR-shən) *noun.* A part or section of a larger whole. —*verb.* To cut or divide into sections or shares. **portioned, portioning.**

por·trait (POR-trit or POR-trayt) *noun.* A painting or photograph of a person.

por·tray (por-TRAY) *verb.* To describe in painting, words, or drama. **portrayed, portraying.**

poppy

porcupine

porpoise

pose (POHZ) *verb.* 1. To stay in one position, as for a photograph. 2. To put into a position: The photographer *posed* us in front of the hotel. 3. To put on a false character or manner. 4. To ask or state: *pose* a question. **posed, posing.** —*noun.* 1. A position. 2. A false manner or character.

posh *adjective.* Elegant; plush.

po·si·tion (pə-ZISH-ən) *noun.* 1. A place: What is the *position* of the satellite? 2. The right place: The director told the cast to get into *position.* 3. A manner of seeing or thinking (of something): What is your dad's *position* regarding the election? 4. State or plight: The boy's *position* is dangerous. 5. Social standing or rank: a *position* of honor. 6. A job or occupation: a high-paying *position.* 7. The way something or someone is arranged or placed: in a sitting *position.* —*verb.* To put in a position. **positioned, positioning.**

pos·i·tive (POZ-ə-tiv) *adjective.* 1. Indicating agreement: a *positive* answer. 2. Sure; having no doubt: I'm *positive* you're wrong. 3. Overly sure of oneself. 4. Stated clearly. 5. Referring to a quantity greater than zero. 6. (Chemistry, physics) Describing the kind of electric charge found on the battery terminal from which current flows. 7. (Grammar) Referring to an adverb or adjective that is not in the comparative or superlative form. —*noun.* Something positive. —**positively** *adverb.*

positive number. Any real number that is greater than zero; any number preceded by a + sign.

pos·se (POSS-ee) *noun.* A group of people organized to help enforce the law. **posses.**

pos·sess (pə-ZESS) *verb.* 1. To own. 2. To have as a characteristic, quality, or feature: Tina *possesses* great beauty. 3. To have inner control of (someone's mind): The woman was said to be *possessed* by evil spirits. **possessed, possessing.**

pos·ses·sion (pə-ZESH-ən) *noun.* 1. Something that is owned or controlled. 2. Ownership or control: *possession* of wealth.

pos·ses·sive (pə-ZESS-iv) *adjective.* 1. Wanting to own or rule or control: a *possessive* parent. 2. (Grammar) Referring to a case of a noun or pronoun that shows ownership or possession: "His" is the *possessive* form of "he." —**possessively** *adverb.*

pos·si·ble (POSS-ə-bəl) *adjective.* Referring to what could happen, be, or be done: It's *possible* that man will someday live on the moon. —**possibility** (poss-ə-BIL-ə-tee) *noun.* —**possibly** *adverb.*

pos·sum (POSS-əm) *noun. See* **opossum.**

post- *prefix.* Indicates: 1. Later, after: *post*date. 2. Behind: *post*dental.

[1]**post** (POHST) *noun.* A piece of wood or metal standing upright in the ground: a fence *post;* a sign *post.* —*verb.* 1. To put on view in a public place: I *posted* the notice on the bulletin board. 2. To put up no-trespassing signs. **posted, posting.**

[2]**post** (POHST) *noun.* 1. A military camp or base. 2. An assigned place: a soldier's *post.* 3. A job, particularly one given by an appointment: a *post* in government. 4. A place where goods are traded. —*verb.* To put up; to offer: *post* a bond. **posted, posting.**

[3]**post** (POHST) *verb.* 1. To mail (a letter). 2. To make aware (of news): Keep me *posted.* **posted, posting.** —*noun.* (British) The postal system.

post·age (POHSS-tij) *noun.* The fee for sending something by mail.

post·al (POHSS-tl) *adjective.* Of or referring to the mail or the post office: *postal* rates.

postal card. A piece of thin cardboard with a postage stamp printed on it, for sending short messages.

postal system. The system by which mail is transported and delivered.

post card Also **postcard.** 1. A piece of thin cardboard, often with a picture on one side, used to send short messages through the mail if a postage stamp is affixed. 2. A postal card.

post·date (pohst-DAYT) *verb.* To put a date on (an item) that is after the true date. **postdated, postdating.**

post·den·tal (pohst-DENT-l) *adjective.* Behind the teeth.

post·er (POHSS-tər) *noun.* A large piece of paper, cardboard, or other material used for advertising, decorating, or giving information.

pos·ter·i·ty (poss-TEHR-ə-tee) *noun.* The people who will be born and live in the future.

postman (POHST-mən) *noun.* A person whose job is delivering mail; a mailman. —**postmen** *plural.*

post·mas·ter (POHST-mass-tər) *noun, masculine.* Also **post·mis·tress** (POHST-miss-triss) *noun, feminine.* The one in charge of a post office.

post office. 1. The organization in charge of the collection and delivery of mail. 2. Any local division of this organization.

post·pone (pohst-POHN) *verb.* To put off (for another time). **postponed, postponing.** —**postponement** *noun.*

post·script (POHST-skript) *noun.* An additional note put on a letter after the signature.

pos·ture (POSS-chər) *noun.* Bearing, body position; manner of standing or moving. —*verb.* To pose. **postured, posturing.**

po·sy (POH-zee) *noun.* A flower. **posies.**

pot *noun.* 1. A rounded container, open on top, flat on the bottom: a cooking *pot.* 2. In certain games, the amount put in or bet by all players. 3. (Slang) Marijuana. —*verb.* 1. To cook or preserve in a pot. 2. To plant in a pot. **potted, potting.**

pot·ash (POT-ash) *noun.* An impure substance containing potassium, used mostly for fertilizers.

po·tas·si·um (pə-TASS-ee-əm) *noun.* A soft, metallic element of a silvery-white color used in soaps and fertilizers.

po·ta·to (pə-TAY-toh) *noun.* 1. A starchy thickened tuber that grows underground and is eaten as a vegetable. 2. The plant on which this tuber grows. **potatoes.**

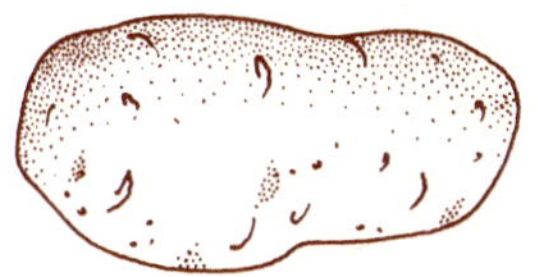

potato

potato chip. A very thin, crisp slice of potato that has been fried and salted.

po·tent (POHT-nt) *adjective.* Strong, powerful; capable of producing a desired effect: The *potent* medicine put me to sleep.

po·ten·tial (pə-TEN-shəl) *adjective.* Possible in the future: a *potential* winner. —*noun.* A quality that exists but isn't in use yet; capability: Steve has the *potential* to be a fine doctor. —**potentially** *adverb.*

po·tion (POH-shən) *noun.* A special drink, as for curing illness or causing a magic effect.

pot·pour·ri (poh-pu-REE) *noun.* A mixture or collection of many different parts.

pot shot. 1. A shot taken at a target in a careless or casual manner or taken at an easy target. 2. An unfriendly or critical remark made to or about someone.

pot·ter (POT-ər) *noun.* A person who makes clay bowls, jugs, cups, and similar items.

pot·ter·y (POT-ə-ree) *noun.* 1. Bowls, dishes, and similar items made of moist clay and baked until hard. 2. The art or process of making pottery. 3. A place where this process is carried on.

pouch (POWCH) *noun.* 1. A small bag. 2. A fold of skin that resembles a sack: kangaroo's *pouch.* **pouches.**

poul·try (POHL-tree) *noun.* Chickens, ducks, turkeys, or other fowl raised for meat or eggs.

pounce (POWNSS) *verb.* To jump or leap (on), especially in order to seize: The lion *pounced* on the zebra. **pounced, pouncing.** —*noun.* A sudden jump or swoop. **pounces.**

[1]**pound** (POWND) *noun.* 1. A unit for measuring weight, equal to 16 ounces. 2. The basic unit of money in England, Ireland, and several other countries.

[2]**pound** (POWND) *verb.* 1. To crush with repeated blows. 2. To strike with hard blows: The messenger *pounded* the castle door. 3. To sound or throb repeatedly: My heart *pounded* after the long run. **pounded, pounding.**

[3]**pound** (POWND) *noun.* A public place for keeping stray animals.

pour (POR) *verb.* 1. To cause to flow: Dad *poured* coffee into his cup. 2. To appear or put forth as rapidly as flowing liquid: The fans *poured* out of the stadium. 3. To rain heavily. **poured, pouring.**

pout (POWT) *verb.* 1. To behave in a moody or disappointed manner. 2. To push out one's lips as an expression of moodiness or disappointment. **pouted, pouting.**

pov·er·ty (POV-ər-tee) *noun.* 1. The condition of being poor or in need. 2. A poor or small quality, amount, or degree: a *poverty* of ideas.

pow·der (POW-dər) *noun.* 1. A substance made up of fine, loose particles, usually formed by the pounding or grinding of a solid material: face *powder;* cleaning *powder.* 2. Gunpowder. —*verb.* 1. To put powder on. 2. To pound or grind into powder: Otto *powdered* the chalk. **powdered, powdering.** —**powdery** (POW-də-ree) *adjective.*

powder horn

powder horn. A hollow animal horn or other container in which gunpowder was once carried by hunters and soldiers.

pow·er (POW-ər) *noun.* 1. Strength; force. 2. Authority: The mayor has the *power* to fire the police chief. 3. The ability to perform some action. 4. Energy: electric *power.* 5. A person, organization, or nation that has great influence or strength: a great naval *power.* 6. A measure of the magnification or enlargement that is provided by binoculars or similar instruments. 7. (Math) The number of times a given number is multiplied by itself: Two to the third *power* is eight. —*verb.* To supply with power. **powered, powering.**

pow·er·ful (POW-ər-fəl) *adjective.* 1. Having great power; mighty. 2. Having great influence or effect. —**powerfully** *adverb.*

pow·er·house (POW-ər-howss) *noun.* 1. A building where electric power is produced. 2. (Informal) A person or group with great power or influence. **powerhouses.**

pow·er·less (POW-ər-liss) *adjective.* Without power; very weak.

power plant. A unit, including buildings and equipment, where some form of power is produced.

pow·wow (POW-wow) *noun.* 1. A special meeting or conference held among North American Indians for making important decisions or plans. 2. A ceremonial tribal feast of North American Indians. 3. (Informal) Any meeting or conference.

prac·ti·ca·ble (PRAK-ti-kə-bəl) *adjective.* 1. Able to be done or carried out: a *practicable* plan. 2. Able to be used: A sled is not *practicable* in the summer.

prac·ti·cal (PRAK-ti-kəl) *adjective.* 1. Able to be done or used successfully or without great difficulty. 2. Sensible; knowing what can be done: Jim is not a dreamer; he is very *practical.* 3. Useful. 4. Related to actual practice rather than to theory or ideas. —**practical joke.** A trick or prank played on a person that makes others laugh at him.

prac·ti·cal·ly (PRAK-tik-lee) *adverb.*

1. Nearly; just about. 2. In a practical manner.

prac·tice (PRAK-tiss) *verb.* 1. To do often or as a habit: We should all *practice* self-control. 2. To do over and over in order to do well or skillfully: *practice* the piano. 3. To work at or pursue (one's profession): Mr. Vail *practices* law. 4. To follow or act on: *Practice* what you preach! **practiced, practicing.** —*noun.* 1. A habit, an often repeated act. 2. An action repeated for the purpose of gaining a skill. 3. The act of doing (something): He put his idea into *practice.* 4. Working at one's profession or the profession itself: law *practice.* **practices.** —**out of practice.** Lacking in skill from failure to keep in training.

prai·rie (PRAIR-ee) *noun.* A large area of grassland with few or no trees or hills. **prairies.**

prairie dog. A rodent that nests in burrows on plains in the U.S. West.

prairie schooner. A covered wagon used by pioneers to travel across America.

praise (PRAYZ) *verb.* 1. To say good things about. 2. To give honor to; worship: *Praise* the Lord! **praised, praising.** —*noun.* 1. Good things said about someone or something. 2. Honor; worship.

praise·wor·thy (PRAYZ-wer-thee) *adjective.* Worthy of praise.

prance (PRANSS) *verb.* 1. To move or spring about on the hind legs. 2. To move or strut in a lively manner. **pranced, prancing.**

prank (PRANGK) *noun.* A trick played out of mischief: Halloween *pranks.*

prat·tle (PRAT-l) *verb.* To talk or chatter foolishly. **prattled, prattling.** —*noun.* Foolish talk; chatter.

pray *verb.* 1. To offer prayers; speak with or appeal to God. 2. To appeal to any supreme being. 3. To ask for in prayer. **prayed, praying.**

prayer (PRAIR) *noun.* 1. A devout plea or appeal to God. 2. An appeal to any supreme being. 3. A special set of words spoken to God or another deity: "The Lord's *Prayer.*" 4. The act of praying.

praying mantis (MAN-tiss). A green or brown insect that feeds on smaller insects. —**praying mantises** or **praying mantes** (MAN-teez) *plural.*

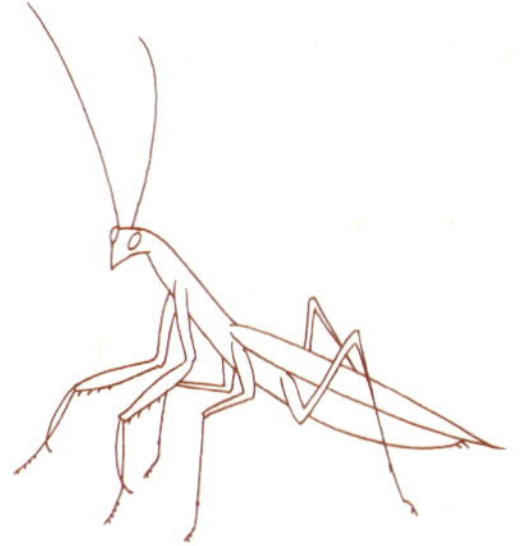

praying mantis

pre- *prefix.* Indicates: 1. Before; at an earlier time: *pre*history; *pre*school. 2. In front or in advance of: *pre*fix.

preach (PREECH) *verb.* 1. To give a sermon or speech about religion. 2. To recommend strongly: The senator *preached* patriotism. 3. To lecture someone or give advice, especially in a bossy manner. **preached, preaching.**

preach·er (PREECH-ər) *noun.* A clergyman or other person who preaches.

pre·car·i·ous (pri-KAIR-ee-əss) *adjective.* Not certain or secure; risky: a *precarious* position on a limb. —**precariously** *adverb.*

pre·cau·tion (pri-KAW-shən) *noun.* An action taken to prevent difficulty or danger before something occurs.

pre·cede (pri-SEED) *verb.* To come ahead of in time, place, or rank: The lightning *preceded* the rain. **preceded, preceding.**

prairie schooner

prec·e·dent (PRESS-ə-dənt) *noun.* An action or decision that can be used later as an example: The Pilgrims' original Thanksgiving set a *precedent* for our national holiday.

pre·ced·ing (pri-SEED-ing) *adjective.* Coming ahead in time, place, or rank.

pre·cept (PREE-sept) *noun.* A rule of conduct; suggestion for moral or correct behavior: "Love thy neighbor as thyself" is a *precept.*

pre·cinct (PREE-singkt) *noun.* 1. A limited area, as of a city. 2. One section of an area for which a police department is responsible. 3. (Usually plural) An area within specific boundaries.

pre·cious (PRESH-əss) *adjective.* 1. Extremely valuable. 2. Beloved; very dear: a *precious* child.

prec·i·pice (PRESS-ə-piss) *noun.* A very steep cliff or section of rock.

pre·cip·i·tate (pri-SIP-ə-tayt) *verb.* 1. To hasten or quicken (a happening): Ralph's insult *precipitated* the quarrel. 2. To hurl or rush down suddenly: The storm *precipitated* heavy rains on the city. 3. To form and fall as moisture, as rain or snow. 4. To sink as solid particles, like silt in a river. **precipitated, precipitating.** —(pri-SIP-ə-tit or pri-SIP-ə-tayt) *adjective.* 1. Hasty; not fully considered: a *precipitate* decision. 2. Sudden and rapid: the *precipitate* plunge of a truck down a hill. **—precipitately** *adverb.*

pre·cip·i·ta·tion (pri-sip-ə-TAY-shən) *noun.* Rain, snow, or other forms of falling moisture.

pre·cise (pri-SIGHSS) *adjective.* 1. Exact; accurate: The *precise* amount of the medicine was 14 drops. 2. Stated clearly; definite: The school rule about lateness is very *precise.* 3. Exact and careful in methods: The waiter was very *precise* in the way he set the table. **—precisely** *adverb.*

pre·ci·sion (pri-SIZH-ən) *noun.* The quality of being precise or exact.

pre·clude (pri-KLOOD) *verb.* To keep from happening; prevent; shut out. **precluded, precluding.**

pre·co·cious (pri-KOH-shəss) *adjective.* Developed or matured earlier than usual: a *precocious* child.

pred·a·tor (PRED-ə-tər or PRED-ə-tor) *noun.* 1. An animal that kills and eats other animals. 2. A person, like a pirate or robber, who lives or gains by stealing from others. **—predatory** (PRED-ə-tor-ee) *adjective.*

pred·e·ces·sor (PRED-ə-sess-ər or PREE-də-sess-ər) *noun.* A person who has gone before in time, especially in a job or position: The new mayor's *predecessor* retired.

pre·dic·a·ment (pri-DIK-ə-mənt) *noun.* A difficult, confusing, or embarrassing situation.

pred·i·cate (PRED-ə-kit) *noun.* (Grammar) The word or words of a sentence that tell something about the subject: In "The eagle flew," "flew" is the *predicate.* **predicates.** —(PRED-ə-kayt) *verb.* To base on a fact or observation: The idea for a cure was *predicated* on study of the disease. **predicated, predicating.**

pre·dict (pri-DIKT) *verb.* To say that something will happen; prophesy: The weatherman *predicted* rain. **predicted, predicting. —prediction** (pri-DIK-shən) *noun.*

pre·dom·i·nant (pri-DOM-ə-nənt) *adjective.* 1. Having power or influence over others; superior: the *predominant* naval power. 2. Most numerous, common, or noticeable: Pink was the *predominant* color in my room. **—predominantly** *adverb.*

pre·dom·i·nate (pri-DOM-ə-nayt) *verb.* To be most influential, common, numerous, or noticeable. **predominated, predominating.**

preen *verb.* 1. To clean or arrange (feathers) with the beak: The swan *preened* its tail. 2. To dress or groom oneself with extreme care. **preened, preening.**

pre·fab·ri·cat·ed (pree-FAB-ri-kay-tid) *adjective.* Built in sections that can be easily transported and put together elsewhere: *prefabricated* houses.

pref·ace (PREF-iss) *noun.* An introduction to a book, speech, or other written composition. **prefaces.** *—verb.* To introduce with or serve as a preface. **prefaced, prefacing.**

pre·fer (pri-FER) *verb.* 1. To like better; regard more highly: Dad *prefers* classical to popular music. 2. To present for study or a decision, as in a court of law: The shopkeeper *preferred* charges against the robber. **preferred, preferring. —preference** (PREF-ər-ənss) *noun.*

pref·er·a·ble (PREF-ər-ə-bəl) *adjective.* More desirable. —**preferably** *adverb.*

pre·fix (pree-FIKS or PREE-fiks) *verb.* To place in front of or before. **prefixed, prefixing.** —(PREE-fiks) *noun.* Letters placed before a word that change or alter its meaning: The *prefix* "un" placed before "happy" changes the meaning of "happy" to "not happy." **prefixes.**

preg·nant (PREG-nənt) *adjective.* 1. Carrying a developing offspring within the body; with child. 2. Full of significance or importance: *pregnant* comments.

pre·his·tor·ic (pree-hiss-TOR-ik) *adjective.* Referring to a time before events were written down.

prej·u·dice (PREJ-ə-diss) *noun.* A slanted or biased opinion based more on emotion than reason: racial *prejudice.* **prejudices.** —*verb.* 1. To create a strong feeling (for or against a person or group) without reason. 2. To damage or injure by some act: Bragging will *prejudice* your chance of getting the job. **prejudiced, prejudicing.**

pre·late (PREL-it) *noun.* A clergyman of high rank. **prelates.**

pre·lim·i·nar·y (pri-LIM-ə-nehr-ee) *adjective.* Coming before the main part of something.

prel·ude (PREL-yood or PREE-lood) *noun.* 1. An introduction or a part that comes before (something): A short speech by the director was a *prelude* to the play. 2. A short musical piece often used as an introduction to a longer piece.

pre·ma·ture (pree-mə-CHUR) *adjective.* Coming too early or before the proper time: a *premature* birth. —**prematurely** *adverb.*

pre·med·i·tate (pree-MED-ə-tayt) *verb.* To plan or think about ahead of time: to *premeditate* a murder. **premeditated, premeditating.** —**premeditation** (pree-med-ə-TAY-shən) *noun.*

pre·mier (pri-MIHR) *noun.* The chief officer of some governments; prime minister.

pre·mière (pri-MIHR) *noun.* The first public presentation. **premières.**

prem·ise (PREM-iss) *noun.* 1. A fact or statement on which a theory or argument is based. 2. (Plural) A place of business; property and the buildings on it. **premises.**

pre·mi·um (PREE-mee-əm) *noun.* 1. Something given as a prize or gift: A towel was the *premium* for buying the new soap. 2. An installment payment on an insurance policy. 3. Esteem, great value. —**at a premium.** Higher in price, usually because of scarcity.

pre·oc·cu·py (pree-OK-yə-pigh) *verb.* To take all the attention of: Practice for next week's swimming meet has *preoccupied* Kathy for weeks. **preoccupied, preoccupying.** —**preoccupation** (pree-ok-yə-PAY-shən) *noun.*

prep. *abbreviation.* 1. Preposition. 2. Preparation. 3. Preparatory.

prep·a·ra·tion (prep-ə-RAY-shən) *noun.* 1. The act of making ready: Mother spent all day in *preparation* for Thanksgiving dinner. 2. (Often plural) Starting acts or plans: *preparations* for a party. 3. A mixture that does a particular job, as a medicine.

pre·par·a·to·ry (pri-PA-rə-tor-ee) *adjective.* Making ready; starting.

pre·pare (pri-PAIR) *verb.* To get ready. **prepared, preparing.**

pre·pay (pree-PAY) *verb.* To pay in advance. **prepaid, prepaying.**

prep·o·si·tion (prep-ə-ZISH-ən) *noun.* (Grammar) A word that shows connection between a noun or pronoun and some other word or words in a sentence: In "the door of a car," "of" is a *preposition.*

prepositional phrase. A group of words that includes a preposition and its object.

pre·pos·ter·ous (pri-POSS-tər-əss) *adjective.* Ridiculous, unreasonable.

pre·scribe (pri-SKRIGHB) *verb.* To give as a rule or direction; to order, especially as a cure or therapy. **prescribed, prescribing.** —**prescription** (pri-SCRIP-shən) *noun.*

pres·ence (PREZ-nss) *noun.* 1. The state of being (somewhere). 2. Nearness: in the *presence* of guests. 3. Poise, bearing: Jack showed great *presence* on the stage.

[1]**pres·ent** (PREZ-ənt) *noun.* The time now; not the past or future. —*adjective.* 1. Referring to or happening in time now. 2. Being near or in view: Maureen was not *present.* 3. (Grammar) Referring to a verb tense that expresses action now: "Go" is the *present* tense; "went" is the past tense.

[2]**pre·sent** (pri-ZENT) *verb.* 1. To introduce. 2. To give: The keys to the city were *presented* to the astronaut. 3. To bring before an audience: *present* a concert. 4. To show or offer in a formal manner: The lawyer *presented* his case. **presented, presenting.** —(PREZ-nt) *noun.* A gift. —**present arms.** To salute with a weapon.

pre·sent·a·ble (pri-ZEN-tə-bəl) *adjective.* Worthy to be offered, shown, or inspected.

pres·en·ta·tion (prez-ən-TAY-shən or pree-zen-TAY-shən) *noun.* 1. A public show or performance. 2. The act of giving or awarding.

pres·ent·ly (PREZ-nt-lee) *adverb.* 1. Soon, in a little while: Tom will be here *presently.* 2. Now: We are *presently* thinking about moving.

present participle. (Grammar) A form of a verb that ends in *ing* and is used with another verb to express continuing action: In "I am going," "going" is a *present participle.*

pres·er·va·tion (prez-ər-VAY-shən) *noun.* Protection from injury, harm, decay, or spoilage.

pre·serve (pri-ZERV) *verb.* 1. To keep from harm or injury. 2. To keep whole, free from damage. 3. To keep from spoiling or decaying by applying a solution or other material: The peaches were *preserved* in brandy. **preserved, preserving.** —*noun.* 1. An area in which animals, forests, or other natural resources are protected. 2. (Usually plural) Fruits kept from spoiling by being cooked with sugar and canned. **preserves.**

pre·side (pri-ZIGHD) *verb.* 1. To rule (over). 2. To act as the head or leader. **presided, presiding.**

pres·i·den·cy (PREZ-ə-dən-see) *noun.* 1. The position of president. 2. The time during which a president serves.

pres·i·dent (PREZ-ə-dənt) *noun.* 1. A person elected or appointed to rule or govern. 2. [Usually capital P] The chief of state, as in the United States. —**presidential** *adjective.*

press *verb.* 1. To squeeze: *press* grapes. 2. To push or put weight (on): The crowd *pressed* Timmy against the wall. 3. To hold tightly; hug. 4. To remove the wrinkles from (clothes); iron. 5. To urge on; to request insistently: The reporters *pressed* the mayor for an answer. 6. To trouble or be troubled by a lack (of something): *pressed* for money. **pressed, pressing.** —*noun.* 1. A device that squeezes or puts pressure on: a wine *press.* 2. A printing press or the place in which a printing press is used. 3. A pushing crowd. 4. Newspapers and magazines and the reporters and editors who create them. 5. Anything that applies pressure.

press agent. A person whose job is to get favorable publicity for some person, group, or business.

press·ing (PRESS-ing) *adjective.* Compelling; urgent.

pres·sure (PRESH-ər) *noun.* 1. The act of pressing or the state of being pressed. 2. A steady weight or push. 3. Compelling force. **pressures.** *—verb.* To apply pressure or force to; urge. **pressured, pressuring.**

pressure group. Any group of people who try to influence lawmakers in favor of their interests.

pres·sur·ize (PRESH-ə-righz) *verb.* 1. To keep air pressure (in an airplane, rocket, or other craft) about the same as it is at ground level. 2. To put pressure on. **pressurized, pressurizing.**

pres·tige (pre-STEEZH or pre-STEEJ) *noun.* Public regard or fame.

pres·to (PRESS-toh) *adverb* (and *adjective*). 1. Quickly, at once. 2. (Music) At a quick pace.

pre·sume (pri-ZOOM) *noun.* 1. To think without proof; suppose. 2. To hazard, dare: ". . . *presume* not God to scan;/ The proper study of mankind is man." (Alexander Pope). 3. To take liberties with: You have *presumed* on my friendship. **presumed, presuming.**

pre·sump·tion (pri-ZUHMP-shən) *noun.* 1. Annoying or offensive nerve, boldness, or pride. 2. A belief held without evidence.

pre·sump·tu·ous (pri-ZUHMP-choo-əss) *adjective.* Too bold, forward, or self-confident.

pre·tend (pri-TEND) *verb.* 1. To make (something or oneself) appear to be what (it or one) isn't. 2. To make believe. 3. To make a claim: *pretend* to a throne. **pretended, pretending.**

pre·tense (PREE-tenss or pri-TENSS) *noun.* 1. Something that seems or claims to be what it isn't: His offer to pay was just *pretense.* 2. An excuse. **pretenses.**

pre·ten·tious (pri-TEN-shəss) *adjective.* 1. Overly showy, flashy: It was *pretentious* of the woman to wear all her jewels at one time. 2. Claiming a high or honored position, especially without reason. 3. Ambitious. **—pretentiously** *adverb.*

pret·ty (PRIT-ee) *adjective.* 1. Pleasant to look at; pleasing. 2. Good or fine, often in a mocking sense: Ollie said "This is a *pretty* mess you've got us into." 3. (Informal) Of a large size or amount: a *pretty* penny. **prettier, prettiest.** *—adverb.* In a way, to a degree: Your cookies are *pretty* good. *—verb.* (Informal) To make attractive. **prettied, prettying.**

pret·zel (PRET-sl) *noun.* A hard, salted and glazed cracker, usually in a knotted or stick shape.

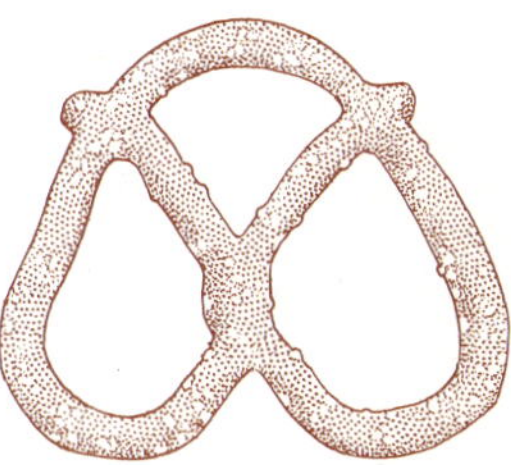

pretzel

pre·vail (pri-VAYL) *verb.* 1. To win or attain a victory. 2. (Used with *on, upon,* or *with*) To persuade or convince. 3. To be most common or widely in use. **prevailed, prevailing.**

prev·a·lent (PREV-ə-lənt) *adjective.* Commonly accepted; happening often or in many places.

pre·vent (pri-VENT) *verb.* To stop, keep (from occurring). **prevented, preventing. —prevention** *noun.*

pre·view (PREE-vyoo) Also **prevue** *noun.* 1. A viewing, as of a play or movie, before the official opening or showing. 2. An ad for a movie or TV show that shows scenes from it.

pre·vi·ous (PREE-vee-əss) *adjective.* Already existing; coming before: a *previous* visit. **—previously** *adverb.*

prey (PRAY) *noun.* 1. A hunted animal sought for food: The hunter stalked his *prey.* 2. A victim of an attack (by a person or misfortune). *—verb.* 1. To seize (animals) for food: Lions *prey* on smaller animals. 2. To rob or attack. 3. To worry, preoccupy: *prey* on the mind. **preyed, preying.**

price (PRIGHSS) *noun.* 1. The amount charged or given (for something). 2. The cost of having or achieving (something): the *price* one pays for success. **prices.** *—verb.* 1. To set a selling amount on. 2. To find out the cost (of something): Mother *priced* several sofas. **priced, pricing.** **—beyond price.** Valued more than any amount of money.

price·less (PRIGHSS-liss) *adjective.* Of a value that cannot be estimated.

prick·le (PRIK-əl) *noun.* 1. A sharp point or thorn. 2. A stinging or tingling feeling. —*verb.* To have a stinging or tingling feeling. **prickled, prickling.** —**prickly** *adjective.*

pride (PRIGHD) *noun.* 1. A self-satisfied feeling because of a deed, accomplishment, or possession. 2. Something that causes good or self-satisfied feelings: Beth's hair is her *pride.* 3. Conceit, being too pleased with oneself: "*Pride* goeth before destruction . . . ." (Proverbs 16:18). —*verb.* To feel good or self-satisfied about. **prided, priding.**

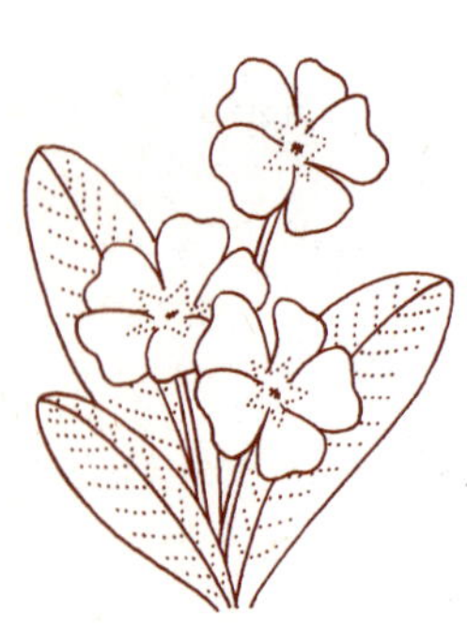

primrose

priest (PREEST) *noun.* A minister or clergyman in certain religions.

prim *adjective.* Overly proper or demure. **primmer, primmest.** —**primly** *adverb.*

pri·ma·ry (PRIGH-mehr-ee) *adjective.* 1. First: *primary* grades. 2. Basic: The *primary* reason for going to school is to learn. —*noun.* An election in which members of a political party name candidates for public office. **primaries.** —**primarily** (prigh-MEHR-ə-lee) *adverb.*

primary color. Any of the colors red, yellow, or blue that form other colors when mixed.

prime (PRIGHM) *noun.* 1. The best: the *prime* of life. 2. A sign (′) used to indicate feet or minutes. 3. (Math) A prime number. **primes.** —*verb.* 1. To prepare (by some action): Dad *primed* the desk for painting with a base coat. 2. To ready for action by filling with a liquid, an explosive, or a fuel: *prime* a pistol. **primed, priming.**

prime meridian. The meridian that goes through Greenwich, England, and from which longitude is measured east and west.

prime minister. The head official of some governments, as Canada.

prime number. A number that can be evenly divided only by itself or 1.

[1]**prim·er** (PRIM-ər) *noun.* 1. A reader; a beginning book for teaching reading. 2. Any book that gives simple or basic instruction.

[2]**prim·er** (PRIGH-mər) *noun.* 1. A device that sets off an explosive. 2. A base coat that prepares a surface for painting.

pri·me·val (prigh-MEE-vəl) *adjective.* From or of a very early time: "This is the forest *primeval.*" (Longfellow).

prim·i·tive (PRIM-ə-tiv) *adjective.* 1. From or of an early or the earliest time, stage, or state: *primitive* man. 2. Without refinement; crude: a *primitive* style of art. —**primitively** *adverb.*

prim·rose (PRIM-rohz) *noun.* 1. A flower, generally of a yellow color, that grows in clusters. 2. The plant on which this flower grows.

prince (PRINSS) *noun.* A man or boy (other than a king) who is a member of a royal family. **princes.**

prin·cess (PRIN-siss or PRIN-sess or prin-SESS) *noun.* A woman or girl (other than a queen) who is a member of a royal family. **princesses.**

prin·ci·pal (PRIN-sə-pəl) *adjective.* Main or chief; most important. —*noun.* 1. The head or leader, as of a school or the cast of a play. 2. A sum of money that earns interest.

prin·ci·ple (PRIN-sə-pəl) *noun.* 1. A basic rule or truth; a general law or thought from which others are developed: the *principles* of justice. 2. A rule that guides a person's conduct: His basic *principle* is to be good and kind. **principles.**

print *noun.* 1. A mark made by reproducing or pressing something on a surface, as a fingerprint or hoof print. 2. Letters or words printed by type. 3. A picture made from a photographic negative. 4. Cloth with a design printed on it: I want some of this *print* for a dress. 5. A copy of a picture or design made by printing. *—verb.* 1. To reproduce letters, words, or pictures on a surface. 2. To publish: More than 20,000 new books are *printed* every year. 3. To write individual letters that look like regular type: *Print* your full name. 4. To make a photograph from a negative. **printed, printing.**

print·er (PRIN-tər) *noun.* A person who works in the printing business.

print·ing (PRIN-ting) *noun.* 1. The act or business of reproducing letters, words, or pictures on a surface. 2. Printed material. 3. Letters or words that look like type but are formed by hand. 4. The number of copies (of a book, magazine, etc.) that are printed at one time. 5. The act of making a photographic print.

printing press. *noun.* A machine for printing words and illustrations on paper.

[1]**pri·or** (PRIGH-ər) *adjective* or *adverb.* Earlier; being or happening before: a *prior* right.

[2]**pri·or** (PRIGH-ər) *noun, masculine* Also **prioress** *noun, feminine.* The person in charge of a religious house called a priory.

pri·or·i·ty (prigh-OR-ə-tee) *noun.* 1. The fact of being earlier or prior: Indians had *priority* in their claims to American land. 2. Greater importance (than something else): Homework has *priority* over TV tonight. **priorities.**

pri·o·ry (PRIGH-ə-ree) *noun.* A religious house, as a convent or a monastery, directed by a prioress or a prior. **priories.**

prism (PRIZ-əm) *noun.* 1. A solid bar of glass or other transparent material whose sides are shaped like a triangle: A *prism* bends light that passes through it and breaks it into the colors of the rainbow. 2. (Geometry) A solid form with sides that are parallelograms and ends that are parallel and of the same shape and size.

pris·on (PRIZ-n) *noun.* A jail; a place where people are locked up as a punishment for crime.

pris·on·er (PRIZ-n-ər or PRIZ-nər) *noun.* A person who is locked up in a prison or is kept somewhere against his will.

pri·va·cy (PRIGH-və-see) *noun.* 1. Secrecy: Let's talk over your idea in *privacy.* 2. The state of being away or apart from other people.

pri·vate (PRIGH-vit) *noun.* A soldier of the lowest rank; in the United States Army, a soldier who ranks below a corporal. **privates.** *—adjective.* 1. For, or belonging to, a particular person or persons; not public. 2. Secret; with no one else present. 3. Not having any public office: a *private* citizen.

pri·va·teer (prigh-və-TIHR) *noun.* 1. A private ship that is armed and has received from a government the right to attack the ships and commerce of an enemy. 2. The commander of such a ship or a member of its crew.

private eye. (Slang) A private detective.

pri·va·tion (prigh-VAY-shən) *noun.* 1. The lack of normal comforts or the basic needs of life. 2. Loss: The closing of our town's only library was a *privation.*

priv·i·lege (PRIV-əl-ij) *noun.* A special right or favor; the right to do a certain thing. **privileges.** *—verb.* To give a special right to. **privileged, privileging.**

prize (PRIGHZ) *noun.* 1. A reward, gift, or honor that is won in a contest. 2. A valuable thing; something worth working hard for. 3. Something captured from the enemy. **prizes.** *—adjective.* 1. Winning or being worthy of a prize: *prize* tomatoes. 2. Awarded as a prize: the *prize* ribbon. 3. Great; outstanding; of great value. *—verb.* To value highly; think a great deal of. **prized, prizing.**

early printing press

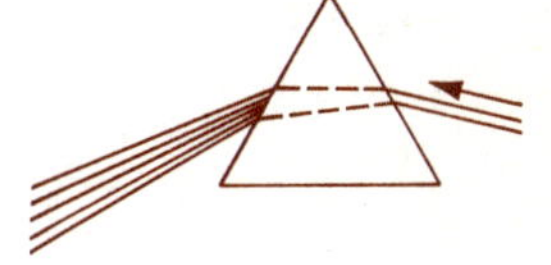
prism

prize fighter. A person who fights in the boxing ring for money; one who boxes as a profession.

pro- *prefix.* Indicates: for; in favor of: *pro-*American.

[1]**pro** (PROH) *adverb.* In favor of: I have said a lot about the plan, both *pro* and con. —*noun.* A reason in favor of: the *pros* and cons.

[2]**pro** (PROH) *noun.* (Slang) A professional; one who works as, or has the skill of, a professional: a hockey *pro.*

prob·a·bil·i·ty (prob-ə-BIL-ə-tee) *noun.* 1. The state of being probable or likely to happen: There is little *probability* of snow tonight. 2. Something that is likely to happen: His election is a distinct *probability.* **probabilities.**

prob·a·ble (PROB-ə-bəl) *adjective.* 1. Believable; likely to happen. 2. Likely to be true: The *probable* reason for her accident was speeding. —**probably** *adverb.*

pro·ba·tion (proh-BAY-shən) *noun.* 1. A testing, or a period of testing, of a person's fitness or conduct. 2. A system of allowing a person who has broken the law to stay out of prison as long as he follows certain rules.

prob·lem (PROB-ləm) *noun.* 1. A thing, person, or situation that is hard to handle: Getting the dog to stop barking is a real *problem.* 2. A question that must be answered or worked out: math *problems.*

pro·ce·dure (prə-SEE-jər) *noun.* 1. A way (to do something): Follow this *procedure* to solve the problem. 2. An established or traditional way of doing business: courtroom *procedure.* **procedures.**

pro·ceed (proh-SEED or prə-SEED) *verb.* 1. To go on or continue after stopping: The next morning he *proceeded* with the job. 2. To begin and carry out an activity: Alice *proceeded* to follow the strange rabbit. **proceeded, proceeding.**

pro·ceed·ing (proh-SEED-ing or prə-SEED-ing) *noun.* 1. An act or a course of action. 2. (Plural) An official record of things done and said at a meeting. 3. (Plural) Action taken in court; a lawsuit or trial.

pro·ceeds (PROH-seedz) *noun, plural.* The total amount of money received from a sale or other business activity; the profit made.

proc·ess (PROSS-ess or PROH-sess) *noun.* 1. A method or way (of doing something): the *process* of baking a cake. 2. A series of changes or actions that are part of a development: the *process* of growing up. 3. The act (of doing something): She was in the *process* of doing her hair. 4. A summons or order to appear in court. **processes.** —*verb.* To prepare, treat, or make in a special way: They *process* old wool before they use it again. **processed, processing.**

pro·ces·sion (prə-SESH-ən) *noun.* A group that moves along in an orderly way: graduation *procession.*

pro·claim (proh-KLAYM or prə-KLAYM) *verb.* To announce publicly and officially. **proclaimed, proclaiming.**

proc·la·ma·tion (prok-lə-MAY-shən) *noun.* The act of proclaiming; a public and official statement.

pro·cure (proh-KYUR or prə-KYUR) *verb.* 1. To get or obtain, especially with some effort: *procure* food. 2. To cause to happen; bring about: He *procured* the freeing of the prisoners. **procured, procuring.**

prod *verb.* 1. To poke with a blunt or pointed thing: The boy *prods* the sheep forward with his stick. 2. To stir up or urge to thought or action: I have to *prod* her to get her to work. **prodded, prodding.** —*noun.* 1. A pointed thing like a stick, used to poke or prod. 2. A nudge or poke; a reminder.

prod·i·gal (PROD-i-gəl) *adjective.* 1. Wasteful; spending in a reckless or careless way: the *prodigal* son.

2. Generous; abundant; giving freely: She is too *prodigal* with her compliments. —*noun.* One who is wasteful. —**prodigally** *adverb.*

pro·di·gious (prə-DIJ-əss) *adjective.* 1. Marvelous. 2. Huge; enormous.

prod·i·gy (PROD-ə-jee) *noun.* 1. Something strange or marvelous; a supernatural sign. 2. A very talented person, especially a young one. **prodigies.**

pro·duce (prə-DOOSS or prə-DYOOSS) *verb.* 1. To show or bring forward: Tom *produced* his new ball. 2. To yield, bring forth, or give birth to: This duck *produces* the most eggs. 3. To make: Foreign countries *produce* many small cars. 4. To cause: Eating too much candy can *produce* an upset stomach. 5. To make ready to show to the public: Our club wants to *produce* a play. **produced, producing.** —(PROD-ooss or PROH-dooss) *noun.* Farm products such as fruits and vegetables.

prod·uct (PROD-əkt) *noun.* 1. Something that is produced; something made or grown: Tobacco is an important *product* in the South. 2. (Math) The answer one gets by multiplying two or more numbers: When you multiply 10 by 2 the *product* is 20.

pro·duc·tion (prə-DUHK-shən or proh-DUHK-shən) *noun.* 1. The act of producing; making or growing: the *production* of a new game. 2. A product or the total of all products: The country's farm *production* is up this year. 3. A work produced for the theater. 4. (Informal) An act that receives more attention or care than it deserves: Don't make such a *production* out of sewing your dress.

pro·duc·tive (prə-DUHK-tiv or proh-DUHK-tiv) *adjective.* Producing or bringing forth much; yielding results: a *productive* worker. —**productively** *adverb.* —**productivity** (proh-duhk-TIV-ə-tee) *noun.*

pro·fane (proh-FAYN or prə-FAYN) *adjective.* 1. Disrespectful of sacred or holy things, especially in speech. 2. Not holy or religious. —*verb.* To treat a holy thing with contempt. **profaned, profaning.** —**profanely** *adverb.*

pro·fan·i·ty (proh-FAN-ə-tee or prə-FAN-ə-tee) *noun.* Profane language; cursing. **profanities.**

pro·fess (prə-FESS or proh-FESS) *verb.* 1. To declare openly: The rebels *professed* their allegiance to the South. 2. To claim; pretend: He *professed* to love the country he was trying to destroy. 3. To declare that one believes (in). **professed, professing.**

pro·fes·sion (prə-FESH-ən) *noun.* 1. Work for which a person needs special education: Law and medicine are *professions.* 2. All the people who do such work: the medical *profession.* 3. The act of declaring openly.

pro·fes·sion·al (prə-FESH-ən-l) *adjective.* 1. Referring to, connected with, engaged in, or appropriate for a profession: Telling a client's secrets is not a *professional* act. 2. Doing a particular thing to earn a living: a *professional* golfer. —*noun.* 1. One who earns his living through athletics. 2. One who earns his living at a profession: Doctors are *professionals.* 3. One who is very good or expert in his field. —**professionally** *adverb.*

pro·fes·sor (prə-FESS-ər) *noun.* A teacher of the highest rank in a college or university.

pro·fi·cient (prə-FISH-ənt) *adjective.* Expert in a subject; skillful. —**proficiently.**

pro·file (PROH-fighl) *noun.* 1. A view of a person's face from the side; a picture of such a view. 2. The outline of anything seen from the side. 3. A short descriptive article about a person. **profiles.**

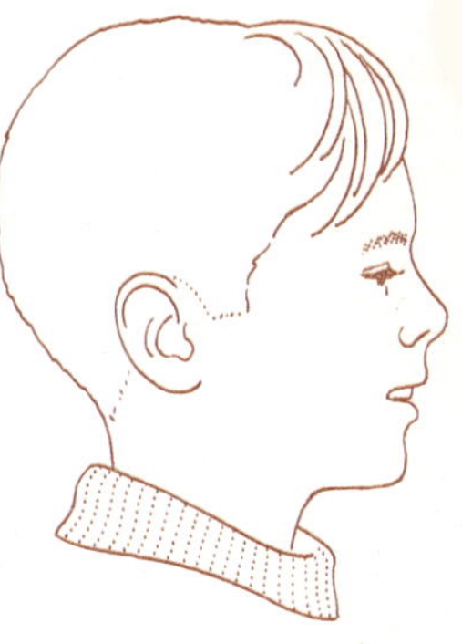
profile

prof·it (PROF-it) *noun.* 1. An advantage, gain, or benefit: There is much *profit* in reading. 2. What is left when the cost is subtracted from the price received. —*verb.* To benefit or gain; be of benefit to: He *profits* by listening to his elders. **profited, profiting.**

prof·it·a·ble (PROF-ə-tə-bəl) *adjective.* Yielding benefit or profit: a *profitable* deal. —**profitably** *adverb.*

pro·found (prə-FOWND or proh-FOWND) *adjective.* 1. Deep; not shallow: She gave a *profound* sigh. 2. Intense; extreme; felt deeply: I have had a *profound* loss. 3. Having deep knowledge, meaning, or understanding: a *profound* person. —**profoundly** *adverb.*

pro·fuse (prə-FYOOSS or proh-FYOOSS) *adjective.* 1. Abundant or plentiful: *profuse* blossoms. 2. Generous; spending freely; extravagant. —**profusely** *adverb.*

pro·fu·sion (prə-FYOO-zhən) *noun.* A large amount or quantity: a *profusion* of ideas.

pro·gram (PROH-gram or PROH-grəm) *noun.* 1. A list of the things that are going to be performed, done, studied, etc. 2. An entertainment or performance: a television *program.* 3. A plan of action or things to be done: a welfare *program.* 4. A series of directions fed into a computer. —*verb.* 1. To schedule or put on a program. 2. To prepare instructions for (a computer). **programed** or **programmed, programing** or **programming.**

prog·ress (PROG-ress) *noun.* Improvement; forward movement; growth. —(prə-GRESS) *verb.* To go forward; move ahead; show improvement. **progressed, progressing.**

pro·gres·sive (prə-GRESS-iv) *adjective.* 1. Showing progress; favoring or bringing improvement: a *progressive* plan. 2. Moving forward or happening step by step: Her *progressive* improvement shows she is working harder. —*noun.* A person who favors political reform or progress. **progressives.** —**progressively** *adverb.*

pro·hib·it (proh-HIB-it) *verb.* 1. Not to allow; forbid by law or regulation. 2. To prevent or stop: A shortage of gas *prohibits* travel. **prohibited, prohibiting.** —**prohibition** (proh-ə-BISH-ən) *noun.*

proj·ect (PROJ-ekt) *noun.* An undertaking or plan: I finished my science *project.* —**pro·ject** (prə-JEKT) *verb.* 1. To point outward; to stick out: The cat's tail *projects* behind her. 2. To plan; foretell or foresee: He *projects* a big increase in the size of our city. 3. To cause to appear on: *project* a filmstrip on a screen. **projected, projecting.**

pro·jec·tile (prə-JEK-təl or prə-JEK-tighl) *noun.* A thing such as a bullet, made to be thrown or shot through the air; anything that is thrown. **projectiles.**

pro·jec·tion (prə-JEK-shən) *noun.* 1. A part that points outward or sticks out. 2. The act of projecting or throwing something on a surface.

pro·jec·tor (prə-JEK-tər) *noun.* A machine that projects pictures on a screen.

pro·lif·ic (prə-LIF-ik) *adjective.* 1. Producing many offspring, as hamsters and rabbits do. 2. Producing much work: a *prolific* writer. —**prolifically** *adverb.*

pro·long (prə-LAWNG) *verb.* To make longer than usual; drag or stretch out: Arguments with the umpire *prolong* the game. **prolonged, prolonging.** —**prolongation** (prə-lawn-GAY-shən) *noun.*

prom·e·nade (prom-ə-NAYD or prom-ə-NAHD) *verb.* 1. To walk in a formal way, as in a procession: The guests at the ball *promenaded* before the queen. 2. To stroll.

promenaded, promenading. —*noun.* 1. Act of promenading. 2. An area for promenading, such as a terrace or boardwalk. **promenades.**

prom·i·nence (PROM-ə-nənss) *noun.* 1. State or condition of being very noticeable or well-known: the President's *prominence.* 2. Something that projects or stands out.

prom·i·nent (PROM-ə-nənt) *adjective.* 1. Projecting; sticking out: Skyscrapers are *prominent* on New York's skyline. 2. Noticeable. 3. Well-known. —**prominently** *adverb.*

prom·ise (PROM-iss) *verb.* 1. To give one's word (that something will be done); to guarantee. 2. To make likely or certain to happen: Black clouds *promise* a storm. **promised, promising.** —*noun.* 1. A guarantee; assurance. 2. A sign of future success: Helen shows *promise* at the piano. **promises.**

prom·is·ing (PROM-iss-ing) *adjective.* Giving hope of good results or future success: a *promising* young ballplayer. —**promisingly** *adverb.*

prom·on·to·ry (PROM-ən-tor-ee) *noun.* A high point of land that projects out into the water; a headland or point. **promontories.**

pro·mote (prə-MOHT) *verb.* 1. To place in a higher class or position: The teacher did not *promote* one student. 2. To act for the growth or success of: *promote* good will. 3. To advertise, or try to sell. **promoted, promoting.** —**promotion** (prə-MOH-shən) *noun.*

prompt *adjective.* Done on time or without delay. —*verb.* 1. To urge to action; inspire. 2. To remind; give a clue to. **prompted, prompting.** —**promptly** *adverb.*

pron. *abbreviation.* 1. Pronoun. 2. Pronunciation.

prone (PROHN) *adjective.* 1. Lying face down: a *prone* position. 2. Having a tendency, habit, or inclination: *prone* to illness.

prong (PRAWNG or PRONG) *noun.* A long projecting part: the *prongs* of a fork. —**pronged** *adjective.*

prong·horn (PRAWNG-horn or PRONG-horn) *noun.* A swift, graceful, horned deer of the Western plains.

pro·noun (PROH-nown) *noun.* A word used in place of a noun, referring to a person, place, or thing.

pro·nounce (prə-NOWNSS) *verb.* 1. To sound out or speak a word or words. 2. To state or declare: The doctor *pronounced* me cured. 3. To speak officially or with authority: The judge will *pronounce* sentence. **pronounced, pronouncing.**

pro·nounced (prə-NOWNST) *adjective.* Shown; spoken clearly or strongly; definite. —**pronouncedly** (prə-NOWN-sid-lee) *adverb.*

pro·nun·ci·a·tion (prə-nuhn-see-AY-shən) *noun.* 1. The manner or act of speaking a word or words. 2. The use of letters or symbols to show how a word is pronounced.

proof *noun.* 1. Evidence (that something is true): My name on the book is *proof* that it's mine. 2. A test to show that something is true or good: "The *proof* of the pudding is in the eating." (Cervantes). 3. A sheet printed to show how type has been set: *proofs* of a book. 4. A trial print from a photographic negative.

-proof *suffix.* Indicates ability to resist: water*proof.*

proof·read (PROOF-reed) *verb.* To read (printed or written material) in order to correct errors. **proofread, proofreading.** —**proofreader** *noun.*

prop *noun.* 1. Something placed beneath or against an object to support it or hold it in position. 2. Any of the incidental objects used in a theatrical production, except costumes and scenery. 3. (Informal) Propeller. —*verb.* 1. To support or hold with a prop or props. 2. To place (an object) so that it is supported. **propped, propping.**

pronghorn

prop·a·gan·da (prop-ə-GAN-də) *noun.* 1. A systematic effort to spread ideas: *Propaganda* against the war failed to stop it. 2. Ideas and beliefs spread by systematic efforts. —**propaganda** *plural.*

prop·a·gan·dize (prop-ə-GAN-dighz) *verb.* To spread ideas and beliefs by systematic efforts. **propagandized, propagandizing.**

prop·a·gate (PROP-ə-gayt) *verb.* 1. To produce offspring or new growth; breed: Rabbits *propagate* quickly. 2. To cause to produce offspring or new growth: You can *propagate* some plants from cuttings. 3. To spread (information or ideas): *Propagate* your faith. 4. To send forth (news or information). **propagated, propagating.** —**propagation** (prop-ə-GAY-shən) *noun.*

pro·pel (prə-PEL) *verb.* To force to move: A gasoline engine *propels* my car. **propelled, propelling.**

pro·pel·lant (prə-PEL-ənt) *noun.* That which propels, specifically, the fuel used in a rocket engine.

pro·pel·ler (prə-PEL-ər) *noun.* Anything that propels, especially a device used to propel an aircraft or a boat, consisting of two or more curved blades set into a hub.

propeller

prop·er (PROP-ər) *adjective.* 1. Suitable; appropriate: the *proper* tool. 2. Polite, mannerly, formal. 3. Moral or modest: *proper* behavior. 4. Indicating a particular person, place, or thing: "Chicago" is a *proper* noun. 5. Strictly speaking: Our barn is not part of the house *proper.* —**properly** *adverb.*

proper fraction. A fraction with a numerator smaller than the denominator: $\frac{2}{3}$ is a *proper* fraction; $\frac{3}{2}$ is an improper fraction.

proper noun. A noun that is capitalized and refers to a person, place, or thing in particular.

prop·er·ty (PROP-ər-tee) *noun.* 1. Anything owned; a possession. 2. A piece of land considered as owned: The *property* next door was sold. 3. (Usually plural) Theater props. 4. A special characteristic: Lead has the *property* of heaviness. **properties.**

proph·e·cy (PROF-ə-see) *noun.* 1. A foretelling of the future by means of supernatural powers. 2. Any prediction: Dick's *prophecy* was that our team would win. 3. Act, process or practice of foretelling the future. **prophecies.**

proph·e·sy (PROF-ə-sigh) *verb.* 1. To foretell the future by means of supernatural powers. 2. To predict: The politician *prophesied* victory for his party. **prophesied, prophesying.**

proph·et (PROF-it) *noun.* 1. One who foretells the future, or tries to do so; one who makes predictions. 2. One who speaks or acts as if inspired by God: Moses was a *prophet.* —**prophetic** (prə-FET-ik) Also **prophetical** *adjective.* —**prophetically** *adverb.*

pro·por·tion (prə-POR-shən) *noun.* 1. The relation of one person, place, or thing to another as to size, extent, amount, or importance; ratio: The *proportion* of clear days to rainy days in June was three to one. 2. Correct relation: In Harry's drawing the arms and legs are not in *proportion.* 3. Amount or number in relation to the whole: The *proportion* of correct answers was high. 4. (Plural) Size; extent: a man of enormous *proportions.* —*verb.* To adjust (related things) to make a relationship correct or proper: *Proportion* Ruth's pay to the work she has completed. **proportioned, proportioning.** —**proportional** *adjective.* —**proportionally** *adverb.*

pro·por·tion·ate (prə-POR-shən-it) *adjective.* In or having the proper proportions. —**proportionately** *adverb.*

pro·pose (prə-POHZ) *verb.* 1. To offer (an idea or plan) for consideration. 2. To offer marriage. **proposed, proposing.** —**proposal** *noun.*

prop·o·si·tion (prop-ə-ZISH-ən) *noun.* 1. An idea or plan offered for consideration; a proposal. 2. A formal statement: Our country is dedicated to the *proposition* that all men are created equal. 3. (Math) A statement to be proved true.

pro·pri·e·tor (prə-PRIGH-ə-tər) *noun.* A person or firm that owns a property or a business: *proprietor* of a hotel.

pro·pri·e·ty (prə-PRIGH-ə-tee) *noun.* 1. Correctness or appropriateness of behavior: The *propriety* of Jack's going to the party without an invitation was doubtful. 2. (Usually plural) Rules of correct or proper behavior. **proprieties.**

pro·pul·sion (prə-PUHL-shən) *noun.* Act of propelling or of being propelled: *Propulsion* of sailboats is done by wind. —**propulsive** *adjective.*

pro·sa·ic (proh-ZAY-ik) *adjective.* Commonplace; dull.

prose (PROHZ) *noun.* Talk or writing that is not poetry; ordinary spoken or written language: The writing in newspapers is mostly *prose.*

pros·e·cute (PROSS-ə-kyoot) *verb.* 1. To bring to trial in a court of law. 2. To carry out to the end; to finish. **prosecuted, prosecuting.**

pros·e·cu·tion (pross-ə-KYOO-shən) *noun.* 1. Act of prosecuting or of being prosecuted; trial in court. 2. Those who are prosecuting: The *prosecution* presented the jury with evidence against the defendant.

pros·e·cu·tor (PROSS-ə-kyoo-tər) *noun.* One who prosecutes; especially an official whose job is to conduct prosecutions, as for a county or state.

pros·pect (PROSS-pekt) *noun.* 1. (Usually plural) Outlook; possibilities for the future: What are the *prospects* for your trip to Europe next summer? 2. A broad view; overlook: The *prospect* from the hilltop was splendid. 3. Someone being considered with regard to his future position or actions: Frank is a strong *prospect* for class president. —*verb.* To search (a region) for mineral deposits: *prospect* for gold. **prospected, prospecting.**

pros·pec·tive (prə-SPEK-tiv) *adjective.* Referring to future events; likely; expected; probable: a *prospective* trip. —**prospectively** *adverb.*

pros·pec·tor (PROSS-pek-tər) *noun.* One who prospects, or searches a region for mineral deposits, such as oil and gold.

pros·per (PROSS-pər) *verb.* 1. To grow in wealth or position; do well: You can *prosper* if you work hard. 2. To grow well; flourish: The farmer's corn *prospered* in the good weather. **prospered, prospering.**

pros·per·i·ty (pross-PEHR-ə-tee) *noun.* State of being prosperous, successful, or wealthy.

pros·per·ous (PROSS-pər-əss) *adjective.* Having prosperity; being successful or wealthy. —**prosperously** *adverb.*

pro·tag·o·nist (proh-TAG-ə-nist) *noun.* The main character of a drama.

pro·tect (prə-TEKT) *verb.* To defend against harm or damage; guard; shelter: Helmets *protect* heads. **protected, protecting.**

pro·tec·tion (prə-TEK-shən) *noun.* 1. Act of protecting, or state of being protected. 2. That which protects.

pro·tec·tive (prə-TEK-tiv) *adjective.* Giving or affording protection; sheltering. —**protectively** *adverb.*

protective coloring. Coloring of an animal's coat that makes it difficult to detect against its natural background and thus protects it against enemies.

pro·te·in (PROH-teen or PROH-tee-in) *noun.* An organic substance that contains nitrogen and is needed for cell growth in animals and plants: Meat, cheese, eggs, and peas are foods that contain *protein.*

pro·test (prə-TEST, proh-TEST, or PROH-test) *verb.* 1. To oppose or resist with strong statements; to object. 2. To state strongly; declare: The man *protested* his innocence. **protested, protesting.** —(PROH-test) *noun.* An objection; demonstration to express disapproval or opposition: the parents' *protest.*

pro·ton (PROH-ton) *noun.* (Physics) An extremely small particle or bit of matter carrying one positive charge of electricity: An atom has at least one *proton* in its nucleus.

pro·to·plasm (PROH-tə-plaz-əm) *noun.* The colorless living matter in all cells of animals and plants.

pro·to·zo·an (proh-tə-ZOH-ən) *noun.* A simple animal that consists of one cell, lives in water, and can usually be seen only with a microscope. —**protozoans** or **protozoa** (proh-tə-ZOH-ə) *plural.* —**protozoan** or **protozoic** *adjective.*

pro·tract (proh-TRAKT) *verb.* To lengthen; drag out: Cynthia *protracted* her visit; she stayed longer than she had planned. **protracted, protracting.**

pro·trac·tor (proh-TRAK-tər) *noun.* (Math) A device for drawing or measuring angles.

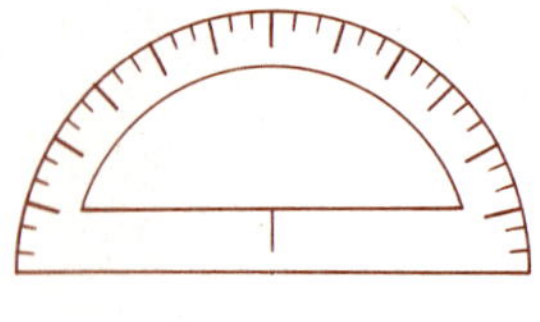
protractor

pro·trude (proh-TROOD) *verb.* To jut or stick out; project: The turtle's head *protruded* from its shell. **protruded, protruding.** —**protrusion** (proh-TROO-shən) *noun.*

proud (PROWD) *adjective.* 1. Having pride; thinking well of oneself; feeling superior. 2. Grand; splendid: a *proud* ship. —**proudly** *adverb.*

prove (PROOV) *verb.* 1. To show to be true or genuine; give proof of. 2. To test; reveal the quality or condition of: A long trip will *prove* your car. 3. Turn out or be found (to be): We hope your illness will not *prove* to be a long one. **proved, proving.**

prov·erb (PROV-erb) *noun.* A short saying often looked upon as a truth: "A stitch in time saves nine" is a *proverb.* —**proverbial** (prə-VER-bee-əl) *adjective.* —**proverbially** *adverb.*

pro·vide (prə-VIGHD) *verb.* 1. To supply, furnish: *provide* food. 2. To give care or support: The man had to *provide* for five children. 3. To take action beforehand: *provide* for the future. 4. To state as a rule or requirement: The Constitution *provides* for a President and a Vice President. **provided, providing.**

pro·vid·ed (prə-VIGHD-id) *conjunction.* On condition that; subject to the rule or understanding that.

prov·i·dence (PROV-ə-dənss) *noun.* 1. Care and aid from God: Only *providence* can save the ship in this raging storm. 2. (Capital P) God. 3. Care for the future: His *providence* will enable him to support himself in his old age.

prov·i·dent (PROV-ə-dənt) *adjective.* Careful about the future; showing providence. —**providently** *adjective.*

prov·i·den·tial (prov-ə-DEN-shəl) *adjective.* Due to God's care or help. —**providentially** *adverb.*

prov·ince (PROV-inss) *noun.* 1. A large division of a country: Alberta is a *province* of Canada. 2. (Plural) Areas far from cities, especially areas considered backward. 3. An area of knowledge or activity: the *province* of science. **provinces.**

pro·vin·cial (prə-VIN-shəl) *adjective.* 1. Relating to a province or provinces: Edmonton is the *provincial* capital of Alberta in Canada. 2. Having the dress or customs of people from the provinces; local or narrow-minded in ideas or outlook: Beverly has never traveled; her outlook is *provincial.* —**provincially** *adverb.*

pro·vi·sion (prə-VIZH-ən) *noun.* 1. A providing or supplying: *provision* of food and clothing. 2. (Plural) Supplies, especially of food. 3. Something done or prepared for the future: Most fathers have life insurance as a *provision* for their families' security. 4. A rule, condition: a *provision* of the Constitution.

pro·vi·sion·al (prə-VIZH-ən-l) *adjective.* Done or provided for a short time only; temporary: a *provisional* government. —**provisionally** *adverb.*

prov·o·ca·tion (prov-ə-KAY-shən) *noun.* Something said or done that causes anger: The shooting was the *provocation* that began the riot.

pro·voc·a·tive (prə-VOK-ə-tiv) *adjective.* Tending to arouse thoughtfulness, curiosity, or anger; stimulating: The rioters shouted *provocative* words at the police. —**provocatively** *adverb.*

pro·voke (prə-VOHK) *verb.* 1. To anger, irritate, or vex: George *provoked* the teacher by continued loud talking. 2. To move or excite to action; cause to happen: *provoke* a fight. **provoked, provoking.**

prow *noun.* The forward part of a boat or ship.

prow·ess (PROW-iss) *noun.* 1. Courage, bravery. 2. Skill, ability.

prowl *verb.* To search quietly; sneak or roam. **prowled, prowling.**

prox·y (PROK-see) *noun.* 1. An agent; one who has the power to vote or act for another. 2. The written permission for such action. **proxies.**

prude (PROOD) *noun.* A narrow-minded person; one who is overly concerned with what is proper or correct. **prudes.** —**prudish** *adjective.* —**prudishly** *adverb.*

pru·dence (PROOD-nss) *noun.* Caution; careful or sensible behavior.

pru·dent (PROOD-nt) *adjective.* Wise, careful, especially where money is concerned: She is a *prudent* shopper. —**prudently** *adverb.*

prune (PROON) *noun.* 1. A dried plum. 2. A kind of plum which can be dried without spoiling. **prunes.** —*verb.* To trim branches off a tree or bush. **pruned, pruning.**

pry (PRIGH) *verb.* 1. To lift or move by using a lever. 2. To snoop; search for information. **pried, prying.**

P.S. *abbreviation.* 1. (Also **p.s.**) Postscript. 2. Public School.

psalm (SAHM) *noun.* 1. A religious poem or song. 2. (Plural, capital P) A book of the Old Testament.

pseu·do (soo-doh) *adjective.* Not real.

pseu·do·nym (soo-də-nim) *noun.* A made-up name, a pen name.

PST *abbreviation.* Pacific Standard Time.

psy·che (SIGH-kee) *noun.* 1. The mind. 2. The soul or spirit rather than the body. **psyches.**

psy·che·del·ic (sigh-kə-DEL-ik) *adjective.* Mind-manipulating; causing one to see and hear things that do not exist, resulting in intense awareness and perception: *psychedelic* colors, *psychedelic* drugs. *See* **acid, LSD.** —**psychedelically** *adverb.*

psy·chi·a·try (si-KIGH-ə-tree) *noun.* The study or treatment of mental illness. —**psychiatrist** *noun.*

psy·chol·o·gy (sigh-KOL-ə-jee) *noun.* 1. The science or study of the minds and behavior of people and animals. 2. The special qualities of mind or behavior of a person or animal. **psychologies.** —**psychologist** *noun.*

psy·cho·sis (sigh-KOH-siss) *noun.* An extreme form of mental illness, characterized by a loss of contact with reality. —**psychoses** (sigh-KOH-seez) *plural.*

pt. *abbreviation.* 1. Pint. 2. Point.

P.T. *abbreviation.* Pacific Time.

PTA *abbreviation.* Parent-Teachers Association.

pter·o·dac·tyl (tehr-ə-DAK-til) *noun.* An extinct flying reptile related to the dinosaur.

PTSA *abbreviation.* Parent-Teachers-Student Association.

prow

prune

pueblo

pub·lic (PUHB-lik) *adjective.* 1. Not private, in the open: a *public* meeting. 2. Of or for all people: *public* transportation. 3. Relating to government: *public* officials. —*noun.* 1. All the people: The *public* should know the facts. 2. A particular group of people; fans: "My *public* is waiting," said the movie star. —**publicly** *adverb.*

public address system. A means of mass oral communication using one or more microphones and amplifiers and, usually, a number of loud-speakers.

pub·li·ca·tion (puhb-li-KAY-shən) *noun.* 1. Something that is published: Newspapers, magazines, and books are *publications.* 2. The act of printing and selling: the *publication* of a diary.

public defender. A lawyer appointed by the state to defend an accused person unable to hire his own lawyer.

public housing. Dwellings owned and rented by the government.

pub·lic·i·ty (puhb-LISS-ə-tee) *noun.* 1. Published or broadcast information: A man running for office needs widespread *publicity.* 2. Public attention: The robbery attracted much *publicity.* 3. The business of distributing news about a person, event, or organization.

public television. Television broadcasting, supported by the government or by private donations, that does not carry commercial messages.

pub·lish (PUHB-lish) *verb.* 1. To make public; tell or make known. 2. To print and sell (books, magazines and the like). **published, publishing.** —**publisher** *noun.*

puck (PUHK) *noun.* A flat disk of hard rubber used as the playing piece in ice hockey.

puck·er (PUK-ər) *verb.* To pull into folds or wrinkles. **puckered, puckering.** —*noun.* A wrinkle.

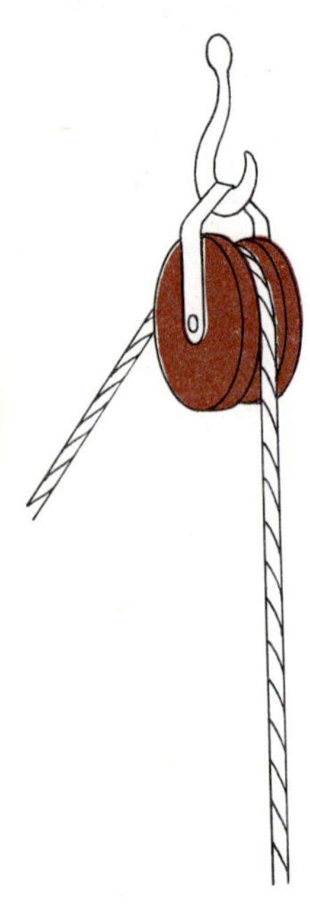
pulley

pud·ding (PUD-ing) *noun.* 1. A soft dessert. 2. One of many baked or cooked mixtures served as food.

pud·dle (PUHD-l) *noun.* A small patch or pool of liquid. **puddles.**

pueb·lo (PWEB-loh) *noun.* 1. An Indian village: Houses in a *pueblo* are built of sun-dried brick and are often placed one on top of another. 2. [Capital P] An Indian of a tribe that lives in such a village. **pueblos.**

puff (PUHF) *verb.* 1. To inflate; or become larger: The blowfish can *puff* itself to three times its normal size. 2. To breathe or blow in short bursts: He *puffed* on the fire to make it burn. 3. To pant as if out of breath. **puffed, puffing.** —*noun.* 1. A short burst of wind, air, or smoke. 2. A soft fluffy pad for putting on powder. 3. A kind of filled pastry. 4. A roll of hair.

puff·y (PUHF-ee) *adjective.* 1. Swollen, enlarged. 2. Light and airy: Cumulus clouds are white and *puffy.* **puffier, puffiest.**

pug nose. A short nose that turns up slightly at the tip.

pull (PUL) *verb.* 1. To use force to draw or move (something) toward oneself: *pull* a sled. 2. To take out or remove: *pull* a tooth. 3. To stretch or tear. 4. To attract: The sound of music *pulled* me to the open door. **pulled, pulling.** —*noun.* 1. The work of moving or drawing: It's a hard *pull* to the top of the hill. 2. A handle or knob: The drawer has brass *pulls.* 3. (Slang) A way of getting special favors: He has *pull* at the candy store because his brother works there. —**pull ahead.** To move out in front of. —**pull through.** To live through; finish successfully.

pul·let (PUL-it) *noun.* A young hen.

pul·ley (PUL-ee) *noun.* A simple device used to change the direction of or to increase a force by passing a line over a grooved wheel.

pull·o·ver (PUL-oh-vər) *noun.* A sweater or other garment which is pulled on over the head.

pulp (PUHLP) *noun.* 1. The soft part of a fruit or vegetable. 2. The inner part of a tooth. 3. Any soft, ground-up mass, especially the mixture from which paper is made. *—verb.* To turn into a soft wet mass. **pulped, pulping.** —**pulpy** *adjective.*

pul·sate (PUHL-sayt) *verb.* 1. To become alternately larger and smaller in a regular rhythm; beat. 2. To quiver or vibrate rhythmically. **pulsated, puslating.**

pulse (PUHLSS) *noun.* 1. The regular beating of the heart: The *pulse* can be felt in the arteries of the body. 2. One such throb or beat. 3. Any movement or action that repeats itself regularly. 4. Public feeling or opinion. **pulses.** *—verb.* To vibrate or beat. **pulsed, pulsing.**

pu·ma (POO-mə) *noun.* An American wildcat; a cougar.

pum·ice (PUHM-iss) *noun.* 1. A soft, spongy stone formed when volcanoes overflow. 2. Powder made from this stone and used for polishing. **pumices.** *—verb.* To polish or make smooth by using pumice. **pumiced, pumicing.**

pum·mel (PUH-məl) *verb.* To beat with the fists.

pump (PUHMP) *noun.* 1. A device for moving a liquid or gas from one place to another through tubes or pipes. 2. A kind of slipper or low shoe that has no laces or other fasteners. *—verb.* 1. To use a pump: *pump* up a tire. 2. To make up-and-down motions like those of a pump handle: Ed *pumped* my hand. 3. To try to get information by asking many questions. **pumped, pumping.**

pump·kin (PUHMP-kin or PUHNG-kin) *noun.* 1. A large orange-colored fruit of the squash family. 2. The vine on which this fruit grows. 3. (Also *adjective*). An orange color.

pun (PUHN) *noun.* A play on words which sound much alike but have different meanings: "Where do sheep get haircuts? At the Baa Baa shop." *—verb.* To make such a joke. **punned, punning.**

punch (PUHNCH) *noun.* 1. A sudden blow with the fist. 2. A tool for making a hole in a material. 3. A sweet drink that is a mixture of juices and other beverages. 4. (Informal) Drive, energy: put *punch* into a speech. **punches.** *—verb.* 1. To hit sharply and quickly. 2. To use a tool to cut holes. 3. To herd (cattle). **punched, punching.**

punc·tu·al (PUHNGK-choo-əl) *adjective.* On time. —**punctually** *adverb.*

punc·tu·ate (PUHNGK-choo-ayt) *verb.* 1. To separate written material into sentences, clauses, and phrases by the use of marks such as commas, colons, and periods. 2. To add importance to (certain words) while speaking: He *punctuates* his speech with motions of his hands. 3. To interrupt again and again: *punctuate* a talk with laughter. **punctuated, punctuating.**

punc·tu·a·tion (puhngk-choo-AY-shən) *noun.* 1. The use of marks, such as commas and periods, in written material to make it easier to read and understand. 2. The mark or marks themselves.

punctuation mark. One of the symbols used in written material to make it easier to read and understand.

punc·ture (PUHNGK-chər) *noun.* A small hole. **punctures.** *—verb.* 1. To make such a hole. 2. To spoil or destroy: *puncture* one's hopes. **punctured, puncturing.**

pun·gent (PUHN-jənt) *adjective.* 1. Sharp or biting to the senses of taste and smell: a *pungent* flavor. 2. Sharp, clever: *pungent* comments. —**pungently** *adverb.*

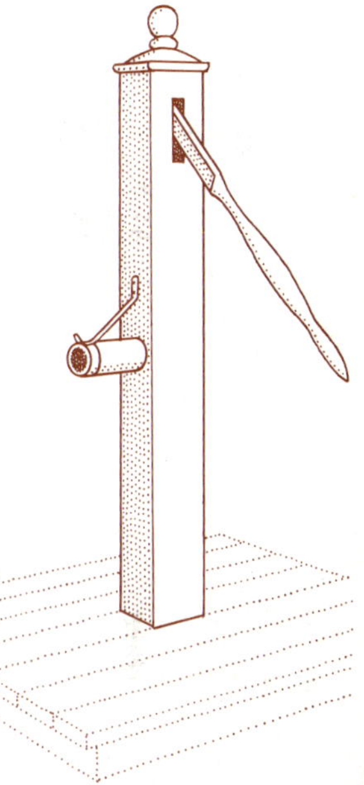
pump

pumpkin

puppets

puppies

pussy willows

pun·ish (PUHN-ish) *verb.* To cause to suffer or pay in some way for doing wrong. **punished, punishing.**

pun·ish·a·ble (PUHN-ish-ə-bəl) *adjective.* Deserving punishment.

pun·ish·ment (PUHN-ish-mənt) *noun.* The act or method of punishing or being punished.

punk (PUHNGK) *noun.* 1. Dry decaying wood and leaves. 2. A substance which burns very slowly without a flame, used to light fireworks. 3. (Slang) A worthless young person.

punt (PUHNT) *noun.* 1. An open boat that is moved through shallow water by means of a long pole. 2. (Football) A quick kick of the ball after it drops from the hands and before it touches the ground. —*verb.* 1. To push a boat along by means of a long pole. 2. (Football) To drop a ball and kick it before it hits the ground. **punted, punting.**

pu·ny (PYOO-nee) *adjective.* Small and weak. —**punily** *adverb.*

pup (PUHP) *noun.* A young dog, wolf, otter, or seal.

pu·pa (PYOO-pə) *noun.* An intermediate stage in the life of certain insects. —**pupae** (PYOO-pee) or **pupas** *plural.*

pu·pil (PYOO-pəl) *noun.* 1. A student. 2. The dark center in the colored portion of the eye.

pup·pet (PUHP-it) *noun.* 1. A figure of a person or animal controlled by strings or by a hand inside the figure. 2. A doll. 3. One whose actions are controlled by another.

pup·py (PUHP-ee) *noun.* A young dog. **puppies.**

pur·chase (PER-chiss) *verb.* To buy or receive in exchange for money, pain, or labor. **purchased, purchasing.** —*noun.* 1. The thing that is bought. 2. An act of buying. 3. A tight hold or grip.

pure (PYUR) *adjective.* 1. Containing only one substance: *pure* gold. 2. Clean, without germs or dirt: *pure* water. 3. Faultless: a *pure* soul. 4. Complete: *pure* chance. **purer, purest.** —**purely** *adverb.*

pure·bred (PYUR-BRED) *adjective.* Referring to an animal whose ancestors are all of the same breed.

purge (PERJ) *verb.* 1. To purify. 2. To rid of wrong or guilt. 3. To cause the bowels to move. **purged, purging.** —*noun.* 1. The act of cleaning or making pure. 2. That which causes the bowels to move.

pur·i·fy (PYUR-ə-figh) *verb.* To clean; make or become pure. **purified, purifying.**

pur·i·tan (PYUR-ət-n) *noun.* 1. A very serious person, one who thinks any kind of pleasure is wrong. 2. [Capital P] A member of the religious group that broke with the Church of England and came to America in the 17th century. —**puritanical** (pyur-ə-TAN-i-kəl) *adjective.*

pu·ri·ty (PYUR-ə-tee) *noun.* 1. Cleanness; freedom from foreign matter or corruption. 2. The state of being innocent.

pur·ple (PER-pəl) *noun.* 1. (Also *adjective*) A color made by mixing red and blue. 2. Clothes of this color worn by noblemen or high-ranking churchmen. **purples.**

pur·port (pər-PORT or PER-port) *verb.* To imply; represent (to be): The man was *purported* to be an honest politician. **purported, purporting.** —(PER-port) *noun.* Sense; meaning; purpose: the *purport* of a remark.

pur·pose (PER-pəss) *noun.* 1. A reason or goal. 2. Use or function. **purposes.** —**on purpose.** With intent; not by chance. —**purposeful** (PER-pəss-fəl) *adjective.* —**purposefully** *adverb.*

purr (PER) *noun.* 1. The low murmur a cat makes when it is happy. 2. Any similar sound. —*verb.* To make such a sound. **purred, purring.**

purse (PERSS) *noun.* 1. A small case or bag for holding money. 2. A woman's pocketbook. 3. Prize money. **purses.** —*verb.* To draw together: *purse* one's lips. **pursed, pursing.**

pur·sue (pər-soo) *verb.* 1. To try to catch; chase. 2. To try for (a certain goal): *pursue* a law career. 3. To involve oneself with: *pursue* a hobby. **pursued, pursuing.**

pur·suit (pər-SOOT) *noun.* 1. A chase; seeking. 2. A hobby, job, or pastime.

pus (PUHSS) *noun.* A yellow-white body fluid that often surrounds an infection.

push *verb.* 1. To apply force on (something) in order to move: *Push* open the door. 2. To urge on. 3. To bump against; shove: Ted always *pushes* to get ahead in line. 4. (Slang) To try to sell: *push* a style. **pushed, pushing.** —*noun.* 1. A shove; forward movement. 2. Ambition; effort. **pushes.**

push·er (PUSH-ər) *noun.* (Slang) Someone who sells drugs illegally.

push·o·ver (PUSH-oh-vər) *noun.* (Slang) 1. One who is easily influenced or defeated. 2. Something very easy to do.

push-up (PUSH-uhp) *noun.* An exercise in which a person who is face down on the floor lifts and lowers his body by straightening and bending his arms.

puss *noun.* 1. (Informal) Also **pussy.** A cat or kitten. 2. (Slang) The face or mouth. **pusses.**

pussy willow. 1. A soft, podlike flower of a gray color that grows in rows on a branch. 2. The bush or small tree on which it grows.

put *verb.* 1. To set or place: *Put* the book on the shelf. 2. To cause (a person or thing) to be in a certain condition: Music *put* the baby to sleep. 3. To subject (to pain, trial, or punishment): His courage was *put* to the test. 4. To guess or approximate: I *put* her age at 14. 5. To charge; impose: *put* a tax on. 6. To say; state: *Put* it simply. 7. To apply; bring in contact with. 8. To go on or forward: *Put* out to sea! **put, putting.** —**put down.** 1. To stop: *put* down a riot. 2. (Slang) To make little of. —**put off.** To delay; postpone. —**put one on.** To fool; play a trick on. —**put over.** To accomplish. —**put up with.** To tolerate; be patient with..

pu·trid (PYOO-trid) *adjective.* 1. Rotting. 2. Disgusting, horrible.

putt (PUHT) *noun.* (Golf) A stroke used when the ball is near the hole. —*verb.* To use such a stroke. **putted, putting.**

put·ter (PUHT-ər) *noun.* (Golf) The club used for putting or the golfer who is putting. —*verb.* To use one's spare time to do simple tasks. **puttered, puttering.**

put·ty (PUHT-ee) *noun.* A clay-like material used to fill holes and cracks and to keep windows in their frames. **putties.** —*verb.* To fill or hold with putty. **puttied, puttying.**

puz·zle (PUHZ-l) *verb.* 1. To confuse, baffle: The secret code *puzzled* me. 2. To try to understand: *puzzle* over a message. **puzzled, puzzling.** —*noun.* 1. A thing that confuses. 2. A game or test of one's thinking powers. **puzzles.**

pyg·my (PIG-mee) Also **pigmy** *noun.* 1. A tiny person or thing. 2. [Capital P] A member of an African or Asian tribe whose adults are no taller than five feet. **pygmies.**

pyr·a·mid (PIHR-ə-mid) *noun.* 1. A solid figure with triangular sides that meet at a point at the top. 2. A monument of this shape. —*verb.* To make or form into a pyramid. **pyramided, pyramiding.**

pyre (PIGHR) *noun.* A mound, as of wood, on which a dead body is burned as a funeral rite. **pyres.**

py·thon (PIGH-thon) *noun.* A very large snake that coils around its prey and squeezes it to death.

pygmies

pyramids

python

Q,q (KYOO) *noun.* The 17th letter of the English alphabet.

qt. *abbreviation.* 1. Quart. 2. Quantity.

quack (KWAK) *noun.* 1. The sound made by a duck. 2. A person who pretends to be a doctor but lacks the training. —*verb.* To make the sound of a duck. **quacked, quacking.**

quad·rant (KWOD-rənt) *noun.* 1. One fourth of a circle. 2. An instrument to measure heights and angles.

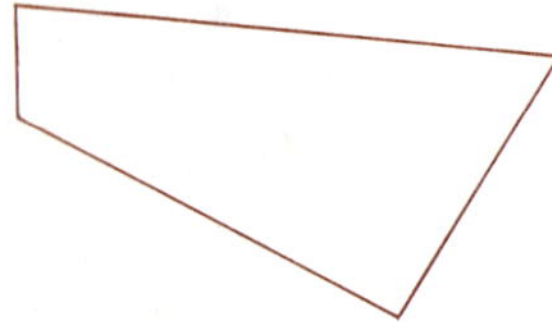

quadrilateral

quad·ri·lat·er·al (kwod-rə-LAT-ər-əl) *noun.* A flat figure having four sides: A square is a *quadrilateral.*

quad·ru·ped (KWOD-ru-ped) *noun.* An animal having four feet: The horse is a *quadruped.*

quad·ru·plet (kwod-RUHP-lit or kwod-ROO-plit) *noun.* One of four offspring born at the same time.

quaff (KWOF or KWAF) *verb.* To drink in large swallows; to gulp. **quaffed, quaffing.**

[1]quail

[1]quail (KWAYL) *noun.* A plump bird with short, strong wings, often hunted for sport or food.

[2]quail (KWAYL) *verb.* To draw back in fright. **quailed, quailing.**

quaint (KWAYNT) *adjective.* Odd, curious; pleasantly old-fashioned: a *quaint* old lady. **quainter, quaintest.** —**quaintly** *adverb.* —**quaintness** *noun.*

quake (KWAYK) *verb.* To shake, tremble: The boy *quaked* with fear. **quaked, quaking.** —*noun.* 1. An earthquake. 2. A shaking or trembling. **quakes.**

qual·i·fi·ca·tion (kwol-ə-fi-KAY-shən) *noun.* 1. Requirement; something that is needed, such as an ability or skill: He has all the *qualifications* for the job. 2. A limit or restriction: He approved my plans with no *qualification.*

qual·i·fy (KWOL-ə-figh) *verb.* 1. To prove able: Campers must be able to swim to *qualify* for the boating course. 2. To limit or change slightly: An adjective is used to *qualify* a noun. **qualified, qualifying.**

qual·i·ty (KWOL-ə-tee) *noun.* 1. A trait or feature that serves to identify a person or thing: Sweetness is a *quality* of sugar. 2. Degree or grade: Prime meat is the best *quality* you can buy. 3. Worth or excellence: a material of the highest *quality.* **qualities.**

qualm (KWAHM) *noun.* 1. Doubt or uncertainty. 2. A guilty feeling: Jon felt *qualms* about skipping school.

quan·da·ry (KWON-dree) *noun.* The state of being undecided or confused. **quandaries.**

quan·ti·ty (KWON-tə-tee) *noun.* 1. Amount, number. 2. A large amount: If you buy eggs in *quantity,* the price per dozen is less. **quantities.**

quar·an·tine (KWOR-ən-teen) *verb.* To isolate to prevent the spreading of a disease: The ship's crew will be *quarantined* because the cook has smallpox. **quarantined, quarantining.** —*noun.* 1. The time during which persons, animals, or plants are held to determine whether they are diseased. 2. The place in which they are held.

quar·rel (KWOR-əl) *noun.* 1. An unpleasant argument or disagreement. 2. A reason for arguing or fighting: She had no *quarrel* with his ideas. —*verb.* To argue or complain.

quarreled or **quarrelled, quarreling** or **quarrelling.**

quar·rel·some (KWOR-əl-səm) *adjective.* Ready for an argument; tending to fight.

quar·ry (KWOR-ee) *noun.* 1. An animal or person that is the object of a hunt or chase. 2. An open mine or pit from which stone or gravel is removed. **quarries.** —*verb.* To cut and remove stones from a quarry. **quarried, quarrying.**

quart (KWORT) *noun.* 1. A unit of liquid measure equal to 2 pints or 32 ounces. 2. A unit of dry measure equal to 2 pints: There are 32 *quarts* in a bushel.

quar·ter (KWOR-tər) *noun.* 1. One-fourth; one of four equal parts. 2. A U.S. coin equal to 25 cents or one-fourth of a dollar. 3. A section of a city: the Italian *quarter.* 4. One of four phases of the moon. 5. One of four time periods in a game such as football. 6. Mercy, kindness: The warden showed the prisoners no *quarter.* 7. (Usually plural) A place to live: He showed the visitors to their *quarters.* —*verb.* 1. To separate or divide into four equal parts. 2. To provide a place to live: The performers were *quartered* at a local hotel. **quartered, quartering.**

quar·ter·back (KWOR-tər-bak) *noun.* (Football) One of four men who play behind the front line: The *quarterback* calls signals for the team.

quar·ter·ly (KWOR-tər-lee) *adjective* and *adverb.* Four times a year, or every three months: We pay our taxes *quarterly.* —*noun.* A magazine, newspaper, or report that is published four times a year. **quarterlies.**

quar·ter·mas·ter (KWOR-tər-mass-tər) *noun.* 1. (Army) An officer in charge of supplies for troops. 2. (Navy) An officer on a ship who steers it and handles signaling equipment.

quar·ter·staff (KWOR-tər-staf) *noun.* A long wooden pole with a metal tip, formerly used as a weapon. —**quarterstaves** (KWOR-tər-stayvz) *plural.*

quar·tet (kwor-TET) Also **quartette** *noun.* 1. A group of four, especially four musicians. 2. A piece of music written for four people to sing or play.

quartz (KWORTS) *noun.* A hard mineral that is usually colorless but may be green, pink, yellow, or purple.

qua·sar (KWAY-zahr) *noun.* (Astronomy) A starlike object located a great distance from the earth: Many *quasars* are known to send out radio waves.

quat·rain (KWOT-rayn) *noun.* Four lines of poetry: A *quatrain* may be a poem in itself or part of a longer poem.

qua·ver (KWAY-vər) *verb.* To shake or tremble. **quavered, quavering.** —*noun.* The act of shaking or trembling.

quay (KEE) *noun.* A dock or wharf, often made of stone or concrete.

queen (KWEEN) *noun.* 1. A female ruler. 2. The wife of a king. 3. Any outstanding woman: a beauty *queen.* 4. The most powerful piece in the game of chess. 5. A pictured playing card, between the jack and the king. 6. A female bee or ant that lays eggs for the entire colony. —**queenly** *adjective.*

queer (KWIHR) *adjective.* 1. Odd; peculiar: a *queer* way of behaving. 2. Subject to suspicion; questionable: Mr. Marner is a *queer* character. **queerer, queerest.** —*verb.* (Slang) To ruin: *queer* someone's chances. **queered, queering.** —**queerly** *adverb.* —**queerness** *noun.*

quell (KWEL) *verb.* 1. To bring to a stop; put down: *quell* a riot. 2. To quiet or make calm: *quell* a baby's fear. **quelled, quelling.**

quarry

quartz

quiver
(definition 2)

quill

quench (KWENCH) *verb.* 1. To satisfy: Water will *quench* your thirst. 2. To put out; extinguish: They used water to *quench* the fire. **quenched, quenching.**

que·ry (KWIHR-ee) *verb.* To ask questions. **queried, querying.** —*noun.* A question. **queries.**

quest (KWEST) *noun.* A search for a particular object or goal. —*verb.* To make a quest. **quested, questing.**

ques·tion (KWESS-chən) *noun.* 1. A sentence that asks for information: "Where are you?" is a *question.* 2. A problem or subject to be talked about and decided: The council will discuss the *question* of trash collection. 3. Uncertainty or doubt: There is some *question* about the weather this weekend. —*verb.* 1. To ask (someone) for information: Mary *questioned* her teacher about the hard problem. 2. To have doubts: Some people *question* the wisdom of space travel. **questioned, questioning.** —**out of the question.** Impossible; not worth discussion: Skipping school today is *out of the question.* —**without question.** Absolutely; without a doubt.

ques·tion·a·ble (KWESS-chən-ə-bəl) *adjective.* Open to doubt or disapproval: a *questionable* practice.

question mark. The punctuation mark (?) used at the end of a sentence that asks for information.

ques·tion·naire (kwess-chə-NAIR) *noun.* A printed or written set of questions used to collect information. **questionnaires.**

queue (KYOO) *noun.* 1. A long braid of hair that hangs down the back. 2. (British) A line of people or vehicles: a *queue* of children in the lunch line. **queues.** —*verb.* (British) (Used with *up*) To form a line: People *queued up* at the bus stop. **queued. queuing.**

quib·ble (KWIB-əl) *verb.* To argue over a small or unimportant matter. **quibbled, quibbling.** —*noun.* An argument over a small matter.

quick (KWIK) *adjective.* 1. Fast, lively: "Jack be nimble,/ Jack be *quick.* . . ." (Nursery rhyme). 2. Fast to react: a *quick* temper. **quicker, quickest.** —*noun.* 1. A tender part: He trimmed his fingernails down to the *quick.* 2. (Rare) The living: "He shall come to judge the *quick* and the dead." (Apostles' Creed). —**quickly** *adverb.* —**quickness** *noun.*

quick·en (KWIK-ən) *verb.* 1. To increase in speed: His pace *quickened* as he neared the finish line. 2. To arouse; stir up: The exciting story *quickened* his pulse. **quickened, quickening.**

quick·sand (KWIK-sand) *noun.* A mass of very fine, wet sand that can suck down animals or people who wander onto it.

quick·sil·ver (KWIK-sil·vər) *noun. See* **mercury.**

quick-wit·ted (KWIK-WIT-id) *adjective.* Clever; intelligent; fast to answer or act.

qui·et (KWIGH-it) *adjective.* 1. Silent, without sound. 2. Calm; peaceful; still: The lake was *quiet* after the storm. 3. Gentle, not noisy. 4. Pale, not bright: The picture is painted in *quiet* colors. **quieter, quietest.** —*noun.* Silence; peace. —*verb.* To become or cause to become calm or silent. **quieted, quieting.** —**quietly** *adverb.* —**quietness** *noun.*

quill (KWIL) *noun.* 1. One of the large feathers found in the wing and tail of a bird. 2. A pen made from such a feather. 3. One of the long sharp spines on the body and tail of the porcupine.

quilt (KWILT) *noun.* A bed covering made of two layers of cloth with filling between and held together by lines of stitching. —*verb.* To sew a quilt or in the pattern of a quilt. **quilted, quilting.**

quince (KWINSS) *noun.* 1. A hard greenish-yellow fruit used for preserves. 2. The tree on which this fruit grows. **quinces.**

qui·nine (KWIGH-nighn) *noun.* A bitter substance made from the bark of a tropical tree and used in medicine for treating malaria.

quin·tes·sence (kwin-TESS-ənss) *noun.* The purest or most typical example (of something): Lincoln was the *quintessence* of honesty.

quin·tet (kwin-TET) Also **quintette** *noun.* 1. A group of five, especially five musicians. 2. A piece of music written for five people to perform.

quin·tu·plet (kwin-TUHP-lit or kwin-TOO-plit) *noun.* One of five offspring born in a single birth.

quip (KWIP) *noun.* A short, witty remark. *—verb.* To make such a remark. **quipped, quipping.**

quirk (KWERK) *noun.* 1. A sudden twist or flourish. 2. A peculiar trait or way of behaving.

quit (KWIT) *verb.* 1. To stop or give up, especially before one has finished: He *quit* the race halfway through. 2. To leave: Rats *quit* a sinking ship. **quit** or **quitted, quitting.** **—call it quits.** To give up or stop.

quite (KWIGHT) *adverb.* 1. Completely: You are *quite* right. 2. (Informal) More than a little; very: Dad was *quite* angry with me for leaving his tools out in the rain.

quit·ter (KWIT-ər) *noun.* One who gives up or stops easily: "Winners never quit and *quitters* never win." (Old saying).

quiv·er (KWIV-ər) *verb.* To shake or cause to shake slightly; tremble: Her lower lip began to *quiver.* **quivered, quivering.** *—noun.* 1. A slight shaking. 2. A case used to hold arrows.

quiz (KWIZ) *verb.* To ask (someone) questions; give a short test (to). **quizzed, quizzing.** *—noun.* A short test. **quizzes.**

quiz show. A program on television or radio in which contestants are asked questions on a wide variety of subjects and in which they win prizes for correct answers.

quiz·zi·cal (KWIZ-i-kəl) *adjective.* 1. Puzzled: a *quizzical* look. 2. Playfully odd: a *quizzical* smile. **—quizzically** *adverb.*

quoit (KWOIT) *noun.* 1. A ring, made of rope or metal. 2. (Plural) A game in which players try to throw such rings over pegs in the ground.

Quonset hut (KWON-sit HUHT). *trademark.* A building, made of pre-shaped pieces of metal and having a curved roof, that can be quickly put together.

quo·rum (KWOR-əm) *noun.* The number of members needed at a meeting to make a legal decision for their organization: Because the senators could not get a *quorum,* they could not vote on the bill.

quo·ta (KWOH-tə) *noun.* A share or amount assigned to any one person, group, or country: I sold my *quota* of tickets.

quo·ta·tion (kwoh-TAY-shən) *noun.* 1. The exact words of a speaker or writer. 2. The act of repeating such words. 3. The current price: The newspaper gives stock *quotations.*

quotation mark. Either of the punctuation marks (“ ”) used to show the beginning or end of a quotation.

quote (KWOHT) *verb.* 1. To repeat the exact words of a speaker or writer. 2. To give (the price of): to *quote* a price for wheat. **quoted, quoting** *—noun.* 1. A quotation. 2. (Plural) Quotation marks. **quotes.**

quotient (KWOH-shənt) *noun.* The number found by dividing one number by another: When 16 is divided by 2, the *quotient* is 8.

quince

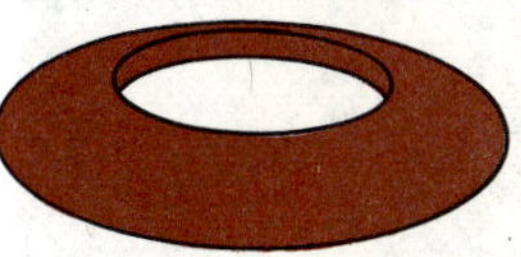
quoit

Quonset huts

rabbit

raccoon

radar

R, r (AHR) *noun.* The eighteenth letter of the English alphabet.

rab·bi (RAB-igh) *noun.* A religious leader or teacher of the Jewish people; the leader of a Jewish synagogue or congregation. **rabbis.**

rab·bit (RAB-it) *noun.* An animal with long ears, a short, stubby tail and soft fur.

rab·ble (RAB-əl) *noun.* 1. A mob; a disorderly crowd. 2. Any group regarded with scorn.

ra·bies (RAY-beez) *noun.* An often fatal disease that causes dogs, wolves, and other animals to go into convulsions: A person who has been bitten by a diseased animal may get *rabies.* Also called "hydrophobia." —**rabid** *adjective.*

rac·coon (ra-KOON) Also **racoon** *noun.* A small, gray animal, with mask-like markings around the eyes and a ringed tail, that comes out mostly at night. Also called "coon." —**raccoons** or **raccoon** *plural.*

[1]**race** (RAYSS) *noun.* A competition; a test of speed; a political contest: a horse *race.* **races.** —*verb.* To run; go swiftly. **raced, racing.**

[2]**race** (RAYSS) *noun.* 1. A large group of people, plants, or animals that have similar physical traits and a common heredity. 2. All of mankind: the human *race.* 3. A group of people with a common characteristic: They were a *race* of honest men. **races.** —**racial** (RAY-shəl) *adjective.* —**racially** *adverb.*

rac·er (RAY-sər) *noun.* 1. A person, animal, or vehicle that races. 2. A kind of snake.

race·track (RAYSS-trak) *noun.* A course where a race takes place, usually inside an oval enclosure.

rack (RAK) *noun.* 1. A stand or shelf with hooks, pegs, or grooves to hold various items: a book *rack.* 2. An instrument used in the Middle Ages to torture people by stretching them. 3. A frame with slats used to hold hay, straw, etc.

rack·et (RAK-it) *noun.* 1. A loud, continuous noise; disturbance. 2. (Informal) A dishonest way of getting money from people: the drug *racket.* 3. (Also **racquet**) A bat with a long handle and an oval frame strung with a network of cord or nylon, used in sports such as tennis.

ra·dar (RAY-dahr) *noun.* An instrument that detects unseen objects and measures their distance and direction through the use of reflected radio waves.

ra·di·ant (RAY-dee-ənt) *adjective.* 1. Glowing, beaming: a *radiant* bride. 2. Coming in the form of rays: *radiant* energy. —**radiance** *noun.* —**radiantly** *adverb.*

ra·di·ate (RAY-dee-ayt) *verb.* 1. To send forth rays; to glow; to shine. 2. To come forth in rays, as light or heat. 3. To spread out from a central point. **radiated, radiating.**

ra·di·a·tion (ray-dee-AY-shən) *noun.* 1. The sending forth of electromagnetic waves. 2. The rays of energy sent forth, as heat from the sun.

ra·di·a·tor (RAY-dee-ay-tər) *noun.* A set of tubes or pipes used in a heating system for radiation of heat.

rad·i·cal (RAD-i-kəl) *noun.* A person who seeks extreme or fundamental change. —*adjective.* Affecting basic principles; fundamental; extreme. —**radically** *adverb.*

ra·di·o (RAY-dee-oh) *noun.* 1. A system of wireless communication by means of electromagnetic waves. 2. An instrument used for sending and receiving sounds by electromagnetic waves. **radios.** —*verb.* To send or communicate by radio. **radioed, radioing.**

ra·di·o·ac·tive (ray-dee-oh-AK-tiv) *adjective.* Giving off rays from atomic nuclei: Radium is *radioactive.* —**radioactivity** (ray-dee-oh-ak-TIV-ə-tee) *noun.*

ra·di·ol·o·gy (ray-dee-OL-ə-jee) *noun.* A branch of medicine which studies and treats certain diseases by using X-rays.

ra·di·om·e·ter (ray-dee-OM-ə-tər) *noun.* An instrument that detects and measures radiation.

rad·ish (RAD-ish) *noun.* A small round or long root with red or white skin.

ra·di·um (RAY-dee-əm) *noun.* A radioactive metallic element discovered by the Curies in 1898.

ra·di·us (RAY-dee-əss) *noun.* 1. A straight line from the center to the outside of a circle. 2. A circular area defined by the length of its radius: There was no building within a *radius* of ten miles from our house. —**radii** (RAY-dee-igh) or **radiuses** *plural.*

raf·fle (RAF-əl) *noun.* A sale in which chances for a prize are sold, the winner being determined by a drawing. **raffles.** —*verb.* To sell by means of a raffle. **raffled, raffling.**

raft *noun.* A floating platform, often made of wood or rubber.

raft·er (RAF-tər) *noun.* A beam or timber that holds up a roof.

rag *noun.* 1. A small piece of old cloth: We wiped the windows with a *rag.* 2. (Plural) Old, worn clothing.

rage (RAYJ) *noun.* 1. Violent anger; fury. 2. (Slang) Fashion; fad. **rages.** —*verb.* To storm; be violently angry. **raged, raging.**

rag·ged (RAG-id) *adjective.* 1. Tattered, torn: *ragged* clothes. 2. Dressed in old clothes; shabby. 3. Rough; with irregular edges: a *ragged* haircut.

rag·weed (RAG-weed) *noun.* A common weed, with small yellow flowers, whose pollen causes hay fever in some people.

raid (RAYD) *noun.* 1. An unexpected and sudden attack or breaking in: a *raid* by enemy soldiers. 2. A sudden breaking in to arrest people: a police *raid.* —*verb.* 1. To attack suddenly. 2. To invade and seize property. **raided, raiding.**

[1]**rail** (RAYL) *noun.* 1. A strip of wood or metal used as part of a fence or barrier: a fence *rail.* 2. (Plural) Parallel metal bars forming a track for trains. 3. Railroad: travel by *rail.*

[2]**rail** (RAYL) *verb.* To complain bitterly. **railed, railing.**

[3]**rail** (RAYL) *noun.* A brownish bird of marshes and swamps.

rail·ing (RAY-ling) *noun.* A barrier or fence made of rails: a porch *railing.*

rail·road (RAYL-rohd) *noun.* 1. A road with tracks or parallel rails for the wheels of trains. 2. The entire system or company operating trains, including buildings, trains, and land.

rai·ment (RAY-mənt) *noun.* Clothing; garments.

rain (RAYN) *noun.* 1. Water falling in drops from the clouds. 2. A shower or downpour. 3. Anything that falls like rain: a *rain* of confetti. —*verb.* 1. To fall from the sky as moisture. 2. To come down like rain. **rained, raining.**

rain·bow (RAYN-boh) *noun.* A curve of colors across the sky made by the sun shining through drops of water.

rain·coat (RAYN-koht) *noun.* A waterproof coat worn as protection from the rain.

rain·drop (RAYN-drop) *noun.* A drop of rain.

raft

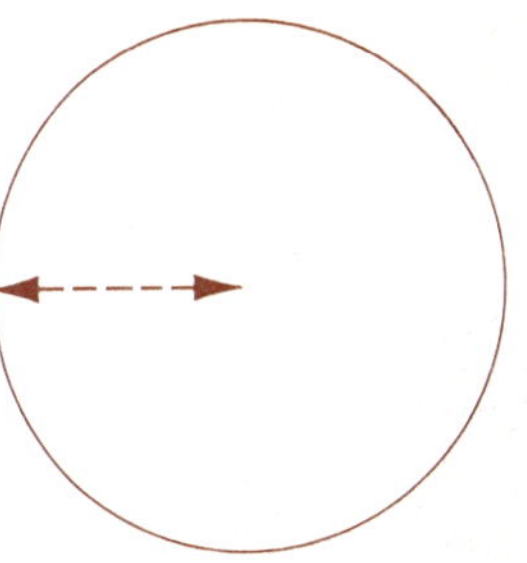

radius

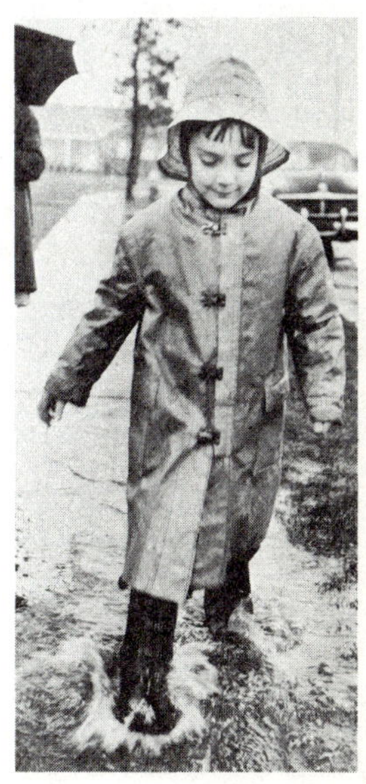

raincoat

rain forest

rakes

rain·fall (RAYN-fawl) *noun.* 1. A downpour of rain. 2. The amount of rain that falls in a particular place during a given time: yearly *rainfall.*

rain forest. A wooded area in the tropics, with heavy rainfall and a moist, hot climate.

rain gauge. Also **rain gage.** A device to measure rainfall.

rain·y (RAY-nee) *adjective.* Having large amounts of rain. **rainier, rainiest.**

raise (RAYZ) *verb.* 1. To lift or put up: She *raised* her hand. 2. To increase in degree or amount: *raise* a price; *raise* one's voice. 3. To grow or cultivate: *raise* carrots. 4. To rear; bring up: *raise* a family. 5. To bring together; collect: *raise* an army. 6. To stir up; cause. 7. To build: They *raised* the barn in one day. 8. To bring up for thought: He *raised* the issue of taxation. **raised, raising.** —*noun.* An increase in salary, amount, or price. **raises.**

rai·sin (RAY-zən) *noun.* A dried grape.

ra·jah (RAH-jə) Also **raja** *noun.* A prince or ruler in India.

rake (RAYK) *noun.* A garden tool with a long handle and a toothed or pronged crossbar at one end. **rakes.** —*verb.* 1. To gather together or smooth with a rake. 2. To search (in) carefully. 3. To spray with gunfire from end to end. **raked, raking.**

ral·ly (RAL-ee) *noun.* A gathering for a purpose; a mass meeting: a football *rally.* **rallies.** —*verb.* 1. To gather around; come together: "*Rally* round the flag, boys." (G. F. Root). 2. To recover health or strength. **rallied, rallying.**

ram *noun.* 1. A male sheep. 2. A machine to batter down walls. —*verb.* 1. To butt; hit with force: They *rammed* into a stone wall. 2. To cram or push down hard: She *rammed* all her papers into her purse. **rammed, ramming.**

ram·ble (RAM-bəl) *verb.* 1. To walk aimlessly; wander. 2. To speak or write in a lengthy, wandering manner. 3. To grow in a wandering way: The roses *rambled* over the fence. **rambled, rambling.** —*noun.* A pleasure walk or stroll. **rambles.**

ram·bunc·tious (ram-BUHNGK-shəss) *adjective.* Very lively; wild; unruly.

ram·i·fi·ca·tion (ram-ə-fə-KAY-shən) *noun.* A side effect; one of the consequences of an action.

ramp *noun.* A sloping road or passageway connecting different levels of a road or building.

ram·page (RAM-payj) *noun.* Violent, angry behavior. **rampages.** —(ram-PAYJ) *verb.* To rage; act wildly. **rampaged, rampaging.**

ram·pant (RAM-pənt) *adjective.* Out of control; unchecked.

ram·part (RAM-pahrt) *noun.* A bank of earth, sometimes with a wall on the top, around a fort: "O'er the *ramparts* we watched." (F. S. Key).

ram·rod (RAM-rod) *noun.* 1. A rod for cleaning the barrel of a gun. 2. A rod for ramming the charge down the barrel of a muzzle-loading gun.

ran *verb. See* **run.**

ranch *noun.* A large farm, especially one for raising cattle or other livestock. **ranches.** —*verb.* To work on or run a ranch. **ranched, ranching.**

ranch house. 1. A one-story house with a low roof. 2. The house on a ranch in which the owner lives.

ran·cid (RAN-sid) *adjective.* Having the unpleasant smell or taste of stale oil or fat; stale.

ran·cor (RANG-kər) *noun.* Hatred; resentment. —**rancorous** *adjective.*

ran·dom (RAN-dəm) *adjective.* With no particular order or pattern; haphazard; aimless: The teacher made a *random* selection of students to collect the tests. —**randomly** *adverb.*

rang *verb. See* **ring.**

range (RAYNJ) *noun.* 1. Extent, area, or limit: Hiring new workers is not within the *range* of the salesman's authority. 2. The distance that anything can travel: the *range* of an airplane. 3. The distance that a gun can fire a bullet or projectile. 4. A chain or series of mountains. 5. A place where guns can be fired at targets for practice. 6. A prairie or other open area where livestock can graze. 7. A stove. **ranges.** —*verb.* 1. To vary or change within certain limits: My marks *range* from C to B+. 2. To roam: The cattle *ranged* about the prairie. 3. To stretch out; extend: The hills *ranged* from one end of the country to the other. **ranged, ranging.**

rang·er (RAYN-jər) *noun.* 1. A warden who watches over or patrols a forest area. 2. A member of a crack military raiding unit: Rogers' *Rangers.*

[1]**rank** (RANGK) *noun.* 1. An official position or grade: the *rank* of corporal. 2. A row, as of soldiers lined up side by side. 3. A high social position: a person of *rank.* 4. One's position or importance as compared with others': a musician of the highest *rank.* 5. (Plural) The army; enlisted men. —*verb.* 1. To hold an official position or rank: Uncle David *ranks* as a captain in the Navy. 2. To place in order: The teams are *ranked* according to their records. 3. To place or arrange in rows. **ranked, ranking.**

[2]**rank** (RANGK) *adjective.* 1. Having a very strong, unpleasant smell or taste. 2. Extreme; complete: a *rank* lie. 3. Growing rapidly and thickly: *rank* weeds.

ran·kle (RANG-kəl) *verb.* To irritate; vex or cause annoyance. **rankled, rankling.**

ran·sack (RAN-sak) *verb.* 1. To search through completely: My sister *ransacked* her closet to find her scarf. 2. To plunder; rob. **ransacked, ransacking.**

ran·som (RAN-səm) *noun.* An amount of money or other payment demanded or given for the release of a captive. —*verb.* To obtain the release of a captive by paying a ransom. **ransomed, ransoming.**

rap *verb.* 1. To strike quickly and lightly; to knock: The teacher *rapped* a ruler against the desk to get our attention. 2. To speak out sharply: *rap* out orders. 3. (Slang) To talk; to converse: The boys *rapped* for hours about sports. **rapped, rapping.** —*noun.* 1. A quick, light striking or knock. 2. (Slang) Undeserved blame, as for a crime: Who took the *rap* for breaking the window?

rap·id (RAP-id) *adjective.* Very quick; swift: a *rapid* pace. —*noun.* (Usually plural) A section of a river or stream where the water runs very swiftly. —**rapidly** *adverb.*

ra·pid·i·ty (rə-PID-ə-tee) *noun.* Swiftness; speed.

ra·pi·er (RAY-pee-ər) *noun.* A light, sharp, pointed sword used for piercing rather than slashing.

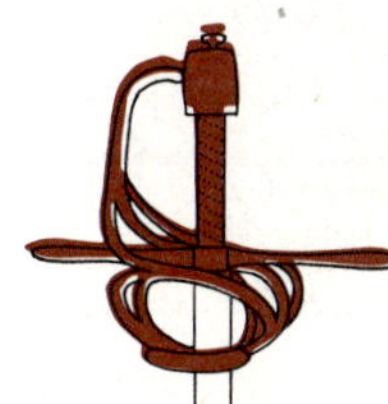

rapier

rap session. (Slang) A time or meeting for exchanging ideas; discussion.

rapt *adjective.* Deeply involved or attracted; engrossed. —**raptly** *adverb.*

rap·ture (RAP-chər) *noun.* A feeling of great joy.

[1]**rare** (RAIR) *adjective.* 1. Not often found or possessed; unusual: *rare* disease. 2. Very special: *rare* talent. 3. Very thin, as air: The air was *rare* at the top of the mountain. **rarer, rarest.** —**rarely** *adverb.*

[2]**rare** (RAIR) *adjective.* Cooked very lightly; close to raw: *rare* meat. **rarer, rarest.** —**rarely** *adverb.*

ras·cal (RASS-kəl) *noun.* 1. A mischievous or playful person. 2. A bad or dishonest person.

[1]**rash** *noun.* 1. An inflammation or spotting of the skin: Measles and chicken pox cause *rashes.* 2. A series or large number of happenings during a particular period: A *rash* of fires was reported during the riot. **rashes.**

[2]rash *adjective.* Inclined to act too quickly or without thinking; reckless: It was *rash* for Bob to skate on the thin ice. **rasher, rashest. —rashly** *adverb.* **—rashness** *noun.*

rasp *verb.* 1. To make a harsh or rough sound: a *rasping* cough. 2. To scrape with a file. 3. To irritate; affect harshly: The sound of squeaking chalk *rasps* on my nerves. **rasped, rasping.** *—noun.* 1. A rough or coarse file. 2. A harsh, rough sound.

raspberry

rasp·ber·ry (RAZ-behr-ee) *noun.* 1. A sweet berry, usually red. 2. The bush or plant on which this fruit grows. **raspberries.**

rat

rat *noun.* 1. A gnawing animal, often destructive, with a long, hairless tail. 2. (Slang) A sneaky or nasty person. *—verb.* (Slang) To betray or give harmful information about someone: The thief *ratted* to the police. **ratted, ratting.**

rate (RAYT) *noun.* 1. A number, amount, or degree in relation to something else, as in miles per hour or dollars per pound. 2. Rank; class: Bill is a first-*rate* pitcher. 3. Price: The farmer sold his grain at the usual *rate.* *—verb.* 1. To rank as to value or position: Our team is *rated* number one in the city. 2. To regard; consider: I *rate* Leo as my best friend. 3. (Informal) Deserve; have a claim to: The new coach *rates* our respect. **rated, rating.**

rattlesnake

rath·er (RATH-ər) *adverb.* 1. More willingly; preferably: I would *rather* sleep than study. 2. Somewhat; *rather* careless. 3. Instead of; more properly: Kathy, *rather* than Jim, should be class president. 4. More correctly: The book costs $1.00 or, *rather,* $1.03.

rat·i·fy (RAT-ə-figh) *verb.* To approve or accept, especially formally: *ratify* a treaty. **ratified, ratifying.**

ra·tio (RAY-shoh or RAY-shee-oh) *noun.* A proportion or relationship between two different numbers or amounts: Boys outnumber girls in our club by a *ratio* of three to one. **ratios.**

ra·tion (RASH-ən or RAY-shən) *noun.* An amount or portion of something, especially if limited or arranged in advance, as of food or fuel: Each sailor received a *ration* of one bowl of beans for supper. *—verb.* To give out in limited amounts; to limit the amount (of something to be given): The government *rationed* coal and oil during the fuel shortage. **rationed, rationing.**

ra·tion·al (RASH-ən-l) *adjective.* 1. Able to reason or think: Humans are *rational* animals. 2. Reasonable; logical. 3. In one's right senses; sane. **—rationally** *adverb.*

ra·tion·al·ize (RASH-ən-l-ighz) *verb.* 1. To justify; make conform to reason. 2. (Psychology) To give one's self and others plausible but inaccurate excuses for behavior. **rationalized, rationalizing. —rationalization** (rash-ən-l-ə-ZAY-shən) *noun.*

rat·tle (RAT-l) *verb.* 1. To make a series of quick sharp sounds: The popcorn *rattled* as it hit the lid of the pan. 2. To move, and rattle as a result: The old car *rattled* over the bumpy road. 3. To talk quickly for a long time: The mayor *rattled* on about votes and taxes. 4. (Informal) To make uneasy; disturb: The booing of the fans *rattled* the young pitcher. **rattled, rattling.** *—noun.* 1. A series of quick, sharp sounds. 2. A baby's toy or other device that rattles. **rattles.**

rat·tle·snake (RAT-l-snayk) *noun.* A poisonous snake with a section at the end of its tail that rattles when it is shaken. **rattlesnakes.**

rau·cous (RAW-kəss) *adjective.* Harsh or rough in sound: The braying of a donkey is a *raucous* sound. **—raucously** *adverb.*

rav·age (RAV-ij) *verb.* To destroy; to ruin: The bombs *ravaged* the enemy village. **ravaged, ravaging.** —*noun.* (Often plural) Destruction; damage: the *ravages* of war. **ravages.**

rave (RAYV) *verb.* 1. To speak in a wild and senseless manner. 2. To speak about very favorably or with great enthusiasm: Dave *raved* about the new movie. **raved, raving.** —*noun.* (Informal) A very favorable or enthusiastic comment or compliment. **raves.**

rav·el (RAV-əl) *verb.* To come undone, as the threads of a fabric: Jim's shirt *raveled* where it was torn. **raveled** or **ravelled, raveling** or **ravelling.**

ra·ven (RAY-vən) *noun.* 1. A large, shiny black bird of the crow family. 2. (Also *adjective*) A black color.

rav·en·ous (RAV-ən-əss) *adjective.* 1. Very hungry. 2. Very greedy. —**ravenously** *adverb.*

ra·vine (rə-VEEN) *noun.* A deep, narrow cut in the earth; a canyon. **ravines.**

ra·vi·o·li (rav-ee-OH-lee) *noun, plural in form but often used with a singular verb.* A food consisting of dough stuffed with ground meat or cheese and covered with sauce.

rav·ish (RAV-ish) *verb.* 1. To seize and take away forcibly. 2. To fill with joy; fascinate. **ravished, ravishing.**

raw *adjective.* 1. Not cooked: *raw* meat. 2. In an original or natural condition; not yet changed by man: *raw* materials. 3. With the skin off; very sore or sensitive: The burn left a *raw* area on his arm. 4. Without training or experience: *raw* beginners. 5. Very cold and damp: *raw* wind. 6. (Slang) Unfair; severe: a *raw* deal.

raw·hide (RAW-highd) *noun.* 1. Cattle hide that is not tanned or treated. 2. A whip or rope made of untanned cattle hide.

[1]**ray** *noun.* 1. A beam or streak of light: sun's *rays.* 2. A beam of electricity, heat, or other energy. 3. A small amount: a *ray* of hope.

[2]**ray** *noun.* A fish with a wide, flat body and long, narrow tail: sting*ray.*

ray·on (RAY-on) *noun.* A silk-like thread or fabric made from cellulose.

raze (RAYZ) *verb.* To destroy totally; tear down: The buildings were *razed* to make room for a new highway. **razed, razing.**

ra·zor (RAY-zər) *noun.* A sharp instrument used for shaving or cutting.

rd. *abbreviation.* 1. Road. 2. Rod.

re (RAY) *noun.* The second note in any standard major or minor scale.

re- *prefix.* Indicates: 1. Again: *re*build; *re*tell. 2. Back: *re*turn.

reach (REECH) *verb.* 1. To be able to touch or grasp: Jim could not *reach* the apples on the tree. 2. To stretch; extend: The rope *reached* from one pole to the other. 3. To arrive at: The plane will *reach* Chicago by noon. 4. To contact; get in touch with. **reached, reaching.** —*noun.* 1. A reaching or stretching out, as of one's hand. 2. The distance that someone or something can reach: The prisoner's *reach* was not long enough to grab the keys. 3. A long, unbroken section: The plane flew over a *reach* of forest.

re·act (ree-AKT) *verb.* 1. To act in answer or in response to some earlier action or condition: Tim *reacted* to his teacher's praise by studying harder. 2. To have a bodily response to an outside influence: The baby *reacted* to the cold with shivers. 3. To undergo a chemical change. **reacted, reacting.** —**reaction** (ree-AK-shən) *noun.*

re·ac·tion·ar·y (ree-AK-shən-ehr-ee) *adjective.* Related to an attitude or policy that is opposed to political change; very conservative. —*noun.* A person who is opposed to change, especially in politics; a very conservative person. **reactionaries.**

re·ac·tor (ree-AK-tər) *noun.* A device or machine in which nuclear energy is produced and controlled.

raven

read (REED) *verb.* 1. To gain meaning from written or printed words: *read* a book. 2. To speak aloud written or printed words: Mother will *read* to Holly. 3. To detect by looking: Dad *read* the disappointment in my expression. 4. To show; indicate: The scale *reads* 3 pounds, 11 ounces. 5. To predict: *read* the future. **read** (RED), **reading, —read between the lines.** To look for or find meanings only hinted at but not stated directly. **—read into.** To see (in a statement) a meaning not expressed.

read·er (REED-ər) *noun.* 1. A person who reads. 2. A book for those learning to read.

reaper

read·y (RED-ee) *adjective.* 1. Prepared for use or action: Tim finds it hard to be *ready* for school on time. 2. Willing. 3. Likely (to do something): We were so naughty that Mother was *ready* to lose her temper. 4. Quick in response: a *ready* laugh. 5. Easily available: Joe has a *ready* store of pencils. **readier, readiest. —readily** *adverb.*

read·y-made (red-ee-MAYD) *adjective.* Made on a large scale for immediate use: *ready-made* clothes.

re·al (REEL) *adjective.* 1. True or actual: a *real* story. 2. Genuine: *real* diamonds.

real estate. Land and everything on it, including buildings and natural resources.

re·al·ism (REE-ə-liz-əm) *noun.* 1. Awareness of things as they are and not as they might be. 2. The act of showing or telling about things in a true-to-life way.

re·al·is·tic (REE-ə-liss-tik) *adjective.* 1. Seeing and thinking of things the way they are: Elaine was *realistic* about money and spent it wisely. 2. True to life: a *realistic* painting. **—realistically** *adverb.*

re·al·i·ty (ree-AL-ə-tee) *noun.* 1. The way things truly are. 2. A fact: The need for sleep is a *reality* of life. **realities.**

re·al·ize (REE-ə-lighz) *verb.* 1. To understand. 2. To make come true. 3. To gain (as a profit). **realized, realizing. —realization** (ree-ə-lə-ZAY-shən) *noun.*

re·al·ly (REE-lee) *adverb.* 1. Truly; actually: When the snow *really* comes, we will be prepared for it. 2. Indeed: *Really,* we ought to be in bed by now.

realm (RELM) *noun.* 1. Kingdom: The king's *realm* was vast. 2. Any region or subject area: the *realm* of art.

ream (REEM) *noun.* 1. A quantity of 500 sheets of paper. 2. (Usually plural) A lot: *reams* of buttons.

reap (REEP) *verb.* 1. To cut or harvest (a crop). 2. To get, as a result of one's actions: Stan *reaped* honors for his schoolwork. **reaped, reaping.**

reap·er (REE-pər) *noun.* A person or machine that cuts or harvests a crop.

re·ap·pear (REE-ə-pihr) *verb.* To come into sight again. **reappeared, reappearing.**

rear (RIHR) *noun.* 1. The back part: the *rear* of a bus. 2. The last part of a military operation: Reinforcements brought up the *rear.* *—adjective.* Of or at the back: the *rear* door. *—verb.* 1. To bring up: Mike was *reared* by his aunt. 2. To lift upright. 3. To build: A new school is being *reared.* 4. To rise above: In the distance, mountains *rear* from the plain. 5. To rise on the hind legs: The horse *reared* in fright. **reared, rearing.**

rear admiral. The naval rank above captain.

re·ar·range (ree-ə-RAYNJ) *verb.* To change the relative positions of: Amy *rearranged* the furniture in her room. **rearranged, rearranging.**

rea·son (REE-zən) *noun.* 1. Cause: *reason* to like him. 2. Explanation: the *reason* why she was late. 3. Clear or logical thinking: Angie used *reason* to figure out the problem. 4. Sanity: Archie lost his *reason.* 5. Good sense or judgment: Her decision showed *reason.* —*verb.* 1. To think logically: Tom *reasoned* out the answer to the new math problem. 2. To discuss logically. **reasoned, reasoning.**

rea·son·a·ble (REE-zən-ə-bəl) *adjective.* 1. Capable of thinking logically or fairly: a *reasonable* person. 2. Fair; moderate or within limits: a *reasonable* price. 3. Sensible: *reasonable* behavior. —**reasonably** *adverb.*

re·as·sure (ree-ə-SHUR) *verb.* 1. To assure again. 2. To lend confidence to: The first robin *reassures* us that spring is on the way. **reassured, reassuring.**

re·bel (ri-BEL) *verb.* 1. To defy or fight against lawful authority: The colonists *rebelled* during the American Revolution. 2. To oppose or be unwilling (to): The baby *rebels* at going to bed. **rebelled, rebelling.** —(REB-əl) *noun.* A person who defies or fights against lawful authority.

re·bel·lion (ri-BEL-yən) *noun.* 1. An uprising against a government. 2. A display of defiance against convention or authority: There was a *rebellion* among the students. **rebellious** (ri-BEL-yəss) *adjective.* —**rebelliously** *adverb.*

re·birth (REE-BERTH) *noun.* 1. Being born again: the *rebirth* of flowers in the spring. 2. A revival.

re·born (REE-BORN) *adjective.* Born anew; feeling as if one were starting over again.

re·bound (ree-BOWND) *verb.* To spring or bounce back: The ball *rebounded* from the wall. **rebounded, rebounding.** —(REE-bownd or ri-BOWND) *noun.* A springing back: Jack caught the ball on a *rebound* from the wall.

re·buff (ri-BUHF) *noun.* A snub; blunt refusal or rejection: A *rebuff* kept Al from offering further help. —*verb.* To refuse or reject bluntly. **rebuffed, rebuffing.**

re·build (ree-BILD) *verb.* To build again. **rebuilt, rebuilding.**

re·buke (ri-BYOOK) *verb.* To scold or reprimand. **rebuked, rebuking.** —*noun.* A scolding or reprimand. **rebukes.**

re·call (ri-KAWL) *verb.* 1. To remember. 2. To call back; order to return: The witness was *recalled.* **recalled, recalling.** —*noun.* The ability to remember: total *recall.*

re·cap·ture (ree-KAP-chər) *verb.* 1. To take or capture again. 2. To remember: *recapture* those happy days. **recaptured, recapturing.**

recd. Also **rec'd.** *abbreviation.* Received.

re·cede (ri-SEED) *verb.* 1. To move back: The tide *recedes* twice a day. 2. To be shaped in a backward or sloping way: His lower jaw *recedes.* **receded, receding.**

re·ceipt (ri-SEET) *noun.* 1. A written acknowledgment that one has received something: Mother signed a *receipt* for the telegram she got. 2. (Usually plural) Money received: The grocer locked the day's *receipts* in his safe. 3. The act of receiving: on *receipt* of the package. 4. A cooking recipe. —*verb.* To sign (a bill) as having been paid: The plumber *receipted* our bill. **receipted, receipting.**

re·ceive (ri-SEEV) *verb.* 1. To accept or take (something): Dottie *received* a birthday present. 2. To experience: He *received* a shock from the broken lamp. 3. To greet or welcome. 4. To hold: A box in church *receives* contributions. 5. To convert electrical impulses into sounds or pictures. **received, receiving.**

re·ceiv·er (ri-SEE-vər) *noun.* 1. A person who receives: The quarterback passed to the *receiver.* 2. Something that receives: The washing machine has a *receiver* for coins. 3. The part of a telephone through which one hears. 4. Someone who deals in stolen articles.

re·cent (REE-sənt) *adjective.* 1. Of late; not far removed in time: In *recent* years, we have seen men on the moon. 2. New; modern: a *recent* issue of a magazine. **—recently** *adverb.*

re·cep·ta·cle (ri-SEP-tə-kəl) *noun.* Any container used to hold things. **receptacles.**

re·cep·tion (ri-SEP-shən) *noun.* 1. Receiving or being received: Tim's *reception* into the club thrilled him. 2. The manner of receiving: The popular speaker received a warm *reception.* 3. A party: a *reception* for new teachers. 4. The condition of sound and pictures as received on radio and television.

re·cess (REE-sess or ri-SESS) *noun.* 1. A period during which regular work stops: school *recess.* 2. A small, hollow space: A statue stood in the *recess* of the wall. **recesses.** *—verb.* To stop for a recess. **recessed, recessing.**

re·ces·sive (ri-SESS-iv) *adjective.* (Biology) Describing one of a pair of inherited traits that is dominated by its partner: *Recessive* factors from both parents produce blue eyes.

rec·i·pe (RESS-ə-pee) *noun.* A set of directions for preparing anything, especially food. **recipes.** *See* **receipt.**

re·cip·i·ent (ri-SIP-ee-ənt) *noun.* One who receives: The *recipient* of the letter turned it over to the police.

re·cip·ro·cal (ri-SIP-rə-kəl) *adjective.* Mutual; cooperative; equally advantageous to each party concerned: *reciprocal* trade. **—reciprocally** *adverb.*

re·cit·al (ri-SIGHT-l) *noun.* 1. A musical or dance entertainment, often given by one person. 2. A detailed telling of a story: Martin's *recital* of his encounter with a bear.

rec·i·ta·tion (ress-ə-TAY-shən) *noun.* 1. The process of reciting a prepared lesson to a teacher. 2. The delivery of a memorized speech or poem before an audience.

re·cite (ri-SIGHT) *verb.* 1. To repeat from memory. 2. To answer, in class, questions on an assigned lesson. **recited, reciting.**

reck·less (REK-liss) *adjective.* Without caution or care for the consequences: a *reckless* driver. **—recklessly** *adverb.*

reck·on (REK-ən) *verb.* 1. To count or calculate: Bob still *reckons* on his fingers. 2. To judge or regard as: He is *reckoned* an honest man. 3. (Informal) To think: The farmer *reckons* three weeks until frost. **reckoned. reckoning.**

reck·on·ing (REK-ən-ing) *noun.* 1. The act of adding or counting. 2. A bill showing what is owed. 3. The payment of a bill. 4. An accounting for actions: day of *reckoning.*

re·claim (ri-KLAYM) *verb.* 1. To turn (wasteland) into an area that can be cultivated: Irrigation *reclaimed* the desert. 2. To make (new products) from discards. 3. To obtain or demand the return of: I *reclaimed* my suitcase from the baggage room. **reclaimed, reclaiming. —reclamation** (rek-lə-MAY-shən) *noun.*

re·cline (ri-KLIGHN) *verb.* To lean back or lie down. **reclined, reclining.**

rec·og·ni·tion (rek-əg-NISH-ən) *noun.* 1. Identification by recollection. 2. The acknowledgment of a claim, status, or position: *recognition* of a government.

rec·og·nize (REK-əg-nighz) *verb.* 1. To know or identify through the senses or knowledge. 2. To acknowledge or admit: Jill *recognizes* her duties at home. 3. To show understanding and approval of: Father *recognized* Tom's efforts at carpentry by the gift of a new saw. **recognized, recognizing.**

re·coil (ri-KOIL) *verb.* 1. To jerk

backward: The rifle *recoiled* when fired. 2. To move backward, as in fear, horror, or disgust. **recoiled, recoiling** —*noun.* The act or process of recoiling.

rec·ol·lect (rek-ə-LEKT) *verb.* To remember. **recollected, recollecting.** —**recollection** *noun.*

rec·om·mend (rek-ə-MEND) *verb.* 1. To speak well and advise the use of: Many people *recommend* the food at the corner restaurant. 2. To advise: An old saying *recommends* an apple a day to keep the doctor away. **recommended, recommending.** —**recommendation** (rek-ə-men-DAY-shən) *noun.*

rec·om·pense (REK-əm-penss) *verb.* 1. To pay; reward: Mother gladly *recompensed* the man who returned her lost wallet. 2. To make a return (for a loss): The insurance company *recompensed* Father when our car was stolen. **recompensed, recompensing.** —*noun.* A payment; reward. **recompenses.**

rec·on·cile (REK-ən-sighl) *verb.* 1. To make up or settle: The judge *reconciled* the quarrel between the two men. 2. To restore to friendship: Mother *reconciled* the angry boys. 3. To make content or resigned: I never can *reconcile* myself to working in this cold room. 4. To make agree: I can't *reconcile* what you say with what I know. **reconciled, reconciling.**

rec·on·noi·ter (ree-kə-NOI-tər or rek-ə-NOI-tər) *verb.* To make a preliminary survey of a territory or place, especially one that an enemy holds. **reconnoitered, reconnoitering.**

re·con·struct (ree-kən-STRUHKT) *verb.* To construct again; rebuild (something) the way it used to be: The Poles *reconstructed* the bombed-out city. **reconstructed, reconstructing.**

re·cord (REK-ərd) *noun.* 1. Information written down and saved: She keeps a *record* of everything the baby says. 2. The deeds of or the things known about something or someone: He had a good *record* as a student. 3. The best performance so far: She holds the *record* for the high jump in her class. 4. A plastic disk made to be played on a phonograph. —(ri-KORD) *verb.* 1. To make a written account of. 2. To put sound in a form that can be played back: He *recorded* my voice on tape. 3. To show or register: This gauge *records* how much oil we use. **recorded, recording.** —**break a record.** To do better than has been done before. —**off the record.** Not to be made public; unofficial. —**on record.** 1. Declared publicly or officially: I want to go *on record* in favor of the new school. 2. Known or set down in a written account.

re·cord·er (ri-KOR-dər) *noun.* 1. A kind of flute. 2. A public official who keeps records. 3. A machine that records: a tape *recorder.*

recorder
(definition 1)

record player. A machine that plays records; a phonograph.

re·count *verb.* 1. (REE-KOWNT) To count again. 2. (ri-KOWNT) To give an account of; tell in some detail: He *recounted* what happened on the way to school. **recounted, recounting.** —*noun.* (REE-kownt) A second counting.

re·course (REE-korss or ri-KORSS) *noun.* 1. A thing to do for help; a resort: My last *recourse* is to ask my father for the money. 2. The person or thing one turns to for help: His *recourse* is the Bible.

re-cover (ree-KUHV-ər) *verb.* To put a new cover on: *re-cover* a chair. **re-covered, re-covering.**

re·cov·er (ri-KUHV-ər) *verb.* 1. To get well. 2. To get back something taken away or lost. 3. To make up for: Can the time I spent away from school be *recovered?* **recovered, recovering.** —**recovery** (ri-KUHV-ə-ree) *noun.*

rec·re·a·tion (rek-ree-AY-shən) *noun.* A pastime, amusement, or sport: My favorite *recreation* is swimming.

rec room. A recreation room; a room where pastimes or amusements are pursued.

re·cruit (ri-KROOT) *noun.* A new member of any group, especially the armed forces. —*verb.* To get new people to join; hire; enlist: The Army needs to *recruit* more nurses. **recruited, recruiting.**

rectangle

rec·tan·gle (REK-tang-gəl) *noun.* A flat figure with four sides and four right angles. **rectangles. —rectangular** (rek-TANG-gyə-lər) *adjective.*

rec·ti·fy (REK-tə-figh) *verb.* 1. To correct; make right: *rectify* an error. 2. To change (an alternating current of electricity) to a direct current. **rectified, rectifying.**

rec·tor (REK-tər) *noun.* 1. A clergyman who heads a parish in certain churches. 2. The head of certain universities or schools.

rec·tum (REK-təm) *noun.* The lowest part of the large intestine.

re·cur (ri-KER) *verb.* 1. To happen or occur again; come back again: The same spelling mistake *recurs* all through your paper. 2. To return in one's talk or thought: Our last vacation *recurs* again and again in my mind. **recurred, recurring.**

re·cy·cle (ree-SIGH-kəl) *verb.* To treat (something) in such a way as to break it down to its original materials for re-use: We should collect all the tin cans so that they may be *recycled.* **recycled, recycling.**

red *noun.* 1. (Also *adjective*) A color like that of blood. 2. A red dye or other coloring matter. 3. [Often capital R] A radical or revolutionary; a Communist. **—in the red.** Showing a loss. **—see red.** To feel very angry.

red blood cell. A blood cell that brings oxygen to all the parts of the body from the lungs.

red·den (RED-n) *verb.* 1. To become or make red. 2. To blush. **reddened, reddening.**

re·deem (ri-DEEM) *verb.* 1. To buy back; get back by returning what one owes: I *redeemed* my ring at the pawnshop. 2. To pay off: It took ten years to *redeem* the mortgage. 3. To turn in for a premium, prize, or money: Mother has hundreds of coupons to *redeem.* 4. To make good; carry out: He always *redeems* his promises. 5. To make up for: Marie's sweet smile *redeems* her careless ways. 6. To save or deliver from sin. **redeemed, redeeming.**

re·demp·tion (ri-DEMP-shən) *noun.* 1. Recovery by payment. 2. Deliverance from sin; salvation.

red-hot (RED-HOT) *adjective.* 1. Glowing: *red-hot* embers. 2. Latest and freshest: *red-hot* gossip. —*noun.* (Slang) A hot dog; frankfurter.

re·dis·cov·er (ree-diss-KUHV-ər) *verb.* 1. To discover again. 2. To take a fresh interest in: Tom has *rediscovered* football and he likes it. **rediscovered, rediscovering.**

re·dress (ri-DRESS) *verb.* To correct; make up for: The boys tried to *redress* the wrongs they had done. **redressed, redressing** —(ri-DRESS or REE-dress) *noun.* The correction of something wrong. **redresses.**

red tape. Official routine which causes delay, especially in business or government.

re·duce (ri-DOOSS or ri-DYOSS) *verb.* 1. To make lower, smaller, or fewer: I want to *reduce* the number of mistakes I make. 2. To change to a different form or state: Burning the wood *reduced* it to ashes. 3. To lower in condition: The long war *reduced* the people to poverty. 4. To lose weight: Proper diet can help you *reduce.* **reduced, reducing.**

re·duc·tion (ri-DUHK-shən) *noun.* 1. A reducing or the state of being reduced: a price *reduction.* 2. A lowering in rank or condition.

red·wood (RED-wud) *noun.* 1. An evergreen tree of California that may grow over 300 feet tall; the sequoia. 2. The brownish-red wood of this tree.

reed *noun.* 1. A tall straight grass with a hollow stem, found in marshy places. 2. A musical pipe made from a reed or another plant. 3. A thin piece of metal, wood, or plastic used in the mouthpiece of a musical (reed) instrument, such as the oboe and clarinet.

[1]**reef** *noun.* A strip of sand, rocks, or coral that is at, or close to, the surface of the water.

[2]**reef** *noun.* A part of a sail that is let out or taken in to control its size. —*verb.* To make a sail smaller by folding or rolling and tying a part of it. **reefed, reefing.**

[1]**ree·fer** (REEF-ər) *noun.* (Slang) A cigarette containing marijuana.

[2]**ree·fer** (REEF-ər) *noun.* A jacket or short coat of thick cloth, worn by sailors.

[1]**reel** *verb.* 1. To stagger or sway, as after a blow. 2. To spin around and around: He felt as if the street were *reeling* around him. 3. To fall back in haste or disorder: The troops *reeled* under the attack. **reeled, reeling.**

[2]**reel** *noun.* 1. A wheel or spool used for winding film, rope, thread, wire, or other materials. 2. The length of material that is usually wound on a single reel. —*verb.* To wind on or off a reel: The fisherman *reels* in his line. —**reel off.** To recite quickly: Joe *reeled off* a long list of places he wanted to visit. **reeled, reeling.**

[3]**reel** *noun.* A lively dance or the music played for such a dance: Virginia *reel.*

re-e·lect (ree-i-LEKT) *verb.* To elect again. **re-elected, re-electing.**

re-en·ter (ree-EN-tər) *verb.* To enter again. **re-entered, re-entering.**

re-en·try (ree-EN-tree) *noun.* 1. A second entry or entering. 2. Re-entering the earth's atmosphere after being in outer space: *Re-entry* heats the surface of the space capsule.

re-entry corridor. The path a spaceship must follow through the atmosphere in order to return safely to a given spot on earth.

re·fer (ri-FER) *verb.* (Used with *to*) 1. To mention; call attention to: Mother often *refers* to her childhood. 2. To turn to for information or help; consult: He often *refers* to his dictionary. 3. To send or direct to for information or help: The teacher *refers* us to the public library. 4. To relay (to someone) for a decision: Let's *refer* the question to your mother. **referred, referring.**

ref·er·ee (ref-ər-EE) *noun.* 1. A person who acts as a judge or umpire in a sport and makes sure that the rules are followed. 2. A person to whom a question is referred for settlement. **referees.** —*verb.* To act as a referee. **refereed, refereeing.**

re·fer·ence (REF-ər-ənss or REF-rənss) *noun.* 1. Mention; the act of calling attention (to): Never make *reference* to her terrible singing voice; it might hurt her feelings. 2. Source of information or quotation: You can find the *reference* in your textbook. 3. Something that one refers to for information, as a book or magazine: An encyclopedia is a work of *reference.* 4. A person who can give information about one's character, ability, and experience: We give the names of *references* when we apply for a job. 5. A statement made by such a person: Dad gave her a fine *reference.* 6. Regard; respect: With *reference* to your question, the answer is "No." **references.**

ref·er·en·dum (ref-ər-EN-dəm) *noun.* The process of offering a law or other proposal to the people for their vote: The *referendum* showed the town was in favor of a new school. —**referenda** (ref-ər-EN-də) or **referendums** *plural.*

redwoods

[2]reel

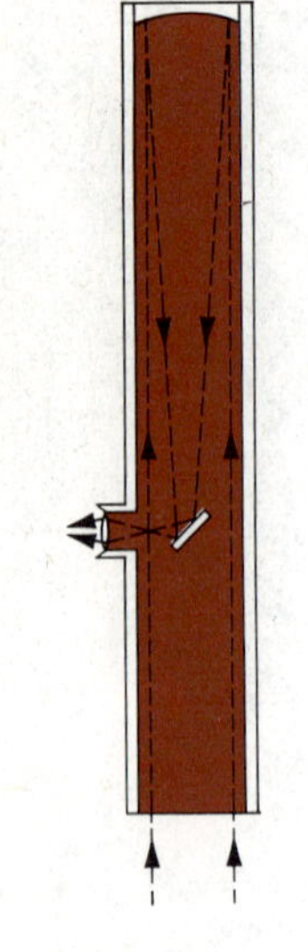
reflecting telescope

re·fill (ree-FIL) *verb.* To fill again. **refilled, refilling.** —(REE-fil) *noun.* Something used to replace a supply or product that has been used up.

re·fine (ri-FIGHN) *verb.* 1. To make or become pure; separate from parts that are not wanted: Oil must be *refined* before we use it. 2. To make or become fine or polished; make better: Listening to educated speakers helps to *refine* one's speech. **refined, refining.**

re·fined (ri-FIGHND) *adjective.* 1. Made pure; freed from parts that are not wanted: *refined* gold. 2. Cultured; having good manners; well-educated.

re·fine·ment (ri-FIGHN-mənt) *noun.* 1. The act of refining or the state of being refined. 2. Fineness of taste, feeling, manners, speech, etc.: He is a person of great *refinement.* 3. A feature added to something to improve it: The new engine has many *refinements.*

re·fin·er·y (ri-FIGHN-ər-ee) *noun.* 1. A place where something, such as oil or gold, is refined or made pure. 2. The machinery used for this purpose. **refineries.**

re·fit (ree-FIT) *verb.* To prepare or supply for use again; make fit again by repairing damages: The ship returned to its home port for *refitting.* **refitted refitting.**

re·flect (ri-FLEKT) *verb.* 1. To give back or form an image of: The still water *reflects* his face. 2. To show: The old movie *reflected* how people dressed in 1920. 3. To throw back, as light or heat: The electric heater *reflects* warmth around it. 4. To show the effect of: My good grades *reflect* many hours of study. 5. To bring, as an honor or compliment: John's excellence in math *reflects* credit on his teacher. 6. To throw blame or doubt (on): Their bad manners *reflect* on their upbringing. 7. To think about in a serious way. **reflected, reflecting.**

reflecting telescope. A telescope in which a curved mirror reflects light to focus the image of a faraway object.

re·flec·tion (ri-FLEK-shən) *noun.* 1. An image created when light rays are thrown or bent back, as from a mirror. 2. A throwing or bouncing back from a surface, particularly of such things as light, heat, or sound. 3. Serious thinking: This difficult problem calls for *reflection.* 4. An idea or thought.

re·flec·tor (ri-FLEK-tər) *noun.* Anything that reflects light, heat, sound, etc.

re·flex (REE-fleks) *noun.* 1. An action not directed by the mind but done in an automatic way: The sudden loud noise made him jump by *reflex.* 2. The power of performing such action: A driver must have good *reflexes* to stop quickly on icy streets. **reflexes.**

re·for·est (ree-FOR-ist) *verb.* To plant trees where others have been destroyed or cut down. **reforested, reforesting. —reforestation** (ree-for-iss-TAY-shən) *noun.*

re·form (ree-FORM or ri-FORM) *verb.* 1. To make better: Jane *reformed* the system of collecting club dues. 2. To do away with wrongdoing or mismanagement. 3. To turn from bad habits: The thief *reformed;* he is now honest. **reformed, reforming.** —*noun.* A change for the better.

ref·or·ma·tion (ref-ər-MAY-shən) *noun.* 1. The act or state of changing for the better. 2. [Capital R] A movement in the 16th century that resulted in the formation of Protestant churches, separate from the Roman Catholic Church.

re·for·ma·to·ry (ri-FOR-mə-tor-ee) *noun.* A place for the confinement and training of young or first-time lawbreakers. **reformatories.**

re·form·er (ri-FOR-mər) *noun.* A person who tries to change things for the better.

re·fract (ri-FRAKT) *verb.* To cause a ray or wave to change direction as it passes from one medium through another of different density. **refracted, refracting.**

refracting telescope. A telescope in which a transparent lens or combination of lenses is used to focus an image.

re·frac·tion (ri-FRAK-shən) *noun.* The bending of light rays (or any other waves) as they pass from a substance of one density to one of a different density: *Refraction* occurs when light passes from a thin medium, such as air, to a thicker medium, such as glass, or vice versa.

[1]**re·frain** (ri-FRAYN) *verb.* To keep oneself (from doing): Helen could not *refrain* from telling the secret. **refrained, refraining.**

[2]**refrain** (ri-FRAYN) *noun.* A part of a song or poem that is repeated.

re·fresh (ri-FRESH) *verb.* 1. To make (someone) feel more lively or less tired: The cool drink *refreshed* me. 2. To revive (by some action): Jane's humming *refreshed* Mother's memory of our camp song. **refreshed, refreshing.** —**refreshing** *adjective.* —**refreshingly** *adverb.*

re·fresh·ments (ri-FRESH-mənts) *noun, plural.* Light food or drink.

re·frig·er·ate (ri-FRIJ-ə-rayt) *verb.* To make or keep (something) cold. **refrigerated, refrigerating.**

re·frig·er·a·tor (ri-FRIJ-ə-ray-tər) *noun.* A cabinet with a machine that keeps food cold.

re·fuel (ree-FYOO-əl) *verb.* 1. To put more fuel in. 2. To take in more fuel. **refueled, refueling.**

ref·uge (REF-yooj) *noun.* 1. A place of shelter or safety: The tree house is Tommy's *refuge* when he's in trouble. 2. Safety or shelter: We sought *refuge* from the storm. 3. Any person or thing that one can rely on for aid: "God is our *refuge.*" (Psalms 46:1). **refuges.**

ref·u·gee (ref-yoo-JEE) *noun.* A person who flees to escape, particularly from punishment for political or religious views, or from war or a natural disaster. **refugees.**

re·fund (ri-FUHND) *verb.* To give back: The grocery clerk *refunded* the deposit on the bottles. **refunded, refunding.** —(REE-fuhnd) *noun.* 1. The act of giving back. 2. The amount given back.

[1]**re·fuse** (ri-FYOOZ) *verb.* To say "no" to; decline: Janet *refused* my offer. **refused, refusing.** —**refusal** *noun.*

[2]**ref·use** (REF-yooss) *noun.* Something thrown away because it is no longer useful or valuable; trash.

re·fute (ri-FYOOT) *verb.* To prove (something) wrong or in error: I can *refute* Chris's statement that the world is flat. **refuted, refuting.** —**refutation** (ref-yoo-TAY-shən) *noun.*

reg. *abbreviation.* 1. Register; registered. 2. Region. 3. Regular.

re·gain (ree-GAYN) *verb.* 1. To take back. 2. To reach or achieve again: *regain* good health. **regained, regaining.**

re·gal (REE-gəl) *adjective.* Referring to or like a king. —**regally** *adverb.*

re·gale (ri-GAYL) *verb.* 1. To amuse: Eddie *regaled* us with stories of his wild adventures. 2. To entertain lavishly. **regaled, regaling.**

re·gard (ri-GAHRD) *verb.* 1. To look at with attention. 2. To think about in a special way: Mother *regards* sewing as an art. 3. To like; admire: *regard* someone highly. 4. To consider; heed. **regarded, regarding.** —*noun.* 1. Respect; admiration: hold someone in high *regard.* 2. Consideration; thought. 3. (Plural) Greetings. 4. Reference: In *regard* to your question, the answer is "Yes."

re·gard·ing (ri-GAHR-ding) *preposition.* Referring to, concerning.

re·gard·less (ri-GAHRD-liss) *adverb.* No matter; in spite (of): I will go *regardless* of what you think. —*adjective.* Careless; unmindful.

refracting telescope

refrigerator

re·gat·ta (ri-GAH-tə or ri-GAT-ə) *noun.* A race or series of races for boats.

re·gent (REE-jənt) *noun.* 1. A person who takes charge of a government when the rightful ruler cannot. 2. A governor of a school, college, or university.

re·gime (ray-ZHEEM or ri-ZHEEM) *noun.* A government, including the people and the system used to make it run. **regimes.**

reg·i·ment (REJ-ə-mənt) *noun.* (Military) A unit of soldiers larger than a battalion.

re·gion (REE-jən) *noun.* 1. A specific section of a larger area of land: the lake *region.* 2. A particular section of the body: the pelvic *region.*

reg·is·ter (REJ-i-stər) *noun.* 1. A record, list, or roll: Please sign the visitors' *register.* 2. A machine that indicates units or totals: a cash *register.* 3. A grill-like device that lets warm or cool air into a room. —*verb.* 1. To list or record: All voters must *register* their names with the Board of Elections. 2. To show or point to: The gas gauge *registers* empty. 3. To display or show (emotion): The boy's face *registered* fear. **registered, registering.**

reins

re·gret (ri-GRET) *verb.* To feel sorry about; be disappointed about: "I *regret* that I have but one life to lose for my country." (Nathan Hale). —*noun.* 1. A feeling of distress, disappointment, or sorrow. 2. (Plural) A message that one will not accept an invitation.

reindeer

re·group (ree-GROOP) *verb.* (Algebra) To change the order of terms in an expression: To factor the expression ax + 6y + 3x + 2ay, one *regroups* the terms as (ax + 3x) + (2ay + 6y).

reg·u·lar (REG-yə-lər) *adjective.* 1. Normal, not unusual: *regular* routine. 2. Arranged in a pleasing or orderly manner: *regular* features. 3. Happening often at evenly spaced times: a *regular* heartbeat. 4. Through and through, complete: Teresa is a *regular* actress. 5. In agreement with established rules or habits: Please follow the *regular* form for heading your test papers. 6. Even, constant: a *regular* speed. 7. (Geometry) Referring to figures with equal sides, faces, and angles. —*noun.* A soldier in an established army: The colonists fought British *regulars.* —**regularity** (reg-yə-LA-rə-tee) *noun.* —**regularly** *adverb.*

reg·u·late (REG-yə-layt) *verb.* 1. To guide or govern (in line with a rule or law): Laws *regulate* the actions of citizens. 2. To change or adjust in order to be in agreement with a standard or rule: The government *regulates* airline fares. 3. To change or adjust in order to make (something) work properly: The carburetor must be *regulated.* **regulated, regulating.**

reg·u·la·tion (reg-yə-LAY-shən) *noun.* 1. A rule or law. 2. The act of guiding, controlling, or adjusting.

re·hearse (ri-HERSS) *verb.* To go over or practice in order to learn or perfect. **rehearsed, rehearsing.**

reign (RAYN) *noun.* 1. The power or authority of a ruler. 2. The period or time during which such power or authority is in effect: the *reign* of Elizabeth I. 3. Authority, control, or influence that is in effect for a period of time: a *reign* of terror. —*verb.* 1. To rule. 2. To be of widespread influence or control. **reigned, reigning.**

rein (RAYN) *noun.* 1. (Often plural) A leather strap used to guide a horse or other animal. 2. Anything that controls or holds back: Lack of money is a *rein* on our activities. —*verb.* To hold back or control. **reined, reining.**

rein·deer (RAYN-dihr) *noun.* A large deer found in Arctic lands. —**reindeer** *plural.*

re·in·force (ree-in-FORSS) *verb.* 1. To make stronger or firmer; give support: Sam *reinforced* the package with cardboard. 2. To send or arrive with more soldiers or equipment. **reinforced, reinforcing. —reinforcement** *noun.*

re·it·er·ate (ree-IT-ə-rayt) *verb.* To say more than once, usually for emphasis: Mother *reiterated* her warning. **reiterated, reiterating. —reiteration** (ree-it-ə-RAY-shən) *noun.*

re·ject (ri-JEKT) *verb.* 1. To refuse or decline: We *rejected* Milly's idea of a cake sale; none of us can bake well. 2. To deny; say "no" to: Mother *rejected* my pleas for a new dress. 3. To throw away: The grocer *rejected* the over-ripe bananas. **rejected, rejecting.** —(REE-jekt) *noun.* Something or someone that has been thrown away or not used because of some imperfection.

re·joice (ri-JOISS) *verb.* To be or make happy or glad. **rejoiced, rejoicing.**

re·join (ree-JOIN) *verb.* To meet or come together again. **rejoined, rejoining.**

re·lapse (ri-LAPS) *verb.* To slip back to a former condition. **relapsed, relapsing.** —*noun.* Backsliding.

re·late (ri-LAYT) *verb.* 1. To tell: *relate* a story. 2. To associate or connect two or more things or people: *relate* smoke with fire. 3. (Informal) To have sympathetic feeling for: I like the way Grandpa *relates* to my friends. **related, relating. —related** *adjective.*

re·la·tion (ri-LAY-shən) *noun.* 1. Kinship. 2. A person who is kin. 3. The way in which two people or things are connected. 4. Reference: in *relation* to your question. 5. The telling of a story or of events.

re·la·tion·ship (ri-LAY-shən-ship) *noun.* Kinship; relation by blood or marriage.

rel·a·tive (REL-ə-tiv) *noun.* A person who is kin. **relatives.** —*adjective.* 1. Being connected with or related to: May's suggestion was not *relative* to the problem. 2. Compared to something else: A temperature of 50 degrees is warm *relative* to one of −11 degrees. **—relatively** *adverb.*

relative humidity. The amount of water vapor in the air expressed as a percentage of the total amount of such moisture the air can hold.

relatively prime numbers. Two numbers that have no factor in common other than 1: 20 and 49 are *relatively prime numbers.*

re·lax (ri-LAKS) *verb.* 1. To make or become loose, or less firm or stiff: *relax* one's grip. 2. To make less strict: *relax* the rules. 3. To rest, stop labor: Sit down and *relax.* 4. To be at ease. **relaxed, relaxing. —relaxation** (ri-lak-SAY-shən) *noun.*

re·lay (REE-lay) *noun.* 1. One person, group, or team that takes over for another. 2. A race in which the individual members from two teams run only a part of the race and are then relieved by other team members. —(ri-LAY) *verb.* To pass along (from one to another): Paul Revere *relayed* the news from town to town. **relayed, relaying.**

relay

re·lease (ri-LEESS) *verb.* 1. To free: *release* from jail. 2. To give up: Dad *released* his claim to the property. **released, releasing.** —*noun.* The act of freeing. **releases.**

rel·e·gate (REL-ə-gayt) *verb.* To allot or assign (usually to an inferior post or duty). **relegated, relegating. —relegation** (rel-ə-GAY-shən) *noun.*

re·lent (ri-LENT) *verb.* To give in, become less stern: Mother *relented* and let us stay up to watch the movie. **relented, relenting.**

re·lent·less (ri-LENT-liss) *adjective.* 1. Firm (in one's stand); without pity. 2. Steady; continuing: *relentless* pursuit. **—relentlessly** *adverb.*

rel·e·vant (REL-ə-vənt) *adjective.* Connected with or related to: The speech was *relevant* to student problems. **—relevantly** *adverb.*

re·li·a·ble (ri-LIGH-ə-bəl) *adjective.* Dependable, able to be counted on. —**reliability** (ri-ligh-ə-BIL-ə-tee) *noun.* —**reliably** *adverb.*

rel·ic (REL-ik) *noun.* 1. Something dating back to the past: Explorers often find *relics* in old caves. 2. A token or remembrance, especially one that belonged to a holy person.

re·lief (ri-LEEF) *noun.* 1. The lessening or removal of pain, worry, or discomfort: Aspirin gives *relief* for some headaches. 2. Anything that lessens or removes pain, worry, or discomfort. 3. Aid, assistance: After the earthquake, *relief* was rushed to the city. 4. Change, replacement; release from duty: *Relief* came after the soldier had been on duty for ten hours. 5. A raised design, as in sculpture or on a map.

relief map

relief map. A map that uses raised surfaces to show differences in altitude.

re·lieve (ri-LEEV) *verb.* 1. To ease or make less, as pain or worry: The medicine *relieved* the pain in his chest. 2. To give aid or assistance: They sent in food and supplies to *relieve* the homeless children. 3. To replace; change, as on duty or shifts: ". . . the Rat, whose turn it was to go on duty, went upstairs to *relieve* Badger . . . ." (Kenneth Grahame). 4. To give variety; set off by contrast: Her brightly printed curtains *relieved* the plain color of the walls. **relieved, relieving.**

re·li·gion (ri-LIJ-ən) *noun.* 1. Belief in or worship of a god or gods, involving respect for basic moral ideals and, usually, belief in a life hereafter. 2. Any formal system of belief in or worship of a god or gods: the Jewish *religion.*

re·li·gious (ri-LIJ-əss) *adjective.* 1. Devout; very devoted to one's religion. 2. Having to do with religion: *religious* music. 3. Strict or careful: The student paid *religious* attention to the teacher's explanation. —**religiously** *adverb.*

re·lin·quish (ri-LING-kwish) *verb.* To surrender; give up; yield. **relinquished, relinquishing.**

rel·ish (REL-ish) *verb.* To enjoy, take pleasure in. **relished, relishing.** —*noun.* 1. Zest, enjoyment. 2. A pleasing taste or flavor: Onions added *relish* to the meat loaf. 3. A spicy vegetable mixture designed to add flavor to other foods. 4. Foods such as celery, olives, or radishes used to add variety to the main meal. **relishes.**

re·luc·tance (ri-LUHK-tənss) *noun.* Unwillingness: *reluctance* to go to bed. —**reluctant** *adjective.* —**reluctantly** *adverb.*

re·ly (ri-LIGH) *verb.* To depend on; have faith in: I *rely* on Dad to wake me in the morning. **relied, relying.** —**reliance** *noun.* —**reliant** *adjective.*

re·main (ri-MAYN) *verb.* 1. To stay; continue in the same place. 2. To stay in the same condition: *remain* healthy. 3. To survive; be left: Only ashes *remained.* 4. To be left (for consideration or to be done): What will happen *remains* to be seen. **remained, remaining.** —**remains** *noun, plural.* 1. A portion that is left: *remains* of a meal. 2. A dead body.

re·main·der (ri-MAYN-dər) *noun.* 1. The portion that is left: Because of the heavy snow, we were dismissed for the *remainder* of the day. 2. (Math) The number that remains when one number is divided by another: When 12 is divided by 5, the *remainder* is 2.

re·mark (ri-MAHRK) *verb.* 1. To comment; say. 2. To note or observe: Ellen *remarked* how thin her aunt had become. **remarked, remarking.** —*noun.* A comment.

re·mark·a·ble (ri-MAHR-kə-bəl) *adjective.* Exceptional; worth remembering for a rare or notable quality: She played the piano with *remarkable* skill. —**remarkably** *adverb.*

re·me·di·al (ri-MEE-dee-əl) *adjective.* Giving aid, helping to improve: *remedial* reading.

rem·e·dy (REM-ə-dee) *noun.* A cure; medicine or treatment offering relief: Swallowing water is sometimes a *remedy* for hiccups. **remedies.** —*verb.* To cure; correct. **remedied, remedying.**

re·mem·ber (ri-MEM-bər) *verb.* 1. To recall; recollect: I always *remember* faces, but I forget names. 2. To keep in mind; not forget: *Remember* that you must go to the dentist today. 3. To think of (someone) on occasions, as with a gift or card: I always *remember* Grandfather on his birthday. 4. To send along greetings: *Remember* me to your mother. **remembered, remembering.**

re·mem·brance (ri-MEM-brənss) *noun.* 1. A recollection, memory. 2. A souvenir, a memento: Tina kept her *remembrances* in a scrapbook.

re·mind (ri-MYND) *verb.* To prompt memory; bring to mind. **reminded, reminding.** —**reminder** *noun.*

rem·i·nisce (rem-ə-NISS) *verb.* To remember, discuss, or write about things from the past. **reminisced, reminiscing.**

re·miss (ri-MISS) *adjective.* Careless; negligent; lax in performance of duty.

re·mit (ri-MIT) *verb.* 1. To send (a payment). 2. To cancel by a pardon: His prison sentence was *remitted.* **remitted, remitting.** —**remittance** *noun.*

rem·nant (REM-nənt) *noun.* What remains; the part left over: *Remnants* of dinner were on the table.

re·mod·el (ree-MOD-l) *verb.* To do over; refashion; redesign: We are *remodeling* our cellar to have a playroom. **remodeled** or **remodelled, remodeling** or **remodelling.**

re·mon·strate (ri-MON-strayt) *verb.* To protest; object. **remonstrated, remonstrating.**

re·morse (ri-MORSS) *noun.* Regret for something done; sorrow for harmful or wrong deeds.

re·mote (ri-MOHT) *adjective.* 1. Far off in time or place; distant. 2. Not closely related: a *remote* cousin. 3. Secluded; located in an isolated place: a *remote* island. 4. Slight: He had only a *remote* idea of who I was. **remoter, remotest.** —**remotely** *adverb.*

re·mov·al (ri-MOOV-əl) *noun.* 1. A taking away: snow *removal.* 2. A change of location: The *removal* of our offices to a new location was a welcome change.

re·move (ri-MOOV) *verb.* 1. To take away; move from one place to another: *Remove* your feet from the chair. 2. To eliminate; do away with: *remove* a wart; *remove* a spot. **removed, removing.**

ren·ais·sance (ren-ə-SAHNSS) *noun.* 1. A rebirth, a reawakening or revival. 2. [Capital R] The period from the 14th through the 16th centuries when there was a rebirth of the arts and learning in Italy and later throughout Europe.

rend *verb.* To tear forcefully; pull apart violently. **rent** or **rended, rending.**

ren·der (REN-dər) *verb.* 1. To give (aid or assistance): *render* a service. 2. To submit or give for consideration: The doctor *rendered* a bill for his services. 3. To cause to be; make: A bad fall *rendered* him an invalid. 4. To give what is due: *render* thanks. **rendered, rendering.**

ren·dez·vous (RON-day-voo or RON-də-voo) *noun.* A meeting or appointment; a fixed time or place to meet. —**rendezvous** (RON-day-vooz) *plural.* —*verb.* To meet at an appointed time and place. **rendezvoused, rendezvousing.**

ren·e·gade (REN-ə-gayd) *noun.* A traitor; someone who breaks away from his own group and joins the other side. **renegades.**

re·new (ri-NOO or ri-NYOO) *verb.* 1. To restore, make like new. 2. To start (efforts) again: He *renewed* his attempt to force the door open. 3. To continue or get again: *renew* a magazine subscription. **renewed, renewing. —renewal** *noun.*

re·nounce (ri-NOWNSS) *verb.* To reject; give up; disown. **renounced, renouncing.**

ren·o·vate (REN-ə-vayt) *verb.* To do over; make new again. **renovated, renovating. —renovation** (ren-ə-VAY-shən) *noun.*

re·nown (ri-NOWN) *noun.* Fame. **—renowned** *adjective.*

[1]**rent** *verb.* 1. To pay a fixed fee to use something: *rent* a car. 2. To allow (someone) use of (something) for a fixed fee: We *rented* our cottage to friends. **rented, renting.** —*noun.* A payment made for the use of something.

[2]**rent** *noun.* A tear or rip. —*verb.* *See* **rend.**

rent·al (RENT-l) *noun.* The fee paid or received as rent.

Rep. *abbreviation.* 1. Representative. 2. Republican. 3. Republic.

re·pair (ri-PAIR) *verb.* 1. To fix, mend: Dad *repaired* the broken door. 2. To correct, make right: Her apology helped to *repair* her thoughtless act. **repaired, repairing.** —*noun.* 1. Work that must be done to fix something: a house that needs *repairs.* 2. A state or condition: in good *repair.*

rep·a·ra·tion (rep-ə-RAY-shən) *noun.* (Often plural) Something done or payment made for damage or losses.

re·past (ri-PAST) *noun.* A meal.

re·pay (ri-PAY) *verb.* To pay back; to return. **repaid, repaying.**

re·peal (ri-PEEL) *verb.* To cancel; withdraw. **repealed, repealing.** —*noun.* Cancellation.

re·peat (ri-PEET) *verb.* 1. To do or say again. 2. To recite from memory. 3. To tell (what has been heard): He *repeated* the story to his friends. **repeated, repeating.**

re·pel (ri-PEL) *verb.* 1. To drive back; hold off: *repel* the invaders. 2. To disgust, offend. **repelled, repelling. —repellent** *noun* and *adjective.*

re·pent (ri-PENT) *verb.* To be sorry; to regret (something done). **repented, repenting. —repentance** *noun.* **—repentant** *adjective.*

re·per·cus·sion (ree-pər-KUHSH-ən) *noun.* A consequence or reaction.

rep·e·ti·tion (rep-ə-TISH-ən) *noun.* The act of doing or saying something more than once.

re·place (ri-PLAYSS) *verb.* 1. To put (something) back: She *replaced* the book on the shelf. 2. To take the place of: For many people television has *replaced* radio. 3. To obtain to take the place of (something or someone): We *replaced* our old sofa with a new one. **replaced, replacing. —replacement** (ri-PLAYSS-mənt) *noun.*

re·play (ree-PLAY) *verb.* To play (something) again: *replay* a record. **replayed, replaying.** —(REE-play) *noun.* The act of replaying or the thing replayed. *See* **instant replay.**

re·plen·ish (ri-PLEN-ish) *verb.* To furnish or fill again: *replenish* a food supply. **replenished, replenishing.**

re·plete (ri-PLEET) *adjective.* Completely filled or supplied.

rep·li·ca (REP-lə-kə) *noun.* 1. A copy of an artistic work, especially one done by the original artist. 2. A faithful copy (of anything). **replicas.**

re·ply (ri-PLIGH) *noun.* An answer. **replies.** —*verb.* (Used with *to*) To answer: *reply* to a question. **replied, replying.**

re·port (ri-PORT) *noun.* 1. An organized account or statement of facts. 2. Rumor; common gossip. —*verb.* 1. To present a report. 2. To present oneself: *Report* to the school office. **reported, reporting.**

re·port·er (ri-POR-tər) *noun.* A person who gathers facts for or writes news stories for publication or broadcast.

re·pose (ri-POHZ) *noun.* 1. A rest, sleep, or period of relaxation. 2. Calm; peace of mind. —*verb.* 1. To lie at rest. 2. To be supported (in or on something). **reposed, reposing.**

rep·re·sent (rep-ri-ZENT) *verb.* 1. To stand for; be a symbol of: The dove *represents* peace. 2. To speak or act for officially: Our senator *represents* us in Congress. 3. To act the part of: In the school pageant, the youngest children *represented* flowers and trees. 4. To describe (something) in hope of convincing: The candidate *represented* himself as the only one capable of doing the job. 5. To depict. **represented, representing.**

rep·re·sen·ta·tion (rep-ri-zen-TAY-shən) *noun.* 1. The act of standing for; the state of being represented: The exhibit had a good *representation* of each grade's work. 2. A likeness or picture. 3. One or more official delegates or agents: Each state has *representation* in Congress.

rep·re·sent·a·tive (rep-ri-ZEN-tə-tiv) *noun.* 1. Someone selected to represent others: Our school sent a *representative* to the conference. 2. A person elected to the lawmaking branch of government. **representatives.** —*adjective.* 1. Describing a government run by elected people. 2. Typical.

re·press (ri-PRESS) *verb.* 1. To curb or hold back: Sue *repressed* her anger. 2. To put down: Police *repressed* the riot. **repressed, repressing.** —**repression** (ri-PRESH-ən) *noun.*

re·prieve (ri-PREEV) *verb.* To delay the punishment of: The governor *reprieved* the condemned man. **reprieved, reprieving.** —*noun.* 1. A delay in punishment. 2. Temporary relief, as from pain. **reprieves.**

rep·ri·mand (REP-rə-mand) *noun.* A severe or formal criticism. —*verb.* To scold. **reprimanded, reprimanding.**

re·pri·sal (ri-PRIGHZ-l) *noun.* Harm or injury done in return for harm suffered; retaliation; revenge.

re·proach (ri-PROHCH) *verb.* To scold: Mother *reproached* Jane for burning the cookies. **reproached, reproaching.** —*noun.* 1. Blame: a word of *reproach.* 2. Disgrace. **reproaches.**

re·proc·ess·ing (ree-PROSS-ess-ing) *noun.* The process of taking waste materials and making them usable.

re·pro·duce (ree-prə-DOOSS or ree-prə-DYOSS) *verb.* 1. To produce again; make a copy of: A telephone *reproduces* sound. 2. To produce young. **reproduced, reproducing.** —**reproductive** (ree-prə-DUHK-tiv) *adjective.*

re·pro·duc·tion (ree-prə-DUHK-shən) *noun.* 1. The act of copying or the state of being copied. 2. The thing copied. 3. The process by which plants and animals produce young.

re·proof (ri-PROOF) *noun.* An expression of blame or rebuke.

re·prove (ri-PROOV) *verb.* To scold. **reproved, reproving.**

rep·tile (REP-til or REP-tighl) *noun.* A cold-blooded animal that has a backbone and moves by creeping or crawling: Snakes, lizards, turtles, and alligators are *reptiles.* **reptiles.**

reptile

re·pub·lic (ri-PUHB-lik) *noun.* A form of government that is run by officials elected by the people.

re·pub·li·can (ri-PUHB-lə-kən) *adjective.* 1. Having to do with a republic: The United States has a *republican* government. 2. In favor of a republican government. 3. [Capital R] Having to do with one of two major political parties in the United States: the *Republican* Party. —*noun.* 1. A person in favor of a republican government. 2. [Capital R] A member of the Republican Party.

re·pu·di·ate (ri-PYOO-dee-ayt) *verb.* 1. To refuse to accept as valid: *repudiate* a treaty. 2. To refuse to acknowledge or pay: *repudiate* debts. 3. To disown or cast off: *repudiate* a son. **repudiated, repudiating.**

re·pulse (ri-PUHLSS) *verb.* 1. To force back; repel: The home team won the game by *repulsing* the visitors' last charge. 2. To drive off by discourtesy or refusal: Her cold manner *repulsed* any attempts at friendliness. **repulsed, repulsing.** —*noun.* A driving off by rudeness. **repulses.**

re·pul·sive (ri-PUHL-siv) *adjective.* Causing distaste, disgust, or dislike; repelling. —**repulsively** *adverb.*

rep·u·ta·ble (REP-yə-tə-bəl) *adjective.* Having a good reputation; honorable. —**reputably** *adverb.*

rep·u·ta·tion (rep-yə-TAY-shən) *noun.* 1. The way others think about a person or thing; name: "A good *reputation* is more valuable than money." (Publilius Syrus). 2. Being known for a single thing: Sally has a *reputation* for being late.

re·pute (ri-PYOOT) *noun.* Reputation. —*verb.* To think of as: The school is *reputed* to be a good one. **reputed, reputing.**

re·quest (ri-KWEST) *verb.* 1. To ask for; show that one wants (something). 2. To ask (that someone do something): The teacher *requested* that Tess clean the blackboard. **requested, requesting.** —*noun.* 1. Something one asks for: Sue's *request* was granted. 2. The act of asking.

re·quire (ri-KWIGHR) *verb.* 1. To need: People *require* warm clothing in cold weather. 2. To demand: The law *requires* all children to attend school. **required, requiring.**

re·quire·ment (ri-KWIGHR-mənt) *noun.* 1. A need. 2. A demand.

req·ui·site (REK-wə-zit) *adjective.* Required; necessary: Bob does not have the *requisite* education for the job he wants. —*noun.* An absolutely necessary requirement: Food is a *requisite* for life. **requisites.**

res·cue (RESS-kyoo) *verb.* To save from danger. **rescued, rescuing.** —*noun.* Deliverance from danger. **rescues.**

re·search (ri-SERCH or REE-serch) *noun.* A methodical search for facts about (something): Jim went to the library to do *research* for his history assignment. **researches.** —*verb.* To study in great detail; investigate (facts). **researched, researching.**

re·sem·blance (ri-ZEM-blənss) *noun.* A likeness; similar appearance.

re·sem·ble (ri-ZEM-bəl) *verb.* To be like; have similar features or qualities: Our new baby is so small she *resembles* a doll. **resembled, resembling.**

re·sent (ri-ZENT) *verb.* To feel indignation and anger about: Bill *resents* having to dress up for company. **resented, resenting.**

re·sent·ment (ri-ZENT-mənt) *noun.* A feeling of anger and injury because of an actual or imagined injustice or insult.

res·er·va·tion (rez-ər-VAY-shən) *noun.* 1. (Usually plural) A holding or keeping back, especially of feeling or opinion: Although Tim didn't say so, he had *reservations* about the whole plan. 2. A limiting condition: Mother said we could go with the *reservation* that we be home by nine. 3. A piece of land set apart by the United States government for a special use: The young Navajo attended a school on his *reservation.* 4. Something held for a person by previous arrangement: Phil had a *reservation* for a seat at the game.

re·serve (ri-ZERV) *verb.* 1. To hold back for future use: Mother *reserves* part of her salary every week for our college education. 2. To keep; set apart: I *reserve* some time each day to play with my dog. **reserved, reserving.** —*noun.* 1. A thing held back for future use: Squirrels have a *reserve* of nuts for the winter. 2. The keeping back of one's full feelings or thoughts. 3. Self-restraint in speech and behavior; coldness. 4. Public land that is held aside: a forest *reserve.* 5. (Often plural) Soldiers kept as reinforcements.

re·served (ri-ZERVD) *adjective.* 1. Kept in reserve; set aside: *reserved* seats. 2. Showing caution or self-restraint. —**reservedly** *adverb.*

res·er·voir (REZ-ər-vwahr) *noun.* 1. A place where water is stored for future use. 2. A reserve; a big supply (of something).

re·side (ri-ZIGHD) *verb.* 1. To live somewhere continuously: My aunt *resides* in Kansas. 2. To be a basic part (of); exist (in): The power to punish *resides* in the courts. **resided, residing.**

res·i·dence (REZ-ə-dənss) *noun.* The house or place in which one lives.

res·i·dent (REZ-ə-dənt) *noun.* 1. A person who lives somewhere on a permanent basis. 2. A doctor who lives in a hospital during part of his training. —*adjective.* 1. Living in a place; dwelling. 2. Living where one works: The boarding school has a *resident* physician.

res·i·den·tial (rez-ə-DEN-shəl) *adjective.* Having to do with a place where people live: *residential* areas.

residual spray. A spray with poisons that remain as a residue and do not dissolve: DDT is a *residual spray.*

res·i·due (REZ-ə-doo or REZ-ə-dyoo) *noun.* The remainder after other parts have been removed: When sea water evaporates, it leaves a *residue* of salt. **residues.**

re·sign (ri-ZIGHN) *verb.* 1. To quit; give up one's job or position. 2. To make (oneself) accept: Elaine was not *resigned* to wearing braces. **resigned, resigning.** —**resignation** (rez-ig-NAY-shən) *noun.*

res·in (REZ-in) *noun.* A yellow or brown sticky material found in some trees, especially pines, and used in making many products.

re·sist (ri-ZIST) *verb.* To strive against; withstand: *resist* the enemy; *resist* laughing. **resisted, resisting.**

re·sist·ance (ri-ZISS-tənss) *noun.* 1. The act of resisting. 2. A secret group that works to free its country from a foreign power. 3. The force that works against an electric current passing through a conductor. —**resistant** *adjective.*

res·o·lute (REZ-ə-loot) *adjective.* Having a firm purpose; determined. —**resolutely** *adverb.*

res·o·lu·tion (rez-ə-LOO-shən) *noun.* 1. A decision to do something: June made a *resolution* to weed her garden each week. 2. Firm determination; being resolute: Abby set about the task with *resolution.* 3. An answer or solution: the *resolution* of a problem. 4. A formal statement of opinion by a group.

re·solve (ri-ZOLV) *verb.* 1. To decide; determine: Elena *resolved* to get up early. 2. To decide by vote. **resolved, resolving.** —*noun.* 1. A thing determined; a decision. 2. Determination: Amy faced the test with *resolve.*

re·solved (ri-ZOLVD) *adjective.* Determined; resolute. —**resolvedly** (ri-ZOL-vid-lee) *adverb.*

res·o·nant (REZ-ə-nənt) *adjective.* Resounding; echoing. —**resonantly** *adverb.*

re·sort (ri-ZORT) *verb.* (Used with *to*) 1. To turn for help or relief: Jane *restorted* to crying when her arguments failed to win her mother over. 2. To go often: Jim *resorts* to the attic when he wants to be alone. **resorted, resorting.** —*noun.* 1. A place where people go for pleasure and recreation: a summer *resort.* 2. The thing or person that one gets help from: Pawning his overcoat was Tom's last *resort.*

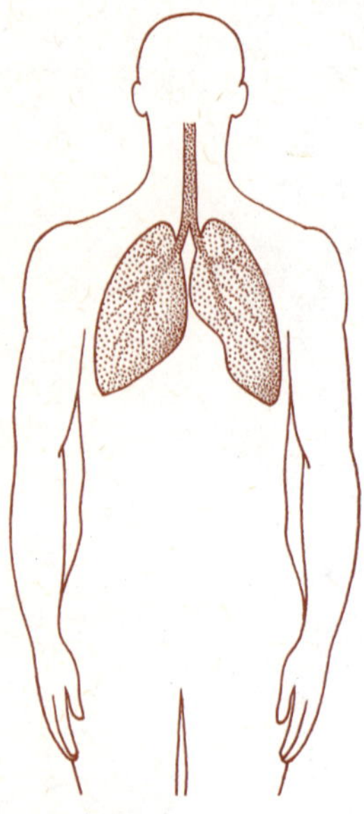
respiratory system

re·sound (ri-ZOWND) *verb.* 1. To be filled (with sound): The auditorium *resounded* with laughter. 2. To sound loudly. **resounded, resounding.**

re·source (REE-sorss) *noun.* 1. A supply that can be used as needed: Forests are an important natural *resource.* 2. The ability to cope with difficulties. 3. Something used for help: A skunk's best defensive *resource* is his odor. **resources.**

re·source·ful (ri-SORSS-fəl) *adjective.* Able to handle problems or situations with ease and ingenuity. **—resourcefully** *adverb.*

re·spect (ri-SPEKT) *verb.* To show or have regard or consideration for: The students *respected* the excellent teacher. **respected, respecting.** *—noun.* 1. Honor; regard; consideration: *respect* for the rights of others. 2. A feature; detail: In one *respect* the general's plan seemed foolish. 3. Reference; relation: I have a suggestion to make with *respect* to your behavior. 4. (Plural) A polite expression of regard or honor: I'd like to pay my *respects* to your father.

re·spect·a·ble (ri-SPEK-tə-bəl) *adjective.* 1. Worthy of respect or regard: The general is a *respectable* old gentleman. 2. Decent; correct: *respectable* conduct. 3. Of fairly good quality: The new pitcher did a *respectable* job for his team. **—respectably** *adverb.*

re·spect·ful (ri-SPEKT-fəl) *adjective.* Showing respect; polite; well-mannered: The girl is *respectful* to her parents. **—respectfully** *adverb.*

re·spect·ing (ri-SPEK-ting) *preposition.* With regard to; about: I want to speak to you *respecting* your conduct.

re·spec·tive (ri-SPEK-tiv) *adjective.* With regard to each one separately; individual: The teams went to their *respective* dressing rooms before the game. **—respectively** *adverb.*

res·pi·ra·tion (ress-pə-RAY-shən) *noun.* Breathing.

res·pi·ra·to·ry (RESS-pə-rə-tor-ee) *adjective.* Related to breathing: Hay fever is a *respiratory* ailment.

respiratory system. The system of organs, including the nose, throat, and lungs, involved in breathing.

res·pite (RESS-pit) *noun.* A brief period of rest or relief: The showers brought a *respite* from the heat.

re·splend·ent (ri-SPLEN-dənt) *adjective.* Shining brightly; having splendor: The Christmas tree was *resplendent* with lights. **—resplendently** *adverb.*

re·spond (ri-SPOND) *verb.* 1. To answer; make a reply. 2. To react to: Sally *responded* to the cold with shivering and chattering teeth. **responded, responding.**

re·sponse (ri-SPONSS) *noun.* 1. An answer; reply. 2. A reaction: Hissing is our cat's *response* to dogs.

re·spon·si·bil·i·ty (ri-spon-sə-BIL-ə-tee) *noun.* 1. The condition of being responsible or obligated: Chris accepted the *responsibility* of caring for his dog. 2. A person or thing for which someone is responsible; an obligation. **responsibilities.**

re·spon·si·ble (ri-SPON-sə-bəl) *adjective.* 1. Having an obligation or duty regarding: Parents are *responsible* for their children. 2. Being the cause of: The broken machine was *responsible* for the loud noise. 3. Involving many duties or requirements: a *responsible* job. 4. Able to accept duties; worthy of trust: The manager gave the important job to his most *responsible* worker. **—responsibly** *adverb.*

re·spon·sive (ri-SPON-siv) *adjective.* Ready or eager to respond or react: Jack was *responsive* to Mother's request for help. **—responsively** *adverb.*

[1]**rest** *noun.* 1. A period or condition of sleep. 2. A period or condition of

relief from activity, labor, or unpleasantness: The workman took a *rest* between tasks. 3. A support: head*rest;* arm*rest.* 4. (Music) A period of silence between notes, or a sign used to indicate such a period. —*verb.* 1. To sleep. 2. To pause from activity or labor; relax. 3. To remain motionless. 4. To lie or lean: The shovel *rested* against the garage. 5. To depend: The team's hopes *rested* on the pitcher. 6. To use a support or resting place for: Dave *rested* his arms on his desk. 7. To be found: The blame for the broken window *rests* with Ralph. **rested, resting.** —**at rest.** 1. Without motion. 2. Dead.

[2]**rest** *noun.* 1. An amount that remains: The *rest* of the soup is cold. 2. (*Singular in form but used with a plural verb*) Those that remain; the others: Four students are to act as monitors; the *rest* are to go to the auditorium. —*verb.* To continue to be: *Rest* assured that we will help you. **rested, resting.**

res·tau·rant (RESS-tə-rənt or RESS-tə-rahnt) *noun.* A place where meals are prepared, sold, and eaten.

rest·ful (REST-fəl) *adjective.* Giving rest or relaxation. —**restfully** *adverb.*

rest·less (REST-liss) *adjective.* 1. Not able to relax or be still: The *restless* man paced up and down the hall. 2. Without rest or sleep: The tourist spent a *restless* night in the noisy hotel. —**restlessly** *adverb.*

re·store (ri-STOR) *verb.* 1. To return to a former state or condition: The old fort was *restored* to the way it looked in colonial times. 2. To return; bring back: Jane's good report *restored* her confidence in herself. **restored, restoring.** —**restoration** (ress-tə-RAY-shən) *noun.*

re·strain (ri-STRAYN) *verb.* To control; keep from (acting or doing): The coach *restrained* his players from arguing with the umpire. **restrained, restraining.**

re·straint (ri-STRAYNT) *noun.* 1. Control, as of feelings or emotions. 2. A thing or situation that restrains or controls: The chain served as a *restraint* to the dog.

re·strict (ri-STRIKT) *verb.* To limit; restrain; hold within bounds. **restricted, restricting.** —**restriction** *noun.*

rest room. A room in a building or other place that contains toilets and wash basins for public use.

re·sult (ri-ZUHLT) *noun.* Something that occurs because of another act or condition: Martha's excellent grade in history was the *result* of hours of study. —*verb.* To occur because of another act or condition: The forest fire *resulted* from the camper's carelessness. **resulted, resulting.**

re·sume (ri-ZOOM) *verb.* To start again, as after an interruption or delay: The ball game *resumed* after the rain. **resumed, resuming.** —**resumption** (ri-ZUHMP-shən) *noun.*

res·ur·rect (rez-ə-REKT) *verb.* 1. To bring back to life. 2. To bring back for new use: Mother *resurrected* some old clothes for us to wear at the Halloween party. **resurrected, resurrecting.**

res·ur·rec·tion (rez-ə-REK-shən) *noun.* 1. A bringing back to life. 2. A bringing back for a new use. 3. [Capital R] The return to life of Jesus Christ after his death on the cross.

re·tail (REE-tayl) *adjective.* Related to the sale of goods in small amounts directly to the public: The *retail* price of a product is higher than the wholesale price paid by a shopkeeper. —*verb.* To sell goods in small amounts. **retailed, retailing.** —**retailer** *noun.*

re·tain (ri-TAYN) *verb.* 1. To keep; continue to have: Mother has *retained* her childhood desire to visit Canada. 2. To hire: *retain* a lawyer. **retained, retaining.**

re·tal·i·ate (ri-TAL-ee-ayt) *verb.* To act in return or in response to an earlier action of another, especially one that is wrong or violent; seek revenge. **retaliated, retaliating.** —**retaliation** (ri-tal-ee-AY-shən) *noun.*

retard (ri-TAHRD) *verb.* To hold back or hinder; delay: The dragging anchor *retarded* the movement of the ship. **retarded, retarding.** —**retardation** (ree-tahr-DAY-shən) *noun.*

re·ten·tion (ri-TEN-shən) *noun.* 1. A retaining; a keeping or remembering. 2. The ability to remember. —**retentive** (ri-TEN-tiv) *adjective.*

ret·i·cent (RET-ə-sənt) *adjective.* Reluctant to speak much; quiet; reserved. —**reticently** *adverb.*

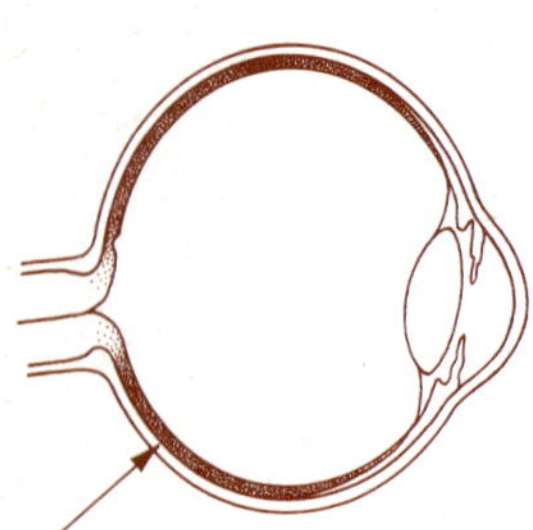

retina

ret·i·na (RET-n-ə) *noun.* A light-sensitive layer of tissue within the eye that receives images of things that are looked at. —**retinas** or **retinae** (RET-n-ee) *plural.*

ret·i·nue (RET-n-oo or RET-n-yoo) *noun.* A group of followers or supporters of an important person: The queen's *retinue* gathered around her throne. **retinues.**

re·tire (ri-TIGHR) *verb.* 1. To leave a job at the end of a career; stop working permanently: The postman *retired* when he reached 65. 2. To remove from a post: The sheriff *retired* his deputy for sleeping on duty. 3. To go to bed. 4. To go aside, as to a quiet area. 5. To retreat. 6. (Baseball) To put out: The pitcher *retired* the side. **retired, retiring.** —**retirement** *noun.*

retrorocket

re·tort (ri-TORT) *noun.* A quick or clever reply. —*verb.* To make a quick or clever reply. **retorted, retorting.**

re·trace (ree-TRAYSS) *verb.* To go over again: The hikers *retraced* their steps. **retraced, retracing.**

re·tract (ri-TRAKT) *verb.* 1. To draw in or back: The cat *retracted* its claws. 2. To take back or deny a statement: Tim *retracted* his insult. **retracted, retracting.**

re·treat (ri-TREET) *verb.* To withdraw; pull back: The troops *retreated* to the other side of the river. **retreated, retreating.** —*noun.* 1. A withdrawal; pulling back, especially of soldiers faced by a stronger force. 2. A place of peace and quiet. 3. A planned time of quiet, as for prayer or study.

re·trieve (ri-TREEV) *verb.* 1. To get back; recover: The fisherman *retrieved* his rod from the water. 2. To get and bring back, especially birds that have been shot. **retrieved, retrieving.**

re·triev·er (ri-TREE-vər) *noun.* Any of many breeds of dogs trained to retrieve game.

ret·ro·ac·tive (ret-roh-AK-tiv) *adjective.* Extending back in time; applying to things that happen before a decision is made or a law passed: The pay raise given in May was *retroactive* to January. —**retroactively** *adverb.*

ret·ro·grade (RET-rə-grayd) *adjective.* 1. Moving backward. 2. Getting worse.

ret·ro·gress (ret-rə-GRESS) *verb.* 1. To go or move backward. 2. To return to an earlier or worse condition. **retrogressed, retrogressing.** —**retrogression** *noun.* —**retrogressive** *adjective.* —**retrogressively** *adverb.*

ret·ro·rock·et (RET-roh-ROK-it) *noun.* A rocket attached to a larger rocket or space vehicle, used to slow it down or reverse its motion.

re·turn (ri-TERN) *verb.* 1. To go or come back. 2. To give, send, or bring back: *return* a book to the library. 3. To respond to with a similar action; repay: Juliet *returned* Romeo's love. **returned, returning.** —*noun.* 1. A going or coming back: The explorer's *return* was greeted with cheers. 2. A giving, sending, or bringing back: Dad was grateful for the *return* of his lost keys. 3. Something that is brought or sent back: All sales final; no *returns* accepted. 4. (Often plural) A profit: The businessman received a large *return* on the money that he invested. 5. (Usually plural) A report: election *returns*. —*adjective*. 1. Related to a going or coming back: *return* trip. 2. Done to pay or give back: After a tennis match in Chicago, the players had a *return* match in Detroit.

re·un·ion (ree-YOON-yən) *noun*. A gathering together again: Members of the football team had a *reunion* five years after they graduated.

re·u·nite (ree-yoo-NIGHT) *verb*. To gather or join together again: The shipwrecked sailors were *reunited* with their shipmates after the rescue. **reunited, reuniting.**

re·us·a·ble (ree-YOOZ-ə-bəl) *adjective*. Able to be used again: a *reusable* bottle.

rev *verb*. (Informal, used with *up*) To increase a motor's speed: The pilot *revved* up the airplane's engines. **revved, revving.** —*noun*. (Informal) A revolution or turning within a motor.

rev. *abbreviation*. 1. Revenue. 2. Revolution. 3. Reverse. 4. [Capital R] Reverend.

re·veal (ri-VEEL) *verb*. 1. To make known something secret or unknown; disclose: The admiral *revealed* the plans for a new submarine. 2. To show; display: Tom took off his hat to *reveal* that he was bald. **revealed, revealing.**

re·veil·le (REV-əl-ee) *noun*. A signal in the morning, as from a bugle or whistle, to wake up soldiers or sailors. **reveilles.**

re·vel (REV-əl) *verb*. 1. To delight in; enjoy: The girls *reveled* in their presents. 2. To take part in a noisy party or other festivity. **reveled** or **revelled, reveling** or **revelling.** —*noun*. A noisy party.

rev·e·la·tion (rev-ə-LAY-shən) *noun*. 1. Something revealed: The spy's true identity was an important *revelation* by the police. 2. The act or process of revealing.

rev·el·ry (REV-əl-ree) *noun*. Loud festivity or celebration. **revelries.**

re·venge (ri-VENJ) *noun*. A doing of harm in return for an earlier action or wrong. **revenges.** —*verb*. To do harm in return for an earlier action or wrong. **revenged, revenging.**

rev·e·nue (REV-ə-noo or REV-ə-nyoo) *noun*. Money that is taken in; income, especially for a government. **revenues.**

re·vere (ri-VIHR) *verb*. To treat or regard with deep respect; honor. **revered, revering.**

rev·er·ence (REV-ər-ənss) *noun*. A feeling or attitude of deep respect: *reverence* for the law. —**reverent** (REV-ər-ənt) *adjective*.

rev·er·end (REV-ər-ənd) *adjective*. [Usually capital R] A title of respect given to clergymen. —*noun*. (Informal) A clergyman.

rev·er·ie (REV-ər-ee) *noun*. A state of pleasant daydreaming.

re·verse (ri-VERSS) *adjective*. 1. Opposite; backward: Ted can name the letters of the alphabet in *reverse* order. 2. Causing movement backwards: The driver shifted into *reverse* gear. —*noun*. 1. The opposite of something: I believe the *reverse* of what she said. 2. A change for the worse: The shop-keeper suffered several *reverses* in his business. 3. The back or opposite side of something. **reverses.** —*verb*. 1. To move or cause to move in an opposite direction: The ship moved backwards when the captain *reversed* the engines. 2. To change or turn to an opposite position: The two teams *reversed* goals during the second quarter. 3. To change a rule or decision: The judge *reversed* the decision of the lower court. **reversed, reversing.**

re·vert (ri-VERT) *verb.* To return to an earlier or less developed state, method, or condition: After months of behaving, Rover has *reverted* to chasing cars. **reverted, reverting.**

re·view (ri-VYOO) *verb.* 1. To look over or study again: We *reviewed* our grammar before the test. 2. To look back or reflect on past events: The television announcer *reviewed* the big plays of the football game. 3. To make a formal inspection: The general *reviewed* the soldiers. 4. To look at, listen to, examine and give opinions about: The critic who *reviewed* the new movie said that it was terrible. **reviewed, reviewing.** —*noun.* 1. A looking over or studying again: a *review* of grammar. 2. A looking back or reflecting on past events. 3. A formal inspection. 4. An article or statement on the quality of a book, play, movie, etc.

rhubarb

re·vile (ri-VIGHL) *verb.* 1. To speak to or about with nasty or insulting language. 2. To scold. **reviled, reviling.**

re·vise (ri-VIGHZ) *verb.* 1. To rewrite or rework so as to correct or make better: *revise* a composition. 2. To change; correct: The admiral *revised* his battle plan. **revised, revising.**

rice

re·viv·al (ri-VIGHV-əl) *noun.* 1. A return to life or consciousness. 2. A return to popularity or common use: the *revival* of an old song. 3. A return to a better attitude or condition: The good news caused a *revival* of our spirits. 4. An increase in religious spirit or a meeting held to inspire such an increase.

re·vive (ri-VIGHV) *verb.* 1. To return to life or consciousness. 2. To bring back to popularity or common use: *revive* the old songs. 3. To return to a better attitude or condition: *revive* our hopes. **revived, reviving.**

re·voke (ri-VOHK) *verb.* To cancel; withdraw: The driver had his license *revoked* because of the accident. **revoked, revoking.**

re·volt (ri-VOHLT) *noun.* An uprising or rebelling against a government or other form of authority. —*verb.* 1. To rebel or rise up against authority: The citizens *revolted* against their hated king. 2. To cause or feel disgust. **revolted, revolting.**

rev·o·lu·tion (rev-ə-LOO-shən) *noun.* 1. A violent overthrow of a government or other form of authority. 2. A complete change: New discoveries have caused a *revolution* in the practice of medicine. 3. A revolving; a moving around a central point. 4. One complete movement around a central point: The earth makes one *revolution* about the sun every 365 days.

rev·o·lu·tion·ar·y (rev-ə-LOO-shən-ehr-ee) *adjective.* Of or related to a revolution or complete change: a *revolutionary* war; a *revolutionary* method of manufacturing. —*noun.* A person who supports or fights in a revolution. **revolutionaries.**

rev·o·lu·tion·ize (rev-ə-LOO-shən-ighz) *verb.* To change completely: The invention of the airplane *revolutionized* methods of travel. **revolutionized, revolutionizing.**

re·volve (ri-VOLV) *verb.* 1. To move around a central point: The earth *revolves* around the sun. 2. To turn; rotate. **revolved, revolving.**

re·volv·er (ri-VOL-vər) *noun.* A hand gun or pistol with a part that turns automatically with each shot in order to make another bullet ready for firing.

re·vul·sion (ri-VUHL-shən) *noun.* A sudden, strong feeling of disgust.

re·ward (ri-WOHRD) *noun.* 1. Something earned or given in return for an action or service: A bicycle was Carl's *reward* for mowing the grass all summer. 2. Money or something else of value offered for the capture of a criminal. —*verb.* To give something to in return for an action or service. **rewarded, rewarding.**

RFD *abbreviation.* Rural free delivery.

rhe·a (REE-ə) *noun.* A large South American bird that resembles an ostrich.

rhesus monkey Also **rhesus** (REE-səss). A small monkey found in India, commonly used in medical experiments. **rhesuses.**

rheu·ma·tism (ROO-mə-tiz-əm) *noun.* A disease that affects the muscles and joints with stiffness and pain.

rhi·noc·er·os (righ-NOSS-ər-əss) *noun.* A very large mammal, found in Africa and Asia, that has thick folds of skin and one or two large horns on its snout. —**rhinoceros** or **rhinoceroses** *plural.*

Rhode Island (ROHD IGH-lənd) *noun.* A New England state in the United States, 13th to ratify the Constitution (1790). —**R.I.** *abbreviation.* Also **RI** for Zip Codes.

rho·do·den·dron (roh-də-DEN-drən) *noun.* An evergreen shrub or tree with white, pink, or purple flowers.

rhom·bus (ROM-bəss) *noun.* A figure that has four sides of equal length with opposite sides parallel and no angles of 90 degrees. —**rhombuses** or **rhombi** (ROM-bigh) *plural.*

rhu·barb (ROO-bahrb) *noun.* 1. A large-leafed plant with long stalks that may be cooked and used in sauces, pies, and desserts. 2. (Slang) A heated quarrel.

rhyme (RIGHM) *noun.* 1. The likeness of sounds at the end of two or more lines of verse. 2. A poem that uses rhyme. **rhymes** —*verb.* To make a rhyme. **rhymed, rhyming.**

rhythm (RITH-əm) *noun.* 1. Any movement that shows a regular pattern, as of rise and fall, short and long beats, or similar combinations: the *rhythm* of the waves, the *rhythm* of heartbeats. 2. A pattern of beats or stressed sounds, as in music or poetry. —**rhythmical** (RITH-mi-kəl) *adjective.* —**rhythmically** *adverb.*

rib *noun.* 1. One of the long, curved bones that run in pairs from the spine around the chest. 2. A structural support that resembles a rib in appearance or function: the *ribs* of an abandoned sailing ship. 3. A cut of meat including a rib bone. —*verb.* 1. To shape or form with ribs or ridges. 2. (Slang) To tease. **ribbed, ribbing.**

rib·bon (RIB-ən) *noun.* 1. A strip of material with finished edges used for tying or decorating, as on a gift or woman's hat. 2. A strip of fabric treated with ink for use in a typewriter or other office machine. 3. A strip of material given as an award: a blue *ribbon.*

rice (RYSS) *noun.* 1. The grain or seeds of a plant widely grown in low, moist ground in warm climates for food. 2. The plant on which this grain grows. —*verb.* To strain potatoes or other food into a form that resembles rice. **riced, ricing.**

rich *adjective.* 1. Wealthy. 2. Full; having or providing plenty: The mountain is *rich* with minerals. 3. Expensive: *rich* gifts. 4. Fertile: *rich* soil. 5. Having many fattening and tasty ingredients: a *rich* dessert. 6. Very pleasing to the senses; deep and mellow: *rich* colors. 7. (Slang) Amusing; funny: a *rich* story. **richer, richest.** —*noun.* Wealthy people as a group. —**richly** *adverb.*

rich·es (RICH-iz) *noun, plural.* Great wealth or possessions.

Richter Scale. A system of measuring the intensity of earthquakes.

rick·ets (RIK-its) *noun, plural in form but often used with a singular verb.* A disease, usually affecting children, that causes softening of the bones because of a lack of proper foods.

rick·et·y (RIK-ə-tee) *adjective.* 1. Very unsteady; shaky: a *rickety* old house. 2. Having rickets.

rhesus monkeys

rhinoceros

Rhode Island
★capital: Providence

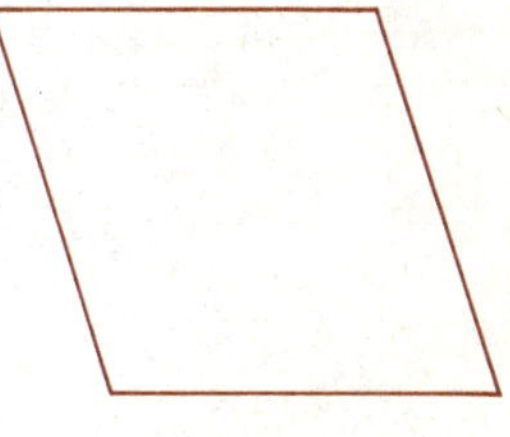

rhombus

rickshaw

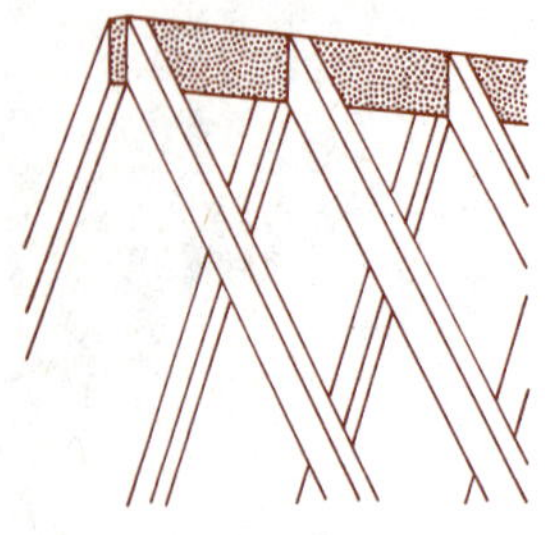
ridgepole

rider

rick·shaw (RIK-shaw) Also **ricksha** *noun.* A two-wheeled, covered vehicle pulled by one or more men, once commonly used for local travel in Oriental countries.

ric·o·chet (rik-ə-SHAY) *verb.* To bounce or skip (off a surface). **ricocheted, ricocheting.**

rid *verb.* To free from something: The Pied Piper *rid* the town of its rats. **rid** or **ridded, ridding.**

rid·dance (RID-ənss) *noun.* Removal. Good *riddance* to bad rubbish.

1 **rid·dle** (RID-l) *noun.* A puzzle; a question that requires cleverness to answer correctly. **riddles.**

2 **rid·dle** (RID-l) *verb.* To make full of holes: The soldiers *riddled* the targets with bullets. **riddled, riddling.**

ride (RIGHD) *verb.* 1. To travel in or on a vehicle: We will *ride* the bus to school. 2. To sit on and control the movement of an animal or machine: Jim knows how to *ride* a horse and a motorbike. 3. To travel on and be supported by: The snowmobile *rides* on rubber treads. 4. To move with riders on board: The large car *rides* smoothly. 5. To float or be carried on: Surfers *ride* the waves toward shore. 6. (Informal) To tease; make fun of: Don't *ride* Otto about his new haircut. **rode, ridden, riding.** —*noun.* 1. A trip; a journey: a bicycle *ride.* 2. A special vehicle or device for riding, as a roller coaster, to provide amusement at a carnival or fair. **rides.**

rid·er (RIGHD-ər) *noun.* 1. One who rides, especially a horseman. 2. An amendment, usually unrelated, to a legislative measure. 3. An amendment to a contract.

ridge (RIJ) *noun.* 1. A long, narrow strip of hilly or elevated land. 2. A long, narrow part along the top (of something): Tex combed the hair along the *ridge* of the horse's neck. 3. The place or line where the upper part of two sloping surfaces join: the *ridge* of a roof. 4. A raised strip along any surface: The rake made *ridges* in the loose soil. **ridges.**

ridge·pole (RIJ-pohl) *noun.* A horizontal beam or support along the top of a roof or similar structure.

rid·i·cule (RID-ə-kyool) *noun.* Words or actions that are meant to make fun of someone or something; mockery. —*verb.* To mock or make fun of someone or something. **ridiculed, ridiculing.**

ri·dic·u·lous (ri-DIK-yə-ləss) *adjective.* Very silly; making no sense; absurd: We laughed at the clown's *ridiculous* behavior. —**ridiculously** *adverb.*

rife (RIGHF) *adjective.* Widespread; happening often: Sickness was *rife* among the survivors of the flood. **rifer, rifest.**

1 **rif·le** (RIGH-fəl) *noun.* A long gun with grooves that cause bullets to spin as they are fired: A *rifle* is aimed and fired with the stock or base against a person's shoulder.

2 **rif·le** (RIGH-fəl) *verb.* To search through and rob; ransack: The pirates *rifled* the captured ship. **rifled, rifling.**

rift *noun.* 1. A break (in friendship): The argument created a *rift* between the two girls. 2. (Geology) A break in the surface of the earth.

rig *verb.* 1. To equip, fit out: to *rig* oneself for camping. 2. To equip with sails: *rig* a ship. 3. (Often used with *up*) To build or make in a hurry: The hikers *rigged* up a temporary shelter when the rain began. 4. To control illegally in order to make a personal gain: The baseball game was *rigged.* **rigged, rigging.** —*noun.* 1. The arrangements of parts of a ship, as the sails and masts. 2. Equipment that is used for a certain purpose: an oil-well *rig.* 3. A horse-drawn vehicle. 4. (Informal) A dress or outfit: a stylish *rig.*

rig·ging (RIG-ing) *noun.* The various

ropes, chains, etc., used to hold up and control parts of a ship, as the sails and masts.

right *adjective.* 1. Good; moral. 2. Correct; true: the *right* answer. 3. Fitting; appropriate: Your blue tie is the *right* one to wear with that suit. 4. In the position or direction that is east when facing north: In America cars travel on the *right* side of the road. 5. Related to the outer side of a fabric meant to be seen or used. —*adverb.* 1. To or on the side opposite the left. 2. In a good or moral manner; justly. 3. In a fitting or appropriate manner. 4. Straight; directly: The sheriff looked *right* at the thief. 5. Completely: The wind blew the papers *right* off the table. 6. At a particular time: Come here *right* this minute. 7. Exactly, in a particular place: Stay *right* here. 8. [Usually capital R] Very, as in certain titles: the *Right* Reverend John Davis. 9. (Informal) Quite; very: Elmer's new pony is *right* handsome. —*noun.* 1. That which is good, moral, or true; a just condition: Our parents taught us to know *right* from wrong. 2. A claim or position to which a person is entitled: the *right* of free speech. 3. The side or area opposite the left. 4. A turn to the side or area opposite the left: Make a *right* at the next corner. 5. [Often capital R] The party or side opposed to change in a political or social situation. —*verb.* 1. To correct; adjust. 2. To make up for or correct something wrong or evil: Uncle George tried to *right* the insult by apologizing to Dad. 3. To put in or return to a straight or standing position: We *righted* the sailboat after the wind tipped it over. **righted, righting.** —**right of way** Also **right-of-way.** 1. The right of one vehicle to move before or in front of another. 2. A route over which one has the right to travel. 3. The land on which a highway, railroad, or similar system is constructed. —**right on!** An expression of approval or encouragement.

right angle. An angle formed by the meeting of perpendicular lines; an angle of 90 degrees: The wall forms a *right angle* with the ceiling.

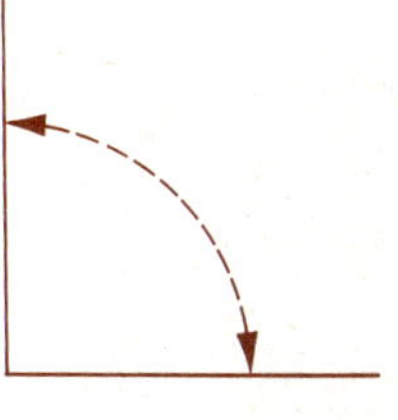
right angle

right·eous (RIGH-chəss) *adjective.* 1. Moral; virtuous: *righteous* behavior. 2. Justified; fitting: *righteous* anger. —**righteously** *adverb.*

right·ful (RIGHT-fəl) *adjective.* Having a proper or lawful claim: the *rightful* owner. —**rightfully** *adverb.*

right-hand (RIGHT-HAND) *adjective.* 1. At or near the right side. 2. Done by or referring to the right hand. 3. Most helpful; dependable: The boss's secretary is his *right-hand* person.

right-hand·ed (RIGHT-HAN-did) *adjective.* 1. Able to do things more easily with the right hand than with the left hand. 2. Designed for use with the right rather than the left hand.

rig·id (RIJ-id) *adjective.* 1. Not bending; inflexible: A telephone pole is *rigid;* a fishing pole is not. 2. Very strict; stern. —**rigidly** *adverb.*

rig·ma·role (RIG-mə-rohl) Also **rigamarole** (RIG-ə-mə-rohl) *noun.* 1. An unnecessarily involved or complicated system or situation: We could not understand the *rigmarole* of instructions on the label. 2. Silly or confusing talk. —**rigmaroles** or **rigamaroles** *plural.*

rig·or (RIG-ər) *noun.* 1. Hardship; difficulty: The explorers suffered from the *rigors* of the Arctic cold. 2. Strictness; harshness.

rig·or·ous (RIG-ər-əss) *adjective.* 1. Strict; harsh: *rigorous* rules. 2. Very exact; precise: The scientist made a *rigorous* examination of the new material. —**rigorously** *adverb.*

rill *noun.* A very small brook.

rim *noun.* 1. An edge or border, especially of a round object: the *rim* of a cup. 2. The outer part of a wheel: An automobile tire is placed on the *rim* of the wheel. *—verb.* To form a border or ring around. **rimmed, rimming.**

rime (RIGHM) *noun. See* **rhyme.**

rind (RYND) *noun.* A tough or thick outer covering: melon *rind.*

[1]**ring** *verb.* 1. To give off the sound made by a bell. 2. To cause or make the sound of a bell: *ring* the doorbell. 3. To fill or be filled with sound: The restaurant *rings* with sounds of celebration. 4. To signal or show especially by sounding a bell: Church bells will *ring* in the new year. **rang, rung** (RUHNG), **ringing.** *—noun.* 1. The sound made by a bell. 2. A special or unusual quality: The old man's words had a *ring* of honesty about them.

[2]**ring** *noun.* 1. A band of metal worn around a finger as an ornament. 2. A circular band, mark, or object: *ring* around the bathtub; key *ring.* 3. Any group of things or people arranged in a circle: a *ring* of trees. 4. A special group or organization, usually devoted to illegal activities: a *ring* of thieves. 5. An area in which fights or other activities are held: boxing *ring.* *—verb.* To form a circle around. **ringed, ringing.**

ring·let (RING-lit) *noun.* A curl of hair, especially a long one.

rink (RINGK) *noun.* 1. An area in which water is frozen for ice skating. 2. A smooth area for roller skating.

rink
(definition 1)

rinse (RINSS) *verb.* 1. To wash out lightly or quickly: The camper *rinsed* his shirt in the stream. 2. To remove soap from with water: After soaking the blouse in suds, Janet *rinsed* it with clear water. **rinsed, rinsing.** *—noun.* 1. A removing of soap with water. 2. A liquid used to tint a person's hair or make it more attractive. **rinses.**

ri·ot (RIGH-ət) *noun.* 1. A wild and destructive demonstration or period of lawlessness. 2. A spectacular display: The fireworks exhibit offered a *riot* of colors to the spectators. 3. (Slang) A very entertaining person or occasion: The new comedian was a *riot.* *—verb.* To take part in a riot. **rioted, rioting.**

rip *verb.* 1. To tear: The dog *ripped* the leg of my trousers. 2. To pull off: Jim *ripped* the tape from the package. **ripped, ripping.** *—noun.* A tear or slash.

ripe (RIGHP) *adjective.* 1. Fully grown or developed; ready for harvest. 2. Developed or prepared to a suitable degree: The time is *ripe* for the army to attack. **riper, ripest.**

rip·en (RIGHP-ən) *verb.* To become or make ripe. **ripened, ripening.**

rip off. (Slang) To steal; to cheat.

rip·ple (RIP-əl) *noun.* 1. A very small wave: The rain caused *ripples* to appear on the pond. 2. A sound resembling that made by a small wave: a *ripple* of applause. **ripples.** *—verb.* To cause or make very small waves: The breeze *rippled* the surface of the pool. **rippled, rippling.**

rip tide. A tide or current that causes great churning or roughness at sea by opposing another current.

rise (RIGHZ) *verb.* 1. To move upward: The elevator *rises* to the top of the building. 2. To move from a lying or a sitting position to a standing position. 3. To make progress toward a higher level or position. 4. To grow or increase, as in amount, strength, or value: Sales *rise* during the Christmas season. 5. To get out of bed. 6. To curve or incline upward: The trail *rises* from the valley to the top of the hill. 7. To grow fuller or higher: Did the cake *rise?* 8. To rebel. 9. To meet the requirements of: *rise* to the occasion. **rose** (ROHZ), **risen** (RIZ-n),

rising. *—noun.* 1. A moving upward: the *rise* of a balloon. 2. Progress toward a higher level or position. 3. Growth or increase, as in amount, strength, or degree: *rise* in prices. 4. A curving or inclining upward. 5. Origin or beginning: Jazz began its *rise* in the South.

risk *noun.* 1. The chance of difficulty, harm, or danger: There is a *risk* that the ice may not support you. 2. A person or thing that could cause trouble: Ralph is a poor *risk;* he cannot be depended upon to keep a secret. *—verb.* 1. To expose to difficulty, harm, or danger: The doctor *risked* his own health to treat the sick people. 2. To make possible some difficulty, harm, or danger. **risked, risking.** —**risky** *adjective.*

rite (RIGHT) *noun.* 1. A customary way of performing a religious ceremony. 2. A formal ceremony.

rit·u·al (RICH-oo-əl) *noun.* A formal ceremony, as a religious service.

ri·val (RIGH-vəl) *noun.* A person or organization that competes with or tries to be better than another: David is Linda's major *rival* for the position of class president. *—verb.* 1. To compete with or try to do better than. 2. To be equal to or about the same as: The traffic in Chicago *rivals* that in New York. **rivaled, rivaling.**

ri·val·ry (RIGH-vəl-ree) *noun.* Competition; trying to surpass: *Rivalry* caused the two boys to work harder. **rivalries.**

riv·er (RIV-ər) *noun.* A very large stream of water that flows in a definite channel and empties into an ocean, lake, or another river.

riv·et (RIV-it) *noun.* A metal pin or bar that is pounded or driven into metal parts to fasten them together. *—verb.* 1. To fasten or attach with rivets. 2. To fasten or attach, as one's attention or sight: The sailor *riveted* his gaze on the distant boat. **riveted, riveting.**

riv·u·let (RIV-yə-lit) *noun.* A tiny stream.

roach (ROHCH) *noun.* 1. An insect pest often found where food is stored or prepared; cockroach. 2. (Slang) A marijuana cigarette.

road (ROHD) *noun.* 1. A route or highway on which trucks, cars, and other vehicles travel. 2. A way or course: "It is a rough *road* that leads to the heights of greatness." (Seneca). —**hit the road.** To travel.

road·bed (ROHD-bed) *noun.* A foundation, usually crushed rock and earth, that supports a road or railroad tracks.

road·run·ner (ROHD-ruhn-ər) *noun.* A crested, long-tailed bird of southwestern United States that is able to run very swiftly.

road·side (ROHD-sighd) *noun.* The area beside a road. *—adjective.* Located beside a road: a *roadside* restaurant.

road·way (ROHD-way) *noun.* 1. A road. 2. The section of a road or highway on which vehicles travel: The car pulled from the *roadway* onto the shoulder.

roam (ROHM) *verb.* To wander; move about without a special direction or destination. **roamed, roaming.**

roar (ROR) *verb.* 1. To make a long, deep, loud sound: The lions *roared.* 2. To shout or cry out with a sound like a roar: The sergeant *roared* orders at the troops. 3. To laugh hard and loud. **roared, roaring.** *—noun.* A long, deep, loud sound.

roast (ROHST) *verb.* 1. To cook, especially meat, in an oven or near a fire. 2. To make very hot: The sun *roasted* the metal roof. 3. To prepare by baking or heating: The coffee beans were *roasted* before they were ground. **roasted, roasting.** *—noun.* A piece of meat that can be or has been roasted.

rob *verb.* To steal or take away from, especially by force. **robbed, robbing.** —**robber** *noun.*

roadrunner

river

robin
(definition 1)

rocking chair

rocket

rob·ber·y (ROB-ər-ee) *noun.* Theft; illegal taking by force. **robberies.**

robe (ROHB) *noun.* 1. A long, full garment worn over other clothing, often as a sign of rank or special position: bishop's *robes.* 2. A bathrobe; a long, full garment worn after bathing or when relaxing. **robes.** —*verb.* To put on a robe; to dress. **robed, robing.**

rob·in (ROB-in) *noun.* 1. A songbird of North America that is grayish brown with a red breast. 2. A small, European bird with a yellow-orange breast.

ro·bot (ROH-bət) *noun.* 1. A machine that resembles a human in appearance and is able to do certain human tasks. 2. A person who does things automatically or without apparent thoughts or feelings.

ro·bust (roh-BUHST or ROH-buhst) *adjective.* Healthy and vigorous; sturdy. —**robustly** *adverb.*

[1]**rock** (ROK) *noun.* 1. A mass or piece of stone: a cliff of *rock.* 2. Something that gives support or strength: "The Lord is my *rock.*" (II Samuel 22:2).

[2]**rock** (ROK) *verb.* 1. To move back and forth or sideways with a steady motion: The woman *rocked* the baby carriage. 2. To sway or shake, often violently: The ship *rocked* in the storm. **rocked, rocking.** —*noun.* 1. A swaying or shaking movement: The sailors could feel the *rock* of the ship. 2. Rock and roll music.

rock and roll. Popular music with a strong beat and elements of the blues as well as of country and western music.

rock·er (ROK-ər) *noun.* 1. A rocking chair. 2. One of the curved sections on which a rocking chair, cradle, or similar object rocks.

rock·et (ROK-it) *noun.* 1. A weapon or other device shaped like a cylinder or tube that moves at high speed, powered by gases that are forced out of one end. 2. A rocket ship. —*verb.* To move or make progress with great speed: The sports car *rocketed* around the racetrack. **rocketed, rocketing.**

rocket ship. A spaceship powered by one or more stages of rocket propulsion.

rocket silo. An underground space or cylinder, built to provide a protected area for storing and launching rockets.

rocking chair. A chair, usually built on two curved bars or rockers, that can be rocked back and forth by someone sitting in it.

rocking horse. A toy horse, built on springs or rockers.

[1]**rock·y** (ROK-ee) *adjective.* 1. Made of rock or having many rocks. 2. Hard as a rock; solid. **rockier, rockiest.**

[2]**rock·y** (ROK-ee) *adjective.* 1. Not steady; easily rocked or swayed: an old rickety, *rocky* desk. 2. Of a difficult or unsteady type or manner: a *rocky* recovery from illness. **rockier, rockiest.**

rod *noun.* 1. A straight, narrow bar, as of wood or metal. 2. A unit of measure equal to 16½ feet. 3. A fishing pole. 4. A bar or staff carried to show or represent authority; scepter. 5. (Slang) A pistol.

rode (ROHD) *verb. See* **ride.**

ro·dent (ROHD-ənt) *noun.* Any of a number of small mammals, such as rats, mice, and rabbits, that use their teeth for gnawing or nibbling.

ro·de·o (ROH-dee-oh or roh-DAY-oh) *noun.* 1. A contest or show at which cowboys compete at roping cattle, riding wild horses, and similar events. 2. A cattle roundup. **rodeos.**

[1]**roe** (ROH) *noun.* The eggs of fish: salmon *roe;* shad *roe.* —**roe** or **roes** *plural.*

[2]**roe** (ROH) Also **roe deer** *noun.* A small deer found in Europe and Asia. —**roe** or **roes** *plural.*

roe·buck (ROH-buhk) *noun.* A male roe deer.

rogue (ROHG) *noun.* 1. A scoundrel or dishonest person. 2. One who is playful in a mischievous way. **—roguish** *adjective.* **—roguishly** *adverb.*

role (ROHL) *noun.* 1. The part played by an actor or actress: the villain's *role.* 2. A person's place or part; an expected or required function: the *role* of peacemaker. **roles.**

roll (ROHL) *verb.* 1. To go or push forward by turning over and over: *Roll* the barrels. 2. To move on rollers or wheels. 3. To wind or gather up into the form of a cylinder or ball: *roll* up a carpet. 4. (Used with *on, away,* or *by*) To move past: Hours *rolled* by. 5. To make progress or move rapidly. 6. To move in waves or billows: The clouds *rolled* across the sky. 7. To move in a circle or curve. 8. To make a deep, loud sound: Thunder *rolled.* 9. To spread out and make flat: The baker *rolled* the cookie dough. 10. To rock. 11. To form into a round or tube shape: *roll* dough into balls. **rolled, rolling.** *—noun.* 1. A rolling. 2. A list of names: the *roll* of those present. 3. Anything rolled into the form of a cylinder. 4. Bread baked in an individual serving. 5. A rocking: *roll* of the ship. 6. A deep loud sound.

roll·er (ROHL-ər) *noun.* 1. A wheel or cylinder on which a vehicle or other object rolls: a table with *rollers* on the bottom. 2. A cylinder on which something is wound or rolled. 3. A cylinder or wheel used to squeeze, spread out, or flatten something: Huge *rollers* pressed the bars of steel into sheet metal. 4. A long, high wave.

roller coaster. A ride at an amusement park in which small cars roll up and down at high speeds over steeply banked tracks.

roller derby. A sporting event in which two teams of roller skaters try to win points by passing each other on an oval rink or track.

roller skate. One of a pair of devices that attach to shoes, equipped with wheels on the bottom for rolling along a smooth surface.

rolling pin. A cylinder with handles, made of wood or other material, used for flattening dough.

ro·ly-po·ly (ROH-lee-POH-lee) *adjective.* Plump; short and chubby.

ro·mance (roh-MANSS or ROH-manss) *noun.* 1. A love affair. 2. A love story. 3. An adventure story. 4. The excitement found in tales of adventure and love. **romances.**

Roman numerals. The style of numbers used in ancient Rome: XIV and DC are *Roman numerals* for 14 and 600.

ro·man·tic (roh-MAN-tik) *adjective.* 1. Like or related to tales or deeds of daring, adventure, and wonder: *romantic* tales about King Arthur. 2. Of or related to love or a love affair. 3. Not practical; more suitable for dreams than for real life: *romantic* notions. *—noun.* A person who has fanciful or romantic ideas. **—romantically** *adverb.*

romp *verb.* 1. To play in a rough and noisy manner. 2. (Slang) To win easily in a race. **romped, romping.** *—noun.* 1. A rough, noisy game or type of play. 2. (Slang) An easy victory.

romp·ers (ROM-pərz) *noun, plural.* Combination pants and blouse for a small child.

roof (ROOF or RUF) *noun.* 1. The covering on the top of a building. 2. The top surface of a variety of things: *roof* of the mouth. *—verb.* To cover with a roof. **roofed, roofing. —raise the roof.** To make a lot of noise; to object violently.

[1]**rook** (RUK) *noun.* A European crow. *—verb.* (Slang) To cheat (someone). **rooked, rooking.**

[2]**rook** (RUK) *noun.* A piece in the game of chess that moves forward or sideways for any distance that is not blocked along a row; a castle.

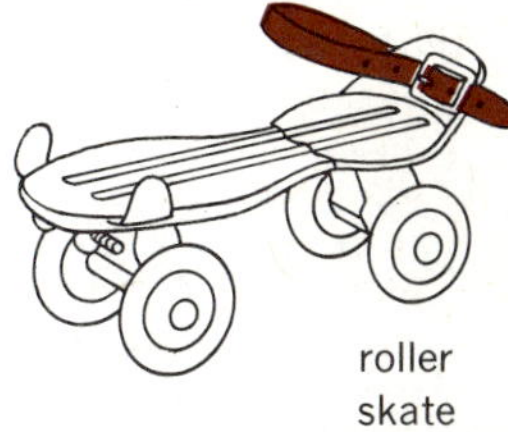

roller skate

roller coaster

roller derby

1	I	18	XVIII
2	II	19	XIX
3	III	20	XX
4	IV	30	XXX
5	V	40	XL
6	VI	49	IL
7	VII	50	L
8	VIII	60	LX
9	IX	70	LXX
10	X	80	LXXX
11	XI	90	XC
12	XII	100	C
13	XIII	200	CC
14	XIV	500	D
15	XV	600	DC
16	XVI	900	CM
17	XVII	1,000	M

Roman numerals

room *noun.* 1. An indoor area enclosed by walls: The house has six *rooms.* 2. Space; area: Is there *room* on the shelf for my package? 3. Students in a classroom: Our *room* is planning a class picnic. 4. Opportunity: There was no *room* for laziness in the busy office. 5. (Plural) Living quarters; dwelling. —*verb.* To live (in); dwell: Ed *rooms* in a dormitory. **roomed, rooming.**

room·mate (ROOM-mayt) *noun.* A person who shares a room or dwelling with another. **roommates.**

room·y (ROOM-ee) *adjective.* Having plenty of space. **roomier, roomiest.** —**roominess** *noun.*

roost *noun.* 1. A perch or bar on which birds can rest, as in a cage. 2. A place with perches on which birds can rest. —*verb.* To rest or sleep, as on a perch or in a shelter: At night the chickens *roosted* in their coop. **roosted, roosting.** —**rule the roost.** To be in command.

rooster
(definition 1)

roost·er (ROOSS-tər) *noun.* 1. An adult, male fowl. 2. The adult male of several types of birds; a cock.

[1]**root** *noun.* 1. The parts of a plant that grow beneath the ground to give support and draw up food and water from the soil. 2. A part that grows beneath the skin: the *roots* of a tooth. 3. Cause; origin: "The very spring and *root* of honesty and virtue lie in good education." (Plutarch). 4. A word from which other words developed or are formed: "Patria" is the Latin *root* for the English word "patriot." 5. (Plural) A feeling or state of being settled and a part of: I have *roots* in this town. 6. (Math) A number that when multiplied by itself a given number of times, yields a particular number: 3 is the square *root* of 9 and the cube *root* of 27. —*verb.* 1. To form roots and grow: The plant *rooted* in the rich soil. 2. To be firmly established; set securely: The desire to win was *rooted* in each member of the team. **rooted, rooting.**

rose

[2]**root** *verb.* 1. To dig or turn up, as with the snout: The pigs *rooted* through the garbage. 2. (Used with *up*) To pull out by the roots; overturn. **rooted, rooting.** —**root out.** 1. To get rid of. 2. To find and reveal or make known.

[3]**root** *verb.* To cheer (for); support. **rooted, rooting.**

rope (ROHP) *noun.* 1. A strong, heavy line made of twisted strands. 2. A lasso. 3. A string of connected objects: a *rope* of flowers. **ropes.** —*verb.* 1. (Usually used with *off*) To put a line or rope around: The police *roped* off the area where the accident occurred. 2. To catch with a line or rope; to lasso. 3. To tie with a line or rope: The workmen *roped* the crates to the truck. 4. (Slang, used with *in* or *into*) To trick; persuade with coaxing or a trick: Several people were *roped* into giving money to the dishonest scheme. **roped, roping.** —**at the end of one's rope.** Having reached a state or situation that is frustrating or hopeless. —**know the ropes.** To be experienced or familiar with a method or procedure.

ro·sa·ry (ROH-zə-ree) *noun.* 1. [Often capital R] A prayer or form of devotion that involves saying a series of shorter prayers. 2. A string of beads used in saying the Rosary.

rose (ROHZ) *noun.* 1. A fragrant flower that grows in a variety of colors. 2. The thorny plant or bush on which this flower grows. 3. (Also *adjective*) A red-pink color. **roses.**

ro·sette (roh-ZET) *noun.* An ornament, decoration, or emblem that resembles a rose, often worn in the lapel.

ros·ter (ROSS-tər) *noun.* A list of the names of members of a group.

ros·trum (ROSS-trəm) *noun.* A raised platform from which speeches are made.

ros•y (ROHZ-ee) *adjective.* 1. Having a red-pink color: *rosy* cheeks. 2. Very pleasant; promising success: a *rosy* future. **rosier, rosiest.**

rot *verb.* To decay; waste away. **rotted, rotting.** —*noun.* 1. Decay; decomposition. 2. Any of a variety of diseases that affect plants or animals. 3. (Informal) Silly talk.

ro•tate (ROH-tayt) *verb.* 1. To turn; move about a central point: The record *rotated* on the phonograph. 2. To change or move according to a plan or pattern: Dad *rotates* the tires on our car. **rotated, rotating.**

ro•ta•tion (roh-TAY-shən) *noun.* 1. A turning or moving about a central point: the *rotation* of the earth. 2. One complete turn; revolution: The record makes about 33 *rotations* each minute. 3. A change or movement according to a plan or pattern: crop *rotation.*

rote (ROHT) *noun.* 1. A process of memorizing, usually without complete understanding: The children learned the song by *rote.* 2. Any routine done without thought.

ro•tor (ROH-tər) *noun.* 1. The set of spinning blades on a helicopter. 2. A turning or spinning part, as on a motor or engine.

rot•ten (ROT-n) *adjective.* 1. Decayed; in a weakened or rotted condition: *rotten* meat; *rotten* planks. 2. Having a strong, unpleasant smell. 3. (Slang) Very bad or unpleasant: It was a *rotten* joke. —**rottenly** *adverb.* —**rottenness** *noun.*

ro•tun•da (roh-TUHN-də) *noun.* A round room, space, or building, especially one covered by a dome: the large *rotunda* beneath the dome of the Capitol Building.

rouge (ROOZH) *noun.* 1. A cosmetic, usually red, used to add color to the cheeks. 2. A reddish powder used to polish metals. **rouges.** —*verb.* To add color, as to the cheeks, with rouge. **rouged, rouging.**

rough (RUHF) *adjective.* 1. Not smooth; uneven. 2. Tough in manner and action: The big fullback is a rough player. 3. Stormy: *rough* weather. 4 Coarse; not fine or soft: Canvas is a *rough* fabric. 5. Not refined; harsh: *rough* speech. 6. Unfinished; not in final form: a *rough* sketch. 7. (Slang) Difficult and unpleasant: a very *rough* time. **rougher, roughest.** —*verb.* 1. To treat roughly; injure. 2. To make rough or uneven. **roughed, roughing.** —*noun.* An area along a golf course where the grass is long and difficult to hit from. —**roughly** *adverb.* —**in the rough.** In a crude or unrefined condition. —**rough it.** To live without one's usual comforts: The boys *roughed it* in the woods.

rough•age (RUHF-ij) *noun.* 1. Rough or coarse foods, as hay or grass for animals. 2. Food elements that are coarse, like certain cereals that add bulk to the diet.

rough•en (RUHF-ən) *verb.* To make or become rough. **roughened, roughening.**

round (ROWND) *adjective.* 1. Having the shape of a ball, circle, or ring. 2. Full; complete: a *round* dozen. 3. Plump; curved. 4. Mellow: the *round* tones of the organ music. 5. Of a whole number; without a fraction. **rounder, roundest.** —*noun.* 1. A series: a *round* of games. 2. A number of things that are served at one time: a *round* of drinks. 3. (Plural) A usual pattern of movements or series of actions: a watchman's *rounds.* 4. A shot or volley from a gun or guns. 5. A unit or period of action during a sporting event: The boxers fought for eight *rounds.* 6. A song in which two or more groups of singers begin singing the words at different times. 7. A cut of beef. 8. Something round in shape. —*verb.* 1. To curve; make or become round: The carpenter *rounded* the edge of the table with

rosary

rotor

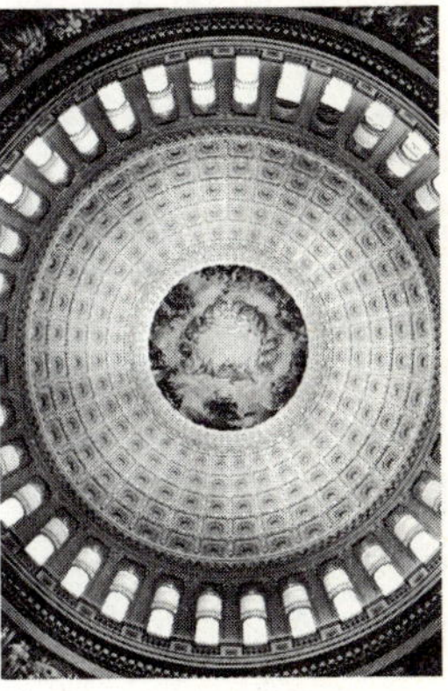

rotunda

a file. 2. To go or turn around: The car *rounded* the corner. **rounded, rounding.** —*adverb.* 1. In a circular or rotating manner; around: The record turned *round* on the phonograph. 2. As part of a pattern or cycle: Christmas comes *round* each December. —*preposition.* 1. All along the edge of; around: The hunters walked *round* the swamp. 2. All about or around: The girl searched *round* the room for her bracelet. —**round off.** To change a number containing a fraction or decimal to the nearest whole number: *Rounding off* 4.25 leaves 4. —**round out.** To complete; fulfill: Let's *round out* the day with a swim. —**round up.** To gather; collect: *round up* cattle.

roundup

round·a·bout (ROWND-ə-bowt) *adjective.* Not direct; not by the shortest route or method: The taxi driver took a *roundabout* way to our house.

round·up (ROWND-uhp) *noun.* 1. A gathering or herding together of cattle. 2. Any gathering or collection, as of people or facts.

rowboat

rouse (ROWZ) *verb.* 1. To make excited; arouse: The speaker's accusations *roused* the crowd to anger. 2. To wake up; make active: The alarm clock *roused* me. **roused, rousing.**

rout (ROWT) *verb.* 1. To cause to retreat or run away, especially in large numbers and in a confused manner: The powerful army *routed* the small enemy force. 2. To defeat by a large margin: The Giants *routed* the Wildcats by a score of 60–0. **routed, routing.** —*noun.* 1. A retreat, especially a large and confused one; a running away. 2. A defeat by a large margin.

row houses

route (ROOT or ROWT) *noun.* 1. A road or way traveled on a regular basis. 2. A journey that follows a regular pattern or involves actions at a series of places: newspaper *route.* **routes.** —*verb.* To send along a road or way traveled on a regular basis. **routed, routing.**

rou·tine (roo-TEEN) *noun.* A method or series of actions done on a regular basis: Dad's morning *routine* includes breakfast, feeding the dog, and reading the paper. **routines.** —*adjective.* 1. Done on a regular basis: *routine* milk deliveries. 2. Uninteresting. —**routinely** *adverb.*

rove (ROHV) *verb.* To wander; roam about. **roved, roving.**

rov·er (ROHV-ər) *noun.* A person who roams, as a hobo; a wanderer.

[1]**row** (ROH) *noun.* A line or column of things, people, animals, or such.

[2]**row** (ROH) *verb.* 1. To use oars to move a boat. 2. To transport (someone or something) by rowing in a boat: The sailors *rowed* the visitor to shore. **rowed, rowing.** —*noun.* A trip made by rowing.

[3]**row** (ROW) *noun.* A loud quarrel; great noise or uproar.

row·boat (ROH-boht) *noun.* A small boat moved by the sweep of oars.

row·el (ROW-əl) *noun.* A small wheel with sharp notches, used on a spur. *See* illustration at **spur.**

row house. One of a number of houses built in a row, similar in appearance, and often joined together side by side.

roy·al (ROI-əl) *adjective.* 1. Related to the position or person of a king, queen, or other monarch: a *royal* court; the *royal* family. 2. Fit for a king or queen; magnificent: a *royal* banquet. —**royally** *adverb.*

roy·al·ty (ROI-əl-tee) *noun.* 1. A person or persons of royal rank. 2. The position or state of a king, queen, or other monarch: *Royalty* has its burdens as well as its privileges. 3. An amount of money paid for the use of a book, play, or other composition done or made by someone else: The drama club had to pay a *royalty* of 75 dollars for the use of the play. **royalties.**

r.p.m. *abbreviation.* Revolutions per minute.

RR *abbreviation.* Railroad.

r.s.v.p. *abbreviation.* Initials of a French phrase "Répondez s'il vous plaît," which means "Reply if you please."

rub (RUHB) *verb.* 1. To move along or against with firmness or pressure: Dave *rubbed* the table with sandpaper. 2. To spread with firmness or pressure: The doctor *rubbed* medicine on my sore shoulder. 3. (Used with *out*) To remove by pressing or scraping with firmness or pressure: The student *rubbed* out the error with his eraser. **rubbed, rubbing.** —*noun.* 1. The act of rubbing: a good *rub* with a towel. 2. A difficulty or drawback. 3. A sharp reproof. **—rub it in.** To remind or make fun of some failure or embarrassment; tease. **—rub the wrong way.** To bother; annoy greatly.

rub·ber (RUHB-ər) *noun.* 1. A flexible, elastic substance made from the sap of certain trees or from synthetic materials. 2. (Usually plural) A rubber covering worn over a shoe in wet weather.

rubber band. A band or ring of rubber used to hold items together.

rub·bish (RUHB-ish) *noun.* 1. Material that is thrown away; trash. 2. (Informal) Nonsense: That silly story is just *rubbish;* don't believe it.

rub·ble (RUHB-əl) *noun.* Broken stone, concrete, or other similar substances: The building became a pile of *rubble* when the bomb exploded.

ru·by (ROO-bee) *noun.* 1. A very valuable, deep red jewel. 2. (Also *adjective*) A deep red color. **rubies.**

rud·der (RUHD-ər) *noun.* A flat device, attached to the rear of a ship, boat, or airplane by hinges and moved in order to change direction.

rud·dy (RUHD-ee) *adjective.* 1. Reddish in color: a *ruddy* apple. 2. Having a healthy, red glow: a *ruddy* complexion. **ruddier, ruddiest. —ruddily** *adverb.* **—ruddiness** *noun.*

rude (ROOD) *adjective.* 1. Not polite; very discourteous. 2. Crude; not fancy: a *rude* cabin. 3. Rough; violent: "The rough *rude* sea." (Shakespeare). **ruder, rudest. —rudely** *adverb.* **—rudeness** *noun.*

ru·di·ment (ROO-də-mənt) *noun.* (Usually plural) A basic principle, idea, or activity: The instructor taught the *rudiments* of tennis.

ru·di·men·ta·ry (roo-də-MEN-tə-ree) *adjective.* 1. Of or related to basic principles, ideas, or activities: *rudimentary* rules of arithmetic. 2. Of or related to a beginning or early stage or form: A tadpole is a *rudimentary* stage of a frog.

rue (ROO) *verb.* To regret; feel sorrow or guilt for. **rued, ruing.**

rue·ful (ROO-fəl) *adjective.* 1. Sorrowful; full of regret. 2. Causing sorrow or regret. **—ruefully** *adverb.*

ruff (RUHF) *noun.* 1. A ring of feathers or fur around the neck of an animal. 2. A fancy, stiff collar once commonly worn by both men and women.

ruf·fi·an (RUHF-ee-ən) *noun.* A rough, rude, or cruel person.

ruf·fle (RUHF-əl) *noun.* 1. A ribbon, piece of fancy cloth, or lace that is pleated or gathered and used for decorating or trimming. 2. A mild disturbance or disorder. **ruffles.** —*verb.* 1. To disturb; agitate: The breeze *ruffled* the field of wheat. 2. To make rough or wrinkled: The cat's fur *ruffled* when the dog barked. 3. To cause annoyance or embarrassment to; to bother. 4. To make or form into ruffles; to pleat. **ruffled, ruffling.**

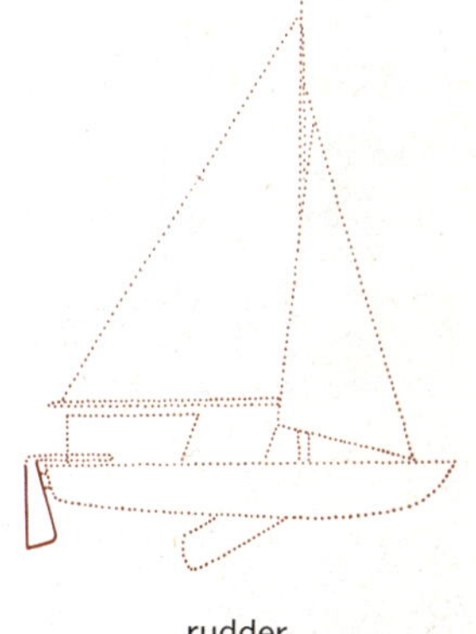
rudder

rugby

rug (RUHG) *noun.* A thick layer of material, usually fabric, used to cover a floor; carpet.

rug·by (RUHG-bee) *noun.* A type of football first played in England.

rug·ged (RUHG-id) *adjective.* 1. Sturdy; tough and strong: The *rugged* fullback scored three touchdowns. 2. Having a very rough, uneven surface: *rugged* mountains. 3. Difficult; harsh: The sailors had a *rugged* voyage during the storm. 4. Not smooth: a *rugged* face. **—ruggedly** *adverb.*

ruins

ruin (ROO-in) *noun.* 1. (Often plural) The remains of something that has decayed or been destroyed: the *ruins* of an old castle. 2. Destruction; decay: The *ruin* of the fort was caused by a great fire. 3. That which causes destruction or decay: A storm was the *ruin* of the old ship. *—verb.* 1. To cause destruction or very great harm. 2. To disturb; spoil: Barbara's black eye *ruins* her appearance. **ruined, ruining.**

ru·in·ous (ROO-i-nəss) *adjective.* Causing ruin or destruction: a *ruinous* flood. **—ruinously** *adverb.*

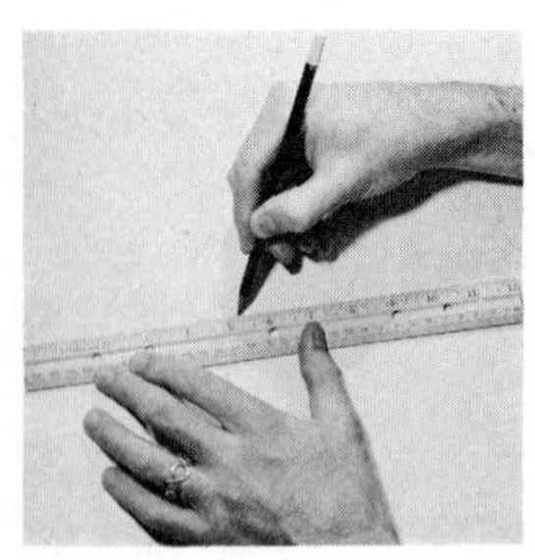

ruler

rule (ROOL) *noun.* 1. A principle or law made to guide or govern people: There is a *rule* against smoking at the museum. 2. A period or state of control or governing: The king's *rule* lasted 40 years. 3. A usual or expected condition or action: Heavy rain is the *rule* here in April. 4. A ruler; an instrument used for measuring length or drawing straight lines. **rules.** *—verb.* 1. To govern or control, as a country or kingdom. 2. To make a formal decision: The court *ruled* that the motorist had to pay a heavy fine. 3. To control or manage. 4. To draw straight lines on: The carpenter *ruled* the board before he sawed it. **ruled, ruling. —as a rule.** Usually. **—rule out.** To exclude; keep from being: The general *ruled out* a new attack.

rul·er (ROOL-ər) *noun.* 1. A person who rules or governs. 2. An instrument used for measuring length or drawing straight lines.

rum (RUHM) *noun.* An alcoholic beverage made from sugar cane or molasses.

rum·ble (RUHM-bəl) *verb.* 1. To make a long, low, thundering sound: The ship's engines *rumbled* as they were started. 2. To move while making such a sound: The old truck *rumbled* over the bumpy road. **rumbled, rumbling.** *—noun.* 1. A long, low, thundering sound: We could hear the *rumble* of the coming storm. 2. (Slang) A fight, especially one between gangs. **rumbles.**

rum·mage (RUHM-ij) *verb.* (Used with through) To search thoroughly, as through piles or masses of things: Dad *rummaged* through the crowded basement looking for his hammer. **rummaged, rummaging.**

rummage sale. An informal sale at which a variety of odd and second-hand items is offered.

rum·my (RUHM-ee) *noun.* A type of card game.

ru·mor (ROO-mər) *noun.* Gossip; a story or information that is spread or discussed without proof that it is true: The report of the soldier's escape is just a *rumor.* *—verb.* To spread or discuss a rumor or unproven report. **rumored, rumoring.**

rump (RUHMP) *noun.* The rear part of an animal where its legs meet its back; buttocks.

rum·ple (RUHM-pəl) *verb.* To wrinkle up; crumple: Jim *rumpled* his paper cup and threw it away. **rumpled, rumpling.** *—noun.* A wrinkle; crease. **rumples.**

rum·pus (RUHM-pəss) *noun.* A noisy disorder; uproar.

run (RUHN) *verb.* 1. To move by rapid actions of the legs. 2. To take part in a race. 3. To flee. 4. To try to win votes for a special job or position: Mayor Blake will *run* for governor. 5. To operate; control; manage: Mr. Thomas *runs* the local bakery. 6. To be in operation or motion: Our washer will not *run.* 7. To go (between places) on a schedule. 8. To flow. 9. To blend, as one color into another: The colors of your blouse will *run* when you wash it. 10. To stretch out; extend; continue: The mountains *run* for miles. 11. To have; be affected by: *run* a high temperature. 12. To make known, as in a newspaper or magazine: The newspaper will *run* a report of the game. **ran, run, running.** —*noun.* 1. A rapid pace or rate of movement: The boys started for home at a *run.* 2. A distance, as of a race, or the time needed to cover a distance: a 600-yard *run.* 3. A score in baseball. 4. A movement of large numbers of fish: a salmon *run.* 5. A regular trip between places, or the time needed to make such a trip. 6. A flow: a *run* of water. 7. A continuous process, situation, or number of actions: a *run* of bad luck. 8. A line or strip of unraveled material: Joan's stocking has a *run* in it. 9. A continuous series of performances: The movie had a long *run.* 10. Permission or freedom to do as one wishes: the *run* of the house. **—a run for one's money.** An activity or competition that offers a real challenge: The mayor's rival gave him *a run for his money* in the last election. **—in the long run.** When all things are considered. **—on the run.** 1. Running away; fleeing. 2. While very active or busy: I don't have time to stay for lunch; I will have to eat *on the run.* **—run across.** To meet or find by accident. **—run away with.** To win by a wide margin.

run•a•bout (RUHN-ə-bowt) *noun.* A small car or boat.

run•a•way (RUHN-ə-way) *adjective.* 1. Running away; escaping. 2. Going off or up rapidly, as with a sudden rise in prices. —*noun.* 1. One who runs away. 2. The act of escaping or running away.

run•back (RUHN-bak) *noun.* (Football) The act of running back after catching a kick or intercepting a forward pass.

run-down (RUHN-down) *adjective.* 1. In a state of disrepair; worn; dilapidated; falling apart: The workman tried to fix the *run-down* barn. 2. Tired; worn out: The doctor was worried by the patient's *run-down* condition. —*noun.* A brief report or summary: The general gave his troops a *run-down* of his battle plan.

rung (RUHNG) *noun.* 1. A bar or rod that forms a step on a ladder. 2. A bar or rod that acts as a support or joins parts on a chair or other piece of furniture.

run•ner (RUHN-ər) *noun.* 1. A person who runs. 2. A bar on which a sled, skate, or other object slides or moves. 3. A messenger, especially in primitive areas: The chief of the tribe sent a *runner* to the next village. 4. A long, narrow tablecloth or carpet. 5. A plant stem that has roots attached to the ground at several places.

run•ning (RUHN-ing) *noun.* The act of moving swiftly, operating, or managing: *running* of a race; *running* of a business. **—in** (or **out of**) **the running.** In (or out of) a position to win or compete successfully: Tom is still *in the running* to be class president.

running mate. A person who runs in an election together with someone who is seeking a more important position: The vice president was the president's *running mate.*

run-of-the-mill (ruhn-əv-th̲ə-MIL) *adjective.* Ordinary; not special.

runt (RUHNT) *noun.* 1. A small, weak offspring or young animal: The *runt* among the newborn pigs died from the chilly weather. 2. A small or weak person.

runway

run·way (RUHN-way) *noun.* 1. A level strip, usually concrete, on which aircraft land and take off. 2. An arm of a stage that extends into the audience's area. 3. A path, ditch, or track along which something moves: The men rolled barrels down the *runway* to the pier.

rup·ture (RUHP-chər) *noun.* 1. A break; a bursting: Too much pressure caused a *rupture* in the air hose. 2. A disorder of the body caused by a break or weakness of supporting tissue. —*verb.* 1. To break open; burst: Freezing weather *ruptured* the water pipe. 2. To experience a break or weakening of body tissue. **ruptured, rupturing.**

ru·ral (RUR-əl) *adjective.* Of or related to the country: Barns are found in *rural* areas. —**rurally** *adverb.*

ruse (ROOZ) *noun.* A trick or scheme.

rye

[1]**rush** (RUHSH) *verb.* 1. To move or act with speed: The frightened animals *rushed* through the forest. 2. To do (something) with haste, often carelessly. 3. To attack suddenly: The police *rushed* the building where the criminals were hiding. **rushed, rushing.** —*noun.* 1. A swift movement or action: The boys' *rush* to the kitchen showed that they were hungry. 2. A doing or acting with haste, often carelessly. 3. A time of great activity or busyness: The store made a large profit during the Christmas *rush.*

[2]**rush** (RUHSH) *noun.* A tall, grasslike plant with a hollow stem that grows in areas near water. **rushes.**

rush hour. A time during the morning or late afternoon when traffic to or from the business district is at its heaviest.

rust (RUHST) *noun.* 1. A reddish-brown powder or scaly coating that forms on iron or steel when it is exposed to moisture or air. 2. Any of several types of plant disease. 3. (Also *adjective*) A reddish-brown color. —*verb.* 1. To become covered with rust; corrode. 2. To become dull or decayed through lack of use: The magician's talents *rusted* after he retired. **rusted, rusting.**

rus·tic (RUHSS-tik) *adjective.* 1. Of or related to the country; rural: the *rustic* beauty of a New England farm. 2. Typical of simple country living; not fancy. —*noun.* A person from a rural area.

rus·tle (RUHSS-l) *verb.* 1. To make a soft, crackling sound like that made by leaves moving in the wind. 2. (Informal) To steal livestock: The thieves *rustled* 30 cows from the ranch. 3. (Informal) To get or prepare quickly: The cook *rustled* up lunch for the hungry workmen. **rustled, rustling.** —*noun.* The sound made by leaves moving in the wind.

rust·y (RUHSS-tee) *adjective.* 1. Covered with rust. 2. Dulled or decayed by lack of use. 3. Having a brownish-red color. **rustier, rustiest.**

rut (RUHT) *noun.* 1. A groove or track, like one made in the ground by a wheel: The wagon left *ruts* in the mud. 2. A regular or routine way of doing or acting, often dull: The old professor is in a *rut;* he teaches the same way year after year. —*verb.* To make grooves or slots in. **rutted, rutting.**

ru·ta·ba·ga (ROO-tə-bay-gə) *noun.* A turnip-like vegetable.

ruth·less (ROOTH-liss) *adjective.* Without mercy; very cruel. —**ruthlessly** *adverb.*

rye (RIGH) *noun.* 1. A widely grown, sturdy grass. 2. The grain from this grass. 3. Flour made from the grain of the rye plant. 4. Whiskey made from the grain of the rye plant.

S, s (ESS) The 19th letter of the English alphabet.

S. *abbreviation.* 1. South, Southern. 2. School. 3. Sea. 4. Sabbath.

-s *suffix.* Used to form the plural of some nouns: boy*s*, girl*s*, house*s*.

sa·ber (SAY-bər) *noun.* A heavy sword with a sharp, curved blade.

sa·ble (SAY-bəl) *noun.* 1. A small mammal with dark, rich fur. 2. The fur of this animal.

sab·o·tage (SAB-ə-tahzh) *noun.* 1. Damage or destruction of factories, power plants, or bridges by enemy agents or by conquered civilians. 2. Any deliberate interference or disruption. *—verb.* To commit acts of sabotage. **sabotaged, sabotaging.**

sac (SAK) *noun.* A pouch-like part of a plant or animal.

sac·cha·rin (SAK-ə-rin) *noun.* A non-fattening chemical sweetener that can be used in place of sugar.

sa·chem (SAY-chəm) *noun.* The chief in some American Indian tribes.

[1]**sack** (SAK) *noun.* A large, strong bag, usually made of coarse cloth. *—verb.* To place in a sack. **sacked, sacking. —hit the sack.** Go to bed.

[2]**sack** (SAK) *verb.* To loot (a captured town). **sacked, sacking.**

sac·ra·ment (SAK-rə-mənt) *noun.* 1. Any of several special religious ceremonies of the Christian Church, such as Baptism or Communion. 2. [Capital S] Holy Communion.

sa·cred (SAY-krid) *adjective.* 1. Holy; related to or used for religious worship. 2. Deserving of respect or special honor. 3. Not to be violated; binding: a *sacred* promise.

sac·ri·fice (SAK-rə-fighss) *noun.* 1. The act of making an offering to God; the thing offered. 2. The giving up of something for a definite purpose; the thing given up. 3. A loss, especially financial loss by selling something at less than true value. **sacrifices.** *—verb.* 1. To make a sacrifice; give up. 2. To sell at a loss. **sacrificed, sacrificing.**

sad *adjective.* 1. Unhappy; having a feeling of sorrow. 2. Causing a feeling of sorrow. **sadder, saddest. —sadly** *adverb.* **—sadness** *noun.*

sad·den (SAD-n) *verb.* To make sad or become sad. **saddened, saddening.**

sad·dle (SAD-l) *noun.* 1. A seat for a rider, as on a horse or bicycle. 2. Anything that has the shape of a saddle: the *saddle* of a hilltop. **saddles.** *—verb.* 1. To put a saddle on (an animal). 2. To burden or load: Sis *saddled* me with doing the dishes. **saddled, saddling.**

saddle shoes. Flat-heeled, laced shoes, often white, with a wide strip of another color over the instep.

safe (SAYF) *adjective.* 1. Not likely to cause harm or danger: *safe* toys. 2. Free from harm or danger: We got home *safe* and sound. 3. Sure; dependable: a *safe* plan. 4. Cautious: a *safe* move. 5. (Baseball) Having touched one of the bases without being tagged out: *safe* at third! **safer, safest.** *—noun.* A heavy metal container for locking up money and valuables. **safes. —safely** *adverb.*

safe·guard (SAYF-gahrd) *noun.* Protection or defense against harm or danger. *—verb.* To protect. **safeguarded, safeguarding.**

safe·keep·ing (SAYF-KEEP-ing) *noun.* Protection; care: Put your valuables in the bank for *safekeeping.*

sable

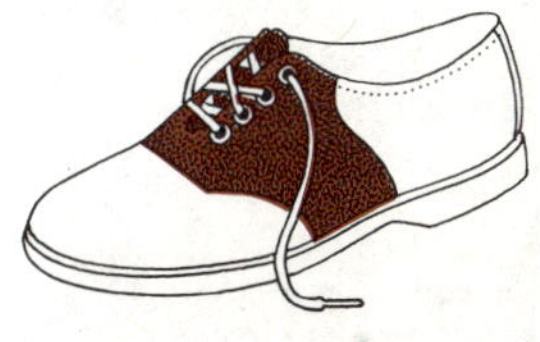

saddle shoe

safety patrol

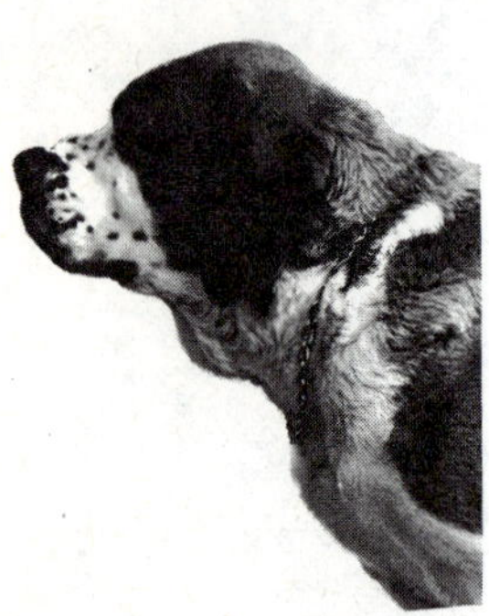
Saint Bernard

Sagittarius

safe·ty (SAYF-tee) *noun.* 1. Condition of being safe; freedom from harm. 2. A device or lock that prevents accidents: a *safety* on a gun. 3. (Football) Downing the ball by an offensive player behind his own goal line. 4. (Football) The defensive back farthest from the opposing team. **safeties.**

safety belt. *See* **seat belt.**

safety patrol. Students trained to direct traffic at school crosswalks.

saf·fron (SAF-rən) *noun.* 1. A part of the crocus flower, yellow-orange in color, that is dried and used as a dye or seasoning. 2. (Also *adjective*) A yellow-orange color.

sag *verb.* 1. To sink or bend. 2. To droop. **sagged, sagging.**

sa·ga (SAH-gə) *noun.* 1. An old Norse story of heroes and their adventures. 2. A long adventure story.

sa·ga·cious (sə-GAY-shəss) *adjective.* Wise and shrewd.

[1]**sage** (SAYJ) *noun.* An old and respected wise man. **sages.** *—adjective.* Wise; thoughtful. **sager, sagest.**

[2]**sage** (SAYJ) *noun.* 1. An herb with silver-green leaves used for seasoning food. 2. Sagebrush.

sage·brush (SAYJ-bruhsh) *noun.* A shrub that grows in the dry areas of western United States.

Sag·it·ta·ri·us (saj-ə-TAIR-ee-əss) *noun.* The ninth sign of the zodiac, also called the "Archer." The time of this sign is from November 22 through December 21.

said (SED) *verb. See* **say.**

sail (SAYL) *noun.* 1. A piece of heavy cloth used on a boat to catch the wind and move the boat along. 2. A trip on a sailboat. 3. Something that looks or acts like a sail. *—verb.* 1. To move (a boat) on water by using a sail or sails. 2. To travel on a ship. 3. To start on an ocean trip. 4. To move through the air: The balloon *sailed* away. **sailed, sailing.**

sail·boat (SAYL-boht) *noun.* A boat moved by a sail or sails.

sail·or (SAYL-ər) *noun.* 1. A man in the Navy. 2. A man who works on a boat or a ship. 3. A straw hat with a flat top. Also called "boater."

saint (SAYNT) *noun.* 1. A person who, after death, is honored for his holiness by a church or religion. 2. A very good person.

Saint Ber·nard (SAYNT bər-NAHRD). A large, powerful dog with dense brown and white hair.

saint·ly (SAYNT-lee) *adjective.* Like a saint; very good or holy. **saintlier, saintliest.**

sake (SAYK) *noun.* 1. Reason; purpose; cause: for the *sake* of peace. 2. Benefit, the good (of): for the *sake* of all of us. **sakes.**

sal·ad (SAL-əd) *noun.* 1. A dish of mixed vegetables, tossed with a dressing. 2. Any mixed dish served with a salad dressing: tuna *salad.*

sal·a·man·der (SAL-ə-man-dər) *noun.* A small amphibious animal that looks like a lizard and lives in damp places.

sal·a·ry (SAL-ə-ree or SAL-ree) *noun.* A set amount of money paid for a period of work. **salaries.**

sale (SAYL) *noun.* 1. An exchange of property or goods for money. 2. An offer of goods at lower than usual prices: I bought my skates on *sale.*

sales·man (SAYLZ-mən) *noun, masculine.* Also **saleswoman** (SAYLZ-wu-mən) *noun, feminine.* A person who earns money by selling goods. **—salesmen, saleswomen** *plural.*

sa·line (SAY-leen or SAY-lighn) *adjective.* Of salt; containing salt.

sa·lin·i·ty (sə-LIN-ə-tee) *noun.* The degree or amount of salt in a solution or compound.

sa·li·va (sə-LIGH-və) *noun.* A tasteless liquid formed in the mouth by certain glands; spit.

sal·i·var·y (SAL-ə-vehr-ee) *adjective.* Referring to or producing saliva.

sal·low (SAL-oh) *adjective.* Having a pale, yellowish skin color, usually associated with poor health.

salm·on (SAM-ən) *noun.* 1. A large food fish caught in northern ocean waters. 2. (Also *adjective*) A yellow-pink or red-orange color. —**salmon** or **salmons** *plural.*

sa·loon (sə-LOON) *noun.* 1. A bar or tavern. 2. A large public room on an ocean liner.

salt (SAWLT) *noun.* 1. A white compound, found in the earth and sea water, used to season or preserve food. 2. Any chemical compound formed by the reaction of an acid and a base. 3. (Informal) An old sailor. —*verb.* To season or preserve with salt. **salted, salting.** —**salt away.** To put away; save up.

salt lick. A block or deposit of salt that animals lick.

salt·wat·er (SAWLT-waw-tər) *adjective.* Of, from, or living in the sea.

salt·y (SAWL-tee) *adjective.* Tasting of or containing salt. **saltier, saltiest.**

sal·u·ta·tion (sal-yə-TAY-shən) *noun.* 1. A greeting or salute. 2. The opening of a letter: "Dear Liz" is the *salutation* of the letter.

sa·lute (sə-LOOT) *verb.* 1. To show honor or respect by raising the hand to the forehead or by firing guns. 2. To greet; wave; show a sign of greeting. **saluted, saluting.** —*noun.* An act of greeting or respect: a *salute* to the flag. **salutes.**

sal·vage (SAL-vij) *verb.* 1. To rescue or retrieve (a ship) after sinking, fire, or shipwreck. 2. To save from destruction or waste: We can *salvage* the bottles for recycling. **salvaged, salvaging.** —*noun.* 1. The act of saving a ship from sinking, fire, etc. or the money or property paid to those who save it. 2. What is saved from destruction or waste.

sal·va·tion (sal-VAY-shən) *noun.* The act of saving or being saved (from evil, danger, or failure).

salve (SAV or SAHV) *noun.* 1. A cream or oil used to sooth the pain of a wound or burn. 2. Anything that is soothing or calming. **salves.** —*verb.* 1. To use or apply a salve. 2. To sooth or calm. **salved, salving.**

SAM Acronym for *s*urface to *a*ir *m*issile; a rocket fired from a ground position against aircraft.

same (SAYM) *adjective.* 1. Identical; not another: She is the *same* teacher I had last year. 2. Similar; alike: Our bicycles are the *same.* 3. Not changing: *same* old thing. —*pronoun.* An identical or similar person or thing: Give her a soda, and I'll have the *same.*

sam·pan (SAM-pan) *noun.* A small, flat-bottomed boat used in the Orient.

sam·ple (SAM-pəl) *noun.* A portion or piece that shows what the whole or rest is like; an example: a *sample* of blood. —*verb.* To try a little; take a sample. **sampled, sampling.**

san·a·to·ri·um (san-ə-TOR-ee-əm) *noun.* (Chiefly British) A sanitarium. —**sanatoriums** or **sanatoria** (san-ə-TOR-ee-ə) *plural.*

sanc·tion (SANGK-shən) *noun.* 1. Permission or approval from someone of authority: the *sanction* of my parents. 2. A penalty to guarantee obedience to the law. —*verb.* To approve or allow; to permit. **sanctioned, sanctioning.**

sanc·tu·ar·y (SANGK-choo-ehr-ee) *noun.* 1. A holy place or building; the part of a church where services are held. 2. A place of safety or of protection. **sanctuaries.**

sand *noun.* Finely ground grains of rocks and seashells found in deserts, beaches, etc. —*verb.* 1. To make smooth or scrape with sand or sandpaper. 2. To spread, sprinkle, or toss sand. **sanded, sanding.**

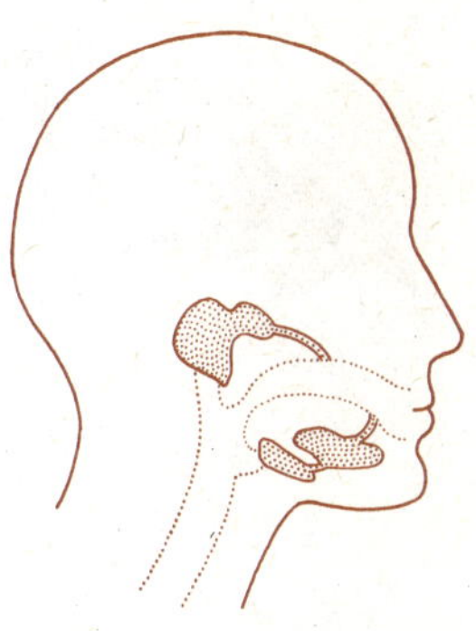

salivary glands

salmon

sampans

sandal

sardines

sari

san·dal (SAND-l) *noun.* 1. A shoe made up of a sole that is fastened to the foot by straps. 2. A lightweight shoe or slipper.

sand·bar (SAND-bahr) *noun.* A ridge or bar of sand in a river or ocean, usually formed by water action.

sand·pa·per (SAND-pay-pər) *noun.* Heavy paper with a sand-like coating on one or both sides, used to smooth rough surfaces.

sand·pi·per (SAND-pigh-pər) *noun.* A small bird with a long thin bill, found near the shore.

sand·stone (SAND-stohn) *noun.* Rock formed mainly of sand and held together by other natural materials, such as clay or lime.

sand·storm (SAND-storm) *noun.* A wind that stirs up gusts of sand.

sand·wich (SAND-wich or SAN-wich) *noun.* Slices of bread between which is a filling such as cheese, meat, or peanut butter. **sandwiches.** —*verb.* To squeeze or confine (between two things). **sandwiched, sandwiching.**

sane (SAYN) *adjective.* 1. Having a healthy mind; not mentally ill. 2. Showing good sense. **saner, sanest.** —**sanely** *adverb.*

sang *verb. See* **sing.**

san·i·tar·i·um (san-ə-TAIR-ee-əm) *noun.* 1. A resort people visit for rest or relaxation. 2. An institution for the care of the chronically ill. —**sanitariums** or **sanitaria** (san-ə-TAIR-ee-ə) *plural.*

san·i·tar·y (SAN-ə-tehr-ee) *adjective.* Clean; healthful; free of germs.

san·i·ta·tion (san-ə-TAY-shən) *noun.* 1. The development and carrying out of methods to improve public health. 2. Sewage disposal.

san·i·ty (SAN-ə-tee) *noun.* The state of having a healthy, sound mind.

sank (SANGK) *verb. See* **sink.**

[1]**sap** *noun.* 1. The juice or liquid that flows in plants and trees. 2. (Slang) A gullible person; a fool.

[2]**sap** *verb.* To weaken or wear away: *sap* one's strength. **sapped, sapping.**

sap·ling (SAP-ling) *noun.* A young tree.

sap·phire (SAF-ighr) *verb.* 1. A blue gem. 2. (Also *adjective*) A deep blue color. **sapphires.**

sar·casm (SAHR-kaz-əm) *noun.* A mocking statement the true meaning of which is just the opposite of its apparent meaning. —**sarcastic** (sahr-KASS-tik) *adjective.* —**sarcastically** *adverb.*

sar·dine (sahr-DEEN) *noun.* A small edible fish of the herring family.

sa·ri (SAH-ree) *noun.* A long piece of lightweight material that is draped about the body to form a garment, mainly worn by the women of India.

[1]**sash** *noun.* A length of ribbon or other material worn about the waist or over the shoulder. **sashes.**

[2]**sash** *noun.* The wooden or metal frame in which the glass of a window or door is set. **sashes.**

sass *noun.* (Informal) Rudeness, disrespect; back talk. —*verb.* To **be** rude to; answer back. **sassed, sassing.** —**sassy** *adjective.*

sat *verb. See* **sit.**

Sa·tan (SAYT-n) *noun.* The devil.

satch·el (SACH-əl) *noun.* A small suitcase or bag.

sat·el·lite (SAT-l-ight) *noun.* 1. A natural or man-made body that revolves around a planet. 2. A nation under the influence or control of another nation. **satellites.**

sat·in (SAT-n) *noun.* A smooth, shiny fabric made of silk, rayon, or nylon.

sat·ire (SAT-ighr) *noun.* 1. The use of humor, mockery, or sarcasm to point out an evil or foolishness. 2. A written work containing such usage. **satires.** —**satirize** (SAT-ə-righz) *verb.*

sat·is·fac·tion (sat-iss-FAK-shən) *noun.* 1. A good feeling as a result of receiving (something) or being fulfilled. 2. Anything that brings a good or happy feeling. 3. A making up (for some loss or injury).

sat·is·fac·to·ry (sat-iss-FAK-tə-ree) *adjective.* 1. Good enough; sufficient: *satisfactory* grades. 2. Fulfilling; pleasing: Winning was very *satisfactory.* —**satisfactorily** *adverb.*

sat·is·fy (SAT-iss-figh) *verb.* 1. To fill (a need or wish): The ice cream *satisfied* my hunger. 2. To give assurance to; to answer. 3. To pay or fulfill. **satisfied, satisfying.**

sat·u·rate (SACH-ə-rayt) *verb.* 1. To make completely wet; to soak. 2. To mix throughout. **saturated, saturating.** —**saturation** (sach-ə-RAY-shən) *noun.*

Sat·ur·day (SAT-ər-dee or SAT-ər-day) *noun.* The seventh day of the week: *Saturday* is the day between Friday and Sunday —**Sat.** *abbreviation.*

Sat·urn (SAT-ərn) *noun.* The planet sixth in distance from the sun.

sat·yr (SAT-ər) *noun.* (Mythology) A Greek demigod with a human body and the legs, horns, and ears of a goat.

sauce (SAWSS) *noun.* 1. A liquid, as gravy or syrup, served with food. 2. Stewed or strained fruit.

sauce·pan (SAWSS-pan) *noun.* A small cooking pan, usually with a long handle and a cover.

sau·cer (SAW-sər) *noun.* A small, almost flat dish used to hold a cup.

sau·cy (SAW-see) *adjective.* 1. Rude or fresh: a *saucy* answer. 2. Lively, jaunty: a *saucy* air. **saucier, sauciest.** —**saucily** *adverb.*

sauer·kraut (SOWR-krowt) *noun.* Cabbage that is shredded, salted, and steeped in its own juice until sour.

saun·ter (SAWN-tər) *verb.* To walk slowly and easily. **sauntered, sauntering.** —*noun.* A slow, easy walk.

sau·sage (SAW-sij) *noun.* Meat (usually pork) that is ground or chopped, flavored, and stuffed into a tube-like case. **sausages.**

sav·age (SAV-ij) *adjective.* 1. Wild; not tame: a *savage* beast. 2. Not civilized or educated; crude: a *savage* tribe. 3. Fierce; cruel: a *savage* blow. —*noun.* 1. An uncivilized person. 2. A cruel person. **savages.** —**savagely** *adverb.* —**savagery** (SAV-ij-ree) *noun.*

sa·van·na (sə-VAN-ə) Also **savannah** *noun.* A flat area, without trees, found in warm climates.

[1]**save** (SAYV) *verb.* 1. To rescue. 2. To keep safe: Jane *saved* all her old dolls in plastic bags. 3. To put away for another time: "A penny *saved* is a penny earned." (Benjamin Franklin). 4. To reduce; lessen: *save* time; *save* work. 5. (Religion) To free from eternal punishment for sin: Christians believe that Christ came to *save* all men. **saved, saving.**

[2]**save** (SAYV) *preposition.* Except: The guests are all here *save* one. —*conjunction.* But.

sav·ing (SAY-ving) *adjective.* 1. Referring to something that saves or rescues. 2. Referring to something that makes up for the lack of other things: Fine photography was the only *saving* quality of the boring movie. 3. Tending not to spend; thrifty: a *saving* person. —*noun.* 1. An act of thrift. 2. (Plural) The amount of money saved.

sav·ior (SAYV-yər) Also **saviour** *noun.* 1. One who saves or keeps from harm. 2. [Capital S] Jesus Christ.

sa·vor (SAY-vər) *noun.* The taste or smell (of something). —*verb.* To taste or smell with pleasure: Charlie *savored* his mother's beef stew. **savored, savoring.**

sa·vor·y (SAY-vər-ee) *adjective.* Pleasant to smell or taste.

[1]**saw** *noun.* A cutting tool whose long blade is edged with teeth-like points. —*verb.* 1. To cut with a saw. 2. To cut as with a saw: Jimmy *sawed* at the meat with a dull knife. **sawed, sawing.**

[2]**saw** *verb. See* **see.**

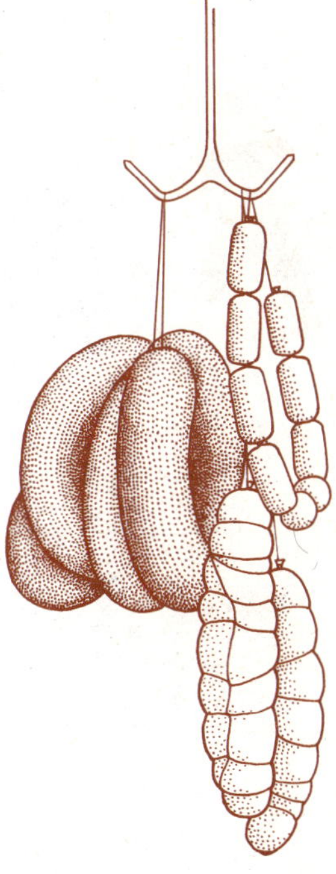
sausage

satyr

sawhorse

saxophone

scale of miles

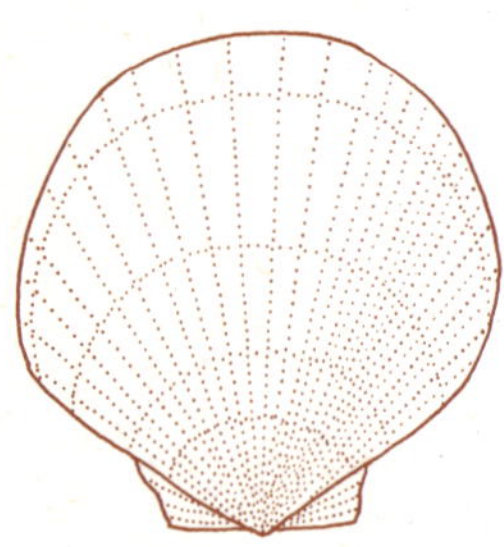

scallop

saw·buck (SAW-buhk) *noun.* 1. A sawhorse. 2. (Slang) A ten-dollar bill.

saw·dust (SAW-duhst) *noun.* The fine, dust-like pieces of wood that are made by sawing or sanding.

saw·horse (SAW-horss) *noun.* A rack for holding wood that is being cut.

saw·mill (SAW-mil) *noun.* A building or business where logs are sawed into lumber.

sax·o·phone (SAK-sə-fohn) *noun.* (Music) A brass, pipe-shaped musical wind instrument with finger keys and a single-reed mouthpiece.

say *verb.* 1. To speak: No one listens to what I *say.* 2. To put into words: You'll *say* you're sorry when you learn the truth! 3. To make a statement; give an opinion: I *say* you're not telling the truth. 4. To speak aloud (something that has been memorized): *say* a speech. 5. To guess or approximate: I'd *say* four inches of snow fell last night. **said, saying.** —*noun.* The chance to speak or give one's opinion: Let me have my *say.* —*adverb.* 1. Almost, about: I'll be ready in, *say,* an hour. 2. For example: If we were to go to, *say,* Utah, how many days would it take?

say·ing (SAY-ing) *noun.* A common or much-used phrase or expression, as a proverb.

scab (SKAB) *noun.* 1. A stiff, crusty covering that forms over a break in the skin. 2. (Informal) One who works while others are on strike.

scab·bard (SKAB-ərd) *noun.* A case or covering for a sword or knife.

scads (SKADZ) *noun, plural.* (Informal) A lot, many: *scads* of people.

scaf·fold (SKAF-əld or SKAF-ohld) *noun.* 1. A temporary supporting structure, usually of wood or metal, put up for workers on high buildings or rooms. 2. A high platform used for executions, usually by hanging.

scald (SKAWLD) *verb.* 1. To burn by a hot liquid or steam. 2. To heat almost to boiling. 3. To clean with boiling water. **scalded, scalding.** —*noun.* A burn from a liquid or steam.

scale (SKAYL) *noun.* 1. One of many hard, flat plates that cover certain animals, especially fish and reptiles. 2. A device for weighing. 3. Degree or extent: In Iowa corn is grown on a large *scale.* 4. The relationship between a map or model and the actual dimensions of what it represents: This map is drawn to a *scale* of one inch to every ten miles. 5. A series of marks for measuring or an instrument having such marks. 6. A sequence of eight musical notes; all notes of an octave. **scales.** —*verb.* 1. To climb: *scale* a ladder. 2. To remove scales from. **scaled, scaling.**

scal·lop (SKOL-əp or SKAL-əp) *noun.* 1. A common marine shellfish with a pair of hinged shells, each deeply grooved or "scalloped": The muscle of some *scallops* is good to eat. 2. Any wavy line or profile suggesting the edge of a scallop shell. —*verb.* 1. To give a wavy edge to: I *scalloped* the edges of my skirt. 2. To bake in a casserole dish with bread crumbs and sauce: *scallop* the tomatoes. **scalloped, scalloping.**

scalp (SKALP) *noun.* 1. The skin of the top and back of the head, where hair normally grows. 2. Any part of the scalp cut or torn off as a battle trophy. —*verb.* To remove the scalp from. **scalped, scalping.**

scal·pel (SKAL-pəl) *noun.* A small knife with a narrow, pointed blade, used in surgery.

scalper (SKALP-ər) *noun.* One who buys tickets or other items in short supply and sells them at a very high price for a quick profit.

scal·y (SKAYL-ee) *adjective.* 1. Covered with scales. 2. Covered with a flaky crust.

scamp (SKAMP) *noun.* A tricky person; a mischief-maker.

scam·per (SKAM-pər) *verb.* To run with quick, darting motions, like a mouse. **scampered, scampering.**

scan (SKAN) *verb.* 1. To examine all parts of with care: He *scanned* my face for some hint of my secret. 2. To measure the rhythm of (a poem): *Scan* the line to see whether it has four beats or five. 3. To read in a hurry. **scanned, scanning.**

scan·dal (SKAND-l) *noun.* 1. Any action that brings disgrace when it becomes known. 2. Public excitement caused by disgraceful action: The mayor resigned because of the *scandal.* 3. Gossip or public talk that hurts one's reputation; slander.

scan·dal·ize (SKAND-l-ighz) *verb.* To shock with disgraceful action. **scandalized, scandalizing.**

scan·dal·ous (SKAND-l-əss) *adjective.* Disgraceful; causing or resulting from scandal. —**scandalously** *adverb.*

scant (SKANT) *adjective.* 1. Not plentiful or abundant; small in amount: In the flooded areas food was *scant.* 2. Not quite full or adequate: The steak was labeled "1 lb." but actually weighed only a *scant* 15 ounces.

scan·ty (SKAN-tee) *adjective.* Scant; in short supply. —**scantier, scantiest.** —**scantily** *adverb.* —**scantiness** *noun.*

scape·goat (SKAYP-goht) *noun.* 1. Among the ancient Hebrews, a ritual goat that was blamed for the people's sins, then driven away. 2. A person, group of people, or thing that is blamed for the wrong-doings of others.

scar (SKAHR) *noun.* 1. A mark left on the skin by a sore or an injury after it heals. 2. A lasting mental or emotional injury resulting from an unhappy experience: People in slums may bear the *scars* of poverty. —*verb.* To form, or cause to form, a scar on. **scarred, scarring.**

scarce (SKAIRSS) *adjective.* Not plentiful; rare. —**scarcer, scarcest.** —**scarceness** *noun.*

scarcely (SKAIRSS-lee) *adverb.* By a small margin; hardly; barely.

scar·ci·ty (SKAIR-sə-tee) *noun.* State of being scarce; a lack: a *scarcity* of food. **scarcities.**

scare (SKAIR) *verb.* 1. To fill with fear; frighten. 2. To become fearful or frightened: You *scare* easily; little things frighten you. **scared, scaring.** —*noun.* Condition of being frightened; state of fear: The skidding car gave them a *scare.* **scares.** —**scarily** *adverb.* —**scary** *adjective.* —**scare up.** To find things that are in short supply.

scare·crow (SKAIR-kroh) *noun.* 1. An object, usually one that looks like a man, set up to scare away crows or other birds, as in a cornfield. 2. Someone who is thin, shabby, or queer-looking.

scarf (SKAHRF) *noun.* 1. A wide strip of cloth worn for warmth or as an ornament around the head, neck, shoulders, or waist; a muffler. 2. A cloth strip used as a cover for a table or dresser; a runner. —**scarfs** or **scarves** (SKAHRVZ) *plural.*

scar·let (SKAHR-lit) *noun.* (Also *adjective*) A bright red color like the blood from arteries.

scarlet fever. A highly contagious disease that produces a red rash, sore throat, and fever.

scat (SKAT) *interjection.* A word hissed sharply and loudly at a small animal, especially a cat, to chase it away. —*verb.* (Informal) To leave or move quickly. **scatted, scatting.**

scat·ter (SKAT-ər) *verb.* 1. To spread around; sprinkle: *scatter* seeds. 2. To move away, or cause to move away, in different directions; disperse: As the truck came down the street, the boys *scattered.* **scattered, scattering.**

scaffold

scarecrow

scat·ter·brain (SKAT-ər-brayn) *noun.* One who acts in a confused, disorganized way. —**scatterbrained** *adjective.*

schnauzer

scav·en·ger (SKAV-in-jər) *noun.* 1. An animal, such as the vulture, that feeds on dead animal or plant matter. 2. One who picks through trash for usable things.

scene (SEEN) *noun.* 1. A view; scenery. 2. The time and place of a drama, book, or movie. 3. One of the parts of an act in a play. 4. Any part of a drama or a book considered as a unit: The appearance of the ghost in "Hamlet" makes an exciting *scene.* 5. A show of bad temper or other strong feeling in public: Father made a *scene* when the waiter spilled the gravy. —**behind the scenes.** Not within view; secret.

scen·er·y (SEEN-ər-ee) *noun.* 1. Screens, doors, hangings, furniture, and other stage properties. 2. Natural features of a landscape: the mountain *scenery* of the Rockies.

scepter

sce·nic (SEE-nik) *adjective.* Relating to the natural features of the landscape, especially those that are beautiful and imposing. —**scenically** *adverb.*

scent (SENT) *noun.* 1. Odor, smell: Foxes have a strong *scent.* 2. A pleasant odor: The *scent* of roses came from the garden. 3. Perfume: Wendy likes her lilac *scent* best. 4. Sense of smell: Hunting dogs must have a sharp *scent.* —*verb.* 1. To smell: The dogs *scented* the deer. 2. To become aware of (something not very noticeable); to suspect: The police *scented* a plot to rob the bank. 3. To give a scent to. **scented, scenting.**

scep·ter (SEP-tər) Also **sceptre** *noun.* The staff carried by a king as a symbol of his high position and power.

sched·ule (SKEJ-ool) *noun.* 1. A list or chart showing the times at which various events will happen or things are to be done: The *schedule* shows that the plane is due at 5:10. 2. A list of items in detail: a price *schedule.* **schedules.** —*verb.* To place on or in a schedule. **scheduled, scheduling.**

scheme (SKEEM) *noun.* 1. A plan of action involving slyness or trickery; a clever plot. 2. An impractical plan or project: wild *schemes* for making money. 3. Any plan of action, especially if complicated. 4. An arrangement or pattern of related things: the color *scheme* of a living room. **schemes.** —*verb.* To prepare or carry out a scheme. **schemed, scheming.**

schnau·zer (SHNOW-zər) *noun.* A dog with short, stiff gray hair, originally bred in Germany.

schol·ar (SKOL-ər) *noun.* 1. A student or pupil, especially one with a strong interest in study and learning. 2. A learned person. —**scholarly** *adjective.*

schol·ar·ship (SKOL-ər-ship) *noun.* 1. Careful study or research: Sam is better in baseball than in *scholarship.* 2. Advanced knowledge; a great deal of learning. 3. A gift or grant of money to help a student pay the expenses of his education.

scho·las·tic (skə-LASS-tik) *adjective.* Referring to performance in studies at school, especially a school below college level: A good *scholastic* record helped Jim to get a college scholarship. —**scholastically** *adverb.*

school (SKOOL) *noun.* 1. An organization of teachers and students, with books and other items devoted to teaching and learning. 2. The experience of attending a school: Bill likes *school* better than doing chores on the farm. 3. The activities of a school: This year *school* will end on June 15. 4. A building or room used for a school: A new junior high *school* will be built next year. 5. An organization that specializes in the teaching of a special kind of knowledge: a *school* of art; a law *school.* 6. A group of persons devoted to a particular set of beliefs or practices: the avant-garde *school* of painting. *—verb.* To teach, educate. **schooled, schooling.**

school board. A group of citizens that directs a local school system.

school·book (SKOOL-buk) *noun.* A book used for teaching in a school; a textbook.

school·boy (SKOOL-boi) *noun.* A boy who attends a school.

school·girl (SKOOL-gerl) *noun.* A girl who attends a school.

school·house (SKOOL-howss) *noun.* A building used as a school, especially a small school building in the country. **schoolhouses.**

school·ing (SKOOL-ing) *noun.* Education in schools or from experience: ". . . all sorts of indoor and outdoor *schooling.*" (R. Frost).

school·mas·ter (SKOOL-mass-tər) *noun.* A male principal or teacher in a school.

school·mate (SKOOL-mayt) *noun.* One who attends school at the same time as someone else. **schoolmates.**

school·room (SKOOL-room) *noun.* A room used for teaching in a school.

school·teach·er (SKOOL-teech-ər) *noun.* A person who teaches in a school.

schoon·er (SKOON-ər) *noun.* A sailing ship with two or more masts.

schwa (SHWAH or SHVAH) *noun.* A symbol (ə) for a vowel sound that is not stressed or accented in a spoken word, such as the *e* in *scraper* or the *a* in *adrift.*

sci·ence (SIGH-ənss) *noun.* 1. The skill or art of learning by observing, testing, and thinking about natural phenomena in an orderly way. 2. A special area of this knowledge: social *science;* natural *science.*

science fiction. Fictional writing that is based on scientific or pseudoscientific facts.

sci·en·tif·ic (sigh-ən-TIF-ik) *adjective.* 1. Relating to science: Bill enjoys *scientific* hobbies such as chemistry. 2. Meeting the standards or tests of science: Astronomers say that astrology is not *scientific.* **—scientifically** *adverb.*

sci·en·tist (SIGH-ən-tist) *noun.* A person highly educated in science who works in some scientific field.

scis·sors (SIZ-ərz) *noun, plural.* A hand tool for cutting, consisting of two sharp-edged blades fastened together by a pivot so that they can be closed together on the material being cut.

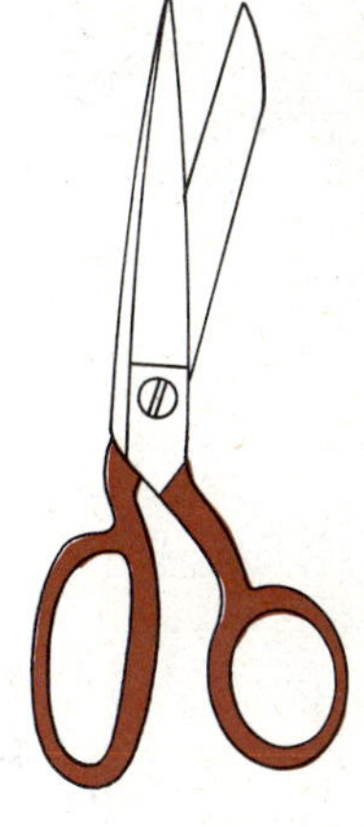

scissors

scoff (SKAWFF or SKOFF) *verb.* To show strong disbelief by scorn or mocking; make fun of: People once *scoffed* at the idea that man could journey to the moon. **scoffed, scoffing.**

scold (SKOHLD) *verb.* 1. To accuse or blame with loud, sharp words: The man *scolded* me for walking on his new grass. 2. To make excited, complaining noises: The blue jays started *scolding* when the cat appeared. **scolded, scolding.** *—noun.* A person who always scolds or finds fault with others.

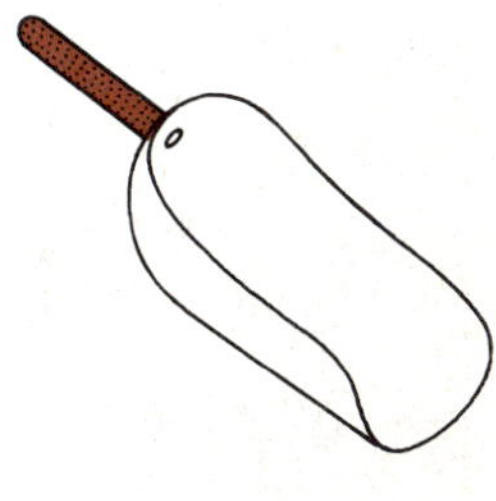

scoop

scoop (SKOOP) *noun.* 1. A spoon-like kitchen tool used for taking up loose material such as sugar, flour, or ice cream. 2. The material that fills a scoop: He took out three *scoops* of cranberries. 3. (Slang) Important or exciting news obtained and published by one newspaper (or other news medium) before others. *—verb.* 1. To lift material out or up, as with a scoop. 2. (Slang) To be ahead of other news media in publishing a piece of news. **scooped, scooping.**

scoot (SKOOT) *verb.* To run hurriedly; dart: The mouse *scooted* under the sofa. **scooted, scooting.**

schooner

scooter

Scorpio

scorpion

scoot·er (SKOOT-ər) *noun.* 1. A child's two-wheeled vehicle that has a footboard and a long handle used for steering. 2. A similar vehicle powered by a motor. 3. A sailboat with runners for travel on ice.

scope (SKOHP) *noun.* Extent; range: The *scope* of our science studies is much wider this year than last.

-scope *suffix.* Indicates a device used for seeing or discovering: tele*scope.*

scorch (SKORCH) *verb.* 1. To burn a little, especially on the outside; singe. 2. To heat to extreme dryness; shrivel with heat: The hot July sun *scorched* our lawn. **scorched, scorching.** —*noun.* A slight burn; extreme dryness or shriveling due to heating.

scorch·er (SKORCH-ər) *noun.* (Slang) A very hot day.

score (SKOR) *noun.* 1. The total number of points won in a game or other contest. 2. A grade on a test. 3. A debt or reckoning: an old *score* to be settled. 4. Reason, account: Karen's manners are not always perfect, but don't reject her on that *score.* 5. The number 20: "Four*score* and seven years ago, our fathers brought forth . . . a new nation. . . ." (Lincoln). 6. A written or printed copy of a musical composition, showing the part to be performed by each voice or instrument. 7. A cut or groove made by a pointed tool, as in leather, wood, or metal. **scores.** —*verb.* 1. To win (points) in a game or contest. 2. To obtain (a certain grade) in a test. 3. To prepare a score for (a musical composition). 4. To achieve: *score* a victory. 5. To mark with cuts or grooves. **scored, scoring.** —**know the score.** (Slang) To be aware (of what is happening).

scorn (SKORN) *verb.* To look upon with contempt as low and unworthy. **scorned, scorning.** —*noun.* 1. Contempt; disdain. 2. An object of scorn: Benedict Arnold became the *scorn* of all patriots. —**scornful** *adjective.* —**scornfully** *adverb.*

Scor·pi·o (SKOR-pee-oh) Also **Scorpius** *noun.* The eighth sign of the zodiac, also called the "Scorpion." The time of this sign is from October 23 through November 21.

scor·pi·on (SKOR-pee-ən) *noun.* A small animal of the spider family that has a poisonous sting at the end of its tail.

scoun·drel (SKOWN-drəl) *noun.* A person without honor or decency; a villain; a rascal.

[1]**scour** (SKOWR) *verb.* 1. To make clean by rubbing, as with a brush or cleanser: Jane *scoured* the frying pan with steel wool. 2. To clean thoroughly. **scoured, scouring.**

[2]**scour** (SKOWR) *verb.* To search quickly and thoroughly: The policemen *scoured* the hotel looking for the stolen jewels. **scoured, scouring.**

scout (SKOWT) *noun.* 1. A person who watches or explores, especially to learn what an enemy's activities are. 2. A person whose job is to discover or give an opinion about people with some special talent: a baseball *scout.* 3. [Capital S] A member of the Boy Scouts, Girl Scouts, or a similar organization. —*verb.* To act or serve as a scout. **scouted, scouting.**

scout·mas·ter (SKOWT-mass-tər) *noun.* An adult who is in charge of a group of Boy Scouts.

scow (SKOW) *noun.* A boat with a flat bottom and square ends, used to carry coal, sand, or similar cargo.

scowl (SKOWL) *verb.* To frown; make an angry or mean look. **scowled, scowling.** —*noun.* An angry or mean look; a frown.

[1]**scrab·ble** (SKRAB-əl) *verb.* 1. To scratch, as in search of something. 2. To struggle. **scrabbled, scrabbling.**

[2]**Scrab·ble** (SKRAB-əl) *trademark.* A game played on a board with

lettered tiles or pieces in which each player earns points for spelling out words with his tiles.

scram (SKRAM) *verb.* (Slang) To get away; leave quickly. **scrammed, scramming.**

scram·ble (SKRAM-bəl) *verb.* 1. To move quickly by running, crawling, or climbing. 2. To struggle or compete for something, often wildly: The children *scrambled* to be first in line. 3. To mix together (as eggs) for cooking. 4. To destroy the orderly arrangement of. **scrambled, scrambling** —*noun.* 1. A quick series of movements, as in running, crawling, or climbing. 2. A frantic struggle to gain or win something: The teams were in a *scramble* for the championship.

[1]**scrap** (SKRAP) *noun.* 1. A small piece; a bit: Tom tore his paper into *scraps.* 2. Leftover or unused material: The old car was torn apart and sold for *scrap.* 3. (Plural) Leftover pieces of food. —*verb.* 1. To put aside; throw away: The general *scrapped* the plan for the new attack. 2. To break up into parts that can be sold or thrown away: The junkman *scrapped* the old car. **scrapped, scrapping.**

[2]**scrap** (SKRAP) *noun.* A fight or quarrel. —*verb.* To fight or quarrel: The boys *scrapped* over which program they would watch. **scrapped, scrapping.** —**scrappy** *adjective.*

scrap·book (SKRAP-buk) *noun.* A book that contains blank pages on which newspaper clippings, pictures, and similar items can be mounted.

scrape (SKRAYP) *verb.* 1. To rub or move across with a sharp or rough object. 2. To remove by rubbing with a sharp or rough object: The workman *scraped* the old paint off the wall. 3. To scratch; rub the skin from: My sister *scraped* her knee when she fell. 4. To make a rough, unpleasant sound by moving or rubbing against: I heard Bob's chair *scrape* the floor when he got up. **scraped, scraping.** —*noun.* A fight or other difficult or unpleasant situation: The man got into a *scrape* with the police when he stole a car. **scrapes.** —**scrape up.** To gather with difficulty, a little at a time.

scratch (SKRACH) *verb.* 1. To make a slight cut or mark on: Bob *scratched* the table when he pushed the heavy bowl across it. 2. To make a cut or mark with fingernails or claws. 3. To scrape with the fingernails, as to stop an itch. 4. To cross out; make a mark through: The student *scratched* out "true" and wrote "false." 5. To remove, as from a race or election: The coach *scratched* his best runner from the mile run. 6. To write or draw quickly or carelessly; to scribble. **scratched, scratching.** —*noun.* 1. A slight cut or mark. 2. A harsh, unpleasant sound made by rubbing or moving over with a hard object: the *scratch* of chalk on the blackboard. **scratches.** —**start from scratch.** To start with nothing or begin with only the basic elements.

scrawl (SKRAWL) *verb.* To write or draw quickly or carelessly; to scribble. **scrawled, scrawling.** —*noun.* Careless or sloppy writing or drawing.

scraw·ny (SKRAW-nee) *adjective.* Very thin; skinny. **scrawnier, scrawniest.**

scream (SKREEM) *verb.* 1. To make a long, sharp cry, as from fear or pain: The girl *screamed* when she saw the rat. 2. To yell or shout: The sergeant *screamed* orders at the troops. **screamed, screaming.** —*noun.* 1. A long, sharp cry. 2. (Slang) A very funny person or event: The clown is a real *scream.*

screech (SKREECH) *verb.* To make a harsh, piercing noise: The train's wheels *screeched* to a stop. **screeched, screeching.** —*noun.* A harsh, piercing noise. **screeches.**

Scouts

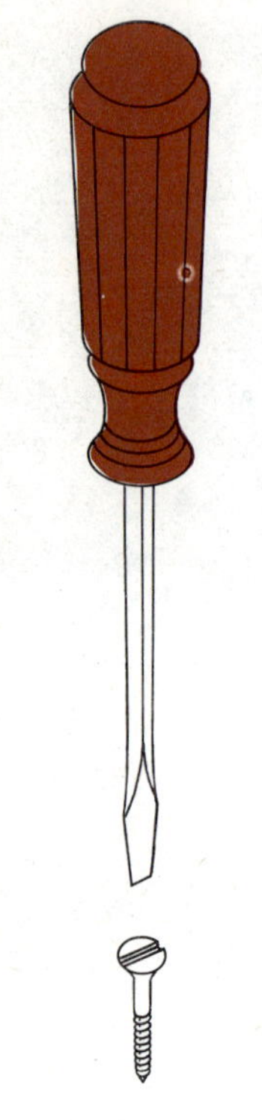
screwdriver and screw

screen (SKREEN) *noun.* 1. An object used to keep something from view or to divide an area: The model stepped behind a *screen* to change her gown. 2. A device made of fine, interwoven wires that is placed within a window frame to keep out insects. 3. Anything that hides or keeps from view: a smoke *screen.* 4. A flat, reflecting surface on which motion pictures or slides are shown. 5. The surface upon which an electronic image is projected: TV *screen.* —*verb.* To shield or keep from view: Heavy clouds *screened* the ships. **screened, screening.**

screw (SKROO) *noun.* 1. A metal, nail-like object that has a spiral thread or ridge winding around its length and is used for fastening things together. 2. A propeller, as on a ship or plane. —*verb.* 1. To fasten or join by twisting or turning: Jim *screwed* the cap back onto the jar. 2. To fasten or attach by a screw. 3. To twist or force into an odd shape: The child *screwed* his face into a frown. **screwed, screwing.**

screw·driver (SKROO-drigh-vər) *noun.* A tool used to turn a screw.

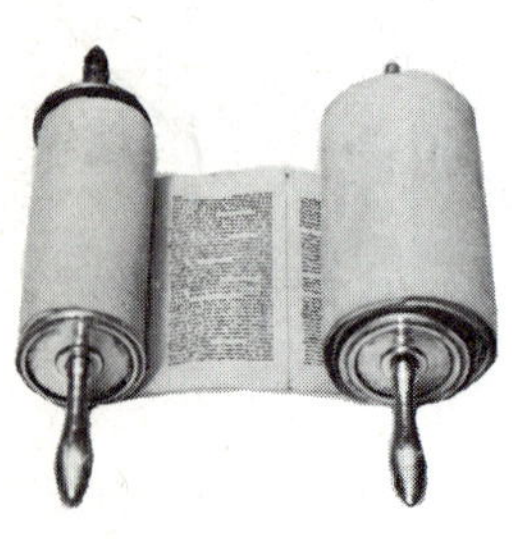
scroll

scrib·ble (SKRIB-əl) *verb.* 1. To write or draw quickly or carelessly; to scrawl. 2. To make marks that do not mean anything. **scribbled, scribbling.** —*noun.* Careless or sloppy writing or drawing; a scrawl.

scribe (SKRIGHB) *noun.* 1. A person whose job is to write or to copy writings. 2. In ancient Israel, a man who taught Jewish law. **scribes.**

scuba

scrim·mage (SKRIM-ij) *noun.* 1. A practice game, especially of football. 2. A struggle; fight. **scrimmages.** —*verb.* To play a practice game, especially in football. **scrimmaged, scrimmaging.**

script (SKRIPT) *noun.* 1. Handwriting: Was Joan's composition typewritten or in *script?* 2. A copy of a play or similar writing.

scroll (SKROHL) *noun.* 1. A roll of paper or similar material used for writing upon. 2. A design or ornament showing a scroll or partly unrolled scroll of paper.

[1]**scrub** (SKRUHB) *verb.* 1. To clean by rubbing hard, as with a mop or brush. 2. (Slang) To cancel; call off: The admiral *scrubbed* the attack. **scrubbed, scrubbing.**

[2]**scrub** (SKRUHB) *noun.* 1. A short undersized tree or shrub. 2. A growth of stunted trees or shrubs. 3. A substitute; anything undersized or inferior: When the first team opened up a big lead, the coach sent in the *scrubs.*

scruff (SKRUHF) *noun.* The nape or back of the neck.

scru·ple (SKROO-pəl) *noun.* 1. An idea based on morality or sense of rightness. 2. A doubt or feeling of guilt about one's acts or decisions. —**scrupulous** (SKROO-pyə-ləss) *adjective.* —**scrupulously** *adverb.*

scu·ba (SKOO-bə) *noun.* Acronym for *s*elf-*c*ontained *u*nderwater *b*reathing *a*pparatus—a device that supplies air to underwater swimmers.

scuff (SKUHF) *verb.* 1. To scrape or drag the feet when walking. 2. To cause a scraped or rough spot on: Tim *scuffed* his new shoes when he tripped. **scuffed, scuffing.** —*noun.* A scraped or rough spot.

scuf·fle (SKUHF-əl) *verb.* 1. To fight or struggle in a confused manner. 2. To shuffle; drag the feet. **scuffled, scuffling.** —*noun.* A confused fight or struggle. **scuffles.**

scull (SKUHL) *noun.* 1. An oar, especially one moved back and forth at the rear of a boat to move it forward. 2. A light, slender rowboat used for racing. —*verb.* To move a boat forward by a scull or sculls. **sculled, sculling.**

sculp·tor (SKUHLP-tər) *noun.* A person who makes sculpture or statues, as from marble or clay. —**sculpt** *verb.*

sculp·ture (SKUHLP-chər) *noun.* 1. The art or process of making statues, as by cutting stone or molding clay. 2. A statue or figure formed by cutting or molding. —*verb.* To make a statue or similar work. **sculptured, sculpturing.**

scum (SKUHM) *noun.* 1. A thin layer of waste matter that floats on top of a liquid: A green *scum* formed on the water in the swamp. 2. Very low or detestable people.

scur·ry (SKER-ee) *verb.* To move quickly; to hurry: The insect *scurried* over the picnic table. **scurried, scurrying.** —*noun.* Hasty movement: We watched the *scurry* of the squirrels when the dog approached.

scur·vy (SKER-vee) *noun.* A disease, brought on by a lack of vitamin C, that causes weakness, bleeding gums, and blemishes on the skin.

[1]**scut·tle** (SKUHT-l) *verb.* To sink (a ship) by letting water in through its side or bottom. **scuttled, scuttling.**

[2]**scut·tle** (SKUHT-l) *noun.* A bucket in which coal is held or carried.

[3]**scut·tle** (SKUHT-l) *verb.* To scamper; scurry. **scuttled, scuttling.**

scythe (SYTH) *noun.* A tool with a long handle and a long, curved metal blade, used for cutting hay or grain. **scythes.**

sea (SEE) *noun.* 1. The salt water that covers most of the earth and forms the oceans. 2. A large body of water, usually salt water: North *Sea*, Mediterranean *Sea*. 3. The surface condition of a body of water; waves: Heavy *seas* forced the small boat to return to port. 4. Something that resembles a sea in size or sweep: a *sea* of wheat.

sea anemone. A simple water animal that looks like a flower.

sea·coast (SEE-kohst) *noun.* Land that borders the sea.

sea·far·er (SEE-fair-ər) *noun.* A sailor or anyone who travels on the sea.

sea gull. A large water bird, usually white or gray and white, with long wings and webbed feet.

sea horse. A small fish with a plated body and a horse-like head.

[1]**seal** (SEEL) *noun.* 1. A design or symbol that is stamped on paper, wax, or other material in order to show official approval or ownership. 2. A device used to stamp an official symbol on something. 3. A paper, stamp, or other item that is marked with an official symbol. 4. Something that closes or keeps out air and water: a *seal* around a window. —*verb.* 1. To stamp or mark with a seal or symbol. 2. To close up; make tight: *seal* a letter. 3. To make definite or official: *seal* a deal with a handshake. **sealed, sealing.**

[2]**seal** (SEEL) *noun.* 1. A large sea mammal that has a sleek body with large flippers. 2. The fur of the seal. —*verb.* To hunt seals. **sealed, sealing.**

sea level. The average level of the sea's surface; used as a reference point in measuring the height of land or the depth of the ocean.

sea lion. A large brown seal of the Northern Pacific coast.

seal·skin (SEEL-skin) *noun.* The skin or fur of the seal.

Sea·ly·ham terrier (SEE-lee-ham TEHR-ee-ər). A dog with white, stiff hair, short legs, and a long head.

seam (SEEM) *noun.* 1. A line formed when pieces of material are sewed or joined together. 2. A layer, as of rock. —*verb.* To form a seam or line. **seamed, seaming.**

sea·man (SEE-mən) *noun.* 1. A sailor. 2. In the Navy, a sailor who is not an officer. —**seamen** *plural.*

sea·man·ship (SEE-mən-ship) *noun.* The skill or ability necessary to operate a boat or ship.

seam·stress (SEEM-striss) *noun.* A woman who makes a living by sewing. **seamstresses.**

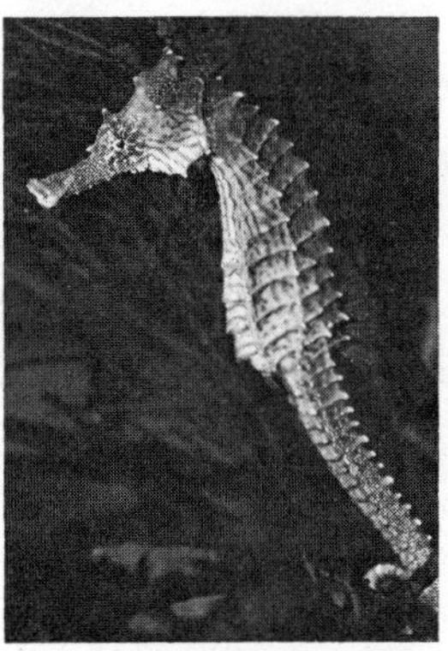
sea horse

seals

Sealyham terrier

seaplane

sea·plane (SEE-playn) *noun.* An airplane that is able to take off and land on water. **seaplanes.**

sea·port (SEE-port) *noun.* A coastal harbor or city with a port where ships can dock.

sear (SIHR) *verb.* 1. To dry up; wither; Autumn *seared* the leaves. 2. To burn or scorch. **seared, searing.**

search (SERCH) *verb.* 1. To look for, to hunt. 2. To examine, look into: *search* one's memory. **searched, searching.** —*noun.* The act of hunting or seeking. **searches.**

searchlight

search·light (SERCH-light) *noun.* A powerful light that can be beamed in any direction.

sea·shell (SEE-shel) *noun.* The shell of a mollusk or other marine organism.

sea·shore (SEE-shor) *noun.* Land bordering the ocean; beach.

sea·sick (SEE-sik) *adjective.* Having an illness caused by the rolling of a ship or boat.—**seasickness** *noun.*

sea·side (SEE-sighd) *noun.* Shore of the ocean; beach. **seasides.**

seaweed

sea·son (SEE-zən) *noun.* 1. One of the four time periods within a year: The four *seasons* are spring, summer, fall, and winter. 2. A time of the year during which there is a special activity: the holiday *season.* —*verb.* 1. To add spice or flavoring: I *season* my food with salt and pepper. 2. To add interest: The old captain *seasoned* his conversation with tales of the sea. 3. To age or allow to dry: It is best to *season* wood before using it. 4. To become adjusted or used to something. **seasoned, seasoning.** —**seasonal** (SEE-zən-l) *adjective.* —**seasonally** *adverb.*

sea·son·ing (SEE-zə-ning) *noun.* A flavoring or spice used to improve the taste of food.

seat (SEET) *noun.* 1. A place to sit; a chair, stool, or bench. 2. The part of the body used for sitting, or the part of clothing that covers it. 3. A position or office: He was elected to a *seat* on the school board. 4. Headquarters or center: a *seat* of national government. 5. Cause or source: the *seat* of trouble. —*verb.* 1. To sit or to help one sit: The waiter *seated* us next to the window. 2. To have places to sit: The church will *seat* 300 people. **seated, seating.**

seat belt. A safety strap used to hold a person in the seat of a vehicle.

sea urchin. A spiny shellfish.

sea·weed (SEE-weed) *noun.* Any of various plants that grow in the sea.

sea·wor·thy (SEE-wer-thee) *adjective.* Fit or safe for travel on water. —**seaworthiness** *noun.*

sec *abbreviation.* A second (unit of time or of measure of angles). —*noun.* (Informal). A moment.

sec. Also **secy.** *abbreviation.* Secretary.

se·cede (si-SEED) *verb.* To withdraw from a group. **seceded, seceding.**

se·ces·sion (si-SESH-ən) *noun.* 1. The act of withdrawing or getting out. 2. [Capital S] The act of 11 Southern states in withdrawing from the Union during the 1860's.

se·clud·ed (si-KLOO-did) *adjective.* 1. Far from others; alone: a *secluded* cottage. 2. Hidden from view.

se·clu·sion (si-KLOO-zhən) *noun.* Privacy; a place away from others.

[1]**sec·ond** (SEK-ənd) *noun.* 1. One of the 60 parts into which a minute is divided. 2. Any very short period of time: It will only take a *second.* 3. (Geometry) One of 60 equal parts in one minute of angular measurement.

[2]**sec·ond** (SEK-ənd) *noun.* 1. An object that is not perfect: The shoe store is having a sale of *seconds.* 2. One who will help if needed: Each of the fighters chose a *second.* —*adjective.* 1. Coming next after first:

second grade. 2. (Music) Referring to a part that is played or sung below the first, or top, line of notes. —*verb.* To support or give aid. **seconded, seconding.** —**secondly** *adverb.* —**second the motion.** In a meeting, to give support to a formal suggestion or motion.

sec·on·dar·y (SEK-ən-dehr-ee) *adjective.* 1. Not first in importance: *secondary* roads. 2. Next in order to first or primary: High schools are called *secondary* schools. —*noun.* (Football) The backfield. **secondaries.**—**secondarily** *adverb.*

sec·ond-class (sek-ənd-KLASS) *adjective.* 1. Not of first quality; inferior. 2. Next below first class.

sec·ond-hand (sek-ənd-HAND) *adjective.* Not new, used first by another: a *second-hand* car. —*adverb.* Not directly from the source: We received the news *second-hand.*

second hand. The hand on a clock or watch that shows the passing of seconds.

second-rate (sek-ənd-RAYT) *adjective.* Not the best; inferior.

se·cre·cy (SEE-krə-see) *noun.* 1. The condition of hiding or being kept hidden. 2. The tendency to conceal.

se·cret (SEE-krit) *noun.* 1. Knowledge that is kept from others: "No one ever keeps a *secret* so well as a child." (Hugo). 2. A mystery: *secrets* of the universe. 3. A successful way or method: The *secret* of good health is taking care of yourself. —*adjective.* 1. Hidden. 2. Keeping to oneself; quiet. 3. Mysterious. 4. Shared by very few: *secret* code. —**secretly** *adverb.*

sec·re·tar·y (SEK-rə-tehr-ee) *noun.* 1. One who writes letters and keeps records for another person or an organization. 2. The head of a department of the government: *Secretary* of the Treasury. 3. A desk with a bookcase on top. **secretaries.**

se·crete (si-KREET) *verb.* 1. To hide (something). 2. To produce and give off (a substance). **secreted, secreting**

se·cre·tion (si-KREE-shən) *noun.* 1. The act of hiding (something). 2. A substance given off by certain plant or animal cells: Tears are a *secretion* from a gland in the eye. 3. The act of forming and giving off such a substance.

sect (SEKT) *noun.* A small group of people holding certain beliefs within a larger group, especially a religious group; a faction.

sec·tion (SEK-shən) *noun.* 1. A part or division. 2. An area of a country, state, or city: They live in the northwest *section* of the city. 3. The inside of a solid object shown by a cut or the drawing of such a cut: The picture shows a *section* of a baseball. 4. A division of land equal to one square mile. —*verb.* To separate or divide: Ropes were used to *section* off the parking lot. **sectioned, sectioning.**

sec·tor (SEK-tər or SEK-tor) *noun.* 1. The part of a circle made by two radii and the arc they cut: A *sector* is shaped like a piece of pie. 2. A zone or area in which a military unit operates. —*verb.* To divide into sectors. **sectored, sectoring.**

sec·u·lar (SEK-yə-lər) *adjective.* Relating to something other than the church or religion: A hymn is sacred music; a show tune is *secular* music. —**secularly** *adverb.*

se·cure (si-KYUR) *adjective.* 1. Safe; free from doubt or fear. 2. Strong, sturdy: The bridge seems *secure.* 3. Fastened tightly: The barn door is *secure.* —*verb.* 1. To tie down; lock, fasten, or otherwise protect from danger. 2. To get: I wish to *secure* a copy of today's paper. 3. To bring about: The senator hopes to *secure* the passage of the bill. 4. To stand behind; guarantee. **secured, securing.** —**securely** *adverb.*

secretary (definition 3)

se·cu·ri·ty (si-KYUR-ə-tee) *noun.* 1. The state of being safe; freedom from fear or doubt. 2. Protection: The guard promised round-the-clock *security.* 3. An object that will be given up if a debt is not paid: He borrowed ten dollars and put up his watch as *security.* 4. (Usually plural) Papers showing ownership, especially of stocks or bonds. **securities.**

se·dan (si-DAN) *noun.* 1. A closed, hard-topped automobile, usually having back and front seats. 2. Formerly, an enclosed chair carried on poles by two or more persons.

sedge

se·date (si-DAYT) *adjective.* Calm and serious. *—verb.* To calm or give a calming medicine (to). **sedated, sedating. —sedately** *adverb.* **—sedation** *noun.* **—sedative** (SED-ə-tiv) *noun* and *adjective.*

Se·der (SAY-dər) *noun.* A Jewish feast celebrated on the first two evenings of Passover in honor of the Israelites' departure from Egypt.

sedge (SEJ) *noun.* A grassy plant that grows on wet ground: *Sedges* are sometimes called "cattails." **sedges.**

sed·i·ment (SED-ə-mənt) *noun.* 1. Solid particles that float in or settle to the bottom of a liquid. 2. Material left behind by wind or water: The delta of a river is built of *sediment.* **—sedimentary** (sed-ə-MEN-tə-ree or sed-ə-MEN-tree) *adjective.*

seesaw

se·di·tion (si-DISH-ən) *noun.* An act that may lead to the overthrow of a government.

se·di·tious (si-DISH-əss) *adjective.* Causing rebellion against a government.

se·duce (si-DOOSS or si-DYOOSS) *verb.* To tempt; encourage (another) to do a wrong thing. **seduced, seducing. —seduction** (si-DUHK-shən) *noun.*

[1]**see** *verb.* 1. To sense by using the eyes: I *see* the moon. 2. To understand: We *see* what you mean. 3. To spend time with, visit. 4. To experience, undergo: *see* much joy. 5. To show the way; go with: Always *see* your guests to the door. 6. To imagine, predict: He *sees* men landing on Jupiter in the next century. 7. To take care or make sure: *See* that the fire is out before leaving camp. 8. Look, notice: *See* the squirrel! 9. To turn or refer to: *See* page 11. **saw, seen, seeing.**

[2]**see** *noun.* The area over which a church bishop has charge. **sees.**

seed *noun.* 1. The part of a plant that is able to produce the offspring or young plant. 2. Any offspring or young. 3. The beginning of anything: the *seed* of an idea. **seeds or seed** *plural.* *—verb.* 1. To plant with seed, sow. 2. To scatter small particles or bits into: The pilot *seeded* the clouds with ice particles to produce rain. 3. To remove the seeds from. 4. (Sports) To arrange a contest so that the best performers do not meet until late in the event. **seeded, seeding. —go to seed.** 1. To ripen fully. 2. To become useless.

seed·case (SEED-kayss) *noun.* A pod or protective covering for a number of seeds. **seedcases.**

seed·ling (SEED-ling) *noun.* A young plant that grows from a seed.

seek *verb.* 1. To search (for); try to find. 2. To try to get: *seek* employment. **sought** (SAWT), **seeking.**

seem *verb.* 1. To appear; have the look of: The dog *seems* to be sick. 2. To appear to be true: It *seems* hot. **seemed, seeming.**

seem·ing (SEE-ming) *adjective.* apparent. **—seemingly** *adverb.*

seen *verb. See* **see.**

seep *verb.* To leak; flow through slowly. **seeped, seeping. —seepage** *noun.*

seer (SIHR) *noun.* One who tells what will happen in the future.

see·saw (SEE-saw) *noun.* A teeter-totter; a board supported in the center on which children ride alternately up and down. *—adjective.* Up-and-down or back-and-forth. *—verb.* 1. To go up and down on a seesaw. 2. To be undecided; to go back and forth from one position to another. **seesawed, seesawing.**

seethe (SEETH) *verb.* 1. To boil or have the appearance of boiling. 2. To be very angry or excited. **seethed, seething.**

seg·ment (SEG-mənt) *noun.* One of the parts into which a thing is divided. *—verb.* To divide or separate into sections: *segment* an orange. **segmented, segmenting.**

seg·re·ga·tion (seg-rə-GAY-shən) *noun.* 1. The act of separating or setting apart. 2. The practice of separating people socially by race or skin color. **—segregate** *verb.*

seismic waves (SIGHZ-mik). The vibrations caused by an earthquake or an underground explosion.

seis·mo·graph (SIGHZ-mə-graf) *noun.* An instrument that records seismic waves giving time, direction, and other details of the movements.

seize (SEEZ) *verb.* 1. To grasp suddenly: He *seized* me by the arm. 2. To capture: The enemy *seized* the fort. 3. To overcome, as with a strong feeling: "Love *seized* me strongly." (Dante). **seized, seizing.**

sei·zure (SEE-zhər) *noun.* 1. The act of grabbing or capturing. 2. An attack of illness: a heart *seizure.*

sel·dom (SEL-dəm) *adverb.* Not often.

se·lect (si-LEKT) *verb.* To pick or choose. **selected, selecting.** *—adjective.* 1. Best; highest in quality. 2. Chosen, preferred.

se·lec·tion (si-LEK-shən) *noun.* 1. The act of choosing. 2. The thing chosen. 3. A collection from which a choice may be made: The furniture store has a large *selection* of tables. 4. A piece of literature or music to be performed: Each piano pupil played one *selection.*

self *noun.* 1. The complete and individual make-up of a person. 2. A person's character or personality: The *self* he showed at work was different from the *self* his family knew. 3. Personal welfare or interests: The miser lived for *self* alone. **—selves** (SELVZ) *plural.*

self- *prefix.* Indicates action referring back to oneself: *self*-criticism.

self-confidence (SELF-KON-fə-dənss) *noun.* Faith in one's own ability.

self-conscious (SELF-KON-shəss) *adjective.* Too aware of one's own appearance and actions; ill at ease. **—self-consciously** *adverb.*

self-control (self-kən-TROHL) *noun.* The ability to handle one's feelings and actions **—self-controlled** *adjective.*

self-employed (self-em-PLOID) *adjective.* Earning a living by oneself; being one's own boss.

self-gov·ern·ment (SELF-GUHV-ərn-mənt) *noun.* Rule by the people; democracy as opposed to dictatorship or rule by another country.

self-im·por·tant (self-im-PORT-nt) *adjective.* Having too high an opinion of one's own importance.

self·ish (SEL-fish) *adjective.* Concerned only with oneself; not considerate of others. **—selfishly** *adverb.* **—selfishness** *noun.*

self-pol·li·na·tion (self-pol-ə-NAY-shən) *noun.* (Botany) The transfer of pollen from a stamen to a stigma on the same plant.

self-re·spect (self-ri-SPEKT) *noun.* A feeling of respect for one's own worth; self-esteem.

self·same (SELF-saym) *adjective.* Identical; the same.

sell (SEL) *verb.* 1. To offer for sale; give in exchange for money. 2. To be offered for sale: Strawberries *sell* at a high price in the winter. **sold** (SOHLD), **selling.** **—sell out.** (Slang) To betray.

selves (SELVZ). *See* **self.**

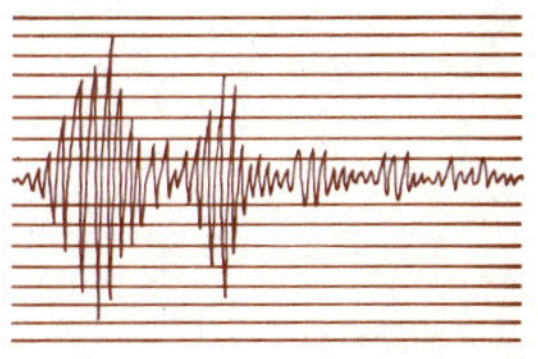

seismograph record

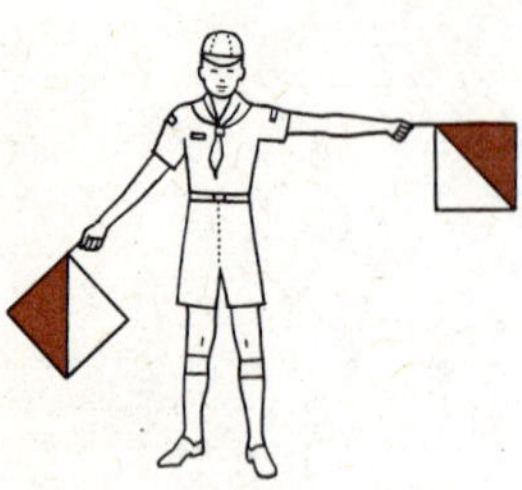
semaphore

sem·a·phore (SEM-ə-for) *noun.* A signal system or device using flags, lights, or arms in various positions to send messages. **semaphores.**

se·mes·ter (sə-MESS-tər) *noun.* Either of two periods of time into which a school year may be divided.

semi- *prefix.* Indicates: 1. Partly; a part of: *semi*conscious. 2. One-half: *semi*circle. 3. Happening two times within a certain period of time: *semi*monthly.

sem·i·cir·cle (SEM-i-ser-kəl) *noun.* Half a circle. **semicircles.**

sem·i·co·lon (SEM-i-koh-lən) *noun.* A mark (;) used to separate complete thoughts within a sentence.

sem·i·nar·y (SEM-ə-nehr-ee) *noun.* 1. A school where people are prepared for religious careers. 2. A private school, especially one for older girls. **seminaries.**

Senate

sem·i·tone (SEM-ee-tohn) *noun. See* **half tone.**

sen·ate (SEN-it) *noun.* 1. An elected group that makes laws. 2. [Capital S] The upper branch of the legislature in some countries and states.

sen·a·tor (SEN-ə-tər) *noun.* 1. An official who is elected to a senate: A *senator* votes on legislation. 2. [Capital S] A member of the United States Senate or the senate of one of the states.

send *verb.* To make someone or something go or be taken from one place to another; convey: *Send* him to the store. **sent, sending.**

sen·ior (SEEN-yər) *adjective.* 1. Identifying the older of two people with the same name, as father and son: Tom Brown, *Senior* is the father of Tom, Junior. 2. Of higher rank, office, or length of service: He is the *senior* man in the business. 3. Referring to the last year of high school or college. —*noun.* 1. One who is older or of higher rank. 2. Someone in the final year of high school or college.

se·ñor (sayn-YOHR) *noun.* The Spanish word for *Mr.* or *sir*, used as a term of address or title: *Señor* Rodrigues is waiting. —**señores** (sayn-YOH-rayss) *plural.*

se·ño·ra (sayn-YOHR-ə) *noun.* The Spanish word for *Mrs.* or *madam.*

se·ño·ri·ta (sayn-yohr-EE-tə) *noun.* The Spanish word for *Miss.*

sen·sa·tion (sen-SAY-shən) *noun.* 1. A mental or bodily feeling. 2. Something that causes a great stir or excitement: The band was a *sensation* in New York.

sen·sa·tion·al (sen-SAY-shən-l) *adjective.* 1. Arousing strong emotions; wonderful; marvelous. 2. Designed or created to be shocking. —**sensationally** *adverb.*

sense (SENSS) *noun.* 1. A feeling; sensation: a *sense* of dread. 2. Judgment; intelligence: common *sense.* 3. A physical ability or function allowing one to be aware of things about him: Our five *senses* are sight, hearing, taste, smell, and touch. 4. A special understanding, awareness, or ability: a *sense* of rhythm. 5. A moral or ethical attitude or feeling: a *sense* of responsibility. 6. Meaning: the *sense* of a word. **senses.** —*verb.* To feel; be aware of; realize. **sensed, sensing.**

sen·si·ble (SEN-sə-bəl) *adjective.* 1. Reasonable; using sound judgment: Be *sensible* and come in out of the rain! 2. Able to receive sensations; aware. —**sensibility** (SEN-sə-BIL-ə-tee) *noun.* —**sensibly** *adverb.*

sen·si·tive (SEN-sə-tiv) *adjective.* 1. Capable of intense feeling; tenderhearted; very aware: Poets are usually *sensitive* people. 2. Easily affected by something: Her throat was *sensitive* to smoke. 3. Easily hurt; touchy: a *sensitive* child. —**sensitively** *adverb.* —**sensitivity** (sen-sə-TIV-ə-tee) *noun.*

sen·so·ry (SEN-sə-ree) *adjective.* Referring to the senses.

sent *verb. See* **send.**

sen·tence (SEN-tənss) *noun.* 1. A series of words expressing a single complete thought and ending with a period, an exclamation point, or a question mark. 2. A prison term or other punishment for wrongdoing determined by a court or judge. **sentences.** *—verb.* To set the terms of punishment: The judge *sentenced* the burglar. **sentenced, sentencing.**

sen·ti·ment (SEN-tə-mənt) *noun.* 1. Feelings of tenderness or affection; a romantic idea or notion. 2. A strong feeling or opinion: There was strong *sentiment* in favor of passage of the bill. 3. A thought or attitude based on emotion rather than reason.

sen·ti·men·tal (sen-tə-MENT-l) *adjective.* 1. Emotional; given to tender feelings and affection. 2. Appealing to romantic, often overemotional feelings: *sentimental* music. **—sentimentally** *adverb.*

sen·ti·nel (SEN-tə-nəl) *noun.* A guard; a soldier on watch duty.

sen·try (SEN-tree) *noun.* A sentinel; one who keeps watch. **sentries.**

se·pal (SEE-pəl) *noun.* In a flower, one of the leaves that form the calyx, which covers the corolla.

sep·a·rate (SEP-ə-rayt) *verb.* 1. To divide by placing a barrier between; be the barrier between. 2. To sort into different groups: Mother *separated* the laundry into five piles. 3. To part; no longer be together. **separated, separating.** —(SEP-ə-rit) *adjective.* 1. Unconnected; not shared; divided. 2. Single; individual. **—separately** *adverb.* **—separation** (sep-ə-RAY-shən) *noun.*

sep·a·ra·tor (SEP-ə-ray-tər) *noun.* A mechanical device for separating cream from milk.

Sep·tem·ber (sep-TEM-bər) *noun.* The ninth month of the year: There are 30 days in *September.* **—Sept.** *abbreviation.*

sep·ul·cher (SEP-əl-kər) *noun.* A burial place; a tomb or grave.

se·quel (SEE-kwəl) *noun.* 1. A new story that comes after an earlier one; a continuation using the same characters in a new plot: "Jo's Boys" is a *sequel* to "Little Women." 2. A consequence; an event that logically follows an earlier one.

se·quence (SEE-kwənss) *noun.* 1. A regular order; set arrangement: She piled the newspapers in *sequence* according to dates. 2. A number of connected incidents: a strange *sequence* of events. **sequences.**

se·quoi·a (si-KWOI-ə) *noun.* A giant evergreen tree of California.

se·ra·pe (sə-RAH-pee) *noun.* A woolen blanket, often fringed, worn over the shoulders as an article of clothing: The *serape* is worn in Mexico and Latin America.

ser·e·nade (sehr-ə-NAYD or SEHR-ə-nayd) *noun.* 1. A song or musical piece performed usually as a romantic offering to a lady. 2. A light, sentimental musical work. **serenades.** *—verb.* To sing or perform a musical piece, especially to a lady. **serenaded, serenading.**

se·rene (si-REEN) *adjective.* 1. Calm; quiet; peaceful. 2. Bright; clear: *serene* as a cloudless sky. **—serenely** *adverb.*

se·ren·i·ty (si-REN-ə-tee) *noun.* Peacefulness; calm; the state of being serene.

serf *noun.* A slave, particularly one who farmed the land for a master during the Middle Ages.

serge (SERJ) *noun.* A durable woolen cloth, often used in men's clothing.

ser·geant (SAHR-jənt) *noun.* 1. A soldier in the military with rank above a corporal but below a lieutenant. 2. A police officer who ranks above a regular policeman.

se·ri·al (SIHR-ee-əl) *noun.* Something presented one part at a time, as a magazine story or a TV drama.

sequoia

serape

se·ries (SIHR-eez) *noun.* A number of similar happenings or related items that follow one another: Our school planned a *series* of folk concerts. —**series** *plural.*

se·ri·ous (SIHR-ee-əss) *adjective.* 1. Grave; critical: a *serious* illness. 2. Thoughtful; solemn: a *serious* expression. 3. Important, momentous: Her first recital was a *serious* occasion. 4. Sincere; in earnest: Are you *serious* about running for office? —**seriously** *adverb.* —**seriousness** *noun.*

ser·mon (SER-mən) *noun.* 1. A speech, usually on religious matters, given by a minister to his congregation. 2. Any serious talk or speech.

ser·pent (SER-pənt) *noun.* A snake, especially a large one.

se·rum (SIHR-əm) *noun.* 1. The yellowish liquid part of the blood that remains after clotting. 2. Fluid from immunized animals used for the prevention or cure of disease. —**serums** or **sera** (SIHR-ə) *plural.*

serv·ant (SER-vənt) *noun.* A person employed to care for someone else's house or to perform personal services, as a maid or chauffeur.

serve (SERV) *verb.* 1. To wait on; take care of: The store clerk *served* his customers promptly. 2. To be useful; provide a needed service: That fire station *serves* the west side of town. 3. To set, place, or pass food before someone. 4. To give or spend time in military service, an elected office, or a prison. 5. To act as; be suitable for: The pile of wood *served* as a ladder. 6. In some ball games, to start the play: Jill *serves* a tennis ball with accuracy and speed. **served, serving.** —*noun.* A play in some sports, as tennis. **serves.** —**serve one right.** To treat justly, especially through deserved punishment or disappointment.

serv·ice (SER-viss) *noun.* 1. Aid or help given to others: You can be of *service.* 2. (Plural) Work done for others: Mother decided that the leaky pipe called for the *services* of a plumber. 3. The military; armed forces. 4. A religious ceremony or a meeting for prayer. 5. Household employment: Mr. Hoskins had a favorite butler in his *service* for many years. 6. A set of dishes or tableware. 7. The act of waiting on someone, as at a restaurant or store. 8. The act of placing the ball in play in tennis, badminton, and other games. **services.** —*verb.* 1. To keep in order; to fix. 2. To provide or supply with a service. **serviced, servicing.**

ser·vice·a·ble (SER-viss-ə-bəl) *adjective.* Able to be used.

ser·vile (SER-vəl or SER-vighl) *adjective.* Acting like a servant or slave; humble or submissive.

ser·vi·tude (SER-və-tood or SER-və-tyood) *noun.* Forced labor or slavery.

ses·sion (SESH-ən) *noun.* 1. A meeting or series of meetings. 2. The period of time during which a meeting or activity takes place. 3. A school day or term: the spring *session.*

set *verb.* 1. To put or place: *Set* the dish on the table. 2. To become firm, change from a liquid to a solid. 3. To arrange in a special way or place in the proper position: *set* a clock. 4. To place or sit on eggs for hatching. 5. To fit words and music together: *set* words to music. 6. To fix or establish: Who *sets* the price of gold? 7. To select type or place it in position: The printers *set* this dictionary in two columns of type. 8. To go out of sight below the horizon: The sun *set.* 9. To plant. **set, setting.** —*noun.* 1. The act or condition of being fixed or in place: the *set* of sails. 2. A group of people or things that belong together: a new *set* of dishes. 3. (Math) An arbitrary collection, as of numbers or things, viewed as a unit. 4. The surroundings or scenery for a play or movie. 5. A piece of equipment made up of many parts: radio and TV *sets.* 6. The way in which a part of the body is carried or held. 7. A young plant or seedling: onion *sets.* —*adjective.* 1. Firm, solid. 2. Established: a *set* time. 3. Ready: Are you *set* to go? —**set down.** Put in writing. —**set forth.** 1. To begin; start out. 2. To declare —**set up.** 1. To arrange. 2. To put in an upright position.

set·back (SET-bak) *noun.* An unexpected stop or difficulty in progress: a *setback* in plans.

set·tee (set-TEE) *noun.* 1. A small couch. 2. A bench with a back.

set·ter (SET-ər) *noun.* Any of a number of breeds of long-haired dogs, trained to find and point to game.

set·ting (SET-ing) *noun.* 1. The act of placing or putting. 2. The silverware and china placed on a dinner table. 3. The place and time in which a story or play unfolds. 4. Stage scenery. 5. The metal frame that holds a jewel. 6. The eggs on which a hen sets. 7. The sinking below the horizon of the sun or the moon. 8. Music written to fit a poem or play.

set·tle (SET-l) *verb.* 1. To come to rest; to sink. 2. To make or become comfortable. 3. To quiet or calm. 4. To come to an agreement; to end (an argument). 5. To pay: *settle* bills. 6. To make a place to live; start a new community. **settled, settling.**

set·tle·ment (SET-l-mənt) *noun.* 1. A new town or village. 2. A movement of people to a place to live: the *settlement* of the West. 3. The end of an argument or disagreement. 4. A community center where people may go for help and recreation. Also called "settlement house."

set·tler (SET-l-ər) *noun.* A person who moves to an undeveloped area or country to live.

sev·en (SEV-ən) *noun* (and *adjective*). The cardinal number after six and before eight; 7.

sev·en·teen (sev-ən-TEEN) *noun* (and *adjective*). The cardinal number after 16 and before 18; 17.

sev·en·teenth (sev-ən-TEENTH) *adjective.* Coming next after 16th; 17th. —*noun.* One of 17 equal parts.

sev·enth (SEV-ənth) *adjective.* Coming next after sixth; 7th. —*noun.* One of seven equal parts.

sev·en·ti·eth (SEV-ən-tee-ith) *adjective.* Coming next after 69th; 70th. —*noun.* One of 70 equal parts.

sev·en·ty (SEV-ən-tee) *noun* (and *adjective*). The cardinal number after 69 and before 71; 70.

sev·er (SEV-ər) *verb.* 1. To cut or separate. 2. To end (a relationship). **severed, severing.**

sev·er·al (SEV-ər-əl) *adjective.* 1. A few, not many. 2. Separate; different. —**severally** *adverb.*

se·vere (sə-VIHR) *adjective.* 1. Strict; stern. 2. Hard; intense: a *severe* storm. 3. Plain; not fancy. 4. Difficult: a *severe* test of strength. **severer, severest.** —**severely** *adverb.* —**severity** (sə-VEHR-ə-tee) *noun.*

sew (SOH) *verb.* 1. To fasten or fix by using a needle and thread. 2. To make stitches by hand or with a sewing machine. **sewed, sewed** or **sewn, sewing.** —**sew up.** (Slang) To finish; make sure of.

sew·age (SOO-ij) *noun.* The waste carried away by a sewer.

sew·er (SOO-ər) *noun.* A drainpipe used to carry away waste material.

sew·ing (SOH-ing) *noun.* 1. The act of making stitches or the stitches themselves. 2. The article being sewed.

sex (SEKS) *noun.* One of two groups into which most living things are divided according to their part in producing offspring: The two *sexes* are male and female. **sexes.** —**sexual** (SEK-shoo-al) *adjective.*

setter

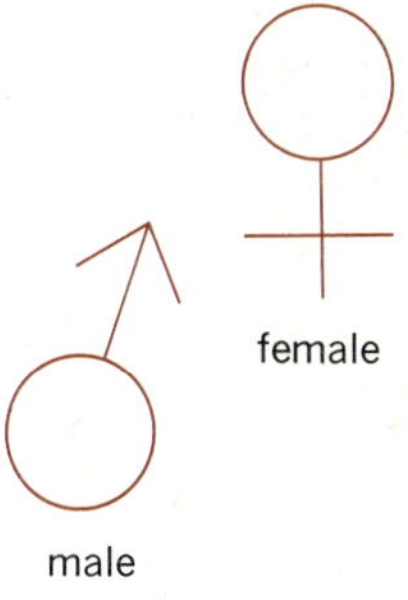

symbols for sex

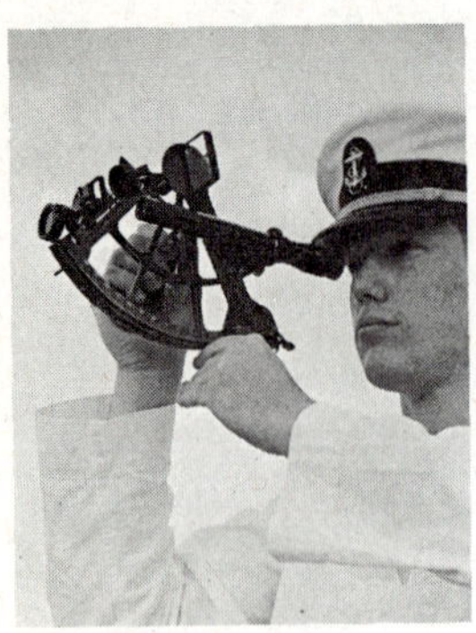

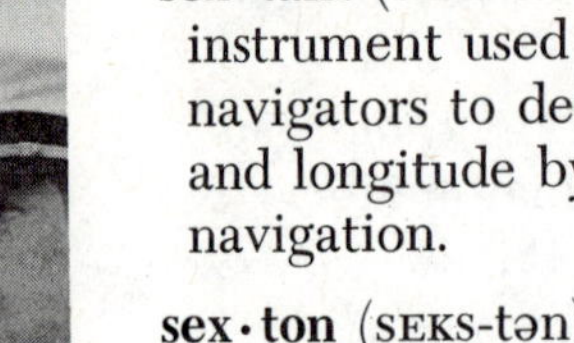

sextant

sex·tant (SEKS-tənt) *noun.* An instrument used primarily by navigators to determine latitude and longitude by celestial navigation.

sex·ton (SEKS-tən) *noun.* The caretaker of a church.

shab·by (SHAB-ee) *adjective.* 1. Ragged or worn-out. 2. Wearing old, worn clothing: a *shabby* tramp. 3. Unpleasant, shameful. **shabbier, shabbiest.** —**shabbily** *adverb.*

shack (SHAK) *noun.* A hut; a small, poorly built house.

shack·le (SHAK-əl) *noun.* 1. A metal band used to hold the ankle or wrist of a prisoner. 2. (Plural) Anything that limits or holds. —*verb.* 1. To fasten with shackles. 2. To hold back; limit (one's freedom). **shackled, shackling.**

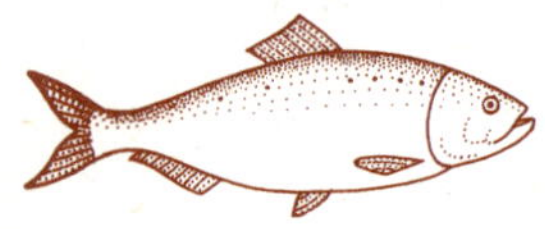

shad

shad *noun.* An Atlantic food fish, usually caught as it swims up European or North American rivers to breed. —**shad** or **shads** *plural.*

shade (SHAYD) *noun.* 1. The darkness or shadow caused when an object cuts off the light from the sun or any other source: the *shade* of a tree. 2. An object used to block or cut off the light: a window *shade.* 3. A ghost. 4. The degree of lightness or darkness of a color: many *shades* of green. 5. Any small difference: a *shade* taller. 6. (Plural, slang) Sunglasses. —*verb.* 1. To shield or protect from light. 2. To darken or apply tints of a color (in a drawing). **shaded, shading.**

shad·ow (SHAD-oh) *noun.* 1. An area from which an object cuts off the light: the *shadow* of a building. 2. The shape of the dark area caused by an object's cutting off of light: "I have a little *shadow* that goes in and out with me." (R. L. Stevenson). 3. A very small amount, a trace: a *shadow* of doubt. 4. (Plural) Darkness caused by the setting of the sun: "*Shadows* of the evening. . . ." (S. Baring-Gould). 5. A ghost. 6. A detective, or one who closely follows the movements of another. —*verb.* 1. To shade; make darker. 2. To follow closely; to trail. **shadowed, shadowing.**

shad·ow·y (SHAD-oh-ee) *adjective.* 1. Shady; like a shadow. 2. Not clear or definite: the *shadowy* outline of a sunken ship beneath the water.

shad·y (SHAYD-ee) *adjective.* 1. In the shadows; cool, dark. 2. Questionable; not to be trusted: a *shady* deal. **shadier, shadiest.** —**shadily** *adverb.*

shaft *noun.* 1. A long, thin part of an object, such as the handle of a rake. 2. A long, thin object, such as a spear or a pole, used in harnessing an animal to a wagon. 3. A beam of light. 4. The stiff, straight part of a feather. 5. The narrow opening to an underground tunnel or mine. 6. A narrow vertical opening in a building: an elevator *shaft.* 7. The part of a machine that carries power from one part to another: a drive *shaft.*

shag·gy (SHAG-ee) *adjective.* 1. Having long coarse hair or fibers. 2. Rough and uneven. **shaggier, shaggiest.** —**shaggily** *adverb.*

shake (SHAYK) *verb.* 1. To move or cause to move with a back-and-forth or up-and-down motion: *Shake* the can of paint. 2. To tremble. 3. To clasp hands with another as in greeting or farewell. 4. To upset or become upset: News of the defeat will *shake* the people. 5. To get rid of: *Shake* the sand from your shoes. **shook** (SHUK), **shaken, shaking.** —*noun.* 1. A drink made by mixing ice cream, flavoring, and milk: a milk *shake.* 2. A movement up and down or from side to side: a *shake* of the head. **shakes.** —**a fair shake.** Fair treatment. —**in a shake.** Soon. —**no great shakes.** Not outstanding.

shak·y (SHAYK-ee) *adjective.* 1. Trembling. 2. Not steady or secure. **shakier, shakiest.** —**shakily** *adverb.*

shale (SHAYL) *noun.* A common kind of rock that is easily split.

shall (SHAL) *verb.* A helping verb used: 1. With "I" or "we" to express the future tense: We *shall* be late if we don't hurry. 2. With other pronouns or nouns to indicate a promise, command, or determination: You *shall* eat your spinach! **should** (SHUD).

shal•low (SHAL-oh) *adjective.* 1. Not deep. 2. Not deep or careful (in thought): "*Shallow* men believe in luck." (Emerson). **shallower, shallowest.** —*noun.* (Often plural) The shallow part of a body of water: We waded in the *shallows.*

sham *adjective.* False, fake: *sham* money. —*noun.* 1. A person or thing that is not genuine. 2. A pillow cover. —*verb.* To pretend. **shammed, shamming.**

sham•ble (SHAM-bəl) *verb.* To walk, dragging the feet; shuffle. **shambled, shambling.** —*noun.* A shuffling walk.

sham•bles (SHAM-bəlz) *noun, plural in form but used with a singular verb.* A state of confusion, disorder: The burglars left the house in a *shambles.*

shame (SHAYM) *noun.* 1. A feeling of embarrassment brought on by doing something wrong. 2. Disgrace or that which causes disgrace: The criminal brought *shame* to his family. 3. A disappointment, sadness: It is a *shame* that she had to leave early. —*verb.* To feel shame or cause another to feel shame. **shamed, shaming.** —**shameful** (SHAYM-fəl) *adjective.* —**shamefully** *adverb.*

sham•poo (sham-POO) *noun.* 1. A special soap or detergent for use in washing the hair. 2. A liquid product used to clean rugs and furniture. 3. The act of using shampoo or having it used: She had a *shampoo* at the beauty shop. **shampoos.** —*verb.* To use shampoo. **shampooed, shampooing.**

sham•rock (SHAM-rok) *noun.* A low-growing form of clover having three leaflets on a single stem; now the national flower of Ireland.

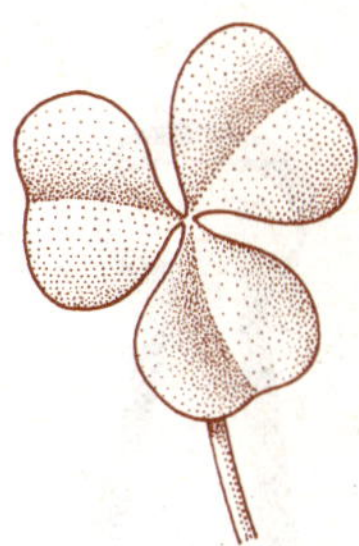
shamrock

shank (SHANGK) *noun.* 1. The part of the leg between the ankle and the knee. 2. The whole leg. 3. A cut of meat from the leg of an animal. 4. The long, slim part of a pin, nail, tool, or utensil. 5. A stem or stalk. 6. The lower part of the shoe under the instep.

shan't (SHANT) *contraction.* A shortening of the words *shall not.*

shan•ty (SHAN-tee) *noun.* A tumbledown hut or shack. **shanties.**

shape (SHAYP) *noun.* 1. Form or outline: The cookies are in the *shape* of hearts. 2. The form of a human body. 3. (Informal) Condition: This building is in bad *shape.* 4. A finished form: to take *shape.* **shapes.** —*verb.* 1. To give or take on a form: *shape* mud into pies. 2. To think out, arrange: *shape* plans for a trip. **shaped, shaping.** —**shape up or ship out.** (Slang) Act right or leave.

shape•ly (SHAYP-lee) *adjective.* Having a form that is pleasing to the eye. **shapelier, shapeliest.**

share (SHAIR) *noun.* 1. A part; the amount given to or by one person. 2. One of the equal portions into which the stock of a company is divided. 3. The sharp blade of a plow. **shares.** —*verb.* 1. To distribute portions. 2. To use, enjoy, or experience with others: *share* a playground. **shared, sharing.**

shark (SHAHRK) *noun.* 1. A large, greedy fish found in oceans: *Sharks* eat other fish and are dangerous to man. 2. A sly or crafty person. 3. (Slang) An expert, usually one who cheats: a card *shark.*

shark

shark•skin (SHAHRK-skin) *noun.* 1. The skin of a shark or the leather made from this skin. 2. A smooth shiny fabric.

[1]**sharp** (SHAHRP) *adjective.* 1. Having a thin edge or a pointed end capable of cutting or piercing.

shears

2. Quick-witted, clever. 3. Abrupt: a *sharp* drop in temperature. 4. Intense; strong: *sharp* pain. 5. Biting, painful: *sharp* wind. 6. (Slang) Good-looking, smart: He wears *sharp* clothes. **sharper, sharpest.** —*noun.* (Music) A note half a tone above a given tone; the sign (♯) indicating such a note. —**sharply** *adverb.*

[2]**sharp** (SHAHRP) *adverb.* 1. Exactly: Be here at two o'clock *sharp.* 2. Alertly: Act *sharp.*

sharp·en (SHAHR-pən) *verb.* 1. To make or improve an edge or point: *sharpen* a pencil. 2. To grow sharper. **sharpened, sharpening.** —**sharpener** *noun.*

shat·ter (SHAT-ər) *verb.* 1. To break or cause to break suddenly into many pieces. 2. To spoil or destroy: The injury *shattered* his plans to play. **shattered, shattering.**

sheep

shave (SHAYV) *verb.* 1. To remove a very thin layer. 2. To use a razor to cut off (hair or whiskers) very close to the skin. 3. To come very close to: The baseball *shaved* the batter's ear. **shaved, shaving.** —*noun.* The act or result of shaving. **shaves.** —**close shave.** A narrow escape.

shaving (SHAYV-ing) *noun.* 1. The act of taking off hair or a thin layer with a sharp tool. 2. (plural) Thin pieces removed by shaving.

shawl *noun.* A large piece of fabric worn over the head or shoulders.

sheep dog

she (SHEE) *pronoun.* A female previously named or indicated: Sally says *she* liked the show.

sheaf (SHEEF) *noun.* 1. A bundle into which wheat, rye, or other grain is tied after cutting. 2. A bundle or collection of things of the same kind: a *sheaf* of paper. —**sheaves** (SHEEVZ) *plural.*

shear (SHIHR) *verb.* 1. To cut with a sharp instrument such as scissors. 2. To trim or cut (off): *shear* wool from sheep. **sheared, sheared** or **shorn, shearing.**

shears (SHIHRZ) *noun, plural.* A cutting tool that works like a pair of scissors.

sheath (SHEETH) *noun.* 1. A cover or case for the blade of a knife or sword. 2. Any cover of this sort.

sheathe (SHEE<u>TH</u>) *verb.* 1. To put (a knife, etc.) into a sheath. 2. To provide with a cover or case: The injured man is *sheathed* in bandages. **sheathed, sheathing.**

[1]**shed** *noun.* A building, usually low and simply built, used for storage or shelter.

[2]**shed** *verb.* 1. To pour out or let fall; drop off: to *shed* tears; to *shed* clothing. 2. To prevent from penetrating: This rain hat *sheds* water. 3. To cause to flow: *shed* blood. 4. To give out: The sun *sheds* light. **shed, shedding.**

she'd (SHEED) *contraction.* A shortened form of the words *she would* or *she had.*

sheen *noun.* Brightness or shininess: New silver coins have a *sheen.*

sheep *noun.* 1. A cud-chewing animal that is raised for its wool and its flesh (mutton). 2. A timid or foolish person. —**sheep** *plural.*

sheep dog. A dog trained to tend and herd sheep.

sheep·ish (SHEEP-ish) *adjective.* 1. Like a sheep; timid or foolish. 2. Bashful, shy, or awkward: a *sheepish* smile. —**sheepishly** *adverb.*

sheep·skin (SHEEP-skin) *noun.* 1. The skin of a sheep, particularly with the wool still on. 2. Leather made from the skin of a sheep. 3. (Informal) A diploma.

[1]**sheer** (SHIHR) *adjective.* 1. So thin that one can almost see through it: a *sheer* fabric. 2. Complete or utter; absolute: *sheer* fatigue. 3. Very steep; extending straight up or down: a *sheer* drop of hundreds of feet. —*adverb* Also **sheerly.** 1. Completely. 2. Very steeply. —**sheerness** *noun.*

[2] **sheer** (SHIHR) *verb.* To turn from a course; to swerve. **sheered, sheering.**

sheet *noun.* 1. A large piece of cloth used to cover a bed or to sleep under. 2. A single piece of paper. 3. A newspaper. 4. A broad, thin piece of anything: a *sheet* of plastic.

sheik (SHEEK or SHAYK) Also **sheikh** *noun.* 1. An Arab official or the head of a tribe. 2. A Moslem leader or person of some importance.

shelf *noun.* 1. A flat, thin piece of wood, metal, plastic, etc., attached to a wall or within a frame and used to hold books or other objects. 2. Something like a shelf, such as a sandbank or a rock ledge. —**shelves** (SHELVZ) *plural.*

shell (SHEL) *noun.* 1. A hard or tough outer covering, as on a clam, nut, or egg. 2. Something light and hollow or shaped like a shell: boat *shell,* pastry *shell,* gun *shell.* 3. The framework of a building. 4. An explosive projectile that is fired from a gun or cannon. —*verb.* 1. To remove the shell from: She *shells* the peanuts. 2. To fire shells at. **shelled, shelling.**

she'll (SHEEL) *contraction.* A shortened form of the words *she will* or *she shall.*

shel·lac (shə-LAK) *noun.* A clear varnish made from a resin and alcohol, used to give a smooth, shiny finish to furniture, cabinets, floors, etc. —*verb.* 1. To coat with shellac. 2. (Slang) To defeat. **shellacked, shellacking.**

shell·fish (SHEL-fish) *noun.* An animal that has a shell and makes its home in water: Clams, oysters, and lobsters are shellfish. —**shellfish** or **shellfishes** *plural.*

shel·ter (SHEL-tər) *noun.* 1. Something that protects one from weather or attack: a *shelter* from the rain. 2. The state of being protected or covered. —*verb.* To give shelter to; protect. **sheltered, sheltering.**

shelve (SHELV) *verb.* 1. To place on a shelf. 2. To put aside: Please *shelve* that subject. **shelved, shelving.**

she·nan·i·gan (shə-NAN-i-gən) *noun.* (Informal, usually plural) Mischief; pranks; tricks.

shep·herd (SHEP-ərd) *noun.* 1. A man who guards and takes care of sheep. 2. A person who guides and takes care of others: "The Lord is my *shepherd.* . . ." (Psalms 23:1). —*verb.* To take care of, as a shepherd does; to guide. **shepherded, shepherding.**

shep·herd·ess (SHEP-ər-diss) *noun.* A girl or woman who guards sheep.

sher·bet (SHER-bit) *noun.* A sweet frozen dessert made with fruit juice, milk or water, and gelatin or egg white.

sher·iff (SHEHR-if) *noun.* The chief law officer of a county.

she's (SHEEZ) *contraction.* A shortened form of the words *she is* or *she has.*

shield (SHEELD) *noun.* 1. A large piece of metal or wood held in front of the body to protect it in combat. 2. Anything that serves to protect. 3. Something in the shape of a shield, as a police officer's badge. —*verb.* To defend or protect. **shielded, shielding.**

shift *noun.* 1. A group of people who work together, or the time that they work: the night *shift.* 2. A change or transfer: a *shift* in jobs. 3. (Football) A switch in backfield positions just before a play starts. —*verb.* 1. To change or move: *shift* gears. 2. To get along: I can *shift* for myself tonight. **shifted, shifting.**

shift·less (SHIFT-liss) *adjective.* Careless; lazy; good-for-nothing. —**shiftlessly** *adverb.*

shift·y (SHIF-tee) *adjective.* Evasive; cunning or sly.

shim·mer (SHIM-ər) *verb.* To shine with a faint unsteady sparkle; gleam faintly. **shimmered, shimmering.** —*noun.* A faint gleam or sparkle.

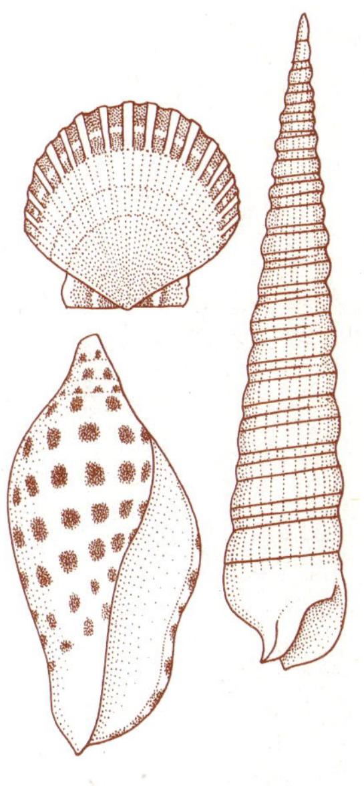

shells

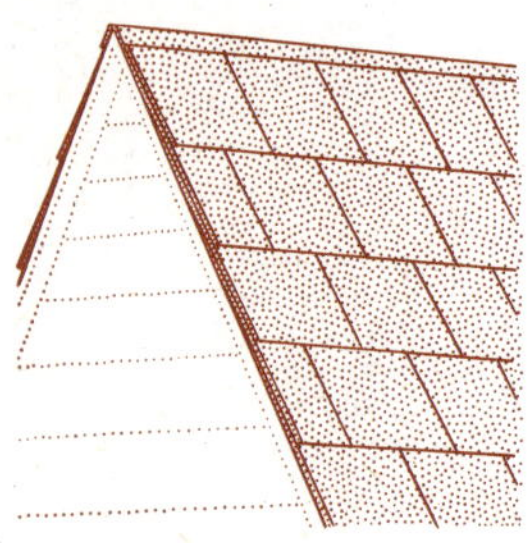
shingles (definition 1)

shoes

shin *noun.* The front part of the leg from the knee to the ankle. *—verb. Also* **shinny.** (Used with *up*) To climb (a rope or pole) by holding tight with one's arms and legs and pulling oneself (up). **shinned, shinning.**

shine (SHIGHN) *verb.* 1. To give light; glow: The moon *shines* bright. 2. To reflect light; be bright: The glasses *shine* in the light. 3. To make bright or polish: *shine* silver. 4. To aim or direct (light). 5. To do very well; be outstanding or brilliant: Jane *shines* in geography. **shone** or **shined, shining.** *—noun.* 1. Brightness or light: the *shine* in her eyes. 2. Polish: a shoe *shine.* 3. Fair weather: I go outside, rain or *shine.*

shin·gle (SHING-gəl) *noun.* 1. A thin piece of wood, asbestos, or slate: *Shingles* are put on in overlapping rows. 2. (Slang) A small signboard outside the office of a doctor, dentist, etc. 3. A woman's close haircut. **shingles.** *—verb.* 1. To put on shingles. 2. To cut the hair close. **shingled, shingling.**

shin·y (SHIGHN-ee) *adjective.* Bright or shining. **shinier, shiniest.**

ship *noun.* 1. A large vessel that goes in deep water. 2. An airship or airplane; a spaceship. 3. The crew of any of these; the passengers: The whole *ship* is talking about the storm. *—verb.* 1. To send: *ship* a package by parcel post. 2. To take a job on a ship. **shipped, shipping.** **—ship out.** To leave.

-ship *suffix.* Indicates: 1. The state of: kin*ship.* 2. The title, level, or office of: intern*ship.* 3. The act, art, or job of: author*ship.*

ship·ment (SHIP-mənt) *noun.* 1. The act of shipping or delivering goods: Pack the goods for *shipment.* 2. The things that are shipped: We received a big *shipment.*

ship·ping (SHIP-ing) *noun.* 1. All the ships of a country, city, port, or other area. 2. The sending of goods from one place to another.

ship·shape (SHIP-shayp) *adjective* and *adverb.* In a neat condition; well-arranged; in good order.

ship·wreck (SHIP-rek) *noun.* 1. The loss or ruin of a ship. 2. A wrecked ship. 3. Ruin or destruction. *—verb.* 1. To wreck. 2. To cause the ruin of. **shipwrecked, shipwrecking.**

ship·yard (SHIP-yahrd) *noun.* A place where ships are made or repaired.

shirk (SHERK) *verb.* To avoid or leave undone. **shirked, shirking.**

shirt (SHERT) *noun.* A garment or undergarment worn on the upper part of the body.

shiv·er (SHIV-ər) *verb.* To shake or tremble with a chill, excitement, or fright. **shivered, shivering.** *—noun.* The act of shaking or trembling.

[1]**shoal** (SHOHL) *noun.* 1. A place in a river or other body of water where the water is shallow. 2. A sandbar that makes water shallow. *—verb.* To become shallow. **shoaled, shoaling.**

[2]**shoal** (SHOHL) *noun.* A large number: a *shoal* of fish.

shock (SHOK) *noun.* 1. A strong, sudden blow or jar: The *shock* of the collision knocked him down. 2. A sudden upset to the mind or feelings: The President's death was a *shock.* 3. The effect on the body caused by an electric current passing through it. 4. A seriously weakened condition of the body caused by sudden injury, bleeding, etc. *—verb.* 1. To disturb greatly. 2. To disgust. 3. To give an electric shock to. **shocked, shocking.**

shocking (SHOK-ing) *adjective.* 1. Very upsetting. 2. Causing horror or disgust. **—shockingly** *adverb.*

shod *verb. See* **shoe.**

shoe (SHOO) *noun.* 1. A covering, often of leather, for the human foot. 2. Something like a shoe in its position, form, or use: horse*shoe.* 3. The part of a brake that presses on a brake drum to slow or stop a wheel. **shoes.** —*verb.* To put shoes on. **shod, shoeing.**

shoe·lace (SHOO-layss) *noun.* A strip of cord or leather used to fasten a shoe; a shoestring. **shoelaces.**

shoe·mak·er (SHOO-may-kər) *noun.* A person who makes or repairs shoes.

shoe·string (SHOO-string) *noun.* A shoelace.

shone (SHOHN) *verb. See* **shine.**

shoo *interjection.* A sound made to scare away chickens or other animals. —*verb.* To scare or drive away by calling "Shoo." **shooed, shooing.**

shook (SHUK) *verb. See* **shake.**

shoot *verb.* 1. To hit or kill with a missile, such as a bullet, fired from a weapon. 2. To send, discharge, or throw rapidly and with force: *shoot* an arrow into the air. 3. To move quickly and suddenly: Oil will soon *shoot* out of the oil well. 4. To push forth: Flowers *shoot* out of the ground in spring. 5. To take pictures with a camera. 6. (Used with *up*) To grow quickly. **shot, shooting.** —*noun.* 1. A shooting match; a hunt. 2. A young plant growth. —**shoot the breeze.** (Slang) To gossip; talk idly.

shooting star. A meteor.

shop *noun.* 1. A small store or business: barber*shop.* 2. A place where a particular kind of work is done: machine *shop.* 3. (Informal) A school course on carpentry and other manual skills. —*verb.* To go to a store to examine or buy things. **shopped, shopping.** —**talk shop.** To talk about one's job or work.

shop·keep·er (SHOP-kee-pər) *noun.* A person who owns or manages a shop.

shop·lift·er (SHOP-lif-tər) *noun.* A person who steals goods from a store.

shop·per (SHOP-ər) *noun.* A person who buys or examines things for sale.

shopping center. A group of stores built together in one area.

[1]**shore** (SHOR) *noun.* The land that borders a body of water. **shores.**

[2]**shore** (SHOR) *verb.* To prop up or support, as with a beam or pole. **shored, shoring.**

shorn *verb. See* **shear.**

short *adjective.* 1. Having little length: a *short* nail. 2. Of little height: a *short* boy. 3. Less than usual in time, distance, or other measure: *short* meeting. 4. (Often used with *of*) Less than the usual or needed amount: Bill was a dollar *short.* 5. Curt; rude. **shorter, shortest.** —*adverb.* 1. Suddenly: The horse stopped *short.* 2. Without reaching: The arrow fell *short* of the target. —*noun.* 1. A short circuit. 2. (Plural) A pair of trousers with the legs ending near or above the knee; also, men's underpants. —*verb.* To cause or have a short circuit. **shorted, shorting.**

short·age (SHOR-tij) *noun.* A lack in quantity or amount: a *shortage* of food. **shortages.**

short·bread (SHORT-bred) *noun.* A type of rich cookie or other pastry.

short·cake (SHORT-kayk) *noun.* A cake made from sweetened biscuit dough and filled and covered with fruit: peach *shortcake.* **shortcakes.**

short·change (short-CHAYNJ) *verb.* 1. To return less money than a customer should receive in change. 2. To give less than should be given: The audience was *shortchanged* when the band played fewer songs than the program promised. **shortchanged, shortchanging.**

short circuit. An electrical circuit, usually accidental, formed when two points on a high-resistance circuit are connected by a low-resistance contact.

short·com·ing (SHORT-kuhm-ing) *noun.* A fault or lack.

short cut. A way that is shorter or more direct than the usual way.

short·en (SHORT-n) *verb.* To make shorter or less in length or time: *shorten* a meeting. **shortened, shortening.**

short·en·ing (SHORT-n-ing or SHORT-ning) *noun.* A fatty substance, such as butter or margarine, used to make pastries rich and flaky.

shorthorn

short·hand (SHORT-hand) *noun.* A system of rapid writing that uses symbols or special marks instead of words.

short·horn (SHORT-horn) *noun.* A breed of cattle that has short horns.

short·ly (SHORT-lee) *adverb.* 1. In a short time; soon: I will finish my work *shortly.* 2. Briefly; curtly; in a few words.

short·sight·ed (SHORT-SIGH-tid) *adjective.* 1. Not able to see distant objects clearly; nearsighted. 2. Not concerned about or able to prepare for the future. —**shortsightedly** *adverb.* —**shortsightedness** *noun.*

short·stop (SHORT-stop) *noun.* (Baseball) A player in the infield between second and third base.

short story. A short fictional tale told in prose.

short wave. A radio wave less than 60 meters long, used mostly for long-distance broadcasting.

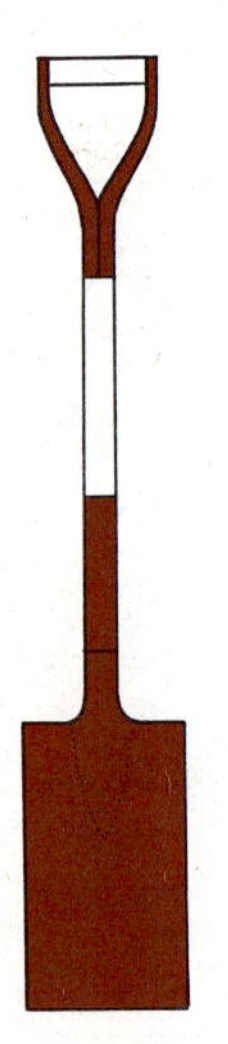

shovel

shot *noun.* 1. A firing or shooting, as of a gun, rocket, or other device: space *shot.* 2. Something that is fired from a weapon, as the pellets contained in a shotgun shell. 3. (Informal) A throw, stroke, or blow: a basketball *shot.* 4. A try; an attempt. 5. An injection: Ed had a polio *shot.* 6. A photograph. 7. A person who shoots: The major is a good *shot.* 8. A heavy metal ball hurled in shot-put competition. —*adjective.* (Slang) Ruined; useless: The motor was *shot.* —**shot in the arm.** Something that gives help, relief, or encouragement.

shot·gun (SHOT-guhn) *noun.* A gun with one or two barrels, used to fire cartridges filled with pellets.

shot-put (SHOT-put) *noun.* A sporting contest in which each competitor tries to throw a heavy metal ball (shot) farther than his opponents.

should (SHUD) *verb. See* **shall.**

shoul·der (SHOHL-dər) *noun.* 1. The part of the body between the neck and the upper arm (in humans) or between the neck and upper foreleg (in animals). 2. The joint connecting the arm with the body. 3. The side of a road. —*verb.* 1. To use the shoulder to push or carry. 2. To carry; take upon oneself: Dad *shoulders* too many of my problems. **shouldered, shouldering.** —**cold shoulder.** A snub.

shoulder blade. One of the two flat, triangular bones that form the rear part of the shoulder.

shouldn't (SHUD-nt) *contraction.* A short form of the words *should not.*

shout (SHOWT) *verb.* To call out in a loud voice; to yell. **shouted, shouting.** —*noun.* A cry or yell.

shove (SHUHV) *verb.* To push roughly. **shoved, shoving.** —*noun.* A push.

shov·el (SHUHV-əl) *noun.* A tool with a long handle and metal scoop used for digging or lifting loose material. —*verb.* 1. To dig, move, or scoop up with a shovel or similar device. 2. To move or push large amounts rapidly: The hungry workmen *shoveled* the stew into their mouths. **shoveled** or **shovelled, shoveling** or **shovelling.**

show (SHOH) *verb.* 1. To put or be within sight; to display: Ted *showed* me his new ball. 2. To point out; to guide or explain. 3. To give; make known: The child *showed* respect for his parents. **showed, showed** or **shown, showing.** —*noun.* 1. A demonstration; display: The army made a *show* of power. 2. An activity at which things are displayed: boat *show.* 3. A movie, play, or similar entertainment. 4. A pretense. —**show off.** To act in a showy or clowning way.

show·case (SHOH-kayss) *noun.* A glass case or cabinet in which things for sale or display are kept. **showcases.**

show·er (SHOW-ər) *noun.* 1. A fall of rain, sleet, or hail. 2. A nozzle that sprays water down on a bather; a bath taken under such a nozzle. 3. A party in honor of a prospective bride. *—verb.* 1. To fall as a shower. 2. To bathe in a shower. **showered, showering.**

show·man (SHOH-mən) *noun.* 1. A person who manages a show. 2. A person who is dramatic in speech or action. —**showmen** *plural.*

shown (SHOHN) *verb. See* **show.**

show·y (SHOH-ee) *adjective.* 1. Fancy or colorful. 2. Attracting attention in a tasteless or flashy manner. **showier, showiest.**

shrank (SHRANGK) *verb. See* **shrink.**

shrap·nel (SHRAP-nəl) *noun.* 1. A large shell loaded with metal fragments or pellets. 2. Fragments of metal or pellets that are scattered with great force when a shell or other weapon explodes. —**shrapnel** *plural.*

shred *noun.* 1. A torn fragment; a scrap. 2. A small amount; trace. *—verb.* To tear or cut into pieces. **shredded** or **shred, shredding.**

shrew (SHROO) *noun.* 1. A small animal that resembles a mouse with a long snout. 2. A bad-tempered woman who quarrels or scolds.

shrewd (SHROOD) *adjective.* Clever; quick-witted. **shrewder, shrewdest.** —**shrewdly** *adverb.*

shriek (SHREEK) *verb.* To make a loud, sharp noise or scream. **shrieked, shrieking.** *—noun.* Such a sound.

shrill (SHRIL) *adjective.* Having a high, sharp sound. **shriller, shrillest.** —**shrilly** *adverb.*

shrimp *noun.* 1. A small shellfish used as food. 2. (Slang) A small person. —**shrimp** or **shrimps** *plural.*

shrine (SHRIGHN) *noun.* A place considered sacred because of a person or event associated with it: The Lincoln Memorial is an American *shrine.* **shrines.**

shrink (SHRINGK) *verb.* 1. To make or become smaller or less: Did the sweater *shrink* when you washed it? 2. To draw back; shy away (from): *shrink* from a dog. **shrank** or **shrunk, shrunk** or **shrunken, shrinking.**

shriv·el (SHRIV-əl) *verb.* To make or become withered or curled up. **shriveled** or **shrivelled, shriveling** or **shrivelling.**

shroud (SHROWD) *noun.* 1. A cloth or sheet in which a body is wrapped for burial. 2. Something that covers or keeps from sight: a *shroud* of fog. *—verb.* To cover or keep from sight. **shrouded, shrouding.**

shrub (SHRUHB) *noun.* A woody plant that has many stems beginning at its base; a bush.

shrub·ber·y (SHRUHB-ər-ee) *noun.* A group or arrangement of shrubs.

shrug (SHRUHG) *verb.* To raise the shoulders briefly, as to show doubt or lack of interest. **shrugged, shrugging.** *—noun.* A brief raising of the shoulders.

shrunk·en (SHRUHNGK-ən) *verb. See* **shrink.**

shuck (SHUHK) *verb.* To remove the husks or coverings from: *shuck* corn. **shucked, shucking.** *—noun.* A husk or covering, as on an ear of corn.

shud·der (SHUHD-ər) *verb.* To tremble suddenly and vigorously. **shuddered, shuddering.** *—noun.* A sudden trembling.

shuf·fle (SHUHF-əl) *verb.* 1. To drag or slide the feet when walking; scuffle. 2. To rearrange the order of, as in mixing cards together. **shuffled, shuffling.** *—noun.* 1. A walk or gait in which the feet drag or slide. 2. A mixing together, as of playing cards.

shuf·fle·board (SHUHF-əl-bord) *noun.* A game in which large disks are pushed along a smooth surface toward an area marked with numbered sections.

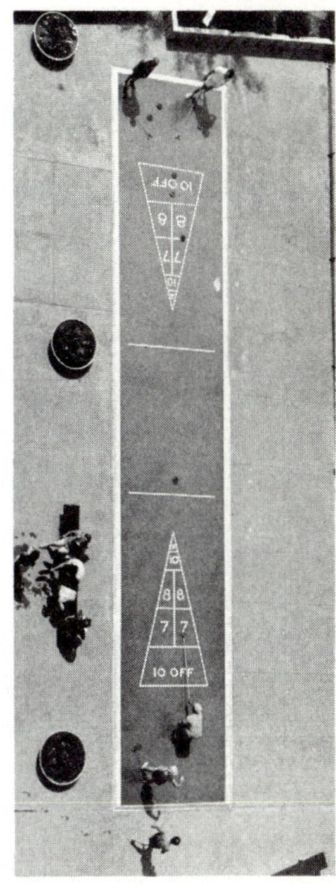

shuffleboard

shrew

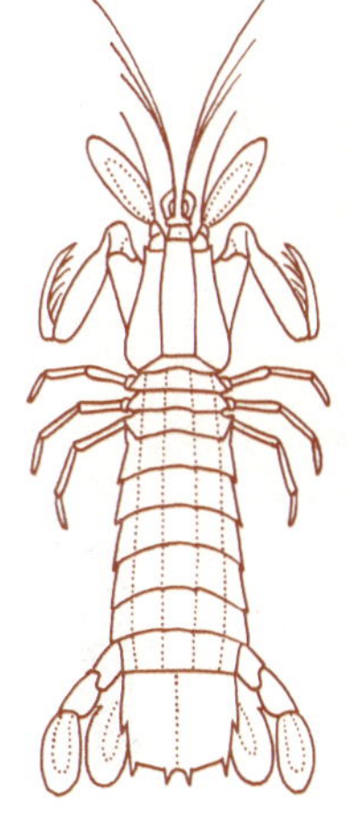
shrimp

shun (SHUHN) *verb.* To avoid; keep away from. **shunned, shunning.**

shush (SHUHSH) *interjection.* Expresses a command or desire for others to be quiet. *—verb.* To silence, as by saying "shush" to. **shushed, shushing.**

shut (SHUHT) *verb.* 1. To move a door, drawer, or other object to close an opening: *Shut* the door. 2. To stop the operation of: The shopkeeper *shut* his store on Christmas. **shut, shutting.** *—adjective.* Closed. **—shut up.** To stop talking; be quiet.

shutters

shut·ter (SHUHT-ər) *noun.* 1. A hinged, door-like covering hung, often in pairs, to protect or decorate a window or doorway. 2. A device that opens and closes an opening in front of a camera lens.

shut·tle (SHUHT-l) *noun.* 1. A device used to move thread back and forth in weaving. 2. A device on a sewing machine that makes the lower thread go back and forth. 3. A train, bus, or airplane that carries passengers back and forth between two points, usually over a short distance. **shuttles.** *—verb.* To move back and forth. **shuttled, shuttling.**

shy (SHIGH) *adjective.* 1. Bashful; not at ease with others. 2. Timid; easily frightened. 3. (Slang) Lacking; without. **shyer** or **shier, shyest** or **shiest.** *—verb.* To turn or move suddenly, as from fear. **shied, shying.** **—shyly** *adverb.* **—shyness** *noun.*

sick (SIK) *adjective.* 1. Ill; having a disease. 2. Having to vomit; nauseated. 3. Of or for a sick person or sickness: *sick* leave. 4. (Used with *of*) Disgusted; annoyed. 5.(Slang) Not wholesome; gruesome. **sicker, sickest.** **—sickness** *noun.*

sick·en (SIK-ən) *verb.* To make or become sick. **sickened, sickening.**

sickle

sick·le (SIK-əl) *noun.* A tool with a short handle and a long, curved blade, used for cutting grass or grain. **sickles.**

sick·ly (SIK-lee) *adjective.* 1. Inclined to be sick; not strong or healthy. 2. Caused by or related to sickness: a *sickly* yellow. **sicklier, sickliest.**

side (SIGHD) *noun.* 1. One of the surfaces between the front and back or top and bottom of an object. 2. Any surface or line of an object or figure: *side* of a triangle. 3. Either surface of a flat object. 4. The right or left part of the body. 5. A location away from a given point: the other *side* of the mountains. 6. The area next to someone or something: The dog sat at my *side.* 7. The persons or groups opposing one another in a contest or battle: Our *side* won. 8. A feature or aspect: the cheerful *side* of the news. 9. A line of descent or ancestry: Dad's *side* of the family. **sides.** *—verb.* To take a position favoring someone or something: He *sided* with me. **sided, siding.**

side·board (SIGHD-bord) *noun.* A piece of dining-room furniture used to hold tablecloths, silverware, etc.

side·line (SIGHD-lighn) Also **side line** *noun.* 1. A line at the side, especially of an athletic field. 2. (Plural) The area just outside such a line. 3. An extra line of business: He breeds dogs as a *sideline.*

side·long (SIGHD-lawng or SIGHD-long) *adjective* and *adverb.* Directed to or toward the side; sideways.

side show. A small show connected with a main one, as at a circus.

side·step (SIGHD-step) *verb.* 1. To avoid by moving to one side: *sidestep* a blow. 2. To avoid (a problem or duty). **sidestepped, sidestepping.**

side·track (SIGHD-trak) *verb.* 1. To turn (a person) aside from something he has in mind: Television *sidetracked* me from studying. 2. To switch (a train) to a sidetrack. **sidetracked, sidetracking.** *—noun.* A short track onto which a train is switched from a main line; a siding.

side·walk (SIGHD-wawk) *noun.* A walk along the side of a street.

side·ways (SIGHD-wayz) Also **sidewise** *adverb.* 1. To the side. 2. From the side. *—adjective.* Toward one side.

sid·ing (SIGH-ding) *noun.* A short section of railroad track, connected by switches to the main track and used for temporary storage of railroad cars.

si·dle (SIGHD-l) *verb.* To move sideways, especially in a sly or stealthy way. **sidled, sidling.**

siege (SEEJ) *noun.* 1. The action of surrounding a fort or town to make it surrender. 2. Any lengthy period, especially of sickness. **sieges.**

si·er·ra (see-EHR-ə) *noun.* A chain of mountains or hills.

si·es·ta (see-ESS-tə) *noun.* A period of rest taken in the afternoon, especially in hot countries.

sieve (SIV) *noun.* A utensil with wire mesh used for straining. **sieves.**

sift *verb.* 1. To separate big or coarse parts from little or fine ones by passing through a sieve: *sift* flour. 2. To pass (through): The sunlight *sifts* through the branches. 3. To examine with care: I must *sift* all he tells me. **sifted, sifting.**

sigh *verb.* 1. To let out a long deep breath, usually when one is sad, tired, or relieved. 2. To long or yearn (for). **sighed, sighing.** *—noun.* The sound of sighing.

sight *noun.* 1. The ability to see with the eyes; vision: Without *sight* we are blind. 2. The act of seeing: It was love at first *sight.* 3. View; the distance that one can see: Suddenly he came into *sight.* 4. Something seen or especially worth seeing. 5. A device used to guide the eye or aim, as a telescopic *sight* on a rifle. *—verb.* 1. To see; catch sight of: *sight* land. 2. To aim; look at through a sight or sights (as on a rifle). **sighted, sighting.**

sight·see·ing (SIGHT-see-ing) *noun.* Touring to see places of interest.

sign (SIGHN) *noun.* 1. A piece of wood, metal, paper, etc., with words or a picture giving information: stop *sign.* 2. A mark or gesture that tells or means something: the secret *sign* of our club. 3. An evidence or trace. *—verb.* To write one's name on: *sign* a letter. **signed, signing. —sign off.** To stop broadcasting, as in television and radio. **—sign up.** 1. To enlist, as in the army. 2. To hire or be hired.

sig·nal (SIG-nəl) *noun.* 1. A sign; a gesture or device that informs or warns. 2. The sound, image, or message sent by radio, television, or telegraph. *—verb.* To make a sign or signal to. **signaled** or **signalled, signaling** or **signalling.**

sig·na·ture (SIG-nə-chur) *noun.* 1. The name of a person written by himself. 2. (Music) A sign that gives the time and key in which a piece is written. **signatures.**

sign·board (SIGHN-bord) *noun.* A board with a sign or notice on it.

sig·nif·i·cance (sig-NIF-i-kənss) *noun.* 1. Meaning: Do you understand the *significance* of this letter? 2. Importance. **—significant** *adjective.* **—significantly** *adverb.*

sig·ni·fy (SIG-nə-figh) *verb.* 1. To mean: What can this sudden darkness *signify?* 2. To make known; express: He *signified* his agreement with a nod. **signified, signifying.**

sign language. A way of saying things by means of gestures: Deaf-mutes express themselves in *sign language.*

si·lence (SIGH-lənss) *noun.* Stillness; quiet. **silences.** *—verb.* To make quiet. **silenced, silencing.**

si·lent (SIGH-lənt) *adjective.* 1. Not speaking, or saying just a little. 2. Quiet; with no noise: The hall is *silent.* 3. Not spoken; not pronounced: In "through" the "gh" is *silent.* 4. Not playing an active or public part: a *silent* partner in a business. **—silently** *adverb.*

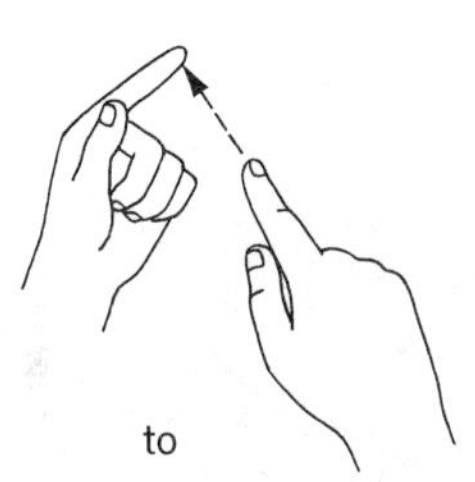

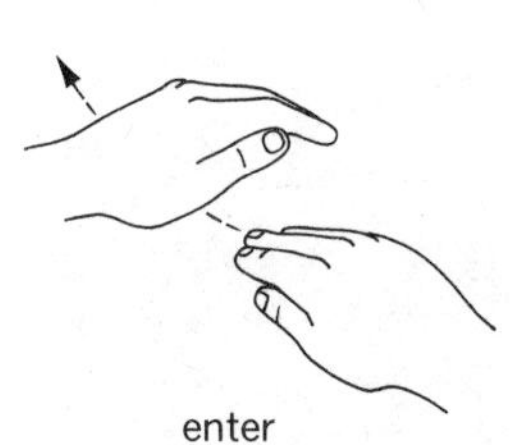

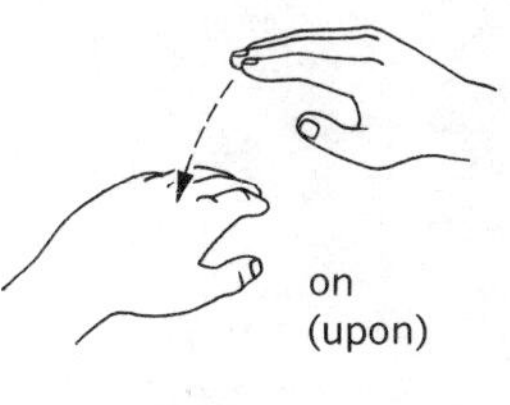

sign language

silhouette

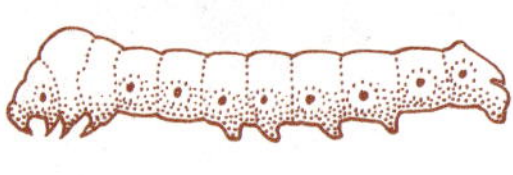
silkworm

silo (definition 1)

sil·hou·ette (sil-oo-ET) *noun.* 1. The outline of a thing (especially a person's head), filled in with black or a color or cut out of black paper. 2. The outline of a person or thing. —*verb.* To make or show as a silhouette. **silhouetted, silhouetting.**

sil·i·con (SIL-i-kon) *noun.* The second commonest chemical element, found only in combination with other substances, such as oxygen.

silk *noun.* 1. A fine, soft thread-like fiber spun by silkworms. 2. Cloth made from this fiber. 3. Anything like silk, as the tassels on corn.

silk·en (SIL-kən) *adjective.* 1. Made of silk: a *silken* robe. 2. Smooth, shining, soft, like silk.

silk·worm (SILK-werm) *noun.* A caterpillar that spins fine, strong silk to make a cocoon.

silk·y (SIL-kee) *adjective.* Of or like silk; shiny, soft, and smooth: *silky* skin. **silkier, silkiest.**

sill (SIL) *noun.* A piece forming the bottom part of the frame of a door, window, or house.

sil·ly (SIL-ee) *adjective.* 1. Foolish; not having good sense: a *silly* fool. 2. (Slang) Stunned or dazed: I will beat him *silly.* **sillier, silliest.** —*noun.* (Slang) One who is silly. **sillies.** —**silliness** *noun.*

si·lo (SIGH-loh) *noun.* 1. An airtight tower in which green food for farm animals is stored. 2. An underground shelter where guided missiles are kept ready for firing. **silos.**

silt *noun.* Fine sand or dirt carried by water and often deposited on the floor of an ocean or river. —*verb.* To fill (up) or become filled with silt. **silted, silting.**

sil·ver (SIL-vər) *noun.* 1. A soft shining white element that is also a precious metal, used to make coins, jewelry, table utensils, etc. 2. Coins made of silver: a handful of *silver.* 3. Table utensils made of silver, such as spoons and knives. 4. Something that looks like silver: hair of *silver.* 5. (Also *adjective*) A grayish-white color. —*verb.* 1. To cover or coat with silver. 2. To make the color of silver. **silvered, silvering.**

sil·ver·smith (SIL-vər-smith) *noun.* A workman who makes things of silver.

sil·ver·ware (SIL-vər-wair) *noun.* Things made of or plated with silver, especially forks, knives, and spoons.

sil·ver·y (SIL-vər-ee) *adjective.* 1. Having the shine or the color of silver. 2. Having a clear sound: The actor speaks in *silvery* tones.

sim·i·lar (SIM-ə-lər) *adjective.* Like; almost the same as something else; alike: My sister and I have *similar* tastes in books. —**similarly** *adverb.*

sim·i·lar·i·ty (sim-ə-LA-rə-tee) *noun.* Likeness; resemblance; a similar feature: Moths and butterflies have many *similarities.* **similarities.**

sim·i·le (SIM-ə-lee) *noun.* A figure of speech, introduced by "like" or "as," that compares two things that are different in many ways: "Like a small gray coffee-pot sits the squirrel." (Humbert Wolfe). **similes.**

sim·mer (SIM-ər) *verb.* 1. To boil or stew gently. 2. To cook just at the boiling point or close to it. 3. To be close to showing (strong emotion or violence): He *simmered* with anger. **simmered, simmering.** —**simmer down.** To calm down.

sim·ple (SIM-pəl) *adjective.* 1. Easy to understand; easy to do. 2. Plain; ordinary; not showy: a *simple* dress. 3. Made up of only one or few parts: a *simple* machine. 4. Natural; sincere. 5. Stupid or weak-minded. **simpler, simplest.**

sim·ple·ton (SIM-pəl-tən) *noun.* A fool; a person who is easily fooled.

sim·plic·i·ty (sim-PLISS-ə-tee) *noun.* 1. The state of being easy to understand or do. 2. Plainness.

3. Naturalness; sincerity. 4. Dullness or folly. **simplicities.**

sim·pli·fy (SIM-plə-figh) *verb.* To make easy or easier; explain in a simple way. **simplified, simplifying.**

sim·ply (SIM-plee) *adverb.* 1. In a clear or easy way: He explains everything *simply.* 2. Plainly. 3. Absolutely; totally: I'm *simply* thrilled with the new car. 4. Just; merely: *simply* telling the truth.

si·mul·ta·ne·ous (sigh-məl-TAY-nee-əss) *adjective.* Happening or existing at the same time. —**simultaneously** *adverb.*

sin *noun.* The breaking of a law of God. —*verb.* 1. To break a religious law. 2. To do something wrong. **sinned, sinning.** —**sinful** (SIN-fəl) *adjective.* —**sinfully** *adverb.*

since (SINSS) *adverb.* Ago; at a time before the present: I lost the money long *since.* —*preposition.* From then till now: Tom has been in the library *since* noon. —*conjunction.* 1. From the time that: It is a long time *since* we went to the movies together. 2. Seeing that; because: *Since* you want the money back, here it is.

sin·cere (sin-SIHR) *adjective.* 1. Truthful; honest: "A friend is a person with whom I may be *sincere.*" (R. W. Emerson). 2. True; genuine. **sincerer, sincerest.** —**sincerely** *adverb.* —**sincerity** (sin-SEHR-ə-tee or sin-SIHR-ə-tee) *noun.*

sin·ew (SIN-yoo) *noun.* 1. A tendon; a tissue that fastens a muscle to a bone. 2. (Plural) The main strength or power: Hospitals, doctors, and nurses are the *sinews* of our health system. —**sinewy** *adjective.*

sing *verb.* 1. To use the voice to make music: *sing* a tune. 2. To make a whistling, humming, or buzzing sound: The wind is *singing* in the willows. 3. To tell or tell about in a song or a poem: He *sings* of the beauty of the countryside. **sang, sung, singing.** —*noun.* (Informal) A gathering of people who sing together.

sing. *abbreviation.* Singular.

singe (SINJ) *verb.* To burn slightly, especially hair or feathers. **singed, singeing.** —*noun.* A light burn.

sing·er (SING-ər) *noun.* A person who sings; especially one who sings for a living.

sin·gle (SING-gəl) *adjective.* 1. Referring to one only: a *single* shoe. 2. Not married. 3. Individual, separate: Every *single* student must attend. —*noun.* 1. An individual person or thing: Can you exchange a five-dollar bill for *singles?* 2. An unmarried person. 3. (Plural) A tennis game in which only one person plays on each side. 4. (Baseball) A hit on which the batter gets to first base. **singles.** —*verb.* 1. (Used with *out*) To pick (one from a group): The teacher *singled* out Barney to make the speech. 2. (Baseball) To hit a single. **singled, singling.** —**singly** *adverb.*

single file. A line in which people or animals follow one another.

sin·gle-hand·ed (sing-gəl-HAN-did) *adjective.* Unassisted; done by one person only. —**single-handedly** *adverb.*

sin·gle-mind·ed (sing-gəl-MIGHN-did) *adjective.* Having only one goal or aim: *single-minded* determination to win. —**single-mindedly** *adverb.*

sin·gu·lar (SING-gyə-lər) *adjective.* 1. One, separate. 2. Odd; peculiar: That was a *singular* thing for him to say! 3. Out of the ordinary; remarkable: a *singular* achievement. 4. (Grammar) Referring to one person or thing: "Child" is *singular;* "children" is plural. —**singularly** *adverb.*

sin·is·ter (SIN-i-stər) *adjective.* 1. Evil, malicious: a *sinister* look. 2. Threatening; acting as an omen of trouble or harm.

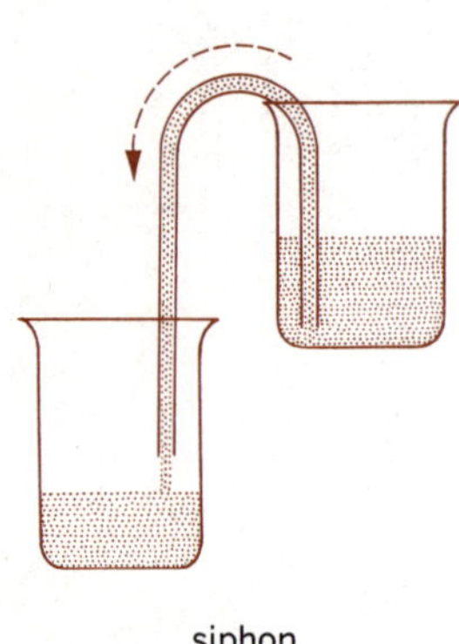

siphon

sisal

skateboard

sink (SINGK) *verb.* 1. To go or be put under a surface, as in water or another liquid. 2. To cause to go under: *sink* a ship. 3. To go down slowly. 4. To dig or put into the ground: *sink* a well. 5. To fail; get worse: Grandpa's health is *sinking* fast. 6. (Informal, used with *in* or *into*) To get through: Algebra just doesn't *sink* into my brain. **sank** or **sunk, sinking.** —*noun.* A water basin, usually with a water faucet and drain connected.

si·nus (SIGH-nəss) *noun.* Open space or pocket, particularly in bones around the nose. **sinuses.**

sip *verb.* To drink a small amount at a time. **sipped, sipping.** —*noun.* A little bit of a drink.

si·phon (SIGH-fən) Also **syphon** *noun.* A U-shaped tube through which the liquid in one container can be drawn into another container by the force of air pressure. —*verb.* To use such a tube. **siphoned, siphoning.**

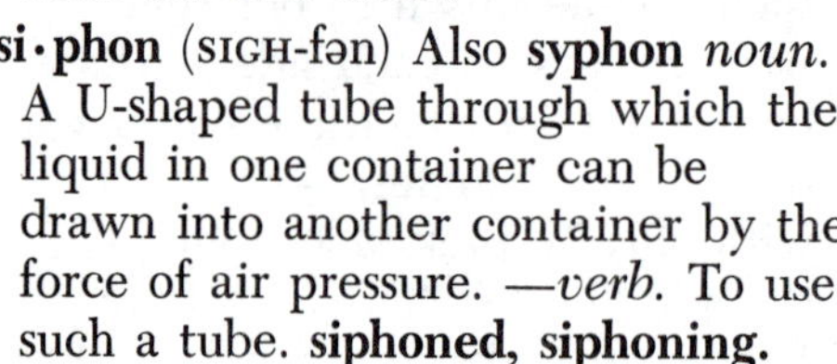

sir (SER) *noun.* 1. A form used to address a man without using his name: Yes, *sir.* 2. [Capital S] An English title for men of rank who are not nobles, as knights: *Sir* Paul.

sire (SIGHR) *noun.* 1. A father or grandfather. 2. A four-legged animal's father. 3. [Capital S] A term of address for a king or other male ruler. **sires.**

si·ren (SIGH-rən) *noun.* 1. A device that gives off a loud sound, usually as a warning. 2. An alluring woman.

sir·up (SIHR-əp) *noun. See* **syrup.**

si·sal (SIGHZ-l) *noun.* A Mexican plant or the fiber from this plant used to make rope and similar products.

sis·ter (SISS-tər) *noun.* 1. A female who has the same mother and father as another person. 2. A woman who is connected with another in some way, as by membership in a group, church, etc. 3. [Capital S] A nun.

sis·ter-in-law (SISS-tər-in-law) *noun.* 1. The sister of one's husband or wife. 2. The wife of one's brother or brother-in-law. —**sisters-in-law** *plural.*

sit *verb.* 1. To rest with the weight of the body on the buttocks, or rear. 2. To cover eggs with the body so as to hatch them. 3. To be located: The cabin *sits* on the edge of the cliff. 4. To pose for a portrait. **sat, sitting.**

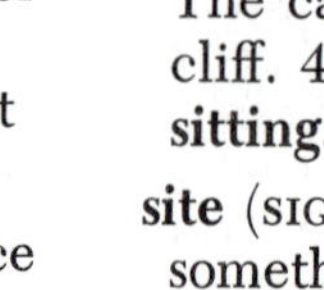

site (SIGHT) *noun.* A place where something is, will be, or was: Gettysburg was the *site* of a great Civil War battle. **sites.**

sit·ting (SIT-ing) *noun.* 1. The act or position of one who sits: a *sitting* for a picture. 2. A time during which one stays seated: She read most of the book in one *sitting.*

sitting room. A small living room or parlor.

sit·u·ate (SICH-oo-ayt) *verb.* To put in a particular place or area: The library will be *situated* in the center of town. **situated, situating.**

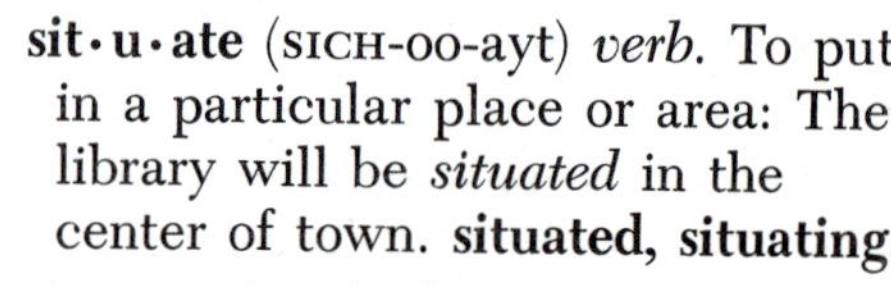

sit·u·a·tion (sich-oo-AY-shən) *noun.* 1. A particular place, state, or condition: a dangerous *situation.* 2. A job or business position.

six (SIKS) *noun* (and *adjective*). The cardinal number after five and before seven; 6.

six·teen (SIK-STEEN) *noun* (and *adjective*). The cardinal number after 15 and before 17; 16.

six·teenth (SIK-STEENTH) *adjective.* Coming next after 15th; 16th. —*noun.* One of 16 equal parts.

sixth (SIKSTH) *adjective.* Coming next after fifth; 6th. —*noun.* One of six equal parts.

six·ti·eth (SIK-stee-ith) *adjective.* Coming next after 59th; 60th. —*noun.* One of 60 equal parts.

six·ty (SIK-stee) *noun* (and *adjective*). The cardinal number after 59 and before 61; 60.

[1] **size** (SIGHZ) *noun.* 1. The measure, dimensions or bulk (of something): the *size* of a room. 2. Relative dimensions of, as of clothing. **sizes.** —*verb.* To make or arrange by size: The manufacturer *sizes* his dresses with even numbers. **sized, sizing.**

[2] **size** (SIGHZ) *noun.* A sticky substance that is used to give a sheen to or to stiffen a material, as paper or cloth. —*verb.* To put size on or treat with size. **sized, sizing.**

siz·zle (SIZ-l) *verb.* To make a hissing sound like fat over a fire: Bacon *sizzles* in the pan. **sizzled, sizzling.**

[1] **skate** (SKAYT) *noun.* A device attached to a shoe that enables the wearer to glide over ice (on blades) or over a surface (on rollers). **skates.** —*verb.* To move on skates. **skated, skating.**

[2] **skate** (SKAYT) *noun.* A saltwater fish with a flat body.

skate·board (SKAYT-bord) *noun.* A piece of wood, with wheels attached underneath, on which the rider places one or both feet and glides along.

skein (SKAYN) *noun.* A long coil or roll of thread or yarn.

skel·e·ton (SKEL-ə-tən) *noun.* 1. The bones as the framework of the body. 2. The framework or outline of something. —**skeletal** *adjective.*

skep·tic (SKEP-tik) *noun.* One who tends to doubt or disagree with accepted ways or opinions. —**skeptical** *adjective.*

sketch (SKECH) *noun.* 1. An outline or rough drawing. 2. A short written work, as a play or story. **sketches.** —*verb.* To make an outline or rough drawing. **sketched, sketching.**

sketch·y (SKECH-ee) *noun.* Not detailed or complete: Ellie gave only a *sketchy* account of what had happened. **sketchier, sketchiest.**

skew (SKYOO) *verb.* To put or turn on a slant. **skewed, skewing.**

ski (SKEE) *noun.* One of two long narrow pieces of wood or spun glass worn on the feet for gliding over snow or water. —*verb.* To travel by means of skis. **skied, skiing.** —**skier** (SKEE-ər) *noun.*

skid *verb.* 1. To slip or slide to the side: The car *skidded* off the icy road. 2. To slide along without rotating or turning. **skidded, skidding.** —*noun.* 1. The act or state of slipping. 2. A platform of wood used to slide or store (something heavy).

skiff (SKIF) *noun.* A small open boat with a flat bottom.

skill (SKIL) *noun.* Capability gained through practice; talent. —**skilled** or **skillful** *adjective.* —**skillfully** *adverb.*

skil·let (SKIL-it) *noun.* A shallow pan with a long handle, used for frying.

skim *verb.* 1. To take (the top layer) off (a liquid): Mother *skimmed* the grease from the soup. 2. To travel over, barely or lightly touching (something): The kite *skimmed* the trees. 3. To read quickly: Dad *skimmed* my report card. **skimmed, skimming.**

skimp *verb.* 1. To hold back; save; economize: *skimp* on lunch. 2. To do quickly without care or using inferior materials: *skimp* on a job. **skimped, skimping.**

skim·py (SKIM-pee) *adjective.* Not enough. **skimpier, skimpiest.**

skin *noun.* 1. The outside covering of man and some animals. 2. The fur from an animal. 3. The outside layer, as of a fruit or vegetable. —*verb.* To remove the skin or part of the skin: *skin* a deer. **skinned, skinning.** —**by the skin of one's teeth.** Barely. —**have a thick skin.** Not caring what others think or say.

skin diving. Swimming underwater with a breathing device and other equipment. —**skin diver** *noun.*

skis

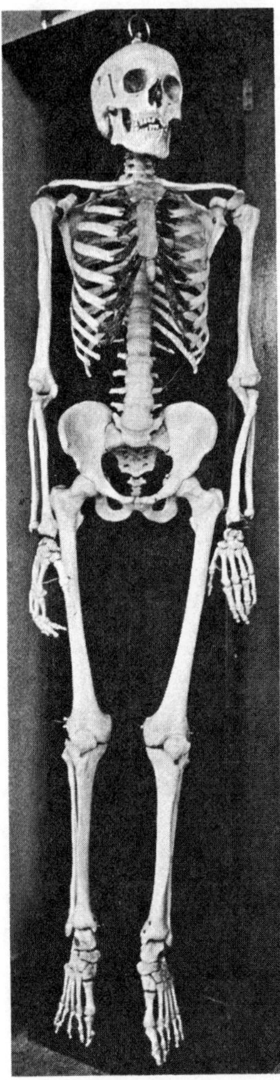

skeleton

skylight

skunk

sky diving

skin·ny (SKIN-ee) *adjective.* Extremely thin. **skinnier, skinniest.**

skin·ny-dip (SKIN-ee-dip) *verb.* To swim in the nude.

skip *verb.* 1. To move in light leaps or jumps. 2. To go from one point or thing to another, missing or omitting what is between. 3. (Informal) To go away in a hurry. **skipped, skipping.** —*noun.* 1. A hopping or jumping movement. 2. An omission or passing over.

ski patrol. A group of skiers assigned to ski certain slopes to aid others who may be injured or in difficulty.

skip·per (SKIP-ər) *noun.* One in charge of a ship or boat; a captain.

skir·mish (SKER-mish) *noun.* A small battle involving few troops. —*verb.* To take part in such a battle. **skirmished, skirmishing.**

skirt (SKERT) *noun.* 1. A piece of clothing that hangs from the waist to the thigh or below. 2. The part of a piece of clothing, as a dress or coat, that hangs from the waist. —*verb.* 1. To be on or go along the boundary of. 2. To avoid: *skirt* an issue. **skirted, skirting.**

skit *noun.* A short, amusing play-like performance.

skulk (SKUHLK) *verb.* To sneak about. **skulked, skulking.**

skull (SKUHL) *noun.* The part of the skeleton that forms the head.

skunk (SKUHNGK) *noun.* 1. A black animal with white streaks down its back that sprays a strong and unpleasant-smelling liquid when annoyed or in danger. 2. (Slang) A mean person.

sky *noun.* 1. The upper atmosphere about the earth. 2. The heavens; the space about the earth including the planets and stars. **skies.**

sky diving. A sport in which one jumps from a plane and does not open his parachute until necessary.

sky·jack (SKY-jak) *verb.* (Informal) To take control by force of an airliner in flight, usually in order to change its destination and often to demand payment of ransom. **skyjacked, skyjacking.**

sky·lark (SKY-lahrk) *noun.* A bird of Europe that sings as it flies. —*verb.* To frolic. **skylarked, skylarking.**

sky·light (SKY-light) *noun.* A glass window-like structure that allows the passage of daylight through a ceiling or roof.

sky·line (SKY-lighn) *noun.* 1. The line where the earth and the sky seem to meet; horizon. 2. The forms of buildings as seen against the sky: The New York City *skyline* is world-famous. **skylines.**

sky·rock·et (SKY-rok-it) *noun.* A firework that explodes into bright sparks after being shot high in the sky.

sky·scrap·er (SKY-skrayp-ər) *noun.* A building so tall it seems to touch, or scrape, the sky.

slab *noun.* A wide, flat, thick piece (of something): a *slab* of stone.

slack (SLAK) *adjective.* 1. Not tight, loose: a *slack* line. 2. Slow; without activity: a *slack* season. 3. Indifferent; slow; careless: *slack* worker. —*noun.* 1. A part that hangs or is loose: the *slack* in the rope. 2. (Plural) Trousers; pants for casual wear.

slack·en (SLAK-ən) *verb.* 1. To go or become slower: The racer's pace *slackened.* 2. To make or become loose. 3. To make or become quieter or less tense. **slackened, slackening.**

slag *noun.* 1. Glass-like matter that remains after the smelting process by which metal is separated from its ore. 2. A kind of lava that remains after a volcano erupts.

slain (SLAYN) *verb.* *See* **slay.**

slake (SLAYK) *verb.* To satisfy: We *slaked* our thirst with water. **slaked, slaking.**

slam *verb.* 1. To close forcefully, making a loud sound: *slam* a door. 2. To hit, place, or throw hard: The batter *slammed* the ball. **slammed, slamming.** —*noun.* 1. An action that produces a loud sound. 2. The sound itself.

slan·der (SLAN-dər) *noun.* A deliberately false statement that does harm to another's reputation. —*verb.* To make such a statement. **slandered, slandering.** —**slanderous** *adjective.*

slang *noun.* Everyday language containing either made-up words (*pooch, nitty-gritty*) or common words used in an uncommon way (*cool it, get lost*): *Slang* is not standard English but is often a means of private communication among friends or associates.

slant *verb.* 1. To slope; not be level: The dunes *slant* to the sea. 2. To report (something) in such a way as to show only one side or viewpoint. **slanted, slanting.** —*noun.* 1. A slope. 2. A particular viewpoint.

slap *verb.* To hit with an open hand or with a flat object. **slapped, slapping.** —*noun.* 1. Such a blow. 2. An insult.

slash *verb.* 1. To cut or slit with a fast long stroke. 2. To make much less; limit greatly. **slashed, slashing.** —*noun.* A long stroke or cut.

slat *noun.* A long, narrow piece of wood or metal.

slate (SLAYT) *noun.* 1. A layered rock that has a smooth, brittle surface, often used as roofing or as a writing surface. 2. (Also *adjective*) A dark gray-blue color. 3. A list of candidates for office. —*verb.* (Informal) To schedule; arrange a time for. **slated, slating.**

slaugh·ter (SLAW-tər) *verb.* 1. To kill (animals) for food. 2. To kill in large numbers. **slaughtered, slaughtering.** —*noun.* killing.

slave (SLAYV) *noun.* 1. A person held against his will to work for another. 2. Anyone ruled by another person, habit, or influence. —*verb.* To work very hard, like a slave. **slaved, slaving.** —**slavish** *adjective.*

slav·er·y (SLAYV-ər-ee or SLAYV-ree) *noun.* 1. The owning of slaves. 2. The condition of being a slave. 3. Very hard, unpleasant work.

slay *verb.* To kill; to murder. **slew** (SLOO), **slain** (SLAYN), **slaying.** —**slaying** *noun.*

sled *noun.* A vehicle with runners attached, used on snow and ice.

sledge (SLEJ) *noun.* A sled, particularly one used for carrying loads.

sledge hammer. A heavy hammer wielded with both hands.

sleek *adjective.* Shiny and smooth. —*verb.* To make neat or smooth. **sleeked, sleeking.**

sleep *noun.* 1. A state during which the body and the mind rest and are unaware of the outside world. 2. A state like sleep. —*verb.* To rest in sleep. **slept, sleeping.**

sleep·er (SLEEP-ər) *noun.* 1. A person asleep. 2. A railroad car in which a passenger can rent a bunk-like bed. 3. (Informal) A little-known play, book, etc., that is unexpectedly successful.

sleep·y (SLEEP-ee) *adjective.* 1. Tired; needing rest. 2. Without activity; quiet: a *sleepy* afternoon. **sleepier, sleepiest.** —**sleepiness** *noun.*

sleet *noun.* 1. Rain that is almost frozen. 2. A combination of rain and snow. —*verb.* To shower partly frozen rain. **sleeted, sleeting.**

sleeve (SLEEV) *noun.* 1. The part of clothing that encases the arm. 2. A case for (something). **sleeves.** —**up (one's) sleeve.** Kept hidden or secret for quick use.

sleigh (SLAY) *noun.* A vehicle, usually horse-drawn, that has runners for travel over snow and ice. —*verb.* To ride in or travel by sleigh. **sleighed, sleighing.**

sled

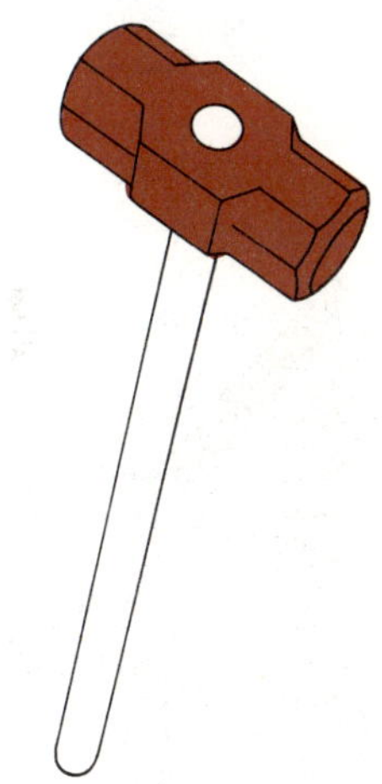

sledge hammer

sleigh

slen·der (SLEN-dər) *adjective.* 1. Slim. 2. Not enough. 3. Not much.

slept *verb. See* **sleep.**

sleuth (SLOOTH) *noun.* (Informal) A detective.

[1]**slew** (SLOO) *verb. See* **slay.**

[2]**slew** (SLOO) Also **slue** *noun.* 1. (Informal) A large quantity or number: a *slew* of people. 2. A twist. —*verb.* To turn or skid. **slewed, slewing.**

slice (SLIGHSS) *noun.* 1. A thin slab or cut (of something): a *slice* of bread. 2. (Slang) A part or share: a *slice* of the profits. 3. (Sports) Hitting a ball so that it curves to the right of its target. **slices.** —*verb.* 1. To cut into slices or portions. 2. To hit a ball so that it curves off its course to the right. **sliced, slicing.**

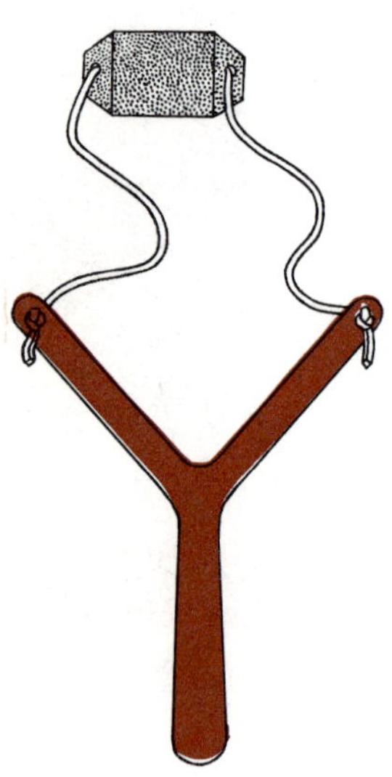

slingshot

slick (SLIK) *adjective.* 1. Shiny or slippery: The icy roads are *slick.* 2. Quick; smart; clever: a *slick* trick of magic. 3. Attractive for the moment or on the surface but having no deep or lasting worth. **slicker, slickest.** —*verb.* 1. To make or make appear to be shiny, smooth, or slippery. 2. (Informal) To tidy (up); make neat. **slicked, slicking.** —**slickly** *adverb.*

slick·er (SLIK-ər) *noun.* 1. A raincoat that has a shiny surface. 2. (Informal) A sophisticated person.

slid *verb. See* **slide.**

slide (SLIGHD) *verb.* To move over a surface without losing contact with it: *Slide* the book across the desk. **slid, sliding.** —*noun.* 1. The act of sliding. 2. A slanted chute, usually found in playgrounds, down which one may slide. 3. A transparent photograph that can be shown on a screen. 4. Rock, dirt, or snow that falls in a mass; an avalanche. **slides.**

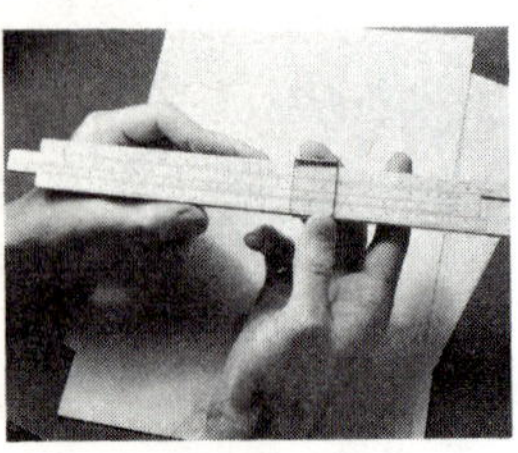

slide rule

slide rule. A device consisting of two scaled rules on which mathematical calculations, such as multiplication and division, are done.

slight *adjective.* 1. Small; little: a *slight* fever. 2. Not very important: The book was of *slight* value. **slighter, slightest.** —*verb.* To snub; be mean to. **slighted, slighting.** —*noun.* A snub. —**slightly** *adverb.*

slim *adjective.* 1. Slender; small in width. 2. Not much; small: There's a *slim* chance that it will rain tomorrow. **slimmer, slimmest.** —**slimly** *adverb.* —**slimness** *noun.* —**slim down.** To lose weight.

slime (SLIGHM) *noun.* Wet, slippery ooze. —**slimy** *adjective.*

sling *noun.* 1. A piece of fabric, leather, or metal, used to hold or lift (something). 2. A weapon made of a strap (or straps) holding a stone or other object that is twirled about and let fly at a target. 3. A wide strip of cloth hung from the neck to support an injured hand or arm. —*verb.* To throw with force. **slung, slinging.**

sling·shot (SLING-shot) *noun.* A piece of wood, metal, or plastic in the shape of a Y fitted with a piece of elastic, used for hurling stones.

slink (SLINGK) *verb.* To move in a sneaky way. **slunk, slinking.**

[1]**slip** *verb.* 1. To move in a quiet, secret way: We tried to *slip* past the guard. 2. To skid, slide, or fall: *slip* on the ice. 3. To put (in, on, or under) secretly or without noise: Ben *slipped* his paper onto the desk. 4. (Informal) To become less alert or strong: Grandpa is *slipping.* **slipped, slipping.** —*noun.* 1. The action of slipping. 2. The place between two piers in which a ship or boat can dock. 3. An important mistake: a *slip* of the tongue. 4. A woman's sleeveless undergarment. —**slip into** or **out of.** To put on or take off (clothes) quickly.

[2]**slip** *noun.* 1. A small bit (of paper). 2. A young, slim person. 3. Part of a plant used for replanting or grafting; a cutting.

slip·per (SLIP-ər) *noun.* A light shoe, generally for wearing in the house.

slip·per·y (SLIP-ə-ree) *adjective.* 1. Slick, causing slipping: a *slippery* road. 2. Sly; unable to be caught or held onto. **slipperier, slipperiest.**

slip·shod (SLIP-SHOD) *adjective.* Done without care; sloppy.

slit *noun.* A long, thin opening or slash. —*verb.* To make a long, thin cut; to split. **slit, slitting.**

sliv·er (SLIV-ər) *noun.* A small, narrow piece (of something) that has been cut or broken off.

slo·gan (SLOH-gən) *noun.* 1. A motto: Teddy Roosevelt's *slogan* was "Speak softly and carry a big stick." 2. A phrase used in advertising.

sloop *noun.* A one-masted sailboat.

slop *verb.* To spill or splash (a liquid): Suzie *slopped* chocolate milk on her dress. **slopped, slopping.** —*noun.* 1. Food that is mushy or has an unappealing look. 2. Very wet mud.

slope (SLOHP) *noun.* A slant: a ski *slope.* **slopes.** —*verb.* To slant (up or down). **sloped, sloping.**

slop·py (SLOP-ee) *adjective.* 1. Wet, slushy; full of or covered with mud. 2. (Informal) Not neat or tidy: a *sloppy* room. 3. (Informal) Done without care. **sloppier, sloppiest.**

sloppy Joe. A dish made of a mixture of hamburger, onion, peppers, and sauce, often served on a bun.

slosh *verb.* To move or splash (in), as in a liquid: The clothes *slosh* around in the washing machine. **sloshed, sloshing.**

slot *noun.* 1. A thin opening or groove: coin *slot.* 2. (Informal) A scheduled time or place: That TV show was moved to a new time *slot.*

slot car. A small model automobile with a tiny electric engine that runs along a slot or track.

sloth (SLOHTH or SLOTH) *noun.* 1. Inactivity; laziness. 2. A slow-moving mammal of South America that lives in trees. —**slothful** *adjective.*

slouch (SLOWCH) *noun.* 1. A stooping or sagging posture. 2. A lazy or incompetent person. **slouches.** —*verb.* To walk, stand, or sit in a stooping way. **slouched, slouching.**

slov·en·ly (SLUHV-ən-lee) *adjective.* Careless, messy. —**slovenliness** *noun.*

slow (SLOH) *adjective.* 1. Not fast; moving or working at a low rate of speed: *slow* traffic. 2. Dull, not quick to learn. 3. Behind time: The clock is *slow.* 4. Not lively; not interesting: a *slow* book. **slower, slowest.** —*adverb.* Also **slowly.** At less speed: Drive *slow* as you pass the school. —*verb.* To make or become slow: Fog *slowed* the traffic. **slowed, slowing.**

slow·poke (SLOH-pohk) *noun.* (Informal) One who moves or acts slowly. **slowpokes.**

slug (SLUHG) *noun.* 1. A slow-moving animal like the snail but without a shell. 2. A heavy blow. 3. A piece of metal used in place of a coin. —*verb.* To hit with the fist or a heavy object. **slugged, slugging.**

slug·gard (SLUHG-ərd) *noun.* A lazy person.

slug·ger (SLUHG-ər) *noun.* (Baseball) A hard-hitting batter.

slug·gish (SLUHG-ish) *adjective.* 1. Dull, lazy. 2. Slow-moving: a *sluggish* stream. —**sluggishly** *adjective.* —**sluggishness** *noun.*

sluice (SLOOSS) *noun.* 1. A ditch used to move water from one place to another. 2. A water trough used for moving logs or washing ore. **sluices.** —*verb.* To wash with a flow of water. **sluiced, sluicing.**

slum (SLUHM) *noun.* A poor, crowded, rundown area. —*verb.* To visit such an area. **slummed, slumming.**

slum·ber (SLUHM-bər) *verb.* 1. To sleep. 2. To be at rest or peace. **slumbered, slumbering.** —*noun.* Sleep.

sloth

sloop

slug (definition 1)

slot cars

slump (SLUHMP) *noun.* A slow period; a drop or fall: The team is in a *slump.* —*verb.* 1. To fall limply. 2. To droop or sag: Jack *slumped* over his desk. **slumped, slumping.**

slung (SLUHNG) *verb. See* **sling.**

slunk (SLUHNGK) *verb. See* **slink.**

slur (SLER) *verb.* 1. To slide over quickly; fail to pronounce clearly: He *slurs* his words. 2. (Music) To sing or play two or more notes smoothly without a break. 3. To make an unkind or insulting remark about. **slurred, slurring.** —*noun.* 1. An insult; unkind remark. 2. (Music) A sign indicating that notes are to be played or sung smoothly, as a phrase.

slush (SLUHSH) *noun.* Melting snow or ice. —**slushy** *adjective.*

sly (SLIGH) *adjective.* 1. Clever, able to fool others. 2. Secret, sneaky. **slier** or **slyer, sliest** or **slyest.** —**slyly** *adverb.* —**slyness** *noun.* —**on the sly.** Secretly.

smack (SMAK) *verb.* 1. To slap; hit with a loud noise. 2. To make a sound with the lips by opening them quickly. 3. To kiss noisily. 4. (Used with *of*) To hint or suggest: Many of Poe's stories *smack* of the supernatural. **smacked, smacking.** —*noun.* 1. The noise or act of slapping or striking something. 2. A loud kiss. 3. The sound made by smacking the lips. 4. A fishing boat. —*adverb.* Directly, straight: My bike ran *smack* into a tree.

small (SMAWL) *adjective.* 1. Little: a *small* child. 2. Unimportant. 3. Mean, not generous. 4. Soft or low: ". . . a still *small* voice." (I Kings 19:12). **smaller, smallest.** —*noun.* People or things that are smaller than the rest: Big fish eat the *small.* —**small talk.** Idle or unimportant conversation.

small·pox (SMAWL-poks) *noun.* A serious contagious disease that causes fever and sores on the skin.

smelter

smart (SMAHRT) *adjective.* 1. Quick-witted, clever, intelligent: a *smart* girl. 2. Fashionable; neat; clean: a *smart* outfit. 3. Lively; quick: a *smart* pace. **smarter, smartest.** —*verb.* To feel or cause pain: The cut *smarts.* **smarted, smarting.** —*noun.* A sharp or stinging pain. —**smartly** *adverb.*

smash *verb.* 1. To break or be broken into pieces. 2. To hit or run (into); crash. **smashed, smashing.** —*noun.* 1. The act or sound of hitting or crashing. 2. (Informal) A big success: The new play is a *smash.* **smashes.**

smat·ter·ing (SMAT-ər-ing) *noun.* A very small amount.

smear (SMIHR) *verb.* 1. To spread or cover (with a soft, moist substance): The baby *smeared* his face with applesauce. 2. (Informal) To defeat, as in a sports event. 3. (Slang) To discredit, especially with untrue charges. **smeared, smearing.** —*noun.* The stain or dirty mark left by a moist substance.

smell (SMEL) *verb.* 1. To sense odors with the nose. 2. To give off an odor: ". . . a rose/ By any other name would *smell* as sweet." (Shakespeare). 3. To give off a bad odor: "Fish and visitors *smell* in three days." (Ben Franklin). **smelled** or **smelt, smelling.** —*noun.* 1. Odor. 2. The ability to sense an odor through the nose. 3. The act of smelling. —**to smell a rat.** To be suspicious.

[1]**smelt** *verb.* To obtain a pure metal by heating metals or their ores to a high temperature. **smelted, smelting.**

[2]**smelt** *noun.* A small fish found in cold waters and used as food.

smelt·er (SMEL-tər) *noun.* 1. A furnace or place used for smelting ores. 2. One who smelts ores.

smile (SMIGHL) *verb.* To grin; turn up the corners of the mouth and look happy. **smiled, smiling.** —*noun.* A happy look caused by turning up the corners of the mouth. **smiles.**

smirk (SMERK) *noun.* A silly smile; one that is not genuine. —*verb.* To smile in a silly way. **smirked, smirking.**

smite (SMIGHT) *verb.* To hit with great strength. **smote** (SMOHT), **smiting.**

smith *noun.* One who shapes metal or repairs metal objects: silver*smith,* gold*smith,* or black*smith.*

smith·y (SMITH-ee or SMITH-ee) *noun.* 1. A blacksmith shop. 2. A blacksmith. **smithies.**

smock (SMOK) *noun.* A loose-fitting garment usually worn to protect one's clothing while working.

smog *noun.* A mixture of smoke and fog. —**smoggy** *adjective.*

smoke (SMOHK) *noun.* 1. A cloud of visible gases released into the air when something burns. 2. Anything that looks like smoke. 3. (Informal) A cigar or cigarette. **smokes.** —*verb.* 1. To give off smoke. 2. To draw in and blow out the gases from a burning cigar, cigarette, or pipe. 3. To preserve or flavor meat or other food by exposing it to smoke. 4. To drive out by smoke. **smoked, smoking.** —**smoky** *adjective.*

smoke·stack (SMOHK-stak) *noun.* A large pipe for discharging smoke.

smol·der (SMOHL-dər) Also **smoulder** *verb.* 1. To burn slowly without a flame. 2. To keep hatred or anger inside one. **smoldered, smoldering.**

smooth (SMOOTH) *adjective.* 1. Flat, level, not rough. 2. Without lumps: *smooth* gravy. 3. Without bumps or jolts: a *smooth* ride. 4. Overly polite; not sincere: a *smooth* talker. —*verb.* To make level or flat by removing wrinkles, bumps, or rough places. **smoothed, smoothing.** —**smoothly** *adverb.* —**smooth the way.** To remove problems or obstacles.

smote (SMOHT) *verb. See* **smite.**

smoth·er (SMUHTH-ər) *verb.* 1. To fail to receive enough air to breathe or to keep another from receiving enough air. 2. To cover thickly: He *smothered* his potatoes with gravy. **smothered, smothering.**

smudge (SMUHJ) *verb.* To soil by smearing with dirt. **smudged, smudging.** —*noun.* 1. A dirty mark. 2. A fire made to fill an area with smoke. **smudges.** —**smudgy** *adjective.*

smug (SMUHG) *adjective.* Too pleased with oneself; self-satisfied. **smugger, smuggest.** —**smugly** *adverb.*

smug·gle (SMUHG-əl) *verb.* 1. To take or bring secretly: Harry *smuggled* the snake into the house. 2. To take in or out of a country illegally. **smuggled, smuggling.** —**smuggler** *noun.*

snack (SNAK) *noun.* 1. A light meal. 2. Food eaten between regular meals. —*verb.* To eat a light meal. **snacked, snacking.**

snag *noun.* 1. A stump or tree hidden or partly hidden under the water. 2. A rough, sharp point extending out from a surface. 3. A pull or tear in a fabric. 4. An unexpected problem: Our plans hit a *snag.* —*verb.* 1. To catch or tear on a snag or rough place. 2. (Informal) To catch quickly: A man in the stands *snagged* the fly ball. **snagged, snagging.**

snail (SNAYL) *noun.* A small, slow-moving animal with a curved shell into which it can withdraw. —**snail's pace.** A very slow speed.

snake (SNAYK) *noun.* 1. A scaly reptile that moves its long, thin, legless body by crawling or looping along the ground. 2. (Informal) A low, sneaky person. **snakes.** —*verb.* To move, curve, or turn along the ground like a snake: The river *snakes* its way to the sea. **snaked, snaking.** —**snaky** *adjective.*

smith

smokestacks

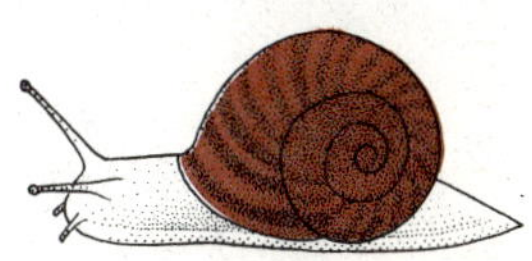
snail

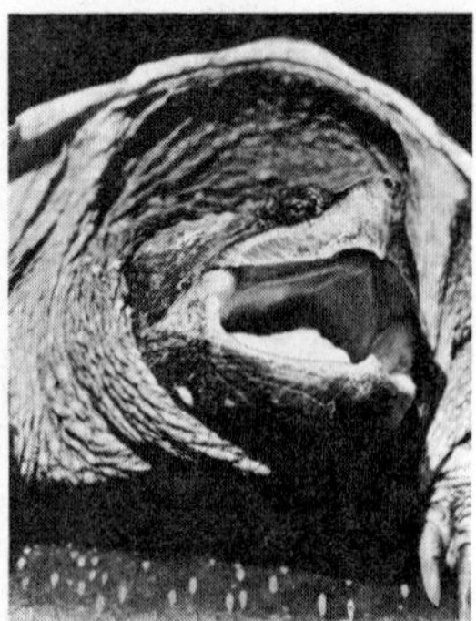
snapping turtle

snare drum

sneakers

snap *verb.* 1. To make or cause to make a sudden sharp noise. 2. To break suddenly. 3. To close quickly, especially the jaws: The dog *snapped* at the mailman. 4. To speak sharply and angrily. 5. To photograph with a camera. **snapped, snapping.** —*noun.* 1. A sudden sharp noise. 2. (Informal) An easy job or school course. 3. A sudden breaking. 4. A quick bite. 5. A fastener on clothing. 6. A crisp cooky: ginger*snap.*

snap·drag·on (SNAP-drag-ən) *noun.* 1. A spike-shaped flower with a series of two connected petals. 2. The plant on which this flower grows.

snapping turtle. A large turtle with strong jaws that lives in American rivers and ponds.

snap·py (SNAP-ee) *adjective.* 1. (Informal) Quick, lively. 2. (Informal) Smart in appearance. 3. Cross, disagreeable. **snappier, snappiest.**

snap·shot (SNAP-shot) *noun.* A small informal or unposed photograph.

snare (SNAIR) *noun.* A trap made with a noose, used to catch small animals and birds. **snares.** —*verb.* To catch in a trap or snare. **snared, snaring.**

snare drum. A small drum with strings across the bottom side.

snarl (SNAHRL) *verb.* 1. To growl and show the teeth. 2. To speak in an angry or unpleasant way. 3. To tangle or cause confusion. **snarled, snarling.** —*noun.* 1. A growl. 2. A tangle or state of confusion.

snatch (SNACH) *verb.* To grasp, grab, or seize suddenly. **snatched, snatching.** —*noun.* 1. The act of taking or grabbing. 2. A small part: *snatches* of conversation. **snatches.**

sneak (SNEEK) *verb.* To move or act in a quiet, secret way: He *sneaked* out. **sneaked, sneaking.** —*noun.* One who acts in a sly, secret way. —**sneaky** *adjective.*

sneak·ers (SNEE-kərz) *noun.* Tennis shoes; cloth shoes with soft soles.

sneer (SNIHR) *verb.* To mock or scorn by the look on one's face or by a remark. **sneered, sneering.** —*noun.* A scornful look or remark.

sneeze (SNEEZ) *verb.* To breathe out suddenly, noisily, and without control. **sneezed, sneezing.** —*noun.* The act or sound of sneezing.

sniff (SNIF) *verb.* 1. To smell by taking breaths through the nose: The dog *sniffed* his food. 2. To breathe in through the nose in short breaths and with a noise. **sniffed, sniffing.** —*noun.* The act or sound of smelling or sniffing.

snif·fle (SNIF-l) *verb.* To sniff repeatedly, as when one is crying or has a cold. **sniffled, sniffling.** —*noun.* 1. The act of sniffling. 2. (Plural, informal) A head cold.

snip *verb.* To cut off quickly in small pieces. **snipped, snipping.** —*noun.* 1. A small piece cut off. 2. The act or sound of snipping.

snipe (SNIGHP) *noun.* A long-billed bird that lives in wet, marshy places. —**snipe** or **snipes** *plural.* —*verb.* 1. To shoot a gun from a hidden location. 2. To hunt snipe. **sniped, sniping.** —**sniper** *noun.*

sniv·el (SNIV-əl) *verb.* 1. To cry or weep. 2. To whine or complain. **sniveled, sniveling.**

snob *noun.* One who looks down on those he considers inferior in position or intelligence.

snoop *verb.* To spy or prowl; look into someone else's business in a sneaky, underhanded way. **snooped, snooping.** —*noun.* One who snoops.

snooze (SNOOZ) *verb.* (Slang) To take a nap; to sleep or doze. **snoozed, snoozing.** —*noun.* A nap.

snore (SNOR) *verb.* To breathe with harsh, noisy sounds while asleep. **snored, snoring.** —*noun.* The sound of snoring.

snork•el (SNOR-kəl) *noun.* 1. A tube or tubes permitting a submarine to take in fresh air while it is under the water. 2. A tube used by a swimmer to get air when his head is under the water. *—verb.* To swim under the water while using a snorkel. Also called "snorkel dive." **snorkeled, snorkeling.**

snort *verb.* 1. To force air through the nose with a sudden harsh sound. 2. To show surprise, dislike, or anger by making such a sound. 3. To make a sound like a snort. **snorted, snorting.** *—noun.* The act or sound of snorting.

snout (SNOWT) *noun.* 1. The long nose of certain kinds of animals, such as the pig. 2. Anything like an animal's snout. 3. (Slang) A person's nose, especially if it is big.

snow (SNOH) *noun.* 1. White flakes that form when vapor forms crystals in the cold air. 2. A fall of such flakes. *—verb.* 1. To fall as snow. 2. (Slang) To charm, flatter, or trick. **snowed, snowing.** —**snow job.** (Slang) Persuasion by excessive flattery.

snow•ball (SNOH-bawl) *noun.* 1. A hard ball made of snow. 2. A bush with small white flowers in large masses like balls. *—verb.* 1. To hit with snowballs; to throw snowballs at. 2. To increase or grow larger rapidly. **snowballed, snowballing.**

snow•drift (SNOH-drift) *noun.* A bank or mass of snow piled up by the wind.

snow•fall (SNOH-fawl) *noun.* 1. A fall of snow. 2. The amount of snow that falls in a given time or place.

snow•flake (SNOH-flayk) *noun.* One small piece or flake of snow.

snow•mo•bile (SNOH-moh-beel) *noun.* A small, open, motorized vehicle made to travel on snow.

snow•plow (SNOH-plow) *noun.* A machine that pushes snow from streets and other outdoor areas.

snow•shoe (SNOH-shoo) *noun.* A wooden frame fitted with leather strips, worn when walking over deep snow. **snowshoes.**

snow•storm (SNOH-storm) *noun.* A storm in which much snow falls.

snow•y (SNOH-ee) *adjective.* 1. Having snow. 2. Covered with snow. 3. White like snow: *snowy* hair.

snub (SNUHB) *verb.* 1. To treat in an unfriendly way; pretend not to see. 2. To check or stop (a rope or cable) suddenly. **snubbed, snubbing.** *—noun.* An unfriendly act.

[1]**snuff** (SNUHF) *verb.* 1. To put out. 2. (Used with *out*) To destroy. 3. To put out a candle by pinching or smothering. **snuffed, snuffing.**

[2]**snuff** (SNUHF) *noun.* Powdered tobacco that is sniffed into the nose, chewed, or placed on the gums. —**up to snuff.** In good condition.

snug (SNUHG) *adjective.* 1. Warm, comfortable, and safe. 2. Tight; close. 3. Small, neat, and orderly: *snug* shops. **snugger, snuggest.**

snug•gle (SNUHG-əl) *verb.* To cuddle; press close or lie close (to) in a loving way. **snuggled, snuggling.**

so (SOH) *adverb.* 1. To such a degree or extent: Do not drink *so* fast. 2. Therefore; for this reason. 3. Very; extremely: I am *so* tired. 4. Likewise; also. 5. Very much: She does carry on *so!* 6. After all: *So* you are going to the game. 7. In this way; as shown: You must throw the ball *so.* 8. As stated (with reference to something already said): She is lame and has been *so* all her life. 9. More or less; approximately: two years or *so.* *—conjunction.* 1. In order that: He walked fast *so* that he'd get home early. 2. And therefore: She did not wear a coat, *so* she is very cold. *—adjective.* True: What he says is simply not *so.* *—interjection.* Expresses surprise: *So!* You did it!

snorkel

snowplow

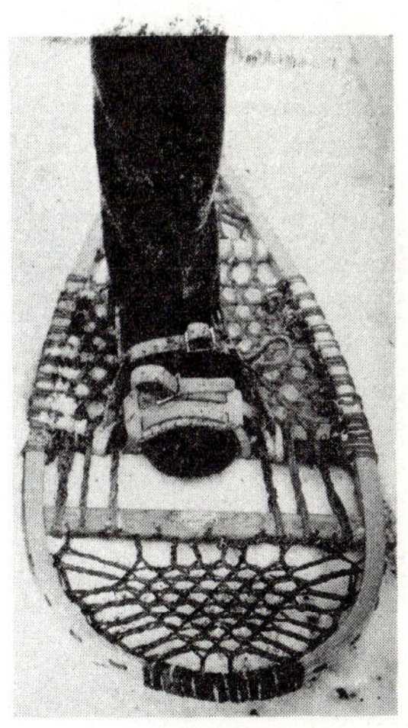

snowshoe

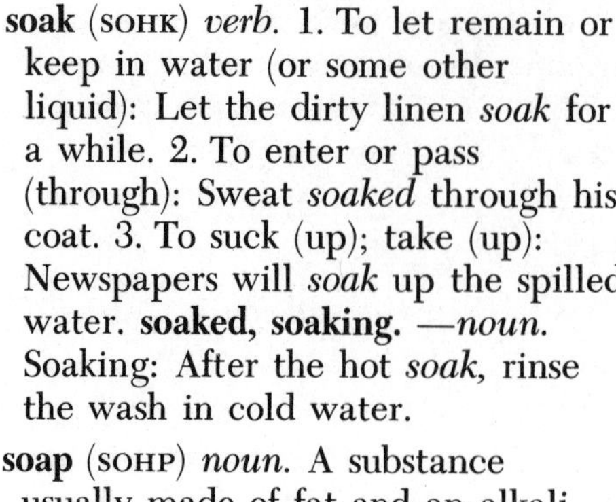

soak (SOHK) *verb.* 1. To let remain or keep in water (or some other liquid): Let the dirty linen *soak* for a while. 2. To enter or pass (through): Sweat *soaked* through his coat. 3. To suck (up); take (up): Newspapers will *soak* up the spilled water. **soaked, soaking.** —*noun.* Soaking: After the hot *soak,* rinse the wash in cold water.

soap (SOHP) *noun.* A substance usually made of fat and an alkali (such as potash) and used for washing. —*verb.* To rub with soap: *Soap* those dirty hands. **soaped, soaping.** —**soapy** *adjective.*

soapbox derby

soapbox derby. A contest in which young people race down a slanting track in motorless cars they have made themselves.

soap·suds (SOHP-suhdz) *noun, plural.* A foaming mixture of soap and water.

soar (SOR) *verb.* 1. To fly high without any movement that can be seen; rise upward in the air: The hawk *soars* to a great height. 2. To rise to a higher level than usual: The price of fresh fruit will *soar* this winter. **soared, soaring.**

sob *verb.* To cry with short quick gasps. **sobbed, sobbing.** —*noun.* The act or sound of sobbing.

so·ber (SOH-bər) *adjective.* 1. Not drunk; not having taken much alcohol: *Sober* drivers have few accidents. 2. Quiet; serious; earnest. 3. Not showy or gay; plain: *sober* dresses. —*verb.* To make or become quiet or sober. **sobered, sobering.** —**soberly** *adverb.* —**soberness** or **sobriety** (soh-BRIGH-ə-tee) *noun.*

so-called (SOH-KAWLD) *adjective.* Commonly called thus, usually implying doubt: His *so-called* friend betrayed Joe.

soccer

soc·cer (SOK-ər) *noun.* A game in which two teams of 11 men each try to hit or kick a round ball into the other team's goal.

so·cia·ble (SOH-shə-bəl) *adjective.* 1. Friendly; liking company: a *sociable* person. 2. Spent in a pleasant way with friends: a *sociable* game of cards. —**sociably** *adverb.*

so·cial (SOH-shəl) *adjective.* 1. Enjoying the company of others; sociable. 2. Having to do with society or people living together in a group: *social* change. 3. Living together in a group: Wasps and bees are *social* insects. 4. Having to do with fashionable society. —*noun.* A party. —**socially** *adverb.*

so·cial·ism (SOH-shəl-iz-əm) *noun.* A social system or plan in which the people as a whole, and not individuals, own and control all the property, factories, and stores, and share in what they produce.

social science. The study of human beings and how they live and work together in large groups: Economics and history are *social sciences.*

social security. A plan of government insurance to provide for retired, disabled, or temporarily unemployed persons and their dependents.

social studies. The study of history, geography, and other social sciences.

so·ci·e·ty (sə-SIGH-ə-tee) *noun.* 1. A group of people who join and work together for a common purpose; an organization. 2. All mankind, especially people of a particular time or place: "The happiness of *society* is the end of government." (John Adams). 3. Companionship. 4. The upper class; rich people.

so·ci·ol·o·gy (soh-see-OL-ə-jee) *noun.* The science or study of society; the study of people living together in groups and their institutions.

[1]**sock** (SOK) *noun.* A short stocking covering the foot, ankle, and part of the lower leg.

[2]**sock** (SOK) (Slang) *verb.* To hit very hard, **socked, socking.** —*noun.* A very hard blow.

sock·et (SOK-it) *noun.* A hollow part into which something is fitted: Screw the bulb into the *socket.*

sod *noun.* The ground cover made by grass and the soil into which its roots grow. —*verb.* To cover ground with sod. **sodded, sodding.**

so·da (SOH-də) *noun.* 1. Sodium carbonate in any of its various forms: baking *soda.* 2. Fizzy, carbonated water used in soft drinks. 3. A sweet drink containing soda water, flavoring, and often ice cream.

soda fountain. A counter at which sodas, ice cream, sandwiches, and other light food and drinks are served.

soda water. Water filled with a gas (carbon dioxide) that makes it bubble.

sod·den (SOD-n) *adjective.* 1. Very wet; completely soaked: *sodden* clothing. 2. Soggy; heavy and doughy: *sodden* biscuits.

so·di·um (SOH-dee-əm) *noun.* A silver-white metallic element that is soft and easily formed into shapes.

sodium chloride. A chemical compound of sodium and chlorine; common salt.

so·fa (SOH-fə) *noun.* An upholstered couch, usually with back and arms.

soft *adjective.* 1. Not hard or stiff; giving way when touched: The ground is *soft* after rain. 2. Not as hard as other things of the same kind: Lead is a *soft* metal. 3. Smooth; not rough or coarse. 4. Pleasant or mild: *soft* breeze. 5. Kind, gentle; soothing: *soft* words. 6. Not harsh or glaring: *soft* light. 7. Low or gentle in sound; not loud: the *soft* ringing of a distant bell. 8. Weak; not strong. 9. Merciful; kind: a *soft* heart. 10. Easy; not needing much effort: a *soft* job. 11. Not severe or hard: a *soft* life. 12. Not containing alcohol: *soft* drinks. 13. Not containing minerals that make it difficult for soap to form suds: *soft* water. 14. (Speech) Having the sound of *c* in *central* and of *g* in *gentle.* **softer, softest.** —**softly** *adverb.* Quietly; gently.

soft·ball (SOFT-bawl) *noun.* 1. A kind of baseball game played with a ball that is bigger and bats that are lighter than the ones used in standard baseball. 2. The ball used in softball.

soft·en (SOF-ən) *verb.* To make or become softer. **softened, softening.**

soft·wood (SOFT-wud) *noun.* 1. Any wood that is fairly soft and easy to cut. 2. A tree that has such wood.

sog·gy (SOG-ee) *adjective.* Soaked; very wet or damp. **soggier, soggiest.**

[1]**soil** *noun.* 1. Dirt; ground; the outer layer of the earth in which plants grow. 2. A region or country: Many of our soldiers died on foreign *soil.*

[2]**soil** *verb.* 1. To become or make dirty: Don't *soil* your clean shirt. 2. To disgrace: The traitor has *soiled* his nation's honor. **soiled, soiling.**

so·journ (SOH-jern) *verb.* To stay for a time in a place: We *sojourned* in the South. **sojourned, sojourning.** —*noun.* A temporary stay.

sol (SOHL) Also **so** (SOH) *noun.* The fifth note in any standard major or minor scale of eight notes.

so·lar (SOH-lər) *adjective.* 1. Having to do with the sun: the *solar* system. 2. Depending on the sun for light or power: a *solar* battery. 3. Measured by the earth's movement around the sun: a *solar* year.

solar flare. A relatively small but intense eruption of light from the atmosphere of the sun.

solar system. The sun and all the objects that revolve around it, such as planets, asteroids, and comets.

sold (SOHLD) *verb.* See **sell.**

sol·der (SOD-ər) *noun.* A metal or alloy that is melted to join or mend other pieces of metal. —*verb.* To

soda fountain

join or mend with solder. **soldered, soldering.**

sol·dier (SOHL-jər) *noun.* A person who serves in an army who is not an officer; an enlisted man.

[1]**sole** (SOHL) *adjective.* Only; without others: I was the *sole* left-hander in my class. —**solely** *adverb.*

[2]**sole** (SOHL) *noun.* 1. The bottom of the foot. 2. The bottom of a shoe, boot, or similar article. —*verb.* To put a sole on a shoe, boot, or similar article. **soled, soling.**

[3]**sole** (SOHL) *noun.* A flatfish similar to a flounder, very popular as seafood. —**sole** or **soles** *plural.*

sol·emn (SOL-əm) *adjective.* 1. Very serious: a *solemn* expression on his face. 2. Formal; performed with dignity: a *solemn* procession of graduates. —**solemnly** *adverb.*

sol·em·ni·ty (sə-LEM-nə-tee) *noun.* 1. Seriousness; formality. 2. A formal ritual or ceremony. **solemnities.**

so·lic·it (sə-LISS-it) *verb.* To try to obtain; seek or ask for, as for aid or money. **solicited, soliciting.**

sol·id (SOL-id) *adjective.* 1. Firm; hard: Some melons were *solid,* but others were soft. 2. Not in the form of a liquid or gas: Ice is water in a *solid* condition. 3. Not hollow. 4. Having height, width, and length: A cube is a *solid* figure; a square is not. 5. Well-built; without flaws: The shaky old shed was not very *solid.* 6. Of one type or color: a *solid* blue auto. 7. Worthy of serious consideration: *solid* plan. 8. Without a break or interruption: a *solid* line of trucks. 9. (Informal) Dependable; worthy of trust and respect: The farmers were *solid* citizens. —*noun.* 1. Something in a solid, rather than a gaseous or liquid, state: Ice is a *solid.* 2. A figure having height, width, and length. —**solidly** *adverb.*

solid figure. (Geometry) Any object that exists in three dimensions, such as a sphere, cube, or pyramid.

so·lid·i·fy (sə-LID-ə-figh) *verb.* To make or become hard or solid: The water *solidified* into ice. **solidified, solidifying.**

sol·i·taire (SOL-ə-tair) *noun.* 1. A card game played by one person. 2. A diamond or other jewel set or mounted by itself, as on a ring.

sol·i·tar·y (SOL-ə-tehr-ee) *adjective.* 1. Living or acting alone: The prospector was a *solitary* old man. 2. Only; sole: The man's license was his *solitary* proof of his age.

sol·i·tude (SOL-ə-tood or SOL-ə-tyood) *noun.* A state of being alone: The forest ranger enjoyed the *solitude* of his life.

so·lo (SOH-loh) *noun.* 1. A piece of music written for a single singer or instrument. 2. Any performance or action done by a single person. **solos.** —*verb.* To perform by oneself, especially to fly a plane alone. **soloed, soloing.**

so·lo·ist (SOH-loh-ist) *noun.* A person who sings or performs some other action by himself.

sol·stice (SOL-stiss) *noun.* Either of two points in the earth's orbit when the sun appears farthest north or south of the equator: In the Northern Hemisphere, the summer *solstice* (about June 22) is the longest day of the year; the winter *solstice* (about December 22) is the shortest day of the year.

sol·u·ble (SOL-yə-bəl) *adjective.* 1. Able to be dissolved: Sugar is *soluble* in water. 2. Able to be solved. —**solubly** *adverb.*

so·lu·tion (sə-LOO-shən) *noun.* 1. The answer (to a problem): the *solution* to a math question. 2. The process of finding an answer or explanation: The *solution* of the crime took many months. 3. A mixture, as of a solid dissolved in a liquid: a *solution* of salt and water. 4. The process of dissolving in a liquid or forming a mixture.

solve (SOLV) *verb.* To find an answer or explanation for. **solved, solving.**

som·ber (SOM-bər) *adjective.* 1. Dark; gloomy: The sky grew *somber.* 2. Depressing; dismal: The funeral was a *somber* affair. —**somberly** *adverb.*

som·bre·ro (som-BRAIR-oh) *noun.* A large, wide-brimmed hat popular in Mexico and South America. **sombreros.**

some (SUHM) *adjective.* 1. Certain, but not named or indicated: *Some* cars have power steering. 2. Of an amount or number that is not named: Please put *some* wood on the fire. 3. (Informal) Outstanding; impressive: Randy is *some* quarterback. —*pronoun.* An amount or number that is not named: *Some* of the food was spoiled. —*adverb.* About; nearly: *Some* 30 runners finished the race.

-some *suffix.* Indicates: 1. An inclination or tendency to: worri*some.* 2. A group or company of: two*some.*

some·bod·y (SUHM-bod-ee) *pronoun.* A person not named; someone: *Somebody* forgot his coat. —*noun.* A person of importance: If you win the race, you will really be *somebody.* **somebodies.**

some·day (SUHM-day) *adverb.* At some vague time in the future.

some·how (SUHM-how) *adverb.* In a manner that is not named or known: We will fix the mower *somehow.*

some·one (SUHM-wuhn) *pronoun.* A person who is not named; somebody.

som·er·sault (SUHM-ər-sawlt) *noun.* A rolling or flipping forward of the body, heels over head, for one full turn. —*verb.* To roll or flip in a *somersault.* **somersaulted, somersaulting.**

some·thing (SUHM-thing) *pronoun.* An object or thing that is not named or known: Dad is looking for *something* in the basement. —*noun.* (Informal) A thing, event, or person of importance: The forest fire was really *something.*

some·time (SUHM-tighm) *adverb.* At a time that is not named or known: I would like to visit Paris *sometime.* —*adjective.* Former: Bob's *sometime* friend is now his enemy.

some·times (SUHM-tighmz) *adverb.* Now and then; one time or another.

some·what (SUHM-hwaht) *adverb.* To some, usually slight, degree: This winter is *somewhat* colder than last. —*noun.* Some amount, degree, or manner: She was *somewhat* of a bore.

some·where (SUHM-hwehr) *adverb.* 1. In or to a place that is not named or known: My teacher went *somewhere* for a rest. 2. In or to some time, quantity, or degree that is not named or known: Karen's weight is *somewhere* around 85 pounds.

son (SUHN) *noun.* A male offspring.

so·nar (SOH-nahr) *noun.* A method of detecting and locating underwater objects with reflected sound waves.

song *noun.* 1. A short piece of music for singing. 2. Any musical sounds: the *song* of a bird. 3. One of various types of poetry: "*Song* of Roland."

song·bird (SONG-berd) *noun.* A bird that is able to make pleasing sounds or songs.

song·ster (SONG-stər) *noun.* A singer.

son·ic (SON-ik) *adjective.* Relating to sound or the speed of sound.

sonic boom. A sound like a thunderclap caused by an airplane flying faster than the speed of sound.

son-in-law (SUHN-in-law) *noun.* The husband of a person's daughter. —**sons-in-law** *plural.*

son·net (SON-it) *noun.* A rhymed poem of 14 lines.

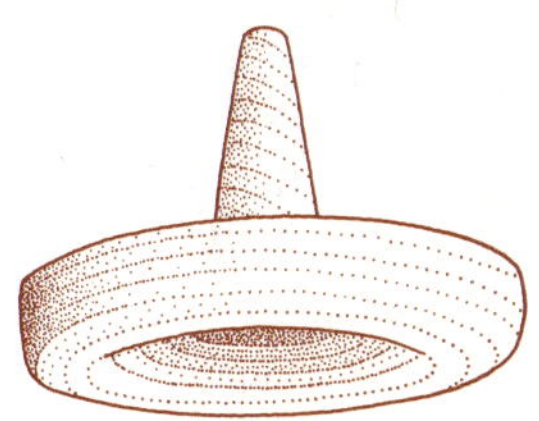

sombrero

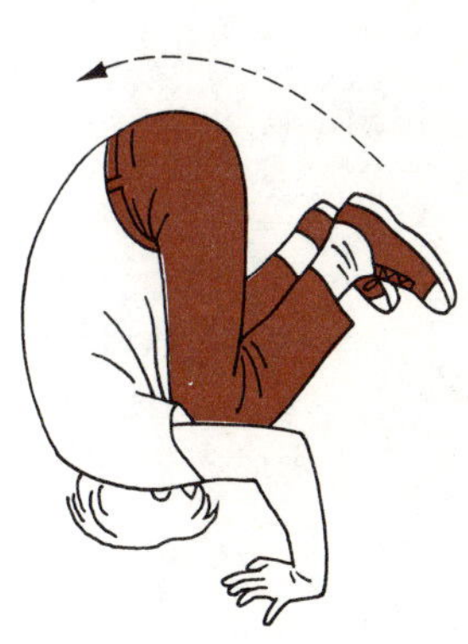

somersault

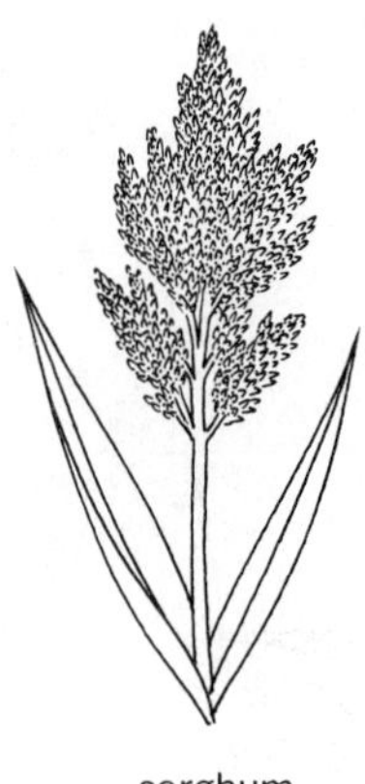
sorghum

so·no·rous (sə-NOR-əss) *adjective.* Having a rich, deep sound. —**sonorously** *adverb.*

soon *adverb.* 1. In a short time: The train will arrive *soon.* 2. Quickly. 3. Early: arrive too *soon.* 4. Willingly; readily: I would just as *soon* stay home as go to an old movie. **sooner, soonest.**

soot *noun.* A fine black substance produced by the burning of coal, oil, or other fuel.

soothe (SOOTH) *verb.* 1. To calm or relax; make comfortable: "Music hath charms to *soothe* the savage breast." (W. Congreve). 2. To relieve from pain or discomfort: A cool cream *soothed* my sunburn. **soothed, soothing.**

sooth·say·er (SOOTH-say-ər) *noun.* A person who claims to be able to predict future events.

so·phis·ti·cat·ed (sə-FISS-ti-kay-tid) *adjective.* 1. Worldly; not childlike. 2. Complicated; involved. —**sophistication** (sə-fiss-ti-KAY-shən) *noun.*

soph·o·more (SOF-ə-mor) *noun.* A student in the second year of high school or college. **sophomores.**

so·pra·no (sə-PRAN-oh) *noun.* 1. The highest singing voice, usually female. 2. A singer, usually female, of soprano range. **sopranos.**

sor·cer·er (SOR-sər-ər) *noun.* A person who is thought or claims to be able to cast spells or perform other magical works with the help of evil spirits; a magician.

sor·cer·y (SOR-sər-ee) *noun.* The power that some persons claim or are supposed to have to cast spells or perform other magical works.

sor·did (SOR-did) *adjective.* 1. Filthy; very shabby or wretched. 2. Morally corrupt; wicked. 3. Selfish; greedy. —**sordidly** *adverb.*

sore (SOR) *adjective.* 1. Tender or painful: Jim's swollen ankle is *sore.* 2. (Informal) Annoyed; angry. 3. Causing pain or unhappiness. a *sore* topic. **sorer, sorest.** —*noun.* A wound, boil, or other place where the body is tender or painful. **sores.** —**sorely** *adverb.* —**soreness** *noun.*

sor·ghum (SOR-gəm) *noun.* 1. A grass or cereal used as food for animals. 2. A syrup made from the stems of sorghum plants.

so·ror·i·ty (sə-ROR-ə-tee) *noun.* A club or organization of girls or women. **sororities.**

[1]**sor·rel** (SOR-əl) *noun.* 1. (Also *adjective*) A reddish-brown color. 2. A reddish-brown horse.

[2]**sor·rel** (SOR-əl) *noun.* A plant with sour leaves which are sometimes used for flavoring, as in salads.

sor·row (SOR-oh) *noun.* 1. Grief; deep sadness. 2. That which causes grief or deep sadness: Many *sorrows* have made his life unhappy. —*verb.* To feel sorrow. **sorrowed, sorrowing.** —**sorrowful** (SOR-oh-fəl) *adjective.* —**sorrowfully** *adverb.*

sor·ry (SOR-ee) *adjective.* 1. Full of regret: I'm *sorry* that I forgot to bring the food. 2. Full of pity or sympathy: Joan felt *sorry* for the tired old man. 3. Causing or worthy of pity; wretched: a *sorry* condition. 4. (Informal) Poor; unsuitable: My clumsy brother is a *sorry* shortstop. **sorrier, sorriest.**

sort *noun.* A kind; type: a lazy *sort* of person. —*verb.* To arrange or separate according to kind or type; classify: Bob *sorted* papers. **sorted, sorting.** —**out of sorts.** In a bad mood; irritable.

SOS 1. A call for help. (Translation of the telegraph code ··· ––– ··· .) 2. Any call for aid or indication of distress.

souf·flé (soo-FLAY) *noun.* A fluffy baked food made by adding whipped egg whites to beaten egg yolks and other ingredients: a cheese *soufflé.* **soufflés.**

sought (SAWT) *verb. See* **seek.**

soul (SOHL) *noun.* 1. The spirit of

man, thought of by many as separate from the body and as the source of thoughts, feelings, and ethics: "Heaven take my *soul*, and England keep my bones." (Shakespeare). 2. An example or model of some quality: "Brevity is the *soul* of wit." (Shakespeare). 3. A person: There wasn't a *soul* at home. 4. (Informal) A spirit or attitude shared and admired by Negroes. —**soul brother** (or **sister**). A male (or female) having a spirit or attitude shared and admired by Negroes.

[1]**sound** (SOWND) *noun.* 1. The sensation received by the ears from vibrations in air, water, etc.; a noise. 2. The manner in which something is stated or understood: The *sound* of the message was disturbing. 3. Hearing distance: within the *sound* of my voice. —*verb.* 1. To make a sound. 2. To seem; appear: *sound* important. 3. To signal or announce: The whistle *sounded* the end of work. **sounded, sounding.**

[2]**sound** (SOWND) *adjective.* 1. In good health. 2. In good condition; sturdy: *sound* timbers. 3. Wise; sensible: *sound* advice. 4. Well-organized; successful and reliable: a *sound* company. 5. Deep; not restless: a *sound* sleep. —**soundly** *adverb.*

[3]**sound** (SOWND) *verb.* 1. To find the depth of a body of water, especially with a weighted line. 2. (Used with *out*) To try to learn what another person's attitudes or ideas are: The reporter *sounded* out the mayor. **sounded, sounding.**

[4]**sound** (SOWND) *noun.* A long body of water joining two larger bodies of water or lying between an island and the mainland.

sound barrier. The sudden increase in wind resistance met by aircraft approaching the speed of sound. Also called "sonic barrier."

sound·proof (SOWND-PROOF) *adjective.* Not allowing sound through. —*verb.* To make so that sound cannot pass through. **soundproofed, soundproofing.**

soup (SOOP) *noun.* A liquid food made by boiling vegetables, meat, or fish.

sour (SOWR) *adjective.* 1. Having a sharp or acid taste: *sour* lemons. 2. Spoiled: *sour* milk. 3. Unpleasant; disagreeable: a *sour* attitude. —*verb.* To make or become spoiled. **soured, souring.** —**sourly** *adverb.*

source (SORSS) *noun.* 1. Any origin or beginning. 2. The beginning of a stream or river. 3. That which supplies information. **sources.**

south (SOWTH) *noun.* 1. The direction opposite north: If you face the rising sun, *south* is to your right. 2. Any area or region to the south. 3. [Capital S] The southern part of the United States. —*adjective.* At or from the south: a *south* wind. —*adverb.* To or toward the south. *See* illustration at **compass.** —**southerly** (SUHTH-ər-lee) *adjective* and *adverb.* —**southern** (SUHTH-ərn) *adjective.*

South America. The continent in the Western Hemisphere lying mainly below the equator.

South Car·o·li·na (SOWTH ka-rə-LIGH-nə) *noun.* A south Atlantic state of the United States, eighth to ratify the Constitution (1788). —**S.C.** *abbreviation.* Also **SC** for Zip Codes.

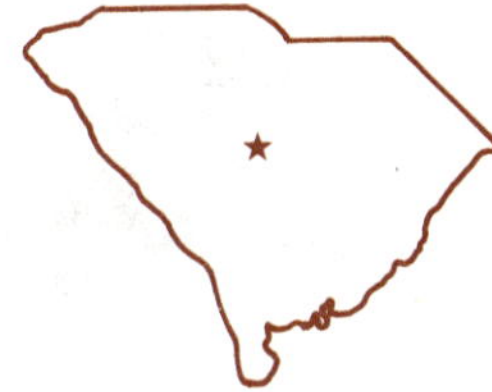

South Carolina
★capital: Columbia

South Da·ko·ta (SOWTH də-KOH-tə) *noun.* A north central state of the United States, 39th or 40th (with North Dakota) to join the Union (1889). —**S. Dak.** *abbreviation.* Also **SD** for Zip Codes.

South Dakota
★capital: Pierre

south·east (sowth-EEST) *noun.* 1. The direction halfway between south and east. 2. Any area or region to the southeast. 3. [Capital S] The states in the southeastern part of the United States. —*adjective* Also **southeastern.** At or from the

space station

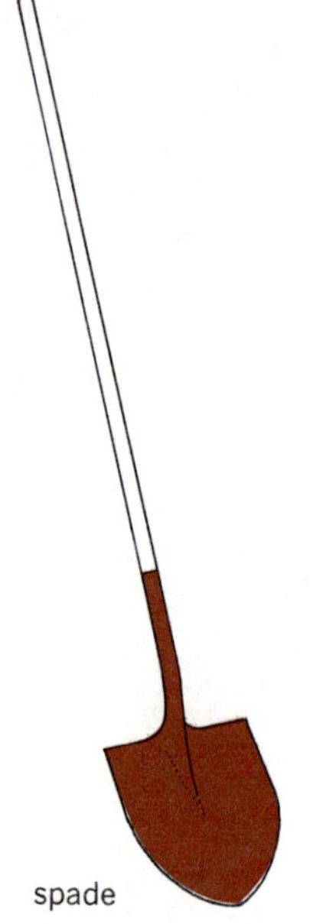
spade

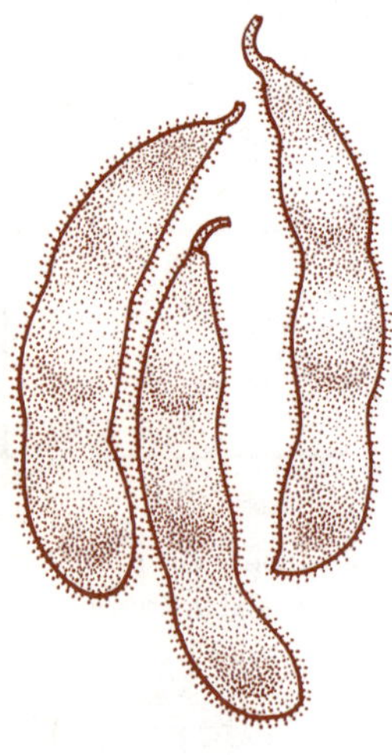
soybeans

southeast. *—adverb.* To or toward the southeast. *See* illustration at **compass.**

southern lights. Flashing lights seen high in the sky south of the equator; also called "aurora australis."

south·paw (SOWTH-paw) *noun.* A left-handed baseball pitcher.

south·west (sowth-WEST) *noun.* 1. The direction between south and west. 2. An area or region to the southwest. 3. [Capital S] The states in the southwestern part of the United States. *—adjective* Also **southwestern.** At or from the southwest. *—adverb.* To or toward the southwest. *See* illustration at **compass.**

sou·ve·nir (SOO-və-NIHR) *noun.* An item bought or saved as a reminder.

sov·er·eign (SOV-ər-ən) *noun.* A ruler; one with supreme power. *—adjective.* 1. Self-governing: a *sovereign* state. 2. Having supreme power. 3. Of the greatest importance. **—sovereignty** *noun.*

[1]**sow** (SOH) *verb.* 1. To plant seed. 2. To scatter. **sowed, sowing.**

[2]**sow** (sow) *noun.* A female pig.

soy·bean (SOI-been) *noun.* 1. A small bean high in food value. 2. The plant on which this bean grows.

spa (SPAH) *noun.* A resort at a spring giving water rich in minerals.

space (SPAYSS) *noun.* 1. The unlimited area in which all things exist. 2. The limited area between two points. 3. The area beyond the earth's atmosphere; the universe. 4. A period of time: the *space* of an hour. **spaces.** *—verb.* To place with spaces between. **spaced, spacing.**

space capsule. A detachable compartment of a vehicle used to carry passengers or equipment on space flights.

space·craft (SPAYSS-kraft) *noun.* A vehicle used for travel outside the earth's atmosphere; a spaceship. **—spacecraft** *plural.*

space probe. An unmanned space flight during which instruments pick up and send back information.

space·ship (SPAYSS-ship) *noun. See* **spacecraft.**

space station. A large spacecraft placed in orbit around the earth and used for research or as a base for other space flights.

space suit. A suit designed to provide pressure, air supply, and other protection in outer space.

spa·cious (SPAY-shəss) *adjective.* Large, roomy. **—spaciousness** *noun.*

spade (SPAYD) *noun.* 1. A small shovel used for digging. 2. A black figure on a suit of playing cards, or a card of that suit. **spades.** *—verb.* To dig with a shovel. **spaded, spading.**

spa·ghet·ti (spə-GET-ee) *noun.* Pasta in the form of long thin strings of dough dried and boiled as food.

span *noun.* 1. The distance between two points. 2. The section between two supports of a bridge or arch. 3. A period of time: "Life is a *span.*" (Aristophanes). *—verb.* To extend across. **spanned, spanning.**

span·gle (SPANG-gəl) *noun.* A small shiny object used for costume decoration.

span·iel (SPAN-yəl) *noun.* Any of many breeds of dogs that are of small-to-medium size and have long, drooping ears and silky hair.

spank (SPANGK) *verb.* To slap with an open hand, especially across the buttocks. **spanked, spanking.**

spank·ing (SPANG-king) *noun.* A slapping, especially with the open hand. *—adjective.* Lively, brisk.

spar (SPAHR) *noun.* A long pole or a supporting piece of wood or metal, as the mast of a ship. *—verb.* 1. To box with light, quick punches. 2. To dispute. **sparred, sparring.**

spare (SPAIR) *verb.* 1. To show mercy, protect. 2. To save from trouble, pain or work. 3. To give up; do without: Can you *spare* a dime? **spared, sparing.** *—adjective.* 1. Thin, lean. 2. Scant, lacking in quantity: a *spare* supper. 3. Extra, held in reserve: *spare* tire. **sparer, sparest.** *—noun.* 1. Something extra. 2. (Bowling) The score made by knocking down 10 pins with the first two balls. **spares.**

spar·ing (SPAIR-ing) *adjective.* Thrifty, saving. **—sparingly** *adverb.*

spark (SPAHRK) *noun.* 1. A bit of burning material, a glowing particle. 2. The flash given off by an electrical discharge. 3. A trace; small bit: a *spark* of enthusiasm. *—verb.* 1. To give off sparks. 2. To put into action: His words *sparked* a plan in my mind. **sparked, sparking.**

spar·kle (SPAHR-kəl) *verb.* 1. To give off or reflect light. 2. To be lively: Her eyes *sparkle* when she is happy. **sparkled, sparkling.** *—noun.* A small flash of light. **sparkles.**

spark plug. A device used in an engine to produce an electrical spark: A *spark plug* ignites fuel.

spar·row (SPA-roh) *noun.* A small bird with gray or brown feathers.

sparse (SPAHRSS) *adjective.* Thin, scanty; not close together. **sparser, sparsest. —sparsely** *adverb.*

spasm (SPAZ-əm) *noun.* A sudden tightening of a muscle or muscles.

[1]**spat** *noun.* 1. A kind of footwear that covers the ankle and top of the shoe. 2. A short argument.

[2]**spat** *verb.* See **spit.**

spat·ter (SPAT-ər) *verb.* To splash or cause to splash in small drops. **spattered, spattering.** *—noun.* The mark or the sound made by a liquid as it spatters.

spat·u·la (SPACH-ə-lə) *noun.* A kitchen tool or utensil with a broad blade that bends easily.

spawn *verb.* 1. To lay eggs or produce young fish or other water animals. 2. To be the source of. **spawned, spawning.**

speak (SPEEK) *verb.* 1. To talk; have the ability to talk: The mute cannot *speak.* 2. To give a speech before a group of people. 3. To be able to use a particular language: Joel can *speak* Spanish. 4. To communicate; tell. **spoke** (SPOHK) **speaking. —speak one's mind.** To give one's own opinion. **—speak up** or **speak out.** 1. To talk louder. 2. To state one's views with confidence.

speak·er (SPEE-kər) *noun.* 1. One who talks, especially before an audience. 2. A loudspeaker. 3. The chairman of a lawmaking body.

spear (SPIHR) *noun.* 1. A weapon that has a sharp, pointed head on the end of a long stick or shaft. 2. The stalk or blade of a plant: asparagus *spears.* *—verb.* To stab or pierce. *spear* a fish. **speared, spearing.**

spear·head (SPIHR-hed) *noun.* 1. The pointed end of a spear. 2. The forward line of a military attack. *—verb.* To lead a military attack or any movement or project. **spear-headed, spearheading.**

spear·mint (SPIHR-mint) *noun.* A plant of the mint family used as flavoring.

spe·cial (SPESH-əl) *adjective.* 1. Outstanding, unusual. 2. Made or planned for one person or purpose. 3. Individual; particular: Coin collecting is his *special* hobby. *—noun.* An event or thing that is different from the usual, such as a sale or an elaborate TV show. **—specially** *adverb.*

spe·cial·ist (SPESH-ə-list) *noun.* One who limits his work or study to a particular field: an eye *specialist.*

spe·cial·ize (SPESH-ə-lighz) *verb.* To concentrate one's interests in a particular field of study or work. **specialized, specializing.**

spatula

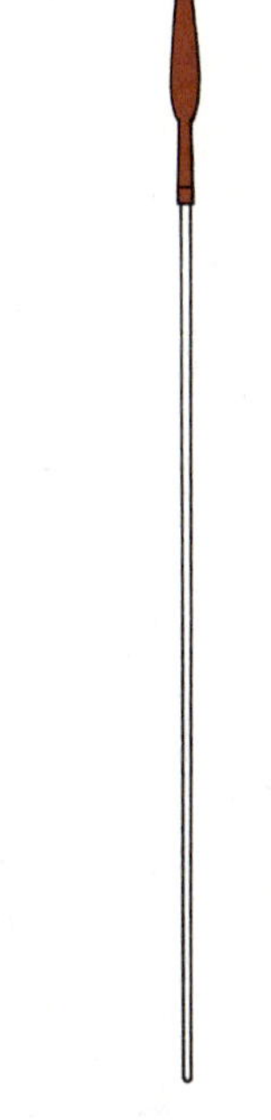
spear

sparrow

spectrum

spe·cial·ty (SPESH-əl-tee) *noun.* 1. Something done especially well. 2. A limited type of work: His *specialty* is repairing old clocks. **specialties.**

spe·cies (SPEE-sheez) *noun.* (Biology) A group of plants or animals so similar to each other that they are able to interbreed and produce offspring. —**species** *plural.*

spe·cif·ic (spə-SIF-ik) *adjective.* Exact, definite: *specific* instructions. —*noun.* Something that is exact or definite. —**specifically** *adverb.*

spec·i·fi·ca·tion (spess-ə-fi-KAY-shən) *noun.* 1. The act of stating exactly. 2. (Usually plural) A plan that includes details such as measurements and materials: He showed us the *specifications* for his new boat.

specific gravity. The comparison between the mass of a given substance and the same volume of a familiar substance: The *specific gravity* of solids and liquids is found by comparing them to water; gases are compared to hydrogen or air.

spec·i·fy (SPESS-ə-figh) *verb.* 1. To state exactly. 2. To include in a detailed description. **specified, specifying.**

spec·i·men (SPESS-ə-mən) *noun.* A sample; an example of a particular thing: butterfly *specimens.*

speck (SPEK) *noun.* 1. A bit or particle: a *speck* of dust. 2. A small dirty spot. —*verb.* To spot or cover with specks. **specked, specking.**

speck·le (SPEK-əl) *noun.* A dot or small spot; a speck. —*verb.* To dot with specks. **speckled, speckling.**

spec·ta·cle (SPEK-tə-kəl) *noun.* 1. A show or display; something unusual to look at. 2. (Plural) Eyeglasses.

spec·tac·u·lar (spek-TAK-yə-lər) *adjective.* Outstanding, remarkable. —**spectacularly** *adverb.*

spec·ta·tor (SPEK-tay-tər) *noun.* One who watches; an onlooker.

speedway

spec·ter (SPEK-tər) *noun.* A ghost.

spec·tro·scope (SPEK-trə-skohp) *noun.* An instrument in which light from a luminous body is separated into colors of the spectrum: Astronomers use the *spectroscope* to determine the chemical elements in stars.

spec·trum (SPEK-trəm) *noun.* The band of different colors or lines produced when light is separated into different wavelengths by passing it through a prism or by other means. —**spectra** or **spectrums** *plural.* —**spectral** *adjective.*

spec·u·late (SPEK-yə-layt) *verb.* 1. To think carefully (about something); to consider. 2. To take a chance (on an unsure business venture) in hopes of making a large profit. **speculated, speculating.** —**speculation** (spek-yə-LAY-shən) *noun.*

sped *verb. See* **speed.**

speech *noun.* 1. The ability to speak or the act of speaking. 2. A talk before a group of people. 3. Talking; communication with others by means of the voice. **speeches.**

speech·less (SPEECH-liss) *adjective.* Not able to speak. —**speechlessly** *adverb.*

speed *noun.* 1. Rate of movement: a *speed* of 20 miles an hour. 2. Swiftness; quickness. —*verb.* 1. To move at a fast pace. 2. (Used with *up*) To go or make go faster; increase the rate (of movement). 3. To drive a car faster than is allowed by law. 4. To help or aid. **sped** or **speeded, speeding.** —**speedy** *adjective.* —**speedily** *adverb.*

speed·om·e·ter (spee-DOM-ə-tər) *noun.* A device that shows how fast one is traveling.

speed·way (SPEED-way) *noun.* A track or road for racing cars.

[1]**spell** (SPEL) *verb.* 1. To say or write out (in proper order) the letters that make up a word. 2. To be a sign of;

mean. **spelled** or **spelt, spelling.**

²**spell** (SPEL) *noun.* 1. A state of being in the control of magic: Because of a *spell,* Sleeping Beauty slept for many years. 2. The word or words that cause such a state. 3. A state of attraction or delight.

³**spell** (SPEL) *noun.* 1. (Informal) A period or time: a hot *spell,* a fainting *spell.* 2. A short time or turn of work: He missed his *spell* as lookout. *—verb.* (Informal) To temporarily relieve (someone) on a job. **spelled, spelling.**

spell·bound (SPEL-bownd) *adjective.* Held fascinated as if by magic.

spell·er (SPEL-ər) *noun.* A book that helps to teach one to spell.

spell·ing (SPEL-ing) *noun.* 1. The act of making up words letter by letter. 2. The way to spell a word: Look up the correct *spelling* in your dictionary. —**spelling bee.** A contest to find the one who can spell the most words correctly.

spend *verb.* 1. To give out, pay, use: I will *spend* my allowance on Mother's birthday present. 2. To exhaust: You will *spend* your strength if you keep rushing like that. 3. To use up or pass (time): *spend* two weeks in the country. **spent, spending.**

spend·thrift (SPEND-thrift) *noun.* One who wastes his money.

spent *verb. See* **spend.**

sperm *noun.* 1. The male cell, or seed, of reproduction. 2. The fluid in which these cells are present.

sperm whale. A whale with a square-shaped snout, valuable for its oil.

spew (SPYOO) *verb.* 1. To throw up; vomit. 2. To throw out; send out forcefully: The smokestack *spewed* black smoke. **spewed, spewing.**

sphere (SFIHR) *noun.* 1. A round object having all points of its surface the same distance from the center; ball; globe. 2. Anything of about this shape: The earth is a *sphere.* 3. The area or conditions in which one lives, works, or socializes. **spheres.** —**spherical** (SFIHR-i-kəl) *adjective.* —**spherically** *adverb.*

sphinx (SFINKS) *noun.* 1. (Ancient Egypt) A figure with the head of a man, hawk, or male sheep, and the body of a lion. 2. (Greek myth) A monster that killed anyone unable to answer its riddle. 3. A person who is very secretive or mysterious. —**sphinxes** or **sphinges** (SFIN-jeez) *plural.*

sphinx (definition 1)

spice (SPYSS) *noun.* 1. A plant with a pleasant, strong smell or taste, used as a food flavoring, as pepper or curry. 2. That which adds flavor or excitement: "Variety's the very *spice* of life." (William Cowper). **spices.** *—verb.* To add spice to. **spiced, spicing.** —**spicy** *adjective.*

spick-and-span (spik-ən-SPAN) *adjective.* 1. Shining, clean and neat. 2. New, never used.

spi·der (SPIGH-dər) *noun.* A small eight-legged animal with a two-part body.

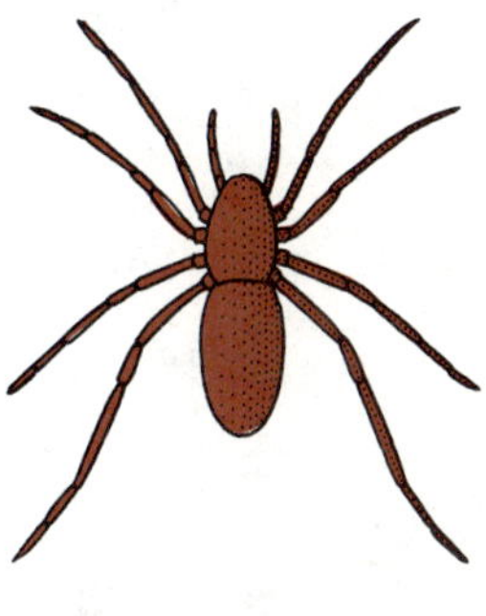

spider

spig·ot (SPIG-ət) *noun.* A faucet.

spike (SPIGHK) *noun.* 1. A large, thick nail. 2. Any sharp, pointed object that sticks out: Tulip *spikes* push up through the earth. **spikes.** *—verb.* 1. To join with a spike or put a spike into. 2. To wound or puncture with a spike. 3. (Slang) To add liquor to: *spike* the punch. **spiked, spiking.** —**spiky** (SPIGH-kee) *adjective.*

spill (SPIL) *verb.* 1. To make or permit (something) to pour or fall (out of a container): Did you *spill* the milk? 2. To cause to run out, as blood. 3. To make fall. 4. (Slang) To tell: *spill* the news. **spilled** or **spilt** (SPILT), **spilling.** *—noun.* 1. The act of spilling or that which is spilled. 2. A fall: Jimmy took quite a *spill* from his bike.

spiral

spinach

spinning wheel

spin *verb.* 1. To make fibers into thread. 2. To make from thread given out by the body: Spiders *spin* webs. 3. To tell or make up: *spin* a tall tale. 4. To turn round and round: *spin* a top. **spun, spinning.** —*noun.* 1. A quick turning motion: a *spin* of the wheel. 2. A short trip.

spin·ach (SPIN-ich) *noun.* A plant with dark green leaves that are used as a vegetable or in salads.

spi·nal (SPIHN-l) *adjective.* 1. Referring to the spine or the area of the body near the spine. 2. Looking like or doing the job of a spine.

spinal column Also **backbone.** A network of bones that extends from the skull to the lowest part of the body's trunk and supports the body as well as enclosing the spinal cord.

spinal cord. A long cord-like piece of nerve tissue that runs from the brain to the base of the spine.

spin·dle (SPIND-l) *noun.* A metal spike on which papers are impaled for safekeeping. —*verb.* To pierce, as with a spindle. **spindled, spindling.**

spine (SPIGHN) *noun.* 1. The spinal column or backbone. 2. That which looks like or does the job of the backbone: the *spine* of a book. 3. A plant or animal part that is sharp and sticks out, as a quill or a thorn.

spine·less (SPIGHN-liss) *adjective.* 1. Not having a spine. 2. Not strong in character or will; cowardly.

spinning wheel. A machine used to make thread or yarn.

spin·ster (SPIN-stər) *noun.* A woman who is not married.

spin·y (SPIGH-nee) *adjective.* 1. Having spines or spikes. 2. Like a spine or spike.

spir·a·cle (SPIGH-rə-kəl or SPIHR-ə-kəl) *noun.* A breathing hole, such as the blowhole of a whale or one of the small openings along the sides of the thorax and abdomen in insects.

spi·ral (SPIGH-rəl) *noun.* 1. A figure in the shape of a coiled spring. 2. That which has such a shape. —*verb.* To move in a spiral path: The leaf *spiraled* down from the tree. **spiraled** or **spiralled, spiraling** or **spiralling.**

spire (SPIGHR) *noun.* The pointed, upper part of something, as of a steeple. **spires.**

spir·it (SPIHR-it) *noun.* 1. An invisible quality that gives life or movement; the soul. 2. A ghost or other supernatural being. 3. The way someone feels (emotionally): in high *spirits.* 4. Active support of or loyalty to: school *spirit.* 5. The underlying meaning: the *spirit* of the law. 6. Liveliness; courage. 7. (Plural) An alcoholic liquor.

spir·it·ed (SPIHR-i-tid) *adjective.* Lively; full of energy: a *spirited* game of ball. —**spiritedly** *adverb.*

spir·i·tu·al (SPIHR-i-choo-əl) *adjective.* 1. Referring to the spirit rather than the body or material objects. 2. Holy; concerned with religion. —*noun.* A religious song of black Americans. —**spiritually** *adverb.*

[1]**spit** *verb.* 1. To force from the mouth: The baby *spits* out food. 2. To force out as if by spitting: The fire *spit* sparks onto the rug. **spat** or **spit, spitting.** —*noun.* Saliva; fluid in one's mouth.

[2]**spit** *noun.* 1. A rod with a sharp, pointed end on which meat is speared for cooking. 2. A point of land reaching out into water.

spite (SPIGHT) *noun.* An evil or mean feeling toward another. —*verb.* To be mean or cruel to. **spited, spiting.** —**in spite of.** Regardless of: We went *in spite of* the rain.

splash *verb.* 1. To splatter or spray (a liquid): I *splashed* ink on my new dress. 2. To scatter water or other liquid by falling, dropping, or moving into or in it: We *splashed* through puddles. **splashed, splashing.**

—*noun.* The sound or act of scattering a large amount of liquid: We heard the *splash* of Tim's dive. **splashes.**

splash·down *noun.* The landing of a space vehicle in water.

splat·ter (SPLAT-ər) *verb.* To spray or splash with a liquid. **splattered, splattering.** —*noun.* The spray itself.

splen·did (SPLEN-did) *adjective.* 1. Very beautiful, magnificent: a *splendid* view. 2. Worthy of praise; very good: a *splendid* report. —**splendidly** *adverb.*

splen·dor (SPLEN-dər) *noun.* 1. A great shine or glow; brilliance. 2. Magnificent display.

splice (SPLIGHSS) *verb.* To join the ends (of two things): Dad *spliced* two short pieces of rope. **spliced, splicing.** —*noun.* A connection made by splicing. **splices.**

splint *noun.* 1. A stiff piece of material, as wood, used to hold (something) in place and prevent movement. 2. A narrow, bendable strip of wood used in basket weaving.

splin·ter (SPLIN-tər) *noun.* A small sharp piece of material broken off from the whole: Sherry got a *splinter* of broken glass in her foot. —*verb.* To break into many thin, sharp pieces: The windshield *splintered* in the crash. **splintered, splintering.**

split *verb.* 1. To cut; separate; divide: Jack *split* the coconut in half. 2. To share, halve: Do you want to *split* a sandwich? **split, splitting.** —*noun.* The action or result of separating or opening: a *split* in the wood.

split-lev·el (SPLIT-lev-əl) *adjective.* Referring to a house in which the floor levels of different rooms are about a half story above or below each other.

spoil *verb.* 1. To damage or harm; ruin: Frost *spoiled* the orange crop. 2. To go bad; decay: Milk will *spoil* if not refrigerated. 3. To overindulge and, as a result, lead (one) to make excessive demands: to *spoil* a baby. **spoiled, spoiling.**

spoils *noun, plural.* 1. Valuables taken by force; booty. 2. (Politics) Favors or privileges won through association with an elected official or party: "To the victor belong the *spoils.*" (William L. Marcy).

spoil·age (SPOI-lij) *noun.* 1. The state or process of spoiling or decaying. 2. That which has been spoiled or the amount spoiled.

[1]**spoke** (SPOHK) *noun.* One of the rods or bars that extend from the center, or hub, of a wheel to the rim.

[2]**spoke** (SPOHK) *verb. See* **speak.**

spo·ken (SPOH-kən) *verb. See* **speak.**

spokes·man (SPOHKS-mən) *noun.* A person who speaks for another person or for a group. —**spokesmen** *plural.*

sponge (SPUHNJ) *noun.* 1. A sea creature whose skeleton is soft and soaks up liquids. 2. A manufactured material that is soft and absorbent like a sponge. 3. (Informal) A person who prefers to borrow from others for his needs. **sponges.** —*verb.* To soak up, wipe, or wash with a sponge. **sponged, sponging.** —**spongy** *adjective.* —**sponge off.** To expect (another person) to support you.

spon·sor (SPON-sər) *noun.* 1. One who supports or takes responsibility for another person, group, event, or activity. 2. A company that pays for a radio or TV program, usually as a means of advertising. 3. A godparent. —*verb.* To act as a sponsor for. **sponsored, sponsoring.**

spon·ta·ne·ous (spon-TAY-nee-əss) *adjective.* Happening naturally, without any outside force or without plan: a *spontaneous* laugh. —**spontaneity** (spon-tə-NEE-ə-tee) *noun.* —**spontaneously** *adverb.*

splashdown

sponge

spool

spoon

spotlight

spook *noun.* (Informal) A ghost. —*verb.* 1. To haunt. 2. To scare. **spooked, spooking.** —**spooky** *adjective.*

spool *noun.* A rounded peg, or cylinder, on which thread or wire is wound.

spoon *noun.* A tool consisting of a small bowl-like scoop with a handle attached, used for stirring food and eating. —*verb.* To take up in a spoon. **spooned, spooning.**

spoonful (SPOON-ful) *noun.* The amount that a spoon can hold. —**spoonfuls** *plural.*

spore (SPOR) *noun.* A single cell of certain plants and animals that can grow into a new plant or animal: Ferns and germs have *spores.* **spores.**

sport *noun.* 1. A game, usually active, that is played for fun, exercise, or money. 2. Play or fun: It is great *sport* to make a snowman. 3. (Slang) A person who takes chances; a likeable or generous person. 4. (Informal) A person as judged in terms of ability to accept defeat or loss: a good *sport,* a poor *sport.* —*verb.* 1. To play or amuse oneself: The kittens *sport* in the grass. 2. To show off; wear in a pleased way. **sported, sporting.** —**in sport.** In jest.

sports·man (SPORTS-mən) *noun.* 1. A person who takes part in sports or is interested in sports. 2. One who is fair, generous, or a good loser. —**sportsmen** *plural.*

spot *noun.* 1. A mark, stain, or speck. 2. A small part that is different from the rest: The bird was a *spot* of red among the green leaves. 3. A bit; a small amount: a *spot* of kindness. 4. A place: a lovely *spot* to visit. 5. A spotlight. —*verb.* 1. To have spots; become spotted; mark with spots. 2. To place; put in position: *spot* men along a route. 3. To pick out; recognize; see. 4. To remove a spot or spots. 5. (Slang) To allow as an advantage: I will *spot* you five points in the next game. **spotted, spotting.** —**on the spot.** 1. At once. 2. In a difficult situation.

spot·light (SPOT-light) *noun.* 1. A light that provides a strong beam, especially in a stage show. 2. Special or public attention. —*verb.* To light up with a spotlight, or as if with one. **spotlighted, spotlighting.**

spot·ty (SPOT-ee) *adjective.* 1. Having spots; marked with spots. 2. Patchy; not regular; not even.

spouse (SPOWSS or SPOWZ) *noun.* A husband or wife.

spout (SPOWT) *noun.* 1. A pipe, lip, or tube through which liquid runs or is poured: A coffee pot has a *spout.* 2. A jet of liquid: the whale's *spout.* —*verb.* 1. To pour; throw out a liquid in a stream or jet. 2. To speak loudly and rapidly. **spouted, spouting.**

sprain (SPRAYN) *verb.* To hurt a muscle or a joint by a sudden wrench or twist. **sprained, spraining.** —*noun.* An injury caused this way.

sprang *verb. See* **spring.**

sprawl *verb.* 1. To lie or sit with arms and legs spread in a careless way. 2. To spread in a way that is awkward. **sprawled, sprawling.** —*noun.* The position of sprawling.

[1]**spray** *noun.* A small branch of a plant with its leaves, flowers, berries, or fruit.

[2]**spray** *noun.* 1. Liquid moving through the air in tiny drops, as when blown from a wave. 2. Anything like a burst or mist of water drops: a *spray* of bullets. 3. An instrument that shoots out a spray. —*verb.* To shoot something in a spray. **sprayed, spraying.**

spread (SPRED) *verb.* 1. To stretch or open (something) out; unfold: *spread* a rug on the floor. 2. To cover with: *spread* peanut butter on bread.

3. To distribute (on a surface). 4. To extend; stretch out: The desert *spreads* for miles. 5. To scatter; travel; be distributed: Bad news *spreads* fast. **spread, spreading.** —*noun.* 1. The act of spreading or extending. 2. The distance between two ends: a wing*spread.* 3. A stretch or extent of land: a *spread* of 1,000 acres. 4. Two facing pages: a magazine *spread.* 5. A cover for a table, bed, or other piece of furniture. 6. Something that is spread on a surface: sandwich *spread.* 7. (Informal) A feast; a meal with many different attractive dishes. —**spread out.** To move farther apart.

spree *noun.* Lively and joyous frolic: buying *spree.* **sprees.**

sprig *noun.* A small shoot or twig of a plant: a *sprig* of mistletoe.

spright·ly (SPRIGHT-lee) *adjective.* Gay; lively; full of spirit. **sprightlier, sprightliest.**

spring *verb.* 1. To jump or leap; move suddenly: *spring* out of bed. 2. (Used with *back*) To resume normal position. 3. To release or set off: *spring* a trap. 4. (Often used with *up*) To grow; shoot up; come into being. 5. To make known suddenly: *spring* a surprise. 6. To split or crack open; bend or warp. **sprang** or **sprung, sprung, springing.** —*noun.* 1. A leap or jump. 2. A coil of metal that can be pushed or pulled out of shape but returns to its original shape when released. 3. Elastic strength; ability to bounce back. 4. The season of the year that comes after winter and before summer: In the Northern Hemisphere, *spring* lasts from about March 22 to June 22. 5. A stream of water coming up from the ground. 6. A beginning; a source.

spring·y (SPRING-ee) *adjective.* Elastic; bouncy; light and lively: a *springy* step. **springier, springiest.**

sprin·kle (SPRING-kəl) *verb.* 1. To scatter in little bits or drops: *Sprinkle* some salt. 2. To scatter from place to place or time to time: Tom *sprinkled* jokes throughout his report. 3. To rain slightly. **sprinkled, sprinkling.** —*noun.* 1. A small amount. 2. A light rain.

sprint *verb.* To run at top speed, usually for a short distance. **sprinted, sprinting.** —*noun.* The act of sprinting; a dash or race at top speed.

sprite (SPRIGHT) *noun.* A fairy or elf.

sprock·et (SPROK-it) *noun.* 1. A tooth on the rim of a wheel, made to fit into a chain that moves or is moved by a wheel. 2. A wheel with such teeth.

sprout (SPROWT) *verb.* 1. To start to grow: Buds *sprout.* 2. To cause to grow or develop: Bushes *sprout* buds. **sprouted, sprouting.** —*noun.* A small new growth from a plant or seed.

spruce (SPROOSS) *noun.* 1. An evergreen tree with needles and cones. 2. The wood of this tree. —*adjective.* Trim, neat. —**spruce up.** To make more attractive.

sprung (SPRUHNG) *verb.* *See* **spring.**

spry (SPRIGH) *adjective.* Quick; moving in a lively way; full of life. **sprier, spriest.**

spud (SPUHD) *noun.* (Slang) A potato.

spun (SPUHN) *verb.* *See* **spin.**

spunk (SPUHNGK) *noun.* (Slang) Braveness; courage.

spur (SPER) *noun.* 1. A metal clip for a horseman's shoe, with a spike or sharp-toothed rowel used to urge a horse to go on. 2. A part that sticks out like a spur, such as the sharp spine on the leg of a cock. 3. Anything that urges a person on: Fame was a *spur.* —*verb.* 1. To stick with spurs. 2. To urge or drive. **spurred, spurring.** —**on the spur of the moment.** Suddenly; without planning.

spruce

spur

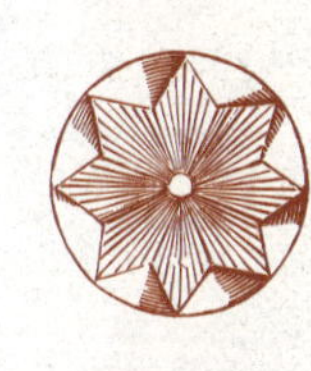

rowels

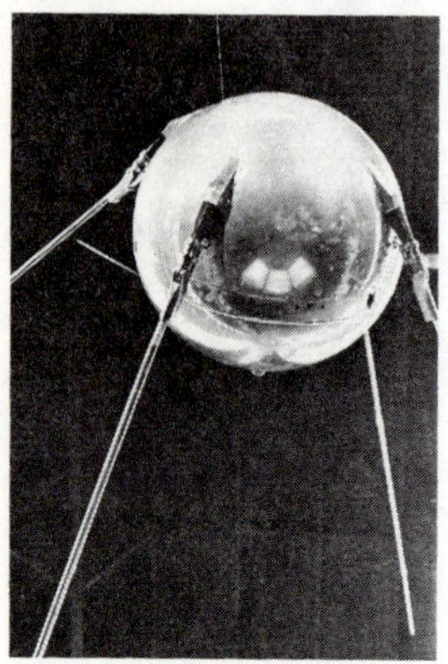
sputnik

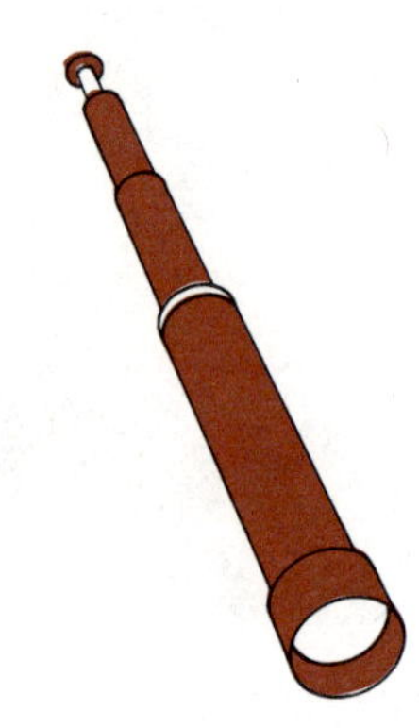
spyglass

square dance

spurn (SPERN) *verb.* To turn down or refuse with scorn. **spurned, spurning.**

spurt (SPERT) *verb.* 1. To shoot out suddenly in a stream (of liquid). 2. To put out extra energy for a short while; show a sudden increase in speed or progress. **spurted, spurting.** —*noun.* 1. A sudden stream; a gush: a *spurt* of flame. 2. A sudden increase of energy or activity for a short while.

sput·nik (SPUHT-nik or SPUT-nik) *noun.* A Russian-made earth satellite, especially the first.

sput·ter (SPUHT-ər) *verb.* 1. To make hissing, spitting noises. 2. To talk or stammer in a way that is hard to understand. **sputtered, sputtering.** —*noun.* Confused, excited talk.

spy (SPIGH) *noun.* 1. A person who secretly watches and listens to other people. 2. A person who finds out a country's military secrets or other information for a foreign government. **spies.** —*verb.* 1. To act as a spy. 2. To catch sight of; to see after searching for. **spied, spying.**

spy·glass (SPIGH-glass) *noun.* A small telescope.

squab (SKWOB) *noun.* A newly hatched pigeon.

squab·ble (SKWOB-əl) *verb.* To quarrel noisily about something of little importance. **squabbled, squabbling.** —*noun.* A noisy quarrel. **squabbles.**

squad (SKWOD) *noun.* 1. A small group of soldiers organized to drill and fight as a unit. 2. A small group organized for some kind of activity: the football *squad.*

squad·ron (SKWOD-rən) *noun.* A group of airplanes, naval ships, or soldiers that operates as a unit.

squal·id (SKWOL-id) *adjective.* Filthy; dirty; miserable: a *squalid* shack.

[1]**squall** (SKWAWL) *verb.* To cry or scream loudly and harshly. **squalled, squalling.** —*noun.* A loud scream.

[2]**squall** (SKWAWL) *noun.* 1. A sudden, strong wind, often with rain, sleet, or snow. 2. (Informal) A brief disturbance.

squal·or (SKWOL-ər) *noun.* A wretched condition; filth; misery.

squan·der (SKWON-dər) *verb.* To waste; spend foolishly: *squander* time. **squandered, squandering.**

square (SKWAIR) *noun.* 1. A shape with four equal sides and four right angles. 2. Anything with this shape or almost this shape. 3. An area in a town or city with a street on each of its four sides. 4. The distance along one side of a square; a city block. 5. A carpenter's tool with two sides that form a right angle. 6. The product of a number multiplied by itself: four is the *square* of two. 7. (Slang) An unsophisticated person: a real *square.* —*adjective.* 1. Having four equal sides and four right angles: a *square* picture frame. 2. Forming a right angle: This corner is *square.* 3. Having a shape that suggests strength: a *square* jaw. 4. Pertaining to a unit of measurement of an area: *square* yard. 5. Even; settled, as an account. 6. Honest, fair: a *square* deal. 7. (Slang) Filling: a *square* meal. 8. (Slang) Having tastes or opinions that are old-fashioned. —*verb.* 1. To make square. 2. To make straight. 3. To settle: *square* a debt. 4. To mark a surface in squares. 5. To fit or agree. 6. To multiply a number by itself. **squared, squaring.** —**squarely** *adverb.*

square dance. A lively dance in which sets of couples form squares.

square root. The number which, when multiplied by itself, produces a given number: 4 is the *square root* of 16.

[1]**squash** (SKWOSH) *noun.* A fruit that grows on a vine and is used as a vegetable. —**squash** or **squashes** *plural.*

[2]**squash** (SKWOSH) *verb.* To crush or mash: The truck *squashed* my hat. **squashed, squashing.** —*noun.* 1. The act or sound of squashing. 2. A game played by hitting a ball against walls with rackets.

squat (SKWOT) *verb.* 1. To crouch; sit on one's heels with bent knees. 2. To settle on someone else's land without any right. 3. To settle on public land in order to become its owner under the law. **squatted, squatting.** —*adjective.* 1. Short and thick: His father is a *squat,* heavy man. 2. In a crouched position.

squaw (SKWAW) *noun.* An American Indian woman, especially a wife.

squawk (SKWAWK) *noun.* 1. A loud harsh noise. 2. (Slang) A noisy complaint. —*verb.* 1. To make a loud harsh noise. 2. (Slang) To complain. **squawked, squawking.**

squeak (SKWEEK) *noun.* A short, sharp sound: *squeak* of a mouse. —*verb.* To make such a sound. **squeaked, squeaking.** —**squeaky** (*adjective.*)

squeal (SKWEEL) *verb.* 1. To make a high-pitched, loud cry, like that of a pig. 2. (Slang) To inform or tattle on. —*noun.* A high-pitched, loud cry. —**squealer** *noun.*

squeeze (SKWEEZ) *verb.* 1. To press hard. 2. To get (out) by pressing: *Squeeze* the juice out of your grapefruit. 3. To force by pressing: Jan *squeezed* her way through the crowd. **squeezed, squeezing.** —*noun.* An act of squeezing; hug; pressure or crush. **squeezes.**

squelch (SKWELCH) *verb.* To suppress; put down. **squelched, squelching.**

squid (SKWID) *noun.* A sea animal with a long, slender body and ten arms. —**squids** or **squid** *plural.*

squint (SKWINT) *verb.* 1. To look with eyes partly closed. 2. To look sideways. **squinted, squinting.**

squire (SKWIGHR) *noun.* 1. A young man who attends a knight and bears his shield and armor. 2. (British) A country gentleman. 3. A title of respect, as for a lawyer or judge. 4. A man who attends or escorts a lady. **squires.** —*verb.* To escort a female. **squired, squiring.**

squirm (SKWERM) *verb.* 1. To twist the body this way and that; wriggle. 2. To feel very embarrassed, sorry, or guilty. **squirmed, squirming.**

squir·rel (SKWER-əl or SKWIHR-əl) *noun.* 1. A small rodent with a long, bushy tail. 2. The fur of this animal.

squirt (SKWERT) *verb.* To spurt; shoot out suddenly in a jet: Water *squirted* from the toy pistol. **squirted, squirting.** —*noun.* 1. The act of squirting. 2. Something used to squirt. 3. A jet or sudden stream of liquid. 4. (Slang) An annoying child; brat.

squish (SKWISH) *noun.* A sound like that made when one walks through deep mud. —*verb.* To make such a sound. **squished, squishing.**

sr. *abbreviation.* Senior.

S.S. *abbreviation.* Steamship.

SST *abbreviation.* Supersonic transport; passenger plane that flies faster than the speed of sound.

St. *abbreviation.* 1. Street. 2. Saint. 3. Strait.

stab *verb.* 1. To wound or pierce with a knife or other pointed object. 2. To offend deeply; hurt the feelings of. **stabbed, stabbing.** —*noun.* 1. A wound made by stabbing. 2. A thrust; a poking into. 3. (Informal) A quick try; attempt: Dan took a *stab* at water skiing.

sta·bil·i·ty (stə-BIL-ə-tee) *noun.* 1. A condition of being steady; firmness: A rowboat has greater *stability* than a canoe. 2. A condition of being long-lasting or unchanging. 3. Reliability; balance and soundness, as of character.

[1]**sta·ble** (STAY-bəl) *noun.* 1. A building in which horses or other

[1]squash

squirrel

SST

stagecoach

stadium

staircase

animals are kept. 2. All of the racehorses that belong to one owner. —*verb.* To put or keep in a stable. **stabled, stabling.**

[2]**sta·ble** (STAY-bəl) *adjective.* 1. Strong, firm, steady: The metal ladder is more *stable* than the wooden one. 2. Long-lasting; unchanging: "No government can remain *stable* in . . . an un*stable* world." (Leon Blum). 3. Reliable; sound: a *stable* product.

stack (STAK) *noun.* 1. A neat pile of hay, straw, or a similar substance. 2. A neat pile of anything: a *stack* of newspapers. 3. A chimney; smokestack. 4. (Plural) The area or shelves in a library where books are kept. —*verb.* 1. To form into a neat pile. 2. To arrange for dishonest purposes: *stack* the cards. 3. To assign (to an airplane) a position to hold while circling before landing. **stacked, stacking.**

sta·di·um (STAY-dee-əm) *noun.* An open area surrounded by tiers or rows of seats: football *stadium.*

staff (STAF) *noun.* 1. A rod or stick: a shepherd's *staff.* 2. A group of assistants or workers, as on a particular job. 3. The set of lines and spaces on which music is written. —*verb.* To fill the positions for a job; select or have workers for: Thirty nurses are needed to *staff* the new hospital. **staffed, staffing.**

stag *noun.* 1. An adult male deer. 2. A male who goes without a date to a dance or other affair. —*adjective.* For men only: a *stag* party.

stage (STAYJ) *noun.* 1. A platform, especially one on which plays are performed. 2. The profession of actors and actresses; the theater. 3. A state or period in a process or journey: Childhood is an early *stage* in human development. 4. One of the major sections of a rocket. 5. The scene or place where an action takes place. 6. A stagecoach. **stages.** —*verb.* 1. To put on (a play or similar performance). 2. To carry out for public view: The workers *staged* a protest. **staged, staging.**

stage·coach (STAYJ-kohch) *noun.* A coach or enclosed wagon pulled by horses and used in former times to carry passengers and mail.

stage-struck (STAYJ-struhk) *adjective.* Filled with a desire to become an actor or an actress.

stag·ger (STAG-ər) *verb.* 1. To stumble or totter; walk or move in an unbalanced manner. 2. To cause to stumble: The boxer's punch *staggered* his opponent. 3. To upset greatly; shock. 4. To arrange at differing times, especially to avoid crowding: Factories *staggered* working hours so that all workers would not arrive at the same time. 5. To arrange at alternate places or positions: The black and red squares are *staggered* on a checkerboard. **staggered, staggering.** —*noun.* A stumbling or reeling.

stag·nant (STAG-nənt) *adjective.* 1. Not flowing or running, as water in a pond. 2. Foul from remaining still: The water in the swamp is *stagnant.* 3. Not active; dull.

stain (STAYN) *noun.* 1. A spot or mark: The spilled ink left a *stain* on Joan's skirt. 2. A liquid used to dye or color something. —*verb.* 1. To spoil or make a spot or mark on. 2. To blemish or spoil, as one's honor or character; dishonor. 3. To color, as with a dye. **stained, staining.**

stair *noun.* 1. (Plural) A series of steps used to climb from one floor in a building to another; staircase. 2. One of the steps in a staircase.

stair·case (STAIR-kayss) *noun.* A flight of stairs. **staircases.**

stair·way (STAIR-way) *noun.* A flight of stairs; staircase.

[1]**stake** (STAYK) *noun.* A pointed rod or stick driven into the ground, as to support a fence or sign. **stakes.**

—*verb.* To fasten with stakes or pegs: *stake* a tent. **staked, staking.** —**stake a claim.** To mark off the boundaries of an area to be used: *stake a claim* on the land. —**pull up stakes.** To leave a place, often permanently.

[2]**stake** (STAYK) *noun.* 1. (Often plural) Something that is bet, as on a game of chance, or the prize for such a game or race. 2. An investment: Dad has a *stake* in the new company. 3. An interest: All men have a *stake* in the conquest of disease. **stakes.** —*verb.* 1. To risk; wager: The gambler *staked* $200 on one roll of the dice. 2. To provide money or supplies (for a venture). **staked, staking.** —**at stake.** Risked or involved, as in a wager or issue. The sick boy's life was *at stake* during the operation.

sta·lac·tite (stə-LAK-tight) *noun.* A mineral deposit that resembles an icicle and is often found hanging from the tops of caves. **stalactites.**

sta·lag·mite (stə-LAG-might or STAL-əg-might) *noun.* A mineral deposit that builds up from the floors of caves. **stalagmites.**

stale (STAYL) *adjective.* 1. Not fresh: *stale* bread. 2. Not showing novelty or imagination; not clever: a *stale* story. 3. Not in best condition; dull: The athlete felt *stale* after his long vacation. **staler, stalest.**

[1]**stalk** (STAWK) *noun.* 1. The stem of certain plants. 2. A part that resembles a plant stem or stalk.

[2]**stalk** (STAWK) *verb.* 1. To pursue in a quiet or stealthy manner: The hunters *stalked* the leopard for hours. 2. To walk in an angry or proud manner. **stalked, stalking.**

[1]**stall** (STAWL) *noun.* 1. A compartment or section for a single animal, as for a horse in a stable. 2. A booth or compartment at which things are shown or sold: one *stall* at the county fair. 3. A bench or seat, as in a church.

[2]**stall** (STAWL) *verb.* 1. To stop or be stopped: *stall* an engine. 2. To slow down a process or avoid an action on purpose: Ron tried to change the subject so as to *stall* my questions. **stalled, stalling.** —*noun.* A delay.

stal·lion (STAL-yən) *noun.* An adult male horse.

stal·wart (STAWL-wərt) *adjective.* 1. Sturdy; strong. 2. Brave or unchanging in seeking a goal. —*noun.* A brave or determined person. —**stalwartly** *adverb.*

sta·men (STAY-mən) *noun.* The part of a flower that bears pollen.

stam·mer (STAM-ər) *verb.* To stutter or falter in speaking. **stammered, stammering.** —*noun.* A stutter.

stamp *noun.* 1. A small label that is glued to a letter or parcel to indicate that postage has been paid. 2. A special mark, seal, or design, as to identify an owner or manufacturer. 3. A tool or machine used to cut out or form, as a pattern or shape. —*verb.* 1. To strike down hard with the sole of the foot. 2. To put a stamp, seal, design, or mark on. 3. To cut out or form, as a pattern or shape: The huge machine *stamped* out metal window frames. **stamped, stamping.**

stam·pede (stam-PEED) *noun.* A sudden and widespread rush or running. —*verb.* To rush or run suddenly in a large group. **stampeded, stampeding.**

stance (STANSS) *noun.* The manner or position in which a person stands.

stand *verb.* 1. To be in an upright position: *stand* in line. 2. To move to or take an upright position: *Stand* when the judge enters. 3. To place or be located: The broom *stands* in the corner. 4. To be a certain height: *stand* four feet tall. 5. To stay whole or in good condition. 6. To be the subject of; experience: *stand* trial. 7. To continue as before: The law still *stands.* 8. To put up with; tolerate: I can't *stand* that

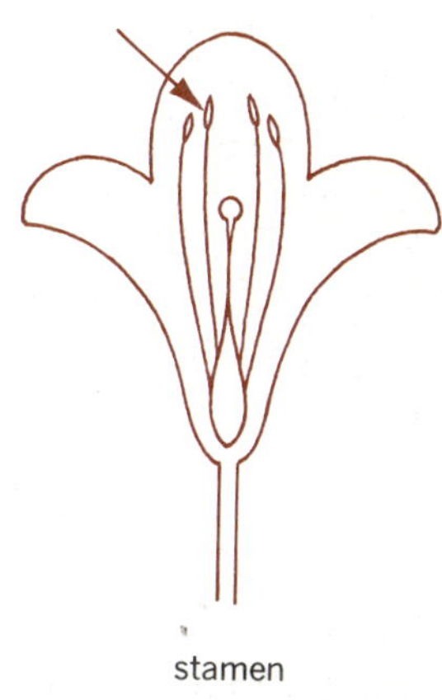
stamen

stalactite and stalagmite

singer. **stood, standing.** —*noun.* 1. The act of standing. 2. A platform or other place where a person stands. 3. A support or device on which something rests: book*stand.* 4. A small, open structure at which items are sold or displayed: refreshment *stand.* 5. A point of view. 6. An engagement or stop for one or more performers: a one-night *stand.* 7. A group or grove of trees or shrubs. 8. A stop or position for fighting or battle. 9. (Plural) Rows of seats for watching a sporting event or other performance: grand*stand.* —**stand off.** To keep at a distance. —**stand up for.** To support or defend. —**stand up to.** To face; oppose or defy.

stan·dard (STAN-dərd) *noun.* 1. A model or rule to which other things are compared: *standards* of good conduct. 2. A flag, banner, or emblem. 3. A pole or other support: The flag waved from its *standard.* —*adjective.* 1. Used as a model or rule to which other things are compared. 2. Established as being reliable: a *standard* textbook. 3. Widely used or available; common: a *standard* car model.

starfish

stan·dard·ize (STAN-dər-dighz) *verb.* To make standard or uniform. **standardized, standardizing.**

stand·point (STAND-point) *noun.* An attitude; point of view.

stand·still (STAND-stil) *noun.* A halt or stop: Work came to a *standstill.*

stank (STANGK) *verb.* See **stink.**

stan·za (STAN-zə) *noun.* A group or unit of lines or verses in a poem.

starling

[1]**sta·ple** (STAY-pəl) *noun.* 1. A short piece of wire that is pressed into papers with a special instrument and holds them together. 2. A U-shaped piece of metal that is hammered into a surface, as to hold an electric cable in place. **staples.** —*verb.* To fasten with a staple. **stapled, stapling.**

[2]**sta·ple** (STAY-pəl) *noun.* 1. A principal crop or item made in an area: Corn is a *staple* in Iowa. 2. An important item kept on hand for a process, as for cooking: Flour and eggs are *staples.* 3. The fiber or strands of cotton, wool, or other materials. **staples.** —*adjective.* Basic; most important.

star (STAHR) *noun.* 1. A heavenly body that is a source of light and other forms of radiated energy. 2. A figure, shape, or symbol, usually with five or six points. 3. A person who is outstanding in sports, acting, singing, or some other activity. —*verb.* 1. To be outstanding. 2. To be the leading actor or actress in a performance. 3. To mark or cover with stars. **starred, starring.** —*adjective.* Outstanding; leading.

star·board (STAHR-bərd) *noun.* The right side of a ship as a person looks toward the bow or front.

starch (STAHRCH) *noun.* 1. A substance found in foods such as potatoes or rice; a white, powdery substance obtained from such foods. 2. Food starch or similar substances that are used to give stiffness to cloth. **starches.** —*verb.* To make (cloth) stiff by using starch. **starched, starching.**

stare (STAIR) *verb.* To look steadily and directly; gaze: Mary *stared* out the window. **stared, staring.** —*noun.* A direct look or gaze.

star·fish (STAHR-fish) *noun.* A small, star-shaped sea animal that has five long arms. —**starfish** or **starfishes** *plural.*

stark (STAHRK) *adjective.* 1. Complete; absolute: *stark* terror. 2. Barren or lonely in appearance. —*adverb.* Completely: *stark* raving mad. —**starkly** *adverb.*

star·light (STAHR-light) *noun.* Light given off by stars.

star·ling (STAHR-ling) *noun.* A very common brown or black bird.

star·lit (STAHR-lit) *adjective.* Lighted by the stars.

star·ry (STAHR-ee) *adjective.* Filled or glowing with stars: *starry* sky. **starrier, starriest.**

start (STAHRT) *verb.* 1. To begin. 2. To begin to act: The engine *started.* 3. To put into operation: *start* an engine. 4. To set up; develop: *start* a lumber business. 5. To move suddenly; jump nervously. **started, starting.** —*noun.* 1. A beginning. 2. A sudden movement; a jerk. 3. A time or place of a beginning.

star·tle (STAHRT-l) *verb.* 1. To cause sudden fright or a nervous movement. 2. To surprise; shock. **startled, startling.**

star·va·tion (stahr-VAY-shən) *noun.* Suffering from not having food.

starve (STAHRV) *verb.* 1. To be ill or die from not having food. 2. To suffer from want or need: *starve* for lack of love. 3. (Informal) To be very hungry. **starved, starving.**

state (STAYT) *noun.* 1. A condition; situation: Joe's room was in a messy *state.* 2. A nation. 3. The governing power or authority of a nation: The *state* has the right to impose taxes. 4. [Often capital S] One of the political units or areas of which a nation is composed. 5. The form of a substance: Ice is water in a solid *state.* **states.** —*verb.* To declare; make known in words: *state* a fact. **stated, stating.**

state·hood (STAYT-hud) *noun.* The condition of existing as a separate nation or state: Alaska was granted *statehood* in 1959.

state·ly (STAYT-lee) *adjective.* 1. Impressive in appearance; majestic. 2. Formal; dignified: *stately* manner. **statlier, statliest.**

state·ment (STAYT-mənt) *noun.* 1. A declaration; something made known in words. 2. A summary or outline of money matters.

states·man (STAYTS-mən) *noun.* A national leader in government or politics. —**statesmen** *plural.*

stat·ic (STAT-ik) *adjective.* Not moving or changing: *static* weather conditions. —*noun.* A crackling noise heard on a radio.

static electricity. Electric charges that are not in motion: *Static electricity* can be produced by friction, as when hair is brushed.

sta·tion (STAY-shən) *noun.* 1. The place where someone or something stands or is put: The crossing guard has a *station* on our block. 2. The building in which something is done or from which action is directed: a fire *station.* 3. A stop for a bus, train, or subway. 4. One's place in society. 5. The place from which radio or TV programs are broadcast. —*verb.* To assign to a place or post. **stationed, stationing.**

station wagon

sta·tion·ar·y (STAY-shən-ehr-ee) *adjective.* 1. Not moving; not movable: The cabinet is *stationary.* 2. Staying the same; unchanging.

sta·tion·er·y (STAY-shən-ehr-ee) *noun.* Paper and envelopes used for letters.

station wagon. An automobile with a rear door and an open storage area behind the rear seat or seats.

sta·tis·tics (stə-TISS-tiks) *noun.* 1. (Used with a singular verb) The gathering, grouping, and interpretation of numerical information. 2. (Used with a plural verb) A collection of numerical data: birth *statistics.*

stat·ue (STACH-oo) *noun.* A solid model or likeness (of something or somebody) that is usually made of wood, stone, clay, or metal and formed by molding, sculpting, or carving. **statues.**

stat·ure (STACH-ər) *noun.* 1. Height in a standing position: tall *stature.* 2. Rank; reputation.

statue

stat·us (STAY-təss or STAT-əss) *noun.* 1. A person's or thing's position in the eyes of the law: draft *status.* 2. One's position in relation to others: Carl's *status* on the team. 3. The way things are at present.

stat·ute (STACH-oot) *noun.* A law or decree. **statutes.**

staunch (STAWNCH or STAHNCH) *adjective.* Loyal; true; firm: a *staunch* friend. —**staunchly** *adverb.*

stave (STAYV) *noun.* A narrow piece of wood that is part of a container, as a barrel. **staves.** —*verb.* 1. To break or put holes in. 2. (Used with *off*) To stop from happening, keep away. **staved, staving.**

[1]**stay** *verb.* 1. To not move: *Stay* where you are. 2. To remain for a time; to pause: We *stayed* overnight in Boston. 3. To check; stop: We *stayed* his anger by telling him a joke. 4. To put off; postpone. 5. To continue; endure: *stay* with a job. **stayed, staying.** —*noun.* 1. The act of stopping. 2. A visit or sojourn. 3. A delay: a *stay* of execution.

[2]**stay** *noun.* 1. A stiff piece of material used in some shirt collars and girdles. 2. A support or prop.

stead (STED) *noun.* The position, place, or job usually held by another: Because Liz was ill, I served refreshments in her *stead.* —**stand one in good stead.** To give an advantage to; to help.

stead·fast (STED-fast) *adjective.* 1. Not moving or changing: *steadfast* opinion. 2. Loyal, true. —**steadfastly** *adverb.* —**steadfastness** *noun.*

stead·y (STED-ee) *adjective.* 1. Firmly placed; secure: a *steady* job. 2. Unwavering; constant: a *steady* gaze. 3. Calm; under control: a *steady* hand. 4. Uninterrupted; regular: a *steady* drip of water. **steadier, steadiest.** —**steadiness** *noun.* —**steadily** *adverb.*

steak (STAYK) *noun.* A slice of meat for broiling or frying.

steamroller

steal (STEEL) *verb.* 1. To take what is not one's own without permission: "Who *steals* my purse *steals* trash." (Shakespeare). 2. To get in a secret or sly way: *steal* a glance. 3. To move in a secret or sly way: *steal* into the house. 4. (Baseball) To take or advance a base without a ball's having been hit. **stole, stolen, stealing.** —*noun.* (Slang) A bargain.

stealth (STELTH) *noun.* Secret or sly action. —**stealthily** *adverb.* —**stealthy** *adjective.*

steam (STEEM) *noun.* 1. Water in a gaseous state. 2. The mist formed by water vapor as it condenses. 3. (Informal) Strength; energy: Let's get up some *steam* and get this job finished. —*verb.* 1. To give off steam. 2. To get power or motion from steam: The boat *steamed* across the lake. 3. To expose to steam: Mother *steamed* my suede shoes. 4. To cook by steam. **steamed, steaming.** —**steamy** *adjective.* —**let off steam.** To express or get rid of strong pent-up feelings.

steam·boat (STEEM-boht) *noun.* A boat powered by steam.

steam engine. An engine that changes steam heat into mechanical energy.

steam·er (STEEM-ər) *noun.* 1. A steamship. 2. A pot or other container in which things are steamed.

steam·roll·er (STEEM-rohl-ər) *noun.* A heavy machine, formerly steam-powered, used to smooth road surfaces.

steam·ship (STEEM-ship) *noun.* A large ship powered by steam.

steed *noun.* A horse.

steel *noun.* A mixture of iron, carbon, and other elements that forms a hard, long-lasting, strong material readily shaped when heated.

steel wool. Fine steel threads that are made into pads used to scour and polish.

[1]**steep** *adjective.* 1. Having a sharp slope or slant. 2. (Slang) Excessive. **steeper, steepest.** —**steeply** *adverb.* —**steepness** *noun.*

[2]**steep** *verb.* To brew or soak: *steep* tea. **steeped, steeping.**

stee·ple (STEE-pəl) *noun.* 1. A tower on top of a building, such as a church. 2. A spire. **steeples.**

steer (STIHR) *verb.* 1. To direct by means of a wheel, oar, or rudder: *steer* a car. 2. To respond to guiding or directing: The car doesn't *steer* well. **steered, steering.** —*noun.* A young male of cattle raised for beef.

[1]**stem** *noun.* 1. The tube-like stalk of a plant. 2. Something like this stalk: a pipe *stem.* 3. The main part of a word to which prefixes and suffixes may be added: "Forget" is the *stem* of the word "unforgettable."

[2]**stem** *verb.* 1. To stop; prevent; hold back: *stem* a leak. 2. To derive (from). **stemmed, stemming.**

sten·cil (STEN-səl) *noun.* A piece of paper, cardboard, or other material, with letters or designs cut into it, that is brushed with ink or paint to reproduce the letters or designs onto material placed below. —*verb.* To mark with a stencil. **stenciled** or **stencilled, stenciling** or **stencilling.**

ste·nog·ra·pher (stə-NOG-rə-fər) *noun.* One who uses shorthand to write down what another says.

step *noun.* 1. An act of walking; moving the foot from one spot to another. 2. The way in which one walks: a light *step.* 3. The pace or rhythm of a group of walkers: Keep in *step.* 4. The length of one step or any short distance. 5. (Plural) Way; course: in his brother's *steps.* 6. One of the levels of a staircase or ladder. 7. A degree in a musical scale. —*verb.* 1. To move one foot after the other. 2. To put the weight of a foot (on): Don't *step* on the dog! 3. To move a little bit or a short distance. **stepped, stepping.** —**step on it.** To go faster. —**watch one's step.** To be careful.

step- *prefix.* Indicates: 1. Relationship through another (previous) marriage of one's husband or wife: *step*son; *step*daughter. 2. Relationship through the remarriage of one's father or mother: *step*mother.

step·lad·der (STEP-lad-ər) *noun.* A lightweight, movable ladder that, when open, has the shape of an *A* with a shelf on the top.

steppe (STEP) *noun.* A very large, very dry plain in Europe and Asia.

ste·re·o (STEHR-ee-oh or STIHR-ee-oh) *noun.* A machine, such as a record player, radio, or tape player, that has stereophonic sound. **stereos.**

ster·e·o·phon·ic (stehr-ee-oh-FON-ik) *adjective.* Referring to the reproduction of sound by using two or more microphones and speakers to achieve a realistic effect.

ster·e·o·type (STEHR-ee-oh-tighp) *noun.* 1. A metal plate used to print the same thing many times. 2. A common, too-simple thought or belief: That Americans are loud, rich, rude people is a *stereotype.* 3. A typical example with no individuality. —**stereotyped** *adjective.*

ster·ile (STEHR-əl) *adjective.* 1. Not able to produce offspring. 2. Free of germs. —**sterility** (stehr-IL-ə-tee) *noun.*

ster·il·ize (STEHR-ə-lighz) *verb.* To make sterile. **sterilized, sterilizing.** —**sterilization** (stehr-il-ih-ZAY-shən) *noun.*

ster·ling (STER-ling) *noun.* 1. Sterling silver, a mixture of 92.5% silver with another metal, as copper. 2. Money in Great Britain. —*adjective.* 1. Made of sterling silver. 2. Of a very high quality.

[1]**stern** *adjective.* 1. Severe; sober. 2. Difficult and unpleasant.

[2]**stern** *noun.* The rear of a vessel.

stepladder

stencil

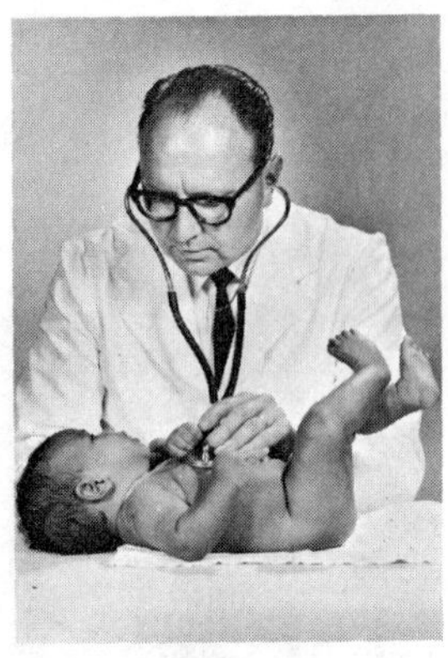
stethoscope

steth·o·scope (STETH-ə-skohp) *noun.* A device for listening to inner body sounds, as in the heart. **stethoscopes.**

stew (STOO or STYOO) *verb.* 1. To cook slowly at a simmer or boil. 2. (Informal) To worry. **stewed, stewing.** —*noun.* A combination of meat or fish and vegetables that has been boiled or simmered slowly. —**in a stew.** Worried.

stew·ard (STOO-ərd or STYOO-ərd) *noun.* 1. A ship's officer in charge of dining arrangements. 2. A man on a ship or airplane whose job is to wait on passengers. 3. A person in charge of another's business.

stew·ard·ess (STOO-ərd-iss or STYOO-ərd-iss) *noun.* A woman on a ship or airplane whose job is to give service to passengers. **stewardesses.**

stick (STIK) *noun.* 1. A long, thin piece of wood, as a branch from a tree. 2. Anything that looks like a stick: a walking *stick.* 3. (Plural, informal) An area of small towns or farms. —*verb.* 1. To put a hole in with a sharp object; pierce. 2. To put on or attach: *stick* a stamp on an envelope. 3. To cling to. 4. To become caught or fixed (in); be unable to continue. 5. To protrude; project: Don't *stick* out your tongue. 6. (Informal) To put the burden (of something) on. **stuck, sticking.** —**stick around.** To stay in a particular place. —**stick it out.** To stay with; endure.

stilts

stick·ball (STIK-bawl) *noun.* A kind of baseball played with a heavy stick and a rubber ball.

stick·y (STIK-ee) *adjective.* 1. Like glue; sticking to things: The baby's hands were *sticky* with jam. 2. Warm and damp. 3. (Informal) Uncomfortable; awkward. **stickier, stickiest.** —**stickiness** *noun.*

stiff (STIF) *adjective.* 1. Not easy to bend or move: *stiff* cardboard. 2. Forceful, strong: a *stiff* wind. 3. Hard, difficult; severe: a *stiff* test. 4. Formal or awkward. **stiffer, stiffest.** —*noun.* (Slang) A dead body. —*adverb.* Completely, entirely: bored *stiff.*

stiff·en (STIF-ən) *verb.* To make or become stiff. **stiffened, stiffening.** —**stiffener** *noun.*

sti·fle (STIGH-fəl) *verb.* 1. To stop or hold back: *stifle* one's laughter. 2. To kill or be killed by smothering. **stifled, stifling.**

stig·ma (STIG-mə) *noun.* 1. A mark or sign of disgrace or dishonor. 2. The upper part of the pistil of a flower, where the pollen is deposited. —**stigmas** or **stigmata** (stig-MAH-tə) *plural.*

stile (STIGHL) *noun.* 1. Steps or stairs that help one go over a fence or wall. 2. A turnstile. **stiles.**

[1]**still** (STIL) *adjective.* 1. Quiet, free from sound: a *still* summer day. 2. Hushed; low in sound: "a *still* small voice." (Kings I). 3. Not moving: "Be *still,* my lad, and sleep." (A. E. Housman). —*noun.* Silence: the *still* of the evening. —*verb.* To stop or calm: I *stilled* Mother's worry by phoning her. **stilled, stilling.** —*adverb.* 1. Without motion. 2. Until now, or some other particular time: I *still* live in a trailer. 3. No matter; nevertheless: Even if it rains, I am *still* going out. —*conjunction.* But; nevertheless.

[2]**still** (STIL) *noun.* A device for distilling liquids.

stilt *noun.* 1. One of two long, thin poles with attached footrests by means of which one can walk high off the ground. 2. Any long, thin poles or posts used to hold (a building) up.

stilt·ed (STILT-əd) *adjective.* Awkward, stiff: *stilted* speech.

stim·u·late (STIM-yə-layt) *verb.* To give energy to; excite. **stimulated, stimulating.** —**stimulant** (STIM-yə-lənt) *noun.*

stim·u·lus (STIM-yə-ləss) *noun.* An

influence that excites to action. —**stimuli** (STIM-yə-ligh) *plural.*

sting *verb.* 1. To pierce or prick (with something sharp): That bee may *sting* you! 2. To cause or feel sharp pain, either mental or physical. **stung, stinging.** —*noun.* 1. The act of stinging. 2. The injury or pain created by stinging.

sting ray. A flat, broad fish with sharp spines.

stin·gy (STIN-jee) *adjective.* 1. Not spending or giving freely. 2. Not much; scanty: a *stingy* portion. **stingier, stingiest.** —**stinginess** *noun.*

stink (STINGK) *verb.* To give off a strong, unpleasant smell. **stank** or **stunk, stinking.** —*noun.* A strong, unpleasant smell.

stint *verb.* To restrict; to limit. **stinted, stinting.** —*noun.* A job done during a certain amount of time: a *stint* in the army.

stir (STER) *verb.* 1. To mix (a liquid or other substance) by moving round and round, as with a spoon. 2. To move slightly. 3. To move quickly or with energy: I must be up and *stirring* early in the morning. 4. (Used with *up*) To start; be the cause of: *stir* up an argument. 5. To arouse strong feeling in: The sad play *stirred* the audience. **stirred, stirring.** —*noun.* 1. The act of stirring. 2. Excitement.

stir·rup (STER-əp or STIHR-əp) *noun.* One of the two loops or rings that hang from each side of a saddle for the rider's feet.

stitch (STICH) *noun.* 1. In sewing, one complete movement of a needle and thread through a fabric. 2. A short section or loop of thread or yarn, as in sewing, knitting, or surgery. 3. A sudden pain. 4. (Informal) A shred; a very small amount. **stitches.** —*verb.* To make stitches in; sew. **stitched, stitching.**

stock (STOK) *noun.* 1. A supply: a *stock* of canned foods. 2. Cattle or other farm animals; livestock. 3. Supply of goods for a business. 4. A base, butt, or handle, as on a gun or tool. 5. The family background of a person; ancestry of any living thing. 6. A share of the ownership in a company, or a paper that proves such ownership. 7. Dramatics, theater: summer *stock.* 8. (Plural) A wooden device in which a person's arms and legs were locked in former times as punishment. 8. Meat broth. —*verb.* 1. To supply with materials. 2. To keep on hand for business purposes. **stocked, stocking.** —*adjective.* 1. Common; regular or typical: a *stock* reply. 2. Usually kept on hand, as for sale: *stock* items. —**take stock.** 1. To count items or supplies a business has on hand. 2. To evaluate or appraise possibilities in a situation.

stock·ade (stok-AYD) *noun.* 1. A fence or barrier, as around a fort, made of stakes driven into the ground side by side. 2. A military prison.

stock car. An automobile of standard make that is equipped with a special engine for racing.

stock·ing (STOK-ing) *noun.* A garment or covering that fits closely over the foot and leg.

stock market. 1. A place or business involved with selling stock in various companies. 2. The price or rate of stock sales: The *stock market* went up today.

stock·y (STOK-ee) *adjective.* Short and thick. **stockier, stockiest.**

stock·yard (STOK-yahrd) *noun.* An enclosed area of pens in which livestock is kept, usually until it is ready to be slaughtered.

[1]**stole** (STOHL) *noun.* 1. A scarf or similar covering, often of fur, worn by women around their shoulders. 2. A narrow band of fabric worn by clergymen over their shoulders.

[2]**stole** (STOHL) *verb. See* **steal.**

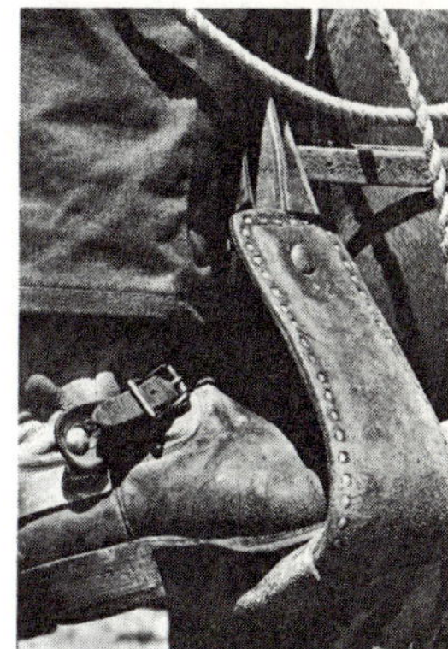

stirrup

stockade

stockyard

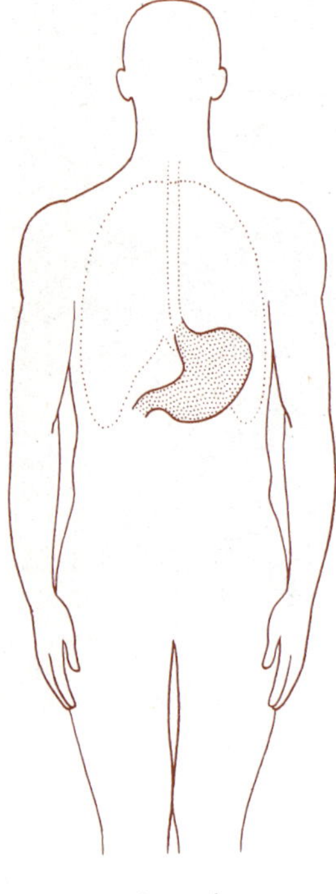
stomach (definition 1)

stom·ach (STUHM-ək) *noun.* 1. The body organ that receives and digests swallowed food. 2. The area in the front of the body between the chest and the hips; abdomen; belly. 3. Inclination; desire: The weary soldiers had no *stomach* for more fighting. *—verb.* To stand or tolerate; put up with. **stomached, stomaching.**

stomach ache. An ache or pain in the stomach, as from overeating.

stomp *verb.* 1. To step or stamp heavily with the bottom of the foot. 2. (Slang) To attack by stamping on or kicking. **stomped, stomping.** *—noun.* 1. A heavy step or stamping. 2. One of a variety of dances.

stone (STOHN) *noun.* 1. Rock: That cliff is a sheet of *stone.* 2. A piece of rock: Don't throw that *stone.* 3. A gem or jewel. 4. A small, hard object that sometimes forms within human organs: gall *stones.* 5. The pit or seed of certain fruits: cherry *stone.* **stones.** *—verb.* 1. To throw stones at. 2. To remove the pits or stones from (fruit). **stoned, stoning.** *—adverb.* Completely: *stone* blind. **—stony** (STOH-nee) *adjective.*

stood (STUD) *verb. See* **stand.**

stool *noun.* 1. A seat with legs but no back or arms, or a similar device for resting one's feet. 2. A bowel movement.

stool pigeon. (Slang) A person who reveals the secrets or actions of others, especially to the police.

stoplight

[1]**stoop** *verb.* 1. To bend over. 2. To let the shoulders bend forward: Don't *stoop;* stand straight. 3. To lower oneself in dignity; act in a base manner: Judy would never *stoop* to cheating. **stooped, stooping.** *—noun.* A bending forward.

[2]**stoop** *noun.* A porch or flight of steps at the entrance to a house.

stop *verb.* 1. To put a halt to. 2. To cease moving, acting, or being. 3. To plug up or block: Fallen leaves *stopped* up the drainpipe. 4. To visit: We *stopped* at Grandmother's house. **stopped, stopping.** *—noun.* 1. A stopping; an end or halt: Work came to a *stop.* 2. A visit; a rest. 3. A location where a bus, train, or other transport regularly picks up or drops off passengers: bus *stop.* 4. A part or device on a musical instrument used to regulate pitch or sound.

stop·light (STOP-light) *noun.* A red traffic light, at which drivers must come to a full stop.

stop·page (STOP-ij) *noun.* 1. A stopping or halt: a work *stoppage.* 2. A clogging: *stoppage* in a pipe.

stop·per (STOP-ər) *noun.* Any device used to plug up an opening, as in a sink.

stop·watch (STOP-woch) *noun.* A special type of watch, used for timing races, that can be stopped and started by pressing a button.

stor·age (STOR-ij) *noun.* 1. The act or condition of storing or putting things away. 2. A place where things are stored.

storage battery. A device that stores and supplies electricity, especially for use in autos.

store (STOR) *noun.* 1. A place where things are sold regularly; a shop. 2. A supply for future use: a *store* of canned foods. 3. A place for storage; storehouse. 4. (Plural) Supplies; stock. **stores.** *—verb.* 1. To save for future use: The squirrel *stored* nuts in the hollow tree. 2. To put in storage. **stored, storing. —in store.** Awaiting: a surprise *in store.* **—set store by.** To have confidence in; regard highly.

store·house (STOR-howss) *noun.* A place in which things are stored; warehouse. **storehouses.**

store·keep·er (STOR-keep-ər) *noun.* A person who manages or owns a store.

store·room (STOR-room) *noun.* A room in which things are stored.

stork *noun.* A large wading bird with long legs, neck, and bill.

storm *noun.* 1. A weather condition marked by strong winds with rain, snow, sleet, or hail, and often thunder and lightning. 2. A sudden outburst: a *storm* of protests. 3. A powerful attack or charge: The large army took the enemy city by *storm.* —*verb.* 1. To be windy, often with rain, snow, sleet, or hail. 2. To express oneself angrily or noisily; to rage. 3. To attack or charge with a powerful force. **stormed, storming.**

storm door. An extra door placed outside of the regular one to keep out wind and cold.

storm·y (STOR-mee) *adjective.* 1. Having or related to storms: *stormy* weather. 2. Marked by anger and confusion: a *stormy* meeting. **stormier, stormiest.**

stor·y (STOR-ee) *noun.* 1. A fictional or made-up writing or account; a tale. 2. An account; telling of events: the *story* of his trip. 3. A lie. 4. A level in a house or other building; floor. **stories.**

stout (STOWT) *adjective.* 1. Fat. 2. Sturdy; strong: *stout* ropes. 3. Courageous; bold: *stout* warriors. **stouter, stoutest.** —*noun.* A strong, dark beer. —**stoutly** *adverb.*

stove (STOHV) *noun.* A device used for cooking foods or providing heat.

stow (STOH) *verb.* To pack or arrange: Bob *stowed* his baseball equipment in the closet. **stowed, stowing.**

stow·a·way (STOH-ə-way) *noun.* A person who hides on a ship, plane, or other transport to get a free trip.

strad·dle (STRAD-l) *verb.* 1. To sit with the legs on either side of: *straddle* a horse. 2. To seem to take both sides in an argument: *straddle* an issue. **straddled, straddling.**

strag·gle (STRAG-əl) *verb.* 1. To fail to keep up; fall behind. 2. To wander or roam in different directions. **straggled, straggling.**

straight (STRAYT) *adjective.* 1. Not bent or curved. 2. In a line; in order: The desks were *straight* when class began. 3. Erect; upright: *straight* posture. 4. Honest; not intended to fool: *straight* talk. 5. Not mixed or diluted: *straight* whiskey. **straighter, straightest.** —*adverb.* 1. Without a bend or curve: Draw the line *straight.* 2. In good order. 3. Erectly: Stand *straight.* 4. Directly: The horse ran *straight* for the barn. 5. Honestly.

straight·en (STRAYT-n) *verb.* 1. To make or become straight. 2. To put in good order: *straighten* a room. **straightened, straightening.**

straight·for·ward (strayt-FOR-wərd) *adjective.* Honest; not intended to fool.

straight·way (STRAYT-way) Also **straightaway** *adverb.* Immediately.

[1]**strain** (STRAYN) *verb.* 1. To injure by too much effort: Ralph *strained* his back when he lifted the log. 2. To make a great effort: The workmen *strained* to lift the piano. 3. To force through a sieve or screen to separate small from large pieces or solid from liquid parts. **strained, straining.** —*noun.* 1. An injury caused by too much effort. 2. Pressure; difficulty: the *strain* of long hours of study.

[2]**strain** (STRAYN) *noun.* 1. A type or kind: a new *strain* of roses. 2. A small amount; trace: a *strain* of selfishness. 3. Family background; ancestry. 4. A melody: *strains* of organ music.

strain·er (STRAY-nər) *noun.* A sieve, screen, or other device for straining.

strait (STRAYT) *noun.* (Often plural) 1. A narrow body of water connecting two larger bodies of water. 2. A situation or position: in dangerous *straits.*

storks

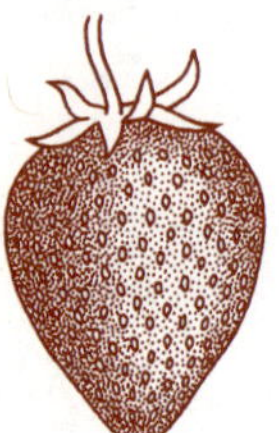
strawberry

stream

[1]**strand** *verb.* 1. To leave or be left alone or in a difficult situation: *stranded* on a desert island. 2. To run aground or be driven aground. **stranded, stranding.** —*noun.* A beach; seashore.

[2]**strand** *noun.* 1. One of the threads or wires that are twisted together to form a cord or rope. 2. Any thread or single, narrow piece: a *strand* of hair; a *strand* of beads.

strange (STRAYNJ) *adjective.* 1. Not known or experienced before: a *strange* city. 2. Odd; peculiar; not normal or usual: *strange* behavior. **stranger, strangest.** —**strangely** *adverb.*

stran·ger (STRAYN-jər) *noun.* 1. A person who is not an acquaintance. 2. A person from outside of a particular area; foreigner: The ship brought *strangers* to the port.

stran·gle (STRANG-gəl) *verb.* 1. To squeeze around the throat; kill by choking. 2. To hold back; stifle: Travel in the city was *strangled* by heavy traffic. **strangled, strangling.**

strap *noun.* 1. A narrow strip of leather or other material used to strengthen things or to hold things in place: The luggage was held on top of the car by heavy *straps.* 2. A belt. —*verb.* 1. To hold in place by fastening with a narrow band. 2. To strike or beat with a belt or similar object. **strapped, strapping.**

strap·ping (STRAP-ing) *adjective.* Tall and sturdy.

stra·ta (STRAY-tə or STRA-tə) *noun.* *See* **stratum.**

strat·a·gem (STRAT-ə-jəm) *noun.* A scheme or plan used to trick, especially to deceive an enemy during war.

stra·te·gy (STRAT-ə-jee) *noun.* The planning and managing of an activity, especially of a war. **strategies.** —**strategic** (strə-TEE-jik) *adjective.* —**strategically** *adverb.*

strat·o·sphere (STRAT-ə-sfihr) *noun.* The layer of the earth's atmosphere that extends from an altitude of about 6 miles to about 30 miles.

stra·tum (STRAY-təm or STRA-təm) *noun.* 1. A layer of a substance, as of rock: a *stratum* of limestone. 2. A level or rank: *stratum* of society. —**strata** or **stratums** *plural.*

straw *noun.* 1. One or many stalks or stems of dried, threshed grain: The calf slept on a bed of *straw.* 2. A slender tube, usually of plastic or waxed paper, used to suck up liquids.

straw·ber·ry (STRAW-behr-ee or STRAW-bə-ree) *noun.* 1. A small, sweet red fruit. 2. The plant on which this fruit grows. **strawberries.**

strawberry shortcake. *See* **shortcake.**

stray *verb.* 1. To wander away from where one should be; roam. 2. To do wrong; be in error. **strayed, straying.** —*noun.* A lost or wandering animal. —*adjective.* 1. Lost; wandering. 2. Scattered; apart from others: *stray* hairs.

streak (STREEK) *noun.* 1. A narrow stripe that is different from the surrounding area: Mother's hair has *streaks* of gray. 2. A particular quality: a mean *streak.* 3. A series of events: a winning *streak.* —*verb.* 1. To make lines or streaks. 2. To move quickly. **streaked, streaking.**

stream (STREEM) *noun.* 1. A body of running water, such as a river or brook. 2. A steady flow (of liquid or gas). 3. A continuous line of objects, words, or thoughts. —*verb.* 1. To flow. 2. To pour out: Smoke *streamed* from the burning plane. 3. To move continuously: The children *streamed* out of the school. 4. To stretch out as in the wind: Her long hair *streamed* over her shoulder. **streamed, streaming.**

stream·er (STREE-mər) *noun.* 1. A narrow flag. 2. A long narrow strip of cloth or paper.

stream·line (STREEM-lighn) *verb.* 1. To design (an object) to move smoothly through air or water. 2. To make more efficient by elimination of unnecessary elements: The expert *streamlined* our business methods. **streamlined, streamlining.**

street *noun.* 1. A public roadway, usually in a city or town. 2. The people who live along such a roadway: Our *street* had a block party.

street·car (STREET-kahr) *noun.* A public passenger car that runs on rails laid along city streets.

strength (STRENGKTH) *noun.* 1. The quality of being mighty or strong; power. 2. Toughness; ability to support weight: Test the *strength* of the ice before you skate on it. **—on the strength of.** Based on.

strength·en (STRENGK-thən) *verb.* To make or become stronger. **strengthened, strengthening.**

stren·u·ous (STREN-yoo-əss) *adjective.* 1. Requiring great energy or effort: a *strenuous* game of tennis. 2. Very active; strong: The doctor has *strenuous* objections to smoking. **—strenuously** *adverb.*

stress *noun.* 1. Pressure or strain: The heavy truck placed too much *stress* on the old bridge. 2. Emphasis: Our coach puts *stress* on daily workouts. 3. Accent: Waltz music has a *stress* on the first beat of each measure. **stresses.** *—verb.* 1. To strain or place pressure on. 2. To place emphasis on; accent. **stressed, stressing.**

stretch (STRECH) *verb.* 1. To extend by pulling: *stretch* a rubber band. 2. To extend in space or time: The desert *stretched* for miles and miles. 3. To spread out or extend: *stretch* one's arms. **stretched, stretching.** *—noun.* 1. The act of stretching. 2. The ability to stretch: This band has lost its *stretch.* 3. A length or section: a *stretch* of bad road. **stretches.**

stretch·er (STRECH-ər) *noun.* A light frame covered with cloth and used for carrying an ill or injured person.

strew (STROO) *verb.* To scatter or spread around, often carelessly. **strewn** or **strewed, strewing.**

strick·en (STRIK-ən) *adjective.* 1. Hit or hurt. 2. Attacked or made to suffer, as from disease or strong feeling.

strict (STRIKT) *adjective.* 1. Stern; demanding obedience: *strict* father. 2. Exact, accurate: *strict* records. 3. Total; unchanging: *strict* secrecy. **stricter, strictest. —strictly** *adverb.*

stride (STRIGHD) *verb.* To walk or run with long steps. **strode, striding.** *—noun.* 1. A long step; the distance covered in one step. 2. Progress: Science has made great *strides.* **strides. —take in stride.** To accept calmly.

strife (STRIGHF) *noun.* 1. War. 2. An argument; a struggle.

strike (STRIGHK) *verb.* 1. To hit. 2. To indicate (the time) by making a hitting sound: The clock *strikes* six. 3. To stop work in an effort to get improvements in pay or working conditions. 4. To cross out or remove: *Strike* that sentence from the record. 5. (Baseball) To swing the bat at and miss a pitched ball. 6. To make burn by rubbing: *strike* a match. 7. To come upon: *strike* gold. 8. To attack: When will the enemy *strike?* 9. To set (out), begin. 10. To make by cutting out or stamping: The U.S. Mint *strikes* coins. 11. To impress suddenly: Maybe a better idea will *strike* us. **struck, striking.** *—noun.* 1. The act of striking. 2. A stopping of work. 3. (Baseball) A well-pitched ball that is not hit by the batter, or any ball that the batter swings at and misses. 4. (Bowling) The score made when ten pins are knocked down by the first ball rolled. 5. A sudden discovery or success. **strikes. —strike it rich.** To become wealthy suddenly.

stretcher

streetcar

strik·ing (STRIGH-king) *adjective.* Outstanding; attracting attention.

string *noun.* 1. A cord or heavy thread. 2. Anything shaped like a string; a set of similar objects threaded together. 3. A line or row. 4. The cord or wire used on certain musical instruments. 5. (Plural) Instruments of the violin family. 6. (Sports) A rank in smaller teams within a large team: first *string.* —*verb.* 1. To hang with a string or wire. 2. To put objects on a string or to add strings to an object. 3. To remove strings (from vegetables). **strung, stringing.** —**pull strings.** To control; get what one wants by using personal influence. —**string along.** To follow; go along with.

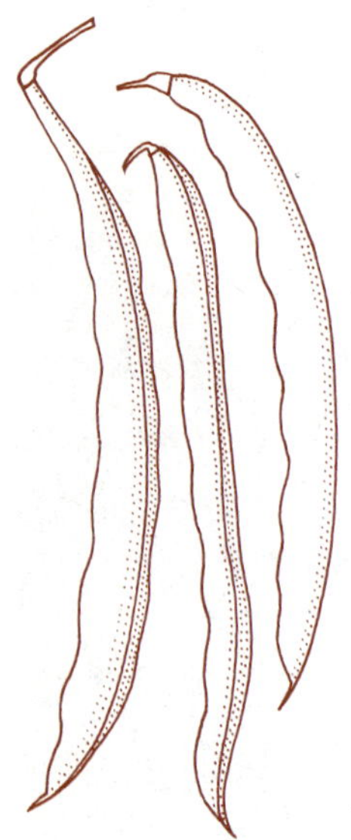

string beans

string bean. 1. A long, narrow green pod, eaten as a vegetable. 2. The plant on which it grows.

stringed instrument. A musical instrument with strings, as a harp.

string·y (STRING-ee) *adjective.* 1. Like string. 2. Having long fibers: *stringy* meat. **stringier, stringiest.**

strip *verb.* 1. To take off the covering or outer layer. 2. To remove one's clothes. 3. To remove from; rob: to *strip* a home. **stripped, stripping.** —*noun.* A long narrow piece.

stripe (STRIGHP) *noun.* 1. A line or long, narrow section that differs from the area that surrounds it. 2. A mark on a uniform that shows rank or years of service. **stripes.** —*verb.* To make or mark with stripes. **striped, striping.**

strip·ling (STRIP-ling) *noun.* A youth.

strip mining

strip mining. A way of mining coal or other minerals by removing layers of the earth's surface.

strive (STRIGHV) *verb.* 1. To fight. 2. To try hard. **strove, striven, striving.**

strode (STROHD) *verb. See* **stride.**

stroke (STROHK) *noun.* 1. The act or sound of striking. 2. A single complete movement, as in swimming. 3. A sudden attack of illness, often causing brain damage: sun*stroke.* 4. A mark, such as one made by a brush or pen. 5. A gentle rubbing with the hand or a brush. **strokes.** —*verb.* To pet; rub gently with the hand or a brush. **stroked, stroking.**

stroll (STROHL) *verb.* To walk slowly. **strolled, strolling.** —*noun.* A slow walk.

stroll·er (STROH-lər) *noun.* 1. One who walks slowly. 2. A low carriage for children.

strong (STRAWNG) *adjective.* 1. Having physical strength or health; powerful. 2. Solid, lasting; able to support weight: a *strong* bridge. 3. Having a powerful effect on the senses; intense: *strong* light. 4. In size or number: Our class sang out, 25 *strong.* **stronger, strongest.** —**strongly** *adverb.*

strong·hold (STRAWNG-hohld) *noun.* 1. A fort. 2. A safe place.

strove (STROHV) *verb. See* **strive.**

struck (STRUHK) *verb. See* **strike.**

struc·ture (STRUHK-chər) *noun.* 1. Something that has been built, such as a building or bridge. 2. The arrangement of parts; way in which something is put together: the *structure* of an atom. **structures.**

strug·gle (STRUHG-əl) *verb.* 1. To fight or wrestle. 2. To move ahead with effort; try hard. **struggled, struggling.** —*noun.* 1. A fight; warfare. 2. A great effort. **struggles.**

strum (STRUHM) *verb.* To move the fingers across lightly, as in playing a stringed instrument. **strummed, strumming.**

strung (STRUHNG) *verb. See* **string.**

strut (STRUHT) *verb.* To walk in a proud way, as if showing off. **strutted, strutting.** —*noun.* 1. A showy way of walking. 2. A piece of supporting framework: *Struts* brace the wings of a light airplane.

stub (STUHB) *verb.* To strike (one's foot or toe) against an object by mistake. **stubbed, stubbing.** —*noun.*

1. A short part left from a larger object: the *stub* of a candle. 2. The end of a ticket or check.

stub·ble (STUHB-əl) *noun.* 1. The short, sharp points of plants left in a field after a crop has been cut. 2. Any short growth, as whiskers.

stub·born (STUHB-ərn) *adjective.* 1. Determined; set in one's ways. 2. Difficult to treat or handle: a *stubborn* cold. —**stubbornly** *adverb.*

stub·by (STUHB-ee) *adjective.* 1. Covered with or made up of stubs. 2. Short and thick: *stubby* fingers. **stubbier, stubbiest.**

stuc·co (STUHK-oh) *noun.* A kind of plaster or cement used on walls. **stuccoes** or **stuccos.** —*verb.* To cover with stucco. **stuccoed, stuccoing.**

stuck (STUHK) *verb.* *See* **stick.**

stuck-up (STUHK-uhp) *adjective.* (Informal) Pleased with oneself; conceited.

stud (STUHD) *noun.* 1. An upright timber that forms part of the framework of a building. 2. A removable clothing button or fastener, often used for decoration. 3. A nail or tack with a head that extends above the surface of the material. 4. A male animal or a group of animals kept for breeding purposes. —*verb.* To decorate or cover as with studs. **studded, studding.**

stu·dent (STOO-dənt or STYOO-dənt) *noun.* 1. A pupil; one who attends school. 2. (Used with *of*) One who studies or follows (a particular subject).

stu·di·o (STOO-dee-oh or STYOO-dee-oh) *noun.* 1. The workshop of a painter, musician, photographer, or other artist. 2. A place for broadcasting radio or TV programs or making movies. **studios.**

stu·di·ous (STOO-dee-əss or STYOO-dee-əss) *adjective.* 1. Devoted to learning. 2. Carefully thoughtful. —**studiously** *adverb.*

stud·y (STUHD-ee) *verb.* 1. To try to learn. 2. To examine or look at carefully. 3. To take a program at school or college. **studied, studying.** —*noun.* 1. The act of trying to learn. 2. The act or result of examining or investigating: a *study* of traffic accidents. 3. A subject or field: Astronomy is the *study* of stars, planets, and outer space. 4. A completed work of literature, art, or music. 5. A room used for reading or studying. **studies.**

stuff (STUHF) *noun.* 1. Substance; any material from which something is made. 2. A mixture of objects: He took a lot of *stuff* out of his pockets. 3. Inner quality or ability: He has the *stuff* to make a good team captain. —*verb.* 1. To fill; pack tightly. 2. To fill with a special mixture or material: *stuff* a turkey. 3. To overeat. 4. To block or stop (up). **stuffed, stuffing.**

stuff·ing (STUHF-ing) *noun.* 1. Material used for filling. 2. A mixture such as bread and seasonings put inside meat before cooking.

stuff·y (STUHF-ee) *adjective.* 1. Lacking fresh air. 2. Having the passages of the nose blocked. 3. (Informal) Dull, formally old-fashioned. **stuffier, stuffiest.** —**stuffily** *adverb.*

stum·ble (STUHM-bəl) *verb.* 1. To trip (over) or run into objects on the ground. 2. To walk in a clumsy way. 3. To fail to speak plainly. 4. To make mistakes. **stumbled, stumbling.** —*noun.* The act of tripping or making a mistake. —**stumble upon.** To come upon by accident.

stump (STUHMP) *noun.* 1. The part of a tree trunk left standing after the upper part has been cut off. 2. The remaining part of anything. 3. (Politics) A platform from which to give speeches. —*verb.* 1. To walk with heavy clumsy steps. 2. To travel from place to place giving political speeches. 3. (Informal) To perplex or baffle. **stumped, stumping.**

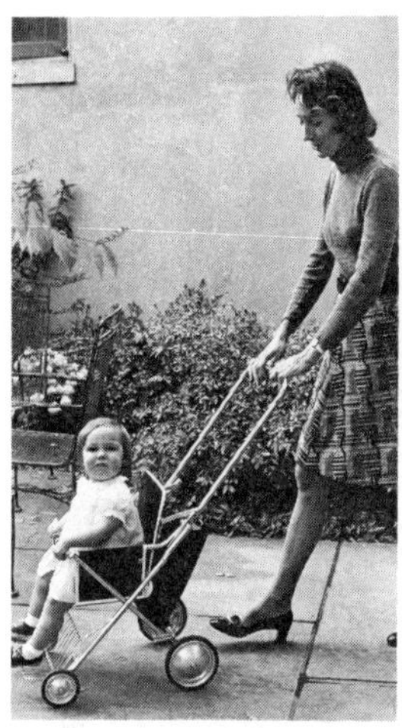

stroller

stun (STUHN) *verb.* 1. To daze; make unconscious. 2. To astonish or surprise greatly. **stunned, stunning.**

stung (STUHNG) *verb. See* **sting.**

stunk (STUHNGK) *verb. See* **stink.**

stun·ning (STUHN-ing) *adjective.* 1. Surprising; upsetting. 2. (Informal) Very beautiful. —**stunningly** *adverb.*

[1]**stunt** (STUHNT) *noun.* 1. A feat requiring unusual skill. 2. A clever trick.

[2]**stunt** (STUHNT) *verb.* To slow or stop the growth of: Heavy winds *stunt* trees by the seashore. **stunted, stunting.**

stu·pe·fy (STOO-pə-figh or STYOO-pə-figh) *verb.* 1. To make dull; numb the senses of. 2. To amaze. **stupefied, stupefying.**

stu·pen·dous (stoo-PEN-dəss or styoo-PEN-dəss) *adjective.* 1. Amazing or astounding. 2. Of surprisingly great size. —**stupendously** *adverb.*

stu·pid (STOO-pid or STYOO-pid) *adjective.* 1. Slow to understand; not bright. 2. Dull and boring. **stupider, stupidest.** —**stupidity** (stoo-PID-ə-tee or styoo-PID-ə-tee) *noun.* —**stupidly** *adverb.*

stu·por (STOO-pər or STYOO-pər) *noun.* A dazed or confused state.

stur·dy (STER-dee) *adjective.* 1. Strong; well built. 2. Healthy or vigorous. **sturdier, sturdiest.** —**sturdiness** *noun.* —**sturdily** *adverb.*

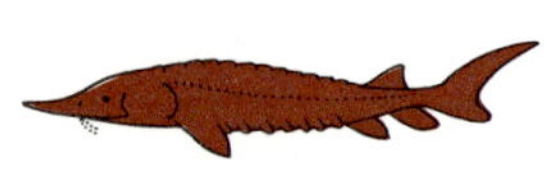
sturgeon

stur·geon (STER-jən) *noun.* A large food fish whose eggs are prized as caviar.

stut·ter (STUHT-ər) *verb.* To speak jerkily, repeating the same sound. **stuttered, stuttering.** —*noun.* The act of stuttering or stammering.

[1]**sty** (STIGH) *noun.* 1. A pigpen. 2. A dirty place. **sties.**

[2]**sty** (STIGH) *noun.* A sore swelling on the edge of the eyelid. **sties.**

style (STIGHL) *noun.* 1. Fashion: dress *styles.* 2. The way in which something is made, said, or done: *style* of writing. **styles.** —*verb.* 1. To design: *style* clothing. 2. To call or name: Joel *styled* himself an artist. **styled, styling.**

styl·ish (STIGH-lish) *adjective.* Fashionable. —**stylishly** *adverb.*

sub (SUHB) *noun.* (Informal) 1. A submarine. 2. A substitute. —*verb.* To act as a substitute. **subbed, subbing.**

sub- *prefix.* Indicates: 1. Under: *sub*way. 2. Lower in position or rank: *sub*committee. 3. Not up to; less than: *sub*standard. 4. A part of a whole: *sub*station.

sub·di·vide (SUHB-də-vighd) *verb.* To divide (especially of land) into smaller parts: *subdivide* property. **subdivided, subdividing.**

sub·due (səb-DOO or səb-DYOO) *verb.* 1. To conquer or overcome. 2. To soften; lower the tone of. **subdued, subduing.**

sub·ject (SUHB-jikt) *noun.* 1. The person, thing, or idea being considered: *subject* of conversation. 2. A person under the rule of a government or ruler: a British *subject.* 3. (Grammar) The word or words in a sentence that identify the performer of an active verb, or the receiver of the action of a passive verb. —*adjective.* 1. Under the power of another: The *subject* people fought for independence. 2. (Used with *to*) Liable or prone: *subject* to allergies. 3. (Used with *to*) Depending on: *subject* to the weather. —(suhb-JEKT) *verb.* 1. To bring under control: *subject* by force. 2. To make liable. 3. To cause to undergo: The company *subjects* new products to tests. **subjected, subjecting.**

sub·junc·tive (səb-JUHNGK-tiv) *adjective.* Naming a form of a verb that expresses something that has not actually occurred: In "If I were king," "were" is in the *subjunctive* mood.

sub·lime (sə-BLIGHM) *adjective.* 1. Noble: *sublime* music. 2. Majestic or lofty: *sublime* mountains.

sub·ma·rine (SUHB-mə-reen) *noun.* 1. A ship designed to travel under water. 2. (Slang) A long sandwich. *See* **grinder.** —*adjective.* Referring to underwater life or work.

sub·merge (səb-MERJ) *verb.* 1. To put or go under water: The submarine *submerged.* 2. To cover with water. **submerged, submerging.**

sub·mis·sive (səb-MISS-iv) *adjective.* Obedient; yielding.

sub·mit (səb-MIT) *verb.* 1. To yield or give (oneself) up to the power of another or others. 2. To give (something) for judgment: Stan *submitted* his paper to the teacher. **submitted, submitting. —submission** (səb-MISH-ən) *noun.*

sub·or·di·nate (sə-BOR-də-nit) *adjective.* 1. Of lower rank or less importance. 2. (Used with *to*) Under the control of: The sergeant was *subordinate* to his lieutenant. —*noun.* A person or thing of less rank or importance than another. **subordinates.** —(sə-BOR-də-nayt) *verb.* To make less important; put in a lower rank: Peter *subordinated* his own wishes to those of his friends. **subordinated, subordinating.**

sub·scribe (səb-SKRIGHB) *verb.* (Used with *to*) 1. To promise to pay or give money: *subscribe* to a fund drive. 2. To agree to take and pay for successive issues of (a publication). 3. To agree to or approve of: He *subscribes* to the principle that all men are created equal. **subscribed, subscribing. —subscription** (səb-SKRIP-shən) *noun.*

sub·se·quent (SUHB-sə-kwənt) *adjective.* Coming after in time or order: The first day of our vacation was rainy, but the *subsequent* days were sunny. **—subsequently** *adverb.*

sub·set (SUHB-set) *noun.* (Math) A set within a set.

sub·side (səb-SIGHD) *verb.* To lessen or quiet down: When the storm *subsides,* we may go out. **subsided, subsiding.**

sub·sid·i·ar·y (səb-SID-ee-ehr-ee) *adjective.* Assisting or helpful; secondary: *subsidiary* income. —*noun.* A business firm that is owned by another firm: The publishing company was the *subsidiary* of a large printing company. **subsidiaries.**

sub·si·dize (SUHB-sə-dighz) *verb.* To help by giving funds to: The government *subsidizes* many experimental programs. **subsidized, subsidizing.**

subsist (səb-SIST) *verb.* To exist or continue to exist. **subsisted, subsisting. —subsistence** *noun.*

sub·soil (SUHB-soil) *noun.* The layer of soil directly beneath the topsoil.

sub·stance (SUHB-stənss) *noun.* 1. Matter; what something is made of. 2. The main or most important part: The *substance* of Tom's speech was citizenship. 3. Wealth or material possessions: a man of *substance.*

sub·stan·tial (səb-STAN-shəl) *adjective.* 1. Strong and solid: a *substantial* building. 2. Real or true. 3. Large or ample: *substantial* improvement. 4. Well-to-do: *substantial* citizen. **—substantially** *adverb.*

sub·sti·tute (SUHB-stə-toot or SUHB-stə-tyoot) *noun.* A person or thing that takes the place of another. —*verb.* (Used with *for*) 1. To use in place of: *substitute* honey for sugar on cereal. 2. To take the place of: He *substituted* for the regular teacher. **substituted, substituting. —substitution** (suhb-stə-TOO-shən or suhb-stə-TYOO-shən) *noun.*

sub·ter·ra·ne·an (suhb-tə-RAY-nee-ən) *adjective.* Underground: *subterranean* caves.

submarine

sub·tle (SUHT-l) *adjective.* 1. Hard to detect; not apparent: a *subtle* flavor. 2. Keen and quick to understand: a *subtle* mind. 3. Clever or sly. **subtler, subtlest.** —**subtly** *adverb.*

sub·tract (səb-TRAKT) *verb.* To take away: Five *subtracted* from nine leaves four. **subtracted, subtracting.**

sub·trac·tion (səb-TRAK-shən) *noun.* The act of taking away: Tom uses *subtraction* to find out how much money he will have left if he spends two dollars.

sub·tra·hend (SUHB-trə-hend) *noun.* The number subtracted from another: In the example ten minus eight, the *subtrahend* is eight.

sub·trop·i·cal (suhb-TROP-i-kəl) *adjective.* Referring to regions near the earth's tropical zone.

subway car

sub·urb (SUHB-ərb) *noun.* A community just outside a city. —**suburban** *adjective.*

sub·way (SUHB-way) *noun.* 1. An underground electric railroad. 2. An underground tunnel.

suc·ceed (sək-SEED) *verb.* 1. To get something done as one wants; reach a desired goal. 2. To follow, come after. **succeeded, succeeding.**

suc·cess (sək-SESS) *noun.* 1. Reaching or getting what one has tried for. 2. A person or thing that succeeds: The operation was a *success.*

suc·cess·ful (sək-SESS-fəl) *adjective.* Having success. —**successfully** *adverb.*

suc·ces·sion (sək-SESH-ən) *noun.* 1. One thing or event after another: a *succession* of accidents. 2. The order in which a person succeeds to an office or the throne: The Vice President is first in *succession* to the Presidency of the United States. 3. The right to succeed to an office or the throne.

suc·ces·sive (sək-SESS-iv) *adjective.* Following one after the other. —**successively** *adverb.*

suc·ces·sor (sək-SESS-ər) *noun.* The person who follows another in a position: George VI was the *successor* to George V of England.

suc·co·tash (SUHK-ə-tash) *noun.* Lima beans and corn cooked together.

suc·cu·lent (SUHK-yə-lənt) *adjective.* Full of juice: a *succulent* pear. —**succulently** *adverb.*

suc·cumb (sə-KUHM) *verb.* (Used with *to*) To give in or yield: *succumb* to temptation. **succumbed, succumbing.**

such (SUHCH) *adjective.* 1. Of a great extent in quality: *such* happiness. 2. Of the same kind; like those referred to: chocolates and other *such* sweets. 3. Whatever: We'll meet at *such* time as you prefer. —*pronoun.* Being the same as something already spoken of: He was sent to jail and died there; *such* is the price of crime.

suck (SUHK) *verb.* 1. To draw (a liquid) into the mouth by suction: He *sucked* his soda through a straw. 2. To take in as though by sucking: The vacuum cleaner *sucks* the dirt from the floor. 3. To keep and move in the mouth to cause to melt: *suck* a piece of candy. **sucked, sucking.** —*noun.* The act of sucking: One *suck* of the drink was enough.

suck·er (SUHK-ər) *noun.* 1. Anything that sucks. 2. A hard candy or lollipop. 3. Any of many fish that feed by sucking. 4. A shoot from a root or branch. 5. (Slang) A person who is easily fooled.

suc·tion (SUHK-shən) *noun.* The act of sucking, as in drawing air out of something to create a vacuum.

sud·den (SUHD-ən) *adjective.* 1. Unexpected or without warning: a *sudden* noise. 2. Fast or quick: a *sudden* movement. —**suddenly** *adverb.* —**all of a sudden.** Unexpectedly.

suds (SUHDZ) *noun, plural.* 1. Soapy water. 2. Foam.

sue (soo) *verb.* 1. To take legal action to right a wrong. 2. To plead or ask: *sue* for mercy. **sued, suing.**

suede (SWAYD) *noun.* A flexible leather with a soft nap.

su·et (soo-it) *noun.* Hard fat from cattle and sheep.

suf·fer (SUHF-ər) *verb.* 1. To have or endure pain, grief, or other discomfort. 2. To experience: *suffer* a sprain. **suffered, suffering.**

suf·fice (sə-FIGHSS) *verb.* To be enough. **sufficed, sufficing.**

suf·fi·cient (sə-FISH-ənt) *adjective.* Enough, adequate; as much as is needed. —**sufficiently** *adverb.*

suf·fix (SUHF-iks) *noun.* A letter or letters added at the end of a word to make another word with a different meaning or function: The *suffix* in "playful" is "ful." **suffixes.**

suf·fo·cate (SUHF-ə-kayt) *verb.* 1. To kill or cause to suffer by depriving of air. 2. To die or suffer from lack of air. **suffocated, suffocating.** —**suffocation** (suhf-ə-KAY-shən) *noun.*

suf·frage (SUHF-rij) *noun.* 1. The right to vote. 2. The act of voting; a vote.

sug·ar (SHUG-ər) *noun.* 1. A sweet substance made from sugar cane or sugar beets. 2. A similar substance made from other plant sap or juice: maple *sugar.* —*verb.* To put sugar on or in. **sugared, sugaring.**

sugar beet. A large white beet used for making common sugar.

sugar cane. A tall grass with thick stems that are the main source of sugar.

sug·gest (səg-JEST or sə-JEST) *verb.* 1. To offer (an idea, plan, etc.); propose: *suggest* a solution to a problem. 2. To express indirectly; to hint at. **suggested, suggesting.**

sug·ges·tion (səg-JESS-chən or sə-JESS-chən) *noun.* 1. A plan or idea suggested; a proposal. 2. An idea or thought expressed indirectly; a hint.

su·i·cide (soo-ə-sighd) *noun.* 1. The act of killing oneself intentionally. 2. A person who kills himself intentionally. **suicides.** —**suicidal** *adjective.*

suit (SOOT) *noun.* 1. A set of clothing made up of two or more parts, such as a coat and trousers or a jacket and skirt. 2. One of the four sets in a deck of playing cards: the diamond *suit.* 3. A legal action taken to obtain justice in a court of law. —*verb.* 1. To make suitable or appropriate; fit; adapt: *Suit* the punishment to the crime. 2. To be appropriate for; satisfy the needs of; be agreeable to. **suited, suiting.**

suit·a·ble (soo-tə-bəl) *adjective.* Right or proper for the need or the occasion; appropriate: *suitable* clothes. —**suitably** *adverb.*

suit·case (SOOT-kayss) *noun.* A small piece of luggage with rectangular sides. **suitcases.**

suite (SWEET) *noun.* 1. A number of connected hotel rooms. 2. A set of furniture: a dining room *suite.* **suites.**

suit·or (soo-tər) *noun.* A man who is courting a woman.

sulfa drug. Any of a group of drugs used to control infections.

sul·fur (SUHL-fər) Also **sulphur** *noun.* A yellow chemical element that is used to make gunpowder, medicine, and sulfuric acid.

sul·fu·ric acid (suhl-FYUR-ik). A thick, oily corrosive liquid used in the manufacture of such products as paint and explosives.

sulk (SUHLK) *verb.* To show anger or resentment by being moody and silent. **sulked, sulking.** —**sulkily** *adverb.* —**sulkiness** *noun.* —**sulky** *adjective.*

sulk·y (SUHL-kee) *noun.* A small, two-wheeled, horse-drawn carriage with a seat for the driver only. **sulkies.**

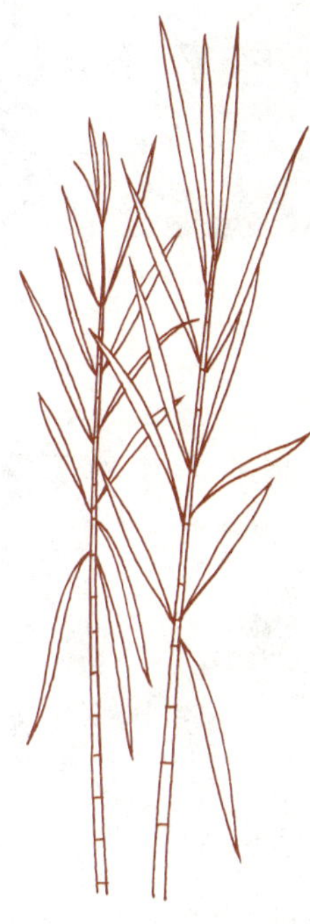

sugar cane

sulky

sumac

sunbonnet

sundial

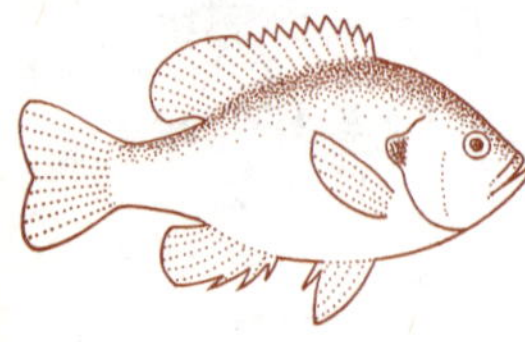
sunfish

sul·len (SUHL-ən) *adjective.* 1. Quietly angry; sulky. 2. Gloomy, dismal: a *sullen* sky. —**sullenly** *adverb.*

sul·tan (SUHL-tən) *noun.* The ruler of a Moslem country.

sul·try (SUHL-tree) *adjective.* Warm, humid, and calm: a *sultry* day. **sultrier, sultriest.**

sum (SUHM) *noun.* 1. The result obtained by adding numbers together; total: The *sum* of 4, 3, and 10 is 17. 2. A problem in arithmetic. 3. An amount of money: a small *sum.* —**sum up.** To repeat the main points.

su·mac (SOO-mak or SHOO-mak) Also **sumach** *noun.* A shrub or small tree having long green leaves that turn red in autumn and long clusters of red berries.

sum·ma·rize (SUHM-ə-righz) *verb.* To state the main points briefly. **summarized, summarizing.**

sum·ma·ry (SUHM-ə-ree) *noun.* A brief statement of the main points; a review. **summaries.**

sum·mer (SUHM-ər) *noun.* The season of the year that comes after spring and before autumn: In the Northern Hemisphere, *summer* lasts from about June 22nd to about September 22nd. —*verb.* To spend the summer: *summer* at the seashore. **summered, summering.**

sum·mit (SUHM-it) *noun.* The highest point; peak; top.

sum·mon (SUHM-ən) *verb.* 1. To command to come: The President *summoned* his cabinet. 2. To order to appear in court. 3. To call up; rouse: *Summon* your courage. **summoned, summoning.**

sum·mons (SUHM-ənz) *noun, plural in form but used with a singular verb.* 1. An order to come. 2. An official order to appear in court. **summonses.**

sump·tu·ous (SUHMP-choo-əss) *adjective.* Lavish and expensive.

sun (SUHN) *noun.* 1. The bright star around which the earth and planets revolve and which gives them light and heat. 2. Sunlight: lie in the *sun.* 3. Any heavenly body like the sun. —*verb.* To lie or place in sunlight. **sunned, sunning.**

sun·beam (SUHN-beem) *noun.* A ray of sunlight.

sun·bon·net (SUHN-bon-it) *noun.* A hat with a wide brim in front for protection against the sun.

sun·burn (SUHN-bern) *noun.* A burning and reddening of the skin caused by excessive exposure to the sun's rays. —*verb.* To burn or become burned by exposure to the sun's rays. **sunburned** or **sunburnt, sunburning.**

sun·dae (SUHN-dee or SUHN-day) *noun.* A dish of ice cream with toppings such as fruit, chocolate, or nuts.

Sun·day (SUHN-dee or SUHN-day) *noun.* The first day of the week: *Sunday* is the day between Saturday and Monday. —**Sun.** *abbreviation.*

sun deck. An open porch or other area for sitting or lying in the sun.

sun·di·al (SUHN-digh-əl) *noun.* A device for telling time from the shadow cast by a pointer on a dial.

sun·down (SUHN-down) *noun.* The time of the setting of the sun.

sun·dry (SUHN-dree) *adjective.* Various; several.

sun·fish (SUHN-fish) *noun.* 1. Any of various small, edible freshwater fishes of North America. 2. A large flat-bodied sea fish with long fins. —**sunfish** or **sunfishes** *plural.*

sun·flow·er (SUHN-flow-ər) *noun.* A plant with a long stem and large yellow flowers with brown centers.

sung (SUHNG) *verb. See* **sing.**

sun·glass·es (SUHN-glass-iz) *noun, plural.* Eyeglasses with tinted glass for protection against sunlight.

sunk (SUHNGK) *verb. See* **sink.**

sunk·en (SUHNG-kən) *adjective.* 1. Hollow; fallen in. 2. In or below the water. 3. Below the surrounding level. —*verb. See* **sink.**

sun·light (SUHN-light) *noun.* Light from the sun. —**sunlit** (SUHN-lit) *adjective.*

sun·ny (SUHN-ee) *adjective.* 1. Lighted by the sun; full of sunshine. 2. Bright and cheerful: a *sunny* smile. **sunnier, sunniest.**

sun porch. A glass-enclosed porch.

sun·rise (SUHN-righz) *noun.* 1. The rising of the sun above the eastern horizon. 2. The hour when the sun rises. **sunrises.**

sun·set (SUHN-set) *noun.* 1. The setting of the sun below the western horizon. 2. The hour when the sun sets.

sun·shine (SUHN-shighn) *noun.* 1. Light from the sun. 2. Cheerfulness; pleasantness.

sun·spot (SUHN-spot) *noun.* Any of the dark spots often seen on the sun when it is viewed through a telescope equipped with a dense filter: *Sunspots* are produced by magnetic disturbances in the sun.

sun·stroke (SUHN-strohk) *noun.* An illness caused by excessive exposure to sunlight or heat.

sun·up (SUHN-uhp) *noun.* Sunrise.

super- *prefix.* Indicates: 1. A place above or over: *super*structure. 2. Higher or greater in size, amount, type, or degree: *super*highway. 3. Out of the ordinary: *super*natural.

su·perb (sə-PERB) *adjective.* 1. Of a fine quality, excellent. 2. Majestic, grand: a *superb* view. —**superbly** *adverb.*

su·per·fi·cial (soo-pər-FISH-əl) *adjective.* 1. Not deep; on the surface: a *superficial* cut. 2. Said with little thought: a *superficial* remark. 3. Hasty, quick: a *superficial* reading. —**superficially** *adverb.*

su·per·high·way (soo-pər-HIGH-way) *noun.* A multi-lane, limited-access, high-speed road.

su·per·in·tend (soo-pər-in-TEND) *verb.* To oversee; direct or manage. **superintended, superintending.**

su·per·in·ten·dent (soo-pər-in-TEND-nt) *noun.* 1. One who manages a building. 2. A person who directs a large organization.

su·pe·ri·or (sə-PIHR-ee-ər) *adjective.* 1. Better than others, greater: a *superior* student. 2. Higher in rank, altitude, or position: a *superior* officer. 3. Haughty or proud in manner. —*noun.* 1. One of higher rank. 2. The person in charge of a convent or monastery.

su·per·la·tive (sə-PER-lə-tiv) *adjective.* 1. Excellent, superb. 2. (Grammar) Expressing the greatest degree of an adjective or adverb: "Best" is the *superlative* form of "good." —*noun.* (Grammar) The form of an adverb or adjective that shows the greatest degree. —**superlatively** *adverb.*

su·per·mar·ket (soo-pər-mahr-kit) *noun.* A large store in which food and household items are sold to customers who serve themselves.

su·per·nat·u·ral (soo-pər-NACH-ə-rəl) *noun.* Something that cannot be explained by known laws of nature. —*adjective.* 1. Relating to other than the natural world. 2. Like a miracle. —**supernaturally** *adverb.*

su·per·no·va (soo-pər-NOH-və) *noun.* An exploding star that shines brilliantly for a few days. —**supernovae** (soo-pər-NOH-vee) *plural.*

su·per·sede (soo-pər-SEED) *verb.* To take the place of, replace. **superseded, superseding.**

su·per·son·ic (soo-pər-SON-ik) *adjective.* Relating to a speed faster than the speed of sound.

su·per·sti·tion (soo-pər-STISH-ən) *noun.* A belief in supernatural meanings and powers of chance events, charms, and taboos. —**superstitious** (soo-pər-STISH-əss) *adjective.* —**superstitiously** *adverb.*

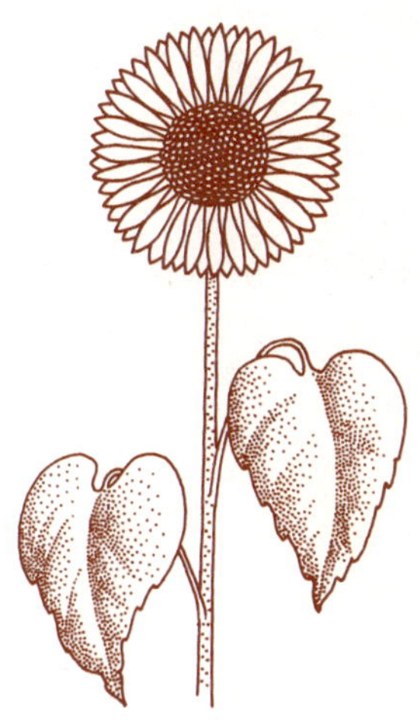
sunflower

su·per·vise (soo-pər-vighz) *verb.* To oversee, direct, or manage. **supervised, supervising.** —**supervision** (soo-pər-VIZH-ən) *noun.*

su·per·vi·sor (soo-pər-vigh-zər) *noun.* One who directs or manages the work of others. —**supervisory** (soo-pər-VIGH-zə-ree) *adjective.*

sup·per (SUHP-ər) *noun.* An evening meal, often light when following a full midday meal.

sup·plant (sə-PLANT) *verb.* To replace, especially to take over another's job or position. **supplanted, supplanting.**

sup·ple (SUHP-əl) *adjective.* 1. Limber, bending easily: *supple* movements. 2. Agreeable, adjusting quickly to new situations. **suppler, supplest.**

sup·ple·ment (SUHP-lə-ment) *verb.* To add to or complete: She *supplements* her diet with vitamins. **supplemented, supplementing.** —(SUHP-lə-mənt) *noun.* 1. Something added to finish or complete something else. 2. An additional section to a printed work: a magazine *supplement* of a newspaper.

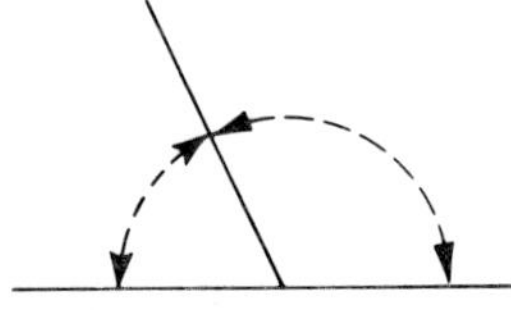

supplementary angles

supplementary angle. An angle that, in combination with another given angle, equals 180 degrees.

sup·pli·cate (SUHP-li-kayt) *verb.* To beg; pray. **supplicated, supplicating.** —**supplication** (suhp-li-KAY-shən) *noun.*

sup·ply (sə-PLIGH) *verb.* To furnish or provide: The school *supplies* pencils. **supplied, supplying.** —*noun.* 1. (Often plural) Goods or stock on hand or needed: Our paper *supplies* are kept in the cupboard. 2. The amount available: The demand for good housing is greater than the *supply.* **supplies.**

sup·port (sə-PORT) *verb.* 1. To hold up, bear the weight of: Wood beams *support* the floor of the house. 2. To provide for, supply money or needs for: My father will *support* me until I find a job. 3. To favor or encourage: What man do you *support* for President? 4. To back up; supply facts for: The lawyer *supported* his claim with photographs. **supported, supporting.** —*noun.* 1. A foundation; something that bears weight: The bridge has stone *supports.* 2. The act of backing or encouraging.

sup·pose (sə-POHZ) *verb.* 1. To assume; imagine or pretend (something is true) for the sake of argument or to prove a point: *Suppose* the wheel had not been invented. 2. To expect or guess: I *suppose* it will rain today. 3. To present as an idea: *Suppose* we think about the plan overnight. **supposed, supposing.**

sup·posed (sə-POHZD) *adjective.* 1. Expected or required: He was *supposed* to go to the dentist today. 2. Believed (usually mistakenly): The *supposed* murderer proved to be innocent. —**supposedly** (suh-POH-zəd-lee) *adverb.*

sup·press (sə-PRESS) *verb.* 1. To hold back: *suppress* a sneeze. 2. To withhold: *suppress* information. 3. To put down: The dictator *suppressed* the uprising. **suppressed, suppressing.** —**suppression** *noun.*

su·prem·a·cy (sə-PREM-ə-see) *noun.* 1. The state or condition of being the best. 2. The position of greatest power: Stalin gained *supremacy* in Russia in 1927.

su·preme (sə-PREEM) *adjective.* 1. Finest, best: His *supreme* moment came when he won the Olympic gold medal. 2. Most powerful or important; above all others: The Constitution is the *supreme* law of our land. 3. Final, extreme: Death in battle is the *supreme* sacrifice. —**supremely** *adverb.*

sure (SHUR) *adjective.* 1. Certain, positive: Are you *sure* you are right? 2. Steady, firm: a *sure* step. 3. Dependable, certain to happen: It is a *sure* thing that the sun will rise tomorrow. **surer, surest.** —*adverb.* (Informal) Of course; certainly.

sure·ly (SHUR-lee) *adverb.* 1. Certainly, without a doubt: "*Surely* goodness and mercy shall follow me all the days of my life. . . ." (Psalms 23:6). 2. Firmly.

surf (SERF) *noun.* Breaking ocean waves or the foam of such waves as they reach the shore. —*verb.* To ride a surfboard: We will *surf* next summer. **surfed, surfing.**

sur·face (SER-fəss) *noun.* 1. The outer layer; the part that is seen: the *surface* of a lake. 2. The appearance rather than the true nature: On the *surface,* the family seemed happy. —*verb.* To come to the top: The submarine *surfaced* near the shore. **surfaced, surfacing.**

surf·board (SERF-bord) *noun.* A long, lightweight board of wood or fiber glass used in riding the waves.

surge (SERJ) *verb.* 1. To rush forward in a wave: Water *surged* over the dam. 2. To move like a wave: The crowd *surged* into the street. 3. To increase suddenly. **surged, surging.** —*noun.* 1. A large wave or group of waves together. 2. A sudden increase: a *surge* of pride. **surges.**

sur·geon (SER-jən) *noun.* A doctor trained to perform operations.

sur·ger·y (SER-jər-ee) *noun.* 1. (Medicine) The repair of ailments or injuries by operations. 2. The room in which operations are performed. 3. The work of a surgeon. **surgeries.** —**surgical** *adjective.* —**surgically** *adverb.*

sur·ly (SER-lee) *adjective.* Crabby, ill-tempered, rude. **surlier, surliest.** —**surlily** *adverb.*

sur·mount (sər-MOWNT) *verb.* 1. To overcome: Lincoln *surmounted* many obstacles. 2. To reach the top of: The prince *surmounted* the palace wall. 3. To be on top of. **surmounted, surmounting.**

sur·name (SER-naym) *noun.* The last, or family, name: Jack's *surname* was Sprat. **surnames.**

sur·pass (sər-PASS) *verb.* To go beyond, be better than: This year's corn crop will *surpass* last year's. **surpassed, surpassing.**

sur·plus (SER-pləss) *adjective.* Excess, more than needed or used. —*noun.* An amount left over. **surpluses.**

sur·prise (sər-PRIGHZ) *verb.* 1. To cause to feel amazement and wonder. 2. To meet, catch, or startle suddenly. 3. To attack or capture without warning: Our army *surprised* the British at Trenton. **surprised, surprising.** —*noun.* 1. An unexpected gift or happening. 2. A feeling of amazement or wonder. **surprises.** —*adjective.* Unexpected.

sur·ren·der (sə-REN-dər) *verb.* 1. To give oneself up, especially under force or pressure: "We shall never *surrender.*" (Winston Churchill). 2. To turn over: *Surrender* your arms. 3. To give up or abandon: *surrender* freedom. **surrendered, surrendering.** —*noun.* The act of giving up or accepting defeat.

sur·rey (SER-ee) *noun.* A light carriage pulled by a horse.

sur·round (sə-ROWND) *verb.* To encircle; enclose or encompass. **surrounded, surrounding.**

sur·round·ings (sə-ROWN-dingz) *noun, plural.* 1. Background; setting: The house has beautiful *surroundings.* 2. Environment; the conditions around one: a child's *surroundings.*

sur·vey (sər-VAY or SER-vay) *verb.* 1. To look over carefully; inspect. 2. To collect information about; study: He *surveyed* the area to learn how many families owned televisions. 3. To make exact land measurements. **surveyed, surveying.** —(SER-vay) *noun.* 1. The act of inspecting, examining, or measuring. 2. The results or record made of such an act.

surfboard

surrey

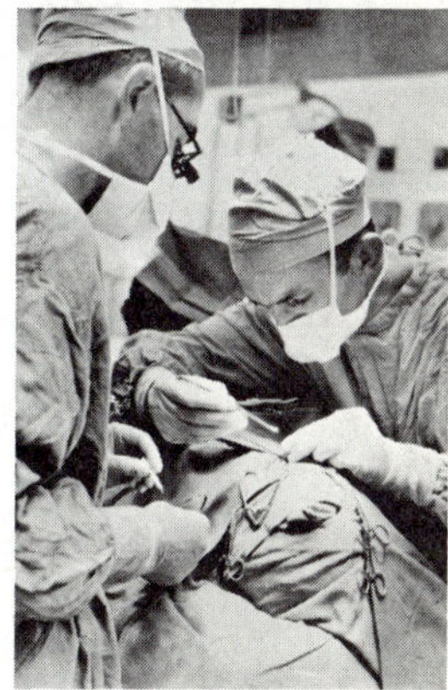

surgeon

sur·vey·or (sər-VAY-ər) *noun.* One who surveys land.

sur·vive (sər-VIGHV) *verb.* 1. To continue to live: Humans cannot *survive* without air and water. 2. To outlive: The dead man's wife and children *survive* him. **survived, surviving.** —**survival** *noun.*

suspenders

sus·cep·ti·ble (sə-SEP-tə-bəl) *adjective.* (Used with *to*) 1. Easily influenced. 2. Sensitive to; apt to be affected by: Most people are *susceptible* to poison ivy. —**susceptibly** *adverb.*

sus·pect (suhss-PEKT) *verb.* 1. To consider to be guilty: We *suspect* the cat of eating the canary. 2. To guess: We *suspect* that someone left the phone off the hook. 3. To doubt: I don't trust him and I *suspect* anything he says. **suspected, suspecting.** —(SUHSS-pekt) *noun.* The one believed to be guilty.

suspension bridge

sus·pend (səss-PEND) *verb.* 1. To hang down: The lamp was *suspended* from the ceiling. 2. To bar temporarily from a school, office, or position, as a form of punishment. 3. To stop for a time; delay or postpone: Work was *suspended* because of the storm. **suspended, suspending.**

sus·pend·ers (səss-PEN-dərz) *noun. plural.* Straps worn over the shoulders and used to hold up trousers or a skirt.

sus·pense (səss-PENSS) *noun.* Uncertainty; concern over the outcome: The monster movie kept us in *suspense.*

[1]swallow

sus·pen·sion (səss-PEN-shən) *noun.* 1. The act of suspending or being suspended. 2. A gas or liquid that has tiny solid particles mixed throughout. 3. The parts of a vehicle, as the springs, that make the ride smooth by cushioning bumps or shocks.

suspension bridge. A bridge that hangs from ropes or cables fastened to high posts or towers at each end.

sus·pi·cion (səss-PISH-ən) *noun.* 1. The act of suspecting; a feeling that something is wrong. 2. A hint or trace: There was a *suspicion* of a smile on her face.

sus·pi·cious (səss-PISH-əss) *adjective.* 1. Causing one to suspect or doubt: *suspicious* conduct. 2. Feeling or expressing suspicion: The night watchman was *suspicious* about the noise. —**suspiciously** *adverb.*

sus·tain (səss-TAYN) *verb.* 1. To suffer; experience: *sustain* a loss. 2. To support the weight of; hold up: Columns *sustain* the heavy roof. 3. To keep up the spirits of; to give courage to: Our cheers *sustain* the team. 4. To keep (something) going; keep up (an activity). 5. To supply with food, clothing, etc.: The money we give *sustains* the orphans. 6. To uphold as correct or true: The higher court *sustains* his claim. **sustained, sustaining.**

sus·ten·ance (SUHSS-tə-nənss) *noun.* Food; nourishment; support.

su·ture (SOO-chər) *noun.* 1. The joining together of the edges of a wound by stitching. 2. The seam made in this way. 3. The line where two bones, especially those of the skull, grow together. **sutures.**

swab (SWOB) *noun.* 1. A mop. 2. A wad of cotton or similar material, usually fastened to the end of a small stick and used to apply medicine. —*verb.* 1. To mop: Sailors *swab* the deck. 2. To apply medicine or clean with a swab. **swabbed, swabbing.**

swag·ger (SWAG-ər) *verb.* 1. To walk or behave in a bold, rude, or showy way; to strut. 2. To brag or boast. **swaggered, swaggering.** —*noun.* A bold or showy way of behaving; a strut.

[1]**swal·low** (SWAHL-oh) *noun.* A small bird with a forked tail.

[2]**swal·low** (SWAHL-oh) *verb.* 1. To

take into the stomach from the mouth through the throat. 2. To move the muscles of the throat as if swallowing, especially when one is upset. 3. To cover over or cause to disappear; use up or destroy: The black night *swallowed* the travelers. 4. To put up with; take without question or resistance: I had to *swallow* Jack's insults. **swallowed, swallowing.** —*noun.* 1. The act of swallowing. 2. The amount one can swallow at one time.

swam *verb. See* **swim.**

swamp (SWAHMP or SWAWMP) *noun.* A marsh; soft, wet land. —*verb.* 1. To sink; flood; fill with water: A big wave *swamped* our boat. 2. To put into deep water; immerse or cover with water. 3. To overcome; flood: Dad's new shop is *swamped* with business. **swamped, swamping.** —**swampy** *adjective.*

swan (SWAHN) *noun.* A large water bird with a long, slender neck, short, webbed feet, and (usually) white feathers.

swap (SWAHP) *verb.* (Slang) To trade; give in exchange. **swapped, swapping.** —*noun.* An exchange.

swarm (SWORM) *noun.* 1. A group of bees that leaves its hive and flies away with a queen to make a new colony in another place. 2. Any large group of insects, especially when flying; any group that suggests such a swarm: a *swarm* of students. —*verb.* 1. To fly off together, as bees to form a new colony. 2. To gather or move in a crowd. 3. To be crowded or filled (with a large group). **swarmed, swarming.**

swar·thy (SWOR-thee) *adjective.* Having a dark skin. **swarthier, swarthiest.**

swat (SWAHT) *verb.* To hit with a hard blow; slap. **swatted, swatting.** —*noun.* A quick, hard blow.

sway *verb.* 1. To swing slowly from side to side, or back and forth. 2. To cause to move: The storm *sways* the trees. 3. To cause (a person) to change his mind; to control or influence. **swayed, swaying.** —*noun.* 1. A swaying from side to side or back and forth: the *sway* of a boat. 2. Rule, control, or influence: under the *sway* of anger.

swear (SWAIR) *verb.* 1. To make a statement with an appeal to God or some other holy being or object, in order to show or confirm the truth of one's statement: He *swears* on the Bible that his words are true. 2. To promise or vow; say in a solemn way. 3. To curse; use profane language. **swore, sworn, swearing.** —**swear in.** To make to take an oath: The court attendant *swears in* the jury.

sweat (SWET) *verb.* 1. To perspire; give off moisture through the skin. 2. To form droplets of water on the surface: The pipes near the furnace always *sweat.* 3. To work very hard, or make to work very hard. 4. (Informal) To worry or be nervous (about something). **sweat** or **sweated, sweating.** —*noun.* 1. Moisture given off through the skin. 2. The droplets of water that collect on a cold surface. 3. A fit of sweating: Running puts me into a *sweat.* 4. (Informal) A fit of worry, impatience, etc.: I am in a *sweat* because I disobeyed my father. —**no sweat.** (Slang; used as an interjection) No trouble or difficulty.

sweat·er (SWET-ər) *noun.* A knitted garment worn on the upper part of the body.

sweat shirt. A heavy pullover with long sleeves, usually made of cotton, and often worn by athletes.

sweat socks. Heavy socks worn by athletes.

sweep *verb.* 1. To clean a surface by brushing, as with a broom. 2. To carry along, move, or destroy with a sweeping movement: A flood can

swamp

swans

sweep away everything in its path. 3. Pass (through or over) quickly: Flames *sweep* through old houses. 4. To touch with a sweeping motion: Her long skirt *sweeps* the floor. 5. To move steadily in an impressive way: The destroyer *sweeps* down upon the tiny fishing boat. 6. To run in a long curve: The coastline *sweeps* northward from here. **swept, sweeping.** —*noun.* 1. The act of sweeping, removing, or cleaning, as with a broom. 2. A steady sweeping action: He saw the *sweep* of their long knives cutting the sugar cane. 3. A stretch: a *sweep* of dense jungle. 4. The reach or range: within the *sweep* of the lights in the prison tower. 5. A boy or man who cleans chimneys.

swift

sweet *adjective.* 1. Having a pleasing taste like sugar or honey. 2. Having a pleasing or likable character. 3. Fresh; not sour or spoiled: *sweet* milk. 4. Not salty: *sweet* butter. **sweeter, sweetest.** —*noun.* 1. (Usually plural) Something sweet, such as candy. 2. Sweet one; darling. —**sweetly** *adverb.*

sweet corn. Corn with a sweet flavor that is eaten by people.

sweet·en (SWEET-n) *verb.* 1. To become or make sweet; add sugar to. 2. To make more pleasant or less difficult. **sweetened, sweetening.**

sweet·en·ing (SWEET-n-ing) *noun.* Something that makes food sweeter.

sweet·heart (SWEET-hahrt) *noun.* A loved person; a good person.

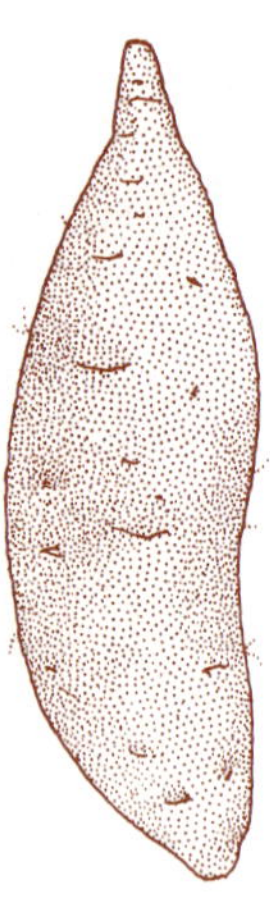

sweet potato

sweet potato. 1. A large yellow root, often sweet in taste, that is cooked and eaten as a vegetable. 2. The vine or plant of this root.

swell (SWEL) *verb.* 1. To become bigger; make bigger: A sprained finger often *swells.* 2. To stick out or bulge out. 3. To become gradually louder; make louder. 4. To become filled (with pride or another emotion). **swelled, swelled** or **swollen, swelling.** —*noun.* 1. A long, large wave or a group of waves. 2. A piece of ground that rises up; a round hill. 3. (Slang) A man who dresses in a fancy way. —*adjective.* (Slang) Fine; excellent.

swel·ter (SWEL-tər) *verb.* To sweat or suffer from heat: *swelter* in the sun. **sweltered, sweltering.**

swept *verb. See* **sweep.**

swerve (SWERV) *verb.* To move away from a straight line: The car *swerved* to the right. **swerved, swerving.** —*noun.* A swerving; a turning aside. **swerves.**

swift *adjective* and *adverb.* 1. Fast; rapid; moving very quickly. 2. Done without delay; happening quickly; acting quickly. **swifter, swiftest.** —*noun.* A small long-winged bird that looks like a swallow and flies very fast. —**swiftly** *adverb.*

swill (SWIL) *noun.* 1. Garbage; slop. 2. A thirsty, greedy gulp or drink. —*verb.* 1. To drink in a thirsty, greedy way. 2. To feed (animals) with swill. **swilled, swilling.**

swim *verb.* 1. To move in water by using the arms and legs or fins and tail. 2. To cross by swimming: *swim* a river. 3. To float in or be covered with: The crackers *swim* in the milk. 4. To be dizzy or confused: Loud noise makes my head *swim.* **swam, swum, swimming.** —*noun.* An act or period of swimming. —**in the swim.** (Slang) Part of the present trend; doing the things that are popular at the time.

swin·dle (SWIND-l) *verb.* To cheat: He *swindled* me out of my money. **swindled, swindling.** —*noun.* A fraud; act of cheating. **swindles.**

swine (SWIGHN) *noun.* 1. A pig, boar, or similar animal. 2. A crude, low person. —**swine** *plural.*

swine·herd (SWIGHN-herd) *noun.* A person who tends pigs or hogs.

swing *verb.* 1. To move back and forth: The tree branches *swing* in the breeze. 2. To move with a free, swaying motion. 3. To move something in a circle or a part of a circle: *Swing* the club around your head. 4. To turn, as a door on hinges. 5. Hang or fasten: *Swing* the rope between these two posts. 6. (Slang) To be executed or killed by hanging. 7. (Slang) To influence, win, or manage as one wants: *swing* an election. **swung, swinging.** —*noun.* 1. The act of swinging. 2. A curving movement. 3. A steady, strong rhythm: the *swing* of a song. 4. A free, swinging movement: They marched along with a cheerful *swing.* 5. A sweeping movement, made to hit: She took a *swing* at me. 6. Anything that swings. 7. A seat, hung from above by chains or ropes, on which one moves back and forth through the air. —**in full swing.** In full action or movement.

swing·er (SWING-ər) *noun.* (Slang) A lively, fun-loving person.

swipe (SWIGHP) (Slang) *noun.* A heavy swinging blow; a sweeping stroke. **swipes.** —*verb.* 1. To hit with such a blow. 2. (Slang) To steal. **swiped, swiping.**

swirl (SWERL) *verb.* 1. To move with a twisting motion; to whirl: The water *swirled* around him. 2. To be affected by dizziness: His head was *swirling.* **swirled, swirling.** —*noun.* 1. A swirling movement. 2. A twist, as of hair or lace; a curl.

swish *verb.* To move with a hissing sound; to rustle. **swished, swishing.** —*noun.* 1. A hissing or swishing sound. 2. A movement that makes a swishing sound. **swishes.**

switch (SWICH) *noun.* 1. A slender stick used for whipping or beating. 2. A stroke or lash. 3. (Electricity) A device for turning a current on or off by making or breaking a circuit. 4. A device for moving a train from one track to another. 5. A change or shift. **switches.** —*verb.* 1. To whip or beat, using a switch. 2. (Used with *on* or *off*) To work (an electric switch). 3. To move (a train) to a different track, using a switch. 4. To change or shift: My father *switched* political parties. 5. To move back and forth like a switch: A horse *switches* his tail to chase the flies away. **switched, switching.**

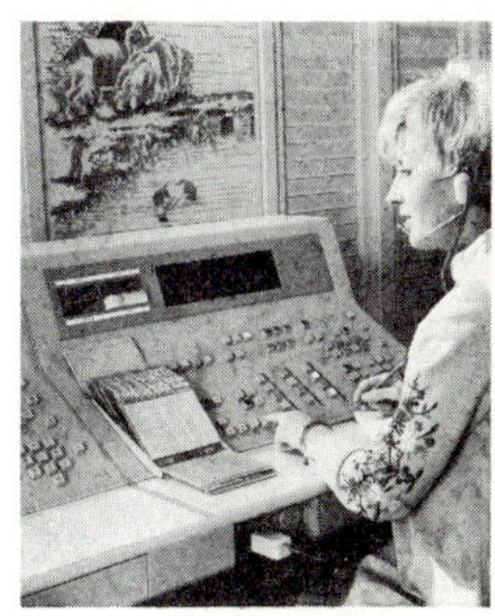
switchboard

switch·board (SWICH-bord) *noun.* A panel or panels containing controls and equipment for handling and using telephone circuits.

swol·len (SWOHL-ən) *verb. See* **swell.**

swoon *verb.* To faint. **swooned, swooning.** —*noun.* A fainting spell.

swoop *verb.* 1. (Used with *down*) To move swiftly through the air: The owl *swooped* down on the mouse. 2. To make a sudden, quick attack: The English warships *swooped* down upon the port. **swooped, swooping.** —*noun.* The act of swooping; a sudden, quick attack.

sword (SORD) *noun.* 1. A weapon with a long sharp blade and a handle. 2. War; military power.

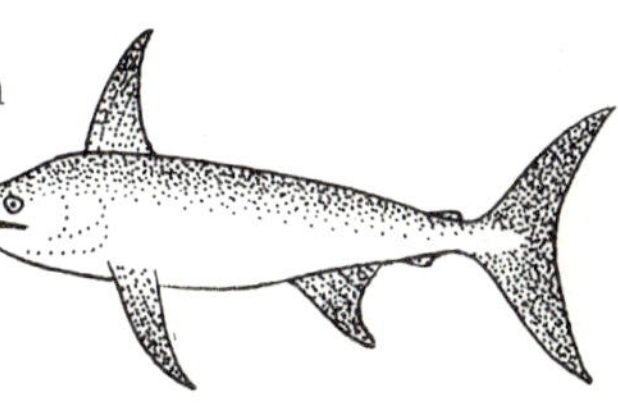
swordfish

sword·fish (SORD-fish) *noun.* A large ocean fish, used for food, whose upper jaw is in the shape of a sword. —**swordfish** or **swordfishes** *plural.*

swords·man (SORDZ-mən) *noun.* 1. A person skilled in the use of the sword. 2. One who uses or is armed with a sword. —**swordsmen** *plural.*

swore (SWOR) *verb. See* **swear.**

swum (SWUHM) *verb. See* **swim.**

swung (SWUHNG) *verb. See* **swing.**

syc·a·more (SIK-ə-mor) *noun.* A large, spreading tree of North America with scaly bark; any of various trees with this name.

sycamore

syl·lab·i·cate (si-LAB-ə-kayt) *verb.* To divide into syllables. **syllabicated, syllabicating.**

syl·la·ble (SIL-ə-bəl) *noun.* 1. A word or a part of a word that is spoken as one sound: The word "up" has one *syllable;* "upset" has two *syllables.* 2. In writing, any of the parts into which a word is divided and between which it may be broken at the end of a line: Centered dots are used to show the *syllables* of the entry words in this dictionary. **syllables.**

sym·bol (SIM-bəl) *noun.* 1. A picture, sign, or object that stands for something else; an emblem: The eagle is a *symbol* of the United States. 2. A letter or other mark that stands for a word or phrase: In math, ÷ is the symbol for "divide." **—symbolic** (sim-BOL-ik) *adjective.* **—symbolically** *adverb.*

sym·met·ry (SIM-ə-tree) *noun.* Balance or likeness in the shape, size, and position of parts that are on the two sides of a center line. **symmetries —symmetrical** (si-MET-ri-kəl) *adjective.* **—symmetrically** *adverb.*

sym·pa·thet·ic (sim-pə-THET-ik) *adjective.* 1. Having or showing sympathy or kindness for others: a *sympathetic* smile. 2. Favorable; approving: The principal is *sympathetic* toward our project. **—sympathetically** *adverb.*

sym·pa·thize (SIM-pə-thighz) *verb.* To feel or show sympathy. **sympathized, sympathizing.**

sym·pa·thy (SIM-pə-thee) *noun.* 1. Sharing with another the same feelings or opinions. 2. Compassion or pity for another's sorrow.

sym·pho·ny (SIM-fə-nee) *noun.* 1. A long piece of music written to be played by a large orchestra. 2. Harmony of sounds, colors, movements, or the like. **symphonies.**

symp·tom (SIM-təm or SIMP-təm) *noun.* A sign of (a sickness or other condition): A running nose is a *symptom* of hay fever.

syn·a·gogue (SIN-ə-gog) *noun.* 1. A place used by Jews for prayer and study of their faith. 2. A group of Jews gathered to pray or study. **synagogues.**

syn·chro·nize (SIN-krə-nighz) *verb.* To operate or cause to operate in unison. **synchronized, synchronizing.**

syn·di·cate (SIN-di-kit) *noun.* 1. An association or organization set up to carry out a particular kind of business. 2. A company that sells articles and comic and political cartoons to a number of newspapers. **syndicates.** *—verb.* (SIN-di-kayt) 1. To form a syndicate. 2. To distribute through such an organization. **syndicated, syndicating.**

syn·o·nym (SIN-ə-nim) *noun.* A word that means the same or nearly the same as another word: "Damp" and "moist" are *synonyms.*

syn·op·sis (si-NOP-sis) *noun.* A short summary or outline. **—synopses** (si-NOP-seez) *plural.*

syn·tax (SIN-taks) *noun.* The way in which words are arranged to form sentences.

syn·thet·ic (sin-THET-ik) *adjective.* 1. Man-made; not occurring in nature. 2. Artificial; not real. **—synthetically** *adverb.*

syr·inge (sə-RINJ) *noun.* A medical tool used to put fluids into the body or draw them out. **syringes.**

syr·up (SIHR-əp) *noun.* A thick, sticky liquid containing sugar and sometimes other flavoring: chocolate *syrup.* **—syrupy** *adjective.*

sys·tem (SISS-təm) *noun.* 1. A method. 2. A network; something made up of many parts. 3. The whole body, or related parts of the body.

sys·tem·at·ic (siss-tə-MAT-ik) *adjective.* 1. Referring to a system; done by a system: a *systematic* search. 2. Orderly; well-organized. **—systematically** *adverb.*

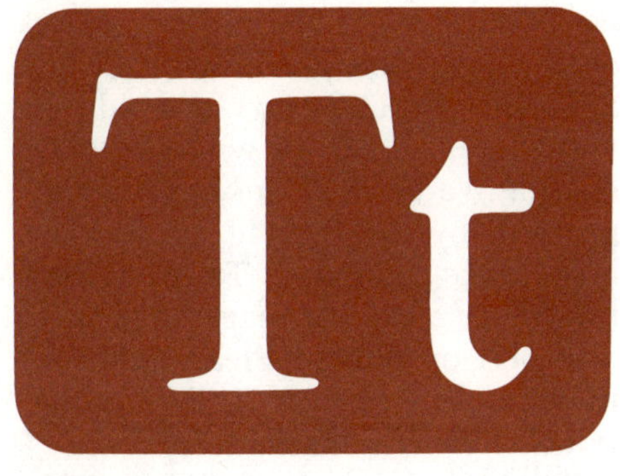

T, t (TEE) *noun.* The 20th letter of the English alphabet. **—to a T.** Exactly: The cap fits *to a T.*

t. *abbreviation.* 1. Teaspoon. 2. (Grammar) Tense. 3. Time.

T. *abbreviation.* 1. Tablespoon. 2. Territory.

tab *noun.* 1. A small flap used for hanging, fastening, identification, or decoration. 2. Money owed; a bill.

tab·er·na·cle (TAB-ər-nak-əl) *noun.* 1. [Often capital T] A portable place of worship carried by the Jews on their journey out of Egypt. 2. A Jewish temple. 3. A building used for worship. **tabernacles.**

ta·ble (TAY-bəl) *noun.* 1. A piece of furniture with one or more legs supporting a flat surface. 2. Food served for a meal: Thanksgiving *table.* 3. Those sitting around a table. 4. A chart or list: *table* of contents. **tables.** *—verb.* 1. To arrange in a list. 2. To put aside or delay decision on. **tabled, tabling.**

ta·ble·cloth (TAY-bəl-kloth) *noun.* A cloth used to cover a table for protection or decoration.

ta·ble·land (TAY-bəl-land) *noun.* A highland with a broad, nearly flat top; a plateau.

ta·ble·spoon (TAY-bəl-spoon) *noun.* 1. A large spoon used for stirring, serving, or measuring. 2. A measure equal to three teaspoons.

tab·let (TAB-lit) *noun.* 1. A pad of paper. 2. A flat piece, as of stone, that bears or is intended to bear inscriptions. 3. Medicine in a hard, flat pill.

ta·boo (tə-BOO or ta-BOO) *noun.* A custom or rule against an activity or idea. **taboos.** *—verb.* To prohibit by rule or code. **tabooed, tabooing.**

tack (TAK) noun. 1. A small nail with a large head. 2. The course of a sailboat in relation to the direction of the wind. 3. The changing of direction of a sailboat. 4. The trend of conduct or action. 5. A long sewing stitch used to hold something temporarily. *—verb.* 1. To hold in place with a small nail. 2. To hold together with long, loose stitches. 3. To put (onto) or add: *Tack* a postscript to your letter. 4. To change a sailboat's direction. **tacked, tacking.**

tack·le (TAK-əl) *verb.* 1. (Football) To jump on or seize in order to stop. 2. To attempt to handle (a difficult task): Can you *tackle* this assignment? **tackled, tackling.** *—noun.* 1. The act of tackling. 2. Equipment needed for certain sports, especially fishing. 3. A series of ropes and pulleys for lifting heavy objects. 4. A position on a football team between guard and end. **tackles.**

ta·co (TAH-koh) *noun.* A Mexican dish, made of a folded tortilla filled with meat or cheese. **tacos.**

tact (TAKT) *noun.* The ability to say or do the right thing, especially in difficult situations. **—tactful** (TAKT-fəl) *adjective.* **—tactfully** *adverb.*

tac·tic (TAK-tik) *noun.* 1. A method or way of working toward a goal. 2. (*Plural in form but used with a singular verb*) The science of military maneuvers, or the use of soldiers and equipment so as to win battles.

tad·pole (TAD-pohl) *noun.* An early stage in the growth of a frog or toad during which it has a long tail and gills and lives in the water; a polliwog. **tadpoles.**

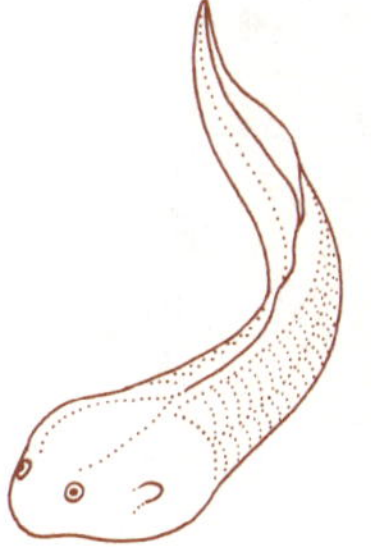
tadpole

taf•fy (TAF-ee) *noun.* A candy made by pulling a cooked sugar or molasses mixture until it becomes very chewy.

tag *noun.* 1. A piece of paper or metal, bearing identification or other information, that is attached to an article; a label. 2. Anything attached or tied on loosely. 3. A name for. 4. A game in which one player, called "it," chases and tags or touches another player, who then becomes "it." *—verb.* 1. To put a tag or label on; give a name to. 2. To touch, as in a game of chase. 3. To follow closely. **tagged, tagging.**

tail (TAYL) *noun.* 1. A body part extending from the back or end of an animal's body. 2. The back or end part of anything; anything formed like a tail: coat*tail.* 3. (Plural) The opposite side of a coin's face; the backside of "heads." 4. (Plural) Very formal evening clothes for a man. *—verb.* (Informal) To secretly follow and watch. **tailed, tailing. —turn tail.** To give up and retreat; run away.

tailgate

tail•gate (TAYL-gayt) *noun.* 1. The gate at the back of a truck or other vehicle that can be lowered or opened for loading. 2. One of the lower gates in a canal lock. **tailgates.** *—verb.* To drive dangerously close behind another vehicle. **tailgated, tailgating.**

tai•lor (TAY-lər) *noun.* One whose job is sewing, repairing, and fitting clothes. *—verb.* 1. To fit or make and adjust for a special group or purpose. 2. To make or mend clothes. **tailored, tailoring.**

tail•spin (TAYL-spin) *noun.* The motion of an airplane falling with its tail moving in circles and its nose pointing toward the ground.

taint (TAYNT) *verb.* To contaminate; pollute; inject an injurious substance into. **tainted, tainting.** *—noun.* 1. A stain or blemish. 2. A trace of a polluting element.

take (TAYK) *verb.* 1. To capture, trap, or win: *take* first place in a race. 2. To pick up and carry or hold with the hands. 3. To win over or charm: We were all *taken* with the pretty baby. 4. To bring into the body: *Take* a drink. 5. To subscribe to: We *take* several magazines. 6. To transport or deliver: Please *take* these books with you. 7. To require: It will *take* two weeks to arrive. 8. To receive or accept. 9. To pick or choose: I'll *take* the red checkers. 10. To make use of; occupy: *take* a bus. 11. To make (a photo of): *Take* a snapshot. 12. To understand: I *take* it that you aren't going. 13. To go or lead (to or toward): Will this highway *take* me to New York? 14. To be affected by: *take* cold. 15. (Slang) To cheat or fool. 16. To subtract: When you *take* 8 from 10, you have 2. **took, taken, taking.** *—noun.* 1. Any instance of taking. 2. The amount or number that is brought in, caught, received, or the like. **—take advantage of.** 1. To use (an opportunity or chance) to the fullest extent. 2. To impose on (another person) for personal gain or profit. **—take after.** 1. To be like in appearance, habits, or behavior. 2. To chase. **—take hold.** To have an effect; settle in or begin to grow; develop roots. **—take in.** 1. To receive, bring in, or admit. 2. To be friendly and helpful to; give a room or bed to. 3. To include. 4. To make (a garment) smaller. 5. To watch or listen carefully; understand. **—take on.** 1. To accept as a challenge; oppose. 2. To undertake, as a burden or difficulty. 3. To give a job or work to. 4. (Informal) To show too much excitement or emotion.

take•off (TAYK-off) *noun.* 1. The act of leaving or going up, as of an airplane or spacecraft. 2. (Informal) A funny imitation of a person.

talc *noun.* A soft, smooth mineral used in dusting powder.

tale (TAYL) *noun.* 1. A story; a relating of events that may or may not be true. 2. A story that is not true; a lie. 3. Gossip. **tales.**

tal·ent (TAL-ənt) *noun.* Natural ability or skill (in a certain field).

tal·ent·ed (TAL-ən-tid) *adjective.* Skillful; having a natural ability.

talent scout. A person whose job is to find people with ability in a certain field, such as acting.

tal·is·man (TAL-iss-mən) *noun.* A good luck charm.

talk (TAWK) *verb.* 1. To communicate by spoken words; speak. 2. To discuss: Let's *talk* money. 3. To gossip. **talked, talking.** —*noun.* 1. A lecture or speech: a *talk* on modern art. 2. A discussion or conference. 3. Gossip. 4. Something or someone gossiped about: the *talk* of the town.

talk·a·tive (TAW-kə-tiv) *adjective.* Speaking very much; always having many things to say.

tall (TAWL) *adjective.* 1. High; not short: a *tall* person. 2. In height: She is three feet *tall.* 3. (Informal) Exaggerated, fanciful: *tall* tales. **taller, tallest.**

tal·low (TAL-oh) *noun.* A hard animal fat, used in candles and soaps.

tall tale. A story that uses exaggeration for fun and excitement.

tal·ly (TAL-ee) *noun.* 1. A counting or record of a score, money, amounts, or such. 2. The sheet or listing of such information. **tallies.** —*verb.* 1. To count or add up a score, money, or such. 2. To write down the amount or score. 3. To agree with or be the same as: Does your answer *tally* with the one on the board? **tallied, tallying.**

tal·on (TAL-ən) *noun.* A long, curved claw found on birds that kill.

ta·ma·le (tə-MAH-lee) *noun.* A Mexican food made of minced meat and red peppers shaped into a long, thin roll, rolled in cornmeal, wrapped in cornhusks, then baked or steamed. **tamales.**

tam·bou·rine (tam-bə-REEN) *noun.* A musical instrument made of a small drum with flat movable metal disks around the rim. **tambourines.**

tambourine

tame (TAYM) *adjective.* 1. No longer wild or ferocious, as an animal trained to live around human beings; gentle. 2. Smooth, calm, or uninteresting; not violent or exciting: a *tame* ride. **tamer, tamest.** —*verb.* 1. To change from wild to gentle and trained. 2. To make calm, or less violent. **tamed, taming.**

tam·per (TAM-pər) *verb.* (Used with *with*) To change, alter, or meddle (with something), usually causing harm. **tampered, tampering.**

tan *verb.* 1. To become darker or brownish in skin color from exposure to the sun. 2. To cure (a skin) into leather by using a chemical. 3. (Informal) To beat or spank. **tanned, tanning.** —*noun* (and *adjective*). 1. A pale, light brown color. 2. A brownish or darkened skin tone caused by the sun.

tan·dem (TAN-dəm) *adverb* (and *adjective*). Having one in back of another, as on a bicycle built for two. —*noun.* A team of horses, bicycle, or other vehicle or arrangement involving two or more animals, things, or persons working one in back of another.

tang *noun.* A sharp, biting quality of a flavor or odor. —**tangy** *adjective.*

tan·gent (TAN-jənt) *noun.* A line that touches a curved line or curved surface without passing through it. —**go off on a tangent.** To change a line of thought or action suddenly.

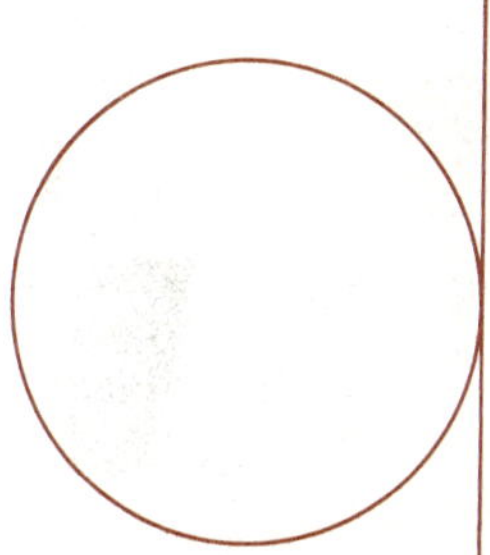
tangent

tan·ger·ine (tan-jə-REEN) *noun.* 1. A small citrus fruit of the orange family with a loose skin that peels easily. 2. The tree on which this fruit grows. 3. (Also *adjective*) A deep red-orange color. **tangerines.**

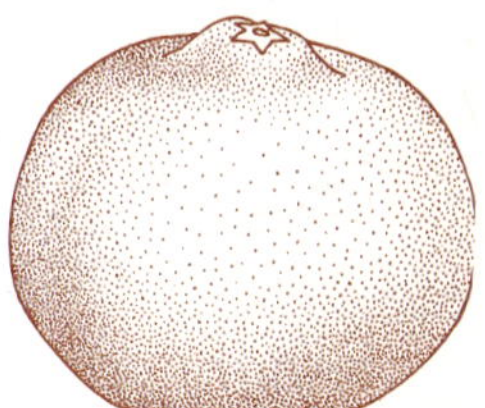
tangerine

tank

tan·gi·ble (TAN-jə-bəl) *adjective.* 1. Able to be appreciated or felt by the sense of touch: Coins are *tangible.* 2. Real; able to be explained or understood exactly. —**tangibly** *adverb.*

tan·gle (TANG-gəl) *verb.* To mix or snarl together so that separation is difficult: The wind has *tangled* my hair. **tangled, tangling.** —*noun.* 1. A mixed-up or confused mess or state: Kevin's clothes were in a *tangle* on the bed. 2. (Informal) A scuffle or disagreement. **tangles.** —**tangle with.** To fight or argue with.

tank (TANGK) *noun.* 1. A holder or container, usually big, for storing gas or liquid: gasoline *tank.* 2. A military vehicle with heavy armor, guns, and belt-like treads. 3. (Slang) A jail cell that holds a number of prisoners.

tapestry

tank·ard (TANG-kərd) *noun.* A large, mug-like cup with a handle and (sometimes) a hinged lid.

tank·er (TANG-kər) *noun.* A ship or other transport for hauling large amounts of liquid, especially oil.

tan·ner (TAN-ər) *noun.* One whose job is tanning hides into leather.

tan·ta·lize (TANT-l-ighz) *verb.* To tempt or tease by holding or placing something just out of reach. **tantalized, tantalizing.**

tan·trum (TAN-trəm) *noun.* A fit or display of bad temper.

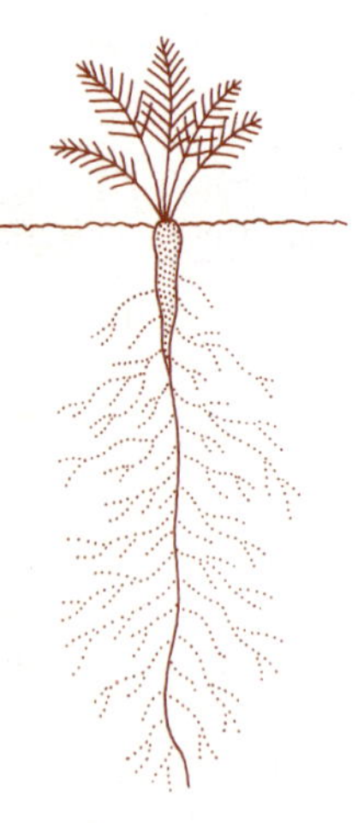
taproot

[1]**tap** *verb.* 1. To hit or pat lightly, usually while making a small clicking sound: *Tap* your fingers to the music. 2. To touch gently: *Tap* me on the arm. **tapped, tapping.** —*noun.* A light touch or pat, or the noise made by it.

[2]**tap** *noun.* 1. A faucet on a pipe from which water or other liquid comes. 2. A stopper or spigot for the hole in a barrel or cask. —*verb.* 1. To draw or drain liquid from. 2. To make a hole in or put a faucet on for drawing off liquid. 3. To make any contact or connection with in order to use: *tap* a supply of energy. **tapped, tapping.**

tape (TAYP) *noun.* 1. A slender strip, long or continuous, as of paper, fabric, or other material, made for various uses: recording *tape.* 2. The ribbon or string pulled across the finish line of a race. **tapes.** —*verb.* 1. To hold together with tape. 2. To record on recording tape. **taped, taping.**

ta·per (TAY-pər) *verb.* 1. To become gradually thinner or smaller at the end. 2. (Used with *off*) To slowly become less; diminish. **tapered, tapering.** —*noun.* 1. A very thin candle. 2. Any gradual lessening.

tape recorder. A device that records sound on magnetic tape.

tap·es·try (TAP-i-stree) *noun.* A thick fabric with designs and figures woven into it, used for wall hangings and upholstery. **tapestries.**

tape·worm (TAYP-werm) *noun.* A very long, thin worm that lives in the intestines of an animal or person.

tap·i·o·ca (tap-ee-OH-kə) *noun.* A substance used for thickening in cooking and for puddings.

ta·pir (TAY-pər or tə-PIHR) *noun.* A large pig-like animal with a downward-curving snout.

tap·root (TAP-root) *noun.* The largest or longest and most important root in a plant, growing downward.

taps *noun, plural.* (Military) A call or signal on a bugle or drums to announce "lights out" or the end of a funeral ceremony.

tar (TAHR) *noun.* 1. A thick, dark, sticky substance used as a waterproof surface for roads and roofs. 2. (Informal) A sailor. —*verb.* To cover with tar. **tarred, tarring.** —**tar and feather.** To cover a person with tar and feathers as a punishment.

ta·ran·tu·la (tə-RAN-chə-lə) *noun.* A large, hairy, poisonous spider.

tar·dy (TAHR-dee) *adjective.* Not on time; late. **tardier, tardiest.** —**tardily** *adverb.* —**tardiness** *noun.*

tar·get (TAHR-git) *noun.* 1. A flat object in the form of a circle marked with rings and used to test one's aim, as with a rifle or a bow and arrow. 2. A person or thing that is the object of an attack or criticism. 3. A goal or aim.

tar·iff (TA-rif) *noun.* A tax or duty on goods coming into or going out of a country.

tar·nish (TAHR-nish) *noun.* A dull coating that forms on metal exposed to air. —*verb.* 1. To become dull or discolored. 2. To spoil; to mar. **tarnished, tarnishing.**

tar·pau·lin (tahr-PAW-lin) *noun.* A piece of waterproof material used as a protective covering.

tar·pon (TAHR-pən) *noun.* A large silvery game fish found along the Atlantic coast—**tarpon** or **tarpons** *plural.*

tar·ry (TA-ree) *verb.* 1. To hesitate; linger, delay. 2. To stay for a time. **tarried, tarrying.**

tart (TAHRT) *adjective.* 1. Sour; sharp: Cherries have a *tart* flavor. 2. Cutting, biting, as an acid remark. **tarter, tartest.** —*noun.* A small open-top pie. —**tartly** *adverb.*

tar·tan (TAHRT-n) *noun.* 1. A plaid wool fabric. 2. A special plaid worn by Scots of the same clan.

tar·tar (TAHR-tər) *noun.* 1. An acidic substance that forms as grape juice turns to wine. 2. A hard material that develops on the teeth.

task *noun.* 1. A bit of work or part of a job, often assigned by another. 2. A hard or unpleasant job. —**to take to task.** To scold or criticize.

tas·sel (TASS-l) *noun.* A hanging decoration made up of a tuft or bunch of thread or string.

taste (TAYST) *noun.* 1. The ability to sense with the tongue the flavor of a substance to tell whether it is sweet, sour, salty, or bitter. 2. Flavor: a sweet *taste.* 3. A small amount, a sample. 4. A personal like or dislike: reading *tastes.* 5. Judgment; manners or behavior. **tastes.** —*verb.* 1. To sense or test flavors in the mouth. 2. To eat or drink a small amount. 3. To have a certain flavor: The soup *tastes* like onions. 4. To try (for the first time). **tasted, tasting.**

taste·ful (TAYST-fəl) *adjective.* Showing good taste. —**tastefully** adverb.

taste·less (TAYST-liss) *adjective.* 1. Lacking flavor. 2. Showing poor taste. —**tastelessly** *adverb.*

tast·y (TAYSS-tee) *adjective.* Flavorful, pleasing to the taste. **tastier, tastiest.**

tat·ter (TAT-ər) *noun.* 1. A rag or scrap of cloth. 2. (Plural) Ragged or ripped clothing.—**tattered** (TAT-ərd) *adjective.*

tat·tle (TAT-l) *verb.* 1. To reveal secrets by carrying tales or gossiping. 2. To chat about unimportant things. **tattled, tattling.**

tat·tle·tale (TAT-l-tayl) *noun.* One who betrays secrets about others. **tattletales.**

tat·too (ta-TOO) *noun.* A permanent picture or design made on the skin by pricking it with a needle and putting in color. **tattoos.** —*verb.* To make designs on the skin with a needle. **tattooed, tattooing.**

taught (TAWT) *verb.* *See* **teach.**

taunt (TAWNT) *verb.* To make fun of; jeer or mock; goad or drive. **taunted, taunting.** —*noun.* An unkind remark or jeer.

Tau·rus (TOR-əss) *noun.* The second sign of the zodiac, also called the "Bull." The time of this sign is from April 21 through May 21.

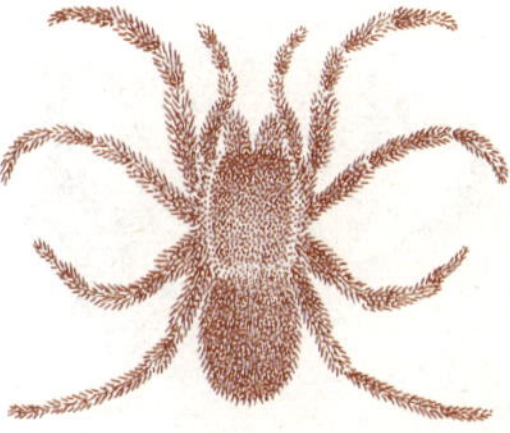
tarantula

tattoo

tarpon

Taurus

teacup

teakettle

teapot

taut (TAWT) *adjective.* 1. Tight, stretched firmly: Keep the kite string *taut.* 2. Strained emotionally: *taut* nerves. 3. In good condition; tidy: a *taut* ship. **tauter, tautest.**

tav·ern (TAV-ərn) *noun.* 1. A country inn. 2. A restaurant or bar serving beer and liquors.

taw·ny (TAW-nee) *noun* (and *adjective*). A light brown or dark yellow color. **tawnier, tawniest.**

tax (TAKS) *noun.* 1. Money collected from individuals or businesses by the government. 2. A burden or extra load. **taxes.** —verb. 1. To require (persons) to pay money to the government. 2. To place a tax on: *tax* gasoline. 3. To strain: The high waves *taxed* the swimmer's strength. **taxed, taxing.** —**taxation** (tak-SAY-shən) *noun.*

tax·i (TAK-see) *noun.* A taxicab. **taxis** —*verb.* 1. To ride in a taxicab. 2. To move (an airplane) along the ground or water under its own power. **taxied, taxiing.**

tax·i·cab (TAK-see-kab) *noun.* A car that carries passengers for money.

TB *abbreviation.* Tuberculosis.

tbs., tbsp. *abbreviation.* Tablespoon.

tea (TEE) *noun.* 1. A bush or small tree grown in countries having a hot, damp climate. 2. The leaves of this plant. 3. A drink made by soaking dried tea leaves or other leaves or herbs in boiling water. 4. (British) A late afternoon meal. 5. (Slang) Marijuana.

teach (TEECH) *verb.* 1. To explain how to: My mother can *teach* you to knit. 2. To give classes or instruction in: *teach* history. 3. To be a professional teacher: My father *teaches.* 4. To cause to learn: A bad sunburn *teaches* one to be careful. **taught, teaching.**

teach·er (TEECH-ər) *noun.* One who helps another to learn.

teach·ing (TEECH-ing) *noun.* 1. The work or profession of helping others learn. 2. (Often plural) Words, rules of conduct, examples.

tea·cup (TEE-kuhp) *noun.* A small cup for drinking tea.

tea·ket·tle (TEE-ket-l) *noun.* A covered pot, with a spout and handle, in which water is boiled. **teakettles.**

teal (TEEL) *noun.* A brightly-colored wild duck. —*noun* (and *adjective*) A dark bluish-green color.

team (TEEM) *noun.* 1. The players on one side in a game. 2. A group of people organized or trained to work together: a *team* of fire fighters. 3. Two or more animals used for pulling. —*verb.* (Often used with *up*) To work together; form a team. **teamed, teaming.**

team·mate (TEEM-mayt) *noun.* A member of the same team.

team·ster (TEEM-stər) *noun.* 1. The driver of a team of animals. 2. The driver of a freight truck.

team·work (TEEM-werk) *noun.* Cooperation; working together.

tea·pot (TEE-pot) *noun.* A pot with a handle and spout, used for brewing and serving tea.

[1]**tear** (TIHR) *noun.* A drop of salty liquid from the eye. —*verb.* To become full of tears. **teared, tearing.** —**in tears.** Weeping.

[2]**tear** (TAIR) *verb.* 1. To rip; separate into pieces by use of force. 2. To hurt or damage, as by snagging or catching: Don't *tear* your jeans on the fence. 3. To rush; move at top speed. **tore, tearing.** —*noun.* The damage or hole caused by tearing. —**tear down.** To take apart; destroy. —**tear into.** To attack.

tear·ful (TIHR-fəl) *adjective.* Sad; filled with or causing tears. —**tearfully** *adverb.*

tear gas. A gas that affects the eyes, causing a flood of tears and (often) temporary blindness.

tease (TEEZ) *verb.* 1. To annoy; to bother; make fun of. 2. To beg or coax (for something). 3. To arrange hair with a special comb. **teased, teasing.** —*noun.* One who teases.

teas·er (TEE-zer) *noun.* 1. A tease. 2. A short part of a coming film designed to attract customers.

tea·spoon (TEE-spoon) *noun.* 1. A small spoon used at the table. 2. A measurement equal to one-third of a tablespoon.

tea·spoon·ful (TEE-spoon-ful) *noun.* The amount one teaspoon will hold.

tech·ni·cal (TEK-ni-kəl) *adjective.* 1. Special, expert; relating to a particular science or occupation. 2. Relating to mechanics or industry: a *technical* school. 3. According to set rules: a *technical* difference. —**technically** *adverb.*

tech·nique (tek-NEEK) *noun.* 1. Method or procedure: a doctor's *technique* for removing tonsils. 2. The degree of skill and ability: The piano student is improving his *technique.* **techniques.**

tech·nol·o·gy (tek-NOL-ə-jee) *noun.* The use of science to serve man in commerce and industry.

teddy bear. A stuffed toy bear.

te·di·ous (TEE-dee-əss) *adjective.* Taking a long time; boring. —**tediously** *adverb.*

tee *noun.* 1. A peg on which a golf ball is placed so it can be hit. 2. A peg on which a football is held for kicking. 3. The area on a golf course from which play begins for each hole. **tees.** —*verb.* To place (a ball) on a tee. **teed, teeing.** —**tee off.** 1. To hit (a golf ball) off a tee. 2. To begin a new project. 3. (Slang) To anger. —**teed off** (Slang) Angry.

teem *verb.* To be full of; to crowd or swarm. **teemed, teeming.**

teen-ag·er (teen-AY-jer) *noun.* A person who is at least 13 and not yet 20 years of age.

teens (TEENZ) *noun, plural.* 1. The numbers ending in the suffix *-teen,* 13 through 19. 2. The years of one's life from 13 through 19.

tee·pee (TEE-pee) *noun. See* **tepee.**

tee·shirt (TEE-shert) *noun. See* **T-shirt.**

tee·ter (TEE-tər) *verb.* To stand or walk unsteadily. **teetered, teetering.**

tee·ter-tot·ter (TEE-tər-tot-ər) *noun.* A seesaw.

teeth *noun. See* **tooth.**

tele- *prefix.* Indicates distance: *tele*scope; *tele*vision.

tel·e·cast (TEL-ə-kast) *noun.* A television broadcast or program. —*verb.* To broadcast or transmit a television program. **telecast** or **telecasted, telecasting.**

tel·e·gram (TEL-ə-gram) *noun.* A message sent by telegraph.

tel·e·graph (TEL-ə-graf) *noun.* A system for sending and receiving messages by electricity over wire. —*verb.* To send a message by electricity over wires. **telegraphed, telegraphing.**

tel·e·me·ter (TEL-ə-mee-tər) *noun.* 1. An instrument for measuring distance. 2. Any of several types of electronic devices used for measuring and sending information, as from a spacecraft.

te·lep·a·thy (tə-LEP-ə-thee) *noun.* A method by which ideas are directly communicated between minds without speech or other sensory contact.

tel·e·phone (TEL-ə-fohn) *noun.* A device or system for carrying conversations by wire over long distances by electronic methods. **telephones.** —*verb.* To call or contact someone by using a telephone. **telephoned, telephoning.**

Tel·e·promp·ter (tel-ə-PROMP-tər) *trademark.* An off-camera electronic device from which television performers can read their lines.

telescope

tel·e·scope (TEL-ə-skohp) *noun.* An instrument that uses lenses to make distant objects seem larger and closer. **telescopes.** —*verb.* To crush or push together, as a series of different sections one into the other: *telescope* a TV aerial to make it shorter. **telescoped, telescoping.**

tel·e·thon (TEL-ə-thon) *noun.* A lengthy, uninterrupted telecast designed to raise money for any of various worthy causes.

Tel·e·type (TEL-ə-tighp) *trademark.* A type of electronic typewriter that transmits messages to a similar machine which types them out.

tel·e·vise (TEL-ə-vighz) *verb.* To send images or pictures by television. **televised, televising.**

tel·e·vi·sion (TEL-ə-vizh-ən) *noun.* 1. A system by which pictures and sound are sent electronically to a device which shows the images on a screen and reproduces the sound. 2. A device that receives and reproduces television images and sounds; a TV set. 3. The business of making and broadcasting television programs.

tell (TEL) *verb.* 1. To explain; express: *Tell* us how this machine works. 2. To relate or make known; inform. 3. To know; recognize: Can you *tell* a cedar tree from a spruce? 4. To order; to command. 5. To have an effect or result: Lack of sleep began to *tell* on Ed. **told, telling.**

temple

tell·er (TEL-ər) *noun.* 1. A worker in a bank who takes in and gives out money. 2. A person who collects and counts ballots, as in a legislature.

Tel·star (TEL-stahr) *noun.* An earth satellite equipped for receiving and sending short-wave radio signals: *Telstar* is used to send television programs and telephone messages between the United States and foreign countries.

temp. *abbreviation.* 1. Temperature. 2. Temporary.

tem·per (TEM-pər) *noun.* 1. The state of one's feelings or attitudes: a gentle *temper.* 2. A state of anger; rage. 3. Control of one's feelings: The coach lost his *temper.* 4. The hardness or flexibility of a metal. —*verb.* 1. To treat a metal to make it hard or flexible. 2. To modify, make less severe. **tempered, tempering.**

tem·per·a·ment (TEM-pər-ə-mənt) *noun.* Disposition; personality: an easygoing *temperament.*

tem·per·a·men·tal (tem-pər-ə-MENT-l) *adjective.* 1. Easily excited or upset; moody. 2. Of or related to temperament or disposition. —**temperamentally** *adverb.*

tem·per·ance (TEM-pər-ənss) *noun.* 1. Moderation; avoidance of extremes; control. 2. Moderation in drinking or the complete avoidance of alcoholic beverages.

tem·per·ate (TEM-pər-it) *adjective.* 1. Moderate; avoiding extremes. 2. Neither too hot nor too cold: a *temperate* climate. 3. Moderate or careful in the use of alcoholic beverages. —**temperately** *adverb.*

Temperate Zone. Either of two areas of the globe located between the tropics and the North or South Polar regions.

tem·per·a·ture (TEM-pər-ə-chər) *noun.* 1. A measure of heat or cold: The *temperature* of the oven is 350°. 2. The degree of heat of a person's body, especially when it is above normal (98.6°F).

tem·pest (TEM-pist) *noun.* 1. A storm with very strong winds. 2. Any wild disturbance. —**tempestuous** (tem-PESS-choo-əss) *adjective.* —**tempestuously** *adverb.*

[1]**tem·ple** (TEM-pəl) *noun.* 1. A building used for the worship of God or of gods. 2. A Jewish temple; synagogue. **temples.**

[2]**tem·ple** (TEM-pəl) *noun.* The flat area on either side of the forehead. **temples.**

tem·po (TEM-poh) *noun.* 1. (Music) The rate of speed at which a piece is played. 2. The pace or rate of speed of any activity. **tempos.**

tem·po·rar·y (TEM-pə-rehr-ee) *adjective.* Not permanent; lasting only a short time. —**temporarily** (tem-pə-RAIR-ə-lee) *adverb.*

tempt *verb.* 1. To encourage to do something, especially something unwise or improper. 2. To dare; to test: *tempt* your luck. 3. To be inclined: *tempted* to quit the team. **tempted, tempting.** —**temptation** (tem-TAY-shən) *noun.*

ten *noun.* The cardinal number after nine and before eleven; 10.

te·na·cious (ti-NAY-shəss) *adjective.* 1. Stubborn; not giving up. 2. Holding firmly: a *tenacious* grip. 3. Able to retain for a long time: a *tenacious* memory. —**tenaciously** *adverb.* —**tenacity** (ti-NASS-ə-tee) *noun.*

ten·ant (TEN-ənt) *noun.* One who pays rent for the use of a building or other property.

[1]**tend** *verb.* To watch over; take care of. **tended, tending.**

[2]**tend** *verb.* To incline or move (toward); be likely (to): Dogs *tend* to chase cars. **tended, tending.**

ten·den·cy (TEN-dən-see) *noun.* An inclination; likelihood: a *tendency* to yawn. **tendencies.**

[1]**ten·der** (TEN-dər) *adjective.* 1. Soft; easily divided or chewed. 2. Sensitive; sore or painful when touched. 3. Gentle; showing love or kindness. 4. Young and not strong: The *tender* new flowers need special care. —**tenderly** *adverb.*

[2]**ten·der** (TEN-dər) *verb.* To offer or present, especially in a formal manner: The students *tendered* their complaints in a petition. **tendered, tendering.** —*noun.* 1. An offer: Our town's *tender* of food to the flood victims was happily accepted. 2. Money: Gold coins were once legal *tender* in the United States.

[3]**tend·er** (TEN-dər) *noun.* 1. A person or thing that tends or watches over. 2. A boat or ship that services or supplies a larger vessel, as with fuel or food.

ten·der·foot (TEN-dər-fut) *noun.* 1. A newcomer to the frontier, ranch life, or other rough life. 2. Any newcomer or inexperienced person. 3. The beginning rank in Boy Scouts. —**tenderfoots** or **tenderfeet** *plural.*

ten·don (TEN-dən) *noun.* One of the bands of tough tissue that joins muscles to bones.

ten·dril (TEN-dril) *noun.* A slender or thread-like part of a climbing plant, such as ivy, that attaches the plant to a surface or object.

ten·e·ment (TEN-ə-mənt) *noun.* 1. An old and run-down apartment building. 2. A building made up of apartments or rooms to rent, or one of the units in such a building.

Ten·nes·see (ten-ə-SEE) *noun.* A southeastern state of the United States, 16th to join the Union (1796). —**Tenn.** *abbreviation.* Also **TN** for Zip Codes.

Tennessee
★capital: Nashville

ten·nis (TEN-iss) *noun.* A game played on a rectangular court by two or four players who use rackets to hit a ball back and forth over a net.

tennis shoes. Shoes of cloth with rubber soles, worn for tennis or play; sneakers.

ten·or (TEN-ər) *noun.* 1. The adult male singing voice above baritone. 2. A male having a tenor voice. 3. The basic meaning; gist.

[1]**tense** (TENSS) *adjective.* 1. Tight; taut. 2. Under strain; nervous. 3. Causing or showing strain or worry: a *tense* discussion. **tenser, tensest.** —*verb.* To make tight or tense. **tensed, tensing.**

[2]**tense** (TENSS) *noun.* The form of a verb that shows the time of an action or state: The past *tense* of the verb "jump" is "jumped."

tennis

tepees

terrapin

terrier

ten·sion (TEN-shən) *noun.* 1. The act or condition of stretching or being stretched: When a fish bites, there is *tension* on the fishing line. 2. Mental strain; nervousness. 3. An uneasy, unfriendly feeling or state.

tent *noun.* A portable shelter made of fabric stretched over a frame. —*verb.* To stay or live in a tent. **tented, tenting.**

ten·ta·cle (TEN-tə-kəl) *noun.* 1. Any of a variety of long, narrow, and flexible body parts of some animals, used for such purposes as feeling or grasping: The octopus uses its *tentacles* for swimming. 2. A narrow, threadlike growth on a plant. **tentacles.**

tenth *adjective.* Coming next after ninth; 10th. —*noun.* One of ten equal parts: A dime is a *tenth* of a dollar.

te·pee (TEE-pee) Also **teepee** *noun.* A cone-shaped tent of animal skins or bark once used by Indians of North America; wigwam. —**tepees** or **teepees** *plural.*

tep·id (TEP-id) *adjective.* Mildly warm; lukewarm. —**tepidly** *adverb.*

term *noun.* 1. A word or phrase: "Adios" is a Spanish *term* for "good-by." 2. A period of time: the school *term.* 3. (Plural) Requirements, as of a contract: the *terms* of a treaty. 4. (Plural) Relationship: on friendly *terms.* 5. (Math) A quantity, as either of two numbers that are added together. —*verb.* To give a name to; to call. **termed, terming.**

ter·mi·nal (TER-mən-l) *noun.* 1. A station on a transportation route, especially one at the end of a line: an airline *terminal.* 2. A point on an electrical circuit where connections can be made. —*adjective.* Of or at the end; final. —**terminally** *adverb.*

ter·mi·nate (TER-mə-nayt) *verb.* To stop. **terminated, terminating.**

ter·mi·nus (TER-mə-nəss) *noun.* 1. An end; final part; goal. 2. A terminal; end of or important stop on a railroad or other transportation line. —**termini** (TER-mə-nigh) or **terminuses** *plural.*

ter·mite (TER-might) *noun.* A small insect that feeds on oils or fats in wood and so can destroy anything made of wood. **termites.**

tern *noun.* A sea bird that looks like a small seagull.

terr. *abbreviation.* Territory.

ter·race (TEHR-iss) *noun.* 1. A flat area on the side or at the top of a slope. 2. A patio or similar paved area next to a house. 3. A row of buildings or a street on the side or at the top of a slope. **terraces.** —*verb.* To make or build a terrace or terraces on: *terrace* a hillside. **terraced, terracing.**

ter·rain (tə-RAYN) *noun.* Land; the surface of an area: The mules climbed over rugged *terrain.*

ter·ra·pin (TEHR-ə-pin) *noun.* Any of a variety of turtles found in North America.

ter·rar·i·um (tə-RA-ree-əm) *noun.* An enclosed container, usually of glass, in which small plants or animals are kept. —**terrariums** or **terraria** (te-RAR-ee-ə) *plural.*

ter·res·tri·al (tə-RESS-tree-əl) *adjective.* 1. Of or related to the earth: The spaceship left its *terrestrial* base and headed for the moon. 2. Of or related to land rather than water. —**terrestrially** *adverb.*

ter·ri·ble (TEHR-ə-bəl) *adjective.* 1. Causing fear or terror; dreadful: a *terrible* accident. 2. Extreme; severe: The *terrible* cold made the hikers turn back. 3. (Informal) Very poor in quality; unpleasant. —**terribly** *adverb.*

ter·ri·er (TEHR-ee-ər) *noun.* Any of several breeds of small dogs bred for hunting burrowing animals.

ter·rif·ic (tə-RIF-ik) *adjective.* 1. Terrible; extreme; causing fear or dismay: A *terrific* explosion destroyed the factory. 2. (Informal)

Excellent; very good. —**terrifically** *adverb.*

ter·ri·fy (TEHR-ə-figh) *verb.* To fill with terror; cause to have extreme fear. **terrified, terrifying.**

ter·ri·to·ry (TEHR-ə-tor-ee) *noun.* 1. An area; region. 2. All of the land and waters that are part of a state or nation. 3. [Capital T] A region that belongs to a nation but has not been made a state. 4. An area assigned to a specific salesman.

ter·ror (TEHR-ər) *noun.* 1. Extreme fear. 2. Someone or something that causes extreme fear.

ter·ror·ize (TEHR-ər-ighz) *verb.* 1. To cause terror in. 2. To control by causing fear. **terrorized, terrorizing.**

terse (TERSS) *adjective.* Brief and easily understood; concise. **terser, tersest** —**tersely** *adverb.*

test *noun.* 1. An examination or trial; a group of questions to be answered or things to be done: a history *test.* 2. An event or way to prove or give evidence of: A close game is a *test* of a team's ability. 3. An analysis; examination: blood *test.* —*verb.* To give a test, trial, or examination to. **tested, testing.**

tes·ta·ment (TESS-tə-mənt) *noun.* 1. A will; a document that indicates how a person's belongings are to be disposed of after his death. 2. [Capital T] Either of the two main divisions of the Bible, the Old *Testament* and the New *Testament.*

tes·ti·fy (TESS-tə-figh) *verb.* 1. To make a statement or act as a witness, especially under oath. 2. To give evidence of: Bill's pitching *testified* to his ability. **testified, testifying.**

tes·ti·mo·ny (TESS-tə-moh-nee) *noun.* 1. Evidence or a statement provided under oath. 2. A proof; evidence or indication.

test tube. A small glass tube, closed at one end, used in chemical experiments.

tet·a·nus (TET-n-əss or TET-nəss) *noun.* A serious disease caused by infection and leading to muscular spasms and, frequently, death. Also called "lockjaw."

teth·er (TETH-ər) *noun.* A rope that is tied to an animal to limit the range of its movements. —*verb.* To tie with a rope. **tethered, tethering.**

Tex·as (TEK-səss) *noun.* A southwestern state in the United States, 28th to join the Union (1845). —**Tex.** *abbreviation.* Also **TX** for Zip Codes.

text (TEKST) *noun.* 1. A textbook. 2. The main part of a book or other printed work. 3. A topic: a speaker's *text.* 4. The words actually used by a writer: Shakespeare's original *text.* 5. A passage from the Bible used as the topic for a sermon.

text·book (TEKST-buk) *noun.* A book used as a basis and necessary guide for classroom study of a subject.

tex·tile (TEKS-tighl or TEKS-til) *noun.* 1. Fabric; woven cloth. 2. Fiber used to make woven fabric. **textiles.**

tex·ture (TEKS-chər) *noun.* 1. The arrangement of the threads or weave of a fabric: rough *texture* of burlap. 2. The structure or the arrangement of parts. **textures.**

¹-th *suffix.* Indicates ordinal numbers: six*th.*

²-th *suffix.* Indicates state or condition: warm*th.*

than (THAN) *conjunction.* 1. Used to introduce the second part of a comparison: A mountain is higher *than* a hill. 2. Used to express the meaning of "further" or "beyond."

thank *verb.* To express gratitude to. **thanked, thanking.** —*noun.* (Plural) Gratitude; appreciation.

thank·ful (THANK-fəl) *adjective.* Grateful. —**thankfully** *adverb.*

thank·less (THANK-liss) *adjective.* 1. Not likely to bring gratitude or thanks: a *thankless* job. 2. Not showing thanks; ungrateful. —**thanklessly** *adverb.*

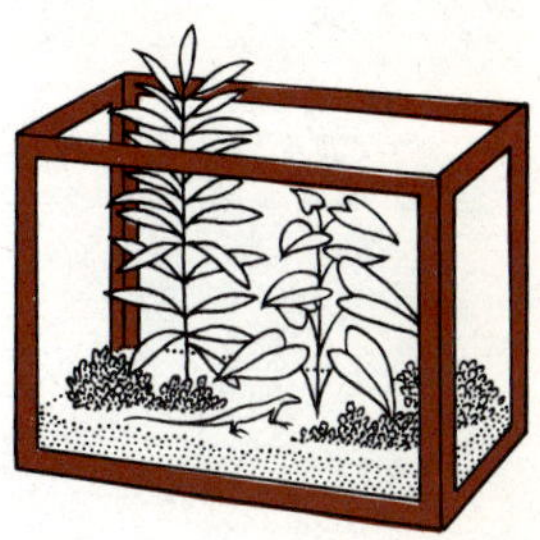

terrarium

Texas
★capital: Austin

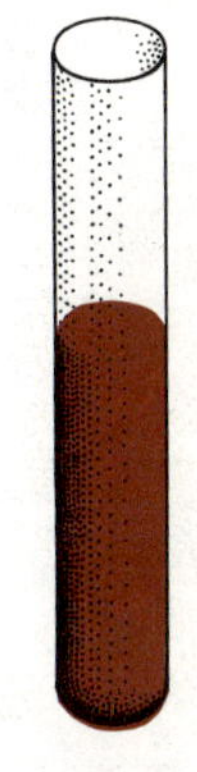

test tube

Thanksgiving Day. A U.S. holiday, celebrated on the fourth Thursday of November, in thanks for God's blessings.

that (THAT) *adjective.* 1. Being the one named, referred to, or known: I am *that* man of whom you spoke. 2. Being the one more distant: You may have this apple, but I want *that* one. **those.** —*pronoun.* 1. The one named, referred to, or known: *That* is the car I saw. 2. The more distant: *That* is our cabin over there; this one is Tom's. 3. Used to introduce a clause: "Something there is *that* doesn't love a wall. . . ." (Robert Frost). —**those** *plural.* —*adverb.* To such a degree: The test wasn't *that* hard. —*conjunction.* Used to begin a clause showing a result, reason, desire, or fact: I thought *that* Jimmy won.

thatch (THACH) *noun.* Straw, grass, or similar material used to make a roof. —*verb.* To cover or make a roof with thatch. **thatched, thatching.**

thaw *verb.* 1. To melt. 2. To become warm enough to melt snow and ice (said of weather): It will *thaw* in early spring. **thawed, thawing.** —*noun.* 1. A thawing. 2. A period of weather warm enough to melt snow and ice.

the (thee before initial vowel of following word; thə before consonant) *article.* Used to indicate a particular person, place, or thing. —*adverb.* Used to indicate a limit or quantity: *The* faster we do our homework, *the* sooner we can watch television.

theater

the·a·ter (THEE-ə-tər) Also **theatre** *noun.* 1. A place where plays, operas, or motion pictures are presented. 2. The profession of actors, actresses, and those who put on plays. 3. A room that is like a theater in design: the hospital's operating *theater.* 4. An area where action takes place: the Pacific *theater* of World War II.

the·at·ri·cal (thee-AT-ri-kəl) *adjective.* 1. Of or related to plays or the theater: a *theatrical* performance. 2. Exaggerated or showy in manner. —**theatrically** *adverb.*

thee (THEE) *pronoun.* (Rare) You: "Shall I compare *thee* to a summer's day?" (Shakespeare).

theft *noun.* A robbery; an act of stealing: The *theft* of the jewels was soon discovered.

their (THAIR) *pronoun, plural* (Also *adjective*). Belonging to two or more beings or things previously named: The cats drank *their* milk.

theirs (THAIRZ) *pronoun, plural.* Something that belongs to two or more beings or things previously named: *Theirs* is the yellow car.

them (THEM) *pronoun, plural.* A form of *they* used as the object of verbs or prepositions: Because Tim and Alice were ill, we sent *them* cards.

theme (THEEM) *noun.* 1. The main topic or idea in a story, play, or other work. 2. A short composition. 3. The main melody in a musical work. **themes.**

them·selves (them-SELVZ or thəm-SELVZ) *pronoun, plural.* A form of *they* used: 1. For emphasis: They built the treehouse *themselves.* 2. When the subject and object of a verb are the same: They have *themselves* to thank. 3. To describe a normal or usual state: The children were not *themselves* today because of the rainy weather.

then (THEN) *adverb.* 1. In a past time: You were younger *then.* 2. Next: First Carol goes, *then* Janice. 3. In that case: If Debby goes, *then* you may go. —*noun.* That time.

thence (THENSS or THENSS) *adverb.* From a particular place, time, or fact: The palace gates opened and the soldiers rode *thence.*

thence·forth (thenss-FORTH or thenss-FORTH) *adverb.* From that time on.

the·ol·o·gy (thee-OL-ə-jee) *noun.* The study of the nature of God, His relationship to man, and religious beliefs and doctrines.

the·o·rem (THEE-ə-rəm or THIHR-əm) *noun.* 1. An idea, rule, or statement that can be proven true. 2. (Math) A statement or proposition that has been or can be proven true.

the·o·ry (THEE-ə-ree or THIHR-ee) *noun.* 1. An unproved explanation based on the available evidence: Columbus believed in the *theory* that the earth is round. 2. The rules, principles, and observations involved in a subject or science rather than the actual practice or activity: the *theory* of art. 3. An idea or opinion: What's your *theory* about life on other planets? **theories.**

there (THAIR) *adverb.* 1. In or at a particular place: Hide *there,* in the closet. 2. To, in the direction, or into a particular place. 3. At a certain time. —*noun.* A particular place. —*interjection.* Expresses an emotion: *There*! Now we are finished.

there·a·bout (thair-ə-BOWT) Also **thereabouts** *adverb.* Nearly, almost.

there·af·ter (thair-AF-tər) *adverb.* From that time on.

there·by (thair-BIGH) *adverb.* By means of.

there·fore (THAIR-for) *adverb* and *conjunction.* For that reason.

there·in (thair-IN or THAIR-in) *adverb.* In a certain place or situation.

ther·mal (THER-məl) *adjective.* Having to do with heat; caused by heat or retaining heat: Scientists in Antarctica stay warm by wearing *thermal* underwear.

ther·mo·graph (THER-mə-graf) *noun.* A thermometer that records temperature changes.

ther·mom·e·ter (thər-MOM-ə-tər) *noun.* An instrument for measuring temperature by degrees.

ther·mo·nu·cle·ar (ther-moh-NOO-klee-ər or ther-moh-NYOO-klee-ər) *adjective.* Referring to a nuclear reaction that takes place at a very high temperature, is produced by the fusion or joining of atomic nuclei, and releases energy, as the explosion of a hydrogen bomb.

thermos (THER-mass) *noun.* A special bottle or container made to keep its contents either hot or cold.

thermos

ther·mo·sphere (THER-mə-sfihr) *noun.* The layer of the atmosphere about 15–50 miles above the earth, between the stratosphere and the ionosphere.

ther·mo·stat (THER-mə-stat) *noun.* Any instrument that automatically regulates temperature.

the·sau·rus (thi-SOR-əss) *noun.* A reference book that contains lists of words that are similar in meaning (synonyms) and of words opposite in meaning (antonyms). —**thesauri** (thi-SOR-igh) or **thesauruses** *plural.*

these (THEEZ) *adjective. See* **this.**

the·sis (THEE-siss) *noun.* 1. An idea or argument, especially a formal one. 2. A paper that develops an idea or point of view, especially one written by a student seeking an advanced college degree. —**theses** (THEE-seez) *plural.*

they (THAY) *pronoun, plural.* Two or more beings or things previously named or indicated: Al and Ed missed school because *they* were sick.

they'd (THAYD) *contraction.* A shortened form of the words *they had* or *they would.*

they'll (THAYL) *contraction.* A shortened form of the words *they will* or *they shall.*

they're (THAIR) *contraction.* A shortened form of the words *they are.*

they've (THAYV) *contraction.* A shortened form of the words *they have.*

thick (THIK) *adjective.* 1. Not thin; with some distance between main surfaces: The swimmers used a *thick* plank for a diving board. 2. (Said of liquids) Having a heavy or dense consistency; not very fluid. 3. With many parts close together; dense: a *thick* forest. 4. Noticeable; very pronounced: a *thick* accent. 5. (Informal) Stupid; stubborn: Dave is too *thick* to understand. 6. (Informal) Close in friendship. **thicker, thickest.** —*noun.* The most active part or place: the *thick* of the fighting. —**thickly** *adverb.*

thick·en (THIK-ən) *verb.* 1. To make or become thicker: Add flour to the gravy to *thicken* it. 2. To make or become more complicated: The mystery *thickens*! **thickened, thickening.**

thick·et (THIK-it) *noun.* A thick clump of bushes or shrubs.

thief (THEEF) *noun.* A person who steals. —**thieves** (THEEVZ) *plural.*

thieve (THEEV) *verb.* To steal. **thieved, thieving.**

thigh *noun.* 1. The part of the human leg between the knee and the hip. 2. The upper part of an animal's leg.

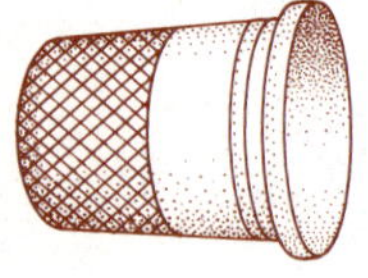

thimble

thim·ble (THIM-bəl) *noun.* A hard protective cap for the finger, worn while hand-sewing. **thimbles.**

thin *adjective.* 1. Not thick: a *thin* wall. 2. Not fat; slender. 3. Not dense; widely spaced: *thin* hair. 4. Quite liquid in form: The soup was too *thin.* 5. Weak, unconvincing: a *thin* excuse. **thinner, thinnest.** —*verb.* To make or become thin. **thinned, thinning.** —**thinly** or **thin** *adverb.*

thine (THIGHN) *pronoun.* (Rare) Possessive of *thou.* ". . . to *thine* own self be true . . . ." (Shakespeare).

thing *noun.* 1. An object. 2. Something not named or recognized: What is that blue *thing?* 3. (Plural) General conditions: How are *things?* 4. A fact; a happening: It's a good *thing* I am here. 5. Act; deed: many *things* to do. 6. (Plural) Clothes; belongings. —**do one's own thing.** (Slang) To do what pleases or is best for oneself.

think *verb.* 1. To use the mind; have an idea or ideas; exercise thought. 2. (Used with *about, over,* or *through*) To reason; work out in the mind: *think* over a problem. 3. To keep in mind; remember: Can you *think* what it was he said? 4. To believe: I *think* so. 5. To imagine; to picture. 6. To consider as probable: I *think* it will rain. **thought, thinking.** —**think better of.** To change one's mind or plans after reconsidering. —**think nothing of.** To consider normal or usual. —**think twice.** To give careful thought. —**think up.** To create in the mind.

third (THERD) *adjective.* Coming next after second; 3rd. —*noun.* One of three equal parts.

thirst (THERST) *noun.* 1. Desire or need for liquid. 2. Any great longing: "Fame is the *thirst* of youth." (Lord Byron). —*verb.* 1. To feel a desire or need for liquid. 2. (Used with *for*) To long for or crave. **thirsted, thirsting.** —**thirsty** (THERSS-tee) *adjective.*

thir·teen (ther-TEEN) *noun* (and *adjective*). The cardinal number after 12 and before 14; 13.

thir·teenth (ther-TEENTH) *adjective.* Coming next after 12th; 13th. —*noun.* One of 13 equal parts.

thir·ti·eth (THER-tee-ith) *adjective.* Coming next after 29th; 30th. —*noun.* One of 30 equal parts.

thir·ty (THER-tee) *noun* (and *adjective*). The cardinal number after 29 and before 31; 30.

this (THISS) *pronoun.* 1. A person, place, or thing just named or near at hand: *This* is a lovely place. 2. Something about to be told: *This* will surprise you. 3. Something nearer than another thing: *This* is mine; the one over there is yours. 4. Now: *This* is the time to strike. —**these** (THEEZ) *plural.* —*adjective.* 1. Being just named or understood: *This* place is nice. 2. Being nearer than another thing: *This* book is mine; yours is upstairs. —*adverb.* To such an amount or extent: I will go only *this* far.

this·tle (THISS-l) *noun.* Any of several prickly, weed-like plants with purple flowers. **thistles.**

thong (THAWNG or THONG) *noun.* 1. A thin strip, as of leather, used for tying or as the lash on a whip. 2. (Plural) Sandals having a thin strap between the first two toes.

tho·rax (THOR-aks) *noun.* 1. The human chest cavity. 2. A similar part of an insect's or animal's body. **thoraxes** or **thoraces** (THOR-ə-seez) *plural.*

thorn (THORN) *noun.* 1. A sharp, pointed growth on a plant. 2. A bush or tree that has thorns. 3. Anything that irritates or hurts like a thorn; a difficulty: a *thorn* in one's side. —**thorny** (THOR-nee) *adjective.*

thor·ough (THER-oh) *adjective.* Complete; covering all possibilities: a *thorough* search. —**thoroughly** *adverb.* —**thoroughness** *noun.*

thor·ough·bred (THER-oh-bred or THER-ə-bred) *adjective.* 1. Pure-blooded, pedigreed as a horse or a dog. 2. (Said of a person) Having the finest qualities of character and behavior. —*noun.* 1. An animal or person of excellence. 2. [Capital T] A particular breed of race horse.

thor·ough·fare (THER-oh-fair) *noun.* 1. A highway or main street. 2. Any through road. **thoroughfares.**

those (THOHZ) *adjective* and *pronoun.* *See* **that.**

thou (THOW) *pronoun, singular.* (Rare) You.

though (THOH) *conjunction.* Even if; in spite of the fact that: *Though* it may rain or snow, the mailman will bring the mail. —*adverb.* In spite of that; nevertheless: It's raining; we'll go, *though.*

thought (THAWT) *noun.* 1. The act of thinking. 2. An idea; possibility; notion: "There is always a comforting *thought* in time of trouble. . . ." (Don Marquis). 3. A way of thinking; a group of ideas: scientific *thought.* —*verb. See* **think.**

thought·ful (THAWT-fəl) *adjective.* 1. Involved with or full of thought: a *thoughtful* look. 2. Kind; considerate: a *thoughtful* act. 3. Showing careful thought: a *thoughtful* answer. —**thoughtfully** *adverb.* —**thoughtfulness** *noun.*

thought·less (THAWT-liss) *adjective.* Without thought; careless; inconsiderate. —**thoughtlessly** *adverb.*

thou·sand (THOW-zənd) *noun* (and *adjective*). The cardinal number after 999 and before 1,001; 1,000.

thou·sandth (THOW-zəndth) *adjective.* Coming next after 999th; 1,000th. —*noun.* One of a thousand equal parts.

thrash *verb.* 1. To beat; give a whipping to. 2. To move (arms and legs) about violently; to toss. 3. To win a complete victory over; to defeat. 4. To thresh. **thrashed, thrashing.** —**thrasher** *noun.* —**thrash out.** To talk over to a conclusion; work out.

thrash·er (THRASH-ər or THRESH-ər) *noun.* A long-tailed American songbird.

thread (THRED) *noun.* 1. A thin string of cotton or other fiber. 2. Anything thin or fine like thread: the *threads* of a spider's web. 3. The ridge on a screw. 4. The connecting idea as in

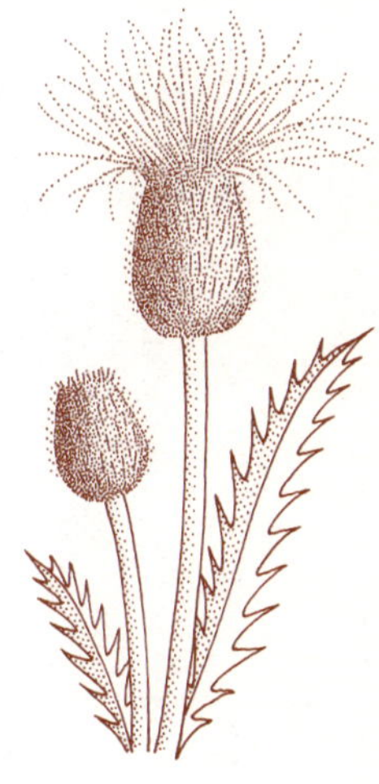
thistle

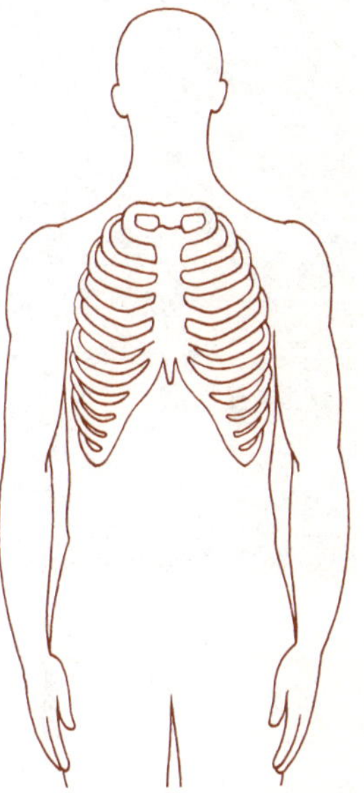
thorax

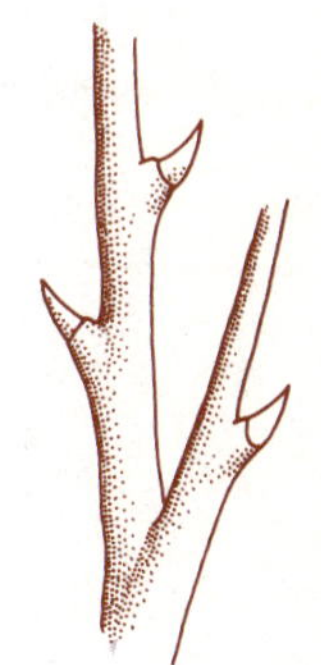
thorns

a story or series of events. —*verb.* 1. To put thread through the eye of (a needle). 2. To move carefully, as through a crowd, a series of obstacles, or dangers: The boat *threaded* its way between the coral reefs. **threaded, threading.**

thread·bare (THRED-bair) *adjective.* 1. Worn; frayed and ragged. 2. Used too often; trite: a *threadbare* excuse.

threat (THRET) *noun.* 1. A warning of intent to do harm. 2. Anything that holds a promise of harm or trouble: the *threat* of war.

threat·en (THRET-n) *verb.* 1. To make a threat; to promise to injure or punish. 2. To suggest or foretell: The black clouds *threaten* rain. **threatened, threatening.**

throne

three *noun* (and *adjective*). The cardinal number after two and before four; 3.

three·fold (THREE-fohld) *adjective.* 1. Having three parts. 2. Three times the size.

three·score (THREE-SKOR) *adjective.* Three times twenty; 60.

thresh *verb.* 1. To separate grain or seeds from a plant by beating or by use of a thresher. 2. To move about wildly; thrash. **threshed, threshing.**

thresh·er (THRESH-ər) *noun.* A machine used to separate grain or seeds from a plant.

thresh·old (THRESH-ohld) *noun.* 1. A doorsill. 2. The beginning: the *threshold* of adventure.

threw (THROO) *verb. See* **throw.**

thrice (THRYSS) *adverb.* Three times.

thrift *noun.* Careful use of money and other resources; ability to save or to avoid waste.

thrif·ty (THRIF-tee) *adjective.* Careful with money. **thriftier, thriftiest.** —**thriftily** *adverb.*

thrill (THRIL) *noun.* 1. A feeling of great excitement. 2. The cause of such excitement: Winning the race was a *thrill.* —*verb.* To feel or cause to feel excitement. **thrilled, thrilling.**

thrive (THRIGHV) *verb.* 1. To do well; prosper. 2. To grow in a healthy way. **throve** (THROHV), **thriving.**

throat (THROHT) *noun.* 1. The front part of the neck containing passages for food and air. 2. Anything that looks like or has the function of a throat: the *throat* of a bottle. —**a lump in the throat.** A feeling of tightness in the throat caused by strong emotion, such as sadness.

throb *noun.* A quivering feeling or movement, as a strong beat of the heart. —*verb.* To move, beat, or vibrate in a steady, pulsing way. **throbbed, throbbing.**

throne (THROHN) *noun.* 1. A special ceremonial chair used by a king or other important person. 2. Royal office; the rights and power of a king or other ruler. **thrones.**

throng *noun.* A crowd; large group. —*verb.* 1. To gather in a crowd. 2. To crowd into; to cluster: People *thronged* the streets, enjoying the fine weather. **thronged, thronging.**

throt·tle (THROT-l) *noun.* 1. The valve that controls the flow of fuel to an engine. 2. A pedal or other control that regulates this valve. **throttles.** —*verb.* 1. To slow down the flow of fuel to an engine. 2. To choke or strangle; to stop or make silent as if by strangling. **throttled, throttling.**

through (THROO) *preposition* (and *adverb*). 1. From the beginning to the end; from one side to another; into and out of: "His answer trickled *through* my head, like water *through* a sieve." (Lewis Carroll). 2. Among or between. 3. In and around: We spent three hours going *through* the museum. 4. Because of; in the name of; by means of: *through* her kindness. —*adjective.* 1. (Informal) Finished: Are you *through* with this book? 2. Traveling without interruption: a *through* train. —*adverb.* All the way, from beginning to end: We drove *through* to Detroit.

through·out (THROO-owt) *preposition* (and *adverb*). In every place or part: "Proclaim liberty *throughout* the land." (Liberty Bell inscription). —*adverb.* At all times or places.

throve (THROHV) *verb. See* **thrive.**

throw (THROH) *verb.* 1. To toss or make go through the air by the motion of the arm. 2. To send out; to project: *throw* a light. 3. To push down or onto the ground, as in a fight. 4. To cause (a person or thing) to go into a certain state: *throw* us into a fit of giggles. 5. To put on or take off in haste: *throw* on a coat. 6. (Informal) To entertain by means of: *throw* a party. 7. (Informal) To let someone else win: *throw* a game. **threw, thrown, throwing.** —*noun.* 1. A fling or toss. 2. How far something can be thrown: a stone's *throw.* —**throw away.** To discard. —**throw off.** To mislead: The skunk can *throw* the hounds *off* the scent. —**throw out.** 1. To discard. 2. To put out forcibly. —**throw up.** To vomit.

thrush (THRUHSH) *noun.* A small, brown songbird. **thrushes.**

thrust (THRUHST) *verb.* 1. To push suddenly or vigorously; to shove: *Thrust* out one's hand. 2. To make a stabbing movement, as with a sword. **thrust, thrusting.** —*noun.* 1. A sudden push or stab. 2. The propelling force produced by a rocket or propeller.

thud (THUHD) *noun.* A dull, heavy sound; a thump. —*verb.* To land or hit with a thud. **thudded, thudding.**

thumb (THUHM) *noun.* 1. The short, thick first digit of the hand. 2. The part of a glove or mitten that fits over the thumb. —**turn thumbs down on.** To refuse or answer "no" to. —**under one's thumb.** In one's control or power.

thump (THUHMP) *noun.* 1. A blow with something heavy or blunt. 2. The dull sound of such a blow. —*verb.* To make a thump; to pound. **thumped, thumping.**

thun·der (THUHN-dər) *noun.* 1. The loud, crackling sound made as air is suddenly expanded by the heat of lightning and then contracted again. 2. Any similar rumbling sound. —*verb.* 1. To produce thunder: The storm *thundered* overhead. 2. To make a sound like thunder: Trucks *thunder* along the highway. 3. To speak with a loud, powerful voice. **thundered, thundering.**

thun·der·bolt (THUHN-dər-bohlt) *noun.* 1. A lightning flash with thunder. 2. A sudden shocking or terrifying event, or the news of it.

thun·der·cloud (THUHN-dər-klowd) *noun.* A dark, thick cloud that may produce lightning and thunder.

thun·der·storm (THUHN-dər-storm) *noun.* A storm with lightning and thunder.

thun·der·struck (THUHN-dər-struhk) *adjective.* Stunned with amazement, as if startled by thunder; shocked.

Thurs·day (THERZ-dee or THERZ-day) *noun.* The fifth day of the week: *Thursday* is the day between Wednesday and Friday. —**Thurs.** *abbreviation.*

thus (THUHSS) *adverb.* 1. In this or that way: Fold up the map *thus.* 2. To this or that extent; so: *Thus* far you are right. 3. As a result; consequently: Pete tries hard; *thus,* he usually gets results.

thwart (THWORT) *verb.* To prevent from doing something. **thwarted, thwarting.** —*noun.* A seat set crosswise in a boat or a canoe.

thy (THIGH) *pronoun.* (Rare) Your.

thyme (TIGHM) *noun.* A small plant of the mint family, with fragrant leaves used for seasoning.

thy·roid (THIGH-roid) *noun.* In man, a gland located in the neck that produces a hormone which regulates food use and body growth.

thrush

thunderclouds

thyme

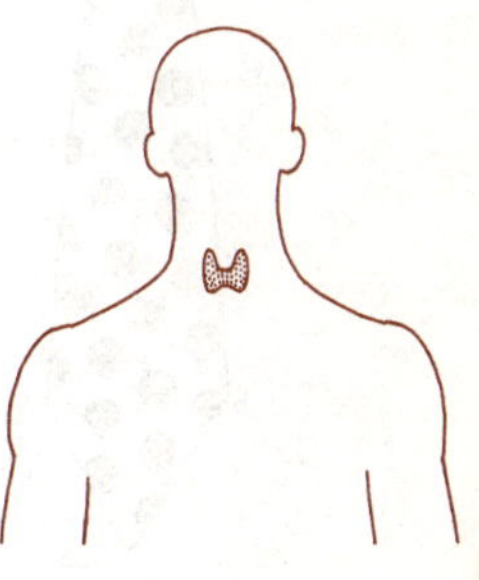
thyroid

thy·self (thigh-SELF) *pronoun.* (Rare) Yourself.

ti (TEE) *noun.* (Music) The seventh note in any standard major or minor scale of eight notes.

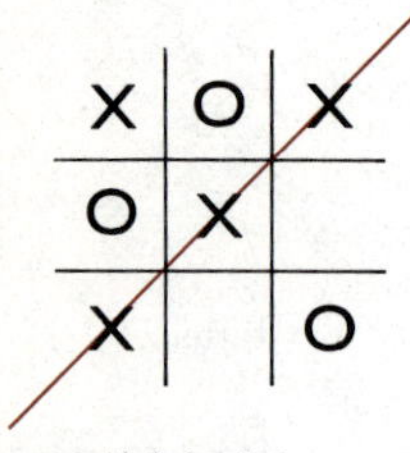
tick-tack-toe

ti·ar·a (tee-AHR-ə) *noun.* 1. A woman's crown in the form of a half circle, usually decorated with jewels or flowers. 2. A triple crown worn by the Pope.

[1]**tick** (TIK) *noun.* 1. One of a series of slight sounds made by a clock or a watch. 2. A small mark, such as a dot, dash, or check mark, made to record, count, or indicate. *—verb.* To make the sound of a tick or ticks, as a clock does. **ticked, ticking.** **—ticked off.** (Slang.) Exasperated. **—tick off.** To check off one by one.

[2]**tick** (TIK) *noun.* Any of various small insects that live by sucking the blood of animals, including man.

tick·et (TIK-it) *noun.* 1. A printed piece of cardboard or paper showing a person's right to attend a performance, ride a train, etc. 2. A tag attached to an article for sale to tell its price and size. 3. A written summons to appear in court, especially for breaking a law: a parking *ticket.* 4. The list of candidates who represent a political party in an election. *—verb.* To mark or record with a ticket; put a ticket on. **ticketed, ticketing.**

bow tie

tick·ing (TIK-ing) *noun.* A strong cloth used to case in feathers or other filling of a pillow or mattress.

tie

tick·le (TIK-əl) *verb.* 1. To touch or stroke lightly so as to cause laughing, twitching, or tingling. 2. To feel a sensation similar to being tickled: My ear *tickles.* 3. To please; to delight or amuse, as with a joke. **tickled, tickling.** *—noun.* 1. The act of tickling. 2. The sensation of being tickled.

tick·lish (TIK-lish) *adjective.* 1. Sensitive to tickling. 2. Likely to become troublesome; needing careful handling: A loud quarrel is a *ticklish* situation.

tick-tack-toe (tik-tak-TOH) Also **tic-tac-toe** *noun.* A game for two players who take turns making marks in a block of nine squares, each trying to get three of his own marks in one row.

tid·al (TIGHD-l) *adjective.* Relating to a tide or tides.

tidal wave. An enormous, far-traveling, destructive ocean wave caused by an earthquake or a storm.

tid·bit (TID-bit) Also **tit·bit** *noun.* A choice bit, as of food or news.

tide (TIGHD) *noun.* 1. The twice-daily rise and fall of sea level along a coast due to the gravitational pull of the moon and the sun on the earth. 2. Any tidelike rising and falling: "There is a *tide* in the affairs of men. . . ." (Shakespeare). *—verb.* (Used with *over*) To carry or help along: Will this loan *tide* you over until next week? **tided, tiding.**

tid·ings (TIGH-dingz) *noun, plural.* Information about events; news.

ti·dy (TIGH-dee) *adjective.* 1. Neat; well arranged; orderly: a *tidy* kitchen. 2. (Informal) Not small; significant; good-sized: a *tidy* sum of money. **tidier, tidiest.** *—verb.* To make neat and orderly: I'll *tidy* up my room. **tidied, tidying.** **—tidily** *adverb.* **—tidiness** *noun.*

tie (TIGH) *verb.* 1. To join (the ends, as of ropes) by means of a knot. 2. To fasten or make secure with a rope or the like: They *tied* the boat to the dock. 3. To confine or restrict: My cold *ties* me to the house. 4. To make the same score as; match in performance: I *tied* Tom for second place. **tied, tying.** *—noun.* 1. Something used for tying, as a rope. 2. A necktie. 3. Any device used to join parts or hold something in place: railroad *ties.* 4. A strong connection; a bond.

5. The outcome of a game or contest in which the contestants make the same score. **ties.**

tier (TIHR) *noun.* Any of several rows or ranks placed one above another: *tiers* of seats in a theater.

ti·ger (TIGH-gər) *noun.* A large, meat-eating mammal of the cat family, having tawny fur with black stripes.

tight *adjective.* 1. Fixed, tied, or bound firmly or securely; not loose. 2. Fitting too closely or snugly: This old shirt is *tight* on me. 3. Not allowing air or water to pass through; not leaky: Is that boat *tight?* 4. Taut; not slack: Keep your line *tight* as you reel in the fish. 5. Difficult: a *tight* situation. 6. Limited; scarce: Jobs are *tight* this year. 7. Stingy; overly careful with one's money. 8. (Slang) Drunk; intoxicated. **tighter, tightest.** —*adverb.* Also **tightly.** Firmly.

tight·en (TIGHT-n) *verb.* To make or become tight or tighter. **tightened, tightening.**

tight·rope (TIGHT-rohp) *noun.* A horizontal, tightly-stretched rope for the use of acrobats. **tightropes.**

tights *noun, plural.* A snug-fitting, elasticized garment, usually covering the body from the waist down.

ti·gress (TIGH-griss) *noun.* A female tiger. **tigresses.**

tile (TIGHL) *noun.* 1. A hard flat piece of baked clay, plastic, asphalt, or stone, used to cover roofs, walls, and floors. 2. A drainpipe of baked clay. **tiles.** —*verb.* To cover with tile; lay tile. **tiled, tiling.**

[1]**till** (TIL) *preposition* and *conjunction.* Until; up to the time of.

[2]**till** (TIL) *verb.* To plow; cultivate: *till* the fields. **tilled, tilling.**

[3]**till** (TIL) *noun.* A cash register; a money drawer, as in a store.

till·er (TIL-ər) *noun.* 1. The lever by which a rudder is moved to steer a boat. 2. One who plows or who cultivates a field.

tilt *verb.* 1. To tip, lean, slant: Don't *tilt* your hat; put it on straight. 2. To charge or fight on horseback with a lance. **tilted, tilting.** —*noun.* 1. State of tilting or being tilted: The flagpole has a slight *tilt.* 2. A tilting contest, as between knights.

tim·ber (TIM-bər) *noun.* 1. Wood prepared in various forms for building. 2. A heavy, wood beam or plank: *Timbers* support the roof. 3. An area covered by trees: My uncle owns 1,000 acres of *timber.* —*verb.* To build or support with timbers. **timbered, timbering.**

tim·ber·line (TIM-bər-lighn) Also **timber line** *noun.* On a mountain, the upper limit beyond which trees cannot grow.

time (TIGHM) *noun.* 1. The period measured by watches, clocks, and calendars during which events occur; duration: How much *time* will you need to do this job? 2. A period of experience: a good *time.* 3. A period of history: This is a *time* of rapid change. 4. (Plural) Conditions or events during a period: "Oh, the *times* they are a-changin." (Bob Dylan). 5. Time required or elapsed, as in a contest: The winner's *time* for the mile run was four minutes. 6. The instant when something happens or is scheduled to happen: At what *time* will you arrive? 7. (Slang) A term in prison. 8. Proper or appropriate moment: This is the *time* to buy strawberries. 9. An instance: This is the second *time* you have been late. 10. A system for measuring or designating time: standard *time;* local *time.* 11. (Music) The manner in which rhythm is organized into measures, such as 2/4 *time* or 3/4 *time.* 12. (Plural) A word equivalent to the multiplication sign meaning "multiplied by" (a certain number):

tiger

tightrope

Two *times* three is six. **times.** —*verb.* 1. To set a time for; to schedule. 2. To measure the duration of (an event): We *timed* the mile run at just four minutes. **timed, timing.** —*adjective.* 1. Adjusted with reference to time, as a *time* bomb. 2. Allowing a period for payment, as a *time* purchase. —**at times.** Now and then. —**behind the times.** Not up to date; old-fashioned. —**for the time being.** For the present; just for now. —**in time.** 1. So as not to be late: *in time* for the flight. 2. Eventually; in due course. 3. According to the rhythm. —**make time.** Do or go rapidly. —**on time.** 1. At or according to the scheduled time: The train is *on time.* 2. With a period of time allowed for payment: Did you buy your new car *on time?* —**time and again** or **time after time.** Repeatedly; over and over again.

time capsule. A box or cylinder containing articles such as newspapers, books, and photographs, placed where it may be found in the future.

time·ly (TIGHM-lee) *adjective.* Occurring or coming at the right time. —**timeliness** *noun.*

time·piece (TIGHM-peess) *noun.* Any instrument for measuring time; a watch or clock. **timepieces.**

time·ta·ble (TIGHM-tay-bəl) *noun.* 1. A list of arrival and departure times, as of buses or planes; a schedule. 2. A list or chart of events showing when they will occur. **timetables.**

tim·id (TIM-id) *adjective.* Without confidence or courage; shy; fearful. —**timidly** *adverb.* —**timidity** (ti-MID-ə-tee) *noun.*

tim·o·rous (TIM-ər-əss) *adjective.* Timid; shy; fearful. —**timorously** *adverb.*

tin *noun.* 1. A silvery-white, soft, metallic element often used in various metal alloys to prevent rusting. 2. A can or other container made of or coated with tin. —*adjective.* Made of tin: *tin* can.

tin·der (TIN-dər) *noun.* Dry material that will start to burn easily and quickly, as paper or twigs; any material that is very flammable.

tine (TIGHN) *noun.* A prong or tip of something: *tine* of a fork. **tines.**

tinge (TINJ) *noun.* 1. A trace of color; tint: At dawn the sky had a *tinge* of pink. 2. Any slight trace, as of taste, smell, feeling, or such: a *tinge* of sadness. **tinges.** —*verb.* To give a tinge to. **tinged, tingeing** or **tinging.**

tin·gle (TING-gəl) *verb.* To feel a slight prickling or stinging sensation as from the cold, a slap, or excitement: My fingers *tingle* from the cold. **tingled, tingling.** —*noun.* A slight prickling or stinging.

tin·ker (TING-kər) *verb.* 1. (Rare) To repair pots and pans. 2. To work on mechanical things, casually or without much skill: *tinker* with the car. **tinkered, tinkering.** —*noun.* A man who travels as a mender of pots and pans. —**tinkerer** *noun.* A casual or clumsy worker.

tin·kle (TING-kəl) *verb.* To make, or cause to make, a small ringing or clinking sound like that of a tiny bell. **tinkled, tinkling.** —*noun.* A light ringing sound. **tinkles.**

tin·sel (TIN-sl) *noun.* 1. Very thin strips of any shiny, inexpensive metal used for decoration: We hang *tinsel* on our Christmas tree. 2. Any cheap, shiny decoration. —*adjective.* 1. Made of tinsel. 2. Cheaply showy.

tint *noun.* 1. One of several different shades of a color: Alice preferred the darker *tint* of green. 2. A trace or slight amount of color; a tinge: Add a *tint* of blue to the white. —*verb.* 1. To color. 2. To color slightly; tinge. **tinted, tinting.**

ti·ny (TIGH-nee) *adjective.* Very small; minute: Our terrier had five *tiny* puppies. **tinier, tiniest.**

-tion *suffix.* Indicates: 1. An action or a series of actions related to: Pronuncia*tion*. 2. A condition: starva*tion*. 3. A thing brought about: transla*tion*.

[1]**tip** *verb.* 1. To turn or slant from the vertical or the horizontal; tilt: *Tip* the pitcher to pour the milk. 2. To lift (a hat) in courtesy to a woman. 3. (Usually used with *over*) To upset; overturn. **tipped, tipping.** —*noun.* 1. A tilt or leaning position. 2. The lifting of one's hat. —**tippy** *adjective.* Tending to tip; unstable.

[2]**tip** *noun.* 1. Extra money given to a service person such as a waiter or porter. 2. A bit of information or advice given secretly: a stock-market *tip*. 3. A glancing touch or tap: a *tip* off the bat. —*verb.* 1. To give a tip to. 2. To strike lightly or glancingly: *tip* a ball with a bat. **tipped, tipping.**

[3]**tip** *noun.* 1. The narrow or pointed end, as of a pencil; a point. 2. The peak or summit, as of a mountain. 3. Something on the end: the metal *tip* on an arrow.

tip·toe (TIP-toh) *noun.* The tip of the toe or toes. **tiptoes.** —*verb.* To walk quietly on the tips of the toes. **tiptoed, tiptoeing.**

tip·top (TIP-top) *noun.* 1. The summit. 2. The best.

[1]**tire** (TIGHR) *verb.* 1. To make or become weary or fatigued: Hard work *tires* me. 2. To exhaust the patience of; bore. **tired, tiring.**

[2]**tire** (TIGHR) *noun.* 1. A tube of rubber and cloth fastened around the wheel of a vehicle and filled with air: A *tire* prevents wear on the wheel and gives easier riding. 2. Iron fastened around a wooden wheel, as on a carriage, to prevent wear. **tires.**

tired (TYRD) *adjective.* Weary; exhausted: *tired* and sleepy children.

tire·less (TIGHR-liss) *adjective.* Active without becoming tired; needing little rest. —**tirelessly** *adverb.*

tire·some (TIGHR-səm) *adjective.* Boring; causing one to be tired. —**tiresomely** *adverb.*

tis·sue (TISH-oo) *noun.* 1. A very light, thin fabric or paper. 2. (Biology) Similar cells in a part of the body or plant: muscle *tissue.*

tithe (TYTH) *noun.* 1. One-tenth. 2. One-tenth of one's earnings or income. **tithes.** —*verb.* To give or pay one-tenth of one's income, as to a church. **tithed, tithing.**

ti·tle (TIGHT-l) *noun.* 1. The name of a book, TV series, or other show or work of art. 2. An owner's legal right to property. 3. A designation of rank or honor. 4. (Sports) A championship. —*verb.* To give a title to. **titled, titling.**

TNT *abbreviation.* Trinitrotoluene.

to (TOO) *preposition.* 1. Toward; in the direction of: Take the road *to* the east. 2. Toward and reaching: He went *to* New York on the plane. 3. On, against: The cars were bumper *to* bumper. 4. As far as: The ship sank *to* the bottom of the sea. 5. Until: Dinner is served from six *to* eight. 6. Before: It's a quarter *to* seven. 7. As compared with: I prefer chocolate *to* vanilla. 8. Going with; for: She lost the directions *to* the puzzle. 9. Turning or changing into: The ship was dashed *to* pieces on the rocks. 10. In pace with; according: They marched *to* the music. 11. Contained in: There are three feet *to* a yard. 12. For the purpose of: "I come *to* bury Caesar. . . ." (Shakespeare). 13. As regards: A toast *to* your success. 14. For: He kept the news *to* himself. 15. A helping word used to form the infinitive of a verb: "*To* go" and "*to* swim" are infinitives. —*adverb.* In the direction, state, or condition (often with the specific word omitted): When he came *to*, the thief was gone. —**to and fro.** Back and forth: The small birds hopped *to and fro*.

tire

toad

toadstools

tobacco

toboggan

toad (TOHD) *noun.* A gray or brown frog-like animal that lives most of its life on land.

toad·stool (TOHD-stool) *noun.* A poisonous mushroom. *See* **mushroom.**

toast (TOHST) *noun.* 1. A piece of bread browned by heat. 2. The act of drinking to the health or in honor of a person or thing. 3. The person thus honored or worthy of such an honor. —*verb.* 1. To brown bread or other food by placing it close to heat or fire. 2. To warm: We *toasted* our toes before the fire. 3. To suggest or drink a toast to a person or thing. **toasted, toasting.**

toast·er (TOHSS-tər) *noun.* A device used for toasting bread or other food.

to·bac·co (tə-BAK-oh) *noun.* 1. A wide-leaved plant of America. 2. The dried cured leaves of this plant used for smoking or chewing. —**tobaccos** or **tobaccoes** *plural.*

to·bog·gan (tə-BOG-ən) *noun.* A long sled made of thin boards curved up at the forward end. —*verb.* 1. To use a toboggan. 2. To slide down rapidly. **tobogganed, tobogganing.**

to·day (tə-DAY) *noun.* 1. This day: *Today* is the tomorrow you worried about yesterday. 2. The present time: the teen-agers of *today.* —*adverb.* 1. On this day: I'll begin *today.* 2. Now.

toe (TOH) *noun.* 1. One of the five digits of the foot. 2. The forward part of a foot covering such as a sock or shoe. 3. Anything like a toe. **toes.** —*verb.* 1. To touch or kick with the toes. 2. To place or point the toe in a certain way. **toed, toeing.** —**on one's toes.** Alert, awake. —**toe the line.** 1. To place the toes on a mark, as in starting a race. 2. To follow rules strictly.

toe·nail (TOH-nayl) *noun.* The tough hard covering on the tip of the toe.

to·ga (TOH-gə) *noun.* A garment worn by early Romans, made of a single piece of cloth draped around the body. **togas.**

to·geth·er (tə-GETH-ər) *adverb.* 1. To or at the same time and place: The students came *together* for a meeting. 2. Touching or next to each other: Clap your hands *together.* 3. With one another: Ham and eggs go well *together.* 4. In agreement: "We must all hang *together* or assuredly we shall all hang separately." (Benjamin Franklin). 5. Combined: Jim had more marbles than all the rest of the boys *together.* —**togetherness** *noun.*

toil *verb.* 1. To work hard. 2. To go forward with effort. **toiled, toiling.** —*noun.* Hard work.

toi·let (TOI-lit) *noun.* 1. A device for getting rid of body wastes by flushing them away with water. 2. A bathroom. 3. The act of washing and dressing.

toilet water. Cologne.

to·ken (TOH-kən) *noun.* 1. A symbol; an indication: This gift is a *token* of our appreciation. 2. A keepsake, something saved as a remembrance. 3. A piece of metal used in place of money: a subway *token.* —**by the same token.** In the same way; likewise. —**token payment.** A small payment that serves as a promise to pay a larger debt.

told (TOHLD) *verb. See* **tell.**

tol·er·a·ble (TOL-ər-ə-bəl) *adjective.* 1. Endurable; able to be withstood: I find this hot weather *tolerable.* 2. Not outstanding. —**tolerably** *adverb.*

tol·er·ance (TOL-ər-ənss) *noun.* 1. The ability to be fair to those whose views, customs, or actions are different from one's own. 2. (Medicine) The natural or acquired ability to resist the effect of (an element, as a drug). 3. (Mechanics) The amount of difference or variation from perfection that can be allowed. **tolerances.**

tol·er·ant (TOL-ər-ənt) *adjective.* 1. Fair to those who differ or disagree. 2. Having the ability to adapt. —**tolerantly** *adverb.*

tol·er·ate (TOL-ə-rayt) *verb.* 1. To allow, permit; put up with: Our teacher will not *tolerate* sloppy work. 2. To recognize the rights of others. 3. To adapt to or be able to bear. **tolerated, tolerating.**

¹toll (TOHL) *verb.* To ring (a bell) slowly with regular strokes. **tolled, tolling.** —*noun.* The sound of a bell rung slowly.

²toll (TOHL) *noun.* 1. A charge or tax: a bridge *toll.* 2. A penalty: Death is the *toll* we pay for war. —**toll call.** A telephone call that costs extra because of distance.

tom·a·hawk (TOM-ə-hawk) *noun.* A hatchet used by North American Indians. —*verb.* To use such a hatchet. **tomahawked, tomahawking.**

to·ma·to (ta-MAY-toh or tə-MAH-toh) *noun.* 1. A plant grown for its juicy fruit. 2. The red fruit of this plant eaten as a vegetable. **tomatoes.**

tomb (TOOM) *noun.* 1. A grave or burying place. 2. A special building or monument for the dead.

tom·boy (TOM-boi) *noun.* A girl who behaves like a boy.

tomb·stone (TOOM-stohn) *noun.* A stone used to mark a grave.

tom·cat (TOM-kat) *noun.* A male cat.

to·mor·row (tə-MOR-oh) *noun.* 1. The day after today. 2. The future. —*adverb.* 1. On the day after today. 2. In the future.

tom-tom (TOM-tom) *noun.* A small drum, beaten with the hands.

ton (TUHN) *noun.* 1. A measure of weight: A long *ton* is equal to 2,240 pounds; a short *ton* is equal to 2,000 pounds. 2. (Informal) A large amount: My books weigh a *ton.*

tone (TOHN) *noun.* 1. A sound made by a voice or a musical instrument. 2. A sound having a definite position on the scale; a note: E is two *tones* above C. 3. A way of speaking or writing: a loving *tone.* 4. Spirit or overall feeling: The *tone* of the meeting was angry. 5. The condition of the body, or a part of the body: muscle *tone.* 6. A color or shade of color. **tones.** —*verb.* 1. To change the color slightly. 2. To adjust the volume of sound: *Tone* it down! 3. To improve the condition of (a muscle). **toned, toning.**

tongs (TONGZ) *noun, plural.* A tool with two long, hinged arms used for picking up or lifting: He moved the burning logs with fire *tongs.*

tongue (TUHNG) *noun.* 1. The movable organ attached to the floor of the mouth that is used in tasting and speaking. 2. The tongue of an animal used as food. 3. Anything shaped like a tongue: *tongue* of a shoe. 4. The movable part of a bell. 5. A language: the English *tongue.* **tongues.** —**on the tip of the tongue.** Almost but not quite remembered.

tongue-tied (TUHNG-tighd) *adjective.* Unable to speak because of shyness or emotion.

tongue twister. A phrase or sentence that is hard to say clearly and quickly: "Black bug's blood" is a *tongue twister.*

ton·ic (TON-ik) *noun.* 1. A medicine to restore health. 2. Anything that makes one feel better or gives strength: The good news was a *tonic.* 3. Quinine water. 4. (Informal) Flavored soda. 5. (Music) The first, or key, note of a scale.

to·night (tə-NIGHT) *noun.* This night; the night that is coming. —*adverb.* On or during this night.

ton·nage (TUHN-ij) *noun.* 1. Weight stated in tons. 2. The capacity of a ship calculated in the number of tons it can safely carry. **tonnages.**

ton·sil (TONSS-l) *noun.* One of a pair of tissue masses found on either side of the throat.

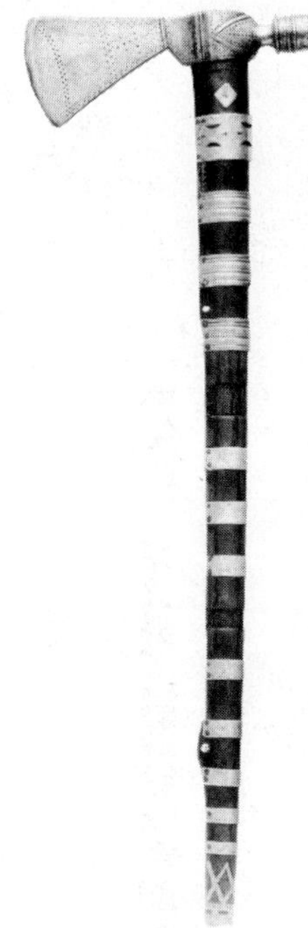
tomahawk

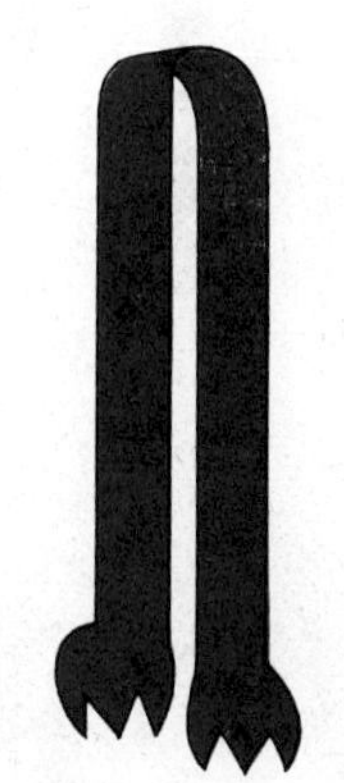
tongs

tom-toms

ton·sil·lec·to·my (ton-sə-LEK-tə-mee) *noun.* An operation to remove tonsils. **tonsillectomies.**

ton·sil·li·tis (ton-sə-LIGH-tiss) *noun.* An illness in which the tonsils are enlarged and inflamed.

too *adverb.* 1. Also. 2. More than is needed or appropriate: *too* much candy. 3. Very. 4. (Informal) Indeed, of course (used to make a statement stronger): You will *too* pay me!

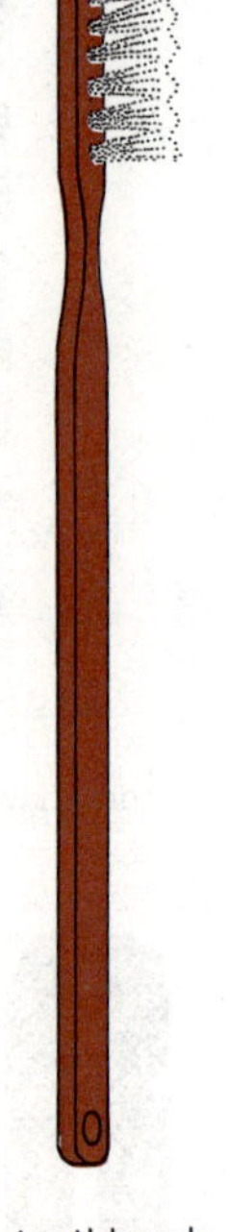

toothbrush

took (TUK) *verb. See* **take.**

tool *noun.* 1. A device used in doing work by hand: plumbing *tools.* 2. Anything necessary to do one's work: An editor's chief *tool* is a blue pencil. 3. Someone who is used unfairly by another. —*verb.* 1. To make or decorate by using a tool: *tool* leather. 2. (Used with *up*) To equip a factory with tools and machinery. **tooled, tooling.**

toot *noun.* The sound made by a short, strong blast of a horn or whistle. —*verb.* To sound such a blast. **tooted, tooting.**

tooth *noun.* 1. A hard, white bonelike structure set in the jaw and used for biting and chewing. 2. The part of any object, such as a comb, gear, saw, or leaf, that looks like a tooth. —**teeth** *plural.* —**put teeth into.** To add force or strength to: *put teeth into* a law. —**sweet tooth.** A liking for sweet foods. —**tooth and nail.** With great strength; roughly.

tooth·brush (TOOTH-bruhsh) *noun.* A small brush used to clean one's teeth. **toothbrushes.**

tooth·pick (TOOTH-pik) *noun.* A small pick or sliver for removing bits of food from between the teeth.

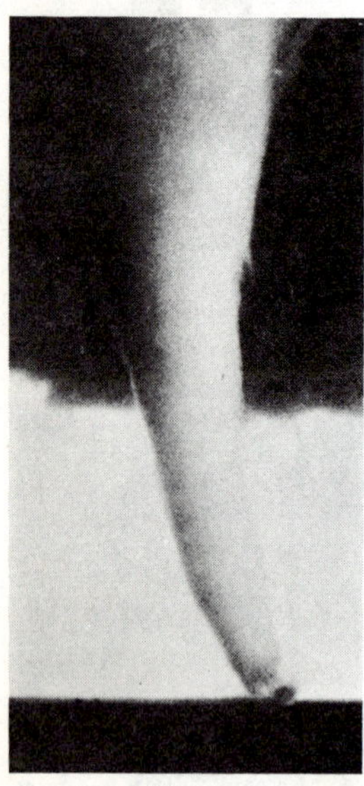

tornado

top *noun.* 1. The highest part of anything: mountain *top.* 2. A lid or covering. 3. The above-ground part of a root-food plant: beet *tops.* 4. A round toy that can be made to spin on a pointed end. 5. At or near the beginning, especially of a sheet of music. 6. (Plural, slang) The best. —*verb.* 1. To be or do better than; beat. 2. To trim (a tree or plant) by removing the top growth. 3. To cap or cover. **topped, topping.** —**top off.** To finish; complete: He *topped off* the meal with a piece of pie.

to·paz (TOH-paz) *noun.* A hard stone found in many colors, used in jewelry. **topazes.**

top·ic (TOP-ik) *noun.* The subject of a spoken or written discussion.

topic sentence. The sentence, usually the first, in a paragraph that gives the main thought of the whole paragraph.

top·knot (TOP-not) *noun.* 1. A crest of hair or feathers. 2. A decoration worn on top of the head.

top·mast (TOP-məst or TOP-mast) *noun.* The mast on a sailing ship that is supported by the lower mast.

to·pog·ra·phy (tə-POG-rə-fee) *noun.* 1. The physical features of an area considered together: *Topography* includes hills, rivers, and lakes as well as roads, canals, and bridges. 2. The study or description of such features. —**topographic** (top-ə-GRAF-ic) *adjective.*

top·ping (TOP-ing) *noun.* A sauce for ice cream or other food.

top·ple (TOP-əl) *verb.* To fall or cause to fall. **toppled, toppling.**

top·soil (TOP-soil) *noun.* The thin upper layer of earth, consisting of rich, dark soil.

top·sy-tur·vy (top-see-TER-vee) *adjective* and *adverb.* 1. Upside-down. 2. Mixed-up; in confusion.

torch *noun.* 1. A flaming light, usually carried by hand. 2. (British) A flashlight. 3. A tool that burns gas to produce a hot flame, used to melt metals and remove paint; a blowtorch. **torches.**

tore (TOR) *verb. See* **tear.**

tor·ment (TOR-ment) *noun.* 1. Torture; terrible suffering of the mind or the body. 2. A source of pain or trouble. —(tor-MENT) *verb.* 1. To cause terrible suffering. 2. To annoy or bother greatly; to trouble. **tormented, tormenting.**

torn *verb. See* **tear.**

tor·na·do (tor-NAY-doh) *noun.* A violent, whirling windstorm with a cloud in the shape of a funnel that usually causes great damage. —**tornadoes** or **tornados** *plural.*

tor·pe·do (tor-PEE-doh) *noun.* 1. A large, underwater missile, shaped like a cigar and loaded with explosives, that travels under its own power to blow up enemy ships. 2. A container or metal case containing explosives. **torpedoes.** —*verb.* To destroy or damage with, or as with, a torpedo. **torpedoed, torpedoing.**

tor·pid (TOR-pid) *adjective.* Sluggish; dull; not moving or feeling. —**torpidly** *adverb.*

tor·rent (TOR-ənt) *noun.* 1. A rushing stream of water. 2. Anything flowing swiftly and wildly like a torrent: a *torrent* of criticism.

tor·rid (TOR-id) *adjective.* Dry or hot; scorching: The weather in the desert is *torrid* in August.

tor·so (TOR-soh) *noun.* The main part, or trunk, of the human body, excluding the arms, legs, neck, and head. **torsos.**

tor·til·la (tor-TEE-yə) *noun.* A thin, round Mexican cornmeal cake, eaten as bread or with a filling.

tor·toise (TOR-təss) *noun.* 1. A turtle, especially one that lives on land. 2. A person who is slow or late.

tortoiseshell (TOR-təss-shel) *noun.* The hard brown and yellow material from the shell of some tortoises, used to make eyeglass frames, combs, and ornaments.

tor·ture (TOR-chər) *noun.* 1. The act of making a person suffer great pain. 2. Any terrible pain or suffering. **tortures.** —*verb.* To make a person suffer physical or mental pain. **tortured, torturing.**

toss *verb.* 1. To throw or heave about; make go up and down: The stormy waves *tossed* the ship. 2. To throw or fling: *Toss* me the ball. 3. To thrash about. 4. To raise in a proud or angry way: *toss* one's head and leave. 5. To throw a coin up to decide a question by which side faces upward when it lands: Let's *toss* for it. 6. To mix lightly until coated with dressing: *toss* the salad. **tossed, tossing.** —*noun.* The act of tossing. **tosses.** —**tossup.** A gamble.

tot *noun.* 1. A small child. 2. A small glass or amount; a drink: a *tot* of rum.

to·tal (TOHT-l) *noun.* The entire amount: Tax is included in the *total.* —*adjective.* 1. Entire; whole: *total* price. 2. Complete: *total* darkness. —*verb.* 1. To add; find the sum of: Please *total* this list of numbers. 2. To reach the sum of; add up to. **totaled, totaling.** —**totally** *adverb.*

tote (TOHT) *verb.* (Slang) 1. To haul; carry by hand: *tote* a suitcase. 2. To carry regularly: Cowboys used to *tote* guns. **toted, toting.**

tote bag. A large handbag, especially one used to carry little packages.

to·tem (TOH-təm) *noun.* An animal, plant, or other natural thing considered to be an ancestor and used as a symbol by a family or tribe. —**totem pole.** A carved and painted pole showing such symbols.

tot·ter (TOT-ər) *verb.* To sway back and forth as if about to fall; to wobble. **tottered, tottering.**

tou·can (TOO-kan) *noun.* A bright-colored tropical American bird with a big beak.

totem pole

toucan

touch (TUHCH) *verb.* 1. To place a finger, hand, or some other part of the body in contact with. 2. To take into the mouth or hands: You haven't *touched* your breakfast. 3. To have to do with; become involved with: He refused to *touch* this business. 4. To get the use of: I can't *touch* the money until I am 21. 5. To be as good as: No one can *touch* him in racing. 6. To harm or spoil a little: The apples were *touched* by the frost. 7. To arouse sympathy or other feeling in: She was *touched* by his kind act. 8. To affect; concern: What *touches* my brother *touches* me. **touched, touching.** —*noun.* 1. A brief physical contact. 2. The ability to sense through the fingers or other body parts what something feels like, whether it is rough or smooth, hot or cold, etc.: Blind people depend on their sense of *touch.* 3. The feel: Silk has a smooth *touch.* 4. Something slight; a small amount: a *touch* of pepper. 5. A special manner or skill: He has not lost his *touch* in telling a story. 6. A way of striking the keys of a musical instrument: She plays the piano with a light *touch.* **touches.** —**in** (or **out of**) **touch.** To be in (or out of) contact (with). —**touch on.** To mention; discuss briefly.

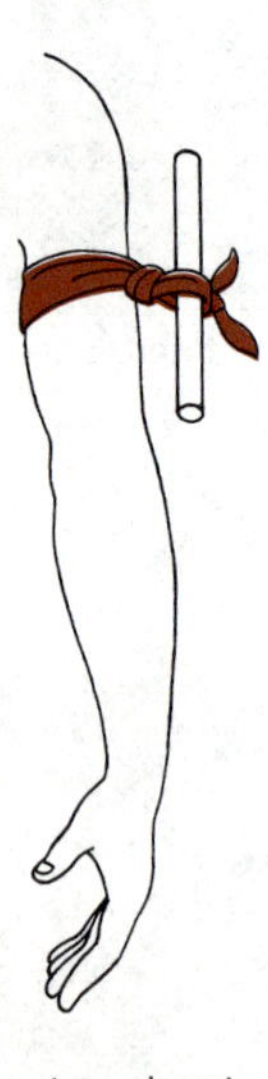
tourniquet

touch·down (TUHCH-down) *noun.* (Football) A score made by advancing the ball across the goal line of the other team.

touch football. A game of football in which the players touch with both hands rather than tackle each other.

touch·ing (TUHCH-ing) *adjective.* Arousing sympathy, sadness, pity, or the like: She cried when she heard my *touching* story.

touch·y (TUHCH-ee) *adjective.* Very sensitive; easily hurt.

tough (TUHF) *adjective.* 1. Strong and able to bend without breaking: Leather is *tough.* 2. Very difficult: a *tough* job. 3. Strong; healthy; hardy: The Marines made him *tough.* 4. Stubborn. 5. Hard to chew or cut: *tough* steak. 6. Rough; violent: There were *tough* towns in the Old West. **tougher, toughest.** —*noun.* A rough person. —**toughly** *adverb.* —**tough luck.** 1. Bad luck; an unlucky break. 2. An expression of sympathy when someone has bad luck.

tour (TUR) *noun.* 1. A personal overall inspection of an area: The children took their parents on a *tour* of the school. 2. A trip from one place to another to give performances: The band is on a *tour* of the Midwest. 3. A sightseeing trip: a *tour* of Europe. 4. A period of being at a certain place or doing special work: a *tour* of duty in Washington. —*verb.* To make a tour; go on a tour through. **toured, touring.**

tour·ist (TUR-ist) *noun.* A person who makes a tour; one who goes to see sights on a vacation. —*adjective.* Not expensive; not as good as first class: to travel *tourist* class.

tour·na·ment (TUR-nə-mənt or TER-nə-mənt) *noun.* 1. A game or a series of games in which teams or individuals compete for the championship. 2. A contest between knights on horseback.

tour·ni·quet (TUR-ni-kit) A device used to stop bleeding from a cut or bite on a limb such as the arm: A simple piece of cloth twisted tightly above a cut serves as a *tourniquet.*

tow (TOH) *verb.* 1. To pull along with a rope, chain, or cable: *tow* a car. 2. To drag: *tow* the bashful boy to the stage. **towed, towing.** —*noun.* 1. The state of pulling or being pulled. 2. A thing that tows or is towed. —**in tow.** Accompanying or being dragged along.

toward (TORD or TWORD) Also **towards** (TORDZ or TWORDZ) *preposition.* 1. In the direction of: Walk *toward* the door, not away. 2. Near; close to: It is getting *toward* the end of the show. 3. For; in order to get: I am saving *toward* a new bike. 4. About; with respect to: He feels friendly *toward* her. 5. Along the way to: a step *toward* victory.

tow·el (TOW-əl) *noun.* A piece of cloth or paper used for drying or wiping.

tow·er (TOW-ər) *noun.* 1. A high, narrow building or such a part of a building: The bells are in the church *tower.* 2. Such a building used as a fort or prison: the *Tower* of London. 3. A person or thing with the qualities of a tower: a *tower* of strength. —*verb.* To stand high or tall: The teacher *towers* above the first graders. **towered, towering.**

town *noun.* 1. A settled area or community smaller than a city but larger than a village. 2. The business center of a town: I have business in *town* today. 3. Something like a town: Prairie dogs live in burrows called *towns.* 4. The people of a town: The whole *town* is talking about him.

town·ship (TOWN-ship) *noun.* 1. A part of a county or state having some powers of local self-government. 2. An area of 36 square miles, one of the main divisions in public land surveys in the United States.

tox·ic (TOK-sik) *adjective.* Poisonous or harmful.

toy (TOI) *noun.* 1. A thing used for play, especially by children. 2. A thing of no real value or great importance; a trinket. 3. Something small: The planes of 20 years ago are *toys* compared to the planes of today. —*verb.* (Used with *with*) To play; amuse oneself: Please don't *toy* with your dinner. **toyed, toying.**

[1]**trace** (TRAYSS) *noun.* 1. A mark, track, or footprint left by a person, animal, or thing. 2. A tiny amount: a *trace* of a smile. **traces.** —*verb.* 1. To track; follow the marks, scent, or trail of: *trace* a missing person. 2. To follow (a path or route): The sailors plan to *trace* the course Columbus followed. 3. To study the development of: We will *trace* the history of the black man. 4. To draw; to outline. 5. To copy (a drawing) by following lines seen through a thin sheet of paper placed over it. **traced, tracing.**

[2]**trace** (TRAYSS) *noun.* One of two straps or ropes attached to the collar of a horse and fastened to a wagon or carriage. **traces.** —**kick over the traces.** To rebel.

tra·che·a (TRAY-kee-ə) *noun.* A tubelike structure in the throat that carries air to the lungs. —**tracheae** (TRAY-kee-ee) or **tracheas** *plural.*

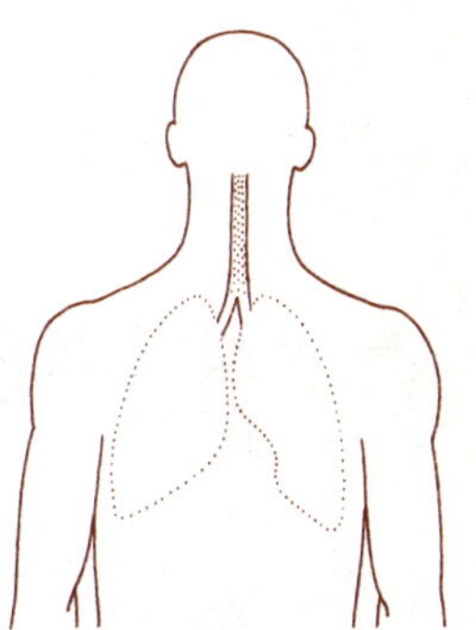
trachea

trac·ing (TRAYSS-ing) *noun.* Something traced or copied, as a map, lettering, or drawing.

track (TRAK) *noun.* 1. A mark or marks left by a person, animal, or thing that has passed: The hunters follow the *tracks* of the lion. 2. Metal rails laid down in pairs for trains or trolleys to run on. 3. A road or course, usually in the form of an oval, built for racing: a race *track.* 4. A path or trail. 5. Sports, such as running and hurdling, that are performed on a track. 6. A moving steel belt such as that on which a bulldozer moves. —*verb.* 1. To follow the marks left by; to trail: We can *track* him through the snow. 2. To follow or hunt until one finds: The police *track* down the robbers. 3. To carry in with the feet and leave: The children *track* snow into the kitchen. **tracked, tracking.** —**make tracks.** (Informal) To depart abruptly. —**on the right track.** Going in the right direction or way.

[1]**tract** (TRAKT) *noun.* A leaflet or booklet, usually political or religious, written to convince people of a certain point of view.

[2]**tract** (TRAKT) *noun.* 1. An area of land. 2. A group of organs or parts of the body that work as a unit to do a certain job: the digestive *tract.*

trac·tion (TRAK-shən) *noun.* 1. Act of pulling, or state of being pulled: *Traction* of logs over rough ground is difficult. 2. Friction between an object and the surface over which it is drawn or driven: *Traction* of auto tires on ice is slight. 3. (Medicine) Any means for maintaining a constant pull on some part of the body for remedial purposes: Harry's broken leg was in *traction* for two weeks.

trac·tor (TRAK-tər) *noun.* 1. A motor-driven vehicle, on wheels or two moving steel tracks, used to haul heavy loads. 2. A truck with a motor and driver's cab but no body, used to pull a trailer.

tractor trailer

tractor trailer. A vehicle made up of a truck with a driver's cab that pulls a detachable trailer. Also called "tractor truck."

trade (TRAYD) *noun.* 1. The business or occupation a person is in: the carpenter's *trade.* 2. All persons engaged in a certain business or kind of work: the book *trade.* 3. The business of buying and selling; commerce: Advertising helps people in *trade* find customers. 4. The customers of a business: the tourist *trade.* 5. The exchange of one thing for another. 6. (Plural) The trade winds. **trades.** —*verb.* 1. To buy and sell; do business. 2. To exchange. 3. To shop (with); buy goods from: I like to *trade* at the neighborhood grocery. **traded, trading.**

trade·mark (TRAYD-mahrk) *noun.* 1. A mark, name, design, or the like used by a business on its products or in its advertising so as to be easily remembered or recognized: A U.S. *trademark* is registered in the United States Patent Office and can be used only by its owner. 2. Something typical of a person or thing: Honesty is Margaret's *trademark.* —*verb.* 1. To put a trademark on something. 2. To register a trademark. **trademarked, trademarking.**

trad·er (TRAYD-ər) *noun.* A merchant or dealer; a person in the business of buying and selling.

trade route. A route used regularly by traders; a sea route followed by merchant ships.

trades·man (TRAYDZ-mən) *noun.* One who buys and sells; a shopkeeper. —**tradesmen** *plural.*

trade union. An association or group of workmen in the same trade, formed to protect jobs and get better wages and working conditions.

trade wind. A steadily blowing wind in the tropics near the equator.

trading post. A store in a frontier settlement where trading is done with natives: In the Old West, Indians brought furs to *trading posts.*

tra·di·tion (trə-DISH-ən) *noun.* 1. The handing down, usually by word of mouth and example, of beliefs, customs, and opinions, from one generation to the next. 2. A belief, custom, or opinion handed down in this way. 3. A principle or standard used as a guide, or a body of such principles and standards: Our country has a *tradition* of equality for all people. —**traditional** *adjective.* —**traditionally** *adverb.*

traf·fic (TRAF-ik) *noun.* 1. The number of people, automobiles, ships, or the like passing along a route: *Traffic* is heavy over the bridge. 2. The movement of such people and things: An accident held up *traffic.* 3. Buying and selling; trading: *Traffic* in drugs is against the law. 4. Dealing; business; exchange of information: We will have no *traffic* with the enemy. —*verb.* To buy; sell; do business; exchange information. **trafficked, trafficking.**

trag·e·dy (TRAJ-ə-dee) *noun.* 1. A very sad event; a piece of extreme bad luck. 2. A serious play, novel, or other work with an unhappy ending; such writing in general.

trag·ic (TRAJ-ik) *adjective.* 1. Very sad; dreadful; causing great harm and grief. 2. Having to do with tragedy. —**tragically** *adverb.*

trail (TRAYL) *verb.* 1. To follow the tracks of; follow behind: *trail* a fox. 2. To drag something along or be drawn along: The bride's long skirt *trails* after her. 3. To follow slowly or lag behind: She is *trailing* the other runners. 4. To spread and root; creep: English ivy *trails* over the ground. 5. To hang down loosely. 6. (Used with *off*) To become fainter or smaller: The old man's voice *trailed* off. 7. To drift: Smoke *trails* from the campfire. **trailed, trailing.** —*noun.* 1. Something that follows along behind: a *trail* of smoke. 2. Something left behind, as a smell or mark: a *trail* of litter. 3. A path.

trail·er (TRAYL-ər) *noun.* 1. One that follows the trail of another; a hunter. 2. A truck body, wagon, or cart that is pulled by an automobile or tractor. 3. A home or office on wheels that can either be moved or set up permanently in a place. 4. A plant that creeps along the ground.

trailer truck. *See* **tractor trailer.**

train (TRAYN) *noun.* 1. A line of railroad cars, joined together and pulled by a locomotive. 2. A moving line of wagons, cars, people, or animals: a camel *train.* 3. A line of connected thoughts, actions, or things. —*verb.* 1. To teach; to drill or exercise (a person or animal) in a skill: *train* a dog. 2. To bring up; form the mind and character of: *Train* a child to respect others. 3. To make or become fit, or ready for a sport: *train* for football. 4. To point or aim. **trained, training.**

train·ing (TRAYN-ing) *noun.* Education and practice in a practical skill, art, sport, or job.

trait (TRAYT) *noun.* A quality, feature, or characteristic.

trai·tor (TRAY-tər) *noun.* One who betrays his country or a cause.

tramp *verb.* 1. To walk or march, especially with a heavy step. 2. (Used with *on*) To step heavily: Don't *tramp* on the flowers! **tramped, tramping.** —*noun.* 1. A traveling beggar or hobo. 2. The sound of heavy steps. 3. A hike: a *tramp* through the woods. 4. A freight ship with no regular route. Also called "tramp steamer."

tram·ple (TRAM-pəl) *verb.* 1. To walk heavily on and crush: The cow *trampled* the garden. 2. To treat in a mean or cruel way: "Accustomed to *trample* on the rights of others, you have lost . . . your own independence." (Lincoln). —**trampled, trampling.**

tram·po·line (TRAM-pə-leen) *noun.* A strong canvas or net stretched in a frame and used as a springboard for tumbling, jumping, and other exercises.

trance (TRANSS) *noun.* A condition in which a person seems to be partly asleep or lost in thought; a daze.

tran·quil (TRAN-kwəl) *adjective.* Quiet; calm; peaceful. —**tranquillity** (tran-KWIL-ə-tee) *noun.* —**tranquilly** *adverb.*

tran·quil·iz·er (TRAN-kwə-lighz-ər) *noun.* A medicine used to soothe the nerves and make one relax.

trans- *prefix.* Indicates: 1. Going from one place to another: *trans*fer. 2. Across or beyond: *trans*continental. 3. Change: *trans*late.

trans·act (tran-ZAKT) *verb.* To do; carry on: *transact* business. **transacted, transacting.** —**transaction** (tran-ZAK-shən) *noun.*

trans·con·ti·nen·tal (transs-kon-tə-NEN-tl) *adjective.* Crossing or going from one side of a continent to the other.

train

trampoline

trans·fer (transs-FER) *verb.* 1. To move or send from one person or place to a different one: I may *transfer* to another class. 2. To give in a legal way, usually for money: *transfer* property. 3. To copy or move (a design, picture, etc.) from one surface to another: Use carbon paper to *transfer* the drawing. 4. To move from one streetcar, bus, airplane, or train to another. **transferred, transferring.** —(TRANSS-fer) *noun.* 1. A person or thing moved from one place to another. 2. A ticket that allows a passenger to transfer to another bus or train.

trans·form (transs-FORM) *verb.* 1. To change in form or appearance: The factory *transforms* coal into energy. 2. To alter in condition, character, etc.: The automobile *transformed* us into a nation of travelers. **transformed, transforming.** —**transformation** (transs-fər-MAY-shən) *noun.*

trans·fu·sion (transs-FYOO-zhən) *noun.* 1. The transfer of the blood of one person or animal to another. 2. A transfer or causing to flow from one to another.

tran·sient (TRAN-shənt) *adjective.* Temporary; staying just a short while: *transient* worker. —*noun.* One who stays only a short while.

transistor (definition 2)

tran·sis·tor (tran-ZISS-tər) *noun.* 1. A tiny electronic device that does the work of a vacuum tube in radios, hearing aids, and other instruments. 2. A radio equipped with transistors.

tran·sit (TRAN-zit) *noun.* 1. A journey or trip; the act of passing through or across: The *transit* of the troops across the river was slow. 2. The carrying or transporting of things: The statue was broken in *transit.* 3. An instrument that surveyors use to measure angles.

tran·si·tion (tran-ZISH-ən) *noun.* The passing or changing from one condition, place, or stage to another.

trans·late (tranz-LAYT) *verb.* 1. To put statements into a different language: *translate* from Spanish to English. 2. To put into other words; explain. 3. To change the form of: We want to *translate* this plan into action. **translated, translating.** —**translation** (tranz-LAY-shən) *noun.*

trans·lu·cent (tranz-LOO-sənt) *adjective.* Allowing light, but not clear images, to pass through: The glass in the shower door is *translucent.*

trans·mis·sion (tranz-MISH-ən) *noun.* 1. The act of sending from one place or person to another: the *transmission* of news. 2. Something that is transmitted. 3. The part of an automobile that transfers power from the motor to the wheels. 4. The sending or carrying of radio and TV waves through space.

trans·mit (tranz-MIT) *verb.* 1. To send from one place to another; transfer: *Transmit* the message by telegraph. 2. To send radio or TV signals. **transmitted, transmitting.**

trans·mit·ter (tranz-MIT-ər) *noun.* 1. A person, machine, or other thing that transmits. 2. The part of a telephone or telegraph by which messages are sent. 3. The device that transmits radio or TV signals.

tran·som (TRAN-səm) *noun.* A narrow, hinged window above another window or a door.

trans·par·ent (transs-PAIR-ənt) *adjective.* 1. Easy to see through: *transparent* tape. 2. Readily detected; obvious: a *transparent* effort to avoid work.

trans·plant (transs-PLANT) *verb.* 1. To dig up and plant in another place: *Transplant* these flowers into a bigger pot. 2. To move (a body organ or tissue) to a different body or part of a body. **transplanted, transplanting.** —(TRANSS-plant) *noun.* 1. The process of transplanting. 2. Something transplanted.

trans·port (transs-PORT) *verb.* 1. To move or carry from one place to another: Trucks *transport* goods. 2. To carry away by strong emotion: The beauty of the mountains *transported* him. **transported, transporting.** —(TRANSS-port) *noun.* 1. Moving or carrying from one place to another; transportation: We use airplanes for *transport.* 2. A plane, truck, bus, car, ship, or any means of moving people or things.

trans·por·ta·tion (transs-pər-TAY-shən) *noun.* 1. Carrying or transporting; being transported. 2. A means of travel or transport: My *transportation* was a shiny new bike. 3. The trade of transporting things or people.

trap *noun.* 1. A device used to catch animals. 2. Something used to catch a person, especially by tricking him: the detectives' *trap.* 3. A U-shaped bend in a drainpipe that lets water pass through to the sewer but keeps out gas. 4. A door in a floor or a roof; a trap door. 5. (Usually plural) Drums and other percussion instruments used in a jazz band. —*verb.* 1. To catch in a trap. 2. To set traps to catch animals. 3. To stop; catch; hold. **trapped, trapping.**

trap door. A door in a floor or a roof.

tra·peze (tra-PEEZ) *noun.* A short horizontal bar hung from two ropes and used by acrobats or athletes.

trap·e·zoid (TRAP-ə-zoid) *noun.* A shape with four sides, only two of which are parallel.

trap·per (TRAP-ər) *noun.* One who traps, especially a person who traps wild animals for their fur.

trap·pings (TRAP-ingz) *noun, plural.* Fancy dress or decorations.

trash *noun.* 1. Rubbish; junk; worthless things. 2. Empty talk; nonsense. —*verb.* (Slang) To vandalize; inflict random damage on intentionally: The mob *trashed* the shopping center.

trav·el (TRAV-əl) *verb.* 1. To go from one place to another; make a trip: *travel* to Europe. 2. To move: Light *travels* faster than sound. **traveled** or **travelled, traveling** or **travelling.** —*noun.* 1. Going from one place to another. 2. (Plural) Trip; journey.

trav·erse (TRAV-ərss or trə-VERSS) *verb.* To go across; pass over or through. **traversed, traversing.**

trawl *noun.* A large net that is dragged along the ocean bottom to gather fish and other sea life. —*verb.* To fish with such a net. **trawled, trawling.**

tray *noun.* A flat piece of metal, wood, or other material, usually with a low rim, used for carrying or holding things: a serving *tray.*

treach·er·ous (TRECH-ər-əss) *adjective.* 1. Not faithful or loyal; not trustworthy. 2. Not reliable; looking safe when it is not: Thin ice can be *treacherous.*

treach·er·y (TRECH-ə-ree) *noun.* 1. Breaking faith; acting in a treacherous way. 2. Treason; disloyalty. **treacheries.**

tread (TRED) *verb.* 1. To walk along or over. 2. To trample; press with the feet. 3. To form with the feet; to beat: Children *tread* a path to the lake. **trod, treading.** —*noun.* 1. Sound or way of walking: a heavy *tread.* 2. The part of a stair on which the foot is set. 3. The part of an automobile tire that touches the road. —**tread water.** To keep afloat by moving the legs as if walking.

tread·le (TRED-l) *noun.* A lever or pedal pressed by the foot to operate a machine like a sewing machine or a grindstone. **treadles.** —*verb.* To work a treadle. **treadled, treadling.**

tread·mill (TRED-mil) *noun.* 1. An apparatus worked by people or animals walking on steps on the rim of a wheel or on an inclined endless belt. 2. Any dull or tiresome job or way of life.

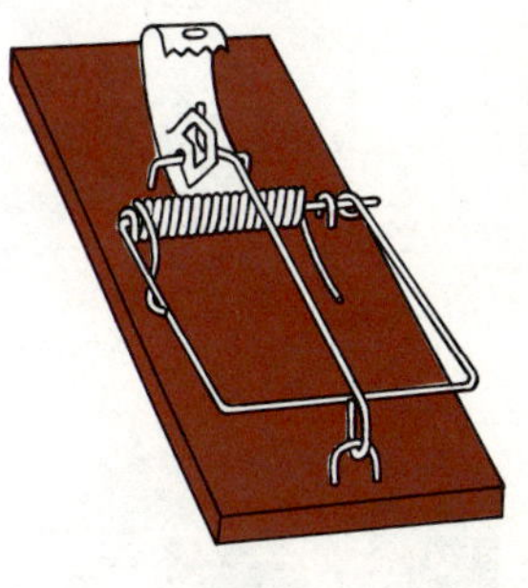
trap

trapezoid

trapeze

trea·son (TREEZ-n) *noun.* The act of betraying one's country; disloyalty.

treas·ure (TREZH-ər) *noun.* 1. Stored-up wealth, such as money, gold, or jewels. 2. A person or thing thought to be precious. *—verb.* To love; value highly. **treasured, treasuring.**

treas·ur·er (TREZH-ər-ər) *noun.* One who handles money matters for a government, club, or other group.

trellis

treas·ur·y (TREZH-ər-ee) *noun.* 1. The money of a club, business, class, or government. 2. [Capital T] The department of a government that prints money, collects taxes, and pays out funds. 3. A place where money or treasure is kept. 4. A collection of things that are valuable.

treat (TREET) *verb.* 1. To act toward; to handle: She *treats* the children with kindness. 2. (Usually used with *as*) To regard and deal with: *Treat* the error as serious. 3. To pay the bill for: They *treated* us to dinner. 4. To care for by medical means: The doctor *treats* many different ailments. 5. To act upon; change in some way: *treat* wood pulp with chemicals to make paper. 6. To deal with in writing or a speech. **treated, treating.** *—noun.* 1. The act of paying for another person's ticket or bill. 2. Something enjoyable.

treat·ment (TREET-mənt) *noun.* 1. An act or way of treating or dealing with: Our crossing guard always gives us good *treatment.* 2. A method of medical care.

trestle

trea·ty (TREE-tee) *noun.* A written agreement between countries: a peace *treaty.* **treaties.**

[1]**treb·le** (TREB-əl) *noun.* 1. The highest voice, part, or instrument in music; soprano. 2. Any high, shrill voice or sound.

[2]**treb·le** (TREB-əl) *adjective.* Three times as much; triple. *—verb.* To make or become three times as much. **trebled, trebling.**

tree *noun.* 1. A tall woody plant with a central trunk from which grow branches with leaves or needles. 2. A bar, beam, or other piece of wood shaped for a particular purpose: a shoe *tree.* 3. A diagram or chart in the form of a tree: a family *tree.* **trees.** *—verb.* To chase and force to climb a tree. **treed, treeing.** **—up a tree.** In a difficult or awkward position.

trek *verb.* To make a trip slowly and with difficulty. **trekked, trekking.** *—noun.* A long, hard trip.

trel·lis (TREL-iss) *noun.* A frame made of crossed sticks that supports plants or vines; a lattice. **trellises.**

trem·ble (TREM-bəl) *verb.* 1. To shiver; shake with fear, cold, or weakness. 2. To shake: Trucks make the house *tremble.* **trembled, trembling.** *—noun.* The condition of trembling.

tre·men·dous (tri-MEN-dəss) *adjective.* 1. Very great; huge. 2. Dreadful; terrible. 3. (Informal) Very good; wonderful. **—tremendously** *adverb.*

trem·or (TREM-ər) *noun.* 1. A bodily trembling or shaking: a *tremor* of excitement. 2. Any trembling movement: an earth *tremor.*

trem·u·lous (TREM-yə-ləss) *adjective.* 1. Shaking or trembling. 2. Timid; fearful. **—tremulously** *adverb.*

trench *noun.* 1. A ditch; a long, narrow opening in the ground. 2. A long ditch, with sandbag or dirt banks, in which soldiers take shelter in war. **trenches.** *—verb.* To dig a trench in. **trenched, trenching.**

trench coat. A loose raincoat with a wide belt and slash pockets.

trend *noun.* A movement, tendency, or direction of activity. *—verb.* To tend. **trended, trending.**

tres·pass (TRESS-pəss or TRESS-pass) *verb.* 1. To go on or across another person's property without permission. 2. To intrude; go further than proper. 3. To sin; do wrong. **trespassed, trespassing.** —*noun.* 1. An act of trespassing. 2. An act of wrongdoing; an offense: "Forgive us our *trespasses*. . . ." (Matthew 6:9).

tress *noun.* 1. A long lock of hair; a braid. 2. (Plural) Long hair. **tresses.**

tres·tle (TRESS-l) *noun.* 1. A movable support made of a bar of wood or metal with a pair of spreading legs attached at each end. 2. A high framework of timber, metal, etc., used to carry railroad tracks or a road over a river or valley. **trestles.**

tri- *prefix.* Indicates: 1. Three: *tri*colored. 2. Every three or every third of: *tri*monthly.

tri·al (TRIGH-əl or TRIGHL) *noun.* 1. A trying or testing. 2. (Law) An examination of facts, conducted in court, to determine the truth of charges or claims. 3. A person or thing that causes difficulty or hardship.

tri·an·gle (TRIGH-ang-gəl) *noun.* A flat figure with three angles and three connected sides. **triangles.**

tri·an·gu·lar (trigh-ANG-gyə-lər) *adjective.* 1. Shaped like a triangle. 2. Having three parts, groups, or members: A *triangular* track meet involves three teams.

tribe (TRYB) *noun.* 1. A group or society of people who have the same ancestors, language, and customs, and who often are united under one leader or chief: The Sioux are an Indian *tribe.* 2. Any group of people, animals, or plants with features in common. **tribes.**

tribes·man (TRYBZ-mən) *noun.* A member of a tribe. —**tribesmen** *plural.*

tri·bu·nal (trigh-BYOO-nl or tri-BYOO-nl) *noun.* A court of justice: The Supreme Court is our highest *tribunal.*

trib·u·tar·y (TRIB-yə-tehr-ee) *noun.* A stream or small river that flows into a larger one. **tributaries.**

trib·ute (TRIB-yoot) *noun.* 1. An action or gift that shows respect, admiration, or gratitude. 2. Money or goods given by one country to another as evidence of obedience and to insure against invasion.

tri·cer·a·tops (trigh-SEHR-ə-tops) *noun.* A plant-eating dinosaur with three horns on its head, one over each eye and one on its nose.

trich·i·no·sis (trik-ə-NOH-siss) *noun.* A disease caused by eating pork that has not been cooked enough.

trick (TRIK) *noun.* 1. An action or plan meant to fool; a scheme. 2. A puzzling or mysterious action that entertains: magic *tricks.* 3. A prank; something done as a joke: Halloween *trick*-or-treat. 4. The method or ability needed to do something: the *trick* of swinging a golf club correctly. 5. In card games, all of the cards played in one round. —*verb.* To fool or deceive. **tricked, tricking.**

trick·er·y (TRIK-ər-ee) *noun.* The using of tricks; deception. **trickeries.**

trick·le (TRIK-əl) *verb.* 1. To flow in drops or a small stream. 2. To move slowly or in small amounts: Cars *trickled* past the wreck. **trickled, trickling.** —*noun.* A small or unsteady flow. **trickles.**

tri·cy·cle (TRIGH-sik-əl) *noun.* A small, three-wheeled vehicle with pedals. **tricycles.**

tri·dent (TRIGHD-nt) *noun.* A spear with three prongs or points.

[1]**tried** (TRIGHD) *verb. See* **try.**

[2]**tried** (TRIGHD) *adjective.* Tested and proved good or useful.

tri·fle (TRIGH-fəl) *noun.* 1. A thing of little importance or value. 2. A small amount, as of time, effort, or money. **trifles.** —*verb.* To treat or use without proper concern: Don't *trifle* with the rules. **trifled, trifling.**

tri·fling (TRIGH-fling) *adjective.* Of little importance or value.

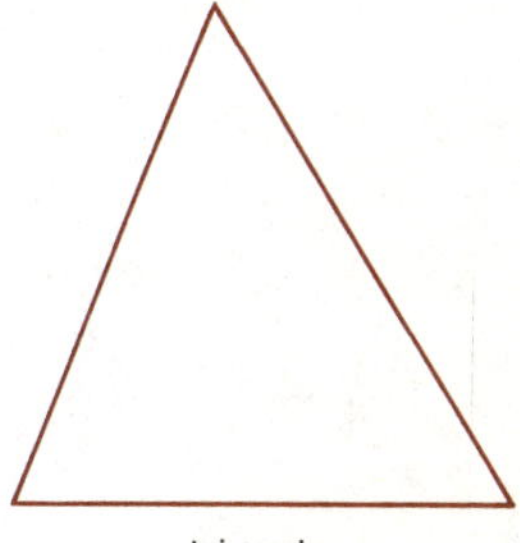
triangle

triceratops

tricycles

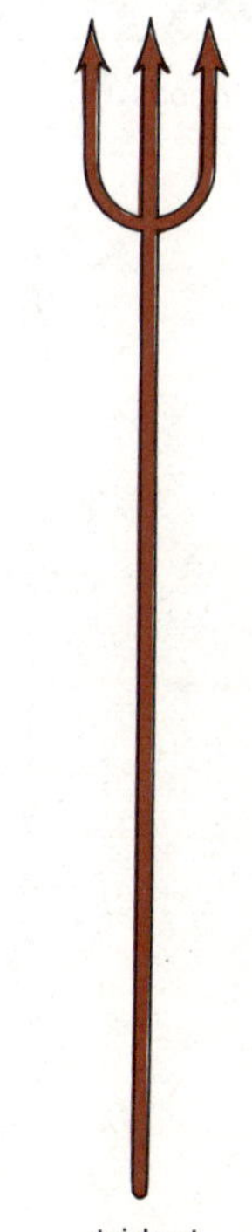
trident

trig·ger (TRIG-ər) *noun.* 1. A narrow lever pulled to fire a gun. 2. Any similar device used to start an action. —*verb.* To start (an action). **triggered, triggering.**

trill (TRIL) *verb.* 1. To sing or utter with a fluttering sound; to warble: The canary *trilled* a song. 2. (Music) To play two adjoining tones in rapid alternation. **trilled, trilling.** —*noun.* 1. A fluttering sound or quality. 2. (Music) The playing of adjoining notes in rapid alternation.

tril·lion (TRIL-yən) *noun.* The cardinal number equal to one thousand billion; 1,000,000,000,000.

tripods

trim *verb.* 1. To cut off small amounts of in order to make neater or more attractive: *trim* hair. 2. To remove excess parts: *trim* fat from steak. 3. To decorate: *trim* a Christmas tree. 4. To adjust (the sails of a ship). 5. To balance (a ship or plane). **trimmed, trimming.** —*noun.* 1. The condition or order of something: in fighting *trim.* 2. Decoration. —*adjective.* Neat. **trimmer, trimmest.** —**trimly** *adverb.*

trim·ming (TRIM-ing) *noun.* 1. Decoration; ornament. 2. (Plural) Parts that go with something else; extras: gravy and other *trimmings* with turkey. 3. (Plural) Parts that are trimmed off. 4. (Slang) A beating.

tri·ni·tro·tol·u·ene (trigh-nigh-troh-TOL-yoo-een) *noun.* A powerful explosive. —**TNT** *abbreviation.*

trin·ket (TRING-kit) *noun.* 1. A small piece of jewelry. 2. A plaything of little value.

tri·o (TREE-oh) *noun.* 1. A group of three. 2. A piece of music sung or played by three performers. 3. Three performers who sing or play as a unit. **trios.**

trip *noun.* 1. A journey: a boat *trip.* 2. A stumble; loss of balance. 3. (Slang) A period when one imagines things under the influence of drugs. —*verb.* 1. To stumble; lose one's balance. 2. To cause to stumble or fall. 3. To move with light, prancing steps: *trip* happily across the yard. 4. To make a mistake or cause to make a mistake. **tripped, tripping.** —**trip up.** To catch in a lie or mistake.

tripe (TRIGHP) *noun.* 1. Stomach walls of oxen or similar animals, used as food. 2. (Slang) Nonsense.

trip·le (TRIP-əl) *adjective.* Having three parts or three times as many or as much: a *triple*-dip ice-cream cone. —*verb.* 1. To multiply by three; increase by three times. 2. (Baseball) To make a three-base hit. **tripled, tripling.** —*noun.* 1. An amount that is three times as much. 2. (Baseball) A three-base hit. **triples.** —**triply** *adverb.*

trip·let (TRIP-lit) *noun.* One of three born at the same birth.

tri·pod (TRIGH-pod) *noun.* A support, stand, or frame having three legs.

trite (TRIGHT) *adjective.* Used too often; common; without newness or interest: a *trite* expression. **triter, tritest.** —**tritely** *adverb.*

tri·umph (TRIGH-əmf) *noun.* A victory. —*verb.* To win a victory. **triumphed, triumphing.**

tri·um·phant (trigh-UHM-fənt) *adjective.* Victorious; successful. —**triumphantly** *adverb.*

triv·i·al (TRIV-ee-əl) *adjective.* Of little importance or value.

trod *verb. See* **tread.**

[1]**troll** (TROHL) *verb.* 1. To fish with a baited line dragged slowly behind a boat. 2. To sing with a full, loud voice. 3. To sing a round, or song in which two or more singers begin singing the same phrases at different times. **trolled, trolling.**

[2]**troll** (TROHL) *noun.* In Scandinavian folklore, a dwarf, elf, or similar imaginary creature.

trol·ley (TROL-ee) *noun.* 1. A streetcar powered by electricity from overhead lines. 2. A basket or other container having wheels that run over a cable or track. 3. A wheeled device that conducts electricity from an electric line to a trolley or other vehicle.

trom·bone (trom-BOHN) *noun.* A brass musical instrument that has a sliding tube by means of which the player changes notes. **trombones.**

troop *noun.* 1. A group of persons, animals, or things. 2. (Usually plural) A body of soldiers. 3. A unit of Boy Scouts or Girl Scouts having an adult leader. *—verb.* To go or walk, usually in a group: The students *trooped* out of the classroom. **trooped, trooping.**

troop·er (TROOP-ər) *noun.* 1. A soldier or policeman who rides on horseback. 2. A state policeman.

tro·phy (TROH-fee) *noun.* An object such as a cup or plaque awarded for or representing a victory or success; a prize. **trophies.**

trop·ic (TROP-ik) *noun.* 1. Either of two imaginary lines, the Tropic of Cancer and the Tropic of Capricorn, that circle the globe north and south of the equator. 2. [Often Capital T] (Plural) The very warm area between the Tropic of Cancer and the Tropic of Capricorn. —**tropical** *adjective.*

Tropic of Cancer. An imaginary circle around the earth $23\frac{1}{2}$ degrees north of and parallel to the equator.

Tropic of Capricorn. An imaginary circle around the earth $23\frac{1}{2}$ degrees south of and parallel to the equator.

tro·pism (TROH-piz-əm) *noun.* (Biology) A response or movement of an organism toward or away from a stimulus, such as light or water: The leaning of a plant toward the sun is an example of *tropism.*

tro·po·sphere (TROH-pə-sfihr) *noun.* The layer of the atmosphere between the earth's surface and the stratosphere; the area where most weather occurs.

trot *noun.* 1. The gait of a horse, faster than a walk, in which a hind leg and the opposite front leg move at about the same time. 2. Any gait faster than a walk but slower than a run. *—verb.* To move or cause to move at a trot. 3. To move briskly; hurry. **trotted, trotting.**

troub·le (TRUHB-əl) *noun.* 1. Difficulty or conflict. 2. Worry; agitation. 3. An effort; work: Please take the *trouble* to wipe your feet. 4. Illness or physical difficulty: ear *trouble.* **troubles.** *—verb.* 1. To cause a problem or difficulty for. 2. To worry; bother. **troubled, troubling.**

troub·le·some (TRUHB-əl-səm) *adjective.* Causing worry or difficulty.

trough (TRAWF or TROF) *noun.* 1. A long, narrow container in which water or food for animals is placed. 2. A rain gutter or other long, narrow object similar in purpose or appearance. 3. A long, narrow space or hollow, as between ridges or waves.

trounce (TROWNSS) *verb.* 1. To beat or whip. 2. To defeat by a wide margin. **trounced, trouncing.**

troupe (TROOP) *noun.* A group, especially of actors, singers, or other performers. **troupes.**

trou·sers (TROW-zərz) *noun, plural.* A garment for covering the body from the waist to the ankles, with divided sections for the legs; slacks; pants.

trout (TROWT) *noun.* Any of a variety of freshwater game fish. —**trout** *plural.*

trow·el (TROW-əl) *noun.* 1. A hand garden tool with a scooplike, pointed blade, used for digging. 2. A hand tool with a flat, pointed blade used for applying and shaping mortar or plaster. *—verb.* To dig or work with a trowel. **troweled, troweling.**

tru·ant (TROO-ənt) *noun.* 1. A student who is absent from school without permission. 2. A person who avoids his work. *—adjective.* Purposely absent; idle. —**truancy** *noun.*

trombone

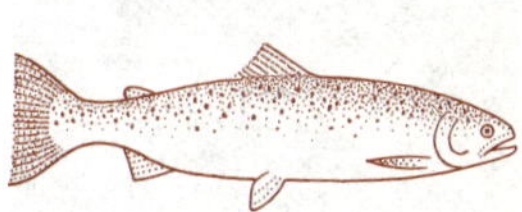
trout

trowel

truce (TROOSS) *noun.* An agreement for a temporary stopping of fighting or a war. **truces.**

[1]**truck** (TRUHK) *noun.* 1. A motor vehicle used to carry heavy loads. 2. Any of various wheeled devices used to move heavy loads. *—verb.* To move by truck. **trucked, trucking.**

[2]**truck** (TRUHK) *noun.* 1. (Informal) Dealings; association: Jim has no *truck* with liars. 2. Vegetables produced for sale.

trudge (TRUHJ) *verb.* To walk, especially wearily or with difficulty: *trudge* up the trail. **trudged, trudging.**

true (TROO) *adjective.* 1. In accord with reality or facts; not false. 2. Loyal; dependable. 3. Real; not pretended: *true* sorrow. 4. Genuine: Which is the *true* king? 5. Accurate, correct. **truer, truest.** *—adverb.* Correctly; accurately.

trumpet

tru·ly (TROO-lee) *adverb.* 1. Truthfully; correctly. 2. Really: "They're only *truly* great who are *truly* good." (George Chapman). 3. Sincerely.

trum·pet (TRUHM-pit) *noun.* 1. (Music) A brass wind instrument with a flared bell and three valves. 2. A sound like that of a trumpet: the *trumpet* of an elephant. 3. Something shaped like a trumpet. *—verb.* 1. To play a trumpet. 2. To make a loud, clear sound like that of a trumpet. 3. To announce loudly. **trumpeted, trumpeting.**

trun·dle (TRUHND-l) *verb.* To roll; move on wheels or rollers. **trundled, trundling.** *—noun.* A caster or roller; a tiny wheel.

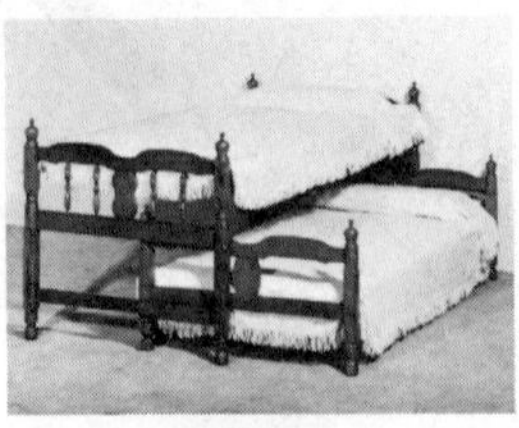
trundle bed

trundle bed. A bed on rollers that can be pushed under a higher bed.

trunk (TRUHNGK) *noun.* 1. A sturdy box or case in which things such as clothing are packed, as for travel or storage. 2. The main stem of a tree. 3. A long snout: an elephant's *trunk.* 4. The human body, not including the head, arms, or legs. 5. A storage compartment in an automobile. 6. (Plural) Short pants worn for athletic activities: swimming *trunks.* **—trunk line.** The most direct or main line in systems such as railroads or telephone switchboards.

truss (TRUHSS) *verb.* 1. To fasten tightly; tie up. 2. To bind (the body of a fowl) for cooking. **trussed, trussing.** *—noun.* 1. A belt-like device used to support a ruptured part of the body. 2. The supporting framework of a bridge or other structure. **trusses.**

trust (TRUHST) *noun.* 1. Faith or confidence in a person, thing, or belief. "In God is our *trust.*" (F. S. Key). 2. Care or charge: Mother left the baby in our *trust.* 3. The object cared for: The baby is our *trust.* 4. (Law) An arrangement by which property is held and managed for the benefit of another; the property itself. 5. Credit; confidence that another will pay. 6. A group of business companies under one management. *—verb.* 1. To have faith or confidence in. 2. To expect: I *trust* the letter will come today. 3. To believe: I *trust* his spelling of the word. 4. To give credit: The ice-cream salesman *trusts* me until tomorrow. 5. (Used with *in* or *to*) To depend on. **trusted, trusting.**

trus·tee (truhss-TEE) *noun.* A person or organization that holds and manages property for another.

trust·ful (TRUHST-fəl) *adjective.* Full of trust; believing. **—trustfully** *adverb.* **—trustfulness** *noun.*

trust·wor·thy (TRUHST-wer-thee) *adjective.* Reliable, dependable; able to be trusted. **—trustworthily** *adverb.* **—trustworthiness** *noun.*

trust·y (TRUHSS-tee) *adjective.* Dependable, reliable. **trustier, trustiest.** *—noun.* A prisoner given special privileges for good behavior.

truth (TROOTH) *noun.* 1. The facts; that which corresponds with actual happenings or events. 2. Honesty or sincerity. 3. A scientific law or accepted principle.

truth·ful (TROOTH-fəl) *adjective.* 1. Given to telling the truth: a *truthful* person. 2. Reliable; based on the truth: a *truthful* story. —**truthfulness** *noun.* —**truthfully** *adverb.*

try (TRIGH) *verb.* 1. To make an effort; attempt. 2. To hear or conduct a trial; place on trial. 3. To strain: Noisy children *try* their mothers' patience. 4. To test: "These are the times that *try* men's souls." (Thomas Paine). **tried, trying.** —*noun.* A trial, effort, or attempt. **tries.** —**try on.** To test by putting on: *Try on* these shoes. —**try out.** To take a test for a job or other activity: *try out* for a part in a play.

T-shirt (TEE-shert) *noun.* A knitted, short-sleeved pullover shirt without a collar.

tsp. *abbreviation.* Teaspoon, teaspoonful.

tsu·na·mi (tsu-NAH-mee) *noun.* A very large wave caused by an active volcano or an earthquake on the ocean floor. Sometimes called "tidal wave."

tub (TUHB) *noun.* 1. A round, open container for holding liquids or soft solids. 2. The amount such a container will hold: a *tub* of water. 3. Anything having a shape like a tub. 4. (Informal) An old or slow-moving boat. 5. A bathtub.

tu·ba (TOO-bə or TYOO-bə) *noun.* (Music) A bass horn; a brass wind instrument with a large bell-shaped end.

tube (TOOB or TYOOB) *noun.* 1. A long, hollow cylinder. 2. Anything shaped like a tube, such as certain organs in the body. 3. A tube-shaped collapsible container having a removable cap: Toothpaste and oil paints come in *tubes.* 4. A sealed, bulb-shaped part of electronic equipment: Lee De Forest invented the vacuum *tube.* 5. (Informal) Television: I saw the news on the *tube.* 6. A rubber air-filled casing used inside some tires. **tubes.** —**tubular** *adjective.*

tu·ber (TOO-bər or TYOO-bər) *noun.* The underground stem of certain plants: The potato is a *tuber.*

tu·ber·cu·lo·sis (tu-ber-kyə-LOH-siss) *noun.* A serious contagious lung disease. —**TB** *abbreviation.*

tub·ing (TOO-bing or TYOO-bing) *noun.* 1. A group or system of tubes. 2. A piece of tube. 3. Something in the shape of a tube.

tuck (TUHK) *noun.* A fold of material, usually stitched in place. —*verb.* 1. To make or sew a fold in material. 2. To put in a safe or out-of-the-way place: *Tuck* your money away. 3. To make secure by pushing the edge or ends in place: *Tuck* in your shirt tail. **tucked, tucking.** —**tuck in.** To put to bed.

Tues·day (TOOZ-dee) *noun.* The third day of the week: *Tuesday* is the day between Monday and Wednesday. —**Tues.** *abbreviation.*

tuft (TUHFT) *noun.* A small bunch of threads, feathers, hair, or such fastened at one end or growing closely together. —*verb.* 1. To decorate or trim with tufts of yarn or thread. 2. To fasten upholstery or quilted pieces with thread at various spots to hold the stuffing in place. **tufted, tufting.**

tug (TUHG) *verb.* 1. To pull hard. 2. To move by dragging or pulling. 3. To tow (a ship) with a tugboat. **tugged, tugging.** —*noun.* 1. A hard pull. 2. A tugboat. 3. A strong force: the *tug* of gravity.

tug·boat (TUHG-boht) *noun.* A small boat with powerful engines, used to move big ships in and out of ports.

T-shirt

tuba

tugboat

tunnel

turban

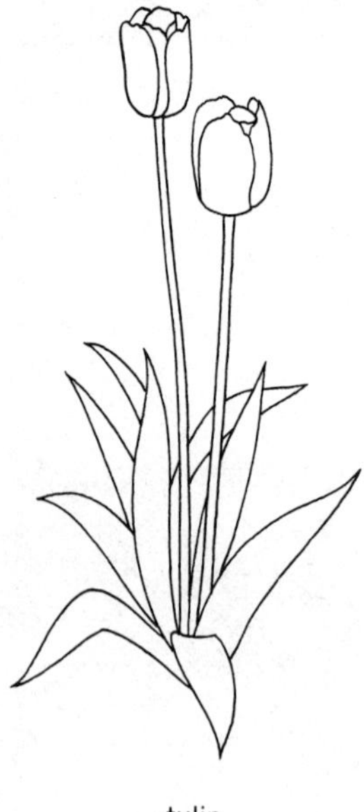
tulip

tug of war. A contest in which two teams pull on opposite ends of a rope, each side trying to pull the other across a middle line.

tu·i·tion (too-ISH-ən) *noun.* 1. The charge made for instruction at a college or private school. 2. Teaching or instruction.

tu·lip (TOO-lip) *noun.* A plant having upright, cup-shaped blossoms.

tum·ble (TUHM-bəl) *verb.* 1. To fall or cause to fall. 2. To do certain gymnastic acts such as somersaults and forward rolls. 3. To mix up or turn over and over: The dryer *tumbles* the clothes. 4. To spill or come out in a disorderly way. 5. (Informal) To catch on: *tumble* to a joke. **tumbled, tumbling.** —*noun.* A fall or spill.

tum·ble-down (TUHM-bəl-down) *adjective.* In need of repair.

tum·bler (TUHM-blər) *noun.* 1. An acrobat; one who does gymnastic tricks. 2. A drinking glass. 3. The movable part of a lock.

tum·ble·weed (TUHM-bəl-weed) *noun.* A plant whose upper branches split off and roll in the wind.

tu·mor (TOO-mər or TYOO-mər) *noun.* A useless and too rapid growth of body tissue.

tu·mult (TOO-məlt) *noun.* 1. The noise and confusion of a crowd. 2. A riot or uprising. 3. A disturbed state of mind or feeling. —**tumultuous** (tə-MUHL-choo-əss) *adjective.* —**tumultuously** *adverb.*

tu·na (TOO-nə) *noun.* A large saltwater food fish. —**tuna** or **tunas** *plural.*

tun·dra (TUHN-drə) *noun.* A treeless plain found in very cold regions of the world.

tune (TOON) *noun.* 1. A melody. 2. The right pitch: Try to sing in *tune.* 3. Agreement: Their plans are in *tune* with ours. **tunes.** —*verb.* 1. To adjust the pitch of: *tune* an instrument. 2. To put in good working order: *tune* an engine. **tuned, tuning.** —**change one's tune.** To change one's attitude or manner. —**to the tune of.** In the amount of. —**tune in.** To adjust a radio or TV set so as to receive a specific program or reach a specific channel or station.

tune-up (TOON-uhp) *noun.* The act of adjusting an engine to put it in good working order.

tung·sten (TUHNG-stən) *noun.* A rare, valuable metal: *Tungsten* makes steel stronger.

tu·nic (TOO-nik) *noun.* 1. A loose-fitting garment worn by ancient Greeks and Romans. 2. A long, straight blouse, usually belted.

tuning fork. A small metal instrument with two prongs, used in tuning musical instruments.

tun·nel (TUHN-l) *noun.* 1. An underground passage. 2. A passage or way through an obstacle, such as a mountain. —*verb.* 1. To make a tunnel. 2. To dig through or beneath something. **tunneled** or **tunnelled, tunneling** or **tunnelling.**

tur·ban (TER-bən) *noun.* 1. A Moslem head covering made by winding a long cloth or scarf around the head. 2. A hat that looks like a turban.

tur·bine (TER-bin) *noun.* 1. A wheel that is turned by the force of a liquid or gas pushing against it. 2. An engine operated by a turbine. **turbines.**

tur·bu·lent (TER-byə-lənt) *adjective.* 1. Full of violent motion or activity: The air is *turbulent* behind a jet plane. 2. Excited, unsettled. —**turbulence** *noun.* —**turbulently** *adverb.*

tu·reen (tu-REEN) *noun.* A large, covered serving dish used for soup or stew.

turf (TERF) *noun.* 1. A layer of earth containing grass and its roots; sod. 2. A racetrack. 3. (Slang) Home ground or territory.

tur·key (TER-kee) *noun.* 1. A large game bird with spreading tail, first found wild in America and now bred for its meat. 2. The meat of this bird: Let's have *turkey* for dinner. 3. (Slang) A person or thing that is a failure. —**talk turkey.** Speak plainly and frankly.

tur·moil (TER-moil) *noun.* State of agitation or commotion; confusion.

turn (TERN) *verb.* 1. To move or cause to move around a central point; rotate or revolve. 2. To change the setting of (a control): *turn* on the light. 3. To become or cause to become; to change: The caterpillar *turns* into a butterfly. 4. To change direction, position, or condition: "Do not *turn* back when you are just at the goal." (Publilius Syrus). 5. To injure by twisting: *turn* an ankle. 6. To make a rounded shape either with a tool or by hand. 7. (Used with *to*) To seek advice or comfort from. 8. (Used with *over*) To transfer. **turned, turning.** —*noun.* 1. A spin or rotation: a *turn* of the wheel. 2. A chance or opportunity: Your *turn* is next. 3. A change in direction, position, or condition: The patient took a *turn* for the better. 4. A surprise; a scare: The wolf howl gave us a *turn.* 5. An act or deed. —**turn down.** To reject or refuse. —**turn in.** 1. To go to bed. 2. To give up or return (an object). —**turn off.** (Slang) To be or cause to be uninterested or disgusted: That song *turns* me *off.* —**turn on.** (Slang) To be or cause to be interested or excited. —**turn out.** 1. To manufacture. 2. To prove to be or come to be. —**turn over in one's mind.** To think about; reflect. —**turn up.** To arrive.

tur·nip (TER-nip) *noun.* A yellowish-white plant root eaten as a vegetable.

turn·out (TERN-owt) *noun.* 1. The act of producing; that which is produced. 2. The number of people attending an event.

turn·over (TERN-oh-vər) *noun.* 1. A small pastry made by folding crust over a filling such as meat or jam. 2. The replacement of persons by others: The hotel has a big *turnover* of guests each week. 3. The amount of business done in a given time. 4. (Sports) The loss of the ball by one team to the other.

turn·pike (TERN-pighk) *noun.* A highway on which tolls are collected. **turnpikes.**

turn·stile (TERN-stighl) *noun.* A post, with four revolving arms, that serves as a gate. **turnstiles.**

tur·pen·tine (TER-pən-tighn) *noun.* 1. The thick, sticky sap of certain pine trees. 2. A clear liquid made from this sap, used to thin paint.

tur·quoise (TER-kwoiz) *noun.* 1. A blue-green stone valued as a gem. 2. (Also *adjective*) A light bluish-green color.

tur·ret (TER-it) *noun.* 1. A small tower. 2. The raised section of a tank, ship, or plane in which the gunner sits.

tur·tle (TERT-l) *noun.* An animal with scaly skin and a soft body covered with a hard shell. **turtles.**

tur·tle·neck (TERT-l-nek) *noun.* 1. A high collar that rolls or folds over and fits snugly around the neck. 2. A pullover with such a collar.

tusk (TUHSK) *noun.* A long, curved tooth (usually one of a pair) of an animal such as the elephant or walrus.

tus·sle (TUHSS-l) *noun.* A struggle or rough fight. **tussles.** —*verb.* To wrestle or struggle (with a person or problem): The boys *tussled* on the lawn. **tussled, tussling.**

turkey

turnpike

turrets

turtle

twins

tu·tor (TOO-tər or TYOO-tər) *verb.* To teach or coach privately. **tutored, tutoring.** —*noun.* A private teacher.

tux·e·do (tuhk-SEE-doh) *noun.* A man's semi-formal dress suit, usually black or dark blue, with satin lapels. —**tuxedos** *plural.*

TV (TEE-VEE) *abbreviation.* Television.

TV dinner. A dinner frozen in a tray, ready to be heated and served.

twain (TWAYN) *noun.* (Rare) Two.

twang *noun.* 1. A sharp, vibrant sound like that of a bowstring or violin string when plucked. 2. A sharp, nasal tone of voice. —*verb.* To make or cause a twang. **twanged, twanging.** —**twangy** *adjective.*

tweed *noun.* 1. A rough woolen fabric, woven in two or more colors. 2. (Plural) Clothes made of tweed.

twelfth *adjective.* Coming next after 11th; 12th. —*noun.* One of 12 equal parts.

twelve (TWELV) *noun* (and *adjective*). The cardinal number after 11 and before 13; 12.

twen·ti·eth (TWEN-tee-ith) *adjective.* Coming next after 19th; 20th. —*noun.* One of 20 equal parts.

twen·ty (TWEN-tee) *noun* (and *adjective*). The cardinal number after 19 and before 21; 20.

twice (TWYSS) *adverb.* 1. Two times. 2. Double: We need *twice* the power we have to move this stone.

twid·dle (TWID-l) *verb.* To twirl or turn in an aimless way: When Tom is thinking, he *twiddles* his thumbs. **twiddled, twiddling.**

twig *noun.* A small shoot that grows from the branch of a tree.

twi·light (TWIGH-light) *noun.* 1. The light of the sky between sunset and full darkness, or between full darkness and sunrise. 2. Partial darkness.

twin *noun.* 1. One of two persons born at the same birth. 2. Either one of two that are exactly or almost alike: Our house is the *twin* of the one next door. —*adjective.* 1. Born at the same birth. 2. Closely alike; identical.

twine (TWIGHN) *noun.* A strong cord made by twisting many threads together. —*verb.* 1. To twist or weave together. 2. To wind around and around, or in and out: Ivy *twines* up the wall. **twined, twining.**

twinge (TWINJ) *noun.* 1. A sudden, sharp pain that quickly goes away. 2. A brief, sharp feeling: a *twinge* of jealousy. **twinges.** —*verb.* To feel such a pain. **twinged, twinging.**

twin·kle (TWING-kəl) *verb.* 1. To shine or gleam with quick flashes; to sparkle; to flicker: "*Twinkle, twinkle,* little star. . . ." (Ann Taylor). 2. To gleam or sparkle: Uncle Bill's eyes *twinkled* as he told his joke. **twinkled, twinkling.** —*noun.* 1. A sparkle: the *twinkle* of lights from the town. 2. A gleam of amusement, as in the eyes.

twirl (TWERL) *verb.* 1. To turn round and round quickly and lightly; spin. 2. To turn suddenly and face the opposite direction. 3. To twine or twist around. **twirled, twirling.** —*noun.* A quick, light turning; a spin. —**twirler** *noun.*

twist *verb.* 1. To turn with a winding motion: To open the door, just *twist* the knob. 2. To twine; wreathe: To make a rope, *twist* pieces of string together. 3. To bend; curve. 4. To change or distort the meaning of: He *twisted* my statement to make it seem silly. 5. To force out of shape: Joe's face was *twisted* with fear. **twisted, twisting.** —*noun.* 1. A winding or twining. 2. A bend, curve, or turn. 3. A change or distortion, as of meaning or shape.

twist·er (TWISS-tər) *noun.* (Informal) A tornado.

twitch (TWICH) *verb.* To make, or cause to make, a short, quick motion, or jerk. **twitched, twitching.** —*noun.* A short, quick motion; a jerk. **twitches.**

twit·ter (TWIT-ər) *verb.* 1. To utter a series of quick, light sounds, as those of a bird; chirp. 2. To flutter or tremble excitedly. **twittered, twittering.** —*noun.* 1. A chirping noise: the *twitter* of swallows. 2. A state of trembling excitement. 3. High-pitched, light laughter or talk.

two (TOO) *noun* (and *adjective*). The cardinal number after one and before three; 2. —**put two and two together.** To draw a conclusion correctly from known facts.

two-bit (TOO-bit) *adjective.* 1. (Informal) Worth two bits (25¢). 2. (Slang) Small in size, worth, or importance.

two-faced (TOO-fayst) *adjective.* 1. Having two faces. 2. Dishonest; not genuine or straightforward.

two·fold (TOO-fohld) *adjective.* 1. Made up of two; double: *twofold* reason. 2. Two times as many; twice as large. —*adverb.* To twice the extent; doubly.

two·some (TOO-səm) *noun.* A couple; two together. **twosomes.**

two-way (TOO-way) *adjective.* 1. Allowing movement or communication in two directions: a *two-way* radio. 2. Involving an exchange between two: a *two-way* relationship.

-ty *suffix.* Indicates: 1. A state or quality: falsi*ty*. 2. Ten times: seven*ty*.

type (TIGHP) *noun.* 1. A group or class of persons or things of a similar kind: the tall, thin *type.* 2. Letters, numbers, and other characters printed or typewritten on paper or some other surface: The *type* on this page is large enough to read easily. 3. (Printing) The piece of metal, plastic, film, or wood bearing the character or characters that are to be printed. —*verb.* 1. To typewrite: *type* a manuscript. 2. To determine the nature or character of: to *type* blood. **typed, typing.**

type·writ·er (TIGHP-right-ər) *noun.* A small hand-operated printing machine having keys that cause letters, numbers, and symbols to be printed on paper. —**typewrite** *verb.* To write with a typewriter.

typewriter

ty·phoid (TIGH-foid) *noun.* A serious, infectious disease caused by germs in food or drink, resulting in high fever and other disorders; also called "typhoid fever."

ty·phoon (tigh-FOON) *noun.* A hurricane, especially one in the western Pacific Ocean.

typ·i·cal (TIP-i-kəl) *adjective.* Characteristic of a certain group or class; of a certain type: Dick is a *typical* athlete; he is strong and competitive. —**typically** *adverb.*

typ·i·fy (TIP-ə-figh) *verb.* To be typical or characteristic of; show all the traits or qualities of. **typified, typifying.**

typ·ist (TIGHP-ist) *noun.* One who operates a typewriter.

ty·ran·no·saur (ti-RAN-ə-sor or tigh-RAN-ə-sor) Also **tyrannosaurus** *noun.* A large flesh-eating dinosaur that walked on its hind legs.

tyrannosaur skeletons

tyr·an·ny (TIR-ə-nee) *noun.* 1. Absolute, harsh, and unjust rule by a king or other authority: Dictatorship is a modern form of *tyranny.* 2. Complete control, particularly when it is harsh or brutal. —**tyrannical** (ti-RAN-i-kəl) *adjective.* —**tyrannically** *adverb.*

tyr·an·nize (TIR-ə-nighz) *verb.* To control or rule completely, often harshly. **tyrannized, tyrannizing.**

ty·rant (TIGH-rənt) *noun.* 1. A ruler who exercises complete control or authority; a cruel ruler. 2. Anyone who dominates other persons cruelly or unfairly.

umbrella

ukulele

U, u (YOO) *noun.* The 21st letter of the English alphabet.

ud·der (UHD-ər) *noun.* The milk-producing organ of some female animals such as cows.

UFO *abbreviation.* Unidentified flying object.

ugh *interjection.* A sound used to indicate dislike or disgust.

ug·ly (UHG-lee) *adjective.* 1. Unpleasant or unattractive in appearance. 2. Displeasing; offensive: an *ugly* sneer. 3. Dangerous: an *ugly* temper. **uglier, ugliest.**

UHF *abbreviation.* (Radio and TV) Ultra-high frequency.

u·ku·le·le (yoo-kə-LAY-lee) *noun.* A musical instrument, originally of Hawaii, that looks like a small guitar with four strings. **ukuleles.**

ul·cer (UHL-sər) *noun.* An inflamed sore on the skin or mucous membrane: a stomach *ulcer.*

ul·ti·mate (UHL-tə-mit) *adjective.* 1. Ending; final: the *ultimate* decision. 2. Most; maximum; highest: the *ultimate* level of achievement. 3. Basic; fundamental: *ultimate* truth. —**ultimately** *adverb.*

ultra- *prefix.* Indicates: ahead; above; beyond: *ultra*modern.

ul·tra·son·ics (uhl-trə-SON-iks) *noun, plural.* The science of sound at frequencies higher than 20,000 vibrations per second, too high for the human ear to hear. —**ultrasonic** *adjective.*

ultraviolet ray. A ray of light below the violet end of the color spectrum with a wavelength so short that the light is invisible to the human eye.

umbilical cord (uhm-BIL-i-kəl). The cordlike structure that joins an unborn baby to his mother and serves to supply food to the baby.

um·brel·la (uhm-BREL-ə) *noun.* A folding frame covered with cloth or plastic, to hold or place above the head as protection from rain or sun.

um·pire (UHM-pighr) *noun.* 1. (Sports) One who rules on plays in a game. 2. One with power to judge or settle an argument or dispute. **umpires.** —*verb.* To act as an umpire. **umpired, umpiring.**

UN, Also **U.N.** *abbreviation.* United Nations.

un- *prefix.* Indicates: 1. Not; the opposite of: *un*believable. 2. The opposite or reverse of an act: *un*do; *un*wind. 3. Lack of: *un*rest.

un·able (uhn-AY-bəl) *adjective.* Not having the ability or power.

un·a·bridged (uhn-ə-BRIJD) *adjective.* Not shortened; of the original size or length: an *unabridged* dictionary.

un·ac·count·a·ble (uhn-ə-KOWN-tə-bəl) *adjective.* 1. Without explanation; mysterious. 2. Not at fault or responsible. —**unaccountably** *adverb.*

un·ac·cus·tomed (uhn-ə-KUHSS-təmd) *adjective.* 1. Not in the habit of; not used to: Jim was shy and *unaccustomed* to speaking up in class. 2. Not familiar or ordinary: an *unaccustomed* route.

u·nan·i·mous (yoo-NAN-ə-məss) *adjective.* 1. Agreed to by all: a *unanimous* decision. 2. In full agreement: The court was *unanimous* in its decision. —**unanimity** (yoo-nə-NIM-ə-tee) *noun.* —**unanimously** *adverb.*

un·armed (uhn-AHRMD) *adjective.* Having no weapons.

un·as·sum·ing (uhn-ə-SOO-ming) *adjective.* Not showy; modest.

un·a·void·a·ble (uhn-ə-VOID-ə-bəl) *adjective.* Not possible to miss, or by-pass: an *unavoidable* accident. —**unavoidably** *adverb.*

un·a·ware (uhn-ə-WAIR) *adjective.* Not alert; not realizing.

un·a·wares (uhn-ə-WAIRZ) *adverb.* By surprise: We were taken *unawares* when guests arrived early.

un·bear·a·ble (uhn-BAIR-ə-bəl) *adjective.* Not possible to endure: *unbearable* pain. —**unbearably** *adverb.*

un·be·com·ing (uhn-bi-KUHM-ing) *adjective.* 1. Unattractive: Shorts are *unbecoming* on some people. 2. Not polite, proper, or suitable for: conduct *unbecoming* an officer. —**unbecomingly** *adverb.*

un·be·liev·a·ble (uhn-bi-LEEV-ə-bəl) *adjective.* Hard to accept; not to be believed: an *unbelievable* story. —**unbelievably** *adverb.*

un·born (uhn-BORN) *adjective.* In the process of developing; not yet born.

un·bound·ed (uhn-BOWN-did) *adjective.* Without limits or bounds.

un·bro·ken (uhn-BROH-kən) *adjective.* 1. Without a break; whole. 2. Without interruption. 3. Not able to be harnessed; wild: an *unbroken* horse.

un·buck·le (uhn-BUHK-əl) *verb.* To unfasten or loosen the buckle of. **unbuckled, unbuckling.**

un·but·ton (uhn-BUHT-n) *verb.* To undo the buttons of. **unbuttoned, unbuttoning.**

un·called-for (uhn-KAWLD-for) *adjective.* 1. Not necessary or needed: The gifts were *uncalled-for* but appreciated. 2. Unfair or improper: *uncalled-for* complaints.

un·can·ny (uhn-KAN-ee) *adjective.* 1. Odd; strange: an *uncanny* feeling. 2. Strong; keen; exceptional: an *uncanny* ability.

un·cer·tain (uhn-SERT-n) *adjective.* 1. Not known. 2. Not sure; undecided. 3. Hard to predict: The weather is *uncertain.* —**uncertainly** *adverb.* —**uncertainty** *noun.*

un·changed (uhn-CHAYNJD) *adjective.* The same; having nothing new or different.

un·civ·i·lized (uhn-SIV-ə-lyzd) *adjective.* 1. Without an established social and cultural way of living. 2. Without culture or refinement.

un·cle (UHNG-kəl) *noun.* 1. The brother of one's mother or father. 2. An aunt's husband. **uncles.**

un·clean (uhn-KLEEN) *adjective.* 1. Dirty. 2. Immoral, not decent.

un·com·fort·a·ble (uhn-KUHM-fər-tə-bəl) *adjective.* 1. Disturbed; not at ease physically: The pea under her mattress made the princess very *uncomfortable.* 2. Not at ease mentally: His stare made us *uncomfortable.* —**uncomfortably** *adverb.*

un·com·mon (uhn-KOM-ən) *adjective.* Unusual; odd, rare, extraordinary. —**uncommonly** *adverb.*

un·com·pro·mis·ing (uhn-KOM-prə-migh-zing) *adjective.* Firm, unbending: *uncompromising* attitude.

un·con·cerned (uhn-kən-SERND) *adjective.* 1. Not concerned; not interested. 2. Not worried or upset. —**unconcernedly** (uhn-kən-SER-nid-lee) *adverb.*

un·con·di·tion·al (uhn-kən-DISH-ən-l) *adjective.* Without any limits or conditions: *unconditional* surrender. —**unconditionally** *adverb.*

un·con·scious (uhn-KON-shəss) *adjective.* 1. Not mentally aware: *unconscious* of danger. 2. In a sleep-like state: He was hit on the head and knocked *unconscious.* 3. Not done on purpose; without thought: It was an *unconscious* reaction. —**unconsciously** *adverb.* —**unconsciousness** *noun.*

un·con·sti·tu·tion·al (uhn-kon-stə-TOO-shən-l) *adjective.* Not provided for or in agreement with a constitution.

un·couth (uhn-KOOTH) *adjective.* 1. Crude; ill-mannered: an *uncouth* remark. 2. Not graceful; clumsy. —**uncouthly** *adverb.*

un·cov·er (uhn-KUHV-ər) *verb.* 1. To remove a lid, top, or cover from. 2. To expose; make known; reveal: Jim Hawkins *uncovered* Long John Silver's plot to mutiny. **uncovered, uncovering.**

un·de·cid·ed (uhn-di-SIGHD-id) *adjective.* 1. Having made no decision. 2. Not settled; open to change. —**undecidedly** *adverb.*

un·de·ni·a·ble (uhn-di-NIGH-ə-bəl) *adjective.* Not possible to contradict; true. —**undeniably** *adverb.*

un·der (UHN-dər) *preposition.* 1. Below in position or place: *under* the covers. 2. Using the disguise of; hidden by: *under* the cover of darkness. 3. Below the top or surface of: *under* the water. 4. Less in degree or amount: *under* ten dollars. 5. Lower than in rank or quality; below in authority: A private is *under* a sergeant. 6. Because of: *under* the circumstances. 7. In a classification or listing: You will find the book listed *under* "Fiction." 8. Subject to or getting the effects of: *under* a doctor's care. —*adverb.* 1. In or into a lower place or position. 2. In a way so as to be covered or surrounded: The wave crashed and swept me *under.* —*adjective.* Lower in place, level, rank, or position.

under- *prefix.* Indicates: 1. Below: *under*ground. 2. Lower in rank or importance: *under*secretary. 3. Lower in amount or degree: *under*privileged.

un·der·brush (UHN-dər-bruhsh) *noun.* Bushes, plants, and vines that grow under tall trees.

un·der·clothes (UHN-dər-klohz) *noun, plural.* The clothes worn next to the body; underwear.

un·der·de·vel·oped (uhn-dər-di-VEL-əpt) *adjective.* 1. Not fully grown; not mature. 2. Lacking modern industry and communications: an *underdeveloped* nation.

un·der·foot (uhn-dər-FUT) *adjective.* 1. Below the feet; underneath: It was muddy *underfoot.* 2. In the way: Our son's dog is always *underfoot.*

un·der·gar·ment (UHN-dər-gahr-mənt) *noun.* A piece of clothing worn under other clothing; underwear.

un·der·go (uhn-dər-GOH) *verb.* To have the experience of: *undergo* an operation. **underwent, undergone, undergoing.**

un·der·ground (UHN-dər-grownd) *adjective* and *adverb.* 1. Beneath the earth's surface: an *underground* tunnel. 2. Secret; hidden: an *underground* organization. 3. Not officially approved or recognized: an *underground* newspaper. —*noun.* 1. A secret organization, usually opposing existing laws or government. 2. A train operating under the streets; a subway system.

Underground Railroad. A system, used in the United States in the 1800's, to help slaves escape to freedom in the North or in Canada.

un·der·growth (UHN-dər-grohth) *noun.* Plants, bushes, and shrubs under trees; underbrush.

un·der·hand·ed (uhn-dər-HAN-did) *adjective.* Sly; sneaky: an *underhanded* trick. —**underhandedly** *adverb.*

un·der·line (UHN-dər-lighn) *verb.* To draw a line under. **underlined, underlining.**

un·der·mine (uhn-dər-MIGHN) *verb.* To make less strong; weaken: His criticisms *undermined* our enthusiasm. **undermined, undermining.**

un·der·neath (uhn-dər-NEETH) *adverb.* 1. Below; beneath. 2. On the lower or under side. *—preposition.* Below; under.

un·der·pass (UHN-dər-pass) *noun.* A road or walk that goes under another road or railroad tracks.

un·der·priv·i·leged (uhn-dər-PRIV-ə-lijd) *adjective.* Lacking social and economic advantages.

un·der·rate (uhn-dər-RAYT) *verb.* To value below true worth. **underrated, underrating.**

un·der·shirt (UHN-dər-shert) *noun.* A shirt worn between the skin and another shirt.

un·der·side (UHN-dər-sighd) *noun.* The part or side underneath.

un·der·stand (uhn-dər-STAND) *verb.* 1. To realize or comprehend; know completely. 2. To know the thoughts and feelings of: My teacher doesn't *understand* me! 3. To be informed: I *understand* you are going away. **understood, understanding.**

un·der·stand·a·ble (uhn-dər-STAND-ə-bəl) *adjective.* Able to be comprehended or sympathized with: Being nervous before a test is *understandable.* **—understandably** *adverb.*

un·der·stand·ing (uhn-dər-STAN-ding) *noun.* 1. The ability to learn, detect, know, or sympathize. 2. Comprehension: It is my *understanding* that you are interested in sports. 3. An agreement: Brian and Tim came to an *understanding* about their problem.

un·der·state (uhn-dər-STAYT) *verb.* To make too little of; play down: *understate* a difficulty. **understated, understating.**

un·der·stud·y (UHN-dər-stuhd-ee) *verb.* 1. To learn the lines of an actor playing a role in order to be able to replace him. 2. To be an understudy to. **understudied, understudying.** *—noun.* One who learns the same part as another. **understudies.**

un·der·take (uhn-dər-TAYK) *verb.* To decide or agree to (do): Dad will *undertake* the raising of funds. **undertook, undertaking, —undertaking** *noun.*

un·der·tak·er (UHN-dər-tay-kər) *noun.* A person who prepares the dead for burial and assists at funerals.

un·der·tone (UHN-dər-tohn) *noun.* 1. A low tone of voice. 2. A partly hidden feeling: There was an *undertone* of anger in Herman's voice. 3. A color seen through other colors. **undertones.**

un·der·tow (UHN-dər-toh) *noun.* A strong current below and opposed to the surface current of the sea.

un·der·wa·ter (UHN-dər-waw-tər) *adjective.* Happening, done, or used under water: *underwater* exploration.

un·der·wear (UHN-dər-wair) *noun.* Clothes worn next to the skin under other clothing.

un·der·went (uhn-dər-WENT) *verb.* *See* **undergo.**

un·de·sir·a·ble (uhn-di-ZIGHR-ə-bəl) *adjective.* Not wanted; offensive: an *undesirable* taste. **—undesirably** *adverb.*

un·do (uhn-DOO) *verb.* 1. To annul; to reverse; cancel: ". . . the power to *undo* the past." (Aristotle). 2. To untie; to free: *undo* a knot. 3. To bring to harm; to ruin. 4. To open: *undo* a package. **undid, undone, undoing.**

un·done (uhn-DUHN) *adjective.* 1. Not finished or done. 2. Brought to harm. 3. Untied; free; open.

un·doubt·ed (uhn-DOWT-id) *adjective.* Held as true. **—undoubtedly** *adverb.*

un·dress (uhn-DRESS) *verb.* To take off clothing. **undressed, undressing.**

un·due (uhn-DOO or uhn-DYOO) *adjective.* 1. Too much: *undue* praise. 2. Not fair; illegal: *undue* punishment. **—unduly** *adverb.*

un·du·late (UHN-ju-layt) *verb.* To move with a flowing motion like a wave: The field of wheat *undulated* in the wind. **undulated, undulating.**

un·dy·ing (uhn-DIGH-ing) *adjective.* Without end; timeless: *undying* devotion.

un·earth (uhn-ERTH) *verb.* 1. To dig up: *unearth* a fossil. 2. To find out by study or search: *unearth* the facts. **unearthed, unearthing.**

un·earth·ly (uhn-ERTH-lee) *adjective.* 1. Apparently not from the earth: an *unearthly* being. 2. Frightening: an *unearthly* scream. 3. Strange; odd: an *unearthly* hairdo.

un·eas·y (uhn-EEZ-ee) *adjective.* Uncomfortable; nervous; disturbed; anxious. —**uneasily** *adverb.* —**uneasiness** *noun.*

un·em·ployed (uhn-em-PLOID) *adjective.* Without work; not having a job. —**unemployment** *noun.*

un·e·qual (uhn-EE-kwəl) *adjective.* 1. Not fair; not even: *unequal* treatment. 2. Not of the same size, time, or amount. 3. (Used with *to*) Not strong or able enough for: *unequal* to a job. —**unequally** *adverb.*

un·e·ven (uhn-EE-vən) *adjective.* 1. Not equal: The lengths of rope were *uneven.* 2. Slanted or bumpy; not level: an *uneven* surface. 3. Unable to be divided evenly by two; odd (said of numbers). —**unevenly** *adverb.* —**unevenness** *noun.*

un·ex·pect·ed (uhn-ik-SPEK-tid) *adjective.* Surprising; arriving or happening without warning: *unexpected* visitors. —**unexpectedly** *adverb.*

un·fail·ing (uhn-FAYL-ing) *adjective.* Unchanging; constant: *unfailing* good humor. —**unfailingly** *adverb.*

un·fair (uhn-FAIR) *adjective.* 1. Unjust; favoring one more than another. 2. Not honest. —**unfairly** *adverb.* —**unfairness** *noun.*

un·faith·ful (uhn-FAYTH-fəl) *adjective.* Not fulfilling a promise or an agreement; without loyalty. —**unfaithfully** *adverb.* —**unfaithfulness** *noun.*

un·fa·mil·iar (uhn-fə-MIL-yər) *adjective.* 1. Foreign; not well known: *unfamiliar* territory. 2. Without knowledge: I am *unfamiliar* with French. —**unfamiliarity** *noun.* —**unfamiliarly** *adverb.*

un·fas·ten (uhn-FASS-n) *verb.* To disconnect; to free or loose: *unfasten* a latch. **unfastened, unfastening.**

un·fa·vor·a·ble (uhn-FAY-vər-ə-bəl) *adjective.* 1. Not good or advantageous: *unfavorable* weather. 2. Opposing: an *unfavorable* vote. —**unfavorably** *adverb.*

un·feel·ing (uhn-FEE-ling) *adjective.* Without sympathy; hardhearted. —**unfeelingly** *adverb.*

un·fit (uhn-FIT) *adjective.* 1. Not qualified; not suitable. 2. In poor physical condition. 3. Not fitting or proper: an *unfit* remark.

un·fold (uhn-FOHLD) *verb.* 1. To open out: *Unfold* the map. 2. To show or reveal gradually. **unfolded, unfolding.**

un·fore·seen (uhn-for-SEEN) *adjective.* Not expected: *unforeseen* problems.

un·for·get·ta·ble (uhn-fər-GET-ə-bəl) *adjective.* Hard or impossible to forget: an *unforgettable* experience. —**unforgettably** *adverb.*

un·for·tu·nate (uhn-FOR-chə-nit) *adjective.* 1. To be regretted; causing bad luck, damage, or harm: an *unfortunate* accident. 2. Having little or no luck: Job was an *unfortunate* man. —*noun.* A person who has little or no luck. **unfortunates.** —**unfortunately** *adverb.*

un·found·ed (uhn-FOWN-did) *adjective.* Not based or founded on facts.

un·friend·ly (uhn-FREND-lee) *adjective.* 1. Cold toward others: an *unfriendly* person. 2. Showing a lack of kindness: an *unfriendly* act. **unfriendlier, unfriendliest.**

un·furl (uhn-FERL) *verb.* To unroll or unfold; open out: *unfurl* a flag. **unfurled, unfurling.**

un·fur·nished (uhn-FER-nisht) *adjective.* Without furniture: an *unfurnished* apartment.

un·gain·ly (uhn-GAYN-lee) *adjective.* Awkward; without grace. **ungainlier, ungainliest.**

un·glued (uhn-GLOOD) *adjective.* (Slang) Very upset emotionally.

un·god·ly (uhn-GOD-lee) *adjective.* 1. Evil; wicked. 2. (Informal) Unbearable; very bad: an *ungodly* mess.

un·grate·ful (uhn-GRAYT-fəl) *adjective.* Not thankful; not showing appreciation. **—ungratefully** *adverb.*

un·guent (UHNG-gwənt) *noun.* A soothing or healing salve.

un·hand (uhn-HAND) *verb.* To free; take one's hands from. **unhanded, unhanding.**

un·hap·py (uhn-HAP-ee) *adjective.* 1. Sad; without joy or laughter. 2. Unlucky: an *unhappy* day. 3. Not appropriate or tactful: an *unhappy* remark. **unhappier, unhappiest. —unhappily** *adverb.* **—unhappiness** *noun.*

un·health·y (uhn-HEL-thee) *adjective.* 1. Bad for one's health: Smoking is *unhealthy.* 2. In poor health. 3. Morally dangerous: *unhealthy* companions. **unhealthier, unhealthiest. —unhealthily** *adverb.* **—unhealthiness** *noun.*

un·heard (uhn-HERD) *adjective.* Not heard or listened to.

un·heard-of (uhn-HERD-uhv) *adjective.* Not done or known before: The Wizard came from the *unheard-of* Land of Oz.

un·hitch (uhn-HICH) *verb.* To untie or unfasten: *Unhitch* the trailer from the car. **unhitched, unhitching.**

un·hook (uhn-HUK) *verb.* To undo the hooks of. **unhooked, unhooking.**

u·ni·corn (YOO-nə-korn) *noun.* A mythical animal, usually drawn as a horse with a horn in the center of its forehead.

unicorn

u·ni·cy·cle (YOO-ni-sigh-kəl) *noun.* A one-wheeled vehicle driven by pushing on pedals. **unicycles.**

unicycle

u·ni·form (YOO-nə-form) *noun.* Identical clothing worn by all the members of a group: a football *uniform.* *—adjective.* The same throughout: a *uniform* design. **—uniformity** (yoo-nə-FOR-mə-tee) *noun.* **—uniformly** *adverb.*

u·ni·fy (YOO-nə-figh) *verb.* To bring or come together as one unit. **unified, unifying.**

un·in·hab·it·ed (uhn-in-HAB-ə-tid) *adjective.* Empty; not lived in.

un·ion (YOON-yən) *noun.* 1. The joining together of two or more things or groups. 2. The result of such joining: a *union* of states. 3. A group of countries joined under one government: the *Union* of South Africa. 4. A marriage. 5. An organization of workers who bargain collectively for better wages and working conditions. 6. A college building that provides facilities for meals, recreation, and other student activities. 7. [Capital U] The United States, especially the federal government at the time of the Civil War.

u·nique (yoo-NEEK) *adjective.* 1. Unlike any other. 2. Having no equal. **—uniquely** *adverb.*

u·ni·son (YOO-nə-sn) *noun.* 1. (Music) Exact sameness of pitch, as of a tone. 2. Harmony; agreement. **—in unison.** As one; all together.

u·nit (YOO-nit) *noun.* 1. One of the parts into which a larger whole can be divided: A syllable is a *unit* of a word. 2. A special part or section, as of a machine: the phonograph *unit* of a stereo set. 3. An exact measurement of amount: An inch is a *unit* of length. 4. One. 5. (Math) The number to the left of the decimal point. 6. A group within a larger group: a *unit* of soldiers.

u·nite (yoo-NIGHT) *verb.* 1. To join or come together as one body; unify. 2. To join or come together in spirit or action: Working together *united* the class. **united, uniting.**

u·ni·ty (YOO-nə-tee) *noun.* 1. The condition or state of being or acting as one. 2. Agreement or harmony.

u·ni·valve (YOO-ni-valv) *noun.* A mollusk with a one-piece shell, such as a snail.

u·ni·ver·sal (yoo-nə-VER-sl) *adjective.* 1. Having to do with the entire world or universe. 2. Affecting or reaching everyone and everything: *universal* peace and good will. —**universally** *adverb.*

u·ni·verse (YOO-nə-verss) *noun.* Everything that exists; the world; the heavens, stars, space, planets, and all they contain.

u·ni·ver·si·ty (yoo-nə-VER-sə-tee) *noun.* 1. An educational institution for advanced studies, having various colleges and awarding a variety of degrees. 2. The buildings, students, and faculty of a university. **universi-ties.**

un·just (uhn-JUHST) *adjective.* Not fair. —**unjustly** *adverb.*

un·kempt (uhn-KEMPT) *adjective.* Messy; poorly groomed; untidy.

un·kind (uhn-KYND) *adjective.* Harsh; lacking good will; thoughtless of others. **unkinder, unkindest.** —**unkindly** *adverb.* —**unkindness** *noun.*

un·known (uhn-NOHN) *adjective.* 1. Unidentified; not known: an *unknown* person. 2. Not famous: an *unknown* poet. —*noun.* 1. That which remains hidden or unable to be seen or known. 2. (Math) An amount whose value is not known; the symbol for such an amount, often *x*, *y*, or *z*.

un·lace (uhn-LAYSS) *verb.* To untie or loosen the strings or laces of. **unlaced, unlacing.**

un·law·ful (uhn-LAW-fəl) *adjective.* Not in accord with the law; illegal. —**unlawfully** *adverb.*

un·less (uhn-LESS) *conjunction.* If it is not a fact that: I won't play *unless* I can be captain.

un·like (uhn-LIGHK) *preposition.* 1. Different from; not the same as: Noisy Jan is *unlike* her quiet sister. 2. Not usual for: It is *unlike* Jan to be sad. —*adjective.* 1. Different: as *unlike* as rain and shine. 2. Unequal, as in ability.

un·like·ly (uhn-LIGHK-lee) *adjective.* Not probable; doubtful. **unliklier, unlikliest.**

un·lim·it·ed (uhn-LIM-i-tid) *adjective.* Without bounds or limitations: *unlimited* time.

un·load (uhn-LOHD) *verb.* 1. To remove (merchandise or supplies) from a truck or other transport. 2. To get rid of. **unloaded, unload-ing.**

un·lock (uhn-LOK) *verb.* 1. To release or unfasten a lock; open with a key. 2. To make free or let go. 3. To find a solution or key to: Nancy tried to *unlock* the mystery. **unlocked, unlocking.**

un·looked-for (uhn-LUKT-for) *adjective.* Not expected; surprising.

un·loose (uhn-LOOSS) *verb.* To undo or loosen; make less tight; release. **unloosed, unloosing.**

un·luck·y (uhn-LUHK-ee) *adjective.* 1. Having bad fortune or bad luck. 2. Brought on by bad luck: an *unlucky* accident. **unluckier, unlucki-est.** —**unluckily** *adverb.*

un·manned (uhn-MAND) *adjective.* Containing no people: an *unmanned* spacecraft.

un·mis·tak·a·ble (uhn-miss-TAYK-ə-bəl) *adjective.* Very clearly seen or understood; obvious: *unmistakable* evidence. —**unmistakably** *adverb.*

un·moved (uhn-MUVD) *adjective.* 1. Showing or having no change of emotion or thought. 2. In the same place; not changed or moved.

un·nat·u·ral (uhn-NACH-ə-rəl) *adjective.* 1. Abnormal; not usual or natural. 2. Evil or perverse; strange. 3. Affected; artificial: *unnatural* manners. —**unnaturally** *adverb.*

un·nec·es·sar·y (uhn-NESS-ə-sehr-ee) *adjective.* 1. Not needed. 2. Not appropriate: *unnecessary* rudeness. —**unnecessarily** (uhn-ness-ə-SEHR-ə-lee) *adverb.*

un·nerve (uhn-NERV) *verb.* To upset; frighten. **unnerved, unnerving.**

un·num·bered (uhn-NUHM-bərd) *adjective.* 1. Not identified by number: The seats are *unnumbered.* 2. Too many to count: *unnumbered* stars.

un·of·fi·cial (uhn-ə-FISH-əl) *adjective.* Not authorized or formal; not official. —**unofficially** *adverb.*

un·pack (uhn-PAK) *verb.* 1. To take things out of (suitcases, trunks, boxes, or the like). 2. To empty, as a suitcase. **unpacked, unpacking.**

un·par·al·leled (uhn-PA-rə-leld) *adjective.* Unique; having no equal.

un·pleas·ant (uhn-PLEZ-nt) *adjective.* Not agreeable; displeasing. —**unpleasantly** *adverb.*

un·pop·u·lar (uhn-POP-yə-lər) *adjective.* Not well liked; not favored or approved of. —**unpopularity** (uhn-pop-yə-LA-rə-tee) *noun.*

un·pre·dict·a·ble (uhn-pri-DIK-tə-bəl) *adjective.* Not possible to foretell; not certain or reliable.

un·pre·pared (uhn-pri-PAIRD) *adjective.* Not ready or equipped.

un·prin·ci·pled (uhn-PRIN-sə-pəld) *adjective.* Without standards, morals, or any such guiding principles.

un·ques·tion·a·ble (uhn-KWESS-chən-ə-bəl) *adjective.* With no doubt or question; definite. —**unquestionably** *adverb.*

un·rav·el (uhn-RAV-əl) *verb.* 1. To undo work such as knitting or weaving. 2. To solve or make (a mystery) clear. **unraveled** or **unravelled, unraveling** or **unravelling.**

un·real (uhn-REE-əl) *adjective.* 1. Imaginary or fanciful; not real. 2. (Slang) Unbelievable or fantastic; unusual. —**unreality** (uhn-ree-AL-ə-tee) *noun.*

un·rea·son·a·ble (uhn-REE-zn-ə-bəl) *adjective.* 1. More than is right or reasonable; too much: an *unreasonable* amount. 2. Not having or showing sense or clear thought: When Joe is angry, he is *unreasonable.* —**unreasonably** *adverb.*

un·re·li·a·ble (uhn-ri-LIGH-ə-bəl) *adjective.* Not dependable.

un·re·served (uhn-ri-ZERVD) *adjective.* 1. Outspoken; open, not quiet: *unreserved* anger. 2. With nothing held back: *unreserved* approval. —**unreservedly** (uhn-ri-ZER-vid-lee) *adverb.*

un·rest (uhn-REST) *noun.* 1. Commotion; confusion or disorder. 2. Nervous uneasiness.

un·ri·valed (uhn-RIGH-vəld) *adjective.* Without competition; having no equal.

un·roll (uhn-ROHL) *verb.* 1. To roll out flat; undo (a roll). 2. To show or reveal. **unrolled, unrolling.**

un·ruf·fled (uhn-RUHF-əld) *adjective.* Calm and composed; not upset.

un·ru·ly (uhn-ROO-lee) *adjective.* Disorderly; hard to make behave: An *unruly* class makes learning difficult.

un·safe (uhn-SAYF) *adjective.* Dangerous. —**unsafely** *adverb.*

un·san·i·tar·y (uhn-SAN-ə-tehr-ee) *adjective.* Not clean or free from germs.

un·sat·is·fac·to·ry (uhn-sat-iss-FAK-tə-ree) *adjective.* Not pleasing; disappointing; unacceptable: an *unsatisfactory* grade on a test. —**unsatisfactorily** *adverb.*

un·schooled (uhn-SKOOLD) *adjective.* 1. Without education or training. 2. Coming naturally, not from instruction: an *unschooled* talent for drawing.

un·screw (uhn-SKROO) *verb.* 1. To unfasten by removing the screws from. 2. To take out or off with a turning motion: *Unscrew* the old light bulb and put in a new one. **unscrewed, unscrewing.**

un·scru·pu·lous (uhn-SKROO-pyə-ləss) *adjective.* Not restrained by known morals, rules, or guiding principles. —**unscrupulously** *adverb.*

un·seal (uhn-SEEL) *verb.* To undo or open (something that has been fastened with a seal or glued together). **unsealed, unsealing.**

un·seat (uhn-SEET) *verb.* 1. To cause to lose one's seat or to fall, particularly from a saddle. 2. To remove from office. **unseated, unseating.**

un·seem·ly (uhn-SEEM-lee) *adjective.* Not proper or pleasant; showing bad manners. **unseemlier, unseemliest.** —**unseemliness** *noun.*

un·sel·fish (uhn-SEL-fish) *adjective.* Thinking of others' welfare or feelings before one's own; generous. —**unselfishly** *adverb.*

un·set·tle (uhn-SET-l) *verb.* To cause to be excited or upset; make nervous. **unsettled, unsettling.**

un·set·tled (uhn-SET-ld) *adjective.* 1. Nervous or upset; not calm. 2. Changeable: *unsettled* weather. 3. Unpaid, as a bill. 4. Not lived in: an *unsettled* desert area.

un·sheathe (uhn-SHEETH) *verb.* To draw or pull (a sword or dagger) from a sheath, scabbard, or other case. **unsheathed, unsheathing.**

un·sight·ly (uhn-SIGHT-lee) *adjective.* Unpleasant to look at; ugly.

un·skilled (uhn-SKILD) *adjective.* 1. Not trained for certain work; without skill. 2. Not requiring skill: Digging ditches is *unskilled* labor.

un·skill·ful (uhn-SKIL-fəl) *adjective.* Without skill; clumsy; awkward. —**unskillfully** *adverb.*

un·sound (uhn-SOWND) *adjective.* 1. Not solid; having defects: an *unsound* building. 2. Not in good health. 3. Not well planned or managed: *unsound* schemes for making money. —**unsoundly** *adverb.*

un·speak·a·ble (uhn-SPEE-kə-bəl) *adjective.* So extreme that it cannot be described: *unspeakable* joy. —**unspeakably** *adverb.*

un·sta·ble (uhn-STAY-bəl) *adjective.* 1. Not stable; likely to tip, turn, fall, or roll. 2. Likely to change: an *unstable* situation on a war front. 3. Changeable; unreliable: an *unstable* person. —**unstably** *adverb.*

un·stead·y (uhn-STED-ee) *adjective.* Not steady; unstable; wavering: The old man was *unsteady* as he walked. —**unsteadily** *adverb.*

un·suit·a·ble (uhn-SOO-tə-bəl) *adjective.* Not proper or fitting: Jeans are *unsuitable* for church. —**unsuitability** (un-soo-tə-BIL-ə-tee) *noun.* —**unsuitably** *adverb.*

un·tan·gle (uhn-TANG-gəl) *verb.* 1. To remove the knots or tangles from. 2. To make clear; solve: to *untangle* a mystery. **untangled, untangling.**

un·think·a·ble (uhn-THING-kə-bəl) *adjective.* Too extreme to be considered or imagined. —**unthinkably** *adverb.*

un·ti·dy (uhn-TIGH-dee) *adjective.* Not neat and clean; disorderly. **untidier, untidiest.** —**untidily** *adverb.* —**untidiness** *noun.*

un·tie (uhn-TIGH) *verb.* 1. To loosen or unfasten (a knot or bow): *Untie* your shoelaces. 2. Release: *Untie* the dog. **untied, untying.**

un·til (uhn-TIL) *preposition.* 1. Up to the time of; till: Dick sat reading *until* dawn. 2. Before: She is not coming *until* Sunday. —*conjunction.* 1. Up to the time that or when:

Don't leave the house *until* I phone you. 2. To the extent, place, or point that: Dick read *until* his eyes ached.

un·time·ly (uhn-TIGHM-lee) *adjective* and *adverb.* Happening or done before the expected or proper time. **untimelier, untimeliest. —untimeliness** *noun.*

un·to (UHN-too) *preposition.* (Rare) To: "Come *unto* me . . . I will give you rest." (Matthew 11:28).

un·told (uhn-TOHLD) *adjective.* 1. Not said or revealed. 2. Too much or too many to express or describe: The war brought *untold* suffering.

un·to·ward (uhn-TORD) *adjective.* 1. Inappropriate. 2. Unfortunate.

un·troub·led (uhn-TRUHB-əld) *adjective.* Calm; peaceful.

un·true (uhn-TROO) *adjective.* 1. Not according to fact; false: It is *untrue* that babies are brought by storks. 2. Not loyal; unfaithful. **—untruth** *noun.*

un·used (uhn-YOOZD) *adjective.* 1. Not used; new. 2. (uhn-YOOST) Not accustomed.

un·u·su·al (uhn-YOO-zhoo-əl) *adjective.* Uncommon; rare. **—unusually** *adverb.*

un·ut·ter·a·ble (uhn-UHT-ər-ə-bəl) *adjective.* Too great or extreme to express or describe: *unutterable* grief. **—unutterably** *adverb.*

un·veil (uhn-VAYL) verb. 1. To uncover: *unveil* a new picture. 2. To reveal: Will Rhoda *unveil* her plans? **unveiled, unveiling.**

un·war·y (uhn-WAIR-ee) *adjective.* Not expecting danger; not watchful or cautious. **unwarier, unwariest. —unwarily** *adverb.*

un·wield·y (uhn-WEEL-dee) *adjective.* Hard to handle or control because of size, shape, or heaviness. **unwieldier, unwieldiest.**

un·will·ing (uhn-WIL-ing) *adjective.* Reluctant; not wanting (to do something): Harry is *unwilling* to go to the dentist. **—unwillingly** *adverb.* **—unwillingness** *noun.*

un·wind (uhn-WYND) *verb.* 1. To undo (something wound); uncoil or become uncoiled: Please *unwind* a yard of thread from that spool. 2. (Informal) To relax; become less tense. **unwound, unwinding.**

un·wise (uhn-WIGHZ) *adjective.* Showing poor judgment; foolish. **unwiser, unwisest. —unwisely** *adverb.*

un·wor·thy (uhn-WER-thee) *adjective.* 1. Unbecoming: Ruth's unkind remark was *unworthy* of her. 2. Not deserving: Mrs. Hightower regards most people as *unworthy* of her attention. **unworthier, unworthiest. —unworthiness** *noun.*

un·wrap (uhn-RAP) *verb.* To remove the wrapping from; open: *unwrap* a package. **unwrapped, unwrapping.**

un·yield·ing (uhn-YEEL-ding) *adjective.* Firm; strong; not submitting or giving in. **—unyieldingly** *adverb.*

up (UHP) *adverb.* 1. Toward a higher position, place, or level: The elevator is going *up.* 2. To a greater degree or amount: Prices are going *up.* 3. Toward a better position or condition: Are you moving *up* in your firm? 4. Into thought or consideration: bring *up* a question. 5. To or into an upright position: stand *up.* 6. Above the horizon or a surface: The sun came *up.* 7. Into pieces: She tore *up* the paper. 8. To a point near or equal (to or with something else): Ann cannot keep *up* with the rest of the class. 9. To a state of completion or fullness: Fill *up* your glass. *—preposition.* 1. From a lower to a higher position in or on: Walk *up* the hill. 2. Along: Walk *up* the street. *—adjective.* 1. In a higher place, level, or degree: a house *up* in the hills. 2. Inclined, moving, or directed upward: the *up* staircase. 3. Ahead: Our team is two games *up* in the tournament. 4. In a position for consideration or action: Our accident case is now *up* in court. 5. Ended; over: "The game is *up.*" (Shakespeare). 6. Out of bed: I was *up* by 6:30. 7. Erect; standing. 8. (Informal) Going on: What's *up?* —*verb.* (Informal) To raise; lift: Why did the stores *up* their prices? **upped, upping.** —**up to.** 1. Equal to; capable of. 2. Doing; scheming: Is Harry *up to* his old tricks again?

up·braid (uhp-BRAYD) *verb.* To scold; criticize severely. **upbraided, upbraiding.**

up·bring·ing (UHP-bring-ing) *noun.* Childhood training and guidance.

up·com·ing (UHP-kuhm-ing) *adjective.* (Informal) Still to come; expected.

up·draft (UHP-draft) *noun.* An upward moving current of air.

up·hill (UHP-HIL) *adverb.* Up the hill; in an upward direction: "Does the road wind *uphill* all the way?" (C. G. Rosetti). —*adjective.* 1. At a higher place; up a hill: The park is an *uphill* climb from here. 2. Difficult; hard to do: an *uphill* task.

up·hold (uhp-HOHLD) *verb.* To maintain; support: *uphold* the Constitution. **upheld, upholding.**

up·hol·ster (uhp-HOHL-stər) *verb.* To put springs in, pad, and cover (furniture) with cloth or other material. **upholstered, upholstering.** —**upholstery** or **upholstering** *noun.*

up·keep (UHP-keep) *noun.* The work, material, and cost of keeping something in good condition.

up·land (UHP-lənd) *noun.* A tract of land higher than land around it.

up·lift (uhp-LIFT) *verb.* 1. To raise. 2. To improve the moral, social, economic, and cultural level of a group or of a society. **uplifted, uplifting.** —(UHP-lift) *noun.* 1. A lifting or raising. 2. An effort to improve social or other conditions.

up·on (ə-PON) *preposition.* On.

up·per (UHP-ər) *adjective.* 1. Higher; nearer the top or head: the *upper* end of the street. 2. Superior; higher in grade, position, or rank: Pamela is in the *upper* half of the class. —*noun.* The part of a boot or shoe to which the sole is attached. —**the upper hand.** The position of control.

up·per·most (UHP-ər-mohst) *adverb* and *adjective.* Highest in position; most important.

up·raise (uhp-RAYZ) *verb.* To raise or lift up. **upraised, upraising.**

up·right (UHP-right) *adjective.* 1. Vertical; straight: The flagpole should be *upright.* 2. Having good character; honest and just: an *upright* man. —*adverb.* Vertically; straight up: Stand *upright.* —*noun.* A part that stands vertically, such as a post supporting a roof.

up·ris·ing (UHP-righ-zing) *noun.* A revolt; rebellion.

up·roar (UHP-ror) *noun.* A loud, confused noise, such as that made by an excited crowd. —**uproarious** (uhp-ROR-ee-əss) *adjective.* —**uproariously** *adverb.*

up·root (uhp-ROOT) *verb.* 1. To pull out (a plant) by the roots. 2. To destroy or wipe out. 3. To remove from the home place with force: War *uproots* many families. **uprooted, uprooting.**

up·set (uhp-SET) *verb.* 1. To tip over; capsize: Don't *upset* this canoe. 2. To disorganize; throw into disorder: Ruth's illness may *upset* our vacation plans. 3. To disturb; to worry. 4. To beat or overcome unexpectedly: Our team *upset* the champions. **upset, upsetting.** —*adjective.* 1. Overturned; capsized. 2. Disorganized; disordered. 3. Disturbed; perturbed. —(UHP-set) *noun.* 1. An upsetting. 2. A state of disorder; disturbed condition. 3. (Sports) A game in which the expected winner loses.

up·shot (UHP-shot) *noun.* The end result; conclusion.

up·side-down (uhp-sighd-DOWN) *adjective.* 1. Turned over so that the top side is down. 2. In complete disorder or confusion.

up·stairs (UHP-STAIRZ) *adverb.* Up the stairs; to or in an upper story: I sleep *upstairs.* —(UHP-stairz) *adjective.* In a place reached by stairs: Our house has three *upstairs* bedrooms. —*noun.* The upper floor or floors.

up·start (UHP-stahrt) *noun.* A person who has risen quickly to wealth or power, especially one who is conceited or vain.

up·stream (UHP-STREEM) *adverb.* Toward the head or origin of a stream; against the current: Paddling *upstream* is a slow job.

up tight Also **up·tight** (UHP-TIGHT) *adjective.* (Slang) Emotionally tense; nervous; anxious.

up-to-date (uhp-tə-DAYT) *adjective.* 1. Extending or including up to the present time: Is your assignment book *up-to-date?* 2. Fitting or appropriate to the present time; not old-fashioned: *up-to-date* ideas.

up·ward (UHP-wərd) Also **upwards** *adverb.* 1. Toward a higher place or level: Sparks from the fire flew *upward.* 2. Toward a higher amount, rank, position, etc.: Prices are moving *upward.* —*adjective.* In or relating to a higher place, rank, level, etc.: prices *upwards* of five dollars.

u·ra·ni·um (yu-RAY-nee-əm) *noun.* A heavy, hard, shiny, metallic element that is radioactive.

U·ra·nus (YU-rə-nəss or yu-RAY-nəss) *noun.* The planet seventh in distance from the sun.

ur·ban (ER-bən) *adjective.* 1. Referring to a city or cities, or having their characteristics: *urban* traffic. 2. Being or living in a city: *urban* workers.

urban renewal. Rebuilding and improvement of buildings, streets, schools, and parks in run-down city areas.

ur·chin (ER-chin) *noun.* 1. A small, mischievous boy. 2. A sea animal with a round shell that has long spikes or spines on it; also called "sea urchin."

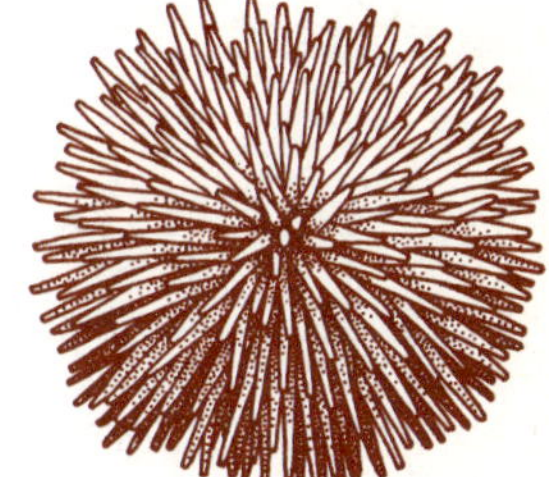

urchin

-ure *suffix.* Indicates: 1. The doing or process of doing: enclos*ure.* 2. A duty or job or the group performing a duty or job: legislat*ure.*

urge (ERJ) *verb.* 1. To encourage earnestly; to push (someone) to action: We *urged* Dad to buy a new car. 2. To present (an idea, plan, or such) earnestly or vigorously; recommend strongly. 3. To push or drive forward: The farmer *urged* the oxen into the field. **urged, urging.** —*noun.* 1. Act of urging. 2. A strong desire (to do something). **urges.**

ur·gent (ER-jənt) *adjective.* Requiring immediate attention or action; of pressing importance: The flood victims have an *urgent* need for food and clothing. —**urgency** (ER-jən-see) *noun.* —**urgently** *adverb.*

u·rine (YUR-in) *noun.* In man and other mammals, the fluid waste produced by the kidneys.

urn (ERN) *noun.* 1. A large vase on a base, especially one used to hold the ashes of a dead person. 2. A container with a faucet, used for making and dispensing tea or coffee.

urn

us (UHSS) *pronoun, plural.* The objective case of *we,* used as a direct object, indirect object, or object of a preposition.

U.S. *abbreviation.* United States.

U.S.A. *abbreviation.* 1. United States of America. 2. United States Army.

us·a·ble (YOO-zə-bəl) Also **useable** *adjective.* Able to be used; fit for use. —**usability** (yoo-zə-BIL-ə-tee) *noun.* —**usably** *adverb.*

us·age (YOO-sij) *noun.* 1. The manner in which something is used; treatment. 2. The way that words are used.

use (YOOZ) *verb.* 1. To put into action; employ for a purpose: The farmer *uses* a shovel to dig. 2. To consume: "*Use* it up, wear it out;/Make it do, or do without." (Anonymous). 3. (Informal) To treat: "Men are *used* as they *use* others." (Bidpai). 4. (Past tense only, followed by infinitive) To be in the habit of: Dad *used* to play football. **used, using.** —(YOOSS) *noun.* 1. A using or being used: The *use* of an ax requires caution. 2. The right to make use of: "The *use* of the sea and air is common to all." (Elizabeth I, Queen of England). 3. Requirement; need: I have no *use* for a second tennis racket. 4. Usefulness: The broken radio is of no *use.* 5. Power or ability to use. 6. Purpose; benefit: What is the *use* of studying Latin? **uses.** —**used** *adjective.* Secondhand, not new: a *used* car. —**used to.** Accustomed to.

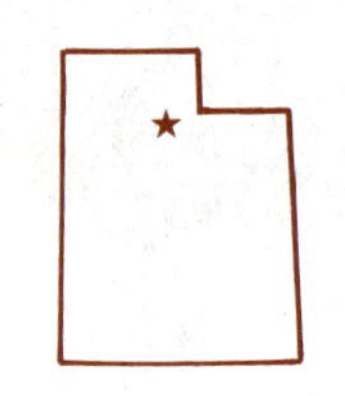

Utah
★capital: Salt Lake City

use·ful (YOOSS-fəl) *adjective.* Able to be used; of value; helpful. —**usefully** *adverb.* —**usefulness** *noun.*

use·less (YOOSS-liss) *adjective.* Not helpful or useful; worthless: Money is *useless* to someone stranded on a desert island. —**uselessly** *adverb.* —**uselessness** *noun.*

ush·er (UHSH-ər) *noun.* A person whose job is to show persons to their seats, as in a theater or church. —*verb.* 1. To escort or show someone to a place. 2. (Used with *in*) To go before as a sign or representative of something that follows: Dark clouds *ushered* in the storm. **ushered, ushering.**

U.S.S.R. *abbreviation.* Union of Soviet Socialist Republics.

u·su·al (YOO-zhoo-əl) *adjective.* Typical or customary; normal. —**usually** *adverb.*

u·surp (yoo-SERP) *verb.* To take over by force without right or authority: The rebels *usurped* the rule of the country. **usurped, usurping.**

U·tah (YOO-taw) *noun.* A western state of the United States, 45th to join the Union (1896). Also **UT** for Zip Codes.

u·ten·sil (yoo-TENSS-l) *noun.* An implement, tool, or container, especially one used in a kitchen.

u·ter·us (YOO-tər-əss) *noun.* An organ in female mammals within which the young form and grow before birth; womb.

u·til·i·ty (yoo-TIL-ə-tee) *noun.* 1. Usefulness: The farmer explained the *utility* of a pitchfork. 2. A service provided to the public, such as water, gas, or electricity. 3. The company providing such a public service. **utilities.** —*adjective.* (Baseball) Able to be used in various positions: a *utility* infielder.

utility room. A room in a building in which necessary machines are kept.

u·til·ize (YOO-tə-lighz) *verb.* To make use of. **utilized, utilizing.**

ut·most (UHT-mohst) *adjective.* 1. Of the greatest degree or amount: a message of *utmost* importance. 2. Farthest: the *utmost* limits of the island. —*noun.* The greatest degree.

u·to·pi·a (yoo-TOH-pee-ə) *noun.* A place or condition of perfection or complete peace and harmony.

[1]**ut·ter** (UHT-ər) *verb.* To say; announce; express: "A thought is often original, though you have *uttered* it a hundred times." (Oliver Wendell Holmes). **uttered, uttering.** —**utterance** *noun.*

[2]**ut·ter** (UHT-ər) *adjective.* Complete; absolute. —**utterly** *adverb.*

V, v (VEE) *noun.* The 22d letter of the English alphabet.

v. *abbreviation.* 1. Verb. 2. Volume. 3. Verse.

va·can·cy (VAY-kən-see) *noun.* 1. An unoccupied house, office, apartment, or hotel room. 2. An unfilled job or position. 3. Emptiness; state of being vacant or unfilled. 4. Lack of thought or intelligence. **vacancies.**

va·cant (VAY-kənt) *adjective.* 1. Empty; not filled or occupied: a *vacant* job; a *vacant* apartment. 2. Free from work: *vacant* time. 3. Without thought or expression: a *vacant* look. —**vacantly** *adverb.*

va·cate (VAY-kayt) *verb.* To leave (a place) empty: *vacate* the house. **vacated, vacating.**

va·ca·tion (vay-KAY-shən) *noun.* A period when one does not work, attend school, or do other duties. —*verb.* To take or spend a vacation. **vacationed, vacationing.**

vac·ci·nate (VAK-sə-nayt) *verb.* To inject a vaccine into, as protection against a disease. **vaccinated, vaccinating.** —**vaccination** (vak-sə-NAY-shən) *noun.*

vac·cine (vak-SEEN) *noun.* 1. A solution containing weakened disease germs that is injected into the body, causing a very slight illness and thus creating an immunity to that particular disease. 2. Such a fluid, injected to protect a person against smallpox. **vaccines.**

vac·u·um (VAK-yoo-əm or VAK-yoom) *noun.* 1. A space that is absolutely empty. 2. A space, as in a light bulb, from which almost all the air has been removed. 3. A vacuum cleaner. —*verb.* To use a vacuum cleaner to clean or remove dirt: *Vacuum* the carpet. **vacuumed, vacuuming.**

vacuum cleaner. An electrical machine that sucks up dirt by creating a vacuum.

vag·a·bond (VAG-ə-bond) *noun.* A homeless wanderer.

va·grant (VAY-grənt) *noun.* A person who wanders from place to place and has no regular home or income; a tramp.

vague (VAYG) *adjective.* Not clear; not definite or sharp: a *vague* idea. **vaguer, vaguest.** —**vaguely** *adverb.*

vain (VAYN) *adjective.* 1. Having too much pride in oneself; conceited. 2. Useless; not successful: a *vain* effort. 3. Worthless; of no value: *vain* promises. **vainer, vainest.** —**vainly** *adverb.*

vale (VAYL) *noun.* A valley. **vales.**

val·en·tine (VAL-ən-tighn) *noun.* A card or a gift sent as a sign of love on St. Valentine's Day. **valentines.**

val·et (VAL-it or va-LAY) *noun.* 1. A manservant who takes care of another man's clothes and performs other personal services. 2. A hotel worker who cleans and presses clothes for the guests.

val·iant (VAL-yənt) *adjective.* Brave; heroic. —**valiantly** *adverb.*

val·id (VAL-id) *adjective.* 1. Founded on facts; reasonable: a *valid* argument. 2. (Law) Binding: A contract is *valid* when it is signed. —**validity** (və-LID-ə-tee) *noun.* —**validly** *adverb.*

val·ley (VAL-ee) *noun.* 1. Land that lies between ranges of mountains or hills. 2. Land lying along a river that drains it: *valley* of the Nile.

valentine

valley

van

val·or (VAL-ər) *noun.* Courage or boldness; bravery. —**valorous** *adjective.*

val·u·a·ble (VAL-yoo-ə-bəl or VAL-yə-bəl) *adjective.* 1. Of great importance and value; highly desirable and useful. 2. Worth a great deal of money: *valuable* property. —*noun.* (Usually plural) Personal belongings or things worth much money. **valuables.**

val·u·a·tion (val-yoo-AY-shən) *noun.* 1. The act of judging how much something is worth: She took her diamond ring to a jeweler for *valuation.* 2. The value or price put on something.

val·ue (VAL-yoo) *noun.* 1. The worth (of something); the quality that makes it valuable: Everyone knows the *value* of an education. 2. Worth in dollars: the *value* of our house. 3. The worth; purchasing power: the *value* of the dollar. 4. (Plural) Beliefs or standards that are important to a person or a society: Are our *values* different from those of our fathers? 5. (Math) The quantity represented by a symbol such as "x": The *value* of "x" is 5. **values.** —*verb.* 1. To estimate the worth of: The jeweler *values* the ring at $750. 2. To hold a high opinion of: We *value* our teacher's friendship. **valued, valuing.**

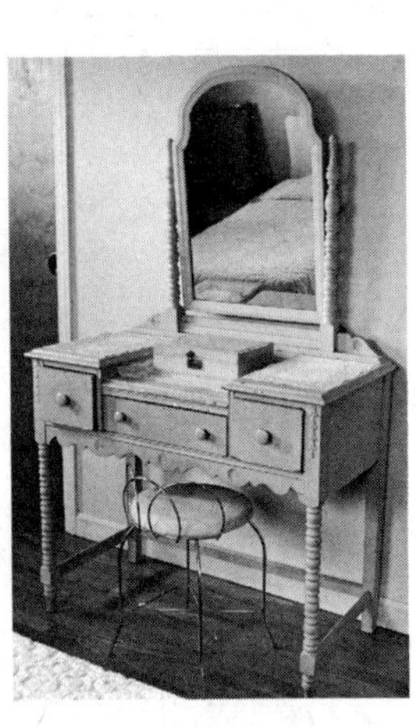
vanity

valve (VALV) *noun.* 1. A movable mechanism that opens and closes to control the flow of gas, liquid, or other material through a pipe or other passageway. 2. In the human body, a membrane, as in the veins, heart, or digestive system, that controls the flow of body liquids. 3. (Music) In a brass wind instrument, device that changes pitch. 4. One of the two movable parts that make up the shell of a clam, oyster, or other mollusk. **valves.**

vam·pire (VAM-pighr) *noun.* 1. In folk stories, a dead person believed to rise from the grave at night to wander about and suck blood from sleeping people. 2. A vampire bat; a tropical bat that feeds on blood.

[1]**van** *noun.* A large closed wagon or truck used to transport goods or animals: We watched men load our furniture into a moving *van.*

[2]**van** *noun.* The forward part of an army or other group that is moving forward; vanguard.

van·dal (VAND-l) *noun.* A person who purposely damages or destroys property. —**vandalism** (VAND-l-iz-əm) *noun.* —**vandalize** (VAND-l-ighz) *verb.*

vane (VAYN) *noun.* 1. A metal figure or object that turns in the direction the wind is blowing; also called "weather vane." 2. A blade of a propeller, electric fan, or windmill. **vanes.**

van·guard (VAN-gahrd) *noun.* 1. The front line troops of an army. 2. The people leading a movement, as in art, literature, or politics.

va·nil·la (və-NIL-ə) *noun.* 1. A flavoring extract used in baking and cooking, especially sweets, made from the pods of an orchid. 2. The tropical plant or the pod of this orchid, called the vanilla "bean."

van·ish (VAN-ish) *verb.* 1. To drop out of sight; disappear suddenly. 2. To go out of existence; die out: Many wild animals may *vanish* if we don't protect them. **vanished, vanishing.**

van·i·ty (VAN-ə-tee) *noun.* 1. Extreme pride in one's appearance, ability, or possessions; conceit. 2. A small dressing table with mirrors. **vanities.**

van·quish (VANG-kwish or VAN-kwish) *verb.* 1. To defeat in battle. 2. To overcome or control (a feeling). **vanquished, vanquishing.**

va·por (VAY-pər) *noun.* 1. Smoke or moisture suspended in the air. 2. A gas formed by heating a liquid.

va·por·iz·er (VAY-pə-righ-zər) *noun.* A device for changing a liquid into a vapor by heating or spraying. —**vaporize** *verb.*

vapour. British form of **vapor.**

var·i·a·ble (VAIR-ee-ə-bəl) *adjective.* 1. Changeable; not steady: The weather will be *variable* today. 2. Able to be changed or varied. —*noun.* A thing or quantity that can vary. —**variably** *adverb.*

var·i·a·tion (vair-ee-AY-shən) *noun.* 1. The act of varying; a change: *variations* in handwriting. 2. The amount or extent of a change: a *variation* of 15 degrees. 3. A different form of a musical theme or tune.

var·ied (VAIR-eed) *adjective.* 1. Of different kinds. 2. Having several different colors.

va·ri·e·ty (və-RIGH-ə-tee) *noun.* 1. A number of different kinds; an assortment. 2. Lack of sameness: "*Variety*'s the very spice of life." (William Cowper). 3. Sort; kind; something different from others of a similar kind: many *varieties* of evergreen trees. **varieties.**

var·i·ous (VAIR-ee-əss) *adjective.* 1. Of different kinds: He has *various* badges on his hat. 2. Separate; individual: She gives prizes to the *various* members of the group. —**variously** *adverb.*

var·nish (VAHR-nish) *noun.* An oil-based paint that gives a smooth, hard coat. **varnishes.** —*verb.* To put varnish on. **varnished, varnishing.**

var·si·ty (VAHR-sə-tee) *noun.* (Sports) A first-string team of a university, college, or school. **varsities.**

var·y (VAIR-ee) *verb.* 1. To make or become different; to change: The temperature does not *vary* much at the equator. 2. To be different: At every age, boys *vary* in height. 3. To introduce changes in: *Vary* the way you pitch the ball. **varied, varying.**

vase (VAYSS or VAYZ) *noun.* A container used as an ornament or to hold flowers. **vases.**

vas·sal (VASS-l) *noun.* 1. In feudal times, a person who held land and received protection from a lord, and in return owed him loyalty and service. 2. A person or country that must serve another.

vast *adjective.* Great or large in size, number, quantity, extent: "the *vast* and furious ocean." (William Bradford). **vaster, vastest.** —**vastly** *adverb.* —**vastness** *noun.*

vat *noun.* A large container or tank for holding liquids.

[1]**vault** (VAWLT) *verb.* To jump (over), especially with the help of one's hands or a pole: He *vaulted* over the counter. **vaulted, vaulting.** —*noun.* A vigorous jump: The cat reached the wall with one *vault.*

[2]vault (definition 4)

[2]**vault** (VAWLT) *noun.* 1. An arched ceiling or roof. 2. A room or space with such a ceiling. 3. Something that is like an arched roof: the starry *vault* of heaven. 4. A strong room for keeping money and other valuables safe. 5. A burial chamber. —*verb.* 1. To cover with a vault. 2. To build in the shape of a vault. **vaulted, vaulting.**

vb. *abbreviation.* Verb.

veal (VEEL) *noun.* The meat of a calf, used for food.

vec·tor (VEK-tər) *noun.* An organism that carries disease germs from one living thing to another: Mosquitoes are the *vectors* of malaria.

veer (VIHR) *verb.* To turn; to shift; to change position or direction: The car *veered* right to avoid the truck. **veered, veering.**

veg·e·ta·ble (VEJ-tə-bəl) *noun.* 1. A plant grown for food and eaten cooked or raw: Spinach and beans are *vegetables.* 2. Any plant: Is it animal, *vegetable,* or mineral?

veg·e·tar·i·an (vej-ə-TAIR-ee-ən) *noun.* A person who eats only vegetables, grains, fruits, and nuts, but no meat.

veg·e·ta·tion (vej-ə-TAY-shən) *noun.* Plant life; all the plants growing in an area: There is little *vegetation* in the desert.

ve·he·ment (VEE-ə-mənt) *adjective.* 1. Full of or showing strong feeling; very emotional. 2. Violent; forceful; angry. —**vehemence** *noun.* —**vehemently** *adverb.*

ve·hi·cle (VEE-i-kəl) *noun.* 1. A means of carrying people or goods, such as an automobile, motorcycle, bus, or sled. 2. A means of expressing something: A poem can be a *vehicle* for one's feelings.

veil (VAYL) *noun.* 1. A piece of very fine, thin cloth like a net, worn by women over the head, sometimes hiding the face. 2. Something that hides like a veil: a *veil* of mist. —*verb.* 1. To cover with a veil. 2. To hide as if with a veil. **veiled, veiling.**

vein (VAYN) *noun.* 1. One of the blood vessels that carry blood back to the heart. 2. One of the long, thin lines or ribs of an insect's wing or a leaf. 3. A crack or seam in the earth or in rock that is filled with a mineral: a *vein* of gold. 4. A streak or stripe of a color, as in marble or other stone. 5. A strain or quality: "A *vein* of poetry exists in the hearts of all men." (Thomas Carlyle).

ventricle

vel·lum (VEL-əm) *noun.* 1. A thin animal skin used as paper in special books. 2. A heavy paper or cloth made to look like vellum.

ve·loc·i·ty (və-LOSS-ə-tee) *noun.* 1. Rate of motion: The spacecraft had a *velocity* of 30,000 miles per hour. 2. Speed: The *velocity* of the car at the time of the crash was 60 miles per hour.

vel·vet (VEL-vit) *noun.* 1. A cloth that has a short, soft, thick pile on one side. 2. Anything soft and smooth like velvet.

vend *verb.* To sell. **vended, vending.** —**vender** or **vendor** *noun.*

ven·er·a·ble (VEN-ər-ə-bəl) *adjective.* Worthy of respect or honor because of age, learning, or position: a *venerable* teacher.

ven·er·ate (VEN-ə-rayt) *verb.* To honor, respect. **venerated, venerating.** —**veneration** (ven-ə-RAY-shən) *noun.*

venge·ance (VEN-jənss) *noun.* A return for a wrong or injury; an act of revenge: The cowboy sought *vengeance* on the man who had shot his friend. —**with a vengeance.** With great force: He hit the ball *with a vengeance.*

ven·i·son (VEN-ə-sən) *noun.* The meat from a deer, eaten as food.

ven·om (VEN-əm) *noun.* 1. Poison, as from a snake or spider. 2. Evil; hatefulness. —**venomous** (VEN-ə-məss) *adjective.*

vent *noun.* An opening; exit; outlet: an air *vent.* —*verb.* 1. To let out; to express: *vent* one's anger. 2. To force through a vent. **vented, venting.**

ven·ti·late (VEN-tl-ayt) *verb.* 1. To allow fresh air to enter: *ventilate* the room. 2. To supply a vent or other opening for the passage of air. **ventilated, ventilating.** —**ventilation** (VEN-tə-LAY-shən) *noun.*

ven·ti·la·tor (VEN-tl-ay-tər) *noun.* A device or opening for allowing fresh air to replace stale air.

ven·tri·cle (VEN-tri-kəl) *noun.* A small enclosed cavity in an organ, as in the heart or brain, especially the two in the heart that receive and send out blood. **ventricles.**

ven·tril·o·quism (ven-TRIL-ə-kwiz-əm) *noun.* A way of making the voice seem to come from a source other than the actual speaker, as from a dummy's or puppet's mouth. —**ventriloquist** (ven-TRIL-ə-kwist) *noun.*

ven·ture (VEN-chər) *noun.* An enterprise that is risky or unsure.

ventures. —*verb.* 1. To risk; take a chance. 2. To take the chance of going: *venture* into the cave. 3. To dare (to give an opinion): I *ventured* to tell Dave that he was wrong. **ventured, venturing.**

Ve·nus (VEE-nəss) *noun.* The planet second in distance from the sun.

ve·ran·da (və-RAN-də) Also **verandah** *noun.* A porch with a roof.

verb *noun.* A word that expresses action, being, or happening.

ver·bal (VER-bəl) *adjective.* 1. Referring to, of, or connected with words. 2. Word for word: a *verbal* quotation. 3. Said rather than written: a *verbal* agreement. 4. Acting as or resembling a verb. —**verbally** *adverb.*

ver·bose (vər-BOHSS) *adjective.* Using too many words; long-winded. —**verbosity** (vər-BOSS-ə-tee) *noun.*

ver·dict (VER-dikt) *noun.* A decision or judgment, such as one made in a court of law by a jury or judge.

verge (VERJ) *noun.* 1. The edge or lip: the *verge* of a cliff. 2. The point, brink: I was on the *verge* of leaving when Uncle Frank arrived. —*verb.* (Usually used with *on* or *upon*) 1. To border: Our town *verges* on a large lake. 2. To come close to: His remarks *verge* on outright insults. **verged, verging.**

ver·i·fy (VEHR-ə-figh) *verb.* 1. To prove to be true: The man's account was *verified* by witnesses. 2. To prove the truth or correctness of: The experiment may *verify* our theory. **verified, verifying.**

ver·i·ly (VEHR-ə-lee) *adverb.* (Rare) Truthfully, surely.

ver·min (VER-min) *noun.* Any small pest, such as a mouse or roach. —**vermin** *plural.*

Ver·mont (vər-MONT) *noun.* A New England state in the United States, 14th to join the Union (1791). —**Vt.** *abbreviation.* Also **VT** for Zip Codes.

ver·sa·tile (VER-sə-tl) *adjective.* 1. Able to do many things well. 2. Able to be used for many things. —**versatility** (ver-sə-TIL-ə-tee) *noun.*

verse (VERSS) *noun.* 1. Poetry: "All that is not prose is *verse.*" (Molière). 2. A line or a stanza of a poem or song. 3. One of the numbered parts of a Bible chapter. **verses.**

versed (VERST) *adjective.* (Used with *in*) Having knowledge of.

ver·sion (VER-zhən) *noun.* 1. A story or account told from a particular point of view: His *version* of the argument differed from yours. 2. A translation: the King James *Version* of the Bible.

ver·sus (VER-səss) *preposition.* In opposition to; against.

ver·te·bra (VER-tə-brə) Any of the bones forming the spinal column. —**vertebrae** (VER-tə-bree) or **vertebras** *plural.*

ver·te·brate (VER-tə-brayt or VER-tə-brit) *noun.* Any animal with a spinal column, as mammals, reptiles, fish, and birds. **vertebrates.** —*adjective.* 1. Having a spinal column. 2. Referring to or like animals with spinal columns.

ver·tex (VER-teks) *noun.* 1. The topmost or highest point. 2. The pointed top of a triangle, opposite the base. 3. The point where two lines meet to form an angle. —**vertexes** or **vertices** (VER-tə-seez) *plural.*

ver·ti·cal (VER-ti-kəl) *adjective.* In a straight up-and-down position: The sides of a house are *vertical.* —**vertically** *adverb.*

ver·y (VEHR-ee) *adverb.* 1. To a great degree: *very* heavy. 2. Exactly: the *very* same person. 3. Actually: the *very* fastest route. —*adjective.* 1. Complete; utter: the *very* top of the hill. 2. Same: She bought the *very* dress I wanted. 3. Slightest; simple: She cried at the *very* mention of her lost doll.

veranda

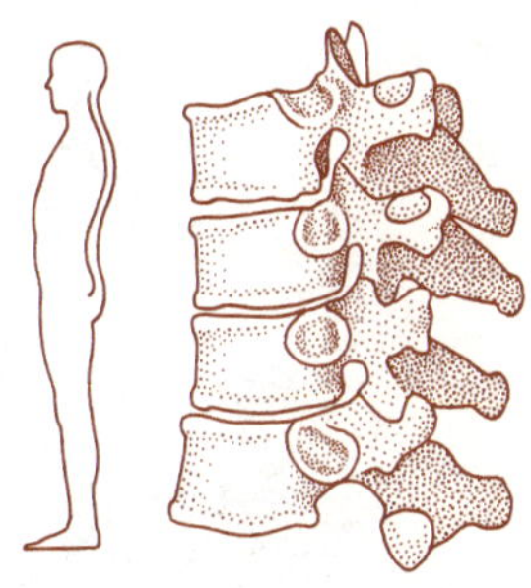
vertebra

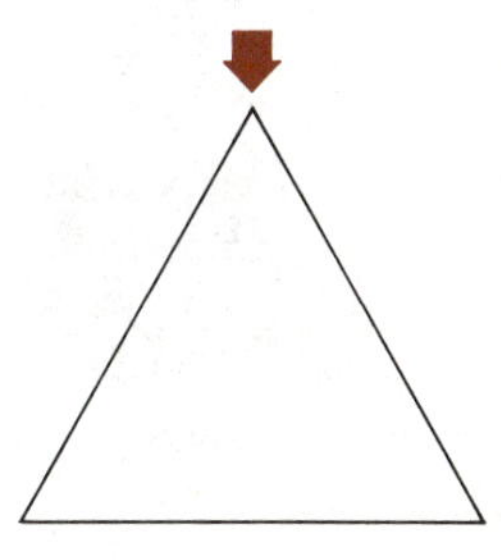
vertex

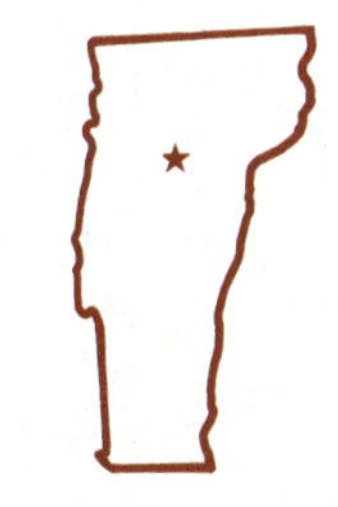
Vermont
★capital: Montpelier

viaduct

vestment

ves·pers (VESS-pərz) *noun, plural.* [Often capital V] A late afternoon or evening prayer service.

ves·sel (VESS-l) *noun.* 1. A container, as a jar or bottle. 2. Any big boat. 3. A part of the body that holds or carries a body fluid: a blood *vessel.*

vest *noun.* A piece of clothing like a short jacket, but without sleeves or collar. —*verb.* 1. To put clothes on, particularly as part of a ceremony: The new judge was *vested* in her robes. 2. (Used with *in*) To give authority to. **vested, vesting.**

ves·ti·bule (VESS-tə-byool) *noun.* An entry hall. **vestibules.**

ves·tige (VESS-tij) *noun.* A bit or sign left by something that no longer exists: Fossils are *vestiges* of prehistoric man. **vestiges.**

vest·ment (VEST-mənt) *noun.* A form of dress used in ceremonies or as a sign of office: a priest's *vestments.*

vet·er·an (VET-ər-ən) *noun.* 1. A person with much experience in a certain field: a *veteran* actor. 2. One who has been in military service.

Veterans Day. A legal holiday in the United States celebrated on the fourth Monday in October, in honor of veterans of the armed forces.

vet·er·i·nar·i·an (vet-ər-ə-NAIR-ee-ən) *noun.* A doctor for animals.

vet·er·i·nar·y (VET-ər-ə-nehr-ee) *adjective.* Referring to the treatment of animal sicknesses and injuries. —*noun.* A doctor for animals.

ve·to (VEE-toh) *noun.* 1. The power of a government executive, particularly a governor or the President, to reject a bill passed by the legislature. 2. The use of such power. **vetoes.** —*verb.* 1. To reject a bill passed by the legislature. 2. To refuse to allow. **vetoed, vetoing.**

vex (VEKS) *verb.* 1. To annoy; bother. 2. To confuse or puzzle: The problem *vexed* me. **vexed, vexing.** —**vexation** (vek-SAY-shən) *noun.*

VHF *abbreviation.* (Radio and TV) Very high frequency.

vi·a (VIGH-ə or VEE-ə) *preposition.* By way of; by means of: We went to New York City *via* Connecticut.

vi·a·duct (VIGH-ə-duhkt) *noun.* A bridge, made up of a number of arches or spans, that carries a road or railroad track across a river, valley, or other road.

vi·al (VIGH-əl) *noun.* A small narrow glass bottle used to hold liquids.

vi·brate (VIGH-brayt) *verb.* 1. To move or make move up and down or back and forth quickly. 2. To make a wavering sound: Tarzan's voice *vibrated* when he pounded his chest. **vibrated, vibrating.** —**vibration** (vigh-BRAY-shən) *noun.*

vic·ar (VIK-ər) *noun.* A clergyman.

vice (VYSS) *noun.* 1. An evil habit or practice: Smoking is her only *vice.* 2. Wickedness or immorality.

vice- *prefix.* Indicates a deputy or substitute for another: *vice*roy.

vice president. 1. (Also **vice-president**) The person next in rank after a president, usually having the power to take over the president's job if necessary. 2. [Capital V and P] The Vice President of the United States.

vice·roy (VYSS-roi) *noun.* A person who governs as a representative of a ruler: The king sent the *viceroy* to rule over the conquered country.

vi·ce ver·sa (VIGH-sə VER-sə). The order being reversed; the other way around as well: Marion likes Tommy and *vice versa.*

vi·cin·i·ty (vi-SIN-ə-tee) *noun.* 1. Nearness. 2. An area or neighborhood: There are not many houses in our *vicinity.* **vicinities.**

vi·cious (VISH-əss) *adjective.* 1. Cruel, mean, evil: a *vicious* crime. 2. Savage: a *vicious* dog. 3. (Informal) Terrible, awful: *vicious* weather. —**viciously** *adverb.* —**viciousness** *noun.*

vic·tim (VIK-tim) *noun.* 1. A person hurt or killed. 2. One who is fooled, cheated, or hurt: the *victim* of our pranks. 3. A living animal or person offered as a sacrifice to a god. —**victimize** *verb.*

vic·tor (VIK-tər) *noun.* The winner; the one who conquers.

vic·to·ri·ous (vik-TOR-ee-əss) *adjective.* 1. Winning, conquering: the *victorious* team. 2. Indicating victory or conquest: a *victorious* smile. —**victoriously** *adverb.*

vic·to·ry (VIK-tə-ree) *noun.* A winning; defeat of those on the opposite side. **victories.**

vid·e·o (VID-ee-oh) *adjective.* Referring to television, particularly to the picture itself. —*noun.* 1. The picture part of a TV broadcast: The *video* is fine, but the sound is poor. 2. Television.

video tape. A magnetic tape on which television sound and pictures are recorded.

vie (VIGH) *verb.* (Used with *for* or *with*) To compete: Barbara *vied* with Jean for the highest grades in the class. **vied, vying.**

view (VYOO) *noun.* 1. A look at; an inspection: a good *view* of my X-rays. 2. Ability or space to see: *view* of the stage. 3. (Plural) Opinions: What are your political *views?* 4. A look; a seeing; a way of thinking about things: a gloomy *view.* 5. A scene: a beautiful *view* of the mountains. —*verb.* 1. To look at; see. 2. To take a close look at; inspect. **viewed, viewing. —point of view.** Attitude; viewpoint.

view·point (VYOO-point) *noun.* 1. Mental attitude. 2. A place from which one can look.

vig·il (VIJ-əl) *noun.* A watch or period of wakefulness, especially when one usually would be asleep.

vig·i·lant (VIJ-ə-lənt) *adjective.* Carefully watchful: the *vigilant* baby sitter. —**vigilantly** *adverb.*

vig·or (VIG-ər) *noun.* Energy; vitality. —**vigorous** (VIG-ər-əss) *adjective.* —**vigorously** *adverb.*

Vi·king (VIGH-king) *noun.* One of the Scandinavian seamen who were pirates and explorers in the eighth to tenth centuries.

vile (VIGHL) *adjective.* 1. Evil; corrupt. 2. Disgusting; extremely unpleasant. 3. Base or low; very mean. 4. Very bad; not suitable. **viler, vilest.** —**vilely** *adverb.*

vil·la (VIL-ə) *noun.* A large, elegant country home or estate.

vil·lage (VIL-ij) *noun.* 1. A group of houses, usually smaller than a town: "Whose woods these are I think I know./His house is in the *village* though." (Robert Frost). 2. The residents of a village. **villages.**

vil·lain (VIL-ən) *noun.* An evil person; scoundrel.

vim *noun.* Vitality or energy.

vin·di·cate (VIN-di-kayt) *verb.* 1. To free from accusation or blame. 2. To show to be correct: *vindicate* a claim. **vindicated, vindicating.**

vin·dic·tive (vin-DIK-tiv) *adjective.* Seeking to revenge a hurt or wrong. —**vindictively** *adverb.*

vine (VIGHN) *noun.* 1. Any of a variety of plants, like ivy and morning-glory, that grow along the ground or upward by clinging to walls, poles, or such. 2. A grapevine.

vin·e·gar (VIN-i-gər) *noun.* A sour liquid made from wine or cider and used in food preparation.

vine·yard (VIN-yərd) *noun.* An area where grapevines are planted.

vin·tage (VIN-tij) *noun.* 1. A crop of grapes or the wine produced from a particular district in one season. 2. The year in which a certain wine is made. 3. The type, style, or period (of any object): The old rifle was of early American *vintage.* —*adjective.* Old or respected; of excellent quality.

vineyard

violet

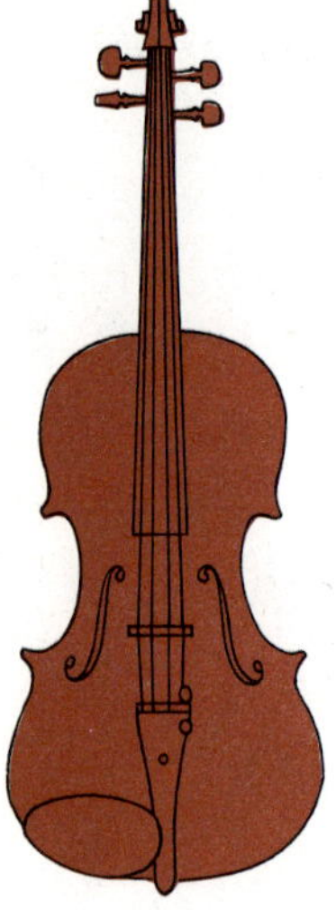
violin

Virginia
★capital: Richmond

Virgo

vi·nyl (VIGHN-l) *noun.* Any of a variety of plastics, somewhat like leather and often used for clothing and for covering furniture.

vi·o·la (vee-OH-lə) *noun.* A musical instrument of the string family that is slightly larger and deeper in tone than a violin.

vi·o·late (VIGH-ə-layt) *verb.* 1. To break, as a rule or law. 2. To disturb or disrupt: *violate* a person's privacy. 3. Treat in a disrespectful manner. **violated, violating.** —**violation** (vigh-ə-LAY-shən) *noun.*

vi·o·lence (VIGH-ə-lənss) *noun.* 1. Force or activity used to cause harm or break a law: the *violence* of an angry mob. 2. Very damaging forcefulness: the *violence* of an earthquake. 3. Strength; intensity: the *violence* of anger.

vi·o·lent (VIGH-ə-lənt) *adjective.* 1. Inclined toward harmful or forceful behavior. 2. Extremely forceful in action: a *violent* storm. 3. Caused by harmful action: a *violent* death. 4. Severe; very great: a *violent* headache. 5. Very noticeable; extreme: a *violent* clash of colors. —**violently** *adverb.*

vi·o·let (VIGH-ə-lit) *noun.* 1. A small, delicate purple, blue, white, or yellow flower. 2. The plant on which this flower grows. 3. (Also *adjective*) A bluish-purple color.

vi·o·lin (vigh-ə-LIN) *noun.* A small musical instrument of the string family, played with a bow.

vi·o·lin·ist (vigh-ə-LIN-ist) *noun.* A person who plays the violin.

vi·o·lon·cel·lo (vee-ə-lən-CHEL-oh) *noun.* A large musical instrument of the string family, played with a bow; cello. **violoncellos.**

vi·per (VIGH-pər) *noun.* 1. A poisonous snake. 2. A treacherous or evil person.

vir·e·o (VIHR-ee-oh) *noun.* A small, grayish or greenish insect-eating bird. **vireos.**

vir·gin (VER-jin) *noun.* 1. A young, unmarried woman; maiden. 2. A person who has never had sexual intercourse. 3. [Capital V] The Virgin Mary, the mother of Jesus. —*adjective.* 1. Unchanged from a natural or original condition; not used: a *virgin* forest. 2. Of or suiting a virgin; modest.

Vir·gin·ia (vər-JIN-yə) *noun.* A south Atlantic state of the United States, 10th to ratify the Constitution (1788). —**Va.** *abbreviation.* Also **VA** for Zip Codes.

Vir·go (VER-goh) *noun.* The sixth sign of the zodiac, also called the "Virgin." The time of this sign is from August 24 to September 23.

vir·tu·al (VER-choo-əl) *adjective.* In effect, though not in fact: The heavy snowstorm made us *virtual* prisoners in our own home. —**virtually** *adverb.*

vir·tue (VER-choo) *noun.* 1. Goodness or uprightness; morality. 2. A special quality or type of goodness: Mercy, courage, and trust are important *virtues.* 3. An advantage. —**virtuous** (VER-choo-əss) *adjective.* —**virtuously** *adverb.*

vi·rus (VIGH-rəss) *noun.* 1. Any of a variety of extremely small bacteria that cause various diseases. 2. Anything that poisons or corrupts the mind or character. **viruses.**

vi·sa (VEE-zə) *noun.* Written permission on a passport to enter or stay within a particular country.

vis·count (VIGH-kownt) *noun.* A nobleman who ranks just above a baron and just below an earl.

vise (VYSS) *noun.* A device with two jaws or matching surfaces that are cranked or screwed together to hold objects firmly in place. **vises.**

vis·i·bil·i·ty (viz-ə-BIL-ə-tee) *noun.* 1. The condition of being visible or able to be seen. 2. Possibility of seeing: *Visibility* in the morning fog was very poor. 3. The distance that a person is able to see clearly: *Visibility* is more than 20 miles on a clear day. **visibilities.**

vis·i·ble (VIZ-ə-bəl) *adjective.* Able to be seen. —**visibly** *adverb.*

vi·sion (VIZH-ən) *noun.* 1. The ability to see; power of sight. 2. An image; something seen in the imagination, as in a dream. "*Visions* of sugar-plums danced in their heads." (Moore). 3. Ability to think or plan with imagination: Centuries ago men of *vision* wrote about trips to the moon. 4. A supernatural sight or appearance: a *vision* of angels.

vis·it (VIZ-it) *noun.* 1. A social call: We had a short *visit* at Grandmother's house. 2. A business or professional call: a doctor's *visit.* 3. A stay: My *visit* to France lasted two weeks. —*verb.* 1. To call upon, as for social or business reasons. 2. To stay as a guest or tourist. 3. To affect or afflict: The family was *visited* by misfortune. **visited, visiting.**

vis·i·tor (VIZ-ə-tər) *noun.* A person who visits; a guest or caller.

vi·sor (VIGH-zər) *noun.* 1. A brim or peak on the front of a hat for shading the eyes. 2. A movable covering for the face in the front of a medieval or ancient helmet.

vis·ta (VISS-tə) *noun.* 1. A view, especially through a long, narrow opening: the *vista* at the end of the tunnel. 2. A long-range mental view: Reading provides us with new *vistas.*

vis·u·al (VIZH-oo-əl) *adjective.* Related to sight or seeing: The eye doctor corrects *visual* problems. —**visually** *adverb.*

vis·u·al·ize (VIZH-oo-əl-ighz) *verb.* To make a mental picture of; imagine. **visualized, visualizing.**

vi·tal (VIGH-tl) *adjective.* 1. Of or related to life or staying alive: The desire for food is a *vital* desire. 2. Essential; of special importance: Is honesty *vital* for success? 3. Full of life or vitality; energetic. —*noun.* (Plural) The heart, lungs, and other organs necessary to life. —**vitally** *adverb.*

vi·tal·i·ty (vigh-TAL-ə-tee) *noun.* 1. Vigor; the quality of being alert or energetic. 2. The power to grow, develop, or live: Good food aids *vitality.*

vi·ta·min (VIGH-tə-mən) *noun.* Any of a number of substances found in foods and essential to good health: *Vitamin* D, found in milk, aids in the growth of strong bones.

vit·re·ous (VIT-ree-əss) *adjective.* 1. Related to or similar to glass: Some plastics are *vitreous* in appearance. 2. Made from glass.

vi·va·cious (vi-VAY-shəss) *adjective.* Full of spirit or vitality; lively: a *vivacious* dance. —**vivaciously** *adverb.*

vi·vac·i·ty (vi-VASS-ə-tee) *noun.* Liveliness; being vivacious.

viv·id (VIV-id) *adjective.* 1. Bright; intense: The noon sky was a *vivid* blue. 2. Clear and lively: The story gave a *vivid* description of the race. —**vividly** *adverb.* —**vividness** *noun.*

vix·en (VIKS-n) *noun.* 1. A female fox. 2. A cross or bad-tempered woman.

vo·cab·u·lar·y (voh-KAB-yə-lehr-ee) *noun.* 1. All the words that a person knows or uses: The professor has a large *vocabulary.* 2. A list of words and their meanings, usually in alphabetical order. **vocabularies.**

vo·cal (VOH-kəl) *adjective.* 1. Of or related to the voice: *Vocal* music is for singing. 2. Speaking freely or loudly: The citizens were *vocal* in supporting the senator. —**vocally** *adverb.*

vocal cords. Folds or bands in the throat that produce sound when they are made tighter or looser as air is breathed out in the process of speaking or singing.

vireo

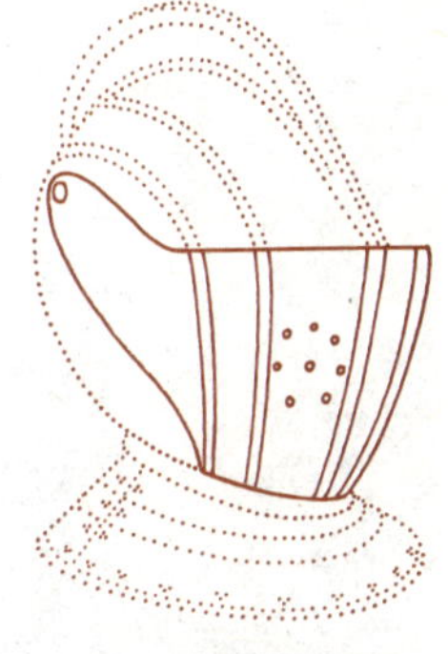

visor
(definition 2)

vo·ca·tion (voh-KAY-shən) *noun.* A career, profession, or occupation.

vo·cif·er·ous (voh-SIF-ər-əss) *adjective.* Noisy; loud and outspoken. —**vociferously** *adverb.*

vogue (VOHG) *noun.* 1. Fashion; style. 2. Popularity of a temporary nature.

voice (VOISS) *noun.* 1. Sounds made in speaking; speech: Billy heard his uncle's *voice.* 2. The quality or nature of speech: a soft *voice.* 3. Something that sounds like speaking: "They hear a *voice* in every wind." (Thomas Gray). 4. A wish or choice; right to decide: Each student has a *voice* in this election. 5. The form of a verb that shows whether its subject acts or receives an action: In "The player kicked the ball," "kicked" is in the active *voice;* in "The ball was kicked," "was kicked" is in the passive *voice.* —*verb.* To speak, utter, or express. **voiced, voicing.**

volleyball

void *adjective.* 1. Lacking; without: The boring speech was *void* of humor. 2. Not in effect; not legally binding: The judge declared the contract *void.* —*noun.* An empty space: a *void* between two high cliffs. —*verb.* To make ineffective; make not binding under the law: *void* a contract or agreement. **voided, voiding.**

voile (VOIL) *noun.* A filmy fabric.

vol·a·tile (VOL-ət-l) *adjective.* 1. Quick to evaporate; easily changed to gas: Fingernail polish remover is *volatile.* 2. Not firm; changing or not staying the same; flighty. 3. Easily angered; violent.

vol·can·ic (vol-KAN-ik) *adjective.* 1. From, like, or relating to a volcano: *volcanic* ash. 2. Violent; easily angered: a *volcanic* temper. —**volcanically** *adverb.*

volcano

vol·ca·no (vol-KAY-noh) *noun.* 1. A crack or opening in the surface of the earth from which hot, liquid rock pours or bursts out. 2. The mound or mountain formed from the outpouring of such a crack. —**volcanoes** or **volcanos** *plural.*

vol·ley (VOL-ee) *noun.* 1. The shooting of several guns at one time; the ammunition so shot at one time. 2. The erupting or shooting forth of similar things at one time: A *volley* of shouts from the grandstand filled the air. 3. (Tennis) The hitting of the ball before it has touched the ground. —*verb.* 1. To shoot all at one time. 2. (Tennis) To hit the ball before it has touched the ground. **volleyed, volleying.**

vol·ley·ball (VOL-ee-bawl) *noun.* 1. A game played by two teams with a lightweight ball nearly the size of a basketball, in which the means of scoring points is hitting the ball to the ground on the opponent's side of the net. 2. The ball with which this game is played.

volt (VOHLT) *noun.* A unit of measurement of electrical power.

volt·age (VOHL-tij) *noun.* Amount of electrical power, given in terms of the number of volts. **voltages.**

vol·u·ble (VOL-yə-bəl) *adjective.* Very talkative. —**volubly** *adverb.*

vol·ume (VOL-yoom or VOL-yəm) *noun.* 1. Capacity or amount of room or space: The *volume* of this bottle is one quart. 2. Any book, but particularly one of a set: *volume* II of an encyclopedia. 3. Amount or loudness of sound, or a knob used to control it: Please turn down the *volume* on your stereo. 4. (Plural) Great quantity or amount. **volumes.**

vo·lu·mi·nous (və-LOO-mə-nəss) *adjective.* 1. Great or large in volume or amount. 2. Having a great many pages or words; enough to fill volumes: *voluminous* letters. —**voluminously** *adverb.*

vol·un·tar·y (VOL-ən-tehr-ee) *adjective.* 1. Done willingly or cooperatively. 2. Willed; conscious: Moving one's toes is a *voluntary* action, while the beating of the heart is involuntary. 3. (Law) Done without force or persuasion. —**voluntarily** (vol-ən-TEHR-ə-lee) *adverb.*

vol·un·teer (vol-ən-TIHR) *verb.* 1. To offer or suggest through one's own desires: Jamie *volunteered* to clean the blackboards. 2. To go into or do by choice: *volunteer* for army service. **volunteered, volunteering.** —*noun.* A person who goes into something or offers his services by choice, without being forced.

vom·it (VOM-it) *verb.* To throw up or expel (through the mouth) undigested food from the stomach, usually because of illness. **vomited, vomiting.** —*noun.* The food so expelled from the stomach.

voo·doo (voo-doo) *noun.* 1. A religion, coming from Africa and still active in Haiti, that uses charms, spells, and other forms of witchcraft. 2. A magic charm or spell used in this religion. 3. A person of this religion believed to have magic powers. **voodoos.**

vo·ra·cious (vor-AY-shəss or və-RAY-shəss) *adjective.* 1. Greedy; extremely or wildly hungry. 2. Having an uncontrolled or extreme desire for something. —**voraciously** *adverb.* —**voracity** (vor-ASS-ə-tee) *noun.*

vor·tex (VOR-teks) *noun.* 1. A circular movement of gas or liquid, as a whirlwind or whirlpool. 2. Any situation which draws things around it toward the core or central part. —**vortexes** or **vortices** (VOR-tə-seez) *plural.*

vote (VOHT) *verb.* 1. To express, whether by voice, signal, or writing, one's opinion or choice, particularly in an election. 2. To decide or put into office by means of voting: Kevin was *voted* class president. **voted, voting.** —*noun.* 1. The showing or expressing of one's opinion, particularly in a formal or official situation. 2. A sign or signal of opinion, such as a piece of paper or ballot: After the election, Marcy and I counted the *votes.* 3. All the votes or ballots, or a special group of them: The farm *vote* is important in the election. **votes.** —**voter** *noun.*

vouch (VOWCH) *verb.* (Used with *for*) To support as true; guarantee. **vouched, vouching.**

vow *verb.* To promise, swear, or declare officially, under oath, or very seriously. **vowed, vowing.** —*noun.* 1. That which is so promised, sworn, or stated; a pledge or promise. 2. An official, legal, or religious pledge: marriage *vows.*

vow·el (vow-əl) *noun.* 1. Generally, a sound of speech made by voicing the flow of breath within the mouth, rather than one made using the lips and teeth. 2. One of the letters which stand for such a sound: The *vowels* in English are *a, e, i, o, u,* and sometimes *y.*

voy·age (VOI-ij) *noun.* A long trip or journey. **voyages.**

vul·gar (VUHL-gər) *adjective.* 1. Not proper; showing poor manners or no taste; crude. 2. Indecent or immoral: *vulgar* pictures. —**vulgarly** *adverb.*

vul·gar·i·ty (vuhl-GA-rə-tee) *noun.* 1. Being improper or without taste or manners; crudeness. 2. Something distasteful, offensive, or improper, as a crude joke. **vulgarities.**

vul·ner·a·ble (VUHL-nər-ə-bəl) *adjective.* 1. Open to attack or danger; in an undefended or unguarded position. 2. Likely to be hurt or injured. 3. Open to blame; likely to be criticized. —**vulnerability** *noun.* —**vulnerably** *adverb.*

vul·ture (VUHL-chər) *noun.* 1. A bird in the hawk family that lives by eating the carcasses of already killed animals. 2. A person who feeds on or profits from the mistakes or bad luck of others. **vultures.**

vulture

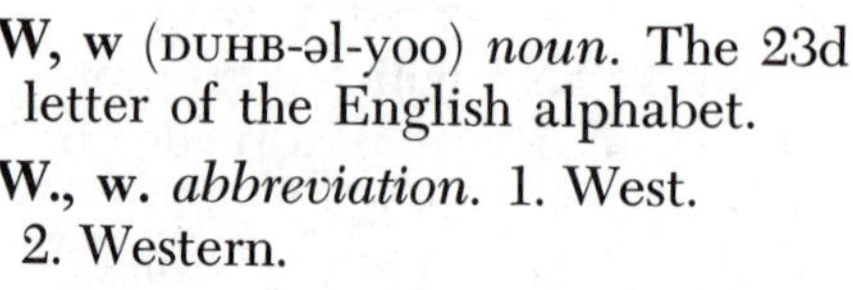

W, w (DUHB-əl-yoo) *noun.* The 23d letter of the English alphabet.

W., w. *abbreviation.* 1. West. 2. Western.

wagon

wad (WOD) *noun.* 1. A crumpled or packed mass, as of cotton or paper. 2. (Informal) A large amount: a *wad* of chewing gum. 3. (Informal) A quantity of money. *—verb.* 1. To roll or crumple into a tight mass. 2. To stuff or pad. **wadded, wadding.**

wad·dle (WOD-l) *verb.* To rock from side to side while walking with short steps like a duck or penguin. **waddled, waddling.** *—noun.* A swaying, duck-like walk.

wade (WAYD) *verb.* 1. To walk through water or something that slows movement. 2. To move or go (through) with difficulty: *wade* through the book. **waded, wading.**

wa·fer (WAY-fər) *noun.* A thin, crisp cracker, cooky, or small piece of candy.

waffle

waf·fle (WOF-əl) *noun.* Pancake batter baked into a crisp, patterned cake on a waffle iron. **waffles.**

waffle iron. An appliance, usually electrical, having two patterned grids that are heated and pressed together to cook the batter between them.

waft (WAHFT or WAFT) *verb.* To float or move gently through the air or on the water. **wafted, wafting.** *—noun.* 1. A gentle puff of air. 2. Something that is wafted, as a smell or sound.

wag *verb.* To move (something) quickly from side to side or up and down: The teacher *wags* her finger at us as a warning. **wagged, wagging.** *—noun.* A playful person.

wage (WAYJ) *noun.* 1. (Often plural) Pay; earnings. 2. (Plural, used with a singular or plural verb) The result of or payment for: "The *wages* of sin is death." (Romans 6:23). **wages.** *—verb.* To be a part of; take part in or carry on: *wage* war. **waged, waging.**

wa·ger (WAY-jər) *noun.* 1. A bet. 2. Something, as money, put up as a bet. *—verb.* To make a bet. **wagered, wagering.**

wag·on (WAG-ən) *noun.* 1. A four-wheeled cart used to carry loads. 2. A delivery truck or station wagon. 3. A small four-wheeled cart used by children.

waif (WAYF) *noun.* A lonely, homeless person or animal.

wail (WAYL) *verb.* 1. To cry or weep out loud. 2. To make a sound similar to such a cry. **wailed, wailing.** *—noun.* A howl or high-pitched cry or a similar sound.

waist (WAYST) *noun.* 1. The part of the body below the ribs and above the hips. 2. The top part of a garment: shirt*waist.* 3. The middle, narrow section of anything.

wait (WAYT) *verb.* 1. (Used with *for*) To stay (in a place) in expectation of (someone or something): *wait* for a plane. 2. To be delayed: My trip to Mexico will have to *wait* until next year. 3. (Informal) To hold off: Don't *wait* dinner for me. **waited, waiting.** *—noun.* A stay or waiting. **—lie in wait.** To stay quiet and hidden in order to make a surprise attack. **—wait on.** 1. To serve or attend. 2. To visit a superior: *wait on* the President. **—wait out.** To stay until (something) is over: *wait* *out* a storm. —**wait up.** To delay going to sleep (for some reason).

wait·er (WAYT-ər) *noun.* A man who serves food or waits on tables.

wait·ress (WAYT-riss) *noun.* A woman who serves food or waits on tables.

waive (WAYV) *verb.* 1. To forfeit or give up of one's own free will: I *waive* my right to vote. 2. To let pass; fail to enforce: The principal *waived* the requirement for a note from home. **waived, waiving.**

[1]**wake** (WAYK) *verb.* 1. (Often used with *up*) To bring or come to consciousness or awareness, as from sleep; to awaken. 2. To excite or arouse. 3. (Often used with *to*) To bring to one's attention or awareness: The accident *woke* them to the danger. **woke, waked** or **woken, waking.** —*noun.* A vigil, especially over a dead body. **wakes.**

[2]**wake** (WAYK) *noun.* 1. A stream of white foamy water left behind a boat or other thing moving through water. 2. Any visible or obvious effect, track, or trail left by something that has passed by. —**in the wake of.** 1. Following soon after. 2. As a result of.

wake·ful (WAYK-fəl) *adjective.* 1. Without sleep or sleepiness: For a *wakeful* evening, drink black coffee. 2. Unable to sleep. —**wakefully** *adverb.* —**wakefulness** *noun.*

wak·en (WAYK-ən) *verb.* To wake. **wakened, wakening.**

walk (WAWK) *verb.* 1. To move by taking steps with the feet. 2. To travel by foot, especially for enjoyment or health. 3. To travel over or through by walking: *walk* the halls. 4. To take for a walk: *walk* the dog. 5. (Baseball) To send or to go to first base when the pitcher has thrown four balls. **walked, walking.** —*noun.* 1. An instance of walking, especially one taken for enjoyment or health. 2. A path on which to walk. 3. The way or speed at which one walks: a graceful *walk.* 4. A gait of a horse in which two feet are always on the ground.

walk·ie-talk·ie (WAWK-ee-TAWK-ee) *noun.* A radio device with batteries, used to transmit voices back and forth over a distance between persons using sets. **walkie-talkies.**

walkie-talkie

wall (WAWL) *noun.* 1. A flat, vertical surface or side used to enclose something or keep something out: "Before I built a *wall* I'd ask to know/What I was walling in or walling out." (Robert Frost). 2. The vertical side of a room. —*verb.* 1. To make walls or surround with walls. 2. To divide or block with a wall. **walled, walling.**

wall·board (WAWL-bord) *noun.* Wood or man-made material formed into large, flat sheets and used for constructing or covering walls.

wal·let (WOL-it) *noun.* A flat case, usually of leather or plastic, used for holding money, particularly bills and cards.

wal·lop (WOL-əp) *verb.* (Informal) 1. To beat or whip hard. 2. To give a sharp blow to. 3. To overcome completely. **walloped, walloping.** —*noun.* A hard blow, or the strength to give one.

wal·low (WOL-oh) *verb.* 1. To roll around in mud. 2. (Used with *in*) To take selfish pleasure or comfort. **wallowed, wallowing.**

wall·pa·per (WAWL-pay-pər) *noun.* A thin, decorative paper or synthetic material used as a wall covering. —*verb.* To hang or cover with wallpaper. **wallpapered, wallpapering.**

wal·nut (WAWL-nuht) *noun.* 1. An edible nut with a hard, wrinkled, light brown shell. 2. The tree on which this nut grows. 3. The wood of this tree, dark brown in color. 4. (Also *adjective*). A dark brown color.

walnut

walrus

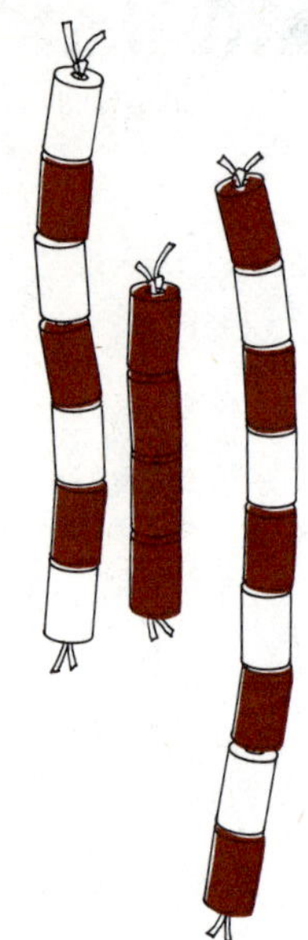
wampum

warbler

wal•rus (WAWL-rəss) *noun.* A sea animal of the seal family, with long tusks, flippers, and a tough hide. —**walruses** or **walrus** *plural.*

waltz (WAWLTS) *noun.* 1. A dance step or pattern having 3/4 time (three beats to a measure). 2. Music written in 3/4 time for this step. **waltzes.** —*verb.* 1. To dance a waltz. 2. To flit around as if dancing: She *waltzed* into the room as if she owned the place. 3. (Used with *through*) To do (something) easily or with little effort: Jan *waltzed* through her homework in no time. **waltzed, waltzing.**

wam•pum (WOM-pəm) *noun.* 1. Small shell beads, strung together, that were used by North American Indians as money and also as jewelry. 2. (Slang) Money.

wan (WON) *adjective.* 1. Without healthy color, usually because of illness or upset. 2. Weak or sickly, as in spirit or action. **wanner, wannest.** —**wanly** *adverb.*

wand (WOND) *noun.* 1. A magic stick or rod, used by fairies and magicians. 2. A long, thin stick used by an orchestra conductor; a baton.

wan•der (WON-dər) *verb.* 1. To walk or travel without purpose or certain direction; roam idly: "I *wandered* lonely as a cloud." (Wordsworth). 2. To become lost. **wandered, wandering.** —**wanderer** *noun.*

wane (WAYN) *verb.* 1. To become less in size or intensity; diminish. 2. To become less in apparent size: a *waning* moon. **waned, waning.** —**on the wane.** Becoming smaller or less intense.

want (WAWNT) *verb.* 1. To desire or wish for. 2. To lack or need: My sweater *wants* a button. 3. To look or hunt for in order to arrest: *wanted* for murder. **wanted, wanting.** —*noun.* 1. A desire or need. 2. A lack or absence (of something). 3. Poverty.

want ad. (Informal) An advertisement in a newspaper or magazine, describing a job, a position, or merchandise offered or needed by the advertiser.

want•ing (WAWN-ting) *adjective.* 1. Lacking or missing. 2. Inadequate. —*preposition.* Without.

wan•ton (WON-tən) *adjective.* 1. Having no regard or care for what is right or good: *wanton* cruelty. 2. Indecent or immoral. —*noun.* One who is wanton. —**wantonly** *adverb.*

war *noun.* 1. A state of armed fighting among states or nations. 2. A feud or long-standing argument. 3. The science of military tactics or strategy. —*verb.* 1. To be involved in or participate in a war. 2. (Used with *on* or *against*) To oppose. **warred, warring.**

war•ble (WOR-bəl) *verb.* 1. To sing with a fluttering sound or a trill: "There's where the birds *warble* sweet in the springtime." (Stephen Foster). 2. To make a sound having a tremor or flutter. **warbled, warbling.** —*noun.* A warbling or a similar sound.

war•bler (WOR-blər) *noun.* 1. A small brightly colored singing bird. 2. Anything that warbles.

ward *noun.* 1. One of a number of sections into which a city is divided for political purposes. 2. A large area or room in a hospital for certain patients: the children's *ward.* 3. An area in a jail or penitentiary. 4. (Law) A person watched over or cared for by someone else, such as a guardian. —**ward off.** To keep or turn away.

-ward, -wards *suffix.* Indicates going in a direction: north*ward.*

war•den (WAWRD-n) *noun.* 1. The keeper or head official in a jail or prison. 2. An official in charge of seeing that specific laws are obeyed: a game *warden.*

ward•robe (WAWRD-rohb) *noun.* 1. One's collection of clothes spoken of together: My *wardrobe* has too few skirts. 2. A portable closet for hanging or storing garments. 3. Theatrical costumes or the place they are kept. **wardrobes.**

ware (WAIR) *noun.* 1. (Used in combination words) Items of similar nature: silver*ware;* hard*ware;* stone*ware.* 2. (Plural) Goods or items for sale. **wares.**

ware•house (WAIR-howss) *noun.* A large storage building. **warehouses.** —*verb.* To store or put into a warehouse. **warehoused, warehousing.**

war•fare (WOR-fair) *noun.* 1. War or the fighting of a war. 2. Battle; any violent conflict. "Life is a struggle, but not a *warfare.*" (J. Burroughs)

war•like (WOR-lighk) *adjective.* 1. Not peaceful; of a fighting nature: a *warlike* tribe. 2. Relating to war; suggesting or leading toward war.

war•lock (WOR-lok) *noun.* A male who performs black magic; a wizard; male equivalent of a witch.

warm *adjective.* 1. Having or feeling a moderate amount of heat. 2. Maintaining or holding heat: *warm* clothes. 3. Showing great feeling: *warm* enthusiasm. 4. Friendly and open: a *warm* personality. 5. Of a color that seems warm (yellows to reds). 6. (Informal) Near or close to being right: That's not the answer, but you're getting *warm*! **warmer, warmest.** —*verb.* 1. To heat; make less cold. 2. To make feel happy or good. **warmed, warming.** —**warmly** *adverb.* —**warm up.** To practice; get into condition by exercising. —**warm-up** *noun.* A practice session.

warm•blood•ed (WAWRM-bluhd-id) *adjective.* Having a constant and warm body temperature that is not affected by environment or surroundings: Snakes are not *warm-blooded;* humans are.

warmth (WORMTH) *noun.* 1. The state of having some heat; being warm. 2. A showing of feeling, such as friendliness.

warn (WORN) *verb.* 1. To notify or tell in advance of possible or known danger. 2. To caution or advise: The dentist *warned* us about eating candy. **warned, warning.**

warn•ing (WOR-ning) *noun.* 1. An indication or telling in advance of possible or known danger. 2. An example or experience that demonstrates a danger: Our near accident was a *warning* to go slower.

warp (WORP) *verb.* 1. To become bent or twisted out of original shape: Left in the rain, the table top *warped.* 2. To make (a boat) move by using a rope attached to something stationary or secure. **warped, warping.** —*noun.* 1. The condition of being bent or twisted from original shape. 2. The threads of a fabric running down its length or long part (crossing threads called the woof). 3. A rope used to move a boat around.

war•rant (WOR-ənt) *noun.* 1. A paper giving the holder legal power to do a certain thing: search *warrant.* 2. Good reason: You are angry at me without *warrant.* —*verb.* 1. To provide a reason for; deserve: Your helpfulness *warrants* a special treat. 2. To prove or guarantee; give support to. **warranted, warranting.**

war•ri•or (WOR-ee-ər) *noun.* One who takes part in a battle or a war.

war•ship (WOR-ship) *noun.* A ship designed for fighting battles.

wart (WORT) *noun.* 1. A small, hard growth on the skin. 2. Something resembling a wart, as a growth on a plant.

war•y (WAIR-ee) *adjective.* 1. Cautious; careful to avoid danger or difficulty. 2. Showing or resulting from caution: a *wary* look. **warier, wariest.** —**warily** *adverb.*

warlock

was (WUHZ) *verb. See* **be.**

wash (WOSH) *verb.* 1. To clean with water. 2. To remove or be removed by rubbing or soaking in water. 3. To flow against: The blue ocean *washed* the sandy shore. 4. (Used with *away*) To remove, erode, or carry. 5. To carry, as on a wave: The tide *washed* the raft onto the beach. 6. (Informal) To remain believable after examination: The robber's story didn't *wash.* **washed, washing.** —*noun.* 1. A washing. 2. Things such as clothes that are washed or are going to be washed. 3. A swirl or rush of water or air, as that made by the propeller of a ship or airplane. 4. A liquid used for medical or cosmetic purposes: eye*wash;* mouth*wash.* 5. A thin paint or similar liquid: white*wash.* 6. A flow of water that carries away a substance, or that which is carried away. 7. A stream bed that has dried up. —**washable** *adjective.* —**wash one's hands of.** To refuse to have anything more to do with.

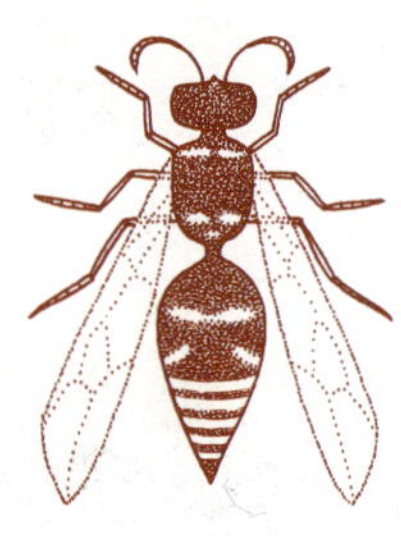
wasp

wash and wear. Needing little or no ironing after washing and drying.

wash·board (WOSH-bord) *noun.* A board with ridges on its surface, on which clothes are rubbed in the process of washing. —*adjective.* Having an uneven surface like a washboard: a *washboard* road.

wash·bowl (WOSH-bohl) *noun.* A bowl or basin used to hold water for washing the face and hands.

wash·er (WOSH-ər) *noun.* 1. A disk, usually of metal or rubber, with a hole in its center, used with nuts and bolts to keep a connection tight or to keep out water. 2. A washing machine.

wash·ing (WOSH-ing) *noun.* 1. Clothes and other things that are washed or going to be washed. 2. A cleaning.

Washington
★capital: Olympia

Wash·ing·ton (WOSH-ing-tən) *noun.* A Pacific state of the United States, 42d to join the Union (1889). —**Wash.** *abbreviation.* Also **WA** for Zip Codes.

Washington, D.C. *See* **District of Columbia.**

Washington's Birthday. A legal holiday in most of the United States, celebrated on the third Monday in February, in honor of George Washington (born February 22, 1732), the first President.

wash·out (WOSH-owt) *noun.* 1. The wearing away or erosion of something by water, as a road by heavy rains. 2. A hole or ditch left by a wearing away with water. 3. (Informal) A failure.

was·n't (WUHZ-nt) *contraction.* A shortened form of *was not.*

wasp (WOSP) *noun.* 1. A flying insect that can give a painful sting. 2. [Capitals WASP] Acronym for White Anglo-Saxon Protestant.

wasp·ish (woss-pish) *adjective.* Cross; ill-tempered. —**waspishly** *adverb.*

waste (WAYST) *noun.* 1. Garbage; anything to be thrown away. 2. Extra; that which is left over. 3. Food and other material that the body does not use or digest and thus eliminates. 4. A careless using up or leaving unused: a *waste* of money. 5. A desert or other empty, unused place. **wastes.** —*verb.* 1. To be careless in using; to use more than is needed. 2. To lose or fail to take: *waste* a chance. **wasted, wasting.** —**lay waste.** To devastate or bring to ruin.

waste·bas·ket (WAYST-bass-kit) *noun.* A basket or container for litter.

waste·ful (WAYST-fəl) *adjective.* Tending to waste or use too much. —**wastefully** *adverb.*

watch (WOCH) *verb.* 1. To look at carefully for a time. 2. To guard; protect: "For some must *watch* while some must sleep." (Shakespeare). 3. (Used with *for*) To look hopefully: to *watch* for a chance.

4. To keep track of; be aware of: A good shopper *watches* prices. **watched, watching.** —*noun.* 1. A small timepiece, often worn on the wrist. 2. A period during which a guard or other person stays alert.

watch·dog (WOCH-dawg) *noun.* A dog trained to guard property.

watch·ful (WOCH-fəl) *adjective.* Watching carefully; alert; cautious. —**watchfully** *adverb.* —**watchfulness** *noun.*

watch·man (WOCH-mən) *noun.* A man who guards a building or other property. —**watchmen** *plural.*

watch·tow·er (WOCH-tow-ər) *noun.* A tower from which guards or others who watch can have a clear and wide view.

watch·word (WOCH-werd) *noun.* 1. A password; a secret word or phrase used to identify oneself. 2. A slogan: "Remember the Alamo" is a famous *watchword* in Texas.

wa·ter (WOT-ər) *noun.* 1. The liquid that makes up oceans, lakes, and streams. 2. (Often plural) A body of water, as an ocean or flood: The ship sailed across the *waters.* 3. A liquid similar to water, as tears. —*verb.* 1. To spray or pour water over: *Water* the roses. 2. To give water to drink: *water* the horses. 3. To give off or fill with water or a similar liquid: Dave's eyes *water* when he peels onions. 4. To mix or weaken with water: *water* the soup. **watered, watering.**

water buffalo. A large mammal that resembles an ox and is often used in Asia and Africa as a work animal.

water color. 1. Paint with a water, rather than oil, base. 2. A painting done with such paint.

wa·ter·course (WOT-ər-korss) *noun.* A river, brook, or its channel.

wa·ter·fall (WOT-ər-fawl) *noun.* A steep fall of a stream of water from a higher to a lower place.

wa·ter·fowl (WOT-ər-fowl) *noun.* A water bird: Ducks are *waterfowl.* —**waterfowl** or **waterfowls** *plural.*

wa·ter·front (WOT-ər-fruhnt) *noun.* The part of a city or other land area that borders a body of water: Ships are tied up along the *waterfront.*

water lily. A large flower, with large, flat, floating leaves, that grows on a water plant.

wa·ter·logged (WOT-ər-logd) *adjective.* Heavily soaked or filled with water.

water main. A big, main water pipe.

wa·ter·mel·on (WOT-ər-mel-ən) *noun.* A large, green melon with sweet red pulp.

water polo. A game played in the water, the object of which is to get a ball into the other team's goal.

wa·ter·pow·er (WOT-ər-pow-ər) *noun.* Power that is or can be produced by moving or falling water: *Waterpower* once turned mill wheels; now it produces electricity.

wa·ter·proof (WOT-ər-proof) *adjective.* Able to prevent water from passing through: a *waterproof* raincoat. —*verb.* To make waterproof: The men *waterproofed* the roof with tar. **waterproofed, waterproofing.** —*noun.* Material that keeps water from passing through.

wa·ter·shed (WOT-ər-shed) *noun.* 1. A ridge or raised area that divides two sections drained by different river systems. 2. A land area drained by a river system.

wa·ter-ski (WOT-ər-skee) *verb.* To skim over water on a special pair of skis while being pulled by a motorboat. **water-skied, water-skiing.** —*noun.* One of a pair of short, wide skis used in water-skiing.

water spaniel. A dog, with curly hair that sheds water, used to retrieve ducks, geese, and other waterfowl.

water lily

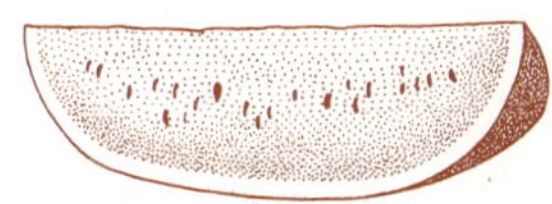

watermelon

water buffalo

water-skiing

wa·ter·spout (WOT-ər-spowt) *noun.* 1. A pipe or tube through which water drains or flows. 2. A funnel-shaped column of water, caused and moved along by a tornado over water.

water table. The level under which the ground is saturated or filled with water.

wa·ter·tight (WOT-ər-tight) *adjective.* 1. Sealed or closed so tight that no water can enter. 2. Having no flaws or weaknesses: a *watertight* excuse.

water vapor. Water in the form of a cool vapor or gas: Fog and mist are *water vapor.*

water wheel

wa·ter·way (WOT-ər-way) *noun.* 1. A river or other body of water through which ships can pass. 2. The bed or channel of a river or other flowing body of water.

water wheel. A large wheel with many blades, turned by moving or falling water.

wa·ter·y (WOT-ər-ee) *adjective.* 1. Of or like water. 2. Wet; moist. 3. Mixed or diluted with water: *watery* soup. **waterier, wateriest.**

watt (WOT) *noun.* A unit of electrical power.

wave (WAYV) *noun.* 1. A moving ridge or bulge of water. 2. A moving shape or ridge that resembles a wave of water: *waves* of clouds. 3. A curl of hair. 4. A moving of the hand back and forth, as in a greeting or farewell. 5. A period during which an activity or condition is especially noticeable: heat *wave.* 6. A sudden surge or movement: a *wave* of fear. 7. An impulse or vibration of energy: sound *waves.* **waves.** *—verb.* 1. To move back and forth: A banner *waved* in the breeze. 2. To move the hand back and forth, as in a greeting or farewell: *wave* good-by. **waved, waving.** —**wavy** *adjective.*

wave length. The distance between similar points on two consecutive waves in a series of impulses or vibrations of energy, as of radio or sound waves.

wa·ver (WAY-vər) *verb.* 1. To sway; move back and forth. 2. To incline first toward one thing and then toward another; be unable to decide. 3. To lose strength; falter. **wavered, wavering.** *—noun.* A fluctuation: There was a *waver* in the speaker's voice.

[1]**wax** (WAKS) *noun.* 1. A yellowish substance made by bees, solid when cold but easily molded when warm. 2. Any of a variety of similar substances: Use *wax* to polish the table. **waxes.** *—verb.* To rub with wax, to polish or protect: Wash and *wax* the car. **waxed, waxing.** —**waxen** *adjective.*

[2]**wax** (WAKS) *verb.* To develop or increase, as in size or amount: The moon *waxes* and wanes. **waxed, waxing.**

way *noun.* 1. A method of doing something: the best *way* to make a fire. 2. A route: the *way* to Boston. 3. A habit; manner of behaving. 4. A detail or respect: In some *ways* I dislike football. 5. A choice; a desire: If I had my *way,* Monday would be a holiday. 6. A distance: a long *way.* 7. A direction: To reach the library, go that *way.* 8. Room to allow movement or passing: Make *way.* 9. A road or path: Jim lives in the house across the *way.* 10. An area; neighborhood: Does this bus go out our *way?* 11. (Informal) Condition: The old house is in a bad *way.* 12. (Plural) A frame or series of timbers on which a ship is built. *—adverb.* (Informal) 1. Far: *way* ahead. 2. Much: *way* better. —**by the way.** Incidentally. —**make one's way.** 1. To travel carefully: The donkey *made its way* along the narrow trail. 2. To support or take care of oneself. —**No way!** (Slang)

Not possible or allowed. —**out of the way.** Away from people or activity. —**under way.** In motion; started. —**way out.** (Slang) Novel; different in an exciting manner; far out.

way·far·er (WAY-fair-ər) *noun.* A person who travels, especially on foot.

way·lay (WAY-lay) *verb.* To ambush; wait for and attack. **waylaid, waylaying.**

way·side (WAY-sighd) *adjective.* By the side of a road: a *wayside* tavern. —*noun.* The area next to a road.

way·ward (WAY-wərd) *adjective.* Unruly; headstrong; willful. —**waywardly** *adverb.*

we (WEE) *pronoun.* Plural used when speaking of oneself and one or more other persons.

weak (WEEK) *adjective.* 1. Without physical strength, endurance, or vitality. 2. Without will power, determination, or moral strength. 3. Easily broken or destroyed: The *weak* rope snapped. 4. Easily defeated or overcome: The *weak* team lost every game. 5. Not convincing or reasonable: a *weak* argument. 6. Not having normal intensity, strength, or effect: a *weak* light. **weaker, weakest.** —**weakly** *adverb.*

weak·en (WEEK-ən) *verb.* To become or make weak. **weakened, weakening.**

weak·ling (WEEK-ling) *noun.* One who is physically or morally weak.

weak·ness (WEEK-niss) *noun.* 1. Lack of strength. 2. A flaw or fault. 3. A special liking or attraction (usually for something one should resist).

wealth (WELTH) *noun.* 1. Riches; large amounts of property or possessions. 2. An abundance; a large or valuable amount: The team has a *wealth* of talent. 3. Natural resources: The oceans are a source of food, minerals, and other *wealth.*

wealth·y (WEL-thee) *adjective.* Rich; having much money or other wealth. **wealthier, wealthiest.**

wean (WEEN) *verb.* 1. To accustom (an infant) to food other than mother's milk. 2. To make (a person) give up an activity or situation. **weaned, weaning.**

weap·on (WEP-ən) *noun.* 1. A device used in fighting or war to cause harm or damage: Rifles, bombs, and tanks are *weapons* of war. 2. Any device used to defeat someone or to get one's own way.

wear (WAIR) *verb.* 1. To have on the body: Did Jane *wear* her blue dress? 2. To show; have: *wear* a happy look. 3. To make by moving or rubbing: Wheels can *wear* ruts in a road. 4. To last; stay in good condition: My boots *wear* well. 5. To pass slowly (said of time): as summer *wears* on. **wore, worn, wearing.** —*noun.* 1. Clothing: men's *wear.* 2. A wearing out or using up: Grease and oil reduce *wear* in a car's engine. —**wear out.** 1. To make or become used up or weakened: Years of use will *wear out* a purse. 2. To make weary: A long race *wears out* the runners.

wea·ri·some (WIHR-ee-səm) *adjective.* Tiresome or boring. —**wearisomely** *adverb.*

wea·ry (WIHR-ee) *adjective.* 1. Tired; exhausted. 2. Wearisome; tiring: a *weary* journey. **wearier, weariest.** —*verb.* To make or become weary; to tire. **wearied, wearying.** —**wearily** *adverb.* —**weariness** *noun.*

wea·sel (WEEZ-l) *noun.* 1. A small, slender mammal with short legs and a long tail. 2. A sly, sneaky person. —**weasel out.** To sneak out of doing something.

weasels

weath·er (WETH-ər) *noun.* The condition of the atmosphere or air in terms of temperature, humidity, wind, and similar features. —*verb.* 1. To become worn or affected by exposure to the weather. 2. To survive; pass through safely: "Here's to the pilot that *weathered* the storm." (G. Canning). **weathered, weathering.** —**under the weather.** (Informal) Not feeling well; sick.

Weather Bureau. An agency of the government that gathers information about the weather in order to keep records, make forecasts, and perform similar tasks.

weath·er·cock (WETH-ər-kok) *noun.* A weather vane shaped like a rooster.

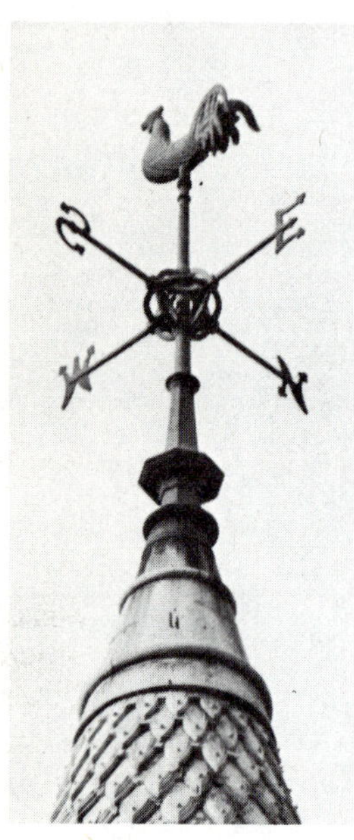

weathercock

weath·er·man (WETH-ər-man) *noun.* A man who forecasts or reports the weather, as on radio or TV. —**weathermen** *plural.*

weather map. A map showing weather conditions in an area at a particular time.

weather vane. A device that turns to show the direction in which the wind is blowing.

weave (WEEV) *verb.* 1. To make (a fabric, basket, or other item) by interlacing or overlapping threads or strips of material. 2. To compose; put together: *weave* a story. 3. To travel or move by winding in and out: *weave* through traffic. **wove** (WOHV) (or **weaved** for number 3), **weaving.** —*noun.* The pattern or method of weaving. **weaves.**

web *noun.* 1. The delicate net-like structure that a spider weaves. 2. A piece of newly woven fabric. 3. A complex arrangement of things; network: a *web* of telephone lines. 4. A complex situation: "Oh, what a tangled *web* we weave,/When first we practice to deceive!" (Sir Walter Scott). 5. A thin membrane that joins the toes of certain water birds.

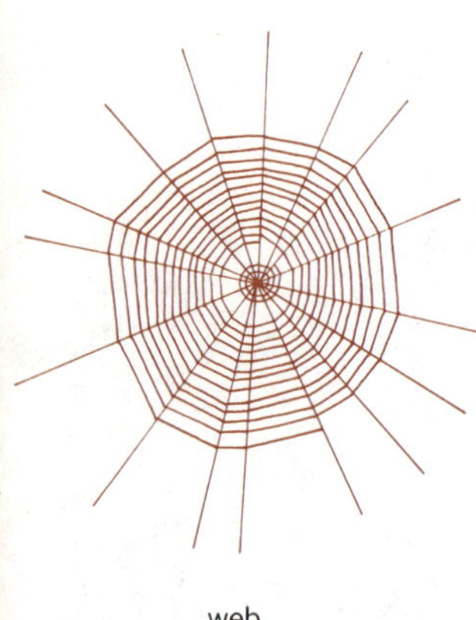
web

wed *verb.* 1. To marry. 2. To join together: The artist *wedded* blue paint and yellow to form green. **wedded, wed** or **wedded, wedding.**

we'd (WEED) *contraction.* A shortened form of the words *we had, we would,* or *we should.*

wed·ding (WED-ing) *noun.* A marriage ceremony.

wedge (WEJ) *noun.* 1. A piece of metal or wood that narrows to a sharp edge and is used with a hammer to split logs, raise heavy loads, and aid in similar tasks. 2. Anything that has the shape of a wedge: a *wedge* of pie. **wedges.** —*verb.* 1. To make (something) fit tightly: The workman *wedged* the stone into place. 2. To force or jam into a small space: Three boys *wedged* into the telephone booth. **wedged, wedging.**

wed·lock (WED-lok) *noun.* Marriage.

Wednes·day (WENZ-dee or WENZ-day) *noun.* The fourth day of the week. *Wednesday* is the day between Tuesday and Thursday. —**Wed.** *abbreviation.*

wee *adjective.* Tiny. **weer, weest.**

weed *noun.* An unwanted plant that harms or interferes with the growth of wanted ones. —*verb.* To remove weeds from. **weeded, weeding.** —**weed out.** To remove (unwanted persons or things).

weed·y (WEE-dee) *adjective.* 1. Full of weeds. 2. Like a weed. 3. Tall and thin; lanky. **weedier, weediest.**

week *noun.* 1. A period of seven days, especially one beginning on Sunday and ending on Saturday. 2. The days or time spent in work during such a seven-day period: Dad works a five-day *week.*

week·day (WEEK-day) *noun.* Any day from Monday through Friday, and sometimes Saturday.

week·end (WEEK-end) *noun.* The period from late Friday through Sunday night.

week·ly (WEEK-lee) *adjective.* Of, for, or related to a week; once a week:

weekly salary. —*adverb.* Once a week; every week. —*noun.* A newspaper or magazine published once a week. **weeklies.**

weep *verb.* 1. To shed tears. 2. To mourn; lament. **wept, weeping.**

weeping willow. A type of willow tree with long, slender, hanging branches.

wee·vil (WEE-vəl) *noun.* A small beetle whose young destroy cotton and other crops.

weigh (WAY) *verb.* 1. To have a certain weight or heaviness: Bill *weighs* 94 pounds. 2. To measure the heaviness of: The butcher *weighed* the beef. 3. To think about the possible effects of (an action). 4. To bear heavily on: Snow *weighed* down the branches. 5. (Used with *on*) To be a difficulty: Poverty *weighed* heavily on the old man. 6. To raise (an anchor). 7. To be considered or counted: The good report will *weigh* in his favor. **weighed, weighing.**

weight (WAYT) *noun.* 1. An amount of heaviness: The *weight* of the package is three pounds. 2. Heaviness; the force of gravity pulling on an object: *Weight* keeps the rock from blowing away. 3. An object used to hold down or pull down something else: a paper*weight.* 4. A carefully measured object that represents an exact weight: a four-ounce *weight.* 5. A burden or strain: the *weight* of responsibility. 6. One of the heavy metal disks on the end of a bar used in weightlifting. 7. Influence; power. —*verb.* 1. To add weight or heavy objects to: The fisherman *weights* his line so the bait will sink. 2. To burden: to *weight* with work. **weighted, weighting.** —**pull one's weight.** To do one's share: Jon more than *pulled his weight* on the work crew.

weight·less (WAYT-liss) *adjective.* 1. Having no weight: A feather is almost *weightless.* 2. Affected by little or no pull of gravity: An astronaut in space flight is almost *weightless.* —**weightlessly** *adverb.* **weightlessness** *noun.*

weight·y (WAY-tee) *adjective.* 1. Heavy. 2. Important: a *weighty* decision. 3. Difficult: a *weighty* problem. **weightier, weightiest.** —**weightily** *adverb.*

weird (WIHRD) *adjective.* 1. Mysterious; suggesting supernatural events: The old hags began a *weird* chant. 2. Odd; unusual. **weirder, weirdest.** —**weirdly** *adverb.*

weird·o (WIHR-doh) *noun.* (Slang) A very odd or strange person or thing. **weirdoes.**

wel·come (WEL-kəm) *adjective.* 1. Gladly or freely given a favor. 2. Received with pleasure: a *welcome* guest. —*verb.* 1. To greet. 2. To receive with pleasure: The farmers *welcomed* the spring rain. **welcomed, welcoming.** —*noun.* A greeting or receiving. —*interjection.* Expresses a friendly greeting or reception. —**wear out one's welcome.** To stay beyond the time during which one's company is wanted.

weld *verb.* 1. To join metal items by applying enough heat to make them soft enough to melt or be hammered together. 2. To join: "Ice and iron cannot be *welded.*" (R. L. Stevenson). **welded, welding.** —*noun.* 1. The act of welding. 2. The spot where metal parts have been welded.

wel·fare (WEL-fair) *noun.* 1. A state of being well-off or in good order; well-being. 2. Public help given to the needy in the form of money, goods, or services.

[1]**well** (WEL) *adverb.* 1. In a good or skillful manner: Marie dances *well.* 2. Thoroughly: Wash your hands *well.* 3. Through close contact; intimately: Do you know Ralph *well?* 4. To a great degree; far: The temperature is *well* below freezing.

5. With good reason: You might *well* be proud of your good behavior. 6. In a prosperous or comfortable manner. **better, best.** —*adjective.* 1. In good health; not sick. 2. In good order or condition. 3. Appropriate; right. **better, best.** —*interjection.* Expresses: 1. Surprise or annoyance. 2. Indecision.

well

[2]**well** (WEL) *noun.* 1. A hole or shaft dug in the ground to get water, oil, or gas. 2. Something that resembles a well in appearance or use: an ink*well.* 3. A source: a *well* of talent. 4. A shaft or opening between the floors of a building, as for stairs or an elevator. —*verb.* To surge: The insult caused anger to *well* up within me. **welled, welling.**

we'll (WEEL) *contraction.* A shortened form of *we will* or *we shall.*

well-be·haved (WEL-bi-HAYVD) *adjective.* Having good or proper manners.

well-be·ing (WEL-BEE-ing) *noun.* A state of being well-off or in good health; welfare.

well-bred (WEL-BRED) *adjective.* Well-mannered; brought up properly.

well-known (WEL-NOHN) *adjective.* Known by many; famous.

well-man·nered (WEL-MAN-ərd) *adjective.* Polite.

well-to-do (wel-tə-DOO) *adjective.* Wealthy; prosperous.

West Virginia
★capital: Charleston

welt *noun.* 1. A bruise or narrow lump on the skin, usually caused by a blow. 2. A strip of leather stitched between the sole and the upper part of a shoe.

wel·ter (WEL-tər) *noun.* A confusing mixture; jumble: a *welter* of clothes, toys, and books. —*verb.* To wallow; roll about. **weltered, weltering.**

wend *verb.* To proceed; go: We *wend* our way to school. **wended, wending.**

went *verb. See* **go.**

wept *verb. See* **weep.**

were (WER) *verb. See* **be.**

we're (WIHR) *contraction.* A shortened form of the words *we are.*

wer·en't (WERNT) *contraction.* A short form of the words *were not.*

were·wolf (WIHR-wulf) *noun.* In legend, a person who can change into a wolf and back again. —**werewolves** (WIHR-wulvz) *plural.*

west *noun.* 1. The direction in which the sun sets; opposite of east. 2. [Capital W] The part of the United States that lies west of the Mississippi River. 3. [Capital W] The countries of western Europe and the Americas. —*adjective.* At or from the west. —*adverb.* To or toward the west. *See* illustration at **compass.**

west·er·ly (WESS-tər-lee) *adjective* and *adverb.* 1. From the west: a *westerly* breeze. 2. Toward the west: a *westerly* voyage.

west·ern (WESS-tərn) *adjective.* 1. In, toward, or from the west. 2. [Often capital W] Of or related to the western part of the United States. —*noun.* [Often capital W] A movie or story about life in the western part of the United States, especially during frontier times.

West Virginia. A south Atlantic state of the United States, 35th to join the Union (1863). —**W. Va.** *abbreviation.* Also **WV** for Zip Codes.

west·ward (WEST-wərd) Also **westwards** (WEST-wərdz) *adjective* and *adverb.* Toward the west.

wet *adjective.* 1. Covered or soaked (with water or another liquid): The fields were *wet* with rain. 2. Not yet dry: The paint is *wet.* 3. Rainy: *wet* weather. **wetter, wettest.** —*verb.* To make or become wet. **wetted, wetting.** —*noun.* Rain; wet weather. —**wetness** *noun.*

wet·lands (WET-landz) *noun, plural.* Marshes, swamps, or similar land.

we've (WEEV) *contraction.* A shortened form of the words *we have.*

whack (HWAK) *verb.* To hit with a loud, sharp sound. **whacked, whacking.** —*noun.* 1. A loud, sharp hit or blow. 2. The noise made by a whack or sharp blow. 3. (Informal) A try; an attempt. —**out of whack.** (Slang) Not working properly.

whale (HWAYL) *noun.* 1. A huge mammal that resembles a fish and lives in the sea. 2. (Informal) Something outstanding or special: a *whale* of a party. —*verb.* To hunt for whales. **whaled, whaling.**

wharf (HWORF) *noun.* A platform or similar structure built along a shore so ships can load and unload cargo. —**wharves** (HWORVZ) or **wharfs** *plural.*

what (HWOT) *pronoun.* 1. Which one; which things: *What* are you wearing? 2. Which kind or type: *What* are those cookies? 3. How much or how large: *What* is your weight? 4. That which: *What* she said was untrue. —*adverb.* Why; in which way: *What* does she care? —*adjective.* 1. Which certain one: *What* day is it? 2. How special or surprising: *What* a great bike!

what·ev·er (hwot-EV-ər or hwuht-EV-ər) *pronoun.* 1. Anything or everything that: Eat *whatever* you like. 2. No matter what: *Whatever* you do, be careful. 3. (Informal) What: *Whatever* did she mean? —*adjective.* 1. No matter what: *Whatever* suggestions the coach gives, obey them. 2. Any: Wrap up *whatever* food is not eaten. 3. Of any type: He refuses to do us any favors *whatever.*

what's (HWOTS) *contraction.* A shortened form of the words *what is.*

wheat (HWEET) *noun.* 1. A grain that is ground into flour for making bread and similar foods. 2. The plant on which this grain grows.

whee (HWEE) *interjection.* Expresses sudden excitement or a thrill.

whee·dle (HWEED-l) *verb.* 1. To coax; persuade by flattery or pleasing words: Jim *wheedles* his sister into doing his work. 2. To get by coaxing or persuading: *wheedle* a favor. **wheedled, wheedling.**

wheel (HWEEL) *noun.* 1. A circular frame or disk that turns on an axle at its center: A bicycle has two *wheels.* 2. A device that is like a wheel in appearance or use: steering *wheel.* 3. (Plural) Forces or operations that control or produce: The *wheels* of progress often turn slowly. 4. (Slang) A person who has much power or influence: Mr. Jones is a big *wheel* in government. 5. (Plural, slang) An automobile: Where are your *wheels?* —*verb.* 1. To move (something) on wheels: *wheel* a baby carriage. 2. To turn (around or aside); rotate or pivot. **wheeled, wheeling.**

wheel·bar·row (HWEEL-ba-roh) *noun.* A container with a single wheel in front and two long handles in back, used for moving heavy loads.

wheel·chair (HWEEL-chair) Also **wheel chair** *noun.* A chair mounted on large wheels in which a disabled person can move or be moved.

wheeze (HWEEZ) *verb.* 1. To breathe with a whistling sound, usually because of sickness. 2. To make a whistling sound. **wheezed, wheezing.** —*noun.* A high, whistling sound. **wheezes.**.

whelk (HWELK) *verb.* Any of a variety of large water snails that are sometimes eaten as food.

whelp (HWELP) *noun.* 1. The young of a dog, lion, or other such animal; cub. 2. A child, often an unruly one. —*verb.* To give birth to (an animal). **whelped, whelping.**

wheat

wheelbarrow

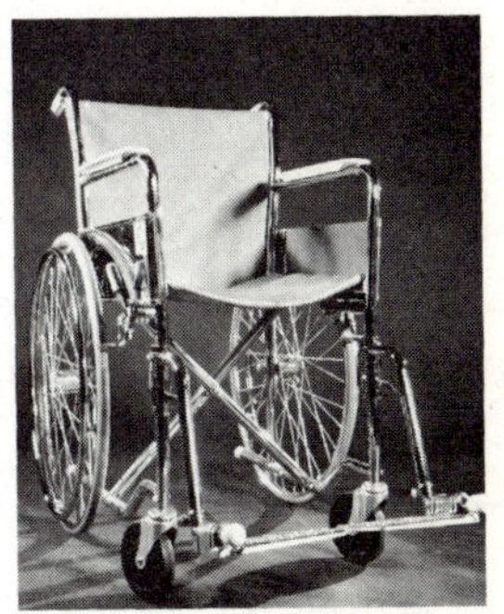
wheelchair

when (HWEN) *adverb.* At what time: *When* did the ship leave? —*conjunction.* 1. At the time that: Work stops *when* the bell rings. 2. Right after which: The firemen had just come from one fire *when* another one started. 3. In spite of the fact that: The boys are playing *when* they should be studying. —*pronoun.* What or which time: Since *when* have you liked to swim? —*noun.* The time that something happens: We learned the *when* and the why of the freeing of the slaves.

whence (HWENSS) *adverb.* (Rare) From what place or source: "And the Lord said unto Satan: *Whence* comest thou?" (Job 1:7).

when·ev·er (hwen-EV-ər) *adverb.* 1. At any time: Let's go hiking *whenever* we can. 2. (Informal) When: *Whenever* will he leave me alone? —*conjunction.* 1. At any time that: Please call me *whenever* you need a friend. 2. Each time: I get hungry *whenever* I think of pie.

where (HWAIR) *adverb.* 1. In or at what place or direction: *Where* is the office? 2. In what condition or state: *Where* would a school be without teachers? 3. From what person, thing, or place: *Where* did he get this money? 4. To what place or direction: "*Where,* oh *where,* has my little dog gone?" (Nursery song). —*conjunction.* 1. At what place or direction: Did you see *where* he hid the card? 2. In a place that: *Where* there's dancing, you'll find music. 3. To a place that or in which: Let's move *where* the children can play safely. —*pronoun.* The place that: *where* the accident occurred. —*noun.* The place or scene: the *where* and when of the robbery.

where·a·bouts (HWAIR-ə-bowts) *noun.* The place where a person or thing is: Do you know Tom's *where-abouts?* —*adverb.* About where: *Whereabouts* is the train station?

where·as (hwair-AZ) *conjunction.* 1. Since it is true that. 2. On the other hand; but: Sally and Susan got their shoes wet, *whereas* we remembered to wear our rubbers.

where·by (hwair-BIGH) *adverb.* By the means or condition of which; because of or through which: I'll set a trap *whereby* we'll catch the thief.

where·on (hwair-ON) *adverb.* On which or on what.

where's (HWAIRZ) *contraction.* A shortened form of *where is.*

where·up·on (HWAIR-ə-pon) *adverb.* Upon which; whereon. —*conjunction.* Then; at or after that time: Dinner was served; *whereupon* we began to eat.

wher·ev·er (hwair-EV-ər) *conjunction.* 1. Any place that: My dog goes *wherever* I go. 2. In any situation that: *Wherever* it is needed, I give my help. —*adverb.* (Informal. Used to make a statement stronger) Where: *Wherever* has that foolish boy gone?

where·with·al (HWAIR-wi<u>th</u>-awl) *noun.* That which is necessary, usually money: I don't have the *wherewithal* to go to the movie.

whet (HWET) *verb.* 1. To make sharp or give a cutting edge to: *whet* a knife. 2. To make stronger or more eager: The smell of dinner cooking *whetted* his appetite. **whetted, whetting.**

wheth·er (HWE<u>TH</u>-ər) *conjunction.* 1. If it is a fact that: Do you know *whether* Bill is sick? 2. Indicating a choice among two (or more) possibilities: *Whether* by bus, train, or foot, I'll make it to your party.

whet·stone (HWET-stohn) *noun.* A stone with a rough surface on which cutting tools are sharpened.

whew (HWOO or HWYOO) *interjection.* Exclamation of relief, tiredness, or wonder.

whey (HWAY) *noun.* The clear, water-like liquid that separates from the curd when milk is soured or made into cheese.

which (HWICH) *pronoun.* 1. What certain one or ones: *Which* seems prettiest to you? 2. Something or a situation that: He forgot his ticket, *which* was very unfortunate. 3. A thing, animal, or happening already named or mentioned: My bicycle, *which* is broken, sits unused in the garage. *—adjective.* What certain one or ones: *Which* bicycle is yours?

which·ev·er (hwich-EV-ər) *adjective.* 1. Any: Wear *whichever* scarf you want. 2. No matter which or what: I got into mud *whichever* way I turned. *—pronoun.* Any one (or ones) that.

whiff (HWIF) *noun.* 1. A puff or light current of air. 2. A sniff or quick breath, as of an odor: One *whiff* and I knew it was apple pie. 3. The odor itself, moving through the air: a *whiff* of newly cut grass.

while (HWIGHL) *noun.* A time; a period of time: Rest for a *while.* *—conjunction.* 1. For the time that: *While* we rested, Jim played his guitar. 2. Even though: *While* he can't sing, he plays very well. 3. On the contrary; whereas: My sister is quiet, *while* I am somewhat noisy. —**while away.** To pass (the time) without care or purpose.

whim (HWIM) *noun.* A sudden urge or desire; a fanciful notion or idea.

whim·per (HWIM-pər) *verb.* 1. To make a soft crying or moaning sound. 2. To complain with a whine. **whimpered, whimpering.** *—noun.* 1. A soft, sobbing cry. 2. An act or instance of whimpering.

whim·si·cal (HWIM-zi-kəl) *adjective.* 1. Light and spontaneous; not serious: *whimsical* stories. 2. Odd; outlandish. —**whimsically** *adverb.*

whine (HWIGHN) *verb.* 1. To make a squealing sound without stopping: The sirens *whined.* 2. To complain in a nagging, annoying manner without stopping. **whined, whining.** *—noun.* 1. A whining sound. 2. Any instance of whining.

whin·ny (HWIN-ee) *verb.* To make a soft neighing sound like that of a horse. **whinnied, whinnying.** *—noun.* A soft neighing sound. **whinnies.**

whip (HWIP) *verb.* 1. To spank or beat, as with a stick. 2. To stir rapidly or beat to an airy, puffy texture: *whip* cream. 3. To do or move with a motion similar to beating or whipping; flap or wave violently: The flags *whipped* in the wind. 4. To act or move quickly: I *whipped* around the corner. 5. (Informal) To overcome; defeat. **whipped, whipping.** *—noun.* 1. A flexible rod or stick, often with a long lash, used for herding or beating animals or humans. 2. A hitting motion made with a whip or similar instrument. 3. A whipped cream or egg-white dessert, usually with a fruit flavoring. —**whip up.** 1. (Informal) Prepare or make quickly: I'll *whip up* some sandwiches. 2. To excite: The speaker *whipped up* the crowd into a frenzy.

whip·lash (HWIP-lash) *noun.* 1. The lash of a whip. 2. A neck injury caused by a sudden snap of the head, as in a rear-end car collision.

whip·pet (HWIP-it) *noun.* A swift racing dog that looks like a greyhound but is smaller.

whip·poor·will (HWIP-ər-wil) *noun.* A brown bird of North America that comes out at night: The *whippoorwill* has a call that sounds like its name.

whir (HWER) *verb.* 1. To make a low purring sound, as of a machine operating smoothly. 2. To move with such a sound. **whirred, whirring.** *—noun.* A low, purring or vibrating sound.

whirl (HWERL) *verb.* 1. To move in circles in the air; twirl: As the dancer spun around, her skirt *whirled.* 2. To go or move very fast. 3. To spin or seem to spin: The loud music and excitement made our heads *whirl.* **whirled, whirling.** *—noun.* 1. A rapid circular

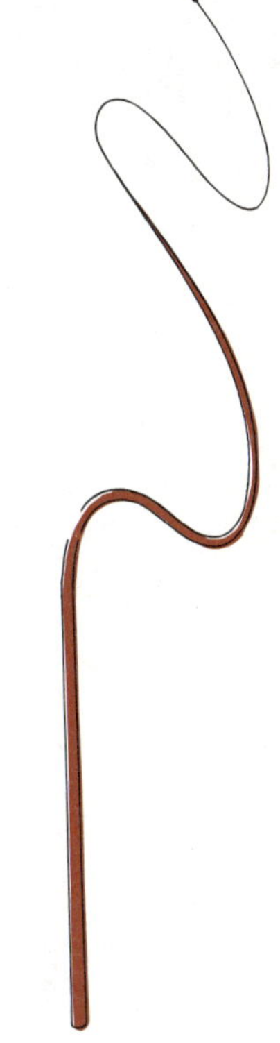
whip

whippet

whippoorwill

movement. 2. A confusing or chaotic situation. 3. A series of happenings: the social *whirl.* 4. A sensation of dizziness, confusion, or such. —**give it a whirl:** To try something.

whirl·pool (HWERL-pool) *noun.* A circular current in a body of water which draws objects to its center.

whirl·wind (HWERL-wind) *noun.* A tornado.

whirl·y·bird (HWER-lee-berd) *noun.* (Slang) Helicopter.

whisk (HWISK) *verb.* 1. (Used with *away, off,* or *out*) To snatch, brush, or move quickly with a sweeping movement: The magician *whisked* away the scarf and there was a chicken! 2. To move lightly or quickly. 3. To beat or whip, as cream. **whisked, whisking.** —*noun.* 1. A sweeping movement. 2. A wire utensil used in cooking for beating a liquid.

whisk·broom (HWISK-broom) *noun.* A small, short-handled broom.

whisk·ers (HWISS-kərz) *noun, plural.* 1. Hair that grows on a man's face; beard. 2. The long hairs around the nose and mouth of dogs, cats and other animals. —**whiskery** *adjective.*

whis·key (HWISS-kee) Also **whisky** *noun.* An alcoholic beverage distilled from grain. —**whiskeys** or **whiskies** *plural.*

whis·per (HWISS-pər) *verb.* 1. To speak very softly. 2. To make a sound similar to a whisper: The leaves *whispered* in the breeze. 3. To gossip or tell secrets. **whispered, whispering.** —*noun.* 1. A soft, breathy sound or speech. 2. Something said in a very quiet way. 3. A secret or bit of gossip.

whistle

whis·tle (HWISS-əl) *verb.* 1. To make a high-pitched, shrill sound by blowing air sharply through puckered lips, the teeth, fingers, or a special instrument. 2. To make musical sounds by changing the position of the lips and tongue while whistling. 3. To call by whistling. 4. To make a high-pitched sound while going or traveling at great speed: The bullet *whistled* toward the target. **whistled, whistling.** —*noun.* 1. A sharp, high-pitched, shrill sound. 2. A metal, plastic, or wooden device that makes a shrill sound when air or steam is forced through it. 3. Any act or instance of whistling.

whit (HWIT) *noun.* (Usually used with *not* or another negative) A tiny bit; the smallest amount.

white (HWIGHT) *noun.* 1. (Also *adjective.*) The opposite of black; the lightest color value: as *white* as snow. 2. The part of something, as an egg or eye, that is clear, white, or light-colored. 3. A person with white or light skin; a Caucasian. 4. (Plural) Clothes of white. **whites.** —*adjective.* 1. Pale or without healthy color. 2. Blameless; without sin, pure. **whiter, whitest.**

white·cap (HWIGHT-kap) *noun.* A wave that has a top of white foam.

white flag. A piece of white cloth that signals a truce, an end to fighting, or a surrender.

whit·en (HWIGHT-n) *verb.* To make white or lighter in color. **whitened, whitening.**

white·wash (HWIGHT-wosh) *noun.* 1. A watery mixture made with lime and other ingredients, used like paint to whiten walls or other surfaces. 2. A covering up, or making less, of wrongdoing. 3. (Informal, sports) The loss of a game without scoring any points. **whitewashes.** —*verb.* 1. To cover or paint with whitewash. 2. To cover up wrongdoing. **whitewashed, whitewashing.**

whith·er (HWI<u>TH</u>-ər) *adverb.* (Rare) To what place, end, or state; wherever: ". . . *whither* thou goest, I will go." (Ruth I:16).

whit·ish (HWIGHT-ish) *adjective.* Almost white in color.

whit·tle (HWIT-l) *verb.* 1. To carve or cut at (something, as wood) with a knife. 2. (Used with *away, down,* or *off*) To lessen or gradually make smaller as if by whittling: We *whittled* down the list to only three items. **whittled, whittling.**

whiz (HWIZ) *verb.* 1. To make a buzzing or zipping sound. 2. To fly past, making such a sound: The ball *whizzed* over the net. **whizzed, whizzing.** —*noun.* 1. A buzzing or zipping sound. 2. Any act or instance of flying past or making such a sound: the *whiz* of bullets. 3. (Slang) A person who shows great talent or ability: My brother is a *whiz* at math. **whizzes.**

who (HOO) *pronoun.* 1. Which or what certain person or group: *Who* came? 2. That, referring to a person already named or mentioned: the girl *who* baby-sits for us.

whoa (HWOH) *interjection.* A command to stop, given to horses.

who·ev·er (hoo-EV-ər) *pronoun.* 1. Any or all persons that; whatever person: *Whoever* wins the race will receive a blue ribbon. 2. No matter what person: *Whoever* it is, I won't talk to him. 3. Who, used to make a sentence stronger: *Whoever* made this delicious pie?

whole (HOHL) *adjective.* 1. Complete; having every part: I bought the *whole* set of books. 2. Not in pieces: a *whole* apple. 3. Well; in good health: a *whole* man. 4. All of; every bit of: He spent his *whole* allowance on books. 5. (Math) Not a fraction: a *whole* number. —*noun.* 1. All parts together; the total. 2. Anything complete or entire: the *whole* of life.

whole·heart·ed (HOHL-HAHR-tid) *adjective.* Sincere; holding nothing back: *wholehearted* thanks. —**wholeheartedly** *adverb.*

whole number. An integer, as 7, 12, or 438; not a fraction or a number with a fraction.

whole·sale (HOHL-sayl) *noun.* The selling of goods in large amounts to a person called a retailer, who then sells them to individuals. —*verb.* To sell goods in large quantities. **wholesaled, wholesaling.** —*adjective.* 1. Sold in a large amount; having to do with such sale. 2. Covering a wide area; general: *wholesale* killing of innocent people.

whole·some (HOHL-səm) *adjective.* 1. Promoting or leading to good physical or mental health. 2. Having or showing good health or character: Ben had a *wholesome* respect for his team's training rules. —**wholesomely** *adverb.*

whol·ly (HOHL-ee) *adverb.* Totally: *wholly* justified; *wholly* burned.

whom (HOOM) *pronoun.* The form of *who* used as the direct object of a verb or the object of a preposition: *Whom* did you call? To *whom* are you speaking?

whom·ev·er (hoom-EV-ər) *pronoun.* The form of *whoever* used as the direct object of a verb or the object of a preposition.

whoop (HOOP or HWOOP) *verb.* 1. To make a loud, hooting yell or shout, usually in joy. 2. To make a severe or prolonged gasp after the coughing typical of whooping cough. **whooped, whooping.** —*noun.* Any such shout or gasp, or a similar sound made by a bird. —**whoop it up.** (Slang) To enjoy a good time with interest and enthusiasm.

whooping cough. A disease of the throat and breathing passages in which the patient has coughing fits followed by severe gasps for breath.

whooping crane. A big bird with long legs and a high, shrill cry.

whooping crane

whoosh (HWOOSH) *verb.* 1. To make a sound like a rush of air: The basketball *whooshed* through the net. 2. To rush or flow out quickly, making such a sound. **whooshed, whooshing.**

wig

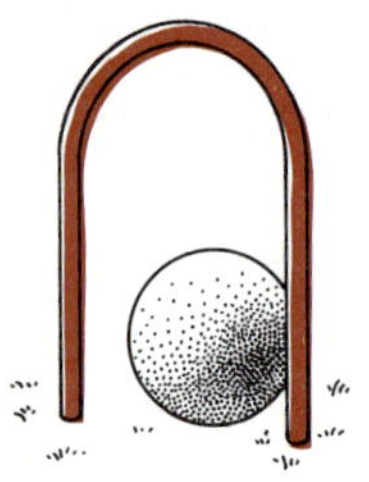
wicket

whop·per (HWOP-ər) *noun.* (Informal) 1. A very large or unusual thing. 2. An exaggeration or lie.

who's (HOOZ) *contraction.* A shortened form of the words *who is* or *who has.*

whose (HOOZ) *pronoun.* Belonging to or having to do with which person or thing: *Whose* car is parked outside? *—adjective.* Belonging to the person or thing mentioned: the boy *whose* bike was stolen.

why (HWIGH) *adverb.* For what reason: *Why* do birds fly south in winter? *—noun.* The cause or explanation: Tell me about the *why* and when of the argument. *—interjection.* Expresses: surprise, disagreement, or reflection: *Why,* of course I didn't do that!

wick (WIK) *noun.* A length of string or fabric in the center of a candle or lamp that draws up the fuel or wax so that a flame can burn steadily.

wick·ed (WIK-id) *adjective.* 1. Very evil or cruel. 2. Painful or harmful: a *wicked* headache. 3. Behaving like a rascal or mischief-maker. 4. (Informal) Impressive or strong: She plays a *wicked* game of chess. **wickeder, wickedest. —wickedly** *adverb.*

wick·er (WIK-ər) *noun.* 1. A narrow, bendable stick from which objects are woven. 2. Objects, such as baskets, chairs or stools, woven from such sticks. *—adjective.* Made with wicker: *wicker* lawn furniture.

wick·et (WIK-it) *noun.* 1. A wire hoop in the game of croquet. 2. A small window, such as one where tickets are sold; a small gate, or door, in a larger one. 3. (Sports) In cricket, the sets of sticks that are used as targets for the ball.

wide (WIGHD) *adjective.* 1. Broad, not narrow: a *wide* board. 2. In distance across: The river is a mile *wide.* 3. Large and varied: a *wide* assortment of fruit. 4. Not close; far: The arrow was *wide* of the target. **wider, widest.** *—adverb* Also **widely.** 1. Over a large area: We looked far and *wide.* 2. All the way; completely: Open the gate *wide.*

wid·en (WIGHD-n) *verb.* To make or become wider. **widened, widening.**

wide·spread (WIGHD-SPRED) *adjective.* 1. Stretched out: *widespread* wings. 2. Over a broad area: *widespread* flood damage.

wid·ow (WID-oh) *noun.* A woman whose husband is dead and who has not married again. *—verb.* To cause (someone) to become a widow. **widowed, widowing.**

wid·ow·er (WID-oh-ər) *noun.* A man whose wife is dead and who has not married again.

width *noun.* 1. The distance across; size: My shoes are narrow in *width.* 2. Something having an exact side-to-side measurement: two *widths* of fabric.

wield (WEELD) *verb.* 1. To use or handle: *wield* an ax. 2. To manage or exercise (strength): Hitler once *wielded* power in Germany. **wielded, wielding.**

wie·ner (WEE-nər) *noun.* A hot dog.

wife (WIGHF) *noun.* A female mate or spouse. **—wives** (WYVZ) *plural.*

wig *noun.* A head covering made of real or false hair.

wig·gle (WIG-əl) *verb.* To squirm; move with short motions from side to side: The caterpillar *wiggles* up a tree. **wiggled, wiggling.** *—noun.* The act of wiggling. **wiggles. —get a wiggle on.** Hurry up.

wig·wag (WIG-wag) *verb.* 1. To wave back and forth. 2. To signal by waving a light or a flag. **wigwagged, wigwagging.**

wig·wam (WIG-wom) *noun.* An Indian tent; a tepee.

wild (WYLD) *adjective.* 1. Living in a natural state, not tamed or cared for by man: *Wild* mushrooms grow in the woods. 2. Not occupied by man: *wild* country. 3. Not civilized.

4. Out-of-control; excited: a *wild* crowd. 5. Unusual, strange: *wild* and crazy ideas. —*adverb* Also **wildly.** Without attention or control: The rancher lets his horses run *wild.* —*noun.* (Usually plural) Wilderness, land not cared for by man: The campers lived in the *wilds.*

wild·cat (WYLD-kat) *noun.* 1. A medium-sized wild animal of the cat family. 2. A person with a quick temper. 3. A well drilled for oil or gas in an area where they are not usually found. —*adjective.* Not legal or approved: a *wildcat* strike.

wil·de·beest (WIL-də-beest) *noun.* A gnu.

wil·der·ness (WIL-dər-niss) *noun.* A wild area; a region left in its natural condition.

wild·fire (WYLD-fighr) *noun.* A fire burning out of control. —**like wildfire.** Rapidly, widely, and uncontrollably.

wild·life (WYLD-lighf) *noun.* Plants or animals in their natural state.

wile (WIGHL) *noun.* 1. A trick. 2. (Usually plural) A sly, cunning manner.

[1]**will** (WIL) *noun.* 1. The mental ability to control one's own actions: He has a *will* of his own. 2. Choice or decision. 3. Determination; strong desire: a *will* to win. 4. Attitude or feeling (toward): "Peace on earth, good *will* to men." (Longfellow). 5. A legal paper stating how one's property is to be distributed after death. —*verb.* 1. To use one's will; decide, choose. 2. To make or try to make happen by power of one's wish or determination: I wish I could *will* the rain away. 3. To grant through a will. **willed, willing.**

[2]**will** (WIL) *verb.* A helping verb used to show: 1. The future tense: We *will* be late for dinner. 2. A command or willingness: All students *will* return library books promptly. 3. Ability to: My Thermos *will* hold four cups. **would.**

will·ful (WIL-fəl) Also **wilful** *adjective.* 1. Stubborn. 2. Deliberate; planned: It was not accidental, but a *willful* act. —**willfulness** *noun.* —**willfully** *adverb.*

will·ing (WIL-ing) *adjective.* Ready or eager: a *willing* helper. —**willingly** *adverb.* —**willingness** *noun.*

wil·low (WIL-oh) *noun.* 1. Any of a variety of trees or shrubs with narrow, pointed leaves. 2. The wood of this plant.

will power. Strong mental control over one's actions.

wilt *verb.* 1. To droop or cause to droop: Cut flowers *wilt* without water. 2. To weaken; lose courage or strength. **wilted, wilting.**

wi·ly (WIGHL-ee) *adjective.* Crafty, sly. **wilier, wiliest.** —**wiliness** *noun.*

win *verb.* 1. To defeat others; to be the victor. 2. To finish first: Who will *win* the race? 3. To gain or get: *win* friends. **won, winning.** —*noun.* The act of winning: an easy *win.*

wince (WINSS) *verb.* To pull back, as if in pain. **winced, wincing.** —*noun.* The act of drawing back.

[1]**wind** *noun.* 1. Air in forceful motion, especially outdoors. 2. Ability to breathe during hard work; breath: Climbing a mountain takes good *wind.* —*verb.* To cause to become short of breath: The steep climb *winded* us. **winded, winding.** —**get wind of.** Discover; become aware of. —**in the wind.** Happening or apt to happen soon.

[2]**wind** (WYND) *verb.* 1. To wrap around and around: *Wind* the yarn into a ball. 2. To wrap, grow, or twist (around or onto something): *Wind* ribbons around the Maypole. 3. To go or be in a twisting uneven way: The path *winds* through the forest. 4. (Often used with *up*) To make (a device) work by twisting or tightening a coil: *wind* up a watch. **wound** (WOWND), **winding.** —*noun.* A twisting or turning. —**wind up.** To finish or end.

wildcat

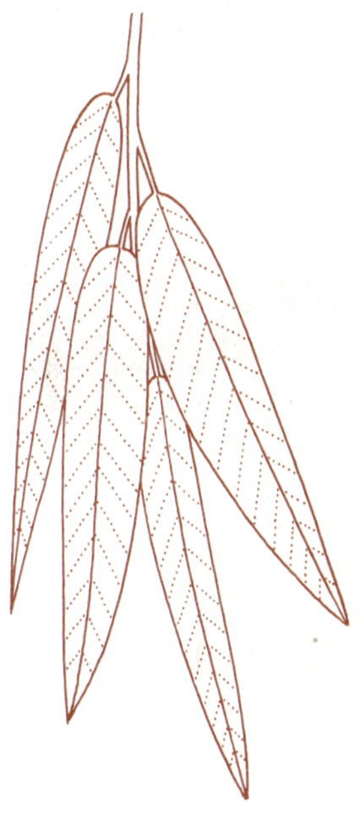
willow

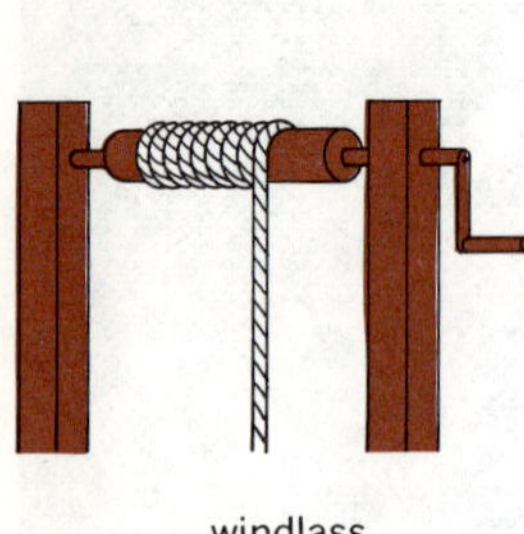
windlass

windmill

wing

wind·break (WIND-brayk) *noun.* Something used to stop the wind; a protection.

Wind·break·er (WIND-brayk-ər) *trademark.* A short, warm jacket.

wind·fall (WIND-fawl) *noun.* 1. Fruit blown down or off by the wind. 2. Unexpected good fortune.

wind instrument. A musical instrument played by blowing through a mouthpiece: The clarinet is a *wind instrument.*

wind·lass (WIND-ləss) *noun.* A special lifting device in which rope is wound around a large spool by turning a crank: The sailors used a *windlass* to raise the anchor.

wind·mill (WIND-mil) *noun.* A mill or machine operated by wind pushing against large blades or sails attached to a turning axle.

win·dow (WIN-doh) *noun.* 1. An opening in a wall to let in light or air. 2. The frame or glass within such an opening.

win·dow·pane (WIN-doh-payn) *noun.* Glass used in a window.

wind·pipe (WIND-pighp) *noun.* The part of the throat through which air reaches the lungs. **windpipes.**

wind·shield (WIND-sheeld) *noun.* The glass or plastic screen that protects the driver and riders in a vehicle.

wind·storm (WIND-storm) *noun.* A storm with high winds.

wind·y (WIN-dee) *adjective.* 1. Having strong winds or breezes. 2. Given to talking: a *windy* salesman. **windier, windiest.** —**windiness** *noun.*

wine (WIGHN) *noun.* 1. A drink made from grape juice that has partly turned to alcohol. 2. A similar drink made from other fruits or plants such as rice or berries. 3. (Also *adjective*) A dark red color.

wing *noun.* 1. One of the two feathered, arm-like parts that birds use in flying. 2. A similar part of a bat, insect, or fish that it uses to fly or glide through the air. 3. Anything shaped or used as a wing; the specially shaped part of an aircraft that provides lift. 4. One section of a building: the science *wing.* 5. Part of an organization, a political party, or a military body. 6. (Theater, often plural) The sides of the stage, not seen by the audience. 7. (Sports) A position on certain teams, such as hockey; also a kind of formation: The team lines up in a single *wing.* —*verb.* 1. To fly: The birds *wing* south. 2. To send or direct: *wing* an arrow. 3. To wound, especially in the arm or wing. **winged, winging.** —**on the wing.** Flying; in a hurry. —**under one's wing.** Protected; in one's care.

winged (WINGD) *adjective.* 1. Having wings. 2. Moving as if by wings; swift.

wing·spread (WING-spred) *noun.* The distance from the tip of one wing to the tip of the other when both are spread out.

wink (WINGK) *verb.* 1. To close and open one eye quickly, often as a message or signal. 2. To close and open both eyes quickly; blink. 3. To shine off and on; twinkle. **winked, winking** —*noun.* 1. The act of winking. 2. A very short time: He was back in a *wink.* 3. A small amount of sleep. —**wink at.** To pretend not to see or notice.

win·ner (WIN-ər) *noun.* A person or thing that wins; victor.

win·ning (WIN-ing) *noun.* 1. The act of coming in first or defeating others. 2. (Plural) Money won through betting. —*adjective.* 1. Victorious. 2. Charming: a *winning* smile.

win·now (WIN-oh) *verb.* 1. To separate the husks from grain by blowing air through it. 2. To separate the good part from the useless. **winnowed, winnowing.** —*noun.* 1. The act of separating. 2. A device for winnowing grain.

win·some (WIN-səm) *adjective.* Sweet; charming. —**winsomely** *adverb.*

win·ter (WIN-tər) *noun.* 1. The coldest season of the year, coming after autumn and before spring: In the Northern Hemisphere, *winter* lasts from about December 22 to March 22. 2. A year: The old man has lived 80 *winters.* —*verb.* To spend the winter: Many birds *winter* in the south. **wintered, wintering.**

win·ter·green (WIN-tər-green) *noun.* 1. A low-growing plant with round evergreen leaves. 2. The oil from the leaves of this plant, used as medicine or flavoring.

win·try (WIN-tree) *adjective.* Like or typical of winter; cold or bleak.

wipe (WIGHP) *verb.* 1. To rub over (with a cloth or hand) as in cleaning: *Wipe* the table. 2. To take off by rubbing: *Wipe* the crumbs away. 3. To dry water or any wet substance from: *Wipe* the dishes. **wiped, wiping.** —*noun.* An act or instance of wiping. —**wipe out.** 1. To destroy completely, leaving nothing. 2. (Informal) To kill. 3. (Slang) To fall off a surfboard.

wire (WIGHR) *noun.* 1. Metal shaped into a continuous thread. 2. A piece of this material. 3. The telegraph system: We learned the news by *wire.* 4. A telegram: We sent Dad a *wire* on his birthday. 5. The finish line at a race. —*verb.* 1. To equip with wire: *wire* a house for electricity. 2. (Informal) To send a telegram. 3. To fasten with wire: *Wire* the gate shut. **wired, wiring.** —**under the wire.** Just in time.

wire·less (WIGHR-liss) *adjective.* Without wire. —*noun.* 1. A communication system that uses radio waves rather than wires. 2. (British) Radio.

wir·y (WIGHR-ee) *adjective.* 1. Like wire: *wiry* hair. 2. Lean and strong. **wirier, wiriest.**

Wis·con·sin (wiss-KAHN-sin) *noun.* A north central state of the United States, 30th to join the Union (1848). **Wis.** or **Wisc.** *abbreviation.* Also **WI** for Zip Codes.

Wisconsin
★capital: Madison

wis·dom (WIZ-dəm) *noun.* 1. Ability to reason carefully and wisely; knowledge. 2. Wise advice: The *wisdom* of the Bible guided us.

wise (WIGHZ) *adjective.* 1. Having superior intelligence: *wise* men. 2. Showing good judgment: a *wise* decision. 3. Having much knowledge. 4. (Slang) Saucily smart: a *wise* guy. **wiser, wisest.** —**wisely** *adverb.* —**get wise to.** To learn about. —**wise up.** (Slang) Get smart.

-wise *suffix.* Indicates: 1. Way, direction, or placement: counterclock*wise.* 2. (Informal) In relation or reference to: time*wise.*

wise·crack (WIGHZ-krak) *noun.* (Slang) A smart remark or joke, usually showing lack of respect. —*verb.* To make such a remark. **wisecracked, wisecracking.**

wish *noun.* 1. A desire or longing. 2. A thing that is desired. **wishes.** —*verb.* 1. To want or long: They *wish* to go to camp. 2. To want (something to happen to someone): We *wish* him a safe trip. 3. To ask or order. **wished, wishing.**

wish·bone (WISH-bohn) *noun.* The Y-shaped breastbone of a bird.

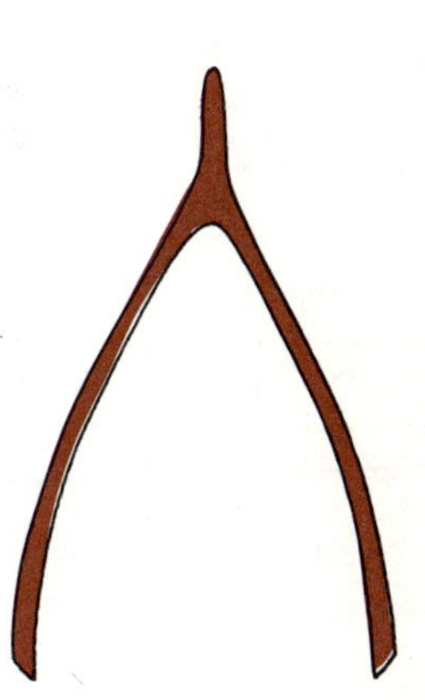
wishbone

wish·ful (WISH-fəl) *adjective.* Having or indicating a desire; hopeful. —**wishfully** *adverb.*

wish·y-wash·y (WISH-ee-wosh-ee) *adjective.* Not firm or purposeful.

wisp *noun.* 1. A tuft; a small bundle: a *wisp* of hair. 2. A thin streak: a *wisp* of smoke. —**wispy** *adjective.*

wisteria

wis·ter·i·a (wiss-TIHR-ee-a) *noun.* 1. Purple or white flowers that grow in clusters. 2. The vine on which these flowers grow.

wist·ful (WIST-fəl) *adjective.* Sad because of an unfulfilled wish. —**wistfully** *adverb.*

wit *noun.* 1. (Often plural) Knowledge; ability; intelligence: Jack used his *wits* in the emergency. 2. A sense of humor: Frank has a sharp *wit.* 3. A person noted for a good sense of humor. —**at wit's end.** Not knowing what to do next.

witch (WICH) *noun.* 1. A woman believed to practice magic or have contact with the devil. 2. A mean, nasty woman.

witch·craft (WICH-craft) *noun.* Magical practices of a witch.

witch doctor. The member of some primitive tribes to whom other members turn for healing.

witch·er·y (WICH-ə-ree) *noun.* 1. Witchcraft. 2. Attraction; allure: "The *witchery* of the soft blue sky!" (Wordsworth).

with (WITH or WITH) *preposition.* 1. In the company of: I went *with* Mary. 2. Near or next to: Put the salt *with* the pepper. 3. In a way showing: She moves *with* grace. 4. Having: Our car came *with* power steering. 5. In the possession or care of: The boy lives *with* his grandparents. 6. Supporting; in favor of: You are *with* me, I hope. 7. Among: Susie is *with* Lois and the other girls. 8. Working for; in the organization of: Mr. Skoda is *with* the Taylor company. 9. By the power or means of; having the help of. 10. In regard to. 11. At the same time as: The fence fell *with* the tree. 12. As a result of: He shook *with* laughter. 13. Against: Marilyn is fighting *with* Nancy. —**with it.** (Slang) Up-to-date, in the know.

with·al (with-AWL) *adverb.* (Rare) 1. In addition. 2. Nevertheless.

with·draw (with-DRAW) *verb.* 1. To remove; take back: *withdraw* a complaint. 2. To move backward; go back: *withdraw* troops. 3. To keep to oneself. **withdrew, withdrawn, withdrawing.**

with·draw·al (with-DRAW-əl) *noun.* 1. The act or state of withdrawing. 2. The act or the result of no longer using an addicting drug.

with·drawn (with-DRAWN) *adjective.* Shy; preferring to be alone.

with·er (WITH-ər) *verb.* 1. To curl or dry up because of a lack of moisture: The plant *withered.* 2. To make ashamed: *wither* with a look. **withered, withering.**

with·hold (with-HOHLD) *verb.* To hold back: *withhold* permission. **withheld, withholding.**

withholding tax. The part of a worker's pay held back by his employer in payment of income tax.

with·in (with-IN) *preposition.* 1. Inside: *within* the town lines. 2. In the limits of: It is not *within* my power to make the arrest. —*adverb.* Inside.

with·out (with-OWT) *preposition.* Not in possession of; not having.

with·stand (with-STAND) *verb.* To resist; put up with: Job was able to *withstand* much suffering. **withstood, withstanding.**

wit·less (WIT-liss) *adjective.* Without intelligence; stupid. —**witlessly** *adverb.*

wit·ness (WIT-niss) *noun.* 1. A person who has seen or heard something: a *witness* to the car accident. 2. A person who testifies in a court. 3. A person who is present at a proceeding in order to be able to tell what happened: My secretary will be a *witness* to the signing of the contract. **witnesses.** —*verb.* 1. To see or hear (something). 2. To make a statement about (some action or situation). **witnessed, witnessing.**

wit·ty (WIT-ee) *adjective.* Having a clever sense of humor. **wittier, wittiest.** —**wittily** *adverb.* —**wittiness** *noun.*

wives (WYVZ) *noun.* *See* **wife.**

wiz·ard (WIZ-ərd) *noun.* 1. A man who practices magic. 2. A very clever person: a *wizard* at math.

wob·ble (WOB-əl) *verb.* To totter; move unsteadily from side to side. **wobbled, wobbling.** —*noun.* A tottering movement. —**wobbly** *adjective.*

woe (WOH) *noun.* 1. Great sadness, grief. 2. Bad luck. —**woeful** *adjective.* —**woefully** *adverb.*

woke (WOHK) *verb.* *See* **wake.**

wolf (WULF) *noun.* A dog-like, meat-eating animal found in northern areas. —**wolves** (WULVZ) *plural.* —*verb.* To eat quickly and hungrily: Reggie *wolfed* his breakfast and rushed off. **wolfed, wolfing.**

wolf·hound (WULF-hownd) *noun.* A large dog bred to hunt wolves.

wolves (WULVZ) *noun.* *See* **wolf.**

wom·an (WUM-ən) *noun.* 1. A mature female human. 2. Mature females thought of as a group. —**women** (WIM-in) *plural.*

wom·an·hood (WUM-ən-hud) *noun.* The state of being a woman.

wom·an·kind (WUM-ən-kynd) *noun.* All women thought of as a group.

wom·an·ly (WUM-ən-lee) *adjective.* Having the qualities or characteristics of a woman. —**womanliness** *noun.*

womb (WOOM) *noun.* *See* **uterus.**

wom·en (WIM-in) *noun.* *See* **woman.**

women's liberation. A movement whose goal is equal opportunities and recognition for women.

won (WUHN) *verb.* *See* **win.**

won·der (WUHN-dər) *noun.* 1. A feeling of surprise, fear, and admiration: Pam looked with *wonder* at the giant balloons. 2. Something that causes such a feeling. 3. A feeling of confusion or doubt. —*verb.* 1. To have a feeling of surprise, fear, and admiration. 2. To be curious, confused, or doubtful: "Twinkle, twinkle, little star, How I *wonder* what you are. . ." (Ann Taylor) **wondered, wondering.**

won·der·ful (WUHN-dər-fəl) *adjective.* 1. Having the ability to cause a feeling of wonder. 2. Marvelous; great: a *wonderful* surprise. —**wonderfully** *adverb.* —**wonderfulness** *noun.*

won·der·ment (WUHN-dər-mənt) *noun.* A state of wonder.

won·drous (WUHN-drəss) *adjective.* Marvelous; wonderful. —**wondrously** *adverb.*

won't (WOHNT) *contraction.* A shortened form of *will not.*

woo *verb.* 1. To try to gain the love of. 2. To seek: Both candidates will *woo* the labor vote. **wooed, wooing.**

wood (WUD) *noun.* 1. The hard, strong substance of trees and shrubs that gives support. 2. This material used for building, furniture, fuel, etc. 3. (Often plural) A forest; a thick growth of many trees.

wood·bine (WUD-bighn) *noun.* One of many types of climbing vines.

wood·chuck (WUD-chuhk) *noun.* A rodent that has short legs and a chubby body and lives in a burrow; a ground hog.

wood·cock (WUD-kok) *noun.* A small brown bird with a long beak.

wood·craft (WUD-kraft) *noun.* Knowledge and ability in things connected with the forest, as hunting or camping.

wood·cut·ter (WUD-kuht-ər) *noun.* A person whose job is cutting wood or trees.

wood·ed (WUD-id) *adjective.* Having many trees: a *wooded* neighborhood.

wolf

wolfhound

woodchuck

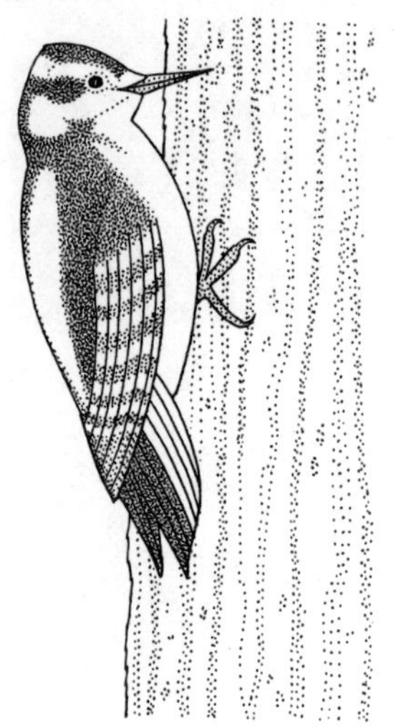
woodpecker

wood·en (WUD-n) *adjective.* 1. Made of wood: a *wooden* statue. 2. Like a piece of wood; stiff; without life: a *wooden* smile. —**woodenly** *adverb.*

wood·land (WUD-lənd or WUD-land) *noun.* A forest; an area with many trees.

wood·peck·er (WUD-pek-ər) *noun.* Any of the many birds with long, hard bills that climb and drill holes in trees looking for insects to eat.

wood·shed (WUD-shed) *noun.* A small building or shed used to store wood.

woods·man (WUDZ-mən) *noun.* A person who lives or works in a forest; a forester, hunter, or woodcutter. —**woodsmen** *plural.*

wood·wind (WUD-wind) *noun.* Any of one group of musical instruments (made originally of wood) that produce sound when air is blown through the mouthpiece: The flute, oboe, and bassoon are *woodwinds.*

wood·work (WUD-werk) *noun.* Something made of wood, particularly the door and window frames and moldings in a house.

wood·y (WUD-ee) *adjective.* 1. Made of or containing wood. 2. Like wood. 3. Having woods. **woodier, woodiest.**

[1]**woof** (WUF) *noun.* A dog's bark or any similar sound.

[2]**woof** (WOOF or WUF) *noun.* The crosswise threads in a woven fabric. *See* **warp.**

wool (WUL) *noun.* 1. The hair of sheep and other animals, like the alpaca, used to make fabric. 2. The fabric made from animal hair, or a garment of wool. —**pull the wool over one's eyes.** To trick or fool.

wool·en (WUL-ən) Also **woollen** *adjective.* Having to do with or made of wool. —*noun, plural.* Fabric or garments made of wool.

wool·ly (WUL-ee) Also **wooly.** *adjective.* 1. Referring to, made of, or covered by wool. 2. Like wool; fuzzy. 3. Without law: the wild and *woolly* West.

word (WERD) *noun.* 1. The smallest sound or group of sounds that stands for an idea: I heard each *word* that she spoke. 2. A written, typed, or printed letter or group of letters that stands for a word: The sentence that I wrote had eight *words.* 3. A promise: Henry gave his *word* that he would keep the secret. 4. A brief talk: Mother wants a *word* with you. 5. A report; news: Is there any *word* about the missing plane? 6. (Plural) A quarrel; argument: The cab drivers had *words.* 7. A command; order. 8. (Plural) Lyrics: the *words* of a song. —**by word of mouth.** By spoken words; through conversation. —**eat one's words.** To take back something that one has said.

word·y (WER-dee) *adjective.* Having or using too many words. **wordier, wordiest.**

wore (WOR) *verb. See* **wear.**

work (WERK) *noun.* 1. Labor; action needed to do or make something: Building a house requires much *work.* 2. A job; employment: Jim is out of *work.* 3. A task, project, or assignment: Finish your *work,* and then you may play. 4. A product; something made or done: The new table is a beautiful piece of *work.* 5. (Plural) Mechanical parts; machinery: the *works* of a watch. 6. (Plural) Actions; behavior: The woman was loved for her kind *works.* 7. (Plural) All of the products or creations of a writer, musician, or other artist: the *works* of Shakespeare. 8. (*Plural in form but used with a singular verb*) A building or plant where something is made or a service is provided: the water *works.* —*verb.* 1. To labor: The plumber *worked* for hours. 2. To hold a job; be employed. 3. To operate; to function: Our TV *works* well. 4. To move slowly or with much effort: The worm *worked* its way across the lawn. 5. To cause: This medicine *works* wonders. 6. To change in condition or position: The wagon's wheel *worked* itself loose. 7. To influence; excite: The insult *worked* Ralph into a fury. 8. To twist, pound, or stretch into shape: The craftsman *worked* the clay into a bowl. 9. To make suitable for growing or being useful: The farmer *worked* his land before planting his crops. 10. To cause to labor: The prospector *worked* his mule hard. **worked, working.**

work·bench (WERK-bench) *noun.* A table at which a mechanic, carpenter, or other craftsman works.

work·book (WERK-buk) *noun.* A book, usually used with a textbook, in which a student can write out answers to questions.

work·er (WER-kər) *noun.* 1. A person who works; employee. 2. A type of bee or other social insect that performs special tasks.

work·ing (WER-king) *adjective.* 1. In operation; able to be used: Is the elevator *working?* 2. Enough to get along with; usable: a *working* knowledge of French.

work·ing·man (WER-king-man) *noun.* A man who works for wages, especially in an industrial or manual job. —**workingmen** *plural.*

work·man (WERK-mən) *noun.* A person who does work, especially physical labor. —**workmen** *plural.*

work·man·ship (WERK-mən-ship) *noun.* The quality of a workman's craft or style.

work·out (WERK-owt) *noun.* 1. A period or time of physical exercise or training: The coach gives the team a *workout* each day. 2. A difficult time or process: Fighting the fire was a *workout* for the firemen.

work·shop (WERK-shop) *noun.* 1. A room or small building where mechanical or other work is done. 2. A meeting or series of meetings to study or discuss a special subject or process: a drama *workshop.*

world (WERLD) *noun.* 1. The earth: There is more water than land on the *world's* surface. 2. The universe: The sun, planets, and stars are all part of our *world.* 3. All of mankind; all of earth's creatures. 4. A special class: the *world* of insects. 5. A special region; area of influence: the English-speaking *world.* 6. A great amount; abundance: a *world* of difference.

world·ly (WERLD-lee) *adjective.* 1. Of or related to the world or the affairs of man. 2. Interested in pleasure rather than in spiritual or religious values. **worldlier, worldliest.**

World Series. A series of baseball games played each fall to decide the champions of American professional baseball.

worm (WERM) *noun.* 1. A small, thin animal with a soft, limbless body that moves by crawling or wriggling. 2. (Slang) A crude or nasty person. 3. (Plural) A disease caused by worms in the intestines. —*verb.* 1. To move like a worm; wriggle or crawl: The boy *wormed* under the fence. 2. (Used with *out of*) To obtain (information, secrets, promises, and such) by persistent or roundabout questioning or pleading: Bob finally *wormed* out of John the truth as to where he had been. 3. To treat an animal in order to remove worms from its intestines. **wormed, worming.**

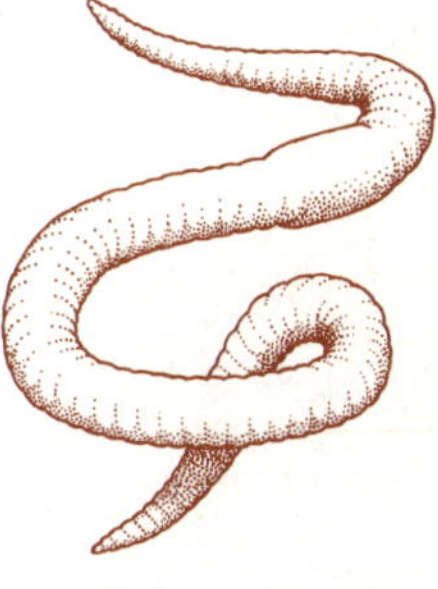
worm

worm·y (WER-mee) *adjective.* 1. Full of worms: *wormy* fruit. 2. Harmed by worms: *wormy* wood. **wormier, wormiest.**

[1]**worn** *verb. See* **wear.**

[2]**worn** *adjective.* 1. Made thin or weak by use. 2. Exhausted.

worn-out (WORN-OWT) *adjective.* 1. No longer able to work or be used: The *worn-out* engine would not start. 2. Exhausted; very tired. 3. Not fresh or original; trite.

wor·ry (WER-ee) *verb.* 1. To feel troubled or concerned (about something). 2. To cause to feel troubled or concerned: Does the coming storm *worry* the sailors? 3. To grasp and shake with the teeth, as a dog does. **worried, worrying.** —*noun.* 1. A troubled feeling; concern or anxiety. 2. Something that causes trouble or concern: The child's sore throat was a *worry* to his parents. **worries.**

worse (WERSS) *adjective. See* **bad.**

wor·ship (WER-ship) *verb.* 1. To honor or adore: *worship* God. 2. To take part in a religious service: Our family *worships* at church each Sunday. 3. To show great love or respect for. **worshiped** or **worshipped, worshiping** or **worshipping.** —*noun.* 1. Honor or adoration, shown especially by taking part in a religious service. 2. Great love or respect.

worst (WERST) *adjective. See* **bad.**

worth (WERTH) *noun.* 1. The value, goodness, or importance (of something or someone). 2. The money value: The *worth* of the radio is 30 dollars. 3. The quantity that can be bought for a certain amount of money: a dollar's *worth* of peaches. —*adjective.* 1. Of the same value as: The ring is *worth* 50 dollars. 2. Having or owning (a certain amount of wealth): The rich man is *worth* over a million dollars. 3. Worthy or deserving of: This theme is *worth* an A.

worth·less (WERTH-liss) *adjective.* Having little or no value or merit; useless. —**worthlessly** *adverb.*

worth·while (WERTH-HWIGHL) *adjective.* Having value or goodness; deserving one's efforts or attention: Studying is a *worthwhile* activity.

wor·thy (WER-thee) *adjective.* 1. Having value, importance, or goodness: a *worthy* cause. 2. Deserving of admiration or honor: a *worthy* gentleman. 3. Meriting. **worthier, worthiest.**

would (WUD) *verb. See* **will.**

would·n't (WUD-nt) *contraction.* A shortened form of *would not.*

[1]**wound** (WOOND) *noun.* 1. An injury that results in the cutting, tearing, or piercing of skin and flesh: The soldier's *wound* was painful. 2. Harm or hurt, as to one's feelings. —*verb.* 1. To injure by cutting, tearing, or piercing the skin and flesh. 2. To harm or hurt, as one's feelings. **wounded, wounding.**

[2]**wound** (WOWND) *verb. See* [2]**wind.**

wove (WOHV) *verb. See* **weave.**

woven (WOH-vən) *verb. See* **weave.**

wow *interjection.* Expression of surprise or a strong reaction: *Wow!* This soup is hot. —*verb.* (Slang) To cause a very favorable reaction in; excite or delight: The singer *wowed* his audience. **wowed, wowing.**

wran·gle (RANG-gəl) *verb.* 1. To quarrel; argue loudly. 2. To herd or gather together cattle or other livestock. **wrangled, wrangling.**

wrap (RAP) *verb.* 1. To enclose within a covering: Will you *wrap* this package? 2. To fold or wind (around): *wrap* tape around the handle. **wrapped** or **wrapt, wrapping.** —*noun.* 1. A coat or other outer garment. 2. A covering or wrapping. —**wrap up.** To finish; bring to an end. —**wrap-up** (RAP-uhp) *noun.* Summary: a *wrap-up* of the game.

wrap·per (RAP-ər) *noun.* 1. A covering; what something is wrapped in: The candy has a paper *wrapper.* 2. A robe or dressing gown.

wrath (RATH) *noun.* Great anger; fury.

wrath·ful (RATH-fəl) *adjective.* Very angry; furious. —**wrathfully** *adverb.*

wreak (REEK) *verb.* (Rare) To inflict; express: The king *wreaked* his anger on the villain by having him sent from the country. **wreaked, wreaking.**

wreath (REETH) *noun.* 1. A ring of plants or flowers twisted together: a holly *wreath.* 2. Something that resembles a wreath; a ring: a *wreath* of clouds. —**wreaths** (REETHZ) *plural.*

wreathe (REETH) *verb.* 1. To decorate with wreaths. 2. To encircle; form a ring around: The clouds *wreathed* the mountain top. 3. To form into a wreath. 4. To cover: The children's faces were *wreathed* with smiles. **wreathed, wreathing.**

wreck (REK) *verb.* 1. To destroy; to ruin: The explosion *wrecked* the factory. 2. To tear down: The workmen *wrecked* the old house. 3. To spoil; cause to fail: Rain *wrecked* our plans for a picnic. **wrecked, wrecking.** —*noun.* 1. A wrecking; destruction: a train *wreck.* 2. The remains of something ruined or wrecked: the *wreck* of an old ship. 3. Someone or something in very poor condition: Jane was a nervous *wreck* before the test.

wreck·age (REK-ij) *noun.* 1. The pieces or what is left of something wrecked or destroyed. 2. A destruction or wrecking; the state of being wrecked.

wreck·er (REK-ər) *noun.* 1. A person who wrecks or destroys old buildings, vehicles, or the like. 2. A truck or other machine used to remove wrecks.

wren (REN) *noun.* Any of a variety of small, brown songbirds with slender beak, rounded wings, and short tail.

wrench (RENCH) *noun.* 1. A tool used for turning or holding nuts, pipes, or other items. 2. A sudden twist or turn: A *wrench* of the branch tore it from the tree. 3. An injury caused by a sudden twist or turn: a painful *wrench* of his ankle. —*verb.* 1. To twist or turn suddenly. 2. To injure by twisting or turning suddenly. 3. To pull away by twisting or turning suddenly: Bill *wrenched* the ball from the other player's hands. **wrenched, wrenching.**

wrest (REST) *verb.* 1. To pull or twist away violently. 2. To seize; take by force: The knights *wrested* power from the king. **wrested, wresting.**

wres·tle (RESS-l) *verb.* 1. To struggle with an opponent, especially in sports, in an effort to force or throw him to the ground. 2. To struggle (with) or try to overcome: *wrestle* with many problems. **wrestled, wrestling.** —**wrestler** *noun.*

wretch (RECH) *noun.* 1. A very unfortunate or unhappy person. 2. A crude or wicked person. **wretches.**

wretch·ed (RECH-id) *adjective.* 1. Very unfortunate or unhappy. 2. In a poor or depressing condition: a *wretched* shack. 3. Crude; wicked. 4. Of very poor quality; terrible: The team played a *wretched* game. —**wretchedly** *adverb.* —**wretchedness** *noun.*

wrig·gle (RIG-əl) *verb.* 1. To twist or squirm; to wiggle: The nervous patient *wriggled* in the dentist's chair. 2. To move by squirming or crawling, as a worm does. 3. (Used with *out*) To escape by crafty or clever means: to *wriggle* out of trouble. **wriggled, wriggling.** —*noun.* A wriggling or squirming.

wring (RING) *verb.* 1. To twist, rub, or squeeze: to *wring* one's hands nervously. 2. (Used with *out*) To twist or squeeze water from: *wring* out a wet towel. 3. To get (from), as by warnings, threats, or force: The detective tried to *wring* the truth from the suspect. **wrung, wringing.**

wrestlers

wreath

wrecker

wring·er (RING-ər) *noun.* A machine or device that presses water from clothes or cloth items.

[1]**wrin·kle** (RING-kəl) *noun.* A small raised line or ridge on a surface that is otherwise smooth: The old shirt had many *wrinkles.* **wrinkles.** —*verb.* 1. To have wrinkles or creases form on a surface: One's skin *wrinkles* after many years. 2. To cause or make wrinkles or creases in: Jack *wrinkles* his nose when he smiles. **wrinkled, wrinkling.**

[2]**wrin·kle** (RING-kəl) *noun.* (Informal) A new or novel process or idea; gimmick. **wrinkles.**

wrist (RIST) *noun.* The joint or part of the body between the hand and the arm.

wrist·band (RIST-band) *noun.* The part of a sleeve that covers the wrist; cuff.

wrist watch. A watch that is attached to a band or bracelet and is worn around the wrist.

writ (RIT) *noun.* (Law) A legal document directed to a public official or private individual ordering or prohibiting a specific action.

write (RIGHT) *verb.* 1. To form letters or words on a surface: *Write* the answers on the blackboard. 2. To set down on paper or put into words a work of literature or music: Did Shakespeare *write* many plays? 3. To tell or send ideas by written words: Tom *writes* to his friend. 4. To earn a living by writing books or other literary works: My brother *writes* for a newspaper. **wrote, written, writing.**

writ·er (RIGH-tər) *noun.* A person who writes books, plays, and the like; an author: My favorite *writer* is Robert Louis Stevenson.

writhe (RYTH) *verb.* To twist or squirm, as with suffering: The injured player *writhed* with pain. **writhed, writhing.**

writ·ing (RIGH-ting) *noun.* 1. (Plural) A book, letter, or other written work: Have you read the *writings* of Mark Twain? 2. Written form: I want his promise in *writing.* 3. The process of forming letters or words on a surface. 4. Handwriting; script: My *writing* is hard to read.

writ·ten (RIT-n) *verb. See* **write.**

wrong (RAWNG) *adjective.* 1. Not correct or true. 2. Not right for the purpose; not suitable: Tom rarely does the *wrong* thing. 3. Immoral; unjust; illegal: To beat an animal is *wrong.* 4. Out of order; not working as it should: Something is *wrong* with the car. 5. Usually turned away; less finished: the *wrong* side of a fabric. —*noun.* An act that is unjust, wicked, or not fair. —*adverb.* In a wrong or mistaken way or direction: You did the assignment *wrong.* —*verb.* To do wrong to; to hurt: He *wrongs* her with his remarks. **wronged, wronging.**

wrong·do·ing (RAWNG-doo-ing) *noun.* Doing wrong; an unlawful act: "The *wrongdoing* of one generation lives into the successive ones." (Hawthorne)

wrong·ful (RONG-fəl) *adjective.* 1. Unjust; unfair: a *wrongful* deed. 2. Not right; unlawful: a *wrongful* ruling. —**wrongfully** *adverb.*

wrote (ROHT) *verb. See* **write.**

wrought (RAWT) *adjective.* 1. Formed; created: a beautifully *wrought* bracelet. 2. Hammered or beaten into shape: a box of *wrought* silver.

wrung (RUHNG) *verb. See* **wring.**

wry (RIGH) *adjective.* 1. Unhappy or twisted: I make a *wry* face when I take medicine. 2. Amusing in a dry, intelligent way; witty. **wrier** or **wryer, wriest** or **wryest.** —**wryly** *adverb.*

Wy·o·ming (wigh-OH-ming) *noun.* A western state of the United States, 44th to join the Union (1890). —**Wyo.** *abbreviation.* Also **WY** for Zip Codes.

Wyoming
★capital: Cheyenne

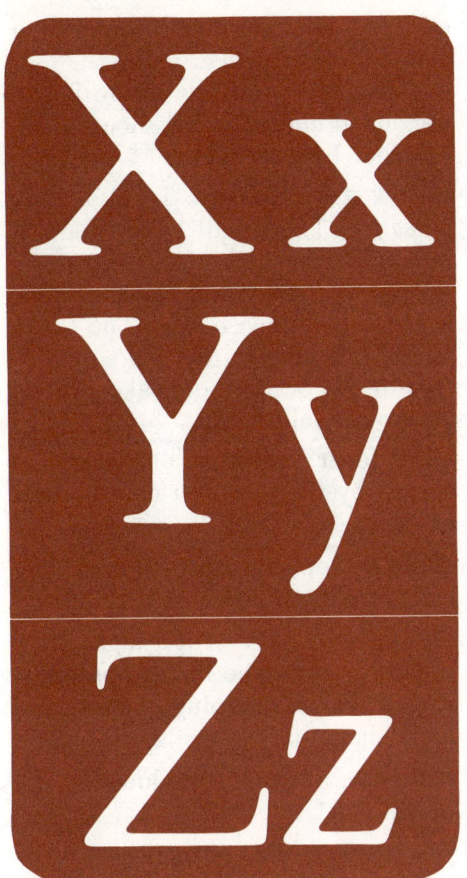

X, x (EKS) *noun.* 1. The 24th letter of the English alphabet. 2. An unknown quantity.

xe·rog·ra·phy (zi-ROG-rə-fee) *noun.* An electrophotographic process for making dry copies of writing and other graphic materials.

Xer·ox (ZIHR-oks) *trademark.* A brand name and trade name of a company that makes photocopiers and other products.

x-ray (EKS-ray) *noun.* 1. Energy radiated as a ray with a short wavelength and a high penetrating power: *X-rays* can be used to treat disease and to photograph bones or foreign matter inside the body. 2. [Capital X] A photograph made by x-rays. *—verb.* To photograph or treat by x-rays. **—x-rayed, x-raying.**

xy·lo·phone (ZIGH-lə-fohn) *noun.* (Music) A percussion instrument made of hard wood bars of different lengths that are struck with small wooden hammers or sticks.

Y, y (WIGH) *noun.* The 25th letter of the English alphabet.

-y, -ey *suffix.* Indicates: 1. The presence of: storm*y*. 2. A relation to or connection with: slim*y*. 3. A state or condition of: thirst*y*. 4. An act, place, or business: mocker*y*; baker*y*. 5. Smallness: kitt*y*.

yacht (YAHT) *noun.* A small vessel used for pleasure cruising or racing. *—verb.* To sail or race on a yacht. **yachted, yachting.**

yacht

yachts·man (YAHTS-mən) *noun.* A person who sails or owns a yacht. **—yachtsmen** *plural.*

Ya·hoo (YAH-hoo) *noun.* A brute; a vulgar person, so-called from the Yahoos in *Gulliver's Travels.*

[1]**yak** *noun.* A longhaired ox of Tibet and Asia.

yak

[2]**yak** *verb.* (Slang) To talk continuously about nothing very important. **yakked, yakking.**

yam *noun.* 1. A starchy orange-colored root, used for food, that is part of a tropical vine. 2. The vine that grows from this root. 3. A variety of sweet potato.

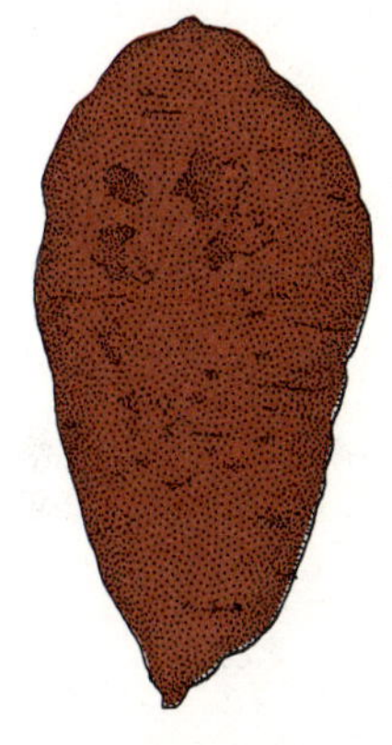
yam

yank (YANGK) *verb.* To jerk; pull suddenly. **yanked, yanking.** *—noun.* A sudden pull; jerk.

yap *verb.* 1. To bark with a high, sharp sound; to yelp. 2. (Slang) To talk in a loud or stupid manner; jabber. **yapped, yapping.** *—noun.* 1. A high, sharp bark; yelp. 2. (Slang) The mouth.

[1]**yard** (YAHRD) *noun.* 1. A unit of measure that equals 3 feet, or 36 inches. 2. A rod attached across a ship's mast to support a sail.

[2]**yard** (YAHRD) *noun.* 1. A plot of ground around or next to a building. 2. An enclosed area used for a special purpose: boat*yard.* 3. An area where railroad trains are made up and cars switched about.

yard·arm (YAHRD-ahrm) *noun.* Either end of a yard or rod that supports a square sail.

xylophone

yard·stick (YAHRD-stik) *noun.* 1. A measuring stick that is 36 inches long. 2. Anything that is used as a standard, or measure of success.

yarn (YAHRN) *noun.* 1. A cord of twisted threads of wool, cotton, or a similar material, used for knitting or weaving. 2. (Informal) A long, involved story or tale.

ye (YEE) *pronoun, plural.* (Rare) You.

yea (YAY) *adverb.* 1. Yes. 2. Indeed; truly. —*noun.* A vote for or in favor of (something): There were 16 *yeas* and 12 nays.

yellow jacket

year (YIHR) *noun.* 1. The period of 365 or 366 days, measured from January 1 through December 31, during which the earth makes a complete revolution around the sun; 12 months. 2. A period of time during which a certain activity takes place: the school *year.* 3. (Plural) Age: Grandfather is very lively for a man of his *years.*

year·book (YIHR-buk) *noun.* A book published each year, especially at a high school or college, that gives information about student activities during the preceding year.

year·ling (YIHR-ling) *noun.* An animal more than one and less than two years old.

year·ly (YIHR-lee) *adjective.* 1. Happening once a year: a *yearly* vacation. 2. Lasting for one year. —*adjective* and *adverb.* Each year; annually: Mr. Bradley plants five acres *yearly.* —*noun.* A magazine or report that comes out once a year. **yearlies.**

yearn (YERN) *verb.* (Used with *for* or *to*) To desire greatly. **yearned, yearning.**

yeast (YEEST) *noun.* 1. Plant cells or fungi used to make baked goods rise or beverages ferment. 2. This substance mixed with flour or meal and pressed into small cakes or packed as a powder in small, sealed envelopes, for use in home baking.

yell (YEL) *verb.* To give a loud cry or call; to shout. **yelled, yelling.** —*noun.* 1. A loud cry; shout. 2. An organized cheer or call shouted together by a group.

yel·low (YEL-oh) *noun.* 1. (Also *adjective*) The bright color of a lemon. 2. The yolk of an egg. —*adjective.* 1. (Slang) Cowardly. 2. Having yellowish skin: The Chinese belong to the *yellow* race. —*verb.* To become or make yellow. **yellowed, yellowing.**

yellow fever. A disease of the tropics spread by the bite of a certain kind of mosquito.

yellow jacket. A wasp or hornet with bright yellow marks.

yelp *verb.* To bark with a high, sharp sound; to yap: The hungry puppies *yelped.* **yelped, yelping.** —*noun.* A high, sharp bark; yap.

[1]**yen** *noun.* (Informal) A longing or desire.

[2]**yen** *noun.* A unit of money in Japan. —**yen** *plural.*

yeo·man (YOH-mən) *noun.* 1. (British) An owner of a small farm. 2. A sailor who acts as a clerk. —**yeomen** *plural.*

yes (YESS) *adverb.* Expresses consent, agreement, or a positive reply; the opposite of *no.* —*noun.* A reply of consent or agreement. **yeses.**

yes·ter·day (YESS-tər-dee) *noun.* 1. The day before today: Today is Tuesday; *yesterday* was Monday. 2. A recent or former time: the songs of *yesterday.* —*adverb.* 1. On the day before the present day. 2. In a former time.

yet *adverb.* 1. Up to now: The work is not *yet* finished. 2. By now: Has Joan left *yet?* 3. But: He was wealthy *yet* unhappy. 4. Even now; still. 5. At some future time: We may win a game *yet.* 6. More so: The prince is rich; the king is *yet* richer. —*conjunction.* Nevertheless:

The people were poor; *yet* they were happy.

yew (YOO) *noun.* 1. An evergreen tree found in Europe, Asia, and America. 2. The wood of the yew tree.

yield (YEELD) *verb.* 1. To produce or provide; give: The field *yielded* a rich crop. 2. To surrender; give way to physical force or pressure. 3. To give way, as to something asked for or owed: The teacher *yielded* to our requests for a holiday. **yielded, yielding.** —*noun.* An amount that is yielded or produced: the *yield* of apples from a tree.

yip *verb.* To bark with a quick, sharp sound; to yap. **yipped, yipping.** —*noun.* A quick, sharp bark.

Y.M.C.A. *abbreviation.* Young Men's Christian Association.

Y.M.H.A. *abbreviation.* Young Men's Hebrew Association.

yo·del (YOHD-l) *verb.* To sing so that the voice flutters or changes from normal to a high shrill sound and back again. **yodeled** or **yodelled, yodeling** or **yodelling.** —*noun.* The sound or act of yodeling.

yo·ga (YOH-gə) *noun.* 1. [Often capital Y] A practice that began in the Orient by which a person tries to reach understanding through quiet thought and relaxation. 2. A program of exercise used to help reach such peace and understanding.

yo·gurt (YOH-gərt) *noun.* A thick, soft food made from curdled milk and often mixed or flavored with fruits.

yoke (YOHK) *noun.* 1. A wooden device used to join together two oxen or other animals, as for plowing. 2. A pair of animals joined together by a yoke. 3. Something that is like a yoke, as for joining things together. 4. Unfair or painful treatment: the *yoke* of slavery. 5. A section of a garment that fits closely around the shoulders (as of a dress) or hips (as of a skirt) from which gathered parts are hung. **yokes.** —*verb.* To join together with a yoke. **yoked, yoking.**

yolk (YOHK) *noun.* The yellow part of an egg.

Yom Kip·pur (yom KIP-ər or yohm ki-PUR) A high holy day of the Jewish religion, observed by fasting and praying.

yon·der (YON-dər) *adverb* and *adjective.* Over there or in that direction.

yore (YOR) *noun.* Ages past; former times.

you (YOO) *pronoun.* A word used in place of the name of a person or persons spoken to: *You* tell me your wish and I'll tell *you* mine.

you'd (YOOD) *contraction.* A shortened form of the words *you had* or *you would.*

you'll (YOOL) *contraction.* A shortened form of the words *you will* or *you shall.*

young (YUHNG) *adjective.* In the early part of life or growth; not old: a *young* dog is a puppy. **younger, youngest.** —*noun.* 1. The offspring of an animal. 2. Young people as a group.

young·ster (YUHNG-stər) *noun.* A young boy or girl; child.

your (YUR) *pronoun* (and *adjective*). Belonging to the person or persons spoken to: Our teacher said, "*Your* reports are due tomorrow."

you're (YUR) *contraction.* A shortened form of the words *you are.*

yours (YURZ) *pronoun.* Something that belongs to the person or persons spoken to: This book is *yours.*

your·self (yur-SELF) *pronoun.* A form of *you* used: 1. For emphasis: Do it *yourself.* 2. When the subject and object of a verb are the same: You got *yourself* into trouble. 3. To describe a normal or usual state: You don't seem *yourself* today.

yew

yoke

zebras

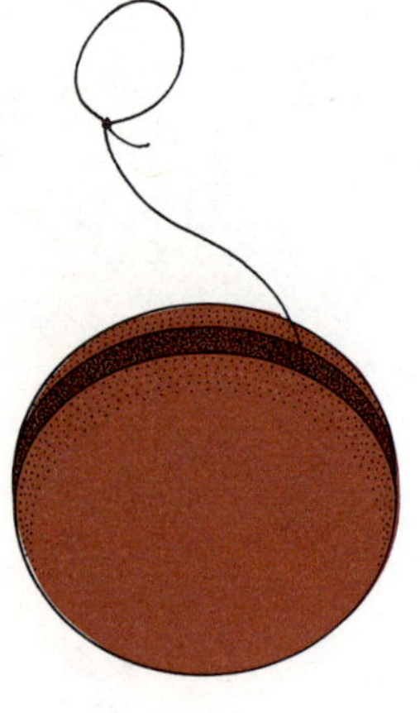
yo-yo

yucca

youth (YOOTH) *noun.* 1. The state or appearance of being young: Her liveliness showed that she had kept her *youth.* 2. A time of being young: Most Americans go to school during their *youth.* 3. A young person, especially a boy. 4. (Used with a plural verb) Young people, considered together: Today's *youth* are healthier than those of a century ago. —**youths** (YOOTHS or YOOTHZ) *plural.*

youth·ful (YOOTH-fəl) *adjective.* 1. Having youth; young. 2. Related to or for young people: Skipping rope is a *youthful* activity. 3. Fresh; vigorous. —**youthfully** *adverb.* —**youthfulness** *noun.*

you've (YOOV) *contraction.* A shortened form of *you have.*

yowl *verb.* To make a prolonged cry or howl. **yowled, yowling.** —*noun.* A prolonged cry or howl.

yo-yo (YOH-yoh) *noun.* A toy made of a round flat spool and a string that is wrapped around the spool so that it can be spun or moved up and down by the person holding the string. **yo-yos.**

yr. *abbreviation.* 1. Year. 2. Your.

yuc·ca (YUHK-ə) *noun.* A tropical plant with large, white flowers and long, pointed leaves.

yule (YOOL) *noun.* [Sometimes capital Y] Christmas.

yule·tide (YOOL-tighd) *noun.* [Sometimes capital Y] The Christmas season.

Y.W.C.A. *abbreviation.* Young Women's Christian Association.

Y.W.H.A. *abbreviation.* Young Women's Hebrew Association.

Z, z (ZEE) *noun.* The twenty-sixth letter of the English alphabet.

zeal (ZEEL) *noun.* Eagerness, great interest: a *zeal* for politics.

zeal·ous (ZEL-əss) *adjective.* Eager, full of interest. —**zealously** *adverb.*

ze·bra (ZEE-brə) *noun.* A horse-like animal of Africa marked with light and dark stripes.

ze·nith (ZEE-nith) *noun.* 1. A point in the sky directly over one's head. 2. The highest point: The pianist was at the *zenith* of his career.

zeph·yr (ZEF-ər) *noun.* 1. A wind from the west. 2. Any gentle breeze: "Soft the *zephyr* blows." (Gray).

zep·pe·lin (ZEP-ə-lin) *noun.* [Often capital Z] A cylindrical airship with a rigid frame.

ze·ro (ZIHR-oh) *noun.* 1. The number or symbol 0. 2. Nothing. 3. The point at which degrees or markings on a scale begin. 4. The lowest point. —**zeros** or **zeroes** *plural.* —*verb.* 1. To close (in on): The hunters *zeroed* in on the animal. 2. To aim directly. **zeroed, zeroing.** —*adjective.* 1. Without any value; nonexisting. 2. (Aviation) So little as to be of no practical use: When visibility is *zero,* pilots fly by instruments.

zest *noun.* Enthusiasm; great enjoyment. —**zestful** *adjective.* —**zestfully** *adverb.*

zig·zag (ZIG-zag) *noun.* 1. The pattern made by a series of back-and-forth motions with sharp turns and angles. 2. One of the marks of such a pattern. —*verb.* To move with or make many sharp turns. **zigzagged, zigzagging.**

zinc (ZINGK) *noun.* A bluish white metal that does not tarnish or rust easily: *Zinc* is often used to coat iron.

zin·ni·a (ZIN-ee-ə) *noun.* 1. A plant grown for its bright flowers. 2. The flower of this plant.

zip *verb.* 1. To move at a very high speed. 2. To fasten by means of a zipper. **zipped, zipping.** —*noun.* 1. A buzzing sound made by something moving very fast. 2. (Informal) Pep, zest.

Zip Also **Zip Code** *noun.* A system designed to speed delivery of mail by the U.S. Postal Service in which each local area is assigned a five-digit code number.

zip·per (ZIP-ər) *noun.* A fastening device having two rows of metal or plastic teeth that are hooked together by means of a sliding tab.

zith·er (ZITH-ər) *noun.* A musical instrument made of a flat sounding-box with many strings stretched across the top.

zo·di·ac (ZOH-dee-ak) *noun.* 1. The unseen path followed through the heavens by the sun, moon, and most planets. 2. The area included in this path divided into 12 parts: The 12 signs of the *zodiac* are named after constellations and are used in astrology.

zone (ZOHN) *noun.* 1. An area having definite boundaries: The Zip Code divides each city into *zones.* 2. One of the major regions of the earth: The five *zones* are North and South Frigid, North and South Temperate, and Torrid. **zones.** —*verb.* To divide into sections for a special reason: *zone* a town. **zoned, zoning.**

zoo *noun.* A place where living, wild (and sometimes domesticated) animals are kept for the public to see. **zoos.**

zo·o·log·i·cal (zoh-ə-LOJ-i-kəl) *adjective.* Relating to animals or animal life. —**zoologically** *adverb.*

zoological garden. A zoo.

zo·ol·o·gy (zoh-OL-ə-jee) *noun.* The science that deals with animals.

zoom *verb.* 1. To move rapidly, especially with a buzzing or humming noise: The race cars *zoom* around the track. 2. To ascend abruptly at a sharp angle: The jet plane *zoomed* skyward. 3. (Photography) To move in quickly toward a subject, or to use a lens with the ability to enlarge the image of the subject. **zoomed, zooming.** —*noun.* The act or sound of zooming.

zwie·back (ZWIGH-bak) *noun.* A sweet, dry toast.

zyz·zy·va (ZIZ-ə-və) *noun.* A tropical, American weevil that destroys plants.

zinnia

zeppelin

zipper

zoo

PHOTOGRAPH CREDITS

The names of the following have been abbreviated throughout this list of credits as indicated:

The Bettmann Archive	B.A.
Culver Pictures, Inc.	C.P.
National Audubon Society	NAS
Photo Researchers	P.R.
United Press International	UPI
Deborah Blish Thomas	D.B.T.

We wish to thank these and all the organizations and individuals listed below for their cooperation and assistance.

page 8 **William Morris,** Philippe Halsman.

aardvark John B. Dobbins from NAS; **aborigine** UPI; **accordion** Curtis A. Reif; **acropolis** George H. Wolfson; **adobe** Library of Congress (Rothstein for FSA); **aerial** UPI; **aerialists** Ed Finley from P.R.; **air conditioner** Curtis A. Reif; **aircraft carrier** UPI; **airport** TWA; **albatross** George Holton from P.R.; **alpaca** A. W. Ambler from NAS; **ambulance** Curtis A. Reif; **amphibian** Textion's Bell Aerosystems Co.; **anaconda** Dade W. Thornton from NAS; **anteater** Jeanne White from NAS; **antelope** Yellowstone National Park; **antlers** Leonard Lee Rue III from NAS; **Aqualung** Curtis A. Reif; **aqueduct** NANA; **ark** B.A.; **armadillo** Leonard Lee Rue III from NAS; **armor** Courtesy of the Metropolitan Museum of Art; **ass** Chuck Abbott from Rapho-Guillumette Pictures; **astronaut** NASA, Manned Spacecraft Center; **atomic bomb** Defense Dept.; **auk** Alvin E. Staffan from NAS.

baboons Leonard Lee Rue III; **badger** Alvin Staffan; **bagpipe** Three Lions; **balcony** Walt Disney Productions; **bald eagle** G. Ronald Austing from NAS; **balloon** N.Y. Daily News; **banjo** Curtis A. Reif; **bareback** Cheetham from P.R.; **barge** Dravo Corp.; **barn** D.B.T.; **baton** Wide World Photos; **beagle** Curtis A. Reif; **bear** Leonard Lee Rue III from NAS; **beaver** Karl H. Maslowski; **belfry** Knotts Berry Farm and Ghost Town; **bison** Allan D. Cruickshank from NAS; **blackboard** H. Armstrong Roberts; **blastoff** Wide World Photos; **blender** D.B.T.; **blimp** Goodyear Tire & Rubber Co.; **blockhouse** C.P.; **bloodhound** Curtis A. Reif; **blowtorch** Standard Oil Co. (N.J.); **boa** Dade W. Thornton from NAS; **boar** Azaria Alon from NAS; **bobcat** Leonard Lee Rue III from NAS; **bobsled** UPI; **bookmobile** D.B.T.; **boxer** Wide World Photos; **boxing** P.R.; **breaker** Pan American World Airways; **bridge** Eastern Photo Service; **brigantine** C.P.; **bronco** Fritz Henle from P.R.; **bronze** Stephanie Dinkins from P.R.; **buggy** C.P.; **bull** Grant Heilman; **bulldogs** Walter Chandoha; **buoy** Jan Hahn; **burnoose** Bernard P. Wolff from P.R.; **bus** Moser & Son; **buzzard** A. W. Ambler from NAS.

cable car Phil Palmer from Monkmeyer; **caboose** Ewing Galloway; **calf** J. C. Allen and Son; **camera** D.B.T.; **camper** D.B.T.; **campus** D.B.T.; **canal** Panama Canal Co.; **canyon** Gene Ahrens; **caribou** Leonard Lee Rue III from NAS; **carousel** Ewing Galloway; **cartwheel** UPI; **cascade** NYSPIX-Commerce; **casserole** Precis; **castle** H. Armstrong Roberts; **cat** Frank's Studio; **cavern** Massie-Missouri Resources Div.; **cemetery** D.B.T.; **centaur** C.P.; **chandelier** Abbie Rowe—Courtesy National Park Service; **chapel** D.B.T.; **chariot** C.P.; **chateau** French Government Tourist Office; **cheerleaders** Bill Stekl from The Middletown Press; **cheetah** Mark Boulton from NAS; **chef** UPI; **chess** D.B.T.; **chickens** Wide World Photo; **chihuahua** UPI; **chimpanzee** Bucky Reeves from NAS; **chipmunk** Alvin Staffan; **choir** D.B.T.; **church** Ewing Galloway; **cirrus** Monkmeyer; **civet** Robert C. Hermes from NAS; **classroom** George Zimbel from P.R.; **clipper** Australian Information Service; **clocks** Westclox, Division of General Time; **clown** Lawrence D. Thornton; **cockatoo** Arthur Ambler from NAS; **cocker spaniel** Kaufmann and Fabry Co.; **coffin** C.P.; **coin** C.P.; **coliseum** UPI; **collie** Curtis A. Reif; **colt** Bob Taylor; **comet** Department of Astronomy, University of Michigan; **command module** NASA, Manned Spacecraft Center; **computer** Philco Corp.; **condor** San Diego Zoo Photo by R. Van Nostrand from P.R.; **conductor** Columbia Broadcasting System; **conning tower** Official U.S. Navy Photo; **constitution** Harris & Ewing; **control tower** A. Devaney, Inc.; **conveyor belt** Florida Citrus Commission; **convict** C. M. Abbott from A. Devaney, N.Y.; **coral** Australian National Travel Association; **cormorant** Allan D. Cruickshank from NAS; **corral** David W. Carson from A. Devaney; **cosmonaut** Novosti from SOVFOTO; **cougar** Hugh M. Halliday from NAS; **cove** Fritz Henle; **covered wagon** B.A.; **cowboy** Bob Taylor; **coyote** Wilford Miller from NAS; **crane** Les Baxter for Port of Toronto; **crater** NASA; **crocodile** Bucky Reeves from NAS; **crossbones** C.P.; **crown** International News Photo; **crow's nest** B.A.; **cumulus** U.S. Weather Bureau; **cyclone** Wide World.

dachshund Jeanne White from NAS; **Dalmatian** Curtis A. Reif; **dam** Bureau of Reclamation; **delta** Fairchild Aerial Surveys, Inc.; **derrick** Sikorsky Aircraft; **desert** Philip Gendreau; **destroyer** U.S. Navy; **dike** Netherland Information Service; **dinghy** Eric M. Sanford; **dirigible** U.S. Navy; **diving bell** U.S. Navy; **diving suit** UPI; **Doberman pinscher** Walter Chandoha; **dolphin** United Press Photo; **dome** A. Devaney, Inc.; **donkey** P. Trelawny from NAS; **dormer** Eric M. Sanford; **drawbridge** UPI; **drill** UPI; **dromedary** UPI; **drum majorette** UPI; **drummer** Ewing Galloway; **duck** Allan D. Cruickshank from NAS; **duckbill** L. H. Newman from NAS; **dune buggy** Ralph Poole.

eclipse UPI; **egret** Allan D. Cruickshank; **elephant** Leonard Lee Rue III from NAS; **elk** C. J. Eckman from NAS; **emu** A. W. Ambler from NAS; **ermine** Karl H. Maslowski from NAS; **escalator** XEP Photo by Robert Taylor; **exchange** UPI; **expressway** Portland Cement Association; **extinguisher** D.B.T.

falcon Walt Disney Productions; **fan** C.P.; **farm** A. Devaney, Inc.; **faun** C.P.; **fawn** Hal H. Harrison; **fence** Harold M. Lambert; **fencing** H. Armstrong Roberts; **ferret** Edward Bonn from NAS; **figurehead** The Whaling Museum, New Bedford, Mass.; **finch** Mitchell Campbell from NAS; **fire engine** D.B.T.; **fire escape** D.B.T.; **fireworks** UPI; **fjord** Norwegian Official Photo Guranger; **flagpole** H. Armstrong Roberts; **flamingo** UPI; **flatboat** Dravo Corp.; **flatcar** Bangor & Aroostook Railroad; **flintlock** C.P.; **folk dance** H. Armstrong Roberts; **football** D.B.T.; **forest ranger** U.S. Forest Service; **fort** B.A.; **fortress** C.P.; **fountain** A. Devaney, Inc.; **fox** G. Ronald Austing from NAS; **freckles** UPI; **freeway** Harold M. Lambert; **freight trains** N.Y. Central System; **frigate** C.P.; **frogmen** Philip D. Rush.

gables John Arms; **galaxy** California Institute of Technology—Mt. Wilson and Palomar Observatories; **galleon** C.P.; **gallows** B.A.; **gantry** U.S. Air Force Photo; **gargoyle** Rapho-Guillumette Pictures; **garter snake** Leonard Lee Rue III from NAS; **gas mask** U.S. Army Photograph; **gazelle** R. Van Nostrand from NAS; **gerbil** Gordon Smith from NAS; **geyser** H. Armstrong Roberts; **ghost town** John Lewis Stage from P.R.; **gibbon** A. W. Ambler from NAS; **giraffe** Wide World; **glacier** U.S. Geological Survey; **gladiator** B.A.; **glass blowing** Corning Glass Works; **glider** Alan Band Associates; **globe** D.B.T.; **gnu** R. Van Nostrand from NAS; **goalie** UPI; **goat** UPI; **go-cart** D.B.T.; **gondola** Bernard G. Silberstein from Rapho-Guillumette Pictures; **goose & goslings** Leonard Lee Rue III; **gopher** Woodrow Goodpaster from NAS; **gorilla** Ringling Bros. Barnum & Bailey Circus; **grandstand** UPI; **gravestone** D.B.T.; **greenhouse** D.B.T.; **grenadier** B.A.; **grizzly bear** Alfred Bailey from NAS; **grosbeak** Karl H. Maslowski; **groundhog** Ewing Galloway; **grouper** Jeanne White from NAS; **grouse** Hal H. Harrison from Monkmeyer; **guillotine** C.P.; **guinea pigs** Walter Chandoha; **guitar** American Music Conference; **gull** Allan D. Cruickshank from NAS.

hamster Gulf Hamstery; **harbor** Laurence Lowry; **harlequin** B.A.; **harp** American Music Conference; **hawk** Fran Hall from NAS; **hedgehog** A. W. Ambler from NAS; **helicopter** Sikorsky Aircraft; **hen** UPI; **heron** Allan D. Cruickshank from NAS; **hieroglyphics** C.P.; **hippopotamus** Ewing Galloway; **hockey** Boston Bruins; **hog** Dave Repp from NAS; **horned toad** Robert H. Wright from NAS; **horses** Grant Heilman; **houseboat** Cris-Craft Corp.; **hummingbird** Allan D. Cruickshank from NAS; **hurdle** UPI; **huskies** Alaska Division of Tourism and Economic Development; **hydrant** D.B.T.; **hydrogen bomb** UPI; **hyena** Gordon Smith from NAS.

ibex R. Van Nostrand from NAS; **ibis** Karl H. Maslowski; **iceberg** U.S. Coast Guard; **iguana** UPI; **incubator** Grant Heilman; **infield** UPI; **ingots** U.S. Steel Corp.; **interstate** Conn. Dept. of Transportation; **island** Peter S. Thacher from P.R.

jack-o'-lantern H. Armstrong Roberts; **jack rabbit** C. E. Stoody from Western Ways; **jaguar** Marvin Newman from ABC-TV; **jockeys** UPI; **judo** UPI; **juggler** P.R.; **jugs** H. Armstrong Roberts; **Jungle gym** Goodyear Tire and Rubber Co.; **junk** Three Lions.

kangaroo UPI; **kayak** U.S. Fish and Wildlife Service, Photo by E. P. Haddon; **kettledrum** American Music Conference; **keyboard** The Washington Post; **kilts** H. Armstrong Roberts; **kimono** UPI; **kite** H. Armstrong Roberts; **kitten** Walter Chandoha.

lace D.B.T.; **ladder** Harold M. Lambert; **lambs** H. Armstrong Roberts; **lamprey** Karl H. Maslowski; **landslide** R. E. Goodman, University of Calif.; **lantern** C.P.; **lasso** Rodeo Information Foundation; **launching pad** NASA; **lemmings** John H. Gerard from NAS; **lemur** Arthur Ambler from NAS; **library** Abington School District; **lifeboats** UPI; **lighthouse** Harold M. Lambert; **liner** Moran Towing & Transportation Co., Inc.; **lion** Leonard Lee Rue III from NAS; **litter** B.A.; **llamas** Wide World; **lobster** Grant Heilman; **lock** Curtis A. Reif; **locomotive** California Western Railroad; **longhorn** Authenticated News; **loon** George A. Smith; **lumberjack** Three Lions; **lunar module** NASA; **lynx** Leonard Lee Rue III.

magpie Allan D. Cruickshank from NAS; **mallard** Authenticated News; **mammoth** Courtesy of the American Museum of Natural History; **marmoset** UPI; **marten** Alfred M. Baily from NAS; **martins** Jack Dermid from NAS; **mask** Courtesy of the American Museum of Natural History; **mastiff** Mary Eleanor Browning from NAS;

matador Las Vegas News Bureau; **meadowlark** J. W. Jackson; **medal** UPI; **megaphone** Harold M. Lambert; **merinos** Frederick Ayer from P.R.; **mermaid** C.P.; **meteor** UPI; **meteorite** Smithsonian Institution; **microscope** American Optical Co.; **Milky Way** Yerkes Observatory; **minarets** UPI; **minibike** UPI; **mink** Karl H. Maslowski; **minstrel** B.A.; **minuteman** C.P.; **mobile home** Mobile Homes Manufacturers Assn.; **mole** John H. Gerard; **mongoose** Lewis Wayne Walker from NAS; **monkeys** Oregon Regional Primate Research Center; **monorail** A. Devaney, Inc.; **moon buggy** NASA; **moon crater** NASA; **moose** Western Ways; **mosaic** Three Lions; **mosque** UPI; **motorboats** H. Armstrong Roberts; **motorcycles** The Washington Post; **mountain goats** Leonard Lee Rue III from NAS; **mountain lion** Dr. Maurice G. Hornocker; **mouse** Leonard Lee Rue III; **mummy** Three Lions; **musket** B.A.; **musk ox** Hugh M. Halliday from NAS; **muskrat** Ohio Conservation Service; **mustangs** Gary Settle from The New York Times.

nebula UPI; **nest** John L. Blackford; **nets** H. Armstrong Roberts; **new moon** Lick Observatory; **nimbostratus** Standard Oil Co. (N.J.); **northern lights** Dewey Bergquist; **nuclear reactor** UPI; **nurse** D.B.T.

obelisk Harold M. Lambert; **observatory** Lick Observatory; **ocelot** Verna R. Johnston from NAS; **octapus** Grant Heilman; **oilwells** Library of Congress; **okapi** R. Van Nostrand; **oppossums** Philip Gendreau; **orangutan** A. W. Ambler from NAS; **orchestra** American Music Conference; **osprey** Leonard Lee Rue III; **ostrich** Mark Boulton; **otter** Ewing Galloway; **outboard motor** Evinrude; **outrigger** George Holton from P.R.; **overpasses** Harold M. Lambert; **owl** UPI; **oxcart** Max and Kit Hunn from NAS; **oxen** Grant Heilman.

paddle wheel Bill Muster for Greene Line Steamers, Inc.; **pagoda** Three Lions; **panda** Wide World Photos; **panther** Arthur W. Ambler from NAS; **parachute** Ted Keplan; **parade** Florida Development Commission—Free Lance Photographers Guild Inc.; **parakeets** Hal Harrison from Grant Heilman; **parasol** B.A.; **parkas** Sam Kimura from P.R.; **parrot** Jeanne White from NAS; **partridge** Karl H. Maslowski; **passenger pigeon** Illinois State Museum; **patrolman** Los Angeles Police Dept.; **peacock** UPI; **peccary** A. W. Ambler from NAS; **pelican** Lovett Williams from NAS; **penguins** National Science Foundation Photo; **Pentagon** Wide World; **petrel** Alvin E. Staffan from NAS; **pewee** G. Ronald Austing from NAS; **pharaoh** Hamilton Wright; **pheasant** Harold M. Lambert; **piano** Steinway & Sons; **piazza** John Phillips from P.R.; **pickup truck** Ford Motor Co.; **pig** Bob Taylor; **pigeons** UPI; **piglets** Bob Taylor; **pintos** David W. Carson from A. Devaney, N.Y.; **planetarium** D.B.T.; **plow** Deere & Co.; **polar bear** Harold M. Lambert; **pole vault** Wide World; **pony express** Public Roads Administration; **poodle** Walter Chandoha; **porcupine** Allan D. Cruickshank from NAS; **porpoise** Charles Meyer from NAS; **powder horn** B.A.; **prairie schooner** Warner Bros. Pictures, Inc.; **printing press** Gladys Muller for The Franklin Institute; **pronghorn** Willis Peterson; **prow** UPI; **pueblo** Mesa Verde National Park; **puppies** UPI; **pygmies** Attilo Getti; **pyramids** B.A.; **python** Dade W. Thornton from NAS.

quail R. Van Nostrand from NAS; **quarry** Philip Gendreau; **Quonset huts** U.S. Army Photograph.

rabbit Bob Taylor; **raccoon** Leonard Lee Rue III; **radar** UPI; **raft** P.R.; **raincoat** National Biscuit Co.; **rain forest** Charlie Ott from NAS; **rakes** Harold M. Lambert; **rat** John H. Gerard from NAS; **rattlesnake** UPI; **raven** Robert C. Hermes from NAS; **reaper** Canadian Government Travel Bureau; **recorder** D.B.T.; **redwoods** Redwood Empire Association; **reel** Harold M. Lambert; **refracting telescope** Yerkes Observatory; **refrigerator** D.B.T.; **reindeer** Eric Hosking from NAS; **reins** F.S.A.; **relay** AAU; **reptiles** Hal Harrison from Grant Heilman; **retrorocket** NASA; **rhesus monkeys** Lynwood Chace from NAS; **rhinoceros** UPI; **rickshaw** UPI; **rider** D.B.T.; **rink** A. Devaney, Inc., N.Y.; **river** Fairchild Aerial Surveys, Inc.; **rocket** U.S. Air Force; **rocking chair** Harold M. Lambert; **roller coaster** Dogpatch U.S.A. Inc.; **roller derby** XEP Photo by Howard Schwach; **rooster** Grant Heilman; **rotor** Sikorsky Aircraft; **rotunda** UPI; **roundup** Bob Taylor; **rowboats** H. Armstrong Roberts; **row houses** Harold M. Lambert; **rugby** D.B.T.; **ruins** Georgia Engelhard—Free Lance Photographers Guild Inc.; **ruler** D.B.T.; **runway** Trans World Airlines.

sable Alfred M. Bailey from NAS; **safety patrol** H. Armstrong Roberts; **Saint Bernard** Curtis A. Reif; **sampans** Richard Harrington from Three Lions; **sari** UPI; **satyr** B.A.; **saxophone** UPI; **scaffold** Janis Groover Boice; **scarecrow** UPI; **scepter** B.A.; **schnauzer** Mary Eleanor Browning from NAS; **schooner** UPI; **Scouts** Girl Scouts of America; **scroll** Jewish Theological Seminary of America; **scuba** UPI; **sea horse** A. W. Ambler from NAS; **seals** BIPS; **Sealyham terrier** Mary Eleanor Browning from NAS; **seaplane** Piper Aircraft Corp.; **searchlight** New York Fire Dept.; **secretary** D.B.T.; **seesaw** Esther Bubley; **Senate** UPI; **sequoia** Grant Heilman; **serape** H. Armstrong Roberts; **setter** Mary Eleanor Browning from NAS; **sextant** U.S. Naval Academy; **shark** P.R.; **sheep dog** Grant Heilman; **shorthorn** Rod Heinrichs/Grant Heilman; **shuffleboard** John Gadja—Free Lance Photographers Guild, Inc.; **shutters** D.B.T.; **skeleton** Dan Bernstein; **skis** UPI; **skunk** John H. Gerard; **sky diving** UPI; **skylight** National Gallery of Art, Washington, D.C.; **sled** Eva Luoma; **sleigh** UPI; **slide rule** D.B.T.; **sloop** Wide World; **slot cars** Stombecker Corp.; **sloth** R. C. Hermes; **smelter** U.S. Steel Corp.; **smith** C.P.; **smokestacks** P.R.; **snapping turtle** John H. Gerard; **snare drum** American Music Conference; **sneakers** Uniroyal, Inc.; **snowplow** Caterpillar Tractor Co.; **snowshoe** Leonard Lee Rue III; **soapbox derby** UPI; **soccer** D.B.T.; **soda fountain** D.B.T.; **space station** North American Rockwell; **speedway** Indianapolis Motor Speedway; **sphinx** H. Armstrong Roberts; **spiral** P.R.; **splashdown** Wide World Photo; **spotlight** D.B.T.; **spur and rowels** C.P.; **sputnik** Tass from SOVFOTO; **square dance** Caplin & Thompson Creative Photography—Free Lance Photographers Guild Inc.; **squirrel** Ewing Galloway; **SST** French Embassy Press and Information Division; **stadium** UPI; **stagecoach** Western Ways Photo; **staircase** Eric M. Sanford; **stalactite and stalagmite** N.M. State Tourist Bureau; **station wagon** D.B.T.; **statue** American Museum of Immigration; **steamroller** H. Armstrong Roberts; **stepladder** D.B.T.; **stethoscope** H. Armstrong Roberts; **stilts** George Pickow from Three Lions; **stirrup** P.R.; **stockade** B.A.; **stockyard** Assn. of American Railroads; **stoplight** D.B.T.; **storks** Black Star; **stream** H. Armstrong Roberts; **streetcar** Los Angeles Times Photo; **stretcher** Bell Helicopter; **strip mining** Billy Davis, The Courier-Journal; **stroller** D.B.T.; **submarine** UPI; **subway** UPI; **sulky** Yonkers Raceway News Photo by Michael Cipriani; **sumac** Hal Harrison from Grant Heilman; **sundial** UPI; **surfboard** P.R.; **surgeon** UPI; **surrey** B.A.; **suspension bridge** Don Knight from A. Devaney; **swamp** U.S.D.A. Photograph; **swans** Josef Scaylea and A. Devaney; **switchboard** A.T. & T. Co.

tailgate D.B.T.; **tambourine** The Washington Post; **tank** H. Armstrong Roberts; **tapestry** The Metropolitan Museum of Art, Gift of John D. Rockefeller, Jr., 1937; **tarpon** Courtesy of the American Museum of Natural History; **tattoo** B.A.; **telescope** Kitt Peck National Observatory; **temple** Japan National Tourist Organization; **tennis** UPI; **tepee** Edmund Y. Lee; **terrapin** Jack Dermid; **terrier** H. Armstrong Roberts; **theater** Friedman-Abeles; **thermos** D.B.T.; **throne** C.P.; **thunderclouds** U.S. Weather Bureau; **tiger** A. Devaney; **tightrope** N.B.C.; **tire** D.B.T.; **toad** Allan D. Cruickshank from NAS; **tobacco** UPI; **toboggan** Eric M. Sanford; **tomahawk** Museum of the American Indian; **tom-tom** Three Lions; **tornado** H. Armstrong Roberts; **totem pole** Division of Economic and Tourist Development, Juneau, Alaska; **toucan** UPI; **tractor trailer** Foto Arts Inc.; **train** Sante Fe Railway; **trampoline** Harold M. Lambert; **transistor** D.B.T.; **trapeze** Wide World; **trellis** H. Armstrong Roberts; **trestle** Gene Ahrens; **tricycle** D.B.T.; **tripods** H. Armstrong Roberts; **trombone** D.B.T.; **trumpet** Gene Badger; **trundle bed** Eric M. Sanford; **tuba** Bob Taylor; **tugboat** Harold M. Lambert; **tunnel** The Port of New York Authority; **turban** H. Armstrong Roberts; **turkey** Leonard Lee Rue III; **turrets** The British Travel Association; **turtle** John H. Gerard; **twins** UPI; **typewriter** D.B.T.; **tyrannosaurs** The American Museum of Natural History.

ukulele American Music Conference; **umbrella** H. Armstrong Roberts; **unicorn** B.A.; **unicycle** UPI; **urn** Courtesy of the Museum of Fine Arts, Boston.

valley H. Armstrong Roberts; **van** Harold M. Lambert; **vanity** D.B.T.; **vault** Chase Manhattan Bank; **veranda** Eric M. Sanford; **vestment** Religious News Service Photo; **viaduct** Three Lions; **vineyard** Almadén Vineyards; **volcano** U.S. Navy Photograph; **volleyball** P.R.; **vulture** Karl Maslowski from NAS.

wagon B.A.; **walkie talkie** Delco Radio Division; **walrus** Leonard Lee Rue III from NAS; **warlock** B.A.; **water buffalo** P.R.; **water-skiing** TVA; **water wheel** H. Armstrong Roberts; **weasels** Karl H. Maslowski; **weathercock** UPI; **well** Peace Corps; **wheat** Merrim from Monkmeyer Press Photo Service; **wheelchair** H. Armstrong Roberts; **whippet** Walter Chandoha; **whooping crane** Allan D. Cruickshank from NAS; **wig** B.A.; **wildcat** Leonard Lee Rue III; **windmill** Adex Advertising Inc. for Netherlands Information Service; **wolf** A. W. Ambler from NAS; **wolfhound** Jeanne White from NAS; **woodchuck** John H. Gerard from NAS; **wrecker** Harold M. Lambert Studios, Inc.; **wrestler** Black Star.

xylophone American Music Conference.

yacht Morris Rosenfeld & Sons; **yak** Bucky and Avis Reeves from NAS; **yoke** B.A.; **yucca** John L. Blackford.

zebra UPI; **zeppelin** B.A.; **zoo** Vivienne from P.R.

Letter Symbols for Sounds

Letters are the symbols we use to represent the sounds we hear in spoken language. Just as one letter symbol can sometimes represent several different sounds, so can one sound be represented by more than one letter symbol. This fact can make spelling a problem, but it's a problem you can solve.

Have you ever tried to look up a word in the dictionary without knowing what letter it starts with? Suppose you are writing about a pet skunk. You want to spell a word that means the same as "odor." You know the word sounds like SENT. But you don't find it in words beginning "se. . . ."

With this kind of puzzle, you will save yourself time by using the chart below. It shows you the different combinations of letters that might be used to represent different sounds. Looking at the symbol for the sound (s) on this chart, you find it might be represented by *sc*. Checking back in the dictionary, you now find that the word you want is *scent*.

If you find you sometimes have trouble with spelling tests, take time now and then to study this chart. Examine a word you have misspelled to make sure first that you have used a letter or letters to stand for every sound in the word. If you have the wrong letter for a sound, study the chart to find out what other letter or letters might be used for that sound.

Letter Symbol for a Sound	**Key Word**	**Letters That May Represent the Sound**
(a)	pat	a, pat; ai, plaid; al, calf; au, laugh; i, meringue
(ah)	far	a, far; aa, bazaar; a-e, are; ah, hurrah; ea, heart
(ai)	air	a-e, bare; ai, air; ea, bear; e-e, there; ei, their
(aw)	jaw	al, chalk; au, fraud; aw, jaw; o, loft; oa, broad; o-e, gone; ou, cough
(ay)	pay	a-e, grate; ai, rain; au, gauge; ay, pay; ea, great; e-e, suede; ee, matinee; ei, rein; eig, reign; et, croquet; ey, obey
(b)	bib	b, bib; bb, hobby
(ch)	church	ch, church; tch, catch; te, righteous; ti, question; tu, stature
(d)	dad	d, dad; dd, ruddy; ed, played
(e)	pet	a, any; ai, again; e, pet; ea, bread; eo, jeopardy; ie, friend
(ee)	bee	e, be; ea, pea; ee, bee; e-e, scheme; ei, seize; ey, key; i, antique; ie, chief; y, merry
(f)	fifteen	f, fifteen; ff, coffee; gh, rough; lf, calf; ph, phone
(g)	gag	g, gag; gg, trigger; gh, ghost; gu, guide; gue, league

(h)	hit	h, hit; wh, whole
(i)	pit	a-e, average; ee, been; i, pit; ie, sieve; ui, build; y, myth
(igh)	sigh	ai, aisle; ay, aye; ei, stein; eigh, height; i, pint; i-e, kite; ie, die; igh, sigh; oi, choir; ui, guide; uy, guy; y, type
(ihr)	pier	eer, beer; ier, pier
(j)	judge	dg, judge; di, soldier; g, giant; j, judge
(k)	kick	c, cob; cc, occupy; ch, ache; ck, kick; k, kick; qu, antique
(l)	lip	l, lip; ll, well
(m)	mum	lm, calm; m, mum; mb, lamb; mm, drummer; mn, solemn
(n)	no	gn, gnat; kn, knit; n, no; nn, flannel; pn, pneumonia
(o)	pot	a, squad; o, pot
(oh)	oh	eau, bureau; ew, sew; oa, oath; o-e, robe; oe, toe; oh, ohm; ough, dough; ow, blow
(oi)	oil	oi, oil; oy, boy
(oo)	boot	ew, blew; o-e, prove; oe, shoe; oo, boot; ou, soup; ough, through; u-e, rude; ue, blue; ui, juice
(ow)	power	ou, count; ow, power
(p)	pop	p, pop; pp, slipper
(r)	rear	r, rear; rh, rhyme; rr, berry; wr, write
(s)	site	c, city; ps, psalms; s, site; sc, scent; ss, puss
(sh)	shoe	c, ocean; ch, chalet; ci, special; sh, shoe; s, sugar; sch, schwa; sci, conscious; si, mansion; ss, mission; ti, motion
(t)	trapped	bt, debt; ed, trapped; pt, pterodactyl; t, trapped; tt, batter; tw, two
(u)	put	o, bosom; oo, book; ou, would; u, put; u-e, lure
(uh)	cut	o, color; oo, flood; ou, tough; u, cut
(v)	valve	f, of; lv, calves; v, valve; ve, have
(w)	win	u, quit; w, win
(y)	yet	i, union; y, yet
(z)	zippers	s, zippers; ss, scissors; x, Xerox; z, zippers; zz, fuzzy
(zh)	pleasure	ge, rouge; s, pleasure; si, decision

Key to Pronunciation

Letter Symbol for a Sound	Key Word and Its Respelling	Letter Symbol for a Sound	Key Word and Its Respelling
(a)	pat (PAT)	**(ng)**	thing (THING)
	barrel (BA-rəl)		finger (FING-gər)
(ah)	far (FAHR)	**(o)**	pot (POT)
(ai)	air (AIR)	**(oh)**	oh, boat (BOHT)
(aw)	jaw (JAW)	**(oi)**	oil (OIL)
(ay)	pay (PAY)	**(oo)**	boot, rule (ROOL)
(b)	bib (BIB)	**(or)**	for (FOR)
(ch)	church (CHURCH)	**(ow)**	power (POW-ər)
(d)	dad (DAD)	**(p)**	pop (POP)
(e)	pet (PET)	**(r)**	rear (RIHR)
(ee)	bee (BEE)	**(s)**	sits (SITS)
(ehr)	berry (BEHR-ee)	**(sh)**	shoe (SHOO)
(er)	term (TERM)	**(ss)**	case (KAYSS)
(f)	fifteen (fif-TEEN)	**(t)**	tapped (TAPT)
(g)	gag (GAG)	**(th)**	thing (THING)
(h)	hit (HIT)	**(<u>th</u>)**	this (<u>TH</u>IS)
(hw)	when (HWEN)	**(u)**	put, book (BUK)
(i)	pit (PIT)	**(uh)**	cut (KUHT)
(igh)	sigh (SIGH)	**(v)**	valve (VALV)
(ihr)	pier (PIHR)	**(w)**	win (WIN)
(j)	judge (JUHJ)	**(y)**	yet (YET)
(k)	kick (KIK)	**(y)**	is also used in place of (igh) before two consonant letters as in child (CHYLD)
(ks)	mix (MIKS)	**(z)**	zippers (ZIP-ərz)
(kw)	quick (KWIK)	**(zh)**	pleasure (PLEZH-ər)
(l)	lip (LIP)		rouge (ROOZH)
	needle (NEED-l)	**(ə)**	represents the sound of any vowel spelling when a syllable is sounded very weakly, as in the first syllable of *a*bout, or the last syllables of it*e*m, gal*lo*p, or foc*u*s, or the middle syllable of char*i*ty.
(m)	mum (MUHM)		
(n)	no (NOH)		
	button (BUHT-n)